Educational Psychology

Educational Psychology

Ninth Edition

~

Anita Woolfolk

The Ohio State University

BOSTON ▪ NEW YORK ▪ SAN FRANCISCO
MEXICO CITY ▪ MONTREAL ▪ TORONTO ▪ LONDON ▪ MADRID ▪ MUNICH ▪ PARIS
HONG KONG ▪ SINGAPORE ▪ TOKYO ▪ CAPE TOWN ▪ SYDNEY

President: Nancy Forsyth
Vice President and Editor-in-Chief, Education: Paul A. Smith
Developmental Editor: Alicia Reilly
Associate Editor: Tom Jefferies
Editorial Assistant: Audrey Stein
Editorial-Production Administrator: Beth Houston
Editorial-Production Services: Kathy Smith
Photo Research: Kathy Smith
Fine Art Research: Helane Prottas
Cover Administrator: Linda Knowles
Composition and Prepress Buyer: Linda Cox
Electronic Composition: Omegatype Typography, Inc.
Text Design: John Walker
Manufacturing Buyer: Andrew Turso
Marketing Manager: Tara Whorf

Library of Congress Cataloging-in-Publication Data

Hoy, Anita Woolfolk
Educational psychology / Anita E. Woolfolk. — 9th ed.
p. cm.
Includes bibliographical references and index.
ISBN: 0-205-36692-9
1. Educational psychology. I. Title

LB1051.W74 2004
370.15—dc21

2002043764

Credits appear on page 669, which constitutes an extension of the copyright page.

Printed in the United States of America
10 9 8 7 6 5 4 3 2 1 07 06 05 04 03

In memory of my grandmother

Anita Marie Wieckert

1902–2002

She gave us all a century of wisdom.

BRIEF CONTENTS

CONTENTS

Chapter 4

Learner Differences and Learning Needs 105

Chapter 5

Culture and Community 153

PART 2 LEARNING AND MOTIVATION

Chapter 6

Behavioral Views of Learning 197

Chapter 7

Cognitive Views of Learning 235

Chapter 8

Complex Cognitive Processes 275

Chapter 9

Social Cognitive and Constructivist Views of Learning 313

Chapter 10

Motivation in Learning and Teaching 349

PART 3 TEACHING

Chapter 11

Creating Learning Environments 395

Chapter 12

Teaching for Academic Learning 431

Chapter 13

Teaching for Self-Regulation, Creativity, and Tolerance 477

PART 4 ASSESSING

Chapter 15

Classroom Assessment 547

Many of you reading this book will be enrolled in an educational psychology course as part of your professional preparation for teaching, counseling, speech therapy, or psychology. The material in this text should be of interest to everyone who is concerned about education and learning, from the nursery school volunteer to the instructor in a community program for adults with disabilities. No background in psychology or education is necessary to understand this material. It is as free of jargon and technical language as possible, and many people have worked to make this edition clear, relevant, and interesting.

Since the first edition of *Educational Psychology* appeared, there have been many exciting developments in the field. The ninth edition continues to emphasize the educational implications and applications of research on child development, cognitive science, learning, and teaching. Theory and practice are not separated, but are considered together; the text shows how information and ideas drawn from research in educational psychology can be applied to solve the everyday problems of teaching. To explore the connections between knowledge and practice, there are many examples, lesson segments, case studies, guidelines, and practical tips from experienced teachers. Throughout the text you will be challenged to think about the value and use of the ideas in each chapter, and you will see principles of educational psychology in action. Professors and students who used the first eight editions found these features very helpful. But what about the new developments?

New in the Ninth Edition

New Chapter: In this edition there is a new chapter on "Teaching for Self-Regulation, Creativity, and Tolerance." Educators are recognizing what parents have known for years—there is more to schooling than academics, and educational psychologists have quite a bit to say about these important nonacademic outcomes. This chapter looks at research on self-regulation and learning to learn, creativity and how to foster it, social–emotional learning and the development of life-coping skills, and finally, teaching for tolerance. The chapter examines cooperative learning, conflict resolution, and classroom communities. The next decade promises to challenge our ability to keep our schools both safe and compassionate. I hope this chapter will help new teachers meet these challenges.

New Topics: Over 430 new citations have been added to this edition to bring prospective teachers the most current information. Topics include the following:

- the brain and learning
- bullying and relational aggression
- working memory and implicit memory
- Section 504 accommodations
- diversity and giftedness
- culture and classroom management
- self-regulation
- goal theory
- culturally relevant pedagogy
- learning strategies
- social cognitive theory and self-efficacy
- problem-based learning and cooperative learning
- interest and emotions in learning
- self-schemas and motivation
- dealing with conflict and violence
- authentic assessment
- high-stakes testing

The Plan of the Book

The introductory chapter begins with you, the prospective teacher, and the questions you may be asking yourself about a teaching career. What is good teaching, and what does it take to become an excellent teacher? How can educational psychology help you to become such a teacher?

Part One, "Students" focuses on the learners. How do they develop mentally, physically, emotionally, and socially, and how do all these aspects fit together? Where do individual differences come from, and what do they mean for teachers? What does it mean to create a culturally compatible classroom, one that makes learning accessible to all students?

Part Two, "Learning and Motivation" looks at learning and motivation from three major perspectives—behavioral, cognitive, and constructivist—with an emphasis on the last two. Learning theories have important implications for instruction at every level. Cognitive research is particularly vital right now and promises to be a wellspring of ideas for teaching in the immediate future.

Part Three, "Teaching" examines how to create learning environments and, then, how to teach, both for academic learning and for self-regulation, creativity, and tolerance. The material in these chapters is based on the most recent research in *real* classrooms.

Part Four, "Assessing" examines many types of testing and grading, providing a sound basis for determining how well students have learned.

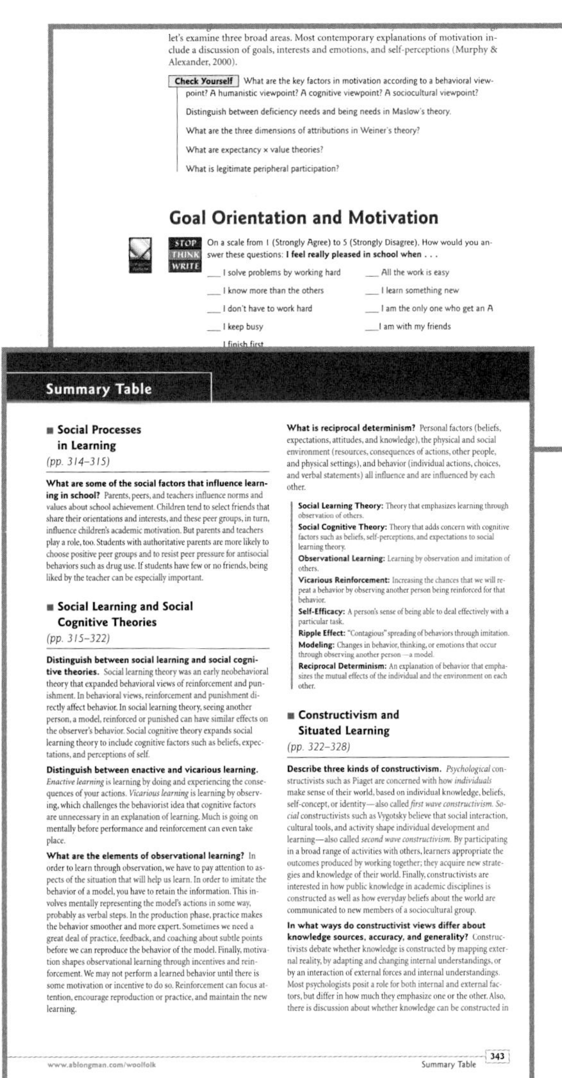

let's examine three broad areas. Most contemporary explanations of motivation include a discussion of goals, interests and emotions, and self-perceptions (Murphy & Alexander, 2000).

Check Yourself What are the key factors in motivation according to a behavioral viewpoint? A humanistic viewpoint? A cognitive viewpoint? A sociocultural viewpoint?

Distinguish between deficiency needs and being needs in Maslow's theory.

What are the three dimensions of attributions in Weiner's theory?

What are expectancy × value theories?

What is legitimate peripheral participation?

Goal Orientation and Motivation

STOP THINK WRITE On a scale from 1 (Strongly Agree) to 5 (Strongly Disagree), How would you answer these questions: **I feel really pleased in school when . . .**

___ I solve problems by working hard
___ I know more than the others
___ I don't have to work hard
___ I keep busy
I finish first
___ All the work is easy
___ I learn something new
___ I am the only one who get an A
___ I am with my friends

Summary Table

■ Social Processes in Learning *(pp. 314–315)*

What are some of the social factors that influence learning in school? Parents, peers, and teachers influence norms and values about school achievement. Children tend to select friends that share their orientations and interests, and these peer groups, in turn, influence children's academic motivation. But parents and teachers play a role, too. Students with authoritative parents are more likely to choose positive peer groups and to resist peer pressure for antisocial behaviors such as drug use. If students have few or no friends, being liked by the teacher can be especially important.

■ Social Learning and Social Cognitive Theories *(pp. 315–322)*

Distinguish between social learning and social cognitive theories. Social learning theory was an early neobehavioral theory that expanded behavioral views of reinforcement and punishment. In behavioral views, reinforcement and punishment directly affect behavior. In social learning theory, seeing another person, a model, reinforced or punished can have similar effects on the observer's behavior. Social cognitive theory expands social learning theory to include cognitive factors such as beliefs, expectations, and perceptions of self.

Distinguish between enactive and vicarious learning. *Enactive learning* is learning by doing and experiencing the consequences of your actions. *Vicarious learning* is learning by observing, which challenges the behaviorist idea that cognitive factors are unnecessary in an explanation of learning. Much is going on mentally before performance and reinforcement can even take place.

What are the elements of observational learning? In order to learn through observation, we have to pay attention to aspects of the situation that will help us learn. In order to imitate the behavior of a model, you have to retain the information. This involves mentally representing the model's actions in some way, probably as verbal steps. In the production phase, practice makes the behavior smoother and more expert. Sometimes we need a great deal of practice, feedback, and coaching about subtle points before we can reproduce the behavior of the model. Finally, motivation shapes observational learning through incentives and reinforcement. We may not perform a learned behavior until there is some motivation or incentive to do so. Reinforcement can focus attention, encourage reproduction or practice, and maintain the new learning.

What is reciprocal determinism? Personal factors (beliefs, expectations, attitudes, and knowledge), the physical and social environment (resources, consequences of actions, other people, and physical settings), and behavior (individual actions, choices, and verbal statements) all influence and are influenced by each other.

Social Learning Theory: Theory that emphasizes learning through observation of others.
Social Cognitive Theory: Theory that adds concern with cognitive factors such as beliefs, self-perceptions, and expectations to social learning theory.
Observational Learning: Learning by observation and imitation of others.
Vicarious Reinforcement: Increasing the chances that we will repeat a behavior by observing another person being reinforced for that behavior.
Self-Efficacy: A person's sense of being able to deal effectively with a particular task.
Ripple Effect: "Contagious" spreading of behaviors through imitation.
Modeling: Changes in behavior, thinking, or emotions that occur through observing another person—a model.
Reciprocal Determinism: An explanation of behavior that emphasizes the mutual effects of the individual and the environment on each other.

■ Constructivism and Situated Learning *(pp. 322–328)*

Describe three kinds of constructivism. *Psychological* constructivists such as Piaget are concerned with how *individuals* make sense of their world, based on individual knowledge, beliefs, self-concept, or identity—also called *first wave constructivism. Social* constructivists such as Vygotsky believe that social interaction, cultural tools, and activity shape individual development and learning—also called *second wave constructivism.* By participating in a broad range of activities with others, learners appropriate the outcomes produced by working together; they acquire new strategies and knowledge of their world. Finally, constructivists are interested in how public knowledge in academic disciplines is constructed as well as how everyday beliefs about the world are communicated to new members of a sociocultural group.

In what ways do constructivist views differ about knowledge sources, accuracy, and generality? Constructivists debate whether knowledge is constructed by mapping external reality, by adapting and changing internal understandings, or by an interaction of external forces and internal understandings. Most psychologists posit a role for both internal and external factors, but differ in how much they emphasize one or the other. Also, there is discussion about whether knowledge can be constructed in

www.ablongman.com/woolfolk

Summary Table 343

Aids to Understanding

At the beginning of each chapter you will find an **Outline** of the key topics with page numbers for quick reference. Then you are confronted with the question "What would you do?" about a real-life classroom situation related to the information in the chapter. By the time you reach the end of the chapter, you should have even more ideas about how to solve the problem raised, so be alert as you read. The chapter then begins with a quick **Overview** along with a list of **Questions** to focus your thinking about the upcoming pages.

Within the chapter, headings point out themes, questions, and problems as they arise, so you can look up information easily. These can also serve as a quick review of important points. When a new term or concept is introduced, it appears in boldface type along with a brief margin definition. These **Key Terms** are also defined in a newly designed **Summary Table** at the end of each chapter. After every major section of the chapter, **Check Yourself** questions ask you to review and apply your knowledge. Can you answer these questions? If not, you might reexamine the material. Throughout the book, graphs, tables, photos, and cartoons have been chosen to clarify and extend the text material—and to add to your enjoyment.

Each chapter ends with a *Summary* of the main ideas and terms keyed to the *Check Yourself* questions in each main heading. This *Summary* is an excellent resource for study and review.

Text Features

As in the previous editions, chapters in the ninth edition include **Guidelines,** the **Teachers' Casebook,** and **Point/Counterpoints.**

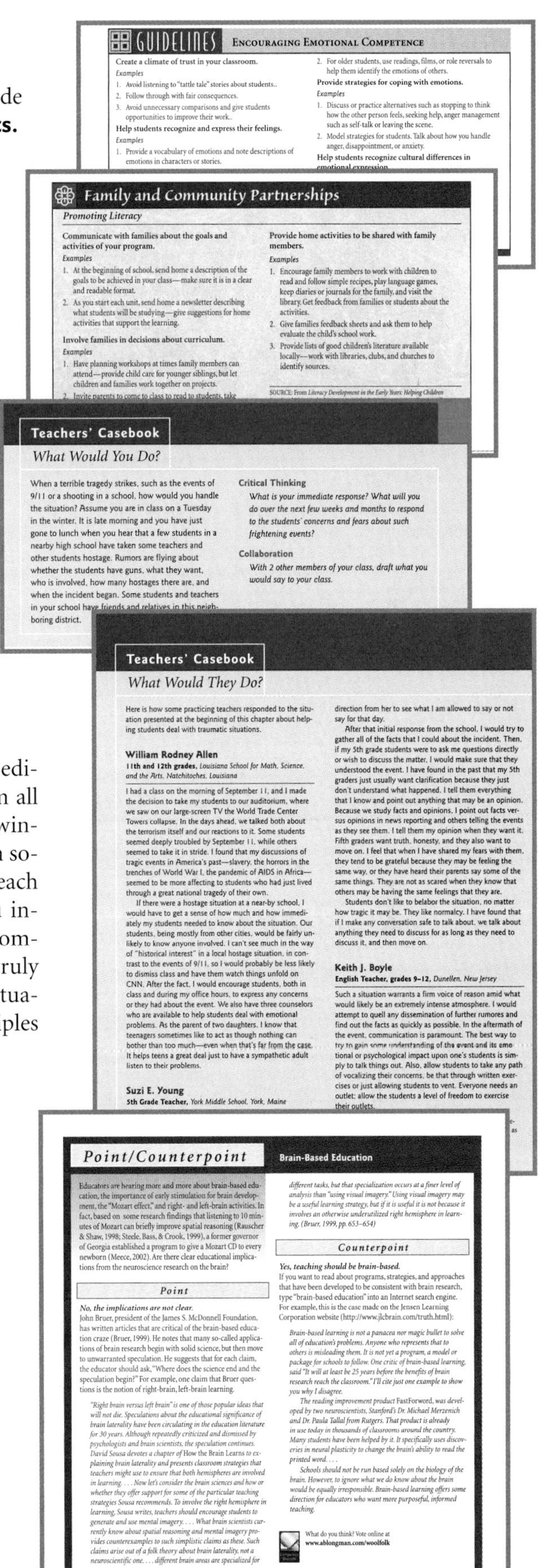

GUIDELINES Encouraging Emotional Competence

Create a climate of trust in your classroom.

Examples

1. Avoid listening to "tattle tale" stories about students..
2. Follow through with fair consequences.
3. Avoid unnecessary comparisons and give students opportunities to improve their work..

Help students recognize and express their feelings.

Examples

1. Provide a vocabulary of emotions and note descriptions of emotions in characters or stories.
2. For older students, use readings, films, or role reversals to help them identify the emotions of others.

Provide strategies for coping with emotions.

Examples

1. Discuss or practice alternatives such as stopping to think how the other person feels, seeking help, anger management such as self-talk or leaving the scene.
2. Model strategies for students. Talk about how you handle anger, disappointment, or anxiety.

Help students recognize cultural differences in emotional expression.

Family and Community Partnerships

Promoting Literacy

Communicate with families about the goals and activities of your program.

Examples

1. At the beginning of school, send home a description of the goals to be achieved in your class—make sure it is in a clear and readable format.
2. As you start each unit, send home a newsletter describing what students will be studying—give suggestions for home activities that support the learning.

Involve families in decisions about curriculum.

Examples

1. Have planning workshops at times family members can attend—provide child care for younger siblings, but let children and families work together on projects.
2. Invite parents to come to class to read to students, take

Provide home activities to be shared with family members.

Examples

1. Encourage family members to work with children to read and follow simple recipes, play language games, keep diaries or journals for the family, and visit the library. Get feedback from families or students about the activities.
2. Give families feedback sheets and ask them to help evaluate the child's school work.
3. Provide lists of good children's literature available locally—work with libraries, clubs, and churches to identify sources.

SOURCE: From *Literacy Development in the Early Years: Helping Children*

Teachers' Casebook

What Would You Do?

When a terrible tragedy strikes, such as the events of 9/11 or a shooting in a school, how would you handle the situation? Assume you are in class on a Tuesday in the winter. It is late morning and you have just gone to lunch when you hear that a few students in a nearby high school have taken some teachers and other students hostage. Rumors are flying about whether the students have guns, what they want, who is involved, how many hostages there are, and when the incident began. Some students and teachers in your school have friends and relatives in this neighboring district.

Critical Thinking

What is your immediate response? What will you do over the next few weeks and months to respond to the students' concerns and fears about such frightening events?

Collaboration

With 2 other members of your class, draft what you would say to your class.

Teachers' Casebook

What Would They Do?

Here is how some practicing teachers responded to the situation presented at the beginning of this chapter about helping students deal with traumatic situations.

William Rodney Allen
11th and 12th grades, *Louisiana School for Math, Science, and the Arts, Natchitoches, Louisiana*

I had a class on the morning of September 11, and I made the decision to take my students to our auditorium, where we saw on our large-screen TV the World Trade Center Towers collapse. In the days ahead, we talked both about the terrorism itself and our reactions to it. Some students seemed deeply troubled by September 11, while others seemed to take it in stride. I found that my discussions of tragic events in America's past—slavery, the horrors in the trenches of World War I, the pandemic of AIDS in Africa—seemed to be more affecting to students who had just lived through a great national tragedy of their own.

If there were a hostage situation at a near-by school, I would have to get a sense of how much and how immediately my students needed to know about the situation. Our students, being mostly from other cities, would be fairly unlikely to know anyone involved. I can't see much in the way of "historical interest" in a local hostage situation, in contrast to the events of 9/11, so I would probably be less likely to dismiss class and have them watch things unfold on CNN. After the fact, I would encourage students, both in class and during my office hours, to express any concerns or they had about the event. We also have three counselors who are available to help students deal with emotional problems. As the parent of two daughters, I know that teenagers sometimes like to act as though nothing can bother than too much—even when that's far from the case. It helps teens a great deal just to have a sympathetic adult listen to their problems.

Suzi E. Young
5th Grade Teacher, *York Middle School, York, Maine*

direction from her to see what I am allowed to say or not say for that day.

After that initial response from the school, I would try to gather all of the facts that I could about the incident. Then, if my 5th grade students were to ask me questions directly or wish to discuss the matter, I would make sure that they understood the event. I have found in the past that my 5th graders just usually want clarification because they just don't understand what happened. I tell them everything that I know and point out anything that may be an opinion. Because we study facts and opinions, I point out facts versus opinions in news reporting and others telling the events as they see them. I tell them my opinion when they want it. Fifth graders want truth, honesty, and they also want to move on. I feel that when I have shared my fears with them, they tend to be grateful because they may be feeling the same way, or they have heard their parents say some of the same things. They are not as scared when they know that others may be having the same feelings that they are.

Students don't like to belabor the situation, no matter how tragic it may be. They like normalcy. I have found that if I make any conversation safe to talk about, we talk about anything they need to discuss for as long as they need to discuss it, and then move on.

Keith J. Boyle
English Teacher, grades 9–12, *Dunellen, New Jersey*

Such a situation warrants a firm voice of reason amid what would likely be an extremely intense atmosphere. I would attempt to quell any dissemination of further rumores and find out the facts as quickly as possible. In the aftermath of the event, communication is paramount. The best way to try to gain some understanding of the event and its emotional or psychological impact upon one's students is simply to talk things out. Also, allow students to take any path of vocalizing their concerns, be that through written exercises or just allowing students to vent. Everyone needs an outlet; allow the students a level of freedom to exercise their outlets.

Point/Counterpoint **Brain-Based Education**

Educators are hearing more and more about brain-based education, the importance of early stimulation for brain development, the "Mozart effect," and right- and left-brain activities. In fact, based on some research findings that listening to 10 minutes of Mozart can briefly improve spatial reasoning (Rauscher & Shaw, 1998; Steele, Bass, & Crook, 1999), a former governor of Georgia established a program to give a Mozart CD to every newborn (Meece, 2002). Are there clear educational implications from the neuroscience research on the brain?

Point

No, the implications are not clear.
John Bruer, president of the James S. McDonnell Foundation, has written articles that are critical of the brain-based education craze (Bruer, 1999). He notes that many so-called applications of brain research begin with solid science, but then move to unwarranted speculation. He suggests that for each claim, the educator should ask, "Where does the science end and the speculation begin?" For example, one claim that Bruer questions is the notion of right-brain, left-brain learning.

> *"Right brain versus left brain" is one of those popular ideas that will not die. Speculations about the educational significance of brain laterality have been circulating in the education literature for 30 years. Although repeatedly criticized and dismissed by psychologists and brain scientists, the speculation continues. David Sousa devotes a chapter of* How the Brain Learns *to explaining brain laterality and presents classroom strategies that teachers might use to ensure that both hemispheres are involved in learning. . . . Now let's consider the brain sciences and how or whether they offer support for some of the particular teaching strategies Sousa recommends. To involve the right hemisphere in learning, Sousa writes, teachers should encourage students to generate and use mental imagery. . . . What brain scientists currently know about spatial reasoning and mental imagery provides counterexamples to such simplistic claims as these. Such claims arise out of a folk theory about brain laterality, not a neuroscientific one. . . . different brain areas are specialized for different tasks, but that specialization occurs at a finer level of analysis than "using visual imagery." Using visual imagery may be a useful learning strategy, but if it is useful it is not because it involves an otherwise underutilized right hemisphere in learning. (Bruer, 1999, pp. 653–654)*

Counterpoint

Yes, teaching should be brain-based.
If you want to read about programs, strategies, and approaches that have been developed to be consistent with brain research, type "brain-based education" into an Internet search engine. For example, this is the case made on the Jensen Learning Corporation website (http://www.jlcbrain.com/truth.html):

> *Brain-based learning is not a panacea nor magic bullet to solve all of education's problems. Anyone who represents that to others is misleading them. It is not yet a program, a model or package for schools to follow. One critic of brain-based learning, said "It will at least be 25 years before the benefits of brain research reach the classroom." I'll cite just one example to show you why I disagree.*
>
> *The reading improvement product* FastForword, *was developed by two neuroscientists, Stanford's Dr. Michael Merzenich and Dr. Paula Tallal from Rutgers. That product is already in use today in thousands of classrooms around the country. Many students have been helped by it. It specifically uses discoveries in neural plasticity to change the brain's ability to read the printed word. . . .*
>
> *Schools should not be run based solely on the biology of the brain. However, to ignore what we do know about the brain would be equally irresponsible. Brain-based learning offers some direction for educators who want more purposeful, informed teaching.*

What do you think? Vote online at **www.ablongman.com/woolfolk**

Guidelines

An important reason for studying educational psychology is to gain skills in solving classroom problems. Often, texts give pages of theory and research findings but little assistance in translating theory into practice. This text is different. Included in every chapter after the first one are several sets of *Guidelines.* These are teaching tips and practical suggestions based on the theory and research discussed in the chapter. Each suggestion is clarified by two or three specific examples. Although the *Guidelines* cannot cover every possible situation, they do provide a needed bridge between knowledge and practice and should help you transfer the text's information to new situations. In addition, every chapter after the first has one set of *Guidelines* that focuses on *Family and Community Partnerships*—an area of growing importance today.

Teachers' Casebook: What Would You Do? What Would They Do?

This highly acclaimed and popular feature from the first eight editions is back. At the end of each chapter, master teachers from all over the country, including many Teacher of the Year award winners, as well as teachers from around the world, offer their own solutions to the problem you encountered at the beginning of each chapter. *Teachers' Casebook: What Would They Do?* gives you insights into the thinking of expert teachers and allows you to compare their solutions to the ones you came up with. Their ideas truly show educational psychology at work in a range of everyday situations. The *Teachers' Casebook* brings to life the topics and principles discussed in each chapter.

Point/Counterpoint

In every chapter, a debate called *Point/ Counterpoint* examines two contrasting perspectives on an important question or controversy related to research or practice in educational psychology; issues such as inclusion, tracking, "paying" kids to learn, zero-tolerance, and character education are examples. Many of the topics considered in these *Point/Counterpoints* have "made the news" recently and are central to the discussions of educational reformers. NEW to this edition are video connections between Point/Counterpoint topics and the *ABC News/Allyn & Bacon Video: Point/Counterpoint,* which provide news clips from ABC's premier news shows.

Chapter 1	What Is Good Teaching?
Chapter 2	Brain-Based Education
Chapter 3	What Should Schools Do to Encourage Students' Self-Esteem?

Chapter 4	Is Tracking an Effective Strategy?
Chapter 5	Do Boys and Girls Learn Differently?
Chapter 6	Should Students Be Rewarded for Learning?
Chapter 7	What's Wrong with Memorizing?
Chapter 8	Should Students Be Allowed to Use Calculators and Spell-Checkers?
Chapter 9	Should Schools Teach Critical Thinking and Problem Solving?
Chapter 10	Does Making Learning Fun Make for Good Learning?
Chapter 11	Is Zero Tolerance a Good Idea?
Chapter 12	Is Homework a Valuable Use of Time?
Chapter 13	Should Schools Teach Character and Compassion?
Chapter 14	Should Tests Be Used to Hold Teachers Accountable?
Chapter 15	Which is Better—Traditional or Authentic Tests?

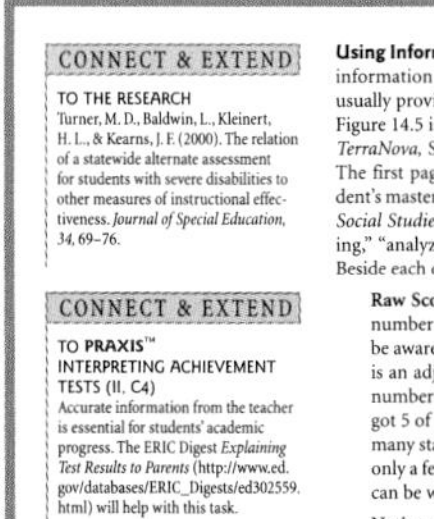

CONNECT & EXTEND

TO THE RESEARCH

Turner, M. D., Baldwin, L., Kleinert, H. L., & Kearns, J. F. (2000). The relation of a statewide alternate assessment for students with severe disabilities to other measures of instructional effectiveness. *Journal of Special Education, 34,* 69–76.

CONNECT & EXTEND

TO **PRAXIS**™ INTERPRETING ACHIEVEMENT TESTS (II, C4)

Accurate information from the teacher is essential for students' academic progress. The ERIC Digest *Explaining Test Results to Parents* (http://www.ed.gov/databases/ERIC_Digests/ed302559.html) will help with this task.

Using Information from a Norm-Referen information can teachers expect from a usually provide individual profiles for each Figure 14.5 is an example of an individual *TerraNova,* Second Edition. Note that the The first page (Performance on Objectives dent's mastery of different objectives in *Rea* *Social Studies.* For example, under *Reading* ing," "analyze text," "evaluate/extend mea Beside each objective are several different w

Raw Score/Number Correct: Under t number of items (out of 100) that Ken be aware, the test probably did not have is an adjusted number based on the a number Ken got right. If there were 10 got 5 of them right, his raw score for th many standardized tests, some of these only a few items each, and the fewer the can be with reliability.

National OPI: The average number co group.

Connect and Extend

Connect and Extend features appear in the margins several times throughout each chapter, linking content to teaching, research, professional journals, students' thinking and prior knowledge, students' teaching philosophy, and to other chapters in the book.

NEW to this edition are Connect and Extend to Your Teaching Portfolio, and Connect and Extend to PRAXIS™.

New Text Features

In addition to these popular features from previous editions, I have added several new elements to every chapter: These features will help you really connect with the knowledge in educational psychology—understanding the information now and also recognizing its value for your future.

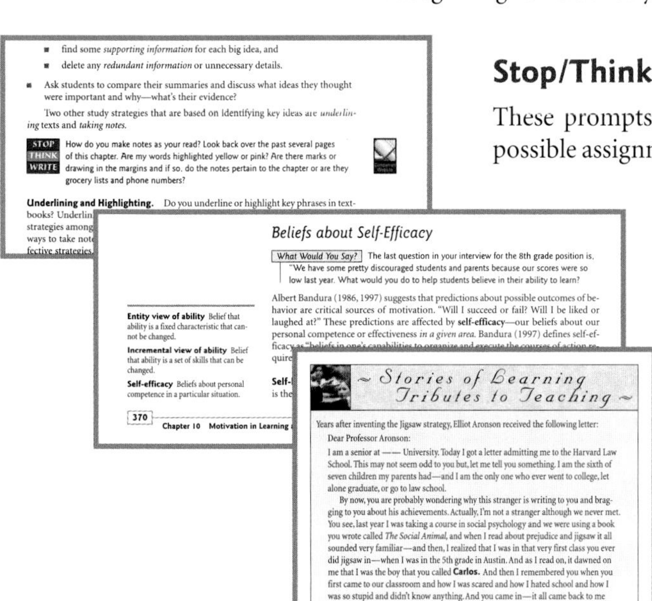

- find some *supporting information* for each big idea, and
- delete any *redundant information* or unnecessary details.

- Ask students to compare their summaries and discuss what ideas they thought were important and why—what's their evidence?

Two other study strategies that are based on identifying key ideas are *underlining* texts and *taking notes.*

STOP THINK WRITE How do you make notes as your read? Look back over the past several pages of this chapter. Are my words highlighted yellow or pink? Are there marks or drawing in the margins and if so, do the notes pertain to the chapter or are they grocery lists and phone numbers?

Underlining and Highlighting. Do you underline or highlight key phrases in textbooks? Underlin strategies among ways to take not fective strategies

Beliefs about Self-Efficacy

What Would You Say? The last question in your interview for the 8th grade position is, "We have some pretty discouraged students and parents because our scores were so low last year. What would you do to help students believe in their ability to learn?

Albert Bandura (1986, 1997) suggests that predictions about possible outcomes of behavior are critical sources of motivation. "Will I succeed or fail? Will I be liked or laughed at?" These predictions are affected by **self-efficacy**—our beliefs about our personal competence or effectiveness *in a given area.* Bandura (1997) defines self-efficacy as "beliefs in one's capabilities to organize and execute the courses of action re- quire

Self- is the

Entity view of ability Belief that ability is a fixed characteristic that cannot be changed.

Incremental view of ability Belief that ability is a set of skills that can be changed.

Self-efficacy Beliefs about personal competence in a particular situation.

370 Chapter 10 Motivation in Learning

~ *Stories of Learning Tributes to Teaching* ~

Years after inventing the Jigsaw strategy, Elliot Aronson received the following letter:

Dear Professor Aronson:

I am a senior at —— University. Today I got a letter admitting me to the Harvard Law School. This may not seem odd to you but, let me tell you something. I am the sixth of seven children my parents had—and I am the only one who ever went to college, let alone graduate, or go to law school.

By now, you are probably wondering why this stranger is writing to you and bragging to you about his achievements. Actually, I'm not a stranger although we never met. You see, last year I was taking a course in social psychology and we were using a book you wrote called *The Social Animal,* and when I read about prejudice and jigsaw it all sounded very familiar—and then, I realized that I was in that very first class you ever did jigsaw in—when I was in the 5th grade in Austin. And as I read on, it dawned on me that I was the boy that you called **Carlos.** And then I remembered you when you first came to our classroom and how I was scared and how I hated school and how I was so stupid and didn't know anything. And you came in—it all came back to me when I read your book—you were very tall—about 6½ feet—and you had a big black beard and you were funny and made us all laugh.

And, most important, when we started to do work in jigsaw groups, I began to realize that I wasn't really that stupid. And the kids I thought were cruel and hostile became my friends and the teacher acted friendly and nice to me and I actually began to love school, and I began to love to learn things and now I'm about to go to Harvard Law School.

You must get a lot of letters like this but I decided to write anyway because let me tell you something. My mother tells me that when I was born I almost died. I was born at home and the cord was wrapped around my neck and the midwife gave me mouth to mouth and saved my life. If she were still alive, I would write to her too, to tell her that I grew up smart and good and I'm going to law school. But she died a few years ago. I'm writing to you because, no less than her, you saved my life too.

SOURCE: From *Nobody left to hate: Teaching compassion after Columbine* by E. Aronson, 2000, New York: Worth, pp. 150–151.

Stop/Think/Write

These prompts provide "minds-on" experiences. They are connected to possible assignments such as interactive journals. The Companion Website allows students to jot down their responses to these prompts and email them to their instructor.

What Would You Say?

Two or three times in every chapter, you are asked how you would answer possible job interview questions based on the text material. These questions were suggested by practicing principals and superintendents around the country.

Stories of Learning/Tributes to Teaching

Every chapter contains a brief story about how a real teacher made a difference in the life of a student. My daughter, a 3rd grade teacher, recently got a phone call from the parents of a former student. The young girl was not expected to live and had asked for Kelly—one of only two people she wanted to see.

The good news is that the girl received a heart transplant and is doing well. The other good news is that her teacher was and is a central part of her life. Each chapter in this book has a story of learning that demonstrates the importance of teachers like Kelly.

Reaching Every Student

In every chapter, this feature provides ideas for assessing, teaching, and motivating all of the students in today's classroom. Some describe teaching strategies to reach students with learning problems. Some explain ways of using technology to reach every student. Others present creative ways to teach complex concepts.

Reaching Every Student

Culturally Responsive Management

Carla Monroe and Jennifer Obidah (2002) studied Ms. Simpson, an African American teacher working with her 8th grade science class. She describes herself as having high expectations for academics and behavior in her classes—so much so that she believed her students perceived her as "mean." Yet she often used humor and dialect to communicate her expectations, as in the following exchange:

Ms. Simpson [addressing the class]: If you know you're going to act the fool just come to me and say, 'I'm going to act the fool at the pep rally,' so I can go ahead and send you to wherever you need to go. [Class laughs.]

Ms. Simpson: I'm real serious. If you know you're having a bad day, you don't want anybody touching you, you don't want nobody saying nothing to you, somebody bump into you you're going to snap—you need to come up to me and say, 'I'm going to snap and I can't go to the pep rally.' [The students start to call out various comments.]

Ms. Simpson: Now, I just want to say I expect you to have the best behavior because you're the most mature students in the building . . . don't make me stop the pep rally and ask the 8th graders to leave.

Edward: We'll have silent lunch won't we? [Class laughs.]

Ms. Simpson: You don't want to dream about what you're going to have. [Class laughs.] Ok, 15 minutes for warm ups. [The students begin their warm-up assignment.]

See the *Reaching Every Student* feature for an example.

Communicating with Families about Classroom Management

As we have seen throughout this book, families are important partners in education. This statement applies to classroom management as well. When parents and teachers share the same expectations and support each other, they can create a more positive classroom environment and more time for learning. The *Family and Community Partnerships Guidelines* on page 424 provide ideas for working with families and the community.

Besides prevention, schools can also establish mentoring programs, conflict resolution training, social skills training, more relevant curricula, and parent and community involvement programs (Padilla, 1992; Parks, 1995). One intervention that seems to be helpful is peer mediation, discussed in Chapter 13.

Check Yourself What does research say about different discipline approaches?

How does culture affect classroom management?

Chapter 1 Creativity in an Urban School
Chapter 2 Scaffolding Learning
Chapter 3 Safety on the Internet
Chapter 4 Higher-Order Comprehension and Severe Learning Disabilities
Chapter 5 Recognizing Giftedness in Bilingual Students
Chapter 6 Students with Learning and Behavior Problems
Chapter 7 A Picture and a Few Hundred Words
Chapter 8 Teaching Them How to Learn
Chapter 9 Lunch Learning
Chapter 10 Bounded Choice
Chapter 11 Culturally Relevant Management
Chapter 12 Resource Rooms, Collaborative Consultation, and Cooperative Teaching
Chapter 13 Learning to Listen
Chapter 14 Accommodations in Testing
Chapter 15 Using Technology to Recognize Improvement

Enhancing Your Expertise with Technology: Professional Development

One section in every chapter describes how to use the World Wide Web to continue learning after you have completed the course and throughout your teaching career; it includes carefully chosen websites and guidance for using them. As a teacher, your education never ends, and with the resources of the Web, you can stay current. This text gives you an excellent library of professional development resources.

Enhancing Your Expertise with Technology

Teaching Every Student

The incident was a small one, but it exemplified many of the issues that teachers face as a result of the nation's demographic changes. Five-year old Emrah, who qualified for the free lunch program, told his teacher that he could eat neither of the two offerings in the school cafeteria that day: sausage with pancakes or deli sub sandwich—because of religious reasons. The teacher contacted the cafeteria manager. The manager said that no accommodations could be made because no other foods were available. (One of the cafeteria workers remarked that "they" should learn to eat what "we" eat.) The incensed teacher finally reached the school district dietician, who resolved the dispute by pointing out that the "ham" in the deli sub sandwich was actually *turkey ham* that Emrah could eat. "I am glad we were able to take care of that problem," said the dietician. "But we can't make accommodations for every ethnic or religious group in the district."

As the nation's school population continues to diversify, incidents like this one (and others far less easily resolved) will certainly arise more and more often. Teachers with expertise about and respect for cultural differences will be able to face these challenges in ways that help students experience genuine acceptance by the school community, leading to increased ethnic pride and motivation to succeed in school.

The Southern Poverty Law Center sponsors the Teaching Tolerance education project (www.tolerance.org) that helps "teachers foster equity, respect and understanding in the classroom and beyond." Its major concern is fair treatment of all people regardless of religious affiliation, gender, race, age, ethnicity, sexual orientation, or physical status. Teaching Tolerance takes a comprehensive approach to achievement of that goal. Here you will find information and resources including:

- current events,
- classroom lesson plans,
- activities to foster teacher self-reflection about tolerance,
- a teacher's forum to share ideas about fostering tolerance in the classroom,
- guidelines and tips for responding to intolerant incidents inside the school, and
- links to other Web sites that promote tolerance.

Perhaps Teaching Tolerance's most interesting—as well as unsettling—feature is its set of Implicit Association Tests (IAT) that measure unconscious bias. These tests might offer you some insight into your own possible hidden biases about race, homosexuality, age, gender, and body image. Teachers alone, of course, cannot create an atmosphere of equity and respect. The sponsors of Teaching Tolerance also provide numerous resources to engage parents and students in efforts to foster tolerance and equity. See what you think of this site. You may very well find it the most disturbing, but useful site that you encounter through this textbook.

Chapter 1 Professional Development
Chapter 2 Language and Literacy Development
Chapter 3 Emotional and Social Development
Chapter 4 Learning about Learning Disabilities
Chapter 5 Teaching Every Student
Chapter 6 Self-Regulation
Chapter 7 Memory Techniques
Chapter 8 Problem Solving
Chapter 9 Thinking Skills
Chapter 10 Motivation to Learn

Chapter 11	Classroom Management
Chapter 12	Questioning Techniques
Chapter 13	Cooperative Learning
Chapter 14	Standardized Testing
Chapter 15	Assessment

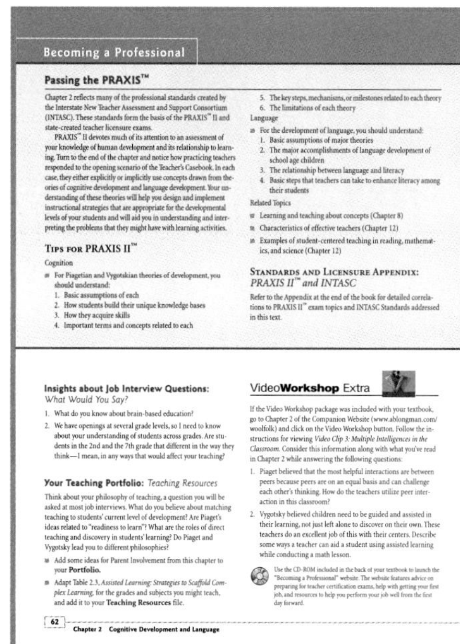

Becoming a Professional

Passing the PRAXIS™

Chapter 2 reflects many of the professional standards created by the Interstate New Teacher Assessment and Support Consortium (INTASC). These standards form the basis of the PRAXIS™ II and state-created teacher licensure exams.

PRAXIS™ II devotes much of its attention to an assessment of your knowledge of human development and its relationship to learning. Turn to the end of the chapter and notice how practicing teachers responded to the opening scenario of the Teacher's Casebook. In each case, they either explicitly or implicitly use concepts drawn from theories of cognitive development and language development. Your understanding of these theories will help you design and implement instructional strategies that are appropriate for the developmental levels of your students and will aid you in understanding and interpreting the problems that they might have with learning activities.

Tips for PRAXIS II™

Cognition

- For Piagetian and Vygotskian theories of development, you should understand:
  1. Basic assumptions of each
  2. How students build their unique knowledge bases
  3. How they acquire skills
  4. Important terms and concepts related to each
  5. The key steps, mechanisms, or milestones related to each theory
  6. The limitations of each theory

Language

- For the development of language, you should understand:
  1. Basic assumptions of major theories
  2. The major accomplishments of language development of school age children
  3. The relationship between language and literacy
  4. Basic steps that teachers can take to enhance literacy among their students

Related Topics

- Learning and teaching about concepts (Chapter 8)
- Characteristics of effective teachers (Chapter 12)
- Examples of student-centered teaching in reading, mathematics, and science (Chapter 12)

Standards and Licensure Appendix: *PRAXIS II™ and INTASC*

Refer to the Appendix at the end of the book for detailed correlations to PRAXIS II™ exam topics and INTASC Standards addressed in this text.

Insights about Job Interview Questions: *What Would You Say?*

1. What do you know about brain-based education?
2. We have openings at several grade levels, so I need to know about your understanding of students across grades. Are students in the 2nd and the 7th grade that different in the way they think—I mean, in any ways that would affect your teaching?

Your Teaching Portfolio: *Teaching Resources*

Think about your philosophy of teaching, a question you will be asked at most job interviews. What do you believe about matching teaching to students' current level of development? Are Piaget's ideas related to "readiness to learn"? What are the roles of direct teaching and discovery in students' learning? Do Piaget and Vygotsky lead you to different philosophies?

- Add some ideas for Parent Involvement from this chapter to your **Portfolio.**
- Adapt Table 2.3, *Assisted Learning: Strategies to Scaffold Complex Learning,* for the grades and subjects you might teach, and add it to your **Teaching Resources** file.

Video**Workshop** Extra

If the Video Workshop package was included with your textbook, go to Chapter 2 of the Companion Website (www.ablongman.com/woolfolk) and click on the Video Workshop button. Follow the instructions for viewing *Video Clip 3: Multiple Intelligences in the Classroom.* Consider this information along with what you've read in Chapter 2 while answering the following questions:

1. Piaget believed that the most helpful interactions are between peers because peers are on an equal basis and can challenge each other's thinking. How do the teachers utilize peer interaction in this classroom?
2. Vygotsky believed children need to be guided and assisted in their learning, not just left alone to discover on their own. These teachers do an excellent job of this with their centers. Describe some ways a teacher can aid a student using assisted learning while conducting a math lesson.

Use the CD-ROM included in the back of your textbook to launch the "Becoming a Professional" website. The website features advice on preparing for teacher certification exams, help with getting your first job, and resources to help you perform your job well from the first day forward.

62 Chapter 2 Cognitive Development and Language

Becoming a Professional

At the end of every chapter, beginning with Chapter 2, is a section called "Becoming a Professional" that gives you guidance for developing a personal study guide for *Passing the PRAXIS™*, or other professional *Licensure Tests* you may be required to take. Marginal notes also direct your attention to material that will be very important in passing licensure examinations. In addition, in *Becoming a Professional,* you will see tips for organizing a professional *Teaching Portfolio* and developing a *Resource File* for your future classrooms.

Standards and Licensure Appendix: Praxis II™ and INTASC

You can refer to this Appendix at the end of the book for detailed correlations to PRAXIS II™ exam topics addressed in the 9th edition of the text.

Student Supplements

Study Guide Designed to help students master the material in the text, the Study Guide includes concept maps, case study applications, lists of key points, exercises with key terms and concepts, practice tests, and explanations of why answers are correct.

Companion Website Students who visit the Companion Website that accompanies the text (ablongman.com/woolfolk) will find many features and activities to help them in their studies: web links and journaling activities; practice tests; an interactive glossary; and vocabulary flash cards. The website features an extended "Teacher's Casebook" with additional audio, video, and text-based cases and activities. The site also contains examples of classroom work created by children in many content areas. Students will be able to assess these artifacts by linking to the discussion and ideas from the main text.

CD Connection to the "Becoming a Professional" Website A new CD-ROM at the back of the text acts as a launcher to the "Becoming a Professional" website. Connected to the text feature of the same name, the website is a tool to help students succeed in the classroom and beyond. The website will help students prepare for teacher certification exams, get their first job, and perform that job well from the first day forward. In addition, the CD-ROM builds on the Appendix in the text by featuring an invaluable set of weblinks correlated to each part of the PRAXIS II™ PLT licensure exam.

VideoWorkshop for *Educational Psychology:* A Course-Tailored Video Learning System www.ablongman.com/videoworkshop is a new way to bring video into your course for maximized learning! This total teaching and learning system includes quality video footage on an easy-to-use CD-ROM plus a Student Learning Guide and an Instructor's Teaching Guide—both with textbook-specific Correlation Grids. The result? A program that brings textbook concepts to life with ease and that helps your students understand, analyze, and apply the objectives of the course. VideoWorkshop is available for your students as a value-pack option with this textbook.

PRAXIS™ Guide Provides information about the PRAXIS II™ tests, which many states require for student certification. The Guide features ten case histories with a series of multiple-choice and short-answer questions echoing those in the actual PRAXIS™ exams.

Research Navigator™ Allyn & Bacon's new Research Navigator™ is the easiest way for students to start a research assignment or research paper. Complete with extensive help on the research process and three exclusive databases of credible and reliable source material including EBSCO's ContentSelect Academic Journal Database, *New York Times* Search by Subject Archive, and "Best of the Web" Link Library, Research Navigator™ helps students quickly and efficiently make the most of their research time.

iSearch: Education This free reference guide includes tips, resources, activities, and URLs to help students use the Internet for their research projects. The first part introduces students to the basics of the Internet and the World Wide Web. The second part includes over thirty Net activities that tie into the content of the text. The third part lists hundreds of education-specific Internet resources. The guide also includes information on how to correctly cite research, and a guide to building an online glossary.

Instructor Supplements

Instructor's Resource Manual The Instructor's Resource Manual includes many ideas and activities to help instructors teach the course. For each chapter it provides: teaching outline, learning objectives, learning activities and handouts (including technology activities and activities for field experiences), discussion questions, and video/Internet resources.

Assessment Package Contains hundreds of challenging questions in multiple-choice, fill-in-the-blank, true/false, short-answer, and case study formats, along with a detailed answer key.

Computerized Test Bank The printed Test Bank is also available electronically through our computerized testing system: TestGen EQ. Instructors can use TestGen EQ to create exams in just minutes by selecting from the existing database of questions, editing questions, or writing original questions.

PowerPoint™ Presentation Ideal for lecture presentations or student handouts, the PowerPoint™ presentation created for this text provides dozens of ready-to-use graphic and text images (available on the Web at ablongman.com/ppt).

ABC News/Allyn & Bacon Video: Point/Counterpoint Containing fifty minutes of ABC News clips from ABC's premier news shows, the video provides a starting point to discuss the issues raised in the *Point/Counterpoint* feature of the main text. An accompanying instructor's guide outlines teaching strategies and provides discussion questions to use with the clips.

Classroom Insights IV Video This two-hour video contains classroom footage illustrating key concepts from *Educational Psychology.*

Allyn & Bacon Transparencies for Educational Psychology IV This updated package includes over 150 full-color acetates.

Digital Media Archive for Education This CD-ROM contains a variety of media elements that instructors can use to create electronic presentations in the classroom. It includes hundreds of original images, as well as selected art from Allyn & Bacon educational psychology texts, providing instructors with a broad selection of graphs, charts, and tables. For classrooms with full multimedia capability, it also contains video segments and Web links.

Student and Instructor Responses You are invited to respond to any aspect of this text. We welcome your feedback. You may wish to criticize the solutions in the *Teachers' Casebook,* for example, or suggest topics or materials you think should be added to future editions. We would also like to know what you think of the text features and student supplements. Please send letters to:

Woolfolk
EDUCATIONAL PSYCHOLOGY, 9/E
Allyn & Bacon
75 Arlington Street Suite 300
Boston, MA 02116

Acknowledgments

During the years I have worked on this book, from initial draft to this most recent revision, many people have supported the project. Without their help, this text simply could not have been written.

Many educators contributed to this project. Carol Weinstein wrote the section in Chapter 11 on spaces for learning. Gypsy Denzine (Northern Arizona University) is responsible for the *Assessment Package* and the answer feedback material that accompanies each item. The *Instructor's Resource Manual* and *PowerPoint*™ *Presentation* were created by Angela O'Donnell (Rutgers University) and the *Study Guide,* by Emilie Johnson (Lindenwood University). The *Companion Website* was created by Richard Giaquinto (St. Francis College) and the *Becoming a Professional* website was created by Mitchell Klett (University of Idaho). The features in every chapter, *Enhancing Your Expertise with Technology,* the *Passing the PRAXIS*™, the marginal notes, and the *Appendix on PRAXIS*™ all were developed by James O'Kelly (Rutgers University). Chapter 7 benefited from the comments of Philip Winne, Nancy Perry, and Angela O'Donnell. Several of the *What Would You Say?* questions were suggested by Dr. Michael DiPaola, former Superintendent of Schools, Pitman, New Jersey (College of William and Mary), Dr. Harry Galinsky, former Superintendent of Schools, Paramus, New Jersey, and Andrea Wong, Principal, Hillside Elementary School, Needham, Massachusetts.

My writing was guided by extensive and thoughtful reviews from the following individuals:

Rebecca P. Cole, *Northern Arizona University*
Alice J. Corkill, *University of Nevada—Las Vegas*
Cheryl C. Durwin, *Southern Connecticut State University*
Daniel P. Hallahan, *University of Virginia*
Steven M. Hoover, *St. Cloud State University*
Young Suk Hwang, *California State University—San Bernardino*

Nancy F. Knapp, *University of Georgia—Athens*
S. Jay Samuels, *University of Minnesota—Twin Cities*
Philip H. Winne, *Simon Fraser University*

Test Bank Reviewers

Melva M. Burke, *East Carolina University*
Gypsy Denzine, *Northern Arizona University*
Steven M. Hoover, *St. Cloud State University*
Beverly M. Klecker, *Morehead State University*
David E. Tanner, *California State University—Fresno*
Linda S. Toth, *California University of Pennsylvania*

Interactive Companion 8/e Reviewers

Pam Angelle, *University of Louisiana—Lafayette*
Steven J. Condly, *University of Central Florida*
Rhoda Cummings, *University of Nevada—Reno*
Julia Harper, *Azusa Pacific University*
Mary F. Maples, *University of Nevada—Reno*
Johnmarshall Reeve, *University of Iowa*

As I made decisions about how to revise this edition, I benefited from the ideas of professors around the country who took the time to complete surveys and answer my questions. Thanks to:

J. Olin Campbell, *Brigham Young University*
Gypsy M. Denzine, *Northern Arizona University*
M. Arthur Garmon, *Western Michigan University*
Tom Kubiszyn, *University of Texas—Austin*
Pamela Manners, *Troy State University*
Elizabeth Reynolds, *University of Idaho*
Catherine Rivoira, *East Carolina University*
Susan Rogers, *Columbus State Community College*
Charles Jeffrey "Jeff" Sandoz, *University of Louisiana—Lafayette*
Marvin Seperson, *Nova Southeastern University*
Anuradhaa Shastri, *SUNY Oneonta*
Gaby van der Giessen, *Fairmont State College*
Bettie Willingham, *Barton College*

Many classroom teachers across the country and around the world contributed their experience, creativity, and expertise to the *Teachers' Casebook.* I have thoroughly enjoyed my association with these master teachers, and I am grateful for the perspective they brought to the book.

William Rodney Allen
Louisiana School for Math, Science, and the Arts
Natchitoches, Louisiana

Jan Andrews
Dulacca State School
Dulacca QLD 4255, Australia

Madya Ayala
Campus Garza Sada
Monterrey, N.L. Mexico

Kelly McElroy Bonin
Klein Oak High School
Spring, Texas

Suzy L. Boswell
Pickens County Middle School
Jasper, Georgia

Keith J. Boyle
Dunellen High School
Dunellen, NJ

Mary Ellen Casey
Snug Harbor Community School
Quincy, Massachusetts

Katie Churchill
Oriole Parke Elementary School
Chicago, Illinois

Maria Cirmia
Hillside School
Needham, Massachusetts

Kathleen Conroy
Rancho Canada Elementary School
Lake Forest, California

Kelly Crockett
Meadowbrook Elementary School
Ft Worth, Texas

Ashley Dodge
Los Angeles Unified School District
Los Angeles, California

Mary Frances Donohoe
Lawton Chiles Elementary
Gainesville, Florida

Margaret Doolan
St. Michael's School
Gordonvale QLD 4865, Australia

Marie C. Enright
Village Elementary School
York Beach, ME

Aimee Fredette
Fisher Elementary School
Walpole, Massachusetts

Pam Gaskill
Riverside Elementary School
Dublin, Ohio

Sandra Gill
Hudson Middle School
Hudson, New York

Linda Glisson
St. James Episcopal Day School
Baton Rouge, Louisiana

Carol Grosberg
Bates School
Wellesley, Massachusetts

Jolita Harper
Weinland Park Elementary School
Columbus, Ohio

Jeff D. Horton
Colton School
Colton, Washington

Kelly L. Hoy
Faber Elementary School
Dunellen, New Jersey

Sue Middleton
St. James Episcopal Day School
Baton Rouge, Louisiana

Julie Mohok
Ponam Primary School
Manus Island, Papua New Guinea

Thomas W. Newkirk
Hamilton Heights Middle School
Arcadia, Indiana

Thomas O'Donnell
Malden High School
Malden, Massachusetts

Alan Osborne
Snug Harbor Community School
Quincy, Massachusetts

Carey Perkson
Brown School
Natick, Massachusetts

Katie Piel
West Park School
Moscow, Idaho

Denise Ready
Snug Harbor Community School
Quincy, Massachusetts

Steven P. Rude
John C. Fremont High School
Los Angeles, California

Ann Sande
Henry Viscardi School
Albertson, New York

Nancy Schaefer
Cincinnati Hills Christian Academy High School
Cincinnati, Ohio

Nancy Sheehan-Melzack
Snug Harbor Community School
Quincy, Massachusetts

Mark H. Smith
Medford High School
Medford, Massachusetts

Richard T. Smith
Harrison Middle School
Yarmouth, Maine

Jacalyn D. Walker
Treasure Mountain Middle School
Park City, Utah

Suzi E. Young
York Middle School
York, Maine

In a project of this size so many people make essential contributions. Robert Tonner, Permissions Coordinator, worked diligently to obtain permissions for the material reproduced in this text and the supplements. The text designer, John Walker, and cover coordinator, Linda Knowles, made the look of this book the best yet. They make it seem easy to produce a beautiful book—it isn't. Kathy Smith, Project Manager, routinely performed minor miracles and held all aspects of the project in her wonderfully ordered and intelligent mind. Beth Houston, Production Administrator, and Elaine Ober, Production Manager, coordinated all aspects of the project, with amazing skill and grace. Somehow they brought sanity to what could have been chaos and fun to what might have been drudgery. Now the book is in the able hands of Tara Whorf, Marketing Manager, Amy Cronin Jordan, Executive Marketing Manager, Kate Conway, Director of Advertising, and their staff. I can't wait to see what they are planning for me now! What a talented and creative group—I am honored to work with them all.

On this edition, I was privileged to work with an outstanding editorial group, Nancy Forsyth, President of Allyn and Bacon, and Paul A. Smith, Vice President, Editor-in-Chief. Their intelligence, creativity, sound judgment, style, and enduring commitment to quality can be seen on every page of this text. They will always have my deepest respect and enduring friendship. I would keep writing forever just to work with them. Audrey Beth Stein, Editorial Assistant, kept everything running smoothly and kept my fax machine and e-mail humming. On this edition I was fortunate again to have the help of Alicia Reilly, an outstanding developmental editor with the perfect combination of knowledge and organizational ability. Once again, she guided this revision in all its many aspects, always staying just ahead of whatever had to happen next, communicating with people around the world—remarkable! The excellent pedagogical supports would not exist without her tireless efforts. The extensive supplements package that accompanies this book was coordinated, with seeming effortlessness, by Tom Jefferies, Associate Editor.

Finally, I want to thank my family and friends for their kindness and support during the long days and nights that I worked on this book. To my family, Marion, Bob, Eric, Suzie, Elsie, Liz, Wayne K., Kelly, Tom, and Mike—you are the greatest.

And finally, to Wayne Hoy, my friend, colleague, inspiration, passion, husband—you are simply the best.

Anita Woolfolk Hoy

CHAPTER

1

Teachers, Teaching, and Educational Psychology

Teachers' Casebook

What Would You Do?

It is your second year as a teacher at the Riverside Combined Campus (Kindergarten–8th grade). The district has just received money from the state and a private foundation to give three awards in your school for "excellence in teaching." The principal wants the teachers' recommendations about how to choose the recipients of these awards, so a committee is formed, composed of experienced teachers and one beginner—you. When the principal asked you to serve on the committee, you felt you had to say yes. All week the Teachers' Lounge has been buzzing with discussion about the awards. Some teachers are suspicious—they fear the decisions will be purely political. Others are glad to see teaching honored. Names are mentioned as "sure winners" and a few teachers who seldom speak to you have become very friendly ever since the committee membership was announced. The first meeting is next week. How will you prepare for it?

Critical Thinking

What do you need to know about teaching to complete this task? What are some indicators of excellent teaching? Do different philosophies of teaching provide different answers to this question? What are your recommendations, and how would you back them up?

Collaboration

With 3 or 4 other members of your class, draw a concept map or web that graphically depicts "good teaching." For an example of a concept map, see "Figure 8.2: Amy's Molecule" in Chapter 8.

If you are like many students, you begin this course with a mixture of anticipation and wariness. Perhaps you are required to take educational psychology as part of a program in teacher education, speech therapy, nursing, or counseling. You may have chosen this class as an elective. Whatever your reason for enrolling, you probably have questions about teaching, schools, students—or even about yourself—that you hope this course may answer. I have written the 9th edition of *Educational Psychology* with questions such as these in mind.

In this first chapter, we begin with education—more specifically, with teaching today. Teachers have been both criticized as ineffective and lauded as the best hope for young people. Do teachers make a difference in students' learning? What characterizes good teaching? Only when you are aware of the challenges and possibilities of teaching and learning today can you appreciate the contributions of educational psychology. After a brief introduction to the world of the teacher, we turn to a discussion of educational psychology itself. How can principles identified by educational psychologists benefit teachers, therapists, parents, and others who are interested in teaching and learning? What exactly is the content of educational psychology, and where does this information come from? By the time you have finished this chapter, you will be in a much better position to answer these questions and many others such as:

- *Does teaching matter?*
- *What is good teaching?*
- *What do expert teachers know?*
- *What are the greatest concerns of beginning teachers?*
- *Why should I study educational psychology?*
- *What roles do theory and research play in this field?*

Atonement (1996) by Tunde Afolayan. Courtesy of the artist and PaintingsDIRECT (http://www.PaintingsDIRECT.com).

Do Teachers Make a Difference?

CONNECT & EXTEND

TO YOUR TEACHING
What are the goals of education, real and ideal? What does it mean to be an educated person? What makes a teacher effective? Describe the most effective teacher you ever had. How do you learn best? What do you hope to gain from this course? Your answers will provide the basis for developing a philosophy of teaching.

Before we consider what defines good teaching, let's examine a more basic question: Does teaching really matter? For a while, some researchers reported findings suggesting that wealth and social status, not teaching, were the major factors determining who learned in schools (e.g., Coleman, 1966). In fact, much of the early research on teaching was conducted by educational psychologists who refused to accept these claims that teachers were powerless in the face of poverty and societal problems (Wittrock, 1986).

How could you decide if teaching makes a difference? You could look to your own experience. Were there teachers who had an impact on your life? Describing teachers who made a difference for him, Harvard professor Robert Coles (1990) said:

> I mention these teachers in my life because, in fact, they continue to be a great big part of it still. Their voices are in my head and are part of my voice, I am sure. Their thoughts and values inform what I consider and call my own thoughts and values. Their example—the things they did, the style of their teaching, the strategies they employed—continue to inform the way I work. (p. 59)

For Robert Coles, the teachers he has had continue to affect his life. But one of the purposes of educational psychology in general and this text in particular is to go beyond individual experiences and testimonies, powerful as they are, to examine larger groups. Three studies speak to the power of teachers in the lives of students. The first followed 179 children from kindergarten through eighth grade. The second was a large-scale policy study of thousands of students and teachers in all 50 of the United States. The final study examined math achievement for students as they moved through 3rd, 4th, and 5th grades.

Teacher-Student Relationships

Bridgett Harme and Robert Pianta (2001) followed all the children in a small school district who entered kindergarten one year and continued in the school district through the 8th grade. The researchers concluded that the quality of the teacher-student relationship in kindergarten (defined in terms of level of conflict with the child, the child's dependency on the teacher, and the teacher's affection for the child) predicted a number of academic and behavioral outcomes through the 8th grade, particularly for students with high levels of behavior problems. Even when the gender, ethnicity, cognitive ability, and behavior ratings of the student were accounted for, the relationship with the teacher still predicted aspects of school success. The researchers concluded that "the association between the quality of early teacher-child relationships and later school performance can be both strong and persistent" (p. 636). Based on the results of this carefully conducted study, it appears that students with significant behavior problems in the early years are less likely to have problems later in school if their teachers are sensitive to their needs and provide frequent, consistent feedback. Read the *Stories of Learning: Tributes to Teaching* feature to put a face on the power of positive teacher-student relationships.

CONNECT & EXTEND

TO THE RESEARCH
For another perspective on teacher quality and teacher preparation, see Borko et al. (2000). Teacher education does matter: A situative view of learning to teach secondary mathematics. *Educational Psychologist, 35,* 193–206.

Teacher Preparation and Quality

Using data from a 50-state survey of policies, state case study analyses, the 1993–94 Schools and Staffing Surveys, and the National Assessment of Educational Progress (NAEP), Linda Darling-Hammond (2000) examined the ways in which teacher qualifications are related to student achievement across states. Her findings indicated that the quality of teachers—as measured by whether the teachers were fully certified and had a major in their teaching field—was related to student performance. In fact, measures of teacher preparation and certification were by far the strongest predictors of

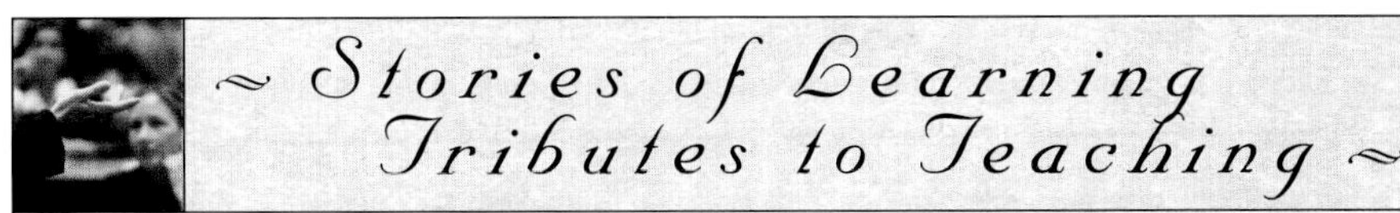

Maggie pulled her four-year-old son's hand a little harder as she hurried him up the sidewalk. A black pickup truck had slowed alongside them.

"Who's that, Mommy?"

"Let's keep walking," Maggie said. Not recognizing the truck, she picked up the pace.

Just then her son tripped on a stray branch and pulled on Maggie to wait. As she stopped, the dark glass of the passenger window rolled down and a young man with sunglasses leaned over to get a better look at the sidewalk couple.

"Mrs. Jensen, is that you?" Maggie looked up, responding with caution to the distantly familiar voice. She scooped up her son and took a cautious step back from the street.

The driver stopped the truck, put it in park, and excitedly ran around to meet her. Taking off his sunglasses so Maggie could see him better, he said with a touch of disappointment, "You don't remember me, do you?"

Apprehension turned to delight as Maggie finally recognized her former student. "Of course I do, **Jay.** You're a hard one to forget."

"I never forgot you, Mrs. Jensen. You're the only one who gave me a chance."

Looking at him she could still see the twelve year old who fought the system. As the big, black truck rolled away, Maggie smiled as she as read his business card, "Jay Getz, Architect."

SOURCE: From *Apples & Chalkdust* by Vicki Carauna. Published by Honor Books. Copyright © 1998 by Vicki Carauna. Adapted with permission of Honor Books, an imprint of Cook Communications Ministries.

student achievement in reading and mathematics, both before and after controlling for student poverty and English language proficiency. For example, look at Table 1.1. All the correlations in the first row of this table are positive and significant. This means that the higher the percentage of teachers with full certification and a major in their teaching field, the higher is their students' achievement in math and in reading. All but one of the correlations in the second row are negative and significant. This indicates that the higher the percentage of teachers who are teaching *outside* of their field, the lower is their students' achievement. So there is evidence that more qualified teachers make a difference in student learning. (Later in the chapter we will look closely at how to interpret these statistics.)

Finally, researchers studied how students are affected by having several effective or ineffective teachers in a row (Sanders & Rivers, 1996). They looked at 5th graders in two large metropolitan school systems in Tennessee. Students who had highly

Table 1.1 Correlations between Teacher Quality Variables and Student Achievement on the National Assessment of Educational Progress (controlling for student poverty).

	Grade 4 Math, 1992	Grade 4 Math, 1996	Grade 8 Math, 1996	Grade 4 Reading, 1992	Grade 4 Reading, 1994
Percent of teachers well-qualified (with full certification and a major in their field)	.71**	.61**	.67**	.80**	.75**
Percent of teachers out of field (with less than a minor in the field they teach)	–.48*	–.44*	–.42*	–.56*	–.33

* $p < .05$
** $p < .01$

SOURCE: From "Teacher Quality and Student Achievement: A Review of State Policy Evidence," by L. Darling-Hammond, 2000, *Educational Policy Analysis Archives, 8,* pp. 1–48. http://epaa.asu.edu/epaa/v8n1/. Copyright © Educational Policy Analysis Archives. Adapted with permission of the EPAA.

effective teachers for 3rd, 4th, and 5th grades scored an average of 83rd percentile on a standardized mathematics achievement test in one district and 96th percentile in the other (99th percentile is the highest possible score). In contrast, students who had the least effective teachers three years in a row averaged 29th percentile in math achievement in one district and 44th percentile in the other—a difference of over 50 percentile points in both cases! Students with average teachers or with a mixture of low, average, and high effectiveness teachers for the three years had math scores between these extremes. Sanders and Rivers concluded that the best teachers encouraged good to excellent gains in achievement for all students, but lower achieving students were the first to benefit from good teaching. The effects of teaching were cumulative and residual—that is, better teaching in a later grade could make up *in part* for less effective teaching in earlier grades, but could not erase all the deficits.

Check Yourself What evidence is there that teachers make a difference?

Well-qualified teachers who establish positive relationships with their students appear to be a powerful force in those students' lives. Students who have problems seem to benefit the most from good teaching—so what is good teaching?

What Is Good Teaching?

What Would You Say? It is your first interview for a teaching position. The principal takes out a pad of paper, a pen, looks intently into your eyes and says, "Tell me what you admired about your favorite teacher. What makes a good teacher?" What will you say?

CONNECT & EXTEND

TO **PRAXIS**™
TEACHER PROFESSIONALISM
(IV, A2)
Begin your own development by reading educational publications. One widely read periodical is *Education Week*. You can access it online at www.edweek.com.

There are hundreds of answers to this question. It has been examined by educators, psychologists, philosophers, novelists, journalists, mathematicians, scientists, historians, policymakers, and parents, to name only a few groups. And good teaching is not confined to classrooms—it occurs in homes and hospitals, museums and sales meetings, therapists' offices and summer camps. In this book, we are primarily concerned with teaching in classrooms, but much of what you will learn applies to other settings as well.

Inside Four Classrooms

To begin our examination of good teaching, let's step inside the classrooms of several outstanding teachers. All the situations that follow are real. The first two teachers worked with my student teachers in local elementary schools. I have chosen them because one of my former colleagues at Rutgers, Carol Weinstein, has written about them in her book on classroom management (Weinstein & Mignano, 2003). The next two are secondary school teachers who have been studied by other educational psychologists.

A Bilingual 1st Grade. There are 25 students in Viviana's class. Most have recently emigrated from the Dominican Republic; the rest come from Nicaragua, Mexico, Puerto Rico, and Honduras. Even though the children speak little or no English when they begin school, by the time they leave in June, Viviana has helped them master the normal 1st-grade curriculum for their district. She accomplishes this by teaching in Spanish early in the year to aid understanding, then gradually introducing English as the students are ready. Viviana does not want her students segregated or labeled as disadvantaged. She encourages them to take pride in their Spanish-speaking heritage while using every available opportunity to support their developing English proficiency.

Viviana's expectations for her students are high, and she makes sure the students have the resources they need. She provides materials—pencils, scissors, crayons—so no child lacks the means to learn. And she supplies constant encouragement. "Viviana's commitment to her students is evident in her 1st-grade bilingual classroom. With an energy level that is rare, she motivates, prods, instructs, models, praises, and captivates her students. . . . The pace is brisk and Viviana clearly has a flair for the dramatic; she uses music, props, gestures, facial expressions, and shifts in voice tone to communicate the material" (Weinstein & Mignano, 2003, p. 14). To know more about her students each year, she visits their homes. For Viviana, teaching is a not just a job; it is a way of life.

A Suburban 5th Grade. Ken teaches 5th grade in a suburban elementary school in central New Jersey. Ken emphasizes "process writing." His students complete first drafts, discuss them with others in the class, revise, edit, and "publish" their work. The students also keep daily journals and often use these to share personal concerns with Ken. They tell him of problems at home, fights, and fears; he always takes the time to respond in writing. The study of science is also placed in the context of the real world. They learn about ocean ecosystems by using a software program called *A Field Trip to the Sea* (Sunburst, 1999). For social studies, the class plays two simulation games that focus on history. One is on coming of age in Native American cultures and the other is on the colonization of America.

CONNECT & EXTEND

TO OTHER CHAPTERS
Ken's process writing, student publishing, and journal writing are examples of a "whole language" approach, discussed in Chapter 12. Ken's "Bill of Rights" is an example of an innovative approach to setting class rules, discussed in Chapter 11.

Throughout the year Ken is very interested in the social and emotional development of his students—he wants them to learn about responsibility and fairness as well as science and social studies. This concern is evident in the way he develops his class rules at the beginning of the year. Rather than specifying dos and don'ts, Ken and his students devise a "Bill of Rights" for the class, describing the rights of the students. These rights cover most of the situations that might need a "rule."

Two Advanced Math Classes. Hilda Borko and Carol Livingston (1989) describe two expert secondary school mathematics teachers. In one lesson for her advanced mathematics class, Ellen had her students identify any three problems about ellipses from their text. She asked if there were any questions or uncertainties about these problems. Ellen answered student questions, worked two of the problems, and then used the three problems to derive all the concepts and equations the students needed to understand the material. Ellen's knowledge of both the subject and her students was so thorough that she could create the explanations and derive the formulas on the spot, no matter which problems the students chose.

Another teacher, Randy, worked with his students' confusion to construct a review lesson about strategies for doing integrals. When one student said that a particular section in the book seemed "haphazard," Randy led the class through a process of organizing the material. He asked the class for general statements about useful strategies for doing integrals. He clarified their suggestions, elaborated on some, and helped students improve others. He asked the students to tie their ideas to passages in the text. Even though he accepted all reasonable suggestions, he listed only the key strategies on the board. By the end of the period, the students had transformed the disorganized material from the book into an ordered and useful outline to guide their learning. They also had a better idea about how to read and understand difficult material.

What do you see in these classrooms? The teachers are committed to their students. They must deal with a wide range of student abilities and challenges: different languages, different home lives, different needs. These teachers must understand their subjects and their students' thinking so well that they can spontaneously create new examples and explanations when students are confused. They must make the most abstract concepts, such as integrals, real and understandable for their particular students. And then there is the challenge of new technologies and techniques. The teachers must use them appropriately to accomplish important goals, not just to entertain the students. The whole time that these experts are navigating through the academic material, they also are taking care of the emotional needs of their students, propping up sagging self-esteem and encouraging responsibility. If we followed these individuals from the first day of class, we would see that they carefully plan and teach the basic procedures for living and learning in their classes. They can efficiently correct and collect homework, regroup students, give directions, distribute materials, collect lunch money, and deal with disruptions—and do all of this while also making a mental note to check why one of their students is so tired.

Viviana, Ken, Ellen, and Randy are examples of expert teachers, the focus of much recent research in education and psychology. For another perspective on the question "What is good teaching?" let's examine this research on what expert teachers know.

CONNECT & EXTEND

TO THE RESEARCH

Another excellent teacher is described in the *Harvard Education Letter.*

Robert Moses, founder of the Algebra Project at the Martin Luther King School in Cambridge, Massachusetts, teaches students the concept of number and sign through a physical event: they go for a ride on a subway. Choosing one subway stop as a starting point, students relate inbound and outbound to positive and negative numbers. They translate their subway ride into mathematical language by considering both the number of stops and their direction. By giving students such experiences before introducing the formal language of algebra, Moses . . . has made math more enjoyable and accessible. (Ruopp & Driscoll, 1990, p. 5)

Expert Knowledge

Expert teachers have elaborate *systems of knowledge* for understanding problems in teaching. For example, when a beginning teacher is faced with students' wrong answers on math or history tests, all the wrong answers may seem about the same—wrong. But for an expert teacher, wrong answers are part of a rich system of knowledge that could include how to recognize several types of wrong answers, the misunderstanding or lack of information behind each kind of mistake, the best way to reteach and correct the misunderstanding, materials and activities that have worked in the past, and several ways to test whether the reteaching was successful (Floden & Klinzing, 1990; Leinhardt, 1988). Peterson and Comeaux (1989) argue that it is the quality of teachers' professional knowledge and their ability to be aware of their own thinking that make them expert. These teachers are **reflective** practitioners.

Expert teachers not only know the content of the subjects they teach, they also know how to relate this content to the world outside the classroom and how to keep students involved in learning.

What do expert teachers know that allows them to be so successful? Lee Shulman (1987) has studied this question, and he has identified seven areas of professional knowledge. Expert teachers know:

1. The academic subjects they teach.
2. General teaching strategies that apply in all subjects (such as the principles of classroom management, effective teaching, and evaluation that you will discover in this book).
3. The curriculum materials and programs appropriate for their subject and grade level.
4. Subject-specific knowledge for teaching: special ways of teaching certain students and particular concepts, such as the best ways to explain negative numbers to lower-ability students.
5. The characteristics and cultural backgrounds of learners.
6. The settings in which students learn—pairs, small groups, teams, classes, schools, and the community.
7. The goals and purposes of teaching.

This is quite a list. Obviously, one course cannot give you all the information you need to teach. In fact, a whole program of courses won't make you an expert. That takes time and experience. But studying educational psychology can add to your professional knowledge because at the heart of educational psychology is a concern with learning wherever it occurs.

No person can learn for another; students create their own knowledge and skills. The teacher's role is to orchestrate materials, tasks, environments, conversations, and explorations that encourage and support learning and the increasing independence of their students. To become such a teacher, you will need to know about your *students* (Part 1 of this book), *learning* (Part 2), *motivating* (Part 3), *teaching* (Part 4), and *assessing* (Part 5). How do you grow from beginning teacher to expert? Can you learn to be an expert teacher, or are really great teachers just born?

Expert teachers Experienced, effective teachers who have developed solutions for common classroom problems. Their knowledge of teaching process and content is extensive and well organized.

Reflective Thoughtful and inventive. Reflective teachers think back over situations to analyze what they did and why and to consider how they might improve learning for their students.

Point/Counterpoint

What Is Good Teaching?

Is good teaching science or art, teacher-centered lecture or student-centered discovery, the application of general theories or the invention of situation-specific practices? Is a good teacher a good explainer or a good questioner, a "sage on the stage" or a "guide by the side"? These debates have raged for years. In your other education classes you probably will encounter criticisms of the scientific, teacher-centered, theory-based, lecturing, sages. You will be encouraged to be artistic, inventive, student-centered, questioning guides. Is this the right path? Let's see what the arguments are.

Point

Teaching is a theory-based science.

Psychologists have spent decades studying how children think and feel, how learning occurs, what influences motivation, and how teaching affects learning. These general and abstract conceptions apply to a wide range of situations—why should teachers have to reinvent all this knowledge? In Chapter 12 you will see one set of teacher characteristics and behaviors that are related to student learning: knowledge, clarity, enthusiasm, and direct or active teaching (Shuell, 1996). An effective teacher reviews, explains, checks for understanding, and reteaches if necessary, always keeping the level or difficulty and the pace just right to keep students learning. Advocates note that ignoring the direct teaching of skills can be detrimental for some children. For example, Harris and Graham (1996) describe the experiences of their daughter Leah in a whole-language/progressive education school, where the teachers successfully developed their daughter's creativity, thinking, and understanding.

> *Skills, on the other hand, have been a problem for our daughter and for other children. At the end of kindergarten, when she had not made much progress in reading, her teacher said she believed Leah had a perceptual problem or a learning disability. Leah began asking what was wrong with her, because other kids were reading and she wasn't. Finally, an assessment was done. (p. 26)*

The testing indicated no learning disability, strong comprehension abilities, and poor word attack skills. Luckily, Leah's parents knew how to teach word attack skills. Direct teaching of these skills helped Leah become an avid and able reader in about six weeks.

Counterpoint

Teaching is an art—a creative reflective process.

Other educators believe that the mark of an excellent teacher is not the ability to apply techniques but the artistry of being reflective—thoughtful and inventive—about teaching (Schon, 1983). Educators who adopt this view tend to be more concerned with how teachers plan, solve problems, create instruction, and make decisions than they are with the specific techniques teachers apply (Borko, 1989; Peterson & Comeaux, 1989). They believe teaching "is specific with respect to task, time, place, participants, and content, and that different subjects vary in those specifics" (Leinhardt, 2001, p. 334). Thus teaching is so complex that it must be invented anew with every new subject and class. And good teachers are not "sages on the stage," spouting knowledge, but rather "guides by their students' sides." Critics of direct, teacher-centered teaching claim that breaking material into small segments, presenting each segment clearly, and reinforcing or correcting, is *transmitting* accurate understandings from teacher to student. The student is viewed as an "empty vessel" waiting to be filled with knowledge, rather than an active constructor of knowledge.

Beware of either/or choices.

Most people agree that teachers must be both technically competent and inventive. They must be able to use a range of strategies, and they must also be able to invent new strategies. They must have some simple routines for managing classes, but they must also be willing and able to break from the routine when the situation calls for change. And teachers need both general theories and situation-specific insights. They need "understandings of students in general—patterns common to particular ages, culture, social class, geography, and gender; patterns in typical student conceptions of the subject matter" (Ball, 1997, p. 773) and they also need to know their own students. "Face to face with actual children who are particular ages and gender, culture and class, teachers must see individuals against a backdrop of sociological and psychological generalizations about groups" (p. 773). The theories you encounter in this text should be used as cognitive tools to help you examine, inspect, and interpret the claims you will hear and read throughout your career (Leinhardt, 2001).

Personally, I hope you all become teachers who both are "sages" about your subject and "on your students' sides" wherever you stand.

What do you think? Vote online at **www.ablongman.com/woolfolk**

Is good teaching an art or a science? See the *Point/Counterpoint* for a closer look at this last question.

CONNECT & EXTEND

TO OTHER CHAPTERS
Teachers' knowledge of their own thinking is an example of metacognitive knowledge, discussed in Chapter 7.

You may be thinking that all this talk about expert teachers and expert knowledge is a bit idealistic and abstract. Right now, you may have other, more down-to-earth, concerns about becoming a teacher. You are not alone!

Beginning Teachers

STOP THINK WRITE Imagine walking into your first day of teaching. List the concerns, fears, and worries you have. What assets do you bring to the job?

Beginning teachers everywhere share many concerns. A review of studies conducted around the world found that beginning teachers regard maintaining classroom discipline, motivating students, accommodating differences among students, evaluating student work, and dealing with parents as the most serious challenges they face. Many teachers also experience what has been called "reality shock" when they take their first job and confront the "harsh and rude reality of everyday classroom life" (Veenman, 1984, p. 143). One source of shock may be that teachers really cannot ease into their responsibilities. On the first day of their first job, beginning teachers face the same tasks as teachers with years of experience. Student teaching, while a critical element, does not really prepare prospective teachers for starting off a school year with a new class. If you listed any of these concerns in the *Stop/Think/Write* box above, you shouldn't be troubled. They come with the job of being a beginning teacher (Borko & Putnam, 1996; Cooke & Pang, 1991; Veenman, 1984).

But even with these concerns, you don't have to wait for years to become a good teacher. I have worked with many students who are excellent, even during their practice teaching experiences. To read about a gifted first year teacher, Esme Codell, see the *Reaching Every Student* feature on the next page.

With experience, most teachers meet the challenges that seem difficult for beginners. They have more time to experiment with new methods or materials. Finally, as confidence grows, seasoned teachers can focus on the *students'* needs. At this advanced stage, teachers judge their success by the successes of their students (Feiman-Nemser, 1983; Fuller, 1969; Putnam & Borko, 1997). Or as Esme's mentor teacher

Teaching is one of the few professions in which a new teacher must assume all of the responsibilities of an experienced "pro" during the first week on the job. Veteran teachers can be an excellent source of information and support during these early weeks.

~ Reaching Every Student ~

Creativity in an Urban School

The following is taken from *Educating Esme: Diary of a Teacher's First Year* by Esme Codell. Here is one day in the life of this gifted 5th grade teacher:

November 2: We are studying inventors. While the kids were at gym I dressed up in an outfit with all sorts of weird stuff sticking out: rubber bands, gum, chocolate chip cookies, lightbulbs, with a tag attached to each item saying who invented it. I wore roller skates, too. The kids loved it when I came rolling down the hall to pick them up! Then we all made a bulletin board of lightbulb cutouts with illustrations of famous discoveries in the middle of each bulb. The board has the heading "Bright Ideas." (Codell, 2001, p. 51)

At the end of the school year, Ms. Codell remembered: I feel like we did a lot of interesting things this year. Some of my favorites: When learning about electricity, we made light-up quiz games. When learning about light, we put on shadow-puppet shows. When learning about medieval history, we built an accurate castle, then decorated it with colored marshmallows and put it in our fairy tale book display. When we learned about air, we had a bubble festival. When learning about Asia, we made sushi. We videotaped commercials to promote our favorite books. We had a book character masquerade party. . . . The kids had checking accounts in a classroom economy. We had a cereal box supermarket, and the kids learned to make change. . . . My kids write the best descriptive compositions. They have international pen pals. They illustrated poetry anthologies. They read and wrote treasure maps. They know all the dances from the 60s. (Codell, 2001, pp. 177–178)

once told her, "The difference between a beginning teacher and an experienced one is that the beginning teacher asks, 'How am I doing?' and the experienced teacher asks, 'How are the children doing?' " (Codell, 2001, p. 191).

Check Yourself What do expert teachers know?

What are the concerns of beginning teachers?

I have talked about good teachers because that is what many of you are planning to become. But all good teaching begins with an understanding of *students* and *learning*—and an understanding of educational psychology.

The Role of Educational Psychology

For as long as educational psychology has existed—about 90 years—there have been debates about what it really is. Some people believe educational psychology is simply knowledge gained from psychology and applied to the activities of the classroom. Others believe it involves applying the methods of psychology to study classroom and school life (Clifford, 1984; Grinder, 1981).

The view generally accepted today is that **educational psychology** is a distinct discipline with its own theories, research methods, problems, and techniques. "Educational psychology is distinct from other branches of psychology because it has the understanding and improvement of education as its primary goal" (Wittrock, 1992, p. 138). Both in the past and today, educational psychologists study learning and teaching and, at the same time, strive to improve educational practice (Pintrich, 2000). But are the findings of educational psychologists really that helpful for teachers? After all, most teaching is just common sense, isn't it? Let's take a few minutes to examine these questions.

CONNECT & EXTEND

TO THE RESEARCH
The Spring 2001 issue of *Educational Psychologist, 36* (2), is devoted to "Educational Psychology: Yesterday, Today, and Tomorrow" with articles about self-regulated learning, classroom management, teacher expectancy effects, program development, and conceptions of learning.

Educational psychology The discipline concerned with teaching and learning processes; applies the methods and theories of psychology and has its own as well.

These students are participating in true "hands-on" cooperative learning. Will their knowledge of science improve using this approach? Are there better ways to learn in biology? Educational research should shed light on questions like these.

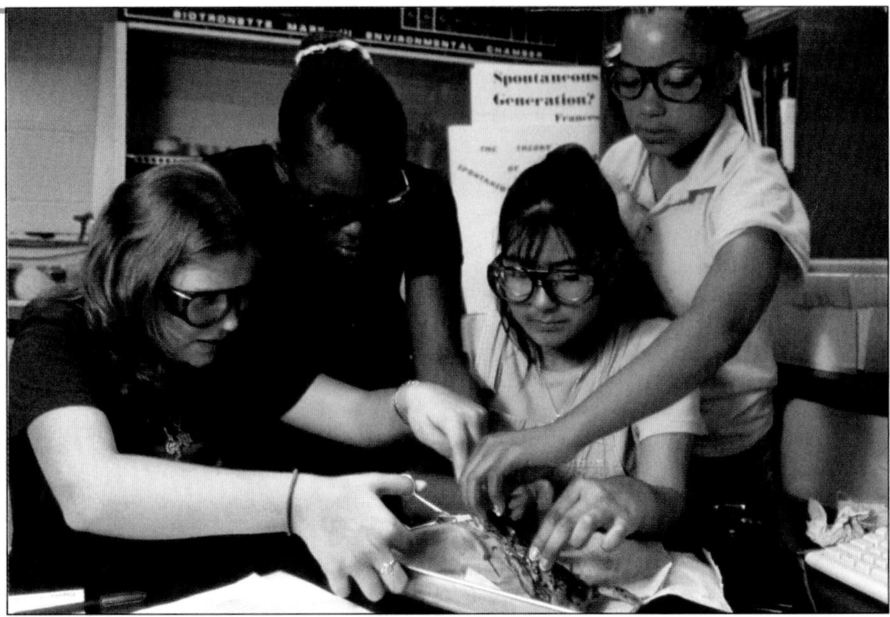

Is It Just Common Sense?

In many cases, the principles set forth by educational psychologists—after spending much thought, time, and money—sound pathetically obvious. People are tempted to say, and usually do say, "Everyone knows that!" Consider these examples:

Taking Turns. What method should a teacher use in selecting students to participate in a primary grade reading class?

Common Sense Answer. Teachers should call on students randomly so that everyone will have to follow the lesson carefully. If a teacher were to use the same order every time, the students would know when their turn was coming up.

Answer Based on Research. Years ago, research by Ogden, Brophy, and Evertson (1977) found that the answer to this question is not so simple. In 1st-grade reading classes, for example, going around the circle in order and giving each child a chance to read led to better overall achievement than calling on students randomly. The critical factor in going around the circle may be that each child gets a chance to participate. Without some system for calling on everyone, many students can be overlooked or skipped. Research suggests there are better alternatives for teaching reading than going around the circle, but teachers should make sure that everyone has the chance for practice and feedback whatever approach is used (Tierney, Readence, & Dishner, 1990). See Chapter 12 for more on teaching reading.

Helping Students. When should teachers provide help for lower achieving students as they do class work?

Common Sense Answer. Teachers should offer help often. After all, these lower achieving students may not know when they need help or may be too embarrassed to ask for help.

Answer Based on Research. Sandra Graham (1996) found that when teachers provide help before students ask, the students and others watching are more likely to conclude that the helped student does not have the ability to succeed. The student is more likely to attribute failures to lack of ability instead of lack of effort. See Chapter 10 for more information on the unintended messages of well-intended teacher actions.

Skipping Grades. Should a school encourage exceptionally bright students to skip grades or to enter college early?

Common Sense Answer. No! Very intelligent students who are a year or two younger than their classmates are likely to be social misfits. They are neither physically nor emotionally ready for dealing with older students and would be miserable in the social situations that are so important in school, especially in the later grades.

Answer Based on Research. Maybe. According to Samuel Kirk and his colleagues (1993), "From early admissions to school to early admissions to college, research studies invariably report that children who have been accelerated have adjusted as well as or better than have children of similar ability who have not been accelerated" (p. 105). Whether acceleration is the best solution for a student depends on many specific individual characteristics, including the intelligence and maturity of the student, and on the other available options. For some students, moving quickly through the material and working in advanced courses with older students is a very good idea. See Chapter 4 for more on adapting teaching to students' abilities.

Obvious Answers? Lily Wong (1987) demonstrated that just seeing research results in writing can make them seem obvious. She selected 12 findings from research on teaching; one of them was the "taking turns" result noted above. She presented six of the findings in their correct form and six in *exactly the opposite form* to college students and to experienced teachers. Both the college students and teachers rated about half of the *wrong* findings as "obviously" correct. In a follow-up study, another group of subjects was shown the 12 findings and their opposites and was asked to pick which ones were correct. For 8 of the 12 findings, the subjects chose the wrong result more often than the right one.

You may have thought that educational psychologists spend their time discovering the obvious. The preceding examples point out the danger of this kind of thinking. When a principle is stated in simple terms, it can sound simplistic. A similar phenomenon takes place when we see a gifted dancer or athlete perform; the well-trained performer makes it look easy. But we see only the results of the training, not all the work that went into mastering the individual movements. And bear in mind that any research finding—or its opposite—may sound like common sense. The issue is not what *sounds* sensible, but what is demonstrated when the principle is put to the test (Gage, 1991).

CONNECT & EXTEND

TO THE RESEARCH
Read and discuss the article by Gage, N. L. (1991). The obviousness of social and educational research results. *Educational Researcher, 20*(1), 10–16. *Focus Questions:* What makes findings in educational research seem "obvious"? What is the danger in this kind of thinking?

Using Research to Understand and Improve Teaching

Quickly, list all the different research methods you can name.

Conducting research to test possible relationships is one of two major tasks of educational psychology. The other is combining the results of various studies into theories that attempt to present a unified view of such things as teaching, learning, and development.

Descriptive Studies. Educational psychologists design and conduct many different kinds of research studies. Some of these are "descriptive," that is, their purpose is simply to describe events in a particular class or several classes. Reports of **descriptive studies** often include survey results, interview responses, samples of actual classroom dialogue, or audio and video records of the class activities.

One descriptive approach, classroom **ethnography**, is borrowed from anthropology. Ethnographic methods involve studying the naturally occurring events in the life of a group and trying to understand the meaning of these events to the people involved. For example, the descriptions of expert high school mathematics teachers in the opening pages of this chapter were taken from an ethnographic study by Borko and Livingston (1989). The researchers made detailed observations in the teachers' classes and analyzed these observations, along with audio recordings and information from interviews with the teachers, in order to describe differences between novice and expert teachers.

In some descriptive studies the researcher uses **participant observation** and works within the class or school to understand the actions from the perspectives of the teacher and the students. Researchers also may employ **case studies.** A case study investigates in depth how a teacher plans courses, for example, or how a student tries to learn specific material.

Correlational Studies. Often the results of descriptive studies include reports of correlations. We will take a minute to examine this concept, because you need a knowledge of correlations to fully understand Table 1.1 and you will encounter many other correlations in the coming chapters. A correlation is a number that indicates both the strength and the direction of a relationship between two events or measurements. **Correlations** range from 1.00 to –1.00. The closer the correlation is to either 1.00 or –1.00, the stronger the relationship. For example, the correlation between height and weight is about .70 (a strong relationship); the correlation between height and number of languages spoken is about .00 (no relationship at all).

The sign of the correlation tells the direction of the relationship. A **positive correlation** indicates that the two factors increase or decrease together. As one gets larger, so does the other. Height and weight are positively correlated because greater height tends to be associated with greater weight. As you saw in Table 1.1, the correlation between the percent of teachers with full teaching credentials and students' math achievement is positive (as the percent of fully credentialed teachers increases, student math achievement increases as well). A **negative correlation** means that increases in one factor are related to decreases in the other. Table 1.1 indicated that as the number of teachers without either a major or a minor in math increases, student math achievement decreases.

It is important to note that correlations do not prove cause and effect (see Figure 1.1). Height and weight are correlated—taller people tend to weigh more than shorter people. But gaining weight obviously does not cause you to grow taller. Knowing a person's weight simply allows you to make a general prediction about that person's height. Educational psychologists identify correlations so they can make predictions about important events in the classroom.

Experimental Studies. A second type of research—**experimentation**—allows educational psychologists to go beyond predictions and actually study cause and effect. Instead of just observing and describing an existing situation, the investigators introduce changes and note the results. First, a number of comparable groups of subjects are created. In psychological research, the term **subjects** generally refers to the people being studied—such as teachers or 8th graders—not to subjects such as math or science. One common way to make sure that groups of subjects are essentially the same is to assign each subject to a group using a random procedure. **Random** means each subject has an equal chance of being in any group.

In one or more of these groups, the experimenters change some aspect of the situation to see if this change or "treatment" has an expected effect. The results in each group are then compared. Usually statistical tests are conducted. When differences are described as **statistically significant,** it means that they probably did not happen

CONNECT & EXTEND

TO REAL LIFE

Perfect positive (1.0) correlation: the radius of a circle and its circumference. Perfect negative (–1.0) correlation: the number of minutes of daylight and the number of minutes of dark each day. Less than perfect positive correlation: the cost of a car and the cost of insuring it. Less than perfect negative correlation: cost of a theater ticket and distance from the stage. Zero correlation: population of India and the winning percentage of the New York Yankees.

Descriptive studies Studies that collect detailed information about specific situations, often using observation, surveys, interviews, recordings, or a combination of these methods.

Ethnography A descriptive approach to research that focuses on life within a group and tries to understand the meaning of events to the people involved.

Participant observation A method for conducting descriptive research in which the researcher becomes a participant in the situation in order to better understand life in that group.

Case study Intensive study of one person or one situation.

Correlations Statistical descriptions of how closely two variables are related.

Positive correlation A relationship between two variables in which the two increase or decrease together. Example: calorie intake and weight gain.

Negative correlation A relationship between two variables in which a high value on one is associated with a low value on the other. Example: height and distance from top of head to the ceiling.

Experimentation Research method in which variables are manipulated and the effects recorded.

Subjects People or animals studied.

Random Without any definite pattern; following no rule.

Statistically significant Not likely to be a chance occurrence.

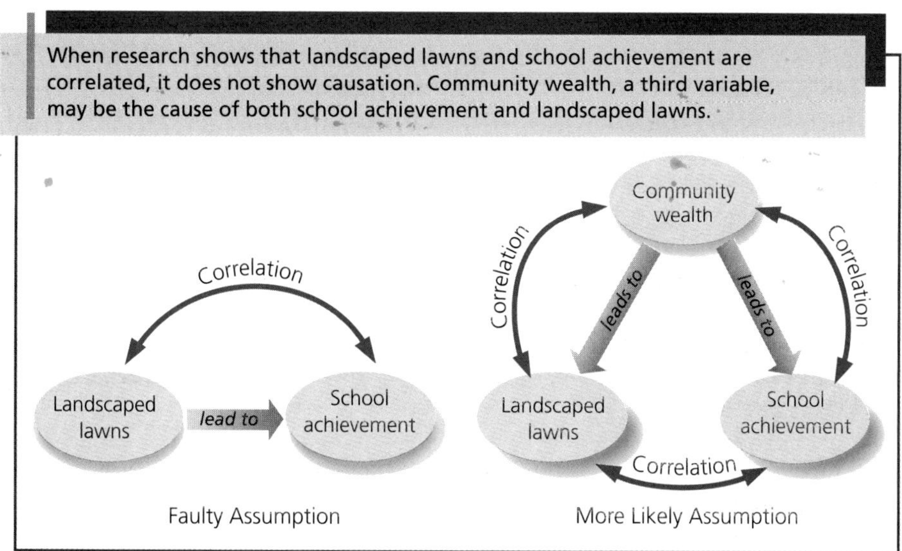

Figure 1.1 Correlations Do Not Show Causation

simply by chance. Look at Table 1.1 again. The $p < .05$ means that these results could happen by chance less than 5 times out of 100, and $p < .01$ means less than 1 time in 100. A number of the studies we will examine attempt to identify cause-and-effect relationships by asking questions such as this: If teachers ignore students who are out of their seats without permission and praise students who are working hard at their desks (cause), will students spend more time working at their desks (effect)?

In many cases, both descriptive and experimental research occur together. The study about "taking turns" by Ogden, Brophy, and Evertson (1977) described at the beginning of this section is a good example. In order to answer questions about the relationship between how students are selected to read in a primary-grade class and their achievement in reading, these investigators first observed students and teachers in a number of classrooms and then measured the reading achievement of the students. They found that having students read in a predictable order was associated, or correlated, with gains in reading scores. With a simple correlation such as this, however, the researchers could not be sure that the strategy was actually causing the effect. In the second part of the study, Ogden and her colleagues asked several teachers to call on each student in turn. They then compared reading achievement in these groups with achievement in groups where teachers used other strategies. This second part of the research was thus an experimental study—specifically, a *field experiment* because it took place in a real classroom setting and not a laboratory.

CONNECT & EXTEND

TO WHAT YOU KNOW

Are the following studies descriptive (D) or experimental (E)? 1. Researchers observe teachers of classes that have high achievement in order to determine how these teachers are alike. 2. Teachers give three groups of impulsive children different types of training to determine which type of training is most effective in reducing impulsivity. 3. Researchers administer IQ tests to a group of boys and girls to determine if there is a relationship between sex and verbal ability. 4. Teachers instruct two similar groups of math students by two different methods to determine which method leads to higher scores on a math achievement test.
Answers: 1. D 2. E 3. D 4. E

Single-Subject Experimental Designs. The goal of **single-subject experimental studies** is to determine the effects of a therapy or teaching method, or other intervention. One common approach is to observe the individual for a baseline period (A) and assess the behavior of interest; try an intervention (B) and note the results; then remove the intervention and go back to baseline conditions (A); and finally reinstate the intervention (B). This form of single-subject design is called an ABAB experiment. For example, a teacher might record how much students are out of their seats without permission during a week-long baseline (A), and then try ignoring those who are up, but praising those who are seated and recording how many are wandering out of their seats for the week (B). Next, the teacher returns to baseline conditions (A) and records results, then reinstates the praise and ignore strategy (B). Years ago, when this very intervention was tested, the praise and ignore strategy proved effective in increasing the time students spent in their seats (Madsen, Becker, Thomas, Koser, & Plager, 1968).

Single-subject experimental studies Systematic interventions to study effects with one person, often by applying and then withdrawing a treatment.

Microgenetic Studies. The goal of microgenetic research is to intensively study cognitive processes in the midst of change—as the change is actually happening. For example, researchers might analyze how children learn a particular strategy for adding two-digit numbers over the course of several weeks. The microgenetic approach has three basic characteristics: (a) researchers observe the entire period of the change—from when it starts to the time it is relatively stable; (b) many observations are made, often using videotape recordings, interviews, and transcriptions of the exact words of the individuals being studied; (c) the behavior that is observed is "put under a microscope," that is, examined moment by moment or trial by trial. The goal is to explain the underlying mechanisms of change—for example, what new knowledge or skills are developing to allow change to take place (Siegler & Crowley, 1991). This kind of research is expensive and time consuming, so often only one or a few children are studied.

The Role of Time in Research. Another distinction is useful in understanding research—a distinction based on time. Many things that psychologists want to study, such as cognitive development, happen over several months or years. Ideally, researchers would study the development by observing their subjects over many years as changes occur. These are called *longitudinal* studies. They are informative, but time consuming, expensive, and not always practical—keeping up with subjects over years as they grow up and move can be impossible. So much research is *cross-sectional,* focusing on groups of children at different ages. For example, to study how children's conceptions of "alive" change from ages 3 to 16, researchers can interview children of several different ages, rather than following the same children for 14 years.

Theories for Teaching. The major goal of educational psychology is understanding teaching and learning; research is a primary tool. Reaching this goal is a slow process. There are very few landmark studies that answer a question once and for all. Human beings are too complicated. Instead, research in educational psychology examines limited aspects of a situation—perhaps a few variables at a time or life in one or two classrooms. If enough studies are completed in a certain area and findings repeatedly point to the same conclusions, we eventually arrive at a **principle.** This is the term for an established relationship between two or more factors—between a certain teaching strategy, for example, and student achievement.

Another tool for building a better understanding of the teaching and learning processes is theory. The common sense notion of theory (as in "Oh well, it was only a theory") is "a guess or hunch." But the scientific meaning of theory is quite different. "A **theory** in science is an interrelated set of concepts that is used to explain a body of data and to make predictions about the results of future experiments" (Stanovich, 1992, p. 21). Given a number of established principles, educational psychologists have developed explanations for the relationships among many variables and even whole systems of relationships. There are theories to explain how language develops, how differences in intelligence occur, and, as noted earlier, how people learn.

Few theories explain and predict perfectly. In this book, you will see many examples of educational psychologists taking different theoretical positions and disagreeing on the overall explanations of such issues as learning and motivation. Because no one theory offers all the answers, it makes sense to consider what each has to offer.

So why, you may ask, is it necessary to deal with theories? Why not just stick to principles? The answer is that both are useful. Principles of classroom management, for example, will give you help with specific problems. A good *theory* of classroom management, on the other hand, will give you a new way of thinking about discipline problems; it will give you tools for creating solutions to many different problems and for predicting what might work in new situations. A major goal of this book is to provide you with the best and the most useful theories for teaching—those that have

CONNECT & EXTEND

TO THE RESEARCH

Killion, J. P., & Todnem, G. R. (1991). A process for personal theory building. *Educational Leadership, 48*(6), 14–16. *Focus Question:* Why do teachers need a personal theory for teaching?

Microgenetic studies Detailed observation and analysis of changes in a cognitive process as the process unfolds over a several day or week period of time.

Principle Established relationship between factors.

Theory Integrated statement of principles that attempts to explain a phenomenon and make predictions.

solid evidence behind them. Although you may prefer some theories over others, consider them all as ways of understanding the challenges teachers face.

Teachers as Researchers. Research also can be a way to improve teaching in one classroom or one school. The same kind of careful observation, intervention, data gathering, and analysis that occurs in large research projects can be applied in any classroom to answer questions such as "Which writing prompts seem to encourage the best descriptive writing in my class?" "When does Kenyon seem to have the greatest difficulty concentrating on academic tasks?" "Would assigning task roles in science groups lead to more equitable participation of girls and boys in the work?" This kind of problem-solving investigation is called **action research.** By focusing on a specific problem and making careful observations, teachers can learn a great deal about both their teaching and their students.

Check Yourself What is educational psychology?

What are correlations and experimental studies?

What are single subject and microgenetic studies?

Distinguish between principles and theories.

What is action research?

CONNECT & EXTEND

TO THE RESEARCH

The Summer 2000 issue of *Educational Psychologist, 35*(3), is devoted to "School Reform and Research in Educational Psychology" with articles about teaching science and mathematics, as well as articles in teacher preparation and professional development.

How This Book Can Help *You* Learn

Years ago, a wonderful principal told me that teachers are the *professional learners* and students are the *amateurs.* She encouraged the teachers in her school to be good guides and learning coaches so that their students would become expert learners too. I tell my class the first day of the semester that I hope they will "take educational psychology personally." If you can become a more expert learner by applying the knowledge from this text about study strategies, motivation, active learning, and understanding, then you will be a better teacher as well.

Structure and Content Supports Learning

Here is how you might use the different elements of the book to help you develop a base of knowledge for use as a student now and as a teacher later.

Getting Ready to Learn. The Chapter Outline gives you a snapshot of the organization of the material to come. Next you encounter a "What would you do?" scenario, asking you to project yourself into a classroom and decide how you would handle a problem situation. As you consider possible actions, you will be confronting issues from the upcoming chapter. So, as you read the chapter, you can check out and perhaps expand your ideas for handling the situation. Reading with a purpose in mind aids comprehension. I hope the "What would you do?" problem gives you good reasons and purposes for reading that tie knowledge in educational psychology to classroom practice.

Aids to Understanding. Throughout the chapters, you will find other aids to understanding and application. Use them fully to get the most from this book. Notice the headings and subheadings as you read. These headings show the structure of the chapter, the main ideas, and the related ideas under each main idea. Many sections ask you to *Stop/Think/Write* about a question that prepares you to better understand the upcoming material. *Key terms* are highlighted in bold first time they are used and defined in the margins. There is a list of key terms and definitions at the end of each chapter along with key issues from each section of the chapter. When you finish reading, test yourself to see if you can briefly explain these terms in your own words, answer the issue question, and apply the information.

Action research Systematic observations or tests of methods conducted by teachers or schools to improve teaching and learning for their students.

In this 9th edition I have added three new features to aid understanding. The first, *Stories of Learning: Tributes to Teaching,* as you have already seen, shows the power of teaching through the eyes of real students—some famous, some not. The second, *Reaching Every Student,* describes strategies for teaching diverse students in today's classrooms. Finally, after each main section of the chapter are *Check Yourself* questioins. As you will learn in this book, frequent reviews improve learning.

Applying Knowledge. If the ideas in this book are to be valuable, they need to be used to think about and act on problems of teaching and learning—both your own and those of your students. That emphasis is clear at the beginning of each chapter when I ask you to consider, "*What would you do?*" Throughout every chapter after this one are *Guidelines,* principles that can be applied in teaching. Each principle includes a few examples. These examples are intended to encourage your thinking about applications. One set of Guidelines focuses on *Families as Partners* in teaching—a very important consideration today. Every chapter also contains a *Point/Counterpoint* debate about a critical issue in educational psychology. You will see that educators do not always agree about the meaning of research findings or how those findings should be applied. These critical issues are tied to possible *Job Interview Questions* that you might encounter. I have polled principals and teachers all over the country to identify these issues and questions. At the end of every chapter after this one is a section called *Becoming a Professional* that gives you guidance for:

- Developing a personal study guide for professional **Licensure Tests** such as the PRAXIS™ series you may be required to take.
- Organizing a professional **Teaching Portfolio.**
- Developing a *Resource File.*

Finally, we return to the "*What would you do?*" situation to see what several experienced teachers around the country would do. Compare your ideas with theirs and with the information in the chapter. Do you agree? What would you add?

CONNECT & EXTEND

TO PRAXIS™
TEACHER PROFESSIONALISM (IV, A1)

Growth as a professional relies on becoming a member of a community of practice, and the national organizations listed here have hundreds of affiliations and chapters across the country that have regular conferences, conventions, and meetings to advance instruction in their areas. Take a look at their websites to get a feel for their approaches to issues related to professionalism.

- National Council of Teachers of English (www.ncte.org)
- International Reading Association (www.reading.org)
- National Science Teachers Association (www.nsta.org)
- National Council for the Social Studies (www.ncss.org)
- National Council of Teachers of Mathematics (www.nctm.org)

Using Web Resources to Enhance Professional Development

In this 9th edition of *Educational Psychology,* I have added a new feature to each chapter, *Enhancing Your Expertise with Technology.* This feature will focus on one or two topics related to the chapter and alert you to Web resources that can enrich your knowledge of those topics. The physical limitations of a book restrict the amount of space that a writer can devote to any feature, but the World Wide Web has no similar limitations. I encourage you to use your favorite search engine (Google, Yahoo, Excite, etc.) and begin to assemble a collection of sites dedicated to your professional development. Here are three steps that you can take to make this a rewarding experience:

Organize. Create an educational psychology folder on your browser and within that folder create a sub-folder for each chapter of this textbook. You will find the resources in these folders invaluable when you are student teaching, participate in job interviews, and face a classroom of students in your first year.

Evaluate. Practically anyone, from an esteemed educator to a leader of a hate group, can create a Web site. As you locate Web resources, make the effort to determine whether the site has the quality to be in your bookmarks or list of favorites. For advice on this activity, download the ERIC Digest, *Guidelines for Evaluating Web Sites* (http://www.ed.gov/databases/ERIC_Digests/ed426440.html).

Share. Over the years I have observed that outstanding teachers develop their high levels of expertise, in part, by borrowing and sharing ideas and materials with each other. Follow those models and share high-quality Web resources with other students and professors.

Licensure Tests In many states, teachers are required to take standardized tests, such as the PRAXIS™ series designed by the Educational Testing Service, in order to be certified or licensed as a teacher.

Teaching Portfolio A depiction of you as a teacher, usually including a curriculum vitae, statement of teaching philosophy, examples of your teaching plans and activities, example assignments and tests, students' work, and even videos or CD excerpts of teaching.

Becoming a Good Beginning Teacher

Becoming an expert teacher takes time and experience, but you can start now by becoming a good beginner. You can develop a repertoire of effective principles and practices for your first years of teaching so that some activities quickly become automatic. You can also develop the habit of questioning and analyzing these accepted practices and your own teaching so you can solve new problems when they arise. You can learn to look behind the effective techniques identified in research to ask: Why did this approach work with these students? What else might be as good or better? The answers to these questions and your ability to analyze the situations are much more important than the specific techniques themselves. As you ask and answer questions, you will be refining your personal theories of teaching.

My goal in writing this book is to help you become an excellent beginning teacher, one who can both apply and improve many techniques. Even more important, I hope this book will cause you to think about students and teaching in new ways, so you will have the foundation for becoming an expert as you gain experience.

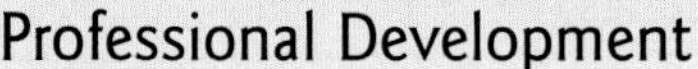

How can this book help you?

By connecting with professional development resources, including those targeted in every chapter of this text under *Enhancing Your Expertise with Technology,* you can continue to improve throughout your career. Here is your first entry.

> **CONNECT & EXTEND**
>
> TO **PRAXIS**™
> REFLECTIVE PRACTICE (IV, A3)
> For a concise description of the benefits and issues related to reflective practices, read *Reflective Practice and Professional Development* (www.ed.gov/databases/ERIC_Digests/ed449120.html).

Enhancing Your Expertise with Technology

Professional Development

Developing expertise as a teacher begins now for you and never ends. Throughout this text you will find sections like this that invite you to develop your expertise as a teacher by exploring the World Wide Web. The development of a good beginning teacher into an expert teacher is surely a learning process. It is also a process of enculturation in which the beginning teacher becomes a member of a community of practice. A key element of this enculturation is professional development. Once often a lonely, haphazard effort that received scant attention, educators and policymakers now realize that sustained, high-quality professional development is an essential component of programs to develop expert teachers.

The World Wide Web has become a force in the professional development of teachers. Many authoritative Web sites exist that provide instructional resources, information about educational research and theory, answers to questions about classroom problems, and opportunities for members of the community of educators to exchange ideas and viewpoints.

As you progress through this book, you will encounter sections that invite you to explore Web sites that can help you develop your expertise as a teacher. For a first exploration it seems appropriate to examine basic principles of professional development. *The Knowledge Loom . . . What Works in Teaching & Learning* (www.knowledgeloom.org) has a set of pages devoted to those principles. For each of the eight principles listed in the site, there are questions to help you consider the implications of a principle, examples of successful implementation of a principle, research summaries, and links for more detailed information.

Before you navigate to this site and begin your exploration, be reminded of several of the themes of this book. These themes include *teachers as:*

- problem solvers,
- members of a learning community,
- designers of instruction,
- reflective thinkers,
- assessors and evaluators of learning,
- learning strategists, and
- users of and sources for research.

When you examine and discuss the principles with other beginning teachers and your instructor, you will no doubt notice these themes—and other significant themes—woven through the questions, examples, and research about professional development you encounter at *The Knowledge Loom.* Revisit these Web pages as you progress through this book and your educational psychology course. As you become more enculturated into the community of educators and move from the periphery of that community toward more central participation, you might find that you have insights, questions, and views of your own that are marks of a more expert teacher.

Summary Table

Do Teachers Make a Difference? (pp. 2–4)

What evidence is there that teachers make a difference? Three studies speak to the power of teachers in the lives of students. The first found that the quality of the teacher-student relationship in kindergarten predicted several aspects of school success through the 8th grade. The second study of thousands of students and teachers in all 50 of the United States found that teacher quality was the strongest predictor of student achievement in mathematics and reading. The final study examined math achievement for students in two large school districts as they moved through 3rd, 4th, and 5th grades. Again, the quality of the teacher made a difference—students who had three high quality teachers in a row were way ahead of students who spent one or more years with less competent teachers.

What Is Good Teaching? (pp. 4–9)

What do expert teachers know? It takes time and experience to become an expert teacher. These teachers have a rich store of well-organized knowledge about the many specific situations of teaching. This includes knowledge about the subjects they teach, their students, general teaching strategies, subject-specific ways of teaching, settings for learning, curriculum materials, and the goals of education.

What are the concerns of beginning teachers? Learning to teach is a gradual process. The concerns and problems of teachers change as they progress. During the beginning years, attention tends to be focused on survival. Maintaining discipline, motivating students, evaluating students' work, and dealing with parents are universal concerns for beginning teachers. Even with these concerns, many beginning teachers bring creativity and energy to their teaching and improve every year. The more experienced teacher can move on to concerns about professional growth and effectiveness with a wide range of students.

Expert Teachers: Experienced, effective teachers who have developed solutions for common classroom problems. Their knowledge of teaching process and content is extensive and well organized.

Reflective: Thoughtful and inventive. Reflective teachers think back over situations to analyze what they did and why and to consider how they might improve learning for their students.

The Role of Educational Psychology (pp. 9–15)

What is educational psychology? The goals of educational psychology are to understand and to improve the teaching and learning processes. Educational psychologists develop knowledge and methods; they also use the knowledge and methods of psychology and other related disciplines to study learning and teaching in everyday situations.

Describe descriptive studies. Reports of descriptive studies often include survey results, interview responses, samples of actual classroom dialogue, or records of the class activities. Ethnographic methods involve studying the naturally occurring events in the life of a group and trying to understand the meaning of these events to the people involved. A case study investigates in depth how a teacher plans courses, for example, or how a student tries to learn specific material.

What are correlations and experimental studies? Correlations allow you to predict events that are likely to occur in the classroom. A correlation is a number that indicates both the strength and the direction of a relationship between two events or measurements. The closer the correlation is to either 1.00 or –1.00, the stronger the relationship. Experimental studies can indicate cause-and-effect relationships and should help teachers implement useful changes. Instead of just observing and describing an existing situation, the investigators introduce changes and note the results.

What are single-subject and microgenetic studies? In single-subject experimental designs, researchers examine the effects of treatments on one person, often by using a baseline/intervention/baseline/intervention or ABAB approach. Microgenetic studies take many detailed observations of subjects to track the progression of change from the very beginning until a process becomes stable.

Distinguish between principles and theories. A principle is an established relationship between two or more factors—between a certain teaching strategy, for example, and student achievement. A theory is an interrelated set of concepts that is used to explain a body of data and to make predictions about the results of future experiments. The principles from research offer a number of possible answers to specific problems, and the theories offer perspectives for analyzing almost any situation that may arise.

What is action research? When teachers or schools make systematic observations or test out methods to improve teaching and learning for their students, they are conducting action research.

Educational Psychology: The discipline concerned with teaching and learning processes; applies the methods and theories of psychology and has its own as well.

Descriptive Studies: Studies that collect detailed information about specific situations, often using observation, surveys, interviews, recordings, or a combination of these methods.

Ethnography: A descriptive approach to research that focuses on life within a group and tries to understand the meaning of events to the people involved.

Participant Observation: A method for conducting descriptive research in which the researcher becomes a participant in the situation in order to better understand life in that group.

Case Study: Intensive study of one person or one situation.

Correlations: Statistical descriptions of how closely two variables are related.

Positive Correlation: A relationship between two variables in which the two increase or decrease together. Example: calorie intake and weight gain.

Negative Correlation: A relationship between two variables in which a high value on one is associated with a low value on the other. Example: height and distance from top of head to the ceiling.

Experimentation: Research method in which variables are manipulated and the effects recorded.

Subjects: People or animals studied.

Random: Without any definite pattern; following no rule.

Statistically Significant: Not likely to be a chance occurrence.

Single-subject Experimental Studies: Systematic interventions to study effects with one person, often by applying and then withdrawing a treatment.

Microgenetic Studies: Detailed observation and analysis of changes in a cognitive process as the process unfolds over a several day or week period of time.

Principle: Established relationship between factors.

Theory: Integrated statement of principles that attempts to explain a phenomenon and make predictions.

Action Research: Systematic observations or tests of methods conducted by teachers or schools to improve teaching and learning for their students.

How This Book Can Help *You* Learn
(pp. 15–17)

How can this book help you? Becoming a good teacher means being a good learner. Much of the information in this text will help you become a more expert learner if you take the ideas personally and apply them to your own life. Take advantage of the book's features—the outlines, overviews, "What would you do?" and Check Yourself questions, organizational headings, Guidelines, key terms, Stories of Learning: Tributes to Teaching, Reaching Every Student, Becoming a Professional, and the Teachers' Casebook—to become an expert learner.

Licensure Tests: In many states, teachers are required to take standardized tests, such as the PRAXIS™ series designed by the Educational Testing Service, in order to be certified or licensed as a teacher.

Teaching Portfolio: A depiction of you as a teacher, usually including a curriculum vitae, statement of teaching philosophy, examples of your teaching plans and activities, example assignments and tests, students' work, and even videos or CD excerpts of teaching.

Enhancing *Your* Expertise with Technology: Professional Development
(p. 17)

The Knowledge Loom: What Works in Teaching & Learning
www.knowledgeloom.org

Other Useful Websites

"The Vent"—a discussion group for new teachers
www.proteacher.com.

Using Technology to Support Alternative Assessment and Electronic Portfolios **http://transition.alaska.edu/www/portfolios.html**

The contact information and website address for every state's Department of Education **http://www.ed.gov/Programs/bastmp/SEA.htm**

Professional Organizations, Magazines, and Journals

Phi Delta Kappan **http://www.pdkintl.org/kappan/kappan.htm**

Theory Into Practice **http://www.coe.ohio-state.edu/TIP**

Educational Psychologist **http://www.nassp.org**

National Board for Professional Teaching Standards
http://www.nbpts.org/

American Educational Research Association has several journals:
http://www.aera.net/

American Psychological Association has many journals:
http://www.apa.org

Becoming a Professional

In every chapter you will see a section called *Becoming a Professional*—a resource for you to use now and in the future. I hope this resource will help you master the knowledge and skill of educational psychology, prepare for the examinations that you probably will have to take to gain your teaching license, get that first teaching job, develop an excellent portfolio, and continue to add to your resources for teaching. For every chapter, *Becoming a Professional* will have the sections described on the next pages.

Passing the PRAXIS™

PRAXIS™/Licensure Test Requirements: *Possible topics and issues*

In this section I will describe connections between the information in the chapter and tests for teachers including PRAXIS™.

Chapter 1 reflects many of the professional standards created by the Interstate New Teacher Assessment and Support Consortium (INTASC). These standards form the basis of the PRAXIS II™ and state-created teacher licensure exams.

Excellent teachers are usually reflective practitioners. They critically examine every aspect of their teaching experiences, display inventiveness in their practices, and continually work to upgrade their knowledge and skills. As a junior member of the committee to recognize "excellence in teaching," you might find it useful for your work as a committee member and your own professional development to learn how nominees for the "excellence in teaching" award approach this professional trait.

PRAXIS II™ recognizes the role of reflective practice in the development of excellent teachers. Reflective practice includes contact with colleagues, membership in professional associations, and review of professional literature as resources, as well as the ability to understand the current views, significant debates, and research about effective teaching practices.

Tips for PRAXIS II™

- Reflective practice and its benefits for professionals: The ERIC Digest *Reflective Practice and Professional Development* (www.ed.gov/databases/ERIC_Digests/ed449120.html) will provide you with information that extends the textbook's presentation about the concepts, techniques, and benefits of reflective practice.
- Developing relationships with professionals: Until you become a teacher, it will be difficult to establish a working relationship with other practitioners. However, you might find these two sites beneficial:
  K–12 Professional Circle
  (http://nces.ed.gov/practitioners/teachers.asp)
  Survival Guide for New Teachers
  (http://www.ed.gov/pubs/survivalguide/)
- Keeping current with educational issues: *Education Week* (www.edweek.com) will keep you up to date about innovations in teaching, policy initiatives, and changes in public laws related to education. These issues are often highly complex. The use of critical thinking skills is essential when making judgments about the information you will encounter in this type of publication.

Related Topics

- Critical thinking skills (Chapter 9)
- Problem solving (Chapter 8)
- Expert knowledge (Chapters 7–8)

Standards and Licensure Appendix: *PRAXIS II™ and INTASC*

Refer to the Appendix at the end of the book for detailed correlations to PRAXIS II™ exam topics and INTASC Standards addressed in this text.

Insights about Job Interview Questions: *What Would You Say?*

We have surveyed principals and superintendents around the country to identify questions that they often ask in job interviews. Those questions related to the chapter just read are included in this section.

Your Teaching Portfolio: *Teaching Resources*

Here I give you ideas for possible additions to a teaching portfolio. Portfolios are increasingly being used during the job interview process and for professional development. If you choose someday to apply for National Board Certification, you will have to present a teaching portfolio.

Video**Workshop** Extra

If the Video Workshop package was included with your textbook, go to Chapter 1 of the Companion Website (www.ablongman.com/woolfolk) and click on the Video Workshop button. Follow the instructions for viewing *Video Clip 1: Teaching Respect.* Consider this information along with what you've read in Chapter 1 while answering the following questions:

1. In what ways does this teacher demonstrate the principles of "expert teaching"?
2. Think of a teacher you had who influenced you. What made this person a good teacher?

Use the CD-ROM included in the back of your textbook to launch the "Becoming a Professional" website. The website features advice on preparing for teacher certification exams, help with getting your first job, and resources to help you perform your job well from the first day forward.

Teachers' Casebook

What Would They Do?

Here is how some practicing teachers responded to the teaching situation presented at the beginning of this chapter about establishing a "Teaching Excellence Award."

Madya Ayala

High School Teacher of Preperatoria Eugenio Garza Lagüera, *Campus Garza Sada, Monterrey, N.L. Mexico*

The first thing that I would propose is to establish a set of selection criteria. We know that all teachers have strengths and weaknesses and what works the best for each of us. The set of evaluation criteria could change from time to time depending on international, national, and local needs and values. These factors would influence the interpretation of a teacher's psychological, pedagogical, and epistemological strengths as well.

Length of experience should not be a factor, only excellence in performance as a teacher. The main objective should be to make teachers aware of what is expected of them and to set the best examples.

Katie Churchill

Third Grade Teacher, *Oriole Parke Elementary School, Chicago, Illinois*

I would prepare for the meeting by researching how other schools have chosen recipients for similar awards in the past. I would recommend that we select different categories of "excellence" to decide who will be nominated for the awards. I would suggest that we choose recipients fairly, based on their teaching abilities. Finally, I would recommend that we have student input regarding which teachers should receive these awards.

Carey Perkson

Second Grade Teacher, *Brown School, Natick, Massachusetts*

I would have a discussion with the experienced teachers before our committee meeting to pinpoint what qualifications we are looking for in our candidates. Establishing a definition of "excellence in teaching" and constructing a list of recommendations should be a priority of the committee to ensure that all committee members are looking for the same qualifications. By constructing a list of key qualities and accomplishments for each nominee, we would be able to assess who would be the most qualified for the award.

Denise Ready

Second Grade Teacher, *Snug Harbor Community School, Quincy, Massachusetts*

My preparation for this meeting would be to come up with the following list of what I believe are indicators of excellent teaching. An excellent teacher:

- Loves children.
- Respects all children and parents under all circumstances.
- Sees potential in all children.
- Motivates students to reach their highest potential.
- Is a spontaneous and creative educator who is able to see a teachable moment and seize the opportunity to go with it.
- Has a sense of humor.

Aimee Fredette

Second Grade Teacher, *Fisher Elementary School, Walpole, Massachusetts*

There are many facets to being an effective teacher, the foremost being that the teacher will reach all children no matter what it takes. Effective teachers will modify curriculum and instruction to allow all ability levels to feel success and to foster a learning environment that builds the self-esteem of their students. This environment and confidence will encourage children to succeed at their own attempts to learn.

Effective teachers, regardless of philosophy, will excite and spark the children's interest. This will help the children to develop their own motivation for learning. I also feel that teachers should fully support the placement of all children into their classroom, regardless of abilities. To be effective, teachers will appropriately modify and implement assignments to meet those levels. A positive learning experience is created with a cooperative relationship among teachers, students, and home.

Go to the Companion Website (www.ablongman.com/woolfolk) for additional case studies including audio and video cases, and examples of student work.

CHAPTER

2

Cognitive Development and Language

Teachers' Casebook

What Would You Do?

The district curriculum guide calls for a unit on poetry, including lessons on *symbolism* in poems. You are concerned that many of your 5th-grade students may not be ready to understand this abstract concept. To test the waters, you ask a few students what a symbol is.

"It's sorta like a big metal thing that you bang together." Tracy waves her hands like a drum major.

"Yeah," Sean adds, "My sister plays one in the high school band."

You realize they are on the wrong track here, so you try again. "I was thinking of a different kind of symbol, like a ring as a symbol of marriage or a heart as a symbol of love, or . . . ."

You are met with blank stares.

Trevor ventures, "You mean like the Olympic torch?"

"And what does that symbolize, Trevor?" you ask.

"Like I said, a torch." Trevor wonders how you could be so dense.

Critical Thinking

What do these students' reactions tell you about children's thinking? How would you approach this unit? What more would you do to "listen" to your students' thinking so you could match your teaching to their level of thinking? How would you give your students concrete experience with symbolism? How will you decide if the students are not developmentally ready for this material?

Collaboration

With 3 or 4 other students in your educational psychology class, plan a lesson about symbolism in poetry that would be appropriate for students in this class. Pair up with another group and teach your lesson.

What is going on with Trevor? In this chapter, you will find out. We begin with a discussion of the general principles of human development and take a brief look at the human brain. Then we will examine the ideas of two of the most influential cognitive developmental theorists, Jean Piaget and Lev Vygotsky. Piaget's ideas have implications for teachers about what their students can learn and when the students are ready to learn it. We will consider important criticisms of his ideas as well. The work of Lev Vygotsky, a Russian psychologist, is becoming more and more influential. His theory highlights the important role teachers and parents play in the cognitive development of the child. Finally, we will explore language development and discuss the role of the school in developing and enriching language skills.

By the time you have completed this chapter, you should be able to answer these questions:

- *What are some general principles of human development?*
- *Is brain-based education effective?*
- *How does children's thinking differ at each of Piaget's four stages of development?*
- *What are the similarities and differences between Piaget's and Vygotsky's ideas about cognitive development?*
- *What are the implications of Piaget's and Vygotsky's theories for teaching students of different ages?*
- *How does language develop during the school years, and what happens if children are learning two languages at once?*

A Definition of Development

The term **development** in its most general psychological sense refers to certain changes that occur in human beings (or animals) between conception and death. The term is not applied to all changes, but rather to those that appear in orderly ways and remain for a reasonably long period of time. A temporary change caused by a brief illness, for example, is not considered a part of development. Psychologists also make a value judgment in determining which changes qualify as development. The changes—at least those that occur early in life—are generally assumed to be for the better and to result in behavior that is more adaptive, more organized, more effective, and more complex (Mussen, Conger, & Kagan, 1984).

Human development can be divided into a number of different aspects. **Physical development,** as you might guess, deals with changes in the body. **Personal development** is the term generally used for changes in an individual's personality. **Social development** refers to changes in the way an individual relates to others. And **cognitive development** refers to changes in thinking.

Many changes during development are simply matters of growth and maturation. **Maturation** refers to changes that occur naturally and spontaneously and that are, to a large extent, genetically programmed. Such changes emerge over time and are relatively unaffected by environment, except in cases of malnutrition or severe illness. Much of a person's physical development falls into this category. Other changes are brought about through learning, as individuals interact with their environment. Such changes make up a large part of a person's social development. But what about the development of thinking and personality? Most psychologists agree that in these areas, both maturation and interaction with the environment (or nature and nurture, as they are sometimes called) are important, but they disagree about the amount of emphasis to place on each.

General Principles of Development

Although there is disagreement about both what is involved in development and the way it takes place, there are a few general principles almost all theorists would support.

1. *People develop at different rates.* In your own classroom, you will have a whole range of examples of different developmental rates. Some students will be larger, better coordinated, or more mature in their thinking and social relationships. Others will be much slower to mature in these areas. Except in rare cases of very rapid or very slow development, such differences are normal and should be expected in any large group of students.
2. *Development is relatively orderly.* People develop abilities in a logical order. In infancy, they sit before they walk, babble before they talk, and see the world through their own eyes before they can begin to imagine how others see it. In school, they will master addition before algebra, Bambi before Shakespeare, and so on. Theorists may disagree on exactly what comes before what, but they all seem to find a relatively logical progression.
3. *Development takes place gradually.* Very rarely do changes appear overnight. A student who cannot manipulate a pencil or answer a hypothetical question may well develop this ability, but the change is likely to take time.

The Brain and Cognitive Development

What Would You Say? You are interviewing for a job in a great district—it is known for innovation. After a few minutes, the principal asks, "Do you know anything about this brain-based education? I've read a lot about that lately." How would you answer?

Development Orderly, adaptive changes we go through from conception to death.

Physical development Changes in body structure and function over time.

Personal development Changes in personality that take place as one grows.

Social development Changes over time in the ways we relate to others.

Cognitive development Gradual orderly changes by which mental processes become more complex and sophisticated.

Maturation Genetically programmed, naturally occurring changes over time.

If you have taken an introductory psychology class, you have read about the brain and nervous system. You probably remember, for example, that there are several different areas of the brain and that certain areas are involved in particular functions. For example, the feathery looking cerebellum coordinates and orchestrates balance and smooth, skilled movements—from the graceful gestures of the dancer to the everyday action of eating without stabbing yourself in the nose with a fork. The cerebellum may also play a role in higher cognitive functions such as learning. The hippocampus is critical in recalling new information and recent experiences, while the amygdala directs emotions. The thalamus is involved in our ability to learn new information, particularly if it is verbal. The reticular formation plays a role in attention and arousal, blocking some messages and sending others on to higher brain centers for processing, and the corpus callosum moves information from one side of the brain to the other (Wood & Wood, 1999; Meece 2002).

The outer 1/8-inch-thick covering of the cerebrum is the wrinkled-looking cerebral cortex—the largest area of the brain. The cerebral cortex accounts for about 85% of the brain's weight in adulthood and contains the greatest number of neurons—the tiny structures that store and transmit information. The cerebral cortex allows the greatest human accomplishments, such as complex problem solving and language. This crumpled sheet of neurons serves three major functions: receiving signals from sense organs (such as visual or auditory signals), controlling voluntary movement, and forming associations. In humans, this area of the brain is much larger than it is in lower animals. The cortex is the last part of the brain to develop, so it is believed to be more susceptible to environmental influences than other areas of the brain. (Berk, 2002; Meece, 2002). Let's see how this part of the brain develops.

CONNECT & EXTEND

TO THE RESEARCH
In the next decade we should see increasing research on the brain, development, learning, and teaching. For example, in 1998, there was a special issue of *Educational Psychology Review* on cognitive neuroscience and education. The authors of this volume emphasized that the brain is a complex collection of systems working together to construct understanding, detect patterns, create rules, and make sense of experience. These systems change over the lifetime as the individual matures and develops.

The Developing Brain: Cerebral Cortex. The cortex develops more slowly than other parts of the brain, and parts of the cortex mature at different rates. The part of the cortex that controls physical motor movement matures first, then the areas that control complex senses such as vision and hearing, and last, the frontal lobe that controls higher-order thinking processes. The temporal lobes of the cortex that play major roles in emotions and language do not develop fully until the high school years and maybe later.

Neuroscientists are just beginning to understand how brain development is related to aspects of adolescence such as risk-taking, decision making, and managing impulsive behaviors. Getting angry or wanting revenge when we are insulted are common human emotions. It is the job of the prefrontal cortex to control these impulses through reason, planning, or delay of gratification. But the impulse inhibiting capacities of the brain are not present at birth (as all new parents quickly discover). Research now indicates that it takes at least two decades for the biological processes of brain development to produce a fully functional prefrontal cortex (Weinberger, 2001). Thus middle and high school students still lack the brain development to balance impulse with reason and planning. Weinberger suggests that parents have to "loan" their children a prefrontal cortex, by helping them set rules and limits and make plans, until the child's own prefrontal cortex can take over. Schools and teachers also can play major roles in cognitive and emotional development if they provide appropriate environments for developing, but sometimes impulsive, brains (Meece, 2002).

This is a simple representation of the left side of the human brain, showing the cerebral cortex. The cortex is divided into different areas, or lobes, each having a variety of regions with different functions. A few of the major functions are indicated here.

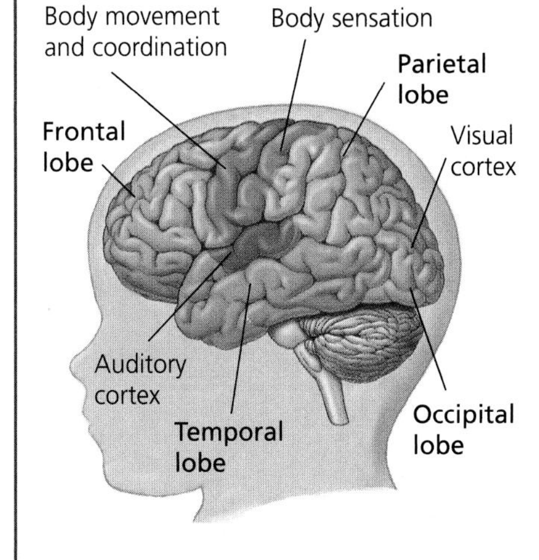

Figure 2.1 A View of the Cerebral Cortex

Specialization and Integration. Different areas of the cortex seem to have different functions, as shown in Figure 2.1. Even though different functions are found in different areas of the brain, these specialized functions are quite specific and elementary. To accomplish more complex functions such as speaking or reading, the various areas of the cortex must work together (Byrnes & Fox, 1998). For example, many areas of the cortex are necessary in processing language. To answer a question, you must first hear it. This involves the primary auditory cortex. Movements controlled by the motor cortex are required to speak your response. Broca's area (near the area that controls the lips, jaw, and tongue) has a role in setting up a grammatically correct way of expressing an idea, and Wernicke's area (near the auditory cortex) is necessary for connecting meaning with particular words. A person with a functioning Broca's area but a damaged Wernicke's area will say meaningless things in a grammatically correct structure. Damage limited to Broca's area, on the other hand, is associated with short, ungrammatical sentences, but the words are appropriate (Anderson, 1995a).

Another aspect of brain functioning that has implications for cognitive development is **lateralization,** or the specialization of the two hemispheres of the brain. We know that each half of the brain controls the opposite side of the body. Damage to the right side of the brain will affect movement of the left side of the body and vice versa. In addition, certain areas of the brain affect particular behaviors. For most of us, the left hemisphere of the brain is a major factor in language processing, and the right hemisphere handles much of the spatial-visual information and emotions (nonverbal information). For some left-handed people, the relationship may be reversed, but for most left-handers there is less hemispheric specialization altogether (Berk, 2002). In addition, females on average seem to show less hemispheric specialization than males (O'Boyle & Gill, 1998). Before lateralization, damage to one part of the cortex often can be overcome as other parts of the cortex take over the function of the damaged area. But after lateralization, the brain is less able to compensate.

These differences in performance by the brain's hemispheres, however, are more relative than absolute; one hemisphere is just more efficient than the other in performing certain functions. Nearly any task, particularly the complex skills and abilities that concern teachers, requires participation of many different areas of the brain in constant communication with each other. For example, the right side of the brain is better at figuring out the meaning of a story, but the left side is where grammar and syntax are understood, so both sides of the brain have to work together in reading. "The primary implication of these findings is that the practice of teaching to 'different sides of the brain' is not supported by the neuroscientific research" (Byrnes & Fox, 1998, p. 310). Thus, beware of educational approaches based on simplistic views of brain functioning—what Keith Stanovich (1998) has called "the left-brain–right-brain nonsense that has inundated education through workshops, inservices, and the trade publications" (p. 420). Remember, no mental activity is exclusively the work of single part of the brain—so there is no such thing as a "right-brained student" unless that individual has had the left hemisphere removed, a rare and radical treatment for some forms of epilepsy.

The Developing Brain: Neurons. About one month after conception, brain development starts. In the tiny tube that is the very beginning of the human brain, neuron cells (nerve cells that store and transfer information) emerge at the amazing rate of 50,000 to 100,000 per second for the next three months or so (McDevitt & Ormrod, 2002). These cells send out axons and dedrites—long arm- and branch-like fibers—to connect with other neuron cells and share information. Look at Figure 2.2; the dendrites on the left of the figure bring information in and the axon in the middle transmits information out through the axon terminals on the right of the figure. The neurons send messages to each other by releasing chemicals that jump across the tiny spaces, called **synapses,** between the dendrites of one neuron and the axons of other neurons.

Lateralization The specialization of the two hemispheres (sides) of the brain cortex.

Synapses The tiny space between neurons—chemical messages are sent across these gaps.

By the time we are born, we have all the neurons we will ever have, about 100 to 200 billion, and each neuron has about 2,500 synapses. However, the fibers that reach out from the neurons and the synapses between the fiber ends increase during the first

Each neuron (nerve cell) includes dendrites that bring in messages and an axon that sends out messages. This is a single neuron, but each neuron is in a network with many others.

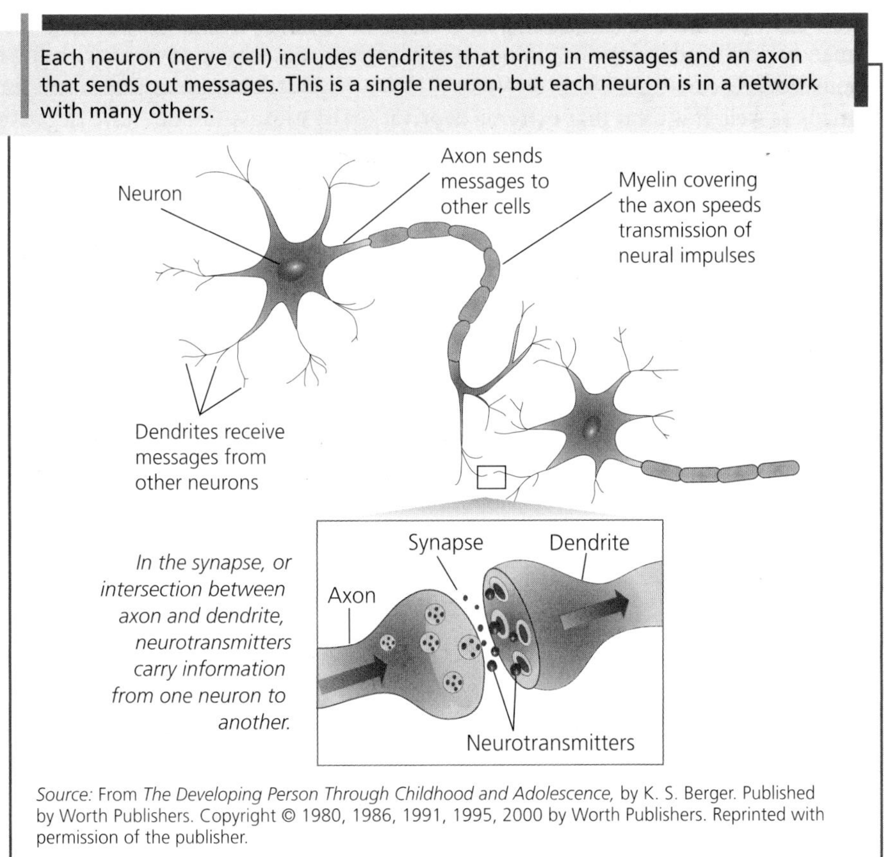

Neuron
Axon sends messages to other cells
Myelin covering the axon speeds transmission of neural impulses
Dendrites receive messages from other neurons
In the synapse, or intersection between axon and dendrite, neurotransmitters carry information from one neuron to another.
Synapse
Dendrite
Axon
Neurotransmitters

Source: From *The Developing Person Through Childhood and Adolescence*, by K. S. Berger. Published by Worth Publishers. Copyright © 1980, 1986, 1991, 1995, 2000 by Worth Publishers. Reprinted with permission of the publisher.

Figure 2.2 A Single Neuron

years of life, perhaps into adolescence. By age two to three, each neuron has around 15,000 synapses; children this age have many more synapses than they will have as adults (McDevitt & Ormrod, 2002). In fact, they are oversupplied with the neurons and synapses that they will need to adapt to their environments. However, only those that are used will survive, and unused neurons will be "pruned" (Diamond & Hobson, 1998).

Two kinds of overproduction and pruning processes take place. One is called *experience-expectant* because synapses are overproduced in certain parts of the brain during certain developmental periods, awaiting (expecting) stimulation. For example, during the first months of life, the brain expects visual and auditory stimulation. If a normal range of sights and sounds occurs, then the visual and auditory areas of the brain develop. But children who are born completely deaf receive no auditory stimulation and, as a result, the auditory processing area of their brains becomes devoted to processing visual information. Similarly, the visual processing area of the brain for children blind from birth becomes devoted to auditory processing (Siegler, 1998). Experience-expectant overproduction and pruning processes are responsible for general development in large areas of the brain.

The second kind of synaptic overproduction and pruning is called *experience-dependent.* Here synaptic connections are formed based on the individual's experiences. New synapses are formed in response to neural activity in very localized areas of the brain when the individual is not successful in processing information. Again, more synapses are produced than will be kept after "pruning." Experience-dependent processes are involved in individual learning.

So stimulation is important in both development (experience-expectant processes) and learning (experience-dependent processes). In fact, animal studies have shown that rats raised in stimulating environments (with toys, tasks for learning, and human handling) develop 25% more synapses than rats who are raised with little stimulation (Greenough, Black, & Wallace, 1987). Early stimulation is important for humans as well. It is clear that extreme deprivation of stimulation can have negative effects on brain development, but extra stimulation will not necessarily improve development for young children who are getting adequate or typical amounts of stimulation (Byrnes & Fox, 1998; Kolb & Whishaw, 1998). So spending money on expensive toys or baby education programs probably provides more stimulation than is necessary.

Even though the brain is developing rapidly during early childhood, learning continues over a lifetime. Early severe stimulus deprivation can have lasting effects, but because of brain plasticity or adaptability, some compensation can overcome deprivation or damage. Of course, many factors besides stimulus deprivation, such as the mother's intake of drugs (including alcohol and caffeine) during pregnancy, toxins in the infant's environment such as lead paint, or poor nutrition, can have direct and dramatic negative effects on brain development.

Another factor that influences thinking and learning is **myelination,** or the coating of neuron fibers with an insulating fatty covering. This process is something like coating bare electrical wires with rubber or plastic. Look at Figure 2.2 and notice the gray coating on the axon. This myelin coating makes message transmission faster and more efficient. Myelination happens quickly in the early years, but continues gradually into adolescence and is the reason the child's brain grows rapidly in size in the first few years of life.

Implications for Teachers. Much has been written lately about brain-based education. Many of these publications for parents and teachers have useful ideas, but beware of suggestions that oversimplify the complexities of the brain. As you can see in the *Point/Counterpoint,* the jury still is out on many of these programs.

Check Yourself What are the different kinds of development?

What are three principles of development?

What is lateralization and why is it important?

What part of the brain is associated with higher mental functions?

We turn next to examine a theory of cognitive development offered by a biologist turned psychologist, Jean Piaget.

Piaget's Theory of Cognitive Development

Can you be in Pittsburgh, Pennsylvania, and the United States all at the same time? Is this a difficult question for you? How long did it take you to answer?

During the past half-century, Swiss psychologist Jean Piaget devised a model describing how humans go about making sense of their world by gathering and organizing information (Piaget, 1954, 1963, 1970a, b). We will examine Piaget's ideas closely, because they provide an explanation of the development of thinking from infancy to adulthood.

According to Piaget (1954), certain ways of thinking that are quite simple for an adult, such as the question above, are not so simple for a child. For example, Piaget asked a 9-year-old:

Myelination The process by which neural fibers are coated with a fatty sheath called *myelin* that makes message transfer more efficient.

Point/Counterpoint

Brain-Based Education

Educators are hearing more and more about brain-based education, the importance of early stimulation for brain development, the "Mozart effect," and right- and left-brain activities. In fact, based on some research findings that listening to 10 minutes of Mozart can briefly improve spatial reasoning (Rauscher & Shaw, 1998; Steele, Bass, & Crook, 1999), a former governor of Georgia established a program to give a Mozart CD to every newborn (Meece, 2002). Are there clear educational implications from the neuroscience research on the brain?

Point

No, the implications are not clear.
John Bruer, president of the James S. McDonnell Foundation, has written articles that are critical of the brain-based education craze (Bruer, 1999). He notes that many so-called applications of brain research begin with solid science, but then move to unwarranted speculation. He suggests that for each claim, the educator should ask, "Where does the science end and the speculation begin?" For example, one claim that Bruer questions is the notion of right-brain, left-brain learning.

> *"Right brain versus left brain" is one of those popular ideas that will not die. Speculations about the educational significance of brain laterality have been circulating in the education literature for 30 years. Although repeatedly criticized and dismissed by psychologists and brain scientists, the speculation continues. David Sousa devotes a chapter of* How the Brain Learns *to explaining brain laterality and presents classroom strategies that teachers might use to ensure that both hemispheres are involved in learning. . . . Now let's consider the brain sciences and how or whether they offer support for some of the particular teaching strategies Sousa recommends. To involve the right hemisphere in learning, Sousa writes, teachers should encourage students to generate and use mental imagery. . . . What brain scientists currently know about spatial reasoning and mental imagery provides counterexamples to such simplistic claims as these. Such claims arise out of a folk theory about brain laterality, not a neuroscientific one. . . . different brain areas are specialized for different tasks, but that specialization occurs at a finer level of analysis than "using visual imagery." Using visual imagery may be a useful learning strategy, but if it is useful it is not because it involves an otherwise underutilized right hemisphere in learning. (Bruer, 1999, pp. 653–654)*

Counterpoint

Yes, teaching should be brain-based.
If you want to read about programs, strategies, and approaches that have been developed to be consistent with brain research, type "brain-based education" into an Internet search engine. For example, this is the case made on the Jensen Learning Corporation website (http://www.jlcbrain.com/truth.html):

> *Brain-based learning is not a panacea nor magic bullet to solve all of education's problems. Anyone who represents that to others is misleading them. It is not yet a program, a model or package for schools to follow. One critic of brain-based learning, said "It will at least be 25 years before the benefits of brain research reach the classroom." I'll cite just one example to show you why I disagree.*
>
> *The reading improvement product* FastForword, *was developed by two neuroscientists, Stanford's Dr. Michael Merzenich and Dr. Paula Tallal from Rutgers. That product is already in use today in thousands of classrooms around the country. Many students have been helped by it. It specifically uses discoveries in neural plasticity to change the brain's ability to read the printed word. . . .*
>
> *Schools should not be run based solely on the biology of the brain. However, to ignore what we do know about the brain would be equally irresponsible. Brain-based learning offers some direction for educators who want more purposeful, informed teaching.*

What do you think? Vote online at **www.ablongman.com/woolfolk**

> What is your nationality?—*I am Swiss.*—How come?—*Because I live in Switzerland.*—Are you also a Genevan?—*No, that's not possible . . . I'm already Swiss, I can't also be Genevan.* (Piaget, 1965/1995, p. 252)

Sometimes all you need to do to teach a new concept is to give students a few basic facts as background. At other times, however, all the facts in the world are useless. The students simply are not ready to learn the concept. Like the nine-year-old above, they may have trouble with classifying one concept (Geneva) as a subset of another (Switzerland). Or their concepts of time may be different from your own. They may think, for example, that they will some day catch up to a sibling in age, or they may confuse the past and the future. Let's examine why.

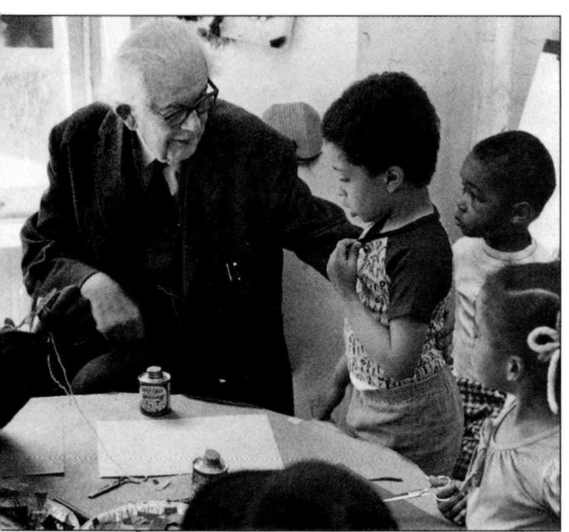

Jean Piaget was a Swiss psychologist whose insightful descriptions of children's thinking changed the way we understand cognitive development.

Influences on Development

As you can see, cognitive development is much more than the addition of new facts and ideas to an existing store of information. According to Piaget, our thinking processes change radically, though slowly, from birth to maturity because we constantly strive to make sense of the world. How do we do this? Piaget identified four factors—biological maturation, activity, social experiences, and equilibration—that interact to influence changes in thinking (Piaget, 1970a). Let's briefly examine the first three factors. We'll return to a discussion of equilibration in the next section.

One of the most important influences on the way we make sense of the world is *maturation,* the unfolding of the biological changes that are genetically programmed. Parents and teachers have little impact on this aspect of cognitive development, except to be sure that children get the nourishment and care they need to be healthy.

Activity is another influence. With physical maturation comes the increasing ability to act on the environment and learn from it. When a young child's coordination is reasonably developed, for example, the child may discover principles about balance by experimenting with a seesaw. Thus, as we act on the environment—as we explore, test, observe, and eventually organize information—we are likely to alter our thinking processes at the same time.

As we develop, we are also interacting with the people around us. According to Piaget, our cognitive development is influenced by *social transmission,* or learning from others. Without social transmission, we would need to reinvent all the knowledge already offered by our culture. The amount people can learn from social transmission varies according to their stage of cognitive development.

Maturation, activity, and social transmission all work together to influence cognitive development. How do we respond to these influences?

Basic Tendencies in Thinking

As a result of his early research in biology, Piaget concluded that all species inherit two basic tendencies, or "invariant functions." The first of these tendencies is toward **organization**—the combining, arranging, recombining, and rearranging of behaviors and thoughts into coherent systems. The second tendency is toward **adaptation,** or adjusting to the environment.

Organization. People are born with a tendency to organize their thinking processes into psychological structures. These psychological structures are our systems for understanding and interacting with the world. Simple structures are continually combined and coordinated to become more sophisticated and thus more effective. Very young infants, for example, can either look at an object or grasp it when it comes in contact with their hands. They cannot coordinate looking and grasping at the same time. As they develop, however, infants organize these two separate behavioral structures into a coordinated higher-level structure of looking at, reaching for, and grasping the object. They can, of course, still use each structure separately (Ginsburg & Opper, 1988; Miller, 2002).

Piaget gave a special name to these structures: **schemes.** In his theory, schemes are the basic building blocks of thinking. They are organized systems of actions or thought that allow us to mentally represent or "think about" the objects and events in our world. Schemes may be very small and specific, for example, the sucking-through-a-straw scheme or the recognizing-a-rose scheme. Or they may be larger and more general—the drinking scheme or the categorizing-plants scheme. As a person's thinking processes become more organized and new schemes develop, behavior also becomes more sophisticated and better suited to the environment.

Organization Ongoing process of arranging information and experience into mental systems or categories.

Adaptation Adjustment to the environment.

Schemes Mental systems or categories of perception and experience.

Adaptation. In addition to the tendency to organize their psychological structures, people also inherit the tendency to adapt to their environment. Two basic processes are involved in adaptation: assimilation and accommodation.

Assimilation takes place when people use their existing schemes to make sense of events in their world. Assimilation involves trying to understand something new by fitting it into what we already know. At times, we may have to distort the new information to make it fit. For example, the first time many children see a skunk, they call it a "kitty." They try to match the new experience with an existing scheme for identifying animals.

Accommodation occurs when a person must change existing schemes to respond to a new situation. If data cannot be made to fit any existing schemes, then more appropriate structures must be developed. We adjust our thinking to fit the new information, instead of adjusting the information to fit our thinking. Children demonstrate accommodation when they add the scheme for recognizing skunks to their other systems for identifying animals.

People adapt to their increasingly complex environments by using existing schemes whenever these schemes work (assimilation) and by modifying and adding to their schemes when something new is needed (accommodation). In fact, both processes are required most of the time. Even using an established pattern such as sucking through a straw may require some accommodation if the straw is of a different size or length than the type you are used to. If you have tried drinking juice from box packages, you know that you have to add a new skill to your sucking scheme—don't squeeze the box or you will shoot juice through the straw, straight up into the air and into your lap. Whenever new experiences are assimilated into an existing scheme, the scheme is enlarged and changed somewhat, so assimilation involves some accommodation.

There are also times when neither assimilation nor accommodation is used. If people encounter something that is too unfamiliar, they may ignore it. Experience is filtered to fit the kind of thinking a person is doing at a given time. For example, if you overhear a conversation in a foreign language, you probably will not try to make sense of the exchange unless you have some knowledge of the language.

Equilibration. According to Piaget, organizing, assimilating, and accommodating can be viewed as a kind of complex balancing act. In his theory, the actual changes in thinking take place through the process of **equilibration**—the act of searching for a balance. Piaget assumed that people continually test the adequacy of their thinking processes in order to achieve that balance.

Briefly, the process of equilibration works like this: If we apply a particular scheme to an event or situation and the scheme works, then equilibrium exists. If the scheme does not produce a satisfying result, then **disequilibrium** exists, and we become uncomfortable. This motivates us to keep searching for a solution through assimilation and accommodation, and thus our thinking changes and moves ahead.

Four Stages of Cognitive Development

What Would You Say? Your interview with the principal seems to be going fairly well. Her next question is, "We have openings at several grade levels, so I need to know about your understanding of students across grades. Are students in the 2nd and the 7th grade that different in the way they think—I mean in any ways that would affect your teaching?

Now we turn to the actual differences that Piaget hypothesized for children as they grow. Piaget's four stages of cognitive development are called sensorimotor, preoperational, concrete operational, and formal operational. Piaget believed that all people pass through the same four stages in exactly the same order. These stages are generally associated with specific ages, as shown in Table 2.1, but these are only general

Assimilation Fitting new information into existing schemes.

Accommodation Altering existing schemes or creating new ones in response to new information.

Equilibration Search for mental balance between cognitive schemes and information from the environment.

Disequilibrium In Piaget's theory, the "out-of-balance" state that occurs when a person realizes that his or her current ways of thinking are not working to solve a problem or understand a situation.

■ Table 2.1 Piaget's Stages of Cognitive Development

Stage	Approximate Age	Characteristics
Sensorimotor	0–2 years	Begins to make use of imitation, memory, and thought. Begins to recognize that objects do not cease to exist when they are hidden. Moves from reflex actions to goal-directed activity.
Preoperational	2–7 years	Gradually develops use of language and ability to think in symbolic form. Able to think operations through logically in one direction. Has difficulties seeing another person's point of view.
Concrete operational	7–11 years	Able to solve concrete (hands-on) problems in logical fashion. Understands laws of conservation and is able to classify and seriate. Understands reversibility.
Formal operational	11–adult	Able to solve abstract problems in logical fashion. Becomes more scientific in thinking. Develops concerns about social issues, identity.

SOURCE: From *Piaget's Theory of Cognitive and Affective Development* (5th ed.), by B. J. Wadsworth. Published by Allyn & Bacon, Boston, MA. Copyright © 1996 by Pearson Education. Adapted by permission of the publisher.

guidelines, not labels for all children of a certain age. Often, people can use one level of thinking to solve one kind of problem and a different level to solve another. Piaget noted that individuals may go through long periods of transition between stages and that a person may show characteristics of one stage in one situation, but characteristics of a higher or lower stage in other situations. Therefore, knowing a student's age is never a guarantee that you know how the child will think (Ginsburg & Opper, 1988; Orlando & Machado, 1996).

Infancy: The Sensorimotor Stage. The earliest period is called the **sensorimotor stage,** because the child's thinking involves seeing, hearing, moving, touching, tasting, and so on. During this period, the infant develops **object permanence,** the understanding that objects exist in the environment whether the baby perceives them or not. As most parents discover, before infants develop object permanence, it is relatively easy to take something away from them. The trick is to distract them and remove the object while they are not looking—"out of sight, out of mind." The older infant who searches for the ball that has rolled out of sight is indicating an understanding that objects still exist even when they are not in view. Recent research, however, suggests that infants as young as 3 to 4 months may know that the object still exists, but they do not have the memory skills to "hold on" to the location of the object or the motor skills to coordinate a search (Baillargeon & DeVos, 1991; Meece, 2002).

A second major accomplishment in the sensorimotor period is the beginning of logical, **goal-directed actions.** Think of the familiar container toy for babies. It is usually plastic, has a lid, and contains several colorful items that can be dumped out and

CONNECT & EXTEND

TO YOUR TEACHING

To experience some of the ways children differ from adults in their thinking, ask children of various ages the following questions:

- What does it mean to be alive?
- Can you name some things that are alive?
- Is the moon alive?
- Where do dreams come from?
- Where do they go?
- Which is farther, to go from the bottom of the hill all the way to the top or go from the top of the hill all the way to the bottom?
- Can a person live in Chicago and in Illinois at the same time?
- Will you be just as old as your big brother some day?
- When is yesterday?
- Where does the sun go at night?

Sensorimotor Involving the senses and motor activity.

Object permanence The understanding that objects have a separate, permanent existence.

Goal-directed actions Deliberate actions toward a goal.

replaced. A 6-month-old baby is likely to become frustrated trying to get to the toys inside. An older child who has mastered the basics of the sensorimotor stage will probably be able to deal with the toy in an orderly fashion by building a "container toy" scheme: (1) get the lid off, (2) turn the container upside down, (3) shake if the items jam, (4) watch the items fall. Separate lower-level schemes have been organized into a higher-level scheme to achieve a goal.

The child is soon able to reverse this action by refilling the container. Learning to reverse actions is a basic accomplishment of the sensorimotor stage. As we will soon see, however, learning to reverse thinking—that is, learning to imagine the reverse of a sequence of actions—takes much longer.

THE FAMILY CIRCUS By Bil Keane

"I can't tell you 'cause I'm wearin' my mittens."

Family Circus, March 12, 2002. Copyright © 2002 Bill Keane, Inc. Reprinted with special permission of King Features Syndicate.

Early Childhood to the Early Elementary Years: The Preoperational Stage. By the end of the sensorimotor stage, the child can use many action schemes. As long as these schemes remain tied to physical actions, however, they are of no use in recalling the past, keeping track of information, or planning. For this, children need what Piaget called **operations,** or actions that are carried out and reversed mentally rather than physically. The stage after sensorimotor is called **preoperational,** because the child has not yet mastered these mental operations but is moving toward mastery.

According to Piaget, the first type of thinking that is separate from action involves making action schemes symbolic. The ability to form and use symbols—words, gestures, signs, images, and so on—is thus a major accomplishment of the preoperational period and moves children closer to mastering the mental operations of the next stage. This ability to work with symbols, such as using the word "bicycle" or a picture of a bicycle to represent a real bicycle that is not actually present, is called the **semiotic function.**

The child's earliest use of symbols is in pretending or miming. Children who are not yet able to talk will often use action symbols—pretending to drink from an empty cup or touching a comb to their hair, showing that they know what each object is for. This behavior also shows that their schemes are becoming more general and less tied to specific actions. The eating scheme, for example, may be used in playing house. During the preoperational stage, we also see the rapid development of that very important symbol system, language. Between the ages of 2 and 4, most children enlarge their vocabulary from about 200 to 2,000 words.

As the child moves through the preoperational stage, the developing ability to think about objects in symbolic form remains somewhat limited to thinking in one direction only, or using *one-way logic.* It is very difficult for the child to "think backwards," or imagine how to reverse the steps in a task. **Reversible thinking** is involved in many tasks that are difficult for the preoperational child, such as the conservation of matter.

Conservation is the principle that the amount or number of something remains the same even if the arrangement or appearance is changed, as long as nothing is added and nothing is taken away. You know that if you tear a piece of paper into several pieces, you will still have the same amount of paper. To prove this, you know that you can reverse the process by taping the pieces back together.

A classic example of difficulty with conservation is found in the preoperational child's response to the following Piagetian task. Leah, a 5-year-old, is shown two identical glasses, both short and wide in shape. Both have exactly the same amount of colored water in them.

Interviewer: Does one glass have more water, or are they the same?

Leah: Same

The experimenter then pours the water from one of the glasses into a taller, narrower glass.

Interviewer: Now, does one glass have more water, or are they the same?

Operations Actions a person carries out by thinking them through instead of literally performing the actions.

Preoperational The stage before a child masters logical mental operations.

Semiotic function The ability to use symbols—language, pictures, signs, or gestures—to represent actions or objects mentally.

Reversible thinking Thinking backward, from the end to the beginning.

Conservation Principle that some characteristics of an object remain the same despite changes in appearance.

Leah: The tall one has more.

Interviewer: How do you know?

Leah: It goes up more here (points to higher level on taller glass).

Notice, by the way, that Leah shows a basic understanding of identity (it's the same water) but not an understanding that the amounts are identical (Ginsburg & Opper, 1988).

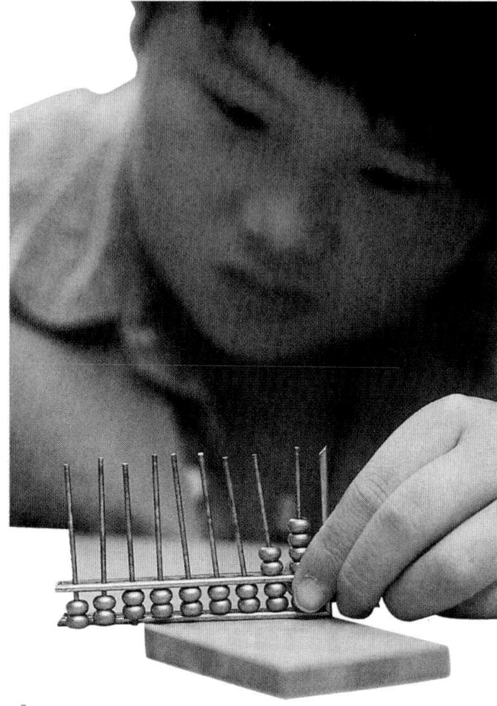

The ability to manipulate concrete objects helps children understand abstract relationships such as the connection between symbols and quantity.

Piaget's explanation for Leah's answer is that she is focusing, or centering, attention on the dimension of height. She has difficulty considering more than one aspect of the situation at a time, or **decentering.** The preoperational child cannot understand that increased diameter compensates for decreased height, because this would require taking into account two dimensions at once. Thus, children at the preoperational stage have trouble freeing themselves from their own perceptions of how the world appears.

This brings us to another important characteristic of the preoperational stage. Preoperational children, according to Piaget, are **egocentric;** they tend to see the world and the experiences of others from their own viewpoint. Egocentric, as Piaget intended it, does not mean selfish; it simply means children often assume that everyone else shares their feelings, reactions, and perspectives. For example, if a little boy at this stage is afraid of dogs, he may assume that all children share this fear. Very young children center on their own perceptions and on the way the situation appears to them. This is one reason it is difficult for these children to understand that your right hand is not on the same side as theirs when you are facing them.

Egocentrism is also evident in the child's language. You may have seen young children happily talking about what they are doing even though no one is listening. This can happen when the child is alone or, even more often, in a group of children—each child talks enthusiastically, without any real interaction or conversation. Piaget called this the **collective monologue.**

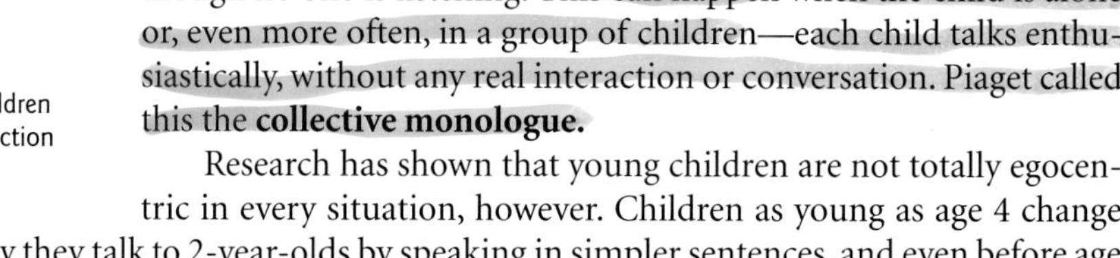

Research has shown that young children are not totally egocentric in every situation, however. Children as young as age 4 change the way they talk to 2-year-olds by speaking in simpler sentences, and even before age 2, children show toys to adults by turning the front of the toy to face the other person. So young children do seem quite able to take the needs and different perspectives of others into account, at least in certain situations (Gelman, 1979; Gelman & Ebeling, 1989). The *Guidelines* give ideas for working with preoperational thinkers.

Later Elementary to the Middle School Years: The Concrete-Operational Stage. Piaget coined the term **concrete operations** to describe this stage of "hands-on" thinking. The basic characteristics of the stage are the recognition of the logical stability of the physical world, the realization that elements can be changed or transformed and still conserve many of their original characteristics, and the understanding that these changes can be reversed.

Look at Figure 2.3 on page 36, which shows examples of the different tasks given to children to assess conservation and the approximate age ranges when most children can solve these problems. According to Piaget, a student's ability to solve conservation problems depends on an understanding of three basic aspects of reasoning: identity, compensation, and reversibility. With a complete mastery of **identity,** the student knows that if nothing is added or taken away, the material remains the same. With an understanding of **compensation,** the student knows that an apparent change in one direction can be compensated for by a change in another direction. That is, if the liquid rises higher in the glass, the glass must be narrower. And with an understanding of **reversibility,** the student can mentally cancel out the change that has been made.

Decentering Focusing on more than one aspect at a time.

Egocentric Assuming that others experience the world the way you do.

Collective monologue Form of speech in which children in a group talk but do not really interact or communicate.

Concrete operations Mental tasks tied to concrete objects and situations.

Identity Principle that a person or object remains the same over time.

Compensation The principle that changes in one dimension can be offset by changes in another.

Reversibility A characteristic of Piagetian logical operations—the ability to think through a series of steps, then mentally reverse the steps and return to the starting point; also called *reversible thinking.*

GUIDELINES Teaching the Preoperational Child

Use concrete props and visual aids whenever possible.

Examples

1. When you discuss concepts such as "part," "whole," or "one-half," use shapes on a felt board or cardboard "pizzas" to demonstrate.
2. Let children add and subtract with sticks, rocks, or colored chips.

Make instructions relatively short, using actions as well as words.

Examples

1. When giving instructions about how to enter the room after recess and prepare for social studies, ask a student to demonstrate the procedure for the rest of the class by walking in quietly, going straight to his or her seat, and placing the text, paper, and a pencil on his or her desk.
2. Explain a game by acting out one of the parts.
3. Show students what their finished papers should look like. Use an overhead projector or display examples where students can see them easily.

Don't expect the students to be consistent in their ability to see the world from someone else's point of view.

Examples

1. Avoid social studies lessons about worlds too far removed from the child's experience.
2. Avoid long lectures on sharing. Be clear about rules for sharing or use of materials, but avoid long explanations of the rationales for the rules.

Be sensitive to the possibility that students may have different meanings for the same word or different words for the same meaning. Students may also expect everyone to understand words they have invented.

Examples

1. If a student protests, "I won't take a nap. I'll just rest!" be aware that a nap may mean something such as "changing into pajamas and being in my bed at home."
2. Ask children to explain the meanings of their invented words.

Give children a great deal of hands-on practice with the skills that serve as building blocks for more complex skills such as reading comprehension.

Examples

1. Provide cut-out letters to build words.
2. Supplement paper-and-pencil tasks in arithmetic with activities that require measuring and simple calculations—cooking, building a display area for class work, dividing a batch of popcorn equally.

Provide a wide range of experiences in order to build a foundation for concept learning and language.

Examples

1. Take field trips to zoos, gardens, theaters, and concerts; invite storytellers to the class.
2. Give students words to describe what they are doing, hearing, seeing, touching, tasting, and smelling.

Another important operation mastered at this stage is **classification.** Classification depends on a student's abilities to focus on a single characteristic of objects in a set and group the objects according to that characteristic. Given 12 objects of assorted colors and shapes, the concrete-operational student can invariably pick out the ones that are round.

More advanced classification at this stage involves recognizing that one class fits into another. A city can be in a particular state or province and also in a particular country, as you probably indicated in your answer to the *Stop/Think/Write* question. As children apply this advanced classification to locations, they often become fascinated with "complete" addresses such as Lee Jary, 5116 Forest Hill Drive, Richmond Hill, Ontario, Canada, North America, Northern Hemisphere, Earth, Solar System, Milky Way, Universe.

Classification is also related to reversibility. The ability to reverse a process mentally now allows the concrete-operational student to see that there is more than one way to classify a group of objects. The student understands, for example, that buttons can be classified by color, then reclassified by size or by the number of holes.

Seriation is the process of making an orderly arrangement from large to small or vice versa. This understanding of sequential relationships permits a student to construct a logical series in which A < B < C (A is less than B is less than C) and so on.

Classification Grouping objects into categories.

Seriation Arranging objects in sequential order according to one aspect, such as size, weight, or volume.

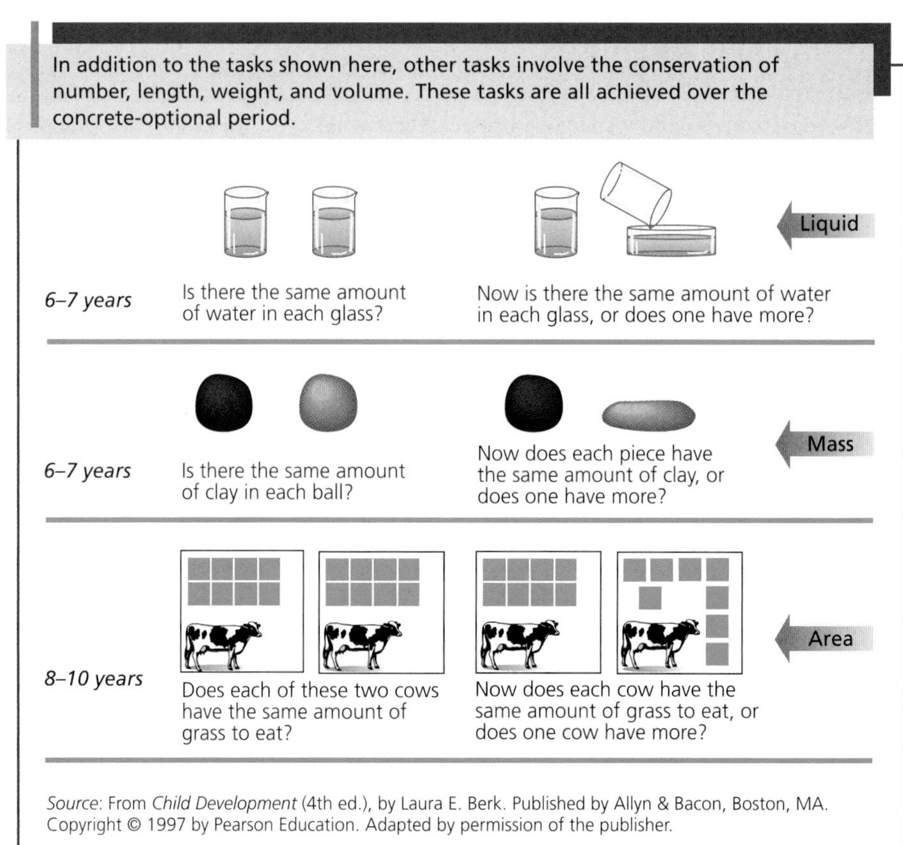

In addition to the tasks shown here, other tasks involve the conservation of number, length, weight, and volume. These tasks are all achieved over the concrete-optional period.
Liquid
6–7 years
Is there the same amount of water in each glass?
Now is there the same amount of water in each glass, or does one have more?
Mass
6–7 years
Is there the same amount of clay in each ball?
Now does each piece have the same amount of clay, or does one have more?
Area
8–10 years
Does each of these two cows have the same amount of grass to eat?
Now does each cow have the same amount of grass to eat, or does one cow have more?
Source: From Child Development (4th ed.), by Laura E. Berk. Published by Allyn & Bacon, Boston, MA. Copyright © 1997 by Pearson Education. Adapted by permission of the publisher.

Figure 2.3 Some Piagetian Conservation Tasks

Unlike the preoperational child, the concrete-operational child can grasp the notion that B can be *larger* than A but *smaller* than C.

With the abilities to handle operations such as conservation, classification, and seriation, the student at the concrete-operational stage has finally developed a complete and very logical system of thinking. This system of thinking, however, is still tied

An important operation mastered during the concrete stage is classification, the ability to focus on a single characteristic of objects in a set and group the objects according to that characteristic.

GUIDELINES Teaching the Concrete-Operational Child

Continue to use concrete props and visual aids, especially when dealing with sophisticated material.

Examples

1. Use time lines in history and three-dimensional models in science.
2. Use diagrams to illustrate hierarchical relationships such as branches of government and the agencies under each branch.

Continue to give students a chance to manipulate and test objects.

Examples

1. Set up simple scientific experiments such as the following involving the relationship between fire and oxygen. What happens to a flame when you blow on it from a distance? (If you don't blow it out, the flame gets larger briefly, because it has more oxygen to burn.) What happens when you cover the flame with a jar?
2. Have students make candles by dipping wicks in wax, weave cloth on a simple loom, bake bread, set type by hand, or do other craft work that illustrates the daily occupations of people in the colonial period.

Make sure presentations and readings are brief and well organized.

Examples

1. Assign stories or books with short, logical chapters, moving to longer reading assignments only when students are ready.
2. Break up a presentation with a chance to practice the first steps before introducing the next.

Use familiar examples to explain more complex ideas.

Examples

1. Compare students' lives with those of characters in a story. After reading *Island of the Blue Dolphins* (the true story of a girl who grew up alone on a deserted island), ask "Have you ever had to stay alone for a long time? How did you feel?"
2. Teach the concept of area by having students measure two rooms in the school that are different sizes.

Give opportunities to classify and group objects and ideas on increasingly complex levels.

Examples

1. Give students slips of paper with individual sentences written on each paper and ask the students to group the sentences into paragraphs.
2. Compare the systems of the human body to other kinds of systems: the brain to a computer, the heart to a pump. Break down stories into components, from the broad to the specific: author; story; characters, plot, theme; place, time; dialogue, description, actions.

Present problems that require logical, analytical thinking.

Examples

1. Use mind twisters, brain teasers, MasterMind, and riddles.
2. Discuss open-ended questions that stimulate thinking: "Are the brain and the mind the same thing?" "How should the city deal with stray animals?" "What is the largest number?"

to physical reality. The logic is based on concrete situations that can be organized, classified, or manipulated. Thus, children at this stage can imagine several different arrangements for the furniture in their rooms before they act. They do not have to solve the problem strictly through trial and error by actually making the arrangements. However, the concrete-operational child is not yet able to reason about hypothetical, abstract problems that involve the coordination of many factors at once. This kind of coordination is part of Piaget's next and final stage of cognitive development.

In any grade you teach, a knowledge of concrete-operational thinking will be helpful. In the early grades, the students are moving toward this logical system of thought. In the middle grades, it is in full flower, ready to be applied and extended by your teaching. In the high school years, it is often used by students whose thinking may not have fully developed to the next stage—the stage of formal operations. The *Guidelines* above should give you ideas for teaching children who can apply concrete operations.

Junior and Senior High: Formal Operations. Some students remain at the concrete-operational stage throughout their school years, even throughout life. However, new experiences, usually those that take place in school, eventually present most students with problems that they cannot solve using concrete operations. What happens when a number of variables interact, as in a laboratory experiment? Then a mental system for controlling sets of variables and working through a set of possibilities is needed. These are the abilities Piaget called **formal operations.**

Companion Website

STOP THINK WRITE

You are packing for long trip, but want to pack light. How many different three-piece outfits (slacks, shirt, jacket) will you have if you include three shirts, three slacks, and three jackets (assuming of course that they all go together in fashion perfection)? Time yourself to see how long it takes to arrive at the answer.

At the level of formal operations, all the earlier operations and abilities continue in force; that is, formal thinking is reversible, internal, and organized in a system of interdependent elements. The focus of thinking shifts, however, from what *is* to what *might be.* Situations do not have to be experienced to be imagined. Ask a young child how life would be different if people did not sleep, and the child might say, "People do sleep!" In contrast, the adolescent who has mastered formal operations can consider contrary-to-fact questions. In answering, the adolescent demonstrates the hallmark of formal operations—**hypothetico-deductive reasoning.** The formal thinker can consider a hypothetical situation (people do not sleep) and reason deductively (from the general assumption to specific implications, such as longer workdays, more money spent on energy and lighting, or new entertainment industries). Formal operations also include inductive reasoning, or using specific observations to identify general principles. For example, the economist observes many specific changes in the stock market and attempts to identify general principles about economic cycles. Formal-operational thinkers can form hypotheses, set up mental experiments to test them, and isolate or control variables in order to complete a valid test of the hypotheses. This kind of reasoning is expected in the later grades (Bjorklund, 1989).

After elementary school, the ability to consider abstract possibilities is critical for much of mathematics and science. Most math is concerned with hypothetical situations, assumptions, and givens: "Let $x = 10$," or "Assume $x^2 + y^2 = z^2$," or "Given two sides and an adjacent angle. . . ." Work in social studies and literature requires abstract thinking, too: "What did Wilson mean when he called World War I the 'war to end all wars'?" "What are some metaphors for hope and despair in Shakespeare's sonnets?" "What symbols of old age does T. S. Eliot use in *The Waste Land*?" "How do animals symbolize human character traits in Aesop's fables?" Desmond Tutu, a respected reformer and religious leader in South Africa, describes a teacher who understood how to teach abstract mathematical concepts, even in classes as large as 80 in the *Stories of Learning/Tributes to Teaching* on page 39.

The organized, scientific thinking of formal operations requires that students systematically generate different possibilities for a given situation. For example, if a child capable of formal operations is asked, "How many different shirt/slacks/jacket outfits can you make using three of each kind of clothing?" the child can systematically identify the 27 possible combinations (did you get it right?). A concrete thinker might name just a few combinations, using each piece of clothing only once. The underlying system of combinations is not yet available.

The ability to think hypothetically, consider alternatives, identify all possible combinations, and analyze one's own thinking has some interesting consequences for adolescents. Since they can think about worlds that do not exist, they often become interested in science fiction. Because they can reason from general principles to specific actions, they often are critical of people whose actions seem to contradict their principles. Adolescents can deduce the set of "best" possibilities and imagine ideal worlds (or ideal parents and teachers, for that matter). This explains why many students at this age develop interests in utopias, political causes, and social issues. They want to design better worlds, and their thinking allows them to do so. Adolescents can also imagine many possible futures for themselves and may try to decide which is best. Feelings about any of these ideals may be strong.

Another characteristic of this stage is **adolescent egocentrism.** Unlike egocentric young children, adolescents do not deny that other people may have different per-

Formal operations Mental tasks involving abstract thinking and coordination of a number of variables.

Hypothetico-deductive reasoning A formal-operations problem-solving strategy in which an individual begins by identifying all the factors that might affect a problem and then deduces and systematically evaluates specific solutions.

Adolescent egocentrism Assumption that everyone else shares one's thoughts, feelings, and concerns.

~ Stories of Learning Tributes to Teaching ~

Reverend **Desmond Tutu** attended a school in South Africa that "had most of the characteristics of a ghetto school; hardly any facilities to mention. I went to the laboratory only once on my five or six years at school, there was a wholly inadequate library and very few recreational and games facilities." The overcrowded classes that routinely had over 80 students were held in a poorly furnished church building. Reverend Tutu notes that math was not his favorite subject—he learned math only because it was compulsory—until he met Mr. Ndebele.

> However, things changed dramatically after Mr. Nimron Ndebele stood in front of the class. He was a middle-sized man with a fine alto voice. He always had a gentle smile playing around his mouth, a very pleasant image, and he made learning his subject so much fun. He always had objects that he used to illustrate what, up to that point, had been cloaked in mystery and unrelieved gloom. He had an extraordinary knack of making the most complicated and abstruse principle seem so straightforward and obvious. Nobody, just nobody, failed his subject in the public state examinations. In fact, many of his students obtained distinctions.
>
> I thank God for Mr. Ndebele and for what he meant for so many of us.
>
> —The Most Reverend Desmond Mpilo Tutu,
> Archbishop of Cape Town, South Africa

SOURCE: From *Mentors, Masters, and Mrs. MacGregor* by J. Bluestein. Published by Health Communications.

ceptions and beliefs; the adolescents just become very focused on their own ideas. They analyze their own beliefs and attitudes. This can lead to what Elkind (1981) calls the sense of an *imaginary audience*—the feeling that everyone is watching. Thus, adolescents believe that others are analyzing them: "Everyone noticed that I wore this shirt twice this week." "The whole class thought my answer was dumb!" "Everybody is going to love my new CD." You can see that social blunders or imperfections in appearance can be devastating if "everybody is watching." Luckily, this feeling of being "on stage" seems to peak in early adolescence by age 14 or 15.

CONNECT & EXTEND

TO YOUR TEACHING
What are the differences (and similarities) between egocentrism in young children and egocentrism in adolescents?

Do We All Reach the Fourth Stage? As we have just seen, most psychologists agree that there is a level of thinking more sophisticated than concrete operations. But the question of how universal formal-operational thinking actually is, even among adults, is a matter of debate. According to Neimark (1975), the first three stages of Piaget's theory are forced on most people by physical realities. Objects really are permanent. The amount of water doesn't change when it is poured into another glass. Formal operations, however, are not so closely tied to the physical environment. They may be the product of experience and of practice in solving hypothetical problems and using formal scientific reasoning. These abilities tend to be valued and taught in literate cultures, particularly in colleges and universities.

Piaget himself (1974) suggested that most adults may be able to use formal-operational thought in only a few areas where they have the greatest experience or interest. So do not expect every student in your junior high or high school class to be able to think hypothetically about all the problems you present. Students who have not learned to go beyond the information given to them are likely to fall by the wayside. Sometimes students find shortcuts for dealing with problems that are beyond their grasp; they may memorize formulas or lists of steps. These systems may be helpful for passing tests, but real understanding will take place only if students are able to go beyond this superficial use of memorization—only, in other words, if they learn

Helping Students to Use Formal Operations

Continue to use concrete-operational teaching strategies and materials.

Examples

1. Use visual aids such as charts and illustrations as well as somewhat more sophisticated graphs and diagrams.
2. Compare the experiences of characters in stories to students' experiences.

Give students the opportunity to explore many hypothetical questions.

Examples

1. Have students write position papers, then exchange these papers with the opposing side and debate topical social issues—the environment, the economy, national health insurance.
2. Ask students to write about their personal vision of a utopia; write a description of a universe that has no sex differences; write a description of Earth after humans are extinct.

Give students opportunities to solve problems and reason scientifically.

Examples

1. Set up group discussions in which students design experiments to answer questions.
2. Ask students to justify two different positions on animal rights, with logical arguments for each position.

Whenever possible, teach broad concepts, not just facts, using materials and ideas relevant to the students' lives.

Examples

1. When discussing the Civil War, consider other issues that have divided the United States since then.
2. Use lyrics from popular songs to teach poetic devices, to reflect on social problems, and to stimulate discussion on the place of popular music in our culture.

to use formal-operational thinking. The *Guidelines* may help you support the development of formal operations with your students.

Check Yourself What are the main influences on cognitive development?

What is a scheme?

As children move from sensorimotor to formal-operational thinking, what are the major changes?

CONNECT & EXTEND

TO **PRAXIS**™ IMPLICATIONS OF PIAGET'S THEORY (I, A2)

The music, physical education, and art teachers in a rural, pre-K to 8 school district work with students who characterize several of Piaget's stages. How should these three teachers adjust their teaching from level to level over the course of a week?

Implications of Piaget's Theory for Teachers

Piaget did not make specific educational recommendations. He was more interested in understanding children's thinking. He did express some general ideas about educational philosophy, however. He believed that the main goal of education should be to help children learn how to learn, and that education should "form not furnish" the minds of students (Piaget, 1969, p. 70). Even though Piaget did not design programs of education based on his ideas, many other people have. For example, the National Association for the Education of Young Children has guidelines for developmentally appropriate education that incorporate Piaget's findings (Bredekamp & Copple, 1997). Piaget has taught us that we can learn a great deal about how children think by listening carefully, by paying close attention to their ways of solving problems. If we understand children's thinking, we will be better able to match teaching methods to children's abilities.

Understanding and Building on Students' Thinking

The students in any class will vary greatly in both their level of cognitive development and their academic knowledge. As a teacher, how can you determine whether students are having trouble because they lack the necessary thinking abilities or because they simply have not learned the basic facts? To do this, Case (1985b) suggests you observe your students carefully as they try to solve the problems you have presented. What kind of logic do they use? Do they focus on only one aspect of the situation? Are they fooled by appearances? Do they suggest solutions systematically or by guessing and forgetting what they have already tried? Ask your students how they tried to solve the problem. Listen to their strategies. What kind of thinking is behind repeated mistakes or problems? The students are the best sources of information about their own thinking abilities (Confrey, 1990a).

An important implication of Piaget's theory for teaching is what Hunt years ago (1961) called "the problem of the match." Students must be neither bored by work that is too simple nor left behind by teaching they cannot understand. According to Hunt, disequilibrium must be kept "just right" to encourage growth. Setting up situations that lead to errors can help create an appropriate level of disequilibrium. When students experience some conflict between what they think should happen (a piece of wood should sink because it is big) and what actually happens (it floats!), they may rethink the situation, and new knowledge may develop.

It is worth pointing out, too, that many materials and lessons can be understood at several levels and can be "just right" for a range of cognitive abilities. Classics such as *Alice in Wonderland,* myths, and fairy tales can be enjoyed at both concrete and symbolic levels. It is also possible for students to be introduced to a topic together, then work individually on follow-up activities matched to their level. Tom Good and Jere Brophy (2003) describe activity cards for three or four ability levels. These cards provide different readings and assignments, but all are directed toward the overall class objectives. One of the cards should be a good "match" for each student.

Activity and Constructing Knowledge

Piaget's fundamental insight was that individuals *construct* their own understanding; learning is a constructive process. At every level of cognitive development, you will also want to see that students are actively engaged in the learning process. In his words:

> Knowledge is not a copy of reality. To know an object, to know an event, is not simply to look at it and make a mental copy or image of it. To know an object is to act on it. To know is to modify, to transform the object, and to understand the process of this transformation, and as a consequence to understand the way the object is constructed. (Piaget, 1964, p. 8)

This active experience, even at the earliest school levels, should not be limited to the physical manipulation of objects. It should also include mental manipulation of ideas that arise out of class projects or experiments (Ginsburg & Opper, 1988). For example, after a social studies lesson on different jobs, a primary-grade teacher might show the students a picture of a woman and ask, "What could this person be?" After answers such as "teacher," "doctor," "secretary," "lawyer," "saleswoman," and so on, the teacher could suggest, "How about a daughter?" Answers such as "sister," "mother," "aunt," and "granddaughter" may follow. This should help the children switch dimensions in their classification and center on another aspect of the situation. Next, the teacher might suggest "American," "jogger," or "blonde." With older children, hierarchical classification might be involved: It is a picture of a woman, who is a human being; a human being is a primate, which is a mammal, which is an animal, which is a life form.

All students need to interact with teachers and peers in order to test their thinking, to be challenged, to receive feedback, and to watch how others work out problems. Disequilibrium is often set in motion quite naturally when the teacher or another student suggests a new way of thinking about something. As a general rule, students should act, manipulate, observe, and then talk and/or write (to the teacher and each other) about what they have experienced. Concrete experiences provide the raw materials for thinking. Communicating with others makes students use, test, and sometimes change their thinking abilities.

Maria Montessori said, "Play is children's work." And in games they learn cooperation, fairness, negotiation, winning, and losing—all important skills for work someday. Without cooperation, there is no game.

The Value of Play

Maria Montessori once noted, and Piaget would agree, "Play is children's work." We saw that the brain develops with stimulation, and play provides some of that stimulation at every age. Babies in the sensorimotor stage learn by exploring, sucking, pounding, shaking, throwing—acting on their environments. Preoperational preschoolers love pretend play and through pretending form symbols, use language, and interact with others. They are beginning to play simple games with predictable rules. Elementary school-age children also like fantasy, but also are beginning to play more complex games and sports, and thus learn cooperation, fairness, negotiation, winning, and losing as well as developing language. As children grow into adolescents, play continues to be part of their physical and social development (Meece, 2002).

Piaget taught us that children do not think like adults. His influence on developmental psychology and education has been enormous, even though recent research has not supported all of his ideas.

Some Limitations of Piaget's Theory

Although most psychologists agree with Piaget's insightful descriptions of *how* children think, many disagree with his explanations of *why* thinking develops as it does.

The Trouble with Stages. Some psychologists have questioned the existence of four separate stages of thinking, even though they agree that children do go through the changes that Piaget described (Gelman & Baillargeon, 1983; Miller, 2002). One problem with the stage model is the lack of consistency in children's thinking. For example, children can conserve number (the number of blocks does not change when they are rearranged) a year or two before they can conserve weight (a ball of clay does not change when you flatten it). Why can't they use conservation consistently? in every situation? Piagetian theorists have tried to deal with these inconsistencies, but not all psychologists are convinced by their explanations (Case, 1998; Orlando & Machado, 1996; Seigler, 1998). In fairness, we should note that in his later work, even Piaget put less emphasis on *stages* of cognitive development and gave more attention to how thinking *changes* through equilibration (Miller, 2002).

Another problem with the idea of separate stages is that, when "viewed from afar, many changes in children's thinking appear discontinuous; when viewed from close up, the same changes often appear as part of a continuous, gradual progression" (Siegler, 1998, p. 55). For example, rather than appearing all at once, object permanence may develop gradually as children's memories develop. The longer you make the infants wait before searching, the older they have to be to succeed—so the problem may be with memory and not with knowing that things still exist when out of sight. Siegler notes that change can be both continuous and discontinuous, as described by a branch of mathematics called *catastrophe theory.* Changes that appear suddenly, like the collapse of a bridge, are preceded by many slowly developing changes such as gradual, continuous corrosion of the metal structures. Similarly, gradually developing changes in children can lead to large changes in abilities that seem abrupt (Fischer & Pare-Blagoev, 2000).

Some psychologists have pointed to research on the brain to support Piaget's stage model. Epstein (1978, 1980) observed changes in rates of growth in brain weight and skull size and changes in the electrical activity of the brain between infancy and adolescence. These growth spurts occur at about the same time as transitions between the stages described by Piaget. Evidence from animal studies indicates that infant rhesus monkeys show dramatic increases in synaptic (nerve) connections throughout the brain cortex at the same time that they master the kinds of sensorimotor problems described by Piaget. This may be true in human infants as well. Transition to the higher cognitive states in humans has also been related to changes in the brain, such as production of additional synaptic connections (Byrnes & Fox, 1998). Thus, there is some neurological evidence for stages.

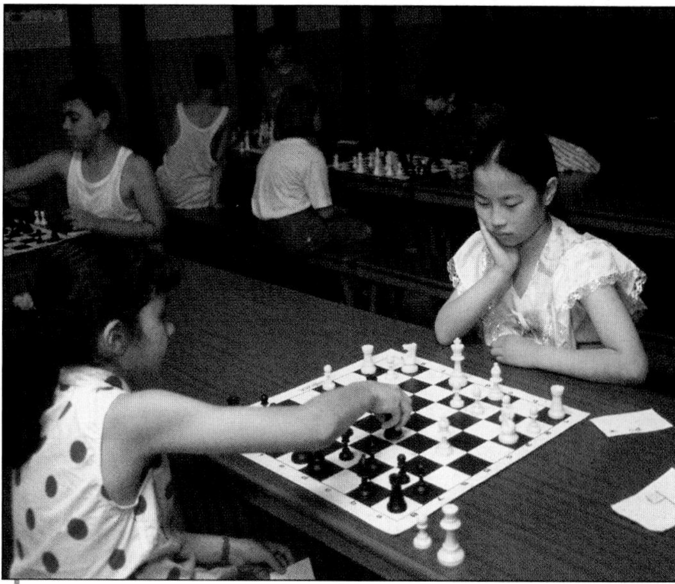

One limitation of Piaget's theory appears to be the underestimation of young children's cognitive abilities. For instance, his theory does not explain how these young girls can play chess at the same level as an adult could.

Underestimating Children's Abilities. It now appears that Piaget underestimated the cognitive abilities of children, particularly younger ones. The problems he gave young children may have been too difficult and the directions too confusing. His subjects may have understood more than they could show on these problems. For example, work by Gelman and her colleagues (Carey & Gelman, 1991; Miller & Gelman, 1983) shows that preschool children know much more about the concept of number than Piaget thought, even if they sometimes make mistakes or get confused. As long as preschoolers work with only three or four objects at a time, they can tell that the number remains the same, even if the objects are spread far apart or clumped close together. In other words, we may be born with a greater store of cognitive tools than Piaget suggested. Some basic understandings, such as the permanence of objects or the sense of number, may be part of our evolutionary equipment, ready for use in our cognitive development.

Piaget's theory does not explain how even young children can perform at an advanced level in certain areas where they have highly developed knowledge and expertise. An expert 9-year-old chess player may think abstractly about chess moves, while a novice 20-year-old player may have to resort to more concrete strategies to plan and remember moves (Seigler, 1998). As John Flavell (1985) noted, "the expert [child] looks very, very smart—very 'cognitively mature'—when functioning in her area of expertise" (p. 83).

Cognitive Development and Information Processing. As you will see in Chapter 7, there are alternative explanations for why children have trouble with conservation and other Piagetian tasks. These explanations focus on the child's developing information processing skills such as attention, memory capacity, and learning strategies. Siegler (1998) proposes that as children grow older, they develop progressively better rules and strategies for solving problems and for thinking logically. Teachers can help students develop their capacities for formal thinking by putting the students in situations that challenge their thinking and reveal the shortcomings of their logic. Siegler's approach is called *rule assessment* because it focuses on understanding, challenging, and changing the rules that students use for thinking.

Some developmental psychologists have devised **neo-Piagetian theories** that retain Piaget's insights about children's construction of knowledge and the general trends in children's thinking, but add findings from information processing about the role of attention, memory, and strategies. For example, Robbie Case (1992, 1998) has devised an explanation of cognitive development suggesting that children develop in

Neo-Piagetian theories More recent theories that integrate findings about attention, memory, and strategy use with Piaget's insights about children's thinking and the construction of knowledge.

stages within specific domains such as numerical concepts, spatial concepts, social tasks, storytelling, reasoning about physical objects, and motor development. As children practice using the schemes in a particular domain (for example, using counting schemes in the number concept area), accomplishing the schemes takes less attention. The schemes become more automatic because the child does not have to "think so hard" about it. This frees up mental resources and memory to do more. The child now can combine simple schemes into more complex ones and invent new schemes when needed (assimilation and accommodation in action).

Within each domain such as numerical concepts or social skills, children move from grasping simple schemes during the early preschool years, to merging two schemes into a unit (between about ages 4 and 6), to coordinating these scheme units into larger combinations, and finally, by about ages 9 to 11, to forming complex relationships that can be applied to many problems (Berk, 2002; Case, 1992, 1998). Children do progress through these qualitatively different stages within each domain, but Case argues that progress in one domain does not automatically affect movement in another. The child must have experience and involvement with the content and the ways of thinking within each domain in order to construct increasingly complex and useful schemes and coordinated conceptual understandings about the domain.

Cognitive Development and Culture. One final criticism of Piaget's theory is that it overlooks the important effects of the child's cultural and social group. Children in Western cultures may master scientific thinking and formal operations because this is the kind of thinking required in Western schools (Artman & Cahan, 1993; Berk, 2002; Geary, 1998). Even basic concrete operations such as classification may not be so basic to people of other cultures. For example, when individuals from the Kpelle people of Africa were asked to sort 20 objects, they created groups that made sense to them—a hoe with a potato, a knife with an orange. The experimenter could not get the Kpelle to change their categories; they said this is how a wise man would do it. Finally the experimenter asked in desperation, "Well, how would a fool do it?" Then the subjects promptly created the four neat classification piles the experimenter had expected—food, tools, and so on (Rogoff & Morelli, 1989).

Check Yourself What is the "problem of the match" described by Hunt?

What is active learning? Why is Piaget's theory of cognitive development consistent with active learning?

What are some limitations of Piaget's theory?

There is another increasingly influential view of cognitive development. Proposed years ago by Lev Vygotsky and recently rediscovered, this theory ties cognitive development to culture.

Vygotsky's Sociocultural Perspective

Psychologists today recognize that the child's culture shapes cognitive development by determining what and how the child will learn about the world. For example, young Zinacanteco Indian girls of southern Mexico learn complicated ways of weaving cloth through informal teachings of adults in their communities. In Brazil, without going to school, children who sell candy on the streets learn sophisticated mathematics in order to buy from wholesalers, sell, barter, and make a profit. Cultures that prize cooperation and sharing teach these abilities early, whereas cultures that encourage competition nurture competitive skills in their children (Bakerman et al., 1990; Ceci & Roazzi, 1994). The stages observed by Piaget are not necessarily "natural" for all children because to some extent they reflect the expectations and activities of Western cultures (Rogoff & Chavajay, 1995).

A major spokesperson for this **sociocultural theory** (also called *sociohistoric*) was a Russian psychologist who died more than 50 years ago. Lev Semenovich Vygotsky was only 38 when he died of tuberculosis, but during that time he produced over 100 books and articles. Some of the translations now available are Vygotsky (1978, 1986, 1987, 1993, 1997). Vyotsky's work began when he was studying learning and development to improve his own teaching (Wink & Putney, 2002). Over his brief lifetime, he wrote about language and thought, the psychology of art, learning and development, and educating students with special needs. His work was banned in Russia for many years because he referenced Western psychologists. But in the past 25 years, with the rediscovery of his work, Vygotsky's ideas about language, culture, and cognitive development have become major influences in psychology and education and have provided alternatives to many of Piaget's theories (John-Steiner & Mahn, 1996; McCaslin & Hickey, 2001; Wink & Putney, 2002).

Lev Vygotsky, shown here with his daughter, elaborated the sociocultural theory of development. His ideas about language, culture, and cognitive development have become major influences in the fields of psychology and education.

Vygotsky believed that human activities take place in cultural settings and cannot be understood apart from these settings. One of his key ideas was that our specific mental structures and processes can be traced to our interactions with others. These social interactions are more than simple influences on cognitive development—they actually create our cognitive structures and thinking processes (Palincsar, 1998). In fact, "Vygotsky conceptualized development as the transformation of socially shared activities into internalized processes" (John-Steiner & Mahn, 1996, p. 192). We will examine two themes in Vygotsky's writings that explain how social processes form learning and thinking: the social sources of individual thinking and the role of tools in learning and development, especially the tool of language (Wertsch, 1991; Wertsch & Tulviste, 1992).

CONNECT & EXTEND

TO THE RESEARCH

See the Spring, 1995 issue of the *Educational Psychologist* for a special issue on "Lev S. Vygotsky and Contemporary Educational Psychology."

The Social Sources of Individual Thinking

Vygotsky assumed that "every function in a child's cultural development appears twice: first, on the social level and later on the individual level; first between people (interpsychological) and then inside the child (intrapsychological)" (1978, p. 57). In other words, higher mental processes appear first between people as they are **co-constructed** during shared activities. Then the processes are internalized by the child and become part of that child's cognitive development. For example, children first use language in activities with others, to regulate the behavior of the others ("No nap!" or "I wanna cookie."). Later, however, the child can regulate her own behavior using private speech ("don't spill"), as you will see in a later section. So, for Vygotsky, social interaction was more than influence, it was the origin of higher mental processes such as problem solving. Consider this example:

> A six-year-old has lost a toy and asks her father for help. The father asks her where she last saw the toy; the child says "I can't remember." He asks a series of questions—did you have it in your room? Outside? Next door? To each question, the child answers, "no." When he says "in the car?" she says "I think so" and goes to retrieve the toy. (Tharp & Gallimore, 1988, p. 14)

Who remembered? The answer is really neither the father nor the daughter, but the two together. The remembering and problem solving was *co-constructed*—between people—in the interaction. But the child may have internalized strategies to use next time something is lost. At some point, the child will be able to function independently to solve this kind of problem. So, like the strategy for finding the toy, higher functions appear first between a child and a "teacher" before they exist within the individual child (Kozulin, 1990).

Here is another example of the social sources of individual thinking. This time the social source is other students and the type of thinking involved is reasoning.

Sociocultural theory Emphasizes role in development of cooperative dialogues between children and more knowledgeable members of society. Children learn the culture of their community (ways of thinking and behaving) through these interactions.

Co-constructed process A social process in which people interact and negotiate (usually verbally) to create an understanding or to solve a problem. The final product is shaped by all participants.

Richard Anderson and his colleagues (2001) studied how 4th graders in small-group classroom discussions appropriate (take for themselves and use) argument strategems that occur in the discussions. An argument strategem is a particular form such as "I think [POSITION] because [REASON]," where the student fills in the position and the reason. For example, a student might say, "I think that the wolves should be left alone because they are not hurting anyone." Another strategy form is "If [ACTION] then [BAD CONSEQUENCE]," as in "If they don't trap the wolves, then the wolves will eat the cows." Other forms manage participation, for example, "What do you think [NAME]?" or "Let [NAME] talk."

Anderson's research identified 13 forms of talk and argument that helped to manage the discussion, get everyone to participate, present and defend positions, and handle confusion. The researchers found that the use of these different forms of talking and thinking *snowballed*—once a useful argument was employed by one student, it spread to other students and the argument strategem form appeared more and more in the discussions. Open discussions—students asking and answering each other's questions—were better than teacher-dominated discussion for the development of these argument forms. Over time, these ways of presenting, attacking, and defending positions could be internalized as mental reasoning and decision making for the individual students.

Both Piaget and Vygotsky emphasized the importance of social interactions in cognitive development, but Piaget saw a different role for interaction. He believed that interaction encouraged development by creating disequilibrium—cognitive conflict—that motivated change. Thus, Piaget believed that the most helpful interactions were those between peers because peers are on an equal basis and can challenge each other's thinking. Vygotsky (1978, 1986, 1987, 1993), on the other hand, suggested that children's cognitive development is fostered by interactions with people who are more capable or advanced in their thinking—people such as parents and teachers (Moshman, 1997; Palinscar, 1998). Of course, as we have seen above, students can learn from both adults and peers.

Cultural Tools and Cognitive Development

Vygotsky believed that **cultural tools,** including real tools (such as printing presses, rulers, abacus—today, we would add PDAs, computers, the Internet) and symbolic tools (such as numbers and mathematical systems, Braille and sign language, maps, works of art, signs and codes, and language) play very important roles in cognitive development. For example, as long as the culture provides only Roman numerals for representing quantity, certain ways of thinking mathematically—from long division to calculus—are difficult or impossible. But if a number system has a zero, fractions, positive and negative values, and an infinite number of numbers, then much more is possible. The number system is a cultural tool that supports thinking, learning, and cognitive development. This symbol system is passed from adult to child through formal and informal interactions and teachings.

Vygotsky emphasized the tools that the culture provides to support thinking. He believed that all higher-order mental processes, such as reasoning and problem solving, are *mediated* by (accomplished through and with the help of) psychological tools, such as language, signs, and symbols. Adults teach these tools to children during day-to-day activities and the children internalize them. Then the psychological tools can help students advance their own development (Karpov & Haywood, 1998). The process is something like this: As children engage in activities with adults or more capable peers, they exchange ideas and ways of thinking about or representing concepts—drawing maps, for example, as a way to represent spaces and places. These co-created ideas are internalized by children. Thus, children's knowledge, ideas, attitudes, and values develop through appropriating or "taking for themselves" the ways of acting and thinking provided by their culture and by the more capable members of their group (Kozulin & Presseisen, 1995).

Cultural tools The real tools (computers, scales, etc.) and symbol systems (numbers, language, graphs) that allow people in a society to communicate, think, solve problems, and create knowledge.

In this exchange of signs and symbols and explanations, children begin to develop a "cultural tool kit" to make sense of and learn about their world (Wertsch, 1991). The kit is filled with physical tools such as pencils or paint brushes directed toward the external world and psychological tools such as problem-solving or memory strategies for acting mentally. Children do not just receive the tools, however. They transform the tools as they construct their own representations, symbols, patterns, and understandings. As we learned from Piaget, children's constructions of meaning are not the same as those of adults. In the exchange of signs and symbols such as number systems, children create their own understandings. These understandings are gradually changed as the children continue to engage in social activities and try to make sense of their world (John-Steiner & Mahn, 1996; Wertsch, 1991).

In Vygotsky's theory, language is the most important symbol system in the tool kit, and it is the one that helps to fill the kit with other tools.

Vygotsky emphasized the tools that particular cultures provide to support thinking, and the idea that children use the tools they're given to construct their own understanding of the physical and social worlds.

The Role of Language and Private Speech

Language is critical for cognitive development. It provides a means for expressing ideas and asking questions, the categories and concepts for thinking, and the links between the past and the future (Das, 1995). When we consider a problem, we generally think in words and partial sentences. Vygotsky thought that

> the specifically human capacity for language enables children to provide for auxiliary tools in the solution of difficult tasks, to overcome impulsive action, to plan a solution to a problem prior to its execution, and to master their own behavior. (Vygotsky, 1978, p. 28)

If we study language across cultures, we see that different cultures need and develop different language tools.

Language and Cultural Diversity. In general, cultures develop words for the concepts that are important to them.

How many different shades of green can you name? If you have access to a purse, check out the different shades of lipstick inside.

In my purse I now have lipsticks called "sheer berry" and "529A" (well, the 99-cent lipsticks have given up on color names). English speaking countries have over 3,000 words for colors. Such words are important in our lives for fashion and home design, artistic expression, films and television, and lipstick and eye shadow choices—to name only a few areas (Price & Crapo, 2002). Other cultures care less about color. For example, the Hanunoo people of Midori Island in the Philippines or the Dani in New Guinea have fewer than five words for colors, even though they can recognize many color variations. Eskimos really don't have hundreds of words for snow, but the Ulgunigamiut Eskimo do have more that 160 words for ice, because they have to recognize ice at different stages of freezing to hunt and live safely in their environment. My mother grew up on a farm in Wisconsin and she can tell you many different words for horse: mare, foal, stallion, gelding, stud, colt, pony, work horse, jumper. Cultures that care about feelings have many word tools to talk about emotion. Think of the variety of words in English for anger (rage, resentment, disgust, pique, wrath, fury, exasperation, ire, hostility, animosity).

Languages change over time to indicate changing cultural needs and values. The Shoshoni Native Americans have one word that means "to make a crunching sound walking on the sand." This word was valuable in the past to communicate about hunting, but today new words describing technical tools have been added to the Shoshoni language, as their life moves away from nomadic hunting. To hear hundreds of new 21st century tool words, listen to techies talk about computers (Price & Crapo, 2002).

Vygotsky placed more emphasis than Piaget on the role of learning and language in cognitive development. In fact, Vygotsky believed that language in the form of private speech (talking to yourself) guides cognitive development.

CONNECT & EXTEND

TO **PRAXIS**™
DISTINCTIONS BETWEEN PIAGET'S AND VYGOTSKY'S THEORIES (I, A2)
Consider how two teachers—one based in Vygotskian theory and one based in Piagetian theory—might differ in their concepts of learning and teaching and the instructional techniques that they might prefer.

Vygotsky's and Piaget's Views Compared. If you have spent much time around young children, you know that they often talk to themselves as they play. Piaget called children's self-directed talk "egocentric speech." He assumed that this egocentric speech is another indication that young children can't see the world through the eyes of others. They talk about what matters to them, without taking into account the needs or interests of their listeners. As they mature, and especially as they have disagreements with peers, Piaget believed, children develop socialized speech. They learn to listen and exchange ideas.

Vygotsky had very different ideas about young children's **private speech.** Rather than being a sign of cognitive immaturity, Vygotsky suggested that these mutterings play an important role in cognitive development by moving children toward self-regulation, the ability to plan, monitor, and guide one's own thinking and problem solving.

Vygotsky believed that self-regulation developed in a series of stages. First the child's behavior is regulated by others, usually parents, using language and other signs such as gestures. For example, the parent says, "No!" when the child reaches toward a candle flame. Next the child learns to regulate the behavior of others using the same language tools. The child says, "No!" to another child who is trying to take away a toy, often even imitating the parent's voice tone. Along with learning to use external speech to regulate others, the child begins to use private speech to regulate her own behavior, saying "no" quietly to herself as she is tempted to touch the flame. Finally the child learns to regulate her own behavior by using silent inner speech (Karpov & Haywood, 1998). This series of steps is another example of how higher mental functions appear first between people as they communicate and regulate each others' behavior, and then emerge again within the individual as cognitive processes.

So children using private speech are communicating—they are communicating with themselves to guide their behavior and thinking. In any preschool room you might hear 4- or 5-year-olds saying, "No, it won't fit. Try it here. Turn. Turn. Maybe this one!" while they do puzzles. As these children mature, their self-directed speech goes underground, changing from spoken to whispered speech and then to silent lip movements. Finally, the children just "think" the guiding words. The use of private speech peaks at around 5 to 7 years of age and has generally disappeared by 9 years of age. Brighter children seem to make this transition earlier (Bee, 1992).

Vygotsky identified this transition from audible private speech to silent inner speech as a fundamental process in cognitive development. Through this process the child is using language to accomplish important cognitive activities such as directing attention, solving problems, planning, forming concepts, and gaining self-control. Research supports Vygotsky's ideas (Berk & Spuhl, 1995; Bivens & Berk, 1990; Diaz & Berk, 1992; Kohlberg, Yaeger, & Hjertholm, 1969). Children tend to use more private speech when they are confused, having difficulties, or making mistakes. Inner speech not only helps us solve problems but also allows us to regulate our behavior. Have you ever thought to yourself something like, "Let's see, the first step is . . ." or "Where did I use my glasses last?" or "If I work to the end of this page, then I can . . ."? You were using inner speech to remind, cue, encourage, or guide yourself. In a really

Private speech Children's self-talk, which guides their thinking and action. Eventually these verbalizations are internalized as silent inner speech.

Table 2.2 Differences between Piaget's and Vygotsky's Theories of Egocentric or Private Speech

	Piaget	Vygotsky
Developmental Significance	Represents an inability to take the perspective of another and engage in reciprocal communication.	Represents externalized thought; its function is to communicate with the self for the purpose of self-guidance and self-direction.
Course of Development	Declines with age.	Increases at younger ages and then gradually loses its audible quality to become internal verbal thought.
Relationship to Social Speech	Negative; least socially and cognitively mature children use more egocentric speech.	Positive; private speech develops out of social interaction with others.
Relationship to Environmental Contexts	—	Increases with task difficulty. Private speech serves a helpful self-guiding function in situations where more cognitive effort is needed to reach a solution.

SOURCE: From "Development of Private Speech among Low-Income Appalachian Children," by L. E. Berk and R. A. Garvin, 1984, *Developmental Psychology, 20*, p. 272.

tough situation, such as taking an important test, you might even find that you return to muttering out loud. Table 2.2 contrasts Piaget's and Vygotsky's theories of private speech. We should note that Piaget accepted many of Vygotsky's arguments and came to agree that language could be used in both egocentric and problem-solving ways (Piaget, 1962).

Self-Talk and Learning. Because private speech helps students to regulate their thinking, it makes sense to allow, and even encourage, students to use private speech in school. Insisting on total silence when young students are working on difficult problems may make the work even harder for them. You may notice when muttering increases—this could be a sign that students need help. One approach, called *cognitive self-instruction,* teaches students to use self-talk to guide learning. For example, students learn to give themselves reminders to go slowly and carefully.

The Role of Learning and Development

Another question in the study of cognitive development concerns the role of learning and development—which one comes first?

Vygotsky's and Piaget's Views Compared. Piaget defined *development* as the active construction of knowledge and *learning* as the passive formation of associations (Siegler, 2000). He was interested in knowledge construction and believed that cognitive development has to come before learning—the child had to be cognitively "ready" to learn. He said that "learning is subordinated to development and not vice-versa" (Piaget, 1964, p. 17). Students can memorize, for example, that Geneva is in Switzerland, but still insist that they cannot be Genevan and Swiss at the same time. True understanding will happen only when the child has developed the operation of *class inclusion*—one category can be included in another. In contrast, Vygotsky believed that learning was an active process that does not have to wait for readiness. In fact, "properly organized learning results in mental development and sets in motion a variety of developmental processes that would be impossible apart form learning" (Vygotsky, 1978, p. 90). He saw learning as a tool in development—learning pulls development up to higher levels and social interaction is a key in learning (Glassman, 2001; Wink & Putney, 2002).

According to Vygotsky, much of children's learning is assisted or mediated by teachers and tools in their environment, and most of this guidance is communicated through language.

Vygotsky's belief that learning pulls development to higher levels means that other people play a significant role in cognitive development.

The Role of Adults and Peers

Vygotsky believed that cognitive development occurs through the child's conversations and interactions with more capable members of the culture—adults or more able peers. These people serve as guides and teachers, providing the information and support necessary for the child to grow intellectually. Thus, the child is not alone in the world "discovering" the cognitive operations of conservation or classification. This discovery is assisted or mediated by family members, teachers, and peers. Most of this guidance is communicated through language, at least in Western cultures. In some cultures, observing a skilled performance, not talking about it, guides the child's learning (Rogoff, 1990). Jerome Bruner called this adult assistance **scaffolding** (Wood, Bruner, & Ross, 1976). The term aptly suggests that children use this help for support while they build a firm understanding that will eventually allow them to solve the problems on their own. The *Reaching Every Student* feature on page 51 gives an example of using scaffolding.

Check Yourself Explain how interpsychological development becomes intrapsychological development.

What are the differences between Piaget's and Vygotsky's perspectives on private speech and its role in development?

Implications of Vygotsky's Theory for Teachers

Scaffolding Support for learning and problem solving. The support could be clues, reminders, encouragement, breaking the problem down into steps, providing an example, or anything else that allows the student to grow in independence as a learner.

There are at least three ways that cultural tools can be passed from one individual to another: imitative learning (where one person tries to imitate the other), instructed learning (where learners internalize the instructions of the teacher and use these instructions to self-regulate), and collaborative learning (where a group of peers strives to understand each other and learning occurs in the process) (Tomasello, Kruger, & Ratner, 1993). Vygotsky was most concerned with instructed learning though direct

Reaching Every Student

Scaffolding Learning

Here is an example of how a teacher named Tamara supported her students' learning about math concepts and problem solving:

> Tamara announces, "To prepare for our museum trip, there's something very important I need to do: Write a check for our entrance fees." She tears a check from a checkbook and holds it up. "It's two dollars a person, and we have twenty-two children. How much would that be?"
>
> When none of the children responds, Tamara modifies her question: "How much for ten people to get into the museum? Let's have ten people stand up so we can see." Tamara asks Kara to tap ten people on the shoulder. After they form a line she continues, "Now, if each ticket costs two dollars and we have ten people, how much will it cost? How could we find out?"
>
> Several children chorus, "We can count by twos!"
>
> Tamara nods and says, "Lets count," as she taps each child in the line. When she reaches "twenty" she asks ten more people to stand. The children continue counting, reaching "forty."
>
> "Now, our last two people. Randy and Michael, please stand up."
>
> A child calls out, "Forty-four dollars in all. That's a lot!" Tamara writes the check, pointing out the dollar signs, followed by numerals 4-4. (Berk, 2001, pp. 186–187)

The scaffolding that Tamara provided—making the problem more concrete, breaking it into steps, using the students as "counters," using the familiar process of counting by twos—allowed her students to understand and solve this problem that they could not solve alone.

teaching or through structuring experiences that support another's learning, but his theory supports the other forms of cultural learning as well. Thus, Vygotsky's ideas are relevant for educators who teach directly and also create learning environments (Das, 1995; Wink & Putney, 2002). One major aspect of teaching in either situation is assisted learning.

CONNECT & EXTEND

TO **PRAXIS**™
IMPLICATIONS OF VYGOTSKY'S THEORY (I, A2)
Make a list of scaffolding techniques that would be appropriate with different instructional levels and content areas. Think of scaffolding techniques that others have used when you learned things outside of school (e.g., sports, hobbies).

Assisted Learning

Vygotsky's theory suggests that teachers need to do more than just arrange the environment so that students can discover on their own. Children cannot and should not be expected to reinvent or rediscover knowledge already available in their cultures. Rather, they should be guided and assisted in their learning—so Vygotsky saw teachers, parents, and other adults as central to the child's learning and development (Karpov & Haywood, 1998).

Assisted learning, or guided participation in the classroom, requires *scaffolding*—giving information, prompts, reminders, and encouragement at the right time and in the right amounts, and then gradually allowing the students to do more and more on their own, as Tamara did with her class. Teachers can assist learning by adapting materials or problems to students' current levels; demonstrating skills or thought processes; walking students through the steps of a complicated problem; doing part of the problem (for example, in algebra, the students set up the equation and the teacher does the calculations or vice versa); giving detailed feedback and allowing revisions; or asking questions that refocus students' attention (Rosenshine & Meister, 1992). Cognitive self-instruction is an example of assisted learning. Cognitive apprenticeships and instructional conversations (Chapter 9) are other examples. Look at Table 2.3 on page 52 for examples of strategies that can be used in any lesson.

How can you know what kind of help to give and when to give it? One answer has to do with the student's zone of proximal development.

Assisted learning Providing strategic help in the initial stages of learning, gradually diminishing as students gain independence.

■ Table 2.3 Assisted Learning: Strategies to Scaffold Complex Learning

- *Procedural facilitators.* These provide a "scaffold" to help students learn implicit skills. For example, a teacher might encourage students to use "signal words" such as who, what, where, when, why, and how to generate questions after reading a passage.
- *Modeling use of facilitators.* The teacher in the above example might model the generation of questions about the reading.
- *Thinking out loud.* This models the teacher's expert thought processes, showing students the revisions and choices the learner makes in using procedural facilitators to work on problems.
- *Anticipating difficult areas.* During the modeling and presentations phase of instructions, for example, the teacher anticipates and discusses potential student errors.
- *Providing prompt or cue cards.* Procedural facilitators are written on "prompt cards" that students keep for reference as they work. As students practice, the cards gradually become unnecessary.
- *Regulating the difficulty.* Tasks involving implicit skills are introduced by beginning with simpler problems, providing for student practice after each step, and gradually increasing the complexity of the task.
- *Providing half-done examples.* Giving students half-done examples of problems and having them work out the conclusions can be an effective way to teach students how to ultimately solve problems on their own.
- *Reciprocal teaching.* Having the teacher and students rotate the role of teacher. The teacher provides support to students as they learn to lead discussions and ask their own questions.
- *Providing checklists.* Students can be taught self-checking procedures to help them regulate the quality of their responses.

SOURCE: From "Effective Teaching Redux," *ASCD Update, 32*(6), p. 5.

CONNECT & EXTEND

TO THE RESEARCH
In Chapter 15 you will read about dynamic assessment—an approach that is consistent with Vygotsky's ideas about the zone of proximal development. For a full description see:

Grigorenko, E. L., & Sternberg, R. J. (1998). Dynamic testing *Psychological Bulletin, 124,* 75–111.

The Zone of Proximal Development

According to Vygotsky, at any given point in development there are certain problems that a child is on the verge of being able to solve. The child just needs some structure, clues, reminders, help with remembering details or steps, encouragement to keep trying, and so on. Some problems, of course, are beyond the child's capabilities, even if every step is explained clearly. The **zone of proximal development** is the area where the child cannot solve a problem alone, but can be successful under adult guidance or in collaboration with a more advanced peer (Wertsch, 1991). This is the area where instruction can succeed, because real learning is possible.

Private Speech and the Zone. We can see how Vygotsky's beliefs about the role of private speech in cognitive development fit with the notion of the zone of proximal development. Often, an adult helps a child to solve a problem or accomplish a task using verbal prompts and structuring. This scaffolding may be gradually reduced as the child takes over the guidance, perhaps first by giving the prompts as private speech and finally as inner speech. Let's move forward to a future day in the life of the girl in the example on page 45 who had lost her toy and listen to her *thoughts* when she realizes that a schoolbook is missing. They might sound something like this:

> "Where's my math book? Used it in class. Thought I put it in my bookbag after class. Dropped my bag on the bus. That dope Larry kicked my stuff, so maybe . . ."

The girl can now systematically search for ideas about the lost book without help from anyone else.

Teaching. Students should be put in situations where they have to reach to understand, but where support from other students or from the teacher is also available. Sometimes the best teacher is another student who has just figured out the problem, because this student is probably operating in the learner's zone of proximal development. Students should be guided by explanations, demonstrations, and work with other students—opportunities for cooperative learning. Having a student work with someone who is just a bit better at the activity would also be a good idea. In addition, students should be encouraged to use language to organize their thinking and to talk

Zone of proximal development Phase at which a child can master a task if given appropriate help and support.

 Applying Vygotsky's Ideas in Teaching

Tailor scaffolding to the needs of students.

Examples

1. When students are beginning new tasks or topics, provide models, prompts, sentence starters, coaching, and feedback. As the students grow in competence, give less support and more opportunities for independent work.
2. Give students choices about the level of difficulty or degree of independence in projects; encourage them to challenge themselves but to seek help when they are really stuck.

Make sure students have access to powerful tools that support thinking.

Examples

1. Teach students to use learning and organizational strategies, research tools, language tools (dictionaries or computer searches), spreadsheets, and word processing programs.
2. Model the use of tools; show students how you use an appointment book or electronic notebook to make plans and manage time, for example.

Capitalize on dialogue and group learning.

Examples

1. Experiment with peer tutoring; teach students how to ask good questions and give helpful explanations.
2. Experiment with cooperative learning strategies described in Chapter 13.

about what they are trying to accomplish. Dialogue and discussion are important avenues to learning (Karpov & Bransford, 1995; Kozulin & Presseisen, 1995; Wink & Putney, 2002). The *Guidelines* give more ideas for applying Vygotsky's ideas.

Check Yourself What is assisted learning, and what role does scaffolding play?

What is a student's zone of proximal development?

Clearly, language plays a major role in learning, inside and outside the classroom. Let's look at this human capability more closely.

The Development of Language

All children in every culture master the complicated system of their native language, unless severe deprivation or physical problems interfere. This knowledge is remarkable. At the least, sounds, meanings, words and sequences of words, volume, voice tone, inflection, and turn-taking rules must all be coordinated before a child can communicate effectively in conversations.

It is likely that many factors—biological and experiential—play a role in language development. We saw earlier that culture plays a major role by determining what language tools are necessary in the life of the people. The important point is that children develop language as they develop other cognitive abilities by actively trying to make sense of what they hear and by looking for patterns and making up rules to put together the jigsaw puzzle of language. In this process, humans may have built-in biases, rules, and constraints about language that restrict the number of possibilities considered. For example, young children seem to have a constraint specifying that a new label refers to a whole object, not just a part. Another built-in bias leads children to assume that the label refers to a class of similar objects. So the child learning about the rabbit is equipped naturally to assume that *rabbit* refers to the whole animal (not just its ears) and that other similar-looking animals are also rabbits (Markman, 1992). Reward and correction play a role in helping children learn correct language use, but the child's thinking in putting together the parts of this complicated system is very important (Rosser, 1994).

CONNECT & EXTEND

TO **PRAXIS**™
LANGUAGE DEVELOPMENT
Familiarize yourself with the basic aspects of language development. Focus on actions that teachers can take to maximize students' language and literacy development.

Diversity in Language: Dual Language Development

In 2000, about six million school-aged children in the United States spoke a language other than English at home. The number grows each year. For example, by 2035, about 50% of the kindergarten children in California will speak languages other than English at home (Winsler, Dias, Espinosa, & Rodriquez, 1999).

Luckily, learning a second language does not interfere with understanding in the first language. In fact, the more proficient the speaker is in the first language, the more quickly she or he will master a second language (Cummins, 1984, 1994). For most children who learn two languages simultaneously as toddlers, there is a period between ages 2 and 3 when they progress more slowly because they have not yet figured out that they are learning two different languages. They may mix up the grammar of the two. But researchers believe that by age 4, if they have enough exposure to both languages, they get things straight and speak as well as native monolinguals, people who speak only one language (Baker, 1993; Reich, 1986). Also, bilingual children may mix vocabularies of the two languages when they speak, but this is not a sign that they are confused because their bilingual parents often intentionally mix vocabularies as well. It takes from three to five years to become truly competent in the second language (Berk, 2002; Bhatia & Richie, 1999).

It appears that there is a critical period for learning accurate language pronunciation. The earlier people learn a second language, the more their pronunciation is near-native. After adolescence it is difficult to learn a new language without speaking with an accent (Anderson & Graham, 1994). However, it is a misconception that young children learn a second language faster than adolescents or adults. In fact, older students go through the stages of language learning faster than young children. Adults have more learning strategies and greater knowledge of language in general to bring to bear in mastering a second language (Diaz-Rico & Weed, 2002). Age is a factor in learning language, but "not because of any critical period that limits the possibility of language learning by adults" (Marinova-Todd, Marshall, & Snow, 2000, p. 28). Kathleen Berger (2003) concludes that the best time to *teach* a second language is during early or middle childhood, but the best time to *learn* on your own through exposure (and to learn native pronunciation) is early childhood.

There is no cognitive penalty for students who learn and speak two languages. In fact, there are benefits. Higher degrees of bilingualism are correlated with increased cognitive abilities in such areas as concept formation, creativity, and cognitive flexibility. In addition, these students have more advanced metalinguistic awareness; for example, they are more likely to notice grammar errors. These findings seem to hold as long as there is no stigma attached to being bilingual and as long as students are not expected to abandon their first language to learn English (Berk, 2002; Bialystok, 1999; Galambos & Goldin-Meadow, 1990; Garcia, 1992; Ricciardelli, 1992). Even though the advantages of bilingualism seem clear, as we will see in Chapter 5, there are strong debates about what these findings should mean for education.

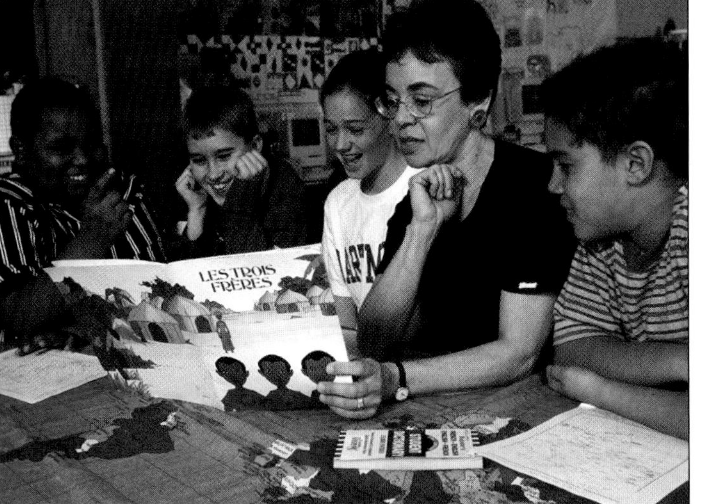

The more proficient speakers are in their first language, the faster they will learn a second language.

Language Development in the School Years

By about age 5 or 6, most children have mastered the basics of their native language. What remains for the school-age child to accomplish?

Pronunciation. The majority of 1st graders have mastered most of the sounds of their native language, but a few may remain unconquered. The *j, v, th,* and *zh* sounds are the last to develop. About 10% of 8-year-olds still have some trouble with *s, z, v, th,* and *zh* (Rathus, 1988). Young children may understand and be able to use many words, but prefer to use the words they can pronounce easily.

"When I say 'runned,' you know I mean 'ran.' Let's not quibble."

Syntax. Children master the basics of word order, or **syntax,** in their native language early. But the more complicated forms, such as the passive voice ("The car was hit by the truck"), take longer to master. By early elementary school, many children can understand the meaning of passive sentences, yet they do not use such constructions in their normal conversations. Other accomplishments during elementary school include first understanding and then using complex grammatical structures such as extra clauses, qualifiers, and conjunctions.

Vocabulary and Meaning. The average 6-year-old has a vocabulary of 8,000 to 14,000 words, growing to about 40,000 by age 11. In fact, some researchers estimate that students in the early grades learn up to 20 words a day (Berger, 2003). School-age children enjoy language games and jokes that play on words. In the early elementary years, some children may have trouble with abstract words such as *justice* or *economy.* They also may not understand the subjunctive case ("If I were a butterfly . . .") because they lack the cognitive ability to reason about things that are not true ("But you aren't a butterfly . . ."). They may take statements literally and thus misunderstand sarcasm or metaphor. Fairy tales are understood concretely simply as stories instead of as moral lessons, for example. Many children are in their preadolescent years before they are able to distinguish being kidded from being taunted or before they know that a sarcastic remark is not meant to be taken literally (Berger, 2003; Gardner, 1982b).

Pragmatics. **Pragmatics** involves the appropriate use of language to communicate. For instance, children must learn the rules of turn-taking in conversation. Young children may appear to take turns in conversations, but if you listen in, you realize that they are not exchanging information, only talk time. In later elementary school, children's conversations start to sound like conversations. Contributions are usually on the same topic. Also, by middle childhood, students understand that an observation can be a command, as in "I see too many children at the pencil sharpener." By adolescence, individuals are very adept at varying their language style to fit the situation. So they can talk to their peers in slang that makes little sense to adults, but marks the adolescent as a member of the group. Yet these same students can speak politely to adults (especially when making requests) and write persuasively about a topic in history (Berk, 2002).

Metalinguistic Awareness. Around the age of 5, students begin to develop **metalinguistic awareness.** This means their understanding about language and how it works becomes explicit. They have knowledge about language itself. They are ready to study and extend the rules that have been implicit—understood but not consciously expressed. This process continues throughout life, as we all become better able to manipulate and comprehend language. One goal of schooling is the development of language and literacy.

Syntax The order of words in phrases or sentences.

Pragmatics The rules for when and how to use language to be an effective communicator in a particular culture.

Metalinguistic awareness Understanding about one's own use of language.

Partnerships with Families. Especially in the early years, the students' home experiences are central in the development of language and literacy (Roskos & Neuman, 1993; Snow, 1993; Whitehurst et al., 1994). In homes that promote literacy, parents and other adults value reading as a source of pleasure, and there are books and other printed materials everywhere. Parents read to their children, take them to

Home environments that emphasize reading as a source of pleasure can be central in children's early development of language and literacy.

bookstores and libraries, limit the amount of television everyone watches, and encourage literacy-related play such as setting up a pretend school or writing "letters" (Pressley, 1996; Roskos & Neuman, 1998; Sulzby & Teale, 1991). Of course, not all homes provide this literacy-rich environment, but teachers can help, as you can see in the *Family and Community Partnerships Guidelines.*

Check Yourself How are humans predisposed to develop language?

What role does learning play?

What are pragmatics and metalinguistic awareness?

Family and Community Partnerships

Promoting Literacy

Communicate with families about the goals and activities of your program.

Examples

1. At the beginning of school, send home a description of the goals to be achieved in your class—make sure it is in a clear and readable format.
2. As you start each unit, send home a newsletter describing what students will be studying—give suggestions for home activities that support the learning.

Involve families in decisions about curriculum.

Examples

1. Have planning workshops at times family members can attend—provide child care for younger siblings, but let children and families work together on projects.
2. Invite parents to come to class to read to students, take dictation of stories, tell stories, record or bind books, and demonstrate skills.

Provide home activities to be shared with family members.

Examples

1. Encourage family members to work with children to read and follow simple recipes, play language games, keep diaries or journals for the family, and visit the library. Get feedback from families or students about the activities.
2. Give families feedback sheets and ask them to help evaluate the child's school work.
3. Provide lists of good children's literature available locally—work with libraries, clubs, and churches to identify sources.

SOURCE: From *Literacy Development in the Early Years: Helping Children Read and Write* (3rd ed.) (pp. 68–70), by L. Morrow. Published by Allyn & Bacon, Boston, MA.

Enhancing Your Expertise with Technology

Language and Literacy Development

Each year in September Jim asks his new kindergartners what they expect to learn in school. The most frequent answer is "To read!" Even 4- and 5-year-olds see that the development of language and literacy skills is a primary mission of schools. It seems obvious to these novice students that language as a focus of learning and the use of language to interact with others will occupy much of their time in the classroom.

In one way or another nearly every educator is a "language teacher," although the mix of concerns may vary by subject matter, grade/age level, or specialty. The important roles of language in the classroom make clear to expert teachers the need to enrich their understanding of language development and their knowledge of effective techniques and strategies that enhance literacy skills.

In the United States there is a national policy to "leave no child behind" in school. If no child is to be left behind, then teachers will have to know how to implement a wide variety of effective classroom practices and techniques; be current with research in literacy development, and recognize the milestones and major trends of language development. This area is so crucial to plans for educational reform and improvement that you will find it useful to build a set of bookmarks or favorites related to it. Start with these three sites and use the questions as cues for exploring each one.

- *Effective Classroom Practices:* Education Place®: (http://www.eduplace.com/rdg/res/literacy/)
- *Research in Literacy Development:* The National Research Center on English Learning & Achievement (http://cela.albany.edu/research.htm)
- *Language Development:* The American Speech-Language-Hearing Association (http://www.asha.org/speech/development/lang_lit.cfm)

Throughout this text you will read about other ways that teachers can encourage language development for both younger and older students. For example, we will discuss bilingual education in Chapter 5, instructional conversations in Chapter 9, and learning to read and write in Chapter 12.

Summary Table

A Definition of Development
(pp. 24–28)

What are the different kinds of development? Human development can be divided into physical development (changes in the body), personal development (changes in an individual's personality), social development (changes in the way an individual relates to others), and cognitive development (changes in thinking).

What are three principles of development? Theorists generally agree that people develop at different rates, that development is an orderly process, and that development takes place gradually.

What is lateralization and why is it important? Lateralization is the specialization of the two sides, or hemispheres, of the brain. The brain begins to lateralize soon after birth. For most people, the left hemisphere is the major factor in language, and the right hemisphere is prominent in spatial and visual processing. Even though certain functions are associated with certain parts of the brain, the various parts and systems of the brain work together to learn and perform complex activities such as reading and to construct understanding.

What part of the brain is associated with higher mental functions? The cortex is a crumpled sheet of neurons that serves three major functions: receiving signals from sense organs (such as visual or auditory signals), controlling voluntary movement, and forming associations. The part of the cortex that controls physical motor movement develops or matures first, then the areas that control complex senses such as vision and hearing, and last the frontal lobe, which controls higher-order thinking processes.

Development: Orderly, adaptive changes we go through from conception to death.

Physical Development: Changes in body structure and function over time.

Personal Development: Changes in personality that take place as one grows.

Social Development: Changes over time in the ways we relate to others.

Cognitive Development: Gradual orderly changes by which mental processes become more complex and sophisticated.

Maturation: Genetically programmed, naturally occurring changes over time.

Lateralization: The specialization of the two hemispheres (sides) of the brain cortex.

Synapses: The tiny space between neurons—chemical messages are sent across these gaps.

Myelination: The process by which neural fibers are coated with a fatty sheath called *myelin* that makes message transfer more efficient.

Piaget's Theory of Cognitive Development
(pp. 28–40)

What are the main influences on cognitive development? Piaget's theory of cognitive development is based on the assumption that people try to make sense of the world and actively create knowledge through direct experience with objects, people, and ideas. Maturation, activity, social transmission, and the need for equilibrium all influence the way thinking processes and knowledge develop. In response to these influences, thinking processes and knowledge develop through changes in the organization of thought (the development of schemes) and through adaptation—including the complementary processes of assimilation (incorporating into existing schemes) and accommodation (changing existing schemes).

What is a scheme? Schemes are the basic building blocks of thinking. They are organized systems of actions or thought that allow us to mentally represent or "think about" the objects and events in our world. Schemes may be very small and specific (grasping, recognizing a square), or they may be larger and more general (using a map in a new city). People adapt to their environment as they increase and organize their schemes.

As children move from sensorimotor to formal-operational thinking, what are the major changes? Piaget believed that young people pass through four stages as they develop: sensorimotor, preoperational, concrete-operational, and formal-operational. In the sensorimotor stage, infants explore the world through their senses and motor activity, and work toward mastering object permanence and performing goal-directed activities. In the preoperational stage, symbolic thinking and logical operations begin. Children in the stage of concrete operations can think logically about tangible situations and can demonstrate conservation, reversibility, classification, and seriation. The ability to perform hypothetico-deductive reasoning, coordinate a set of variables, and imagine other worlds marks the stage of formal operations.

Organization: Ongoing process of arranging information and experience into mental systems or categories.

Adaptation: Adjustment to the environment.

Schemes: Mental systems or categories of perception and experience.

Assimilation: Fitting new information into existing schemes.

Accommodation: Altering existing schemes or creating new ones in response to new information.

Equilibration: Search for mental balance between cognitive schemes and information from the environment.

Disequilibrium: In Piaget's theory, the "out-of-balance" state that occurs when a person realizes that his or her current ways of thinking are not working to solve a problem or understand a situation.

Sensorimotor: Involving the senses and motor activity.
Object Permanence: The understanding that objects have a separate, permanent existence.
Goal-Directed Actions: Deliberate actions toward a goal.
Operations: Actions a person carries out by thinking them through instead of literally performing the actions.
Preoperational: The stage before a child masters logical mental operations.
Semiotic Function: The ability to use symbols—language, pictures, signs, or gestures—to represent actions or objects mentally.
Reversible Thinking: Thinking backward, from the end to the beginning.
Conservation: Principle that some characteristics of an object remain the same despite changes in appearance.
Decentering: Focusing on more than one aspect at a time.
Egocentric: Assuming that others experience the world the way you do.
Collective Monologue: Form of speech in which children in a group talk but do not really interact or communicate.
Concrete Operations: Mental tasks tied to concrete objects and situations.
Identity: Principle that a person or object remains the same over time.
Compensation: The principle that changes in one dimension can be offset by changes in another.
Reversibility: A characteristic of Piagetian logical operations—the ability to think through a series of steps, then mentally reverse the steps and return to the starting point; also called *reversible thinking.*
Classification: Grouping objects into categories.
Seriation: Arranging objects in sequential order according to one aspect, such as size, weight, or volume.
Formal Operations: Mental tasks involving abstract thinking and coordination of a number of variables.
Hypothetico-Deductive Reasoning: A formal-operations problem-solving strategy in which an individual begins by identifying all the factors that might affect a problem and then deduces and systematically evaluates specific solutions.
Adolescent Egocentrism: Assumption that everyone else shares one's thoughts, feelings, and concerns.

Implications of Piaget's Theory for Teachers

(pp. 40–44)

What is the "problem of the match" described by Hunt? The "problem of the match" is that students must be neither bored by work that is too simple nor left behind by teaching they cannot understand. According to Hunt, disequilibrium must be carefully balanced to encourage growth. Situations that lead to errors can help create an appropriate level of disequilibrium.

What is active learning? Why is Piaget's theory of cognitive development consistent with active learning? Piaget's fundamental insight was that individuals *construct* their own understanding; learning is a constructive process. At every level of cognitive development, students must be able to incorporate information into their own schemes. To do this, they must act on the information in some way. This active experience, even at the earliest school levels, should include both physical manipulation of objects and mental manipulation of ideas. As a general rule, students should act, manipulate, observe, and then talk and/or write about what they have experienced. Concrete experiences provide the raw materials for thinking. Communicating with others makes students use, test, and sometimes change their thinking abilities.

What are some limitations of Piaget's theory? Piaget's theory has been criticized because children and adults often think in ways that are inconsistent with the notion of invariant stages. It also appears that Piaget underestimated children's cognitive abilities. Alternative explanations place greater emphasis on students' developing information processing skills and ways teachers can enhance their development. Piaget's work is also criticized for overlooking cultural factors in child development.

Neo-Piagetian Theories: More recent theories that integrate findings about attention, memory, and strategy use with Piaget's insights about children's thinking and the construction of knowledge.

Vygotsky's Sociocultural Perspective

(pp. 44–50)

Explain how interpsychological development becomes intrapsychological development. Higher mental processes appear first between people as they are co-constructed during shared activities. As children engage in activities with adults or more capable peers, they exchange ideas and ways of thinking about or representing concepts. These co-created ideas are internalized by children. Thus children's knowledge, ideas, attitudes, and values develop through appropriating, or "taking for themselves," the ways of acting and thinking provided by their culture and by the more capable members of their group.

What are the differences between Piaget's and Vygotsky's perspectives on private speech and its role in development? Vygotsky's sociocultural view asserts that cognitive development hinges on social interaction and the development of language. As an example, Vygotsky describes the role of children's self-directed talk in guiding and monitoring thinking and problem solving, while Piaget suggested that private speech was an indication of the child's egocentrism. Vygotsky, more than Piaget, emphasized the significant role played by adults and more able peers in children's learning. This adult assistance provides early support while students build the understanding necessary to solve problems on their own later.

Sociocultural Theory: Emphasizes role in development of cooperative dialogues between children and more knowledgeable members of society. Children learn the culture of their community (ways of thinking and behaving) through these interactions.

Co-constructed Process: A social process in which people interact and negotiate (usually verbally) to create an understanding or to solve a problem. The final product is shaped by all participants.

Cultural Tools: The real tools (computers, scales, etc.) and symbol systems (numbers, language, graphs) that allow people in a society to communicate, think, solve problems, and create knowledge.

Private Speech: Children's self-talk, which guides their thinking and action. Eventually these verbalizations are internalized as silent inner speech.

Scaffolding: Support for learning and problem solving. The support could be clues, reminders, encouragement, breaking the problem down into steps, providing an example, or anything else that allows the student to grow in independence as a learner.

Implications of Vygotsky's Theory for Teachers

(pp. 50–53)

What is assisted learning, and what role does scaffolding play? Assisted learning, or guided participation in the classroom, requires scaffolding—giving information, prompts, reminders, and encouragement at the right time and in the right amounts, and then gradually allowing the students to do more and more on their own. Teachers can assist learning by adapting materials or problems to students' current levels, demonstrating skills or thought processes, walking students through the steps of a complicated problem, doing part of the problem, giving detailed feedback and allowing revisions, or asking questions that refocus students' attention.

What is a student's zone of proximal development? At any given point in development there are certain problems that a child is on the verge of being able to solve and others that are beyond the child's capabilities. The zone of proximal development is the area where the child cannot solve a problem alone, but can be successful under adult guidance or in collaboration with a more advanced peer.

Assisted Learning: Providing strategic help in the initial stages of learning, gradually diminishing as students gain independence.

Zone of Proximal Development: Phase at which a child can master a task if given appropriate help and support.

The Development of Language

(pp. 53–56)

How are humans predisposed to develop language? What role does learning play? Children develop language as they develop other cognitive abilities by actively trying to make sense of what they hear, looking for patterns, and making up rules. In this process, built-in biases and rules may limit the search and guide the pattern recognition. Reward and correction play a role in helping children learn correct language use, but the child's thought processes are very important.

What are pragmatics and metalinguistic awareness? Pragmatics is knowledge about how to use language—when, where, how, and to whom to speak. Metalinguistic awareness begins around age 5 or 6 and grows throughout life.

Syntax: The order of words in phrases or sentences.

Pragmatics: The rules for when and how to use language to be an effective communicator in a particular culture.

Metalinguistic Awareness: Understanding about one's own use of language.

Enhancing Your Expertise with Technology

(p. 57)

Effective Classroom Practices: Education Place®
(http://www.eduplace.com/rdg/res/literacy/)

The National Research Center on English Learning & Achievement
(http://cela.albany.edu/research.htm)

The American Speech-Language-Hearing Association
(http://www.asha.org/speech/development/lang_lit.cfm)

Other Useful Websites

A collection of child development websites
http://www.ume.maine.edu/~cofed/eceol/guide.html

In Search of . . . Brain-Based Education. Online article in *Phi Delta Kappan* **http://www.pdkintl.org/kappan/kbru9905.htm**

Practical applications of current brain research from educators K. Nunley and G. Van Tassell **http://www.brains.org/**

ERIC documents on brain-based learning, selected by the Association for Curriculum and Supervision Development
http://www.ascd.org/educationnews/eric/brainabs.html

Southwest Educational Development Laboratory site on "How Can Research on the Brain Inform Education?"
http://www.sedl.org/scimath/compass/v03n02/brain.html

Organizations

The National Academy of Child Development: NACD is an international organization of parents and professionals dedicated to helping children and adults reach their full potential. The site includes resources for parents and links to research articles.
http://www.nacd.org/

American Academy of Child and Adolescent Psychiatry: This organization helps families understand the developmental, emotional, and behavioral disorders affecting children and adolescents.
http://www.aacap.org/

Passing the PRAXIS™

Chapter 2 reflects many of the professional standards created by the Interstate New Teacher Assessment and Support Consortium (INTASC). These standards form the basis of the PRAXIS™ II and state-created teacher licensure exams.

PRAXIS™ II devotes much of its attention to an assessment of your knowledge of human development and its relationship to learning. Turn to the end of the chapter and notice how practicing teachers responded to the opening scenario of the Teacher's Casebook. In each case, they either explicitly or implicitly use concepts drawn from theories of cognitive development and language development. Your understanding of these theories will help you design and implement instructional strategies that are appropriate for the developmental levels of your students and will aid you in understanding and interpreting the problems that they might have with learning activities.

Tips for PRAXIS II™

Cognition

- For Piagetian and Vygotskian theories of development, you should understand:
  1. Basic assumptions of each
  2. How students build their unique knowledge bases
  3. How they acquire skills
  4. Important terms and concepts related to each
  5. The key steps, mechanisms, or milestones related to each theory
  6. The limitations of each theory

Language

- For the development of language, you should understand:
  1. Basic assumptions of major theories
  2. The major accomplishments of language development of school age children
  3. The relationship between language and literacy
  4. Basic steps that teachers can take to enhance literacy among their students

Related Topics

- Learning and teaching about concepts (Chapter 8)
- Characteristics of effective teachers (Chapter 12)
- Examples of student-centered teaching in reading, mathematics, and science (Chapter 12)

Standards and Licensure Appendix: *PRAXIS II™ and INTASC*

Refer to the Appendix at the end of the book for detailed correlations to PRAXIS II™ exam topics and INTASC Standards addressed in this text.

Insights about Job Interview Questions: *What Would You Say?*

1. What do you know about brain-based education?
2. We have openings at several grade levels, so I need to know about your understanding of students across grades. Are students in the 2nd and the 7th grade that different in the way they think—I mean, in any ways that would affect your teaching?

Your Teaching Portfolio: *Teaching Resources*

Think about your philosophy of teaching, a question you will be asked at most job interviews. What do you believe about matching teaching to students' current level of development? Are Piaget's ideas related to "readiness to learn"? What are the roles of direct teaching and discovery in students' learning? Do Piaget and Vygotsky lead you to different philosophies?

- Add some ideas for Parent Involvement from this chapter to your **Portfolio.**
- Adapt Table 2.3, *Assisted Learning: Strategies to Scaffold Complex Learning,* for the grades and subjects you might teach, and add it to your **Teaching Resources** file.

Video**Workshop** Extra

If the Video Workshop package was included with your textbook, go to Chapter 2 of the Companion Website (www.ablongman.com/woolfolk) and click on the Video Workshop button. Follow the instructions for viewing *Video Clip 3: Multiple Intelligences in the Classroom.* Consider this information along with what you've read in Chapter 2 while answering the following questions:

1. Piaget believed that the most helpful interactions are between peers because peers are on an equal basis and can challenge each other's thinking. How do the teachers utilize peer interaction in this classroom?
2. Vygotsky believed children need to be guided and assisted in their learning, not just left alone to discover on their own. These teachers do an excellent job of this with their centers. Describe some ways a teacher can aid a student using assisted learning while conducting a math lesson.

Use the CD-ROM included in the back of your textbook to launch the "Becoming a Professional" website. The website features advice on preparing for teacher certification exams, help with getting your first job, and resources to help you perform your job well from the first day forward.

Teachers' Casebook

What Would They Do?

Here is how some practicing teachers responded to the teaching situation presented at the beginning of this chapter about teaching abstract concepts such as "symbol."

Linda Glisson and Sue Middleton

Fifth Grade Team Teachers, *St. James Episcopal Day School, Baton Rouge, Louisiana*

To begin the lesson, I would have the students use a dictionary to define the word *symbolism* (root word—*symbol*) to discover that it means "something that stands for or represents something else." I would then give them a brief "across the curriculum" exercise in ways they incorporate symbols and symbolism into their thinking every day. For example: (social studies, American history): The American flag is just a piece of cloth. Why then do we recite a pledge to it? Stand at attention when it passes in a parade? What does it stand for? (English, literature—fables and fairy tales): What does the wolf usually represent (stand for)? The lion? The lamb? (Art): What color stands for a glorious summer day? Evil? Goodness and purity? I would continue with math symbols, scientific symbols, and music symbols and lead the students toward contributing other examples such as symbols representing holidays. I would then tell them about their own examples of symbolism that I had recorded. The students' participation in and enthusiasm for the exercises would serve to determine whether they were ready for the material.

Madya Ayala

High School Teacher of Preperatoria Eugenio Garza Lagüera, *Campus Garza Sada, Monterrey, N.L. Mexico*

Since the students' experience is concrete, they respond using corporal symbols that they can relate to. Thus, rather than using verbal analogies, I would use visual images, which are more concrete. For example, I would use familiar examples, such as a heart drawn on the blackboard, and then ask the students what the heart represents. I would also take the opportunity to invert this approach. For example, I would ask students to think about the beach, and then ask them to represent it with one symbol.

Carol Grosberg

Fifth Grade Teacher, *Bates School, Wellesley, Massachusetts*

It has been my experience that students at the 5th grade level are capable of understanding and actually enjoy learning about homonyms, homophones, and homographs. After giving these students an explanation about the difference between them, I would challenge them to create a list of as many of them as they can.

After I was confident that my students understood the idea of words with multiple meanings, I hope that they would know that a symbol and a cymbal are yet another pair of words that fit into this category.

Dr. Nancy Sheehan-Melzack

Art and Music Teacher, *Snug Harbor Community School, Quincy, Massachusetts*

Even very young children can recognize symbols *if* the symbol is presented first and the explanation required second. A drawing of an octagon on a pole has always elicited the answer, "A stop sign," whenever I have shown it. Children recognize symbols, but the teacher needs to work from their concrete knowledge to the more abstract concept, and there are a great many symbols in their daily life on which one can draw. Children as young as 1st graders can recognize traffic sign shapes, letters of the alphabet, and numbers, and further recognize that they stand for directions, sounds, and how many. When they talk about these very common symbols, they can also realize they all use them for the same meaning.

Valerie A. Chilcoat

Fifth/Sixth Grade Advanced Academics, *Glenmount School, Baltimore, Maryland*

Concrete examples of symbolism must come from the students' own world. Street signs, especially those with pictures and not words, are a great example. These concrete symbols, however, are not exactly the same as symbolism used in poetry. The link has to be made from the concrete to the abstract. Silly poetry is one way to do this. It is motivating to the students to read or listen to, and it can provide many examples of one thing acting as another. This strategy can also be used in lower grades to simply expose children to poetry containing symbolism.

Go to the Companion Website (www.ablongman.com/woolfolk) for additional case studies including audio and video cases, and examples of student work.

CHAPTER

3 Personal, Social, and Moral Development

Teachers' Casebook

What Would You Do?

You have seen it before, but this year the situation in your middle school classroom seems especially vicious. A clique of popular girls has made life miserable for several of their former friends—now rejected. The old friends have committed the social sins of not fitting in—they wear the wrong clothes or aren't pretty enough or aren't interested in boys yet. To keep the status distinctions clear between themselves and "the others," the popular girls spread gossip about their former friends, often disclosing the intimate secrets revealed when the "out" girls and the "in" girls were *best* friends, only a few months ago. Today you discover that Stephanie, one of the rejected girls, has written a long, heart-bearing e-mail to her former best friend Alison, asking why Alison is "acting so mean." The now-popular Alison forwarded the e-mail to the entire school and Stephanie is humiliated. She has been absent for three days since the incident.

Critical Thinking

How would you respond to each of the girls? Would you say anything to your other students? What? In your teaching, are there ways you can address the issues raised by this situation? Reflecting on your years in school, were your experiences more like those of Alison or Stephanie?

Collaboration

With 3 or 4 other students in your class, role play a talk with Stephanie, Alison, or their families. Take turns playing the different roles in your group.

Schooling involves more than cognitive development. As you remember your years in school, what stands out—memories about academic knowledge or memories of feelings, friendships, and fears? In this chapter we examine personal, social, and moral development.

We begin with the work of Erik Erikson, whose comprehensive theory provides a framework for studying personal and social development. Next, we explore ideas about how we come to understand ourselves and others. What is the meaning of the self-concept, and how is it shaped? How do our views of others change as we grow? What factors determine our views about morality? What can teachers do to foster such personal qualities as honesty, cooperation, empathy, resilience, and self-esteem? We then consider the three major influences on children's personal and social development: families, peers, and schools. Families today have gone through many transitions, and these changes affect the roles of teachers.

We end the chapter by examining several of the risks that confront students today—such as child abuse, eating disorders, and drugs.

By the time you have completed this chapter, you should be able to answer these questions:

- *What are Erikson's stages of psychosocial development, and are there any implications of his theory for teaching?*
- *How can teachers foster genuine and appropriate self-esteem in their students?*
- *What are the roles of peers, cliques, and friendships in students' lives?*
- *What are Kohlberg's stages of moral reasoning, and what are some of the challenges to his work?*
- *What encourages cheating and aggression in classrooms, and how can teachers respond to each problem?*
- *What can teachers do to support students as they face challenges and risks today?*

Erik Erikson proposed a theory of psychosocial development that describes tasks to be accomplished at different stages of life.

The Work of Erikson

Like Piaget, Erik Erikson did not start out as a psychologist. In fact, Erikson never graduated from high school. He spent his early adult years studying art and traveling around Europe. A meeting with Sigmund Freud in Vienna led to an invitation from Freud to study psychoanalysis. Erikson then emigrated to America to practice his profession and to escape the threat of Hitler.

In his influential *Childhood and Society* (1963), Erikson offered a basic framework for understanding the needs of young people in relation to the society in which they grow, learn, and later make their contributions. His later books, *Identity, Youth, and Crisis* (1968) and *Identity and the Life Cycle* (1980), expanded on his ideas. Although Erikson's approach is not the only explanation of personal and social development, I have chosen it to organize our discussion because Erikson's **psychosocial** theory emphasized the emergence of the self, the search for identity, the individual's relationships with others, and the role of culture throughout life.

Like Piaget, Erikson saw development as a passage through a series of stages, each with its particular goals, concerns, accomplishments, and dangers. The stages are interdependent: Accomplishments at later stages depend on how conflicts are resolved in the earlier years. At each stage, Erikson suggests that the individual faces a **developmental crisis**—a conflict between a positive alternative and a potentially unhealthy alternative. The way in which the individual resolves each crisis will have a lasting effect on that person's self-image and view of society. We will look briefly at all eight stages in Erikson's theory—or, as he called them, the "eight ages of man." Table 3.1 presents the stages in summary form.

Table 3.1 Erikson's Eight Stages of Psychosocial Development

Stages	Approximate Age	Important Event	Description
1. Basic trust versus basic mistrust	Birth to 12–18 months	Feeding	The infant must form a first loving, trusting relationship with the caregiver or develop a sense of mistrust.
2. Autonomy versus shame/doubt	18 months to 3 years	Toilet training	The child's energies are directed toward the development of physical skills, including walking, grasping, controlling the sphincter. The child learns control but may develop shame and doubt if not handled well.
3. Initiative versus guilt	3 to 6 years	Independence	The child continues to become more assertive and to take more initiative but may be too forceful, which can lead to guilt feelings.
4. Industry versus inferiority	6 to 12 years	School	The child must deal with demands to learn new skills or risk a sense of inferiority, failure, and incompetence.
5. Identity versus role confusion	Adolescence	Peer relationships	The teenager must achieve identity in occupation, gender roles, politics, and religion.
6. Intimacy versus isolation	Young adulthood	Love relationships	The young adult must develop intimate relationships or suffer feelings of isolation.
7. Generativity versus stagnation	Middle adulthood	Parenting/Mentoring	Each adult must find some way to satisfy and support the next generation.
8. Ego integrity versus despair	Late adulthood	Reflection on and acceptance of one's life	The culmination is a sense of acceptance of oneself and a sense of fulfillment.

SOURCE: From *Psychology* (5th ed.), by Lester A. Lefton. Published by Allyn & Bacon, Boston, MA. Copyright © 1994 by Pearson Education. Reprinted by permission of the publisher.

The Preschool Years: Trust, Autonomy, and Initiative

Children need opportunities to learn things for themselves in order to develop a sense of initiative.

Erikson identifies *trust versus mistrust* as the basic conflict of infancy. According to Erikson, the infant will develop a sense of trust if its needs for food and care are met with comforting regularity and responsiveness from caregivers. In this first year, infants are in Piaget's sensorimotor stage and are just beginning to learn that they are separate from the world around them. This realization is part of what makes trust so important: Infants must trust the aspects of their world that are beyond their control (Bretherton & Waters, 1985; Isabella & Belsky, 1991).

Erikson's second stage, ***autonomy** versus shame and doubt*, marks the beginning of self-control and self-confidence. Young children begin to assume important responsibilities for self-care such as feeding, toileting, and dressing. During this period parents must tread a fine line; they must be protective—but not overprotective. If parents do not maintain a reassuring, confident attitude and do not reinforce the child's efforts to master basic motor and cognitive skills, children may begin to feel shame; they may learn to doubt their abilities to manage the world on their own terms. Erikson believes that children who experience too much doubt at this stage will lack confidence in their own abilities throughout life.

For Erikson, the next stage of "***initiative*** adds to autonomy the quality of undertaking, planning, and attacking a task for the sake of being active and on the move" (Erikson, 1963, p. 255). The challenge of this period is to maintain a zest for activity and at the same time understand that not every impulse can be acted on. Again, adults must tread a fine line, this time in providing supervision without interference. If children are not allowed to do things on their own, a sense of guilt may develop; they may come to believe that what they want to do is always "wrong." The *Guidelines* on page 68 suggest ways of encouraging initiative.

Elementary and Middle School Years: Industry versus Inferiority

In the early school years, students are developing what Erikson calls a sense of **industry.** They are beginning to see the relationship between perseverance and the pleasure of a job completed. The crisis at this stage is *industry versus inferiority.* For children in modern societies, the school and the neighborhood offer a new set of challenges that must be balanced with those at home. Interaction with peers becomes increasingly important as well. The child's ability to move between these worlds and to cope with academics, group activities, and friends will lead to a growing sense of competence. Difficulty with these challenges can result in feelings of inferiority. The second *Guidelines* on page 68 gives ideas for encouraging industry.

Adolescence: The Search for Identity

Have you decided on your career? What alternatives did you consider? Who or what was influential in shaping your decision?

CONNECT & EXTEND

TO **PRAXIS**™
ERIKSON'S PSYCHOSOCIAL THEORY OF DEVELOPMENT (I, A1, 2)
The school population spans four stages of Erikson's theory. Identify the major crisis of each of these stages. How can teachers support positive resolution of each of these stages? What are implications for positive resolution of these crises?

Psychosocial Describing the relation of the individual's emotional needs to the social environment.

Developmental crisis A specific conflict whose resolution prepares the way for the next stage.

Autonomy Independence.

Initiative Willingness to begin new activities and explore new directions.

Industry Eagerness to engage in productive work.

GUIDELINES Encouraging Initiative in Preschool Children

Encourage children to make and to act on choices.

Examples

1. Have a free-choice time when children can select an activity or game.
2. As much as possible, avoid interrupting children who are very involved in what they are doing.
3. When children suggest an activity, try to follow their suggestions or incorporate their ideas into ongoing activities.
4. Offer positive choices: instead of saying, "You can't have the cookies now," ask, "Would you like the cookies after lunch or after naptime?"

Make sure that each child has a chance to experience success.

Examples

1. When introducing a new game or skill, teach it in small steps.
2. Avoid competitive games when the range of abilities in the class is great.

Encourage make-believe with a wide variety of roles.

Examples

1. Have costumes and props that go along with stories the children enjoy. Encourage the children to act out the stories or make up new adventures for favorite characters.
2. Monitor the children's play to be sure no one monopolizes playing "teacher," "Mommy," "Daddy," or other heroes.

Be tolerant of accidents and mistakes, especially when children are attempting to do something on their own.

Examples

1. Use cups and pitchers that make it easy to pour and hard to spill.
2. Recognize the attempt, even if the product is unsatisfactory.
3. If mistakes are made, show students how to clean up, repair, or redo.

The central issue for adolescents is the development of an **identity** that will provide a firm basis for adulthood. The individual has been developing a sense of self since infancy. But adolescence marks the first time that a conscious effort is made to answer the now-pressing question "Who am I?" The conflict defining this stage is *identity versus role confusion.* Identity refers to the organization of the individual's drives, abilities, beliefs, and history into a consistent image of self. It involves deliberate choices and decisions, particularly about work, values, ideology, and commitments to people and ideas (Marcia, 1987; Penuel & Wertsch, 1995). If adolescents fail to integrate all these aspects and choices, or if they feel unable to choose at all, role confusion threatens.

Identity The complex answer to the question, "Who am I?"

Identity Statuses. James Marcia has suggested that there are four identity alternatives for adolescents, depending on whether they have *explored* options and made

GUIDELINES Encouraging Industry

Make sure that students have opportunities to set and work toward realistic goals.

Examples

1. Begin with short assignments, then move on to longer ones. Monitor student progress by setting up progress checkpoints.
2. Teach students to set reasonable goals. Write down goals and have students keep a journal of progress toward goals.

Give students a chance to show their independence and responsibility.

Examples

1. Tolerate honest mistakes.
2. Delegate to students tasks such as watering class plants, collecting and distributing materials, monitoring the computer lab, grading homework, keeping records of forms returned, and so on.

Provide support to students who seem discouraged.

Examples

1. Use individual charts and contracts that show student progress.
2. Keep samples of earlier work so students can see their improvements.
3. Have awards for most improved, most helpful, most hardworking.

commitments (Marcia, 1991, 1994, 1999). The first is **identity achievement.** This means that after exploring the realistic options, the individual has made choices and is committed to pursuing them. It appears that few students achieve this status by the end of high school; students who attend college may take a bit longer to decide. But even during college, about 80% of students change their majors at least once. And some adults may achieve a firm identity at one period in their lives, only to reject that identity and achieve a new one later. So identity, once achieved, may not be unchanging for everyone (Stephen, Fraser, & Marcia, 1992; Waterman, 1992).

Identity foreclosure is commitment without exploration; foreclosed adolescents have not experimented with different identities or explored a range of options, but simply committed themselves to the goals, values, and lifestyles of others, usually their parents but sometimes cults or extremist groups. **Identity diffusion,** on the other hand, occurs when individuals do not explore or commit. They reach no conclusions about who they are or what they want to do with their lives; they have no firm direction. Adolescents experiencing identity diffusion may be apathetic and withdrawn, with little hope for the future, or they may be openly rebellious (Berger & Thompson, 1995; Kroger, 1995).

Finally, adolescents in the midst of struggling with choices are experiencing what Erikson called a **moratorium.** Erikson used the term moratorium to describe exploration with a delay in commitment to personal and occupational choices. This delay is very common, and probably healthy, for modern adolescents. Erikson believed that adolescents in complex societies have an *identity crisis* during moratorium. Today, the period is no longer referred to as a crisis because, for most people, the experience is a gradual exploration rather than a traumatic upheaval (Grotevant, 1998).

Consequences of Different Statuses. Both identity achievement and moratorium are considered healthy alternatives. The natural tendency of adolescents to "try on" identities, experiment with lifestyles, and commit to causes is an important part of establishing a firm identity. But adolescents who can't get past either the identity diffusion or foreclosure stage have difficulties adjusting. For example, identity-diffused adolescents and young adults often give up, trust their lives to fate, or go along with the crowd, so they are more likely to abuse drugs (Archer & Waterman, 1990). Foreclosed adolescents tend to be rigid, intolerant, dogmatic, and defensive (Frank, Pirsch, & Wright, 1990). Schools that give adolescents experiences with community service, real-world work, internships, and mentoring foster identity formation (Cooper, 1998). The *Guidelines* on page 70 suggest other approaches.

CONNECT & EXTEND

TO OTHER CHAPTERS

Relate this information to concepts you learned in Chapter 2. For example, what aspects of formal-operational thought are helpful (or perhaps necessary) in achieving identity formation? Can you think of people who seem to have established their identity, but who do not seem to have achieved the formal-operational stage? Is identity formation necessarily a conscious process?

Beyond the School Years

The crises of Erikson's stages of adulthood all involve the quality of human relations. The first of these stages is *intimacy versus isolation.* Intimacy in this sense refers to a willingness to relate to another person on a deep level, to have a relationship based on more than mutual need. Someone who has not achieved a sufficiently strong sense of identity tends to fear being overwhelmed or swallowed up by another person and may retreat into isolation. The next stage is *generativity versus stagnation.* **Generativity** extends the ability to care for another person and involves caring and guidance for the next generation and for future generations. While generativity frequently refers to having and nurturing children, it has a broader meaning. Productivity and creativity are essential features. The last of Erikson's stages is *integrity versus despair,* coming to terms with death. Achieving **integrity** means consolidating your sense of self and fully accepting its unique and now unalterable history. Those unable to attain a feeling of fulfillment sink into despair.

Erikson's work helped start the life-span development approach, and his theories have been especially useful in understanding adolescence. But feminists have criticized his notion that identity precedes intimacy, because their research indicates that for women,

Identity achievement Strong sense of commitment to life choices after free consideration of alternatives.

Identity foreclosure Acceptance of parental life choices without consideration of options.

Identity diffusion Uncenteredness; confusion about who you are and what you want.

Moratorium Identity crisis; suspension of choices because of struggle.

Generativity Sense of concern for future generations.

Integrity Sense of self-acceptance and fulfillment.

GUIDELINES Supporting Identity Formation

Give students many models for career choices and other adult roles.

Examples

1. Point out models from literature and history. Have a calendar with the birthdays of eminent women, minority leaders, or people who made a little-known contribution to the subject you are teaching. Briefly discuss the person's accomplishments on his or her birthday.
2. Invite guest speakers to describe how and why they chose their professions. Make sure all kinds of work and workers are represented.

Help students find resources for working out personal problems.

Examples

1. Encourage them to talk to school counselors.
2. Discuss potential outside services.

Be tolerant of teenage fads as long as they don't offend others or interfere with learning.

Examples

1. Discuss the fads of earlier eras (neon hair, powdered wigs, love beads).
2. Don't impose strict dress or hair codes.

Give students realistic feedback about themselves.

Examples

1. When students misbehave or perform poorly, make sure they understand the consequences of their behavior—the effects on themselves and others.
2. Give students model answers or show them other students' completed projects so they can compare their work to good examples.
3. Since students are "trying on" roles, keep the roles separate from the person. You can criticize behavior without criticizing the student.

identity achievement is fused with achieving intimacy (Miller, 2002). With Erikson's theory of psychosocial development as a framework, we can now examine several aspects of personal and social development that are issues throughout childhood and adolescence.

Check Yourself Why is Erikson's theory considered a psychosocial perspective?

What are Erikson's stages of psychosocial development?

Understanding Ourselves and Others

What is self-concept? How do we come to understand other people and ourselves? How do we develop a sense of right and wrong—and do these beliefs affect our behavior? You will see that these areas follow patterns similar to those noted in Chapter 2 for cognitive development. Children's understandings of themselves are concrete at first, and then become more abstract. Early views of self and friends are based on immediate behaviors and appearances. Children assume that others share their feelings and perceptions. Their thinking about themselves and others is simple, segmented, and rule-bound, not flexible or integrated into organized systems. In time, children are able to think abstractly about internal processes—beliefs, intentions, values, and motivations. With these developments in abstract thinking, then, knowledge of self, others, and situations can incorporate more abstract qualities (Berk, 2002; Harter, 1998).

Self-Concept and Self-Esteem

STOP THINK WRITE How strongly do you agree or disagree with these statements?

On the whole I am satisfied with myself.

I feel that I have a number of good qualities.

I wish I could have more respect for myself.

At times I think that I am no good at all.

I certainly feel useless at times.

I take a positive attitude toward myself.

Interest in the self in psychology has grown steadily. In 1970, about 1 in every 20 publications in psychology was related to the self. By 2000, the ratio was 1 in every 7 (Tesser, Stapel, & Wood, 2002). We focus on one aspect of self—self-concept, considered by many psychologists to be the foundation of both social and emotional development (Davis-Kean & Sandler, 2001).

When you encountered Stephanie's situation at the beginning of this chapter, was the idea of self-concept part of your analysis? The term self-concept is part of our everyday conversation. We talk about people who have a "low" self-concept or individuals whose self-concept is not "strong," as if self-concept were fluid levels in a car or a muscle to be developed. These actually are misuses of the term. In psychology, **self-concept** generally refers to "the composite of ideas, feelings, and attitudes people have about themselves" (Hilgard, Atkinson, & Atkinson, 1979, p. 605). We could consider self-concept to be our attempt to explain ourselves to ourselves, to build a scheme (in Piaget's terms) that organizes our impressions, feelings, and attitudes about ourselves. But this model or scheme is not permanent, unified, or unchanging. Our self-perceptions vary from situation to situation and from one phase of our lives to another.

Self-concept and self-esteem are often used interchangeably, even though they have distinct meanings. Self-concept is a cognitive structure—a belief about who you are, for example, a belief that you are a good basketball player. **Self-esteem** is an affective reaction—an judgment about who you are, for example, feeling good about your basketball skills. If people evaluate themselves positively—if they "like what they see"—we say that they have high *self-esteem* (Pintrich & Schunk, 2002). The questions in the *Stop/Think/Write* box above are taken from a widely used measure of self-esteem (Rosenberg, 1979; Hagborg, 1993). You can see the evaluative judgments in the items.

The Structure of Self-Concept. Look at Figure 3.1 on page 72 and notice that the general view of self is made up of other, more specific concepts, including the non-academic self-concept, self-concept in English, and self-concept in mathematics. Recent research indicates that self-concept for artistic abilities is another separate area (Vispoel, 1995). These self-concepts at the second level are themselves made up of more specific, separate conceptions of the self, such as conceptions about physical ability and appearance, relations with peers, and relations with family (particularly parents) (Byrne & Shavelson, 1996; Yeung, McInerney, Russell-Bowie, Suliman, Chui, & Lau, 2000). These conceptions are based on many experiences and events, such as sports performance, assessment of body, friendships, artistic abilities, contributions to community groups, and so on.

The hierarchical structure of self-concept shown in Figure 3.1 is strongest for early adolescents. Older adolescents and adults seem to have separate, specific self-concepts, but these are not necessarily integrated into an overall self-concept. Perhaps young adolescents, faced with the challenges of different academic subjects in school and the "life task" of forming an identity, try to integrate across their many "selves" to achieve that identity. Adults are not actively involved in *all* the academic domains (math, science, social studies) and can define themselves in terms of their current interests and activities, so self-concept is more situation-specific in adults (Byrne & Worth Gavin, 1996; Pintrich & Schunk, 2002).

One important way self-concept affects learning in school is through course selection. Think back to high school. When you had a chance to choose courses, did you pick your worst subjects—those where you felt least capable? Probably not. Herbert Marsh and Alexander Yeung (1997) examined how 246 boys in early high school in Sydney, Australia, chose their courses. Academic self-concept for a particular subject (mathematics, science, etc.) was the most important predictor of course selection—more important than previous grades in the subject or overall self-concept. In fact, having a positive self-concept in a particular subject was an even bigger factor in selecting courses when self-concept in other subjects was low. The courses selected in high school put students on a path toward the

CONNECT & EXTEND

TO YOUR TEACHING

William Glasser talks about self-concept in terms of failure and success identities. Loneliness, apathy, and withdrawal or delinquency characterizes the "failure identity"; the "success identity" is characterized by the ability to give and receive love, and the feeling of doing something that is important to self or others. (Glasser, W. [1969]. *Schools without failure.* New York: Harper and Row.) Given these characteristics, what kind of experiences can a teacher provide to help a student change from a failure identity to a success identity, that is, develop a more positive self-concept?

Self-concept Our perceptions about ourselves.

Self-esteem The value each of us places on our own characteristics, abilities, and behaviors.

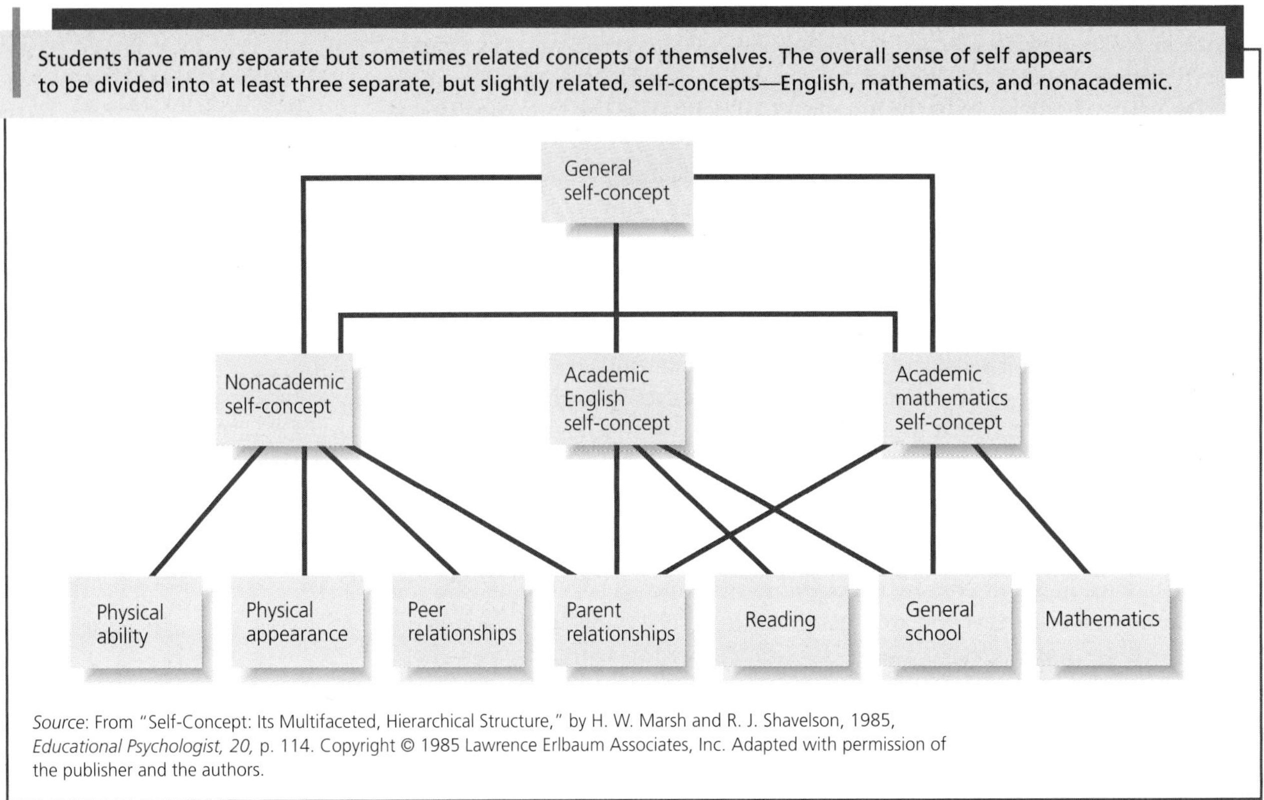

Figure 3.1 Structure of Self-Concept

future, so self-concepts about particular academic subjects can be life-changing influences.

How Self-Concept Develops. The self-concept evolves through constant self-evaluation in different situations. Children and adolescents are continually asking themselves, in effect, "How am I doing?" They gauge the verbal and nonverbal reactions of significant people—parents and other family members in the early years and friends, schoolmates, and teachers later—to make judgments (Harter, 1998).

Young children tend to make self-concept appraisals based on their own improvement over time. A recent study followed 60 students in New Zealand from the time they started school until the middle of their third year (Chapman, Tunmer, & Prochnow, 2000). In the first 2 months of school, differences on reading self-concept began to develop, based on the ease or difficulty students had learning to read. Students who entered school with good knowledge about sounds and letters learned to read more easily and developed more positive reading self-concepts. Over time, differences in the reading performance of students with high and low reading self-concepts grew even greater. Thus, the early experiences with the important school task of reading had strong impact on self-concept.

As they move toward middle school, students compare their performance with their own standards—their performance in math to their performance in English and science, for example, to form self-concepts in these areas. If math is their best subject, their math self-concept may be the most positive, even if their actual performance in math is poor. But social comparisons are becoming more influential, too, at least in Western cultures. Students' self-concepts in math are shaped by how their performance compares to that of other students in their math classes (Marsh, 1994; Pintrich & Schunk, 2002). Students who are strong in math in an average school feel better about their math skills than students of equal ability in high-achieving schools do.

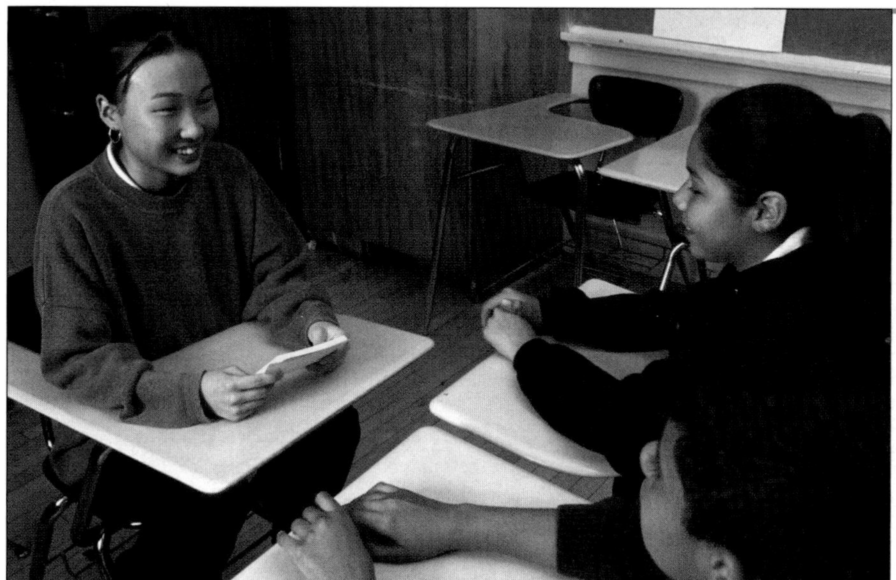

Although it is not certain whether one is the cause of the other, high self-esteem and favorable school experiences seem to be closely related.

Marsh (1990; Marsh, Kong, Hau, 2000) calls this the "Big-Fish-Little-Pond Effect." Participation in a gifted and talented program seems to have an opposite "Little-Fish-in-a-Big-Pond" effect—students who participate in gifted programs, compared to similar students who remain in regular classes, tend to show *declines* in academic self-concepts over time, but no changes in nonacademic self-concepts (Marsh, Chessor, Craven, & Roche, 1995).

School Life and Self-Esteem

We turn now to self-esteem—the students' evaluations and feelings about themselves. For teachers, there are at least two questions to ask about self-esteem: (1) How does self-esteem affect a student's behavior in school? (2) How does life in school affect a student's self-esteem? As you can see from the *Point/Counterpoint* on page 74, the school's role in student self-esteem has been hotly debated.

In answer to the first question, it appears that students with higher self-esteem are somewhat more likely to be successful in school (Marsh, 1990), although the strength of the relationship varies greatly, depending on the characteristics of the students and the research methods used (Ma & Kishor, 1997; Marsh & Holmes, 1990). In addition, higher self-esteem is related to more favorable attitudes toward school, more positive behavior in the classroom, and greater popularity with other students (Cauley & Tyler, 1989; Metcalfe, 1981; Reynolds, 1980). Of course, as we discussed in Chapter 1, knowing that two variables are related (correlated) does not tell us that one is causing the other. It may be that high achievement and popularity lead to self-esteem, or vice versa. In fact, it probably works both ways (Marsh, 1987; Pintrich & Schunk, 2002).

What about the second question of how school affects self-esteem: Is school important? A study that followed 322 6th-grade students for two years would say yes. Hoge, Smit, and Hanson (1990) found that students' satisfaction with school, their sense that classes were interesting and that teachers cared, and teacher feedback and evaluations influenced students' self-esteem. In physical education, teachers' opinions were especially powerful in shaping students' conceptions of their athletic abilities. Being placed in a low-ability group or being held back in school seems to have a negative impact on students' self-esteem, but learning in collaborative and cooperative settings seems to have a positive effect (Covington, 1992; Deci & Ryan, 1985). Interestingly, special programs such as "Student of the Month" or admission to advanced math classes had little effect on self-esteem. (Relate this to the "Big-Fish-Little-Pond Effect.")

CONNECT & EXTEND

TO **PRAXIS**™
SELF-ESTEEM (I, A2)
Understand the bidirectional effects of school life and self-esteem on each other. What can teachers do to enhance students' self-esteem?

Point/Counterpoint

What Should Schools Do to Encourage Students' Self-Esteem?

More than 2,000 books about how to increase self-esteem have been published. Schools and mental health facilities continue to develop self-esteem programs (Slater, 2002). James Beane (1991) begins his article on the school's role in self-esteem, "Sorting Out the Self-Esteem Controversy," with this statement: "In the '90s, the question is not whether schools should enhance students' self-esteem, but how they propose to do so" (p. 25). The attempts to improve students' self-esteem have taken three main forms: personal development activities such as sensitivity training; self-esteem programs where the curriculum focuses directly on improving self-esteem; and structural changes in schools that place greater emphasis on cooperation, student participation, community involvement, and ethnic pride.

Point

The self-esteem movement has problems.

Many of the self-esteem courses are commercial packages—costly for schools but without solid evidence that they make a difference for students (Crisci, 1986; Leming, 1981). As Beane notes, "Saying 'I like myself and others' in front of a group is not the same as actually feeling that way, especially if I am only doing it because I am supposed to. Being nice has a place in enhancing self-esteem, but it is not enough" (p. 26). Some people have accused schools of developing programs where the main objective is "to dole out huge heaping of praise, regardless of actual accomplishments" (Slater, 2002, p. 45).

Sensitivity training and self-esteem courses share a common conceptual problem. They assume that we encourage self-esteem by changing the individual's beliefs, making the young person work harder against the odds. But what if the student's environment is truly unsafe, debilitating, and unsupportive? Some people have overcome tremendous problems, but to expect everyone to do so "ignores the fact that having positive self-esteem is almost impossible for many young people, given the deplorable conditions under which they are forced to live by the inequities in our society" (Beane, 1991, p. 27). Worse yet, some psychologists are now contending that low self-esteem is not a problem, whereas high self-esteem may be. For example, they contend, people with high self-esteem are more willing to inflict pain and punishment on others (Slater, 2002).

Because many attempts to encourage self-esteem have been superficial, commercial, and filled with "pop psychology," the self-esteem movement has become an easy target for critics in magazine articles.

Counterpoint

The self-esteem movement has promise.

Beyond the "feel-good psychology" of some aspects of the self-esteem movement is a basic truth: "Self-esteem is a central feature of human dignity and thus an inalienable human entitlement. As such, schools and other agencies have a moral obligation to help build it and avoid debilitating it" (Beane, 1991, p. 28). If we view self-esteem accurately as a product of our thinking and our actions—our values, ideas, and beliefs as well as our interactions with others—then we see a significant role for the school. Practices that allow authentic participation, cooperation, problem solving, and accomplishment should replace policies that damage self-esteem, such as tracking and competitive grading.

Beane (1991) suggests four principles to guide educators:

> *First, being nice is surely a part of this effort, but it is not enough. Second, there is a place for some direct instruction regarding affective matters, but this is not enough either. Self-esteem and affect are not simply another school subject to be placed in set-aside time slots. Third, the negative affect of "get tough" policies is not a promising route to self-esteem and efficacy. This simply blames young people for problems that are largely not of their own making. Fourth, since self-perceptions are powerfully informed by culture, comparing self-esteem across cultures without clarifying cultural differences is distracting and unproductive. (pp. 29–30)*

Psychologist Lauren Slater (2002) in her article, "The Trouble with Self-Esteem" suggests we rethink self-esteem and move toward honest self-appraisal that will lead to self-control:

> *Maybe self-control should replace self-esteem as a primary peg to reach for. . . . Ultimately, self-control need not be experienced as a constriction; restored to its original meaning, it might be experienced as the kind of practiced prowess an athlete or artist demonstrates, muscles not tamed but trained, so that the leaps are powerful, the spine supple and the energy harnessed and shaped. (p. 47)*

What do you think? Vote online at **www.ablongman.com/woolfolk**

SOURCE: From "The Trouble with Self-Esteem," by L. Slater, *The New York Times Magazine,* February 3, 2002, pp. 44–47 and "Sorting Out the Self-Esteem Controversy," by J. A. Beane, 1991, *Educational Leadership, 49*(1), pp. 25–30.

■ Table 3.2	Suggestions for Encouraging Self-Esteem

1. Value and accept all pupils, for their attempts as well as their accomplishments.
2. Create a climate that is physically and psychologically safe for students.
3. Become aware of your own personal biases (everyone has some biases) and expectations.
4. Make sure that your procedures for teaching and grouping students are really necessary, not just a convenient way of handling problem students or avoiding contact with some students.
5. Make standards of evaluation clear; help students learn to evaluate their own accomplishments.
6. Model appropriate methods of self-criticism, perseverance, and self-reward.
7. Avoid destructive comparisons and competition; encourage students to compete with their own prior levels of achievement.
8. Accept a student even when you must reject a particular behavior or outcome. Students should feel confident, for example, that failing a test or being reprimanded in class does not make them "bad" people.
9. Remember that positive self-concept grows from success in operating in the world *and* from being valued by important people in the environment.
10. Encourage students to take responsibility for their reactions to events; show them that they have choices in how to respond.
11. Set up support groups or "study buddies" in school and teach students how to encourage each other.
12. Help students set clear goals and objectives; brainstorm about resources they have for reaching their goals.
13. Highlight the value of different ethnic groups—their cultures and accomplishments.

SOURCES: Information from "Improving Students' Self-Esteem," by J. Canfield, 1990, *Educational Leadership*, *48*(1), pp. 48–50; *Teacher Behavior and Student Self-Concept*, by M. M. Kash and G. Borich, 1978, Menlo Park, CA: Addison-Wesley; "The Development of Self-Concept," by H. H. Marshall, 1989, *Young Children*, *44*(5), pp. 44–51.

Over 100 years ago, William James (1890) suggested that self-esteem is determined by how *successful* we are in accomplishing tasks or reaching goals we *value*. If a skill or accomplishment is *not* important, incompetence in that area doesn't threaten self-esteem. Susan Harter (1990) has found evidence that James was right. Children who believe an activity is important and who feel capable in that area have higher self-esteem than students who think the activity is important, but question their competence. Students must have legitimate success on tasks that matter to them. The way individuals explain their successes or failures also is important. Students must attribute their successes to their own actions, not to luck or to special assistance, in order to build self-esteem.

Teachers' feedback, grading practices, evaluations, and communication of caring for students can make a difference in how students feel about their abilities in particular subjects. But the greatest increases in self-esteem come when students grow more competent in areas they value—including the social areas that become so important in adolescence. *Thus, a teacher's greatest challenge is to help students achieve important understandings and skills.* Given this responsibility, what can teachers do? The recommendations in Table 3.2 are a beginning.

Gender, Ethnicity, and Self-Esteem

What Would You Say? As part of the interview process for a job in a middle school, you are asked the following: "What would you do to help all your students feel good about themselves?"

Younger children tend to have positive and optimistic views of themselves. In one study, over 80% of the 1st graders surveyed thought they were the best students in class. As they mature, students become more realistic, but many are not accurate judges of their own abilities (Paris & Cunningham, 1996). In fact, some students suffer from "illusions of incompetence"—they seriously underestimate their own competence (Phillips & Zimmerman, 1990). Gender and ethnic stereotypes can play roles here.

Diversity and Self-Esteem. A recent study followed 761 middle-class, primarily European American students from 1st grade through high school (Jacobs, Lanza, Osgood, Eccles, & Wigfield, 2002). It is difficult to get longitudinal data, so this is a valuable study. In 1st grade, girls and boys had comparable perceptions of their own abilities in language arts, but boys felt significantly more competent in math and sports. As you can see in Figure 3.2, competence beliefs declined for both boys and girls across the grades, but boys fell faster in math so that by high school, math competence beliefs were about the same for boys and girls. In language arts, boys' competence ratings fell more sharply than those of girls after 1st grade, but both leveled off during high school. In sports, both boys and girls dropped, but boys remained significantly more confident in their competence in sports throughout the entire 12 years. Other studies have also found that girls tend to see themselves as more able than boys in reading and close friendships; boys are more confident about their abilities in math and athletics (Cole, Martin, Peeke, Seroczynski, & Fier, 1999; Eccles, Wigfield, & Schiefele, 1998; Wilgenbusch & Merrell, 1999). For most ethnic groups (except African Americans), males are more confident about their abilities in math and science. Differences between males and females generally are small but consistent across studies (Grossman & Grossman, 1994; Kling, Hyde, Showers, & Buswell, 1999). Unfortunately, there are no long-term studies of other ethnic groups, so these patterns may be limited to European Americans.

How do students feel about themselves in general during the school years? Jean Twenge and Keith Campbell (2001) analyzed over 150 samples of students from studies conducted between 1968 and 1994, looking at general self-esteem, not subject-specific competence. They found that self-esteem decreased slightly for both girls and boys in the transition to junior high. Then boys' general self-esteem increased dramatically during high school while girls' self-esteem stayed about the same, leaving girls with significantly lower general self-esteem than boys by the end of high school. When these results are examined together with the findings by Jacobs et al. above that boys and girls differ in their academic self-concepts in various subjects and Marsh and Yeung's (1997) results that academic self-concept influences course selection, it seems that many students make decisions about courses that forever limit their options in life, and often these decisions are not based on ability but instead on "illusions of incompetence."

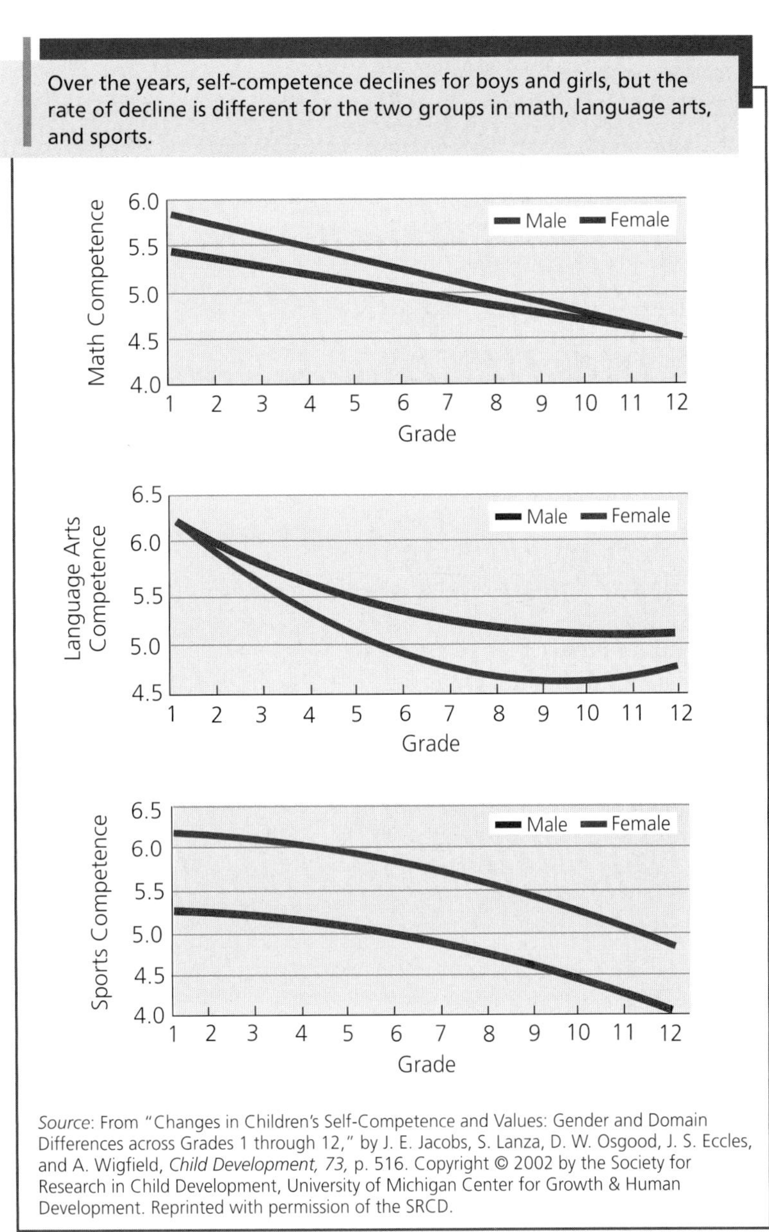

Source: From "Changes in Children's Self-Competence and Values: Gender and Domain Differences across Grades 1 through 12," by J. E. Jacobs, S. Lanza, D. W. Osgood, J. S. Eccles, and A. Wigfield, *Child Development, 73,* p. 516. Copyright © 2002 by the Society for Research in Child Development, University of Michigan Center for Growth & Human Development. Reprinted with permission of the SRCD.

Figure 3.2 Gender Differences in Changes in Self-Competence over the School Years

Personal and Collective Self-Esteem. To this point we have discussed self-esteem as a purely individual characteristic. A number of psychologists have suggested that there is another basis for self-worth and identity called the *collective self,* or the self as a member of a family, peer group, ethnic heritage, class, or team (Wright & Taylor, 1995). Perhaps our self-esteem is influenced by both individual qualities and by **collective self-esteem**—a sense of the worth of the groups to which we belong. When students are faced with daily reminders, subtle or blatant, that their ethnic or family group has less status and power, the basis for collective self-esteem can erode.

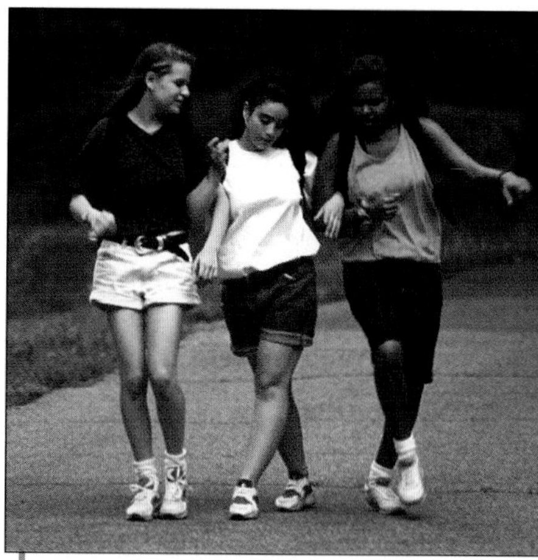

Studies indicate that self-esteem decreases slightly for both boys and girls in the transition to middle school. However, during the high school years, boys' self-esteem increases dramatically, while girls' self-esteem stays about the same.

Some early research on children's perceptions seemed to indicate that ethnic minority group children internalized negative stereotypes. When confronted with a light-skinned doll and a dark-skinned doll, African American children tended to choose the light-skinned doll as prettier and better on a number of dimensions (Clark & Clark, 1939). Similar findings were reported for Mexican American children (Weiland & Coughlin, 1979), Chinese American children (Aboud & Skerry, 1984), and Canadian Native children (Corenblum & Annis, 1987). However, many of these studies didn't ask the children *why* they preferred the light-skinned dolls. Some psychologists suggest that the children are simply indicating that they understand the power and status differences that surround them. The children do not think less of themselves—their self-esteem is high—but they know that majority group members tend to have more wealth and power (Spencer & Markstrom-Adams, 1990).

For all students, pride in family and community is part of the foundation for a stable identity and collective self-esteem. Because ethnic minority students are members of both a majority culture and a subculture, it is sometimes difficult for them to establish a clear identity. Values, learning styles, and communication patterns of the students' subculture may be inconsistent with the expectations of the school and the larger society. Embracing the values of mainstream culture may seem to require rejecting ethnic values. Ethnic minority students have to "sift through two sets of cultural values and identity options" to achieve a firm identity, so they may need more time to explore possibilities (Markstrom-Adams, 1992, p. 177). In the process of establishing identity, individuals may pass through several stages (Frable, 1997):

- being unaware of, denying, or devaluing ethnic identity;
- being challenged by conflicts and discrimination to confront and examine ethnicity;
- being immersed in a particular ethnic or racial consciousness;
- appreciating their ethnicity;
- integrating their ethnicity into a full and complex bicultural identity.

Special efforts to encourage **ethnic pride** are particularly important so students examining their identities do not get the message that differences are deficits (Spencer & Markstrom-Adams, 1990). Each of us has an ethnic heritage. When majority adolescents are knowledgeable and secure about their own heritage, they are also more respectful of the heritage of others. Thus, exploring the ethnic roots of all students should foster both self-esteem and acceptance of others (Rotherham-Borus, 1994).

There is a particular aspect of ethnic heritage and pride that affects schooling—language. In Chapter 5 we will examine bilingual education in greater depth. But while we are talking about self-esteem, consider the results of a study of the impact of heritage language on personal and collective self-esteem by Stephen Wright and Donald Taylor (1995). These researchers found that when Canadian Native (Inuit) children were educated in their heritage language for the first three years of school, they had more positive personal and collective self-esteem than the Canadian Native children in the same school who received second-language instruction (English or French) from kindergarten on. When schools value the language of all students, ethnic pride and collective self-esteem may be enhanced.

One very important group membership for all students is their family. A study by John Fantuzzo, Gwendolyn Davis, and Marika Ginsburg (1995) capitalized on the power of families to improve students' self-esteem. The *Family and Community Partnerships*

Collective self-esteem Beliefs about the worth of the groups you belong to.

Ethnic pride A positive self-concept about one's racial or ethnic heritage.

Family and Community Partnerships

Building Self-Esteem

1. Work with families to co-create methods for family involvement. Offer a range of possible participation methods. Make sure the plans are realistic and fit the lives of the families.
2. Maintain regular home–school contact through telephone calls or notes. If a family has no telephone, identify a contact person (relative or friend) who can take messages. If literacy is a problem, use pictures, symbols, and codes for written communication.
3. Make all communications positive, emphasizing growth, progress, and accomplishments.
4. With the families, design family–student celebrations of the student's efforts and successes (a movie, special meal, trip to the park or library, going out for ice cream or pizza).
5. On a regular basis, send home a note in word or picture form that describes the student's progress. Ask families to indicate how they celebrated the success and to return the note.
6. Follow up with a telephone call to discuss progress, answer questions, solicit family suggestions, and express appreciation for the families' contributions.
7. Encourage families to visit the classroom.

SOURCE: From "Effects of Parent Involvement in Isolation or in Combination with Peer Tutoring on Student Self-Concept and Mathematics Achievement," by J. Fantuzzo, G. Davis, and M. Ginsburg, *Journal of Educational Psychology, 87,* pp. 272–281.

Guidelines list the strategies from their study that proved effective in increasing self-esteem and mathematics achievement for the 4th- and 5th-grade African American urban-school students who participated.

The Self and Others

As we seek our own identity and form images of ourselves, we are also seeking and forming ways understanding the "significant others" around us. How do we learn to interpret what others are thinking and feeling?

Intention. Around the age of 2, children have a sense of intention, at least of their own intentions. They will announce, "I wanna peanut butter sandwich." They can say firmly, "I didn't break it on purpose!" By 2 or 3 years old, children extend the understanding of intention to others. Older preschoolers who get along well with their peers are able to separate intentional from unintentional actions and react accordingly. For example, they will not get angry when another child accidentally knocks over their block tower. But aggressive children have more trouble assessing intention. They are likely to attack anyone who topples their tower, even accidentally (Berk, 2002; Dodge & Somberg, 1987). As children mature, they are more able to assess and consider the intentions of others.

Taking the Perspective of Others. Very young children don't understand that other people have different feelings and experiences. But this **perspective-taking ability** develops over time until it is quite sophisticated in adults. Robert Selman (1980) has developed a stage model to describe the development of perspective-taking. As children mature and move toward formal-operational thinking, they take more information into account and realize that different people can react differently to the same situation. Sometime between the ages of 10 to 15, most children develop the ability to analyze the perspectives of several people involved in a situation from the viewpoint of an objective bystander. Finally, older adolescents and adults can even imagine how different cultural or social values would influence the perceptions of the bystander. Even though children move through these stages, there can be great variation among children of the same age. Students who have difficulty taking the perspective of others may feel little remorse when they mistreat peers or adults. Some coaching in perspective-taking from the teacher might help (Berk, 2002).

Perspective-taking ability Understanding that others have different feelings and experiences.

■ Table 3.3	Emotional Competence Skills

Here are eight skills that make up emotional competence:

1. Awareness of your own emotions, including understanding that you can feel multiple emotions at the same time.
2. Ability to read emotions in others, even taking into account cultural differences in emotional expression.
3. Ability to talk about emotions with appropriate vocabulary.
4. Capacity for empathy and sympathy with others.
5. Knowing that outward emotional expression may not match inner feelings in yourself or in others.
6. Capacity to cope with negative emotions and manage stress in ways that are adaptive—not harmful to yourself or others.
7. Awareness that relationships are defined in part by how emotions are expressed within them and that different kinds of relationships (parent-child, employer-employee, close friends, acquaintances, etc.) involve different kinds of appropriate expressions.
8. Capacity for emotional self-efficacy—feeling that overall, your emotions fit your own beliefs about emotional balance and your own moral sense.

SOURCE: From *The Development of Emotional Competence,* by Carolyn Saarni. Published by Guilford Publications, Inc. Copyright © 2002 by Guilford Publications, Inc. Adapted with permission of the publisher.

Emotional Competence. Understanding intentions and taking the perspective of others are elements in the development of emotional competence or the ability to understand and manage emotional situations. Carolyn Saarni (2002) says that "we demonstrate emotional competence when we emerge from an emotion-eliciting encounter with a sense of having accomplished what we set out to do" (p. 3). Table 3.3 describes eight skills of emotional competence.

How can teachers help students develop emotional competence? The *Guidelines* give some ideas. In Chapter 13 we look at teaching strategies and programs that encourage emotional competence.

Check Yourself Distinguish between self-concept and self-esteem.

How do self-concept and self-esteem change as children develop?

How do perspective-taking skills change as students mature?

What are the skills involved in emotional competence?

GUIDELINES Encouraging Emotional Competence

Create a climate of trust in your classroom.

Examples

1. Avoid listening to "tattle tale" stories about students.
2. Follow through with fair consequences.
3. Avoid unnecessary comparisons and give students opportunities to improve their work.

Help students recognize and express their feelings.

Examples

1. Provide a vocabulary of emotions and note descriptions of emotions in characters or stories.
2. Be clear and descriptive about your own emotions.
3. Encourage students to write in journals about their own feelings. Protect the privacy of these writing (see trust above).

Help students recognize emotions in others.

Examples

1. For young children, "Look at Chandra's face. How do you think she feels when you say those things?"
2. For older students, use readings, films, or role reversals to help them identify the emotions of others.

Provide strategies for coping with emotions.

Examples

1. Discuss or practice alternatives such as stopping to think how the other person feels, seeking help, anger management such as self-talk or leaving the scene.
2. Model strategies for students. Talk about how you handle anger, disappointment, or anxiety.

Help students recognize cultural differences in emotional expression.

Examples

1. Have students write about or discuss how they show emotions in their family.
2. Teach students "check it out"—ask the other people how they are feeling.

CONNECT & EXTEND

TO YOUR PHILOSOPHY

The June 3, 1996 issue of *U.S. News & World Report* had a cover story titled "How to Raise a Moral Child: Let's Hear It for Honesty, Self-Discipline, and Empathy" (pp. 52–59). This is an interesting mix of research and opinion and a good discussion starter.

CONNECT & EXTEND

TO **PRAXIS**™
MORAL DEVELOPMENT (I, A2)

Moral issues can have an important impact on the classroom. Identify major issues related to moral development and explain what a teacher can do to appropriately address these issues.

Moral Development

Some of the earliest moral issues in classrooms involve dividing and sharing materials or **distributive justice** (Damon, 1994). For young children (ages 5 to 6), fair distribution is based on *equality;* thus, teachers often hear, "Keshawn got more than I did—that's not fair!" In the next few years, children come to recognize that some people should get more based on *merit*—they worked harder or performed better. Finally, around age 8, children are able to take need into account and reason based on *benevolence,* so they can understand that some students may get more time or resources from the teacher because those students have special needs.

Another area that involves moral development is an understanding of rules. If you have spent time with young children, you know that there is a period when you can say, "Eating in the living room is not allowed!" and get away with it. For young children, rules simply exist. Piaget (1965) called this the state of **moral realism.** At this stage, the child of 5 or 6 believes that rules about conduct or rules about how to play a game are absolute and can't be changed. If a rule is broken, the child believes that the punishment should be determined by how much damage is done, not by the intention of the child or by other circumstances. So accidentally breaking three cups is worse than intentionally breaking one, and in the child's eyes, the punishment for the three-cup offense should be greater.

As children interact with others, develop perspective-taking emotional abilities, and see that different people have different rules, there is a gradual shift to a **morality of cooperation.** Children come to understand that people make rules and people can change them. When rules are broken, both the damage done and the intention of the offender are taken into account. These developmental changes and others are reflected in Kohlberg's theory of moral development, based in part on Piaget's ideas.

Kohlberg's Stages of Moral Development

A man's wife is dying. There is one drug that could save her, but it is very expensive, and the druggist who invented it will not sell it at a price low enough for the man to buy it. Finally, the man becomes desperate and considers stealing the drug for his wife. What should he do, and why?

Lawrence Kohlberg (1963, 1975, 1981) proposed a detailed sequence of stages of **moral reasoning,** or judgments about right and wrong. He divided moral development into three levels: (1) preconventional, where judgment is based solely on a person's own needs and perceptions; (2) conventional, where the expectations of society and law are taken into account; and (3) postconventional, where judgments are based on abstract, more personal principles that are not necessarily defined by society's laws. Look at Table 3.4 to see how each of these three levels is then subdivided into stages. Can you find your reasons for your answer to the *Stop/Think/Write* question above in Table 3.4?

Kohlberg has evaluated the moral reasoning of both children and adults by presenting them with **moral dilemmas,** or hypothetical situations in which people must make difficult decisions and give their reasons. At level 1 (preconventional), the child's answer to the drug dilemma above might be, "It is wrong to steal because you might get caught." This answer reflects the child's basic egocentrism. The reasoning might be: "What would happen to me if I stole something? I might get caught and punished."

At level 2 (the conventional level), the subject is able to look beyond the immediate personal consequences and consider the views, and especially the approval, of others. Laws, religious or civil, are very important and are regarded as absolute and unalterable. One answer stressing adherence to rules is, "It is wrong to steal because it is against the law." Another answer, placing high value on loyalty to family and loved

Distributive justice Beliefs about how to divide materials or privileges fairly among members of a group; follows a sequence of development from equality to merit to benevolence.

Moral realism Stage of development wherein children see rules as absolute.

Morality of cooperation Stage of development wherein children realize that people make rules and people can change them.

Moral reasoning The thinking process involved in judgments about questions of right and wrong.

Moral dilemmas Situations in which no choice is clearly and indisputably right.

■ Table 3.4 Kohlberg's Theory of Moral Reasoning

Level 1. Preconventional Moral Reasoning

Judgment is based on personal needs and others' rules.

Stage 1	Punishment–Obedience Orientation Rules are obeyed to avoid punishment. A good or bad action is determined by its physical consequences.
Stage 2	Personal Reward Orientation Personal needs determine right and wrong. Favors are returned along the lines of "You scratch my back, I'll scratch yours."

Level 2. Conventional Moral Reasoning

Judgment is based on others' approval, family expectations, traditional values, the laws of society, and loyalty to country.

Stage 3	Good Boy–Nice Girl Orientation Good means "nice." It is determined by what pleases, aids, and is approved by others.
Stage 4	Law and Order Orientation Laws are absolute. Authority must be respected and the social order maintained.

Level 3. Postconventional Moral Reasoning

Stage 5	Social Contract Orientation Good is determined by socially agreed-upon standards of individual rights. This is a morality similar to that of the U.S. Constitution.
Stage 6*	Universal Ethical Principle Orientation Good and right are matters of individual conscience and involve abstract concepts of justice, human dignity, and equality.

*In later work Kohlberg questioned whether Stage 6 exists separately from Stage 5.

SOURCE: From "The Cognitive-Developmental Approach to Moral Education," by L. Kohlberg, 1975, *Phi Delta Kappan*, *56*, p. 671. Adapted by permission of the *Journal of Philosophy*.

ones but still respecting the law, is, "It's right to steal because the man means well—he's trying to help his wife. But he will still have to pay the druggist when he can or accept the penalty for breaking the law."

At level 3 (the postconventional level), an answer might be, "It is not wrong to steal because human life must be preserved. The worth of a human life is greater than the worth of property." This response considers the underlying values that might be involved in the decision. Abstract concepts are no longer rigid, and, as the name of this level implies, principles can be separated from conventional values. A person reasoning on this level understands that what is considered right by the majority may not be considered right by an individual in a particular situation. Rational, personal choice is stressed.

CONNECT & EXTEND

TO YOUR TEACHING

In a classroom discussion about stealing, the teacher finds that many students express the opinion that it is all right to steal if you don't get caught. How should a teacher respond? Would the race, culture, gender, or socioeconomic status of the student influence the teacher's response?

Agnes's moral dilemma. How would you rate her reasoning?

From *Agnes,* May 7, 2002. © 2002 Tony Cochran. Reprinted with permission of the Creators Syndicate.

Moral reasoning is related to both cognitive and emotional development. As we have seen, abstract thinking becomes increasingly important in the higher stages of moral development, as children move from decisions based on absolute rules to those based on abstract principles such as justice and mercy. The ability to see another's perspective, to judge intentions, and to imagine alternative bases for laws and rules also enters into judgments at the higher stages.

Alternatives to Kohlberg's Theory

Even though there is evidence that the different levels of reasoning identified by Kohlberg do form a hierarchy, with each stage an advancement in reasoning over the one before (Boom, Brugman, & van der Heijden, 2001), the stage theory has been criticized. First, in reality, the stages do not seem to be separate, sequenced, and consistent. People often give reasons for moral choices that reflect several different stages simultaneously. Or a person's choices in one instance may fit one stage and his or her decisions in a different situation may reflect another stage. When asked to reason about helping someone else versus meeting their own needs, both children and adolescents reason at higher levels than when they are asked to reason about breaking the law or risking punishment (Arnold, 2000; Eisenberg et al., 1987; Sobesky, 1983).

Second, in everyday life, making moral choices involves more reasoning. Emotions, competing goals, relationships, and practical considerations all affect choices. People may be able to reason at higher levels, but make choices at lower levels based on these other factors (Carpendale, 2000). Kohlberg emphasized cognitive reasoning about morality, but overlooked other aspects of moral maturity, such as character and virtue, that operate to solve moral problems in everyday life (Walker & Pitts, 1998).

Cultural Differences in Moral Reasoning. Another criticism of Kohlberg's stage theory is that stages 5 and 6 in moral reasoning are biased in favor of Western, male values that emphasize individualism. In cultures that are more family-centered or group-oriented, the highest moral value might involve putting the opinions of the group before decisions based on individual conscience. There has been much disagreement over the "highest" moral stage. Kohlberg himself questioned the applicability of stage 6. Few people other than trained philosophers reason naturally or easily at this level. Kohlberg (1984) suggested that for all practical purposes, stages 5 and 6 might be combined.

Diversity in Reasoning: The Morality of Caring

Carol Gilligan has challenged traditional conceptions of moral development with her work on the "ethic of care."

One of the most hotly debated criticisms of Kohlberg's theory is that the stages are biased in favor of males and do not represent the way moral reasoning develops in women, because the stage theory was based on a longitudinal study of men only (Gilligan, 1982; Gilligan & Attanucci, 1988). Carol Gilligan (1982) has proposed a different sequence of moral development, an "ethic of care." Gilligan suggests that individuals move from a focus on self-interest to moral reasoning based on commitment to specific individuals and relationships, and then to the highest level of morality based on the principles of responsibility and care for all people.

The highest stage in Kohlberg's theory of moral development involves decisions based on universal principles of justice and fairness. Reasoning based on caring for others and maintaining relationships is scored at a lower level. Many of Kohlberg's early studies of moral reasoning found that most men progressed to stages 4 and 5 by adulthood, while most women "stayed" at stage 3. This makes it appear as if women are morally challenged. But recent studies find few significant differences between men and women, or boys and girls, in their level of moral reasoning as measured by Kohlberg's procedures (Eisenberg, Martin, & Fabes, 1996; Turiel, 1998).

In order to study moral reasoning as it actually happens in real life, and to get an idea about the basis for decisions, Walker and his colleagues (Walker, 1991; Walker, Pitts, Hennig, & Matsuba, 1995) asked children, adolescents, and adults to describe a personal moral problem and analyze a traditional moral dilemma. For both types of problems, males and females revealed both a morality of caring and a concern with justice. Andrew Garrod and his colleagues (1990) used fables to study the moral reasoning of 1st, 3rd, and 5th graders and found that there were no differences between the moral reasoning of boys and girls in the 1st and 3rd grades. However, a few 5th-grade boys (but no girls) suggested solutions involving violence or tricks. So justice and caring seem to be important bases for moral reasoning for both genders. Even though men and women both seem to value caring and justice, there is some evidence that in everyday life, women feel more guilty about violating caring norms (being inconsiderate or untrustworthy) and men feel more guilty when they show violent behaviors (fighting or damaging property) (Williams & Bybee, 1994). Women are somewhat more likely to use a care orientation, but both men and women *can* use both orientations (Skoe, 1998).

Caring for students and helping students learn to care has become a theme for many educators. For example, Nel Noddings (1995) urged that "themes of care" be used to organize the curriculum. Possible themes include "Caring for Self," "Caring for Family and Friends," and "Caring for Strangers and the World." Using the theme of "Caring for Strangers and the World," there could be units on crime, war, poverty, tolerance, ecology, or technology. Table 3.5 shows how a focus on crime and caring for strangers could be integrated into several high school classes.

In the last years of his life, Kohlberg was studying moral behavior in schools. We turn to that topic now.

CONNECT & EXTEND

TO YOUR OWN PHILOSOPHY
Moral action does not necessarily follow directly from moral judgment. But is it necessary for moral judgment to precede moral action? That is, can a person behave in a moral way even if he or she cannot make a cognitive statement about how one "should" behave?

Moral Behavior

As people move toward higher stages of moral reasoning, they also evidence more sharing, helping, and defending of victims of injustice. This relationship between moral reasoning and moral behavior is not very strong, however (Berk, 2002). Many other factors besides reasoning affect behavior. Three important influences on moral

Table 3.5 Using "Caring for Strangers and the World" as a Teaching Theme

As part of a unit on "Caring for Strangers and the World," high school students examine the issue of crime in several classes. In every class, the study of aspects of crime would be continually tied to the theme of caring and to discussions of safety, responsibility, trust in each other and in the community, and commitment to a safer future.

Subject	Elements
Mathematics	Statistics: Gather data on the location and rates of crimes, ages of offenders, and costs of crime to society. Is there a correlation between severity of punishment and incidence of crime? What is the actual cost of a criminal trial?
English and Social Studies	Read *Oliver Twist.* Relate the characters to their social and historical context. What factors contributed to crime in 19th century England? Read popular mysteries. Are they literature? Are they accurate depictions of the criminal justice system?
Science	Genetics: Are criminal tendencies heritable? Are there sex differences in aggressive behavior? Are women less competent than men in moral reasoning (and why did some social scientists think so)? How would you test this hypothesis?
Arts	Is graffiti art really art?

SOURCE: From "Teaching Themes of Care," by Nel Noddings, *Phi Delta Kappan, 76,* pp. 675–679. Copyright © 1995 Nel Noddings. Reprinted with permission of the author.

Over time, children learn to internalize moral principles such as compassion and justice and adopt them for themselves.

behavior are modeling, internalization, and self-concept. First, children who have been consistently exposed to caring, generous adult models will tend to be more concerned for the rights and feelings of others (Lipscomb, MacAllister, & Bregman, 1985). Second, most theories of moral behavior assume that young children's moral behavior is first controlled by others through direct instruction, supervision, rewards and punishments, and correction. But in time, children **internalize** the moral rules and principles of the authority figures who have guided them; that is, children adopt the external standards as their own. If children are given reasons they can understand when they are corrected—particularly reasons that highlight the effects of actions on others—then they are more likely to internalize moral principles. They learn to behave morally even when "no one is watching" (Berk, 2002; Hoffman, 2000).

Finally, we must integrate moral beliefs and values into our total sense of who we are, our self-concept.

> The tendency for a person to behave morally is largely dependent on the extent to which moral beliefs and values are integrated in the personality, and in one's sense of self. The influence our moral beliefs have on our lives, therefore, is contingent on the personal importance that we as individuals attach to them—we must identify and respect them as our own. (Arnold, 2000, p. 372)

Let's consider several moral issues that arise in classrooms, beginning with aggression and violence.

What Would You Say? As part of the interview process for a job in a high school, you are asked the following: "Tell me how you could tell if there might be violence among students in our school. What are the warning signs?"

Aggression. There are several forms of aggression. The most common form is **instrumental aggression,** which is intended to gain an object or privilege, such as shoving to get in line first or snatching a toy from another child. The intent is to get what you want, not to hurt the other child, but the hurt may happen anyway. A second kind is **hostile aggression**—inflicting intentional harm. Hostile aggression can be either the **overt aggression** of threats or physical attacks (as in, "I'm gonna beat you up!") or **relational aggression,** which involves threatening or damaging social relationships (as in, "I'm never going to speak to you again!"). Boys are more likely to use overt aggression and girls, like Alison in the opening case, are more likely to use relational aggression (Berk, 2002). Aggression should not be confused with assertiveness, which means affirming or maintaining a legitimate right. As Helen Bee (1981) explains, "A child who says, 'That's my toy!' is showing assertiveness. If he bashes his playmate over the head to reclaim it, he has shown aggression" (p. 350).

Modeling plays an important role in the expression of aggression (Bandura, Ross, & Ross, 1963). Children who grow up in homes filled with harsh punishment and family violence are more likely to use aggression to solve their own problems (Emery, 1989; Holden & Ritchie, 1991). One very real source of aggressive models is found in almost every home in America—television. In the United States, 82% of TV programs have at least some violence. The rate for children's programs is especially high—an average of 32 violent acts per hour, with cartoons being the worst. And in over 70% of the violent scenes, the violence goes unpunished (Mediascope, 1996; Waters, 1993). Most children spend more time watching television than they do in any other activity except sleep (Timmer, Eccles, & O'Brien, 1988).

You can reduce the negative effects of TV violence by stressing three points with your students: Most people do not behave in the aggressive ways shown on television; the violent acts on TV are not real, but are created by special effects and stunts; and

Internalize Process whereby children adopt external standards as their own.

Instrumental aggression Strong actions aimed at claiming an object, place, or privilege—not intended to harm, but may lead to harm.

Hostile aggression Bold, direct action that is intended to hurt someone else; unprovoked attack.

Overt aggression A form of hostile aggression that involves physical attack.

Relational aggression A form of hostile aggression that involves verbal attacks and other actions meant to harm social relationships.

there are better ways to resolve conflicts—these are the ways most real people use to solve their problems (Huessmann, Eron, Klein, Brice, & Fischer, 1983). Also, avoid using TV viewing as a reward or punishment because that makes television even more attractive to children (Slaby et al., 1995). But television is not the only source of violent models. Many popular films and video games are also filled with graphic depictions of violence, often performed by the "hero." Students growing up in the inner cities see gang violence. Newspapers, magazines, and the radio are filled with stories of murders, rapes, and robberies. In some preschools the children don't play "Mommy" and "Daddy"; they pretend to sell "nickel bags" of heroin (really bags of ground-up chalk) to their playmates.

CONNECT & EXTEND

TO THE RESEARCH
Galen, B. R., & Underwood, M. K. (1997). A developmental investigation of social aggression among children. *Developmental Psychology, 33,* 589–600.

Bullies. Aggressive children tend to believe that violence will be rewarded, and they use aggression to get what they want. They are more likely to believe that violent retaliation is acceptable: "It's OK to shove people when you're mad" (Egan, Monson, & Perry, 1998). Seeing violent acts go unpunished probably affirms and encourages these beliefs. In addition to being surrounded by violence and believing that violent "pay back" is appropriate when you are insulted or harmed, some children, particularly boys, have difficulty reading the intentions of others (Zelli, Dodge, Lochman, & Laird, 1999). As we saw earlier, they assume another child "did it on purpose" when their block tower is toppled, they are pushed on the bus, or some other mistake is made. Retaliation follows and the cycle of aggression continues.

Helping children handle aggression can make a lasting difference in their lives. For example, one study in Finland found that teacher-rated aggression at age 8 predicted school adjustment problems in early adolescence and long-term unemployment in adulthood (Kokko & Pulkkinen, 2000). Sandra Graham (1996) has successfully experimented with approaches that help aggressive, 5th- and 6th-grade African American boys become better judges of others' intentions. Strategies include engaging in role play, participating in group discussions of personal experiences, interpreting social cues from photographs, playing pantomime games, making videos, and writing endings to unfinished stories. The boys in the 12-session training group showed clear improvement in reading the intentions of others and responding with less aggression.

Relational Aggression. Insults, gossip, exclusion, taunts—all these are forms of relational aggression, sometimes called *social aggression* because the intent is to harm social connections. Both boys and girls take part in relational aggression, but after 2nd or 3rd grade, girls tend to engage in relational aggression more than boys. This may be because as girls become aware of gender stereotypes, they push their overt aggression underground into verbal, not physical, attacks. This type of aggression can be even more damaging than overt physical aggression—both to the victim and the aggressor. Victims, like Stephanie in the chapter opening, can be devastated. Relational aggressors can be viewed as even more problematic than physical aggressors by teachers and other students (Berger, 2003; Crick, Casas, & Mosher, 1997). As early as preschool, children need to learn how to negotiate social relations without resorting to aggression.

Victims. Some students tend to be bullies; other children are victims. Studies from Europe and the United States indicate that about 10% of children are chronic victims—the constant targets for physical or verbal attacks. These victims tend to have low self-esteem and they feel anxious, lonely, insecure, and unhappy. They often are prone to crying and withdrawal; when attacked, generally they won't defend themselves. Recent research suggests that victims may blame themselves for their situation. They believe that they are rejected because they have character flaws that they cannot change or control—no wonder they are depressed and helpless! The situation is worse for young adolescent victims whose peers seem to have little sympathy for them. Children who have been chronic victims through elementary and middle school are more

CONNECT & EXTEND

TO THE RESEARCH
Graham, S. (1998). Self-blame and peer victimization in middle school: An attributional analysis. *Developmental Psychology, 34,* 587–599.

depressed and more likely to attempt suicide as young adults (Graham, 1998; Hodges & Perry, 1999). In the past years we have seen tragic consequences when bullied students turned guns on their tormentors in schools in the United States and in Europe.

There is a second kind of victim—highly emotional and hot-tempered students who seem to provoke aggressive reactions from their peers. Members of this group, about 10% to 15% of students, are rejected by almost all peers and have few friends (Pellegrini, Bartini, & Brooks, 1999). The *Guidelines* may give you ideas for handling aggression and encouraging cooperation.

When Aggression Leads to Violence. About one-third of all injury-related deaths are the result of interpersonal violence—and young people are often the victims or the attackers in these violent acts (Peterson & Newman, 2000). Teachers and students need to know the warning signs of potential dangers. Table 3.6 describes two kinds of signs—immediate warning and potential problems. For more information, go to the Companion Website that takes you to the American Psychological Association resources in youth violence: http://helping.apa.org/warningsigns/.

Cheating. Early research indicates that cheating seems to have more to do with the particular situation than with the general honesty or dishonesty of the individual (R. Burton, 1963). A student who cheats in math class is probably more likely to cheat in other classes, but may never consider lying to a friend or taking candy from the store. Most students will cheat if the pressure to perform well is great and the chances of being caught are slim. In one study, about 60% of middle school students and 70% of high school students believed that cheating was a serious problem in their school (Evans & Craig, 1990). In 1996, Steinberg reported that 66% of the adolescents in his study admitted to cheating on a test in the last year.

There are some individual differences in cheating. Most studies of adolescent and college-age students find that males are more likely to cheat than females and lower achieving students are more likely to cheat than higher achievers. Students focusing

Dealing with Aggression and Encouraging Cooperation

Present yourself as a nonaggressive model.

Examples

1. Do not use threats of aggression to win obedience.
2. When problems arise, model nonviolent conflict-resolution strategies (see Chapter 13).

Ensure that your classroom has enough space and appropriate materials for every student.

Examples

1. Prevent overcrowding.
2. Make sure prized toys or resources are plentiful.
3. Remove or confiscate materials that encourage personal aggression, such as toy guns.

Make sure students do not profit from aggressive behaviors.

Examples

1. Comfort the victim of aggression and ignore the aggressor.
2. Use reasonable punishment, especially with older students.

Teach directly about positive social behaviors.

Examples

1. Incorporate lessons on social ethics/morality through reading selections and discussions.
2. Discuss the effects of antisocial actions such as stealing, bullying, and spreading rumors.

Provide opportunities for learning tolerance and cooperation.

Examples

1. Emphasize the similarities among people rather than the differences.
2. Set up group projects that encourage cooperation.

Coach victimized children to be more assertive.

Examples

1. Provide models and encouragement—role play appropriate self defense.
2. Build self-esteem by building skills and knowledge.
3. Seek help for students who seem especially isolated and victimized.

■ Table 3.6	Recognizing the Warning Signs of Violence
The following lists were developed by the American Psychological Association. Other resources are available at: http://helping.apa.org/warningsigns/	
If you see these immediate warning signs, violence is a serious possibility:	**If you notice the following signs over a period of time, the potential for violence exists:**
■ loss of temper on a daily basis	■ a history of violent or aggressive behavior
■ frequent physical fighting	■ serious drug or alcohol use
■ significant vandalism or property damage	■ gang membership or strong desire to be in a gang
■ increase in use of drugs or alcohol	■ access to or fascination with weapons, especially guns
■ increase in risk-taking behavior	■ threatening others regularly
■ detailed plans to commit acts of violence	■ trouble controlling feelings like anger
■ announcing threats or plans for hurting others	■ withdrawal from friends and usual activities
■ enjoying hurting animals	■ feeling rejected or alone
■ carrying a weapon	■ having been a victim of bullying
	■ poor school performance
	■ history of discipline problems or frequent run-ins with authority
	■ feeling constantly disrespected
	■ failing to acknowledge the feelings or rights of others

SOURCE: From "Warning Signs." Copyright © 1996 by the American Psychological Association. Adapted with permission of the APA. For more information, consult the website—http://helping.apa.org/warningsigns

on performance goals (making good grades, looking smart) as opposed to learning goals, and students with a low sense of academic self-efficacy (a belief that they probably can't do well in school) are likely to cheat. Students also are particularly likely to cheat when they are behind or "cramming for tests" or when they believe that their teachers do not care about them. But the sad fact is that cheating by all groups has increased over the past 20 years (Jensen, Arnett, Feldman, & Cauffman, 2002; Murdock, Hale, & Weber, 2001; Newstead, Franklyn-Stokes, & Armstead, 1996).

The implications for teachers are straightforward. To prevent cheating, try to avoid putting students in high-pressure situations. Make sure they are well prepared for tests, projects, and assignments so they can do reasonably well without cheating. Focus on learning and not on grades. Make extra help available for those who need it. Be clear about your policies in regard to cheating, and enforce them consistently. Help students resist temptation by monitoring them carefully during testing. And separate the cheating behavior from your relationship with the student while you build authentic caring connections with your students.

Check Yourself What are the key differences among the preconventional, conventional, and postconventional levels of moral reasoning?

Describe Gilligan's levels of moral reasoning.

What influences moral behavior?

Socialization: Family, Peers, and Teachers

Socialization The ways in which members of a society encourage positive development for the immature individuals of the group.

Socialization is the process by which the mature members of a society, such as parents and teachers, influence the beliefs and behaviors of children, enabling them to fully participate in and contribute to the society. In this section we will consider three of the most important influences on the development and socialization of children: family, peers, and teachers.

American Families Today

CONNECT & EXTEND

TO **PRAXIS**™
FAMILIES (I, B6)
Understand the influence of families, their culture and values on student learning.

The most appropriate expectation to have about your students' families is no expectation at all. Increasingly, students today have only one or no sibling, or they may be part of **blended families,** with stepbrothers or stepsisters who move in and out of their lives. Some of your students may live with an aunt, with grandparents, with one parent, in foster or adoptive homes, or with an older brother or sister. The best advice is to drop the phrases "your parents" and "your mother and father" and to speak of "your family" when talking to students.

Today in the United States, about 72% of the women with school-aged children are employed (U.S. Bureau of Labor Statistics, 2000). Given the number of children who live in single-parent homes (about 25%) and the number of homes where both parents work, your students are likely to be alone or unsupervised much of the time outside school. In fact, the growing number of these *latchkey children* has prompted many schools to offer before- and after-school programs.

Divorce. The divorce rate in the United States is the highest in the world, over a third higher than the second-ranked nation, Great Britain (Berk, 2002). And as too many of us know from experiences in our own families, separation and divorce are stressful events for all participants, even under the best circumstances. The actual separation of the parents may have been preceded by years of conflict in the home or may come as a shock to all, including friends and children. During the divorce itself, conflict may increase as property and custody rights are being decided.

After the divorce, more changes may disrupt the children's lives. The parent who has custody may have to move to a less expensive home, find new sources of income, go to work for the first time, or work longer hours. For the child, this can mean leaving behind important friendships in the old neighborhood or school, just when support is needed the most. It may mean having just one parent, who has less time than ever to be with the children. About two-thirds of parents remarry and half of them divorce again, so there are more adjustments ahead for the children (Furstenburg & Cherlin, 1991; Nelson, 1993). In some divorces there are few conflicts, ample resources, and the continuing support of friends and extended family. But divorce is never easy for anyone.

Effects of Divorce. The first two years after the divorce seem to be the most difficult period for both boys and girls. During this time, children may have problems in school or just skip school, lose or gain an unusual amount of weight, develop difficulties sleeping, and so on. They may blame themselves for the breakup of their family or hold unrealistic hopes for a reconciliation (Hetherington, 1999; Pfeffer, 1981). Long-term adjustment is also affected. Boys tend to show a higher rate of behavioral and interpersonal problems at home and in school than either girls in general or boys from intact families. Girls may have trouble in their dealings with males. They may become more sexually active or have difficulties trusting males. However, living with one fairly content, if harried, parent may be better than living in a conflict-filled situation with two unhappy parents. And adjustment to divorce is an individual matter; some children respond with increased responsibility, maturity, and coping skills (Amato, Loomis, & Booth, 1995; Berk, 2002). Over time, about 75% to 80% of children in divorced families adapt and become reasonably well adjusted (Hetherington & Kelly, 2002). See the *Guidelines* for ideas about how to help students in these situations.

Peer Relationships and Peer Cultures

Blended families Parents, children, and stepchildren merged into families through remarriages.

Friendships are central to students' lives. When there has been a falling-out or an argument, when one child is not invited to a sleep-over, when rumors are started and

GUIDELINES Helping Children of Divorce

Take note of any sudden changes in behavior that might indicate problems at home.

Examples

1. Be alert to physical symptoms such as repeated headaches or stomach pains, rapid weight gain or loss, fatigue or excess energy.
2. Be aware of signs of emotional distress such as moodiness, temper tantrums, difficulty in paying attention or concentrating.
3. Let parents know about the students' signs of stress.

Talk individually to students about their attitude or behavior changes. This gives you a chance to find out about unusual stress such as divorce.

Examples

1. Be a good listener. Students may have no other adult willing to hear their concerns.
2. Let students know you are available to talk, and let the student set the agenda.

Watch your language to make sure you avoid stereotypes about "happy" (two-parent) homes.

Examples

1. Simply say "your families" instead of "your mothers and fathers" when addressing the class.
2. Avoid statements such as "We need volunteers for room mother" or "Your father can help you."

Help students maintain self-esteem.

Examples

1. Recognize a job well done.
2. Make sure the student understands the assignment and can handle the workload. This is not the time to pile on new and very difficult work.
3. The student may be angry with his or her parents, but may direct the anger at teachers. Don't take the student's anger personally.

Find out what resources are available at your school.

Examples

1. Talk to the school psychologist, guidance counselor, social worker, or principal about students who seem to need outside help.
2. Consider establishing a discussion group, led by a trained adult, for students going through a divorce.

Be sensitive to both parents' rights to information.

Examples

1. When parents have joint custody, both are entitled to receive information and attend parent-teacher conferences.
2. The noncustodial parent may still be concerned about the child's school progress. Check with your principal about state laws regarding the noncustodial parent's rights.

pacts are made to ostracize someone (as with Alison and Stephanie at the beginning of the chapter), the results can be devastating. Even when students begin to mature and know intellectually that rifts will soon be healed, they may still be emotionally crushed by temporary trouble in the friendship.

Beyond the immediate trauma of friendship failures, peer relationships play a significant role in healthy personal and social development. There is strong evidence that adults who had close friends as children have higher self-esteem and are more capable of maintaining intimate relationships than adults who had lonely childhoods. The characteristics of friends and the quality of the friendships matter too. Having stable, supportive relationships with friends who are socially competent and mature enhances social development, especially during difficult times such as parents' divorce or transition to new schools (Hartup & Stevens, 1999). Adults who were rejected as children tend to have more problems, such as dropping out of school or committing crimes (Coie et al., 1995; Coie & Dodge, 1998).

Peer relationships in the school years appear to play a significant role in self-esteem, success in school, and success in adult life.

Who Is Likely to Have Problems with Peers? Students who are aggressive, withdrawn, and inattentive-hyperactive are more likely to be rejected. But classroom context matters too, especially for aggressive or withdrawn students. In classrooms where the general level of aggression is high, being aggressive is less likely to lead to peer rejection. And in classrooms where solitary play and work are more common, being withdrawn is not as likely to lead to rejection. Thus, part of rejection is being too different from the norm. Also, prosocial behaviors such as sharing, cooperating, empathy, and friendly interactions are associated with peer acceptance, no matter what the classroom context. Many aggressive and withdrawn students lack these social skills; inattentive-hyperactive students often misread social cues or have trouble controlling impulses, so their social skills suffer too (Stormshak, Bierman, Bruschi, Dodge, & Coie, 1999). A teacher should be aware of how each student gets along with the group. Are there outcasts? Do some students play the bully role? Careful adult intervention can often correct such problems, especially at the middle elementary-school level.

Peer Cultures. Recently psychologists have studied the powerful role of peer culture in children's development. Peer cultures are groups of students who have a set of "rules"—how to dress, talk, style their hair. The group determines which activities, music, or other students are in or out of favor. For example, when Jessica, a popular high school student, was asked to explain the rules that her group lives by, she had no trouble:

> OK. No. 1: clothes. You cannot wear jeans any day but Friday, and you cannot wear a ponytail or sneakers more than once a week. Monday is fancy day—like black pants or maybe you bust out with a skirt. You have to remind people how cute you are in case they forgot over the weekend. No. 2: parties. Of course we sit down and discuss which ones we're going to because there is no point in getting all dressed up for a party that's going to be lame. (Talbot, 2002, p. 28)

These peer cultures encourage conformity to the group rules. When another girl in Jessica's group wore jeans on Monday, Jessica confronted her: "Why are you wearing jeans today? Did you forget it was Monday?" (Talbot, 2002, p. 28). Jessica explained that the group had to suspend this "rebel" several times, not allowing her to sit with the group at lunch.

To see the power of peers, we have to look at situations where the values and interests of parents clash with those of peers, and then see whose influence dominates. In these comparisons, peers usually win. For example, differences between black and white achievement vanish when you take peer culture into account (Tavris, 1998). But not all aspects of peer cultures are bad or cruel. The norms in some groups are positive and support achievement in school. Peer cultures are more powerful in defining issues of style and socializing. Parents and teachers still are influential in matters of morality, career choice, and religion (Harris, 1998).

New Roles for Teachers

CONNECT & EXTEND

TO THE RESEARCH

The entire March 2001 issue of the *Journal of School Psychology* is devoted to schools and mental health.

When we consider the high rate of divorce and the power of peer relationships for children, we see that teachers today are dealing with issues that once stayed outside the walls of the school. The first and most important task of the teacher is to educate, but student learning suffers when there are problems with personal and social development.

Teachers are sometimes the best source of help for students facing emotional or interpersonal problems. When students have chaotic and unpredictable home lives, they need a caring, firm structure in school. They need teachers who set clear limits, are consistent, enforce rules firmly but not punitively, respect students, and show genuine concern. As a teacher, you can be available to talk about personal problems without requiring that your students do so. One of my student teachers gave a boy in her class a journal entitled "Very Hard Thoughts" so that he could write about his parents' divorce. Sometimes he talked to her about the journal entries, but at other times he just recorded his feelings. The student teacher was very careful to respect the boy's privacy about his writings. In Chapter 13 you will learn about strategies and programs for helping students develop socially and emotionally. For now, the *Guidelines* give some ideas.

GUIDELINES Supporting Personal and Social Development

Help students examine the kinds of dilemmas they are currently facing or will face in the near future.

Examples

1. In elementary school, discuss sibling rivalries, teasing, stealing, prejudice, treatment of new students in the class, and behavior toward classmates with disabilities.
2. In high school, discuss cheating, letting friends drive when they are intoxicated, conforming to be more popular, and protecting a friend who has broken a rule.

Help students see the perspectives of others.

Examples

1. Ask a student to describe his or her understanding of the views of another, then have the other person confirm or correct the perception.
2. Have students exchange roles and try to "become" the other person in a discussion.

Help students make connections between expressed values and actions.

Examples

1. Follow a discussion of "What should be done?" with "How would you act? What would be your first step? What problems might arise?"
2. Help students see inconsistencies between their values and their own actions. Ask them to identify inconsistencies, first in others, then in themselves.

Safeguard the privacy of all participants.

Examples

1. Remind students that in a discussion they can "pass" and not answer questions.
2. Intervene if peer pressure is forcing a student to say more than he or she wants to.
3. Don't reinforce a pattern of telling "secrets."

Make sure students are really listening to each other.

Examples

1. Keep groups small.
2. Be a good listener yourself.
3. Recognize students who pay careful attention to each other.

Make sure that as much as possible your class reflects concern for moral issues and values.

Examples

1. Make clear distinctions between rules based on administrative convenience (keeping the room orderly) and rules based on moral issues.
2. Enforce standards uniformly. Be careful about showing favoritism.

SOURCE: From "What Criteria Should Public School Moral Education Programs Meet?" by J. W. Eiseman, *Oxford Review of Education, 7,* pp. 226–227. http://www.tandf.co.uk/journals

Check Yourself What challenges face children whose parents are divorced?

Why are peer relations important?

What are peer cultures?

Challenges for Children

What Would You Say? Your interview for a teaching position at a new school is going well when the department chair asks a question you were not expecting: "Tell me what you could do to help entering students make the transition to this school when it opens?"

In the next few pages we examine a number of challenges children face as they mature. Many of these challenges are all too modern and have put students at great risk today. We will end by considering just a few of these risks.

Navigating Transitions

Do you remember your first day of school? I remember getting my list of required school supplies (Big Chief tablet, #2 pencils, . . .). I bought them at the Rexall drug store that gave a free milk shake with your school supply purchase. By the time my daughter started school, the free milk shakes were gone—we all were watching our cholesterol. The transition to 1st grade is a critical time, one that can begin a journey toward life-long learning.

Between the ages of 5 and 7, when most children are entering school, cognition is developing rapidly. The transition to 1st grade is a critical time—one that can begin a journey toward life-long learning.

Young Children: Starting School. Between the ages of 5 and 7 when most children start school, cognitive development is proceeding rapidly. Children can process more information faster and their memory spans are increasing. They are moving from preoperational to concrete operational thinking. As these internal changes progress, the children are spending hours every weekday in the new physical and social world of school. They must now reestablish Erikson's stages of psychosocial development in the unfamiliar school setting. They must learn to trust new adults, act autonomously in this more complex situation, and initiate actions in ways that fit the new rules of school. At the same time, the new psychosocial challenge of industry versus inferiority looms large. The child must master new skills and work toward new goals, while being compared to others and risking failure.

The way children cope with these challenges has implications for the rest of their school experience. Two of the best predictors of dropping out of school are low grade point average by the 3rd grade and being held back in one of the primary grades (Paris & Cunningham, 1996). Children who do well in the 1st grade are on their way to achievement, while those who flounder are on a path toward difficulty. The achievement test score differences among students from high and low socioeconomic groups in 1st grade are relatively small, but by the 6th grade, the differences have tripled. "How well students do in the primary grades matters more for their future success than does their school performance at any other time" (Entwisle & Alexander, 1998, p. 354).

What can be done to make the transition to school positive? Research points to a few answers. First, quality preschool and full-day kindergarten experiences are critical for helping children, especially children from low-income homes, to do well in 1st grade. Children who achieve in 1st grade do better in later grades, so the time to make a difference is early. Programs such as Reading Recovery and Success for All are based on early and intensive intervention. Continuity helps children become successful students, so staying in the same school for kindergarten and 1st grade, with the same peers and teachers can be helpful. In Chapter 11, you will learn about teaching students directly how to accomplish school rules and procedures. Teachers, administrators, families, and community leaders can work together to make the transition to school positive for all children (Mangione & Speth, 1998; Paris & Cunningham, 1996).

Students in the Middle Grades: Another Transition. There are many different age configurations in schools today, but most students move from elementary to middle school or junior high between the 5th and 7th grades—a time developmental psychologists call "early adolescence" (Sandrock, 1996). Again, cognitive processes are expanding as the students develop capabilities for abstract thinking and for understanding the perspectives of others. But even greater changes are taking place in the students' physical development as they approach puberty. The students bring their new cognitive abilities and their changing bodies to the psychosocial task of identity—exploring possible selves. Who am I? Who do I want to become and who do I fear becoming? During the middle grades, students are more likely to describe themselves in terms of psychological and social traits such as "moody," "loyal," or "depressed" and political or religious orientation such as Jewish, Muslim, Christian, conservative, or libertarian. Their sense of self becomes more differentiated, so they know that they have many capabilities and limitations. Quite a bit is going on.

In the transition to middle school, students confront an increased focus on grades and performance as well as more competition on all fronts—academic, social, and athletic. Just when they are eager to make decisions and assume more independence, these developing minds encounter more required rules, courses, and assignments. They move from a close connection with one teacher all year to more impersonal relations with many teachers in many different subjects across the year (Murdock, Hale, & Weber, 2001; Rudolph, Lambert, Clark, & Kurlakowsky, 2001).

And their world outside school is changing, too. The Carnegie Council on Adolescent Development's (1995) report, *Great Transitions: Preparing Adolescents for a New Century,* describes five changes that create a complex context for growing up today. First, as we saw earlier, the number of divorces and working parents in many countries means that young adolescents spend less time with adults and more time with peers or watching television. Second, the job future for many adolescents is grim as the world shifts to a knowledge-based economy, where a high school degree is not enough to earn a good salary. Why work hard in school if you will have the same dead-end job offered to a school drop-out? Third, adolescents go through puberty earlier and assume adult roles later than previous generations. It is a strain, to say the least, to be sexually mature but socially restricted for a long time. Fourth, adolescents are surrounded by media—television, films, videos, and music—that influence their expectations, fears, and values. And finally, the world has become more diverse. About one-third of American adolescents today are of non-European descent.

So, with developing minds and identities and bodies, young adolescents must navigate the transition to the middle grades in an uncertain world. What are the results? One of the most common findings is that overall self-concept and self-esteem decline in early adolescence, as do assessments of competence in academic and nonacademic areas. During the middle school or junior high years, students grow more self-conscious (remember, adolescent egocentrism and Elkind's imaginary audience discussed in Chapter 2). At this age, feelings of self-worth are more closely tied to physical appearance and social acceptance, so these years can be exceedingly difficult for students such as Stephanie, described at the opening of this chapter (Wigfield, Eccles, & Pintrich, 1996). When young adolescents move from being the most mature and highest status students in a small, familiar elementary school to being the bottom of the chain in a large, impersonal junior or senior high school, there may be negative consequences (Graber & Brooks-Gunn, 1996; Lord, Eccles, & McCarthy, 1994; Meece, 1997; Wigfield, Eccles, MacIver, Rueman, & Midgley, 1991).

What can teachers do to make these transitions easier for middle grade students? The middle school movement is one attempt to structure schools to meet the needs of this developmental period. Some of the features of middle grade schools are interdisciplinary teams of teachers who work with a "pod" or cohort of students; integrated curricula that take into account the personal concerns of the students and build learning tasks around these concerns; advisory programs that pair every student with a teacher/advisor; and special-interest exploratory classes such as photography or computers. One more element relates to you, the teacher. Middle grade schools should have teachers who are knowledgeable about and like young adolescents (Muth & Alvermann, 1999).

CONNECT & EXTEND

TO **PRAXIS**™
HUMAN DEVELOPMENT (I, A2)
Explain how development in one domain (e.g., physical, emotional) can affect development in other domains.

Children and Youth at Risk

It is a difficult time to become an adult. Many of the challenges children face threaten their safety as well as their personal and social development. We will consider only a few of the risks that students encounter. Teachers can play a role in helping students cope with these situations. In the first area—child abuse—teachers have legal responsibilities to consider.

CONNECT & EXTEND

TO THE RESEARCH
The May 1999 and the May 2000 issues of *The Elementary School Journal* are entirely devoted to the non-subject-matter outcomes of school such as social-emotional development, self-regulation, physical activity, and service learning.

Child Abuse. Accurate information about the number of abused children in the United States is difficult to find; most experts agree that an enormous number of cases go unreported (Children's Defense Fund, 2002). In 1998, 3.1 million cases were reported, an increase of 132% over the level in the 1980s. Of course, parents are not the only people who abuse children. Siblings, other relatives, and even teachers have been responsible for the physical and sexual abuse of children. And today, there is another source of abuse—the Internet. The *Reaching Every Student* feature presents a set of guidelines to give to students to protect them from Internet predators.

As a teacher, you must alert your principal, school psychologist, or school social worker if you suspect abuse. In all 50 states, the District of Columbia, and the U.S. territories, the law requires certain professionals, often including teachers, to report suspected cases of child abuse. The legal definition of abuse has been broadened in many states to include neglect and failure to provide proper care and supervision. Most laws also protect teachers who report suspected neglect in good faith (Beezer, 1985). Be sure that you understand the laws in your state or province on this important issue as well as your own moral responsibility. At least five children die of abuse or neglect each day in the United States, in many cases because no one would "get involved" (Thompson & Wyatt, 1999). The *Stories of Learning/Tributes to Teaching* tells how one teacher made a difference.

What should you look for as indicators of abuse? Table 3.7 lists possible indicators.

■ Table 3.7 Indicators of Child Abuse

The following are some of the signs of abuse. Not every child with these signs is abused, but these indicators should be investigated.

	Physical Indicators	Behavioral Indicators	
Physical Abuse	■ Unexplained bruises (in various stages of healing), welts, human bite marks, bald spots ■ Unexplained burns, especially cigarette burns or immersion-burns (glovelike) ■ Unexplained fractures, lacerations, or abrasions	■ Self-destructive ■ Withdrawn and aggressive—behavioral extremes ■ Uncomfortable with physical contact ■ Arrives at school early or stays late, as if afraid	■ Chronic runaway (adolescents) ■ Complains of soreness or moves uncomfortably ■ Wears clothing inappropriate to weather, to cover body
Physical Neglect	■ Abandonment ■ Unattended medical needs ■ Consistent lack of supervision ■ Consistent hunger, inappropriate dress, poor hygiene ■ Lice, distended stomach, emaciation	■ Regularly displays fatigue or listlessness, falls asleep in class ■ Steals food, begs from classmates ■ Reports that no caretaker is at home	■ Frequently absent or tardy ■ Self-destructive ■ School dropout (adolescents)
Sexual Abuse	■ Torn, stained, or bloodied underclothing ■ Pain or itching in genital area ■ Difficulty walking or sitting ■ Bruises or bleeding in external genitalia ■ Venereal disease ■ Frequent urinary or yeast infections	■ Withdrawn, chronic depression ■ Excessive seductiveness ■ Role reversal, overly concerned for siblings ■ Poor self-esteem, self-devaluation, lack of confidence ■ Peer problems, lack of involvement ■ Massive weight change ■ Suicide attempts (especially adolescents)	■ Hysteria, lack of emotional control ■ Sudden school difficulties ■ Inappropriate sex play or premature understanding of sex ■ Threatened by physical contact, closeness ■ Promiscuity

SOURCE: From "Supporting Victims of Child Abuse" by T. Bear, S. Schenk, and L. Buckner, *Educational Leadership, 50*(4). Copyright © 1993 by the American Association for Supervision and Curriculum Development. Reprinted with permission from ASCD. All rights reserved.

~ Reaching Every Student ~

Safety on the Internet

Provide these guidelines to your students so they can protect themselves when using the Internet.

1. Never give identifying data such as your name, address, phone number, school name, and so on to anyone on the Internet unless you check with a parent or teacher first.
2. Never share your password with anyone, even a best friend.
3. Never tell anyone on-line where you will be or what you will be doing at a certain time without a parent or teacher's permission.
4. Never give out your picture over the Internet.
5. Choose a name that is not your own name for an E-mail address.
6. Check with a parent or teacher before you enter a chat room.
7. Never agree to meet in person anyone whom you have met on the Internet. If someone asks to meet you, tell a parent or a teacher.
8. If you receive pictures or messages that make you uncomfortable, tell an adult at home or school immediately.
9. If someone makes suggestive comments to you on the Internet stop talking to him or her immediately. Tell an adult at home or at school.
10. Never fill out a questionnaire or give a credit card number on-line without checking with a parent or teacher.
11. If you unintentionally pull up nude or obscene pictures, tell someone immediately.
12. Never open or respond to an E-mail message from someone you do not know.
13. Be open with parents or teachers about what you are accessing on the Internet.
14. Be careful when anyone offers you anything free on the Internet.
15. Do not do things on-line that you would hesitate to do in real life.

SOURCE: From *When Children Are Abused: An Educator's Guide To Intervention,* by Cynthia Crosson-Tower. Published by Allyn & Bacon, Boston, MA. Copyright © 2002 by Pearson Education. Reprinted by permission of the publisher. See also Hughes, 1998; Monteleone, 1998; http://encarta.msn.com/schoolhouse/safetyasp; and http://www.missingkids.com.

~ Stories of Learning Tributes to Teaching ~

David was not an easy child to like, but Garth Nobel did. David was hyperactive and demanded a good deal of attention. Other teachers told Nobel that David got on their nerves. But David loved gym class. Or was it Garth Nobel's patience and kindness that he enjoyed? For whatever reason, David was always the first to arrive at class and put his whole self into whatever game or activity was asked of him. He wasn't necessarily a team player. In fact, he stayed away from the other children when he was not engaged in an activity. He never dressed with the others or palled around with them. But it was not until David was injured one day in a rather exuberant game of basketball, that Garth Nobel suspected anything. When he lifted David's shirt to check for injuries, he could not believe what he saw. Numerous ugly bruises and burns transversed the boys chest. The different stages of healing made it clear that they were inflicted over a period of time.

"What happened to you, Dave?" Nobel breathed, almost in a whisper. At first, tears ran silently down the boy's face. And then he began to sob, deep heart-wrenching sobs that were hard for the teacher to witness.

"My Dad . . ." Sobbed David but he could not continue. Instead he hugged Garth Nobel with a desperateness that the young and caring teacher would never forget.

He would later learn that David's father had beaten him so badly over the last few years that he had caused internal damage. But that day, Garth Nobel knew that David needed an advocate—someone who cared and could help this boy through the perils that his future would bring. Years later, David would return to see Nobel with sincere thanks and admiration for standing by him over the next few years when David would be removed from his abusive home and placed in a foster home.

SOURCE: From *When Children Are Abused: An Educator's Guide To Intervention,* by Cynthia Crosson-Tower. Published by Allyn & Bacon, Boston, MA. Copyright © 2002 by Pearson Education. Reprinted by permission of the publisher.

It has always been difficult to navigate the adolescent years, but today the waters seem more dangerous than ever. We will touch on only a few challenges.

Eating Disorders. Adolescents going through the changes of puberty are very concerned about their bodies. This has always been true, but today, the emphasis on fitness and appearance makes adolescents even more likely to worry about how their bodies "measure up." For some, the concern becomes excessive. One consequence is eating disorders such as **bulimia** (binge eating) and **anorexia nervosa** (self-starvation), both of which are much more common in females than in males. Bulimics often binge, eating an entire gallon of ice cream or a whole cake. Then, to avoid gaining weight, they force themselves to vomit, or they use strong laxatives, to purge themselves of the extra calories. Bulimics tend to maintain a normal weight, but their digestive systems can be permanently damaged.

Anorexia is an even more dangerous disorder, for anorexics either refuse to eat or eat practically nothing while often exercising obsessively. In the process they may lose 20% to 25% of their body weight, and some (about 5% to 10%) literally starve themselves to death. Anorexic students may appear pale, have brittle fingernails, and have fine dark hairs developing all over their bodies. They are easily chilled because they have so little fat to insulate their bodies. They often are depressed, insecure, moody, and lonely. Girls may stop having their menstrual period. These eating disorders often begin in adolescence and are becoming more common—about 1% of adolescent girls become anorexic (Rice & Dolgin, 2002). These students usually require professional help—don't ignore the warning signs. Again, a teacher may be the person who begins the chain of help for students with these tragic problems.

Drug Abuse. Modern society makes growing up a very confusing process. Notice the messages from films and billboards. "Beautiful," popular people drink alcohol and smoke cigarettes with little concern for their health. We have over-the-counter drugs for almost every common ailment. Coffee wakes us up, and a pill helps us sleep. And then we tell students to "say no!" to drugs.

For many reasons, not just because of these contradictory messages, drug use has become a problem for students. Accurate statistics are hard to find, but estimates from the National Center for Education Statistics indicate that 92% of high school seniors report some experience with alcohol—with 66% using it in the past month. About 20% of seniors are daily smokers, and 30% have tried at least one illegal drug. Throughout the mid-1900s, drug use among 12- to 18-year-olds gradually increased (Lerner & Galambos, 1998).

What can be done about drug use among our students? First, we should distinguish between experimentation and abuse. Many students try something at a party but do not become regular users. The best way to help students who have trouble saying no appears to be through peer programs that teach them how to say no assertively. The successful programs also teach general social skills and build self-esteem; are located in schools but run by community agencies; give intensive caring adult attention to individual students; and provide opportunities for work experiences (Lerner & Galambos, 1998). Also, the older students are when they experiment with drugs, the more likely they are to make responsible choices, so helping younger students say no is a clear benefit.

Suicide. The suicide rate among males has tripled in the past 30 years. Suicide often comes as a response to life problems—problems that parents and teachers sometimes dismiss. There are many warning signs that trouble is brewing. Watch for changes in eating or sleeping habits, weight, grades, disposition, activity level, or interest in friends or activities that were once fun. Students at risk sometimes suddenly give away prized possessions such as stereos, CDs, clothing, or pets. They may seem depressed or hyperactive and may say things like "Nothing matters anymore," "You won't have to worry about me anymore," or "I wonder what dying is like." They may start miss-

Bulimia Eating disorder characterized by overeating, then getting rid of the food by self-induced vomiting or laxatives.

Anorexia nervosa Eating disorder characterized by very limited food intake.

■ Table 3.8	Myths and Facts about Suicide
Myth:	People who talk about suicide don't kill themselves.
Fact:	Eight out of ten people who commit suicide tell someone that they're thinking about hurting themselves before they actually do it.
Myth:	Only certain types of people commit suicide.
Fact:	All types of people commit suicide—male and female, young and old, rich and poor, country people and city people. It happens in every racial, ethnic, and religious group.
Myth:	When a person talks about suicide, you should change the subject to get his or her mind off it.
Fact:	You should take them seriously. Listen carefully to what they are saying. Give them a chance to express their feelings. Let them know you are concerned. And help them get help.
Myth:	Most people who kill themselves really want to die.
Fact:	Most people who kill themselves are confused about whether they want to die. Suicide is often intended as a cry for help.

SOURCE: From *Changing Bodies, Changing Lives: A Book for Teens on Sex and Relationships* (p. 142), by R. Bell, 1980, New York: Random House.

ing school or quit doing work. It is especially dangerous if the student not only talks about suicide, but also has a plan for acting.

If you suspect that there is a problem, talk to the student directly. One feeling shared by many people who attempt suicide is that no one really takes them seriously. "A question about suicide does not provoke suicide. Indeed, teens (and adults) often experience relief when someone finally cares enough to ask" (Range, 1993, p. 145). Be realistic, not poetic, about suicide. Ask about specifics, and take the student seriously. Also, be aware that teenage suicides often occur in clusters. After one student acts or when stories about a suicide are reported in the media, other teens are more likely to copy the suicide (Lewinsohn, Rohde, & Seeley, 1994; Rice & Dolgin, 2002). Table 3.8 lists common myths and facts about suicide.

This has been a brief, selective look at the needs of children. In Chapter 13 we will look at teaching strategies and approaches for supporting social and emotional development.

Check Yourself What are key transitions for students?

What are some danger signs of child abuse, eating disorders, and potential for suicide?

Enhancing Your Expertise with Technology

Emotional and Social Development

During her first round of parent-teacher conferences at the middle school, Susan recognized a pattern: She and the parents would discuss a child's academic progress in the marking period, and then the conversation would shift toward social and emotional issues. The parents were concerned about how emotional and social factors affect academic progress, and about the school's influences on their children's emotional and social growth. Susan was surprised at the number of concerns that parents brought up . . . bullying, peer relationships, body image, eating disorders—just to mention a few worries.

When you consider the amount of time that students spend in school from the years of early childhood through adolescence, you see why teachers need a high level of knowledge about human development and expertise in the application of that knowledge. For example, are the ill-kempt appearance and surliness of a 13-year-old typical within the bounds of normal behavior or are they signs of possible depression? How should you handle the tantrum of a 1st grader, and what could a tantrum indicate? Teachers at all levels, preschool through high school, need to create classroom and school climates that promote students' social and emotional growth. They should be able to identify student behaviors and attitudes that undermine that growth. Teachers must possess the knowledge and skills necessary to address such problems effectively in conjunction with the appropriate support professionals (e.g., guidance counselor, psychologist, psychiatrist).

As I hope you have done in the previous chapters, you will find it valuable to collect and maintain an organized set of bookmarks or favorites about social and emotional development on your Web browser. Use the sites listed here as a foundation for your collections. The topics below are examples that you can investigate at these sites. (I have selected these topics based on my experiences as a parent and as a professional educator. Your experiences may differ considerably from mine. What other topics might you include?) To judge the quality of the information offered, take the perspective of a first-year teacher who encounters these situations and seeks guidance. Many sites have forums, "ask the expert" links, bulletin boards, and newsletters that will help you stay current with research about emotional and social development. You might be inclined to focus exclusively on the age levels that you intend to work with as an educator. Please set aside that inclination, especially when learning about human development. Recall that Erikson emphasized the interdependence of the stages of psychosocial development—the way conflicts are resolved at one stage strongly influences resolutions at successive stages.

Early Childhood and Middle Childhood

Shyness	Making friends
Separation anxiety	Nightmares/sleep problems
Fears/phobias	Reluctant speakers

- Child Psychology Development Index (http://psychology.about.com/cs/child/) drSpock (www.drspock.com)
- KidsHealth for Parents (http://kidshealth.org/parent/emotions/)
- Parent Soup (http://www.parentsoup.com/)

Adolescence

Depression	Parent/child tensions
Suicide	Delinquency
Substance abuse	Eating disorders

- American Academy of Child & Adolescent Psychiatrists (http://www.aacap.org/)
- Center for Adolescent Studies (http://education.indiana.edu/cas/)
- Child Development Institute (http://www.childdevelopmentinfo.com/)
- Connect for Kids (http://www.connectforkids.org/)
- Resources on Adolescent Development (http://www.indiana.edu/~iuepsyc/topics/r_ado.htm)

The Work of Erikson

(pp. 66–70)

Why is Erikson's theory considered a psychosocial perspective? Erikson was interested in the ways that individuals developed psychologically to become active and contributing members of society. He believed that all humans have the same basic needs and that each society must accommodate those needs. Erikson's emphasis on the relationship between society and the individual is a psychosocial theory of development—a theory that connects personal development (psycho) to the social environment (social).

What are Erikson's stages of psychosocial development? Erikson believed that people go through eight life stages between infancy and old age, each of which involves a central crisis. Adequate resolution of each crisis leads to greater personal and social competence and a stronger foundation for solving future crises. In the first two stages, an infant must develop a sense of trust over mistrust and a sense of autonomy over shame and doubt. In early childhood, the focus of the third stage is on developing initiative and avoiding feelings of guilt. In the child's elementary school years, the fourth stage involves achieving a sense of industry and avoiding feelings of inferiority. In the fifth stage, identity versus role confusion, adolescents consciously attempt to solidify their identity. According to Marcia, these efforts may lead to identity achievement, foreclosure, diffusion, or moratorium. Erikson's three stages of adulthood involve struggles to achieve intimacy, generativity, and integrity.

Psychosocial: Describing the relation of the individual's emotional needs to the social environment.

Developmental Crisis: A specific conflict whose resolution prepares the way for the next stage.

Autonomy: Independence.

Initiative: Willingness to begin new activities and explore new directions.

Industry: Eagerness to engage in productive work.

Identity: The complex answer to the question: "Who am I?"

Identity Achievement: Strong sense of commitment to life choices after free consideration of alternatives.

Identity Foreclosure: Acceptance of parental life choices without consideration of options.

Identity Diffusion: Uncenteredness; confusion about who one is and what one wants.

Moratorium: Identity crisis; suspension of choices because of struggle.

Generativity: Sense of concern for future generations.

Integrity: Sense of self-acceptance and fulfillment

Understanding Ourselves and Others

(pp. 70–79)

Distinguish between self-concept and self-esteem. Both self-concept and self-esteem are beliefs about the self. Self-concept is our attempt to build a scheme that organizes our impressions, feelings, and attitudes about ourselves. But this model is not permanent. Self-perceptions vary from situation to situation and from one phase of our lives to another. Self-esteem is an evaluation of who you are. If people evaluate themselves positively, we say that they have high self-esteem. Self-concept and self-esteem are often used interchangeably, even though they have distinct meanings. Self-concept is a cognitive structure and self-esteem is an affective evaluation.

How do self-concept and self-esteem change as children develop? Self-concept (definition of self) and self-esteem (valuing of self) become increasingly complex, differentiated, and abstract as we mature. Self-concept evolves through constant self-reflection, social interaction, and experiences in and out of school. Students develop a self-concept by comparing themselves to personal (internal) standards and social (external) standards. The self-esteem of middle and junior high school students becomes more tied to physical appearance and social acceptance. High self-esteem is related to better overall school experience, both academically and socially. Gender and ethnic stereotypes are significant factors as well.

How do perspective-taking skills change as students mature? An understanding of intentions develops as children mature, but aggressive students often have trouble understanding the intentions of others. Social perspective-taking also changes as we mature. Young children believe that everyone has the same thoughts and feelings they do. Later, they learn that others have separate identities and therefore separate feelings and perspectives on events.

What are the skills involved in emotional competence? Emotionally competent individuals are aware of their own emotions and the feeling of others—realizing that inner emotions can differ from outward expressions. They can talk about and express emotions in ways that are appropriate for their cultural group. They can feel empathy for others in distress and also cope with their own distressing emotions—they can handle stress. Emotionally competent individuals know that relationships are defined in part by how emotions are communicated within the relationship. All these skills come together to produce a capacity for emotional self-efficacy.

Self-Concept: Our perceptions about ourselves.

Self-Esteem: The value each of us places on our own characteristics, abilities, and behaviors.

Collective Self-Esteem: Beliefs about the worth of the groups you belong to.

Ethnic Pride: A positive self-concept about one's racial or ethnic heritage.

Perspective-Taking Ability: Understanding that others have different feelings and experiences.

Moral Development
(pp. 80–87)

What are the key differences among the preconventional, conventional, and postconventional levels of moral reasoning? Kohlberg's theory of moral development includes three levels: (1) a preconventional level, where judgments are based on self-interest; (2) a conventional level, where judgments are based on traditional family values and social expectations; and (3) a postconventional level, where judgments are based on more abstract and personal ethical principles. Kohlberg has evaluated the moral reasoning of both children and adults by presenting them with moral dilemmas, or hypothetical situations in which people must make difficult decisions. Critics suggest that Kohlberg's view does not account for possible sex differences in moral reasoning or differences between moral reasoning and moral behavior.

Describe Gilligan's levels of moral reasoning. Carol Gilligan has suggested that because Kohlberg's stage theory was based on a longitudinal study of men only, it is very possible that the moral reasoning of women and the stages of women's development were not adequately represented. She has proposed an "ethic of care." Gilligan believes that individuals move from a focus on self-interests to moral reasoning based on commitment to specific individuals and relationships, and then to the highest level of morality based on the principles of responsibility and care for all people. Women are somewhat more likely to use a care orientation, but studies also show that both men and women *can* use both orientations.

What influences moral behavior? Adults first control young children's moral behavior through direct instruction, supervision, rewards and punishments, and correction. In time, children internalize the moral rules and principles of the authority figures who have guided them. If children are given reasons—particularly reasons that highlight the effects of actions on others—they can understand when they are corrected and then they are more likely to internalize moral principles. A second important influence on the development of moral behavior is modeling. Children who have been consistently exposed to caring, generous adult models will tend to be more concerned for the rights and feelings of others. The world and the media provide many negative models of behavior. Some schools have adopted programs to increase students' capacity to care for others. In schools, cheating and aggression are two common behavior problems that involve moral issues. After preschool, boys are more likely to engage in overt aggression, girls in relational aggression.

Distributive Justice: Beliefs about how to divide materials or privileges fairly among members of a group; follows a sequence of development from equality to merit to benevolence.

Moral Realism: Stage of development wherein children see rules as absolute.

Morality of Cooperation: Stage of development wherein children realize that people make rules and people can change them.

Moral Reasoning: The thinking process involved in judgments about questions of right and wrong.

Moral Dilemmas: Situations in which no choice is clearly and indisputably right.

Internalize: Process whereby children adopt external standards as their own.

Instrumental Aggression: Strong actions aimed at claiming an object, place, or privilege—not intended to harm, but may lead to harm.

Hostile Aggression: Bold, direct action that is intended to hurt someone else; unprovoked attack.

Overt Aggression: A form of hostile aggression that involves physical attack.

Relational Aggression: A form of hostile aggression that involves verbal attacks and other actions meant to harm social relationships.

Socialization: Family, Peers, and Teachers
(pp. 87–91)

What challenges face children whose parents are divorced? During the divorce itself, conflict may increase as property and custody rights are being decided. After the divorce, the custodial parent may have to move to a less expensive home, find new sources of income, go to work for the first time, or work longer hours. For the child, this can mean leaving behind important friendships in the old neighborhood or school just when support is needed the most, having only one parent who has less time than ever to be with the children, or adjusting to new family structures when parents remarry.

Why are peer relations important? Peer relationships play a significant role in healthy personal and social development. There is strong evidence that adults who had close friends as children have higher self-esteem and are more capable of maintaining intimate relationships than adults who had lonely childhoods. Adults who were rejected as children tend to have more problems, such as dropping out of school or committing crimes.

What are peer cultures? Groups of students develop their own norms for appearance and social behavior. At times, these group norms run counter to teachers' goals for students. Group loyalties can lead to rejection for some students, leaving them upset and unhappy.

Socialization: The ways in which members of a society encourage positive development for the immature individuals of the group.

Blended Families: Parents, children, and stepchildren merged into families through remarriages.

■ Challenges for Children

(pp. 91–97)

What are key transitions for students? Transition to kindergarten or 1st grade requires new social roles—children must fit into the group and learn to be students. Evaluation is built into school and success is not guaranteed. In school, children are compared to each other. How well students do in the primary grades matters more for their future success than does their school performance at any other time. The next transition is to middle school, just as students are undergoing great physical and cognitive changes. When young adolescents move from being the most mature and highest status students in a small, familiar elementary school to being the bottom of the chain in a large, impersonal junior high school, there may be negative consequences such as loss of self-esteem.

What are some danger signs of child abuse, eating disorders, and potential for suicide? Signs of abuse or neglect include unexplained bruises, burns, bites, or other injuries and fatigue, depression, frequent absences, poor hygiene, inappropriate clothing, problems with peers and many others. Teachers must report suspected cases of child abuse and can be instrumental in helping students cope with other risks as well. Anorexic students may appear pale, have brittle fingernails, and have fine dark hairs developing all over their bodies. They are easily chilled because they have so little fat to insulate their bodies. They often are depressed, insecure, moody, and lonely. Girls may stop having their menstrual period. Students at risk of suicide may show changes in eating or sleeping habits, weight, grades, disposition, activity level, or interest in friends. They sometimes suddenly give away prized possessions such as stereos, CDs, clothing, or pets. They may seem depressed or hyperactive and may start missing school or quit doing work. It is especially dangerous if the student not only talks about suicide, but also has a plan for action.

Bulimia: Eating disorder characterized by overeating, then getting rid of the food by self-induced vomiting or laxatives.

Anorexia Nervosa: Eating disorder characterized by very limited food intake.

■ Enhancing Your Expertise with Technology

(pp. 97–98)

Early Childhood and Middle Grades

Child Psychology Development Index
(http://psychology.about.com/cs/child/)

drSpock **(www.drspock.com)**

KidsHealth for Parents
(http://kidshealth.org/parent/emotions/)

Parent Soup **(http://www.parentsoup.com/)**

Adolescence

American Academy of Child & Adolescent Psychiatrists
(http://www.aacap.org/)

Center for Adolescent Studies
(http://education.indiana.edu/cas/)

Child Development Institute
(http://www.childdevelopmentinfo.com/)

Connect for Kids **(http://www.connectforkids.org/)**

Resources on Adolescent Development
(http://www.indiana.edu/~iuepsyc/topics/r_ado.htm)

Other Useful Websites

http://www.ume.maine.edu/~cofed/eceol/guide.html

Mental Health Net **http://mhnet.org/**

American Foundation for Suicide Prevention **http://afsp.org/**

Government Health Links
http://www.uhs.wisc.edu/government.html

The Department of Health and Human Services: Children's Bureau: This is an excellent general resource.
http://acf.dhhs.gov/programs/cb/policy.htm

Childhelp: To get information about child protection or to find out how to report suspected abuse. **800-4-A-Child**

American Academy of Child and Adolescent Psychiatry: This organization helps families understand the developmental, emotional, and behavioral disorders affecting children and adolescents.
http://www.aacap.org/

Mental Health Net **http://mhnet.org/**

American Foundation for Suicide Prevention **http://afsp.org/**

Government Health Links
http://www.uhs.wisc.edu/government.html

American Psychological Association resources in youth violence.
http://helping.apa.org/warningsigns/

Alcoholics Anonymous: AA is an organization that helps people with alcohol problems. **http://www.aa.org**

Al-Anon/Alateen: This organization provides support for the family members of alcoholics. **http://www.al-anon.org**

Becoming a Professional

Passing the PRAXIS™

Chapter 3 reflects many of the professional standards created by the Interstate New Teacher Assessment and Support Consortium (INTASC). These standards form the basis of the PRAXIS II™ and state-created teacher licensure exams.

Whether you will be dealing with kindergartners with separation anxieties, work-weary high school seniors, or—as in this case—cliques in a middle school, you will find that students are far more than mere learners. They bring every personal, social, emotional, and moral triumph, disappointment, and challenge—past and present—into the classroom with themselves, and those factors will influence your teaching and their learning.

Most licensure examinations, including PRAXIS II™, will require you to be knowledgeable about the personal, emotional, social, moral, and physical development of students. The situation described in the casebook demonstrates why that knowledge is essential for teachers. Here you encountered actions and attitudes that, if managed poorly, could have serious long-term negative consequences inside and outside the classroom for all the involved students.

Tips for PRAXIS II™

Understand the major concepts and progressions related to:

- Erikson's theory of psychosocial development
- Piaget's and Kohlberg's perspectives on moral development
- Gilligan's theory of caring

Design or choose strategies that:

- support optimal social and emotional development of students
- help students cope with major life transitions and challenges to safety, physical, and mental health
- help students build a sense of self-concept and self-esteem

Recognize signs or behaviors that indicate:

- eating disorders
- drug abuse
- child abuse
- potential for suicide
- sexual abuse

Related Topics

- Student motivation to learn (Chapter 10)
- Classroom management techniques (Chapters 6, 11)
- Promoting cooperation among students (Chapter 13)
- Teaching every student (Chapter 5)

Standards and Licensure Appendix: *PRAXIS II™ and INTASC*

Refer to the Appendix at the end of the book for detailed correlations to PRAXIS II™ exam topics and INTASC Standards addressed in this text.

Insights about Job Interview Questions: *What Would You Say?*

1. What would you do to help all your students feel good about themselves?
2. How you could tell if there might be violence among students in our school? What are the warning signs?
3. What could you do to help entering students make the transition to this school when it opens?

Your Teaching Portfolio: *Teaching Resources*

Think about your philosophy of teaching, a question you will be asked at most job interviews. What do you believe about teaching values and moral behavior? How can you support the development of genuine and well-founded self-esteem in your students? (Consult Table 3.3 for ideas.)

Add some ideas for parent involvement from this chapter to your **Portfolio.**

Adapt Table 3.5, *Using "Caring for Strangers and the World" as a Teaching Theme,* for the grades and subjects you might teach and add it to your **Teaching Resources** file.

Add Table 3.3, *Emotional Competence Skills,* Table 3.6, *Recognizing the Warning Signs of Violence* and Table 3.7, *Indicators of Child Abuse,* to your **Teaching Resources** file.

Video**Workshop** Extra

If the VideoWorkshop package was included with your textbook, go to Chapter 3 of the Companion Website (www.ablongman.com/woolfolk) and click on the VideoWorkshop button. Follow the instructions for viewing *Video Clip 2: Social Skills Development.* Consider this information along with what you've read in Chapter 3 while answering the following questions:

1. How does a student conflict resolution team help students learn appropriate positive social skills? Describe an instance, other than a playground conflict, in which this kind of intervention would be helpful.
2. Name two principles discussed in your textbook that are demonstrated in this video, and explain how they apply to this scenario.

Use the CD-ROM included in the back of your textbook to launch the "Becoming a Professional" website. The website features advice on preparing for teacher certification exams, help with getting your first job, and resources to help you perform your job well from the first day forward.

Teachers' Casebook

What Would They Do?

Here is how some practicing teachers responded to the situation presented at the beginning of this chapter about cliques in middle school, and the difficulties some students face with "fitting in."

Jacalyn D. Walker

8th Grade Science Teacher, *Treasure Mountain Middle School, Park City, Utah*

Never work in a vacuum. This is especially important in a middle school or junior high school. Work with your school counselor, other grade level teachers, and parents. If you are doing this, you will have several options for dealing with this problem. You cannot fake caring about 12, 13, and 14 year olds. They can spot a fake. You must be working with this age group because you truly like them as people. You appreciate their humor and their abilities. With a caring, trusting, and respectful relationship, students will be open to your help and guidance. Parents are often not involved in the classroom at these grade levels, but there are great programs available to get parents involved.

Nancy Schaefer

Grades, 9–12, Cincinnati Hills Christian Academy High School, *Cincinnati, Ohio*

I would first make a phone call to Stephanie's home. Under the guise of calling about assignments because of the days she has missed, I would talk to one of her parents or guardians. My first goal would be to find out if the parents are aware of the situation. Sometimes girls like Stephanie are too embarrassed to tell their parents the whole story or even any of the real story. The parents might know that something is wrong, but not the details. I would try to find out how much the parents know. If the parents did not know the entire story, my next thought would be to get Stephanie on the phone and try to help her tell her parents. Letting the adults around her know what has happened can relieve some of the shame she might be feeling.

I would then meet with Stephanie and one or more of her parents, to plan Stephanie's transition back to school. If there is a school counselor, he or she might also be involved in this conversation. The adults in the conversation would help Stephanie come up with a plan for how she will handle possible difficult situations: face-to-face encounters with Allison, encounters with other old "friends," mean messages that might be sent to Stephanie during the school day, or comments made to her by other students. We would help her think through these situations and practice how she could respond. I would also help facilitate arrangements for a safe place and person at school, which she could access for a few days, until she is comfortable at school again. This would be a place and a person that Stephanie could go to if the situation becomes too overwhelming and she wants to escape the pressure. If the problem seems to warrant extra measures, I could talk to Stephanie's teachers to work on rearranging groups or seating to move the girls away from each other or to foster other friendships for Stephanie. We could also make arrangements for an older, respected student to talk to Stephanie. Since almost everyone has stories about unfaithful friends, Stephanie might benefit from talking with a freshman or sophomore about that person's experiences and how they made new friends. Finally, I would try to arrange a brief and supervised meeting between Stephanie and Allison. Allowing an encounter to happen in a controlled environment would provide Stephanie an outlet to voice her hurt, without her having to resort to inappropriate actions. Whether this happens before she comes back to school, on her first day back to school, or few days after her return would depend on the volatility of the situation.

During all of this, I would want to make sure that someone was also working with Allison, to prevent the escalation of events. This may be an administrator responsible for discipline, if school rules were violated, or the school counselor, or another teacher with a good relationship with Allison. I would encourage the involvement of Allison's parents, especially if this were not the first vicious episode.

Marie C. Enright

Special Education Teacher, *Village Elementary School, York Beach, ME*

This middle school girl clique thing is a tough one. At this age girls seem to love to talk about themselves and each other. There is a lot of following the crowd even when most of the individuals don't agree with what is being said or done. Very few in a class want to stand out or stand up for fairness and kindness.

I would first call in Alison, the mean one, with others of her crowd including those I feel would be sympathetic to Stephanie. I would say the reason I asked Alison is because I thought they were friends. (If I could remain honest without disclosing that I know about the email, hopefully the email story would come up in the discussion.) Since they had been friends until recently, a teacher doesn't have to keep up with the groups.

Out of this discussion, I think and hope would come some offers to call or otherwise connect with Stephanie. Perhaps an apology would ensue. And the least the girls would come away with an understanding of how much they can be hurting each other's feelings and a sense that they have the power and ability to reverse these hurtful actions with some honest talk and kind actions.

Go to the Companion Website (www.ablongman.com/woolfolk) for additional case studies including audio and video cases, and examples of student work.

CHAPTER

4 Learner Differences and Learning Needs

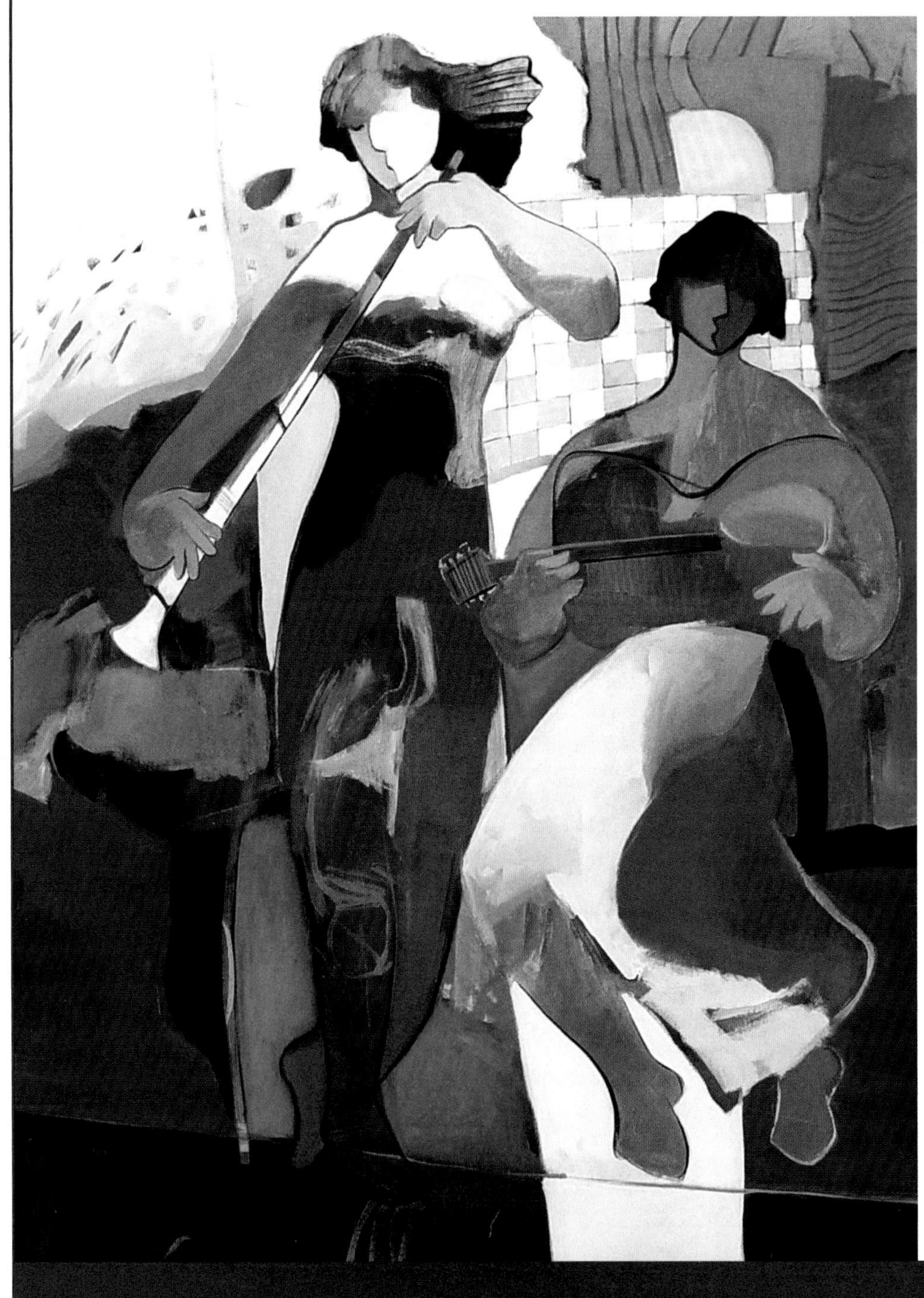

Teachers' Casebook

What Would You Do?

Stuffed in your (undersized) mailbox in the school office is a large, official-looking envelope. There seems to be one in almost every box. Inside are computer printouts with the results of the fall testing, including scores on a group test of intelligence for all the 7th- and 8th-grade students in your advisory section. Also in your box are notes from two parents who must have already heard that the test results are in. They want to meet with you to see their child's scores, and especially, as one parent put it, "To find out how smart Jason really is." You look at the printouts and at the notes, wondering what you should do with the results.

Critical Thinking

How will you use this information? What do the intelligence test scores tell you about your students? How would you respond to the notes from the parents; will you share the scores with them?

Collaboration

With two or three other students in your class, plan and present a role play showing what you would do and how you would communicate with the parents. How would you prepare for the conversations? What would you ask or say?

To answer the questions above, you need an understanding of individual differences. So far, we have talked little about individuals. We have discussed principles of development that apply to everyone—stages, processes, conflicts, and tasks. Our development as human beings is similar in many ways, but not in every way. Even among members of the same family, there are marked contrasts in appearance, interests, abilities, and temperament, and these differences have important implications for teaching. In addition, recent changes in federal legislation mean that you probably will have at least one student with special needs in your class, whatever grade you teach. We explore both prevalent and less frequently occurring learning problems that students may have. As we discuss each problem area, we will consider how a teacher might recognize problems, seek help, and plan instruction. By the time you have completed this chapter, you should be able to answer these questions:

- *What are the potential problems in categorizing and labeling students?*
- *What is your personal concept of intelligence?*
- *What is your stance on ability grouping?*
- *Should you adapt lessons for students with varying learning styles?*
- *What are the implications of the Individuals with Disabilities Act (IDEA) for your teaching? What about Section 504?*
- *In your classroom, how will you identify and teach students with hearing, vision, language, and behavior problems, specific learning disabilities, as well as those who are gifted?*

We begin with an issue that affects any discussion of individual differences—language and labeling.

When labels take precedence over individual characteristics, the labels themselves constitute a handicap. Stereotypes about people who use wheelchairs might interfere with recognition of this young man's other characteristics and his individuality.

Language and Labeling

Every child is a distinctive collection of talents, abilities, and limitations. In that sense, they all are "exceptional." But some students are called **exceptional students** because they have learning disabilities, communication disorders, emotional or behavioral disorders, mental retardation, physical disabilities, impaired vision or difficulties hearing, autism, traumatic brain injury, or special abilities and talents. Even though we will use these terms throughout the chapter, a caution is in order: Labeling students is a controversial issue.

A label does not tell which methods to use with individual students. For example, few specific "treatments" automatically follow from a "diagnosis" of mental retardation; many different teaching strategies and materials are appropriate. Further, the labels can become self-fulfilling prophecies. Everyone—teachers, parents, classmates, and even the students themselves—may see a label as a stigma that cannot be changed. Finally, labels are mistaken for explanations, as in, "Mitchell gets into fights because he has a behavior disorder." "How do you know he has a behavior disorder?" "Because he gets into fights."

On the other hand, some educators argue that for younger students, at least, being labeled as "special" protects the child. For example, if classmates know a student has mental retardation (sometimes called a cognitive disability), they will be more willing to accept his or her behaviors. Of course, labels still open doors to some special programs, useful information, special technology and equipment, or financial assistance. Labels probably both stigmatize and help students (Heward & Orlansky, 1992; Keogh & MacMillan, 1996).

Person-First Language. This caution about labeling also applies to many of the common descriptions heard in schools every day. Today many people object to labels such as "mentally retarded student" or "at-risk student" because describing a complex person with one or two words implies that the condition labeled is the most important aspect of the person. Actually, the individual has many abilities, and to focus on the disability is to misrepresent the individual. An alternative is "person-first" language or speaking of "students with mental retardation" or "students placed at risk." Here, the emphasis is on the students first, not on the special challenges they face. Other examples suggested by Meece (2002, p. 317) are:

Exceptional students Students who have abilities or problems so significant that they require special education or other services to reach their potential.

A student with a learning disability	NOT	A learning disabled student
Students receiving special education	NOT	Special education students
A person with epilepsy	NOT	An epileptic
A child with a physical disability	NOT	A crippled child

Disabilities and Handicaps. One more distinction in language is important. A **disability** is just what the word implies—an inability to do something specific such as see or walk. A **handicap** is a disadvantage in certain situations. Some disabilities lead to handicaps, but not in all contexts. For example, being blind (a visual disability) is a handicap if you want to drive a car. But blindness is not a handicap when you are composing music or talking on the telephone. Stephen Hawking, the greatest living physicist, sufferers from Lou Gehrig's disease and no longer can walk or talk. He once said that he is lucky that he became a theoretical physicist "because it is all in the mind. So my disability has not been a serious handicap." It is important that we do not *create* handicaps for people by the way we react to their disabilities. Some educators have suggested that we drop the word "handicap" altogether because the source of the word is demeaning. *Handicap* came from the phrase "cap-in-hand," used to describe people with disabilities who once were forced to beg just to survive (Hardman, Drew, & Egan, 1999).

Check Yourself What are the advantages of and problems with labels?

What is person-first language?

Distinguish between a disability and a handicap.

In the next section we consider a concept that has provided the basis for many labels—intelligence.

Individual Differences in Intelligence

Because the concept of intelligence is so important in education, so controversial, and so often misunderstood, we will spend quite a few pages discussing it. Let us begin with a basic question.

What Does Intelligence Mean?

Who was the most intelligent person in your high school? Write down a name and the first 4 or 5 words that come to mind when you see that person in your mind's eye. What made you pick this individual?

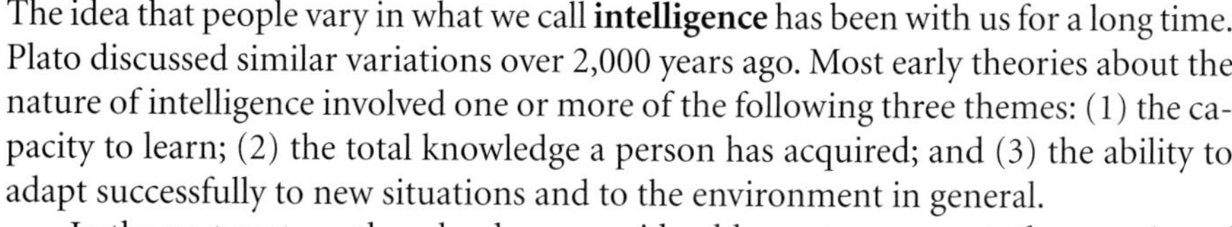

The idea that people vary in what we call **intelligence** has been with us for a long time. Plato discussed similar variations over 2,000 years ago. Most early theories about the nature of intelligence involved one or more of the following three themes: (1) the capacity to learn; (2) the total knowledge a person has acquired; and (3) the ability to adapt successfully to new situations and to the environment in general.

In the past century, there has been considerable controversy over the meaning of intelligence. Thirteen psychologists in 1921 and 24 psychologists in 1986 met to discuss intelligence. Both times, every psychologist had a different view about the nature of intelligence (Neisser et al., 1996; Sternberg & Detterman, 1986). Both times, about half of the experts mentioned higher-level thinking processes such as abstract reasoning and problem solving as important aspects of intelligence. The 1986 definitions added metacognition and executive processes (monitoring your own thinking), the interaction of knowledge with mental processes, and the cultural context—what

Disability The inability to do something specific such as walk or hear.

Handicap A disadvantage in a particular situation, sometimes caused by a disability.

Intelligence Ability or abilities to acquire and use knowledge for solving problems and adapting to the world.

CONNECT & EXTEND

TO THE RESEARCH

Here are a few current ideas about the meaning of intelligence:

- goal-directed adaptive behavior
- ability to solve novel problems
- ability to acquire and think with new conceptual systems
- problem-solving ability
- planning and other metacognitive skills
- memory access speed
- what people think intelligence is
- what IQ tests measure
- the ability to learn from bad teaching

is valued by the culture—as elements of intelligence. But in 1921 and again in 1986, the psychologists disagreed about the structure of intelligence—whether it is a single ability or many separate abilities (Gustafsson & Undheim, 1996; Louis, Subotnik, Breland, & Lewis, 2000; Sattler, 2001; Sternberg & Kaufman, 1998).

Intelligence: One Ability or Many? Some theorists believe intelligence is a basic ability that affects performance on all cognitively oriented tasks from computing mathematical problems to writing poetry or solving riddles. Evidence for this position comes from study after study finding moderate to high positive correlations among all the different tests that are designed to measure separate intellectual abilities (Carroll, 1993; McNemar, 1964). What could explain these results? Charles Spearman (1927) suggested there is one mental attribute, which he called *g* or general intelligence, that is used to perform any mental test, but that each test also requires some specific abilities in addition to *g*. For example, memory for a series of numbers probably involves both *g* and some specific ability for immediate recall of what is heard. Spearman assumed that individuals vary in both general intelligence and specific abilities, and that together these factors determine performance on mental tasks.

Another view that has stood the test of time is Raymond Cattell and John Horn's theory of fluid and crystallized intelligence (Cattell, 1963; Horn, 1998). **Fluid intelligence** is mental efficiency that is essentially culture-free and nonverbal. This aspect of intelligence increases until adolescence because it is grounded in brain development, then declines gradually with age. (Every year it gets harder for me to write that sentence!) Fluid intelligence is sensitive to injuries. In contrast, **crystallized intelligence,** the ability to apply culturally approved problem-solving methods, can increase throughout the life span because it includes the learned skills and knowledge such as vocabulary, facts, and how to hail a cab, make a quilt, or study in college. By *investing fluid intelligence* in solving problems, we *develop our crystallized intelligence,* but many tasks in life such as mathematical reasoning draw on both fluid and crystallized intelligence (Hunt, 2000; Sattler, 2001).

The most widely accepted view today is that intelligence, like self-concept, has many facets and is a hierarchy of abilities, with general ability at the top and more specific abilities at lower levels of the hierarchy (Sternberg, 2000). Earl Hunt summarized the current thinking about the structure of intelligence this way:

> After almost a century of such research, that structure is pretty well-established. There is considerable agreement for the bottom two levels of a three-tiered lattice model of intelligence. At the bottom are elementary information-processing actions, and immediately above them are eight or so secondary abilities. These are more broadly defined capabilities, such as holding and accessing information in short- and long-term memory and, most importantly, the trio of 'intellectual' abilities: crystallized intelligence . . . , fluid intelligence . . . , and visual-spatial reasoning ability [which] may be just the most visible of several abilities to manipulate information coded in a particular sensory modality. (Hunt, 2000, p. 123)

Look at Figure 4.1 to see an example of this three-level view of intelligence. John Carroll (1997) identifies one general ability, a few broad abilities (such as fluid and crystallized abilities, learning and memory, visual and auditory perception, processing speed) and at least 70 specific abilities such as language development, memory span, and simple reaction time. General ability may be related to the maturation and functioning of the frontal lobe of the brain, while specific abilities may be connected to other parts of the brain (Byrnes & Fox, 1998).

Multiple Intelligences. In spite of the correlations among the various tests of different abilities, some psychologists insist that there are several separate mental abilities (Gardner, 1983; Guilford, 1988). According to Gardner's (1983, 1999) **theory of multiple intelligences,** there are at least eight separate intelligences: linguistic (verbal), musical,

Fluid intelligence Mental efficiency, nonverbal abilities grounded in brain development.

Crystallized intelligence Ability to apply culturally approved problem-solving methods.

Theory of multiple intelligences In Gardner's theory of intelligence, a person's eight separate abilities: logical-mathematical, verbal, musical, spatial, bodily-kinesthetic, interpersonal, intrapersonal, and naturalist.

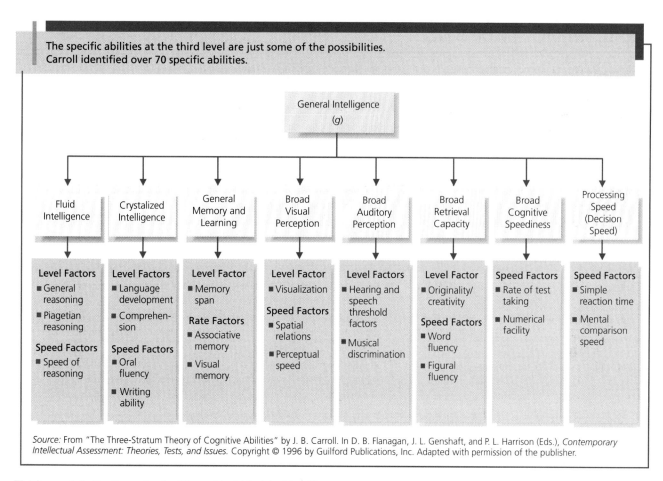

The specific abilities at the third level are just some of the possibilities. Carroll identified over 70 specific abilities.

General Intelligence (*g*)

Fluid Intelligence	Crystalized Intelligence	General Memory and Learning	Broad Visual Perception	Broad Auditory Perception	Broad Retrieval Capacity	Broad Cognitive Speediness	Processing Speed (Decision Speed)
Level Factors ■ General reasoning ■ Piagetian reasoning **Speed Factors** ■ Speed of reasoning	**Level Factors** ■ Language development ■ Comprehension **Speed Factors** ■ Oral fluency ■ Writing ability	**Level Factor** ■ Memory span **Rate Factors** ■ Associative memory ■ Visual memory	**Level Factor** ■ Visualization **Speed Factors** ■ Spatial relations ■ Perceptual speed	**Level Factors** ■ Hearing and speech threshold factors ■ Musical discrimination	**Level Factor** ■ Originality/creativity **Speed Factors** ■ Word fluency ■ Figural fluency	**Speed Factors** ■ Rate of test taking ■ Numerical facility	**Speed Factors** ■ Simple reaction time ■ Mental comparison speed

Source: From "The Three-Stratum Theory of Cognitive Abilities" by J. B. Carroll. In D. B. Flanagan, J. L. Genshaft, and P. L. Harrison (Eds.), *Contemporary Intellectual Assessment: Theories, Tests, and Issues.* Copyright © 1996 by Guilford Publications, Inc. Adapted with permission of the publisher.

Figure 4.1 An Example of a Hierarchical Model of Intelligence

spatial, logical-mathematical, bodily-kinesthetic (movement), interpersonal (understanding others), intrapersonal (understanding self), and naturalist (observing and understanding natural and human-made patterns and systems) (see Table 4.1 on page 110). Gardner stresses that there may be more kinds of intelligence—eight is not a magic number. Recently he has speculated that there may be a spiritual intelligence and an existential intelligence or the abilities to contemplate big questions about the meaning of life (Gardner, 1999). Gardner bases his notion of separate abilities on evidence that brain damage (from a stroke, for example) often interferes with functioning in one area, such as language, but does not affect functioning in other areas. Also, individuals may excel in one of these eight areas but have no remarkable abilities in the other seven.

What are these intelligences? Gardner (1998, 1999) contends that an intelligence is the ability to solve problems and create products or outcomes that are valued by a culture. Varying cultures and eras of history place different values on the eight intelligences. A naturalist intelligence is critical in farming cultures, whereas verbal and mathematical intelligences are important in technological cultures. In addition, Gardner believes that intelligence has a biological basis. Intelligence "is a biological and psychological potential; that potential is capable of being realized to a greater or lesser extent as a consequence of the experiential, cultural, and motivational factors that affect a person" (1998, p. 62).

Howard Gardner's theory of multiple intelligences proposes that there are several kinds of intelligences, and that they may be affected by culture, biology, and other factors.

Gardner's multiple intelligence theory has not received wide acceptance in the scientific community, even though it has been embraced by many educators. Some critics suggest that several of intelligences are really talents (bodily-kinesthetic skill, musical ability) or personality traits (interpersonal ability). Other "intelligences" are

■ Table 4.1	Eight Intelligences	
Howard Gardner's theory of multiple intelligences suggests that there are eight kinds of human abilities. An individual might have strengths or weaknesses in one or several areas.		
Intelligence	**End States**	**Core Components**
Logical-mathematical	Scientist Mathematician	Sensitivity to, and capacity to discern, logical or numerical patterns; ability to handle long chains of reasoning.
Linguistic	Poet Journalist	Sensitivity to the sounds, rhythms, and meanings of words; sensitivity to the different functions of language.
Musical	Composer Violinist	Abilities to produce and appreciate rhythm, pitch, and timbre; appreciation of the forms of musical expressiveness.
Spatial	Navigator Sculptor	Capacities to perceive the visual-spatial world accurately and to perform transformations on one's initial perceptions.
Bodily-kinesthetic	Dancer Athlete	Abilities to control one's body movements and to handle objects skillfully.
Interpersonal	Therapist Salesman	Capacities to discern and respond appropriately to the moods, temperaments, motivations, and desires of other people.
Intrapersonal	Person with detailed, accurate self-knowledge	Access to one's own feelings and the ability to discriminate among them and draw on them to guide behavior; knowledge of one's own strengths, weaknesses, desires, and intelligence.
Naturalist	Botanist Farmer Hunter	Abilities to recognize plants and animals, to make distinctions in the natural world, to understand systems and define categories (perhaps even categories of intelligence).

SOURCE: From "Multiple Intelligences Go to School," by H. Gardner and T. Hatch, *Educational Researcher, 18*(8), p. 6. Copyright © 1989 by the American Educational Research Association. Reproduced by permission of the publisher. Also *Educational Information and Transformation,* edited by J. Kane. Published by Prentice Hall. Copyright © 2002 by Prentice Hall. Reprinted by permission of Pearson Education, Inc., Upper Saddle River, NJ.

not new at all. Many researchers have identified verbal and spatial abilities as elements of intelligence. In addition, the eight intelligences are not independent; there are correlations among the abilities. In fact, logical-mathematical and spatial intelligences are highly correlated (Sattler, 2001). So, these "separate abilities" may not be so separate after all. Recent evidence linking musical and spatial abilities has prompted Gardner to consider that there may be connections among the intelligences (Gardner, 1998). Stay tuned for more developments.

Gardner (1998) has responded to critics by identifying a number of myths and misconceptions about multiple intelligence theory and schooling. One is that intelligences are the same as learning styles (Gardner doesn't believe that people actually have consistent learning styles). Another misconception is that multiple intelligence theory disproves the idea of *g*. Gardner does not deny the existence of a general ability, but does question how useful *g* is as an explanation for human achievements.

CONNECT & EXTEND

TO PRAXIS™
MULTIPLE INTELLIGENCES (I, B1)
Many teachers erroneously assume that they must address each of the eight intelligences in each lesson they design. What are some of the realistic implications of the theory for classroom instructions?

Multiple Intelligences Go to School. An advantage of Gardner's perspective is that it expands teachers' thinking about abilities and avenues for teaching, but the theory has been misused. Some teachers embrace a simplistic version. They include every "intelligence" in every lesson, no matter how inappropriate. Table 4.2 lists some misuses and positive applications of Gardner's work.

Even though many teachers and schools are enthusiastic about Gardner's ideas, there is not yet strong research evidence that adopting a multiple intelligences approach will enhance learning. In one of the few carefully designed evaluations, Callahan, Tomlinson, and Plucker (1997) found no significant gains in either achievement or self-concept for students who participated in START, a multiple intelligences approach to identifying and promoting talent in students who were at risk of failing. Learning is still hard work, even if there are multiple paths to knowledge. Perry Klein

Triarchic theory of intelligence A three-part description of the mental abilities (thinking processes, coping with new experiences, and adapting to context) that lead to more or less intelligent behavior.

■ **Table 4.2** Misuses and Applications of Multiple Intelligence Theory

Recently Howard Gardner described these negative and positive applications of his theory. The quotes are his words on the subject.

Misuses:

1. **Trying to teach all concepts or subjects using all intelligences:** "There is no point in assuming that every subject can be effectively approached in at least seven ways, and it is a waste of effort and time to attempt to do this."
2. **Assuming that it is enough just to apply a certain intelligence, no matter how you use it:** For bodily-kinesthetic intelligence, for example, "random muscle movements have nothing to do with the cultivation of the mind."
3. **Using an intelligence as a background for other activities**, such as playing music while students solve math problems. "The music's function is unlikely to be different from that of a dripping faucet or humming fan."
4. **Mixing intelligences with other desirable qualities:** For example, interpersonal intelligence "is often distorted as a license for cooperative learning," and intrapersonal intelligence "is often distorted as a rationale for self-esteem programs."
5. **Direct evaluation or even grading of intelligences without regard to context:** "I see little point in grading individuals in terms of how 'linguistic' or how 'bodily-kinesthetic' they are."

Good uses:

1. **The cultivation of desired capabilities:** "Schools should cultivate those skills and capabilities that are valued in the community and in the broader society."
2. **Approaching a concept, subject matter, discipline in a variety of ways:** Schools try to cover too much. "It makes far more sense to spend a significant amount of time on key concepts, generative ideas, and essential questions and to allow students to become familiar with these notions and their implications."
3. **The personalization of education:** "At the heart of the MI perspective—in theory and in practice—inheres in taking human difference seriously."

SOURCE: "Reflections on Multiple Intelligences: Myths and Messages," by H. Gardner, 1998. In A. Woolfolk (Ed.), *Readings in Educational Psychology* (2nd ed.) (pp. 64–66), Boston: Allyn & Bacon. Copyright © 1998 by Phi Delta Kappan.

(2002) argues that the multiple intelligence theory is too broad to tell teachers how to teach. "For instance, the knowledge that basketball relies on 'bodily-kinesthetic intelligence' tells a coach nothing about the skills her players need to learn" (p. 228).

Intelligence as a Process

As you can see, the theories of Spearman, Cattell and Horn, Carroll, and Gardner tend to describe how individuals differ in the *content* of intelligence—different abilities. Recent work in cognitive psychology has emphasized instead the thinking *processes* that may be common to all people. How do humans gather and use information to solve problems and behave intelligently? New views of intelligence are growing out of this work.

Robert Sternberg's (1985, 1990) **triarchic theory of intelligence** is a cognitive process approach to understanding intelligence. As you might guess from the name, this theory has three parts—analytic, creative, and practical (see Table 4.3 on page 112).

Analytic/componential intelligence involves the mental processes of the individual that lead to more or less intelligent behavior. These processes are defined in terms of components—elementary information processes that are classified by the functions

Albert Einstein experienced uneven success in his school years, and his genius in science and mathematics did not appear until his teen years. He represents the vast differences that can exist among individual students.

■ Table 4.3 Sternberg's Triarchic Theory of Intelligence

Sternberg suggests that intelligent behavior is the product of applying thinking strategies, handling new problems creatively and quickly, and adapting to contexts by selecting and reshaping our environment.

	Analytic Componential Intelligence	Creative Experiential Intelligence	Practical Contextual Intelligence
Definition	Ability to think abstractly, process information; verbal abilities.	Ability to formulate new ideas and combine unrelated facts; creativity—ability to deal with novel situations and make new solutions automatic.	Ability to adapt to a changing environment and shape the environment to make the most of opportunities—problem solving in specific situations.
Examples	Solving analogies or syllogisms, learning vocabulary.	Diagnosing a problem with a car engine; finding resources for a new project.	Taking your telephone off the hook or putting a "do not disturb" sign on the door to limit distractions while studying.

they serve and by how general they are. Metacomponents perform higher-order functions such as planning, strategy selection, and monitoring. Executing the strategies selected is handled by *performance components.* Gaining new knowledge is performed by *knowledge-acquisition components,* such as separating relevant from irrelevant information as you try to understand a new concept (Sternberg, 1985).

Some components are specific; that is, they are necessary for only one kind of task, such as solving analogies. Other components are very general and may be necessary in almost every cognitive task. For example, metacomponents are always operating to select strategies and keep track of progress. This may help to explain the persistent correlations among all types of mental tests. People who are effective in selecting good problem-solving strategies, monitoring progress, and moving to a new approach when the first one fails are more likely to be successful on all types of tests. Metacomponents may be a modern-day version of Spearman's *g.*

The second part of Sternberg's triarchic theory, *creative/experiential intelligence,* involves coping with new experiences. Intelligent behavior is marked by two characteristics: (1) **insight,** or the ability to deal effectively with novel situations, and (2) **automaticity**—the ability to become efficient and automatic in thinking and problem solving. Thus intelligence involves solving new problems as well as quickly turning new solutions into routine processes that can be applied without much cognitive effort.

The third part of Sternberg's theory, *practical/contextual intelligence,* highlights the importance of choosing to live and work in a context where success is likely, adapting to that context, and reshaping it if necessary. Here, culture is a major factor in defining successful choice, adaptation, and shaping. For example, abilities that make a person successful in a rural farm community may be useless in the inner city or at a country club in the suburbs. People who are successful often seek situations in which their abilities will be valuable, then work hard to capitalize on those abilities and compensate for any weaknesses. Thus, intelligence in this third sense involves practical matters such as career choice or social skills. In a recent field study in a Russian city, Elena Grigorenko and Robert Sternberg (2001) found that adults with higher practical and analytical intelligence coped better mentally and physically with the stresses caused by rapid changes in that part of the world.

Practical intelligence is made up mostly of action-oriented **tacit knowledge.** This tacit knowledge is more likely to be learned during everyday life than through formal schooling—it is "knowing how" rather than "knowing that" (Sternberg, Wagner, Williams, & Horvath, 1995). Recently, however, Sternberg and his colleagues have designed a program for developing practical intelligence for school success by teaching

Insight The ability to deal effectively with novel situations.

Automaticity The result of learning to perform a behavior or thinking process so thoroughly that the performance is automatic and does not require effort.

Tacit knowledge Knowing how rather than knowing that—knowledge that is more likely to be learned during everyday life than through formal schooling.

students effective strategies for reading, writing, homework, and test taking (Sternberg & Kaufman, 1998; Williams et al., 1996).

How Is Intelligence Measured?

What is the capital of France? How are an inch and a mile alike? What does *obstreperous* mean? Repeat these numbers backwards: 8 5 7 3 0 2 1 9 7. In what two ways is a lamp better than a candle? If a suit sells for 1/2 of the regular price at $123, what was the original cost of the suit? These items, taken from Sattler (2001, p. 222) are similar to the verbal questions from a common individual intelligence test for children. Another part of the test asks the child to tell what is missing in a picture, put pictures in order to tell a story, copy a design using blocks, assemble part of a puzzle, complete mazes, and copy symbols.

Even though psychologists do not agree about what intelligence is, they do agree that intelligence, as measured by standard tests, is related to learning in school. Why is this so? It has to do in part with the way intelligence tests were first developed.

Binet's Dilemma. In 1904, Alfred Binet was confronted with the following problem by the minister of public instruction in Paris: How can students who will need special teaching and extra help be identified early in their school careers, before they fail in regular classes? Binet was also a political activist, very concerned with the rights of children. He believed that having an objective measure of learning ability could protect students from poor families who might be forced to leave school because they were the victims of discrimination and assumed to be slow learners.

CONNECT & EXTEND

TO **PRAXIS**™
INTELLIGENCE TESTING (II, C1,4)
The public often misunderstands intelligence testing. Be prepared to respond to questions about the appropriate uses of intelligence tests. What are some inappropriate uses of these tests?

Binet and his collaborator Theodore Simon wanted to measure not merely school achievement, but the intellectual skill students needed to do well in school. After trying many different tests and eliminating items that did not discriminate between successful and unsuccessful students, Binet and Simon finally identified 58 tests, several for each age group from 3 to 13. Binet's tests allowed the examiner to determine a **mental age** for a child. A child who succeeded on the items passed by most 6-year-olds, for example, was considered to have a mental age of 6, whether the child was actually 4, 6, or 8 years old.

The concept of **intelligence quotient,** or **IQ,** was added after Binet's test was brought to the United States and revised at Stanford University to give us the Stanford-Binet test. An IQ score was computed by comparing the mental-age score to the person's actual chronological age. The formula was

$$\text{Intelligence Quotient} = \text{Mental Age/Chronological Age} \times 100$$

The early Stanford-Binet test has been revised four times, most recently in 1986 (Thorndike, Hagen, & Sattler, 1986). The practice of computing a mental age has proven to be problematic because IQ scores calculated on the basis of mental age do not have the same meaning as children get older. To cope with this problem, the concept of deviation IQ was introduced. The **deviation IQ** score is a number that tells exactly how much above or below the average a person scored on the test, compared to others in the same age group.

CONNECT & EXTEND

TO OTHER CHAPTERS
The deviation IQ score takes into account variations in performance at different ages by calculating individual deviation from the age-group average. This idea is discussed more fully in Chapter 14.

Group versus Individual IQ Tests. The Stanford-Binet is an individual intelligence test. It has to be administered to one student at a time by a trained psychologist and takes about two hours. Most of the questions are asked orally and do not require reading or writing. A student usually pays closer attention and is more motivated to do well when working directly with an adult.

Psychologists also have developed group tests that can be given to whole classes or schools. Compared to an individual test, a group test is much less likely to yield an accurate picture of any one person's abilities. When students take tests in a group, they may do poorly because they do not understand the instructions, because they have

Mental age In intelligence testing, a score based on average abilities for that age group.

Intelligence quotient (IQ) Score comparing mental and chronological ages.

Deviation IQ Score based on statistical comparison of an individual's performance with the average performance of others in that age group.

This boy is trying to arrange the red and white blocks so that they match the pattern. His performance is timed. This subtest of the Wechsler Intelligence Scale for children assesses spatial ability.

trouble reading, because their pencils break or they lose their place on the answer sheet, because other students distract them, or because the answer format confuses them (Sattler, 2001). As a teacher, you should be very wary of IQ scores based on group tests.

What Does an IQ Score Mean?

Most intelligence tests are designed so that they have certain statistical characteristics. For example, the average score is 100; 50% of the people from the general population who take the tests will score 100 or above, and 50% will score below 100. About 68% of the general population will earn IQ scores between 85 and 115. Only about 16% will receive scores below 85, and only 16% will score above 115. Note, however, that these figures hold true for White, native-born Americans whose first language is Standard English. Whether IQ tests should even be used with ethnic minority-group students is hotly debated. The *Guidelines* below will help you interpret IQ scores realistically.

Intelligence and Achievement. Intelligence test scores predict achievement in schools quite well, at least for large groups. For example, the correlation is about .4 to .5 between school grades and scores on a popular individual intelligence test, the revised Wechsler Intelligence Scale for Children (WISC-III). Correlations between standardized achievement test and intelligence test scores are higher, around .5 to .7 (Sattler, 2001; Walberg, 1984). This isn't surprising because the tests were designed to predict school achievement. Remember, Binet threw out test items that did not discriminate between good and poor students.

Do people who score high on IQ tests achieve more in life? Here the answer is less clear. There is evidence that *g*, or general intelligence, correlates with "real-world academic, social, and occupational accomplishments" (Ceci, 1991), but there is great

GUIDELINES: Interpreting IQ Scores

Check to see if the score is based on an individual or a group test. Be wary of group test scores.

Examples

1. Individual tests include the Wechsler Scales (WPPSI, WISC-III, WAIS-III, WAIS Abbreviated), the Stanford-Binet, the McCarthy Scales of Children's Abilities, the Woodcock-Johnson Psycho-Educational Battery, the Kaufman Assessment Battery for Children, the Kaufman Adolescent and Adult Intelligence Test (KAIT), and the Das-Naglieri Cognitive Assessment System.
2. Group tests include the Cognitive Abilities Test (CogAT—formerly the Lorge-Thorndike Intelligence Tests), the Analysis of Learning Potential, the Kuhlman-Anderson Intelligence Tests, the Otis-Lennon School Abilities Test (formerly the Otis-Lennon Intelligence Test), and the School and College Ability Tests (SCAT).

Remember that IQ tests are only estimates of general aptitude for learning.

Examples

1. Ignore small differences in scores among students.
2. Bear in mind that even an individual student's scores may change over time for many reasons, including measurement error.
3. Be aware that a total score is usually an average of scores on several kinds of questions. A score in the middle or average range may mean that the student performed at the average on every kind of question or that the student did quite well in some areas (for example, on verbal tasks) and rather poorly in other areas (for example, on quantitative tasks).

Remember that IQ scores reflect a student's past experiences and learning.

Examples

1. Consider these scores to be predictors of school abilities, not measures of innate intellectual abilities.
2. If a student is doing well in your class, do not change your opinion or lower your expectations just because one score seems low.
3. Be wary of IQ scores for minority students and for students whose first language was not English. Even scores on "culture-free" tests are lower for students placed at risk.

debate about the size and meaning of these correlations (*Current Directions in Psychological Science,* 1993; McClelland, 1993). People with higher intelligence-test scores tend to complete more years of school and to have higher-status jobs. However, when the number of years of education is held constant, IQ scores and school achievement are not highly correlated with income and success in later life. Other factors such as motivation, social skills, and luck may make the difference (Goleman, 1995; Neisser et al., 1996; Sternberg & Wagner, 1993).

Intelligence: Heredity or Environment? Nowhere has the nature-versus-nurture debate raged so hard as in the area of intelligence. Should intelligence be seen as a potential, limited by our genetic makeup? Or does intelligence simply refer to an individual's current level of intellectual functioning, as influenced by experience and education? In fact, it is almost impossible to separate intelligence "in the genes" from intelligence "due to experience." Today, most psychologists believe that differences in intelligence are due to both heredity and environment, probably in about equal proportions for children (Petrill & Wilkerson, 2000). "Genes do not fix behavior. Rather they establish a range of possible reactions to the range of possible experiences that the environment can provide" (Weinberg, 1989, p. 101). And environmental influences include everything from the health of a child's mother during pregnancy to the amount of lead in the child's home to the quality of teaching a child receives.

As a teacher, it is especially important for you to realize that cognitive skills, like any other skills, are always improveable. *Intelligence is a current state of affairs,* affected by past experiences and open to future changes. Even if intelligence is a limited potential, the potential is still quite large, and a challenge to all teachers. For example, Japanese and Chinese students know much more mathematics than American students, but their intelligence test scores are quite similar. This superiority in math probably is related to differences in the way mathematics is taught and studied in the three countries and to the self-motivation skills of many Asian students (Baron, 1998; Stevenson & Stigler, 1992).

Check Yourself What is *g*?

What is Gardner's view of intelligence and his position on *g*?

What are the elements in Sternberg's theory of intelligence?

How is intelligence measured and what does an IQ score mean?

Now that you have a sense of what intelligence means, let's consider how to handle cognitive ability differences in teaching.

Ability Differences and Teaching

What Would You Say? You are interviewing for a job in a new middle school, scheduled to open this fall. After about 4 minutes of small talk, the curriculum supervisor says to you, "We have been having some heated debates in this district about ability grouping and tracking. Where do you stand on those issues?"

In this section we consider alternatives for handling differences in academic ability. By the time you finish this section, especially the *Point/Counterpoint* on page 117, you should have an answer to the question above. Is ability grouping a solution to the challenge of ability differences?

Between-Class Ability Grouping

When whole classes are formed based on ability, the process is called **between-class ability grouping** or **tracking,** a common practice in secondary schools and some

Between-class ability grouping/tracking System of grouping in which students are assigned to classes based on their measured ability or their achievements.

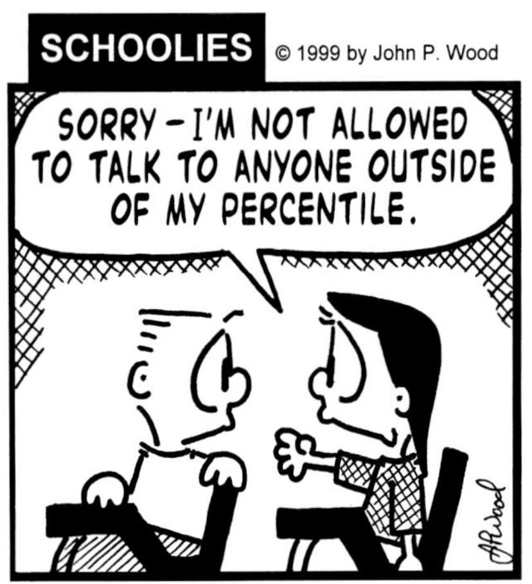

SCHOOLIES
© 1999 by John P. Wood
SORRY - I'M NOT ALLOWED TO TALK TO ANYONE OUTSIDE OF MY PERCENTILE.

Schoolies © 1999 John P. Wood. Reprinted with permission.

elementary schools as well. Many high schools have "college prep" courses and "general" courses or high-, middle-, and low-ability classes in a particular subject. Although this seems on the surface to be an efficient way to teach, research has consistently shown that segregation by ability may benefit high-achieving students, but it causes problems for low-achieving students (Garmon, Nystrand, Berends, & LePore, 1995; Oakes & Wells, 1998; Robinson & Clinkenbeard, 1998; Slavin, 1987, 1990).

Low-ability classes tend to receive lower-quality instruction in general. Teachers emphasize lower-level objectives and routine procedures, with less academic focus. Often there are more student behavior problems and, along with these problems, increased teacher stress and decreased enthusiasm. These differences in instruction and the teachers' negative attitudes may mean that low expectations are communicated to the students. Attendance may drop along with self-confidence. The lower tracks often have a disproportionate number of minority-group and economically disadvantaged students, so ability grouping, in effect, becomes segregation in school. Possibilities for friendships become limited to students in the same ability range. Assignments to classes are often made on the basis of group IQ tests instead of tests in the subject area itself. However, group IQ tests are not good guides for what someone is ready to learn in a particular subject area (Corno & Snow, 1986; Garmon, Nystrand, Berends, & LePore, 1995; Kulik & Kulik, 1982; Slavin, 1987, 1990).

Recently there has been a movement for **untracking** or teaching all students in mixed ability groups, but providing extra help for those who struggle and enrichment for those who learn quickly (Corno, 1995; Oakes & Wells, 2002). Jeannie Oakes and Amy Wells (2002) described several different ways to teach effectively in secondary schools without tracking.

- Eliminate remedial courses and have one regular and one advanced track.
- Offer honors assignment options or challenge pull-out activities within each course.
- Require all students to take a common core of classes, then allow self-selection into advanced classes after the core.
- Encourage minority group students to enroll in advanced placement courses.
- Provide additional times during intercessions when struggling students can get extra help.
- Providing tutoring before and after school.
- Staff a homework help center with teachers, parents, and community volunteers.
- Instead of "dumbing down" content, teach students learning strategies for dealing with difficult material.

Not everyone agrees that untracking is a good idea. This movement has been more successful at the elementary than the secondary level. The *Point/Counterpoint* looks at both sides.

There are two exceptions to the general finding that between-class ability grouping leads to lower achievement. The first is found in honors or gifted classes, where high-ability students tend to perform better than comparable students in regular classes (Kulik & Kulick, 1997). The second exception is the **nongraded elementary schools** and the related Joplin Plan. In a nongraded school, student of several ages (for example, 6, 7, and 8) are together in one class, but they are flexibly grouped within the class for instruction based on achievement, motivation, or interest in different subjects. This cross-grade grouping seems to be effective for students of all abilities as long as the grouping allows teachers to give more direct instruction to the groups. When cross-age grouping is used to implement individualized instruction, the effects are much less positive (Linley, 1999; Gutierrez & Slavin, 1992).

Untracking Redesigning schools to teach students in classes that are not grouped by ability.

Nongraded elementary school/The Joplin Plan Arrangement wherein students are grouped by ability in particular subjects, regardless of their ages or grades.

Point/Counterpoint

Is Tracking an Effective Strategy?

Tracking students into different classes or strands (college prep, vocational, remedial, gifted, etc.) has been standard procedure in many schools for a long time, but does it work? Critics say tracking is harmful while supporters claim it is useful, even though it presents challenges.

Point

Tracking is harmful and should be eliminated.
According to Tom Loveless, writing in the April 1999 issue of *Educational Leadership,* "Prominent researchers and prestigious national reports have argued that tracking stands in the way of equal educational opportunity." (p. 28)

Loveless goes on to cite the work of Braddock and Slavin (1993); Carnegie Council on Adolescent Development (1995); Oakes (1985); and Wheelock (1992)—all of whom make the argument against tracking. What is the basis for these claims? Surprisingly, the evidence is not clear or direct. For example, a few well-done and carefully designed studies found that tracking increases the gap between high and low achievers by depressing the achievement of low-track students and boosting the achievement of high track students (Gamoran, 1987; Kerckhoff, 1986). And Gamoran also found that the achievement gap between low- and high-track students is greater than the gap between students who drop out of school and students who graduate. Because low-income students and students of color are overrepresented in the lower tracks, they suffer the greatest harm from tracking and should benefit the most from the elimination of tracking (Oakes, 1990; Oakes & Wells, 2002). Is this likely?

Counterpoint

Eliminating tracking will hurt many students.
Researchers who have looked closely at tracking believe that tracking may be harmful for some students some of the time, but not for all students and not all of the time. First, as most people agree, tracking seems to have positive effects for the high-track students. Gifted programs, honors classes, and advanced placement classes seem to work (Fuchs, Fuchs, Hamlett, & Karns, 1998; Robinson & Clinkenbeard, 1998). No one, especially parents, wants to eliminate the positive effects of these programs. And the chance of being assigned to a high track is 10% greater for African American students (Gamoran & Mare, 1989), so detracking could be a special disservice to these students.

What would happen if schools were detracked? Loveless (1999) identifies some possible hidden costs. First, results of a large national study suggest that when low-track 10th graders are assigned to heterogeneous classes rather than low tracks, they gain about 5 percentage points in achievement. So far, so good. But average students lose 2 percentage points when put into heterogeneous classes and high-ability students lose about 5 points.

> *The achievement gap is indeed narrowed, but apparently at the expense of students in regular and high tracks, representing about 70% of 10th graders in the United States. (Loveless, 1999, p. 29)*

Another consequence of detracking is *bright flight*—the withdrawal of the brightest students from the schools. Both African American and White parents distrust mixed ability classes to meet the needs of their children (Public Agenda Foundation, 1994).

In some classes, using a mixed ability structure seems to hinder the achievement of all students. For example, students in heterogeneous algebra classes don't learn as much as students in tracked classes—whatever the ability level of the students (Epstein & MacIver, 1992). And a meta-analysis of student self-esteem found that students in low-track classes did *not* have lower self-esteem than students in heterogeneous classes (Kulik & Kulik, 1997).

So what is the answer? As usual, it is more complicated than simply detracking versus tracking. Careful attention to every student's achievement may mean different answers at different times.

What do you think? Vote online at **www.ablongman.com/woolfolk**

In the **Joplin Plan,** students stay in their regular mixed ability grade level classes, but are regrouped across grade levels for reading. A reading group might therefore have students from several grades, all working on the same reading level. *But be sensible about cross-age grouping.* Mixing 3rd, 4th, and 5th graders for math or reading class based on what they are ready to learn makes sense. Sending a large 4th grader to the 2nd grade, where he is the only older student and stands out like a sore thumb, isn't likely to work well. Also, when cross-age classes are created just because there are too few students for one grade and not in order to better meet the students' learning needs, the results are not positive (Veenman, 1997).

Within-Class Ability Grouping

You are preparing a unit on habitats for your students. You decide to do as your old educational psychology professor recommended and give an alternate form of the final unit test as a pretest to find out what the students already know about the subject. After you reassure them that the test won't be graded—you just want an idea about where to go in developing the lesson—the students settle in and seem to take the task seriously. Looking over the papers that night, you are dismayed. A quarter of the students make over 90% on the "final." Quite a few get around half of the questions and problems right, but the rest of the class is clueless. The next day, when you ask Shanequa why she did so well on the test, she explains that in science class last year her group (and several others) chose habitats as the focus of their special project work. You stare at your lesson plans and realize that they fit practically no one in this class. What will you do?

Differences like the ones illustrated above are common in most schools and classrooms. If you decided to simply forge ahead and teach the same material in the same way to your entire class, you would not be alone. One study found that in 46 different classrooms, 84% of the activities were the same for high achieving and average achieving students (Westberg, Archambault, Dobyns, & Slavin, 1993). Differences in student prior knowledge are a major challenge for teachers, especially in subjects that build on previous knowledge and skills such as math and science (Loveless, 1998).

Today many elementary school classes are grouped for reading, and some are grouped for math, even though there is no clear evidence that this **within-class ability grouping** is superior to other approaches. Thoughtfully constructed and well taught ability groups in math and reading can be effective, but other approaches such as cooperative learning are available too. The point of any grouping strategy should be to provide appropriate challenge and support—that is, to reach children within their "zone of proximal development" (Vygotsky, 1997).

Many people are strongly against ability groupings of any kind. After reading the above section and the *Point/Counterpoint,* you should be able to determine your position on ability grouping and tracking—and answer the interview question at the beginning of this section. If you ever decide to use homogeneous small groups in your class, the *Guidelines* should make the approach more effective (Good & Brophy, 1997; Slavin, 1987).

Check Yourself What are the problems with between-class ability grouping?

What are the alternatives available for grouping in classes?

Cognitive and Learning Styles

What Would You Say? Describe a learning activity that you have planned for a class and ways that you have accommodated individual learning styles or needs.

In this section we examine individual differences that have very little to do with intelligence but can influence students' learning in school. These differences have been called *cognitive styles* or *learning styles.* Be aware that you may hear these terms used interchangeably. In general, educators prefer the term *learning styles,* and include many kinds of differences in this broad category. Psychologists tend to prefer the term *cognitive styles,* and limit their discussion to differences in the ways people process information (Bjorklund, 1989).

CONNECT & EXTEND

TO **PRAXIS**™
LEARNING/COGNITIVE STYLES (I, B1)
Familiarize yourself with the major issues involved with learning and cognitive styles, and understand their implications for classroom practice.

Cognitive Styles

The notion of cognitive styles is fairly new. It grew out of research on how people perceive and organize information from the world around them. Differences in **cognitive style** have to do with "characteristic modes of perceiving, remembering,

Within-class ability grouping System of grouping in which students in a class are divided into two or three groups based on ability in an attempt to accommodate student differences.

Cognitive styles Different ways of perceiving and organizing information.

GUIDELINES Grouping by Achievement

Form and reform groups on the basis of students' *current performance* in the subject being taught.

Examples

1. Use scores on the most recent reading assessments to establish reading groups, and rely on current math performance to form math groups.
2. Change group placement frequently when students' achievement changes.

Discourage comparisons between groups and encourage students to develop a whole-class spirit.

Examples

1. Don't seat groups together outside the context of their reading or math group.
2. Avoid naming ability groups—save the names for mixed-ability or whole-class teams.

Group by ability for one or, at the most, two subjects.

Examples

1. Make sure there are many lessons and projects that mix members from the groups.
2. Experiment with learning strategies in which cooperation is stressed (described in Chapter 11).
3. Keep the number of groups small (two or three at most) so that you can provide as much direct teaching as possible—leaving students alone for too long leads to less learning.

Make sure teachers, methods, and pace are adjusted to fit the needs of the group.

Examples

1. Organize and teach groups so that low-achieving students get appropriate extra instruction—not just the same material again.
2. Experiment with alternatives to grouping. There are alternatives to within-class grouping that appear more effective for some subjects. DeWayne Mason and Tom Good (1993) found that supplementing whole-class instruction in math with remediation and enrichment for students when they needed it worked better than dividing the class into two ability groups and teaching these groups separately.

thinking, problem solving, and decision making, reflective of information-processing regularities that develop . . . around underlying personality trends" (Messick, 1994, p. 122) and not with intelligence. For example, certain individuals respond very quickly in most situations. Others are more reflective and slower to respond, even though both types of people may be equally knowledgeable about the task at hand.

Field Dependence and Field Independence. In the early 1940s, Herman Witkin became intrigued by the observation that certain airline pilots would fly into a bank of clouds and fly out upside down, without realizing that they had changed position. His research on how people separate one factor from the total visual field identified the cognitive styles of field dependence and field independence (Davis, 1991; Witkin, Moore, Goodenough, & Cox, 1977).

People who are **field dependent** tend to perceive a pattern as a whole, not separating one element from the total visual field. They have difficulty focusing on one aspect of a situation, picking out important details, analyzing a pattern into different parts, or monitoring their use of strategies to solve problems. They tend to work well in groups, have a good memory for social information, and prefer subjects such as literature and history. **Field-independent** people, on the other hand, are more likely to monitor their own information processing. They perceive separate parts of a total pattern and are able to analyze a pattern according to its components. They are not as attuned to social relationships as field-dependent people, but they do well in math and science, where their analytical abilities pay off.

Students approach problems in different ways. Some may need help learning to pick out important features and to ignore irrelevant details. They may seem lost in less-structured situations and need clear, step-by-step instructions. Other students may be great at organizing but less sensitive to the feelings of others and not as effective in social situations.

Impulsive and Reflective Cognitive Styles. Another aspect of cognitive style is impulsivity versus reflectiveness. An **impulsive** student works very quickly but makes

Field dependence Cognitive style in which patterns are perceived as wholes.

Field independence Cognitive style in which separate parts of a pattern are perceived and analyzed.

Impulsive Characterized by cognitive style of responding quickly but often inaccurately.

CONNECT & EXTEND

TO YOUR TEACHING PORTFOLIO
When students fail a grade or a course, they are often "recycled" through the same material on the assumption that repetition will produce learning. Use the concept of cognitive style to argue against this practice.

many mistakes. The more **reflective** student, on the other hand, works slowly and makes fewer errors. As with field dependence/independence, impulsive and reflective cognitive styles are not highly related to intelligence within the normal range. However, as children grow older, they generally become more reflective, and for school-age children, being more reflective does seem to improve performance on school tasks such as reading (Kogan, 1983; Smith & Caplan, 1988).

Students can learn to be more reflective, however, if they are taught specific strategies. One that has proved successful in many situations is **self-instruction,** described in Chapter 6. This approach capitalizes on the beneficial use of private speech described by Vygotsky (Meichenbaum, 1986). Another possibility is learning scanning strategies. For example, students taking multiple-choice tests might be encouraged to cross off each alternative as they consider it, so that no possibilities will be ignored. They might work in pairs and talk about why each possibility is right or wrong. Just slowing down is not enough. These students must be taught effective strategies for solving the problem at hand by considering each reasonable alternative. I have also encountered several bright students who seem too reflective. They turn 30 minutes of homework into an all-night project.

Learning Styles and Preferences

Learning styles are approaches to learning and studying. Although many different learning styles have been described, one theme that unites most of the styles is differences between deep and surface approaches to processing information in learning situations (Snow, Corno, & Jackson, 1996). Individuals who have a *deep-processing approach* see the learning activities as a means for understanding some underlying concepts or meanings. They tend to learn for the sake of learning and are less concerned about how their performance is evaluated, so motivation plays a role as well. Students who take a *surface-processing* approach focus on memorizing the learning materials, not understanding them. These students tend to be motivated by rewards, grades, external standards, and the desire to be evaluated positively by others. Of course, the situation can encourage deep or surface processing, but there is evidence that individuals have tendencies to approach learning situations in characteristic ways (Biggs, 2001; Pintrich & Schrauben, 1992; Tait & Entwistle, 1998).

When, where, and how do you study best? Do you like to have music playing? Eat while you study? Make outlines or notes or draw pictures to help you remember? See the CW activity to take a learning styles test for yourself.

What Are Learning Preferences? Since the late 1970s, a great deal has been written about differences in students' learning preferences (Dunn, 1987; Dunn & Dunn, 1978, 1987; Gregorc, 1982; Keefe, 1982). Workshops and in-service training sessions around the country focus on this topic. Learning preferences are usually called *learning styles* in these workshops, but I believe preference is a more accurate label. **Learning preferences** are individual preferences for particular learning modes and environments. They could be preferences for where, when, with whom, or with what lighting, food, or music you like to study. Think for a minute about how you learn best. I like to study and write during large blocks of time, late at night. I usually make some kind of commitment or deadline every week so that I have to work in long stretches to finish the work before that deadline. Then I take a day off. When I plan or think, I have to see my thinking in writing. I have a colleague who draws diagrams of relationships when she listens to a speaker or plans a paper. You may be similar or very different, but we all may work effectively.

There are a number of instruments for assessing students' learning preferences Be aware, however, that many lack evidence of reliability and validity (Stahl, 2002).

Reflective Characterized by cognitive style of responding slowly, carefully, and accurately.

Self-instruction Talking oneself through the steps of a task.

Learning styles Characteristic approaches to learning and studying.

Learning preferences Preferred ways of studying and learning, such as using pictures instead of text, working with other people versus alone, learning in structured or in unstructured situations, and so on.

People are different, and it is good practice to recognize and accommodate individual differences. It is also good practice to present information in a variety of ways through more than one modality, but it is not wise to categorize learners and prescribe methods solely on the basis of tests with questionable technical qualities. . . . The idea of learning styles is appealing, but a critical examination of this approach should cause educators to be skeptical. (Snider, 1990, p. 53)

Teachers can make options available to accommodate individual preferences. Having quiet, private corners as well as large tables for working; comfortable cushions as well as straight chairs; brightly lighted desks along with darker areas; headphones for listening to music as well as earplugs; structured as well as open-ended assignments; information available from videos and tapes as well as in books—all these options will allow students to work and learn in their preferred mode at least some of the time.

Cautions. Some proponents of learning styles believe that students learn more when they study in their preferred setting and manner (Dunn, Beaudry, & Klavas, 1989; Dunn & Dunn, 1987). And there is evidence that very bright students need less structure and prefer quiet, solitary learning (Torrance, 1986). But most educational psychologists are skeptical about the value of learning preferences. "The reason researchers roll their eyes at learning styles research is the utter failure to find that assessing children's learning styles and matching to instructional methods has any effect on their learning" (Stahl, 2002, p. 99). So before you try to accommodate all your students' learning styles, remember that students, especially younger ones, may not be the best judges of how they should learn. Sometimes students, particularly students who have difficulty, prefer what is easy and comfortable; real learning can be hard and uncomfortable. Sometimes students prefer to learn in a certain way because they have no alternatives; it is the only way they know how to approach the task. These students may benefit from developing new—and perhaps more effective—ways to learn.

Check Yourself Distinguish between cognitive style and learning preference.

Should teachers match instruction to individual learning styles?

Thus far we have focused mostly on teachers' responses to the varying abilities and styles of students. For the rest of the chapter we will consider what can interfere with learning. It is important for all teachers to be aware of these issues because laws and policy changes over the past 25 years have expanded teachers' responsibilities in working with all students.

CONNECT & EXTEND

TO THE RESEARCH

There are a number of instruments for assessing students' learning preferences. *The Learning Style Inventory* by Renzulli and Smith (1978) asks students to indicate preferences for different types of instruction, such as lecture, discussion, projects, games, and so on. *The Learning Style Inventory* by Dunn, Dunn, and Price (1984) measures preferences for 23 elements of the instructional program, including the immediate environment (temperature, noise level, etc.); emotional involvement (motivational strategies, structure, etc.); social support (working alone or with others, etc.); physical characteristics (time of day, visual versus auditory materials, etc.); and psychological inclinations (impulsive or reflective, global or analytic, etc.). The *Learning Style Profile* (Keefe & Monk, 1986) is a 126-item test based on a broad definition of learning style that includes cognitive, affective, and physiological differences.

Changes in the Law: Integration and Inclusion

Have you ever had the experience of being the only one in a group who had trouble doing something? How would you feel if every day in school you faced the same kind of difficulty, while everyone else seemed to find the work easier than you? What kind of support and teaching would you need to keep trying?

In 1975, a law was passed that began revolutionary changes in the education of children with disabilities. The Education for All Handicapped Children Act (Public Law 94-142) required states to provide "a free, appropriate public education for every child between the ages of 3 and 21 (unless state law does not provide free public education to children 3 to 5 or 18 to 21 years of age) regardless of how, or how seriously, he may be handicapped." In 1986, PL 99-457 extended the requirement for a free, appropriate education

CONNECT & EXTEND

TO THE RESEARCH

The Winter 1996 issue of *Theory Into Practice* is devoted to "The Inclusive School: The Continuing Debate." See http://www.coe.ohio-state.edu/TIP. This journal is especially for educators.

to all children ages 3 to 5 with handicaps, even in states that do not have public schooling for children this age. Also in the mid-1980s, some special educators and educational policymakers suggested that regular and special education should be merged so that regular teachers would have to take even more responsibility for the education of exceptional students. This movement is called the **regular education initiative.**

In 1990, PL 94-142 was amended by the **Individuals with Disabilities Education Act (IDEA).** This legislation replaced the word "handicapped" with "disabled," and expanded the services for students with disabilities. Also in 1990, the **Americans with Disabilities Act (ADA)** extended civil rights protection in employment, transportation, public accommodations, state and local government, and telecommunications to people with disabilities. In 1997, IDEA was reauthorized with some new sections as PL 105-17. A major change was that the general education classroom teacher became a member of the team that writes the student's Individualized Education Program (IEP), described below. Stay tuned—changes are likely to continue. See the CW activity or www.ed.gov/offices/OSERS/Policy/ for current information.

Let's examine the requirements in these laws. There are three major points of interest to teachers: the concept of "least restrictive placement"; the individualized education program (IEP); and the protection of the rights of students with disabilities and their parents.

CONNECT & EXTEND

TO **PRAXIS**™
INDIVIDUAL EDUCATION PROGRAMS (IEP) (I, B3)
When you sign an IEP, you are signing an important educational and legal document. Be sure that you can explain the purpose of an IEP, identify its components, and describe the kind of information that can be contained in one.

Least Restrictive Placement

The laws require states to develop procedures for educating each child in the **least restrictive placement**—a setting that is as normal as possible. Earlier interpretations of this requirement led to **mainstreaming**—bringing exceptional students into general educational settings when the students could meet expectations for that setting—for example, allowing them to participate in recess or art or music (Friend & Bursuck, 2002). In most schools students with severe disabilities were not integrated into regular classes; but in some districts there is a movement toward **full inclusion**—integrating all students, even those with severe disabilities, into regular classes.

Advocates of inclusion believe that students with disabilities can benefit from involvement with their nondisabled peers and should be educated with them in their regular home-district school, even if doing so means changes in educational requirements, special aids, services, and training or consultation for the regular teaching staff (Stainback & Stainback, 1992). However, some researchers caution that inclusion classrooms are not the best placement for every child. For example, Naomi Zigmond and her colleagues (1995) report that only about half of the students with learning disabilities in their study of six full-inclusion elementary schools were able to benefit.

Individualized Education Program

The drafters of the laws recognized that each student is unique and may need a specially tailored program to make progress. The **Individualized Education Program, or IEP,** is written by a team that includes the student's teacher or teachers, a qualified school psychologist or special education supervisor, the parent(s) or guardian(s), and (when possible) the student. The program must be updated each year and must state in writing:

1. The student's present level of functioning.
2. Goals for the year and short-term measurable instructional objectives leading to those goals.
3. A list of specific services to be provided to the student and details of when those services will be initiated.
4. A description of how fully the student will participate in the regular school program.
5. A schedule telling how the student's progress toward the objectives will be evaluated and approximately how long the services described in the plan will be needed.

Regular education initiative An educational movement that advocates giving regular education teachers, not special education teachers, responsibility for teaching mildly (and sometimes moderately) handicapped students.

Individuals with Disabilities Education Act (IDEA) Amendment to PL 94-142.

Americans with Disabilities Act (ADA) Legislation prohibiting discrimination against persons with disabilities in employment, transportation, public access, local government, and telecommunications.

Least restrictive placement Placement of each child in as normal an educational setting as possible.

Mainstreaming Teaching children with disabilities in regular classes for part or all of their school day.

Full inclusion The integration of all students, including those with severe disabilities, into regular classes.

Individualized Education Program (IEP) Annually revised program for an exceptional student, detailing present achievement level, goals, and strategies, drawn up by teachers, parents, specialists, and (if possible) the student.

6. Beginning at age 16 (and as young as 14 for some students), a statement of needed transitional services to move the student toward further education or work in adult life.

Figure 12.3 on page 468 is an excerpt from the IEP of a 9-year-old girl with mild retardation.

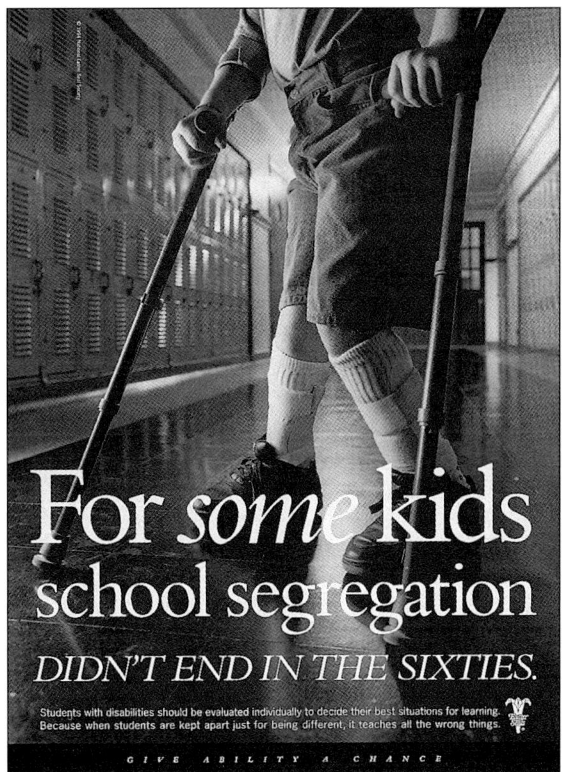

For some kids
school segregation
DIDN'T END IN THE SIXTIES.
Students with disabilities should be evaluated individually to decide their best situations for learning.
Because when students are kept apart just for being different, it teaches all the wrong things.
GIVE ABILITY A CHANCE

The latter portion of the 20th century has seen the doors of the general education system open to students of all abilities.

The Rights of Students and Families

Several stipulations in these laws protect the rights of parents and students. Schools must have procedures for maintaining the confidentiality of school records. Testing practices must not discriminate against students from different cultural backgrounds. Parents have the right to see all records relating to the testing, placement, and teaching of their child. If they wish, parents may obtain an independent evaluation of their child. Parents may bring an advocate or representative to the meeting at which the IEP is developed. Students whose parents are unavailable must be assigned a surrogate parent to participate in the planning. Parents must receive written notice (in their native language) before any evaluation or change in placement is made. Finally, parents have the right to challenge the program developed for their child, and are protected by due process of law. If you have conferences with your student's family, following the suggestions in the *Family and Community Partnerships Guidelines* can make the meetings more effective.

Family and Community Partnerships

Productive Conferences

Plan and prepare for a productive conference.

Examples

1. Have a clear purpose and gather the needed information. If you want to discuss student progress, have work samples.
2. Send home a list of questions and ask families to bring the information to the conference.

Sample questions from Friend and Bursuck (2002) are:

1. What is your child's favorite class activity?
2. Does your child have worries about any class activities? If so, what are they?
3. What are your priorities for your child's education this year?
4. What questions do you have about your child's education in my class this year?
5. How could we at school help make this the most successful year ever for your child?
6. Are there any topics you want to discuss at the conference that I might need to prepare for? If so, please let me know.
7. Would you like other individuals to participate in the conference? If so, please give me a list of their names.
8. Is there particular school information you would like me to have available? If so, please let me know.

During the conference, create and maintain an atmosphere of collaboration and respect.

Examples

1. Arrange the room for private conversation. Put a sign on your door to avoid interruptions. Meet around a conference table for better collaboration. Have tissues available.
2. Address families as "Mr." and "Ms.," not "Mom" and "Dad" or "Grandma." Use students' names.
3. Listen to families' concerns and build on their ideas for their children.

After the conference, keep good records and follow up on decisions.

Examples

1. Make notes to yourself and keep them organized.
2. Summarize any actions or decisions in writing and send a copy to the family and any other teachers or professionals involved.
3. Communicate with families on other occasions, especially when there is good news to share.

Check Yourself Describe the main legal requirements that pertain to students with disabilities.

We turn now to the challenges your students may face.

Prevalent Problems and Mild Disabilities

Look at Table 4.4. You will see that almost 3 million students served under IDEA have specific learning disabilities and another 1 million have speech and language impairments. If you add children with mental retardation and students with emotional problems, that totals about 90% of the students served. With recent changes in the laws and new, more inclusive policies, you are likely to have children from all these categories in your classes.

Almost one-half of all students receiving some kind of special education services in the public schools are diagnosed as having learning disabilities—by far the largest category of students with disabilities.

Students with Learning Disabilities

CONNECT & EXTEND

TO THE RESEARCH

The January 2001 issue of *The Elementary School Journal* is edited by Russell Gersten and Sharon Vaughn and is entirely devoted to "Instructional Interventions for Students with Learning Disabilities." Topics include teaching expressive writing, literacy, self-concept, and higher order learning.

How do you explain a student who struggles to read, write, spell, or learn math, even though he or she does not have mental retardation, emotional problems, or educational disadvantages and has normal vision, hearing, and language capabilities? One explanation is that the student has a **learning disability.** This is a relatively new and controversial category of exceptional students. There is no fully agreed upon definition. A recent text on learning disabilities lists a dozen definitions (Hallahan, Kauffman, & Lloyd, 1999). The National Joint Committee on Learning Disabilities (1989), a group of parents and professionals, proposes the following definition:

> Learning disabilities is a general term that refers to a heterogeneous group of disorders manifested by significant difficulties in the acquisition and use of

■ Table 4.4 Students Age 6–21 Served under IDEA, by Disability Category: 1998–1999

Disability	Number	Percentage
Specific learning disabilities	2,81 7,148	50.8
Speech and language impairments	1,074,548	19.4
Mental retardation	611,076	11.0
Emotional disturbance	463,262	8.4
Multiple disabilities	107,763	1.9
Hearing impairments	70,883	1.4
Orthopedic impairments	69,495	1.1
Other health impairments	220,831	1.2
Visual impairments	26,132	0.5
Autism	53,576	1.0
Deaf-blindness	1,609	>0.1
Traumatic brain injury	12,933	0.2
Developmental delay	11,910	0.2
All disabilities	5,541,166	

SOURCE: U.S. Department of Education, Office of Special Education Programs, Data Analysis System (DANS), cited in the *Twenty-Second Annual Report to Congress on the Implementation of the Individuals with Disabilities Education Act* (2000), pp. 11–21.

Learning disability Problem with acquisition and use of language; may show up as difficulty with reading, writing, reasoning, or math.

listening, speaking, reading, writing, reasoning, or mathematical abilities. These disorders are intrinsic to the individual, presumed to be due to central nervous system dysfunction, and may occur across the life span. (p. 1)

This definition eliminates references to older terms such as *brain injury* or *minimal brain dysfunction,* and indicates that learning disabilities may pose a lifelong challenge. Most definitions agree that students with learning disabilities are at least average in intelligence, but have significant academic problems and perform significantly below what would be expected.

Some educators and psychologists believe the learning disability label is overused and abused. They suggest that many of the students called learning disabled are really slow learners in average schools, average learners in high-achieving schools, students with second-language problems, or students who are behind in their work because they are absent or changed schools often (Gartner & Lipsky, 1987).

Student Characteristics. Students with learning disabilities are not all alike. The most common characteristics are specific difficulties in one or more academic areas; poor coordination; problems paying attention; hyperactivity and impulsivity; problems organizing and interpreting visual and auditory information; disorders of thinking, memory, speech, and hearing; and difficulties making and keeping friends (Hallahan & Kauffman, 2003; Hunt & Marshall, 2002). As you can see, many students with other disabilities (such as attention deficit disorder) and many normal students may have some of the same characteristics. To complicate the situation even more, not all students with learning disabilities will have these problems, and few will have all of the problems. One student may be three years behind in reading but above grade level in math, while another student may have the opposite strengths and weaknesses and a third may have problems with organizing and studying that affect almost all subject areas.

Most students with learning disabilities have difficulties reading. Table 4.5 on page 126 lists some of the most common problems and signs. These difficulties appear to be caused by problems with relating sounds to letters that make up words, making spelling hard as well (Stanovich, 1994; Willcutt et al., 2001). Math, both computation and problem solving, is the second most common problem area for students with learning disabilities. The writing of some of these students is virtually unreadable, and their spoken language can be halting and disorganized. Students with learning disabilities often lack effective ways of approaching academic tasks. They don't know how to focus on the relevant information, get organized, apply learning strategies and study skills, change strategies when one isn't working, or evaluate their learning. They tend to be passive learners, in part because they don't know *how* to learn. Working independently is especially trying, so homework and seatwork are often left incomplete (Hallahan, Kauffman, & Lloyd, 1999).

Early diagnosis is important so that students with learning disabilities do not become terribly frustrated and discouraged. The students themselves do not understand why they are having such trouble, and they may become victims of **learned helplessness.** This condition was first identified in learning experiments with animals. The animals were put in situations where they received punishment (electric shocks) that they could not control. Later, when the situation was changed and they could have escaped the shocks or turned them off, the animals didn't even bother trying (Seligman, 1975). They had learned to be helpless victims. Students with learning disabilities may also come to believe that they cannot control or improve their own learning. This is a powerful belief. The students never exert the effort to discover that they can make a difference in their own learning, so they remain passive and helpless.

Students with learning disabilities may also try to compensate for their problems and develop bad learning habits in the process, or they may begin avoiding certain subjects out of fear of not being able to handle the work. To prevent these things from happening, the teacher should refer the students to the appropriate professionals in the school as early as possible.

CONNECT & EXTEND

TO YOUR TEACHING/PORTFOLIO

Dolgins, J., Myers, M., Flynn, P. A., & Moore, J. (1984, February). How do we help the learning disabled? *Instructor,* 29–36.

- Allow assignments to be typed, taped, or dictated.
- Have material to be copied or directions on the child's desk rather than on the board.
- Increase the time allowed or decrease the amount of writing.
- Omit handwriting as a criterion for evaluating reports.
- Construct tests that require minimal writing, such as multiple-choice or matching.
- Tape selections that a child cannot read, but can comprehend.
- Provide opportunities for group projects, peer tutoring, contracts, and/or learning centers.
- Write summaries of reading assignments.
- Decrease the number of spelling words required at one time.
- To increase exposure, use spelling words that are also required in reading or science.
- Avoid spelling as a criterion for evaluating assignments.
- Require fewer math problems for an assignment.
- Allow the use of calculators or other manipulative aids.
- Provide concrete examples.

CONNECT & EXTEND

TO OTHER CHAPTERS

The concept of learned helplessness will be discussed again in Chapter 5 as one explanation for the lower achievement of children of poverty and again in Chapter 9 as a factor influencing motivation.

Learned helplessness The expectation, based on previous experiences with a lack of control, that all one's efforts will lead to failure.

■ Table 4.5 Reading Habits and Errors of Students with Learning Disabilities

Do any of your students show these signs? They could be indications of learning disabilities.

Poor Reading Habits

- Frequently loses his or her place
- Jerks head from side to side
- Expresses insecurity by crying or refusing to read
- Prefers to read with the book held within inches from face
- Shows tension while reading; such as reading in a high-pitched voice, biting lips, and fidgeting

Word Recognition Errors

- Omitting a word (e.g., "He came to the park," is read, "He came to park")
- Inserting a word (e.g., "He came to the [beautiful] park")
- Substituting a word for another (e.g., "He came to the *pond*")
- Reversing letters or words (e.g., *was* is read *saw*)
- Mispronouncing words (e.g., *park* is read *pork*)
- Transposing letters or words (e.g., "The dog ate fast," is read, "The dog fast ate")
- Not attempting to read an unknown word by breaking it into familiar units
- Slow, laborious reading, less than 20 to 30 words per minute

Comprehension Errors

- Recalling basic facts (e.g., cannot answer questions directly from a passage)
- Recalling sequence (e.g., cannot explain the order of events in a story)
- Recalling main theme (e.g., cannot give the main idea of a story)

SOURCE: From *Child and Adolescent Development for Educators,* by J. L. Meece. Published by McGraw-Hill.

Teaching Students with Learning Disabilities. There is also controversy over how best to help these students. A promising approach seems to be to emphasize study skills and methods for processing information in a given subject such as reading or math. Many of the principles of cognitive learning from Chapters 7 and 8 can be applied to help all students improve their attention, memory, and problem-solving abilities (Sawyer, Graham, & Harris, 1992). The Kansas Learning Strategies Curriculum is one example of this approach (Deshler & Schumaker, 1986).

In teaching reading, a combination of teaching letter-sound (phonological) knowledge and word identification strategies appears to be effective. For example, Maureen Lovett and her colleagues (Lovett et al., 2000) in Canada taught students with severe reading disabilities to use the four different word identification strategies: (1) word identification by analogy, (2) seeking the part of the word that you know, (3) attempting different vowel pronunciations, and (4) "peeling off" prefixes and suffixes in a multisyllabic word. Teachers worked one-to-one with the students to learn and practice these four strategies along with analysis of word sounds and blending sounds into words (phonological knowledge). Direct teaching of skills and strategies is especially important for students with reading disabilities. And the teaching does not have to focus on low-level skills. Joanna Williams and her colleagues (2002) describe a system for teaching students with severe learning disabilities how to identify the theme in a literature story. *Reaching Every Student* describes the approach.

Students with Communication Disorders

From the ages of 6 to 11, students with communication disorders are the second largest group served by special education. They make up about 19% of students

Reaching Every Student

Higher Order Comprehension and Severe Learning Disabilities

Joanna Williams (2002) developed the *Theme Identification Program* to help middle school students with severe learning disabilities understand and use the abstract idea of themes in literature. Teachers taught 12 different lessons using 12 stories. Briefly (see the article for more detail) the process for each lesson was:

Prereading: defining a theme, discussing the value of themes, drawing on students' personal experiences.

Reading: the teacher reads the story and inserts questions while reading to help students connect what they know to the story. At the end of the reading, the class discusses the main point in the story and the teacher reads a summary highlighting the points.

Discussing Using the Theme Scheme: The teacher and students discuss the important information using six organizing questions. The first four questions focused on the story content:

- Who was the main character?
- What was her/his problem?
- What did she/he do?
- What happened at the end of the story?

The last two questions encouraged students to make judgments in order to identify a theme:

- Was what happened good or bad?
- Why was it good or bad?

Identifying the Theme: Students then state the theme in a standard format:

- [The main character] learned that she (he) should (not) ____________.
- We should (not) ____________.
- The theme of the story is ____________.

Application of Theme: the students learn to ask three questions to generalize the theme:

- Can you name someone who should (not) ____________?
- When is it important for (that person) to do (or not do) ____________?
- In what situation will this help?

Multimodal Activity: Every lesson after the first one included a role-play of the story theme where the students acted out the characters in the story, an art activity to show the theme, or a music activity such as writing a rap song that communicated the theme.

Review: a recap of the Theme Scheme and a preview of the next lesson.

For a summary of research about teaching higher order skills to students with learning disabilities, see "Research on Interventions for Adolescents with Learning Disabilities: A Meta-analysis of Outcomes Related to Higher-order Processing," by H. L. Swanson, 2001, *The Elementary School Journal, 101,* 332–348.

receiving services. Language disorders may arise from many sources, because so many different aspects of the individual are involved in learning language. A child with a hearing impairment will not learn to speak normally. A child who hears inadequate language at home will learn inadequate language. Children who are not listened to, or whose perception of the world is distorted by emotional problems, will reflect these problems in their language development. Because speaking involves movements, any impairment of the motor functions involved with speech can cause language disorders. And because language development and thinking are so interwoven, any problems in cognitive functioning can affect ability to use language.

Speech Disorders. Students who cannot produce sounds effectively for speaking are considered to have a **speech disorder.** About 5% of school-age children have some form of speech impairment. Articulation problems and stuttering are the two most common problems.

Articulation disorders include substituting one sound for another (*thunthine* for *sunshine*), distorting a sound (*shoup* for *soup*), adding a sound (*ideer* for *idea*), or omitting sounds (*po-y* for *pony*) (Smith, 1998). Keep in mind, however, that most children are 6 to 8 years old before they can successfully pronounce all English sounds

Speech disorder Inability to produce sounds effectively for speaking.

Articulation disorders Any of a variety of pronunciation difficulties, such as the substitution, distortion, or omission of sounds.

Communication skills are an important component of a student's IEP. Adaptations like the speech talker shown in this photo help students with communication disorders participate in general education activities.

in normal conversation. The sounds of the consonants *l,r,y,s,* and *z* and the consonant blends *sh, ch, zh,* and *th* are the last to be mastered. Also, there are dialect differences based on geography that do not represent articulation problems. A child in your class from New England might say "ideer" for "idea" but have no speech impairment.

Stuttering generally appears between the ages of 3 and 4. It is not yet clear what causes stuttering, but it can lead to embarrassment and anxiety for the sufferer. In about 50% of cases, stuttering disappears during early adolescence (Wiig, 1982). If stuttering continues more than a year or so, the child should be referred to a speech therapist. Early intervention is critical (Onslow, 1992).

Voicing problems, a third type of speech impairment, include speaking with an inappropriate pitch, quality, or loudness or in a monotone (Hallahan & Kauffman, 2003). A student with any of these problems should be referred to a speech therapist. Recognizing the problem is the first step. Be alert for students whose pronunciation, loudness, voice quality, speech fluency, expressive range, or rate is very different from that of their peers. Pay attention also to students who seldom speak. Are they simply shy, or do they have difficulties with language?

Language Disorders. Language differences are not necessarily language disorders. Students with language disorders are those who are markedly deficient in their ability to understand or express language, compared with other students of their own age and cultural group (Owens, 1999). Students who seldom speak, who use few words or very short sentences, or who rely only on gestures to communicate should be referred to a qualified school professional for observation or testing. Table 4.6 gives ideas for promoting language development for all students.

Students with Mental Retardation

According to the American Association on Mental Deficiency (AAMD Ad Hoc Committee on Terminology and Classification, 1992, p. 5), **mental retardation** refers to:

> substantial limitations in present intellectual functioning. It is characterized by significantly subaverage intellectual functioning existing concurrently with related limitations in two or more of the following applicable adaptive skill areas: communication, self-care, home living, social skills, community use,

Voicing problems Inappropriate pitch, quality, loudness, or intonation.

Mental retardation Significantly below-average intellectual and adaptive social behavior, evident before age 18.

self-direction, health and safety, functional academics, leisure, and work. Mental retardation manifests before age 18.

Intellectual function is usually measured by IQ tests with a cutoff score of 70 to 75 as one indicator of retardation. But an IQ score below the 70 to 75 range is *not* enough to diagnose a child as having mental retardation. There must also be problems with adaptive behavior, day-to-day independent living, and social functioning. This caution is especially important when interpreting the scores of students from different cultures. Defining retardation based on test scores alone can create what some critics call "6-hour retardates"—students who are seen as retarded only for the part of the day they attend school.

Only about 1% to 1.5% of the population fit the AAMD's definition of having retardation in both intellectual functioning and adaptive behavior (Hallahan & Kauffman, 2003). For years, retardation was further divided into mild, moderate, severe, and profound levels, with each level keyed to a particular range of IQ scores. Most school districts still use this system. However, the IQ ranges are not perfect predictors of individuals' abilities to function, so the AAMR now recommends a classification scheme based on the amount of support that a person requires to function at his or her highest level. Table 4.7 summarizes this new classification system.

As a regular teacher, you may not have contact with children needing extensive or pervasive support unless your school is participating in a full inclusion program for exceptional students (described earlier in this chapter), but you probably will work with children with mild retardation. In the early grades, these students may simply learn more slowly than their peers. They need more time and more practice

Table 4.6 Encouraging Language Development

- Talk about things that interest children.
- Follow the children's lead. Reply to their initiations and comments. Share their excitement.
- Don't ask too many questions. If you must, use questions such as *how did/do . . . , why did/do . . . ,* and *what happened . . .* that result in longer explanatory answers.
- Encourage children to ask questions. Respond openly and honestly. If you don't want to answer a question, say so and explain why. (*I don't think I want to answer that question; it's very personal.*)
- Use a pleasant tone of voice. You need not be a comedian, but you can be light and humorous. Children love it when adults are a little silly.
- Don't be judgmental or make fun of children's language. If you are overly critical of children's language or try to catch and correct all errors, they will stop talking to you.
- Allow enough time for children to respond.
- Treat children with courtesy by not interrupting when they are talking.
- Include children in family and classroom discussions. Encourage participation and listen to their ideas.
- Be accepting of children and of their language. Hugs and acceptance can go a long way.
- Provide opportunities for children to use language and to have that language work for them to accomplish their goals.

SOURCE: From *Language Disorders* (3rd ed.), by Robert E. Owens, Jr. Published by Allyn & Bacon, Boston, MA. Copyright © 1999 by Pearson Education. Reprinted by permission of the publisher.

Table 4.7 AAMR Classification Scheme for Mental Retardation

This new scheme for classification is based on the level of support a student would need to function as completely as possible.

Intermittent	Supports on an "as needed basis." Characterized by episodic nature, person not always needing the support(s), or short-term supports needed during life-span transitions (e.g., job loss or an acute medical crisis). Intermittent supports may be high or low intensity when provided.
Limited	An intensity of supports characterized by consistency over time and time-limited but not of an intermittent nature, may require fewer staff members and less cost than more intense levels of support (e.g., time-limited employment training or transitional supports during the school-to-adult period).
Extensive	Supports characterized by regular involvement (e.g., daily) in at least some environments (such as work or home) and not time-limited (e.g., long-term home living support).
Pervasive	Supports characterized by their constancy, high intensity, provided across environments; potential life-sustaining nature. Pervasive supports typically involve more staff members and intrusiveness than do extensive or time-limited supports.

SOURCE: From *Mental Retardation: Definition, Classification, and Systems of Support,* by AARM Ad Hoc Committee on Terminology and Classification, 1992. Copyright © 1992 by the American Association of Mental Retardation. Reprinted with permission from the AAMR.

It is more common today to have children with retardation in general education classrooms.

to learn and have difficulty transferring learning from one setting to another or putting small skills together to accomplish a more complex task. The *Guidelines* list suggestions for teaching students with below-average general intelligence.

Learning goals for many students with mental retardation between the ages of 9 and 13 include basic reading, writing, arithmetic, learning about the local environment, social behavior, and personal interests. In junior and senior high school, the emphasis is on vocational and domestic skills, literacy for living (using the telephone book; reading signs, labels, and newspaper ads; completing a job application), job-

GUIDELINES Teaching Students with Mild Retardation

1. Determine readiness: However little a child may know, he or she is ready to learn a next step.
2. State and present objectives simply.
3. Base specific learning objectives on an analysis of the child's learning strengths and weaknesses.
4. Present material in small, logical steps. Practice extensively before going on to the next step.
5. Work on practical skills and concepts based on the demands of adult life.
6. Do not skip steps. Students with average intelligence can form conceptual bridges from one step to the next, but children with retardation need every step and bridge made explicit. Make connections for the student. Do not expect him or her to "see" the connections.
7. Be prepared to present the same idea in many different ways.
8. Go back to a simpler level if you see the student is not following.
9. Be especially careful to motivate the student and maintain attention.
10. Find materials that do not insult the student. A junior high boy may need the low vocabulary of "See Spot run," but will be insulted by the age of the characters and the content of the story.
11. Focus on a few target behaviors or skills so you and the student have a chance to experience success. Everyone needs positive reinforcement.
12. Be aware that students with retardation must overlearn, repeat, and practice more than children of average intelligence. They must be taught how to study, and they must frequently review and practice their newly acquired skills in different settings.
13. Pay close attention to social relations. Simply including students with retardation in a regular class will not guarantee that they will be accepted or that they will make and keep friends.

related behaviors such as courtesy and punctuality; health self-care; and citizenship skills. Today there is a growing emphasis on **transition programming**—preparing the student to live and work in the community. As you saw earlier in the chapter, the law requires that schools design an IEP, or individualized educational program, for every disabled child. An ITP, or individualized transition plan, may be part of the IEP for students with retardation (Hallahan & Kauffman, 2003).

Students with Emotional or Behavioral Disorders

Students with emotional and behavioral disorders can be among the most difficult to teach in a regular class and a source of concern for many prospective teachers (Avramidis, Bayliss, & Burden, 2000). Behavior becomes a problem when it deviates so greatly from what is appropriate for the child's age group that it significantly interferes with the child's own growth and development and/or the lives of others. Clearly, deviation implies a difference from some standard, and standards of behavior differ from one situation, age group, culture, and historical period to another. Thus, what passes for team spirit in the football bleachers might be seen as disturbed behavior in a bank or restaurant. In addition, the deviation must be more than a temporary response to stressful events; it must be consistent across time and in different situations.

Quay and Peterson (1987) describe six dimensions of emotional/behavioral disorders. Children who have *conduct disorders* are aggressive, destructive, disobedient, uncooperative, distractible, disruptive, and persistent. They have been corrected and punished for the same misbehavior countless times. The adults and even the other children in their lives dislike many of these children. The most successful strategies for helping these children are the behavior management approaches described in Chapter 6. These students need very clear rules and consequences, consistently enforced. The future is not promising for students who never learn to control their behavior and who also fail academically. Waiting for the students to "outgrow" their problems is seldom effective (O'Leary & Wilson, 1987; Theodore, Bray, Kehle, & Jenson, 2001).

CONNECT & EXTEND

TO OTHER CHAPTERS
In Chapter 12, you will find ideas for dealing with mild to moderate behavior problems.

Children who are extremely anxious, withdrawn, shy, depressed, and hypersensitive, who cry easily and have little confidence, are said to have an *anxiety-withdrawal disorder.* These children have few social skills and consequently very few friends. The most successful approaches with them appear to involve the direct teaching of social skills (Cohen, 1999; Gresham, 1981).

The third category is *attentional problems immaturity.* Characteristics include a short attention span, frequent daydreaming, little initiative, messiness, and poor coordination. If an immature student is not too far behind others in the class, she or he may respond to the behavior management strategies described in Chapter 6. But if these approaches fail or if the problem is severe, you should consult the school psychologist, guidance counselor, or another mental health professional. Related to this dimension is the category of *motor excess.* These students are restless and tense; they seem unable to sit still or stop talking. You can see that these children share many characteristics of ADHD.

The fifth category of behavior disorders is *socialized aggression.* Students in this group are often members of gangs. They may steal or vandalize because their peer culture expects it.

Finally, some students exhibit *psychotic behavior.* You are not likely to work with many of these students. Their behavior may be bizarre, and they may express very farfetched ideas. These six categories are very general. If you are concerned about the behavior of one of your students, it is best to consult the school psychologist or guidance counselor.

Many exceptional students—those with learning disabilities, mental retardation, or ADHD, for example—may have emotional or behavioral problems as well as they

Transition programming Gradual preparation of exceptional students to move from high school into further education or training, employment, or community involvement.

GUIDELINES Disciplining Students with Emotional Problems

Be careful not to violate due process rights of students—students and parents must know the behaviors expected and the consequences for misbehavior.

Examples

1. Communicate expectations clearly and in writing.
2. Ask parents and students to sign a copy of the classroom rules.
3. Post rules and consequences in class and on a class Web page.

Be very careful with severe punishments that remove students from class for a long time. These constitute a change in the child's educational program (IEP) and require due process.

Examples

1. Suspensions of more than 10 days require due process.
2. Prolonged periods of time-out (in-school suspension) may require due process.

Punishments for students with severe emotional problems must serve a clear educational purpose.

Examples

1. Give a rationale for punishment or correction that ties an action to student's learning or the learning of others in the class.
2. Use written behavior contracts that include a rationale.

Make sure the rule and the punishment are reasonable.

Examples

1. Consider the student's age and physical condition.
2. Does the punishment match the offense and the way others in the class are treated?
3. Do other teachers handle similar situations in the same way?
4. Try less intrusive punishments first. Be patient. Move to more severe actions only when less severe procedures fail.

Keep good records and work collaboratively so all involved are informed.

Examples

1. Document the punishment of all students in a journal or log. List what precipitated the punishment, what procedures were used, how long the punishment lasted, the results, modifications to the punishment, and new results.
2. Note meetings with families, special education teachers, and the principal.
3. Make any changes involving management plans with families and other teachers.

Always use positive consequences in conjunction with negative ones.

Examples

1. If students lose points for breaking rules, give them ways to regain points through positive behavior.
2. Recognize genuine accomplishment and small steps—DON'T say, "Well it's about time you . . . ."

struggle in school. In Chapter 13 we will consider how to help all students cope with social and emotional challenges that threaten both their own learning and the learning of others in the classroom.

Because students with emotional and behavioral disorders frequently break rules and push the limits, teachers often find themselves disciplining the students. Be aware that there have been court rulings on disciplining students with serious emotional problems (Yell, 1990). The *Guidelines* above may help when you are faced with these situations.

Check Yourself What is a learning disability?

What are the most common communication disorders?

What defines mental retardation?

What are the best approaches for students with emotional problems?

No set of teaching techniques will be effective for every child. You should work with the special education teachers in your school to design appropriate instruction for individual students. Also, you will need to continue your professional development in this area throughout your teaching career. The next section gives you one way.

Enhancing Your Expertise with Technology

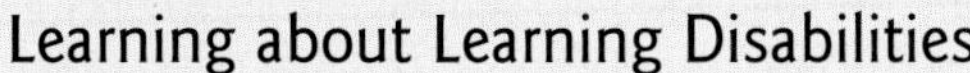

Learning about Learning Disabilities

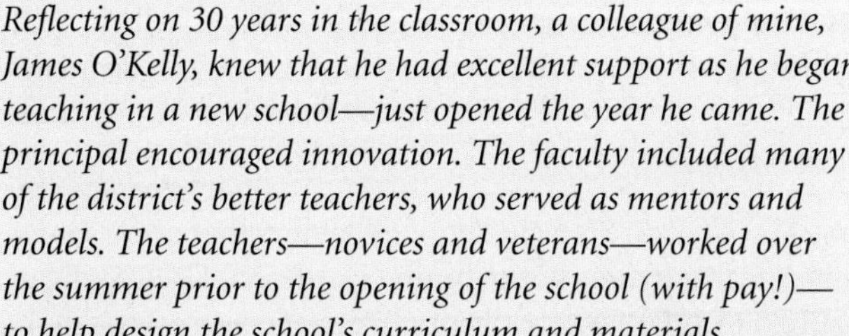

Reflecting on 30 years in the classroom, a colleague of mine, James O'Kelly, knew that he had excellent support as he began teaching in a new school—just opened the year he came. The principal encouraged innovation. The faculty included many of the district's better teachers, who served as mentors and models. The teachers—novices and veterans—worked over the summer prior to the opening of the school (with pay!)—to help design the school's curriculum and materials.

Despite all this support, the most difficult challenge that Jim faced was his work with children with learning disabilities. How could seemingly typical 6th graders be unable to comprehend a simple paragraph, misapply the few steps for the solution of a math problem, or confuse simple oral directions? How should these students be graded? What accommodations could be made for them? Advice from the principal and veteran teachers helped somewhat, as did coursework at a local college. Nevertheless, finding answers was not easy.

Since Jim entered the classroom, the laws, court decisions, public attitudes, and research about learning disabilities have changed dramatically. Future teachers will be expected to be far more knowledgeable about learning disabilities than teachers in the past. LD Online (www.ldonline.org) can provide help with these challenges. It has a variety of resources that will expand your knowledge about this important topic. You will find descriptions and characteristics of specific learning disabilities, autobiographical accounts by people who have experienced learning difficulties, a bulletin board where people exchange information and questions, an archived column in which a child psychiatrist answers questions, and more. Here are a few questions that you might explore at LD Online:

- How can teachers' attributions about academic achievement affect the ways they interact with students with learning disabilities?
- How can teachers structure the classroom environment to enhance the academic achievement experiences of their students with learning disabilities?
- What can a teacher do to facilitate home-school collaboration for students with ADHD?
- What are the main issues involved in the use of assistive technologies to support the learning of children with learning disabilities?
- What instructional strategies can I use to assist students with various specific learning disabilities?

Each of these questions relates to one or more topics found in this textbook: attribution theory, classroom environment, home-school communication, ADHD, assistive technologies, and instructional strategies. As you encounter other major themes and concepts in this textbook, go to LD Online to see how they relate to learning disabilities.

Less Prevalent Problems and More Severe Disabilities

In this section we meet students with more severe disabilities. In your first years of teaching you may encounter only a few of these students, but you still can make a difference in their lives.

Students with Health Impairments

Some students must have special devices such as braces, special shoes, crutches, or wheelchairs to participate in a normal school program. If the school has the necessary architectural features, such as ramps, elevators, and accessible rest rooms, and if teachers allow for the physical limitations of students, little needs to be done to alter the usual educational program. Two other health impairments you may encounter are cerebral palsy and seizure disorders.

Cerebral Palsy and Multiple Disabilities. Damage to the brain before or during birth or during infancy can cause a child to have difficulty moving and coordinating his or her body. The problem may be very mild, so the child simply appears a bit

> **CONNECT & EXTEND**
>
> **TO YOUR TEACHING/PORTFOLIO**
> Students with AIDS can have many of the problems discussed in this chapter: mental retardation, attention-deficit/hyperactiviy disorder, seizures, neurological impairments similar to cerebral palsy, behavior disorders, and so on. Most states have policies that emphasize the education of children with AIDS in the regular classroom.

clumsy, or so severe that voluntary movement is practically impossible. The most common form of **cerebral palsy** is characterized by **spasticity** (overly tight or tense muscles). Many children with cerebral palsy also have secondary handicaps (Kirk, Gallagher, & Anastasiow, 1993). In the classroom, these secondary handicaps are the greatest concern—and these are generally what the regular teacher can help with most. For example, many children with cerebral palsy also have visual impairments, speech problems, or mild mental retardation. The strategies described in this chapter should prove helpful in such situations.

Seizure Disorders (Epilepsy). A seizure is a cluster of behaviors that occurs in response to abnormal neurochemical activities in the brain (Hardman, Drew, & Egan, 1999). The effects of the seizure depend on where the discharge of energy starts in the brain and how far it spreads. People with **epilepsy** have recurrent seizures, but not all seizures are the result of epilepsy; temporary conditions such as high fevers or infections can also trigger seizures. Seizures take many forms and differ with regard to the length, frequency, and movements involved. A partial or absence seizure involves only a small part of the brain, whereas a generalized or tonic-clonic seizure includes much more of the brain.

Most **generalized seizures** (once called *grand mal*) are accompanied by uncontrolled jerking movements that ordinarily last two to five minutes, possible loss of bowel or bladder control, and irregular breathing, followed by a deep sleep or coma. On regaining consciousness, the student may be very weary, confused, and in need of extra sleep. Most seizures can be controlled by medication. If a student has a seizure accompanied by convulsions in class, the teacher must take action so the student will not be injured. The major danger to a student having such a seizure is getting hurt by striking a hard surface during the violent jerking.

Stay calm and reassure the rest of the class. Do not try to restrain the child's movements; you can't stop the seizure once it starts. Lower the child gently to the floor, away from furniture or walls. Move hard objects away. Loosen scarves, ties, or anything that might make breathing difficult. Turn the child's head gently to the side, put a soft coat or blanket under the student's head. Never put anything in the student's mouth—it is NOT true that people having seizures can swallow their tongues. Don't attempt artificial respiration unless the student does not start breathing again after the seizure stops. Find out from the student's parents how the seizure is usually dealt with. If one seizure follows another and the student does not regain consciousness in between, if the student is pregnant or has a medical ID that does not say "epilepsy, seizure disorder," if there are signs of injury, or if the seizure goes on for more than 5 minutes, get medical help right away (Friend & Bursuck, 2002). For more ideas and information, see the Epilepsy Foundation of America website at www.efa.org/answerplace.

Not all seizures are dramatic. Sometimes the student just loses contact briefly. The student may stare, fail to respond to questions, drop objects, and miss what has been happening for 1 to 30 seconds. These were once called *petit mal,* but they are now referred to as **absence seizures** and can easily go undetected. If a child in your class appears to daydream frequently, does not seem to know what is going on at times, or cannot remember what has just happened when you ask, you should consult the school psychologist or nurse. The major problem for students with absence seizures is that they miss the continuity of the class interaction—these seizures can occur as often as 100 times a day. If their seizures are frequent, students will find the lessons confusing. Question these students to be sure they are understanding and following the lesson. Be prepared to repeat yourself periodically.

Cerebral palsy Condition involving a range of motor or coordination difficulties due to brain damage.

Spasticity Overly tight or tense muscles, characteristic of some forms of cerebral palsy.

Epilepsy Disorder marked by seizures and caused by abnormal electrical discharges in the brain.

Generalized seizure A seizure involving a large portion of the brain.

Absence seizure A seizure involving only a small part of the brain that causes a child to lose contact briefly.

Students Who Are Deaf and Hard of Hearing

You will hear the term, "hearing impaired," to describe these students, but the deaf community and researchers object to the term "hearing impaired," so I will use their preferred terms, deaf and hard of hearing. The number of deaf students has been declining over the past three decades, but when the problem does occur, the consequences for learning are serious (Hunt & Marshall, 2002). Signs of hearing problems are turning one ear toward the speaker, favoring one ear in conversation, or misunderstanding conversation when the speaker's face cannot be seen. Other indications include not following directions, seeming distracted or confused at times, frequently asking people to repeat what they have said, mispronouncing new words or names, and being reluctant to participate in class discussions. Take note particularly of students who have frequent earaches, sinus infections, or allergies.

In the past, educators have debated whether oral or manual approaches are better for children who are deaf or hard of hearing. Oral approaches involve speech reading (also called lip reading) and training students to use whatever limited hearing they may have. Manual approaches include sign language and finger spelling. Research indicates that children who learn some manual method of communicating perform better in academic subjects and are more socially mature than students who are exposed only to oral methods. Today, the trend is to combine both approaches (Hallahan & Kauffman, 2003).

Another perspective suggests that people who are deaf are part of a different culture with a different language, values, social institutions, and literature. Hunt and Marshall (2002) quote one deaf professional: "How would women like to be referred to as male-impaired, or whites like to be called black-impaired? I'm not impaired; I'm deaf!" (p. 348). From this perspective, a goal is to help deaf children become bilingual and bicultural, to be able to function effectively in both cultures. Technological innovations such as teletypewriters in homes and public phones and the many avenues of communication through e-mail and the Internet have expanded communication possibilities for all people, including those with hearing problems.

Students with Low Vision and Blindness

In the United States only about 1 child in 1,000 has visual impairments so serious that special educational services are needed. Most of this group needing special services is classified as having **low vision.** This means they can read with the aid of a magnifying glass or large-print books. A small group of students, about 1 in every 2,500, is **educationally blind.** These students must use hearing and touch as the predominant learning channels (Kirk, Gallagher, & Anastasiow, 1993).

Students who have difficulty seeing often hold books either very close to or very far from their eyes. They may squint, rub their eyes frequently, or complain that their eyes burn or itch. The eyes may actually be swollen, red, or encrusted. Students with vision problems may misread material on the chalkboard, describe their vision as being blurred, be very sensitive to light, or hold their heads at an odd angle. They may become irritable when they have to do deskwork or lose interest if they have to follow an activity happening across the room (Hunt & Marshall, 2002). Any of these signs should be reported to a qualified school professional.

Special materials and equipment that help these students to function in regular classrooms include large-print typewriters; software that coverts printed material to speech or to braille; personal organizers (like a Palm) that have talking appointment books or address books; variable-speed tape recorders (allowing teachers to make time-compressed tape recordings, which speed up the rate of speech without changing the voice pitch); special calculators; the abacus; three-dimensional maps, charts, and models; and special measuring devices. For students with visual problems, the quality of the print is often more important than the size, so watch out for hard-to-read handouts and blurry copies. The Instructional Materials Reference Center of the American Printing House for the Blind (1839 Frankfort Avenue, Louisville, KY 40206) has catalogs of instructional materials for students with visual impairments.

Low vision Vision limited to close objects.

Educationally blind Needing Braille materials in order to learn.

■ **Table 4.8** Making a Referral

1. Contact the student's parents. It is very important that you discuss the student's problems with the parents *before* you refer.
2. Before making a referral, check *all* the student's school records. Has the student ever:
   - had a psychological evaluation?
   - qualified for special services?
   - been included in other special programs (e.g., for disadvantaged children; speech or language therapy)?
   - scored far below average on standardized tests?
   - been retained?

   Do the records indicate:
   - good progress in some areas, poor progress in others?
   - any physical or medical problem?
   - that the student is taking medication?
3. Talk to the student's other teachers and professional support personnel about your concern for the student. Have other teachers also had difficulty with the student? Have they found ways of dealing successfully with the student? Document the strategies that you have used in your class to meet the student's educational needs. Your documentation will be useful as evidence that will be helpful to or be required by the committee of professionals who will evaluate the student. Demonstrate your concern by keeping written records. Your notes should include items such as:
   - exactly what you are concerned about
   - why you are concerned about it
   - dates, places, and times you have observed the problem
   - precisely what you have done to try to resolve the problem
   - who, if anyone, helped you devise the plans or strategies you have used
   - evidence that the strategies have been successful or unsuccessful

Remember that you should refer a student only if you can make a convincing case that the student may have a handicapping condition and probably cannot be served appropriately without special education. Referral for special education begins a time-consuming, costly, and stressful process that is potentially damaging to the student and has many legal ramifications.

SOURCE: From *What Should I Know about Special Education? Answers for Classroom Teachers,* by P. L. Pullen & J. M. Kauffman, 1987. Copyright © 1987 PRO-ED, Austin, Texas. Reprinted by permission.

The arrangement of the room is also an issue. Students with visual problems need to know where things are, so consistency matters—a place for everything and everything in its place. Leave plenty of space for moving around the room and make sure to monitor possible obstacles and safety hazards such as trash cans in aisles and open cabinet doors. If you rearrange the room, give students with visual problems a chance to learn the new layout. Make sure the students have a buddy for fire drills or other emergencies (Friend & Bursuck, 2002).

If you decide that students in your class might benefit from special services, the first step is making a referral. How would you begin? Table 4.8 guides you through the referral process. In Chapter 12, when we discuss effective teaching, we will look at more ways to reach all your students.

Check Yourself How can schools accommodate the needs of physically disabled students?

How would you handle a seizure in class?

What are some signs of hearing and visual impairment?

Not all students who need special accommodations in school are covered by IDEA or eligible for the services provided by the law. But these students' educational needs may be covered by Section 504 of the Vocational Rehabilitation Act of 1973. We turn to these students now.

Section 504 Protections for Students

As a consequence of the civil rights movement in the 1960s and 1970s, the federal government passed the Vocational Rehabilitation Act of 1973. Section 504 of that law prevents discrimination against people with disabilities in any program that receives federal money, such as public schools.

Through **Section 504,** all school age children are ensured an equal opportunity to participate in school activities. The definition of "disability" is broad in Section 504. If a student has a condition that substantially limits participation in school, then the school still must develop a plan for giving that student access to education, even though the school gets no extra funds. To get assistance through Section 504, students must be assessed, often by a team, and a plan developed. Unlike IDEA however, there are fewer rules about how this must happen, so individual schools design their own procedures (Friend & Bursuck, 2002). Look at Table 4.9 to see an example of the kinds of accommodations that might be made for a student. Many of these ideas seem to be "just good teaching." But I have been surprised to see how many teachers won't let students use calculators or tape recorders because "they should learn do it like everyone else!"

Two major groups are considered for Section 504 accommodations: students with medical or health needs such as diabetes, drug addition, severe allergies, communicable diseases, temporary disabilities resulting from accidents, or alcoholism, and students with ADHD. We will take some time to explore the second group because teachers must spend quite a bit of time with these students.

■ Table 4.9 Examples of Accommodations Under Section 504

The types of accommodations that can be written into a Section 504 plan are almost without limit. Some accommodation may relate to physical changes in the learning environment (for example air filters are installed to remove allergens). However, many students who have Section 504 plans have functional impairments related to their learning or behavior, and their needs are somewhat similar to those of students with disabilities. The following is a sample of instructional accommodations that could be incorporated into a Section 504 plan:

- Seat the student nearest to where the teacher does most of his/her instruction.
- Have the student sit next to a peer who can help as needed.
- Seat the student away from the distractions of doorways or windows.
- Fold assignments in half so that the student is less overwhelmed by the quantity of work.
- Make directions telegraphic, that is, concise and clear.
- Allow use of a calculator or tape recorder.
- Use voice recognition software on the computer for written assignments.
- Mark right answers instead of wrong answers.
- Send a set of textbooks to be left at home so that the student does not have to remember to bring books from school.
- Provide books on tape so that the student can listen to assignments instead of reading them.

If you review these items, you can see that many of them just make good instructional sense. They are effective instructional practices that help learners with special needs succeed in your classroom.

SOURCE: From *Including Students with Special Needs: A Practical Guide for Classroom Teachers* (3rd ed.), by Marilyn Friend & William D. Bursick. Published by Allyn & Bacon, Boston, MA. Copyright © 2002 by Pearson Education. Adapted by permission of the publisher.

Students with Hyperactivity and Attention Disorders

What Would You Say? If a student is struggling with time management and organization issues, what kind of accommodations would you provide?

You probably have heard and may even have used the term "hyperactivity." The notion is a modern one; there were no hyperactive children 50 to 60 years ago. Such children, like Mark Twain's Huckleberry Finn, were seen as rebellious, lazy, or "fidgety" (Nylund, 2000). Today, if anything, the term is applied too often and too widely. Many student teachers in my program have classes with 5 or 6 students diagnosed as "hyperactive," and in one class, there are 10 students with that diagnosis. Actually, hyperactivity is not one particular condition; it is "a set of behaviors—such as excessive restlessness and short attention span—that are quantitatively and qualitatively different from those of children of the same sex, mental age, and SES [socioeconomic status]" (O'Leary, 1980, p. 195).

Today most psychologists agree that the main problem for children labeled hyperactive is directing and maintaining attention, not simply controlling their physical activity. The American Psychiatric Association has established a diagnostic category called **attention-deficit/hyperactivity disorder (ADHD)** to identify children with this problem. Table 4.10 on page 138 lists some indicators of ADHD used by this group.

Children with ADHD are not only more physically active and inattentive than other children, they also have difficulty responding appropriately and working steadily toward goals (even their own goals); and they may not be able to control their behavior on command, even for a brief period. The problem behaviors are generally evident in all situations and with every teacher. It is difficult to know how many children should be classified as hyperactive. The most common estimate is 3% to 5% of the elementary school population (Friend & Bursuck, 2002; Sagvolden, 1999). More boys

Section 504 A part of civil rights law that prevents discrimination against people with disabilities in programs that receive federal funds, such as public schools.

Attention-deficit/hyperactivity disorder Current term for disruptive behavior disorders marked by overactivity, excessive difficulty sustaining attention, or impulsiveness.

■ Table 4.10	Indicators of ADHD: Attention-Deficit/Hyperactivity Disorder

Do any of your students show these signs? They could be indications of ADHD.

Problems with *Inattention*

- Fails to give close attention to details or makes careless mistakes
- Has difficulty sustaining attention in tasks or play activities
- Does not seem to listen when spoken to directly
- Does not follow through on instructions and fails to finish schoolwork (not due to oppositional behavior or failure to understand instructions)
- Has difficulty organizing tasks or activities
- Avoids, dislikes, or is reluctant to engage in tasks that require sustained mental effort (such as schoolwork or homework)
- Loses things necessary for tasks or activities
- Is easily distracted by extraneous stimuli
- Is forgetful in daily activities

Problems with *Impulse Control*

- Blurts out answers before questions have been completed
- Has difficulty awaiting his/her turn
- Interrupts or intrudes on others in conversations or games

Hyperactivity

- Fidgets with hands or feet or squirms in seat
- Leaves seat in classroom or in other situations in which remaining seated is expected
- Runs about or climbs excessively in situations in which it is inappropriate (in adolescents may be limited to subjective feelings of restlessness)
- Has difficulty playing or engaging in leisure activities quietly
- Talks excessively
- Acts as if "driven by a motor" and cannot remain still

SOURCE: From *Diagnostic and Statistical Manual of Mental Disorders,* Fourth Edition (DSM-IV) (pp. 83–84), 1994, Washington, DC: American Psychiatric Association. Adapted with permission from the *Diagnostic and Statistical Manual of Mental Disorders,* Fourth Edition. Copyright © 1994 American Psychiatric Association.

than girls are identified as hyperactive. Just a few years ago, most psychologists thought that ADHD diminished as children entered adolescence, but now there are some researchers who believe that the problems can persist into adulthood (Hallowell & Ratey, 1994). Adolescence—with the increased stresses of puberty, transition to middle or high school, more demanding academic work, and more engrossing social relationships—can be an especially difficult time for students with ADHD (Taylor, 1998).

Treating and Teaching Students with ADHD

Today there is an increasing reliance on drug therapy for ADHD. In fact, from 1990 to 1998, there was a 700% increase in the production of Ritalin in the United States (Diller, 1998). Ritalin and other prescribed drugs such as Dexedrine and Cylert are stimulants, but in particular dosages they tend to have paradoxical effects on many children with ADHD: Short-term effects include possible improvements in social behaviors such as cooperation, attention, and compliance. Research suggests that about 80% of children with ADHD are more manageable when on medication. But for many there are negative side effects such as increased heart rate and blood pressure, interference with growth rate, insomnia, weight loss, and nausea (Friend & Bursuck, 2002; Panksepp, 1998; Weiss & Hechtman, 1993). In addition, little is known about the long-term effects of drug therapy. There also is no evidence that the drugs lead to improvement in academic learning or peer relationships, two areas where children with ADHD have great problems. Because students appear to improve dramatically in their behavior, parents and teachers, relieved to see change, may

Are we overusing drugs?

Mike Smith reprinted by permission of United Features Syndicate, Inc.

assume the problem has been cured. It hasn't. The students still need special help in learning.

One approach to helping students with attention deficits is based on the behavioral principles described in Chapter 6. Long assignments may overwhelm students with attention deficits, so give them a few problems or paragraphs at a time with clear consequences for completion. Another promising approach combines instruction in learning and memory strategies with motivational training. The goal is to help students develop the "skill and will" to improve their achievement (Paris, 1988). They are also encouraged to be persistent and to see themselves as "in control" (Reid & Borkowski, 1987).

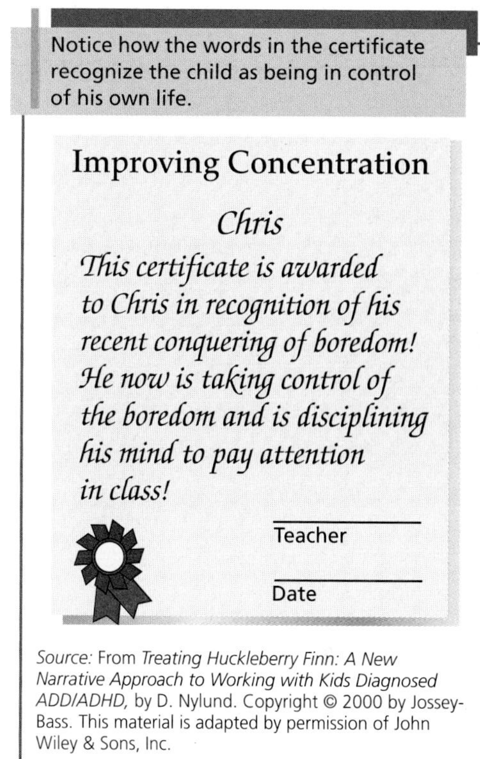

Notice how the words in the certificate recognize the child as being in control of his own life.
Improving Concentration
Chris
This certificate is awarded to Chris in recognition of his recent conquering of boredom! He now is taking control of the boredom and is disciplining his mind to pay attention in class!
Teacher
Date

Source: From *Treating Huckleberry Finn: A New Narrative Approach to Working with Kids Diagnosed ADD/ADHD,* by D. Nylund. Copyright © 2000 by Jossey-Bass. This material is adapted by permission of John Wiley & Sons, Inc.

Figure 4.2 Conquering Boredom: Putting Students in Charge

The notion of being in control is part of a new therapy strategy for dealing with ADHD, one that stresses personal agency. David Nylund (2000) describes this type of therapy that has important implications for teachers. Rather than treating the problem child, Nylunds' idea is to enlist the child's strengths to conquer the child's problems—put the child in control. New metaphors for the situation are developed. Rather than seeing the problems as inside the child, Nylund helps everyone see ADHD, Trouble, Boredom, and other enemies of learning as outside the child—demons to be conquered or unruly spirits to be enlisted in the service of what *the child* wants to accomplish. The focus is on solutions. The steps of the **SMART** approach are:

Separating the problem of ADHD from the child

Mapping the influence of ADHD on the child and family

Attending to the exceptions to the ADHD story

Reclaiming special abilities of children diagnosed with ADHD

Telling and celebrating the new story. (Nylund, 2000, p. xix)

As a teacher, you can look for times when the student is engaged—even short times. What is different about these times? Discover the student's strengths and allow yourself to be amazed by them. Make changes in your teaching that support the changes the student is trying to make. Nylund gives the following example: Chris (age 9) and his teacher, Ms. Baker, became partners in putting Chris in control of his concentration in school. Ms. Baker moved Chris's seat to the front of the room. The two designed a subtle signal to get Chris back on track and Chris organized his messy desk. These sound like some of the Section 504 accommodations in Table 4.9. When Chris's concentration improved, Chris received the award shown in Figure 4.2 at a party in his honor. Chris described how he was learning to listen in class: "You just have to have a strong mind and tell ADHD and Boredom not to bother you" (Nylund, 2000, p. 166). Here are suggestions that came from students working with Nylund, telling how their teachers can help them gain control:

Use lots of pictures (visual clues) to help me learn.

Recognize cultural and racial identity.

Know when to bend the rules.

Notice when I am doing well.

Don't tell the other kids that I am taking Ritalin.

Offer us choices.

Don't just lecture—it's boring!

Realize that I am intelligent.

Let me walk around the classroom.

Don't give tons of homework.

More recess!

Be patient.

The above methods should be thoroughly tested with the student before drugs are used. Even if students in your class are on medication, it is critical that they also learn the academic and social skills they will need to survive. Again, this will not happen by itself, even if behavior improves with medication (Friend & Bursuck, 2002).

CONNECT & EXTEND

TO **PRAXIS**™
ADHD (I, B2)
A new student's parent calls you to tell you that a neurologist has diagnosed her child with ADHD. What typical behaviors can you expect from the student? What can you do to support that student's development?

Check Yourself What is Section 504?

What is ADHD, and how is it handled in school?

We end the chapter with another group that has special needs, but is not covered by IDEA or Section 504—highly intelligent or talented students.

Students Who Are Gifted and Talented

Consider this situation, a true story.

> Latoya was already an advanced reader when she entered 1st grade in a large urban school district. Her teacher noticed the challenging chapter books Latoya brought to school and read with little effort. After administering a reading assessment, the school's reading consultant confirmed that Latoya was reading at the 5th grade level. Latoya's parents reported with pride that she had started to read independently when she was 3 years old and "had read every book she could get her hands on." (Reis et al., 2002)

In her struggling urban school, Latoya received no particular accommodations, and by 5th grade, she was still reading at just above the 5th grade level. Her 5th grade teacher had no idea that Latoya had ever been an advanced reader.

Latoya is not alone. There is a group of students with special needs that is often overlooked by the schools: the **gifted and talented.** In the past, providing an enriched education for extremely bright or talented students was seen as undemocratic and elitist. Now there is a growing recognition that gifted students are being poorly served by most public schools. A national survey found that more than one-half of all gifted students do not achieve in school at a level equal to their ability (Tomlinson-Keasey, 1990). In 1988, the federal government passed the Gifted and Talented Students Education Act that recognized that these students need special services, but the law did not require states to provide services that would enable students like Latoya to get an appropriate education.

Who Are These Students?

There are many definitions of gifted because individuals can have many different gifts. Remember that Gardner (1983) identified eight separate "intelligences" and Sternberg (1985) suggests a triarchic model. Renzulli and Reis (1991) have a different three-part conception of giftedness: above-average general ability, a high level of creativity, and a high level of task commitment or motivation to achieve. One of the most inclusive definitions comes from the U.S. Department of Education (1993):

> Children and youth with outstanding talent perform or show the potential for performing at remarkably high levels of accomplishment when compared with others of their age, experience, or environment. These children and youth exhibit high capability in intellectual, creative, and/or artistic areas, possess an unusual leadership capacity, or excel in specific academic fields. They require services or activities not ordinarily provided by the schools. Outstanding talents are present in children and youth from all cultural groups, across all economic strata, and in all areas of human endeavor. (p. 26)

Truly gifted children are not the students who simply learn quickly with little effort. The work of gifted students is original, extremely advanced for their age, and potentially of lasting importance. These children may read fluently with little instruction by age 3 or 4. They may play an musical instrument like a skillful adult, turn a visit to the grocery store into a mathematical puzzle, and become fascinated with algebra when their friends are having trouble carrying in addition (Winner, 2000). Recent

Gifted student A very bright, creative, and talented student.

~ Stories of Learning Tributes to Teaching ~

Charelle is an African American student in the third grade, on free lunch, homeless for much of the year, and much loved and supported by both parents. Her mother is a housekeeper in a local hospital. Her father "flips burgers" (her words) at a fast-food restaurant. Now in housing in a different school zone, Charelle still attends the school in which she began, because her mother makes the long bus ride with Charelle, continuing on to her own job via public transportation. Charelle is often as much as an hour late for class because of the extended bus ride, but when she arrives in her classroom, she becomes immediately absorbed in her schoolwork. Charelle's teacher feels the long ride seems worthwhile to Charelle's parents because the school has been nurturing to the family, and that Project START "may have been the icing on the cake (that kept them coming)."

Charelle seems to be hungry, not so much for food as for knowledge. She often asks for extra schoolwork to do at home. Her current teacher calls her "a joy. I feel lucky to have her in my class. There are few children intrinsically motivated like Charelle. . . . She's a real big ham. She would act out anything. She's just kind of bright and bubbly and effervescent and gregarious. . . . She writes. She loves to tell stories. She's a good leader in a group. . . . Not as a forceful leader, but she coaches, like, 'Well, maybe we should do this.' She's blown the doors off math in here. I have her well into fourth-grade math." Charelle's second-grade teacher echoes, "She's very talented in writing and reading. She is very creative, good in art, good in all subjects." The teacher points out a piece of Charelle's artwork, which is permanently displayed in the school corridor.

SOURCE: From "Challenging Expectations: Case Studies of High Potential, Culturally Diverse Young Children," by C. Tomlinson, C. Callahan, and K. Lelli, *Gifted Child Quarterly, 41*(2), pp. 5–17.

conceptions widen the view of giftedness to include attention to the children's culture, language, and exceptionalities (Association for the Gifted, 2001). These newer conceptions are more likely to identify children like Charelle in the *Stories of Learning/ Tributes to Teaching* feature.

What do we know about these remarkable individuals? A classic study of the characteristics of the academically and intellectually gifted was started decades ago by Lewis Terman and colleagues (1925, 1947, 1959; Holahan & Sears, 1995). This huge project is following the lives of 1,528 gifted males and females and will continue until the year 2010. The subjects all have IQ scores in the top 1% of the population (140 or above on the Stanford-Binet individual test of intelligence). They were identified on the basis of these test scores and teacher recommendations.

Terman and colleagues found that these gifted children were larger, stronger, and healthier than the norm. They often walked sooner and were more athletic. They were more emotionally stable than their peers and became better-adjusted adults than the average. They had lower rates of delinquency, emotional difficulty, divorce, drug problems, and so on. Of course, the teachers in Terman's study who made the nominations may have selected students who were better adjusted initially.

What Is the Origin of These Gifts? For years, researchers have debated the nature/nurture question about people with extraordinary abilities and talents. As usual, there is evidence that it takes both. Studies of prodigies and geniuses in many fields document that deep and prolonged practice is necessary to achieve at the highest levels. For example, it took Newton 20 years to move from his first ideas to his ultimate contribution (Howe, Davidson, & Sloboda, 1998; Winner, 2000).

I remember listening to the early reports of Bloom's study of talent (1982). His research team had interviewed, among others, the top tennis players in the world,

CONNECT & EXTEND

TO THE RESEARCH

A follow-up of Terman subjects 60 years later found that Terman's subjects who were popular and outgoing as children were less likely to maintain serious intellectual interests as adults. The authors of the study speculate that an active social life may divert interest away from intellectual pursuits (Tomlinson-Keasey & Little, 1990). In fact, gifted children tend to be introverted—they don't mind being alone and may even need solitude to develop their talents (Winner, 2000). Every path has its benefits and its liabilities for the individual.

IQ tests are still seen as a reliable predictor of academic giftedness; however, there may also be other ways for students to demonstrate their special abilities.

their coaches, parents, siblings, and friends. One coach said that he would make a suggestion, and a few days later the young athlete would have mastered the move. Then the parents told how the child had practiced that move for hours on end after getting the coach's tip. So, focused, intense practice plays a role. Also, the families of prodigies tend to be child-centered and to devote hours to supporting the development of their child's gifts. Bloom's research team described tremendous sacrifices made by families: rising before dawn to drive their child to a coach in another city, working two jobs, or even moving the whole family to another part of the country to find the best teachers. The children responded to the family's sacrifices by working harder and the families responded to the child's hard work by sacrificing more—an upward spiral of investment and achievement.

But hard work will never make me a world class tennis player or a Newton. There is a role for nature as well. The children studied by Bloom showed early and clear talent in the areas they later developed. As children, great sculptors were constantly drawing and mathematicians were fascinated with dials, gears, and gauges. Parents' investments in their children came after the children showed early high-level achievement (Winner, 2000). Recent research suggests that gifted children, at least those with extraordinary abilities in mathematics, music, and visual arts, may have unusual brain organization—which can have both advantages and disadvantages. Giftedness in mathematics, music, and visual arts appears to be associated with superior visual-spatial abilities and enhanced development of the right side of the brain. Children with these gifts are also more likely not to have right-hand dominance and to have language related-problems. These brain differences are evidence that "gifted children, child prodigies, and savants are not made from scratch but are born with unusual brains that enable rapid learning in a particular domain" (Winner, 2000, p. 160).

What Problems Do the Gifted Face? In spite of Bloom's and Terman's findings, it would be incorrect to say that every gifted student is superior in adjustment and emotional health. In fact, gifted adolescents, especially girls, are more likely to be depressed and to report social and emotional problems (Berk, 2002). Many difficulties confront a gifted child, including boredom and frustration in school as well as isolation (sometimes even ridicule) from peers. Schoolmates may be consumed with baseball or worried about failing math, while the gifted child is fascinated with Mozart, focused on a social issue, or totally absorbed in computers, drama, or geology. Gifted children may be impatient with friends, parents, and even teachers who do not share their interests or abilities. Because their language is well developed, they may be seen as show-offs when they are simply expressing themselves. They are sensitive to expectations and feeling of others, so these students may be very vulnerable to criticisms and taunts. Because they are goal-directed and focused, they may seem stubborn and uncooperative. Their keen sense of humor can be used as a weapon against teachers and other students. Adjustment problems seem to be greatest for the most gifted, those in the highest range of academic ability (e.g., above 180 IQ) (Hardman, Drew, & Egan, 1999; Keogh & MacMillan, 1996; Robinson & Clinkenbeard, 1998).

Strategies for Identifying and Teaching Gifted Students

Identifying gifted children is not always easy and teaching them well may be even more challenging. Many parents provide early educational experiences for their children. Even very advanced reading in the early grades does not guarantee that students will still be outstanding readers years later (Mills & Jackson, 1990). In junior high and high school, some very able students deliberately earn lower grades, making their abilities even harder to recognize. Girls are especially likely to hide their abilities (Berk, 2002).

Recognizing Gifts and Talents. Teachers are successful only about 10% to 50% of the time in picking out the gifted children in their classes (Fox, 1981). These seven questions, taken from an early study of gifted students, are still good guides today (Walton, 1961):

- Who learns easily and rapidly?
- Who uses a lot of common sense and practical knowledge?
- Who retains easily what he or she has heard?
- Who knows about many things that the other children don't?
- Who uses a large number of words easily and accurately?
- Who recognizes relations and comprehends meanings?
- Who is alert and keenly observant and responds quickly?

Based on Renzulli and Reis's (1991) definition of giftedness, we might add:

- Who is persistent and highly motivated on some tasks?
- Who is creative, often has unusual ideas, or makes interesting connections?

Group achievement and intelligence tests tend to underestimate the IQs of very bright children. Group tests may be appropriate for screening, but they are not appropriate for making placement decisions. Many psychologists recommend a case study approach to identifying gifted students. This means gathering many kinds of information, test scores, grades, examples of work, projects and portfolios, letters or ratings from teachers, self-ratings, and so on (Renzulli & Reis, 1991; Sisk, 1988). Especially for recognizing artistic talent, experts in the field can be called in to judge the merits of a child's creations. Science projects, exhibitions, performances, auditions, and interviews are all possibilities. Creativity tests such as those described in Chapter 13 may identify some children not picked up by other measures, particularly minority students who may be at a disadvantage on the other types of tests (Maker, 1987). Remember, students with remarkable abilities in one area may have much less impressive abilities in others. In fact, there may be up to 180,000 students in American schools who are gifted and learning disabled (Davis & Rimm, 1985).

Teaching Gifted Students. Some educators believe that gifted students should be accelerated—moved quickly through the grades or through particular subjects. Other

CONNECT & EXTEND

TO THE RESEARCH

The September 2001 issue of *Psychology in the Schools* has several articles on identifying and teaching underrepresented gifted students.

CONNECT & EXTEND

TO THE RESEARCH

There are three groups of students who are underrepresented in gifted education programs: women, students with learning disabilities, and students living in poverty (Stormont, Stebbins, & Holliday, 2001).

GIRLS AND GIFTEDNESS

As young girls develop their identities in adolescence, they often reject being labeled as gifted—being accepted and popular—"fitting in" may become more important than achievement (Stormont et al., 2001; Basow & Rubin, 1999).

How can teachers reach girls with gifts? Here are some ideas:

- Notice when girls' test scores seem to decline in middle or high school.
- Encourage assertiveness, achievement, high goals, and demanding work from all students.
- Provide models of achievement through speakers, internships, or readings.
- Look for and support gifts in arenas other than academic achievement.

GIFTED STUDENTS WITH LEARNING DISABILITIES: TWICE-EXCEPTIONAL

Here are some ideas for supporting twice-exceptional students (McCoach, Kehle, Bray, & Siegle, 2001):

- Identify these students by looking longitudinally at achievement.
- Remediate skill deficits, but also identify and develop talents and strengths.
- Provide emotional support; it is important for all students, but especially for this group.
- Help students learn to compensate directly for their learning problems, and assist them in "tuning in" to their own strengths and difficulties.

GIFTED STUDENTS WHO LIVE IN POVERTY

Health problems, lack of resources, homelessness, fears about safety and survival, frequent moves, responsibilities for the care of other family members all make achievement in school more difficult. To identify student with gifts:

- Use alternative assessment, teacher nomination, and creativity tests.
- Be sensitive to cultural differences in values about cooperative or solitary achievement (Ford, 2000).
- Use multicultural strategies to encourage both achievement and the development of racial identities.

educators prefer enrichment—giving the students additional, more sophisticated, and more thought-provoking work, but keeping them with their age-mates in school. Actually, both may be appropriate (Torrance, 1986). Look at Table 4.11 to see examples of how content can be modified through acceleration, enrichment, sophistication, and novelty.

Many people object to acceleration, but most careful studies indicate that truly gifted students who begin primary, elementary, junior high, high school, college, or even graduate school early do as well as, and usually better than, nongifted students who are progressing at the normal pace. Social and emotional adjustment does not appear to be impaired. Gifted students tend to prefer the company of older playmates and may be miserably bored if kept with children of their own age. Skipping grades may not be the best solution for a particular student, but it does not deserve the bad name it has received (Jones & Southern, 1991; Kulik & Kulik, 1984; Richardson & Benbow, 1990). An alternative to skipping grades is to accelerate students in one or two particular subjects or allow concurrent enrollment in advanced placement courses, but keep them with peers for most classes (Robinson & Clinkenbeard, 1998). For students who are extremely advanced intellectually (for example, those scoring 160 or higher on an individual intelligence test), the only practical solution may be to accelerate their education (Hunt & Marshall, 2002; Keogh & MacMillan, 1996).

Teaching methods for gifted students should encourage abstract thinking (formal-operational thought), creativity, reading of high-level and original texts, and independence, not just the learning of greater quantities of facts. One approach that does *not* seem promising with gifted students is cooperative learning in mixed ability groups. Gifted students tend to learn more when they work in groups with other high ability peers (Fuchs, Fuchs, Hamlett, & Karns, 1998; Robinson & Clinkenbeard, 1998). In working with gifted and talented students, a teacher must be imaginative, flexible, tolerant, and unthreatened by the capabilities of these students. The teacher must ask: What do these children need most? What are they ready to learn? Who can help me to challenge them? Challenge and support are critical for all students. But challenging students who know more than anyone else in the school about history or music or science or math can be a challenge! Answers might come from faculty members at nearby colleges, retired professionals, books, museums, or older students. Strategies might be as simple as letting the child do math with the next grade. Other options are summer institutes; courses at nearby colleges; classes with local artists, musicians, or dancers; independent research projects; selected classes in high school for younger students; honors classes; and special-interest clubs (Mitchell, 1984).

Table 4.11 Examples of How to Modify Content for Students with Gifts and Talents

	Subject			
Modification	**Math**	**Science**	**Language Arts**	**Social Studies**
Acceleration	Algebra in fifth grade	Early chemistry and physics	Learning grammatical structure early	Early introduction to world history
Enrichment	Changing bases in number systems	Experimentation and data collecting	Short story and poetry writing	Reading biographies for historical insight
Sophistication	Mastering the laws of arithmetic	Learning the laws of physics	Mastering the structural properties of plays, sonnets, and so on	Learning and applying the principles of economics
Novelty	Probability and statistics	Science and its impact on society	Rewriting Shakespeare's tragedies with happy endings	Creating future societies and telling how they are governed

SOURCE: From *Teaching the Gifted Child* (4th ed.), by James J. Gallagher & Shelagh Gallagher. Published by Allyn & Bacon, Boston, MA. Copyright © 1994 by Pearson Education. Adapted by permission of the publisher.

In the midst of providing challenge, don't forget the support. We all have seen the ugly sights of parents, coaches, or teachers forcing the joy out of their talented students by demanding practice and perfection beyond the child's interest. Just as we should not force children to stop investing in their talent ("Oh, Michaelangelo, quit fooling with those sketches and go outside and play"), we also should avoid destroying intrinsic motivation with heavy doses of pressure and external rewards.

Check Yourself What are the characteristics of gifted students?

Is acceleration a useful approach with gifted students?

Summary Table

Language and Labeling
(pp. 106–107)

What are the advantages of and problems with labels? Labels and diagnostic classifications of exceptional students can easily become both stigmas and self-fulfilling prophecies, but they can also open doors to special programs and help teachers develop appropriate instructional strategies.

What is person-first language? "Person-first" language ("students with mental retardation," "students placed at risk," etc.) is an alternative to labels that describe a complex person with one or two words, implying that the condition labeled is the most important aspect of the person. With person-first language, the emphasis is on the students first, not on the special challenges they face.

Distinguish between a disability and a handicap. A disability is an inability to do something specific such as see or walk. A handicap is a disadvantage in certain situations. Some disabilities lead to handicaps, but not in all contexts. Teachers must avoid imposing handicaps on disabled learners.

Exceptional Students: Students who have abilities or problems so significant that they require special education or other services to reach their potential.
Disability: The inability to do something specific such as walk or hear.
Handicap: A disadvantage in a particular situation, sometimes caused by a disability.

Individual Differences in Intelligence
(pp. 107–115)

What is *g*? Spearman suggested there is one mental attribute, which he called *g* or general intelligence, that is used to perform any mental test, but that each test also requires some specific abilities in addition to *g*. A current version of the general plus specific abilities theory is Carroll's work identifying a few broad abilities (such as learning and memory, visual perception, verbal fluency) and at least 70 specific abilities.

What is Gardner's view of intelligence and his position on *g*? Gardner contends that an intelligence is a biological and psychological potential to solve problems and create outcomes that are valued by a culture. These intelligences are realized to a greater or lesser extent as a consequence of the experiential, cultural, and motivational factors. The intelligences are: linguistic, musical, spatial, logical-mathematical, bodily-kinesthetic, interpersonal, intrapersonal, naturalist, and perhaps existential. Gardner does not deny the existence of *g*, but does question how useful *g* is as an explanation for human achievements.

What are the elements in Sternberg's theory of intelligence? Sternberg's triarchic theory of intelligence is a cognitive process approach to understanding intelligence: Analytic/componential intelligence involves mental processes that are defined in terms of components: metacomponents, performance components, and knowledge-acquisition components. Creative/experiential intelligence involves coping with new experiences through insight and automaticity. Practical/contextual intelligence involves choosing to live and work in a context where success is likely, adapting to that context, and reshaping it if necessary. Practical intelligence is made up mostly of action-oriented tacit knowledge learned during everyday life.

How is intelligence measured and what does an IQ score mean? Intelligence is measured through individual tests (Stanford-Binet, Wechsler, etc.) and group tests (Lorge-Thorndike, Analysis of Learning Potential, School and College Ability Tests, etc.). Compared to an individual test, a group test is much less likely to yield an accurate picture of any one person's abilities. The average score is 100. About 68% of the general population will earn IQ scores between 85 and 115. Only about 16% of the population will receive scores below 85 or above 115. These figures hold true for White, native-born Americans whose first language is Standard English. Intelligence predicts success in school, but is less predictive of success in life when level of education is taken into account.

Intelligence: Ability or abilities to acquire and use knowledge for solving problems and adapting to the world.

Fluid Intelligence: Mental efficiency, nonverbal abilities grounded in brain development

Crystallized Intelligence: Ability to apply culturally approved problem-solving methods.

Theory of Multiple Intelligences: In Gardner's theory of intelligence, a person's eight separate abilities: logical-mathematical, verbal, musical, spatial, bodily-kinesthetic, interpersonal, intrapersonal, and naturalist.

Triarchic Theory of Intelligence: A three-part description of the mental abilities (thinking processes, coping with new experiences, and adapting to context) that lead to more or less intelligent behavior.

Insight: The ability to deal effectively with novel situations.

Automaticity: The result of learning to perform a behavior or thinking process so thoroughly that the performance is automatic and does not require effort.

Tacit Knowledge: Knowing how rather than knowing that—knowledge that is more likely to be learned during everyday life than through formal schooling.

Mental Age: In intelligence testing, a score based on average abilities for that age group.

Intelligence Quotient (IQ): Score comparing mental and chronological ages.

Deviation IQ: Score based on statistical comparison of individual's performance with the average performance of others in that age group.

Ability Differences and Teaching

(pp. 115–118)

What are the problems with between-class ability grouping? Academic ability groupings can have both disadvantages and advantages for students and teachers. For low-ability students, however, between-class ability grouping generally has a negative effect on achievement, social adjustment, and self-esteem. Teachers in low achievement classes tend to emphasize lower-level objectives and routine procedures, with less academic focus. Often there are more student behavior, increased teacher stress, lowered expectations, and decreased enthusiasm. Ability grouping can promote segregation within schools.

What are the alternatives available for grouping in classes? Cross-age grouping by subject can be an effective way to deal with ability differences in a school. Within-class ability grouping, if handled sensitively and flexibly, can have positive effects, but alternatives such as cooperative learning may be better.

Between-Class Ability Grouping/Tracking: System of grouping in which students are assigned to classes based on their measured ability or their achievements.

Untracking: Redesigning schools to teach students in classes that are not grouped by ability.

Nongraded Elementary School/The Joplin Plan: Arrangement wherein students are grouped by ability in particular subjects, regardless of their ages or grades.

Within-Class Ability Grouping: System of grouping in which students in a class are divided into two or three groups based on ability in an attempt to accommodate student differences.

Cognitive and Learning Styles

(pp. 118–121)

Distinguish between cognitive style and learning preference. Cognitive styles are characteristic modes of perceiving, remembering, thinking, problem solving, and decision making. They reflect information-processing regularities that develop around underlying personality trends such as a tendency for deep or surface processing of information. Learning preferences are individual preferences for particular learning modes and environments. Even though cognitive styles and learning preferences are not related to intelligence or effort, they may affect school performance.

Should teachers match instruction to individual learning styles? Results of some research indicate that students learn more when they study in their preferred setting and manner, but most research does not show a benefit. Many students would do better to develop new—and perhaps more effective—ways to learn.

Cognitive Styles: Different ways of perceiving and organizing information.

Field Dependence: Cognitive style in which patterns are perceived as wholes.

Field Independence: Cognitive style in which separate parts of a pattern are perceived and analyzed.

Impulsive: Characterized by cognitive style of responding quickly but often inaccurately.

Reflective: Characterized by cognitive style of responding slowly, carefully, and accurately.

Self-Instruction: Talking oneself through the steps of a task.

Learning Styles: Characteristic approaches to learning and studying.

Learning Preferences: Preferred ways of studying and learning, such as using pictures instead of text, working with other people versus alone, learning in structured or in unstructured situations, and so on.

Changes in the Law: Integration and Inclusion

(pp. 121–124)

Describe the main legal requirements that pertain to students with disabilities. Public Law 94-142 (1975) requires that each exceptional learner or student with special needs be educated in the least restrictive environment according to an individualized education program (IEP). The law also protects the rights of students with special needs and their parents. Public Law 99-457 extends the 94-142 law to preschool-age children, and IDEA, the Individuals with Disabilities Education Act, extends services to include transition programming for exceptional learners 16 years old and older. IDEA was reauthorized in 1997, and the classroom teacher was added to the IEP planning group.

Regular Education Initiative: An educational movement that advocates giving regular education teachers, not special education teachers, responsibility for teaching mildly (and sometimes moderately) handicapped students.

Individuals with Disabilities Education Act (IDEA): Amendment to PL 94-142.

Americans with Disabilities Act (ADA): Legislation prohibiting discrimination against persons with disabilities in employment, transportation, public access, local government, and telecommunications.

Least Restrictive Placement: Placement of each child in as normal an educational setting as possible.

Mainstreaming: Teaching children with disabilities in regular classes for part or all of their school day.

Full Inclusion: The integration of all students, including those with severe disabilities, into regular classes.

Individualized Education Program (IEP): Annually revised program for an exceptional student, detailing present achievement level, goals, and strategies, drawn up by teachers, parents, specialists, and (if possible) the student.

Prevalent Problems and Mild Disabilities

(pp. 124–132)

What is a learning disability? Specific learning disabilities involve significant difficulties in the acquisition and use of listening, speaking, reading, writing, reasoning, or mathematical abilities. These disorders are intrinsic to the individual, presumed to be the result of central nervous system dysfunction, and may occur across the life span. Students with learning disabilities may become victims of learned helplessness when they come to believe that they cannot control or improve their own learning and therefore cannot succeed. A focus on learning strategies often helps students with learning disabilities.

What are the most common communication disorders? Common communication disorders include speech impairments (articulation disorders, stuttering, and voicing problems) and oral language disorders. If these problems are addressed early, great progress is possible.

What defines mental retardation? Before age 18, students must score below about 70 on a standard measure of intelligence and must have problems with adaptive behavior, day-to-day independent living, and social functioning.

What are the best approaches for students with emotional problems? Methods from applied behavioral analysis and direct teaching of social skills are two useful approaches.

Learning Disability: Problem with acquisition and use of language; may show up as difficulty with reading, writing, reasoning, and math.

Learned Helplessness: The expectation, based on previous experiences with a lack of control, that all one's efforts will lead to failure.

Speech disorder: Inability to produce sounds effectively for speaking.

Articulation Disorders: Any of a variety of pronunciation difficulties, such as the substitution, distortion, or omission of sounds.

Voicing Problems: Inappropriate pitch, quality, loudness, and intonation.

Mental Retardation: Significantly below-average intellectual and adaptive social behavior, evident before age 18.

Transition Programming: Gradual preparation of exceptional students to move from high school into further education or training, employment, or community involvement.

Enhancing Your Expertise with Technology: Learning about Learning Disabilities

(p. 133)

LD Online **www.ldonline.org**

Other Useful Websites

A collection of child development websites **http://www.ume.maine.edu/~cofed/eceol/guide.html**

Listing of technical assistance documents from the Office of Special Education **http://www.state.sd.us/state/executive/deca/special/taguide.htm**

Introduction to multiple intelligences **http://edweb.gsn.org/edref.mi.intro.html**

Project Zero **http://pzweb.harvard.edu**

Teaching to the 7 Multiple Intelligences **http://ns1.iols.net/users/berolart/GRPWEBPG.HTM**

National Education Association's Policy on Inclusion **http://www.nea.org/publiced/idea/ideaplcy.html**

IDEA law (Individuals with Disabilities Education Act) **http://www.ed.gov/offices/OSERS/IDEA/the_law.html**

Profiles of Children with Disabilities **http://nces.ed.gov/pubs97/97254.html**

Disability-Related Resources on the Web **http://www.thearc.org/misc/dislnkin.html**

Organizations

The Office of Special Education: You can find information on new legislation and new resources on this site. This is an excellent general resource. **http://teach.virginia.edu/curry/dept/cise/ose/new.html**

The National Academy of Child Development (NACD): An international organization of parents and professionals dedicated to helping

children and adults reach their full potential. The site includes resources for parents and links to research articles.
http://www.nacd.org/

National Association for Attention Deficit Disorder
http://www.add.org/

Learning Disabilities Association **http://www.ldanatl.org/**

Children and Adults with Attention Deficit Disorders (C.H.A.D.D.).
http://chadd.org/

To take a learning styles test, go to: **http://www2.ncsu.edu/unity/lockers/users/f/felder/public/ILSdir/ilsweb.html**

To take an intelligence test, go to either: **http://www.iqtest.com/**
http://www.queendom.com/tests/iq/index.html

Less Prevalent Problems and More Severe Disabilities

(pp. 133–136)

How can schools accommodate the needs of physically disabled students? If the school has the necessary architectural features, such as ramps, elevators, and accessible rest rooms, and if teachers allow for the physical limitations of students, little needs to be done to alter the usual educational program. Identifying a peer to help with movements and transitions can be useful.

How would you handle a seizure in class? Do not restrain the child's movements. Lower the child gently to the floor, away from furniture or walls. Move hard objects away. Turn the child's head gently to the side, put a soft coat or blanket under the student's head, and loosen any tight clothing. Never put anything in the student's mouth. Find out from the student's parents how the seizure is usually dealt with. If one seizure follows another and the student does not regain consciousness in between or if the seizure goes on for more than 5 minutes, get medical help right away.

What are some signs of hearing and visual impairment? Signs of hearing problems are turning one ear toward the speaker, favoring one ear in conversation, or misunderstanding conversation when the speaker's face cannot be seen. Other indications include not following directions, seeming distracted or confused at times, frequently asking people to repeat what they have said, mispronouncing new words or names, and being reluctant to participate in class discussions. Take note particularly of students who have frequent earaches, sinus infections, or allergies. Holding books very close or far away, squinting, rubbing eyes, misreading the chalkboard, and holding the head at an odd angle are possible signs of visual problems.

Cerebral Palsy: Condition involving a range of motor or coordination difficulties due to brain damage.

Spasticity: Overly tight or tense muscles, characteristic of some forms of cerebral palsy.

Epilepsy: Disorder marked by seizures and caused by abnormal electrical discharges in the brain.

Generalized Seizure: A seizure involving a large portion of the brain.

Absence Seizure: A seizure involving only a small part of the brain that causes a child to lose contact briefly.

Low Vision: Vision limited to close objects.

Educationally Blind: Needing Braille materials in order to learn.

Section 504 Protections for Students

(pp. 136–140)

What is Section 504? Section 504 is a part of the Vocational Rehabilitation Act of 1973 that prevents discrimination against people with disabilities in any program that receives federal money, such as public schools. Through Section 504, all school age children are ensured an equal opportunity to participate in school activities. The definition of "disability" is broad in Section 504.

What is ADHD and how is it handled in school? Attention-deficit/hyperactivity disorder (ADHD) is the term used to describe individuals of any age with hyperactivity and attention difficulties. Use of medication to address ADHD is controversial, but currently on the rise. For many students there are negative side effects. In addition, little is known about the long-term effects of drug therapy. There also is no evidence that the drugs lead to improvement in academic learning or peer relationships. Two promising approaches are behavior modification and techniques that combine instruction in learning and memory strategies with motivational training. The SMART approach that focuses on the abilities of children in another possibility.

Section 504: A part of civil rights law that prevents discrimination against people with disabilities in programs that receive federal funds, such as public schools.

Attention-Deficit/Hyperactivity Disorder: Current term for disruptive behavior disorders marked by overactivity, excessive difficulty sustaining attention, or impulsiveness.

Students Who Are Gifted and Talented

(pp. 140–145)

What are the characteristics of gifted students? Gifted students learn easily and rapidly and retain what they have learned; use common sense and practical knowledge; know about many things that the other children don't; use a large number of words easily and accurately; recognize relations and comprehend meaning; are alert and keenly observant and respond quickly; are persistent and highly motivated on some tasks; and are creative or make interesting connections. Teachers should make special efforts to support underrepresented gifted students—girls, students who also have learning disabilities, and children living in poverty.

Is acceleration a useful approach with gifted students? Many people object to acceleration, but most careful studies indicate that truly gifted students who are accelerated do as well as, and usually better than, nongifted students who are progressing at the normal pace. Gifted students tend to prefer the company of older playmates and may be bored if kept with children their own age. Skipping grades may not be the best solution for a particular student, but for students who are extremely advanced intellectually (with a score of 160 or higher on an individual intelligence test), the only practical solution may be to accelerate their education.

Gifted Student: A very bright, creative, and talented student.

Becoming a Professional

Passing the PRAXIS™

Chapter 4 reflects many of the professional standards created by the Interstate New Teacher Assessment and Support Consortium (INTASC). These standards form the basis of the PRAXIS II™ and state-created teacher licensure exams.

This chapter opens with what is often the singular event of the school year: the release of standardized test scores to teachers, parents, and students. Hidden within rows and columns of statistics are much of what veteran teachers know about learner differences. If we could work backwards in time over the school year, we would see thousands of decisions and actions based on knowledge of intelligence, academic ability, grouping practices, learning disabilities, giftedness, creativity, physical disabilities, and state and federal legislation. These decisions, of course, were influenced by experience and reflection, but even the newest member of the profession can possess the basic knowledge to make sound decisions most of the time.

Tips for PRAXIS II™

Explain the effects of legislation on public education:

- Americans with Disabilities Act
- Individuals with Disabilities Act
- Section 504
- Individualized Education Plans
- Inclusion, Mainstreaming, and Least Restrictive Environment

Understand views of intelligence and describe its measurement:

- Types of intelligence tests and their uses
- Multiple intelligences
- Interpreting intelligence scores
- Modifications to testing

Accommodate the needs of students with exceptionalities:

- Attention-Deficit/Hyperactivity Disorder
- Visual, speech, and physical difficulties
- Learning disabilities
- Mental retardation

Related Topics

- Standardized testing (Chapter 14)
- Effective teaching in inclusive classrooms (Chapter 12)
- Ethnic and racial differences in school achievement (Chapter 5)
- Creating culturally compatible classrooms (Chapter 5)

Standards and Licensure Appendix: *PRAXIS II™ and INTASC*

Refer to the Appendix at the end of the book for detailed correlations to PRAXIS II™ exam topics and INTASC Standards addressed in this text.

Insights about Job Interview Questions: *What Would You Say?*

1. Describe a learning activity that you have planned for a class and ways that you have accommodated individual learning styles or needs.
2. If a student is struggling with time management and organization issues, what kind of accommodations would you provide?
3. We have been having some heated debates in this district about ability grouping and tracking. Where do you stand on those issues?

Your Teaching Portfolio: *Teaching Resources*

- Use Table 4.6 "Encouraging Language Development" to generate ideas for developing students' language and add these to your **Portfolio.**
- For your **Portfolio,** develop a lesson plan that appropriately uses Gardner's work on multiple intelligences.
- Add Table 4.8, "Making a Referral" to your **Portfolio.**
- Add Tables 4.3, 4.4, 4.5, 4.6, 4.7, and 4.8 to your file of **Teaching Resources.**

Video**Workshop** Extra

If the VideoWorkshop package was included with your textbook, go to Chapter 4 of the Companion Website (www.ablongman.com/woolfolk) and click on the VideoWorkshop button. Follow the instructions for viewing *Video Clip 3: Individual Differences.* Consider this information along with what you've read in Chapter 4 while answering the following questions:

1. What are these teachers doing, or what should they be doing, to adapt the lesson for students with varying learning styles?
2. How does this method of teaching allow for the needs of gifted students as well as learning challenged students?

Use the CD-ROM included in the back of your textbook to launch the "Becoming a Professional" website. The website features advice on preparing for teacher certification exams, help with getting your first job, and resources to help you perform your job well from the first day forward.

Teachers' Casebook

What Would They Do?

Here is how some practicing teachers responded to the teaching situation presented at the beginning of this chapter about discussing IQ scores with parents.

Kelly L. Hoy

Third Grade Teacher, *Faber Elementary School, Dunellen, New Jersey*

Disclosing individual information about standardized tests is always a ticklish problem. Of course, parents want to know as much as they can about their children, but there are dangers of misinterpreting or misusing information, categorizing and stereotyping children, and individual comparisons. I would be very careful about disclosing the specifics of IQ test scores to parents.

I certainly would meet with the parents who have written to explain the reasons for IQ testing in our school. Tests are aids to teachers to help us understand how to deal more effectively with our students—to challenge them, to help them, and to have high, but realistic expectations of them. For those parents who persist in wanting to know the results of an IQ test, in an individual conference I would sketch the meaning of IQ and emphasize the notion of multiple intelligences. I would avoid simple numbers and gross indices such as "your child has an IQ of 115." Rather, I would focus on the strengths of the student as I discussed the student's intelligence profile. All of my explanations would be in general terms, such as "your child is better than most of his peers in coping with new experiences, but about average in solving abstract word problems." Again, I would emphasize the positive and use other results to provide suggestions to parents about what they could do to help in areas in which the student seemed less advanced.

Jeff D. Horton

Seventh–Twelfth Grade Teacher, *Colton School, Colton, Washington*

For the most part, intelligence testing can give some information about groups of students. It also can tell where individual students are positioned compared to a group. However, these tests are usually not a good instrument for determining how "smart" a student is or can be.When presenting intelligence test scores to parents, it is important to be clear about what the information does and does not say. Parents should also be informed that they will be comparing their son's or daughter's score(s) against a group, not against individual students. This point is very important. Often teachers will be asked to compare one student's work with that of another student. This should never be done. Each student is unique and has a variety of abilities and limitations. Teachers must look at the individual abilities, skills, and knowledge of the student being assessed, as well as that student's effort in the subject(s) being taught. If the parent wants to see the actual scores, it may be wise to have the school's counselor or an administrator available to help explain the results.

Thomas W. Newkirk

Eighth Grade English Teacher, *Hamilton Heights Middle School, Arcadia, Indiana*

Reports in regard to the success of my students and especially of my advisory students are important and deserve my full attention. Hopefully such reports, together with my own observations and the observations of my colleagues, give me insight in helping my students realize their potential. Obviously, the more information I have, the more insight I am likely to have, and I would try to avoid basing any judgment on a single observation or report.

When I met with the parents to discuss their child's achievement, I would review the types of questions asked on the test, share my own opinions based upon daily observations, and emphasize that test results are only one measure of intelligence.

Amy Neal

Ninth Grade Teacher, *Katy High School, Katy, Texas*

After I read the test results, I would call each parent. I would arrange a time for them to come to the school to meet with me and their child's guidance counselor. At that meeting, we would discuss the results of the test and the validity of the test. I would explain to the parents that as a special education teacher, I use intelligence tests as a guide to a student's intellectual ability, but the scores are not a measure of "how smart a student really is."

Elizabeth Chouinard

Fourth Grade Teacher, *MacGregor Elementary School, Houston, Texas*

I would cautiously analyze the test results and compare them to other information on the child, such as performance on other tests and classroom experiences. I would share the test results with parents of the children involved. However, I would caution them about possible sources of error in testing. I would also share other pertinent information with the parents that might present a more accurate rating of their child's intelligence level.

Go to the Companion Website (www.ablongman.com/woolfolk) for additional case studies including audio and video cases, and examples of student work.

CHAPTER

5

Culture and Community

Teachers' Casebook

What Would You Do?

There are students from four different ethnic groups in the middle school "pod" you are working with this year. Last week, the principal added a student with pretty severe emotional/behavioral problems and a student with cerebral palsy to the group as part of an experiment in full inclusion. The boy with cerebral palsy is in a wheelchair and has some difficulties with language and hearing. Students from each of the four ethnic groups seem to stick together, never making friends with students from "outside." When you ask people to work together for projects, the divisions are strictly on ethnic lines. Many of the subgroups communicate in their native language—one you don't understand—and you assume that often the joke is on you because of the looks and laughs directed your way. Clarise, the emotionally disturbed student, is making matters worse by telling ethnic jokes to anyone who will listen in a voice loud enough to be overheard by half the class. There are rumors of an ambush after school to "teach Clarise a lesson." You agree that she—and the whole class for that matter—needs a lesson, but not this kind.

Critical Thinking

How would you handle the situation? How would you teach the class to help the students feel more comfortable together? What are your first goals in working on this problem? How will these issues affect the grade levels you will teach?

Collaboration

With 4 or 5 other members of your class, brainstorm as many reasonable ways as you can of addressing this situation. Come to consensus on the two best ways and present them to the class, with your rationale for why these are good choices.

The face of American classrooms is changing. The same can be said for many countries today. In this chapter we examine the many cultures that form the fabric of our society. We begin by tracing the schools' responses to different ethnic and cultural groups and consider the concept of multicultural education. With a broad conception of culture as a basis, we then examine three important dimensions of every student's identity: social class, ethnicity, and gender. Then we turn to a consideration of language and bilingual education. The last section of the chapter presents three general principles for teaching every student.

By the time you have completed this chapter you should be able to answer these questions:

- *What is the difference between the melting pot and multicultural education?*
- *What is* culture *and what groups make up your own cultural identity?*
- *Why does the school achievement of low-income students often fall below that of middle- and upper-income students?*
- *What are some examples of conflicts and compatibilities between home and school cultures?*
- *What is the school's role in the development of gender differences?*
- *What is effective teaching in bilingual classrooms?*
- *What are examples of culturally relevant pedagogy that fit the grades and subjects you will teach?*

Dancing (1998) by Gladys Barbot Desmangles. Courtesy of the artist and PaintingsDIRECT (http://www.PaintingsDIRECT.com).

Today's Multicultural Classrooms

CONNECT & EXTEND

TO **PRAXIS**™ MULTICULTURAL EDUCATION (III, B)
Know the major dimensions of multicultural education. Describe how these dimensions influence each other.

Who are the students in American classrooms today? Here are a few statistics:

- One in four Americans under the age of 18 lives in poverty. For children under age 3, the number is one in three. Nearly 50% of all African American children are poor.
- The number of children in poverty in the United States is almost 50% higher than in *any other developed Western nation* and 5 to 8 times higher than in many prominent industrialized nations.
- Children growing up in poverty are twice as likely to be retained in a grade, drop out of school, or experience a violent crime.
- One in three children lives with a single parent, usually a working mother.
- In 2000, 62% of the students in the public schools were White, 17% were African American, 16% were Hispanic, 4% were Asian, and 1% were Native American.
- By the year 2020, over 66% of all school-age children in the United States will be African American, Asian, Hispanic, or Native American—many the children of new immigrants.
- By 2050, there will be no majority race or ethnicity in the United States; every American will be a member of a minority group (Banks, 2002; Duncan & Brooks-Gunn, 2000; Grant & Sleeter, 1989; Halford, 1999; McLoyd, 1998; Meece & Kurtz-Costes, 2001; Payne & Biddle, 1999).

CONNECT & EXTEND

TO THE RESEARCH
See Banks, J. et al. (2001). Diversity within unity: Essential principles for teaching and learning within a multicultural society. *Phi Delta Kappan, 83,* 196–212, for a synthesis of research on diversity and education.

Individuals, Groups, and Society

Since the beginning of the 20th century, a flow of immigrants has entered the United Kingdom, Western Europe, Canada, Australia, the United States, and many other developed countries. These new immigrants were expected to assimilate—that is, to enter the cultural **melting pot** and become like those who had arrived earlier. For years, the goal of American schools was to be the fire under the melting pot. Immigrant children who spoke different languages and had different religious and cultural heritages were expected to come to the schools, master standard English, and learn to become mainstream Americans.

In the 1960s and 1970s, some educators suggested that minority group and poor students had problems in school because they had not fully "melted" or assimilated into mainstream American life. The students were described as "culturally disadvantaged" or "culturally handicapped." The assumption of this **cultural deficit model** was that the students' home culture was inferior because it had not prepared them to fit into the schools. Today most people reject the idea of cultural deficits. They believe that no culture is deficient, but rather that there may be incompatibilities between the student's home culture and the expectations of the school (Gallimore & Goldenberg, 2001).

Also during the 1960s and 1970s, there was growing concern for civil and human rights and an increasing sense among many ethnic groups that they did not want to assimilate completely into mainstream American society. Rather, they wanted to maintain their culture and identity while still being a respected part of the larger society. Multiculturalism was the goal.

Today there are many definitions of and disagreements about multiculturalism. In an interview for *Educational Leadership* (Halford, 1999), Ronald Takaki states that multiculturalism in the United States is simply "serious scholarship that includes all American peoples" (p. 9) and acknowledges that "when we look around us, we realize that not all of us came from Europe. Many came from Africa and Latin America, and others were already here in North America" (p. 9).

Melting pot A metaphor for the absorption and assimilation of immigrants into the mainstream of society so that ethnic differences vanish.

Cultural deficit model A model that explains the school achievement problems of ethnic minority students by assuming that their culture is inadequate and does not prepare them to succeed in school.

Multicultural education is one response to the increasing diversity of the school population as well as to the growing demand for equality for all groups. An examination of the alternative approaches to multicultural education is beyond the scope of an educational psychology text, but be aware that there is no general agreement about the "best" approach.

Multicultural education Education that teaches the value of cultural diversity.

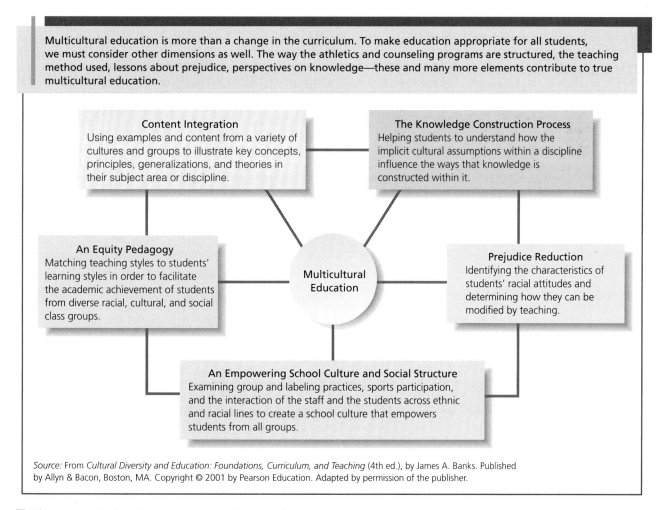

James Banks (2002) suggests that multicultural education has five dimensions, as shown in Figure 5.1. Many people are familiar only with the dimension of *content integration,* using examples and content from a variety of cultures when teaching a subject. Because they believe that multicultural education is simply a change in curriculum, some teachers assume that it is irrelevant for subjects such as science and mathematics. But if you consider the other four dimensions—helping students understand how knowledge is influenced by beliefs, reducing prejudice, creating social structures in schools that support learning and development for all students, and using teaching methods that reach all students—then you will see that this view of multicultural education is relevant to all subjects and all students.

Multicultural education rejects the idea of the melting pot and supports a society that values diversity (Banks, 1997, 2002; Sleeter, 1995). Let's take a closer look at the differences that make up the mosaic of cultural diversity.

Multicultural education is more than a change in the curriculum. To make education appropriate for all students, we must consider other dimensions as well. The way the athletics and counseling programs are structured, the teaching method used, lessons about prejudice, perspectives on knowledge—these and many more elements contribute to true multicultural education.

Content Integration
Using examples and content from a variety of cultures and groups to illustrate key concepts, principles, generalizations, and theories in their subject area or discipline.
The Knowledge Construction Process
Helping students to understand how the implicit cultural assumptions within a discipline influence the ways that knowledge is constructed within it.
An Equity Pedagogy
Matching teaching styles to students' learning styles in order to facilitate the academic achievement of students from diverse racial, cultural, and social class groups.
Multicultural Education
Prejudice Reduction
Identifying the characteristics of students' racial attitudes and determining how they can be modified by teaching.
An Empowering School Culture and Social Structure
Examining group and labeling practices, sports participation, and the interaction of the staff and the students across ethnic and racial lines to create a school culture that empowers students from all groups.

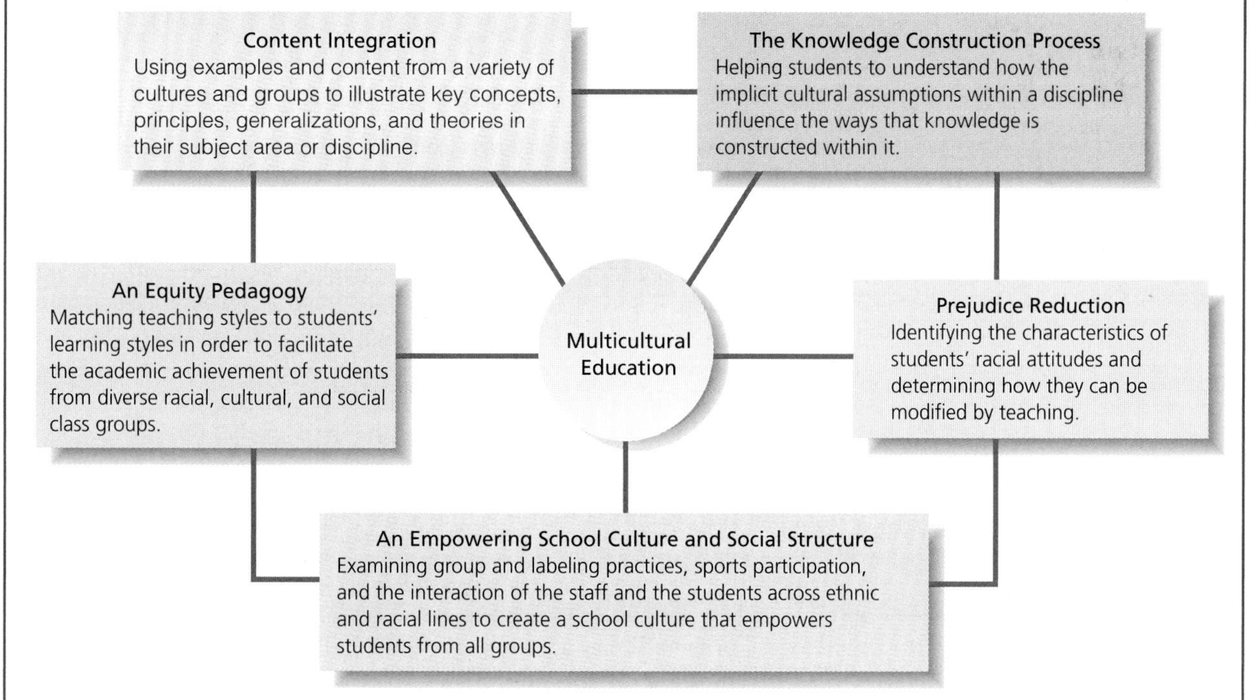

Source: From *Cultural Diversity and Education: Foundations, Curriculum, and Teaching* (4th ed.), by James A. Banks. Published by Allyn & Bacon, Boston, MA. Copyright © 2001 by Pearson Education. Adapted by permission of the publisher.

■ **Figure 5.1** Banks's Dimensions of Multicultural Education

American Cultural Diversity

Take a quick break from reading and turn on the television. (Don't do this if you will not come back to reading until next Tuesday!). Find a channel with commercials (I know, it is harder to find one without). Listen to about 15 commercials. For each one, is the voice or the character in the ad a male or a female? White, African American, Latino, Asian? Old or young? Privileged or poor? Do a quick tally of how many instances you observe in each category.

CONNECT & EXTEND

TO THE RESEARCH

- The Spring 1998 issue of *Theory Into Practice* is devoted to "Preparing Teachers for Cultural Diversity." See http://www.coe.ohio-state.edu/TIP This journal is especially for educators.
- See the *Review of Educational Research,* Spring 2000, for a whole issue on cultural competence and teaching.
- See *Educational Leadership,* Vol. 60, Number 4 (2003) for an entire issue on "Equity and Opportunity."

In this text we take a broad interpretation of culture and multicultural education, so we will examine social class, race, ethnicity, and gender as aspects of diversity. We begin with a look at the meaning of culture. Many people associate this concept with the "cultural events" section of the newspaper—art galleries, museums, Shakespeare, classical music, and so on. Culture has a much broader meaning; it embraces the whole way of life of a group of people.

Culture and Group Membership. There are many definitions of **culture.** An article in the 1998 *Annual Review of Psychology* described seven views: Culture as core societal values, as context and customs, as power and social position, as intergroup relations and social identities, as tools and practices, as social capital or wealth, and as psychological capabilities to navigate borders in diverse societies (Cooper & Denner, 1998). Most definitions include the knowledge, rules, traditions, beliefs, and values that guide behavior in a particular group of people (Betancourt & Lopez, 1993). The group creates a culture—a program for living—and communicates the culture to members. Thus people are members of groups, they are not members of cultures. Groups can be defined along regional, ethnic, religious, racial, gender, social class, or other lines. Each of us is a member of many groups, so we all are influenced by many different cultures. Sometimes the influences are incompatible or even contradictory. For example, if you are a feminist but also a Roman Catholic, you may have trouble reconciling the two different cultures' beliefs about the ordination of women as priests. Your personal belief will be based, in part, on how strongly you identify with each group (Banks, 1994).

There are many different cultures, of course, in every modern country. In the United States, students growing up in a small rural town in the Deep South are part of a cultural group that is very different from that of students in a large urban center or students in a West Coast condo. In Canada, students living in the suburbs of Toronto certainly differ in a number of ways from students growing up in a Montreal high-rise apartment or on a farm in Quebec. Within those small towns in the Deep South or Quebec, the child of a gas station attendant grows up in a different culture from the child of the town doctor or dentist. Individuals of African, Asian, Hispanic, Native American, or European descent have distinctive histories and traditions. The experiences of males and females are different in most ethnic and economic groups. Everyone living within a particular country shares many common experiences and values, especially because of the influence of the mass media. But other aspects of their lives are shaped by differing cultural backgrounds.

Cautions in Interpreting Cultural Differences. Before we examine the bases for cultural differences, two cautions are necessary. First, we will consider social class, ethnicity, and gender separately, because much of the available research focuses on only one of these variables. Of course, real children are not just African American, or middle class, or female; they are complex beings and members of many groups.

The second caution comes from James Banks (1993), who has written several books on multicultural education:

> Although membership in a gender, racial, ethnic, social-class, or religious group can provide us with important clues about an individual's behavior, it cannot enable us to predict behavior. . . . *Membership in a particular group does not determine behavior but makes certain types of behavior more probable.* (pp. 13–14)

Culture The knowledge, values, attitudes, and traditions that guide the behavior of a group of people and allow them to solve the problems of living in their environment.

Keep this in mind as you read about characteristics of economically disadvantaged students or Asian Americans or males. The information we will examine reflects tendencies and probabilities. It does not tell you about the specific students you will teach. For example, if a minority group student in your class consistently arrives late, it may be that the student has a job before school or must walk a long distance, or even that he or she dreads school.

Socioeconomic status (SES) Relative standing in the society based on income, power, background, and prestige.

Check Yourself Distinguish between the "melting pot" and multiculturalism.

What is multicultural education?

What is culture?

Social Class Differences

The term used by sociologists for variations in wealth, power, and prestige is **socioeconomic status,** or **SES.** In modern societies, levels of wealth, power, and prestige are not always consistent. Some people—for instance, university professors—are members of professions that are reasonably prestigious but provide little wealth or power. Other people have political power even though they are not wealthy. No single variable, not even income, is an effective measure of SES. In spite of these inconsistencies, most researchers identify four general levels of SES: upper, middle, working, and lower classes. The main characteristics of these four levels are summarized in Table 5.1. As you watched the commercials (*Stop/Think/Write* on page 156), how many people did you see who appeared to be lower SES?

Social class is a significant dimension of cultural differences, often overpowering other differences such as ethnicity or gender. For example, upper-class Anglo-Europeans, African Americans, and Hispanic Americans typically find that they have more in common with each other than they have with lower-class individuals from their own ethnic groups (Gollnick & Chinn, 1994).

CONNECT & EXTEND

TO **PRAXIS**™
ECONOMIC CONDITIONS/
SOCIOECONOMIC STATUS (SES)
(IV, B2)
Be aware of the possible effects of socioeconomic status on student achievement. Consider what steps teachers can take to minimize those effects.

Table 5.1 Selected Characteristics of Different Social Classes

	Upper Class	**Middle Class**	**Working Class**	**Lower Class**
Income	$160,000+	$80,000–$160,000 (1/2) $40,000–$80,000 (1/2)	$25,000–$40,000	Below $25,000
Occupation	Corporate, professional, family money	White-collar, skilled blue-collar	Blue-collar	Minimum-wage unskilled labor
Education	Prestigious colleges and professional schools	High school, college, or professional school	High school	High school or less
Home ownership	At least one home	Usually own home	About half own a home	No
Health coverage	Full	Usually	Limited	No
Neighborhoods	Exclusive or comfortable	Comfortable	Modest	Deteriorating
Afford children's college	Easily	Usually	Seldom	No
Political power	National, state, or local	State or local	Limited	No

SOURCE: Information from *Sociology* (9th ed.) (pp. 276–280), by J. J. Macionis, 2003, Saddle River, NJ: Prentice-Hall. Copyright © 2003 by Prentice-Hall.

CONNECT & EXTEND

TO YOUR TEACHING PORTFOLIO
Gabelko, N. H. & Sosniak, L. A. (2002). Someone just like me: When academic engagement trumps race, class, and gender. *Phi Delta Kappan, 83,* 400–405.

Being Poor

About one in four Americans under the age of 18 lives in poverty, defined in 2002 by the United States Department of Health and Human Services as an income of $18,100 for a family of four ($22,630 in Alaska and $20,820 in Hawaii). The United States has the highest rate of poverty for children of all developed nations, as much as five to eight times higher than other industrialized countries. And almost half of these children can be classified as living in deep poverty—in families with incomes 50% below the poverty threshold. Recently, there seem to be improvements. In 2000, the number of families in poverty was the lowest in 21 years—about 6.2 million (U.S. Census Bureau, September 25, 2001).

The majority of these poor children, about 65%, are White, because the total number of poor White families is greater than any other ethnic group. But even though the total number of poor African American and Hispanic American children is smaller than the number of poor White children, the percentages are higher. According to the 2000 United States Census, about 21% of all Hispanic American families and 22% of all African American families live in poverty. Compare this to an overall poverty rate of 11% for all families in the United States.

CONNECT & EXTEND

TO THE RESEARCH
See two issues of *Educational Leadership* with special sections on "Reaching for Equity," December 1997/January 1998 (Vol. 55, No. 4) and "Race, Class, and Culture," April 1999 (Vol. 56, No. 7).

SES and Achievement

There are many relationships between SES and school performance. For example, it is well documented that high-SES students of all ethnic groups show higher average levels of achievement on test scores and stay in school longer than low-SES students (Conger, Conger, & Elder, 1997; McLoyd, 1998). Poverty during a child's preschool years appears to have the greatest negative impact. Unfortunately, families with young children are the most likely to be poor because young parents have the lowest paying jobs or no jobs at all (Bronfenbrenner, McClelland, Wethington, Moen, & Ceci, 1996). And the longer the child is in poverty, the stronger the impact on achievement. For example, even when we take into account parents' education, the chance that children will be retained in grades or placed in special education increases by 2% to 3% for every year the children live in poverty (Sherman, 1994).

What are the effects of low socioeconomic status that might explain the lower school achievement of these students? Many factors maintain a cycle of poverty. Poor health care for mother and child, limited resources, family stress, interruptions in schooling, exposure to violence, overcrowding, homelessness, discrimination, and other factors lead to school failures, low-paying jobs—and another generation born in poverty. Garcia (1991) and McLoyd (1998) describe other possible explanations. Let's take a closer look at each of them.

Poor Health Care. Families in poverty have less access to good prenatal and infant health care and nutrition. Over half of all adolescent mothers receive no prenatal care at all. Poor mothers and adolescent mothers are more likely to have premature babies, and prematurity is associated with many cognitive and learning problems. Children in poverty are more likely to be exposed to legal drugs (nicotine, alcohol) and illegal drugs (cocaine, heroin) before birth. Children whose mothers take drugs during pregnancy can have problems with organization, attention, and language skills. Children who live in older houses with lead paint and lead-soldered pipes, which exist in many inner city areas, have greater concentrations of lead in their blood. This lead poisoning is associated with lower school achievement and long-term neurological impairment (McLoyd, 1998). Also, when parents have more physical and emotional problems, there tend to be more conflicts between parents and children—because stress levels are high (Duncan & Brooks-Gunn, 2000).

Low Expectations—Low Self-Esteem. Because low-SES students may wear old clothes, speak in a dialect, or be less familiar with books and school activities, teachers and other students may assume that these students are not bright. The teacher may avoid calling on them to protect them from the embarrassment of giving wrong answers or because they make the teacher uncomfortable. The children come to believe that they aren't very good at schoolwork (Elrich, 1994). The following true story shows how powerful this effect on academic self-concept can be. Terrence Quinn, principal of an elementary school in New York, spends his mornings serving coffee and doughnuts in a welfare hotel six blocks from his school, trying to convince parents to send their children to school.

> Last spring, Jacqueline, a 6th-grader who had lived at the hotel, was selected as the school's valedictorian. One month before the official announcement, she entered Quinn's office and asked to speak to him in private. "Can someone on welfare actually be the valedictorian?" she asked. (Reed & Sautter, 1990, p. K2)

CONNECT & EXTEND

TO OTHER CHAPTERS
The concepts of teacher expectation effects and self-fulfilling prophecies are very important in a consideration of cultural differences in the classroom. These concepts are discussed fully in Chapter 12.

Learned Helplessness. Low-SES children may be the victims of learned helplessness, described in the previous chapter. That is, low-SES students (or any students who fail continually) may come to believe that doing well in school is impossible. Many of their friends and relatives never finished school, so it seems normal to quit. In fact, about one-fourth of children from poor families drop out of school (Bennett, 1995). Without a high school diploma, these students find few rewards awaiting them in the work world. Many available jobs barely pay a living wage. If the head of a family of three works full time at the minimum wage, the family's income will still be below the poverty line. Low-SES children, particularly those who also encounter racial discrimination, "become convinced that it is difficult if not impossible for them to advance in the mainstream by doing well in school" (Goleman, 1988).

CONNECT & EXTEND

TO OTHER CHAPTERS
The concept of learned helplessness was discussed in Chapter 4 as one explanation for the lower achievement of students with learning disabilities and will be discussed again in Chapter 10 as a factor influencing motivation.

Peer Influences and Resistance Cultures. Some researchers have suggested that low-SES students may become part of a **resistance culture.** To members of this culture, making it in school means selling out and trying to act "middle class." In order to maintain their identity and their status within the group, low-SES students must reject the behaviors that would make them successful in school—studying, cooperating with teachers, even coming to class (Bennett, 1995; Ogbu, 1987, 1997). John Ogbu linked identification in a resistance culture to poor Latino American, Native American, and African American groups, but similar reactions have been noted for poor White students both in the United States and in England (Willis, 1977) and high school students in Papua New Guinea (Woolfolk Hoy, Demerath, & Pape, 2002). This is not to say that all low-SES students resist achievement. Adolescents whose parents value academic achievement tend to select friends who also share those values (Berndt & Keefe, 1995) and many young people, like Jacqueline described above, are high achievers in spite of either their economic situation or negative peer influences (O'Connor, 1997). And we should not forget that some aspects of schooling—competitive grading, public reprimands, stressful testing and assignments, and repetitive work that is too hard or too easy—can encourage resistance in all students (Okagaki, 2001).

Tracking. Another explanation for the lower achievement of many low-SES students is that these students experience **tracking** and therefore have a different academic socialization; that is, they are actually taught differently (Oakes, 1990b). If they are tracked into "low-ability" or "general" classes, they may be taught to memorize and be passive. Middle-class students are more likely to be encouraged to think and create in their classes (Anyon, 1980). When low-SES students receive an inferior education, their academic skills are inferior and their life chances are limited. Adam Gamoran (1987) found that the achievement differences between low-track and high-track students were greater than the differences between high school dropouts and graduates. In an interview with Marge Scherer (1993), Jonathan Kozol described the cruel predictive side of tracking:

> [T]racking is so utterly predictive. The little girl who gets shoved into the low reading group in 2nd grade is very likely to be the child who is urged to take

CONNECT & EXTEND

TO OTHER CHAPTERS
Related information on the effects of ability grouping and tracking appears in Chapter 4.

Resistance culture Group values and beliefs about refusing to adopt the behaviors and attitudes of the majority culture.

Tracking Assignment to different classes and academic experiences based on achievement.

CONNECT & EXTEND

TO THE RESEARCH
For two different opinions about the "Success for All" approach to helping low achieving students, see "At Odds: Success for All," a special section in *Phi Delta Kappan,* vol. 83, no. 6, pp. 463–471.

cosmetology instead of algebra in the 8th grade, and most likely to be in vocational courses, not college courses, in the 10th grade, if she hasn't dropped out by then. (p. 8)

Childrearing Styles. The oldest explanation for the academic problems of low-SES children is that their home environment does not give them the head start in school provided by middle- and upper-class homes. For example, studies have shown that middle-class mothers talk more; give more verbal guidance; help their children understand the causes of events, make plans, and anticipate consequences; direct their children's attention to the relevant details of a problem; and, rather than impose solutions, encourage children to solve problems themselves (Hess & Shipman, 1965; Hoffman, 1984). Contrast these two interactions as a mother works with a child on a puzzle:

"No, that piece goes here!"

"What shape is that piece? Can you find a spot that is straight like the piece? Yes, that's straight, but look at the color. Does the color match? No? Look again for a straight, red piece. Yes—try that one. Good for you! You finished the corner."

By assisting their children in these ways, mothers are actually following Vygotsky's advice to provide intellectual support, or scaffolding, in the children's zone of proximal development, as we discussed in Chapter 2. You can see how the second approach is more likely to encourage learning concepts (straight, shape, color, corner, match) and problem solving. Hess and McDevitt (1984) studied mothers and children over an eight-year period and found evidence that this "teaching as opposed to telling" style is related to higher achievement test scores for children ages 4 through 12.

You should be wary, however, of prejudging families based on their socioeconomic status. Recent research indicates that higher control parenting is linked to better grades for Asian and African American students (Glasgow, Dornbusch, Troyer, Steinberg, & Ritter, 1997). Parenting that is strict and directive, with clear rules and consequences, combined with high levels of warmth and emotional support, is associated with higher academic achievement for inner-city children (Jarrett, 1995). Differences in cultural values and in the danger of neighborhoods may make more parental control useful and appropriate (Smetana, 2000).

Home Environment and Resources. Families in poverty seldom have access to high quality preschool care for their young children. Research has shown that such high quality care enhances cognitive and social development (Duncan & Brooks-Gunn, 2000). Other research has focused on the home and neighborhood resources of families—books, computers, libraries, trips, museums, and so on. These home and neighborhood resources seem to have the greatest impact on children's achievement when school is not in session—during the summer or before students enter school. For example, Entwisle, Alexander, and Olson (1997) found that low-SES and high-SES students made comparable gains in reading and math when schools were open, but the low-SES students lost ground during summer while the high-SES students continued to improve academically. Another study found that lack of emotional support and cognitive stimulation in the home accounted for one-third to one-half of the disadvantages in verbal, reading, and math skills of poor children in a national study (Korenman, Miller, & Sjaastad, 1995).

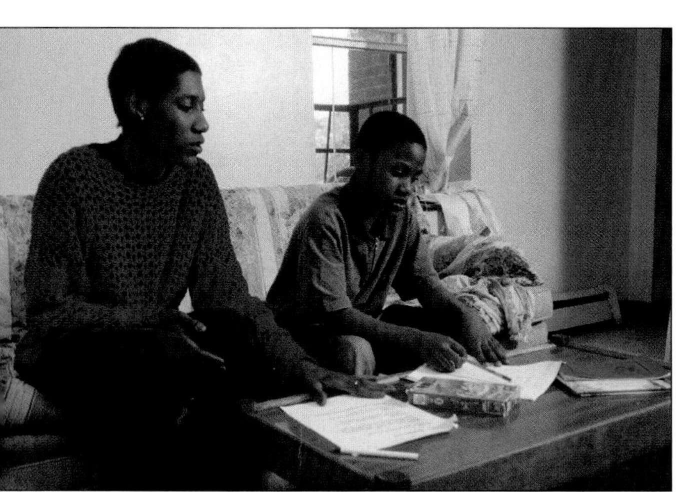

When families stress the value of reading, studying, and learning, their children are usually at an advantage in school.

Again, not all low-income families lack resources. Many of these families provide rich learning environments for their children. When parents of any SES level support and encourage their children—by reading to them, providing books and educational toys, taking the children to the library, making time and space for learning—the children tend to become better, more enthusiastic readers (Morrow, 1983; Peng & Lee, 1992; Shields, Gordon, & Dupree, 1983). White (1982) found that the actual behaviors of the parents were more predictive of their children's school achievement than income level or parents' occupation.

Check Yourself What is SES?

What is the relationship between SES and school achievement?

Ethnic and Racial Differences

Ethnicity is used to refer to "groups that are characterized in terms of a common nationality, culture, or language" (Betancourt & Lopez, 1993, p. 631). This shared sense of identity may be based on geography, religion, race, or language. We all have some ethnic heritage, whether our background is Italian, Jewish, Ukrainian, Hmong, Chinese, Japanese, Navajo, Hawaiian, Puerto Rican, Cuban, Hungarian, German, African, or Irish—to name only a few. **Race,** on the other hand, is defined as "a category composed of men and women who share biologically transmitted traits that are defined as socially significant" such as skin color or hair texture (Macionis, 1991, p. 308). Depending on the traits you measure and the theory you follow, there are between 3 and 300 races. In effect, race is a label people apply to themselves and to others based on appearances. There are no biologically pure races (Betancourt & Lopez, 1993).

Sociologists sometimes use the term **minority group** to label a group of people that receives unequal or discriminatory treatment. Strictly speaking, however, the term refers to a numerical minority compared to the total population. Referring to particular racial or ethnic groups as "minorities" is technically incorrect in some situations, because in certain places the "minority" group is actually the majority, for example, African Americans in Chicago or Mississippi. So the practice of referring to people as "minorities" because of their racial or ethnic heritage has been criticized because it is misleading.

CONNECT & EXTEND

TO THE RESEARCH
See *Educational Psychologist,* Winter 2001. This entire issue is devoted to "Schooling of Ethnic Minority Children and Youth." The guest editors are Judith Meece and Beth Kurtz-Costes.

The Changing Demographics: Cultural Differences

Between 1981 and 1990, the number of immigrants entering the United States was the largest ever. By the year 2020, almost two-thirds of the school-age population will be from African American, Asian, Latina/Latino, or other ethnic groups (Meece & Kurtz-Costes, 2001).

Ricardo Garcia (1991) compares culture to an iceberg. One-third of the iceberg is visible; the rest is hidden and unknown. The visible signs of culture, such as costumes and marriage traditions, represent only a small portion of the differences among cultures. Many of the differences are "below the surface." They are implicit, unstated, even unconscious biases and beliefs (Casanova, 1987; Kagan, 1983).

Cultures differ in rules for conducting interpersonal relationships, for example. In some groups, listeners give a slight affirmative nod of the head and perhaps an occasional "uh huh" to indicate they are listening carefully. But members of other cultures listen without giving acknowledgment, or with eyes downcast, as a sign of respect. In some cultures, high-status individuals initiate conversations and ask the questions, and low-status individuals only respond. In other cultures, the pattern is reversed.

Cultural influences are widespread and pervasive. Some psychologists even suggest that culture defines intelligence. For example, physical grace is essential in Balinese social life, so the ability to master physical movements is a mark of intelligence in that culture. Manipulating words and numbers is important in Western societies, so in these cultures such skills are indicators of intelligence (Gardner, 1983). But it would

CONNECT & EXTEND

TO **PRAXIS**™
THE LARGER COMMUNITY
(IV, B1,3)
Familiarize yourself with the predicted changes in the U.S. population over the next several decades. How are those changes likely to affect education? What can schools and teachers do to adjust positively to those changes?

Ethnicity A cultural heritage shared by a group of people.

Race A group of people who share common biological traits that are seen as self-defining by the people of the group.

Minority group A group of people who have been socially disadvantaged—not always a minority in actual numbers.

The visible signs of cultural differences represent only a small portion of the differences among cultures. Many are "below the surface" and have more to do with beliefs and attitudes about life.

be wrong to assume that every member of a cultural group is identical in beliefs, actions, or values. Eugene Garcia (2002) suggests that culture is "attributes that are made available to members of a group, but may not be shared by all members" (p. 93).

Cultural Conflicts. The differences between cultures may be very obvious, such as holiday customs, or they may be very subtle, such as how to get your turn in conversations. The more subtle and unconscious the difference, the more difficult it is to change or even recognize (Casanova, 1987). Cultural conflicts are usually about below-the-surface differences, because when subtle cultural differences meet, misunderstandings are common. Thus, the members of a different culture may be misperceived as rude, slow, or disrespectful.

CONNECT & EXTEND

TO OTHER CHAPTERS
This issue was considered in Chapter 3 when ethnic pride was discussed.

For example, Erickson and Shultz (1982) studied school counselors working with both students from the same culture and students from different cultures. The researchers found that the culturally different students did not nod and say "uh huh" as they listened to the counselors. Not having received this expected feedback, the counselors assumed that the culturally different students had not understood, and so the counselors repeated their remarks in simpler form. Again no nod, so the counselors simplified and repeated once more. When the students were interviewed afterwards, many said that the counselors had made them feel stupid. In fact, the counselors had decided that these students were not very bright. Neither participant realized that a subtle cultural difference in how to listen was probably to blame for the impressions. In contrast, when students and counselors shared the same background, discussions proceeded smoothly, without the cycles of simplifying and repeating. The students knew the counselors' tacit rules for listening, because both counselor and student had learned from the same teacher—their common culture.

CONNECT & EXTEND

TO THE RESEARCH
In the Chinese tradition, achievement is seen as dependent more on concentration, effort, and persistence than on talent. Centuries ago, Xu Gan, a revered Chinese scholar, said, "Will is the teacher of study and talent is the follower of study. If a person has no talent, [achievement] is possible. But if a person has no will, it is not worth talking about study" (Hess, Chih-Mei, & McDevitt, 1987, p. 180).

Cultural Compatibility. Not all cultural differences lead to clashes, however. A study comparing mothers in the People's Republic of China, Chinese American mothers, and Caucasian American mothers found dramatic differences in beliefs about motivation and the value of education (Hess, Chih-Mei, & McDevitt, 1987). For example, the mothers from the Republic of China attributed school failure to lack of effort more often than the Caucasian American mothers. The Chinese American mothers were in the middle, attributing failure to lack of effort more often than the Caucasian American mothers but less often than the Republic of China mothers.

This does not mean that all Chinese American children are perfectly equipped for the American school, however. Children may perform well on tests and assignments but feel uncomfortable in social situations, where subtle rules for interacting are not second nature to them (Casanova, 1987; Yee, 1992).

Ethnic and Racial Differences in School Achievement

A major concern in schools is that some ethnic groups consistently achieve below the average for all students. This pattern of results tends to hold for all standardized achievement tests, but the gaps have been narrowing over the past two to three decades. Level of educational attainment is improving too, as you can see in Figure 5.2. In 2000, 94% of Whites, 87% of African Americans, and 63% of Hispanic students between ages 25 and 29 had graduated from high school. But Whites still complete high school and college more frequently than African Americans and Hispanics.

Although there are consistent differences among ethnic groups on tests of cognitive abilities, most researchers agree that these differences are mainly the legacy of discrimination, the product of cultural mismatches, or a result of growing up in a low-SES environment. Because many minority group students are also economically disadvantaged, it is important to separate the effects of these two sets of influences on school achievement. When we compare students from different ethnic and racial groups who are all at the same SES level, then their achievement differences diminish (Gleitman, Fridlund, & Reisberg, 1999; Scarr & Carter-Saltzman, 1982).

CONNECT & EXTEND

TO OTHER CHAPTERS
Strategies for motivating minority group students are discussed in Chapter 10.

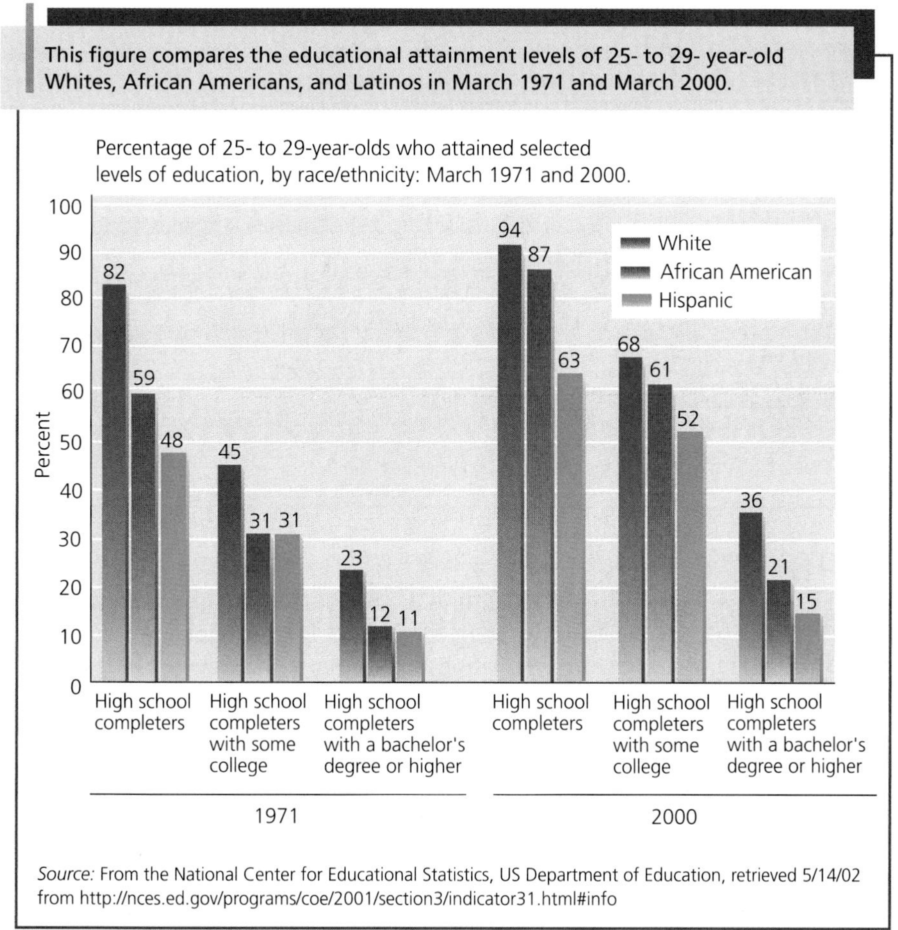

Figure 5.2 Educational Attainment

Family and Community Partnerships

Building Learning Communities

Joyce Epstein (1995) describes six types of family/school/community partnerships. The following guidelines are based on her six categories:

Parenting partnerships: Help all families establish home environments to support children as students.

Examples

1. Offer workshops, videos, courses, family literacy fairs, and other informational programs to help parents cope with parenting situations that they identify as important.
2. Establish family support programs to assist with nutrition, health, and social services.
3. Find ways to help families share information with the school about the child's cultural background, talents, and needs—learn from the families.

Communication: Design effective forms for school-to-home and home-to-school communication.

Examples

1. Make sure communications fit the needs of families. Provide translations, visual support, large print—whatever is needed to make communication effective.
2. Visit families in their territory after gaining their permission. Don't expect family members to come to school until a trusting relationship is established.
3. Balance messages about problems with communications of accomplishments and positive information.

Volunteering: Recruit and organize parent help and support.

Examples

1. Do an annual postcard survey to identify family talents, interests, times available, and suggestions for improvements.
2. Establish a structure (telephone tree, etc.) to keep all families informed. Make sure families without telephones are included.
3. If possible, set aside a room for volunteer meetings and projects.

Learning at home: Provide information and ideas for families about how to help children with schoolwork and learning activities.

Examples

1. Provide assignment schedules, homework policies, and tips on how to help with schoolwork without doing the work.
2. Get family input into curriculum planning—have idea and activity exchanges.
3. Send home learning packets and enjoyable learning activities, especially over holidays and summers.

Decision-making partnerships: Include families in school decisions, developing family and community leaders and representatives.

Examples

1. Create family advisory committees for the school with parent representatives.
2. Make sure all families are in a network with their representative.

Community partnerships: Identify and integrate resources and services from the community to strengthen school programs, family practices, and student learning and development.

Examples

1. Have students and parents research existing resources—build a database.
2. Identify service projects for students—explore service learning.
3. Identify community members who are school alumni and get them involved in school programs.

SOURCE: Excerpt from pp. 704–705, "School/Family/Community Partnerships: Caring for Children We Share," by J. L. Epstein, *Phi Delta Kappan, 76,* pp. 701–712.

How can you get to know the cultures of your students? The *Family and Community Partnerships Guidelines* give some ideas. Later in this chapter, we will explore other ways to make classrooms compatible with the home cultures of students. First, however, we need to see some of the effects of cultural conflicts and discrimination on student achievement.

The Legacy of Discrimination

What Would You Say? As part of your interview for a job in a very diverse middle school, the lead teacher for one of the home-based sections asks: "Describe how your life experiences will contribute to our goal to create an active anti-racist school system."

When we considered explanations for why low-SES students have trouble in school, we listed the low expectations and biases of teachers and fellow students. This has been the experience of many ethnic minority students as well. Imagine that the child described below is your own. What would you do?

> Almost forty years ago, in the city of Topeka, Kansas, a minister walked hand in hand with his seven-year-old daughter to an elementary school four blocks from their home. Linda Brown wanted to enroll in the 2nd grade, but the school refused to admit her. Instead, public school officials required her to attend another school two miles away. This meant that she had to walk six blocks to a bus stop, where she sometimes waited half an hour for the bus. In bad weather, Linda Brown would be soaking wet by the time the bus came; one day she became so cold at the bus stop that she walked back home. Why, she asked her parents, could she not attend the school only four blocks away? (Macionis, 1991, p. 307)

Her parents' answer to this question, with the help of other concerned families, was to file a suit challenging the school policy. You know the outcome of *Brown* v. *the Board of Education of Topeka.* "Separate but equal" schools for Black children were declared inherently unequal. Even though segregation in schools became illegal in 1954, about two-thirds of all African American students still attend schools where members of minority groups make up at least 50% of the student body. For about one-third of all Black students, this figure is over 90% (Schofield, 1991). This is because segregation in housing and neighborhoods persists and because some areas have drawn school boundary lines deliberately to separate school enrollments along racial lines (Calmore, 1986; Kantor & Lowe, 1995).

Years of research on the effects of desegregation have mostly shown that legally mandated integration is not a quick solution to the detrimental effects of centuries of racial inequality. Too often, minority group students are resegregated in low-ability tracks even in integrated schools. Simply putting people in the same building does not mean that they will come to respect each other or even that they will experience the same quality of education (Pettigrew, 1998; Schofield, 1991). But when minority group students are moved into high quality schools with a substantial proportion of middle-class peers and when these integrations start in early elementary school, the ethnic minority students benefit. They are more likely to achieve higher grades, attend integrated colleges, and earn more money as adults than comparable students who stayed in segregated schools. The quality of the school probably is the major factor influencing these positive outcomes (Schofield, 1995; Wells & Crain, 1994).

What is the legacy of unequal treatment and discrimination?

Nine-year-old Linda Brown, the plaintiff in *Brown* v. *Topeka Board of Education*.

The Development of Prejudice. The word *prejudice* is closely related to the word *prejudge*. **Prejudice** is a rigid and irrational generalization—a prejudgment—about an entire category of people (Macionis, 1994). Prejudice may be positive or negative;

Doonesbury BY GARRY TRUDEAU

Prejudice Prejudgment, or irrational generalization about an entire category of people.

that is, you can have positive as well as negative irrational beliefs about a group, but the word usually refers to negative attitudes. Prejudice may target people in particular racial, ethnic, religious, political, geographic, or language groups, or it may be directed toward the sex or sexual orientation of the individual. Racial prejudice is pervasive. The United States is a racist society, and this racism is not confined to one group (Clark, Anderson, Clark, & Williams, 1999).

There are many theories about how and why prejudice develops, but no complete explanation of prejudice (Duckitt, 1992). Current explanations combine personal and social factors. Extreme prejudice may develop as part of an **authoritarian personality**—a person who rigidly conforms to conventional values and believes that society is naturally competitive, with the "better" people rightly reaping the rewards (Duckitt, 1992, 1994; Macionis, 1994). A related source of prejudice is the human tendency to divide the social world into two categories—*us* and *them* or the *in-group* and the *out-group*. These divisions may be made on the basis of race, religion, sex, age, ethnicity, or even athletic team membership. We tend to see members of the out-group as inferior and different from us, but similar to each other—"they all look alike" (Lambert, 1995).

But prejudice is more than a personality trait or a tendency to form in-groups—it is also a set of cultural values. Children learn about valued traits and characteristics from their families, friends, teachers, and the world around them. Think back to your analysis of commercials—did you observe many women or people of color? For years, most of the models presented in books, films, television, and advertising were middle- and upper-class European Americans. People of different ethnic and racial backgrounds were seldom the "heroes" (Gerbner, Gross, Signorelli, & Morgan, 1986). This is changing. In 2002, the Oscar awards for best actress and best actor went to African Americans, but Denzel Washington won for his portrayal of a villain.

List 3 traits most characteristic of:

College freshmen ______________________

Politicians ______________________

Athletes ______________________

Buddhists ______________________

Members of the National Rifle Association ______________________

Prejudice is difficult to combat because it can be part of our thinking processes. You saw in Chapter 2 that children develop *schemas*—organized bodies of knowledge—about objects, events, and actions. We have schemas that organize our knowledge about drinking from a straw, people we know, the meaning of words, and so on. We can also form schemas about groups of people. When I were to asked you to list the traits most characteristic of college freshmen, politicians, athletes, Buddhists, and members of the National Rifle Association, you probably could generate a list. That list would show that you have a **stereotype**—a schema—that organizes what you know about the group (Wyler, 1988).

As with any schema, we use our stereotype to make sense of the world. You will see in Chapter 7 that having a schema allows you to process information more quickly and efficiently, but it also allows you to distort information to make it fit your schema better (Macrae, Milne, & Bodenhausen, 1994). This is the danger in racial and ethnic stereotypes. We notice information that confirms or agrees with our stereotype—our schema—and miss or dismiss information that does not fit. For example, if a juror has a negative stereotype of Asian Americans and is listening to evidence in the trial of an Asian American, the juror may interpret the evidence more negatively. The juror may actually forget testimony in favor of the defendant but remember more damaging testimony. Information that fits the stereotype is even processed more quickly (Anderson, Klatzky, & Murray, 1990; Baron, 1998).

Authoritarian personality Rigidly conforming to the belief that society is naturally competitive, with "better" people reaping its rewards.

Stereotype Schema that organizes knowledge or perceptions about a category.

Continuing Discrimination. Prejudice consists of attitudes, feelings, and beliefs (usually negative) about an entire category of people. **Discrimination** is unequal treatment of particular categories of people. Clearly, ethnic Americans face prejudice and discrimination in subtle or blatant ways every day. One of the most discouraging findings I encountered while writing this chapter is that less than 10% of the scientists, engineers, and mathematicians in the United States are either African American or Hispanic American—whereas more than 20% of the total population is from one of these groups. Even though their attitudes toward science and math are more favorable than those of White students, Black and Hispanic students begin to lose out in science and math as early as elementary school. They are chosen less often for gifted classes and acceleration or enrichment programs. They are more likely to be tracked into "basic skills" classes. As they progress through junior high, high school, and college, their paths take them farther and farther out of the pipeline that produces our scientists. If they do persist and become scientists or engineers, they, along with women, will still be paid less than Whites for the same work (National Science Foundation, 1996).

There is another problem caused by stereotypes and prejudice that can undermine academic achievement—stereotype threat.

CONNECT & EXTEND

TO **PRAXIS**™
RACIAL BIAS (IV, B4)
Describe the possible effects of racial discrimination and bias on minority students. What can teachers and schools do to address the lingering effects of this discrimination?

Stereotype Threat

Stereotype threat is an "apprehensiveness about confirming a stereotype" (Aronson, 2002, p. 282). The basic idea is that when stereotyped individuals are in situations where the stereotype applies, they bear an extra emotional and cognitive burden. The burden is the possibility of confirming the stereotype, either in the eyes of others or in their own eyes. Thus when girls are asked to solve complicated mathematics problems, for example, they are at risk of confirming widely held stereotypes that girls are inferior to boys in mathematics. It is not necessary that the individual even believe the stereotype. All that matters is that the person is *aware* of the stereotype and *cares about performing* well enough to disprove its unflattering implications (Aronson, Lustina, Good, Keough, Steele, & Brown, 1999). What are the results of stereotype threat? Recent research provides answers that should interest all teachers.

Short-Term Effects: Test Performance. In the short run, the fear that you might confirm a negative stereotype can induce test anxiety and undermine performance. In a series of experiments, Joshua Aronson, Claude Steele, and their colleagues have demonstrated that when African American or Latino college students are put in situations that induce stereotype threat, their performance suffers (Aronson, 2002; Aronson & Salinas, 1998; Aronson, Steele, Salinas, & Lustina, 1999; Steele & Aronson, 1995). For example, African American and White undergraduate subjects in an experiment at Stanford University were told that the test they were about to take would precisely measure their verbal ability. A similar group of subjects was told that the purpose of the test was to understand the psychology of verbal problem solving and not to assess individual ability. As shown in Figure 5.3 on page 168, when the test was presented as diagnostic of verbal ability, the African American students solved about half as many problems as the White students. In the non-threat situation, the two groups solved about the same number of problems.

All groups, not just minority group students, can be susceptible to stereotype threat. In another study, the subjects were White male college students who were very strong in mathematics. One group was told that the test they were taking would help experimenters determine why Asian students performed so much better than Whites on that particular test. Another group just took the test. The group that faced the stereotype threat of confirming that "Asians are better in math" scored significantly lower on the test (Aronson et al., 1999).

Discrimination Treating particular categories of people unequally.

Stereotype threat The extra emotional and cognitive burden that your performance in an academic situation might confirm a stereotype that others hold about you.

When African American college students were told that they were taking a test that would diagnose their verbal ability (stereotype threat), they solved about one-half as many problems as another group of African American students who were not told the test would assess ability. The performance of Caucasian students was not affected by the threat conditions.

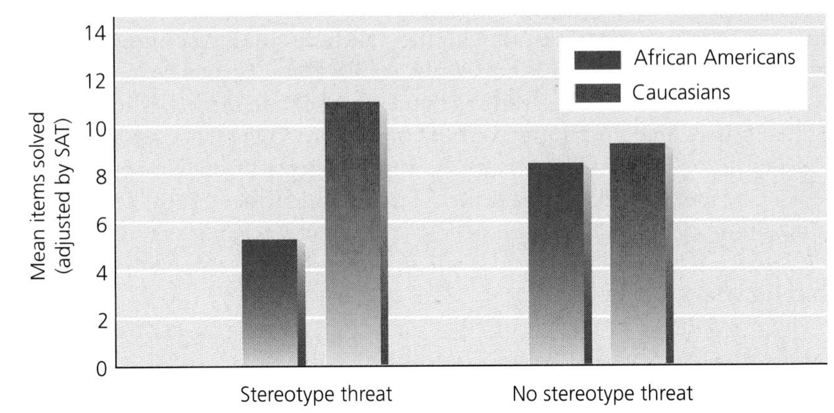

Source: From "The Effect of Stereotype Threat on the Standardized Test Performance of College Students," by J. Aronson, C. P. Steele, M. F. Salinas, and M. J. Lustina. In Elliot Aronson (Ed.), *Readings about the Social Animal* (4th ed.) © 1973, 1977, 1981, 1984, 1988, 1992, 1995, 1999 by Worth Publishers. Adapted by permission of the publisher.

Figure 5.3 The Impact of Stereotype Threat on College Students' Standardized Test Performance

How does stereotype threat affect test performance? One link is anxiety. Some studies have found higher levels of anxiety among African American elementary school and middle school students compared to White students. And higher anxiety is correlated with lower scores on tests. But does stereotype threat actually cause anxiety and does anxiety actually lead to lower scores? Jason Osborne (2001) studied a large representative national sample of White, African American, and Latino high school seniors who took achievement tests and tests of anxiety at the same time. The White students scored significantly higher, but anxiety played a role in those differences. Even after controlling for prior achievement in school, anxiety explained almost one-third of the racial differences in the scores. Anxiety and distraction appeared to be the main problems in the studies of college students, too. The African American students were more likely to be thinking about the stereotypes as they tried to work (Spencer, Steele, & Quinn, 1999).

Long-Term Effects: Disidentification. As we will see in Chapter 10, students often develop self-defeating strategies to protect their self-esteem about academics. They withdraw, claim to not care, exert little effort—they *disidentify* or psychologically disengage from success in the domain and claim "math is for nerds" or "school is for losers." There is evidence that African Americans are more likely than Whites to disidentify with academics (Major & Schmader, 1998; Ogbu, 1997). Once students define academics as "uncool," it is unlikely they will exert the effort needed for real learning.

Combating Stereotype Threat. Stereotypes are pervasive and difficult to change. Rather than wait for changes, it may be better to acknowledge that these images exist, at least in the eyes of many, and give students ways of coping with the stereotypes. In Chapter 10 we will discuss test anxiety and how to overcome the negative effects of anxiety. Many of those strategies are appropriate for helping students resist stereotype threat.

Aronson (2002) demonstrated the powerful effects of changing beliefs about intelligence. In their study, African American and White undergraduates were asked to write letters to "at-risk" middle school students to encourage them to persist in school. Some of the undergraduates were given evidence that intelligence is *improveable* and encouraged to communicate this information to their pen pals. Others were given information about multiple intelligences, but not told that these multiple abilities can be improved. The middle school students were not real, but the process of writing persuasive letters about improving intelligence proved powerful. The African American college students, and the White students to a lesser extent, who were encouraged to believe that intelligence can be improved had higher grade point averages and reported greater enjoyment of and engagement in school when contacted at the end of the next school quarter. Thus, believing that intelligence can be improved might inoculate students against stereotype threat.

Check Yourself Distinguish between ethnicity and race.

How can ethnicity affect school performance?

Distinguish among prejudice, discrimination, and stereotype threat.

In the next section we examine another difference that is the source of stereotypes—gender.

Girls and Boys: Differences in the Classroom

What Would You Say? You are interviewing for a job in a 2nd/3rd grade in an affluent district. After a few questions, the principal asks, "Do you believe that boys and girls learn differently?" How would you answer?

While I was proofreading this very page for a previous edition, riding cross-country on a train, the conductor stopped beside my seat. He said, "I'm sorry, dear, for interrupting your homework, but do you have a ticket?" I had to smile at his (I'm sure unintended) sexism. I doubt that he made the same comment to the man across the aisle writing on his legal pad. Like racial discrimination, messages of sexism can be subtle. In this section we will examine how men and women are socialized and the role of teachers in providing an equitable education for both sexes.

Gender-Role Identity

Men and women are different. Years of research on personality indicates that men *on average* are more assertive, active, and aggressive in their actions. Women are more extroverted, anxious, compliant, emotionally sensitive, and dependent; their aggressions are expressed more in relationships (Berk, 2002; Eisenberg & Fabes, 1998). There also appear to be some differences in verbal and spatial abilities between the sexes. The origins and meanings of these differences are hotly debated. Gender-role identity is part of the discussion.

CONNECT & EXTEND

TO THE RESEARCH
For a lively debate on the terminology of gender and sex, see the March 1993 issue of *Psychological Science.*

The word *gender* usually refers to traits and behaviors that a particular culture judges to be appropriate for men and for women. In contrast, *sex* refers to biological differences (Brannon, 2002; Deaux, 1993). **Gender-role identity** is the image each individual has of himself or herself as masculine or feminine in characteristics—a part of self-concept. People with a "feminine" identity would rate themselves high on characteristics usually associated with females, such as "sensitive" and low on characteristics traditionally associated with males, such as "forceful." Most people see themselves in gender-typed terms, as high on *either* masculine or feminine characteristics.

Gender-role identity Beliefs about characteristics and behaviors associated with one sex as opposed to the other.

Gender schemas often have become barriers to success when boys and girls avoid activities not associated with their gender. Recognizing these potential barriers has allowed children's choices to become less gender-driven.

Some children and adults, however, are more **androgynous**—they rate themselves high on *both* masculine and feminine traits. They can be forceful or sensitive, depending on the situation. Recently, some psychologists have suggested that measures of androgyny actually assess *instrumental* (goal-directed) and *expressive* (social-emotional) traits, not masculine and feminine traits (Spence & Buckner, 2000).

How do gender-role identities develop? It is likely that biology plays a role. Very early, hormones affect activity level and aggression, with boys tending to prefer active, rough, noisy play. Play styles lead young children to prefer same-sex play partners with similar styles, so by age 4, children spend three times as much play time with same-sex playmates as with opposite-sex playmates and by age 6, the ratio is 11 to 1 (Benenson, 1993; Maccoby, 1998). Of course, these are averages and individuals do not always fit the average. In addition, many other factors—social and cognitive—affect gender-role identity.

Both parents play more roughly and vigorously with sons than they do with daughters. Parents tend to touch male infants more at first; later, they keep male toddlers at a greater distance than females (Jacklin, DiPietro, & Maccoby, 1984). Parents are more likely to react positively to assertive behavior on the part of their sons and emotional sensitivity in their daughters (Brody, 1999; Fagot & Hagan, 1991). Through their interactions with family, peers, teachers, and the environment in general, children begin to form **gender schemas,** or organized networks of knowledge about what it means to be male or female (see Figure 5.4). Gender schemas help the children make sense of the world and guide their behavior. So a young girl whose schema for "girls" includes "girls play with dolls and not with trucks" or "girls can't be scientists" will pay attention to, remember, and interact more with dolls than trucks, and she may avoid science activities (Berk, 2002: Liben & Signorella, 1993; Martin & Little, 1990).

Gender-Role Stereotyping in the Preschool Years. Different treatment of the sexes and gender-role stereotyping continue in early childhood. Researchers have

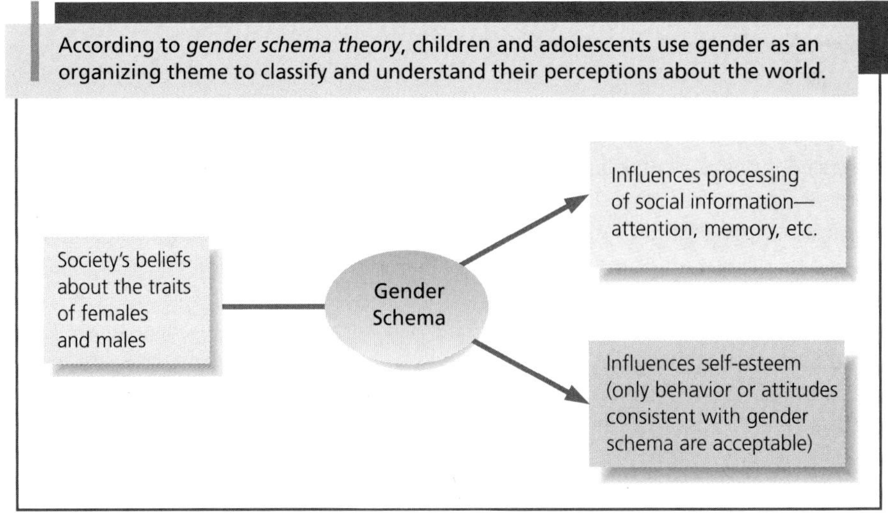

According to *gender schema theory*, children and adolescents use gender as an organizing theme to classify and understand their perceptions about the world.
Society's beliefs about the traits of females and males
Gender Schema
Influences processing of social information—attention, memory, etc.
Influences self-esteem (only behavior or attitudes consistent with gender schema are acceptable)

Figure 5.4 Gender Schema Theory

Androgynous Having some typically male and some typically female characteristics apparent in one individual.

Gender schemas Organized networks of knowledge about what it means to be male or female.

found that boys are given more freedom to roam the neighborhood, and they are not protected for as long a time as girls from potentially dangerous activities such as playing with sharp scissors or crossing the street alone. Parents quickly come to the aid of their daughters, but are more likely to insist that their sons handle problems themselves. Thus, independence and initiative seem to be encouraged more in boys than in girls (Brannon, 2002; Block, 1983; Fagot, Hagan, Leinbach, & Kronsberg, 1985).

And then there are the toys! Walk through any store's toy section and see what is offered to girls and boys. Dolls and kitchen sets for girls and toy weapons for boys have been with us for decades, but what about even more subtle messages? Margot Mifflin went shopping for a toy for her 4-year-old that was not gender-typed and found a Wee Waffle farm set. Then she discovered that "the farmer plugged into a round hole in the driver's seat of the tractor, but the mother—literally a square peg in a round hole—didn't" (Mifflin, 1999, p. 1). But we cannot blame the toy makers alone. Adults buying for children favor gender-typed toys and fathers tend to discourage young sons from playing with "girl's" toys (Brannon, 2002).

By age 4 or 5, children have developed a gender schema that describes what clothes, games, toys, behaviors, and careers are "right" for boys and girls—and these ideas can be quite rigid (Brannon, 2002). Many of my student teachers are surprised when they hear young children talk about gender roles. Even in this era of great progress toward equal opportunity, a preschool girl is more likely to tell you she wants to become a nurse than to say she wants to be an engineer. After she had given a lecture on the dangers of sex stereotyping in schools, a colleague of mine brought her young daughter to her college class. The students asked the little girl, "What do you want to be when you grow up?" The child immediately replied, "A doctor," and her professor/mother beamed with pride. Then the girl whispered to the students in the front row, "I really want to be a nurse, but my Mommy won't let me." Actually, this is a common reaction for young children. Preschoolers tend to have more stereotyped notions of sex roles than older children, and all ages seem to have more rigid and traditional ideas about male occupations than about what females do (Martin, 1989).

Gender Bias in the Curriculum. During the elementary school years, children continue to learn about what it means to be male or female. Unfortunately, schools often foster these **gender biases** in a number of ways. Most of the textbooks produced for the early grades before 1970 portrayed both males and females in stereotyped roles. One study found that there were four times more stories about male characters than about females; in addition, the females tended to be shown in the home, behaving passively and expressing fear or incompetence (*Women on Words and Images*, 1975).

Publishers have established guidelines to prevent these problems, but it still makes sense to check your teaching materials for stereotypes. For example, even though children's books now have an equal number of males and females as central characters, there still are more males in the titles and the illustrations, and the characters (especially the boys) continue to behave in stereotypic ways. Boys are more aggressive and argumentative, and girls are more expressive and affectionate. Girl characters sometimes cross gender roles to be more active, but boy characters seldom show "feminine" expressive traits (Brannon, 2002; Evans & Davies, 2000). Videos, computer programs, and testing materials also often feature boys more than girls (Meece, 2002).

Another "text" that students read long before they arrive in your classroom is television. Remember the commercial count break I asked you to take earlier? (No—you can't take another one here.) A content analysis of television commercials found that White male characters were more prominent than any other group. Even when only the actor's voice could be heard, men were 10 times more likely to narrate commercials. And the same pattern of men as the "voice of authority" on television

CONNECT & EXTEND

TO **PRAXIS**™
GENDER BIAS (IV, B4)
There has been much debate in the news media over possible gender bias in schools. What can you as a teacher do to reduce or eliminate gender bias and its effects?

CONNECT & EXTEND

TO YOUR TEACHING PORTFOLIO
Do you consider commercials an influence on the development of sex roles?

Gender biases Different views of males and females, often favoring one gender over the other.

CONNECT & EXTEND

TO **PRAXIS**™
CULTURAL AND GENDER DIFFERENCES IN THE CLASSROOM (III, B)
What are the sources of possible miscommunication between students and teachers in the classroom because of cultural or gender differences? Identify steps a teacher can take to minimize such problems.

occurred in the United Kingdom, Europe, Australia, and Asia. Women were more likely than men to be shown as dependent on men and often were depicted at home (Brannon, 2002). So, before and after going to school, students are likely to encounter texts that overepresent males.

Sex Discrimination in Classrooms. There has been quite a bit of research on teachers' treatment of male and female students. One of the best documented findings of the past 25 years is that teachers interact more with boys than with girls. This is true from preschool to college. Teachers ask more questions of males, give males more feedback (praise, criticism, and correction), and give more specific and valuable comments to boys. As girls move through the grades, they have less and less to say. By the time students reach college, men are twice as likely to initiate comments as women (Bailey, 1993; Sadker & Sadker, 1994, 1986b; Wingate, 1986). The effect of these differences is that from preschool through college, girls, on the average, receive 1,800 fewer hours of attention and instruction than boys (Sadker, Sadker, & Klein, 1991). Of course, these differences are not evenly distributed. Some boys, generally high-achieving White students, receive more than their share, whereas high-achieving girls receive the least teacher attention. Minority group boys, like girls, tend to receive much less attention from the teacher.

The imbalances of teacher attention given to boys and girls are particularly dramatic in math and science classes. In one study, boys were questioned in science class 80% more often than girls (Baker, 1986). Teachers wait longer for boys to answer and give more detailed feedback to the boys (Meece, 2002; Sadker & Sadker, 1994). Boys also dominate the use of equipment in science labs, often dismantling the apparatus before the girls in the class have a chance to perform the experiments (Rennie & Parker, 1987).

Stereotypes are perpetuated in many ways, some obvious, some subtle. Boys with high scores on standardized math tests are more likely to be put in the high-ability math group than girls with the same scores. Guidance counselors, parents, and teachers often do not protest at all when a bright girl says she doesn't want to take any more math or science courses, but when a boy of the same ability wants to forget about math or science, they will object. More women than men are teachers, but men tend to be the administrators, coaches, and advanced math and science teachers. In these subtle ways, students' stereotyped expectations for themselves are reinforced (Sadker & Sadker, 1994).

Sex Differences in Mental Abilities

From infancy through the preschool years, most studies find few differences between boys and girls in overall mental and motor development or in specific abilities. During the school years and beyond, psychologists find no differences in general intelligence on the standard measures—these tests have been designed and standardized to minimize sex differences. However, scores on some tests of specific abilities show sex differences. For example, from elementary through high school, girls score higher than boys on tests of reading and writing and fewer girls require remediation in reading (Berk, 2002, Halpern, 2000). Diane Halpern and Mary LaMay (2000) summarized the research:

> Although there are no sex differences in general intelligence, reliable differences are found on some tests of cognitive abilities. Many of the tasks that assess the ability to manipulate visual images in working memory show an advantage for males, whereas many of the tasks that require retrieval from long-term memory and the acquisition and use of verbal information show a female advantage. Large effects favoring males are also found on advanced tests of mathematical achievement, especially with highly select samples. Males are also overrepresented in some types of mental retardation. (p. 229)

It is clear that academically gifted boys perform better than girls on advanced mathematics tests. In a special program to identify advanced mathematics students, the Scholastic Assessment Test is given to 7th and 8th graders who seem gifted in mathematics. Results of over 40,000 tests so far indicate that boys are twice as likely as girls to score above 500 and 13 times as likely to score above 700 on that test. In fact, the scores of males tend to be more variable in general, so there are more males than females with very high *and* very low scores on tests (Berk, 2002; Willingham & Cole, 1997). Even with these test score differences, however, girls tend to get higher grades than boys in mathematics classes (Halpern, 2000).

In another area, males have the clear advantage. When we look at the results of Advanced Placement tests, we see that boys are almost 7% more likely than girls to earn a score of 4 or 5 that earns college credit at most institutions. This means that thousands of girls have to start with more basic courses in college, take the extra time, pay the extra money, and perhaps not reach the advanced levels needed for some careers. One study found that the major reasons for the differences could be traced to the girls' lack of interest in the subjects and lower self-concept in the areas tested, particularly science and mathematics (Ackerman, Bowen, Beier, & Kanfer, 2001). All teachers need to be sure that both girls and boys realize the value of advanced knowledge in opening doors to advanced education.

What is the basis for the differences? The answers are complex. For example, males on average are better on tests that require mental rotation of a figure in space, prediction of the trajectories of moving objects, and navigating. Some researchers argue that evolution has favored these skills in males (Buss, 1995; Geary, 1995, 1999) but others relate these skills to males' more active play styles and to their participation in athletics (Linn & Hyde, 1989; Newcombe & Baenninger, 1990; Stumpf, 1995).

There is a caution, however. In most studies of sex differences, race and socioeconomic status are not taken into account. When racial groups are studied separately, African American females outperform African American males in high school mathematics; there is little or no difference in the performance of Asian American girls and boys in math or science (Grossman & Grossman, 1994; Yee, 1992).

CONNECT & EXTEND

TO THE RESEARCH

See Latham, A. S. (1998). Gender differences on assessments. *Educational Leadership, 55*(4), 88–89.

Eliminating Gender Bias

There is some evidence that teachers treat girls and boys differently in mathematics classes. For example, some elementary school teachers spend more academic time with boys in math and with girls in reading. In one study, high school geometry teachers directed most of their questions to boys, even though the girls asked questions and volunteered answers more often. Several researchers have found that some teachers tend to accept wrong answers from girls, saying, in effect, "Well, at least you tried." But when boys give the wrong answer, the teachers are more likely to say, "Try harder! You can figure this out." These messages, repeated time and again, can convince girls that they just aren't cut out for mathematics ("Girls' Math Achievement," 1986; Horgan, 1995). If you are like a few of the student teachers I have supervised who "really hate math," please don't pass this attitude on to your students. You may have been the victim of sex discrimination yourself. The *Guidelines* on page 174 provide additional ideas about avoiding sexism in your teaching. Some are taken from Rop (1997/1998).

Some popular authors have argued that boys and girls learn differently and that schools tend to reward the passive, cooperative behaviors of girls (Gurian, 2001). Other people believe that schools "shortchange" girls and "fail to be fair" (AAUW, 1991; Sadker & Sadker, 1995). The *Point/Counterpoint* on page 175 examines these issues.

CONNECT & EXTEND

TO YOUR TEACHING PORTFOLIO

- Sadker, D. (1998). Gender equity: still knocking at the classroom door. *Educational Leadership, 56*(7), 22–27.
- Special section on Gender Equity, *Phi Delta Kappan,* Vol. 84, No. 3, 2002, pp. 235–245.

Check Yourself What is gender-role identity?

How do gender-role identities develop?

Are there sex differences in cognitive abilities?

GUIDELINES Avoiding Sexism in Teaching

Check to see if textbooks and other materials you are using present an honest view of the options open to both males and females.

Examples

1. Are both males and females portrayed in traditional and nontraditional roles at work, at leisure, and at home?
2. Discuss your analyses with students, and ask them to help you find sex role biases in other materials—magazine advertising, TV programs, news reporting, for example.

Watch for any unintended biases in your own classroom practices.

Examples

1. Do you group students by sex for certain activities? Is the grouping appropriate?
2. Do you call on one sex or the other for certain answers—boys for math and girls for poetry, for example?
3. Monitor your metaphors. Ask students to "tackle the problem" and also to "cook up a solution."

Look for ways in which your school may be limiting the options open to male or female students.

Examples

1. What advice is given by guidance counselors to students in course and career decisions?
2. Is there a good sports program for both girls and boys?
3. Are girls encouraged to take advanced placement courses in science and mathematics? Boys in English and foreign languages?

Use gender-free language as much as possible.

Examples

1. Do you speak of "law-enforcement officer" and "mail carrier" instead of "policeman" and "mailman"?
2. Do you name a committee "head" instead of a "chairman"?

Provide role models.

Examples

1. Assign articles in professional journals written by female research scientists or mathematicians.
2. Have recent female graduates who are majoring in science, math, engineering or other technical fields come to class to talk about college.
3. Create electronic mentoring programs for both male and female students to connect them with adults working in areas of interest to the students.

Make sure all students have a chance to do complex, technical work.

Examples

1. Experiment with same-sex lab groups so girls do not always end up as the secretaries, boys as the technicians.
2. Rotate jobs in groups or randomly assign responsibilities.

Language Differences in the Classroom

In the classroom, quite a bit happens through language. Communication is at the heart of teaching, but as we have seen in this chapter, culture affects communication. In this section, we will examine two kinds of language differences—dialect differences and bilingualism.

CONNECT & EXTEND

TO THE RESEARCH
See the Autumn 2000 issue of *Theory Into Practice* on "Children and Languages in School." See http://www.coe.ohio-state.edu/TIP. This journal is especially for educators.

Dialects

A **dialect** is a language variation spoken by a particular ethnic, social, or regional group and is an element of the group's collective identity (Ogbu, 1999). The rules for a language define how words should be pronounced, how meaning should be expressed, and the ways the basic parts of speech should be put together to form sentences. Dialects appear to differ in their rules in these areas, but it is important to remember that these differences are not errors. Each dialect within a language is just as logical, complex, and rule-governed as the standard form of the language (often called **standard speech**). An example of this is the use of the double negative. In Standard English, the redundancy of the double negative is not allowed. But in many dialects, such as Black American English, just as in many other languages (for instance, Russian, French, Spanish, and Hungarian), the double negative is required by the grammatical rules. To say "I don't want anything" in Spanish, you must literally say, "I don't want nothing," or "No quiero nada."

Dialect Rule-governed variation of a language spoken by a particular group.

Standard speech The most generally accepted and used form of a given language.

Point/Counterpoint — Do Boys and Girls Learn Differently?

As we have seen, there are a number of documented sex differences in mental abilities. Do these translate into different ways of learning and thus different needs in the classroom?

Point

Yes, boys and girls learn differently.

Since at least the 1960s, there have been questions about whether schools serve boys well. Accusations that schools were trying to destroy "boys culture" and forcing "feminine, frilly content" on boys caused some public concern (Connell, 1996). More recently, according to Connell:

> *Discrimination against girls has ended, the argument runs. Indeed, thanks to feminism, girls have special treatment and special programs. Now, what about the boys? It is boys who are slower to learn to read, more likely to drop out of school, more likely to be disciplined, more likely to be in programs for children with special needs. In school it is girls who are doing better, boys who are in trouble—and special programs for boys that are needed. (1996, p. 207)*

In their book, *Boys and Girls Learn Differently,* Michael Gurian and Patricia Henley (2001) make a similar argument that boys and girls need different teaching approaches. Reviewing the book for The Men's Resource Network, J. Steven Svoboda (2001) writes:

> *Our schools seem to be creating overt depression in girls and covert depression in boys. Through violence, male hormones and brains cry out for a different school promoting closer bonding, smaller classes, more verbalization, less male isolation, better discipline, and more attention to male learning styles. Most of all, boys need men in their schools. (90% of elementary teachers are female.) They need male teachers, male teaching assistants, male volunteers from the parents or grandparents, and older male students. Peer mentoring across grades helps everybody involved.*

For girls, Gurian and Henley recommend developing their leadership abilities, encouraging girls to enjoy healthy competition, providing extra access to technology, and helping them understand the impact of the media on their self-images.

Counterpoint

No, differences are too small or inconsistent to have educational implications.

Many of Gurian and Henley's claims about sex differences in learning are based on sex differences in the brain. But John Bruer (1999) cautions that

> *Although males are superior to females at mentally rotating objects, this seems to be the only spatial task for which psychologists have found such a difference. Moreover, when they do find gender differences, these differences tend to be very small. . . . The scientific consensus among psychologists and neuroscientists who conduct these studies is that whatever gender differences exist may have interesting consequences for the scientific study of the brain, but they have no practical or instructional consequences.*

In fact, there are boys who thrive in schools and boys who do not; girls who are strong in mathematics and girls who have difficulties; boys who excel in languages and those who do not. There is some evidence that the activities used to teach math may make a difference for girls. Elementary age girls may do better in math if they learn in cooperative as opposed to competitive activities. Certainly it makes sense to balance both cooperative and competitive approaches so that students who learn better each way have equal opportunities (Fennema & Peterson, 1988).

What do you think? Vote online at **www.ablongman.com/woolfolk**

Dialects and Pronunciation. Another area in which nonstandard dialects differ from Standard English is pronunciation, which can lead to spelling problems. In Black American English and in Southern dialects, for instance, there is less attention paid to pronouncing the ends of words than in Standard English. A lack of attention to final consonants, such as *s*, can lead to failure to indicate possession, third-person singular verbs, and plurals in the standard way. So *John's book* might be *John book,* and words such as *thinks, wasps,* and *lists* may be difficult to pronounce. When endings are not pronounced, there are more *homonyms* (words that sound alike but have different meanings) in the student's speech than the unknowing teacher may expect; *spent* and *spend* might sound alike, for example. Even without the confusions caused by dialect differences, there are many homonyms in English. Usually, special attention is given to words such as these when they come up in the spelling lesson. If teachers are aware of the special homonyms in student dialects, they can teach these differences directly.

Dialects and Teaching. What does all of this mean for teachers? How can they cope with linguistic diversity in the classroom? First, they can be sensitive to their own possible negative stereotypes about children who speak a different dialect. Taylor (1983) found that teachers who held negative attitudes toward "Black English" gave lower ratings for reading comprehension to students using that dialect, even when the accuracy of the students' performance was the same as that of Standard English speakers. Second, teachers can ensure comprehension by repeating instructions using different words and by asking students to paraphrase instructions or give examples.

CONNECT & EXTEND

TO THE RESEARCH
Harvard Graduate School of Education (1991, November/December). Kids who speak Spanish: Schools that help them learn. *Harvard Education Newsletter, 7*(6), 1–4. *Focus Question:* What are the characteristics of schools that help Spanish-speaking students learn?

But what about the use of home language in the classroom? The best teaching approach seems to be to focus on understanding the children and to accept their dialect as a valid and correct language system, but to teach as an alternative the standard form of English (or whatever the dominant language is in your country). For example, Lisa Delpit (1995) describes Martha Demientieff, a Native Alaskan teacher of Athabaskan children in a small village. The teacher's goal is for her students to become fluent in both their dialect, which she calls "Heritage English," and the "Formal English" of employers and others outside the village. She explains to her students that people outside the village will judge them by the way they talk and write. She goes on to explain:

> We have to feel sorry for them because they have only one way to talk. We're going to learn two ways to say things. . . . One will be our Heritage way. The other will be Formal English. Then when we go to get jobs, we'll be able to talk like those people who only know and can only listen to one way. Maybe after we get the jobs we can help them to learn how it feels to have another language, like ours, that feels so good. We'll talk like them when we have to, but we'll always know our way is best. (p. 41)

Moving between two speech forms is called **code-switching**—something we all have learned to do. Sometimes the code is formal speech for educational or professional communication. Sometimes the code is informal for talk among friends and family. Sometimes the codes are different dialects. Even young children recognize variations in codes. Lisa Delpit (1995) describes the reaction of one of her first grade students to her very first reading lesson. After she carefully recited the memorized introduction from the teacher's manual, a student raised his hand and asked, "Teacher, how come you talkin' like a white person? You talkin' just like my momma talk when she get on the phone."

Learning the standard speech is easy for most children whose original language is a dialect, as long as they have good models, clear instruction, and opportunities for authentic practice. The *Guidelines* give other ideas.

CONNECT & EXTEND

TO YOUR TEACHING PORTFOLIO
Is the increasing cultural plurality of the United States making the learning of foreign languages (namely, Spanish) more important in U.S. schools than was the case in the past?

Bilingualism

Bilingualism is a topic that sparks heated debates and touches many emotions. One reason is the changing demographics discussed earlier in this chapter. About 5% of all school-age children speak a language other than English at home (Meece & Kurtz-Costes, 2001). In the past 10 years, there has been a 65% increase in the number of Spanish speaking students and almost a 100% increase in students who speak Asian languages. In some states almost one-fourth of all students speak a first language other than English—usually Spanish (Gersten, 1996a). By 2050, about one-fourth of the United States population is expected to be Latina/o (Yetman, 1999).

Two terms that you will see associated with bilingualism are **English as a second language (ESL)**, describing classes for students whose primary language is not English, and **limited English proficiency (LEP)**, referring to students whose English skills are limited.

What Does Bilingualism Mean? There are disagreements about the meaning of *bilingualism*. Some definitions focus exclusively on a language-based meaning: Bilingual people, or bilinguals, speak two languages. But this limited definition minimizes

Code-switching Successful switching between cultures in language, dialect, or nonverbal behaviors to fit the situation.

Bilingualism Speaking two languages fluently.

English as a second language (ESL) Designation for programs and classes to teach English to students who are not native speakers of English.

Limited English proficiency (LEP) Descriptive term for students who have limited mastery of English.

GUIDELINES Dialects in the Classroom

1. Become familiar with features of the students' dialect. This will allow you to understand students better and to distinguish a reading miscue (a noncomprehension feature) from a comprehension error. Students should not be interrupted during the oral reading process. Correction of comprehension features is best done after the reading segment.
2. Allow students to listen to a passage or story first. This can be done in two ways: (a) finish the story and then ask comprehension questions, or (b) interrupt the story at key comprehension segments and ask students to predict the outcome.
3. Use predictable stories, which can be familiar episodes in literature, music, or history. They can be original works or experiential readers.
4. Use visual aids to enhance comprehension. Visual images, whether pictures or words, will aid word recognition and comprehension.
5. Use "cloze procedure" deletions to focus on vocabulary and meaning. Cloze procedures are selected deletions of words from a passage in order to focus on a specific text feature. *Examples:* (a) The little red hen found an ear of corn. The little red _______ said, "Who will dry the ear of _______?" (vocabulary focus) (b) Today I feel like a (*noun*). (grammar focus) (c) There was a (*pain*) in the pit of his stomach. (semantic focus)
6. Allow students to retell the story or passage in various speech styles. Have students select different people to whom they would like to retell the story (family member, principal, friend), and assist them in selecting synonyms most appropriate to each audience. This allows both teacher and student to become language authorities.
7. Integrate reading, speaking, and writing skills whenever possible.
8. Use the computer (if available) as a time-on-task exercise. The computer can effectively assist in teaching the reading techniques of skimming (general idea), scanning (focused reference), reading for comprehension (mastery of total message), and critical reading (inference and evaluation).
9. Teach students directly how to switch between home and school dialects.
10. Give practice with feedback and correction in using school dialect. All learning takes practice.

SOURCE: From *Comprehensive Multicultural Education, Theory and Practice* (2nd ed.) (pp. 234–235), by C. I. Bennett. Copyright © 1990 by Allyn and Bacon. Also "Beyond Language: Ebonics, Proper English, and Identity in a Black-American Speech Community," by J. U. Ogbu, *American Educational Research Journal, 36*, p. 178. Copyright © by American Educational Research Association. Adapted with permission of the publisher.

the significant problems that bilingual students face. Consider the words of these two students:

> A 9th-grade boy, who recently arrived in California from Mexico: "There is so much discrimination and hate. Even from other kids from Mexico who have been here longer. They don't treat us like brothers. They hate even more. It makes them feel more like natives. They want to be American. They don't want to speak Spanish to us; they already know English and how to act. If they are with us, other people will treat them more like wetbacks, so they try to avoid us." (Olsen, 1988, p. 36)
>
> A 10th-grade Chinese-American girl who had been in America for several years: "I don't know who I am. Am I the good Chinese daughter? Am I an American teenager? I always feel I am letting my parents down when I am with my friends because I act so American, but I also feel that I will never really be an American. I never feel really comfortable with myself anymore." (Olsen, 1988, p. 30)

The experiences of these two students show that there is more to being bilingual than just speaking two languages. You must also be able to move back and forth between two cultures while still maintaining a sense of your own identity (Hakuta & Garcia, 1989). Being bilingual and bicultural means mastering the knowledge necessary to communicate in two cultures as well as dealing with potential discrimination. As a teacher, you will have to help your students learn all these skills. And often, being bilingual causes students to appear less capable in the classroom, as they struggle to master two languages. The *Reaching Every Student* feature gives ideas about how to recognize giftedness in students who are learning English.

Becoming Bilingual. Proficiency in a second language has two separate aspects: face-to-face communication (known as "contextualized language skills") and academic

CONNECT & EXTEND

TO PROFESSIONAL JOURNALS
Thomas, W. P., & Collier, V. P. (1998). Two languages are better than one. *Educational Leadership, 55*(4), 23–27. This article makes the case that native and non-native speakers of English benefit greatly from learning together in two languages.

~ Reaching Every Student ~

Recognizing Giftedness in Bilingual Students

To identify gifted bilingual students, you can use a case study or portfolio approach in order to collect a variety of information, including interviews with parents and peers, formal and informal assessments, samples of student work and perfomances, and student self-assessments. The following checklist might add useful information.

_____ Learn English quickly
_____ Takes risks in trying to communicate in English
_____ Practices English skills by him- or herself
_____ Initiates conversations with native English speakers
_____ Does not frustrate easily
_____ Is curious about new words or phrases and practices them
_____ Questions word meanings; for example, "How can a bat be an animal and also something you use to hit a ball?"
_____ Looks for similarities between words in their native language and English
_____ Is able to modify his or her language for less capable English speakers
_____ Uses English to demonstrate leadership skills; for example, uses English to resolve disagreements and to facilitate cooperative learning groups
_____ Prefers to work independently or with students whose level of English proficiency is higher than his or hers
_____ Is able to express abstract verbal concepts with a limited English vocabulary
_____ Is curious about American culture
_____ Is able to use English in a creative way; for example, can make puns, poems, jokes, or original stories in English
_____ Becomes easily bored with routine tasks or drill work
_____ Has a great deal of curiosity
_____ Is persistent; sticks to a task
_____ Has good physical coordination
_____ Is independent and self-sufficient
_____ Has a long attention span
_____ Becomes absorbed with self-selected problems, topics, and issues
_____ Retains, easily recalls, and uses new information
_____ Demonstrates social maturity, especially in the home or community

SOURCE: From *Researching New Horizons: Gifted and Talented Education for Culturally and Linguistically Diverse Students,* by Jaime A. Castellano and Eva I. Diaz. Published by Allyn & Bacon, Boston, MA. Copyright © 2002 by Pearson Education. Adapted by permission of the publisher.

uses of language such as reading and doing grammar exercises ("decontextualized language skills") (Snow, 1987). It takes students about two to three years in a good-quality program to be able to communicate face-to-face in a second language, but mastering decontextualized, academic language skills in the new language takes five to seven years. So students who seem in conversation to "know" a second language may still have great difficulty with complex schoolwork in that language (Cummins, 1994; Ovando, 1989). Here is how one Spanish-speaking student, who went on to earn a doctoral degree and teach at a university, described her struggles with texts in college:

> I could not understand why I was doing so poorly. After all, my grammar and spelling were excellent. It took me a long time to realize that the way text is organized in English is considerably different from the way text is organized in a romance language, Spanish. The process involved a different set of rhetorical rules which were grounded in cultural ways of being. I had never heard of the thesis statement, organizational rules, cohesion, coherence, or other features of discourse. (Sotillo, 2002, p. 280)

There are a number of misconceptions about becoming bilingual. Table 5.2 summarizes a few of these taken from Brice (2002).

Bilingual Education. Virtually everyone agrees that all citizens should learn the official language of their country. But when and how should instruction in that lan-

Table 5.2 Myths about Bilingual Students

In the following table, L1 means the original language and L2 means the second language.

Myth	Truth
Learning a second language (L2) takes little time and effort.	Learning English as a second language takes 2–3 years for oral and 5–7 years for academic language use.
All language skills (listening, speaking, reading, writing) transfer from L1 to L2.	Reading is the skill that transfers most readily.
Code-switching is an indication of a language disorder.	Code-switching indicates high-level language skills in both L1 and L2.
All bilinguals easily maintain both languages.	It takes great effort and attention to maintain high-level skills in both languages.
Children do not lose their first language.	Loss of L1 and underdevelopment of L2 are problems for second language learners (**semilingual** in L1 and L2).
Exposure to English is sufficient for L2 learning.	To learn L2, students need to have a reason to communicate, access to English speakers, interaction, support, feedback, and time.
To learn English, students' parents need to speak only English at home.	Children need to use both languages in many contexts.
Reading in L1 is detrimental to learning English.	Literacy-rich environments in either L1 or L2 support development of necessary prereading skills.
Language disorders must be identified by tests in English.	Children must be tested in both L1 and L2 to determine language disorders.

SOURCE: From *The Hispanic Child: Speech, Language, Culture, and Education,* by Alejandro E. Brice. Published by Allyn & Bacon, Boston, MA. Copyright © 2002 by Pearson Education. Adapted by permission of the publisher.

guage begin? Here the debate is bitter at times, but it is clear the United States has not solved the problem. For example, "Spanish-speaking students—*even when taught and tested in Spanish*—still score at the [bottom] 32nd percentile in relation to a national comparison group (taught and tested in English)" (Goldenberg, 1996, p. 353).

Is it better to teach non–English-speaking and limited-English-proficiency students to read first in their native language or to begin reading instruction in English? Do these children need some oral lessons in English before reading instruction can be effective? Should other subjects, such as mathematics and social studies, be taught in the primary (home) language until the children are fluent in English? On these questions there are two basic positions, which have given rise to two contrasting teaching approaches, one that focuses on making the *transition* to English as quickly as possible and the other that attempts to *maintain* or improve the native language and use the native language as the primary teaching language until English skills are more fully developed.

Proponents of the first approach—*transition*—believe that English ought to be introduced as early as possible; they argue that valuable learning time is lost if students are taught in their native language. Most bilingual programs today follow this line of thinking. Proponents of *native-language maintenance instruction,* however, raise four important issues (Gersten, 1996b; Goldenberg, 1996; Hakuta & Garcia, 1989). First, children who are forced to try to learn math or science in an unfamiliar language are bound to have trouble. What if you had been forced to learn fractions or biology in a second language that you had studied for only a semester? Some psychologists believe students taught by this approach may become **semilingual,** that is, they are not proficient in either language. Being semilingual may be

Semilingual Not proficient in any language; speaking one or more languages inadequately.

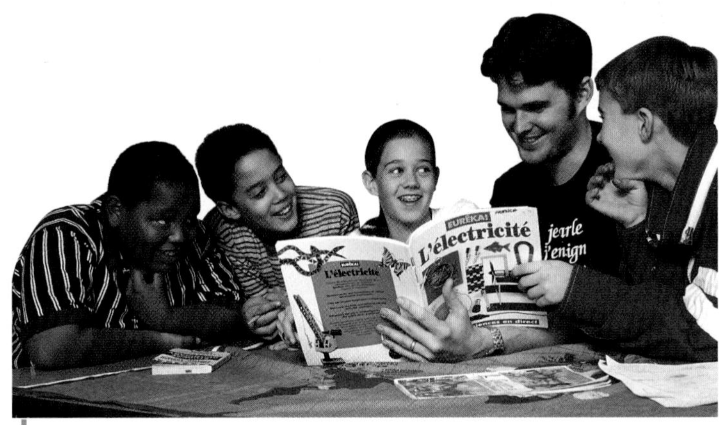

While most people agree that all citizens should learn the official language of their country, how this should be accomplished in school remains a very controversial question.

one reason the dropout rate is so high for low-SES Latino students (Ovando & Collier, 1998).

Second, students may get the message that their home languages (and therefore, their families and cultures) are second class. You saw the seeds of these feelings in the stories of the two students at the beginning of this section. Third, the academic content (math, science, history, etc.) that students learn in their native language is learned—they do not forget the knowledge and skills when they are able to speak English.

Fourth is what Kenji Hakuta (1986) calls a "paradoxical attitude of admiration and pride for school-attained bilingualism on the one hand and scorn and shame for home-brewed immigrant bilingualism on the other" (p. 229). Ironically, by the time students have mastered academic English and let their home language deteriorate, they reach secondary school and are encouraged to learn a second language. Hakuta (1986) suggests that the goals of the educational system could be the development of *all students* as functional bilinguals. One new approach to reaching this goal is to create classes that mix students who are learning a second language with students who are native speakers. The goal is for both groups to become fluent in both languages (Snow, 1986). My daughter spent a summer in such a program in Quebec and was ahead in every French class after that. For truly effective bilingual education, we will need many bilingual teachers. If you have a competence in another language, you might want to develop it fully for your teaching.

CONNECT & EXTEND

TO **PRAXIS**™
BILINGUAL ISSUES (IV, B4)
Identify the major issues related to the debate over bilingual education. Explain the major approaches to bilingual education, and describe steps that a teacher can take to promote the learning and language acquisition of non-English speaking students.

Research on Bilingual Programs. It is difficult to separate politics from practice in the debate about bilingual education. It is clear that high quality bilingual education programs can have positive results. Students improve in the subjects that were taught in their native language, in their mastery of English, and in self-esteem as well (Crawford, 1997; Hakuta & Gould, 1987; Wright & Taylor, 1995). English as a second language (ESL) programs seem to have positive effects on reading comprehension (Fitzgerald, 1995). But attention today is shifting from debate about general approaches to a focus on effective teaching strategies. As you will see many times in this book, a combination of clarity of learning goals and direct instruction in needed skills—including learning strategies and tactics, teacher- or peer-guided practice leading to independent practice, authentic and engaging tasks, opportunities for interaction and conversation that are academically focused, and warm encouragement from the teacher—seems to be effective (Chamot & O'Malley, 1996; Gersten, 1996b; Goldenberg, 1996). Table 5.3 is a set of constructs for promoting learning and language acquisition that capture many of these methods for effective instruction.

Table 5.3 Ideas for Promoting Learning and Language Acquisition

Effective teaching for students in bilingual and ESL classrooms combines many strategies—direct instruction, mediation, coaching, feedback, modeling, encouragement, challenge, and authentic activities.

1. Structures, frameworks, scaffolds, and strategies
   - Provide support to students by "thinking aloud," building on and clarifying input of students
   - Use visual organizers, story maps, or other aids to help students organize and relate information
2. Relevant background knowledge and key vocabulary concepts
   - Provide adequate background knowledge to students and informally assess whether students have background knowledge
   - Focus on key vocabulary words and use consistent language
   - Incorporate students' primary language meaningfully
3. Mediation/feedback
   - Give feedback that focuses on meaning, not grammar, syntax, or pronunciation
   - Give frequent and comprehensible feedback
   - Provide students with prompts or strategies
   - Ask questions that press students to clarify or expand on initial statements
   - Provide activities and tasks that students can complete
   - Indicate to students when they are successful
   - Assign activities that are reasonable, avoiding undue frustration
   - Allow use of native language responses (when context is appropriate)
   - Be sensitive to common problems in second language acquisition
4. Involvement
   - Ensure active involvement of all students, including low-performing students
   - Foster extended discourse
5. Challenge
   - Implicit (cognitive challenge, use of higher-order questions)
   - Explicit (high but reasonable expectations)
6. Respect for—and responsiveness to—cultural and personal diversity
   - Show respect for students as individuals, respond to things students say, show respect for culture and family, and possess knowledge of cultural diversity
   - Incorporate students' experiences into writing and language arts activities
   - Link content to students' lives and experiences to enhance understanding
   - View diversity as an asset, reject cultural deficit notions

SOURCE: From "Literacy Instruction for Language-Minority Students: The Transition Years," by R. Gersten, 1996, *The Elementary School Journal, 96,* pp. 241–242. Copyright © 1996 by the University of Chicago Press. Adapted with permission.

Check Yourself What are the origins of language differences in the classroom?

What is bilingual education?

We have dealt with a wide range of differences in this chapter. How can teachers provide an appropriate education for all their students? One response is to make the classroom compatible with the students' cultural heritage. Such a classroom is described as being culturally compatible.

Creating Culturally Compatible Classrooms

The goal of creating **culturally compatible classrooms** is to eliminate racism, sexism, and ethnic prejudice while providing equal educational opportunities for all students. Roland Tharp (1989) states that "two decades of data on cultural issues in classroom interactions and school outcomes have accumulated. When schools are changed, children's experiences and achievement also change" (p. 349). Tharp outlines several dimensions of classrooms that can be tailored to fit the needs of students. Three dimensions are social organization, learning style, and sociolinguistics.

Culturally compatible classrooms Classrooms in which procedures, rules, grouping strategies, attitudes, and teaching methods do not cause conflicts with the students' culturally influenced ways of learning and interacting.

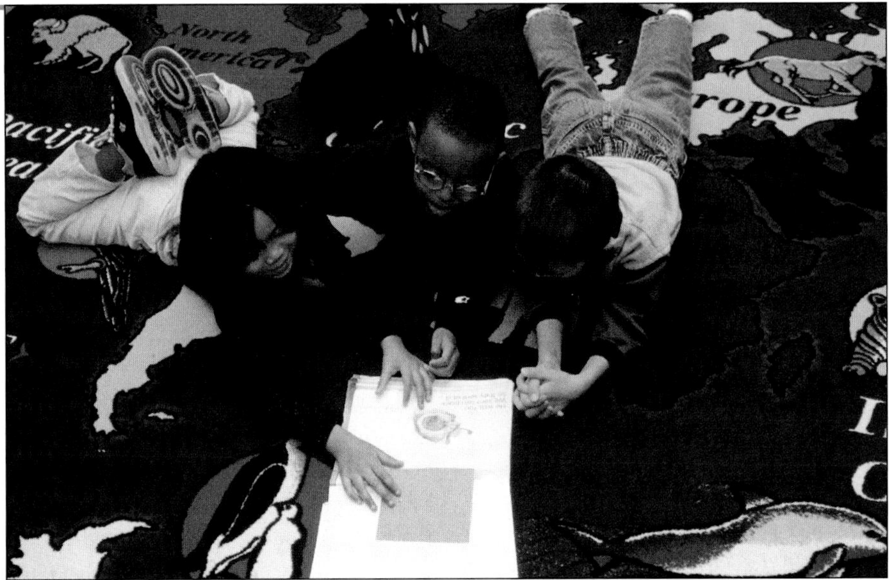

A major goal of creating culturally compatible classrooms is to encourage mutual respect among students from all backgrounds.

Social Organization

CONNECT & EXTEND

TO YOUR TEACHING PORTFOLIO

Menkart, D. J. (1999). Deepening the meaning of heritage months. *Educational Leadership, 56*(7), 19–21. This article discusses how to get past foods and festivals to increase students' understandings of heritage.

Tharp (1989) states that "a central task of educational design is to make the organization of teaching, learning, and performance compatible with the social structures in which students are most productive, engaged, and likely to learn" (p. 350). Social structure or social organization in this context means the ways people interact to accomplish a particular goal. For example, the social organization of Hawaiian society depends heavily on collaboration and cooperation. Children play together in groups of friends and siblings, with older children often caring for the younger ones. When cooperative work groups of four or five boys and girls were established in Hawaiian classrooms, student learning and participation improved (Okagaki, 2001). The teacher worked intensively with one group while the children in the remaining groups helped each other. But when the same structure was tried in a Navajo classroom, students would not work together. These students are socialized to be more solitary and not to play with the opposite sex. By setting up same-sex working groups of only two or three Navajo students, teachers encouraged them to help each other.

Learning Styles

Some psychologists have found ethnic group differences in students' cognitive styles. You may remember from the previous chapter that cognitive styles are the ways that individuals typically process information. The following are a few examples.

CONNECT & EXTEND

TO PROFESSIONAL JOURNALS

O'Neil, J. (1990). Link between style, culture proves divisive. *Educational Leadership, 48*(2), 8. *Focus Question:* Why do some educators argue against linking learning styles to cultural differences?

Possible Differences. Results of some research suggest that Mexican Americans tend to be field dependent, preferring holistic, concrete, social approaches to learning. Because being field independent is related to achievement in mathematics, the tendency to be field dependent may interfere with performance in mathematics if it is taught in the usual abstract, analytical way (Buenning & Tollefson, 1987). Other researchers have suggested that Hispanic American students are more oriented toward family and group loyalty. This may mean that these students prefer cooperative activities and dislike being made to compete with fellow students (Garcia, 1992; Vasquez, 1990).

Bennett (1999) summarizes research that suggests the learning styles of African Americans may be inconsistent with teaching approaches in most schools. Some of the characteristics of this learning style are a visual/global rather than a verbal/analytic approach; a preference for reasoning by inference rather than formal logic; a focus on people and relationships; a preference for energetic involvement in several activities simultaneously rather than routine, step-by-step learning; a tendency to approximate numbers, space and time; and a greater dependence on nonverbal communication. To capitalize on these learning styles, Hale-Benson (1986) recommends the following strategies with young African American children:

Use appropriate nonverbal cues, gestures, and eye contact.

Allow equal "talking time" for teacher and students.

Emphasize small-group learning and hands-on contact with the teacher.

Use a variety of learning activities that include movement, games, poetry, and music.

Native Americans also appear to have a more global, visual style of learning. For example, Navajo students prefer hearing a story all the way through to the end before discussing parts of the story. Teachers who stop to ask questions seem odd to these students and interrupt the learning process (Tharp, 1989). Also, these students sometimes show strong preferences for learning privately, through trial and error, rather than having their mistakes made public (Vasquez, 1990).

There has been little research on the learning styles of Asian Americans, perhaps because they are seen as "successful minorities." Some educators suggest that Asian children tend to value teacher approval and to work well in structured, quiet learning environments where there are clear goals and social support (Manning & Baruth, 1996). But there are dangers in stereotyping Asian and Asian American students as quiet, hardworking, and passive. Suzuki (1983) suggests that this practice "tends to reinforce conformity and stifle creativity. Asian and Pacific American students, therefore, frequently do not develop the ability to assert and express themselves verbally and are channeled in disproportionate numbers into the technical/scientific fields. As a result, many Asian and Pacific American students . . . are overly conforming, and have their academic and social development narrowly circumscribed" (p. 9).

Suzuki's cautions are echoed by many critics of the research on ethnic differences in learning styles (Yee, 1992).

Cautions about Learning Styles Research. In considering this research on learning styles, you should keep two points in mind. First, the validity of some of the learning styles research has been strongly questioned, as we saw in the previous chapter. Second, there is a heated debate today about whether identifying ethnic group differences in learning styles and preferences is a dangerous, racist, sexist exercise. In our society we are quick to move from the notion of "difference" to the idea of "deficits" and stereotypes (Gordon, 1991; O'Neil, 1990a). I have included the information about learning style differences because I believe that, used sensibly, this information can help you better understand your students.

It is dangerous and incorrect, however, to assume that every individual in a group shares the same learning style. The best advice for teachers is to be sensitive to individual differences in all your students and to make available alternative paths to learning. Never prejudge how a student will learn best on the basis of assumptions about the student's ethnicity or race. Get to know the individual.

CONNECT & EXTEND

TO YOUR TEACHING PORTFOLIO

For a concise discussion of cultural styles and the possible clashes of styles in classrooms, see Hilliard, A. G., III (1989). Teachers and cultural styles in a pluralistic society. *NEA Today, 7*(6), 65–69. Hilliard notes: "[T]he misunderstanding of behavioral styles leads teachers to mistake achievement in academic areas such as creative expression. . . . Many teachers from Eurocentric cultures have a linear storytelling style. Many African-American children, on the other hand, exhibit a spiraling storytelling style with many departures from an initial point, but a return to make a story whole. Many teachers of these children are unable to follow the children's coherent stories. Some teachers even believe that the children's stories have no coherence at all. Some lose patience with the children and indicate that they are doing badly." (p. 69)

Sociolinguistics

Sociolinguistics is the study of "the courtesies and conventions of conversation across cultures" (Tharp, 1989, p. 351). A knowledge of sociolinguistics will help you understand why communication sometimes breaks down in classrooms. The classroom is a special setting for communicating; it has its own set of rules for when, how, to whom, about what subject, and in what manner to use language. Sometimes the sociolinguistic skills of students do not fit the expectations of teachers or counselors, as we saw earlier.

Sociolinguistics The study of the formal and informal rules for how, when, about what, to whom, and how long to speak in conversations within cultural groups.

CONNECT & EXTEND

TO THE RESEARCH

See Cultural differences in the classroom. (1988, March). *Harvard Education Letter, 2*(2), 1–4. This article describes the KEEP program and Shirley Heath's project in the Piedmont Carolinas and offers four conclusions:

1. Interaction is the key to learning, and language is the key to interaction. "When teachers in both projects became aware of specific communication and interaction skills children were developing in their homes, they adapted classroom practice to build on these skills. In addition, teachers specifically demonstrated respect for the language of their students" (p. 3).
2. Academic standards and teacher expectations for students should not be lowered. Standard English skills were still emphasized in both projects but without devaluing the children's own dialect.
3. Schools can work with local colleges, parents, and other community members to learn more about students' home cultures.
4. By attending to students' cultures, teachers can expand and improve their teaching skills. The new ways of teaching developed in the two projects proved helpful for all the students in the classes, not just those from different cultures.

Participation Structures. In order to be successful, students must know the communication rules; that is, they must understand the pragmatics of the classroom—when, where, and how to communicate. This is not such an easy task. As class activities change, rules change. Sometimes you have to raise your hand (during the teacher's presentation), but sometimes you don't (during storytime on the rug). Sometimes it is good to ask a question (during discussion), but other times it isn't so good (when the teacher is reprimanding you). These differing activity rules are called **participation structures,** and they define appropriate participation for each class activity. Most classrooms have many different participation structures.

To be competent communicators in the classroom, students sometimes have to read very subtle, nonverbal cues telling them which participation structures are currently in effect. For example, in one classroom, when the teacher stood in a particular area of the room, put her hands on her hips, and leaned forward at the waist, the children in the class were signaled to "stop and freeze," look at the teacher, and anticipate an announcement (Shultz & Florio, 1979).

Sources of Misunderstandings. Some children are simply better than others at reading the classroom situation because the participation structures of the school match the structures they have learned at home. The communication rules for most school situations are similar to those in middle-class homes, so children from these homes often appear to be more competent communicators. They know the unwritten rules. Students from different cultural backgrounds may have learned participation structures that conflict with the behaviors expected in school. For example, one study found that the home conversation style of Hawaiian children is to chime in with contributions to a story. In school, however, this overlapping style is viewed as "interrupting." When the teachers in one school learned about these differences and made their reading groups more like their students' home conversation groups, the young Hawaiian children in their classes improved in reading (Au, 1980; Tharp, 1989).

The source of misunderstanding can be a subtle sociolinguistic difference, such as how long the teacher waits to react to a student's response. White and Tharp (1988) found that when Navajo students in one class paused in giving a response, their Anglo teacher seemed to think that they were finished speaking. As a result, the teacher often unintentionally interrupted students. In another study, researchers found that Pueblo Indian students participated twice as much in classes where teachers waited longer to react. Waiting longer also helps girls to participate more freely in math and science classes (Grossman & Grossman, 1994).

It seems that even students who speak the same language as their teachers may still have trouble communicating, and thus learning school subjects, if their knowledge of pragmatics does not fit the school situation. What can teachers do? Especially in the early grades, you should make communication rules for activities clear and explicit. Do not assume students know what to do. Use cues to signal students when changes occur. Explain and demonstrate appropriate behavior. I have seen teachers show young children how to use their "inside voice," "six-inch voice," or "whisper voice." One teacher said and then demonstrated, "If you have to interrupt me while I'm working with other children, stand quietly beside me until I can help you." Be consistent in responding to students. If students are supposed to raise their hands, don't call on those who break the rules. In these ways you teach students how to learn in school.

Culturally Relevant Pedagogy

In the last 20 years, several researchers have focused on teachers who are especially successful with students of color and students in poverty (Bennett, 1999; Delpit, 1995; Ladson-Billings, 1994, 1995; Moll, Amanti, Neff, & Gonzalez, 1992). The work of Gloria Ladson-Billings (1990, 1992, 1995) is a good example. For three years she studied excellent teachers in a California school district that served an African American

Participation structures The formal and informal rules for how to take part in a given activity.

community. In order to select the teachers, she asked parents and principals for nominations. Parents nominated teachers who respected them, created enthusiasm for learning in their children, and understood their children's need to operate successfully in two different worlds—the home community and the White world beyond. Principals nominated teachers who had few discipline referrals, high attendance rates, and high standardized test scores. Ladson-Billings was able to examine in depth 8 of the 9 teachers who were nominated by *both parents and principals.*

Based on her research, Ladson-Billings developed a conception of teaching excellence that encompasses, but also goes beyond, considerations of sociolinguistics or social organizations. She uses the term **culturally relevant pedagogy** to describe teaching that rests on three propositions.

CONNECT & EXTEND

TO THE RESEARCH

The Summer 1995 issue of *Theory Into Practice* is devoted to "Culturally Relevant Teaching." See http://www.coe.ohio-state.edu/TIP. This journal is especially for educators.

Students Must Experience Academic Success. "Despite the current social inequities and hostile classroom environments, students must develop their academic skills. The ways those skills are developed may vary, but all students need literacy, numeracy, technological, social, and political skills in order to be active participants in a democracy" (Ladson-Billings, 1995, p. 160).

Develop/Maintain Their Cultural Competence. As they become more academically skilled, students still retain their cultural competence. "Culturally relevant teachers utilize students' culture as a vehicle for learning" (Ladson-Billings, 1995, p. 161). For example, one teacher used "non-offensive" rap music to teach about literal and figurative meaning, rhyme, alliteration, and onomatopoeia in poetry. Another brought in a community expert known for her sweet potato pies to work with students. Follow-up lessons included investigations of George Washington Carver's sweet potato research, numerical analyses of taste tests, marketing plans for selling pies, and research on the educational preparation needed to become a chef.

Develop a Critical Consciousness to Challenge the Status Quo. In addition to developing academic skills while retaining cultural competence, excellent teachers help students "develop a broader sociopolitical consciousness that allows them to critique the social norms, values, mores, and institutions that produce and maintain social inequities" (Ladson-Billings, 1995, p. 162). For example, in one school students were upset that their textbooks were out of date. They mobilized to investigate the funding formulas that allowed middle-class students to have newer books, wrote letters to the newspaper editor to challenge these inequities, and updated their texts with current information from other sources.

Ladson-Billings (1995) noted that many people have said her three principles "are just good teaching." She agrees that she is describing good teaching, but questions "why so little of it seems to be occurring in classrooms populated by African American students" (p. 159). Geneva Gay (2000) uses the term *culturally responsive teaching* to describe a similar approach that uses the "cultural knowledge, prior experiences, frames of reference, and performance styles of ethnically diverse students to make learning encounters more relevant to and effective for them. It *teaches to and through* the strengths of these students. It is culturally *validating and affirming*" (p. 29).

The qualities described by Delpit and Gay are evident in a study of the common themes and characteristics of schools that were valued by African American families during the time of segregation in the South (Siddle Walker, 2001). Exemplary African American teachers are described repeatedly by their students as having high expectations and a demanding teaching style. They insisted that students learn and refused to lower their standards, even if it meant working extra hours with students after school. Consistent with the research on teacher quality described in Chapter 1, these exemplary teachers often had more education than White teachers in the same states. The teachers also were respected members of the community who cared deeply about the children in their classes, as you can see in the story of Vivian Gunn Morris, now a professor of education, in the *Stories of Learning/Tributes to Teaching* feature.

Culturally relevant pedagogy Excellent teaching for students of color that includes academic success, developing/maintaining cultural competence, and developing a critical consciousness to challenge the status quo.

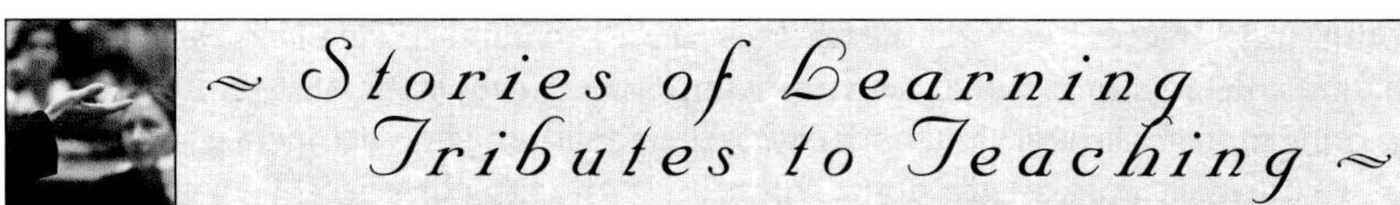

For me, caring was personified by **Mrs. Willie Mae Thompson,** my home economics teacher. Mrs. Thompson was like a third mother to me—third only to my biological mother and favorite aunt (Earline). As with my friends, we lived in the same neighborhood (as did most of our teachers and principals). Most families attended one of the four Black churches in the community. Hence, many of the teachers also taught us in Sunday school as well. We were welcome to Mrs. Thompson's anytime and could visit without calling. So it is no surprise that home economics was probably my favorite subject (if I had to choose a favorite). I liked being able to immediately apply what I learned. Because of home economics, my family enjoyed (or suffered) my preparation of foods in new and different ways. School broadened my horizons about different ways of doing things. Thanks to Mrs. Thompson, I made most of my own clothes after taking home economics in seventh grade. But I was also fortunate to have many other outstanding and caring teachers as well.

At the risk of painting an overly idyllic portrait of my school experience, let me point out that children were pretty much the same as they are today. Bullying seems to be a common school experience and is part of my memories as well. In first grade, some of my classmates decided to bully me and threw rocks at me on my way home from school. I reported the incident to Mrs. Magnolia Watkins, my first-grade teacher. Mrs. Watkins intervened and it never happened again.

SOURCE: From "No More Cotton Picking: African American Voices from a Small Southern Town," by Vivian Gunn Morris and C. L. Morris. In Gloria Swindler Boutte (Ed.), *Resounding Voices: School Experiences of People from Diverse Ethnic Backgrounds.* Published by Allyn & Bacon, Boston, MA.

Check Yourself What are the elements of a culturally compatible classroom? What is culturally relevant pedagogy?

Bringing It All Together: Teaching Every Student

What Would You Say? As the interview continues for the Middle School position, the next question is, "Describe the things you do for students to indicate you have feelings for them." What would you say?

The goal of this chapter is to give you a sense of the diversity in today's and tomorrow's schools and to help you meet the challenges of teaching in a multicultural classroom. How will you understand and build on all the cultures of your students? How will you deal with many different languages? Here are three general teaching principles to guide you in finding answers to these questions.

CONNECT & EXTEND

TO THE RESEARCH
For an entire volume devoted to educating students who face challenges, see Stringfield, S., & Land, D. (2002). *Educating at-risk students: Yearbook of the National Society for the Study of Education* (NSSE) (Vol. 2). Chicago, IL: University of Chicago Press.

Know Your Students

Nothing you read in a chapter on cultural differences will teach you enough to understand the lives of all your students. If you can take other courses in college or read about other cultures, I encourage you to do it. But reading and studying are not enough. You should get to know your students' families and communities. Elba Reyes, a successful bilingual teacher for special needs children, describes her approach:

> Usually I find that if you really want to know a parent, you get to know them on their own turf. This is key to developing trust and understanding the parents' perspective. First, get to know the community. Learn where the local grocery store is and what the children do after school. Then schedule a home visit at a time that is convenient for the parents. . . . The home environment is not usually as ladened with failure. I sometimes observed the child being successful in the home, for example, riding a bicycle or helping with dinner. (Bos & Reyes, 1996, p. 349)

Try to spend time with students and parents on projects outside school. Ask parents to help in class or to speak to your students about their jobs, their hobbies, or the history and heritage of their ethnic group. In the elementary grades, don't wait until a student is in trouble to have the first meeting with a family member. Watch and listen to the ways that your students interact in large and small groups. Have students write to you, and write back to them. Eat lunch with one or two students. Spend some nonteaching time with them.

Respect Your Students

From knowledge ought to come respect for your students' learning strengths—for the struggles they face and the obstacles they overcome. For a child, genuine acceptance is a necessary condition for developing self-esteem. Sometimes the self-image and occupational aspirations of minority children actually decline in their early years in public school, probably because of the emphasis on majority culture values, accomplishments, and history. By presenting the accomplishments of particular members of an ethnic group or by bringing that group's culture into the classroom (in the form of literature, art, music, or any cultural knowledge), teachers can help students maintain a sense of pride in their cultural group. This integration of culture must be more than the "tokenism" of sampling ethnic foods or wearing costumes. Students should learn about the socially and intellectually important contributions of the various groups. There are many excellent references that provide background information, history, and teaching strategies for different groups of students (e.g., Banks, 1997, 1999, 2002; Bennett, 1999; Irvine & Armento, 2001; Ladson-Billings, 1995).

CONNECT & EXTEND

TO YOUR TEACHING PORTFOLIO
Midobuche, E. (1999). Respect in the classroom: Reflections of a Mexican-American educator. *Educational Leadership, 56*(7), 80–83. The story of the early school experiences of a Spanish-speaking child in an all-English world.

Teach Your Students

The most important thing you can do for your students is teach them to read, write, speak, compute, think, and create. Too often, goals for low-SES or minority group students have focused exclusively on basic skills. Students are taught words and sounds, but the meaning of the story is supposed to come later. Knapp, Turnbull, and Shields (1990, p. 5) make these suggestions:

- Focus on meaning and understanding from beginning to end—for example, by orienting instruction toward comprehending reading passages, communicating important ideas in written text, or understanding the concepts underlying number facts.
- Balance routine skill learning with novel and complex tasks from the earliest stages of learning.
- Provide context for skill learning that establishes clear reasons for needing to learn the skills.
- Influence attitudes and beliefs about the academic content areas as well as skills and knowledge.
- Eliminate unnecessary redundancy in the curriculum (e.g., repeating instruction in the same mathematics skills year after year).

One area of teaching that often places students at risk is the use of technology. Many students have limited access to technology at home or in their communities. For example, almost 33% of White students use computers in their homes, compared to about 10% for African American and Hispanic students (Brown, 2000).

And finally, teach students directly about how to be students. In the early grades this could mean directly teaching the courtesies and conventions of the classroom: how to get a turn to speak, how and when to interrupt the teacher, how to whisper, how to get help in a small group, how to give an explanation that is helpful. In the later grades it may mean teaching the study skills that fit your subject. You can ask students to learn "how we do it in school" without violating principle number two above—respect your students. Ways of asking questions around the kitchen table at home may be different from ways of asking questions in school, but students can learn both ways, without deciding that either way is superior. The *Guidelines* give more ideas.

Check Yourself How can teachers create classroom environments in which all students can learn?

GUIDELINES Culturally Relevant Teaching

Experiment with different grouping arrangements to encourage social harmony and cooperation.

Examples

1. Try "study buddies" and pairs.
2. Organize heterogeneous groups of four or five.
3. Establish larger teams for older students.

Provide a range of ways to learn material to accommodate a range of learning styles.

Examples

1. Give students verbal materials at different reading levels.
2. Offer visual materials—charts, diagrams, models.
3. Provide tapes for listening and viewing.
4. Set up activities and projects.

Teach classroom procedures directly, even ways of doing things that you thought everyone would know.

Examples

1. Tell students how to get the teacher's attention.
2. Explain when and how to interrupt the teacher if students need help.
3. Show which materials students can take and which require permission.
4. Demonstrate acceptable ways to disagree with or challenge another student.

Learn the meaning of different behaviors for your students.

Examples

1. Ask students how they feel when you correct or praise them. What gives them this message?
2. Talk to family and community members and other teachers to discover the meaning of expressions, gestures, or other responses that are unfamiliar to you.

Emphasize meaning in teaching.

Examples

1. Make sure students understand what they read.
2. Try storytelling and other modes that don't require written materials.
3. Use examples that relate abstract concepts to everyday experiences; for instance, relate negative numbers to being overdrawn in your checkbook.

Get to know the customs, traditions, and values of your students.

Examples

1. Use holidays as a chance to discuss the origins and meaning of traditions.
2. Analyze different traditions for common themes.
3. Attend community fairs and festivals.

Help students detect racist and sexist messages.

Examples

1. Analyze curriculum materials for biases.
2. Make students "bias detectives," reporting comments from the media.
3. Discuss the ways that students communicate biased messages about each other and what should be done when this happens.
4. Discuss expressions of prejudice such as anti-Semitism.

Enhancing Your Expertise with Technology

Teaching Every Student

The incident was a small one, but it exemplified many of the issues that teachers face as a result of the nation's demographic changes. Five-year old Emrah, who qualified for the free lunch program, told his teacher that he could eat neither of the two offerings in the school cafeteria that day: sausage with pancakes or deli sub sandwich—because of religious reasons. The teacher contacted the cafeteria manager. The manager said that no accommodations could be made because no other foods were available. (One of the cafeteria workers remarked that "they" should learn to eat what "we" eat.) The incensed teacher finally reached the school district dietician, who resolved the dispute by pointing out that the "ham" in the deli sub sandwich was actually turkey ham that Emrah could eat. "I am glad we were able to take care of that problem," said the dietician. "But we can't make accommodations for every ethnic or religious group in the district."

As the nation's school population continues to diversify, incidents like this one (and others far less easily resolved) will certainly arise more and more often. Teachers with expertise about and respect for cultural differences will be able to face these challenges in ways that help students experience genuine acceptance by the school community, leading to increased ethnic pride and motivation to succeed in school.

The Southern Poverty Law Center sponsors the Teaching Tolerance education project (www.tolerance.org) that helps "teachers foster equity, respect and understanding in the classroom and beyond." Its major concern is fair treatment of all people regardless of religious affiliation, gender, race, age, ethnicity, sexual orientation, or physical status. Teaching Tolerance takes a comprehensive approach to achievement of that goal. Here you will find information and resources including:

- current events,
- classroom lesson plans,
- activities to foster teacher self-reflection about tolerance,
- a teacher's forum to share ideas about fostering tolerance in the classroom,
- guidelines and tips for responding to intolerant incidents inside the school, and
- links to other Web sites that promote tolerance.

Perhaps Teaching Tolerance's most interesting—as well as unsettling—feature is its set of Implicit Association Tests (IAT) that measure unconscious bias. These tests might offer you some insight into your own possible hidden biases about race, homosexuality, age, gender, and body image. Teachers alone, of course, cannot create an atmosphere of equity and respect. The sponsors of Teaching Tolerance also provide numerous resources to engage parents and students in efforts to foster tolerance and equity. See what you think of this site. You may very well find it the most disturbing, but useful site that you encounter through this textbook.

Today's Multicultural Classrooms
(pp. 154–157)

Distinguish between the "melting pot" and multiculturalism. Statistics point to increasing cultural diversity in American society. Old views—that minority group members and immigrants should lose their cultural distinctiveness and assimilate completely in the American "melting pot" or be regarded as culturally deficient—are being replaced by new emphases on multiculturalism, equal educational opportunity, and the celebration of cultural diversity.

What is multicultural education? According to the multicultural ideal, America should be transformed into a society that values diversity. James Banks suggests that multicultural education has five dimensions: integrating content, helping students understand how knowledge is influenced by beliefs, reducing prejudice, creating social structures in schools that support learning and development for all students, and using teaching methods that reach all students.

What is culture? There are many conceptions of culture, but most include the knowledge, rules, traditions, attitudes, and values that guide behavior in a particular group of people—culture is a program for living. Everyone is a member of many cultural groups, defined in terms of geographic region, nationality, ethnicity, race, gender, social class, and religion. Membership in a particular group does not determine behavior or values, but makes certain values and kinds of behavior more likely. Wide variations exist within each group.

Melting Pot: A metaphor for the absorption and assimilation of immigrants into the mainstream of society so that ethnic differences vanish.

Cultural Deficit Model: A model that explains the school achievement problems of ethnic minority students by assuming that their culture is inadequate and does not prepare them to succeed in school.

Multicultural Education: Education that teaches the value of cultural diversity.

Culture: The knowledge, values, attitudes, and traditions that guide the behavior of a group of people and allow them to solve the problems of living in their environment.

Social Class Differences
(pp. 157–161)

What is SES? Socioeconomic status (SES) is a term used by sociologists for variations in wealth, power, and prestige. Socioeconomic status is determined by several factors—not just income—and often overpowers other cultural differences. No single variable is an effective measure of SES, but most researchers identify four general levels of SES: upper, middle, working, and lower classes. The main characteristics of these four levels are summarized in Table 5.1. The majority of children in poverty are White, but a disproportionate number of African American and Hispanic American children live in poverty.

What is the relationship between SES and school achievement? Socioeconomic status and academic achievement are closely related. High-SES students of all ethnic groups show higher average levels of achievement on test scores and stay in school longer than low-SES students. Poverty during a child's preschool years appears to have the greatest negative impact. And the longer the child is in poverty, the stronger the impact on achievement. Why is there a correlation between SES and school achievement? Low-SES students may suffer from inadequate health care, teachers' lowered expectations of them, low self-esteem, learned helplessness, participation in resistance cultures, school tracking, and understimulating childrearing styles and home environments. A striking finding is that low-SES children lose academic ground outside school over the summer while higher-SES children continue to advance.

Socioeconomic Status (SES): Relative standing in the society based on income, power, background, and prestige.

Resistance Culture: Group values and beliefs about refusing to adopt the behaviors and attitudes of the majority culture.

Tracking: Assignment to different classes and academic experiences based on achievement.

Ethnic and Racial Differences
(pp. 161–169)

Distinguish between ethnicity and race. Ethnicity (culturally transmitted behavior) and race (biologically transmitted physical traits) are socially significant categories people use to describe themselves and others. Minority groups (either numerically or historically unempowered) are rapidly increasing in population.

How can ethnicity affect school performance? Conflicts between groups can arise from differences in culture-based beliefs, values, and expectations. Cultural conflicts are usually about below-the-surface differences, because when subtle cultural differences meet, misunderstandings are common. Students in some cultures learn attitudes and behaviors that are more consistent with school expectations. Differences among ethnic groups in cognitive and academic abilities are largely the legacy of racial segregation and continuing prejudice and discrimination.

Distinguish among prejudice, discrimination, and stereotype threat. Prejudice is a rigid and irrational generalization—a prejudgment—about an entire category of people. Prejudice may target people in particular racial, ethnic, religious, political, geographic, or language groups, or it may be directed toward the sex or sexual orientation of the individual. Discrimination is unequal treatment of particular categories of people. Stereotype threat is the extra emotional and cognitive burden that your performance in an academic situation might confirm a stereotype that others hold about you. It is not necessary that the individual even believe the stereotype. All that matters is that the person is *aware* of the stereotype and *cares about performing* well enough to disprove its unflattering implications. In the short run, the fear that you might confirm a negative stereotype can induce test anxiety and undermine performance. Over time, experiencing stereotype threat may lead to disidentification with schooling and academic achievement.

Ethnicity: A cultural heritage shared by a group of people.

Race: A group of people who share common biological traits that are seen as self-defining by the people of the group.

Minority Group: A group of people who have been socially disadvantaged—not always a minority in actual numbers.

Prejudice: Prejudgment, or irrational generalization about an entire category of people.

Authoritarian Personality: Rigidly conforming to the belief that society is naturally competitive, with "better" people reaping its rewards.

Stereotype: Schema that organizes knowledge or perceptions about a category.

Discrimination: Treating particular categories of people unequally.

Stereotype Threat: The extra emotional and cognitive burden that your performance in an academic situation might confirm a stereotype that others hold about you.

Girls and Boys: Differences in the Classroom

(pp. 169–174)

What is gender-role identity? Gender-role identity is the image each individual has of himself or herself as masculine or feminine in characteristics—a part of self-concept. People with a "feminine" identity would rate themselves high on characteristics usually associated with females, such as "sensitive" or "warm," and low on characteristics traditionally associated with males, such as "forceful" and "competitive." Most people see themselves in gender-typed terms; however, some children and adults are more androgynous—they rate themselves high on *both* masculine and feminine traits.

How do gender-role identities develop? Biology (hormones) plays a role, as does the differential behavior of parents and teachers toward male and female children. Through their interactions with family, peers, teachers, and the environment in general, children begin to form gender schemas, or organized networks of knowledge about what it means to be male or female. Research shows that gender-role stereotyping begins in the preschool years and continues through gender bias in the school curriculum and sex discrimination in the classroom. Teachers often unintentionally perpetuate these problems.

Are there sex differences in cognitive abilities? Some measures on IQ and SAT tests have shown sex-linked differences, especially in verbal and spatial abilities and mathematics. Males seem to be superior on tasks that require mental rotation of objects and females are better on tasks that require acquisition and use of verbal information. Research on the causes of these differences has been inconclusive, except to indicate that academic socialization and teachers' treatment of male and female students in mathematics classes do play a role. Teachers can use many strategies for reducing gender bias.

Gender-Role Identity: Beliefs about characteristics and behaviors associated with one sex as opposed to the other.

Androgynous: Having some typically male and some typically female characteristics apparent in one individual.

Gender Schemas: Organized networks of knowledge about what it means to be male or female.

Gender Biases: Different views of males and females, often favoring one gender over the other.

Language Differences in the Classroom

(pp. 174–181)

What are the origins of language differences in the classroom? Language differences among students include dialects, bilingualism, and culture-based communication styles. Dialects are not inferior languages and should be respected, but Standard English should be taught for academic contexts. Dialects often affect the pronunciation of words, so teachers have to be able to distinguish a mistake from a dialect difference in oral language. Student who speak in dialect and students who are bilingual often use code switching to communicate in different groups.

What is bilingual education? Bilingual students speak a first language other than English, learn English as a second language, may have some degree of limitation in English proficiency, and also must often struggle with social adjustment problems relating to biculturalism. While there is much debate over the best way to help bilingual students master English, studies show it is best if they are not forced to abandon their first language. The more proficient students are in their first language, the faster they will master the second. Mastering academic language skills in any new language takes five to seven years.

Dialect: Rule-governed variation of a language spoken by a particular group.
Standard Speech: The most generally accepted and used form of a given language.
Code-switching: Successful switching between cultures in language, dialect, or nonverbal behaviors to fit the situation.
Bilingualism: Speaking two languages fluently.
English as a Second Language (ESL): Designation for programs and classes to teach English to students who are not native speakers of English.
Limited English Proficiency (LEP): Descriptive term for students who have limited mastery of English.
Semilingual: Not proficient in any language; speaking one or more languages inadequately.

Creating Culturally Compatible Classrooms

(pp. 181–186)

What are the elements of a culturally compatible classroom? Culturally compatible classrooms are free of racism, sexism, and ethnic prejudice and provide equal educational opportunities for all students. Dimensions of classroom life that can be modified to that end are social organization, learning style formats, and participation structures. Teachers, however, must avoid stereotypes of culture-based learning styles and must not assume that every individual in a group shares the same style. Communication may break down in classrooms because of differences in sociolinguistic styles and skills. Teachers can directly teach appropriate participation structures and be sensitive to culture-based communication rules.

What is culturally relevant pedagogy? Gloria Ladson-Billings developed a conception of teaching excellence that encompasses considerations of sociolinguistics or social organizations, but goes beyond them. She uses the term *culturally relevant pedagogy* to describe teaching that rests on three propositions: Students must experience academic success, develop/maintain their cultural competence, and develop a critical consciousness to challenge the status quo.

Culturally Compatible Classrooms: Classrooms in which procedures, rules, grouping strategies, attitudes, and teaching methods do not cause conflicts with the students' culturally influenced ways of learning and interacting.
Sociolinguistics: The study of the formal and informal rules for how, when, about what, to whom, and how long to speak in conversations within cultural groups.
Participation Structures: The formal and informal rules for how to take part in a given activity.
Culturally Relevant Pedagogy: Excellent teaching for students of color that includes academic success, developing/maintaining cultural competence, and developing a critical consciousness to challenge the status quo.

Bringing It All Together: Teaching Every Student

(pp. 186–188)

How can teachers create classroom environments in which all students can learn? To help create compatible multicultural classrooms, teachers must know and respect all their students, have high expectations of them, and teach them what they need to know to succeed.

Enhancing Your Expertise with Technology: Teaching Tolerance

(p. 189)

The Southern Poverty Law Center Teaching Tolerance education project at www.tolerance.org provides resources to help teachers create an atmosphere of tolerance and respect in their classrooms.

Other Useful Websites

Clearinghouse for Multicultural and Bilingual Education
http://www.weber.edu/MBE/htmls/MBE-resource.html

Community Learning Network: A Canadian site with information on multiculturalism **http://www.cln.org/**

Partnerships for family involvement in education
http://pfie.ed.gov/

Pulling together: A collection of resources for educators in rural schools **http://www.ncrel.org/rural/**

Multicultural curriculum and instructional resources
http://www.cln.org/subjects/mc.html

Modified Fennema-Sherman Attitude: An assessment of attitudes toward mathematics
http://www.woodrow.org/teachers/math/gender/08scale.html

National Multicultural Institute: The mission is to increase knowledge, awareness, and respect among people of different racial, ethnic, and cultural backgrounds.
http://www.nmci.org/index.htm

The Southern Poverty Law Center sponsors the Teaching Tolerance education project. **www.tolerance.org**

Resources on Women and Mathematics
http://forum.swarthmore.edu/library/ed_topics/equity_women/

Language and Literacy Effective Classroom Practices: Education Place® **http://www.eduplace.com/rdg/res/literacy/**

Research in Literacy Development: The National Research Center on English Learning & Achievement
http://cela.albany.edu/research.htm

Language Development: The American Speech-Language-Hearing Association **http://www.asha.org/speech/development/lang_lit.cfm**

To read Ms. Mifflin's entire article, see:
www.salon.com/mwt/feature/1999/12/13/toys/

Becoming a Professional

Passing the PRAXIS™

Chapter 5 reflects many of the professional standards created by the Interstate New Teacher Assessment and Support Consortium (INTASC). These standards form the basis of the PRAXIS II™ and state-created teacher licensure exams.

A classroom should be a community of learners, and the community described in the Teacher's Casebook is fractured along several lines. Divisions and attitudes that undermine the goal of that community—learning—must be addressed fairly, firmly, and tactfully. As the leader of that community, your practices and attitudes will be major factors that determine whether that community moves toward your goal.

In PRAXIS II™ you will be presented with scenarios and questions that will test your knowledge of the increasingly complex learning communities that teachers and students inhabit. You will be challenged to implement strategies and practices that foster learning for each of the varied students who are in that community with you.

Tips for PRAXIS II™

Recognize the influences that ethnicity, socioeconomic status, and community values may have on:

- Student-teacher relationships/parent-teacher relationships
- Student learning styles
- Academic achievement
- Attitudes, self-esteem, and expectations for success
- Opportunities for quality educational experiences

Understand the influences that gender may have on:

- Teachers' attention to students
- Differences in mental abilities

Devise strategies that:

- Eliminate sexist teaching practices
- Promote positive school-home relationships
- Support English acquisition in non-English speaking students
- Reduce or eliminate racial and ethnic stereotypes and biases

Related Topics

- Gender, ethnicity, and self-esteem (Chapter 3)
- Socialization: family, peers, and teachers (Chapter 3)
- Self-schemas (Chapter 3)
- Teacher expectations (Chapter 12)
- Creating a positive learning environment (Chapter 11)

Standards and Licensure Appendix: *PRAXIS II™ and INTASC*

Refer to the Appendix at the end of the book for detailed correlations to PRAXIS II™ exam topics and INTASC Standards addressed in this text.

Insights about Job Interview Questions: *What Would You Say?*

1. Describe the things you do for students to indicate you have feelings for them.
2. Describe how your life experiences will contribute to our goal to create an active anti-racist school system.
3. Do you believe that boys and girls learn differently?

Your Teaching Portfolio: *Teaching Resources*

- What is your stance on multicultural education? On tracking? Add these ideas to your philosophy of teaching statement.
- Include ideas for the integration of multicultural material.
- Add Table 5.3 "Ideas for Promoting Learning and Language Acquisition" to your **Teaching Resources** file.
- Use the *Family and Community Partnerships Guidelines* to brainstorm ideas for family involvement in helping your students "take their learning home."

Video**Workshop** Extra

If the VideoWorkshop package was included with your textbook, go to Chapter 5 of the Companion Website (www.ablongman.com/woolfolk) and click on the VideoWorkshop button. Follow the instructions for viewing *Video Clip 6: Teaching in Bilingual Classrooms.* Consider this information while answering the following questions:

1. The teacher in this multicultural classroom teaches in English, but asks other students to translate when necessary. There are two schools of thought on teaching ESL students that focus on the transition to English. What are they, and which approach does this teacher favor?
2. What are some ways a teacher can overcome the language barrier in a multicultural classroom?

Use the CD-ROM included in the back of your textbook to launch the "Becoming a Professional" website. The website features advice on preparing for teacher certification exams, help with getting your first job, and resources to help you perform your job well from the first day forward.

Teachers' Casebook

What Would They Do?

Here is how some practicing teachers responded to the teaching situation presented at the beginning of this chapter about bringing together a class with many conflicts and cliques.

Mary Frances Donohoe

Fifth Grade Teacher, *Lawton Chiles Elementary, Gainesville, Florida*

Students must learn to respect themselves and others. Respect should be taught, modeled, and practiced throughout the school year. A short daily activity that engages students in reflecting, talking about, and practicing respect constantly reinforces this concept. At the end of each week, students are asked to nominate a citizen of the week. They should give reasons why they have nominated this person and the teacher should respond with positive comments. Students can cast a secret ballot, or the teacher may decide based on his or her observation. The citizen of the week is announced at the end of the day, her name is placed on a recognition board, and she is given a reward commensurate with age. Middle school students like to receive certificates excusing them from a homework assignment.

For example, the allegory *The Terrible Things*, by Eve Bunting, stimulates students' thinking about and understanding prejudice. Early in the school year, I read this to students and encourage them to respond by writing individually, sharing with others at their table, and finally with a whole class discussion.

Thomas W. Newkirk

Eighth Grade Teacher, *Hamilton Heights Middle School, Arcadia, Indiana*

The members of the class need lessons that both celebrate their differences and recognize their similarities. Assigning students to homogeneous groups to report to the class about their cultures may eliminate some misconceptions students have. Assigning students to heterogeneous groups may encourage them to work with people from "outside." Introducing the class to E. L. Konigsburg's *The View from Saturday*, as well as to other notable examples of young adult literature could provide topics for class discussion and could help students understand the contributions each member of the class has to offer. Hopefully these activities would reduce the tension in the classroom and would eliminate the audience for Clarise's ethnic jokes. Certainly Clarise cannot be allowed to make the class uncomfortable for anyone.

Ann Sande

Third Grade Teacher, *Henry Viscardi School, Albertson, New York*

In order to break down the barriers separating ethnic groups I would assign two children from different groups to perform a desirable task. It might be working together to find information on the computer's encyclopedia or the Internet and reporting it back to the class, or preparing materials for the class science experiments. The children need to "see" each other in new ways and to learn to appreciate each other's strengths and talents beyond preconceived notions.

Modeling behavior is critical. When a group of students is speaking in another language and seemingly laughing at me I would "call them on it." I would express my dislike of the behavior in a firm manner and reiterate that it is unacceptable within our class community. By doing so, it gives the students another way and the appropriate language to deal with the objectionable behavior displayed by Clarise. I might also suggest that, as a fun activity, the entire class try to learn a language that is not part of the curriculum; we might learn some American Sign Language together.

Steven P. Rude

Guidance Counselor, *John C. Fremont High School, Los Angeles, California*

I would request that the school psychologist or special education teacher come to my class to prepare the class for the arrival of their new fellow students. I would also encourage the students with disabilities to explain their own individual differences in their own way. There are many classroom activities that encourage students to explore and acknowledge their own differences, whether it be the color of their skin or the type of disability they possess. I would expect to review the Individual Education Plan for each of the students involved in the transition. Also, it would be helpful to know what behavior interventions work for the emotionally disturbed child and what teaching methods are most effective for the student with cerebral palsy. I would speak with the parents of these children to explore their expectations and past experiences in inclusive settings. There would also need to be teacher's aides available to help the special education students and to assist in communicating with the children who do not speak English. The inclusion of special education students into the classroom is a challenge, but it can ultimately encourage acceptance across all lines, including ethnicities and exceptionalities.

Go to the Companion Website (www.ablongman.com/woolfolk) for additional case studies including audio and video cases, and examples of student work.

CHAPTER

6

Behavioral Views of Learning

Teachers' Casebook

What Would You Do?

You were hired in January to take over the class of a teacher who moved away. This is a great district and a terrific school. If you do well, you might be in line for a full-time opening next fall. As you are introduced around the school, you get a number of sympathetic looks and many—too many—offers of help: "Let me know if I can do anything for you."

As you walk toward the class, you begin to understand why so many teachers volunteered their help. You hear the screaming when you are still halfway down the hall. "Give it back, it's MINE!" "No way—come and get it!" "I hate you." A crashing sound follows as a table full of books hits the floor. The first day is a nightmare. Evidently the previous teacher had no management system—no order. Several students walk around the room while you are talking to the class, interrupt you when you are working with a group, torment the class goldfish, and open their lunches (or those of other students) for a self-determined, mid-morning snack. Others listen, but ask a million questions off the topic. Simply taking roll and introducing the first activity takes an hour. You end the first day exhausted and discouraged, losing your voice and your patience.

Critical Thinking

How would you approach the situation? Which problem behaviors would you tackle first? Would giving rewards or administering punishments be useful in this situation? Why or why not?

Collaboration

With two other members of your class, role play an orientation meeting between this new teacher and the mentor teacher assigned to help. How should the mentor prepare the new teacher for the assignment? What plans could be made to handle the situation?

We begin this chapter with a general definition of learning that takes into account the opposing views of different theoretical groups. We will highlight one group, the behavioral theorists, in this chapter; another major group, the cognitive theorists, in Chapters 7 and 8; and then look at current social cognitive views and constructivism in Chapter 9.

Our discussion in this chapter will focus on three behavioral learning processes: contiguity, classical conditioning, and operant conditioning, with the greatest emphasis on the last process. After examining the implications of applied behavior analysis for teaching, we look at two recent directions in behavioral approaches to learning—self-management and cognitive behavior modification.

By the time you have completed this chapter, you should be able to answer these questions:

- *What is learning?*
- *What are the similarities and differences among contiguity, classical conditioning, and operant conditioning?*
- *What are examples of four different kinds of consequences that can follow any behavior, and what effect each is likely to have on future behavior?*
- *How could you use applied behavior analysis (group consequences, token economies, contingency contracts) to solve common academic or behavior problems?*
- *What is cognitive behavior modification, and how does it apply to teaching?*

Understanding Learning

When we hear the word *learning*, most of us think of studying and school. We think about subjects or skills we intend to master, such as algebra, Spanish, chemistry, or karate. But learning is not limited to school. We learn every day of our lives. Babies learn to kick their legs to make the mobile above their cribs move, teenagers learn the lyrics to all their favorite songs, middle-aged people like me learn to change their diet and exercise patterns, and every few years we all learn to find a new style of dress attractive when the old styles (the styles we once loved) go out of fashion. This last example shows that learning is not always intentional. We don't try to like new styles and dislike old ones; it just seems to happen that way. We don't intend to become nervous when we hear the sound of a dentist's drill or when we step onto a stage, yet many of us do. So what is this powerful phenomenon called learning?

Learning: A Definition

In the broadest sense, **learning** occurs when experience causes a relatively permanent change in an individual's knowledge or behavior. The change may be deliberate or unintentional, for better or for worse, correct or incorrect, and conscious or unconscious (Hill, 2002). To qualify as learning, this change must be brought about by experience—by the interaction of a person with his or her environment. Changes simply caused by maturation, such as growing taller or turning gray, do not qualify as learning. Temporary changes resulting from illness, fatigue, or hunger are also excluded from a general definition of learning. A person who has gone without food for two days does not learn to be hungry, and a person who is ill does not learn to run more slowly. Of course, learning plays a part in how we respond to hunger or illness.

Our definition specifies that the changes resulting from learning are in the individual's knowledge or behavior. While most psychologists would agree with this statement, some tend to emphasize the change in knowledge, others the change in behavior. Cognitive psychologists, who focus on changes in knowledge, believe learning is an internal mental activity that cannot be observed directly. As you will see in the next chapter, cognitive psychologists studying learning are interested in unobservable mental activities such as thinking, remembering, and solving problems (Schwartz, Wasserman, & Robbins, 2002).

The psychologists discussed in this chapter, on the other hand, favor **behavioral learning theories.** The behavioral view generally assumes that the outcome of learning is change in behavior and emphasizes the effects of external events on the individual. Some early behaviorists such as J. B. Watson took the radical position that because thinking, intentions, and other internal mental events could not be seen or studied rigorously and scientifically, these "mentalisms," as he called them, should not even be included in an explanation of learning. Before we look in depth at behavioral explanations of learning, let's step into an actual classroom and note the possible results of learning.

Learning Is Not Always What It Seems

After weeks of working with her cooperating teacher in an 8th-grade social studies class, Elizabeth was ready to take over on her own. As she moved from behind the desk to the front of the room, she saw another adult approach the classroom door. It was Mr. Ross, her supervisor from college. Elizabeth's neck and facial muscles suddenly became very tense and her hands trembled.

"I've stopped by to observe your teaching," Mr. Ross said. "This will be my first of six visits. I couldn't reach you last night to tell you."

Elizabeth tried to hide her reaction, but her hands trembled as she gathered the notes for the lesson.

Learning Process through which experience causes permanent change in knowledge or behavior.

Behavioral learning theories Explanations of learning that focus on external events as the cause of changes in observable behaviors.

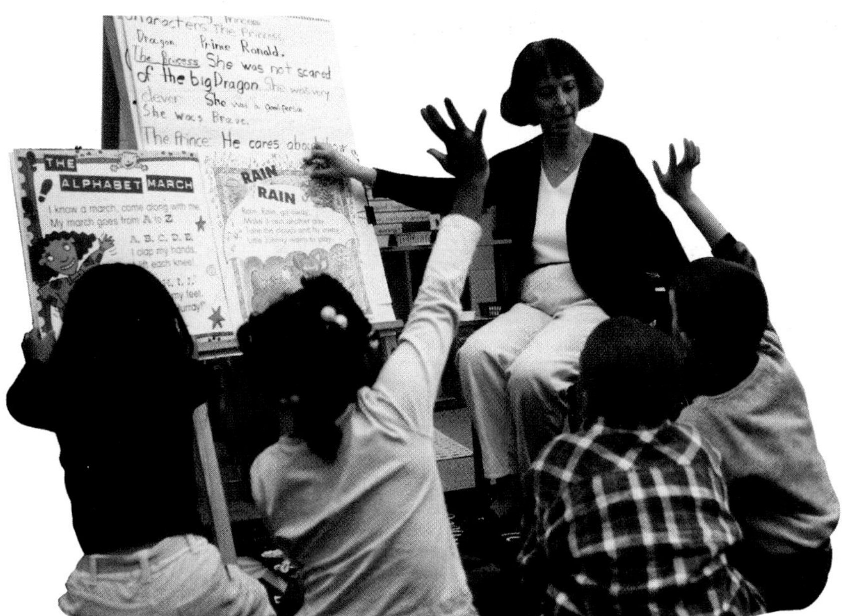

What is learning? Behavioral theorists emphasize the role of outside stimuli, focusing on behavior and observable responses.

"Let's start today with a kind of game. I will say some words, then I want you to tell me the first words you can think of. Don't bother to raise your hands. Just say the words out loud, and I will write them on the board. Don't all speak at once, though. Wait until someone else has finished to say your word. Okay, here is the first word: Slavery."

"Civil War." "Lincoln." "Freedom." "Emancipation Proclamation." The answers came very quickly, and Elizabeth was relieved to see that the students understood the game.

"All right, very good," she said. "Now try another one: South."

"South Carolina." "South Dakota." "South Street Seaport," "No, the Confederacy, you dummy." "*Gone with the Wind.*" "Clark Gable." With this last answer, a ripple of laughter moved across the room.

"Clark Gable!" Elizabeth sighed dreamily. "*Gone with the Wind* was on television last week." Then she laughed too. Soon all the students were laughing. "Okay, settle down," Elizabeth said. "Here is another word: North."

"Bluebellies." The students continued to laugh. "Yellowbellies." "Belly-dancers." More laughter and a few appropriate gestures.

"Just a minute," Elizabeth pleaded. "These ideas are getting a little off base!"

"Off base? Baseball," shouted the boy who had first mentioned Clark Gable. He stood up and started throwing balls of paper to a friend in the back of the room, simulating the style of Roger Clemens.

"The Atlanta Braves." "No, the Mets." "Shea Stadium." "Hot dogs." "Popcorn." "Movies." "DVDs," "*Gone with the Wind.*" "Clark Gable." The responses now came too fast for Elizabeth to stop them. For some reason, the Clark Gable line got an even bigger laugh the second time around, and Elizabeth suddenly realized she had lost the class.

"Okay, because you know so much about the Civil War, close your books and take out a pen," Elizabeth said, obviously angry. She passed out the worksheet that she had planned as a cooperative, open-book project. "You have 20 minutes to finish this test!"

"You didn't tell us we were having a test!" "This isn't fair!" "We haven't even covered this stuff yet!" "I didn't do anything wrong!" There were moans and disgusted looks, even from the most mellow students. "I'm reporting you to the principal; it's a violation of students' rights!"

This last comment hit hard. The class had just finished discussing human rights as preparation for this unit on the Civil War. As she listened to the protests, Elizabeth felt terrible. How was she going to grade these "tests"? The first section of the worksheet involved facts about events during the Civil War, and the second section asked students to create a news-style program interviewing ordinary people touched by the war.

"All right, all right, it won't be a test. But you do have to complete this worksheet for a grade. I was going to let you work together, but your behavior this morning tells me that you are not ready for group work. If you can complete the first section of the sheet working quietly and seriously, you may work together on the second section." Elizabeth knew that her students would like to work together on writing the script for the news interview program.

Elizabeth was afraid to look back at her supervisor. What was he writing on his observation form?

It appears, on the surface at least, that very little learning of any sort was taking place in Elizabeth's classroom. In fact, Elizabeth had some good ideas, but she also made some mistakes in her application of learning principles. We will return to this episode later in the chapter to analyze various aspects of what took place. To get us started, three events can be singled out, each possibly related to a different learning process.

First, Elizabeth's hands trembled when her college supervisor entered the room. Second, the students were able to associate the words *Carolina* and *Dakota* with the word *South*. Third, one student continued to disrupt the class with inappropriate responses. The three learning processes represented are classical conditioning, contiguity, and operant conditioning. In the following pages we will examine these three kinds of learning, starting with contiguity.

Check Yourself Define learning.

CONNECT & EXTEND

TO **PRAXIS**™
LEARNING BY ASSOCIATION
(I, A1)
Quite a bit of classroom learning can be attributed to contiguity (i.e., learning by association). What are some things that you might have learned because your teacher paired certain stimuli (e.g., names of the letters of the alphabet)?

Early Explanations of Learning: Contiguity and Classical Conditioning

One of the earliest explanations of learning came from Aristotle (384–322 B.C.). He said that we remember things together (1) when they are similar, (2) when they contrast, and (3) when they are *contiguous*. This last principle is the most important, because it is included in all explanations of *learning by association*. The principle of **contiguity** states that whenever two or more sensations occur together often enough, they will become associated. Later, when only one of these sensations (a **stimulus**) occurs, the other will be remembered too (a **response**) (Rachlin, 1991; Wasserman & Miller, 1997).

Some results of contiguous learning were evident in Elizabeth's class. When she said "South," students associated the words "Carolina" and "Dakota." They had heard these words together many times. Other learning processes may also be involved when students learn these phrases, but contiguity is a factor. Contiguity also plays a major role in another learning process best known as *classical conditioning*.

Contiguity Association of two events because of repeated pairing.

Stimulus Event that activates behavior.

Response Observable reaction to a stimulus.

Pavlov's Dilemma and Discovery: Classical Conditioning

STOP THINK WRITE Close your eyes and focus on a vivid image of the following:

The smell of French fries cooking. The taste of chocolate fudge.
A time you were really embarrassed in school. The sound of a dentist's drill.

What did you notice as you formed these images?

If you are like me, imagining the sound of the dentist's drill tightens your neck muscles. I can actually salivate when I imagine salty fries or smooth rich chocolate (especially because it is 11:57 PM and I am hungry). The first embarrassing school incident I remembered was falling flat as I did a cartwheel in front of the whole high school. A small cringe still accompanies the memory. **Classical conditioning** focuses on the learning of *involuntary* emotional or physiological responses such as fear, increased muscle tension, salivation, or sweating. These sometimes are called **respondents** because they are automatic responses to stimuli. Through the process of classical conditioning, humans and animals can be trained to react involuntarily to a stimulus that previously had no effect—or a very different effect—on them. The stimulus comes to *elicit,* or bring forth, the response automatically.

Classical conditioning was discovered by Ivan Pavlov, a Russian physiologist, in the 1920s. In his laboratory, Pavlov was plagued by a series of setbacks in his experiments on the digestive system of dogs. He was trying to determine how long it took a dog to secrete digestive juices after it had been fed, but the intervals of time kept changing. At first, the dogs salivated in the expected manner while they were being fed. Then the dogs began to salivate as soon as they saw the food. Finally, they salivated as soon as they saw the scientist enter the room. The white coats of the experimenters and the sound of their footsteps all *elicited* salivation. Pavlov decided to make a detour from his original experiments and examine these unexpected interferences in his work.

In one of his first experiments, Pavlov began by sounding a tuning fork and recording a dog's response. As expected, there was no salivation. At this point, the sound of the tuning fork was a **neutral stimulus** because it brought forth no salivation. Then Pavlov fed the dog. The response was salivation. The food was an **unconditioned stimulus (US)** because no prior training or "conditioning" was needed to establish the natural connection between food and salivation. The salivation was an **unconditioned response (UR),** again because it occurred automatically—no conditioning required.

Using these three elements—the food, the salivation, and the tuning fork—Pavlov demonstrated that a dog could be conditioned to salivate after hearing the tuning fork. He did this by contiguous pairing of the sound with food. At the beginning of the experiment, he sounded the fork and then quickly fed the dog. After Pavlov repeated this several times, the dog began to salivate after hearing the sound but before receiving the food. Now the sound had become a **conditioned stimulus (CS)** that could bring forth salivation by itself. The response of salivating after the tone was now a **conditioned response (CR).**

Generalization, Discrimination, and Extinction

Pavlov's work also identified three other processes in classical conditioning: *generalization, discrimination,* and *extinction* (Hill, 2002). After the dogs learned to salivate in response to hearing one particular sound, they would also salivate after hearing similar tones that were slightly higher or lower. This process is called **generalization** because the conditioned response of salivating generalized or occurred in the presence of similar stimuli. Pavlov could also teach the dogs **discrimination**—to respond to one tone but not to others that are similar—by making sure that food always followed only one tone, not any others. **Extinction** occurs when a conditioned stimulus (a particular tone) is presented repeatedly but is not followed by the unconditioned stimulus (food). The conditioned response (salivating) gradually fades away and finally is "extinguished"—it disappears altogether.

If you think that Pavlovian conditioning is of historical interest only, consider this excerpt from a story I read this morning in *USA Today* describing an advertising campaign for products aimed at "Gen Y," those people born between 1977 and 1994:

Classical conditioning Association of automatic responses with new stimuli.

Respondents Responses (generally automatic or involuntary) elicited by specific stimuli.

Neutral stimulus Stimulus not connected to a response.

Unconditioned stimulus (US) Stimulus that automatically produces an emotional or physiological response.

Unconditioned response (UR) Naturally occurring emotional or physiological response.

Conditioned stimulus (CS) Stimulus that evokes an emotional or physiological response after conditioning.

Conditioned response (CR) Learned response to a previously neutral stimulus.

Generalization Responding in the same way to similar stimuli.

Discrimination Responding differently to similar, but not identical stimuli.

Extinction Gradual disappearance of a learned response.

> Mountain Dew executives have their own term for this [advertising strategy]: the Pavlovian connection. By handing out samples of the brand at surfing, skateboard and snowboard tournaments, "There's a Pavlovian connection between the brand and the exhilarating experience," says Dave Burwich, a top marketing executive at Pepsi, which makes Mountain Dew. (Horovitz, April 22, 2002, p. B2)

Maybe they could hand out math homework too!

It is possible that many of our emotional reactions to various situations are learned in part through classical conditioning. For example, Elizabeth's trembling hands when she saw her college supervisor might be traced to previous unpleasant experiences. Perhaps she had been embarrassed during past evaluations of her performance, and now just the thought of being observed elicits a pounding heart and sweaty palms. Pavlov's findings and those of other researchers who have studied classical conditioning have implications for teachers as well as marketing managers. Remember that emotions and attitudes as well as facts and ideas are learned in classrooms. This emotional learning can sometimes interfere with academic learning. Procedures based on classical conditioning also can be used to help people learn more adaptive emotional responses, as the *Guidelines* suggest.

Check Yourself How does a neutral stimulus become a conditioned stimulus? Discriminate between generalization and discrimination.

CONNECT & EXTEND

TO **PRAXIS**™
BASICS OF OPERANT CONDITIONING (I, A1)
Be able to explain learning from the behavioral perspective. Incorporate concepts of *reward* and *punishment* into your explanation. Have a firm grasp of the effects of reinforcement schedules on learning.

Operant Conditioning: Trying New Responses

So far we have concentrated on the automatic conditioning of involuntary responses such as salivation and fear. Clearly, not all human learning is so automatic and unintentional. Most behaviors are not *elicited* by stimuli; they are *emitted* or voluntarily enacted. People actively "operate" on their environment to produce different kinds of

GUIDELINES: Applying Classical Conditioning

Associate positive, pleasant events with learning tasks.

Examples

1. Emphasize group competition and cooperation over individual competition. Many students have negative emotional responses to individual competition that may generalize to other learning.
2. Make division drills fun by having students decide how to divide refreshments equally, then letting them eat the results.
3. Make voluntary reading appealing by creating a comfortable reading corner with pillows, colorful displays of books, and reading props such as puppets (see Morrow & Weinstein, 1986, for more ideas).

Help students to risk anxiety-producing situations voluntarily and successfully.

Examples

1. Assign a shy student the responsibility of teaching two other students how to distribute materials for map study.
2. Devise small steps toward a larger goal. For example, give ungraded practice tests daily, and then weekly, to students who tend to "freeze" in test situations.
3. If a student is afraid of speaking in front of the class, let the student read a report to a small group while seated, then read it while standing, then give the report from notes instead of reading it verbatim. Next, move in stages toward having the student give a report to the whole class.

Help students recognize differences and similarities among situations so they can discriminate and generalize appropriately.

Examples

1. Explain that it is appropriate to avoid strangers who offer gifts or rides but safe to accept favors from adults when parents are present.
2. Assure students who are anxious about taking college entrance exams that this test is like all the other achievement tests they have taken.

consequences. These deliberate actions are called **operants.** The learning process involved in operant behavior is called **operant conditioning** because we learn to behave in certain ways as we operate on the environment.

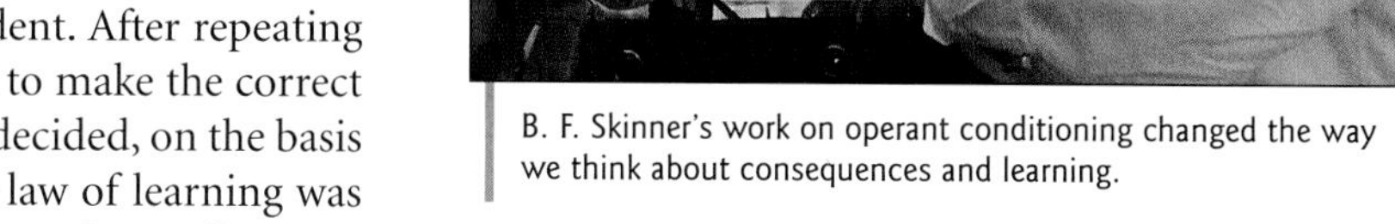

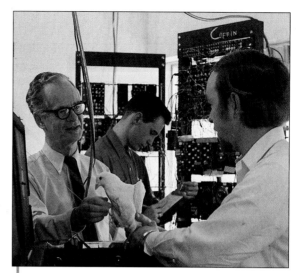

B. F. Skinner's work on operant conditioning changed the way we think about consequences and learning.

The Work of Thorndike and Skinner

Edward Thorndike and B. F. Skinner both played major roles in developing knowledge of operant conditioning. Thorndike's (1913) early work involved cats that he placed in puzzle boxes. To escape from the box and reach food outside, the cats had to pull out a bolt or perform some other task; they had to act on their environment. During the frenzied movements that followed the closing of the box, the cats eventually made the correct movement to escape, usually by accident. After repeating the process several times, the cats learned to make the correct response almost immediately. Thorndike decided, on the basis of these experiments, that one important law of learning was the *law of effect:* Any act that produces a satisfying effect in a given situation will tend to be repeated in that situation. Because pulling out a bolt produced satisfaction (access to food), cats repeated that movement when they found themselves in the box again.

Thorndike thus established the basis for operant conditioning, but the person generally thought to be responsible for developing the concept is B. F. Skinner (1953). Skinner began with the belief that the principles of classical conditioning account for only a small portion of learned behaviors. Many human behaviors are operants, not respondents. Classical conditioning describes only how existing behaviors might be paired with new stimuli; it does not explain how new operant behaviors are acquired.

Behavior, like response or action, is simply a word for what a person does in a particular situation. Conceptually, we may think of a behavior as sandwiched between two sets of environmental influences: those that precede it (its **antecedents**) and those that follow it (its **consequences**) (Skinner, 1950). This relationship can be shown very simply as antecedent–behavior–consequence, or A–B–C. As behavior is ongoing, a given consequence becomes an antecedent for the next ABC sequence. Research in operant conditioning shows that operant behavior can be altered by changes in the antecedents, the consequences, or both. Early work focused on consequences, often using rats or pigeons as subjects.

Types of Consequences

Think back over teachers you have had who used rewards or punishments. *Try to remember different types of rewards:*

Concrete rewards (stickers, food, prizes, certificates) ____________

Activity rewards (free time, puzzles, free reading) ____________

"Exemption" rewards (no homework, no weekly test) ____________

Social rewards (praise, recognition) ____________

What about punishments?

Loss of privileges (sit where you want, work with friends) ____________

Fines (lost points, grades, money) ____________

Extra work (homework, laps, push-ups) ____________

Operants Voluntary (and generally goal-directed) behaviors emitted by a person or an animal.

Operant conditioning Learning in which voluntary behavior is strengthened or weakened by consequences or antecedents.

Antecedents Events that precede an action.

Consequences Events that follow an action.

According to the behavioral view, consequences determine to a great extent whether a person will repeat the behavior that led to the consequences. The type and timing of consequences can strengthen or weaken behaviors. We will look first at consequences that strengthen behavior.

Reinforcement. Although **reinforcement** is commonly understood to mean "reward," this term has a particular meaning in psychology. A **reinforcer** is any consequence that strengthens the behavior it follows. So, by definition, *reinforced behaviors increase in frequency or duration.* Whenever you see a behavior persisting or increasing over time, you can assume the consequences of that behavior are reinforcers for the individual involved. The reinforcement process can be diagrammed as follows:

		CONSEQUENCE		EFFECT
Behavior	→	Reinforcer	→	Strengthened or repeated behavior

We can be fairly certain that food will be a reinforcer for a hungry animal, but what about people? It is not clear why an event acts as a reinforcer for an individual, but there are many theories about why reinforcement works. For example, some psychologists suggest that reinforcers satisfy needs, while other psychologists believe that reinforcers reduce tension or stimulate a part of the brain (Rachlin, 1991). Whether the consequences of any action are reinforcing probably depends on the individual's perception of the event and the meaning it holds for her or him. For example, students who repeatedly get themselves sent to the principal's office for misbehaving may be indicating that something about this consequence is reinforcing for them, even if it doesn't seem desirable to you. By the way, Skinner did not speculate about why reinforcers increase behavior. He believed that it was useless to talk about "imaginary constructs" such as meaning, habits, needs, or tensions. Skinner simply described the tendency for a given operant to increase after certain consequences (Hill, 2002; Skinner, 1953, 1989).

There are two types of reinforcement. The first, called **positive reinforcement,** occurs when the behavior produces a new stimulus. Examples include pecking on the red key producing food for a pigeon, wearing a new outfit producing many compliments, or falling out of your chair producing cheers and laughter from classmates.

Notice that positive reinforcement can occur even when the behavior being reinforced (falling out of a chair) is not "positive" from the teacher's point of view. In fact, positive reinforcement of inappropriate behaviors occurs unintentionally in many classrooms. Teachers help maintain problem behaviors by inadvertently reinforcing them. For example, Elizabeth may have unintentionally reinforced problem behavior in her class by laughing the first time the boy answered, "Clark Gable." The problem behavior may have persisted for other reasons, but the consequence of Elizabeth's laughter could have played a role.

When the consequence that strengthens a behavior is the *appearance* (addition) of a new stimulus, the situation is defined as positive reinforcement. In contrast, when the consequence that strengthens a behavior is the *disappearance* (subtraction) of a stimulus, the process is called **negative reinforcement.** If a particular action leads to avoiding or escaping an **aversive** situation, the action is likely to be repeated in a similar situation. A common example is the car seatbelt buzzer. As soon as you attach your seatbelt, the irritating buzzer stops. You are likely to repeat this action in the future because the behavior made an aversive stimulus disappear. Consider students who continually "get sick" right before a test and are sent to the nurse's office. The behavior allows the students to escape aversive situations—tests—so getting "sick" is being maintained, in part, through negative reinforcement. It is negative because the stimulus (the test) disappears; it is reinforcement because the behavior that caused the stimulus to disappear (getting "sick") increases or repeats. It is also possible that classical conditioning plays a role. The students may have been conditioned to experience unpleasant physiological reactions to tests.

The "negative" in negative reinforcement does not imply that the behavior being reinforced is necessarily negative. The meaning is closer to that of "negative" numbers—

CONNECT & EXTEND

TO YOUR TEACHING

To become aware of the prevalence of reinforcement in daily life, keep a log, noting every time you give or receive reinforcement. Look for positive and negative reinforcement and also record the kind of schedule operating. Another possibility is to note reinforcement and schedules in a field placement classroom or even in college classes. What examples of reinforcement are present in your education classes?

CONNECT & EXTEND

TO YOUR TEACHING

Positive reinforcement: Praise for good grades, bonus points on tests, a class pizza party when everyone makes above 85 on the weekly spelling test. *Negative reinforcement:* Removing a stone from your shoe; calling on a child who is madly waving his hand and shouting, "I know, I know!" (you are negatively reinforced because the noise stops); wearing a certain pair of shoes on trips to avoid aching feet; saying "I'm really sorry" to your spouse to avoid his or her anger. *Presentation punishment:* Running extra laps; reprimands; bad grades; corporal punishment. *Removal punishment:* Fines; being grounded; missing recess; not being allowed to go on the field trip; getting fired.

Reinforcement Use of consequences to strengthen behavior.

Reinforcer Any event that follows a behavior and increases the chances that the behavior will occur again.

Positive reinforcement Strengthening behavior by presenting a desired stimulus after the behavior.

Negative reinforcement Strengthening behavior by removing an aversive stimulus when the behavior occurs.

Aversive Irritating or unpleasant.

something is subtracted. Associate *positive* and *negative* reinforcement with *adding* or *subtracting* something following a behavior that strengthens the behavior.

Punishment. Negative reinforcement is often confused with punishment. The process of reinforcement (positive or negative) always involves strengthening behavior. **Punishment,** on the other hand, involves *decreasing or suppressing behavior.* A behavior followed by a punisher is *less* likely to be repeated in similar situations in the future. Again, it is the effect that defines a consequence as punishment, and different people have different perceptions of what is punishing. One student may find suspension from school punishing, while another student wouldn't mind at all. The process of punishment is diagrammed as follows:

		CONSEQUENCE		EFFECT
Behavior	→	Punisher	→	Weakened or decreased behavior

Like reinforcement, punishment may take one of two forms. The first type has been called Type I punishment, but this name isn't very informative, so I use the term **presentation punishment.** It occurs when the appearance of a stimulus following the behavior suppresses or decreases the behavior. When teachers assign demerits, extra work, running laps, and so on, they are using presentation punishment. I call the other type of punishment (Type II punishment) **removal punishment** because it involves removing a stimulus. When teachers or parents take away privileges after a young person has behaved inappropriately, they are applying removal punishment. With both types, the effect is to decrease the behavior that led to the punishment. Figure 6.1 summarizes the processes of reinforcement and punishment.

CONNECT & EXTEND

TO YOUR TEACHING
Recall an instance of punishment that you have experienced at some time during your life. What were your feelings when you were being punished? List the feelings. (Negative feelings, such as embarrassment, resentment, hurt, anger, etc., probably will account for 90% of the responses.) Does the punishment work? What are some other negative effects of punishment? If punishment is ineffective and also produces negative side effects, why do so many teachers rely on it so much?

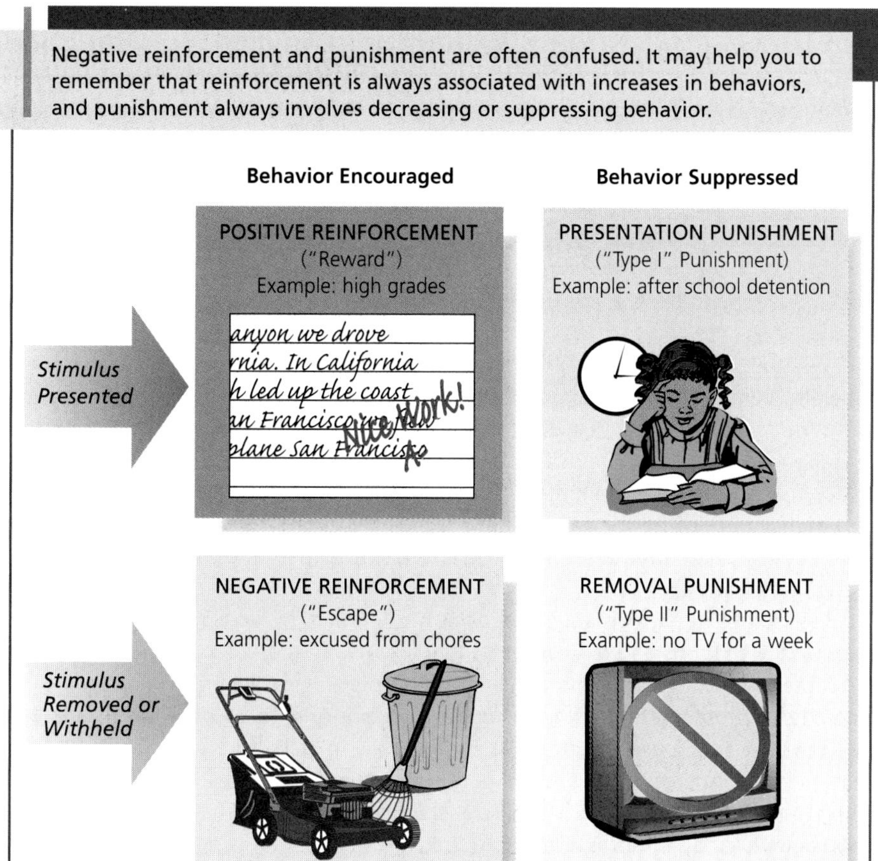

Figure 6.1 Kinds of Reinforcement and Punishment

Punishment Process that weakens or suppresses behavior.

Presentation punishment Decreasing the chances that a behavior will occur again by presenting an aversive stimulus following the behavior; also called Type I punishment.

Removal punishment Decreasing the chances that a behavior will occur again by removing a pleasant stimulus following the behavior; also called Type II punishment.

Table 6.1 Reinforcement Schedules

Schedule	Definition	Example	Response Pattern	Reaction When Reinforcement Stops
Continuous	Reinforcement after every response	Turning on the television	Rapid learning of response	Very little persistence; rapid disappearance of response
Fixed-interval	Reinforcement after a set period of time	Weekly quiz	Response rate increases as time for reinforcement approaches, then drops after reinforcement	Little persistence; rapid drop in response rate when time for reinforcement passes and no reinforcer appears
Variable-interval	Reinforcement after varying lengths of time	Pop quizzes	Slow, steady rate of responding; very little pause after reinforcement	Greater persistence; slow decline in response rate
Fixed-ratio	Reinforcement after a set number of responses	Piece work Bake sale	Rapid response rate; pause after reinforcement	Little persistence; rapid drop in response rate when expected number of responses are given and no reinforcer appears
Variable-ratio	Reinforcement after a varying number of responses	Slot machines	Very high response rate; little pause after reinforcement	Greatest persistence; response rate stays high and gradually drops off

Reinforcement Schedules

When people are learning a new behavior, they will learn it faster if they are reinforced for every correct response. This is a **continuous reinforcement schedule.** Then, when the new behavior has been mastered, they will maintain it best if they are reinforced intermittently rather than every time. An **intermittent reinforcement schedule** helps students to maintain skills without expecting constant reinforcement.

There are two basic types of intermittent reinforcement schedules. One—called an **interval schedule**—is based on the amount of time that passes between reinforcers. The other—a **ratio schedule**—is based on the number of responses learners give between reinforcers. Interval and ratio schedules may be either *fixed* (predictable) or *variable* (unpredictable). Table 6.1 summarizes the five possible reinforcement schedules (the continuous schedule and the four kinds of intermittent schedules).

What are the effects of different schedules? Speed of performance depends on control. If reinforcement is based on the number of responses you give, then you have more control over the reinforcement: The faster you accumulate the correct number of responses, the faster the reinforcement will come. A teacher who says, "As soon as you complete these ten problems correctly, you may go to the student lounge," can expect higher rates of performance than a teacher who says, "Work on these ten problems for the next 20 minutes. Then I will check your papers and those with ten correct may go to the lounge."

Persistence in performance depends on unpredictability. Continuous reinforcement and both kinds of fixed reinforcement (ratio and interval) are quite predictable. We come to expect reinforcement at certain points and are generally quick to give up when the reinforcement does not meet our expectations. To encourage persistence of response, variable schedules are most appropriate. In fact, if the schedule is gradually changed until it becomes very "lean"—meaning that reinforcement occurs only after many responses or a long time interval—then people can learn to work for extended periods without any reinforcement at all. Just watch gamblers playing slot machines to see how powerful a lean reinforcement schedule can be.

Reinforcement schedules influence how persistently we will respond when reinforcement is withheld. What happens when reinforcement is completely withdrawn?

CONNECT & EXTEND

TO YOUR TEACHING PORTFOLIO
When a teacher decides to begin ignoring a behavior that he or she wants to extinguish, there is frequently an increase in the behavior for a short time before it decreases. How do you explain this phenomenon?

Continuous reinforcement schedule Presenting a reinforcer after every appropriate response.

Intermittent reinforcement schedule Presenting a reinforcer after some but not all responses.

Interval schedule Length of time between reinforcers.

Ratio schedule Reinforcement based on the number of responses between reinforcers.

Extinction. In classical conditioning, we saw that the conditioned response was extinguished (disappeared) when the conditioned stimulus appeared but the unconditioned stimulus did not follow (tone, but no food). In operant conditioning, a person or an animal will not persist in a certain behavior if the usual reinforcer is withheld long enough. The behavior will eventually be extinguished (stop). For example, if you go for a week without selling even one magazine door-to-door, you may give up. Removal of reinforcement altogether leads to extinction. The process may take a while, however, as you know if you have tried to extinguish a child's tantrums by withholding your attention. Often the child wins—you give up ignoring and instead of extinction, intermittent reinforcement occurs. This, of course, may encourage even more persistent tantrums in the future.

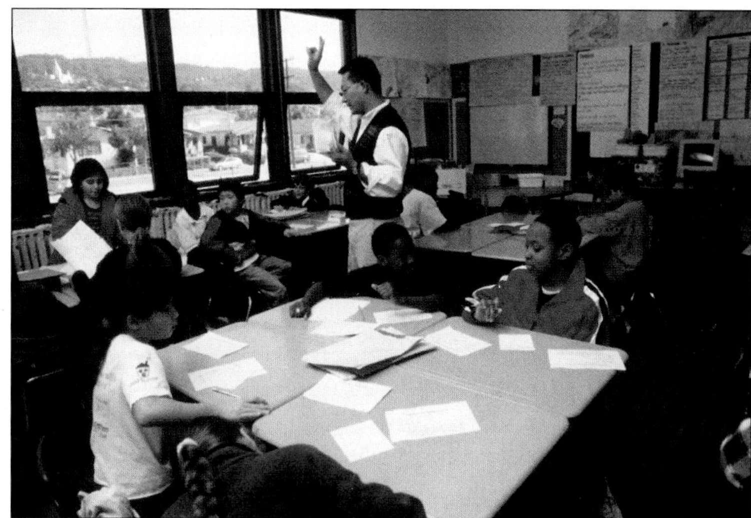

This teacher uses a visual cue to prompt his students to quiet down in class.

Antecedents and Behavior Change

In operant conditioning, antecedents—the events preceding behaviors—provide information about which behaviors will lead to positive consequences and which will lead to negative ones. Skinner's pigeons learned to peck for food when a light was on, but not to bother when the light was off, because no food followed pecking when the light was off. In other words, they learned to use the antecedent light as a cue to discriminate the likely consequence of pecking. The pigeons' pecking was under **stimulus control,** controlled by the discriminative stimulus of the light. You can see that this idea is related to discrimination in classical conditioning, but here we are talking about voluntary behaviors such as pecking, not reflexes such as salivating.

We all learn to discriminate—to read situations. When should you ask to borrow your roommate's car, after a major disagreement or after you both have had a great time at a party? The antecedent cue of a school principal standing in the hall helps students discriminate the probable consequences of running or attempting to break into a locker. We often respond to such antecedent cues without fully realizing that they are influencing our behavior. But teachers can use cues deliberately in the classroom.

Cueing. By definition, **cueing** is the act of providing an antecedent stimulus just before a particular behavior is to take place. Cueing is particularly useful in setting the stage for behaviors that must occur at a specific time but are easily forgotten. In working with young people, teachers often find themselves correcting behaviors after the fact. For example, they may ask students, "When are you going to start remembering to . . . ?" Such reminders often lead to irritation. The mistake is already made, and the young person is left with only two choices, to promise to try harder or to say, "Why don't you leave me alone?" Neither response is very satisfying. Presenting a nonjudgmental cue can help prevent these negative confrontations. When a student performs the appropriate behavior after a cue, the teacher can reinforce the student's accomplishment instead of punishing the student's failure.

Prompting. Sometimes students need help in learning to respond to a cue in an appropriate way so the cue becomes a discriminative stimulus. One approach is to

CONNECT & EXTEND

TO YOUR TEACHING

Examples of stimulus control: I found myself (more than once) about to turn into my old office parking lot, even after my department had been moved to a new building across town. The old cues kept me heading automatically to the old office. Another example is the supposedly true story of a getaway car driver in a bank robbery who sped through town, only to be caught by the police when she dutifully stopped at a red light. The stimulus of the red light had come to have automatic control.

CONNECT & EXTEND

TO YOUR TEACHING PORTFOLIO

Suggest the cues or prompts you would use to elicit the following behaviors: (1) the class looks at you to hear your directions; (2) the students open their books to the assigned page when the bell rings; (3) the students give you their full attention when you are making an important point; and (4) a student walks instead of running to the door when the dismissal bell rings.

Stimulus control Capacity for the presence or absence of antecedents to cause behaviors.

Cueing Providing a stimulus that "sets up" a desired behavior.

By using this checklist, students are reminded how to be effective tutors. As they become more proficient, the checklist may be less necessary.

Remember to...

____ 1. Have the lesson ready.

____ 2. Talk clearly.

____ 3. Be friendly.

____ 4. Tell the student when the answer is right.

____ 5. Correct mistakes. STOP! Give the right answer. Have the student do it.

____ 6. Praise good work!

____ 7. Make the lesson fun.

____ 8. Do not give TOO MUCH help.

____ 9. Fill out the daily sheet.

____ 10. Can you add a suggestion?

Source: From *Achieving Educational Excellence: Behavior Analysis for School Personnel* (Figure, p. 89), by B. Sulzer-Azaroff and G. R. Mayer, 1994, San Marcos, CA: Western Image, P.O. Box 427. Copyright © 1994 by Beth Sulzer-Azaroff and G. Roy Mayer. Reprinted by permission of the authors.

Figure 6.2 Written Prompts: A Peer-Tutoring Checklist

provide an additional cue, called a **prompt,** following the first cue. There are two principles for using a cue and a prompt to teach a new behavior (Becker, Engelmann, & Thomas, 1975). First, make sure the environmental stimulus that you want to become a cue occurs immediately before the prompt you are using, so students will learn to respond to the cue and not rely only on the prompt. Second, fade the prompt as soon as possible so students do not become dependent on it.

An example of cueing and prompting is providing students with a checklist or reminder sheet. Figure 6.2 is a checklist for the steps in peer tutoring. Working in pairs is the cue; the checklist is the prompt. As students learn the procedures, the teacher may stop using the checklist, but may remind the students of the steps. When no written or oral prompts are necessary, the students have learned to respond appropriately to the environmental cue of working in pairs—they have learned how to behave in tutoring situations. However, the teacher should continue to monitor the process, recognize good work, and correct mistakes. Before a tutoring session, the teacher might ask students to close their eyes and "see" the checklist, focusing on each step. As students work, the teacher could listen to their interactions and continue to coach students as they improve their tutoring skills.

CONNECT & EXTEND

TO **PRAXIS**™
ANTECEDENTS (I, A1)
Understand how antecedents can affect learning. Be particularly familiar with the effective uses of prompting and cueing.

Prompt A reminder that follows a cue to make sure the person reacts to the cue.

Applied behavior analysis The application of behavioral learning principles to understand and change behavior.

Behavior modification Systematic application of antecedents and consequences to change behavior.

Check Yourself What defines a consequence as a reinforcer? As a punisher?

Negative reinforcement is often confused with punishment. How are they different?

How can you encourage persistence in a behavior?

What is the difference between a prompt and a cue?

Applied Behavior Analysis

Applied behavior analysis is the application of behavioral learning principles to change behavior. The method is sometimes called **behavior modification,** but this term has negative connotations for many people and is often misunderstood (Alberto & Troutman, 2003; Kaplan, 1991; Kazdin, 2001).

Ideally, applied behavior analysis requires clear specification of the behavior to be changed, careful measurement of the behavior, analysis of the antecedents and reinforcers that might be maintaining inappropriate or undesirable behavior, interventions based on behavioral principles to change the behavior, and careful measurement of changes. In research on applied behavior analysis, an ABAB (described in Chapter 1) design is common. That is, researchers take a baseline measurement of the behavior (A), then apply the intervention (B), then stop the intervention to see if the behavior goes back to the baseline level (A), and then reintroduce the intervention (B).

In classrooms, teachers usually cannot follow all the ABAB steps, but they can do the following:

1. Clearly specify the behavior to be changed and note the current level. For example, if a student is "careless," does this mean 2, 3, 4, or more computation errors for every 10 problems?
2. Plan a specific intervention using antecedents, consequences, or both. For example, offer the student one extra minute of computer time for every problem completed with no errors.
3. Keep track of the results, and modify the plan if necessary.

Let's consider some specific methods for accomplishing step 2—the *intervention.*

CONNECT & EXTEND

TO PRAXIS™ APPLIED BEHAVIOR ANALYSIS (I, C4)
When teachers need to change inappropriate or ineffective classroom behaviors that have not changed in response to standard behavioral techniques (e.g., response cost), they often employ applied behavior analysis. Familiarize yourself with the steps in developing and implementing an intervention based on that technique.

Methods for Encouraging Behaviors

As we discussed earlier, to encourage behavior is to reinforce it. There are several specific ways to encourage existing behaviors or teach new ones. These include praise, the Premack principle, shaping, and positive practice.

CONNECT & EXTEND

TO THE RESEARCH
For an up-to-date look at applied behavior analysis, see: Kazdin, A. E. (2001). *Behavior modification in applied settings* (6th ed.). Belmont, CA: Wadsworth and Alberto, P. A., & Troutman, A. C. (2003). *Applied behavior analysis for teachers* (6th ed.). Saddle River, NJ: Prentice-Hall.

Reinforcing with Teacher Attention. Based on early work such as that of Madsen, Becker, and Thomas (1968) demonstrating that teachers can improve student behavior by ignoring rule-breakers and praising students who are following the rules, many psychologists advised teachers to "accentuate the positive"—liberally praise students for good behavior while ignoring mistakes and misbehavior. This *praise-and-ignore approach* can be helpful, but we should not expect it to solve all classroom management problems. Several studies have shown that disruptive behaviors persist when teachers use positive consequences (mostly praise) as their only classroom management strategy (McGoey & DuPaul, 2000; Pfiffner & O'Leary, 1987; Sullivan & O'Leary, 1990).

There is a second consideration in using praise. The positive results found in research occur when teachers carefully and systematically praise their students. Unfortunately, praise is not always given appropriately and effectively. Merely "handing out compliments"

Praise can be an effective technique for class management and the encouragement of learning if it is used only as a sincere recognition of well-defined behavior.

Using Praise Appropriately

Be clear and systematic in giving praise.

Examples

1. Make sure praise is tied directly to appropriate behavior.
2. Make sure the student understands the specific action or accomplishment that is being praised. Say, "You returned this poster on time and in good condition," not, "You were very responsible."

Recognize genuine accomplishments.

Examples

1. Reward the attainment of specified goals, not just participation.
2. Do not reward uninvolved students just for being quiet and not disrupting the class.
3. Tie praise to students' improving competence or to the value of their accomplishment. Say, "I noticed that you double-checked all your problems. Your score reflects your careful work."

Set standards for praise based on individual abilities and limitations.

Examples

1. Praise progress or accomplishment in relation to the individual student's past efforts.
2. Focus the student's attention on his or her own progress, not on comparisons with others.

Attribute the student's success to effort and ability so the student will gain confidence that success is possible again.

Examples

1. Don't imply that the success may be based on luck, extra help, or easy material.
2. Ask students to describe the problems they encountered and how they solved them.

Make praise really reinforcing.

Examples

1. Don't attempt to influence the rest of the class by singling out some students for praise. This tactic frequently backfires, because students know what's really going on. In addition, you risk embarrassing the student you have chosen to praise.
2. Don't give undeserved praise to students simply to balance failures. It is seldom consoling and calls attention to the student's inability to earn genuine recognition.

will not improve behavior. To be effective, praise must (1) be contingent on the behavior to be reinforced, (2) specify clearly the behavior being reinforced, and (3) be believable (O'Leary & O'Leary, 1977). In other words, the praise should be sincere recognition of a well-defined behavior so students understand what they did to warrant the recognition. Teachers who have not received special training often violate these conditions (Brophy, 1981). Ideas for using praise effectively, based on Brophy's extensive review of the subject, are presented in the *Guidelines* above.

Some psychologists have suggested that teachers' use of praise tends to focus students on learning to win approval rather than on learning for its own sake. Perhaps the best advice is to be aware of the potential dangers of the overuse or misuse of praise and to navigate accordingly.

Selecting Reinforcers: The Premack Principle. In most classrooms, there are many readily available reinforcers other than teacher attention, such as the chance to talk to other students or feed the class animals. However, teachers tend to offer these opportunities in a rather haphazard way. Just as with praise, by making privileges and rewards directly contingent on learning and positive behavior, the teacher may greatly increase both learning and desired behavior.

A helpful guide for choosing the most effective reinforcers is the **Premack principle,** named for David Premack (1965). According to the Premack principle, a high-frequency behavior (a preferred activity) can be an effective reinforcer for a low-frequency behavior (a less-preferred activity). This is sometimes referred to as "Grandma's rule": First do what I want you to do, then you may do what you want to do. Elizabeth used this principle in her class when she told them they could work together on their Civil War news program after they quietly completed the first section of the worksheet on their own.

Premack principle Principle stating that a more-preferred activity can serve as a reinforcer for a less-preferred activity.

If students didn't have to study, what would they do? The answers to this question may suggest many possible reinforcers. For most students, talking, moving around the room, sitting near a friend, being exempt from assignments or tests, reading magazines, using the computer, or playing games are preferred activities. The best way to determine appropriate reinforcers for your students may be to watch what they do in their free time.

For the Premack principle to be effective, the low-frequency (less preferred) behavior must happen first. In the following dialogue, notice how the teacher loses a perfect opportunity to use the Premack principle:

Students: Oh, no! Do we have to work on grammar again today? The other classes got to discuss the film we saw in the auditorium this morning.

Teacher: But the other classes finished the lesson on sentences yesterday. We're almost finished too. If we don't finish the lesson, I'm afraid you'll forget the rules we reviewed yesterday.

Students: Why don't we finish the sentences at the end of the period and talk about the film now?

Teacher: Okay, if you promise to complete the sentences later.

"Hey, wait a minute! You're cleaning erasers as a punishment? I'm cleaning erasers as a reward!"

(© 1991 Tony Saltzmann)

Discussing the film could have served as a reinforcer for completing the lesson. As it is, the class may well spend the entire period discussing the film. Just as the discussion becomes fascinating, the teacher will have to end it and insist that the class return to the grammar lesson.

Some teachers use questionnaires such as the one in Table 6.2 to identify effective reinforcers for their students. Remember, what works for one student may not be right for another. And students can get "too much of a good thing"; reinforcers can lose their potency if they are overused. See the *Stories of Learning/Tributes to Teaching* feature on page 212 to read how one educator remembers the positive practices of her teacher over a half-century ago.

Shaping. What happens when students continually fail to gain reinforcement because they simply cannot perform a skill in the first place? Consider these examples:

- A 4th-grade student looks at the results of the latest mathematics test. "No credit on almost half of the problems again because I made one dumb mistake in each problem. I hate math!"
- A 10th-grade student tries each day to find some excuse for avoiding the softball game in gym class. The student cannot catch a ball and now refuses to try.

Table 6.2 What Do You Like? Reinforcement Ideas from Students

Name ______________________ **Grade** ________ **Date** ____________

Please answer all the questions as completely as you can.

1. The school subjects I like best are:
2. Three things I like most to do in school are:
3. If I had 30 minutes' free time at school each day to do what I really liked, it would be:
4. My two favorite snacks are:
5. At recess I like most to (three things):
6. If I had $1 to spend on anything, I would buy:
7. Three jobs I would enjoy in the class are:
8. The two people I most like to work with in school are:
9. At home I really enjoy (three things):

SOURCE: From *Modification of Child and Adolescent Behavior* (3rd ed.), by G. Blackman and A. Silberman. Published by Wadsworth, Belmont, CA. Copyright © 1979 by Wadsworth Publishing Co. Reprinted with permission of the publisher.

~ Stories of Learning Tributes to Teaching ~

My third-grade teacher taught a really comprehensive program. She was a good model. . . . She brought in home economics, she read stories, she did all kinds of things that made you know that you could do anything in the world.

I can remember hearing about New York City from her reading a book, and I got the idea back then: "One of these days, I'm going to go to New York City."

She talked about the high-rise apartments and the elevators, and I could just feel myself going up the elevators and coming down, and I'd never seen an elevator before, growing up in rural Mississippi!

She was the kind who always gave you incentives for doing something. She would take two people from the class, either weekly or monthly, to go to her house for a meal. She had all kinds of ways you could earn that privilege—maybe by coming to school every day, by doing your work every day, or by being a good citizen; all kinds of things. It was possible for everybody to earn that nice gift. You didn't have to be an A student, you could always do other things. I am sure that she had it set up so that every student got a chance to go to her house during the school year. The way she had it fixed, everybody was a winner; nobody would lose. When we went to her house, we would help her to prepare the meal. She would teach us how to set the table because we didn't have the silver at home to do it. She taught us that you put the fork on the left and the knife and the spoon on the right.

—Virgie Binford, Educational Consultant, Richmond Virginia

SOURCE: From *Mentors, Masters, and Mrs. MacGregor* (pp. 229–230) by J. Bluestein. Copyright © 1995 by Health Communications. Adapted by permission of the publisher.

In both situations the students are receiving no reinforcement for their work because the end product of their efforts is not good enough. A safe prediction is that the students will soon learn to dislike the class, the subject, and perhaps the teacher and school in general. One way to prevent this problem is the strategy of **shaping,** also called **successive approximations.** Shaping involves reinforcing progress instead of waiting for perfection.

In order to use shaping, the teacher must break down the final complex behavior the student is expected to master into a number of small steps. One approach identifying the small steps is **task analysis,** originally developed by R. B. Miller (1962) to help the armed services train personnel. Miller's system begins with a definition of the final performance requirement, what the trainee (or student) must be able to do at the end of the program or unit. Then the steps that will lead to the final goal are specified. The procedure simply breaks skills and processes down into subskills and subprocesses.

Consider an example of task analysis in which students must write a position paper based on library research. If the teacher assigned the position paper without analyzing the task in this way, what could happen? Some of the students might not know how to do computer searching. They might search through one or two encyclopedias, then write a summary of the issues based only on the encyclopedia articles. Another group of students might know how to use computers, tables of contents, and indexes, but have difficulty reaching conclusions. They might hand in lengthy papers listing summaries of different ideas. Another group of students might be able to draw conclusions, but their written presentations might be so confusing and grammatically incorrect that the teacher could not understand what they were trying to say. Each of the groups would have failed in fulfilling the assignment, but for different reasons.

A task analysis gives a picture of the logical sequence of steps leading toward the final goal. An awareness of this sequence can help teachers make sure that students have the necessary skills before they move to the next step. In addition, when students have difficulty, the teacher can pinpoint problem areas.

CONNECT & EXTEND

TO **PRAXIS**™
ENCOURAGING/DISCOURAGING BEHAVIORS (I, B2)
Understand the appropriate uses of techniques to encourage or discourage various classroom behaviors. Know the limitations and problems associated with these types of interventions.

Shaping Reinforcing each small step of progress toward a desired goal or behavior.

Successive approximations Small components that make up a complex behavior.

Task analysis System for breaking down a task hierarchically into basic skills and subskills.

GUIDELINES ENCOURAGING POSITIVE BEHAVIORS

Make sure you recognize positive behavior in ways that students value.

Examples

1. When presenting class rules, set up positive consequences for following rules as well as negative consequences for breaking rules.
2. Recognize honest admissions of mistakes by giving a second chance: "Because you admitted that you copied your paper from a book, I'm giving you a chance to rewrite it."
3. Offer desired rewards for academic efforts, such as extra recess time, exemptions from homework or tests, or extra credit on major projects.

When students are tackling new material or trying new skills, give plenty of reinforcement.

Examples

1. Find and comment on something right in every student's first life drawing.
2. Reinforce students for encouraging each other. "French pronunciation is difficult and awkward at first. Let's help each other by eliminating all giggles when someone is brave enough to attempt a new word."

After new behaviors are established, give reinforcement on an unpredictable schedule to encourage persistence.

Examples

1. Offer surprise rewards for good participation in class.
2. Start classes with a short, written extra-credit question. Students don't have to answer, but a good answer will add points to their total for the semester.
3. Make sure the good students get compliments for their work from time to time. Don't take them for granted.

Use cueing to help establish new behaviors.

Examples

1. Put up humorous signs in the classroom to remind students of rules.
2. At the beginning of the year, as students enter class, call their attention to a list on the board of the materials they should have with them when they come to class.

Make sure all students, even those who often cause problems, receive some praise, privileges, or other rewards when they do something well.

Examples

1. Review your class list occasionally to make sure all students are receiving some reinforcement.
2. Set standards for reinforcement so that all students will have a chance to be rewarded.

Establish a variety of reinforcers.

Examples

1. Let students suggest their own reinforcers or choose from a "menu" of reinforcers with "weekly specials."
2. Talk to other teachers or parents about ideas for reinforcers.

Use the Premack principle to identify effective reinforcers.

Examples

1. Watch what students do with their free time.
2. Notice which students like to work together. The chance to work with friends is often a good reinforcer.

Krumboltz and Krumboltz (1972) have described the following three methods of shaping: (1) reinforce each subskill, (2) reinforce improvements in accuracy, and (3) reinforce longer and longer periods of performance or participation. Many behaviors can be improved through shaping, especially skills that involve persistence, endurance, increased accuracy, greater speed, or extensive practice to master. Because shaping is a time-consuming process, however, it should not be used if success can be attained through simpler methods such as cueing.

Positive Practice. A strategy for helping students replace one behavior with another is **positive practice.** This approach is especially appropriate for dealing with academic errors. When students make a mistake, they must correct it as soon as possible and practice the correct response (Gibbs & Luyben, 1985; Kazdin, 1984). The same principle can be applied when students break classroom rules. Instead of being punished, the student might be required to practice the correct alternative action.

The *Guidelines* above summarize approaches encouraging positive behavior.

Coping with Undesirable Behavior

No matter how successful you are at accentuating the positive, there are times when you must cope with undesirable behavior, either because other methods fail or because the

Positive practice Practicing correct responses immediately after errors.

CONNECT & EXTEND

TO YOUR TEACHING PORTFOLIO
Examples of negative reinforcement: A 10th-grade teacher tells her class that those students who turn in sloppy, careless work will have to use their free-choice time to redo it. A 1st-grade teacher tells an angry boy that he must sit by the tree until he feels able to rejoin the kickball game without arguing.

behavior itself is dangerous and calls for direct action. For this purpose, negative reinforcement, satiation, reprimands, and punishment all offer possible solutions.

Negative Reinforcement. Recall the basic principle of negative reinforcement: If an action stops or avoids something unpleasant, then the action is likely to occur again in similar situations. Negative reinforcement was operating in Elizabeth's classroom. When she gave in to the moans and complaints of her class and canceled the test, her behavior was being negatively reinforced. She escaped the unpleasant student comments by changing her assignment, but students may have learned to complain more in the future through negative reinforcement.

Negative reinforcement may also be used to enhance learning. To do this, you place students in mildly unpleasant situations so they can "escape" when their behavior improves. Consider these examples:

> *Teacher to a 3rd-grade class:* "When the supplies are put back in the cabinet and each of you is sitting quietly, we will go outside. Until then, we will miss our recess."
>
> *High school teacher to a student who seldom finishes in-class assignments:* "As soon as you complete the assignment, you may join the class in the auditorium. But until you finish, you must work in the study hall."

Actually, a true behaviorist might object to calling these examples of negative reinforcement because too much student thinking and understanding is required to make them work. Teachers cannot treat students like lab animals, delivering a mild shock to their feet until they give a right answer, then turning off the shock briefly. But teachers can make sure that unpleasant situations improve when student behavior improves.

You may wonder why the examples above are not considered punishment. Surely staying in during recess or not accompanying the class to a special program is punishing. But the focus in each case is on strengthening specific behaviors (putting away supplies or finishing in-class assignments). The teacher strengthens (reinforces) the behaviors by removing something aversive *as soon as the desired behaviors occur.* Because the consequence involves removing or "subtracting" a stimulus, the reinforcement is negative.

Negative reinforcement also gives students a chance to exercise control. Missing recess and staying behind in study hall are unpleasant situations, but in each case the students retain control. As soon as they perform the appropriate behavior, the unpleasant situation ends. In contrast, punishment occurs after the fact, and a student cannot so easily control or terminate it.

There are several rules for negative reinforcement: Describe the desired change in a positive way. Don't bluff. Make sure you can enforce your unpleasant situation. Follow through despite complaints. Insist on action, not promises. If the unpleasant situation terminates when students promise to be better next time, you have reinforced making promises, not making changes (Krumboltz & Krumboltz, 1972; O'Leary, 1995).

CONNECT & EXTEND

TO YOUR TEACHING PORTFOLIO
Satiation: A 6th-grade teacher discovered one of his students making paper airplanes during an independent work time. He gave that student a stack of paper and told her to continue making airplanes until the stack of paper was gone. The student thought it was great fun for the first 10 minutes, but then she got weary and wanted to stop. After this experience, this student made better use of her independent work times.

Satiation Requiring a person to repeat a problem behavior past the point of interest or motivation.

Satiation. Another way to stop problem behavior is to insist that students continue the behavior until they are tired of doing it. This procedure, called **satiation,** should be applied with care. Forcing students to continue some behaviors may be physically or emotionally harmful or even dangerous.

An example of an appropriate use of satiation is related by Krumboltz and Krumboltz (1972). In the middle of a 9th-grade algebra class, the teacher suddenly noticed four students making all sorts of unusual motions. In response to persistent teacher questioning, the students finally admitted they were bouncing imaginary balls. The teacher pretended to greet this idea with enthusiasm and suggested the whole class do it. At first, there was a great deal of laughing and joking. After a minute this stopped, and one student even quit. The teacher, however, insisted that all the students continue. After 5 minutes and a number of exhausted sighs, the teacher allowed the students to stop. No one bounced an imaginary ball in that class again.

Teachers also may allow students to continue some action until they stop by themselves, if the behavior is not interfering with the rest of the class. A teacher can do this by simply ignoring the behavior. Remember that responding to an ignorable behavior may actually reinforce it.

In using satiation, a teacher must take care not to give in before the students do. It is also important that the repeated behavior be the one you are trying to end. If the algebra teacher above had insisted that the students write, "I will never bounce imaginary balls in class again" 500 times, the students would have become satiated with writing rather than with bouncing balls.

Reprimands. In the *Junction Journal,* my daughter's elementary-school newspaper, I read the following lines in a story called "Why I Like School," written by a 4th grader: "I also like my teacher. She helps me understand and learn. She is nice to everyone. . . . I like it when she gets mad at somebody, but she doesn't yell at them in front of the class, but speaks to them privately."

A study by Dan O'Leary and his associates examined the effectiveness of soft, private **reprimands** versus loud, public reprimands in decreasing disruptive behavior (O'Leary, Kaufman, Kass, & Drabman, 1970). Reprimanding a problem student quietly so that only the student can hear seems to be much more effective. When the teacher in the study spoke to offenders loudly enough for the entire class to hear, the disruptions increased or continued at a constant level. Some students enjoy public recognition for misbehavior. If reprimands are not used too often, and if the classroom is generally a positive, warm environment, then students usually respond quickly (Kaplan, 1991; Van Houten & Doleys, 1983).

Response Cost. The concept of **response cost** is familiar to anyone who has ever paid a fine. For certain infractions of the rules, people must lose some reinforcer (money, time, privileges). In a class, the concept of response cost may be applied in a number of ways. The first time a student breaks a class rule, the teacher gives a warning. The second time, the teacher makes a mark beside the student's name in the grade book. The student loses 2 minutes of recess for each mark accumulated. For older students, a certain number of marks might mean losing the privilege of working in a group or going on a class trip.

Social Isolation. One of the most controversial behavioral methods for decreasing undesirable behavior is the strategy of **social isolation,** often called **time out** from reinforcement. The process involves removing a highly disruptive student from the classroom for 5 to 10 minutes. The student is placed in an empty, uninteresting room alone. It seems likely that the factor that actually decreases behavior is the punishment of brief isolation from other people (O'Leary & O'Leary, 1976). A trip to the principal's office or confinement to a chair in the corner of the regular classroom does not have the same effect as sitting alone in an empty room.

Some Cautions. Punishment in and of itself does not lead to any positive behavior. Thus, whenever you consider the use of punishment, you should make it part of a two-pronged attack. The first goal is to carry out the punishment and suppress the undesirable behavior. The second goal is to make clear what the student should be doing instead and to provide reinforcement for those desirable actions. Thus, while the problem behaviors are being suppressed, positive alternative responses are being strengthened. The *Guidelines* on page 216 give ideas for using punishment for positive purposes.

Check Yourself What are the steps in applied behavior analysis?

How can the Premack principle help you identify reinforcers?

When is shaping an appropriate approach?

What are some cautions in using punishment?

CONNECT & EXTEND

TO YOUR TEACHING PORTFOLIO

Soft reprimands: During reading in Miss McCormick's 1st-grade class, she noticed that Kenny wasn't concentrating on his book. She was working with a group at the time and could have called out, "Kenny, you'd better get back to work. You're not concentrating," but she decided this would embarrass him as well as disturb the concentration of others. Instead, Miss McCormick walked over to him, asked him a couple of questions about the story, and asked him to let her know how the story ended. She achieved her goal without causing embarrassment, and she provided Kenny with an impetus and motive to concentrate on his story again.

Reprimands Criticisms for misbehavior; rebukes.

Response cost Punishment by loss of reinforcers.

Social isolation Removal of a disruptive student for 5 to 10 minutes.

Time out Technically, the removal of all reinforcement. In practice, isolation of a student from the rest of the class for a brief time.

GUIDELINES Using Punishment

Try to structure the situation so you can use negative reinforcement rather than punishment.

Examples

1. Allow students to escape unpleasant situations (completing additional workbook assignments, weekly tests of math facts) when they reach a level of competence.
2. Insist on actions, not promises. Don't let students convince you to change the terms of the agreement.

Be consistent in your application of punishment.

Examples

1. Avoid in advertently reinforcing the behavior you are trying to punish. Keep confrontations private, so that students don't become heroes for standing up to the teacher in a public showdown.
2. Let students know in advance the consequences of breaking the rules by posting major class rules for younger students or outlining rules and consequences in a course syllabus for older students.
3. Tell students they will receive only one warning before punishment is given. Give the warning in a calm way, then follow through.
4. Make punishment as unavoidable and immediate as is reasonably possible.

Focus on the students' actions, not on the students' personal qualities.

Examples

1. Reprimand in a calm but firm voice.
2. Avoid vindictive or sarcastic words or tones of voice. You might hear your own angry words later when students imitate your sarcasm.
3. Stress the need to end the problem behavior instead of expressing any dislike you might feel for the student.

Adapt the punishment to the infraction.

Examples

1. Ignore minor misbehaviors that do not disrupt the class, or stop these misbehaviors with a disapproving glance or a move toward the student.
2. Don't use homework as a punishment for misbehaviors such as talking in class.
3. When a student misbehaves to gain peer acceptance, removal from the group of friends can be effective, because this is really time out from a reinforcing situation.
4. If the problem behaviors continue, analyze the situation and try a new approach. Your punishment may not be very punishing, or you may be inadvertently reinforcing the misbehavior.

CONNECT & EXTEND

TO **PRAXIS**™
TEACHING AND MANAGEMENT (I, A1; II, A3; I,C4)
Identify major approaches to teaching and classroom management that are based on behavioral principles. Understand the advantages and disadvantages of each.

Behavioral Approaches to Teaching and Management

The behavioral approach to learning has made several important contributions to instruction, including systems for specifying learning objectives (we will look at this topic in Chapter 12 when we discuss planning), mastery learning techniques, and class management systems such as group consequences, token economies, and contingency contracts. These approaches are useful when the goal is to learn *explicit information* or change *behaviors* and when the material is *sequential* and *factual.*

First let's consider one element that is part of every behavioral learning program—specific practice of correct behaviors. Contrary to popular wisdom, practice does not make *perfect.* Instead, practice makes *permanent* the behaviors practiced, so practicing accurate behaviors is important. Describing Tiger Woods in a *Newsweek* article, Devin Gordon (2001) said,

> Tiger's habit of pounding golf ball after golf ball long into the twilight—often during tournament play—has already become part of his legend. During his so-called slump earlier this year, Woods claimed he was simply working on shots he would need for the Masters in April. People rolled their eyes. Until he won the Masters. (p. 45)

Last week (I am writing this paragraph in April, 2002), he won the Masters again. No doubt he had continued specific practice of the shots he would need.

As an example of a behavioral teaching approach, consider mastery learning.

Mastery Learning

Mastery learning is based on the assumption that given enough time and the proper instruction, most students can master any learning objective (Bloom, 1968; Guskey & Gates, 1986). To use the mastery approach, a teacher must break a course down into small units of study. Each unit might involve mastering several specific objectives. "Mastery" usually means a score of 80% to 90% on a test or other assessment. The teacher informs the students of the objectives and the criteria for meeting each one. Students who do not reach the minimum level of mastery or who reach this minimum but want to improve their performance (thus raising their grade) can recycle through the unit. When they are ready, they take another form of the unit test.

The challenge in mastery learning is providing the appropriate extra help for students who don't attain mastery. There are many possibilities. Students can work with peer tutors or aides inside or outside class or they can get extra help from their team members in cooperative groups. If no extra time or staff is available, mastery learning can be adapted to a regular class time frame. For example, after explaining the mastery approach, the teacher teaches the lessons, then gives an ungraded assessment to determine students' levels of understanding. Those who have reached the mastery level are given enrichment activities such as independent or group work, computer simulations, research projects, or creative problems to solve. Those who need more help work with the teacher on corrective instruction (Block & Anderson, 1975). The Keller Plan, also called the Personalized System of Instruction (PSI), is a form of mastery learning used most often in college (Sherman, Ruskin, & Semb, 1982).

Many of the systematic applications of behavioral principles focus on classroom management. For two examples that successfully applied behavioral principles to improve behaviors of students with special needs, see *Reaching Every Student: Students with Learning and Behavior Problems* on page 218.

Mastery learning Teaching approach in which students must learn one unit and pass a test at a specified level before moving to the next unit.

Good behavior game Arrangement where a class is divided into teams and each team receives demerit points for breaking agreed-upon rules of good behavior.

Group consequences Rewards or punishments given to a class as a whole for adhering to or violating rules of conduct.

Group Consequences

A teacher can base reinforcement for the class on the cumulative behavior of all members of the class, usually by adding each student's points to a class or a team total. The **good behavior game** is an example of this approach. A class is divided into two teams. Specific rules for good behavior are cooperatively developed. Each time a student breaks one of the rules, that student's team is given a mark. The team with the fewest marks at the end of the period receives a special reward or privilege (longer recess, first to lunch, and so on). If both teams earn fewer than a preestablished number of marks, both teams receive the reward. Most studies indicate that even though the game produces only small improvements in academic achievement, it can produce definite improvements in the behaviors listed in the good behavior rules.

You can also use **group consequences** without dividing the class into teams; that is, you can base reinforcement on the behavior of the whole class. Wilson and Hopkins (1973) conducted a study using group consequences to reduce noise levels. Radio music served effectively as the reinforcer for students in a family and consumer science class. Whenever noise in the class was below a predetermined level, students could listen to the radio; when the noise exceeded the level, the radio was turned off. Given the success of this simple method, such a procedure might be considered in any class where music does not interfere with the task at hand.

Rules, consequences, and rewards are posted in this elementary school classroom to serve as reminders about appropriate behavior.

However, caution is needed using group approaches. The whole group should not suffer for the misbehavior or mistakes

~ Reaching Every Student ~

Students with Learning and Behavior Problems

Students with severe behavior problems are some of the most difficult challenges for teachers. Two studies show how behavioral principles can be useful in helping these students.

Lea Theodore and her colleagues (2001) worked with the teacher of five adolescent males who were diagnosed as having severe emotional disorders. A short list of clear rules was established (e.g., no obscene words, comply with teacher's requests within 5 seconds, no verbal putdowns). The rules were written on index cards taped to each student's desk. The teacher had a checklist on his desk with each student's name to note any rule breaking. This checklist was easily observable, so students could monitor their own and each others' performance. At the end of the 45-minute period, a student chose a "criterion" from a jar. The possible criteria were: performance of the whole group, student with the highest score, student with the lowest score, the average of all students, or a random single student. If the student or students selected to be the criterion had 5 checks or fewer for rule breaking, then the whole class got a reward, also chosen randomly from a jar. The possible rewards were things like a soda, a bag of chips, candy bars, or a late-to-class pass. An ABAB design was used—baseline, two-week intervention, two-week withdrawal of intervention, and two-week return to group consequences. All students showed clear improvement in following the rules when the reward system was in place, as you can see in the chart for one of the students below. Students liked the approach and the teacher found it easy to implement.

In the second study, Kara McGoey and George DuPaul (2000) worked with teachers in three preschool classrooms to address problem behaviors of four students diagnosed as having Attention-Deficit/Hyperactive Disorder. The teachers tried both a token reinforcement program (students earned small and large buttons on a chart for following class rules), and a response cost system (students began with 5 small buttons and one large button per activity each day and lost buttons for not following rules). Both procedures were effective in lowering rule breaking, but the teachers found the response cost system easier to implement.

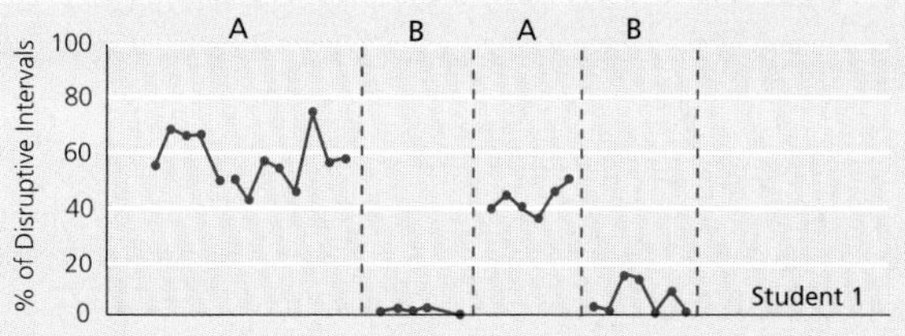

SOURCE: For details of both of these approaches see: "Randomization of Group Contingencies and Reinforcers to Reduce Classroom Disruptive Behavior" by L. A. Theodore, M. A. Bray, T. J. Kehle, & W. R. Jenson, 2001, *Journal of School Psychology, 39,* 267–277 and "Token Reinforcement and Response Cost Procedures: Reducing Disruptive Behavior of Preschool Children with Attention-Deficit/Hyperactive Disorder" by K. E. McGoey & G. J. DuPaul, 2000, *School Psychology Quarterly, 15,* 330–343.

of one individual if the group has no real influence over that person (Epanchin, Townsend, & Stoddard, 1994; Jenson, Sloane, & Young, 1988). I saw an entire class break into cheers when the teacher announced that one boy was transferring to another school. The chant "No more points! No more points!" filled the room. The "points" referred to the teacher's system of giving one point to the whole class each time anyone broke a rule. Every point meant 5 minutes of recess lost. The boy who was transferring had been responsible for many losses. He was not very popular to begin with, and the point system, though quite effective in maintaining order, had led to rejection and even greater unpopularity.

Peer pressure in the form of support and encouragement, however, can be a positive influence, as you saw in the *Reaching Every Student* feature above. Group consequences are recommended for situations in which students care about the approval of their peers (Theodore, Bray, Kehle, & Jenson, 2001). If the misbehavior of several students seems to be encouraged by the attention and laughter of other students, then group consequences could be helpful. Teachers might show students how to give support and constructive feedback to classmates. If a few students seem to enjoy sabotaging the system, those students may need separate arrangements.

Token Reinforcement Programs

Have you ever participated in a program where you earned points or credits that you could exchange for a reward? Are you a member of a frequent flyer club or do you get points on your credit card? Do you collect Subway Club stamps (my husband has hundreds right now)? Do you get one free movie for every 10 rentals? Does being a part of such a program affect your buying habits? How? Go to http://www.bookitprogram.com/ and see a reading incentive club for pizza eaters.

Often it is difficult to provide positive consequences for all the students who deserve them. A **token reinforcement system** can help solve this problem by allowing all students to earn tokens for both academic work and positive classroom behavior. The tokens may be points, checks, holes punched in a card, chips, play money, or anything else that is easily identified as the student's property. Periodically the students exchange the tokens they have earned for some desired reward (Kazdin, 2001; Alberto & Troutman, 2003).

Depending on the age of the student, the rewards could be small toys, school supplies, free time, special class jobs, or other privileges. When a "token economy," as this kind of system is called, is first established, the tokens should be given out on a fairly continuous schedule, with chances to exchange the tokens for rewards often available. Once the system is working well, however, tokens should be distributed on an intermittent schedule and saved for longer periods of time before they are exchanged for rewards.

Another variation is to allow students to earn tokens in the classroom and then exchange them for rewards at home. These plans are very successful when parents are willing to cooperate. Usually a note or report form is sent home daily or twice a week. The note indicates the number of points earned in the preceding time period. The points may be exchanged for minutes of television viewing, access to special toys, or private time with parents. Points can also be saved up for larger rewards such as trips. Do not use this procedure, however, if you suspect the child might be severely punished for poor reports.

Token reinforcement systems are complicated and time-consuming. Generally, they should be used in only three situations: to motivate students who are completely uninterested in their work and have not responded to other approaches; to encourage students who have consistently failed to make academic progress; and to deal with a class that is out of control. Some groups of students seem to benefit from token economies more than others. Students with mental retardation, children who have failed often, students with few academic skills, and students with behavior problems all seem to respond to the concrete, direct nature of token reinforcement.

Before you try a token system, you should be sure that your teaching methods and materials are right for the students. Sometimes class disruptions or lack of motivation indicate that teaching practices need to be changed. Maybe the class rules are unclear or are enforced inconsistently. Maybe the text is too easy or too hard. Maybe the pace is wrong. If these problems exist, a token system may improve the situation temporarily, but the students will still have trouble learning the academic material (Jenson, Sloane, & Young, 1988).

Contingency Contract Programs

In a **contingency contract** program, the teacher draws up an individual contract with each student, describing exactly what the student must do to earn a particular privilege or reward. In some programs, students participate in deciding on the behaviors to be reinforced and the rewards that can be gained. The negotiating process itself can be an educational experience, as students learn to set reasonable goals and abide by the terms of a contract. And, if students participate in setting the goals, they often are more committed to reaching them (Locke & Latham, 1990; Pintrich & Schunk, 2002).

Token reinforcement system System in which tokens earned for academic work and positive classroom behavior can be exchanged for some desired reward.

Contingency contract A contract between the teacher and a student specifying what the student must do to earn a particular reward or privilege.

The teacher and student agree on the due dates for each assignment, marking them in blue on the chart. Each time an assignment is turned in, the date of completion is marked in black on the chart. As long as the actual completion line is above the planned completion line, the student earns free time or other contracted rewards.

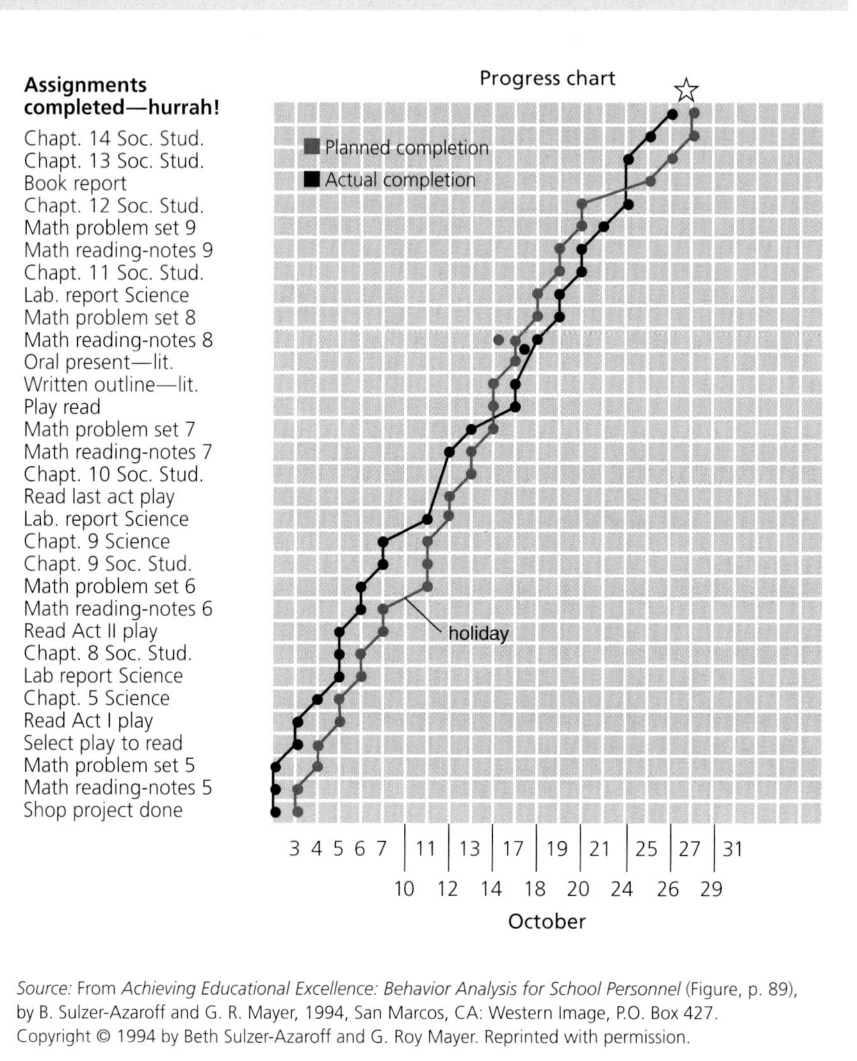

Source: From *Achieving Educational Excellence: Behavior Analysis for School Personnel* (Figure, p. 89), by B. Sulzer-Azaroff and G. R. Mayer, 1994, San Marcos, CA: Western Image, P.O. Box 427. Copyright © 1994 by Beth Sulzer-Azaroff and G. Roy Mayer. Reprinted with permission.

Figure 6.3 A Contingency Contract for Completing Assignments

An example of a contract for completing assignments that is appropriate for intermediate and upper-grade students is presented in Figure 6.3. This chart serves as a contract, assignment sheet, and progress record. Information about progress can support student motivation (Schunk, 2000). Something like this might even help you keep track of assignments and due dates in your college classes.

The few pages devoted here to token reinforcement and contingency contracts can offer only an introduction to these programs. If you want to set up a large-scale reward program in your classroom, you should probably seek professional advice. Often the school psychologist, counselor, or principal can help.

Check Yourself What is mastery learning?

Describe the managerial strategies of group consequences, token programs, and contracts.

Recent Approaches: Self-Regulation and Cognitive Behavior Modification

What Would You Say? The Physical Therapy unit where you are interviewing is a state-of-the-art facility. You feel as though the interview for a patient-educator position is going well. Your next question is: "One of our biggest problems here, and in most rehabilitation centers for that matter, is getting our clients to stick to an exercise program. What ideas do you have for helping these clients maintain their prescribed regimens?"

A recent application of behavioral views of learning emphasizes **self-management**—helping students gain control of their own learning. As you will see throughout this book, the role of students in their own learning is a major concern of psychologists and educators today. This concern is not restricted to any one group or theory. Different areas of research and theory all converge on one important idea, that responsibility and the ability to learn rest within the student. No one can learn for someone else (Mace, Belfiore, & Hutchinson, 2001; Manning & Payne, 1996; Winne, 1995; Zimmerman, 1990).

Behavioral psychologists became interested in self-management because they found students taught with classic behavioral methods seldom generalized their learning to new situations. For example, in my dissertation research I found that inattentive students could learn to pay excellent attention to lessons in a small group, but when they returned to the regular classroom, they did not take their new skill back with them (Woolfolk & Woolfolk, 1974). Many behavioral psychologists decided that generalization would be encouraged if students became partners in the behavior change procedures. About this same time, Donald Meichenbaum (1977) was having success teaching impulsive students to "talk themselves through" tasks, so there was evidence that students could benefit from what Meichenbaum termed "cognitive behavior modification" (Manning, 1991).

CONNECT & EXTEND

TO YOUR TEACHING PORTFOLIO
Concern with self-management is not restricted to any one group or theory. Psychologists who study Vygotsky's ideas about cognitive development (Chapter 2) are involved, as are cognitive psychologists interested in learning strategies (Chapters 7 and 8) and motivational psychologists pointing to self-regulation as a critical factor in motivation (Chapters 10 and 13).

Self-Management

If one goal of education is to produce people who are capable of educating themselves, then students must learn to manage their own lives, set their own goals, and provide their own reinforcement. In adult life, rewards are sometimes vague and goals often take a long time to reach. Think about how many small steps are required to complete an education and find your first job. Life is filled with tasks that call for this sort of self-management (Kanfer & Gaelick, 1986).

Students may be involved in any or all of the steps in implementing a basic behavior change program. They may help set goals, observe their own work, keep records of it, and evaluate their own performance. Finally, they can select and deliver reinforcement. Such involvement can help students master all the steps so they can perform these tasks in the future (Kaplan, 1991).

Goal Setting. It appears that the goal-setting phase is very important in self-management (Pintrich & Schunk, 2002; Reeve, 1996). In fact, some research suggests that setting specific goals and making them public may be the critical elements of self-management programs. For example, S. C. Hayes and his colleagues identified college students who had serious problems with studying and taught them how to set specific study goals. Students who set goals and announced them to the experimenters performed significantly better on tests covering the material they were studying than students who set goals privately and never revealed them to anyone (Hayes, Rosenfarb, Wulfert, Munt, Korn, & Zettle, 1985).

Higher standards tend to lead to higher performance (McLaughlin & Gnagey, 1981). Unfortunately, student-set goals have a tendency to reflect lower and lower expectations. Teachers can help students maintain high standards by monitoring the goals set and reinforcing high standards. In one study, a teacher helped 1st-grade

Self-management Use of behavioral learning principles to change your own behavior.

students raise the number of math problems they set for themselves to work on each day by praising them whenever they increased their objective by 10%. The students maintained their new, higher work standards, and the improvements even generalized to other subjects (Price & O'Leary, 1974).

CONNECT & EXTEND

TO YOUR TEACHING PORTFOLIO
A study conducted by Mark Morgan (1985. Self-monitoring of attained subgoals in private study. *Journal of Educational Psychology, 77,* 623–630) combined goal setting, self-recording, and self-evaluation. Morgan taught self-monitoring strategies to all the students in the required educational psychology course at his college. The students who set specific short-term objectives for each study unit and monitored their progress toward the objectives outperformed the students who simply monitored study time, even though the students who monitored their time actually spent more hours studying!

Monitoring and Evaluating Progress. Students may also participate in the monitoring and evaluation phases of a behavior change program (Mace, Belfiore, & Hutchinson, 2001). Some examples of behaviors that are appropriate for self-monitoring are the number of assignments completed, time spent practicing a skill, number of books read, number of problems correct, and time taken to run a mile. Tasks that must be accomplished without teacher supervision, such as homework or private study, are also good candidates for self-monitoring. Students keep a chart, diary, or checklist recording the frequency or duration of the behaviors in question.

A progress record card can help older students break down assignments into small steps, determine the best sequence for completing the steps, and keep track of daily progress by setting goals for each day. The record card itself serves as a prompt that can be faded out (Jenson, Sloane, & Young, 1988). Completing homework is a problem for students in almost any grade. Here is a checklist, taken from Belfiore, & Hornyak (1998) to help students manage their homework:

1. *Did I turn in yesterday's homework?*
2. *Did I write all homework assignments in my notebook?*
3. *Is all the homework in the homework folder?*
4. *Are all my materials to complete my homework with me?*
5. *Begin Homework*
6. *Are all homework papers completed?*
7. *Did someone check homework to make sure it was completed?*
8. *After checking, did I put all homework back in folder?*
9. *Did I give this paper to teacher?* (p. 190).

Self-evaluation is somewhat more difficult than simple self-recording because it involves making a judgment about quality. Students can evaluate their behavior with reasonable accuracy, especially if they learn standards for judging a good performance or product. For example, Sweeney, Salva, Cooper, and Talbert-Johnson (1993) taught secondary students how to evaluate their handwriting for size, slant, shape, and spacing. One key to accurate self-evaluation seems to be periodically checking students' assessments and giving reinforcement for accurate judgments. Older students may learn accurate self-evaluation more readily than younger students. Again, bonus points can be awarded when the teachers' and students' evaluations match (Kaplan, 1991). I have worked with one teacher who found that his 8th-grade science class could learn to give themselves fair and accurate grades when he used such a system.

Self-correction can accompany self-evaluation. Students first evaluate, then alter and improve their work, and finally compare the improvements to the standards again (Mace, Belfiore, & Hutchinson, 2001).

CONNECT & EXTEND

TO YOUR TEACHING PORTFOLIO
There is one student in your class who is never prepared to do his work. He doesn't have a pencil, has misplaced his book, left his homework at home, doesn't understand the assignment, forgot to buy notebook paper, and so on. The result of all this is that he seldom hands in his homework assignments. How would you approach this problem? Develop several alternative strategies, such as reward and punishment, shaping, or self-management.

Self-Reinforcement. The last step in self-management is **self-reinforcement.** There is some disagreement, however, as to whether this step is actually necessary. Some psychologists believe that setting goals and monitoring progress alone are sufficient and that self-reinforcement adds nothing to the effects (Hayes et al., 1985). Others believe that rewarding yourself for a job well done can lead to higher levels of performance than simply setting goals and keeping track of progress (Bandura, 1986). If you are willing to be tough and really deny yourself something you want until your goals are reached, then perhaps the promise of the reward can provide extra incentive for work. With that in mind, you may want to think of some way to reinforce yourself when you finish reading this chapter. A similar approach helped me write the chapter in the first place.

Self-reinforcement Providing yourself with positive consequences, contingent on accomplishing a particular behavior.

Family and Community Partnerships

Student Self-Management

Introduce the system to parents and students in a positive way.

Examples

1. Invite family participation and stress possible benefits to all family members.
2. Consider starting the program just with volunteers.
3. Describe how you use self-management programs yourself.

Help families and students establish reachable goals.

Examples

1. Have examples of possible self-management goals for students such as starting homework early in the evening, or keeping track of books read.
2. Show families how to post goals and keep track of progress. Encourage everyone in the family to work on a goal.

Give families ways to record and evaluate their child's progress (or their own).

Examples

1. Divide the work into easily measured steps.
2. Provide models of good work where judgments are more difficult, such as in creative writing.
3. Give families a record form or checklist to keep track of progress.

Encourage families to check the accuracy of student records from time to time, and help their children to develop forms of self-reinforcement.

Examples

1. Have many checkups when students are first learning, and fewer later.
2. Have siblings check one another's records.
3. Where appropriate, test the skills that students are supposed to be developing at home and reward students whose self-evaluations match their test performances.
4. Have students brainstorm ideas with their families for rewarding themselves for jobs well done.

At times, families can be enlisted to help their children develop self-management abilities. Working together, teachers and parents can focus on a few goals and, at the same time, support the growing independence of the students. The *Family and Community Partnerships Guidelines* give some ideas.

Sometimes, teaching students self-management can solve a problem for teachers and provide fringe benefits as well. For example, the coaches of a competitive swim team with members aged 9 to 16 were having difficulty persuading swimmers to maintain high work rates. Then the coaches drew up four charts indicating the training program to be followed by each member and posted the charts near the pool. The swimmers were given the responsibility of recording their numbers of laps and completion of each training unit. Because the recording was public, swimmers could see their own progress and that of others, give and receive congratulations, and keep accurate track of the work units completed. Work output increased by 27%. The coaches also liked the system because swimmers could begin to work immediately without waiting for instructions (McKenzie & Rushall, 1974).

Cognitive Behavior Modification and Self-Instruction

Self-management generally means getting students involved in the basic steps of a behavior change program. **Cognitive behavior modification** adds an emphasis on thinking and self-talk. For this reason, many psychologists consider cognitive behavior modification more a cognitive than a behavioral approach. I present it here because it serves as a bridge to Chapters 7 and 8 on cognitive learning.

As noted in Chapter 2, there is a stage in cognitive development when young children seem to guide themselves through a task using private speech. They talk to themselves, often repeating the words of a parent or teacher. In cognitive behavior modification, students are taught directly how to use **self-instruction.** Meichenbaum (1977) outlined the steps:

Cognitive behavior modification Procedures based on both behavioral and cognitive learning principles for changing your own behavior by using self-talk and self-instruction.

Self-instruction Talking oneself through the steps of a task.

1. An adult model performs a task while talking to him- or herself out loud (cognitive modeling).
2. The child performs the same task under the direction of the model's instructions (overt, external guidance).
3. The child performs the task while instructing him- or herself aloud (overt, self-guidance).
4. The child whispers the instructions to him- or herself as he/she goes through the task (faded, overt self-guidance).
5. The child performs the task while guiding his/her performance via private speech (covert self-instruction). (p. 32)

Brenda Manning and Beverly Payne (1996) list four skills that can increase student learning: *listening, planning, working,* and *checking.* How might cognitive self-instruction help students develop these skills? One possibility is to use personal booklets or class posters that prompt students to "talk to themselves" about these skills. For example, one 5th-grade class designed a set of prompts for each of the four skills and posted the prompts around the classroom. The prompts for listening included "Does this make sense?" "Am I getting this?" "I need to ask a question now before I forget." "Pay attention!" "Can I do what he's saying to do?" Planning prompts were, "Do I have everything together?" "Do I have my friends tuned out for right now?" "Let me get organized first." "What order will I do this in?" "I know this stuff!" Posters for these and the other two skills, working and checking, are shown in Figure 6.4. Part of the power

These four posters were designed by a 5th-grade class to help them remember to use self-instruction. Some of the reminders reflect the special world of these preadolescents.

Poster 1

While Listening:

1. Does this make sense?
2. Am I getting this?
3. I need to ask a question now before I forget.
4. Pay attention.
5. Can I do what he's saying to do?

Poster 3

While Working:

1. Am I working fast enough?
2. Stop staring at my girlfriend and get back to work.
3. How much time is left?
4. Do I need to stop and start over?
5. This is hard for me, but I can manage.

Poster 2

While Planning:

1. Do I have everything together?
2. Do I have my friends tuned out for right now?
3. Let me get organized first.
4. What order will I do this in?
5. I know this stuff!

Poster 4

While Checking:

1. Did I finish everything?
2. What do I need to recheck?
3. Am I proud of this work?
4. Did I write all the words? Count them.
5. I think I finished. I organized myself. Did I daydream too much?

Source: From *Self-Talk for Teachers and Students: Metacognitive Strategies for Personal and Classroom Use* (p. 125), by Brenda H. Manning & Beverly D. Payne. Published by Allyn & Bacon, Boston, MA. Copyright © 1996 by Pearson Education. Adapted by permission of the publisher.

Figure 6.4 Posters to Remind Students to "Talk Themselves Through" Listening, Planning, Working, and Checking in School of this process is in getting students involved in thinking about and creating their own guides and prompts. Having the discussion and posting the ideas makes students more self-aware and in control of their own learning.

Actually, cognitive behavior modification as it is practiced by Meichenbaum and others has many more components than just teaching students to use self-instruction. Meichenbaum's methods also include dialogue and interaction between teacher and student, modeling, guided discovery, motivational strategies, feedback, careful matching of the task with the student's developmental level, and other principles of good teaching. The student is even involved in designing the program (Harris, 1990; Harris & Pressley, 1991). Given all this, it is no surprise that students do seem to generalize the skills developed with cognitive behavior modification to new learning situations (Harris, Graham, & Pressley, 1992).

Check Yourself What are the steps in self-management?

Enhancing Your Expertise with Technology

Self-Regulation

Jim found it exhausting, but very satisfying, to serve as Cherie's mentor during her first year as a teacher. They met each morning for about 15 minutes, frequently talked at lunchtime, and always met after the last class to analyze the day. Often, the conversations focused on an unexpected event such as a distressing comment made by a student about a situation at home. Cherie, however, usually had an agenda: How do you prepare for parent-teacher conferences? Who offers high-quality science workshops? In many ways, Cherie was teaching herself about the profession, and Jim was her resource manual.

Cherie is an example of a self-regulated learner. She identified gaps in her knowledge, set goals, and located resources for her learning. She organized her time to effectively achieve her goals. She, along with her mentor, evaluated her progress toward the goals. In this chapter and the next four, we examine several theoretical perspectives that strongly influence classroom practices. These perspectives often differ starkly in their assumptions about learning and the roles of students and teachers. However, all these perspectives find some common ground affirming the importance of self-regulated learning—and an expert teacher is by necessity a highly self-regulated learner.

A key attribute of a self-regulated learner is the effective use of resources. The AskERIC Web site (http://ericir.syr.edu) is one of the most comprehensive, up-to-date, and authoritative educational resources that you will find anywhere in any medium. The AskERIC home page provides you with a hint of the vast breadth of disciplines that comprise the field of education. You will see sections devoted to counseling, educational technology, educational management, librarianship, and many more.

There are three features that beginning teachers will find immediately useful. The first is the link to a collection of lesson plans that not only includes plans for a variety of subject areas, but also provides guidelines for writing plans that complement the guidelines you will find in this textbook. Second, the *Ask an ERIC Expert* link puts you in contact with one of ERIC's information specialists, who will respond to you within two days and provide resources that you can use to research your question. Third, the *Question Archive* is composed of a set of questions that have been previously answered by ERIC specialists. Many of these questions are the type that novice teachers would typically ask.

As you explore AskERIC, be sure to navigate to its collection of ERIC Digests (http://www.ed.gov/databases/ERIC_Digests/index/). Each digest (there are more than 2500 of them) is a brief report on a current topic of interest to the educational community. Among the many topics addressed in a recent set of digests were gifted education, children with exceptional needs, home schooling, problem-based learning, and child development. Perhaps the best way to discover the full potential of this resource-rich site is to sign up for the *AskERIC Update Newsletter.* You will receive an emailed newsletter on the first day of the month that advises you of additions and revisions to AskERIC.

Problems and Issues

The preceding sections provide an overview of several strategies for changing classroom behavior. However, you should be aware that these strategies are tools that may be used responsibly or irresponsibly. What, then, are some issues you should keep in mind?

Criticisms of Behavioral Methods

What Would You Say? During your job interview, the principal asks, "A teacher last year got in trouble for bribing his students with homework exemptions to get them to behave in class. What do you think about using rewards and punishments in teaching?" What do you say?

While you think about your answer to this question, look at the *Point/Counterpoint* on "Should Students Be Rewarded for Learning?" to see two different perspectives. Properly used, the strategies in this chapter can be effective tools to help students learn academically and grow in self-sufficiency. Effective tools, however, do not automatically produce excellent work. The indiscriminate use of even the best tools can lead to difficulties. Critics of behavioral methods point to two basic problems that may arise.

Some psychologists fear that rewarding students for all learning will cause them to lose interest in learning for its own sake (Deci, 1975; Deci & Ryan, 1985; Kohn, 1993, 1996; Lepper & Greene, 1978; Lepper, Keavney, & Drake, 1996; Ryan & Deci, 1996). Studies have suggested that using reward programs with students who are already interested in the subject matter may, in fact, cause students to be less interested in the subject when the reward program ends, as you can see in the *Point/Counterpoint.* In addition, there is some evidence that praising students for being intelligent when they succeed can undermine their motivation if they do not perform as well the next time. After they fail, students who had been praised for being smart may be less persistent and enjoy the task less compared to students who had been praised earlier for working hard (Mueller & Dweck, 1998).

Just as you must take into account the effects of a reward system on the individual, you must also consider the impact on other students. Using a reward program or giving one student increased attention may have a detrimental effect on the other students in the classroom. Is it possible that other students will learn to be "bad" in order to be included in the reward program? Most of the evidence on this question suggests that using individual adaptations such as reward programs does not have any adverse effects on students who are not participating if the teacher believes in the program and explains the reasons for using it to the nonparticipating students. After interviewing 98 students in grades 1 through 6, Cindy Fulk and Paula Smith (1995) concluded that "Teachers may be more concerned about equal treatment of students than students are" (p. 416). If the conduct of some students does seem to deteriorate when their peers are involved in special programs, many of the same procedures discussed in this chapter should help them return to previous levels of appropriate behavior (Chance, 1992, 1993).

Ethical Issues

The ethical questions related to the use of the strategies described in this chapter are similar to those raised by any process that seeks to influence people. What are the goals? How do these goals fit with those of the school as a whole? What effect will a strategy have on the individuals involved? Is too much control being given to the teacher, or to a majority?

Goals. The strategies described in this chapter could be applied exclusively to teaching students to sit still, raise their hands before speaking, and remain silent at all other times (Winett & Winkler, 1972). This certainly would be an unethical use of the techniques. It is true that a teacher may need to establish some organization and order, but stopping with improvements in conduct will not ensure academic learning. On

Point/Counterpoint

Should Students Be Rewarded for Learning?

For years educators and psychologists have debated whether students should be rewarded for school work and academic accomplishments. In the early 1990s, Paul Chance and Alfie Kohn exchanged opinions in several issues of *Phi Delta Kappan* (March 1991; November 1992; June 1993). Then, Judy Cameron and W. David Pierce (1996) published an article on reinforcement in the *Review of Educational Research* that precipitated extensive criticisms and rebuttals in the same journal from Mark Lepper, Mark Keavney, Michael Drake, Alfie Kohn, Richard Ryan, and Edward Deci. Many of the same people exchanged opinions in the November 1999 issue of *Psychological Bulletin.* What are the arguments?

Point

Students are punished by rewards.

Alfie Kohn (1993) argues that "Applied behaviorism, which amounts to saying, 'do this and you'll get that,' is essentially a technique for controlling people. In the classroom it is a way of doing things *to* children rather than working *with* them" (p. 784). He contends that rewards are ineffective because when the praise and prizes stop, the behaviors stop too. After analyzing 128 studies of extrinsic rewards, Edward Deci, Richard Koestner, and Richard Ryan (1999) concluded that "tangible rewards tend to have a substantial effect on intrinsic motivation, with the limiting conditions we have specified. Even when tangible rewards are offered as indicators of good performance, they typically decrease intrinsic motivation for interesting activities" (pp. 658–659).

The problem with rewards does not stop here. According to Kohn, rewarding students for learning actually makes them less interested in the material:

> *All of this means that getting children to think about learning as a way to receive a sticker, a gold star, or a grade—or even worse, to get money or a toy* for *a grade, which amounts to an extrinsic motivator for an extrinsic motivator—is likely to turn learning from an end into a means. Learning becomes something that must be gotten through in order to receive the reward. Take the depressingly pervasive program by which children receive certificates for pizzas when they have read a certain number of books. John Nicholls of the University of Illinois comments, only half in jest, that the likely consequence of this program is "a lot of fat kids who don't like to read." (p. 785)*

Counterpoint

Learning should be rewarding.

According to Paul Chance (1993):

> *Behavioral psychologists in particular emphasize that we learn* by *acting on our environment. As B. F. Skinner put it: "[People] act on the world, and change it, and are changed in turn by the consequences of their actions." Skinner, unlike Kohn, understood that people learn best in a responsive environment. Teachers who praise or otherwise reward student performance provide such an environment. . . . If it is immoral to let students know they have answered questions correctly, to pat students on the back for a good effort, to show joy at a student's understanding of a concept, or to recognize the achievement of a goal by providing a gold star or a certificate—if this is immoral, then count me a sinner. (p. 788)*

Do rewards undermine interest? In their review of research, Cameron and Pierce (1994) concluded, "When tangible rewards (e.g., gold star, money) are offered contingent on performance on a task [not just on participation] or are delivered unexpectedly, intrinsic motivation is maintained" (p. 49). In a later review of research, Eisenberg, Pierce, and Cameron (1999) added that "Reward procedures requiring specific high task performance convey a task's personal or social significance, increasing intrinsic motivation" (p. 677). Even psychologists such as Edward Deci and Mark Lepper who suggest that rewards might undermine intrinsic motivation agree that rewards can also be used positively. When rewards provide students with information about their growing mastery of a subject or when the rewards show appreciation for a job well done, then the rewards bolster confidence and make the task more interesting to the students, especially students who lacked ability or interest in the task initially. Nothing succeeds like success. As Chance points out, if students master reading or mathematics with the support of rewards, they will not forget what they have learned when the praise stops. Would they have learned without the rewards? Some would, but some might not. Would you continue working for a company that didn't pay you, even though you liked the work? Will freelance writer Alfie Kohn, for that matter, lose interest in writing because he gets paid fees and royalties?

What do you think? Vote online at **www.ablongman.com/woolfolk**

the other hand, in some situations, reinforcing academic skills may lead to improvements in conduct. Whenever possible, emphasis should be placed on academic learning. Academic improvements generalize to other situations more successfully than do changes in classroom conduct.

Strategies. Punishment can have negative side effects: It can serve as a model for aggressive responses, and it can encourage negative emotional reactions. Punishment is unnecessary and even unethical when positive approaches, which have fewer potential dangers, might work as well. When simpler, less-restrictive procedures fail, then more complicated procedures should be tried.

A second consideration in the selection of a strategy is the impact of the strategy on the individual student. For example, some teachers arrange for students to be rewarded at home with a gift or activities based on good work in school. But if a student has a history of being severely punished at home for bad reports from school, a home-based reinforcement program might be very harmful to that student. Reports of unsatisfactory progress at school could lead to increased abuse at home.

Check Yourself What are the main criticisms of behavioral approaches?

Understanding Learning

(pp. 198–200)

Define learning. Although theorists disagree about the definition of learning, most would agree that learning occurs when experience causes a change in a person's knowledge or behavior. Behavioral theorists emphasize the role of environmental stimuli in learning and focus on behavior—observable responses. Behavioral learning processes include contiguity learning, classical conditioning, and operant conditioning.

Learning: Process through which experience causes permanent change in knowledge or behavior.

Behavioral Learning Theories: Explanations of learning that focus on external events as the cause of changes in observable behaviors.

Early Explanations of Learning: Contiguity and Classical Conditioning

(pp. 200–202)

How does a neutral stimulus become a conditioned stimulus? In classical conditioning, which was discovered by Pavlov, a previously neutral stimulus is repeatedly paired with a stimulus that evokes an emotional or physiological response. Later, the previously neutral stimulus alone evokes the response—that is, the neutral stimulus is conditioned to bring forth a conditioned response. The neutral stimulus has become a conditioned stimulus.

Discriminate between generalization and discrimination. Conditioned responses are subject to the processes of generalization and discrimination. After animals or people learn to respond to one particular stimulus, they may also have similar responses to other stimuli that are similar to the original one. This process is called *generalization* because the conditioned response has generalized or occurred in the presence of similar stimuli. Discrimination is learning to make distinctions—to respond to one stimulus but not to others that are similar.

Contiguity: Association of two events because of repeated pairing.

Stimulus: Event that activates behavior.

Response: Observable reaction to a stimulus.

Classical Conditioning: Association of automatic responses with new stimuli.

Respondents: Responses (generally automatic or involuntary) elicited by specific stimuli.

Neutral Stimulus: Stimulus not connected to a response.

Unconditioned Stimulus (US): Stimulus that automatically produces an emotional or physiological response.

Unconditioned Response (UR): Naturally occurring emotional or physiological response.

Conditioned Stimulus (CS): Stimulus that evokes an emotional or physiological response after conditioning.

Conditioned Response (CR): Learned response to a previously neutral stimulus.

Generalization: Responding in the same way to similar stimuli.

Discrimination: Responding differently to similar, but not identical stimuli.

Extinction: Gradual disappearance of a learned response.

Operant Conditioning: Trying New Responses

(pp. 202–208)

What defines a consequence as a reinforcer? As a punisher? In Skinner's operant conditioning people learn through the effects of their deliberate responses. For an individual, the effects of consequences following an action may serve as reinforcers or punishers. A consequence is defined as a reinforcer if it strengthens or maintains the response that brought it about, whereas a consequence is defined as a punishment if it decreases or suppresses the response that brought it about.

Negative reinforcement is often confused with punishment. How are they different? The process of reinforcement (positive or negative) always involves strengthening behavior. The teacher strengthens (reinforces) desired behaviors by removing something aversive *as soon as the desired behaviors occur.* Because the consequence involves removing or "subtracting" a stimulus, the reinforcement is negative. Punishment, on the other hand, involves *decreasing or suppressing behavior.* A behavior followed by a "punisher" is *less* likely to be repeated in similar situations in the future.

How can you encourage persistence in a behavior? Ratio schedules (based on the number of responses) encourage higher rates of response, and variable schedules (based on varying numbers of responses or varying time intervals) encourage persistence of responses.

What is the difference between a prompt and a cue? A cue is an antecedent stimulus just before a particular behavior is to take place. A prompt is an additional cue following the first cue. Make sure the environmental stimulus that you want to become a cue occurs immediately before the prompt you are using, so students will learn to respond to the cue and not rely only on the prompt. Then, fade the prompt as soon as possible so students do not become dependent on it.

Operants: Voluntary (and generally goal-directed) behaviors emitted by a person or an animal.

Operant Conditioning: Learning in which voluntary behavior is strengthened or weakened by consequences or antecedents.

Antecedents: Events that precede an action.

Consequences: Events that follow an action.

Reinforcement: Use of consequences to strengthen behavior.

Reinforcer: Any event that follows a behavior and increases the chances that the behavior will occur again.

Positive Reinforcement: Strengthening behavior by presenting a desired stimulus after the behavior.

Negative Reinforcement: Strengthening behavior by removing an aversive stimulus when the behavior occurs.

Aversive: Irritating or unpleasant.

Punishment: Process that weakens or suppresses behavior.

Presentation Punishment: Decreasing the chances that a behavior will occur again by presenting an aversive stimulus following the behavior; also called Type I punishment.

Removal Punishment: Decreasing the chances that a behavior will occur again by removing a pleasant stimulus following the behavior; also called Type II punishment.

Continuous Reinforcement Schedule: Presenting a reinforcer after every appropriate response.

Intermittent Reinforcement Schedule: Presenting a reinforcer after some but not all responses.

Interval Schedule: Length of time between reinforcers.

Ratio Schedule: Reinforcement based on the number of responses between reinforcers.

Stimulus Control: Capacity for the presence or absence of antecedents to cause behaviors.

Cueing: Providing a stimulus that "sets up" a desired behavior.

Prompt: A reminder that follows a cue to make sure the person reacts to the cue.

Applied Behavior Analysis

(pp. 209–216)

What are the steps in applied behavior analysis? The steps are: (1) Clearly specify the behavior to be changed and note the current level. (2) Plan a specific intervention using antecedents, consequences, or both. (3) Keep track of the results, and modify the plan if necessary.

How can the Premack principle help you identify reinforcers? The Premack principle states that a high-frequency behavior (a preferred activity) can be an effective reinforcer for a low-frequency behavior (a less-preferred activity). The best way to determine appropriate reinforcers for your students may be to watch what they do in their free time. For most students, talking, moving around the room, sitting near a friend, being exempt from assignments or tests, reading magazines, or playing games are preferred activities.

When is shaping an appropriate approach? Shaping helps students develop new responses a little at a time, so shaping is useful for building complex skills, working toward difficult goals, and increasing persistence, endurance, accuracy, or speed. Because shaping is a time-consuming process, however, it should not be used if success can be attained through simpler methods such as cueing.

What are some cautions in using punishment? Punishment in and of itself does not lead to any positive behavior. Thus, whenever you consider the use of punishment, you should make it part of a two-pronged attack. First, carry out the punishment and suppress the undesirable behavior. Second, make clear what the student should be doing instead and provide reinforcement for those desirable actions. Thus, while the problem behaviors are being suppressed, positive alternative responses are being strengthened.

Applied Behavior Analysis: The application of behavioral learning principles to understand and change behavior.

Behavior Modification: Systematic application of antecedents and consequences to change behavior.

Premack Principle: Principle stating that a more-preferred activity can serve as a reinforcer for a less-preferred activity.

Shaping: Reinforcing each small step of progress toward a desired goal or behavior.

Successive Approximations: Small components that make up a complex behavior.

Task Analysis: System for breaking down a task hierarchically into basic skills and subskills.

Positive Practice: Practicing correct responses immediately after errors.

Satiation: Requiring a person to repeat a problem behavior past the point of interest or motivation.

Reprimands: Criticisms for misbehavior; rebukes.

Response Cost: Punishment by loss of reinforcers.

Social Isolation: Removal of a disruptive student for 5 to 10 minutes.

Time Out: Technically, the removal of all reinforcement. In practice, isolation of a student from the rest of the class for a brief time.

Behavioral Approaches to Teaching and Management

(pp. 216–220)

What is mastery learning? To use mastery learning, a teacher must break a course down into small units of study. Each unit might involve mastering several specific objectives. "Mastery" usually means a score of 80% to 90% on a test or other assessment. The teacher informs the students of the objectives and the criteria for meeting each one. Students who do not reach the minimum level of mastery or who reach this minimum but want to improve their performance can recycle through the unit. When they attain the mastery score, they move to the next unit.

Describe the managerial strategies of group consequences, token programs, and contracts. Using group consequences involves basing reinforcement for the whole class on the behavior of the whole class. In token programs, students earn tokens (points, checks, holes punched in a card, chips, etc.) for both academic work and positive classroom behavior. Periodically the students exchange the tokens they have earned for some desired reward. In a contingency contract program, the teacher draws up an individual contract with each student, describing exactly what the student must do to earn a particular privilege or reward. A teacher must use these programs with caution, emphasizing learning and not just "good" behavior.

Mastery Learning: Teaching approach in which students must learn one unit and pass a test at a specified level before moving to the next unit.

Good Behavior Game: Arrangement where a class is divided into teams and each team receives demerit points for breaking agreed-upon rules of good behavior.

Group Consequences: Rewards or punishments given to a class as a whole for adhering to or violating rules of conduct.

Token Reinforcement System: System in which tokens earned for academic work and positive classroom behavior can be exchanged for some desired reward.

Contingency Contract: A contract between the teacher and a student specifying what the student must do to earn a particular reward or privilege.

■ Recent Approaches: Self-Regulation and Cognitive Behavior Modification

(pp. 221–225)

What are the steps in self-management? Students can apply behavior analysis on their own to manage their own behavior. Teachers can encourage the development of self-management skills by allowing students to participate in setting goals, keeping track of progress, evaluating accomplishments, and selecting and giving their own reinforcers. Teachers can also use cognitive behavior modification, a behavior change program described by Meichenbaum in which students are directly taught how to use self-instruction.

Self-Management: Use of behavioral learning principles to change your own behavior.

Self-Reinforcement: Providing yourself with positive consequences, contingent on accomplishing a particular behavior.

Cognitive Behavior Modification: Procedures based on both behavioral and cognitive learning principles for changing your own behavior by using self-talk and self-instruction.

Self-Instruction: Talking oneself through the steps of a task.

■ Enhancing Your Expertise with Technology: Self-Regulation

(p. 225)

AskERIC Web site **(http://ericir.syr.edu)**

ERIC Digests **(http://www.ed.gov/databases/ERIC_Digests/index/)**

Other Useful Websites

The Risks of Rewards
http://www.ed.gov/databases/ERICDigests/ed376990.html

Classroom Management
http://scholar.coe.uwf.edu.pacee/steps/tutorial/classmanagement/main.htm#section4

Behaviorism **http://utm.edu/research/iep/b/behavior/htm**

Operant Learning
http://chiron.valdosta.edu.whuitt/col/behsys/operant.html

Theories of Learning **http://tip.psychology.org/**

■ Problems and Issues

(pp. 225–228)

What are the main criticisms of behavioral approaches? The misuse or abuse of behavioral learning methods is unethical. Critics of behavioral methods also point out the danger that reinforcement could decrease interest in learning by overemphasizing rewards and could have a negative impact on other students. Teachers can use behavioral learning principles appropriately and ethically.

Becoming a Professional

Passing the PRAXIS™

Chapter 6 reflects many of the professional standards created by the Interstate New Teacher Assessment and Support Consortium (INTASC). These standards form the basis of the PRAXIS II™ and state-created teacher licensure exams.

Whether you begin your teaching career on the first day of the school year in your own classroom or as a mid-year substitute, the earliest public indicators of your teaching competence often will be the conduct of your students and your classroom management skills. As you read and discuss this chapter, you will encounter many principles of behaviorism that you can employ to foster appropriate classroom conduct and to establish effective routines and procedures. These principles also may be used to explain some of the learning that occurs in classrooms, and it is useful in understanding the complex factors that motivate students to learn. (Do you remember how the daily calendar review in kindergarten helped you learn to recognize numerals and the names of days and months? Did any of your elementary school teachers participate in book-reading reward programs that were sponsored by corporations?) Look for PRAXIS II™ to test your knowledge of behaviorism to address many common classroom situations.

Tips for PRAXIS II™

Understand the basic assumptions and contributions of these behaviorists:

- Pavlov
- Watson
- Thorndike
- Skinner

Determine appropriate behavioral techniques to:

- Establish efficient classroom routines and procedures
- Foster appropriate classroom conduct
- Help students monitor and regulate learning

Understand basic processes of operant conditioning and their roles in learning, including:

- Antecedents and consequences
- Types of reinforcement and reinforcement schedules
- Punishment
- Shaping

Related Topics

- Social learning and social cognitive theories (Chapter 9)
- Behavioral approaches to motivation (Chapter 10)
- Rules and procedures (Chapter 11)
- Objectives for learning (Chapter 12)
- Teacher-centered instruction (Chapter 12)

Standards and Licensure Appendix: *PRAXIS II™ and INTASC*

Refer to the Appendix at the end of the book for detailed correlations to PRAXIS II™ exam topics and INTASC Standards addressed in this text.

Insights about Job Interview Questions: *What Would You Say?*

1. The Physical Therapy unit where you are interviewing is a state-of-the-art facility. You feel as though the interview for a patient-educator position is going well. Your next question is: "One of our biggest problems here, and in most rehabilitation centers for that matter, is getting our clients to stick to an exercise program. What ideas do you have for helping these clients maintain their prescribed regimens?"
2. During your job interview, the principal asks, "A teacher last year got in trouble for bribing his students with homework exemptions to get them to behave in class. What do you think about using rewards and punishments in teaching?" What do you say?

Your Teaching Portfolio: *Teaching Resources*

- What is your stance on using extrinsic reinforcement and punishment in teaching? Be prepared to answer questions about these issues in your interviews.
- Use Table 6.2 "Reinforcement Ideas from Students" to generate ideas for appropriate reinforcers for students you will teach and include these ideas in your **Portfolio.**
- Add Figures 6.2 "Written Prompts: A Peer Tutoring Checklist," 6.3 "A Contingency Contract for Completing Assignments," and 6.4 "Posters to Remind Students to 'Talk Themselves Through' Listening, Planning, Working, and Checking in School" to your **Teaching Resources** file.

Use the CD-ROM included in the back of your textbook to launch the "Becoming a Professional" website. The website features advice on preparing for teacher certification exams, help with getting your first job, and resources to help you perform your job well from the first day forward.

Teachers' Casebook

What Would They Do?

Here is how some practicing teachers responded to the teaching situation presented at the beginning of this chapter about a class out of control.

Richard T. Smith

Fifth Grade Teacher, *Harrison Middle School, Yarmouth, Maine*

Begin "Day Two" with a class meeting, with all students sitting quietly in a circle. The teacher begins with a tennis ball in her hand. The teacher has the ball so she has the floor—she explains her expectation of her students in order to conduct a class. The ball is passed and each student is given a chance to explain what he or she needs from fellow classmates and the teacher. After everybody has spoken, they begin to make a list of classroom expectations, consequences, and privileges. You know what the kids expect and they know what to expect from you. These rules should be photocopied and taped to their desks, reminding students of behaviors, rewards, and consequences.

Kathleen Conroy

Third Grade Teacher, *Rancho Canada Elementary School, Lake Forest, California*

If I were hired in January to take over a class that had no management system, I would start the class as if it were day one with my own system of rules, expectations, and consequences. We would create the needed classroom expectations together so that students felt part of this process. Then we would go through how to enforce these expectations. I would put up a colored chart with our class-created rules, and another corresponding chart with the consequences if rules are broken. I would put up all the students' names and newly assigned numbers on a series of different colored cards, and explain that this system of behavior is a reward system. If all the rules are followed, then they earn different privileges by collecting stamps for being on task. These would be passed out on a daily or weekly basis.

Katie Churchill

Third Grade Teacher, *Oriole Parke Elementary School, Chicago, Illinois*

I believe that it is extremely important to be firm when entering a new classroom. I would enter the classroom the next morning and make the students aware that I will enforce classroom rules and expectations and that I will contact parents if any behavior problems persist. I would have my students help me choose a set of classroom rules that are reasonable so the rules will have more meaning to the students. I would make it clear that the students are in charge of their own behavior and consequences. The students will know exactly what is expected of them and what will happen if they disobey any of the rules. I would consistently follow through with the prescribed consequences. I also would keep the students busy with material that interests them.

Anne Worth

Fourth Grade Teacher, *Clardy School, Kansas City, Missouri*

Have the students share their ideas about what rules are necessary at school and what a working classroom sounds and looks like. Try to call only on those who raise their hands and compliment those who do follow the rules. Before you begin this discussion say, "I think it is important that we establish the rules we will follow together, so for the next ten minutes we will share ideas about school rules. Please raise your hand to be called on so that everyone gets a chance to share." When the list is complete, or if the list needs additions, the teacher can add some basics.

Using a behavior tool such as marbles in a jar, the teacher can set up a system instantly. Tell the class that when each of the rules is followed, a marble will be dropped in the jar. When the jar is full there will be 15 minutes of free time. Drop a marble each time something good happens in the class. Hopefully by the end of the day or the next there will be a reward and you can begin to control the class and do some teaching.

Brenda Miller

Second Grade Teacher, *Yucca Elementary School, Alamogordo, New Mexico*

I would introduce this class to a reward system using classroom "bucks" and a "store" of items to be open each Friday. I would ask parents for various items to be sold in the store, such as toys, pencils, notepads, markers, and toiletries. I would describe the behaviors I expected to see and reward each good behavior with a "buck."

I believe rewards would be more useful at first because most children see discipline as negative, and this class has already seen too much negativism. After my reward system was established I would enlist the help of my students to determine the classroom rules. The key to the reward system's working is to be consistent, generous, and fair. I would price my items higher in the store and give "bucks" away often in reinforcement of good behavior. On the day of store I would have two students (different each week) be the shopkeepers. This reward system teaches responsibility, math, cooperation, and communication. I use this in my second grade classroom with much success.

Go to the Companion Website (www.ablongman.com/woolfolk) for additional case studies including audio and video cases, and examples of student work.

CHAPTER

7

Cognitive Views of Learning

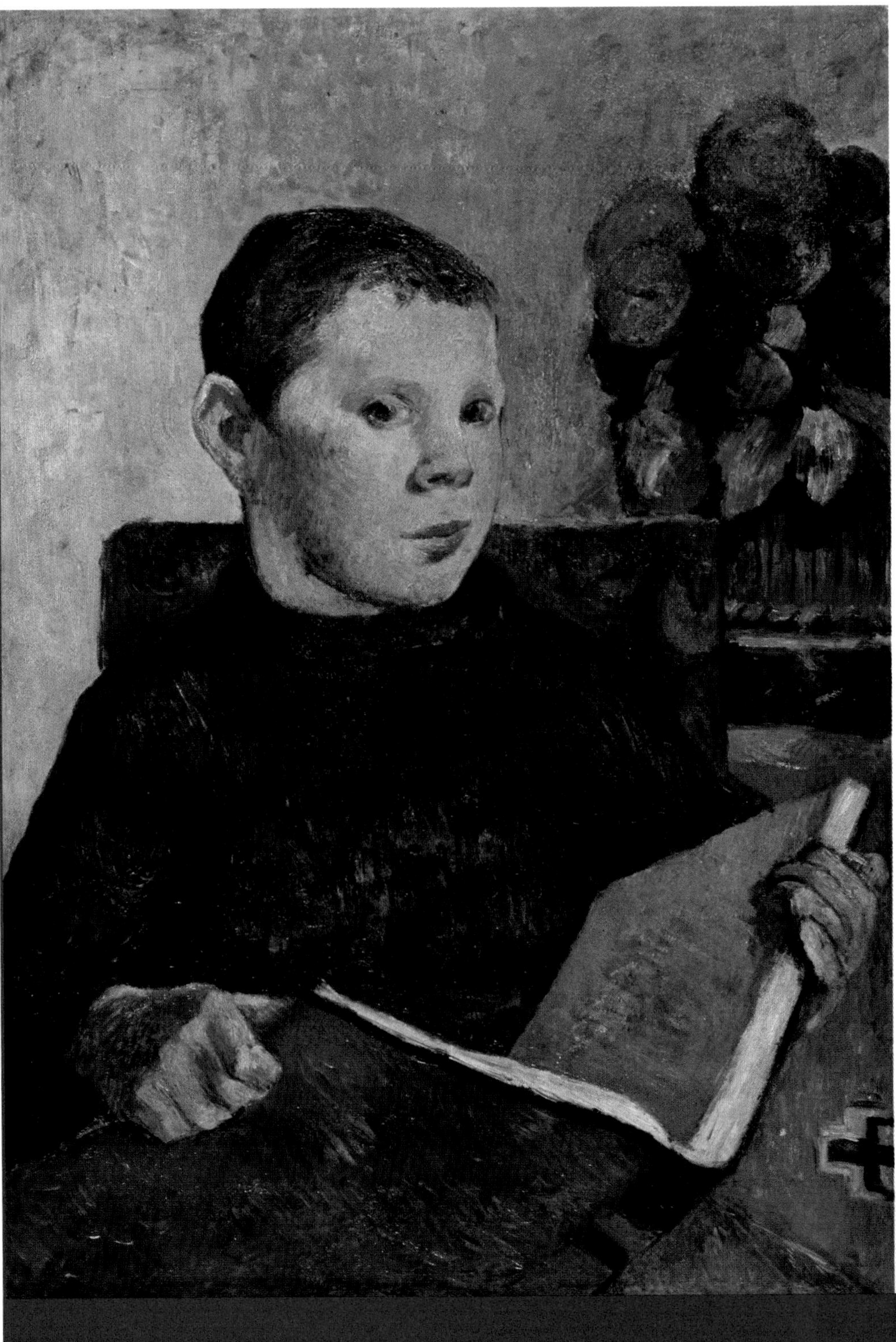

Teachers' Casebook

What Would You Do?

The students in your senior history classes seem to equate understanding with memorizing. They prepare for each unit test by memorizing the exact words of the textbook. Even the best students seem to think that flash cards are the only learning strategy possible. In fact, when you try to get them to think about history by reading some original sources, debating issues in class, or examining art and music from the time period you are studying, they rebel. "Will this be on the test?" "Why are we looking at these pictures—will we have to know who painted them and when?" "What's this got to do with history?" Even the students who participate in the debates seem to use words and phrases straight from the textbook without knowing what they are saying.

Critical Thinking

What do these students "know" about history? What are their beliefs and expectations, and how do these affect their learning? Why do you think they insist on using the rote memory approach? How would you teach your students to learn in this new way? How will these issues affect the grade levels you will teach?

Collaboration

With 2 or 3 other people in your class, talk about teachers you've had who helped you develop deep knowledge about a topic. How did they guide your thinking to move past memorizing to a more complete understanding?

In this chapter we turn from behavioral theories of learning to the cognitive perspective. This means a shift from "viewing the learners and their behaviors as products of incoming environmental stimuli" to seeing the learners as "sources of plans, intentions, goals, ideas, memories, and emotions actively used to attend to, select, and construct meaning from stimuli and knowledge from experience" (Wittrock, 1982, pp. 1–2). We will begin with a discussion of the general cognitive approach to learning and memory and the importance of knowledge in learning. To understand memory, we will consider a widely accepted cognitive model, information processing, which suggests that information is manipulated in different storage systems. Next we will explore metacognition, a field of study that may provide insights into individual and developmental differences in learning. Then we turn to ideas about how teachers can help their students become more knowledgeable. By the time you have completed this chapter, you should be able to answer these questions:

- *What is the role of knowledge in learning?*
- *What is the human information processing model of memory?*
- *What are declarative, procedural, and conditional knowledge?*
- *How do perception, attention, schemas, and scripts influence learning and remembering?*
- *Why do students forget what they have learned?*
- *What is the role of metacognition in learning and remembering?*
- *What are the stages in the development of cognitive skills?*

Elements of the Cognitive Perspective

CONNECT & EXTEND

TO OTHER CHAPTERS
Two different models of instruction based on principles of cognitive learning—Bruner's discovery learning and Ausubel's expository teaching—are described in Chapter 8.

The cognitive perspective is both the oldest and the youngest member of the psychological community. It is old because discussions of the nature of knowledge, the value of reason, and the contents of the mind date back at least to the ancient Greek philosophers (Hernshaw, 1987). From the late 1800s until several decades ago, however, cognitive studies fell from favor and behaviorism thrived. Then, research during World War II on the development of complex human skills, the computer revolution, and breakthroughs in understanding language development all stimulated a resurgence in cognitive research. Evidence accumulated indicating that people plan their responses, use strategies to help themselves remember, and organize the material they are learning in their own unique ways (Miller, Galanter, & Pribram, 1960; Shuell, 1986). Educational psychologists became interested in how people think, learn concepts, and solve problems (e.g., Ausubel, 1963; Bruner, Goodnow, & Austin, 1956).

Interest in concept learning and problem solving soon gave way, however, to interest in how knowledge is represented in the mind and particularly how it is remembered. Remembering and forgetting became major topics for investigation in cognitive psychology in the 1970s and 1980s, and the information processing model of memory dominated research.

Today, there is renewed interest in learning, thinking, and problem solving. The **cognitive view of learning** can be described as a generally agreed-upon philosophical orientation. This means that cognitive theorists share basic notions about learning and memory. Most importantly, cognitive psychologists assume that mental processes exist, that they can be studied scientifically, and that humans are active participants in their own acts of cognition (Ashcraft, 2002).

Comparing Cognitive and Behavioral Views

Cognitive view of learning A general approach that views learning as an active mental process of acquiring, remembering, and using knowledge.

The cognitive and behavioral views differ in their assumptions about what is learned. According to the cognitive view, knowledge is learned, and changes in knowledge make changes in behavior possible. In the behavioral view, the new behaviors themselves are learned (Shuell, 1986). Both behavioral and cognitive theorists believe reinforcement is important in learning, but for different reasons. The strict behaviorist maintains that reinforcement strengthens responses; cognitive theorists see reinforcement as a source of feedback about what is likely to happen if behaviors are repeated or changed—as a source of information.

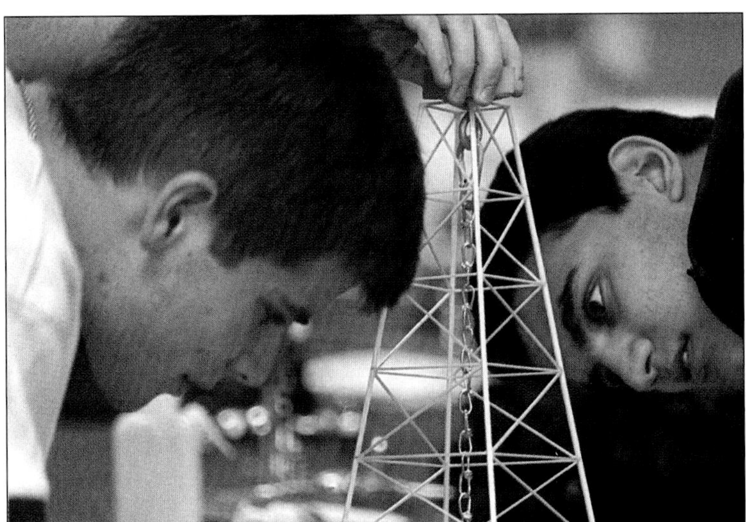

The cognitive view sees learning as an active process in which learners, rather than simply "receiving" knowledge, seek new information to solve problems and reorganize what they already know to achieve new insights.

The cognitive view sees learning as "transforming significant understanding we already have, rather than simple acquisitions written on blank slates" (Greeno, Collins, & Resnick, 1996, p. 18). Instead of being passively influenced by environmental events, people actively choose, practice, pay attention, ignore, reflect, and make many other decisions as they pursue goals. Older cognitive views emphasized the *acquisition* of knowledge, but newer approaches stress its *construction* (Anderson, Reder, & Simon, 1996; Greeno, Collins, & Resnick, 1996; Mayer, 1996).

The methods of cognitive and behavioral researchers also differ. Much of the work on behavioral learning principles has been with animals in controlled laboratory settings. The goal is to identify a few general laws of learning that apply to all higher organisms—including humans, regardless of age, intelligence, or other individual differences. Cognitive psychologists, on the other hand, study a wide range of learning situations. Because of their focus on individual and developmental differences in cognition, they have not been as concerned with general laws of learning. This is one of the reasons that there is no single cognitive model or theory of learning representative of the entire field.

The Importance of Knowledge in Learning

Quickly, list 10 terms that pertain to educational psychology. Now list 10 terms that relate to ceramic engineering.

Unless you are studying ceramic engineering, it probably took you longer to list 10 terms from that field than from educational psychology. Some of you may still be asking, "What is ceramic engineering anyway?" Your answers depend on your knowledge of ceramic engineering. (*Hint:* Think fiber optics, ceramic teeth and bones, ceramic semi-conductors for computers, heat-shielding tiles for space shuttles. . . .)

Knowledge is the outcome of learning. When we learn the history of cognitive psychology, the products of ceramic engineering, or the rules of tennis, we know something new. However, knowledge is more than the end product of previous learning; it also guides new learning. The cognitive approach suggests that one of the most important elements in the learning process is what the individual brings to new learning situations. What we already know "is a scaffold that supports the construction of all future learning" (Alexander, 1996, p. 89)—knowledge determines to a great extent what we will pay attention to, perceive, learn, remember, and forget (Dochy, Segers, & Buehl, 1999; Greeno, Collins, & Resnick, 1996).

A study by Recht and Leslie (1988) shows the importance of knowledge in understanding and remembering new information. These psychologists identified junior high school students who were either very good or very poor readers. They tested the students on their knowledge of baseball and found that knowledge of baseball was not related to reading ability. So the researchers were able to identify four groups of students: *good readers/high baseball knowledge, good readers/low baseball knowledge, poor readers/high baseball knowledge, and poor readers/low baseball knowledge.* Then students in all four groups read a passage describing a baseball game and were tested in a number of ways to see if they understood and remembered what they had read.

The results demonstrated the power of knowledge. Poor readers who knew baseball remembered more than good readers with little baseball knowledge and almost as much as good readers who knew baseball. Poor readers who knew little about baseball remembered the least of what they had read. Thus a good basis of knowledge can be more important than good reading skills in understanding and remembering—but extensive knowledge plus good reading skills are even better.

General and Specific Knowledge. Knowledge in the cognitive perspective includes both subject specific understandings (math, history, soccer, etc.) and general cognitive abilities, such as planning, solving problems, and comprehending language (Greeno, Collins, & Resnick, 1996). So, there are different kinds of knowledge. Some is **domain-specific knowledge** that pertains to a particular task or subject. For example, knowing that the shortstop plays between second and third base is specific to the domain of baseball. Some knowledge, on the other hand, is general—it applies to many different situations. For example, **general knowledge** about how to read or write or use a word processor is useful in and out of school. Of course, there is no absolute line between general and domain-specific knowledge. When you were first learning to read, you may have studied specific facts about the sounds of letters. At that time, knowledge about letter sounds was specific to the domain of reading. But

Domain-specific knowledge Information that is useful in a particular situation or that applies mainly to one specific topic.

General knowledge Information that is useful in many different kinds of tasks; information that applies to many situations.

now you can use both knowledge about sounds and the ability to read in more general ways (Alexander, 1992; Schunk, 2000).

Declarative, Procedural, and Conditional Knowledge. Another way of categorizing knowledge is as declarative, procedural, or conditional (Paris & Cunningham, 1996; Paris, Lipson, & Wixson, 1983). **Declarative knowledge** is knowledge that can be declared, through words and symbol systems of all kinds—Braille, sign language, dance or musical notation, mathematical symbols, and so on (Farnham-Diggory, 1994). Declarative knowledge is "knowing that" something is the case. The history students in the opening "What Would You Do?" situation were focusing exclusively on declarative knowledge about history. The range of declarative knowledge is tremendous. You can know very specific facts (the atomic weight of gold is 196.967), or generalities (leaves of some trees change color in autumn), or personal preferences (I don't like lima beans), or rules (to divide fractions, invert the divisor and multiply). Small units of declarative knowledge can be organized into larger units; for example, principles of reinforcement and punishment can be organized in your thinking into a theory of behavioral learning (Gagné, Yekovich, & Yekovich, 1993).

Procedural knowledge is "knowing how" to do something such as divide fractions or clean a carburetor—procedural knowledge is knowledge in action. It must be demonstrated. Notice that repeating the rule "to divide fractions, invert the divisor and multiply" shows *declarative* knowledge—the student can state the rule. But to show *procedural* knowledge, the student must act. When faced with a fraction to divide, the student must divide correctly. Students demonstrate procedural knowledge when they translate a passage into Spanish or correctly categorize a geometric shape or craft a coherent paragraph.

Conditional knowledge is "knowing when and why" to apply your declarative and procedural knowledge. Given many kinds of math problems, it takes conditional knowledge to know when to apply one procedure and when to apply another to solve each problem. It takes conditional knowledge to know when to read every word in a text and when to skim. For many students, conditional knowledge is a stumbling block. They have the facts and can do the procedures, but they don't seem to apply what they know at the appropriate time.

Table 7.1 shows that we can combine our two systems for describing knowledge. Declarative, procedural, and conditional knowledge can be either general or domain-specific.

Check Yourself Contrast cognitive and behavioral views of learning in terms of what is learned and the role of reinforcement.

How does knowledge affect learning?

To be used, knowledge must be remembered. What do we know about memory?

Table 7.1 Kinds of Knowledge

	General Knowledge	Domain-Specific Knowledge
Declarative	Hours the library is open Rules of grammar	The definition of "hypotenuse" The lines of the poem "The Raven"
Procedural	How to use your word processor How to drive	How to solve an oxidation-reduction equation How to throw a pot on a potter's wheel
Conditional	When to give up and try another approach When to skim and when to read carefully	When to use the formula for calculating volume When to rush the net in tennis

Declarative knowledge Verbal information; facts; "knowing that" something is the case.

Procedural knowledge Knowledge that is demonstrated when we perform a task; "knowing how."

Conditional knowledge "Knowing when and why" to use declarative and procedural knowledge

Information processing The human mind's activity of taking in, storing, and using information.

The Information Processing Model of Memory

There are a number of theories of memory, but the most common are the information processing explanations (Ashcraft, 2002; Hunt & Ellis, 1999; Sternberg, 1999). We will use this well-researched framework for examining learning and memory.

An Overview of the Model

Early **information processing** views of memory used the computer as a model. Like the computer, the human mind takes in information, performs operations on it to change its form and content, stores the information, retrieves it when needed, and generates responses to it. Thus, processing involves gathering information and organizing it in relation to what you already know, or *encoding;* holding information, or *storage;* and getting at the information when needed, or *retrieval.* The whole system is guided by *control processes* that determine how and when information will flow through the system.

For most cognitive psychologists, the computer model is only a metaphor for human mental activity. But other cognitive scientists, particularly those studying artificial intelligence, try to design and program computers to "think" and solve problems like human beings (Anderson, 1995a; Schunk, 2000). Some theorists suggest that the operation of the brain resembles a large number of very slow computers, all operating in parallel (at the same time), with each computer dedicated to a different, specific task (Ashcraft, 2002).

Figure 7.1 is a schematic representation of a typical information processing model of memory, derived from the ideas of several theorists (Atkinson & Shiffrin,

CONNECT & EXTEND

TO YOUR TEACHING/PORTFOLIO
Consider these proverbs about memory taken from Klatzky, R. L. (1984). *Memory and awareness: An information processing perspective.* New York: Freeman, p. 122.

On Learning

- Learning teacheth more in one year than experience in twenty. (Roger Ascham)
- What we have to learn to do, we learn by doing. (Aristotle)

On Memory

- The true art of memory is the art of attention. (Samuel Johnson)
- A man's memory may almost become the art of continually varying and misrepresenting his past, according to his interests in the present. (George Santayana)

On Forgetting

- The mind is slow in unlearning what it has been long in learning. (Seneca)
- Soon learnt, soon forgotten. (Proverb)
- Out of sight, out of mind. (Proverb)
- An injury is much sooner forgotten than an insult. (Lord Chesterfield)

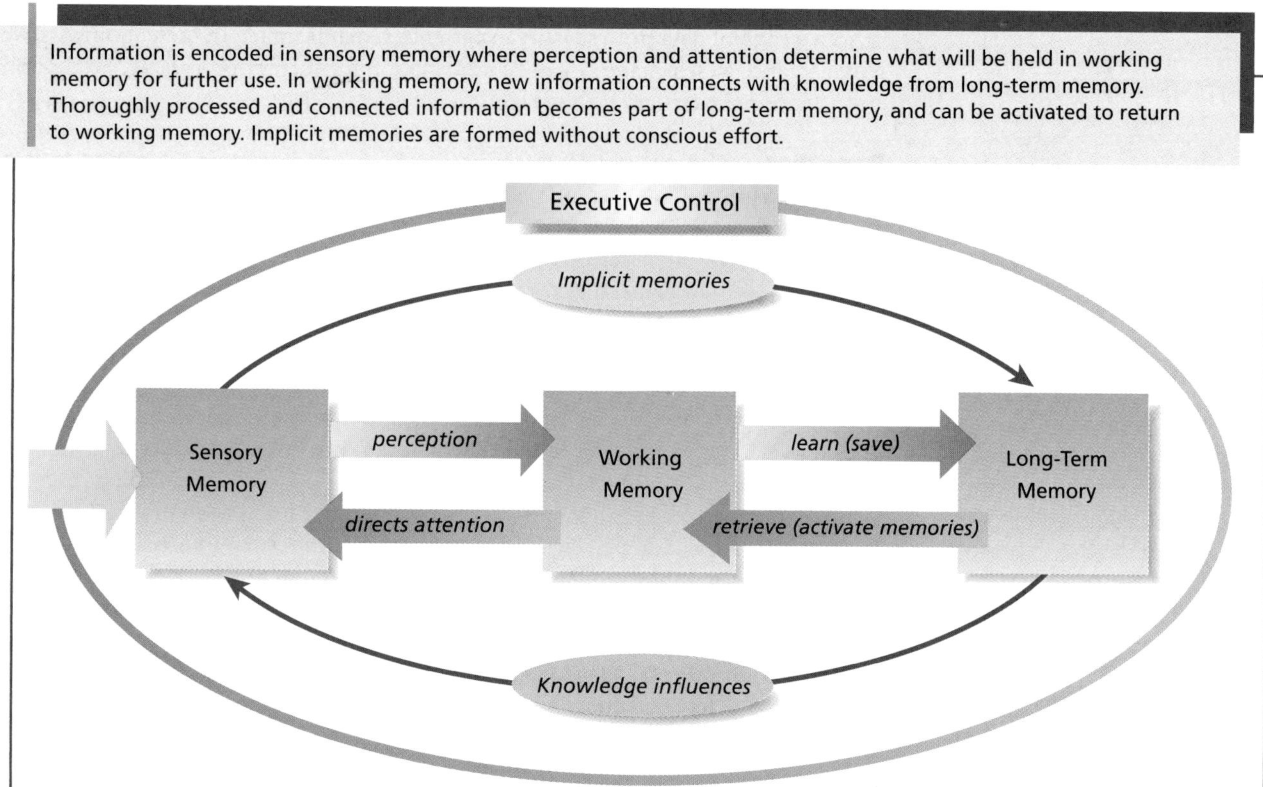
Information is encoded in sensory memory where perception and attention determine what will be held in working memory for further use. In working memory, new information connects with knowledge from long-term memory. Thoroughly processed and connected information becomes part of long-term memory, and can be activated to return to working memory. Implicit memories are formed without conscious effort.
Executive Control
Implicit memories
Sensory Memory
perception
directs attention
Working Memory
learn (save)
retrieve (activate memories)
Long-Term Memory
Knowledge influences

■ **Figure 7.1** The Information Processing System

1968; Neisser, 1976; R. Gagné, 1985). In order to understand this model, let's examine each element.

Sensory Memory

Stimuli from the environment (sights, sounds, smells, etc.) constantly bombard our body's mechanisms for seeing, hearing, tasting, smelling, and feeling. **Sensory memory** is the initial processing that transforms these incoming stimuli into information so we can make sense of them. Even though sights and sounds may last only fractions of a second, the transformations (information) that represent these sensations are briefly held in the *sensory register* or *sensory information store* so that this initial processing can take place (Bruning, Schraw, & Ronning, 1999).

Capacity, Duration, and Contents of Sensory Memory. The *capacity* of sensory memory is very large, and can take in more information than we can possibly handle at once. But this vast amount of sensory information is fragile in *duration*. It lasts between one and three seconds.

Wave a pencil (or your finger) back and forth before your eyes while you stare straight ahead. What exactly do you see? Pinch your arm and let go. What do you feel just after you let go?

You just experienced this brief holding of sensory information in your own sensory register. You could see a trace of the pencil after the actual stimulus has been removed and feel the pinch after you let go. The sensory register held information about the stimuli very briefly after the actual stimulus had left (Lindsay & Norman, 1977).

The information *content* of sensory memory resembles the sensations from the original stimulus. Visual sensations are coded briefly by the sensory register as images, almost like photographs. Auditory sensations are coded as sound patterns, similar to echoes. It may be that the other senses also have their own codes. Thus, for a second or so, a wealth of data from sensory experience remains intact. In these moments, we have a chance to select and organize information for further processing. Perception and attention are critical at this stage.

Perception. The process of detecting a stimulus and assigning meaning to it is called **perception.** This meaning is constructed based on both physical representations from the world and our existing knowledge. For example, consider these marks: **I3**. If asked what the letter is, you would say "B." If asked what the number is, you would say "13." The actual marks remain the same; their meaning changes in keeping with your expectation to recognize a number or a letter. To a child without appropriate knowledge to perceive either a number or a letter, the marks would probably be meaningless (F. Smith, 1975).

Some of our present-day understanding of perception is based on studies conducted in Germany (and later in the United States) early in this century by psychologists called *Gestalt theorists.* **Gestalt,** which means "pattern" or "configuration" in German, refers to people's tendency to organize sensory information into patterns or relationships. Instead of perceiving bits and pieces of unrelated information, we usually perceive organized, meaningful wholes. Figure 7.2 presents a few Gestalt principles.

The Gestalt principles are reasonable explanations of certain aspects of perception, but they are not the whole story. There are two other kinds of explanations in information processing theory for how we recognize patterns and give meaning to sensory events. The first is called *feature analysis,* or **bottom-up processing** because the stimulus must be analyzed into features or components and assembled into a meaningful pattern "from the bottom up." For example, a capital letter A consists of two relatively straight lines joined at a 45-degree angle and a horizontal line through the middle. Whenever we see these features, or anything close enough,

Sensory memory System that holds sensory information very briefly.

Perception Interpretation of sensory information.

Gestalt German for *pattern* or *whole;* Gestalt theorists hold that people organize their perceptions into coherent wholes.

Bottom-up processing Perceiving based on noticing separate defining features and assembling them into a recognizable pattern.

Gestalt principles of perception explain how we "see" patterns in the world around us.

a. Figure-ground
What do you see? Faces or a vase? Make one figure—the other ground.

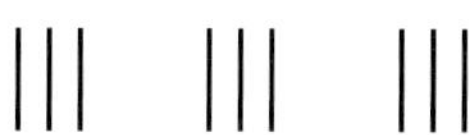

b. Proximity
You see these lines as 3 groups because of the proximity of the lines.

c. Similarity
You see these lines as an alternating pattern because of the similarity in height of lines.

d. Closure
You perceive a circle instead of dotted curved lines.

Source: From *Learning Theories: An Educational Perspective* (2nd ed.), by D. H. Schunk. Published by Prentice Hall. Copyright © 1996 by Prentice Hall. Reprinted by permission of Pearson Education, Inc., Upper Saddle River, NJ.

Figure 7.2 Examples of Gestalt Principles

including, A, *A*, **A**, A, *A*, and A, we recognize an A (Anderson, 1995a). This explains how we are able to read words written in other people's handwriting.

If all perception relied only on feature analysis, learning would be very slow. Luckily, humans are capable of another type of perception based on knowledge and expectation often called **top-down processing.** To recognize patterns rapidly, in addition to noting features, we use what we already know about the situation—what we know about words or pictures or the way the world generally operates. For example, you would not have seen the marks above as the letter A if you had no knowledge of the Roman alphabet. So, what you know also affects what you are able to perceive. The role of knowledge in perception is represented by the arrows pointing left in Figure 7.1 from long-term memory (stored knowledge), to working memory and then to sensory memory.

The Role of Attention. If every variation in color, movement, sound, smell, temperature, and so on ended up in working memory, life would be impossible. By paying **attention** to selected stimuli and ignoring others, we limit the possibilities that we will process. What we pay attention to is guided to a certain extent by what we already know and what we need to know, so attention is involved in and influenced by all three memory processes in Figure 7.1

But attention takes effort and is a limited resource. I imagine you have to work a bit to pay attention to these words about attention! We can pay attention to only one cognitively demanding task at time (Anderson, 1995a). For example, when I was learning to drive, I couldn't listen to the radio and drive at the same time. After some practice, I could listen, but I had to turn the radio off when traffic was heavy. After years of practice, I can plan a class, listen to the radio, and carry on a conversation as I drive. This is possible because many processes that initially require attention and concentration become automatic with practice. Actually, **automaticity** probably is a matter of degree; we are not completely automatic, but rather more or less automatic in our performances depending on how much practice we have had and the situation. For example, even experienced drivers might become very attentive and focused during a blinding blizzard (Anderson, 1995a).

Attention and Teaching. The first step in learning is paying attention. Students cannot process information that they do not recognize or perceive. Many factors in the classroom influence student attention. Eye-catching or startling displays or actions

CONNECT & EXTEND

TO **PRAXIS**™
ATTENTION (I, A1)
Attention has an important place in instructional activities. What steps can a teacher take to gain and maintain student attention during instruction.

CONNECT & EXTEND

TO THE RESEARCH
Flavell (1985) described four aspects of attention in developing children:

1. *Controlled:* Develop longer attention spans and ability to focus on important details, ignoring minor ones.
2. *Tailored to task:* Older children focus attention on most difficult material being learned (Berk, 2002).
3. *Directive:* They develop a feel for cues (teacher's voice, gestures) telling them when/how to direct their attention.
4. *Self-monitoring:* They learn to decide if they are using the right strategy, and to change if it's not working.

Top-down processing Perceiving based on the context and the patterns you expect to occur in that situation.

Attention Focus on a stimulus.

Automaticity The ability to perform thoroughly learned tasks without much mental effort.

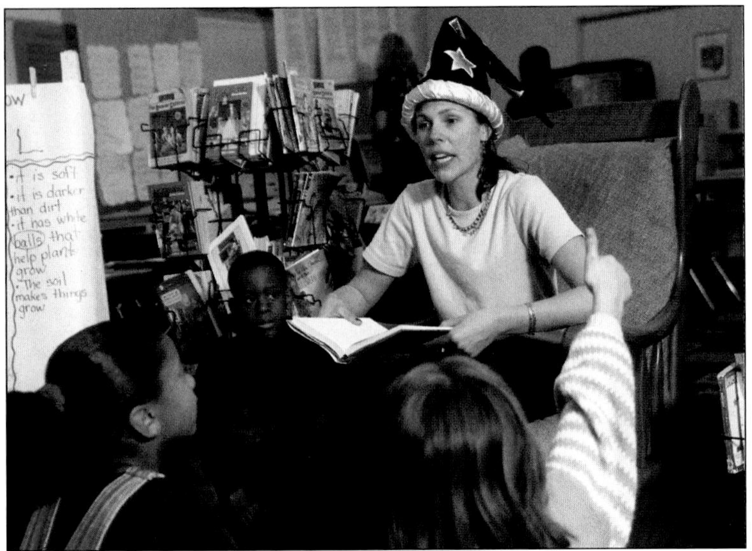

Teachers must first be able to gain and maintain their students' attention, especially in learning situations that may be less inherently interesting. Lessons might be introduced with an eye-catching or startling display to "grab" students.

can draw attention at the beginning of a lesson. A teacher might begin a science lesson on air pressure by blowing up a balloon until it pops. Bright colors, underlining, highlighting of written or spoken words, calling students by name, surprise events, intriguing questions, variety in tasks and teaching methods, and changes in voice level, lighting, or pacing can all be used to gain attention. And students have to maintain attention—they have to stay focused on the important features of the learning situation. The *Guidelines* offer additional ideas for capturing and maintaining students' attention.

Working Memory

The information in sensory memory is available for further processing, as soon as it is noticed and transformed into patterns of images or sounds (or perhaps other types of sensory codes). **Working memory** is "the temporary storage of information that is being processed in any range of cognitive tasks" (Baddeley, 1986, p. 43). Working memory is the "workbench" of the memory system, the interface where new information is held temporarily and combined with knowledge from long-term memory. Working memory "contains" what you are thinking about at the moment. For this reason, some psychologists consider the

GUIDELINES: Gaining and Maintaining Attention

Use signals.

Examples

1. Develop a signal that tells students to stop what they are doing and focus on you. Some teachers move to a particular spot in the room, flick the lights, tap the table, or play a chord on the class piano.
2. Avoid distracting behaviors such as tapping a pencil while talking that interfere with both signals and attention to learning.
3. Give short, clear directions before, not during, transitions.

Make sure the purpose of the lesson or assignment is clear to students.

Examples

1. Write the goals or objectives on the board and discuss them with students before starting. Ask students to summarize or restate the goals.
2. Explain the reasons for learning, and ask students for examples of how they will apply their understanding of the material.
3. Tie the new material to previous lessons—show an outline or map of how the new topic fits with previous and upcoming material.

Incorporate variety, curiosity, and surprise.

Examples

1. Arouse curiosity with questions such as "What would happen if . . . ?"
2. Create shock by staging an unexpected event such as a loud argument just before a lesson on communication.
3. Alter the physical environment by changing the arrangement of the room or moving to a different setting.
4. Shift sensory channels by giving a lesson that requires students to touch, smell, or taste.
5. Use movements, gestures, and voice inflection—walk around the room, point, and speak softly and then more emphatically. (My husband has been known to jump up on his desk to make an important point in his college classes!)

Ask questions and provide frames for answering.

Examples

1. Ask students why the material is important, how they intend to study, and what strategies they will use.
2. Give students self-checking or self-editing guides that focus on common mistakes or have them work in pairs to improve each other's work—sometimes it is difficult to pay attention to your own errors.

working memory to be synonymous with "consciousness" (Sweller, van Merrienboer, & Paas, 1998). Unlike sensory memory or long-term memory, working memory capacity is very limited—something many of your professors seem to forget as they race through a lecture while you work to hold and process the information.

You may have heard the term **short-term memory.** This was an earlier name for the brief memory component of the information processing system. Short-term memory is not exactly the same as working memory. Working memory includes both temporary storage and active processing—the workbench of memory—where active mental effort is applied to new and old information. But short-term memory usually means just storage, the immediate memory for new information that can be held about 15 to 20 seconds (Baddeley, 2001). Early experiments suggested that the capacity of short-term memory was only about 5 to 9 separate new items at once (Miller, 1956). Later we will see that this limitation can be overcome using strategies such as chunking or grouping, but the 5 to 9 limit generally holds true in everyday life. It is quite common to remember a new phone number after looking it up, as you walk across the room to make the call. But what if you have two phone calls to make in succession? Two new phone numbers (14 digits) probably cannot be stored simultaneously.

A current view of working memory is that it is composed of at least three elements: the central executive that controls attention and other mental resources (the "worker" of working memory), the phonological loop that holds verbal and acoustical (sound) information, and the visuospatial sketchpad for visual and spatial information.

Solve this problem from Ashcraft (2002, p. 186) and pay attention to how you go about the process:

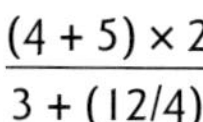

$$\frac{(4 + 5) \times 2}{3 + (12/4)}$$

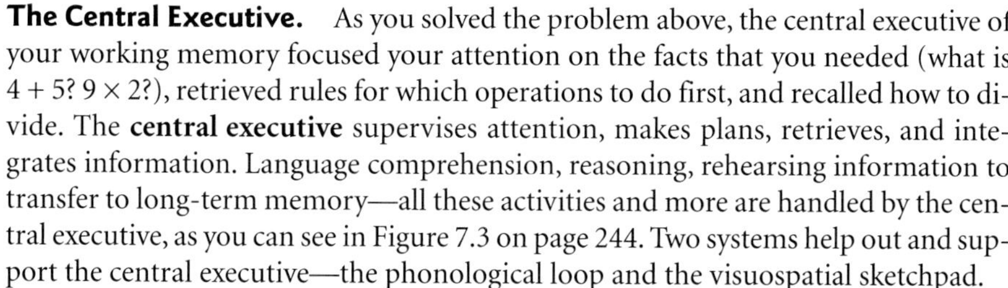

The Central Executive. As you solved the problem above, the central executive of your working memory focused your attention on the facts that you needed (what is 4 + 5? 9 × 2?), retrieved rules for which operations to do first, and recalled how to divide. The **central executive** supervises attention, makes plans, retrieves, and integrates information. Language comprehension, reasoning, rehearsing information to transfer to long-term memory—all these activities and more are handled by the central executive, as you can see in Figure 7.3 on page 244. Two systems help out and support the central executive—the phonological loop and the visuospatial sketchpad.

The Phonological Loop. The **phonological loop** is a system for rehearsing words and sounds for short-term memory. It is the place you put the "18" (4 + 5 = 9 × 2 = 18) from the top line of the problem above while you calculated the 3 + (12/4) on the bottom of the problem. Baddeley (1986, 2001) suggests that we can hold as much in the phonological loop as we can rehearse (say to ourselves) in 1.5 to 2 seconds. The 7-digit telephone number fits this limitation. But what if you tried to hold these 7 words in mind: *disentangle appropriation gossamer anti-intellectual preventative forclosure documentation* (Gray, 2002)? Besides being a mouthful, these words take longer than 2 seconds to rehearse and are more difficult to hold in working memory than 7 single digits or 7 short words.

Remember—put in your working memory—that we are discussing temporarily holding *new information.* In daily life we certainly can hold more than 5 to 9 bits or 1.5 seconds of information at once. While you are dialing that 7-digit phone number you just looked up, you are bound to have other things "on your mind"—in your memory—such as how to use a telephone, whom you are calling, and why. You don't have to pay attention to these things; they are not new knowledge. Some of the processes, such as dialing the phone, have become automatic. However, because of the working memory's limitations, if you were in a foreign country and were attempting to use an unfamiliar telephone system, you might very well have trouble remembering

Working memory The information that you are focusing on at a given moment.

Short-term memory Component of memory system that holds information for about 20 seconds.

Central executive The part of working memory that is responsible for monitoring and directing attention and other mental resources.

Phonological loop Part of working memory. A memory rehearsal system for verbal and sound information of about 1.5 to 2 seconds.

The central executive system is the pool of mental resources for such cognitive activities as focusing attention, reasoning, and comprehension. The phonological loop holds verbal and sound information, and the visuospatial sketchpad holds visual and spatial information. The system is limited and can be overwhelmed if information is too much or too difficult.

WORKING MEMORY

Central Executive
(Pool of mental resources)

Activities:
Initiate control and decision processes
Reasoning, language comprehension
Transfer information to long-term memory via rehearsal, recoding

Phonological loop
(Short-term buffer)

Activities:
Recycling items for immediate recall
Articulatory processes
(Executive's resources are drained if articulation task is difficult)

Visuospatial sketchpad

Activities:
Visual imagery tasks
Spatial, visual search tasks
(Executive's resources are drained if imagery or spatial task is difficult)

Source: From *Cognition* (3rd ed.), by M. H. Ashcraft. Published by Prentice Hall. Copyright © 2002 by Prentice Hall. Reprinted by permission of Pearson Education, Inc., Upper Saddle River, NJ.

■ **Figure 7.3** Three Parts of Working Memory

the phone number because your central executive was trying to figure out the phone system at the same time. Even a few bits of new information can be too much to remember if the new information is very complex or unfamiliar or if you have to integrate several elements to make sense of a situation (Sweller, van Merrienboer, & Paas, 1998).

The Visuospatial Sketchpad. Now try this problem from Gray (2002).

STOP THINK WRITE If you rotate a *p* 180 degrees, do you get a *b* or a *d*?

Most people answer the question above by creating a visual image of a "p" and rotating it. The **visuospatial sketchpad** is the place where you manipulated the image (after your central executive retrieved the meaning of "180 degrees," of course). Working in the visuospatial sketchpad has some of the same aspects as actually looking at a picture or object. If you have to solve the "p" problem and also pay attention to an image on a screen, you will be slowed down just like you would be if you had to look back and forth between two different objects. But if you had to solve the "p" problem while repeating digits, there is little slow down. You can use your phonological loop and your visuospatial sketchpad at the same time, but each is quickly filled and easily overburdened. In fact, each kind of task—verbal and visual—appears to happen in different areas of the brain. As we will see later, there are some individual differences in the capacities of these systems, too (Ashcraft, 2002; Gray, 2002).

Visuospatial sketchpad Part of working memory. A holding system for visual and spatial infromation.

Duration and Contents of Working Memory. It is clear that the *duration* of information in the working memory system is short, about 5 to 20 seconds unless you keep rehearsing the information or process it some other way. It may seem to you that a memory system with a 20-second time limit is not very useful but, without this system, you would have already forgotten what you read in the first part of this sentence before you came to these last few words. This would clearly make understanding sentences difficult.

The *contents* of information in working memory may be in the form of sounds and images that resemble the representations in sensory memory, or the information may be structured more abstractly, based on meaning.

Retaining Information in Working Memory. Because information in working memory is fragile and easily lost, it must be kept activated to be retained. Activation is high as long as you are focusing on information, but activation decays or fades quickly when attention shifts away. Holding information in working memory is like keeping a series of plates spinning on top of poles in a circus act. The performer gets one plate spinning, moves to the next plate, and the next, but has to return to the first plate before it slows down too much and falls off its pole. If we don't keep the information "spinning" in working memory—keep it activated—it will "fall off" (Anderson, 1995a, 1995b). When activation fades, forgetting follows, as shown in Figure 7.4. To keep information activated in working memory for longer than 20 seconds, most people keep rehearsing the information mentally.

There are two types of rehearsal (Craik & Lockhart, 1972). **Maintenance rehearsal** involves repeating the information in your mind. As long as you repeat the information, it can be maintained in working memory indefinitely. Maintenance rehearsal is useful for retaining something you plan to use and then forget, such as a phone number or a location on a map.

Elaborative rehearsal involves connecting the information you are trying to remember with something you already know, with knowledge from long-term memory. For example, if you meet someone at a party whose name is the same as your brother's, you don't have to repeat the name to keep it in memory, you just have to make the association. This kind of rehearsal not only retains information in working memory but helps move information from short-term to long-term memory. Rehearsal is a process the central executive controls to manage the flow of information through the information processing system.

The limited capacity of working memory can also be somewhat circumvented by the process of **chunking.** Because the number of bits of information, not the size of each bit, is a limitation for working memory, you can retain more information if you can group individual bits of information. For example, if you have to remember the

CONNECT & EXTEND

TO **PRAXIS**™
MEMORY AND INSTRUCTION (II, A1)
To maximize the learning derived from instructional activities, a teacher should be aware of the characteristics of working memory. Consider the techniques or tactics a teacher can employ that complement those characteristics.

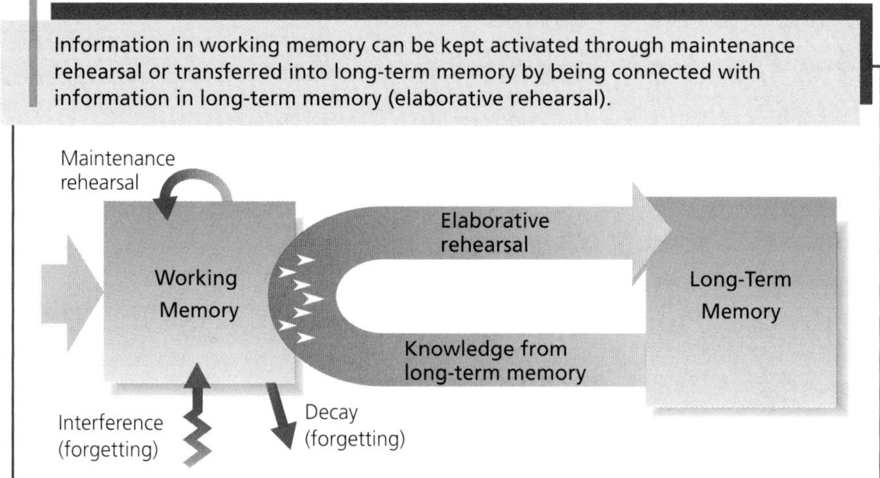

Information in working memory can be kept activated through maintenance rehearsal or transferred into long-term memory by being connected with information in long-term memory (elaborative rehearsal).
Maintenance rehearsal
Working Memory
Elaborative rehearsal
Long-Term Memory
Knowledge from long-term memory
Interference (forgetting)
Decay (forgetting)

Figure 7.4 Working Memory

Maintenance rehearsal Keeping information in working memory by repeating it to yourself.

Elaborative rehearsal Keeping information in working memory by associating it with something else you already know.

Chunking Grouping individual bits of data into meaningful larger units.

Maintenance rehearsal—going over something several times—can be an effective way to remember, or memorize, larger amounts of information such as lines in a play, at least temporarily. Whether the information will be remembered long into the future depends on other factors as well.

six digits 3, 5, 4, 8, 7, and 0, it is easier to put them together into three chunks of two digits each (35, 48, 70) or two chunks of three digits each (354, 870). With these changes, there are only two or three bits of information rather than six to hold at one time. Chunking helps you remember a telephone number or a social security number (Bruning, Schraw, & Ronning, 1999).

Forgetting. Information may be lost from working memory through interference or decay (see Figure 7.4). Interference is fairly straightforward: Processing new information interferes or gets confused with old information. As new thoughts accumulate, old information is lost from working memory. Information is also lost by time **decay.** If you don't continue to pay attention to information, the activation level decays (weakens) and finally drops so low that the information cannot be reactivated—it disappears altogether.

Actually, forgetting is very useful. Without forgetting, people would quickly overload their working memories and learning would cease. Also, it would be a problem if you remembered permanently every sentence you ever read, every sound you ever heard, every picture you ever saw . . . you get the idea. Finding a particular bit of information in all that sea of knowledge would be impossible. It is helpful to have a system that provides temporary storage and that "weeds out" some information from everything you experience.

Check Yourself Compare declarative, procedural, and conditional knowledge.

Give two explanations for perception.

What is working memory?

We turn next to long-term memory. Because this is such an important topic for teachers, we will spend quite a bit of time on it.

Long-Term Memory: The Goal of Teaching

Working memory holds the information that is currently activated, such as a telephone number you have just found and are about to dial. **Long-term memory** holds the information that is well learned, such as all the other telephone numbers you know.

Capacity, Duration, and Contents of Long-Term Memory

Decay The weakening and fading of memories with the passage of time.

Long-term memory Permanent store of knowledge.

There are a number of differences between working and long-term memory, as you can see in Table 7.2. Information enters working memory very quickly. To move information into long-term storage requires more time and a bit of effort. Whereas the capacity of working memory is limited, the capacity of long-term memory appears

■ Table 7.2	Working and Long-Term Memory				
Type of Memory	**Input**	**Capacity**	**Duration**	**Contents**	**Retrieval**
Working	Very fast	Limited	Very brief: 5–20 sec.	Words, images, ideas, sentences	Immediate
Long-Term	Relatively slow	Practically unlimited	Practically unlimited	Propositional networks, schemata, productions, episodes, perhaps images	Depends on representation and organization

SOURCE: From *Comprehension and Learning: A Conceptual Framework for Teachers*, by F. Smith, 1975, New York: Holt, Rinehart, and Winston. Copyright © Holt, Rinehart, and Winston. Adapted with permission of the author.

to be, for all practical purposes, unlimited. In addition, once information is securely stored in long-term memory, it can remain there permanently. Our access to information in working memory is immediate because we are thinking about the information at that very moment. But access to information in long-term memory requires time and effort. Recently, some psychologists have suggested that there are not two separate memory stores (working and long-term). Rather, working memory is the part of long-term memory that works on (processes) currently activated information—so working memory is more about processing than storage (Wilson, 2001).

Allan Paivio (1971, 1986; Clark & Paivio, 1991) suggests that information is stored in long-term memory as either visual images or verbal units, or both. Psychologists who agree with this point of view believe that information coded both visually and verbally is easiest to learn (Mayer & Sims, 1994). This may be one reason why explaining an idea with words and representing it visually in a figure, as we do in textbooks, has proved helpful to students. For example, Richard Mayer and his colleagues (Mayer, 1999, 2001; Mautone & Mayer, 2001) have found that illustrations like the one in the *Reaching Every Student* feature on page 248 are helpful in improving students' understanding of science concepts. Paivio's ideas have some support, but critics contend that the capacity of the brain is not large enough to store all the images we have seen or can imagine. They suggest that many images are actually stored as verbal codes and then translated into visual information when an image is needed (Schunk, 2000).

Another recent addition to the information processing model is the notion of long-term working memory (Kintsch, 1998). **Long-term working memory** holds the retrieval structures and strategies that pull from long-term memory the information needed at the moment. As you develop knowledge and expertise in an area, you create efficient long-term working memory structures for solving problems in that area. So long-term working memory involves a set of domain-specific access tools that improve as you gain expertise in that domain.

Most cognitive psychologists distinguish two categories of long-term memory, explicit and implicit, with subdivisions under each category, as shown in Figure 7.5 on page 249. **Explicit memory** is knowledge from long-term memory that can be recalled and consciously considered. We are aware of these memories—we know we have remembered them. **Implicit memory,** on the other hand, is knowledge that we are not conscious of recalling, but that influences behavior or thought without our awareness. These different kinds of memory are associated with different parts of the brain (Ashcraft, 2002).

Long-term working memory Holds the strategies for pulling information from long-term memory into working memory.

Explicit memory Long-term memories that involve deliberate or conscious recall.

Implicit memory Knowledge that we are not conscious of recalling, but influences behavior or thought without our awareness.

Semantic memory Memory for meaning.

Explicit Memories: Semantic and Episodic

From Figure 7.5 on page 249 you will see that explicit memories can be either semantic or episodic. **Semantic memory,** very important in schools, is memory for meaning, including words, facts, theories, and concepts—declarative knowledge. These

~ Reaching Every Student ~

A Picture and a Few Hundred Words

Is a picture worth 1000 words in teaching? Richard Mayer (1999, 2001) has studied this question for several years and found that the right combination of pictures and words can make a significant difference in students' learning. Mayer's cognitive theory of multimedia learning includes three ideas:

- *Dual Coding:* Visual and verbal materials are processed in different systems (Clark & Paivio, 1991)
- *Limited Capacity:* Working memory for verbal and visual material is severely limited (Baddeley, 2001).
- *Generative Learning:* Meaningful learning happens when students focus on relevant information and generate or build connections (Mayer, 1999).

The problem? How to build complex understandings that integrate information from visual (pictures, diagrams, graphs, films) and verbal (text, lecture) sources, given the limitations of working memory. The answer? Make sure the information is available at the same time or in focused small bites. Here are two examples:

In one study Mayer and Gallini (1990) used three kinds of texts to explain how a bicycle pump works. One text used only words, the second had pictures that just showed the parts of the brake system and the steps, and the third (this one improved student learning and recall) showed both the "on" and the "off" states of the pumps with labels for each step, like the following:

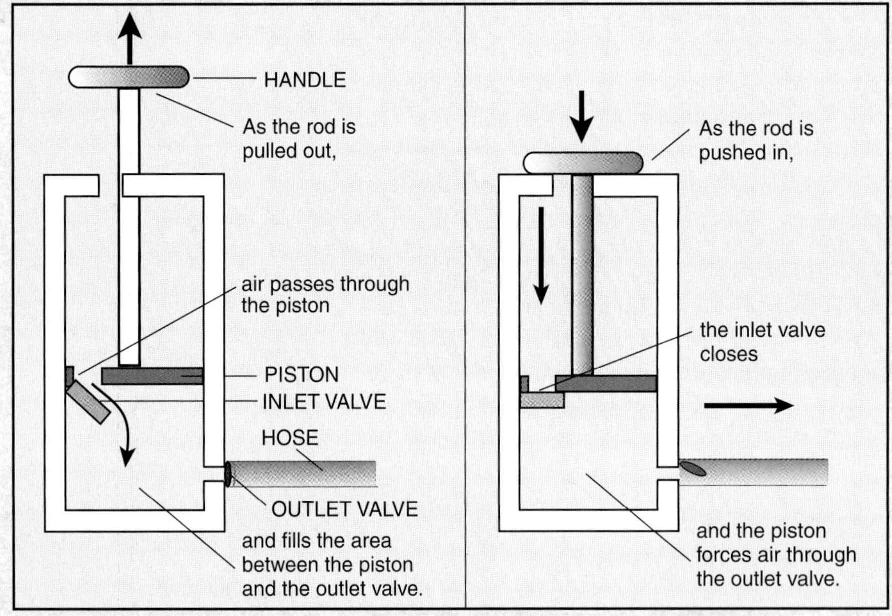
HANDLE
As the rod is pulled out,
air passes through the piston
PISTON
INLET VALVE
HOSE
OUTLET VALVE
and fills the area between the piston and the outlet valve.
As the rod is pushed in,
the inlet valve closes
and the piston forces air through the outlet valve.

The second study involved a 140-second multimedia presentation on cloud to ground lightning. The presentation was an animation showing the 16 steps in the production of lightning, beginning with moist air moving over the land from the ocean and ending with a flash of lightning. There were five different modes for the presentation:

1. Concurrent, with animation showing the 16 steps and narration explaining the process at the same time,
2. the full 140-second animated illustration followed by the full verbal narration describing the process,
3. the full narration first and then the full animation,
4. small bites—one step at a time of the process shown first in animation followed by narration,
5. small bites—one step at a time of the process with narration first and then animation.

Students who saw the *concurrent* or either of the *small bites* presentations performed significantly better on several kinds of tests about lightning. Mayer suggests that the learning was better because students had both the visual and the verbal information at the same time or close enough to the same time that they could hold it in working memory. Waiting through the entire narration before you get the animation or vice versa puts too much strain on working memory—you can't remember the pictures of step 5 when you finally hear the explanation later.

The moral of the story? Give students multiple ways to understand—pictures and explanations. But don't overload working memory—"package" the visual and verbal information together in bite-size (or memory-size) pieces.

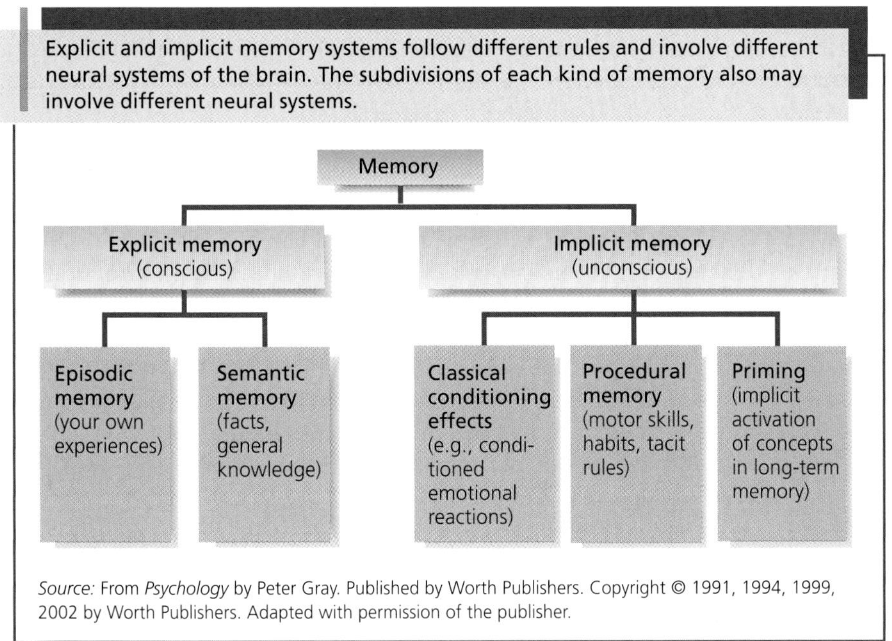
Explicit and implicit memory systems follow different rules and involve different neural systems of the brain. The subdivisions of each kind of memory also may involve different neural systems.
Memory
Explicit memory (conscious)
Implicit memory (unconscious)
Episodic memory (your own experiences)
Semantic memory (facts, general knowledge)
Classical conditioning effects (e.g., conditioned emotional reactions)
Procedural memory (motor skills, habits, tacit rules)
Priming (implicit activation of concepts in long-term memory)
Source: From Psychology by Peter Gray. Published by Worth Publishers. Copyright © 1991, 1994, 1999, 2002 by Worth Publishers. Adapted with permission of the publisher.

Figure 7.5 Long-Term Memory: Explicit and Implicit

memories are not tied to particular experiences and are stored as *propositions, images,* and *schemas.*

Propositions and Propositional Networks. A *proposition* is the smallest unit of knowledge that can be judged true or false. The statement, "Ida borrowed the antique tablecloth" has two propositions:

1. Ida borrowed the tablecloth.
2. The tablecloth is an antique.

Propositions that share information, such as the two above that share information about the tablecloth (Ida borrowed the tablecloth and the tablecloth is an antique) are linked in what cognitive psychologists call **propositional networks.** It is the meaning, not the exact words or word order, that is stored in the network. The same propositional network would apply to the sentence: "The antique tablecloth was borrowed by Ida." The meaning is the same, and it is this *meaning* that is stored in memory as a set of relationships.

It is possible that most information is stored and represented in propositional networks. When we want to recall a bit of information, we may translate its meaning (as represented in the propositional network) into familiar phrases and sentences, or mental pictures. Also, because propositions are networked, recall of one bit of information can trigger or *activate* recall of another. We are not aware of these networks, for they are not part of our conscious memory (Anderson, 1995a). In much the same way, we are not aware of underlying grammatical structure when we form a sentence in our own language; we don't have to diagram a sentence in order to say it.

Images. **Images** are representations based on the structure or appearance of the information (Anderson, 1995a). As we form images (like you did in the "p" problem), we try to remember or recreate the physical attributes and spatial structure of information. For example, when asked how many windowpanes are in their living room, most people call up an image of the windows "in their mind's eye" and count the panes—the more panes, the longer it takes to respond. If the information were represented only in a proposition such as "my living room has seven window panes," then everyone would take about the same time to answer, whether the number

Propositional network Set of interconnected concepts and relationships in which long-term knowledge is held.

Images Representations based on the physical attributes—the appearance—of information.

Schemata (singular, **schema**) Basic structures for organizing information; concepts.

was 1 or 24 (Mendell, 1971). However, as we saw earlier, researchers don't agree on exactly how images are stored in memory. Some psychologists believe that images are stored as pictures; others believe we store propositions in long-term memory and convert to pictures in working memory when necessary.

There probably are features of each process involved—some memory for images and some verbal or propositional descriptions of the image. Seeing images "in your mind's eye" is not exactly the same as seeing the actual image. It is more difficult to perform complicated transformations on mental images than on real images (Matlin & Foley, 1997). For example, if you had a plastic "p," you could very quickly rotate it. Rotating mentally takes more time for most people. Nevertheless, images are useful in making many practical decisions such as how a sofa might look in your living room or how to line up a golf shot. Images may also be helpful in abstract reasoning. Physicists, such as Faraday and Einstein, report creating images to reason about complex new problems. Einstein claimed that he was visualizing chasing a beam of light and catching up to it when the concept of relativity came to him (Kosslyn & Koenig, 1992).

CONNECT & EXTEND

TO **PRAXIS**™
PRIOR KNOWLEDGE (I, A1)
Prior knowledge strongly influences how we build and reorganize new knowledge. Be familiar with the role of schema and propositional networks in the construction of knowledge and how they affect learning.

Schemas. Propositions and single images are fine for representing single ideas and relationships, but often our knowledge about a topic combines images and propositions. To explain this kind of complex knowledge, psychologists developed the idea of a schema (Gagné, Yekovich, & Yekovich, 1993). **Schemas** (sometimes called *schemata*) are abstract knowledge structures that organize vast amounts of information. A schema (the singular form) is a pattern or guide for representing an event, concept, or skill. For example, Figure 7.6 is a partial representation of a schema for knowledge about an "antique."

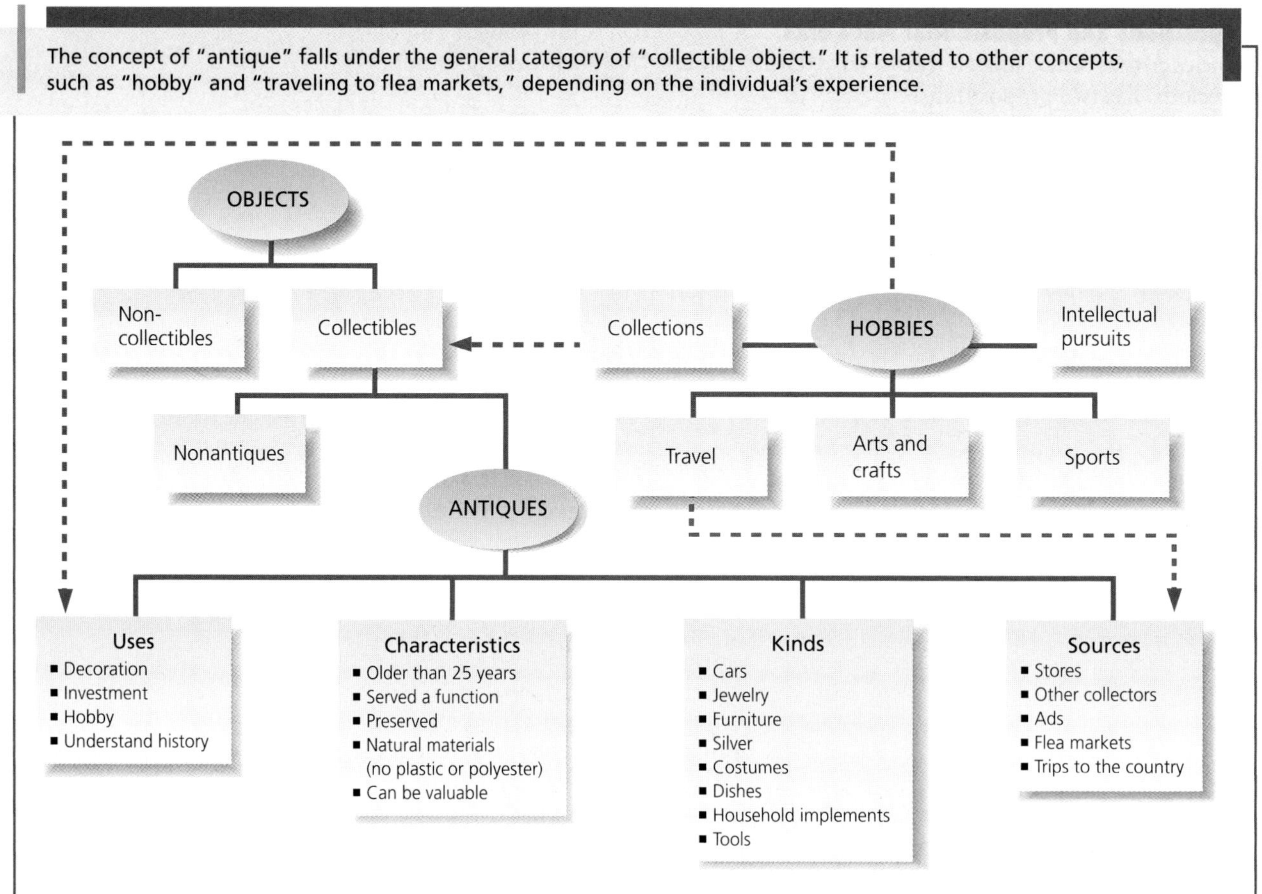

Figure 7.6 A Schema for "Antique"

The schema tells you what features are typical of a category, what to expect about an object or situation. The pattern has "slots" that are filled with specific information as we apply the schema in a particular situation. And schemas are personal. For example, my schema of an antique is less richly developed than the schema of an antique collector. You encountered a very similar concept of scheme in the discussion of Piaget's theory of cognitive development in Chapter 2.

When you hear the sentence, "Ida borrowed the antique tablecloth," you know even more about it than the two propositions. This is because you have schemas about borrowing, tablecloths, antiques, and maybe even Ida herself. You know without being told, for example, that the lender does not have the tablecloth now, because it is in Ida's possession, and that Ida has an obligation to return the tablecloth to the lender (Gentner, 1975). None of this information is explicitly stated, but it is part of our schema for the meaning of "borrow." Other schemas allow you to infer that the cloth is not plastic (if it is a real antique) and that Ida has probably invited guests for a meal. If you actually knew Ida, your schema about her may even allow you to predict how promptly the cloth will be returned and in what condition.

CONNECT & EXTEND

TO YOUR TEACHING/PORTFOLIO
How can schemas about differences among individuals, groups, and social contexts determine how new information about people and situations is interpreted?

Another type of schema, a **story grammar** (sometimes called a schema for text or story structure) helps students to understand and remember stories (Gagné, Yekovich, & Yekovich, 1993; Rumelhart & Ortony, 1977). A story grammar could be something like this: murder discovered, search for clues, murderer's fatal mistake identified, trap set to trick suspect into confessing, murderer takes bait . . . mystery solved! In other words, a story grammar is a typical general structure that could fit many specific stories. To comprehend a story, we select a schema that seems appropriate. Then we use this framework to decide which details are important, what information to seek, and what to remember. It is as though the schema is a theory about what should occur in the story. The schema guides us in "interrogating" the text, pointing to the specific information we expect to find so that the story makes sense. If we activate our "murder mystery schema," we may be alert for clues or a murderer's fatal mistake (Resnick, 1981). Without an appropriate schema, trying to understand a story, textbook, or classroom lesson is a very slow, difficult process, something like finding your way through a new town without a map. A schema representing the typical sequence of events in an everyday situation is called a **script** or an *event schema*. Children as young as 3 have basic scripts for the familiar events in their lives (Nelson, 1986).

What Would You Say? During your interview, the supervisor for the primary grades asks you, "What is your script for a typical day? Tell me how a good day should go in terms of what you would plan and how much time you would give to each segment of your day."

Storing knowledge of the world in schemas and scripts has advantages and disadvantages. A schema can be applied in many contexts, depending on what part of the schema is relevant. You can use what you know about antiques, for example, to plan trips to antique shops, decide if a particular article is worth the price asked, or enjoy a museum display. Having a well-developed schema about Ida lets you recognize her (even as her appearance changes), remember many of her characteristics, and make predictions about her behavior. But it also allows you to be wrong. You may have incorporated incorrect or biased information into your schema of Ida. For example, if Ida is a member of an ethnic group different from yours and if you believe that group is dishonest, you may assume that Ida will keep the tablecloth. In this way, racial and ethnic stereotypes can function as schemas for misunderstanding individuals and for racial discrimination (Sherman & Bessenoff, 1999).

The second kind of explicit memory is episodic. We turn to that now.

Episodic Memory. Memory for information tied to a particular place and time, especially information about the events or episodes of your own life, is called **episodic memory.** Episodic memory is about events we have experienced, so we often can explain *when* the event happened. In contrast, we usually can't describe when we

Story grammar Typical structure or organization for a category of stories.

Script Schema or expected plan for the sequence of steps in a common event such as buying groceries or ordering take-out pizza.

Episodic memory Long-term memory for information tied to a particular time and place, especially memory of the events in a person's life.

acquired a semantic memory. For example, you may have a difficult time remembering when you developed semantic memories for the meaning of the word "injustice," but you can easily remember a time that you felt unjustly treated. Episodic memory also keeps track of the order of things, so it is also a good place to store jokes, gossip, or plots from films.

Implicit Memories

Look back at Figure 7.5. You see that there are three kinds of implicit or out-of-awareness memories: classical conditioning, procedural memory, and priming effects. In classical conditioning, as we saw in Chapter 6, some out-of-awareness memories may cause you to feel anxious as you take a test or make your heart rate increase when you hear a dentist's drill.

The second type of implicit memory is memory for skills, habits, and how to do things, called **procedural memory.** It may take a while to learn a procedure—such as how to ski, serve a tennis ball, or factor an equation—but once learned, this knowledge tends to be remembered for a long time. Procedural memories are represented as *condition-action rules,* sometimes called productions. **Productions** specify what to do under certain conditions: If A occurs, then do B. A production might be something like, "If you want to snow ski faster, lean back slightly," or "If your goal is to increase student attention and a student has been paying attention a bit longer than usual, then praise the student." People can't necessarily state all their condition-action rules, and don't even know that they are following these rules, but they act on them nevertheless. The more practiced the procedure, the more automatic the action and the more implicit the memory (Anderson, 1995a).

Fill in these blanks: ME _ _ _ _

The final type of implicit memory involves **priming** or activating information that already is in long-term memory through some out-of-awareness process. You might have seen an example of priming in the fill-in-the-blank question above. If you wrote MEMORY instead of MENTOR or MEMBER, or METEOR or other ME words, then priming may have played a role because the word "memory" has occurred many times in this chapter. Priming may be the fundamental process for retrieval as associations are activated and spread through the memory system (Ashcraft, 2002).

CONNECT & EXTEND

TO YOUR TEACHING/PORTFOLIO See the Teachers' Casebook for practicing teachers' ideas about how to help students retain and retrieve information.

Storing and Retrieving Information in Long-Term Memory

Just what is done to "save" information permanently—to create explicit and implicit memories? How can we make the most effective use of our practically unlimited capacity to learn and remember? *The way you learn information in the first place*—the way you process it in working memory at the outset—strongly affects its recall later. One important requirement is that you integrate new information with knowledge already stored in long-term memory as you construct an understanding. Here *elaboration, organization,* and *context* play a role.

Elaboration is adding meaning to new information by connecting with already existing knowledge. In other words, we apply our schemas and draw on already existing knowledge to construct an understanding. Frequently we change our existing knowledge in the process. We often elaborate automatically. For example, a paragraph about an historic figure in ancient Rome tends to activate our existing knowledge about that period; we use the old knowledge to understand the new.

Procedural memory Long-term memory for how to do things.

Productions The contents of procedural memory; rules about what actions to take, given certain conditions.

Priming Activating a concept in memory or the spread of activation from one concept to another.

Elaboration Adding and extending meaning by connecting new information to existing knowledge.

Material that is elaborated when first learned will be easier to recall later. First, as we saw earlier, elaboration is a form of rehearsal. It keeps the information activated in working memory long enough to have a chance for the new information to be linked with knowledge in long-term memory. Second, elaboration builds extra links to existing knowledge. The more one bit of information or knowledge is associated with other bits, the more routes there are to follow to get to the original bit. To put it another way, you have several "handles" or priming/retrieval cues to "pick up" or recognize the information you might be seeking (Schunk, 2000).

The more students elaborate new ideas, the more they "make them their own," the deeper their understanding and the better their memory for the knowledge. We help students to elaborate when we ask them to translate information into their own words, create examples, explain to a peer, draw or act out the relationships, or apply the information to solve new problems. Of course, if students elaborate new information by developing misguided explanations, these misconceptions will be remembered too.

Organization is a second element of processing that improves learning. Material that is well organized is easier to learn and to remember than bits and pieces of information, especially if the information is complex or extensive. Placing a concept in a structure will help you learn and remember both general definitions and specific examples. The structure serves as a guide back to the information when you need it. For example, Table 7.1 organizes information about types of knowledge; Table 7.2 gives an organized view of the capacity, duration, contents, and retrieval of information from working and long-term memory; and Figure 7.6 organizes my (limited) knowledge about antiques.

Context is a third element of processing that influences learning. Aspects of physical and emotional context—places, rooms, moods, who is with us—are learned along with other information. Later, if you try to remember the information, it will be easier if the current context is similar to the original one. Context is a kind of prime that activates the information. This has been demonstrated in the laboratory. Students who learned material in one type of room performed better on tests taken in a similar room than they did on tests taken in a very different-looking room (Smith, Glenberg, & Bjork, 1978). So studying for a test under "testlike" conditions may result in improved performance. Of course, you can't always go back to the same place or a similar one in order to recall something. But if you can picture the setting, the time of day, and your companions, you may eventually reach the information you seek.

CONNECT & EXTEND

TO **PRAXIS**™
MEMORY AND RECALL (I, A1)
Cognitivists emphasize the role that elaboration, organization, and context have in effective encoding of information into long-term memory. Be aware of techniques that make use of those processes.

Levels of Processing Theories. Craik and Lockhart (1972) first proposed their **levels of processing theory** as an alternative to short-/long-term memory models, but levels of processing is particularly related to the notion of elaboration described above. Craik and Lockhart suggested that what determines how long information is remembered is *how extensively* the information is analyzed and connected with other information. The more completely information is processed, the better are our chances of remembering it. For example, according to the levels of processing theory, if I ask you to sort pictures of dogs based on the color of their coats, you might not remember many of the pictures later. But if I ask you to rate each dog on how likely it is to chase you as you jog, you probably would remember more of the pictures. To rate the dogs, you must pay attention to details in the pictures, relate features of the dogs to characteristics associated with danger, and so on. This rating procedure requires "deeper" processing and more focus on the *meaning* of the features in the photos.

Retrieving Information from Long-Term Memory. When we need to use information from long-term memory, we search for it. Sometimes the search is conscious, as when you see a friend approaching and search for her name. At other times locating and using information from long-term memory is automatic, as when you dial a telephone or solve a math problem without having to search for each step, or the word "memory" pops to mind when you see ME _ _ _ _. Think of long-term memory

Organization Ordered and logical network of relations.

Context The physical or emotional backdrop associated with an event.

Levels of processing theory Theory that recall of information is based on how deeply it is processed.

as a huge shelf full of tools (skills, procedures) and supplies (knowledge, schemas) ready to be brought to the workbench of working memory to accomplish a task. The shelf (long-term memory) stores an incredible amount, but it may be hard to find what you are looking for quickly. The workbench (working memory) is small, but anything on it is immediately available. Because it is small, however, supplies (bits of information) sometimes are lost when the workbench overflows or when one bit of information covers (interferes with) another (E. Gagné, 1985).

The size of the network in long-term memory is huge, but only small parts from it are activated at any one time. Only the information we are currently thinking about is in working memory. Information is retrieved in this network through **activation spreading.** When a particular proposition or image is active—when we are thinking about it—other closely associated knowledge can be *primed* or activated as well, and activation can spread through the network (Anderson, 1993; Gagné, Yekovich, & Yekovich, 1993). Thus, as I focus on the propositions, "I'd like to go for a drive to see the fall leaves," related ideas such as, "I should rake leaves," and "The car needs an oil change," come to mind. As activation spreads from the "car trip" to the "oil change," the original thought, or active memory, disappears from working memory because of the limited space. So **retrieval** from long-term memory is partly through the spreading of activation from one bit of knowledge to related ideas in the network. We often use this spreading in reverse to retrace our steps in a conversation, as in, "Before we got onto the topic of where to get the oil changed, what were we talking about? Oh yes, seeing the leaves." The learning and retrieving processes of long-term memory are diagrammed in Figure 7.7.

In long-term memory, the information is still available, even when it is not activated, even when you are not thinking about it at the moment. If spreading activation does not "find" the information we seek, then we might still come up with an answer through **reconstruction,** a cognitive tool or problem-solving process that makes use of logic, cues, and other knowledge to *construct* a reasonable answer by filling in any missing parts (Koriat, Goldsmith, & Pansky, 2000). Sometimes reconstructed recollections are incorrect. For example, in 1932, F. C. Bartlett conducted a series of famous studies on remembering stories. He read a complex, unfamiliar Native-American tale to students at England's Cambridge University and, after various lengths of time, asked the students to recall the story. Stories the students recalled were generally shorter than the original and were translated into the concepts and language of the Cambridge student culture. The story told of a seal hunt, for instance,

We activate information from long-term memory to help us understand new information in working memory. With mental work and processing (elaboration, organization, context) the new information can be stored permanently in long-term memory. Forgetting is caused by interference and time decay.

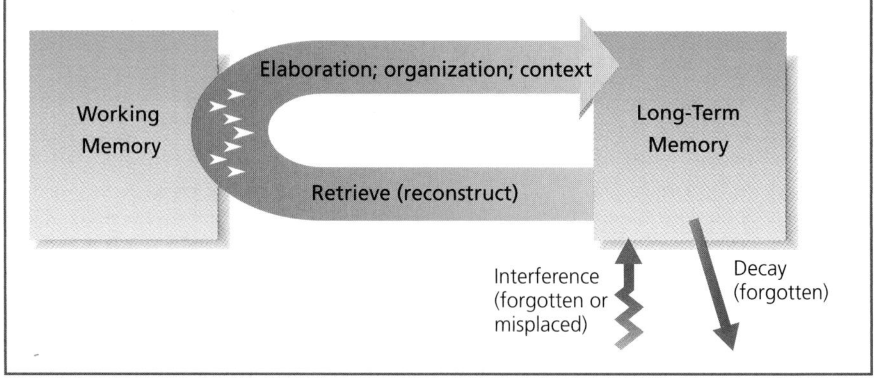

Figure 7.7 Long-Term Memory

Activation spreading Retrieval of pieces of information based on their relatedness to one another. Remembering one bit of information activates (stimulates) recall of associated information.

Retrieval Process of searching for and finding information in long-term memory.

Reconstruction Recreating information by using memories, expectations, logic, and existing knowledge.

but many students remembered (reconstructed) a "fishing trip," an activity closer to their experiences and more consistent with their schemas.

One area where reconstructed memory can play a major role is eyewitness testimony. Elizabeth Loftus and her colleagues have conducted a number of studies showing that misleading questions or other information during questioning can affect memory. For example, in a classic study, Loftus and Palmer (1974) showed subjects slides of a car wreck. Later, the experimenters asked some subjects, "How fast were the cars going when they *hit* each other?" while other subjects who saw the same slides were asked, "How fast were the cars going when they *smashed* into each other?" The difference in verbs was enough to bias the subjects' memories—the "hit" subjects estimated the cars were traveling an average of 34 miles per hour, but the "smashed" subjects estimated almost 41 miles per hour. And one week later, 32% of the "smashed" subjects remembered seeing broken glass at the scene of the wreck, while only 14% of the "hit" subjects remembered glass. (There was no broken glass visible in any of the slides.)

Forgetting and Long-Term Memory. Information lost from working memory before it has a chance to integrate into the network of long-term memory truly disappears. No amount of effort or searching will bring it back. But information stored in long-term memory may be available, given the right cues. Some people believe that nothing is ever lost from long-term memory; however, research casts doubts on this assertion (Schwartz, Wasserman, & Robbins, 2002).

What Would You Say? As part of your interview, the principal says, "We have to cover so much material to get our students ready for the state assessments. What would you do to help your students remember what they have learned in your classes?"

Information appears to be lost from long-term memory through time decay and **interference.** For example, memory for Spanish–English vocabulary decreases for about 3 years after a person's last course in Spanish, then stays level for about 25 years, then drops again for the next 25 years. One explanation for this decline is that neural connections, like muscles, grow weak without use. After 25 years, it may be that the memories are still somewhere in the brain, but they are too weak to be reactivated (Anderson, 1995a, 1995b). And some neurons simply die. Finally, newer memories may interfere with or obscure older memories, and older memories may interfere with memory for new material.

Even with decay and interference, long-term memory is remarkable. In a review of almost 100 studies of memory for knowledge taught in school, George Semb and John Ellis (1994) concluded that, "contrary to popular belief, students retain much of the knowledge taught in the classroom" (p. 279). It appears that teaching strategies that encourage student engagement and lead to higher levels of *initial* learning (such as frequent reviews and tests, elaborated feedback, high standards, mastery learning, and active involvement in learning projects) are associated with longer retention. The *Guidelines* on page 256 give applications of information processing for teaching.

Check Yourself How is information represented in long-term memory, and what role do schemas play?

What learning processes improve long-term memory?

Why do we forget?

Metacognition, Regulation, and Individual Differences

One question that intrigues many cognitive psychologists is why some people learn and remember more than others. For those who hold an information processing view,

Interference The process that occurs when remembering certain information is hampered by the presence of other information.

GUIDELINES Using Information Processing Ideas in the Classroom

Make sure you have the students' attention.

Examples

1. Develop a signal that tells students to stop what they are doing and focus on you. Make sure students respond to the signal—don't let them ignore it. Practice using the signal.
2. Move around the room, use gestures, and avoid speaking in a monotone.
3. Begin a lesson by asking a question that stimulates interest in the topic.
4. Regain the attention of individual students by walking closer to them, using their names, or asking them a question.

Help students separate essential from nonessential details and focus on the most important information.

Examples

1. Summarize instructional objectives to indicate what students should be learning. Relate the material you are presenting to the objectives as you teach: "Now I'm going to explain exactly how you can find the information you need to meet Objective One on the board—determining the tone of the story."
2. When you make an important point, pause, repeat, ask a student to paraphrase, note the information on the board in colored chalk, or tell students to highlight the point in their notes or readings.

Help students make connections between new information and what they already know.

Examples

1. Review prerequisites to help students bring to mind the information they will need to understand new material: "Who can tell us the definition of a quadrilateral? Now, what is a rhombus? Is a square a quadrilateral? Is a square a rhombus? What did we say yesterday about how you can tell? Today we are going to look at some other quadrilaterals."
2. Use an outline or diagram to show how new information fits with the framework you have been developing. For example, "Now that you know the duties of the FBI, where would you expect to find it in this diagram of the branches of the U.S. government?"
3. Give an assignment that specifically calls for the use of new information along with information already learned.

Provide for repetition and review of information.

Examples

1. Begin the class with a quick review of the homework assignment.
2. Give frequent, short tests.
3. Build practice and repetition into games, or have students work with partners to quiz each other.

Present material in a clear, organized way.

Examples

1. Make the purpose of the lesson very clear.
2. Give students a brief outline to follow. Put the same outline on an overhead so you can keep yourself on track. When students ask questions or make comments, relate these to the appropriate section of the outline.
3. Use summaries in the middle and at the end of the lesson.

Focus on meaning, not memorization.

Examples

1. In teaching new words, help students associate the new word to a related word they already understand: "*Enmity* is from the same base as *enemy*. . . ."
2. In teaching about remainders, have students group 12 objects into sets of 2, 3, 4, 5, 6, and ask them to count the "leftovers" in each case.

part of the answer lies in the executive control processes shown in Figure 7.1. **Executive control processes** guide the flow of information through the information processing system. We have already discussed a number of control processes, including attention, maintenance rehearsal, elaborative rehearsal, organization, and elaboration. These executive control processes are sometimes called *metacognitive skills,* because they can be intentionally used to regulate cognition.

Metacognitive Knowledge and Regulation

Donald Meichenbaum and his colleagues describe **metacognition** as people's "awareness of their own cognitive machinery and how the machinery works" (Meichenbaum, Burland, Gruson, & Cameron, 1985, p. 5). Metacognition literally means cognition about cognition—or knowledge about knowing and learning. This metacognitive knowledge is used to monitor and regulate cognitive processes such as reasoning, comprehension, problem solving, learning, and so on (Metcalfe & Shimamura, 1994). Because people differ in their metacognitive knowledge and skills, they

CONNECT & EXTEND

TO THE RESEARCH
See the entire issue of *Learning and Individual Differences* (1996, #4) on individual differences in metacognition.

differ in how well and how quickly they learn (Brown, Bransford, Ferrara, & Campione, 1983; Morris, 1990).

Metacognition involves three kinds of knowledge: declarative knowledge about yourself as a learner, the factors that influence your learning and memory, and the skills, strategies, and resources needed to perform a task—knowing *what* to do; procedural knowledge or knowing *how* to use the strategies; and conditional knowledge to ensure the completion of the task—knowing *when* and *why* to apply the procedures and strategies (Bruning, Schraw, & Ronning, 1999). Metacognition is the strategic application of this declarative, procedural, and conditional knowledge to accomplish goals and solve problems (Schunk, 2000).

Metacognition involves *choosing* the best way to approach a learning task. Students with good metacognitive skills set goals, organize their activities, select among various approaches to learning, and change strategies if needed.

Metacognitive knowledge is used to regulate thinking and learning (Brown, 1987; Nelson, 1996). There are three essential skills that allow us to do this: planning, monitoring, and evaluating. *Planning* involves deciding how much time to give to a task, which strategies to use, how to start, what resources to gather, what order to follow, what to skim and what to give intense attention to, and so on. *Monitoring* is the on-line awareness of "how I'm doing." Monitoring entails asking, "Is this making sense? Am I trying to go too fast? Have I studied enough?" *Evaluating* involves making judgments about the processes and outcomes of thinking and learning. "Should I change strategies? Get help? Give up for now? Is this paper (painting, model, poem, plan, etc.) finished?"

Of course, we don't have to be metacognitive all the time. Some actions become routine. Metacognition is most useful when tasks are challenging, but not too difficult. Then planning, monitoring, and evaluating can be helpful. And even when we are planning, monitoring, and evaluating, these processes are not necessarily conscious, especially in adults. We may use them automatically without being aware of our efforts (Perner, 2000). Experts in a field may plan, monitor, and evaluate as second nature; they have difficulty describing their metacognitive knowledge and skills (Bargh & Chartrand, 1999; Reder, 1996).

Individual Differences in Metacognition

Some differences in metacognitive abilities are the result of development. As children grow older they are more able to exercise executive control over strategies. For example, they are more able to determine if they have understood instructions (Markman, 1977, 1979) or if they have studied enough to remember a set of items (Flavell, Friedrichs, & Hoyt, 1970). Metacognitive abilities begin to develop around ages 5 to 7 and improve throughout school (Flavell, Green, & Flavell, 1995; Garner, 1990). In her work with 1st and 2nd graders, Nancy Perry found that asking students two questions helped them become more metacognitive. The questions were "What did you learn about yourself as a reader/writer today?" and "What did you learn that you can do again and again and again?" When teachers asked these questions regularly during class, even young students demonstrated fairly sophisticated levels of metacognitive understanding and action (Perry et al., 2000).

Not all differences in metacognitive abilities have to do with age or maturation. There is great variability even among students of the same developmental level, but these differences do not appear to be related to intellectual abilities. In fact, superior

CONNECT & EXTEND

TO **PRAXIS**™
METACOGNITION (I, A1)
Often the difference between two students—one a successful learner, and the other a struggling learner—is the effective use of metacognitive processes. Identify strategies that teachers can use to enhance the role of metacognition in instruction.

Executive control processes Processes such as selective attention, rehearsal, elaboration, and organization that influence encoding, storage, and retrieval of information in memory.

Metacognition Knowledge about our own thinking processes.

metacognitive skills can compensate for lower levels of ability, so these metacognitive skills can be especially important for students who often have trouble in school (Schunk, 2000; Swanson, 1990).

Some individual differences in metacognitive abilities are probably caused by biological differences or by variations in learning experiences. Students can vary greatly in their ability to attend selectively to information in their environment. In fact, many students diagnosed as learning disabled actually have attention disorders (Hallahan & Kauffman, 2003), particularly with long tasks (Pelham, 1981).

Individual Differences and Working Memory

As you might expect, there are both developmental and individual differences in working memory. Let's examine a few. First, try this:

Read the following sentences and words in caps out loud once:

For many years my family and friends have been working on the farm. SPOT

Because the room was stuffy, Bob went outside for some fresh air. TRAIL

We were fifty miles out to sea before we lost sight of the land. BAND

Now cover the sentences and answer these questions (be honest):

Name the words that were in all caps. Who was in the stuffy room? Who worked on the farm?

You have just taken a few items from a test of working memory span (Engle, 2001). The test required you to both process and store—process the meaning of the sentences and store the words (Ashcraft, 2002). How did you do?

Developmental Differences. Research indicates that young children have very limited working memories, but their memory span improves with age. It is not clear whether these differences are the result of changes in memory *capacity* or improvements in *strategy* use. Case (1985a, 1985b) suggests that the total amount of "space" available for processing information is the same at each age, but young children must use quite a bit of this space to remember how to execute basic operations, such as reaching for a toy, finding the right word for an object, or counting. Using a new operation takes up a large portion of the child's working memory. Once an operation is mastered, however, there is more working memory available for short-term storage of new information. For very young children, biology may play a role too. As the brain and neurological system of the child mature, processing may become more efficient so that more working-memory space is available.

As children grow older, they develop more effective strategies for remembering information. About age 4, children begin to understand that "remembering" means recalling something from the past. Before age 4, children think remembering means what they see or know now and forgetting means not knowing (Perner, 2000). Most children spontaneously discover rehearsal around age 5 or 6. Siegler (1998) describes a 9-year-old boy who witnessed a robbery, then mentally repeated the license number of the getaway car until he could give the number to the police. Younger children can be taught to rehearse, and will use the strategy effectively as long as they are reminded. But they will not apply the strategy spontaneously. Children are 10 to 11 years old before they have adult-like working memories.

According to Case (1985a, 1985b), young children often use reasonable but incorrect strategies to solve problems because of their limited memories. They try to simplify the task by ignoring important information or skipping steps to reach a correct solution. This puts less strain on memory. For example, when comparing quantities, young children may consider only the height of the water in a glass, not the diameter of the glass, because this approach demands less of their memory. According to Case, this explains young children's inability to solve the classic Piagetian conservation problem. (See Figure 2.3 on page 36.)

There are several developmental differences in how students use organization, elaboration, and knowledge to process information in working memory. Around age 6, most children discover the value of using *organizational strategies* and by 9 or 10, they use these strategies spontaneously. So, given the following words to learn:

couch, orange, rat, lamp, pear, sheep, banana, rug, pineapple, horse, table, dog

an older child or an adult might organize the words into three short lists of furniture, fruit, and animals. Younger children can be taught to use organization to improve memory, but they probably won't apply the strategy unless they are reminded. Children also become more able to use elaboration as they mature, but this strategy is developed late in childhood. Creating images or stories to remember ideas is more likely for older elementary school students and adolescents (Siegler, 1998).

Individual Differences. Besides developmental differences, there are other individual variations in working memory and these differences have implications for learning. For example, the correlation between scores on a test of working memory span (like the one you just took in the Stop/Think/Write exercise) and the verbal portion of the Scholastic Assessment Test (SAT) are about .59. But there is no correlation between the SAT and simple short term-memory span (repeating digits). If a task requires controlled attention, then working memory span probably is a factor in performing that task (Ashcraft, 2002).

Some people seem to have more efficient working memories than others (Cariglia-Bull & Pressley, 1990; Di Vesta & Di Cintio, 1997; Jurden, 1995), and differences in working memory may be associated with giftedness in math and verbal areas. For example, subjects in one research study were asked to remember lists of numbers, the locations of marks on a page, letters, and words (Dark & Benbow, 1991). Subjects who excelled in mathematics remembered numbers and locations significantly better than subjects talented in verbal areas. The verbally talented subjects, on the other hand, had better memories for words. Based on these results, Dark and Benbow believe that basic differences in information processing abilities play a role in the development of mathematical and verbal talent.

Individual Differences and Long-Term Memory

The major individual difference that affects long-term memory is knowledge. When students have more *domain-specific declarative* and *procedural knowledge,* they are better at learning and remembering material in that domain (Alexander, 1997). Think about what it is like to read a very technical textbook in an area you know little about. Every line is difficult. You have to stop and look up words or turn back to read about concepts you don't understand. It is hard to remember what you are reading because you are trying to understand and remember at the same time. But with a good basis of knowledge, learning and remembering become easier; the more you know, the easier it is to know more. This is true in part because having knowledge improves strategy use. Another factor is related to developing domain knowledge and remembering it—interest. To develop expert understanding and recall in a domain requires the "continuous interplay of skill (i.e., knowledge) and thrill (i.e., interest)" (Alexander, Kulikowich, & Schulze, 1994, p. 334).

Check Yourself What are the three metacognitive skills?

Describe some individual differences in metacognition.

How can using better metacognitive strategies improve children's working and long-term memories?

CONNECT & EXTEND

TO YOUR TEACHING/PORTFOLIO
What is the memory strategy used in each of the following examples?

a. In order to help children remember the symbol for the number eight, the teacher makes a snowman out of the figure 8 while telling a story about the snowman with eight buttons who lives for eight days.
b. To remember that Bismarck is the capital of North Dakota, a student imagines N.D. on a biscuit.
c. To help students remember how to spell "separate," the teacher says, "There is a rat in separate."
d. A student lists the products of Alabama so that the first letters spell CAPS—for cotton, apples, paper products, and soybeans.
e. Columbus sailed the ocean blue in fourteen hundred and ninety-two.
f. To remember a grocery list, Mrs. Tarent imagines cheese on her TV, limes on the sofa, milk on the table, beans in the wicker basket, and tomatoes on the stove.
g. The teacher uses a time line to show the major events before, during, and after the Vietnam War.
h. Students are asked to compare their present home chores with chores they might have if they lived during Civil War times.

Now that we have examined the information processing explanation of how knowledge is represented and remembered, let's turn to the really important question: How can teachers support the development of knowledge?

Becoming Knowledgeable: Some Basic Principles

Understanding a concept such as "antique" involves *declarative knowledge* about characteristics and images as well as *procedural knowledge* about how to apply rules to categorize specific antiques. We will discuss the development of declarative and procedural knowledge separately, but keep in mind that real learning is a combination and integration of these elements.

Development of Declarative Knowledge

Within the information processing perspective, to learn declarative knowledge is really to integrate new ideas with existing knowledge and construct an understanding. As you have seen, people learn best when they have a good base of knowledge in the area they are studying. With many well-elaborated schemas and scripts to guide them, new material makes more sense, and there are many possible spots in the long-term memory network for connecting new information with old. But students don't always have a good base of knowledge. In the early phases of learning, students of any age must grope around the landscape a bit, searching for landmarks and direction. Even experts in an area must use some learning strategies when they encounter unfamiliar material or new problems (Alexander, 1996, 1997; Garner, 1990; Perkins & Salomon, 1989; Shuell, 1990).

What are some possible strategies? Perhaps the best single method for helping students learn is to make each lesson as meaningful as possible.

Making It Meaningful. Meaningful lessons are presented in vocabulary that makes sense to the students. New terms are clarified through ties with more familiar words and ideas. Meaningful lessons are well organized, with clear connections between the different elements of the lesson. Finally, meaningful lessons make natural use of old information to help students understand new information through examples or analogies.

The importance of meaningful lessons is emphasized below in an example presented by Smith (1975).

Look at the three lines below. Begin by covering all but the first line. Look at it for a second, close the book, and write down all the letters you remember. Then repeat this procedure with the second and third lines.

1. KBVODUWGPJMSQTXNOGMCTRSO
2. READ JUMP WHEAT POOR BUT SEEK
3. KNIGHTS RODE HORSES INTO WAR

Each line has the same number of letters, but the chances are great that you remembered all the letters in the third line, a good number of letters in the second line, and very few in the first line. The first line makes no sense. There is no way to organize it in a brief glance. Working memory is simply not able to hold and process all that information quickly. The second line is more meaningful. You do not have to see each letter because your long-term memory brings prior knowledge of spelling rules and vocabulary to the task. The third line is the most meaningful. Just a glance and you can probably remember all of it because you bring to this task prior knowledge

A useful and effective way to learn is to use new information. Making information meaningful is important and often is the greatest challenge for teachers.

not only of spelling and vocabulary but also of rules about syntax and probably some historical information about knights (they didn't ride in tanks). This sentence is meaningful because you have existing schemas for assimilating it. It is relatively easy to associate the words and meaning with other information already in long-term memory (Sweller, van Merrienboer, & Paas, 1998).

The challenge for teachers is to make lessons less like learning the first line and more like learning the third line. Although this may seem obvious, think about the times when *you* have read a sentence in a text or heard an explanation from a professor that might just as well have been KBVODUWGPJMSQTXNOGMCTRSO. But remember, attempts to change the ways that students are used to learning—moving from memorizing to meaningful activities as in the opening "What Would You Do?" situation—are not always greeted with student enthusiasm. Students may be concerned about their grades; at least when memorization gains an A, they know what is expected. Meaningful learning can be riskier and more challenging. In Chapters 8, 9, and 12 we will examine a variety of ways in which teachers can support meaningful learning and understanding. For now, see how one teacher made learning meaningful for her new students in *Stories of Learning/Tributes to Teaching* on page 262.

When information has little inherent meaning, *mnemonic strategies* build in meaning by connecting what is to be learned with established words or images.

Mnemonics. **Mnemonics** are systematic procedures for improving memory. Many of these mnemonic strategies use imagery (Atkinson et al., 1999; Levin, 1994; McCormick & Levin, 1987).

The **loci method** derives its name from the plural of the Latin word *locus*, meaning "place." To use loci, you must first imagine a very familiar place, such as your own house or apartment, and pick out particular locations. Every time you have a list to remember, the same locations serve as "pegs" to "hang" memories. Simply place each item from your list in one of these locations. For instance, let's say you want to remember to buy milk, bread, butter, and cereal at the store. Imagine a giant bottle of milk blocking the entry hall, a lazy loaf of bread sleeping on the living room couch, a stick of butter melting all over the dining room table, and cereal covering the kitchen floor. When you want to remember the items, all you have to do is take an imaginary walk through your house. Other **peg-type mnemonics** use a standard list of words (one is bun, two is shoe . . .) as pegs. Then the items to be remembered are linked to the pegs through images or stories. The rhyming primes the list of pegs.

CONNECT & EXTEND

TO **PRAXIS**™

MEMORY STRATEGIES (II, A1)

Medical students often use mnemonics to remember the vast amounts of information they encounter in their studies. Be familiar with the major mnemonic methods and the kinds of information that they are most suitable for.

Mnemonics Techniques for remembering; also, the art of memory.

Loci method Technique of associating items with specific places.

Peg-type mnemonics Systems of associating items with cue words.

~ Stories of Learning Tributes to Teaching ~

Susan lived in what seemed to be a normal upper middle-class home, but her abusive father caused problems for the entire family. It was difficult for her to devote attention to school work. Susan thought she was just dumb, but she enjoyed art and dance and had the strong support of many family members. When her mother divorced and moved the family to another state, Susan encountered some wonderful teachers who captured her imagination and capitalized on her talents. Susan went on to earn a Ph.D in early childhood education and counseling—using her experiences as a resilient child to help others. She describes her her senior English teacher.

> The most exciting thing about my move was starting over academically. I was placed in a superior English class that year and I was also in pretty good classes across the board.
>
> I'll never forget the first time I heard my English teacher, Mr. Borders, teach. I was sitting in class, and, for the first time in my life, I was able to really listen, pay attention, and focus on what the teacher was saying. It was an overwhelming experience and a wonderful feeling. I felt like the top of my head was off and everything that had previously clouded my brain and life was being lifted. I could use my brain like it was supposed to be used. There was a sense of quiet where I was free to think and process information without worrying about what was happening at home or how my mom was doing.
>
> I began getting excited about learning. In fact, I liked learning because Mr. Borders, my "Superior English" teacher, made it exciting. He also introduced me to project work. I was able to make a Shakespearean character for one of my projects. I loved doing this project. I remember the great detail I took to make this character look authentic. I also saw myself excelling academically even though I thought I wasn't supposed to be smart. I was also drawing my cousin's lab pictures for her college biology class. Of course, art was one of my gifts and it didn't take brains to do this, I thought, but, nevertheless, I felt proud. So, I began to surprise my mom as well as myself.

SOURCE: From "Hidden Lives: Examining the Lives of Resilient European American Children," by S. G. Hendley. In Gloria Swindler Boutte (Ed.), *Resounding Voices: School Experiences of People from Diverse Ethnic Backgrounds.* Published by Allyn & Bacon, Boston, MA.

Acronym Technique for remembering names, phrases, or steps by using the first letter of each word to form a new, memorable word.

Chain mnemonics Memory strategies that associate one element in a series with the next element.

Keyword method System of associating new words or concepts with similar-sounding cue words and images.

Rote memorization Remembering information by repetition without necessarily understanding the meaning of the information.

Serial-position effect The tendency to remember the beginning and the end but not the middle of a list.

Part learning Breaking a list of rote learning items into shorter lists.

Distributed practice Practice in brief periods with rest intervals.

Massed practice Practice for a single extended period.

If you need to remember information for long periods of time, an acronym may be the answer. An **acronym** is a form of abbreviation—a word formed from the first letter of each word in a phrase, for example, HOMES to remember the Great Lakes (Huron, Ontario, Michigan, Erie, Superior). Another method forms phrases or sentences out of the first letter of each word or item in a list, for example, Every Good Boy Does Fine to remember the lines on the G clef—E, G, B, D, F. Because the words must make sense as a sentence, this approach also has some characteristics of **chain mnemonics,** methods that connect the first item to be memorized with the second, the second item with the third, and so on. In one type of chain method, each item on a list is linked to the next through some visual association or story. Another chain-method approach is to incorporate all the items to be memorized into a jingle such as "i before e except after c."

The mnemonic system that has been most extensively researched in teaching is the **keyword method.** Joel Levin and his colleagues use a mnemonic (the *3 Rs*) to teach the keyword mnemonic method:

- *recode* the to-be-learned vocabulary item as a more familiar, concrete keyword—this is the keyword;
- *relate* the keyword clue to the vocabulary item's definition through a sentence;
- *retrieve* the desired definition.

For example, to remember that the English word *carlin* means *old woman,* you might recode *carlin* as the more familiar keyword *car.* Then make up a sentence such as *The old woman was driving a car.* When you are asked for the meaning of the word *carlin,* you think of the keyword *car,* which triggers the sentence about the car and the *old woman,* the meaning. (Jones, Levin, Levin, & Beitzel, 2000).

The keyword method has been used extensively in foreign language learning. For example, the Spanish word *carta* (meaning "letter") sounds like the English word "cart." Cart becomes the keyword: You imagine a shopping cart filled with letters on its way to the post office, or you make up a sentence such as "The cart full of letters tipped over" (Pressley, Levin, & Delaney, 1982). A similar approach has been used to help students connect artists with particular aspects of their paintings. For example, students are told to imagine that the heavy dark lines of paintings by Rouault are made with a *ruler* (Rouault) dipped in black paint (Carney & Levin, 2000). Figure 7.8 is an example of using mnemonic pictures as aids in learning complicated science concepts (Carney & Levin, 2002).

"How many times must I tell you—it's 'cat' before 'temple' except after 'slave.'"

(By permission of Bo Brown, From *Phi Delta Kappan*)

One problem, however, is that the keyword method does not work well if it is difficult to identify a keyword for a particular item. Many words and ideas that students need to remember are quite a challenge to associate with keywords (Hall, 1991; Pressley, 1991). Also, vocabulary learned with keywords may be easily forgotten if students are given keywords and images instead of being asked to supply the words and images. When the teacher provides the memory links, these associations may not fit the students' existing knowledge and may be forgotten or confused later, so remembering suffers (Wang & Thomas, 1995; Wang, Thomas, & Ouelette, 1992). Younger students have some difficulty forming their own images. For them, memory aids that rely on auditory cues—rhymes such as "Thirty days hath September . . ." seem to work better (Willoughby, Porter, Belsito, & Yearsley, 1999).

Many teachers use a mnemonic system to quickly learn their students' names. Until we have some knowledge to guide learning, it may help to use some mnemonic approaches to build vocabulary and facts. Not all educators agree, as is noted in the *Point/Counterpoint* on page 264.

Rote Memorization. *Very few things need to be learned by rote.* The greatest challenge teachers face is to help students think and understand, not just memorize. Unfortunately, many students, including those in the scenario opening this chapter, see **rote memorizing** and learning as the same thing (Iran-Nejad, 1990).

However, on rare occasions we have to memorize something word-for-word, such as lines in a song, poem, or play. How would you do it? If you have tried to memorize a list of items that are all similar to one another, you may have found that you tended to remember items at the beginning and at the end of the list but forgot those in the middle. This is called the **serial-position effect. Part learning,** breaking the list into smaller segments, can help prevent this effect, because breaking a list into several shorter lists means there will be fewer middle items to forget.

Another strategy for memorizing a long selection or list is the use of **distributed practice.** A student who studies Hamlet's soliloquy intermittently throughout the weekend will probably do much better than a student who tries to memorize the entire speech on Sunday night. Studying for an extended period is called **massed practice.** Massed practice leads to fatigue and lagging motivation. Distributed practice gives time for deeper processing and the chance to move information into long-term memory (Mumford, Costanza, Baughman, Threlfall, & Fleishman, 1994). What is forgotten after one session can be relearned in the next with distributed practice.

This illustration tells a story that provides a frame for remembering and pegs for hanging the concept names in the biological subdivision of angiosperms.

To remember that the subdivision **angiosperms** includes the class **dicotyledons**, which in turn includes the three orders **rubales**, **sapindales**, and **rosales**, study the picture of the angel with the pet **dinosaur** that is walking up the **Rubik's cubes** so that he can lick the sweet **sap** that drips down from the **rose** tree.

Source: From "Pictorial Illustrations Still Improve Students' Learning From Text," by R. N. Carney and J. R. Levin, *Educational Psychology Review, 14.* Copyright © 2002 by Kluwer Academic Publishers. Reprinted with permission of the publisher and authors.

Figure 7.8 Using Mnemonics to Promote Learning Complex Concepts

Point/Counterpoint — What's Wrong with Memorizing?

For years students have relied on memorization to learn vocabulary, procedures, steps, names, and facts. Is this a bad idea?

Point

Rote memorization creates inert knowledge.
Years ago William James (1912) described the limitations of rote learning by telling a story about what can happen when students memorize but do not understand:

> *A friend of mine, visiting a school, was asked to examine a young class in geography. Glancing at the book, she said: "Suppose you should dig a hole in the ground, hundreds of feet deep, how should you find it at the bottom—warmer or colder than on top?" None of the class replying, the teacher said: "I'm sure they know, but I think you don't ask the question quite rightly. Let me try." So, taking the book, she asked: "In what condition is the interior of the globe?" And received the immediate answer from half the class at once. "The interior of the globe is in a condition of igneous fusion." (p. 150)*

The students had memorized the answer, but they had no idea what it meant. Perhaps they didn't understand the meaning of "interior," "globe," or "igneous fusion." At any rate, the knowledge was useful to them only when they were answering test questions, and only then when the questions were phrased exactly as they had been memorized. Students often resort to memorizing the exact words of definitions when they have no hope for actually understanding the terms or when teachers count off for definitions that are not exact.

Most recently, Howard Gardner has been a vocal critic of rote memorization and a champion of "teaching for understanding." In an interview in *Phi Delta Kappan* (Siegel & Shaughnessy, 1994), Gardner says:

> *My biggest concern about American education is that even our better students in our better schools are just going through the motions of education. In* The Unschooled Mind, *I review ample evidence that suggests an absence of understanding—the inability of students to take knowledge, skills, and other apparent attainments and apply them successfully in new situations. In the absence of such flexibility and adaptability, the education that the students receive is worth little. (pp. 563–564)*

Counterpoint

Rote memorization can be effective.
Memorization may not be such a bad way to learn new information that has little inherent meaning, such as foreign language vocabulary. Alvin Wang, Margaret Thomas, and Judith Ouellette (1992) compared learning Tagalog (the national language of the Philippines) using either rote memorization or the keyword approach. The keyword method is a way of creating connections and meaning for associating new words with existing words and images. In their study, even though the keyword method led to faster and better learning initially, long-term forgetting was *greater* for students who had used the keyword method than for students who had learned by rote memorization.

There are times when students must memorize and we do them a disservice if we don't teach them how. Every discipline has its own terms, names, facts, and rules. As adults, we want to work with physicians who have memorized the correct names for the bones and organs of the body or the drugs needed to combat particular infections. Of course, they can look up some information or research certain conditions, but they have to know where to start. We want to work with accountants who give us accurate information about the new tax codes, information they probably had to memorize because it changes from year to year in ways that are not necessarily rational or meaningful. We want to deal with computer sales people who have memorized their stock and know exactly which printers will work with our computer. Just because something was learned through memorization does not mean it is inert knowledge. The real question, as Gardner points out above, is whether you can *use* the information flexibly and effectively to solve new problems.

What do you think? Vote online at **www.ablongman.com/woolfolk**

Becoming an Expert: Development of Procedural and Conditional Knowledge

Experts in a particular field have a wealth of domain-specific knowledge, that is, knowledge that applies specifically to their area or domain. This includes *declarative knowledge* (facts and verbal information), *procedural knowledge* (how to perform various cognitive activities), and *conditional knowledge* (knowing when and why to apply what they know). In addition, it appears that experts have developed their *long-term working memories* in the domain and can quickly access relevant knowledge and strategies for solving problems in that domain.

Another characteristic distinguishes experts from novices. Much of the expert's declarative knowledge has become "proceduralized," that is, incorporated into routines they can apply automatically without making many demands on working memory. Explicit memories have become implicit and out-of-awareness. Skills that are applied without conscious thought are called **automated basic skills.** An example is shifting gears in a standard transmission car. At first you had to think about every step, but as you became more expert (if you did), the procedure became automatic. But not all procedures can be automatic, even for experts in a particular domain. For example, no matter how expert you are in driving, you still have to consciously watch the traffic around you. This kind of conscious procedure is called a *domain-specific strategy.* Automated basic skills and domain-specific strategies are learned in different ways (Gagné, Yekovich, & Yekovich, 1993).

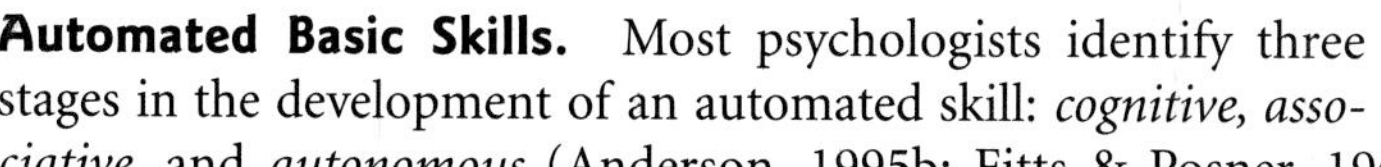

What Would You Say? As part of your interview, the department chair asks, "What are the basic skills for your students—the foundations of their more advanced learning—and how would you teach them?"

Driving a car employs both automated basic skills and domain-specific strategies.

Automated Basic Skills. Most psychologists identify three stages in the development of an automated skill: *cognitive, associative,* and *autonomous* (Anderson, 1995b; Fitts & Posner, 1967). At the *cognitive stage,* when we are first learning, we rely on declarative knowledge and general problem-solving strategies to accomplish our goal. For example, to learn to assemble a bookshelf, we might try to follow steps in the instruction manual, putting a check beside each step as we complete it to keep track of progress. At this stage we have to "think about" every step and perhaps refer back to the pictures of parts to see what a "4-inch metal bolt with lock nut" looks like. The load on working memory is heavy. There can be quite a bit of trial-and-error learning at this stage when, for example, the bolt we chose doesn't fit.

At the *associative stage,* individual steps of a procedure are combined or "chunked" into larger units. We reach for the right bolt and put it into the right hole. One step smoothly cues the next. With practice, the associative stage moves to the *autonomous stage,* where the whole procedure can be accomplished without much attention. So if you assemble enough bookshelves, you can have a lively conversation as you do, paying little attention to the assembly task. This movement from the cognitive to the associative to the autonomous stage holds for the development of basic cognitive skills in any area, but science, medicine, chess, and mathematics have been most heavily researched.

What can teachers do to help their students pass through these three stages and become more expert? In general, it appears that two factors are critical: *prerequisite knowledge* and *practice with feedback.* First, if students don't have the essential prior knowledge (schemas, skills, etc.), the load on working memory will be too great. In order to compose a poem in a foreign language, for example, you must know some of the vocabulary and grammar of that language, and you must have some understanding of poetry forms. To learn the vocabulary, grammar, *and* forms as you also try to compose the poem would be too much.

Second, practice with feedback allows you to form associations, recognize cues automatically, and combine small steps into larger condition-action rules or *productions.* Even from the earliest stage, some of this practice should include a simplified version of the whole process in a real context. Practice in real contexts helps students

CONNECT & EXTEND

TO **PRAXIS**™
DEVELOPING BASIC SKILLS (II, A3)
Efficient and effective performance as a learner requires the automatic use of basic skills. Describe what teachers can do to help students develop automatic basic skills.

Automated basic skills Skills that are applied without conscious thought.

Domain-specific strategies Consciously applied skills to reach goals in a particular subject or problem area.

learn not only *how* to do a skill but also *why* and *when* (Collins, Brown, & Newman, 1989; Gagné, Yekovich, & Yekovich, 1993). Of course, as every athletic coach knows, if a particular step, component, or process is causing trouble, that element might be practiced alone until it is more automatic, and then put back into the whole sequence, to lower the demands on working memory (Anderson, Reder, & Simon, 1996).

Domain-Specific Strategies. As we saw earlier, some procedural knowledge, such as monitoring the traffic while you drive, is not automatic because conditions are constantly changing. Once you decide to change lanes, the maneuver may be fairly automatic, but the decision to change lanes was conscious, based on the traffic conditions around you. **Domain-specific strategies** are these consciously applied skills that organize thoughts and actions to reach a goal. To support this kind of learning, teachers need to provide opportunities for practice in many different situations—for example, practice reading with newspapers, package labels, magazines, books, letters, operating manuals, and so on. In the next chapter's discussion of problem solving and study strategies, we will examine other ways to help students develop domain-specific strategies. For now, let's turn to a consideration of how students can develop strategies for learning outside school.

Learning Outside School

The last several sections of this chapter have described many ideas for helping students become knowledgeable—memory strategies, mnemonics, metacognitive skills such as planning or monitoring comprehension, and cognitive skills. Some students have an advantage in school because they learn these strategies and skills at home. The *Family and Community Partnerships Guidelines* give ideas for working with families to give all your students more support and practice developing these skills.

Check Yourself Describe three ways to develop declarative knowledge.

Describe some procedures for developing procedural knowledge.

Family and Community Partnerships

Organizing Learning

Give families specific strategies to help their children practice and remember.

Examples

1. Develop "super learner" homework assignments that include material to be learned and a "parent coaching card" with a description of a simple memory strategy—appropriate for the material—that parents can teach their child.
2. Provide a few comprehension check questions so a family member can review reading assignments and check the child's understanding.
3. Describe the value of distributed practice and give family members ideas for how and when to work skills practice into home conversations and projects.

Ask family members to share their strategies for organizing and remembering.

Examples

1. Create a family calendar.
2. Encourage planning discussions in which family members help students break large tasks into smaller jobs, identify goals, and find resources.

Discuss the importance of attention in learning.

Examples

1. Encourage families to create study spaces for children away from distractions.
2. Make sure parents know the purpose of homework assignments.

Enhancing Your Expertise with Technology

Memory Techniques

At this point in the semester my hunch is that you are busy taking exams, writing term papers or reports, and working on a long-term project or two for your various courses. If that's the case, you will probably enjoy a brief diversion from your workload, and you'd appreciate some help remembering efficiently and effectively what you are learning in those courses.

Set aside your class notes, study guides, and textbooks, and navigate to NASA's Applied Cognition game page (http://human-factors.arc.nasa.gov/cognition/tutorials/index.html). Here is a set of five memory games. Take a few minutes and play with each game. After you've played them, try to match a game on the left with a principle of human memory on the right:

Game	Memory Principle
1. Penny Recognition	A. Reconstruction
2. The Mnenomicizer	B. Organization
3. Human Memory: Recall	C. Interference
4. Interference	D. Meaningfulness
5. Short Term Memory: Encoding and Rehearsal	E. Elaboration

(See answers below.)

These games demonstrate several of the characteristics of memory that you encountered in this chapter: reconstruction, organization, meaningfulness, interference, and elaboration. Knowledge of these characteristics, and their implications for learning and teaching, will enhance your own expertise as a student now and as a teacher later. Insights about the nature of memory have inspired many techniques for enhancing the storage and retrieval of information. Medical students, for example, need to remember thousands of physical structures, processes, diseases, drugs, and pathogens (just to mention a few)—and understand the relationships among them. It would be nearly impossible to learn this information by simple rehearsal, so these students often rely on memory techniques for that purpose. (To see what I mean, go to a search engine and enter "medical mnemonics" in the search box.)

You might find that a disciplined, practiced use of the memory techniques presented at Mind Tools (http://www.mindtools.com) will serve you as well as they serve future surgeons. A key to success in any field is the use of the right tool at the right time. Mind Tools has a set of memory tools for a variety of purposes: ordered lists, long lists, short lists, grouped information, names, and numbers. There also is a clear description of how and when to use each technique, examples, and advice about effectively using a technique. Now might be the time for you to check out the page that explains how to remember information for a test.

When it comes to learning about memory techniques, remember that the most effective way to help someone learn is to keep things meaningful. As you examine the various techniques, think about when you might use particular ones, and how they are based on what we know about the nature of memory.

Answers to quiz: 1A, 2E, 3B, 4C, 5D.

Summary Table

■ Elements of the Cognitive Perspective

(pp. 236–238)

Contrast cognitive and behavioral views of learning in terms of what is learned and the role of reinforcement. Cognitive learning theorists focus on the human mind's active attempts to make sense of the world. In the cognitive view, knowledge is learned, and changes in knowledge make changes in behavior possible. In the behavioral view, the new behaviors themselves are learned. Both behavioral and cognitive theorists believe reinforcement is important in learning, but for different reasons. The strict behaviorist maintains that reinforcement strengthens responses; cognitive theorists see reinforcement as a source of feedback about what is likely to happen if behaviors are repeated or changed—as a source of information.

How does knowledge affect learning? The cognitive approach suggests that one of the most important elements in the learning process is knowledge the individual brings to the learning situation. Knowledge is the outcome of learning and a guide that shapes new learning. What we already know determines to a great extent what we will pay attention to, perceive, learn, remember, and forget.

Cognitive View of Learning: A general approach that views learning as an active mental process of acquiring, remembering, and using knowledge.

Domain-Specific Knowledge: Information that is useful in a particular situation or that applies mainly to one specific topic.

General Knowledge: Information that is useful in many different kinds of tasks; information that applies to many situations.

Declarative Knowledge: Verbal information; facts; "knowing that" something is the case.

Procedural Knowledge: Knowledge that is demonstrated when we perform a task; "knowing how."

Conditional Knowledge: "Knowing when and why" to use declarative and procedural knowledge.

■ The Information Processing Model of Memory

(pp. 239–246)

Compare declarative, procedural, and conditional knowledge. Declarative knowledge is knowledge that can be declared, usually in words or other symbols. Declarative knowledge is "knowing that" something is the case. Procedural knowledge is "knowing how" to do something; procedural knowledge must be demonstrated. Conditional knowledge is "knowing when and why" to apply your declarative and procedural knowledge.

Give two explanations for perception. The Gestalt principles are valid explanations of certain aspects of perception, but there are two other kinds of explanations in information processing theory for how we recognize patterns and give meaning to sensory events. The first is called *feature analysis,* or *bottom-up processing,* because the stimulus must be analyzed into features or components and assembled into a meaningful pattern. The second type of perception, *top-down processing,* is based on knowledge and expectation. To recognize patterns rapidly, in addition to noting features, we use what we already know about the situation.

What is working memory? Working memory is both short-term storage in the phonological loop and visuospatial sketchpad and processing guided by the central executive—it is the workbench of conscious thought. To keep information activated in working memory for longer than 20 seconds, people use maintenance rehearsal (mentally repeating) and elaborative rehearsal (making connections with knowledge from long-term memory). This kind of rehearsal also helps move new information to long-term memory. The limited capacity of working memory can also be somewhat circumvented by the control process of chunking.

Information Processing: The human mind's activity of taking in, storing, and using information.

Sensory Memory: System that holds sensory information very briefly.

Perception: Interpretation of sensory information.

Gestalt: German for *pattern* or *whole;* Gestalt theorists hold that people organize their perceptions into coherent wholes.

Bottom-Up Processing: Perceiving based on noticing separate defining features and assembling them into a recognizable pattern.

Top-Down Processing: Perceiving based on the context and the patterns you expect to occur in that situation.

Attention: Focus on a stimulus.

Automaticity: The ability to perform thoroughly learned tasks without much mental effort.

Working Memory: The information that you are focusing on at a given moment.

Short-Term Memory: Component of memory system that holds information for about 20 seconds.

Central Executive: The part of working memory that is responsible for monitoring and directing attention and other mental resources.

Phonological Loop: Part of working memory. A memory rehearsal system for verbal and sound information of about 1.5 to 2 seconds.

Visuospatial Sketchpad: Part of working memory. A holding system for visual and spatial information.

Maintenance Rehearsal: Keeping information in working memory by repeating it to yourself.

Elaborative Rehearsal: Keeping information in working memory by associating it with something else you already know.

Chunking: Grouping individual bits of data into meaningful larger units.

Decay: The weakening and fading of memories with the passage of time.

Long-Term Memory: The Goal of Teaching

(pp. 246–255)

How is information represented in long-term memory, and what role do schemas play? Long-term memory seems to hold an unlimited amount of information for a very long time. Memories may be explicit (semantic or episodic) or implicit (procedural, classical conditioning, or priming). In long-term memory, bits of information may be stored and interrelated in terms of propositional networks or images and in schemas that are data structures that allow us to represent large amounts of complex information, make inferences, and understand new information.

What learning processes improve long-term memory? The way you learn information in the first place affects its recall later. One important requirement is to integrate new material with knowledge already stored in long-term memory using elaboration, organization, and context. Another view of memory is the levels of processing theory, in which recall of information is determined by how completely it is processed.

Why do we forget? Information lost from working memory truly disappears, but information stored in long-term memory may be available, given the right cues. Information appears to be lost from long-term memory through time decay (neural connections, like muscles, grow weak without use) and interference (newer memories may interfere with or obscure older memories, and older memories may interfere with memory for new material).

Long-Term Memory: Permanent store of knowledge.
Long-Term Working Memory: Holds the strategies for pulling information from long-term memory into working memory.
Explicit Memory: Long-term memories that involve deliberate or conscious recall.
Implicit Memory: Knowledge that we are not conscious of recalling, but influences behavior or thought without our awareness.
Semantic Memory: Memory for meaning.
Propositional Network: Set of interconnected concepts and relationships in which long-term knowledge is held.
Images: Representations based on the physical attributes—the appearance—of information.
Schemata (singular, **Schema**): Basic structures for organizing information; concepts.
Story Grammar: Typical structure or organization for a category of stories.
Script: Schema or expected plan for the sequence of steps in a common event such as buying groceries or ordering take-out pizza.
Episodic Memory: Long-term memory for information tied to a particular time and place, especially memory of the events in a person's life.
Procedural Memory: Long-term memory for how to do things.
Productions: The contents of procedural memory; rules about what actions to take, given certain conditions.
Priming: Activating a concept in memory or the spread of activation from one concept to another.
Elaboration: Adding and extending meaning by connecting new information to existing knowledge.
Organization: Ordered and logical network of relations.
Context: The physical or emotional backdrop associated with an event.
Levels of Processing Theory: Theory that recall of information is based on how deeply it is processed.
Activation Spreading: Retrieval of pieces of information based on their relatedness to one another. Remembering one bit of information activates (stimulates) recall of associated information.
Retrieval: Process of searching for and finding information in long-term memory.
Reconstruction: Recreating information by using memories, expectations, logic, and existing knowledge.
Interference: The process that occurs when remembering certain information is hampered by the presence of other information.

Metacognition, Regulation, and Individual Differences

(pp. 255–260)

What are the three metacognitive skills? The three metacognitive skills used to regulate thinking and learning are planning, monitoring, and evaluation. Planning involves deciding how much time to give to a task, which strategies to use, how to start, and so on. Monitoring is the on-line awareness of "how I'm doing." Evaluating involves making judgments about the processes and outcomes of thinking and learning and acting on those judgments.

Describe some individual differences in metacognition. As children develop cognitively, they are more able to exercise executive control and use strategies. Also, some individual differences in metacognitive abilities probably are caused by biological differences or by variations in learning experiences. Students can vary greatly in their ability to attend selectively to information in their environment, plan, and execute strategies. They also differ in working memory span.

How can using better metacognitive strategies improve children's working and long-term memories? Younger children can be taught to use organization to improve memory, but they probably won't apply the strategy unless they are reminded. Children also become more able to use elaboration as they mature, but this strategy is developed late in childhood. Creating images or stories to remember ideas is more likely for older elementary school students and adolescents.

Executive Control Processes: Processes such as selective attention, rehearsal, elaboration, and organization that influence encoding, storage, and retrieval of information in memory.

Metacognition: Knowledge about our own thinking processes.

Becoming Knowledgeable: Some Basic Principles

(pp. 260–266)

Describe three ways to develop declarative knowledge. Declarative knowledge develops as we integrate new information with our existing understanding. The most useful and effective way to learn and remember is to understand and use new information. Making the information to be remembered meaningful is important and often is the greatest challenge for teachers. Mnemonics are memorization aids: They include peg-type approaches such as the loci method, acronyms, chain mnemonics, and the keyword method. A powerful but limiting way to accomplish this is rote memorization, which can best be supported by part learning and distributed practice.

Describe some procedures for developing procedural knowledge. Automated basic skills and domain-specific strategies—two types of procedural knowledge—are learned in different ways. There are three stages in the development of an automated skill: cognitive (following steps or directions guided by declarative knowledge), associative (combining individual steps into larger units), and autonomous (where the whole procedure can be accomplished without much attention). Prerequisite knowledge and practice with feedback help students move through these stages. Domain-specific strategies are consciously applied skills of organizing thoughts and actions to reach a goal. To support this kind of learning, teachers need to provide opportunities for practice and application in many different situations.

Mnemonics: Techniques for remembering; also, the art of memory.

Loci Method: Technique of associating items with specific places.

Peg-Type Mnemonics: Systems of associating items with cue words.

Acronym: Technique for remembering names, phrases, or steps by using the first letter of each word to form a new, memorable word.

Chain Mnemonics: Memory strategies that associate one element in a series with the next element.

Keyword Method: System of associating new words or concepts with similar-sounding cue words and images.

Rote Memorization: Remembering information by repetition without necessarily understanding the meaning of the information.

Serial-Position Effect: The tendency to remember the beginning and the end but not the middle of a list.

Part Learning: Breaking a list of rote learning items into shorter lists.

Distributed Practice: Practice in brief periods with rest intervals.

Massed Practice: Practice for a single extended period.

Automated Basic Skills: Skills that are applied without conscious thought.

Domain-Specific Strategies: Consciously applied skills to reach goals in a particular subject or problem area.

Enhancing Your Expertise with Technology: Memory Techniques

(p. 267)

NASA's Applied Cognition game page **(http://human-factors.arc.nasa.gov/cognition/tutorials/index.html)**

Mind Tools **(http://www.mindtools.com)**

Other Useful Websites

Metacognition and Reading to Learn
http://www.ed.gov/databases/ERIC_Digests/ed376427.html

Metacomprehension
http://www.ed.gov/databases/ERIC_Digests/ed250670.html

Overview of metacognition
http://www.ncrel.org/skrs/areas/issues/students/learning/lr1metn.htm

Learn To: provides thousands of step-by-step tutorials on a variety of skills. **www.learn2.com**

Mindtools **http://www.psychwww.com/mtsite/**

Organizations

Wolf-Trap Institute for Early Learning Through the Arts: organization to help early childhood professionals use the arts as part of their care and instruction of young children. The Institute is accessible on the web by going to the main site for Wolf Trap and then selecting Education.
http://www.wolf-trap.org/

An interactive site sponsored by Wolf-Trap called *Artsplay*
http://www.wolf-trap.org/

Becoming a Professional

Passing the PRAXIS™

The predicament that you face in the Teachers' Casebook demonstrates the interconnected nature of the topics of educational psychology. Ask yourself these questions: Am I able to call these students self-regulated learners? What do they understand about the value and demands of the learning tasks that I have presented to them? How extensive is their set of sophisticated learning strategies? Research based on the cognitive perspective addresses these topics and many more.

Knowledge of human memory and learning has influenced nearly every aspect of classroom practice from the design of curricula and tests to the design of textbooks and instructional software. PRAXIS II™ will assess your knowledge of the contributions of the cognitive perspective.

Tips for PRAXIS II™

Understand how memory and recall are affected by:

- The limitations, capacities, and capabilities of the various structures of human memory (e.g., memory stores)
- The manner in which humans process information
- Prior knowledge of a topic
- Metacognitive/executive control processes

Explain how students and teachers can enhance learning through the use of:

- Elaboration and mnemonic devices
- Organized presentations
- Study tools that organize information (e.g., outlines, concept maps)
- Meaningful learning and instructional activities

Related Topics

- Common elements of the constructive perspective (Chapter 9)
- Cognitive approaches to motivation (Chapter 10)
- Teaching concepts through exposition (Chapter 8)
- Objectives for learning (Chapter 12)
- Flexible and creative planning—using taxonomies (Chapter 12)

Standards and Licensure Appendix: *PRAXIS II™ and INTASC*

Refer to the Appendix at the end of the book for detailed correlations to PRAXIS II™ exam topics and INTASC Standards addressed in this text.

Insights about Job Interview Questions: *What Would You Say?*

1. As part of your interview, the principal says, "We have to cover so much material to get our students ready for the state assessments. What would you do to help your students remember what they have learned in your classes?"
2. During your interview, the supervisor for the primary grades asks you, "What is your script for a typical day? Tell me how a good day should go in terms of what you would plan and how much time you would give to each segment of your day."
3. As part of your interview, the department chair asks, "What are the basic skills for your students—the foundations of their more advanced learning—and how would you teach them?"

Your Teaching Portfolio: *Teaching Resources*

- Use the section on the differences between behavioral and cognitive approaches to learning to refine your teaching philosophy. How will you answer the job interview question, "What is your theory of learning and why?"
- Use the section on mnemonics to generate ideas for helping your students learn key vocabulary in science or social studies subjects and include these ideas in your **Teaching Resources** file.
- Are there mnemonics such as the one in Figure 7.8 that would help your students learn important relationships?

Video**Workshop** Extra

If the VideoWorkshop package was included with your textbook, go to Chapter 7 of the Companion Website (www.ablongman.com/woolfolk) and click on the VideoWorkshop button. Follow the instructions for viewing *Video Clip 7: Memory.* Consider this information along with what you've read in Chapter 7 while answering the following questions:

1. During the lesson on the skeletal system, what activities do the students use to enhance their long-term memory of the concepts? Use the terminology from this chapter in answering this question.
2. When you first read this chapter, what type of memory were you utilizing? What type of memory did these students use when they answered the teacher's questions?

Use the CD-ROM included in the back of your textbook to launch the "Becoming a Professional" website. The website features advice on preparing for teacher certification exams, help with getting your first job, and resources to help you perform your job well from the first day forward.

Teachers' Casebook

What Would They Do?

Here is how some practicing teachers responded to the teaching situation presented at the beginning of this chapter about history students intent on memorizing.

Mark Smith

Ninth–Twelfth Grade Teacher, *Medford High School, Medford, Massachusetts*

The students in this class have always used memorization, and although they have probably been somewhat successful in the past, there comes a point where learners must get into higher-level thinking. Because this is a senior history class and many of these students will be heading off to college, they must be taught different ways of learning and thinking.

A critical piece of learning is being able to debate a topic and do so with a convincing argument. If I were the teacher in this class and the students were so worried about tests and grades, I would add more oral presentations and writing assignments that make the students think about the facts and try to analyze the information. Knowing facts and details in history is not as important as understanding how they affected the present and why the past is important for today and tomorrow.

Madya Ayala

High School Teacher of Preperatoria Eugenio Garza Lagüera, *Campus Garza Sada, Monterrey, N.L. Mexico*

I observe that there are two existing conflicts. First, the students' available cognitive strategies (memorizing) don't fit the assigned task (higher-level thinking). Second, the students can't see connections between current situations and past events. For the first conflict I would use cognitive strategies such as mind mapping, schemas, comparative tables, and other advanced organizers that would enable students to learn the material.

Second, I recommend establishing a relation between past and present realities by focusing students' attention on an important event from the past and asking them to link it to an international, national, local, or even a social problem that is happening in school. Drama is a very interesting way of involving students because it gives them the opportunity to feel and experience any historic action. They could represent what "really" happens in making decisions and living the consequences. On the other hand they can change the facts and analyze how history could have changed if different decisions had been made. This is an active and constructivist approach.

Ashley Dodge

Ninth and Tenth Grade Teacher, *Los Angeles Unified School District, Los Angeles, California*

These students are obviously using strategies that have worked for them in the past (memorization and regurgitation of facts and dates), but they have not developed any critical thinking skills. Many students are very successful with these techniques up to a certain point. They become obsessed with learning only what is necessary to pass the class.

In order to give these students the opportunity to see history as something more than a time line, I would announce to the class that for the next unit, there would be no test. Instead, we would create projects reflective of the era. Perhaps we would produce a play, a fashion show with period clothing, or a festival. Some students may wish to construct a city at the time being studied, focusing on the differences in the city as it was then compared to now. The students would need to use the information in the text to incorporate their ideas into their projects, but it would not need to be memorized. They would be graded on both the originality and the quality of their work, and the project grade would count as two unit grades.

Mitchell D. Klett

Twelfth Grade Teacher, *A.C. New Middle School, Springs, Texas*

Students need to understand that the events of the past have a profound influence on the world today. The adage, "those who don't know history are doomed to repeat it," rings true. As their teacher, I would emphasize cause-and-effect relationships throughout history and compare them with one another. By focusing on the causes of specific events, such as revolutions caused by economic rifts, students can better understand the cyclic nature of these types of revolutions. Events such as the French Revolution and the Russian Revolution could be examined through inquiry learning, group discussion, or role playing. Students could be given the opportunity to explore the nature of revolutions and apply what they have learned to new situations.

Thomas O'Donnell

Social Studies Chairperson, Grades 7–12, *Malden High School, Malden, Massachusetts*

To help students break out of rote thinking I would test them on comprehension and assess them on that basis. Once they realize what the goal is, they will switch their approach in order to achieve success. I would also teach them to recognize any word in the reading that assumes "a truth" or accepts only one explanation of events. Finally, I would train students to ask Who? What? Where? How? and Why? for all situations.

Go to the Companion Website (www.ablongman.com/woolfolk) for additional case studies including audio and video cases, and examples of student work.

CHAPTER

8

Complex Cognitive Processes

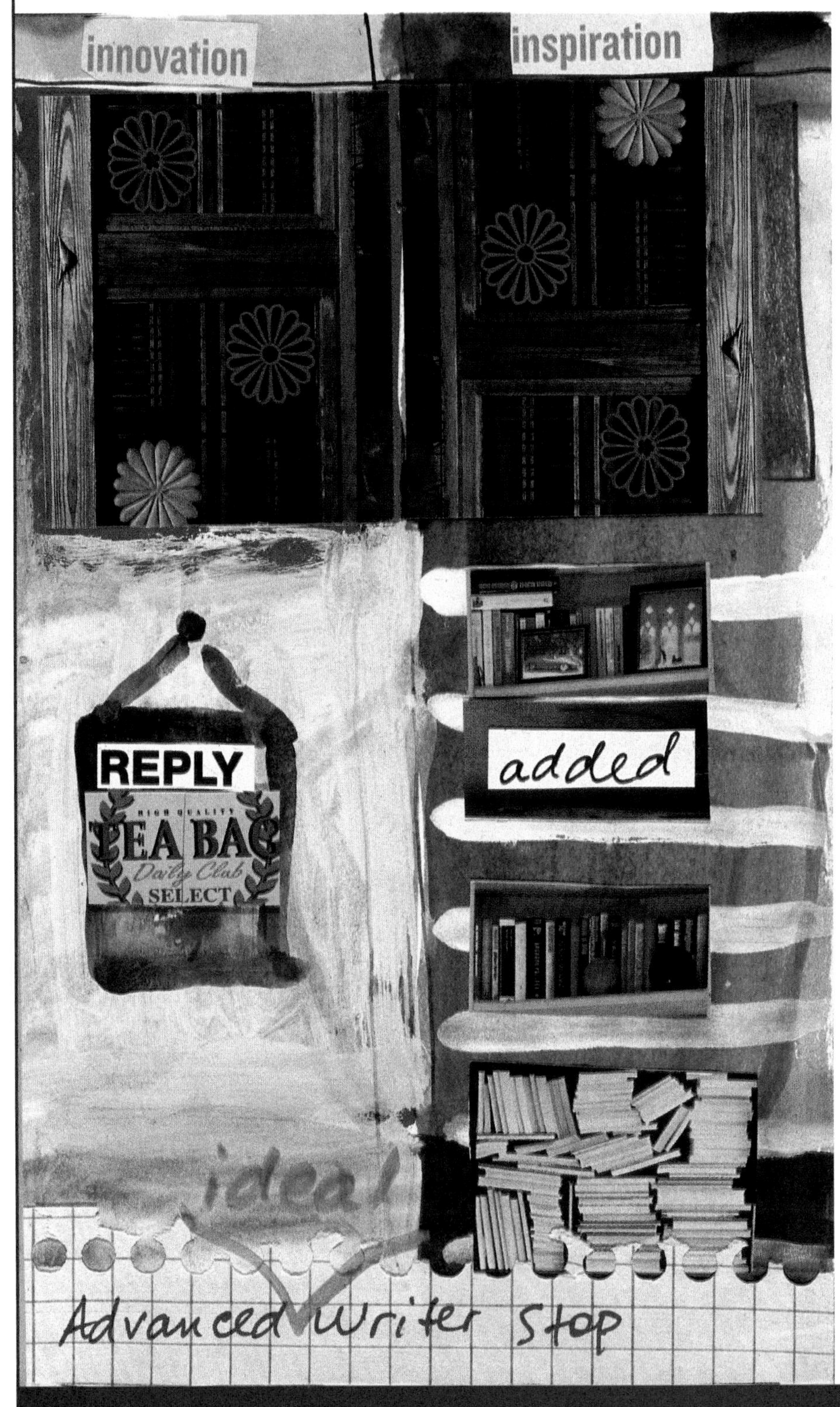

Teachers' Casebook

What Would You Do?

You have just finished reading the journals and projects from the discovery lesson on magnets, and you are depressed. In almost every working group, only one or two students seemed to "get it." The rest just drew pictures that were vaguely related to the unit or copied from the readings (or from the students who got it). You had taken the activities from a good "hands-on" science book and you thought the objectives and directions were clear. You know many students will be upset with the grades you are about to give.

Critical Thinking

What might have happened to make this lesson so unsuccessful? What will you do now with these projects? How could you make similar discovery activities more productive in the future?

Collaboration

With three or four members of your class, design a discovery lesson in your area that is consistent with the principles of cognitive learning from Chapter 7 and is more likely to be successful than the less than "magnetic" lesson above.

In the previous chapter we focused on the development of knowledge—how people make sense of and remember information and ideas. In this chapter we consider complex cognitive processes that lead to understanding. Understanding is more than memorizing. It is more than retelling in your own words. Understanding involves appropriately *transforming* and *using* knowledge, skills, and ideas. These understandings are considered "higher-level cognitive objectives" in a commonly used system of educational objectives (Anderson & Krathwohl, 2001; Bloom, Engelhart, Frost, Hill, & Krathwohl, 1956). We will focus on the implications of cognitive theories for the day-to-day practice of teaching.

Because the cognitive perspective is a philosophical orientation and not a unified theoretical model, teaching methods derived from it are varied. In this chapter, we will first examine three important areas in which cognitive theorists have made suggestions for learning and teaching: concept learning, problem solving, and learning strategies and tactics. Finally, we will explore the question of how to encourage the transfer of learning from one situation to another to make learning more useful.

By the time you have completed this chapter, you should be able to answer these questions:

- *What are the characteristics of a good lesson for teaching a key concept in your subject area?*
- *What are the steps in solving complex problems ?*
- *What are the roles of problem representation, algorithms, and heuristics in problem solving?*
- *How could you apply new learning strategies and tactics to prepare for tests and assignments in your current courses?*
- *What are three ways a teacher might encourage positive transfer of learning?*

Learning and Teaching about Concepts

STOP THINK WRITE What makes a cup a cup? List the characteristics of cupness. What is a fruit? Is a banana a fruit? Is a tomato a fruit? How about a squash? A watermelon? A sweet potato? An olive? How did you learn what makes a fruit a fruit?

Most of what we know about cups and fruits and the world involves concepts and relations among concepts (Ashcraft, 2002). But what exactly is a concept? A **concept** is a category used to group similar events, ideas, objects, or people. When we talk about a particular concept such as *student,* we refer to a category of people who are similar to one another—they all study a subject. The people may be old or young, in school or not; they may be studying baseball or Bach, but they can all be categorized as students. Concepts are abstractions. They do not exist in the real world. Only individual examples of concepts exist. Concepts help us organize vast amounts of information into manageable units. For instance, there are about 7.5 million distinguishable differences in colors. By categorizing these colors into some dozen or so groups, we manage to deal with this diversity quite well (Bruner, 1973).

CONNECT & EXTEND

TO THE RESEARCH
Howard Gardner (1993b) defines understanding as:

> the capacity to take knowledge, skills, and concepts and apply them appropriately in new situations. If someone only parrots back what he or she has been taught, we do not know whether the individual understands. If that person applies the knowledge promiscuously, regardless of whether it is appropriate, then I would not say he or she understands either. . . . But if that person knows where to apply and where not to apply, and can do it to new situations, he or she understands. (p. 2)

Views of Concept Learning

In early research, psychologists assumed that concepts share a set of **defining attributes,** or distinctive features. For example, books all contain pages that are bound together in some way (but what about electronic "books"?). The defining attributes theory of concepts suggests that we recognize specific examples by noting key required features.

Since about 1970, however, these views about the nature of concepts have been challenged (Ashcraft, 2002). Although some concepts, such as equilateral triangle, have clear-cut defining attributes, most concepts do not. Take the concept of *party.* What are the defining attributes? You might have difficulty listing these attributes, but you probably recognize a party when you see or hear one (unless, of course we are talking about political parties, or the other party in a lawsuit, where the sound might not help you recognize the "party"). What about the concept of *bird*? Your first thought might be that birds are animals that fly. But is an ostrich a bird? What about a penguin? A bat?

CONNECT & EXTEND

TO YOUR TEACHING/PORTFOLIO
According to Piaget, a person cannot think in abstract terms until the stage of formal operations is reached. How then can a child learn abstract concepts such as "yesterday" and "happy"? Can abstract concepts be taught through the use of prototypes?

Prototypes and Exemplars. Current conceptions of concept learning suggest that we have in our minds a prototype of a party and a bird—an image that captures the essence of each concept. A **prototype** is the best representative of its category. For instance, the best representative of the "birds" category for many North Americans might be a robin (Rosch, 1973). Other members of the category may be very similar to the prototype (sparrow) or similar in some ways but different in others (chicken, ostrich). At the boundaries of a category, it may be difficult to determine if a particular instance really belongs. For example, is a telephone "furniture"? Is an elevator a "vehicle"? Is an olive a "fruit"? Whether something fits into a category is a matter of degree. Thus, categories have fuzzy boundaries. Some events, objects, or ideas are simply better examples of a concept than others (Ashcraft, 2002).

Another explanation of concept learning suggests that we identify members of a category by referring to exemplars. **Exemplars** are our actual memories of specific birds, parties, furniture, and so on that we use to compare with an item in question to see if that item belongs in the same category as our exemplar. For example, if you see a strange steel-and-stone bench in a public park, you may compare it to the sofa in your living room to decide if the uncomfortable-looking creation is still for sitting or if it has crossed a fuzzy boundary into "sculpture."

Prototypes probably are built from experiences with many exemplars. This happens naturally because episodic memories of particular events tend to blur together over time, creating an average or typical sofa prototype from all the sofa exemplars you have experienced (Schwartz & Reisberg, 1991).

Concept A general category of ideas, objects, people, or experiences whose members share certain properties.

Defining attributes Distinctive features shared by members of a category.

Prototype Best representative of a category.

Exemplar A specific example of a given category that is used to classify an item.

Concepts and Schemas. In addition to prototypes and exemplars, there is a third element involved when we recognize a concept—our schematic knowledge related to the concept. How do we know that counterfeit money is not "real" money, even though it perfectly fits our "money" prototype and exemplars? We know because of its history. It was printed by the "wrong" people. So our understanding of the concept of money is connected with concepts of crime, forgery, the federal treasury, and many others.

CONNECT & EXTEND

TO **PRAXIS**™
TEACHING CONCEPTS (II, A2)
Teachers devote much effort to the development of concepts that are vital in learning subject matter and skills. Understand the major approaches to teaching concepts and be able to describe their strengths and limitations.

Strategies for Teaching Concepts

What Would You Say? You are interviewing for a job in a school that serves many immigrant families. The principal asks, "How would you teach abstract concepts to a student who just arrived from Somalia and can't even read in her native language, much less English?"

Both prototypes and defining attributes are important in learning. Children first learn many concepts in the real world from the best examples or prototypes, pointed out by adults (Tennyson, 1981). But when examples are ambiguous (is an olive a fruit?), we may consult the defining attributes to make a decision. Olives are foods with seeds in the edible parts, which matches the defining attributes for fruits, so they must be fruits, even though are not typical or prototypic fruits (Schunk, 2000).

Like the learning of concepts, the teaching of concepts can combine both defining attributes and prototypes. One approach to teaching about concepts is called *concept attainment*—a way of helping students construct an understanding of specific concepts and practice thinking skills such as hypothesis testing (Joyce, Weil, & Calhoun, 2000; Klausmeier, 1992).

An Example Concept-Attainment Lesson. Here is how a 5th-grade teacher helped his students learn about a familiar concept and practice thinking skills at the same time (Eggen & Kauchak, 2001, pp. 148–151). The teacher began a lesson by saying that he had an idea in mind and wanted students to "figure out what it is." He placed two signs on a table—"Examples" and "Nonexamples." Then he placed an apple in front of the "Examples" sign and a rock in front of the "Nonexamples" sign. He asked his students, "What do you think the idea might be?" "Things we eat" was the first suggestion. The teacher wrote "HYPOTHESES" on the board and, after a brief discussion of the meaning of "hypotheses," listed "things we eat" under this heading. Next he asked for other hypotheses—"living things" and "things that grow on plants" came next. After some discussion about plants and living things, the teacher brought out a tomato for the "Examples" side and a carrot for the "Nonexamples." Animated reconsideration of all the hypotheses followed these additions and a new hypothesis—"red things"—was suggested. Through discussion of more examples (peach, squash, orange) and nonexamples (lettuce, artichoke, potato), the students narrowed their hypothesis to "things with seeds in the parts you eat." The students had "constructed" the concept of "fruit"—foods with seeds in the edible parts (or, a more advanced definition, any engorged ovary, such as a pea pod, nut, tomato, pineapple, or the edible part of the plant developed from a flower).

"City children have trouble with the concept of harvest."

(© Martha Campbell—From *Phi Delta Kappan*)

Lesson Components. Whatever strategy you use for teaching concepts, you will need four components in any lesson: examples and nonexamples, relevant and irrelevant attributes, the name of the concept, and a definition (Joyce, Weil, & Calhoun, 2000). In addition, visual aids such as pictures, diagrams, or maps can improve learning of many concepts (Anderson & Smith, 1987; Mayer, 2001).

Examples: More examples are needed in teaching complicated concepts and in working with younger or less knowledgeable students. Both examples and nonexamples (sometimes called positive and negative instances) are necessary to make the boundaries of the category clear. A discussion of why a bat (nonexample) is not a bird will help students define the boundaries of the bird concept.

Relevant and Irrelevant Attributes: The ability to fly, as we've seen, is not a relevant attribute for classifying animals as birds. Even though many birds fly, some birds do not (ostrich, penguin), and some nonbirds do (bats, flying squirrels). The ability to fly would have to be included in a discussion of the bird concept, but students should understand that flying alone does not define an animal as a bird.

Name: Simply learning a label does not mean the person understands the concept, although the label is necessary for the understanding. In the example above, students probably already used the "fruit" name, but may not have understood that tomatoes, squash, and avocados are fruits.

Definition: A good definition has two elements: a reference to any more general category for the new concept, and a statement of the new concept's defining attributes (Klausmeier, 1976). For example, a fruit is food (general category) with seeds in the edible parts (defining attributes). An equilateral triangle is a plane, a simple, closed figure (general category), with three equal sides and three equal angles (defining attributes). This kind of definition helps place the concept in a schema of related knowledge.

In teaching some concepts, "a picture is worth a thousand words"—or at least a few hundred, as we saw in Chapter 7. Seeing and handling specific examples, or pictures of examples, helps young children learn concepts. For students of all ages, the complex concepts in history, science, and mathematics can often be illustrated in diagrams or graphs. For example, Anderson and Smith (1983) found that when their students just read about the concept of light, only 20% could understand the role of reflected light in our ability to see objects. But when the students worked with diagrams such as the one in Figure 8.1, almost 80% understood the concept.

Illustrations can help students grasp a difficult concept.

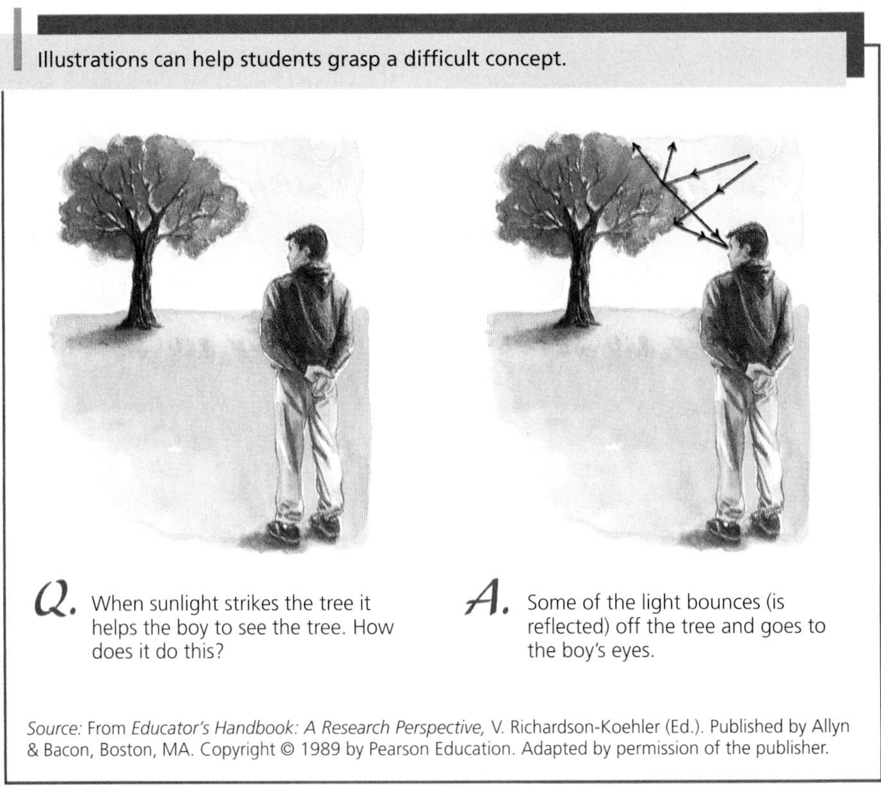

Q. When sunlight strikes the tree it helps the boy to see the tree. How does it do this?
A. Some of the light bounces (is reflected) off the tree and goes to the boy's eyes.

Source: From *Educator's Handbook: A Research Perspective*, V. Richardson-Koehler (Ed.). Published by Allyn & Bacon, Boston, MA. Copyright © 1989 by Pearson Education. Adapted by permission of the publisher.

Figure 8.1 Understanding Complex Concepts

Undergeneralization Exclusion of some true members from a category; limiting a concept.

Overgeneralization Inclusion of nonmembers in a category; overextending a concept.

Concept mapping Student's diagram of his or her understanding of a concept.

■ **Table 8.1** Phases of the Concept Attainment Model

There are three main phases in concept attainment teaching. First the teacher presents examples/nonexamples and students identify the concept, then the teacher checks for understanding, and finally students analyze their thinking strategies.

Phase One: Presentation of Data and Identification of Concept	Phase Two: Testing Attainment of the Concept	Phase Three: Analysis of Thinking Strategies
Teacher presents labeled examples.	Students identify additional unlabeled examples as yes or no.	Students describe thoughts.
Students compare attributes in positive and negative examples.	Teacher confirms hypotheses, names concept, and restates definitions according to essential attributes.	Students discuss role of hypotheses and attributes.
Students generate and test hypotheses.	Students generate examples.	Students discuss type and number of hypotheses
Students state a definition according to the essential attributes.		

SOURCE: From *Models of Teaching* (6th ed.), by Bruce Joyce and Marsha Weils. Published by Allyn & Bacon, Boston, MA. Copyright © 2000 by Pearson Education. Reprinted by permission of the publisher.

Lesson Structure. The fruit lesson above is an example of good concept teaching for several reasons. First, it is more effective to examine examples and nonexamples before discussing attributes or definitions (Joyce, Weil, & Calhoun, 2000). Start your concept lesson with prototypes, or best examples, to help the students establish the category. The teacher above began with the classic fruit example, an apple, then moved to less typical examples such as tomatoes and squash. These examples show the wide range of possibilities the category includes and the variety of irrelevant attributes within a category. Including fruits that have one seed or many, have a sweet taste or not, are different colors, and have thick or thin skin, will prevent **undergeneralization,** or the exclusion of some foods, such as squash, from their rightful place in the category fruit.

Nonexamples should be very close to the concept, but miss by one or just a few critical attributes. For instance, sweet potatoes and rhubarb are *not* fruits, even though sweet potatoes are sweet and rhubarb is used to make pies. Including nonexamples will prevent **overgeneralization,** or the inclusion of substances that are not fruits.

After the students seem to have grasped the concept under consideration, it is useful to ask them to think about the ways that they formed and tested their hypotheses. Thinking back helps students develop their metacognitive skills and shows them that different people approach problems in different ways (Joyce, Weil, & Calhoun, 2000). Table 8.1 summarizes the stages of concept teaching.

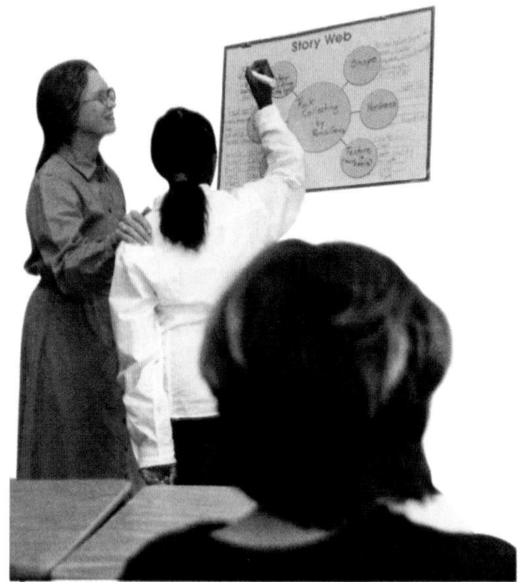

In creating this story web, the students are increasing their reading comprehension skills and using their knowledge of literary elements.

Extending and Connecting Concepts. Once students have a good sense of a concept, they should use it. This might mean doing exercises, solving problems, writing, reading, explaining, or any other activity that requires them to apply their new understanding. This will connect the concept into the students' web of related schematic knowledge. One approach that you may see in some texts and workbooks for students above the primary grades is **concept mapping** (Novak & Musonda, 1991). Students "diagram" their understanding of the concept, as Amy has in Figure 8.2 on page 280. Amy's map shows a reasonable understanding of the concept of "molecule," but also indicates that Amy holds one misconception. She thinks that there is no space between the molecules in solids.

CONNECT & EXTEND

TO **PRAXIS**™
CONCEPT MAPPING (II, A2)
For advice and additional information about the creation and use of concept maps, go to the website *Graphic Organizers* (http://www.graphic.org/concept.html).

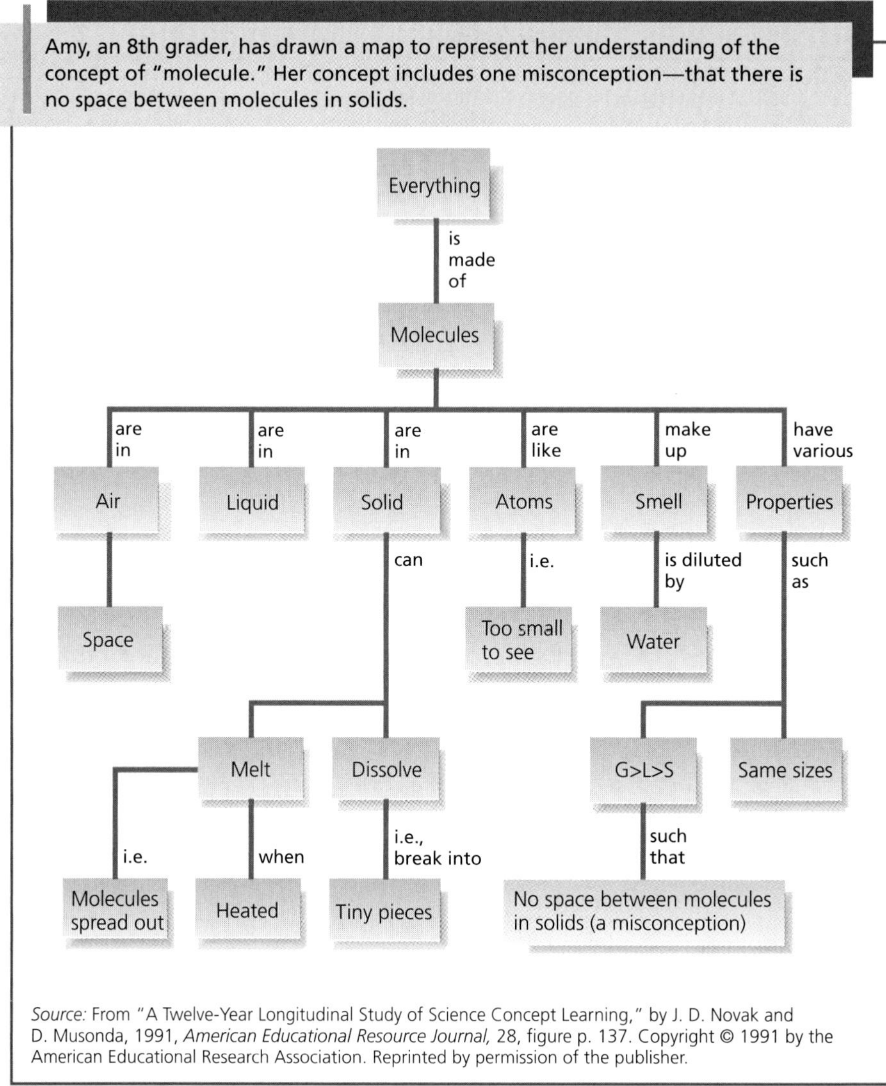

Source: From "A Twelve-Year Longitudinal Study of Science Concept Learning," by J. D. Novak and D. Musonda, 1991, *American Educational Resource Journal,* 28, figure p. 137. Copyright © 1991 by the American Educational Research Association. Reprinted by permission of the publisher.

Figure 8.2 Amy's Molecule

Teaching Concepts through Discovery

CONNECT & EXTEND

TO YOUR TEACHING/PORTFOLIO
See the "Teachers' Casebook" for ideas about how to conduct discovery lessons so that everyone, not just the brightest or quickest, makes discoveries.

Jerome Bruner's early research on thinking (Bruner, Goodnow, & Austin, 1956) stirred his interest in educational approaches that encourage concept learning and the development of thinking. Bruner's work emphasized the importance of understanding the structure of a subject being studied, the need for active learning as the basis for true understanding, and the value of inductive reasoning in learning.

Structure and Discovery. Subject structure refers to the fundamental ideas, relationships, or patterns of the field—the essential information. Because structure does not include specific facts or details about the subject, the essential structure of an idea can be represented simply as a diagram, set of principles, or formula. According to Bruner, learning will be more meaningful, useful, and memorable for students if they focus on understanding the structure of the subject being studied.

In order to grasp the structure of information, Bruner believes, students must be active—they must identify key principles for themselves rather than simply accepting teachers' explanations. This process has been called **discovery learning.** In discovery learning, the teacher presents examples and the students work with the

Discovery learning Bruner's approach, in which students work on their own to discover basic principles.

GUIDELINES Applying Bruner's Ideas

Present both examples and nonexamples of the concepts you are teaching.

Examples

1. In teaching about mammals, include people, kangaroos, whales, cats, dolphins, and camels as examples, and chickens, fish, alligators, frogs, and penguins as nonexamples.
2. Ask students for additional examples and nonexamples.

Help students see connections among concepts.

Examples

1. Ask questions such as these: What else could you call this apple? (Fruit.) What do we do with fruit? (Eat.) What do we call things we eat? (Food.)
2. Use diagrams, outlines, and summaries to point out connections.

Pose a question and let students try to find the answer.

Examples

1. How could the human hand be improved?
2. What is the relation between the area of one tile and the area of the whole floor?

Encourage students to make intuitive guesses.

Examples

1. Instead of giving a word's definition, say, "Let's guess what it might mean by looking at the words around it."
2. Give students a map of ancient Greece and ask where they think the major cities were.
3. Don't comment after the first few guesses. Wait for several ideas before giving the answer.
4. Use guiding questions to focus students when their discovery has led them too far astray.

examples until they discover the interrelationships—the subject's structure. Thus, Bruner believes that classroom learning should take place through **inductive reasoning,** that is, by using specific examples to formulate a general principle. The concept attainment lesson on fruit above used this approach.

Discovery in Action. An inductive approach requires **intuitive thinking** on the part of students. Bruner suggests that teachers can nurture this intuitive thinking by encouraging students to make guesses based on incomplete evidence and then to confirm or disprove the guesses systematically (Bruner, 1960). After learning about ocean currents and the shipping industry, for example, students might be shown old maps of three harbors and asked to guess which one became a major port. Then they could check their guesses through systematic research. Unfortunately, educational practices often discourage intuitive thinking by punishing wrong guesses and rewarding safe, but uncreative answers.

A distinction is usually made between discovery learning, in which the students work on their own to a very great extent, and **guided discovery,** in which the teacher provides some direction. Unguided discovery is appropriate for preschool children, but in a typical elementary or secondary classroom, unguided activities usually prove unmanageable and unproductive. For these situations, guided discovery is preferable. Students are presented with intriguing questions, baffling situations, or interesting problems: Why does the flame go out when we cover it with a jar? Why does this pencil seem to bend when you put it in water? What is the rule for grouping these words together? Instead of explaining how to solve the problem, the teacher provides the appropriate materials and encourages students to make observations, form hypotheses, and test solutions. The *Guidelines* should help you apply Bruner's suggestions.

CONNECT & EXTEND

TO **PRAXIS**™
REASONING (II, A1)
Be able to distinguish between inductive and deductive reasoning. Explain the role that each plays in the learning of concepts.

CONNECT & EXTEND

TO **PRAXIS**™
DISCOVERY LEARNING (I, A1)
Many teachers, especially in mathematics and science, believe that meaningful learning in their areas is best supported by discovery learning. Be prepared to answer questions about the assumptions, techniques, strengths, and limitations of this instructional strategy.

Inductive reasoning Formulating general principles based on knowledge of examples and details.

Intuitive thinking Making imaginative leaps to correct perceptions or workable solutions.

Guided discovery An adaptation of discovery learning, in which the teacher provides some direction.

Expository teaching Ausubel's method—teachers present material in complete, organized form, moving from broadest to more specific concepts.

Meaningful verbal learning Focused and organized relationships among ideas and verbal information.

Teaching Concepts through Exposition

In contrast to Bruner, David Ausubel's (1963, 1977, 1982) believed that people acquire knowledge primarily through reception rather than through discovery. Concepts, principles, and ideas are presented and understood, not discovered.

Ausubel's **expository teaching** model stresses what is known as **meaningful verbal learning**—verbal information, ideas, and relationships among ideas, taken

Expository teaching methods present information to learners in an organized, "finished" form, rather than having them discover it themselves.

together. Rote memorization is not meaningful learning, because material learned by rote is not *connected* with existing knowledge. In this approach, teachers present materials in a carefully organized and sequenced form. Ausubel believes that learning should progress, not inductively as Bruner recommends, but using **deductive reasoning:** from the general to the specific.

Advance Organizers. Ausubel's strategy always begins with an **advance organizer.** This is an introductory statement broad enough to encompass all the information that will follow. The organizers can serve three purposes: They direct your attention to what is important in the coming material; they highlight relationships among ideas that will be presented; and they remind you of relevant information you already have.

In general, advance organizers fall into one of two categories, *comparative* and *expository* (Joyce, Weil, & Calhoun, 2000; Mayer, 1984). Each fulfills an important function. Comparative organizers *activate* (bring into working memory) already existing schemas. They remind you of what you already know, but may not realize is relevant. A comparative advance organizer for a history lesson on revolutions might be a statement that contrasts military uprisings with the physical and social changes involved in the Industrial Revolution; you could also compare the common aspects of the French, English, Mexican, Russian, Iranian, and American revolutions (Salomon & Perkins, 1989).

In contrast, *expository organizers* provide *new* knowledge that students will need to understand the upcoming information. In an English class, you might begin a large thematic unit on rites of passage in literature with a very broad statement of the theme and why it has been so central in literature—something like, "A central character coming of age must learn to know himself or herself, often makes some kind of journey of self-discovery, and must decide what in the society is to be accepted and what rejected."

CONNECT & EXTEND

TO **PRAXIS**™
ADVANCE ORGANIZERS (II, A3)
The advance organizer is an important element in many teacher-centered/expository approaches to instruction. Be able to explain the role of the advance organizer in these approaches, and identify the basic types of organizers.

The general conclusion of research on advance organizers is that they do help students learn, especially when the material to be learned is quite unfamiliar, complex, or difficult (Corkill, 1992; Mayer, 1984; Morin & Miller, 1998), if two conditions are met. First, to be effective, the organizer must be understood by the students. This was demonstrated dramatically in a study by Dinnel and Glover (1985). They found that instructing students to paraphrase an advance organizer—which, of course, requires them to understand its meaning—increased the effectiveness of the organizer. Second, the organizer must really be an organizer: It must indicate relations among the basic concepts and terms that will be used. No amount of student processing can make a bad organizer more effective. Concrete models, diagrams, or analogies seem to be especially good organizers (Mayer 1983a, 1984; Robinson, 1998).

Steps in an Expository Lesson. After the advance organizer, the next step is to present content in terms of similarities and differences using specific examples, perhaps provided by the students themselves. Assume you are teaching the coming-of-age theme in literature, using *The Diary of Anne Frank* and *The Adventures of Huckleberry Finn.* As the students read, you might ask them to compare the central character's growth, state of mind, and position in society with characters from other novels, plays, and films (connect to students' prior knowledge). Then students can compare Anne Frank's inner journey with Huck Finn's trip down the Mississippi. As comparisons are made, you should underscore the goal of the lesson and elaborate the advance organizer.

The best way to point out similarities and differences is with examples. Huck Finn's and Anne Frank's dilemmas must be clear. Finally, when all the material has been presented, ask students to discuss how the examples can be used to expand on the original advance organizer. The phases of expository teaching are summarized in Figure 8.3.

Expository teaching is more developmentally appropriate for students at or above later elementary school, that is, around the 5th or 6th grade (Luiten, Ames, & Ackerson, 1980). The *Guidelines* below should help you follow the main steps in expository teaching.

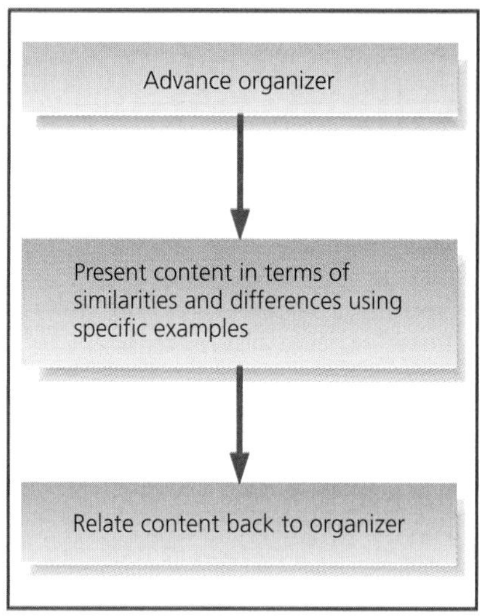

Figure 8.3 Phases of Expository Teaching

Teaching Concepts in Diverse Classrooms

A recent approach to teaching concepts that also emphasizes connections with prior knowledge is called **analogical instruction** (Bulgren, Deshler, Schumaker, & Lenz, 2000). This approach has proved helpful for teaching scientific or cultural knowledge in heterogeneous secondary classes that include students who are less academically prepared and students with learning disabilities. In secondary classrooms, as the amount and complexity of content increases, these students are especially at risk for failure. The goal of analogical instruction is to identify knowledge that these students already have in memory that can be used as a starting point for learning the new, complex material. Analogies have long been used in problem solving, as you will see in the next section, but until recently studies of analogies in teaching content have been rare.

Check Yourself Distinguish between prototypes and exemplars.

What are the four elements needed in concept teaching?

What are the key characteristics of Bruner's discovery learning?

What are the stages of Ausubel's expository teaching?

How can you teach concepts through analogies?

Deductive reasoning Drawing conclusions by applying rules or principles; logically moving from a general rule or principle to a specific solution.

Advance organizer Statement of inclusive concepts to introduce and sum up material that follows.

Analogical instruction Teaching new concepts by making connections (analogies) with information that the student already understands.

Problem Solving

What Would You Say? You're interviewing with the district superintendent for a position as a school psychologist. The man is known for his unorthodox interview questions. He hands you a pad of paper and a ruler and says, "Tell me, what is the exact thickness of a single sheet of paper?"

GUIDELINES Applying Ausubel's Ideas

Use advance organizers.

Examples

1. English: Shakespeare used the social ideas of his time as a framework for his plays—*Julius Caesar, Hamlet,* and *Macbeth* dealt with concepts of natural order, a nation as the human body, etc.
2. Social studies: Geography dictates economy in preindustrialized regions or nations.
3. History: Important concepts during the Renaissance were symmetry, admiration of the classical world, the centrality of the human mind.

Use a number of examples.

Examples

1. In mathematics class, ask students to point out all the examples of right angles that they can find in the room.
2. In teaching about islands and peninsulas, use maps, slides, models, postcards.

Focus on both similarities and differences.

Examples

1. In a history class, ask students to list the ways in which the North and South were alike and different before the Civil War.
2. In a biology class, ask students how they would transform spiders into insects or an amphibian into a reptile.

CONNECT & EXTEND

TO THE RESEARCH

Vosniadou, S., & Schommer, M. (1988). Explanatory analogies can help children acquire information from expository text. *Journal of Educational Psychology, 80,* 524–536. This article describes the results of an experiment in which analogies were used to help young children learn new information from science texts. For example, "an infection is like a war," "a stomach is like a blender," etc. Results showed that children in the analogy condition communicated more information than those in the control condition. Implication: Analogies can facilitate learning.

CONNECT & EXTEND

TO THE RESEARCH

You might want to note that, although interest in problem solving is great today, many of the early ideas of John Dewey are consistent with the recent emphasis on teaching students to be effective problem solvers.

This is a true story—I was asked the paper thickness question in an interview years ago. The answer was to measure the thickness of the entire pad and divide by the number of pages in the pad. I got the answer and the job, but what a tense moment that was. I suppose the superintendent was interested in my ability to solve problems.

A **problem** has an initial state (the current situation), a goal (the desired outcome), and a path for reaching the goal (including operations or activities that move you toward the goal). Problem solvers often have to set and reach subgoals as they move toward the final solution. For example, if your goal is to drive to the beach, but at the first stop sign you skid through the intersection, you may have to reach a subgoal of fixing your brakes before you can continue toward the original goal (Schunk, 2000). Also, problems can range from well-structured to ill-structured, depending on how clear-cut the goal is and how much structure is provided for solving the problem. Most arithmetic problems are well-structured, but finding the right college major is ill-structured—many different solutions and paths to solutions are possible. Life presents many ill-structured problems.

Problem solving is usually defined as formulating new answers, going beyond the simple application of previously learned rules to achieve a goal. Problem solving is what happens when no solution is obvious—when, for example, you can't afford new brakes for that car that skidded on the way to the beach (Mayer & Wittrock, 1996). Some psychologists suggest that most human learning involves problem solving (Anderson, 1993).

Problem Solving: General or Domain-Specific?

There is a debate about problem solving. Some psychologists believe that effective problem-solving strategies are specific to the problem area. That is, the problem-solving strategies in mathematics are unique to math, the strategies in art are unique to art, and so on. The other side of the debate claims that there are some general problem-solving strategies that can be useful in many areas.

There is evidence for both sides of the argument. In their research with 8- to 12-year olds, Robert Kail and Lynda Hall (1999) found that both domain-specific and general factors affected performance on arithmetic word problems. The influences were *arithmetic knowledge*—assessed by the time needed and errors produced in solving simple addition and subtraction problems—and *general information-processing skills,* including reading and information processing time and, to a lesser extent, memory span.

It appears that people move between general and specific approaches, depending on the situation and their level of expertise. Early on, when we know little about a problem area or domain, we may rely on general learning and problem-solving strategies to make sense of the situation. As we gain more domain-specific knowledge (particularly procedural knowledge about how to do things in the domain), we consciously apply the general strategies less; our problem solving becomes more automatic. But if we encounter a problem outside our current knowledge, we may return to relying on general strategies to attack the problem (Alexander, 1992, 1996; Perkins & Salomon, 1989; Shuell, 1990).

Let's consider general problem-solving strategies first. Think of a general problem-solving strategy as a beginning point, a broad outline. Such strategies usually have five stages (Derry, 1991; Derry & Murphy, 1986; Gallini, 1991; Gick, 1986). John Bransford and Barry Stein (1993) use the acronym IDEAL to identify the five steps:

I *Identify* problems and opportunities.

D *Define* goals and represent the problem.

E *Explore* possible strategies.

A *Anticipate* outcomes and *Act.*

L *Look* back and *Learn.*

Problem Any situation in which you are trying to reach some goal and must find a means to do so.

Problem solving Creating new solutions for problems.

We will examine each of these steps because they are found in many approaches to problem solving.

Identifying: Problem Finding

The first step, identifying that a problem exists and treating the problem as an opportunity, begins the process. This is not always straightforward. There is a story describing tenants who were angry about the slow elevators in their building. Consultants hired to "fix the problem" reported that the elevators were no worse than average and that improvements would be very expensive. Then one day, as the building supervisor watched people waiting impatiently for an elevator, he realized that the problem was not slow elevators but the fact that people were bored; they had nothing to do while they waited. When the boredom problem was identified and seen as an opportunity to improve the "waiting experience," the simple solution of installing a mirror by the elevator on each floor eliminated complaints.

Identifying the problem is a critical first step. Research indicates that people often hurry through this important step and "leap" to naming the first problem that comes to mind ("the elevators are too slow!"). Experts in a field are more likely to spend time carefully considering the nature of the problem (Bruning, Schraw, & Ronning, 1999). Finding a solvable problem and turning it into an opportunity is the process behind many successful inventions, such as the ball point pen, garbage disposal, appliance timer, alarm clock, self-cleaning oven, and thousands of others.

Once a *solvable* problem is identified, what next?

CONNECT & EXTEND

TO **PRAXIS**™
PROBLEM SOLVING (II, A1)
Be prepared to identify the steps in the general problem-solving process. Describe the techniques that students can employ to build useful representations of problems.

Defining Goals and Representing the Problem

Let's take a real problem: The machines designed to pick tomatoes are damaging the tomatoes. What should we do? If we represent the problem as a faulty machine design, then the goal is to improve the machine. But if we represent the problem as a faulty design of the tomatoes, then the goal is to develop a tougher tomato. The problem-solving process follows two entirely different paths, depending on which representation and goal are chosen (Bransford & Stein, 1993). To represent the problem and set a goal, you have to *focus attention* on relevant information, *understand* the words of the problem, and *activate the right schema* to understand the whole problem.

If you have black socks and white socks in your drawer, mixed in the ratio of four to five, how many socks will you have to take out to make sure of having a pair the same color (adapted from Sternberg & Davidson, 1982)?

Focusing Attention. Representing the problem often requires finding the relevant information and ignoring the irrelevant details. For example, what information was relevant in solving the above sock problem? Did you realize that the information about the four-to-five ratio of black socks to white socks is irrelevant? As long as you have only two different colors of socks in the drawer, you will have to remove only three socks before two of them have to match.

Understanding the Words. The second task in representing a story problem is understanding the meaning of the words and sentences (Mayer, 1983a, 1983b, 1992). For example, the main stumbling block in representing many word problems is the students' understanding of *part-whole relations* (Cummins, 1991). Students have trouble figuring out what is part of what, as is evident in this dialogue between a teacher and a 1st grader:

Teacher: Pete has three apples. Ann also has some apples. Pete and Ann have nine apples altogether. How many apples does Ann have?

CONNECT & EXTEND

TO OTHER CHAPTERS

Piaget (Chapter 2) identified children's difficulties with part-whole relations years ago when he asked questions such as, "There are six daisies and two daffodils; are there more daisies or flowers?" Young children usually answer, "Daisies!"

Student: Nine.

Teacher: Why?

Student: Because you just said so.

Teacher: Can you retell the story?

Student: Pete had three apples. Ann also had some apples. Ann had nine apples. Pete also has nine apples. (Adapted from De Corte & Verschaffel, 1985, p. 19)

The student interprets "altogether" (the whole) as "each" (the parts).

Understanding the Whole Problem. The third task in representing a problem is to assemble all the relevant information and sentences into an accurate understanding or translation of the total problem. Even if you understand every sentence, you may still misunderstand the problem as a whole. Consider this example.

Two train stations are 50 miles apart. At 2 P.M. one Saturday afternoon, two trains start toward each other, one from each station. Just as the trains pull out of the stations, a bird springs into the air in front of the first train and flies ahead to the front of the second train. When the bird reaches the second train it turns back and flies toward the first train. The bird continues to do this until the trains meet. If both trains travel at the rate of 25 miles per hour and the bird flies at 100 miles per hour, how many miles will the bird have flown before the trains meet? (Posner, 1973)

Your interpretation of the problem is called a *translation* because you translate the problem into a schema that you understand. If you translate this as a *distance* problem and set a goal ("I have to figure out how far the bird travels before it meets the oncoming train and turns around, then how far it travels before it has to turn again, and finally add up all the trips back and forth . . ."), then you have a very difficult task on your hands. But there is a better way to structure the problem. You can represent it as a question of *time* and focus on the time the bird is in the air. The solution could be stated like this:

> The trains are going the same speed so they will meet in the middle, 25 miles from each station. This will take *one hour* because they are traveling 25 mph. In an hour, the bird will cover 100 miles because it is flying at 100 miles per hour. Easy!

Research shows that students can be too quick to decide what a problem is asking. Once a problem is categorized—"Aha, it's a distance problem!"—a particular schema is activated. The schema directs attention to relevant information and sets up expectations for what the right answer should look like (Kalyuga, Chandler, Tuovinen, & Sweller, 2001; Reimann & Chi, 1989).

When students lack the necessary schemas to represent problems, they often rely on surface features of the situation and represent the problem incorrectly, like the student who wrote "15 + 24 = 39" as the answer to, "Joan has 15 bonus points and Louise has 24. How many more does Louise have?" This student saw two numbers and the word "more," so he applied the *add to get more* procedure. When students use the wrong schema, they overlook critical information, use irrelevant information, and may even misread or misremember critical information so that it fits the schema. But when students use the proper schema to represent a problem, they are less likely to be confused by irrelevant information or tricky wording, such as *more* in a problem that really requires *subtraction* (Resnick, 1981). Figure 8.4 gives examples of different ways students might represent a simple mathematics problem.

Translation and Schema Training. How can students improve translation and schema selection? To answer this question, we often have to move from general to area-specific problem-solving strategies because schemas are specific to content areas. In mathematics, for example, it appears that students benefit from seeing many

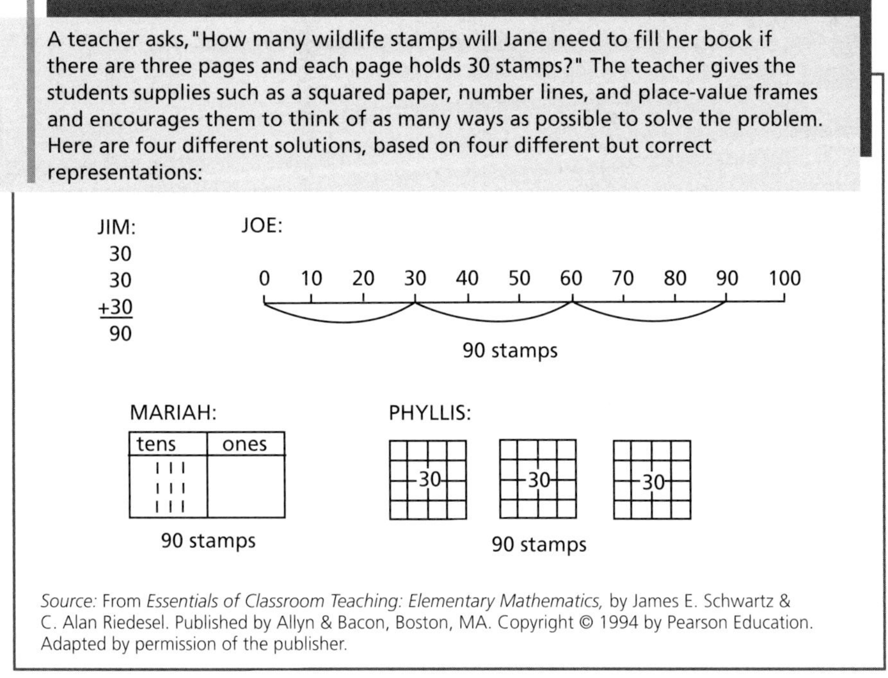

A teacher asks, "How many wildlife stamps will Jane need to fill her book if there are three pages and each page holds 30 stamps?" The teacher gives the students supplies such as a squared paper, number lines, and place-value frames and encourages them to think of as many ways as possible to solve the problem. Here are four different solutions, based on four different but correct representations:
JIM:
30
30
+30
90
JOE:
0 10 20 30 40 50 60 70 80 90 100
90 stamps
MARIAH:
tens
ones
90 stamps
PHYLLIS:
30
30
30
90 stamps

Source: From *Essentials of Classroom Teaching: Elementary Mathematics,* by James E. Schwartz & C. Alan Riedesel. Published by Allyn & Bacon, Boston, MA. Copyright © 1994 by Pearson Education. Adapted by permission of the publisher.

Figure 8.4 Four Different Ways to Represent a Problem

different kinds of example problems worked out correctly for them. The common practice of showing students a few examples, then having students work many problems on their own, is less effective. Especially when problems are unfamiliar or difficult and when students have less knowledge, worked-out examples are helpful (Cooper & Sweller, 1987). When students are learning, worked examples should deal with one source of information at a time (Marcus, Cooper, & Sweller, 1996). Ask students to compare examples. What is the same about each solution? What is different? Why?

The same procedures may be effective in areas other than mathematics. Adrienne Lee and Laura Hutchinson (1998) found that undergraduate students learned more when they had examples of chemistry problem solutions that were annotated to show an expert problem solver's thinking at critical steps. In Australia, Slava Kalyuga et al. (2001) found that worked examples helped apprentices to learn about electrical circuits when the apprentices had less experience in the area. Asking students to reflect on the examples helped too; thus both explanation and reflection can make worked examples more effective.

How else might students develop the schemas they will need to represent problems in a particular subject area? Mayer (1983b) has recommended giving students practice in the following: (1) recognizing and categorizing a variety of problem types; (2) representing problems—either concretely in pictures, symbols, or graphs, or in words; and (3) selecting relevant and irrelevant information in problems.

The Results of Problem Representation. There are two main outcomes of the problem representation stage of problem solving, as shown in Figure 8.5 on page 288. If your representation of the problem suggests an immediate solution, your task is done. In one sense, you haven't really solved a new problem, you have simply recognized the new problem as a "disguised" version of an old problem that you already know how to solve. This has been called **schema-driven problem solving.** In terms of Figure 8.5, you have taken the *schema-activated route* and have proceeded directly to a solution. But what if you have no existing way of solving the problem or if your activated schema fails? Time to search for a solution!

Schema-driven problem solving Recognizing a problem as a "disguised" version of an old problem for which one already has a solution.

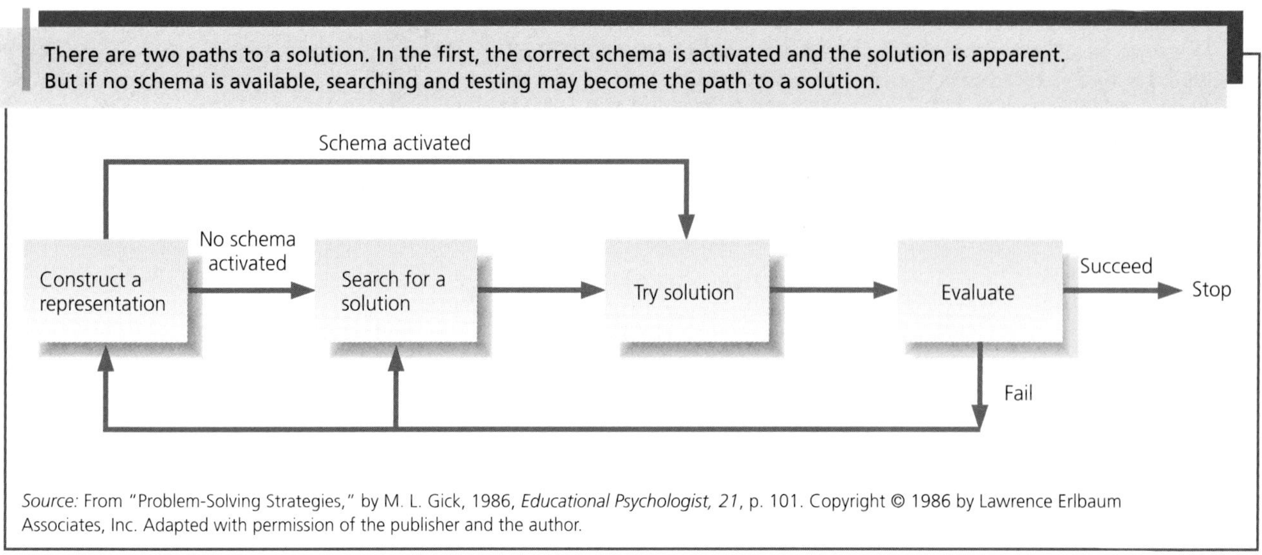
There are two paths to a solution. In the first, the correct schema is activated and the solution is apparent. But if no schema is available, searching and testing may become the path to a solution.
Schema activated
No schema activated
Construct a representation
Search for a solution
Try solution
Evaluate
Succeed
Stop
Fail
Source: From "Problem-Solving Strategies," by M. L. Gick, 1986, Educational Psychologist, 21, p. 101. Copyright © 1986 by Lawrence Erlbaum Associates, Inc. Adapted with permission of the publisher and the author.

Figure 8.5 Diagram of the Problem-Solving Process

Exploring Possible Solution Strategies

If you do not have existing schemas that suggest an immediate solution, then you must take the *search-based route* indicated in Figure 8.5. Obviously, this path is not as efficient as activating the right schema, but sometimes it is the only way. In conducting your search for a solution, you have available two general kinds of procedures: algorithmic and heuristic.

Algorithms. An **algorithm** is a step-by-step prescription for achieving a goal. It usually is domain-specific; that is, it is tied to a particular subject area. In solving a problem, if you choose an appropriate algorithm and implement it properly, a right answer is guaranteed. Unfortunately, students often apply algorithms haphazardly. They try first this, then that. They may even happen on the right answer, but not understand how they found it. For some students, applying algorithms haphazardly could be an indication that formal operational thinking and the ability to work through a set of possibilities systematically, as described by Piaget, is not yet developed.

Many problems cannot be solved by algorithms. What then?

Heuristics. A **heuristic** is a general strategy that might lead to the right answer. Because many of life's problems (careers, relationships, etc.) are not straightforward and have ill-defined problem statements and no apparent algorithms, the discovery or development of effective heuristics is important (Korf, 1999). Let's examine a few.

In **means-ends analysis,** the problem is divided into a number of intermediate goals or subgoals and then a means of solving each intermediate subgoal is figured out. For example, writing a 20-page term paper can loom as an insurmountable problem for some students. They would be better off breaking this task into several intermediate goals, such as selecting a topic, locating sources of information, reading and organizing the information, making an outline, and so on. As they attack a particular intermediate goal, they may find that other goals arise. For example, locating information may require that they find someone to refresh their memory about using the library computer search system. Keep in mind that psychologists have yet to discover an effective heuristic for students who are just starting their term paper the night before it is due.

A second aspect of means-ends analysis is *distance reduction,* or pursuing a path that moves directly toward the final goal. People tend to look for the biggest differ-

Algorithm Step-by-step procedure for solving a problem; prescription for solutions.

Heuristic General strategy used in attempting to solve problems.

Means-ends analysis Heuristic in which a goal is divided into subgoals.

Working-backward strategy Heuristic in which one starts with the goal and moves backward to solve the problem.

Analogical thinking Heuristic in which one limits the search for solutions to situations that are similar to the one at hand.

Verbalization Putting your problem-solving plan and its logic into words.

ence between the current state of affairs and the goal and then search for a strategy that reduces the difference. We resist taking detours or making moves that are indirect as we search for the quickest way to reach the goal. So when you realize that reaching the goal of completing a term paper may require a detour of relearning the library computer search system, you may resist at first because you are not moving directly and quickly toward the final goal (Anderson, 1993).

Some problems lend themselves to a **working-backward strategy,** in which you begin at the goal and move back to the unsolved initial problem. Working backward is sometimes an effective heuristic for solving geometry proofs. It can also be a good way to set intermediate deadlines ("Let's see, if I have to submit this chapter in three weeks, then it has to be in the mail by the 28th, so I should have a first draft by the 11th").

Another useful heuristic is **analogical thinking** (Copi, 1961), which limits your search for solutions to situations that have something in common with the one you currently face. When submarines were first designed, for example, engineers had to figure out how battleships could determine the presence and location of vessels hidden in the depths of the sea. Studying how bats solve an analogous problem of navigating in the dark led to the invention of sonar.

One of the advantages of having students work in groups in problem-solving situations is that they will be called on to explain their proposed solutions to one another. Putting solutions into words usually improves problem solving.

Analogical reasoning can lead to faulty problem solving too. When they were first learning to use a word processor, some people used the analogy of the typewriter and failed to take advantage of the features of a computer. It seems that people need knowledge in both the problem domain and the analogy domain in order to use an analogy effectively (Gagné, Yekovich, & Yekovich, 1993).

Putting your problem-solving plan into words and giving reasons for selecting it can lead to successful problem solving (Cooper & Sweller, 1987; Lee & Hutchinson, 1998). You may have discovered the effectiveness of this **verbalization** process accidentally, when a solution popped into your head as you were explaining a problem to someone else.

Anticipating, Acting, and Looking Back

What Would You Say? You are interviewing with chair of the department. She asks, "What do you think about letting students use calculators and spell checkers? Do you think this is making learning too easy?"

After representing the problem and exploring possible solutions, the next step is to select a solution and *anticipate the consequences.* For example, if you decide to solve the damaged tomato problem by developing a tougher tomato, how will consumers react? If you take time to learn a new graphics program to enhance your term paper (and your grade), will you still have enough time to finish the paper?

After you choose a solution strategy and implement it, evaluate the results by checking for evidence that confirms or contradicts your solution. Many people tend to stop working before reaching the best solution and simply accept an answer that works in some cases. In mathematical problems, evaluating the answer might mean applying a checking routine, such as adding to check the result of a subtraction problem or, in a long addition problem, adding the column from bottom to top instead of top to bottom. Another possibility is estimating the answer. For example, if the computation was 11×21, the answer should be around 200, because 10×20 is 200. A student who reaches an answer of 2,311 or 23 or 562 should quickly realize these answers cannot be correct. Estimating an answer is particularly important when students rely on calculators or computers, because they cannot go back and spot an error in the figures. See the *Point/Counterpoint* on page 290 for opinions on the use of technology in checking answers.

CONNECT & EXTEND

TO YOUR TEACHING/PORTFOLIO

Guidelines for encouraging problem solving in children:

1. Provide problems, not just solutions.
2. Encourage viewing problems from different angles.
3. Make sure students have necessary background information.
4. Make sure students understand the problem.
   - Make accurate and useful representation.
   - Math: ensure linguistic comprehension, use problem schemas.
   - Understand through associations and analogies.
5. Help students tackle the problem systematically.
   - Verbalize
   - Describe and compare.
   - Practice with worked-out examples.
   - Watch for "bugs" in math.

Point/Counterpoint

Should Students Be Allowed to Use Calculators and Spell Checkers?

Not all educators believe that teachers should allow students to use calculators and other technical tools for performing operations and proofing work.

Point

Calculators and spell checkers are crutches that harm learning.

When I polled my graduate class[1] of experienced teachers and principals, I got some opinions such as: "When students are given calculators to do math in the early grades, most of them never learn rudimentary mathematical concepts; they only learn to use the calculator" and "To learn math, students need repetition and practice on the concepts to remember the operations—calculators get in the way." In a summary of the issue online, Nancy Ayres (http://www.math.twsu.edu/history/topics/calculators.html#calc) noted, "David Gelernter, professor of computer science at Yale University, believes calculators should be totally eliminated from the classroom. He feels that allowing children to use calculators produces adults who can't do basic arithmetic, doomed to wander through life in a numeric haze. In 1997, California legislation would prohibit the use of calculators in schools prior to the sixth grade. Whereas, the state of Virginia purchased 200,000 graphing calculators to be used by all middle school and high school math students." In terms of word processing, results of the 1997 National Assessment of Educational Progress (1997) indicated that even though the use of word processors by 11th graders increased from 19% in 1984 to 96%, the average writing scores of 11th graders declined during those years.

Counterpoint

Calculators and spell checkers support learning.

Just because students learned mathematics in the past with paper-and-pencil procedures and practice does not mean that this is the best way to learn. Today, we have to consider each teaching situation on a case-by-case basis to determine if paper-and-pencil procedures or technology or some combination provides the best way to learn (Waits & Demana, 2000). For example, in the Third International Mathematics and Science Study (TIMSS, 1998), on every test at the advanced level, students who said that they used calculators in their daily math coursework performed much better than students who rarely or never used calculators. In fact, rather than eroding basic skills, the research on calculators over the past decade has found that using calculators has positive effects on students' problem solving skills and attitudes toward math (Waits & Demana, 2000).

What about word processors and spelling checkers? Pricilla Norton and Debra Sprague (2001) suggest that "no other technology resource has had as great an impact on education as word processing" (p. 78). They list the following effects: Word processing enhances learners' perceptions of themselves as "real" writers, lets students reflect on the thinking that goes on behind the writing, facilitates collaborative writing, and helps students be more critical and creative in their writing. In my class, an advisor working with undergraduate engineering students pointed out another plus for technology: "We have many international students who have an average to good command of English. . . . In my opinion, they need Spellcheck to catch the errors as well as to 'teach' them the corrected form. Spellcheck is at times a nuisance to us by questioning everything, but I think it's very helpful to ESL students and for general proofreading purposes."

What do you think? Vote online at **www.ablongman.com/woolfolk**

[1]Thanks to Ohio State students Debbie Lanam and Charles Page for sharing their ideas.

Factors That Hinder Problem Solving

STOP THINK WRITE You enter a room. There are two ropes suspended from the ceiling. You are asked by the experimenter to tie the two ends of the ropes together and are assured that the task is possible. On a nearby table are a few tools, including a hammer and pliers. You grab the end of one of the ropes and walk toward the other rope. You immediately realize that you cannot possibly reach the end of the other rope. You try to extend your reach using the pliers but still cannot grasp the other rope. What can you do? (Maier, 1933)

CONNECT & EXTEND

TO YOUR TEACHING/PORTFOLIO
A student was given the problem "Find the value of x and y that solves both equations":

$$8x + 4y = 28 \quad 4x + 2y = 10$$

The student quickly responded $x = 2$, $y = 3$, correctly addressing the first problem, but neglecting to check the solution on the second. How could you help the student be more reflective?

Functional Fixedness. This problem can be solved by using an object in an unconventional way. If you tie the hammer or the pliers to the end of one rope and start swinging it like a pendulum, you will be able to catch it while you are standing across the room holding the other rope, as shown in Figure 8.6. You can use the weight of

In the two-string problem, the subject must set one string in motion in order to tie both strings together.

Figure 8.6 Overcoming Functional Fixedness

the tool to make the rope come to you instead of trying to stretch the rope. People often fail to solve this problem, because they seldom consider unconventional uses for materials that have a specific function. This difficulty is called **functional fixedness** (Duncker, 1945). Problem solving requires seeing things in new ways. In your everyday life, you may often exhibit functional fixedness. Suppose a screw on a dresser-drawer handle is loose. Will you spend 10 minutes searching for a screwdriver? Or will you think to use another object not necessarily designed for this function, such as a ruler edge or a dime to fix it?

Response Set. Another block to effective problem solving is **response set.**

In each of the four matchstick arrangements below, move only one stick to change the equation so that it represents a true equality such as V = V.

V = VII   VI = XI   XII = VII   VI = II

You probably figured out how to solve the first example quite quickly. You simply move one matchstick from the right side over to the left to make VI = VI. Examples two and three can also be solved without too much difficulty by moving one stick to change the V to an X or vice versa. But the fourth example (taken from Raudsepp & Haugh, 1977) probably has you stumped. To solve this problem you must change your response set or switch schemas, because what has worked for the first three problems will not work this time. The answer here lies in changing from Roman numerals to Arabic numbers and using the concept of square root. By overcoming response set, you can move one matchstick from the right to the left to form the symbol for square root; the solution reads $\sqrt{1} = 1$, which is simply the symbolic way of saying that the square root of 1 equals 1.

The Importance of Flexibility. Functional fixedness and response set point to the importance of flexibility in understanding problems. If you get started with an inaccurate or inefficient representation of the true problem, it will be difficult—or at least very time-consuming—to reach a solution (Wessells, 1982). Sometimes it is helpful to "play" with the problem. Ask yourself: "What do I know? What do I need to know to answer this question? Can I look at this problem in other ways?" Try to think conditionally rather than rigidly and divergently rather than convergently. Ask, "What could this be?" instead of "What is it?" (Benjafield, 1992).

Functional fixedness Inability to use objects or tools in a new way.

Response set Rigidity; tendency to respond in the most familiar way.

CONNECT & EXTEND

TO YOUR TEACHING/PORTFOLIO
The following five heuristics that might help students solve college math problems are from Schoenfeld, A. H. (1979). Explicit heuristic training as a variable in problem solving performance. *Journal for Research in Mathematics Education, 10,* 173–187.

1. Draw a diagram, if possible.
2. If the problem has an "N" that takes on integer values, try substituting numbers such as 1, then 2, then 3, then 4 for the "N," and look for a pattern in the results.
3. If you are trying to prove a statement, for example, "If X is true, then Y is true," try proving the contrapositive, "If X is false, then Y is false," or try assuming the statement you want to prove is false and look for a contradiction.
4. Try solving a similar problem with fewer variables.
5. Try to set up subgoals.

Insight Sudden realization of a solution.

If you open your mind to multiple possibilities, you may have what the Gestalt psychologists called an insight. **Insight** is the sudden reorganization or reconceptualization of a problem that clarifies the problem and suggests a feasible solution. The supervisor described earlier, who suddenly realized that the problem in his building was not slow elevators but impatient, bored tenants, had an insight that allowed him to reach the solution of installing mirrors by the elevators.

Effective Problem Solving: What Do the Experts Do?

Most psychologists agree that effective problem solving is based on an ample store of knowledge about the problem area. In order to solve the matchstick problem, for example, you had to understand Roman and Arabic numbers as well as the concept of square root. You also had to know that the square root of 1 is 1. Let's take a moment to examine this expert knowledge.

Expert Knowledge. The modern study of expertise began with investigations of chess masters (Simon & Chase, 1973). Results indicated that masters can quickly recognize about 50,000 different arrangements of chess pieces. They can look at one of these patterns for a few seconds and remember where every piece on the board was placed. It is as though they have a "vocabulary" of 50,000 patterns. Michelene Chi (1978) demonstrated that 3rd- through 8th-grade chess experts had a similar ability to remember chess piece arrangements. For all the masters, patterns of pieces are like words. If you were shown any word from your vocabulary store for just a few seconds, you would be able to remember every letter in the word in the right order (assuming you could spell the word).

But a series of letters arranged randomly is hard to remember, as you saw in Chapter 7. An analogous situation holds for chess masters. When chess pieces are placed on a board randomly, masters are no better than average players at remembering the positions of the pieces. The master's memory is for patterns that make sense or could occur in a game.

A similar phenomenon occurs in other fields. There may be an intuition about how to solve a problem based on recognizing patterns and knowing the "right moves" for those patterns. Experts in physics, for example, organize their knowledge around central principles, whereas beginners organize their smaller amounts of physics

Experts have a rich store of declarative, procedural, and conditional knowledge. While basic intelligence is certainly a factor, hard work and practice are also required to become an expert in any given field.

knowledge around the specific details stated in the problems (Ericsson, 1999). For instance, when asked to sort physics problems from a textbook in any way they wanted, novices sorted based on superficial features such as the kind of apparatus mentioned—a lever or a pulley—whereas the experts grouped problems according to the underlying physics principle needed to solve the problem, such as Boyle's or Newton's laws (Hardiman, Dufresne, & Mestre, 1989).

In addition to representing a problem very quickly, experts know what to do next. They have a large store of productions or condition-action schemas about what action to take in various situations. Thus, the steps of understanding the problem and choosing a solution happen simultaneously and fairly automatically (Ericsson & Charness, 1999). Of course, this means that they must have many, many schemas available. A large part of becoming an expert is simply acquiring a great store of *domain knowledge* or knowledge that is particular to a field (Alexander, 1992). To do this, you must encounter many different kinds of problems in that field, see problems solved by others, and practice solving many yourself. Some estimates are that it takes 10 years or 10,000 hours of study to become an expert in most fields (Simon, 1995).

Experts' rich store of knowledge is *elaborated* and *well practiced,* so that it is easy to retrieve from long-term memory when needed (Anderson, 1993). Experts can use their extensive knowledge to *organize* information for easier learning and retrieval. Compared to 4th-graders with little knowledge of soccer, 4th-graders who were soccer experts learned and remembered far more new soccer terms, even though the abilities of the two groups to learn and remember nonsoccer terms were the same. The soccer experts organized and clustered the soccer terms to aid in recall (Schneider & Bjorklund, 1992). Even very young children who are experts on a topic can use strategies to organize their knowledge. To get an example of the use of category knowledge about dinosaurs, I called my nephews, Lucas and Geoffrey (4 and 3 years old at the time). They promptly ran down the list of large and small plant- and meat-eating dinosaurs (their organizing categories), from the well-known stegosaurus (large, plant eater) to the less familiar ceolophysis (small, meat eater).

With organization comes planning and monitoring. Experts spend more time analyzing problems, drawing diagrams, breaking large problems down into subproblems, and making plans. Whereas a novice might begin immediately—writing equations for a physics problem or drafting the first paragraph of a paper, experts plan out the whole solution and often make the task simpler in the process. As they work, experts monitor progress, so time is not lost pursuing dead ends or weak ideas (Gagné et al., 1993).

Chi, Glaser, and Farr (1988) summarize the superior capabilities of experts. Experts (1) perceive large, meaningful patterns in given information, (2) perform tasks quickly and with few errors, (3) deal with problems at a deeper level, (4) hold more information in working and long-term memories, (5) take a great deal of time to analyze a given problem, and (6) are better at monitoring their performance. When the area of problem solving is fairly well defined, such as chess or physics or computer programming, then these skills of expert problem solvers hold fairly consistently. But when the problem-solving area is less well defined and has fewer clear underlying principles, such as problem solving in economics or psychology, then the differences between experts and novices are not as clear-cut (Alexander, 1992).

Novice Knowledge. Studies of the differences between experts and novices in particular areas have revealed some surprising things about how novices understand and misunderstand a subject. Physics again provides many examples. Most beginners approach physics with a great deal of misinformation, partly because many of their intuitive ideas about the physical world are wrong. Most elementary school children believe that light helps us see by brightening the area around objects. They do not realize that we see an object because the light is reflected by the object to our eyes. This concept does not fit with the everyday experience of turning on a light and "brightening" the dark area. Researchers from the Elementary Science Project at Michigan State University found that even after completing a unit on light in which

CONNECT & EXTEND

TO YOUR TEACHING/PORTFOLIO
Brainstorm about intuitive models in other fields besides science and mathematics. What are some common misconceptions about cultural differences, history, government, or educational psychology?

GUIDELINES Problem Solving

Ask students if they are sure they understand the problem.

Examples

1. Can they separate relevant from irrelevant information?
2. Are they aware of the assumptions they are making?
3. Encourage them to visualize the problem by diagramming or drawing it.
4. Ask them to explain the problem to someone else. What would a good solution look like?

Encourage attempts to see the problem from different angles.

Examples

1. Suggest several different possibilities yourself, and then ask students to offer some.
2. Give students practice in taking and defending different points of view on an issue.

Help students develop systematic ways of considering alternatives.

Examples

1. Think out loud as you solve problems.
2. Ask, "What would happen if . . . ?"
3. Keep a list of suggestions.

Teach heuristics.

Examples

1. Ask students to explain the steps they take as they solve problems.
2. Use analogies to solve the problem of limited parking in the downtown area. How are other "storage" problems solved?
3. Use the working backward strategy to plan a party.

Let students do the thinking; don't just hand them solutions.

Examples

1. Offer individual problems as well as group problems, so that each student has the chance to practice.
2. Give partial credit if students have good reasons for "wrong" solutions to problems.
3. If students are stuck, resist the temptation to give too many clues. Let them think about the problem overnight.

materials explicitly stated the idea of reflected light and vision, most 5th-grade students—about 78%—continued to cling to their intuitive notions. But when new materials were designed that directly confronted the students' misconceptions, only about 20% of the students failed to understand (Eaton, Anderson, & Smith, 1984).

It seems quite important for science teachers to understand their students' intuitive models of basic concepts. If the students' intuitive model includes misconceptions and inaccuracies, then the students are likely to develop inadequate or misleading representations of a problem. (You should note that some researchers don't use the term "misconception," but refer to *naïve* or *intuitive conceptions* to describe students' beginning knowledge in an area.) In order to learn new information and solve problems, students must sometimes "unlearn" common-sense ideas (Joshua & Dupin, 1987). Changing your intuitive ideas about concepts involves motivation too. Pintrich, Marx, and Boyle (1993) suggest that four conditions are necessary for people to change basic concepts: (1) Students have to be dissatisfied with the current concept; that is, their existing concept must be seen as inaccurate, incomplete, or not useful. (2) Students must understand the new concept. (3) The new concept must be plausible—it must fit in with what the students already know. (4) The new concept must be fruitful—it must be seen as useful in solving problems or answering questions.

The *Guidelines* above give some ideas for helping students become expert problem solvers.

Check Yourself What are the steps in the general problem-solving process?

Why is the representation stage of problem solving so important?

Describe factors that can interfere with problem solving.

What are the differences between expert and novice knowledge in a given area?

How do misconceptions interfere with learning?

Enhancing Your Expertise with Technology

Problem Solving

If you look at the teacher's guide for any recently developed mathematics or science program, you are certain to see a pair of words: problem solving. (And you will see this pairing often.) This encounter between you and these two words is not by chance. Forces and innovations in our culture are often reflected in school curricula. Changes in the nature of work and business, the potential benefits of emerging technologies, and research in psychology have increased the press on teachers, beginning as early as preschool, to nurture the inquiry and problem-solving skills of their students in all academic areas.

Problem solving, of course, is far more than a mere term. Early in this chapter's section on problem solving I noted that there is a major debate about whether effective problem solving strategies are general or domain-specific, and we examined one general solving approach, IDEAL, in detail. In order to develop your expertise in the area of problem solving, it would be useful to examine problem solving in more detail from a domain-specific perspective—or more accurately from two domains. Mathematics and science are domains in which educational psychologists have extensively researched basic processes of problem solving, and teachers have traditionally designed strategies to enhance problem-solving skills in these areas.

The Eisenhower National Clearinghouse (ENC) (http://www.enc.org/topics/inquiry/) provides rich sets of resources and information about problem solving in mathematics and science. When you reach its home page, you will notice that problem solving is one of the major sections of the site. As you navigate through that section, you might find it refreshing to see that the clearinghouse incorporates knowledge from two major sources: practitioners (i.e., expert teachers) and researchers (i.e., educational psychologists).

As you grow in expertise as teacher, you will see the interrelated nature of various areas of educational psychology. The ENC section about problem solving illustrates that point well. There you will find articles and information about problem solving and the following areas:

questioning techniques
problem-based learning
peer learning
creativity
thematic units
communities of learners
student discourse
learning with technology

A visit to the ENC Web site should be valuable to you whether you are interested in mathematics, science, or any other major discipline. Problem solving is not the sole domain of mathematics and science educators, of course. Each discipline has unique contributions to make toward solving the problems of contemporary life.

Becoming an Expert Student: Learning Strategies and Study Skills

What Would You Say? As part of your interview, the department chair asks, "Many of our students go on to high-pressure colleges and don't seem to know how to study when they don't have daily homework deadlines. How would you help them prepare to handle the heavy work load in those institutions?"

Most teachers will tell you that they want their students to "learn how to learn." Years of research indicate that using good learning strategies helps students learn and that these strategies can be taught (Hamman, Berthelot, Saia, & Crowley, 2000). But were you taught "how to learn"? Powerful and sophisticated learning strategies and study skills are seldom taught directly until high school or even college, so students have little practice with these powerful strategies. In contrast, early on students usually discover repetition and rote learning on their own, so they have extensive practice with these strategies. And, unfortunately, some teacher think that memorizing is learning (Hofer & Pintrich, 1997; Woolfolk Hoy & Murphy, 2001). This may explain why many students cling to flash cards and memorizing—they don't know what else to do to learn (Willoughby, Porter, Belsito, & Yearsley, 1999).

As we saw in Chapter 7, the way something is learned in the first place greatly influences how readily we remember and how appropriately we can apply the

CONNECT & EXTEND

TO THE RESEARCH

Willoughby, T., Porter, L., Belsito, L., & Yearsley, T. (1999). Use of elaboration strategies by grades two, four, and six. *Elementary School Journal, 99,* 221–231.

This study tested the effectiveness of verbal elaboration (answer why each fact is true), imagery (create a metal picture), and keyword (create a mental picture using the keywords provided) in helping 2nd, 4th, and 6th grade Canadian students remember information from stories. Verbal elaboration worked for all three grades, especially when the students had some prior knowledge related to the stories. Imagery was more helpful than elaborations for older students when the students lacked prior knowledge about the story content, but 2nd graders needed support to use imagery.

knowledge later. First, students must be *cognitively engaged* in order to learn—they have to focus attention on the relevant or important aspects of the material. Second, they have to *invest effort,* make connections, elaborate, translate, organize, and reorganize in order to *think and process deeply*—the greater the practice and processing, the stronger the learning. Finally, students must *regulate and monitor* their own learning—keep track of what is making sense and notice when a new approach is needed. The emphasis today is on helping students develop effective learning strategies and tactics that *focus attention and effort, process information deeply,* and *monitor understanding.* Some students will develop good strategies for organizing and learning on their own, but most need help.

CONNECT & EXTEND

TO **PRAXIS**™
LEARNING STRATEGIES (I, A1)
For suggestions about their effective use, take a look the study skills site developed by the Virginia Polytechnic Institute (http://www.ucc.vt.edu/stdysk/stdyhlp.html).

Learning Strategies and Tactics

Learning strategies are ideas for accomplishing learning goals, a kind of overall plan of attack. **Learning tactics** are the specific techniques that make up the plan (Derry, 1989). Your strategy for learning the material in this chapter might include the tactics of using mnemonics to remember key terms, skimming the chapter to identify the organization, and then writing answers to possible essay questions. Your use of strategies and tactics reflects metacognitive knowledge. Researchers have identified several important principles:

CONNECT & EXTEND

TO OTHER CHAPTERS
- The guidelines for study skills apply to everyone who wishes to become an expert learner and involve the metacognitive abilities and executive control processes discussed in Chapter 7.
- See Chapter 7 for a discussion of declarative, procedural, and conditional knowledge.

1. Students must be exposed to a number of *different strategies,* not only general learning strategies but also very specific tactics, such as the graphic strategies described later in this chapter.

2. Students should be taught *conditional knowledge* about when, where, and why to use various strategies (Pressley, 1986). Although this may seem obvious, teachers often neglect this step. A strategy is more likely to be maintained and employed if students know when, where, and why to use it.

3. Students may know when and how to use a strategy, but unless they also *develop the desire to employ these skills,* general learning ability will not improve. Several learning strategy programs (Borkowski, Johnston, & Reid, 1986; Dansereau, 1985) include a motivational training component. In Chapter 10 we look more closely at this important issue of motivation.

4. Students should receive *direct instruction in schematic knowledge;* this is often an important component of strategy training. In order to identify main ideas—a critical skill for a number of learning strategies—you must have an appropriate schema for making sense of the material. It will be difficult to summarize a paragraph about ichthyology, for example, if you don't know much about fish. Table 8.2 summarizes several tactics for learning declarative (verbal) knowledge and procedural skills (Derry, 1989).

CONNECT & EXTEND

TO YOUR TEACHING/PORTFOLIO
Weinstein, C., Ridley, D. S., Dahl, T., & Weber, E. S. (1988/1989). Helping students develop strategies for effective learning. *Educational Leadership, 46*(4), 17–19.

Examples of elaboration strategies:
What is the main idea of this story?
If this principle were not true, what would that imply?
What does this remind me of?
How could I use this information in the project I am working on?
How could I represent this in a diagram?
How do I feel about the author's opinion?
How could I put this in my own words?
What might be an example of this?
If I were going to interview the author, what would I ask her?
How does this apply to my life?

Deciding What Is Important. You can see from the first entry in Table 8.2, that learning begins with focusing attention—deciding what is important. But distinguishing the main idea from less important information is not always easy. Often students focus on the "seductive details" or the concrete examples, perhaps because they are more interesting (Dole, Duffy, Roehler, & Pearson, 1991; Gardner, Brown, Sanders, & Menke, 1992). You may have had the experience of remembering a joke or an intriguing example from a lecture, but not being clear about the larger point the professor was trying to make. Finding the central idea is especially difficult if you lack prior knowledge in an area and the amount of new information provided is extensive. Teachers can give students practice using signals in texts such as headings, bold words, outlines, or other indicators to identify key concepts and main ideas. Teaching students to summarize material can be helpful too (Lorch, Lorch, Ritchey, McGovern, & Coleman, 2001).

Summaries. Creating summaries can help students learn, but students have to be taught how to summarize (Byrnes, 1996; Dole et al., 1991; Palincsar & Brown, 1984).

Table 8.2 Examples of Learning Tactics

	Examples	Use When?
Tactics for Learning Verbal Information	1. Attention Focusing	
	■ Making outlines, underlining	With easy, structured materials; for good readers
	■ Looking for headings and topic sentences	For poorer readers; with more difficult materials
	2. Schema Building	
	■ Story grammars	With poor text structure, goal is to encourage active comprehension
	■ Theory schemas	
	■ Networking and mapping	
	3. Idea Elaboration	
	■ Self-questioning	To understand and remember specific ideas
	■ Imagery	
Tactics for Learning Procedural Information	1. Pattern Learning	
	■ Hypothesizing	To learn attributes of concepts
	■ Identifying reasons for actions	To match procedures to situations
	2. Self-instruction	
	■ Comparing own performance to expert model	To tune, improve complex skills
	3. Practice	
	■ Part practice	When few specific aspects of a performance need attention
	■ Whole practice	To maintain and improve skill

SOURCE: Based on "Putting Learning Strategies to Work," by S. Derry, 1989, *Educational Leadership, 47*(5), pp. 5–6.

Jeanne Ormrod (1999, p. 333) summarizes these suggestions for helping students create summaries:

- Begin doing summaries of short, easy, well-organized readings. Introduce longer, less organized, and more difficult passages gradually.
- For each summary, ask students to
  - find or write a *topic sentence* for each paragraph or section,
  - identify *big ideas* that cover several specific points,
  - find some *supporting information* for each big idea, and
  - delete any *redundant information* or unnecessary details.
- Ask students to compare their summaries and discuss what ideas they thought were important and why—what's their evidence?

Two other study strategies that are based on identifying key ideas are *underlining* texts and *taking notes.*

How do you make notes as you read? Look back over the past several pages of this chapter. Are my words highlighted yellow or pink? Are there marks or drawing in the margins and if so, do the notes pertain to the chapter or are they grocery lists and phone numbers?

Underlining and Highlighting. Do you underline or highlight key phrases in textbooks? Underlining and note taking are probably two of the most commonly used strategies among college students. Yet few students receive any instruction in the best ways to take notes or underline, so it is not surprising that many students use ineffective strategies. One common problem is that students underline or highlight too

Learning strategies General plans for approaching learning tasks.

Learning tactics Specific techniques for learning, such as using mnemonics or outlining a passage.

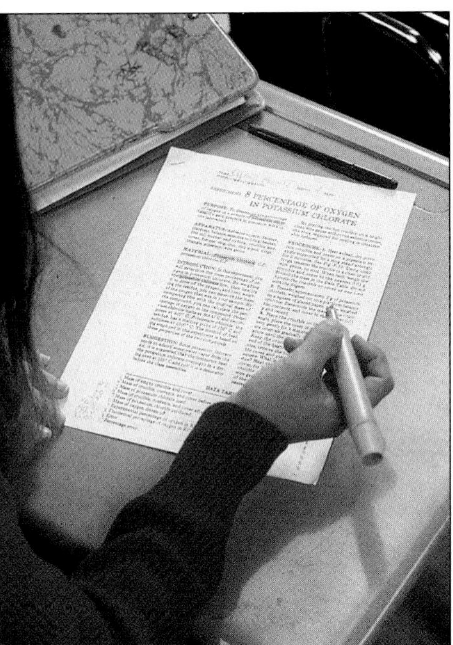

One common problem students have in studying is underlining or highlighting too much. Studies that limit how much students are allowed to highlight correlate this strategy with higher learning.

much. It is far better to be selective. In studies that limit how much students can underline—for example, only one sentence per paragraph—learning has improved (Snowman, 1984). In addition to being selective, you also should actively transform the information into your own words as you underline or take notes. Don't rely on the words of the book. Note connections between what you are reading and other things you already know. Draw diagrams to illustrate relationships. Finally, look for organizational patterns in the material and use them to guide your underlining or note taking (Irwin, 1991; Kiewra, 1988).

Taking Notes. As you sit in class, filling your notebook with words or furiously trying to keep up with a lecturer, you may wonder if taking notes makes a difference. It does, if used well:

- Taking notes focuses attention during class and helps encode information so it has a chance of making it to long-term memory. In order to record key ideas in your own words, you have to translate, connect, elaborate, and organize. Even if students don't review notes before a test, taking them in the first place appears to aid learning, especially for those who lack prior knowledge in an area. Of course, if taking notes distracts you from actually listening to and making sense of the lecture, then note taking may not be effective (DiVesta & Gray, 1972; Kiewra, 1989; Van Meter, Yokoi, & Pressley, 1994).
- Notes provide extended external storage that allows you to return and review. Students who use their notes to study tend to perform better on tests, especially if they take many high quality notes—more is better as long as you are capturing *key ideas, concepts,* and *relationships,* not just intriguing details (Kiewra, 1985, 1989).
- Expert students match notes to their anticipated use and modify strategies after tests or assignments; use personal codes to flag material that is unfamiliar or difficult; fill in holes by consulting relevant sources (including other students in the class); record information verbatim only when a verbatim response will be required. In other words, they are strategic about taking and using notes (Van Meter, Yokoi, & Pressley, 1994).

To help students organize their note taking, some teachers provide matrices or maps. When students are first learning to use these maps, you might fill in some of the spaces for them. If you use maps and matrices with your students, encourage them to exchange their filled-in maps and explain their thinking to each other.

Visual Tools for Organizing

READS A five-step reading strategy: *Review* headings; *Examine* boldface words; *Ask,* "What do I expect to learn?"; *Do* it—Read; *Summarize* in your own words.

PQ4R A method for studying text that involves six steps: *Preview, Question, Read, Reflect, Recite, Review.*

CAPS A strategy that can be used in reading literature: *Characters, Aim* of story, *Problem, Solution.*

KWL A strategy to guide reading and inquiry: Before—What do I already *know?* What do I *want* to know? After—What have I *learned?*

To use underlining and note taking effectively, you must identify main ideas. In addition, effective use of underlining and note taking depends on an understanding of the *organization* of the text or lecture—the connections and relationships among ideas. Some visual strategies have been developed to help students with this key element (Van Meter, 2001). There is some evidence that creating graphic organizers such as maps or charts is more effective than outlining in learning from texts (Robinson, 1998; Robinson & Kiewra, 1995). "Mapping" relationships by noting causal connections, comparison/contrast connections, and examples improved recall. Davidson (1982) suggested that students compare one another's "maps" and discuss the differences. Amy's molecule (Figure 8.2) is a hierarchical graphic depiction of the relationships among concepts. There are other ways to visualize organization such as *Venn diagrams* showing how ideas or concepts overlap or *tree diagrams* showing how ideas branch off each other. Timelines organize information in sequence and are useful in classes such as history or geology.

Reading Strategies

As we saw above, effective learning strategies and tactics should help students focus attention, invest effort (elaborate, organize, summarize, connect, translate) so they process information deeply, and monitor their understanding. There are a number of strategies that support these processes in reading. Many use mnemonics to help students remember the steps involved. For example, one strategy for any grade above later elementary is **READS:**

CONNECT & EXTEND

TO OTHER CHAPTERS
Direct instruction in learning strategies is especially important for students with learning disabilities, as described in Chapter 4.

- **R** *Review* headings and subheadings
- **E** *Examine* boldface words
- **A** *Ask,* "What do I expect to learn?"
- **D** *Do* it—Read!
- **S** *Summarize* in your own words. (Friend & Bursuck, 1996).

READS is similar to a well-known strategy you might have encountered in school, called **PQ4R** (Thomas & Robinson, 1972):

CONNECT & EXTEND

TO THE RESEARCH
See Peterson, D. & Van Der Wege, C. (2002). Guiding children to be strategic readers. *Phi Delta Kappan, 83,* 437–440.

Preview. Survey the major topics and sections and set a purpose for reading.

Question. For each major section, write questions that are related to your reading purposes. One way is to turn the headings and subheadings into questions.

Read. At last! The questions you have formulated can be answered through reading.

Reflect. While you are reading, try to think of examples or create images of the material. Elaborate and try to make connections between what you are reading and what you already know.

Recite. After reading each section, sit back and think about your initial purposes and questions. Can you answer the questions without looking at the book?

Review. Effective review incorporates new material more thoroughly into your long-term memory. As study progresses, review should be cumulative, including the sections and chapters you read previously.

A strategy that can be used in reading literature is **CAPS:**

- **C** Who are the *characters*?
- **A** What is the *aim* of the story?
- **P** What *problem* happens?
- **S** How is the problem *solved*?

Many of the cooperating teachers I work with use a strategy called **KWL** to guide reading and inquiry in general. This general frame can be used with most grade levels. The steps are:

- **K** What do I already *know* about this subject?
- **W** What do I *want* to know?
- **L** At the end of the reading or inquiry, what have I *learned*?

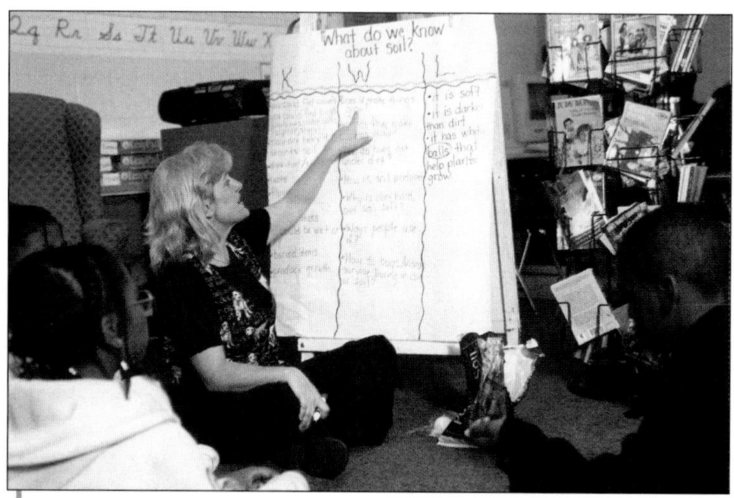

One cooperative learning strategy used by many teachers to guide reading and inquiry is called KWL: What do I know? What do I want to know? What have I learned?

~ *Reaching Every Student* ~

Teaching Them How to Learn

Here is how one teacher used modeling and discussion to teach the KWL strategy. After reviewing the steps, the teacher models an example and a nonexample of using KWL to learn about "crayons."

Teacher: What do we do now that we have a passage assigned to read? First, I brainstorm, which means I try to think of anything I already know about the topic and write it down.

The teacher writes on the board or overhead known qualities of crayons, such as "made of wax," "come in many colors," "can be sharpened," "several different brands."

Teacher: I then take this information I already know and put it into categories, like "what crayons are made of" and "crayon colors." Next, I write down any questions I would like to have answered during my reading, such as "Who invented crayons? When were they invented? How are crayons made? Where are they made?" At this point, I'm ready to read, so I read the passage on crayons. Now I must write down what I learned from this passage. I must include any information that answers the questions I wrote down before I read and any additional information. For example, I learned that colored crayons were first made in the United States in 1903 by Edwin Binney and E. Harold Smith. I also learned that the Crayola Company owns the company that made the original magic markers. Last, I must organize this information into a map so I can see the different main points and any supporting points.

At this point, the teacher draws a map on the chalkboard or overhead.

Teacher: Let's talk about the steps I used and what I did before and after I read the passage.

A class discussion follows.

Teacher: Now I'm going to read the passage again, and I want you to evaluate my textbook reading skills based on the KWL Plus strategy we've learned.

The teacher then proceeds to demonstrate the strategy *incorrectly.*

Teacher: The passage is about crayons. Well, how much can there really be to know about crayons besides there are hundreds of colors and they always seem to break in the middle? Crayons are for little kids, and I'm in junior high so I don't need to know that much about them. I'll just skim the passage and go ahead and answer the question. Okay, how well did I use the strategy steps?

The class discusses the teacher's inappropriate use of the strategy.

SOURCE: From *Including Students with Special Needs: A Practical Guide for Classroom Teachers* (3rd ed.), by Marilyn Friend & William D. Bursick. Published by Allyn & Bacon, Boston, MA. Copyright © 2002 by Pearson Education. Adapted by permission of the publisher.

CONNECT & EXTEND

TO YOUR TEACHING/PORTFOLIO
This teacher uses both examples and nonexamples to teach the concept of KWL. This is consistent with what you learned about teaching concepts earlier in this chapter.

CONNECT & EXTEND

TO YOUR TEACHING/PORTFOLIO
"The greatest enemy of understanding is coverage. As long as you are determined to cover everything, you actually ensure that most kids are not going to understand." Howard Gardner in Brandt, R. (1993). On teaching for understanding: A Conversation with Howard Gardner. *Educational Leadership, 50*(7), 7.

No matter what strategies you use, students have to be taught how to use them. Direct teaching, explanation, modeling, and practice with feedback are necessary. Direct teaching of learning and reading strategies is especially important for students with learning challenges and students whose first language is not English (Friend & Bursuck, 2002). The *Reaching Every Student* feature is an example of teaching the KWL strategy.

Anderson (1995a) suggests several reasons why strategies such as PQ4R or READS are effective. First, following the steps makes students more aware of the organization of a given chapter. How often have you skipped reading headings entirely and thus missed major clues to the way the information was organized? Next, these steps require students to study the chapter in sections instead of trying to learn all the information at once. This makes use of distributed practice. Creating and answering questions about the material forces students to process the information more deeply and with greater elaboration (Doctorow, Wittrock, & Marks, 1978; Hamilton, 1985).

The *Guidelines* on the next page provide a summary of ideas about studying.

Applying Learning Strategies

Assuming students have a repertoire of powerful learning strategies, will they use them? Several conditions must be met (Ormrod, 1999). First, of course, the learning task must be appropriate. Why would students use more complex learning strategies when the task set by the teacher is to "learn and return" the exact words of the text or lecture? Here memorizing will be rewarded and the best strategies involve distributed practice and perhaps mnemonics (described in Chapter 7). But we hope that

GUIDELINES Becoming an Expert Student

Make sure you have the necessary declarative knowledge (facts, concepts, ideas) to understand new information.

Examples

1. Keep definitions of key vocabulary available as you study.
2. Review required facts and concepts before attempting new material.

Find out what type of test the teacher will give (essay, short answer), and study the material with that in mind.

Examples

1. For a test with detailed questions, practice writing answers to possible questions.
2. For a multiple-choice test, use mnemonics to remember definitions of key terms.

Make sure you are familiar with the organization of the materials to be learned.

Examples

1. Preview the headings, introductions, topic sentences, and summaries of the text.
2. Be alert for words and phrases that signal relationships, such as *on the other hand, because, first, second, however, since.*

Know your own cognitive skills and use them deliberately.

Examples

1. Use examples and analogies to relate new material to something you care about and understand well, such as sports, hobbies, or films.
2. If one study technique is not working, try another—the goal is to stay involved, not to use any particular strategy.

Study the right information in the right way.

Examples

1. Be sure you know exactly what topics and readings the test will cover.
2. Spend your time on the important, difficult, and unfamiliar material that will be required for the test or assignment.
3. Keep a list of the parts of the text that give you trouble and spend more time on those pages.
4. Process the important information thoroughly by using mnemonics, forming images, creating examples, answering questions, making notes in your own words, and elaborating on the text. Do not try to memorize the author's words—use your own.

Monitor your own comprehension.

Examples

1. Use questioning to check your understanding.
2. When reading speed slows down, decide if the information in the passage is important. If it is, note the problem so you can reread or get help to understand. If it is not important, ignore it.
3. Check your understanding by working with a friend and quizzing one another.

SOURCE: From "Research Synthesis on Study Skills" by B. B. Armbruster and T. H. Anderson. *Educational Leadership, 39.*

there are few of these kinds of tasks in contemporary teaching, so if the task is understanding, not memorizing, what else is necessary?

Valuing Learning. The second condition for using sophisticated strategies is that students must care about learning and understanding. They must have goals that can be reached using effective strategies (Zimmerman & Schunk, 2001). I was reminded of this one semester when I enthusiastically shared with my educational psychology class an article from the newspaper, *USA Today,* about study skills. The gist of the article was that students should continually revise and rewrite their notes from a course, so that by the end, all their understanding could be captured in one or two pages. Of course, the majority of the knowledge at that point would be reorganized and connected well with other knowledge. "See," I told her class, "these ideas are real—not just trapped in texts. They can help you study smarter in college." After a heated discussion, one of the best students said in exasperation, "I'm carrying 18 hours—I don't have time to *learn* this stuff!" She did not believe that her goal—to survive the 18 hours—could be reached by using time-consuming study strategies.

Effort and Efficacy. The student above also was concerned about effort. The third condition for applying learning strategies is that students must believe the effort and investment required to apply the strategies are *reasonable,* given the likely return

(Winne, 2001). And of course, students must believe that they are capable of using the strategies, that is they must have self-efficacy for using the strategies to learn the material in question (Schunk, 2000). This is related to another condition. Students must have a base of knowledge and/or experience in the area. No learning strategies will help students accomplish tasks that are completely beyond their current understandings.

Epistemological Beliefs. Finally, what students believe about knowledge and learning (their epistemological beliefs) will influence the kinds of strategies that they use.

How would you answer these questions taken from Chan & Sachs (2001)?

1. The most important thing in learning math is to: (a) remember what the teacher has taught you, (b) practice lots of problems, (c) understand the problems you work on.

2. The most important thing you can do when trying to do science is (a) faithfully do the work the teacher tells you, (b) try to see how the explanation makes sense, (c) try to remember everything you are supposed to know.

3. If you wanted to know everything there is about something, say animals, how long would you have to study it? (a) less than a year if you study hard, (b) about one or two years, (c) forever.

4. As you learn more and more about something (a) the questions get more and more complex, (b) the questions get easier and easier, (c) the questions all get answered.

Using questions like those above, researchers have identified several dimensions of epistemological beliefs (Chan & Sachs, 2001; Schommer, 1997; Schommer-Aikins, 2002; Schraw & Olafson, in press). For example:

- *Structure of Knowledge:* Is knowledge in a field a simple set of facts or a complex structure of concepts and relationships?
- *Stability/Certainty of Knowledge:* Is knowledge fixed or evolving over time?
- *Ability to Learn:* Is the ability to learn fixed (based on innate ability) or changeable?
- *Speed of Learning:* Can we gain knowledge quickly or does it take time to develop knowledge?
- *Nature of learning:* Does learning mean memorizing facts passed down from authorities and keeping the facts isolated, or developing your own integrated understandings?

CONNECT & EXTEND

TO THE RESEARCH

Garner, R. (1990). When children and adults do not use learning strategies: Toward a theory of settings. *Review of Educational Research, 60,* 517–530.

Students' beliefs about knowing and learning affect their use of learning strategies. For example, if you believe that knowledge should be gained quickly, you are likely to try one or two quick strategies (read the text once, spend 2 minutes trying to solve the word problem) and then stop. If you believe that learning means developing integrated understandings, you will process the material more deeply, connect to existing knowledge, create your own examples, or draw diagrams, and generally elaborate the information to make it your own (Hofer & Pintrich, 1997; Kardash & Howell, 2000). In one study, elementary school students (grades 4 and 6), who believed that learning is understanding, processed science texts more deeply than students who believed that learning is reproducing facts (Chan & Sachs, 2001). The questions about learning in the *Stop/Think/Write* box above were used in that study to assess the students' beliefs. The answers associated with a belief in complex, evolving, knowledge that takes time to understand and grows from active learning are 1c, 2b, 3c, and 4a.

Check Yourself Distinguish between learning strategies and tactics.

What key functions do learning strategies play?

Describe some procedures for developing learning strategies.

When will students apply learning strategies?

Teaching for Transfer

Think back for a moment to a class in one of your high school subjects that you have not studied college. Imagine the teacher, the room, the textbook. Now remember what you actually learned in class. If it was a science class, what were some of the formulas you learned? Oxidation reduction? Boyle's law?

If you are like most of us, you may remember that you learned these things, but you will not be quite sure exactly what you learned. Were those hours wasted? These questions are about the transfer of learning. We turn to that important topic next. Let's begin with a definition of transfer.

Whenever something previously learned influences current learning or when solving an earlier problem affects how you solve a new problem, **transfer** has occurred (Mayer & Wittrock, 1996). If students learn a mathematical principle in one class and use it to solve a physics problem days or weeks later in another class, then transfer has taken place. However, the effect of past learning on present learning is not always positive. *Functional fixedness* and *response set* (described earlier in this chapter) are examples of negative transfer because they are attempts to apply familiar but *inappropriate* strategies to a new situation.

A Contemporary View of Transfer

Gavriel Salomon and David Perkins (1989) describe two kinds of transfer, termed low-road and high-road transfer. **Low-road transfer** "involves the spontaneous, automatic transfer of highly practiced skills, with little need for reflective thinking" (p. 118). The key to low-road transfer is practicing a skill often, in a variety of situations, until your performance becomes automatic. So if you worked one summer for a temporary secretarial service and were sent to many different offices to work on all kinds of computers, by the end of the summer you probably would be able to handle most machines easily. Your practice with many machines would let you transfer your skill automatically to a new situation.

High-road transfer, on the other hand, involves consciously applying abstract knowledge learned in one situation to a different situation. This can happen in one of two ways. First, you may learn a principle or a strategy, intending to use it in the future—*forward-reaching* transfer. For example, if you plan to apply what you learn in anatomy class this semester to work in a life-drawing course you will take next semester, you may search for principles about human proportions, muscle definition, and so on. Second, when you are faced with a problem, you may look back on what you have learned in other situations to help you in this new one—*backward-reaching* transfer. Analogical thinking is an example of this kind of transfer. You search for other, related situations that might provide clues to the current problem.

The key to high-road transfer is *mindful abstraction,* or the deliberate identification of a principle, main idea, strategy, or procedure that is not tied to one specific problem or situation but could apply to many. Such an abstraction becomes part of your metacognitive knowledge, available to guide future learning and problem solving. Table 8.3 on page 304 summarizes the types of transfer.

Transfer Influence of previously learned material on new material.

Low-road transfer Spontaneous and automatic transfer of highly practiced skills.

High-road transfer Application of abstract knowledge learned in one situation to a different situation.

■ Table 8.3	Kinds of Transfer	
	Low-Road Transfer	**High-Road Transfer**
Definition	Automatic transfer of highly practiced skill	Conscious application of abstract knowledge to a new situation
Key Conditions	Extensive practice Variety of settings and conditions Overlearning to automaticity	Mindful focus on abstracting a principle, main idea, or procedure that can be used in many situations
Examples	Driving many different cars Finding your gate in an airport	Applying PQ4R in reading texts Applying procedures from math in designing a page layout for the school newspaper

CONNECT & EXTEND

TO **PRAXIS**™
TRANSFER OF LEARNING
Successful transfer of learning from the school to other contexts is evidence of superior instruction. What can teachers do to optimize transfer of knowledge and skills to the broader world?

Teaching for Positive Transfer

Years of research and experience show that students will master new knowledge, problem-solving procedures, and learning strategies, but they will not use them unless prompted or guided. For example, studies of real-world mathematics show that people do not always apply math procedures learned in school to solve practical problems in their homes or grocery stores (Lave, 1988; Lave & Wenger, 1991). This happens because learning is *situated,* that is, learning happens in specific situations. We learn solutions to particular problems, not general all-purpose solutions that can fit any problem. Because knowledge is learned as a tool to solve particular problems, we may not realize that the knowledge is relevant when we encounter a problem that seems different, at least on the surface (Driscoll, 2000; Singley & Anderson, 1989). How can you make sure your students will use what they learn, even when situations change?

What Is Worth Learning? First you must answer the question "What is worth learning?" The learning of basic skills such as reading, writing, computing, cooperating, and speaking will definitely transfer to other situations, because these skills are necessary for later work both in and out of school—writing job applications, reading novels, paying bills, working on a team, locating and evaluating health care services, among others. All later learning depends on positive transfer of these basics to new situations.

Teachers must also be aware of what the future is likely to hold for their students, both as a group and as individuals. What will society require of them as adults? As a child growing up in Texas in the 1950s and 1960s, I studied nothing about computers, even though my father was a computer systems analyst; yet now I spend hours at my Mac. Computer programming and word processing were not part of my high school curriculum, but learning to use a slide rule was taught. Now calculators and computers have made this skill obsolete. Undoubtedly changes as extreme and unpredictable as these await the students you will teach. For this reason, the general transfer of principles, attitudes, learning strategies, and problem solving will be just as important to these students as the specific transfer of basic skills.

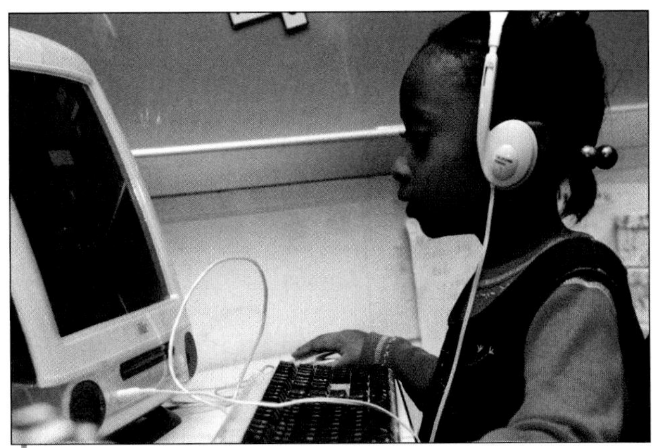

A challenge for all learners and educators is to be sure that knowledge acquired in school will be applicable to real-life situations or problems. Will this girl's technology skills be applicable years from now?

How Can Teachers Help? To have something to transfer, students must first learn and understand. Students will be more likely to transfer information to new situations if they have been actively involved in the learning process. They must be encouraged to form abstrac-

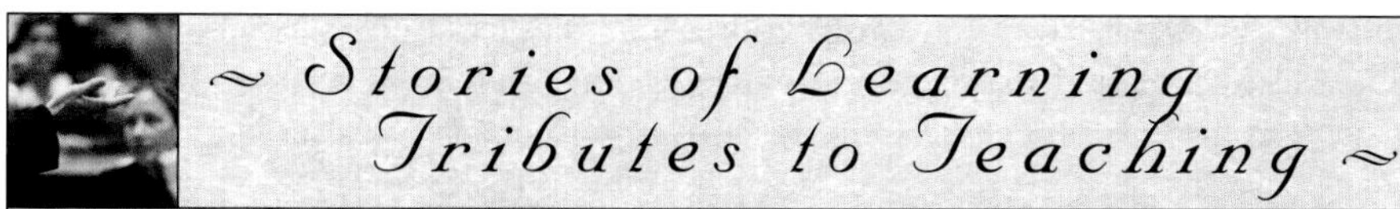

Esme Codell, a first-year teacher in an urban school, describes how she helped her students learn and succeed in a real-world task that was especially difficult for them—public speaking.

May 12

Storyteller's Workshop is going well. I got a small grant. After school a couple of times a week, I train about a dozen children to give dramatic performances of folktales. I specifically picked children who are particularly shy or challenged in reading or speaking. We went on a field trip to see a professional storyteller, and they all own copies of the books they are going to perform. For the past six weeks I've been training them, modeling for them, and—to some extent—pressuring them. I had them go "on tour" to other classes during school hours to help them gain confidence and to get feedback. We are hosting a school-wide storytelling festival in less than two weeks.

Maurissa didn't want to perform for the fourth grade. Her dark skin paled to the color of ash, she was so afraid. I sent her with Ruben and Latoya, to watch and support her. She begged me not to make her go. Secretly, I wondered if she would throw up. But I literally pushed her out the door anyway and told her not to return until the mission-was accomplished, that I knew she could do it. She came back fifteen minutes later—I should say leapt in—smiling broadly, her color back to normal.

"I did it! I did a beautiful job." She burst out laughing and crying at the same time, and we embraced.

Rochelle, another shy girl I sent out, returned breathing heavily. "You were right! The kids did join in on the repeated lines." I'm so proud of their successes. I know in the face of the wide world these are small victories, but sometimes a little song is sweet to hear, even if an orchestra is more accomplished.

SOURCE: From Codell, 2001, pp. 156–158.

tions that they will apply later. For example, Salomon and Perkins (1989) give this advice for teaching history:

> [The] history teacher can introduce direct discussion of contemporary events. To provoke forward-reaching transfer, the teacher can select an episode in history and encourage students to seek contemporary analogs. To provoke backward-reaching transfer, the teacher can choose a current phenomenon . . . and urge students to reach into their historical repertoires for analogies and disanalogies. (p. 136)

Greater transfer can also be ensured by **overlearning,** practicing a skill past the point of mastery. Many of the basic facts students learn in elementary school, such as the multiplication tables, are traditionally overlearned. Overlearning helps students retrieve the information quickly and automatically when it is needed. See the *Stories of Learning/Tributes to Teaching* feature for an example of active engagement and overlearning.

There is one last kind of transfer that is especially important for students—the transfer of the learning strategies we encountered in the previous section. Learning strategies and tactics are meant to be applied across a wide range of situations, but this often does not happen, as you will see below.

Stages of Transfer for Strategies. Sometimes students simply don't understand that a particular strategy applies in new situations or they don't know how to adapt it to fit. As we saw above, they may think the strategy takes too much time (Schunk, 2000).

Gary Phye (1992, 2001; Phye & Sanders, 1994) suggests we think of the transfer of learning strategies as a tool to be used in a "mindful" way to solve academic problems. He describes three stages in developing strategic transfer. In the *acquisition phase,*

CONNECT & EXTEND

TO YOUR TEACHING/PORTFOLIO
Why is information that is overlearned resistant to forgetting? Do we overlearn all information that is practiced and rehearsed?

Overlearning Practicing a skill past the point of mastery.

students should not only receive instruction about a strategy and how to use it, but they should also rehearse the strategy and practice being aware of when and how they are using it. In the *retention phase,* more practice with feedback helps students hone their strategy use. In the *transfer phase,* the teacher should provide new problems that can be solved with the same strategy, even though the problems appear different on the surface. To enhance motivation, point out to students how using the strategy will help them solve many problems and accomplish different tasks. These steps help build both procedural and conditional knowledge—how to use the strategy as well as when and why.

Newly mastered concepts, principles, and strategies must be applied in a wide variety of situations. Positive transfer is encouraged when skills are practiced under authentic conditions, similar to those that will exist when the skills are needed later. Students can learn to write by corresponding with e-mail pen pals in other countries. They can learn historical research methods by researching their own families. Some of these applications should involve complex, ill-defined, unstructured problems, because many of the problems to be faced in later life, in school and out, will not come to students complete with instructions. The *Family and Community Partnerships Guidelines* give ideas for enlisting the support of families in encouraging transfer.

This chapter has covered quite a bit of territory, partly because the cognitive perspective has so many implications for instruction. Although they are varied, you can see that most of the cognitive ideas for teaching concepts, problem-solving skills, and learning strategies emphasize the role of the student's prior knowledge and the need for active, mindful learning.

Check Yourself What is transfer?

Distinguish between low-road and high-road transfer.

Family and Community Partnerships

Promoting Transfer

Keep families informed about their child's curriculum so they can support learning.

Examples

1. At the beginning of units or major projects, send a letter summarizing the key goals, a few of the major assignments, and some common problems students have in learning the material for that unit.
2. Ask parents for suggestions about how their child's interests could be connected to the curriculum topics.
3. Invite parents to school for an evening of "strategy learning"—have the students teach their family members one of the strategies they have learned in school.

Give families ideas for how they might encourage their children to practice, extend, or apply learning from school.

Examples

1. To extend writing, ask parents to encourage their children to write letters or e-mail to companies or civic organizations asking for information or free products. Provide a shell letter form for structure and ideas and include addresses of companies that provide free samples or information.
2. Ask family members to include their children in some projects that require measurement, halfing or doubling recipes, or estimating costs.
3. Suggest students work with grandparents to do a family memory book. Combine historical research and writing.

Show connections between learning in school and life outside.

Examples

1. Ask families to talk about and show how they use the skills their children are learning in jobs, hobbies, or community involvement projects.
2. Ask family members to come to class to demonstrate how they use reading, writing, science, math, or other knowledge in their work.

Make families partners in practicing learning strategies.

Examples

1. Focus on one learning tactic at a time—ask families to simply remind their children to use a particular tactic with homework that week.
2. Develop a lending library of books and videotapes to teach families about learning strategies.
3. Give parents a copy of the Becoming an Expert Student Guidelines on page 301, rewritten for your grade level.

Learning and Teaching about Concepts
(pp. 276–283)

Distinguish between prototypes and exemplars. Concepts are categories used to group similar events, ideas, people, or objects. A prototype is the best representative of its category. For instance, the best representative of the "birds" category for many Americans might be a robin. Exemplars are our actual memories of specific birds and so on that we use to compare with an item in question to see if that item belongs in the same category as our exemplar. We probably learn concepts from prototypes or exemplars of the category, understand in terms of our schematic knowledge, and then refine concepts through our additional experience of relevant and irrelevant features.

What are the four elements needed in concept teaching? Lessons about concepts include four basic components: concept name, definition, attributes, and examples (along with nonexamples). The concept attainment model is one approach to teaching concepts that asks students to form hypotheses about why particular examples are members of a category and what that category (concept) might be.

What are the key characteristics of Bruner's discovery learning? In discovery learning, the teacher presents examples and the students work with the examples until they discover the interrelationships—the subject's structure. Bruner believes that classroom learning should take place through inductive reasoning, that is, by using specific examples to formulate a general principle. Encouraging inductive thinking in this way is sometimes called the eg-rule method.

What are the stages of Ausubel's expository teaching? Ausubel believes that learning should progress deductively: from the general to the specific, or from the rule or principle to examples. After presenting an advance organizer, the next step in a lesson using Ausubel's approach is to present content in terms of basic similarities and differences, using specific examples. Finally, when all the material has been presented, ask students to discuss how the examples can be used to expand on the original advance organizer.

How can you teach concepts through analogies? By identifying known information that relates to a new concept, teachers and students can map the analogies between the known and the new, then summarize an understanding of the new concept by explaining the similarities and differences between the known and the new concepts.

Concept: A general category of ideas, objects, people, or experiences whose members share certain properties.

Defining Attributes: Distinctive features shared by members of a category.

Prototype: Best representative of a category.

Exemplar: A specific example of a given category that is used to classify an item.

Undergeneralization: Exclusion of some true members from a category; limiting a concept.

Overgeneralization: Inclusion of nonmembers in a category; overextending a concept.

Concept Mapping: Student's diagram of his or her understanding of a concept.

Discovery Learning: Bruner's approach, in which students work on their own to discover basic principles.

Inductive Reasoning: Formulating general principles based on knowledge of examples and details.

Intuitive Thinking: Making imaginative leaps to correct perceptions or workable solutions.

Guided Discovery: An adaptation of discovery learning, in which the teacher provides some direction.

Expository Teaching: Ausubel's method—teachers present material in complete, organized form, moving from broadest to more specific concepts.

Meaningful Verbal Learning: Focused and organized relationships among ideas and verbal information.

Deductive Reasoning: Drawing conclusions by applying rules or principles; logically moving from a general rule or principle to a specific solution.

Advance Organizer: Statement of inclusive concepts to introduce and sum up material that follows.

Analogical Instruction: Teaching new concepts by making connections (analogies) with information that the student already understands.

Problem Solving
(pp. 283–294)

What are the steps in the general problem-solving process? Problem solving is both general and domain-specific. The five stages of problem solving are contained in the acronym IDEAL: *I*dentify the problem, *D*efine goals and represent the problem, *E*xplore possible strategies, *A*nticipate outcomes and *A*ct, *L*ook back and *L*earn.

Why is the representation stage of problem solving so important? To represent the problem accurately, you must understand both the whole problem and its discrete elements. Schema training may improve this ability. The problem-solving process follows entirely different paths, depending on what representation and goal are chosen. If your representation of the problem suggests an immediate solution, the task is done; the new problem is recognized as a "disguised" version of an old problem with a clear solution. But if there is no existing way of solving the problem or if the activated schema fails, then students must search for a solution. The application of algorithms and heuristics—such as means-ends analysis, analogical thinking, working backward, and verbalization—may help students solve problems.

Describe factors that can interfere with problem solving. Factors that hinder problem solving include functional fixedness or rigidity (response set). These disallow the flexibility needed to represent problems accurately and to have insight into solutions.

What are the differences between expert and novice knowledge in a given area? Expert problem solvers have a rich store of declarative, procedural, and conditional knowledge. They organize this knowledge around general principles or patterns that apply to large classes of problems. They work faster, remember relevant information, and monitor their progress better than novices.

How do misconceptions interfere with learning? If the students' intuitive model includes misconceptions and inaccuracies, then the students are likely to develop inadequate or misleading representations of a problem. In order to learn new information and solve problems, students must sometimes "unlearn" commonsense ideas.

Problem: Any situation in which you are trying to reach some goal and must find a means to do so.
Problem Solving: Creating new solutions for problems.
Schema-Driven Problem Solving: Recognizing a problem as a "disguised" version of an old problem for which one already has a solution.
Algorithm: Step-by-step procedure for solving a problem; prescription for solutions.
Heuristic: General strategy used in attempting to solve problems.
Means-Ends Analysis: Heuristic in which a goal is divided into subgoals.
Working-Backward Strategy: Heuristic in which one starts with the goal and moves backward to solve the problem.
Analogical Thinking: Heuristic in which one limits the search for solutions to situations that are similar to the one at hand.
Verbalization: Putting your problem-solving plan and its logic into words.
Functional Fixedness: Inability to use objects or tools in a new way.
Response Set: Rigidity; tendency to respond in the most familiar way.
Insight: Sudden realization of a solution.

Enhancing Your Expertise with Technology: Problem Solving

(p. 295)

The Eisenhower National Clearinghouse
http://www.enc.org/topics/inquiry/

Other Useful Websites

Wolf-Trap Institute for Early Learning Through the Arts
http://www.wolf-trap.org/

Problem Solving In Early Childhood Classrooms
http://www.ed.gov/databases/ERIC_Digests/ed355040.html

Teaching Problem Solving—Secondary School Science
http://www.ed.gov/databases/ERIC_Digests/ed309049.html

Mindtools
http://www.psychwww.com/mtsite/

Becoming an Expert Student: Learning Strategies and Study Skills

(pp. 295–303)

Distinguish between learning strategies and tactics. Learning strategies are ideas for accomplishing learning goals, a kind of overall plan of attack. Learning tactics are the specific techniques that make up the plan. A strategy for learning might include several tactics such as mnemonics to remember key terms, skimming to identify the organization, and then writing answers to possible essay questions. Use of strategies and tactics reflects metacognitive knowledge.

What key functions do learning strategies play? Learning strategies help students *become cognitively engaged*—focus attention on the relevant or important aspects of the material. Second, they encourage students to *invest effort,* make connections, elaborate, translate, organize, and reorganize in order to *think and process deeply*—the greater the practice and processing, the stronger the learning. Finally, strategies help students *regulate and monitor* their own learning—keep track of what is making sense and notice when a new approach is needed.

Describe some procedures for developing learning strategies. Expose students to a number of different strategies, not only general learning strategies but also very specific tactics, such as the graphic strategies. Teach conditional knowledge about when, where, and why to use various strategies. Develop motivation to use the strategies and tactics by showing students how their learning and performance can be improved. Provide direct instruction in content knowledge needed to use the strategies.

When will students apply learning strategies? If they have appropriate strategies, students will apply them if they are faced with a task that requires good strategies, value doing well on that task, think the effort to apply the strategies will be worthwhile, and believe that they can succeed using the strategies. Also, to apply deep processing strategies, students must assume that knowledge is complex and takes time to learn and that learning requires their own active efforts.

Learning Strategies: General plans for approaching learning tasks.
Learning Tactics: Specific techniques for learning, such as using mnemonics or outlining a passage.
READS: A five-step reading strategy: *Review* headings; *Examine* boldface words; *Ask,* "What do I expect to learn?"; *Do* it—Read; *Summarize* in your own words.
PQ4R: A method for studying text that involves six steps: *Preview, Question, Read, Reflect, Recite, Review.*
CAPS: A strategy that can be used in reading literature: *Characters, Aim* of story, *Problem, Solution.*
KWL: A strategy to guide reading and inquiry: Before—What do I already *know*? What do I *want* to know? After—What have I *learned*?

■ Teaching for Transfer
(pp. 303–306)

What is transfer? Transfer occurs when a rule, fact, or skill learned in one situation is applied in another situation; for example, applying rules of punctuation to write a job application letter. Transfer also involves applying to new problems the principles learned in other, often dissimilar situations.

Distinguish between low-road and high-road transfer. Transfer involving spontaneity and automaticity in familiar situations has been called *low-road transfer. High-road transfer* involves reflection and conscious application of abstract knowledge to new situations. Teachers can promote thinking and learning skills by teaching for mastery and for the positive, general transfer of knowledge. In addition, teachers can help students transfer learning strategies by teaching strategies directly, providing practice with feedback, and then expanding the application of the strategies to new and unfamiliar situations.

Transfer: Influence of previously learned material on new material.
Low-Road Transfer: Spontaneous and automatic transfer of highly practiced skills.
High-Road Transfer: Application of abstract knowledge learned in one situation to a different situation.
Overlearning: Practicing a skill past the point of mastery.

Becoming a Professional

Passing the PRAXIS™

Chapter 8 reflects many of the professional standards created by the Interstate New Teacher Assessment and Support Consortium (INTASC). These standards form the basis of the PRAXIS II™ and state-created teacher licensure exams.

In this chapter's Teachers' Casebook you used a discovery lesson to help your students develop their concepts of magnetism. The lesson failed. The disappointment from a failed lesson is an emotion that nearly all teachers experience. Less capable teachers often become frustrated, and they may quickly abandon an instructional format or learning approach. Outstanding teachers often become reflective, and they seek answers to questions like the ones posed in the Teachers' Casebook.

As you become more knowledgeable about teaching through experience, study, and reflection, you can expect to develop a sophisticated set of instructional strategies. In many circumstances, discovery will certainly be the wisest instructional format. However, few teachers are purists, and you might find exposition to be a wiser choice in other circumstances—and elsewhere you might stress problem-solving skills or strategies. And you should always be concerned with how the learning will transfer to other situations.

Tips for PRAXIS II™

Focus on each of these major topics:

Discovery learning and expository teaching:

- Basic assumptions
- Inductive reasoning/deductive reasoning
- Appropriate uses/principles of implementation

Problem solving:

- General problem-solving strategies/heuristics and algorithms
- The value of problem representation
- Factors that impede problem solving

Learning strategies

- Basic principles of teaching these strategies
- Cognitive processes involved in various strategies
- Appropriate uses of different strategies

Transfer of learning

- Types of transfer/promoting transfer

Related Topics

- Cooperative learning (Chapter 13)
- Direct instruction (Chapter 12)
- Inquiry learning (Chapter 9)
- Critical thinking (Chapter 9)

Standards and Licensure Appendix: *PRAXIS II™ and INTASC*

Refer to the Appendix at the end of the book for detailed correlations to PRAXIS II™ exam topics and INTASC Standards addressed in this text.

Insights about Job Interview Questions: *What Would You Say?*

1. How would you teach abstract concepts to a student who just arrived from Somalia and can't even read in her native language, much less English?
2. Many of our students go on to high-pressure colleges and don't seem to know how to study when they don't have daily homework deadlines. How would you help them prepare to handle the heavy work load in those institutions?
3. What do you think about letting students use calculators and spell checkers? Do you think this is making learning too easy?

Your Teaching Portfolio: *Teaching Resources*

- Use Table 8.2 plus the section titled *Learning Strategies and Tactics* to generate ideas for appropriate learning strategies and tactics for the students you will teach.
- Add Figures 8.3, "Phases of Expository Teaching," Figure 8.7, "A Map To Guide Note Taking," and Table 8.2 on Learning Strategies to your file of **Teaching Resources.**
- Use the *Family and Community Partnerships Guidelines* to brainstorm ideas for family involvement in helping your students "take their learning home."

Video**Workshop** Extra

If the VideoWorkshop package was included with your textbook, go to Chapter 8 of the Companion Website (www.ablongman.com/woolfolk) and click on the VideoWorkshop button. Follow the instructions for viewing *Video Clip 12: Managing Technology in the Classroom.* Consider this information along with what you've read in Chapter 8 while answering the following questions:

1. Computers can be a useful problem-solving tool, but they can also be misused. How do you, as a teacher, determine when to use the computer to help teach concepts or solve problems, and when not to? Give examples.
2. Choose a concept in a subject area of your choice, and design a lesson in which you use technology to facilitate learning.

Use the CD-ROM included in the back of your textbook to launch the "Becoming a Professional" website. The website features advice on preparing for teacher certification exams, help with getting your first job, and resources to help you perform your job well from the first day forward.

Teachers' Casebook

What Would They Do?

Here is how some practicing teachers responded to the teaching situation presented at the beginning of this chapter about a discovery lesson that went wrong.

Maria Cirma

Fifth Grade Teacher, *Hillside School, Needham, Massachusetts*

I would hand back the graded lessons and projects and would encourage my students to discuss with me in an open forum how they feel they did on their finished projects. I am always honest about their performance and achievements and urge them to reflect on their own efforts, difficulties, and feelings of success. I would let them know that I am questioning the assignment itself and need their help to improve on it for future classes. In a way, they are the best source for this information because they experienced the assignment firsthand.

We would discuss how the lesson could be approached differently and if directions, criteria, and expectations were clear enough to follow. This is their opportunity to help me rewrite the assignment. It's also a way to model self-evaluation, which is an important tool for students and teachers to utilize, because it aids in the learning process, helps build on prior knowledge, and enables us to move forward in our work. Many students will want the opportunity to redo the assignment because of their personal investment. They'll be more productive and will have a healthier attitude toward their own learning.

Jan Andrews

Teaching Principal, Years Four–Seven, *Dulacca State School, Dulacca QLD 4255, Australia*

I do not believe that the failure of the lesson could be the fault of the science book but that the approach was new to the students and they were unable to adapt themselves to it successfully. The projects would not be marked but handed back to the students. Those who "got it" would have their projects and journals used as examples. I would explain to the students the process that I had intended them to go through and what I expected them to "discover." Then I would take the class through simple exercises that would help them when next participating in a discovery lesson.

Kate McMenemy

Fifth Grade Teacher, *St. Ignatius Primary School, Grove Crescent, Toowong, Australia*

Many aspects of this lesson could have contributed to students' poor reports.

A. With a graded report as an outcome, one lesson (particularly a discovery lesson) is not adequate. Guided discovery would be more effective.
B. It may well be that the students were not skilled in group work. My students need to display adequate signs of social skills, cooperation, teamwork, and interest in working as a group before I consider using this form of learning.
C. Rather than marking the projects, I would consider an apology for my lack of leadership and hence their lack of success.

Wendy Merefield-Ward

Teacher-Librarian, *Payne Road State School, The Gap QLD 4061, Australia*

Why was it so unsuccessful? I would ask myself the following questions:

- Did I clearly and concisely communicate what I wanted to all of the students?
- Did the students have enough experience with group work to cope with the task?
- Were the groups effective in size and composition?
- Did the tasks include a variety of learning experience to cater to differing learning styles?
- Were the students given enough time and resources to complete the task?
- Was the task interesting and relevant?

Find the negatives in the answers and address them.

Jennifer Hudson Thomas

Armidale High School, Armidale, Australia

It is fairly obvious that the science material that I chose did not engage the learners, no matter how well it was researched, presented, and taught. It would seem that it was fairly purposeless learning for this group of students. How discouraging! Maybe it is time to negotiate with the class the science topics that they are interested in pursuing. With choice and ownership for their learning on their side, meaningful and productive units of work could then be developed. Following the successful completion of a number of student-chosen science topics, my confidence and that of the students may allow a return to the more abstract and challenging learning required to understand magnetism.

Go to the Companion Website (www.ablongman.com/woolfolk) for additional case studies including audio and video cases, and examples of student work.

CHAPTER

9

Social Cognitive and Constructivist Views of Learning

Teachers' Casebook

What Would You Do?

You have finally landed a job teaching English and writing in a high school. The first day of class, you discover that a number of students appear to have limited English proficiency. You make a mental note to meet with them to determine how much and what kind of reading they can handle. To get a sense of the class's interest, you ask them to write a "review" of the last book they read, as if they were on TV doing a "Book Beat" program. There is a bit of grumbling, but the students seem to be writing, so you take a few minutes to try to talk with one of the students who has trouble with English.

That night you look over the "book reviews." Either the students are giving you a hard time, or no one has read anything lately. Several students mention a text from another class, but their reviews are one sentence evaluations—usually containing the words "lame" or "useless" (often misspelled). In stark contrast are the papers of three students—they are a pleasure to read, worthy of publication in the school literary magazine (if there were one), and reflect a fairly sophisticated understanding of some good literature.

Critical Thinking

How would you adapt your plans for this group? What will you do tomorrow? What teaching approaches do you think will work with this class? How will you work with the three students who are more advanced?

Collaboration

With two or three other students in your class, redesign the assignment to get students more engaged. How could you prepare them to use what they know to succeed on this assignment?

For the past three chapters we have analyzed different aspects of learning. We considered behavioral and information processing explanations of what and how people learn. We have examined complex cognitive processes such as concept learning and problem solving. These explanations of learning focus on the individual and what is happening in his or her "head." Recent perspectives have called attention to two other aspects of learning that are critical—social and cultural factors. In this chapter we look at the role of other people and the cultural context in learning.

Two general theoretical frames include social and cultural factors as major elements. The first, social learning/social cognitive views, began as an extension and expansion of behavioral theories. The second, sociocultural constructivist theories, have roots in cognitive perspectives. Rather than debating the merits of each approach, we will consider the contributions of different models of instruction, grounded in different theories of learning. Don't feel that you must choose the "best" approach—there is no such thing. Even though theorists argue about which model is best, most excellent teachers apply all the approaches as appropriate.

By the time you have completed this chapter, you should be able to answer these questions:

- *What are the elements of social cognitive theory?*
- *In what situations might a teacher use modeling?*
- *What are three constructivist perspectives on learning?*
- *How could you incorporate inquiry, problem-based learning, instructional conversations, and cognitive apprenticeships in your teaching?*

Social Processes in Learning

When you consider the English class in the Teachers' Casebook, do you think about social and cultural influences on the students' learning? Reading and books seem to have very different meanings for various students in the class. And the students probably have seen different models of reading in their lives outside school. In the following pages we will discuss how people learn through interactions with others and how observation, modeling, dialogue, and culture affect learning—all are increasingly important topics in educational psychology. Over as decade ago, Jerome Bruner, who pioneered the study of individual concept learning, said, "I have come increasingly to recognize that learning in most settings is a communal activity, a sharing of culture" (1986, p. 27).

Let's consider three social influences on students—parents, peers, and teachers.

Parents, Peers, and Teachers

Think back to high school—did you have friends in any of these groups: normals, populars, brains, jocks, partyers, druggies, others? What were the main "crowds" at your school? How did your friends influence you?

Laurence Steinberg and his colleagues have studied the role of parents, peers, and community contexts in school achievement (Steinberg, 1998, 1996; Durbin, Darling, Steinberg, & Brown, 1993). Based on a three-year study that surveyed 20,000 students in nine high schools in Wisconsin and California, Steinberg concluded that about 40% of these students were just going through the motions of learning. When they were in class, they were not really paying attention or trying very hard to learn. About 90% had copied someone else's homework and 66% had cheated on a test within the last year. Steinberg claims that this lack of investment is due in part to peer pressure. "For a large number of adolescents, peers—not parents—are the chief determinants of how intensely they are invested in school and how much effort they devote to their education" (1998, p. 331). Results of his research indicate that peers provide incentives for certain activities and ridicule others, which creates a school culture that affects the way the teachers behave. One in every five students said that their friends make fun of people who tried to do well in school. When asked what crowd they would most like to belong to:

> [F]ive times as many students say the "populars" or "jocks" as say the "brains." Three times as many say they would rather be "partyers" or "druggies" than "brains." And of all the crowds, the "brains" were least happy with who they are—nearly half wished they were in a different crowd. (Steinberg, 1998, p. 332)

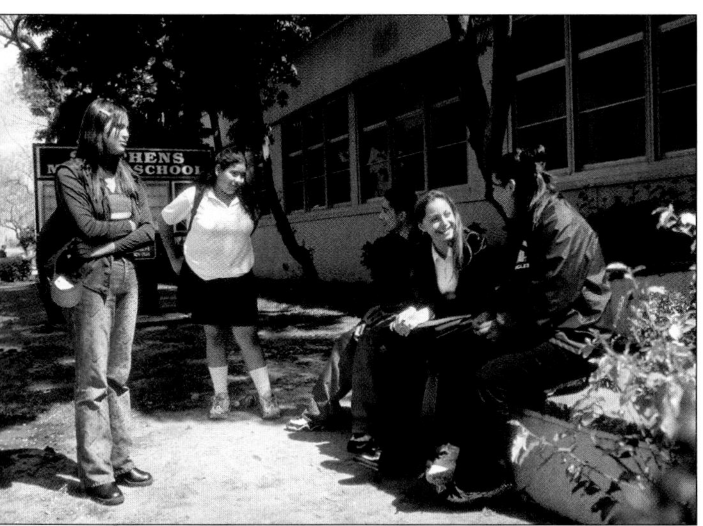

Children tend to select friends that share their orientations and interests, and these peer groups in turn influence children's academic motivation. The degree to which children are influenced by their peers is partly related to how involved their parents are in their daily lives.

But parents and teachers play a role too. When 3,407 9th- through 12th-grade European American students described their parents' styles and their peer-group orientation, adolescents who characterized their parents as authoritative (demanding but responsive, rational, and democratic) were more likely to favor well-rounded crowds that rewarded both adult- and peer-supported norms such as "normals" and "brains." Students, especially girls, who characterized their parents as uninvolved were more likely to be oriented toward "partyers" and "druggies" that did not endorse adult values. Finally, boys with indulgent parents were more likely to be oriented toward fun-cultures such as "partyers" (Durbin, Darling, Steinberg, & Brown, 1993). In fact, adolescents with authoritative parents are more likely to respond to peer pressure to do well in school and less likely to be swayed by peer pressure to use drugs or alcohol, especially when their friends also have authoritative parents (Collins, Maccoby, Steinberg, Hetherington, & Bornstein, 2000).

Children are not randomly assigned to friendship groups, cliques, and crowds. In elementary school, children tend to select friends who share their orientation toward school (Wentzel, 1999). A study by Jill Hamm (2000) comparing friendship patterns of African, Asian, and European American adolescents found that all three groups chose friends who were similar (but not identical) in substance use and somewhat similar in academic orientation. African Americans were more likely than the other two groups to select friends who were similar in terms of ethnic identity, however.

There also is some evidence that academic achievement is less valued in African American peer groups than in Asian or European American groups (Steinberg, Dornbusch, & Brown, 1992; Wentzel & Battle, 2001). But we have to be careful about research that overlooks possible individual and group differences. For example, when European, Hispanic, and African American adolescents were asked to nominate peers they most admired, respected, and wanted to be like, girls in all three groups and European American boys nominated high achieving peers. In contrast, African American and Hispanic American boys nominated low achieving boys as most admired (Graham, Taylor, & Hudley, 1998).

When children do not have friends or have few friends, parents and teachers can play an important role in supporting school achievement. Kathryn Wentzel and her colleagues have found that perceived support from teachers is related to positive motivation for learning and adjustment in school for students (Wentzel & Battle, 2001). In addition, being liked by teachers can offset the negative effects of peer rejection in middle school. And students who have few friends, but are not rejected—simply ignored by other students—can remain well-adjusted academically and socially when they are liked and supported by teachers. Often these students are highly motivated to learn (Wentzel, 1999). See the *Stories of Learning/Tributes to Teaching* feature on page 316 for one example.

Check Yourself What are some of the social factors that influence learning in school?

Observation and modeling play a role in peer influence. The first perspective we will examine that adds social considerations to an explanation of learning is the work of Albert Bandura (1977, 1986, 1997). In the early 1960s he demonstrated that people can learn by observing the actions and consequences of others.

Social Learning and Social Cognitive Theories

Bandura's early work on learning was grounded in the behavioral principles of reinforcement and punishment described in Chapter 6. However, Bandura challenged and expanded behavioral conceptions of learning. He believed that the traditional behavioral views were accurate—but incomplete—because they gave only a partial explanation of learning. Behavioral views overlooked important elements, particularly the social influences on learning. Bandura's early work focused on social *behaviors,* and was labeled **social learning theory;** it was considered a *neobehavioral* approach (Bandura, 1977; Hill, 2002).

To explain some limitations of the behavioral model, Bandura distinguishes between the *acquisition of knowledge* (learning) and the *observable performance based on that knowledge* (behavior). In other words, Bandura suggests that we all may know more than we show. An example is found in one of Bandura's early studies (1965). Preschool children saw a film of a model kicking and punching an inflatable "Bobo" doll. One group saw the model rewarded for the aggression, another group saw the

Social learning theory Theory that emphasizes learning through observation of others.

~ Stories of Learning Tributes to Teaching ~

The impact of teachers has been captured powerfully in works of fiction. The following story shows both the impact of teachers and the dangers of acting on negative expectations (discussed in Chapter 12). It is adapted from a longer version of this story, available at http://www.saintjohnonline.com/centennialschool/cs_inspirations.html. The teacher, **Miss Thompson,** encountered **Teddy** in her second year of teaching fifth grade. He was dirty and had a strange smell. He fell farther and farther behind. She remembered:

> While I did not actually ridicule the boy, my attitude was obviously quite apparent to the class, for he quickly became the class "goat," the outcast: the unlovable and the unloved. He knew I didn't like him, but he didn't know why. . . . All I know is that he was a little boy no one cared about, and I made no effort on his behalf. I knew that Teddy would never catch up in time to be promoted to the sixth grade level. To justify myself, I went to his cumulative folder. First grade: Teddy shows promise by work and attitude, but has poor home situation. Second grade: Teddy could do better. Mother terminally ill. He receives little help at home. Third grade: Teddy is a pleasant boy. Helpful, but too serious. Slow learner. Mother passed away end of the year. Fourth grade: Very slow, but well behaved. Father shows no interest. Well, they had passed him four times, but he will certainly repeat fifth grade! Do him good! I said to myself.
>
> And then the last day before the holiday arrived. Many gifts were heaped underneath our little tree, waiting for the big moment. . . . As I removed the last bit of masking tape from the brown paper on Teddy's gift, two items fell to my desk: a gaudy rhinestone bracelet with several stones missing and a small bottle of dime-store cologne-half empty.
>
> I could hear the snickers and whispers as I placed the bracelet on my wrist. "Teddy, would you help me fasten it?" He smiled shyly as he fixed the clasp, and I held up my wrist for all of them to admire. There were a few hesitant ooh's and ahh's, but as I dabbed the cologne behind my ears, all the little girls lined up for a dab behind their ears.
>
> When all the students had left, Teddy walked up to me. "You smell just like my mom," he said softly. "Her bracelet looks real pretty on you too. I'm glad you liked it." He left quickly. I locked the door, sat down at my desk, and wept, resolving to make up to Teddy what I had deliberately deprived him of—a teacher who cared. I stayed every afternoon with Teddy from the end of holidays until the last day of school. Sometimes we worked together. Sometimes he worked alone while I drew up lesson plans or graded papers. Slowly but surely he caught up with the rest of the class. In fact, his final averages were among the highest in the class.
>
> I did not hear from Teddy until seven years later, when his first letter appeared in my mailbox.
>
> "Dear Miss Thompson,
> I just wanted you to be the first to know, I will be graduating second in my class next month.
> Very Truly Yours, Teddy Stallard"

Four years later, Teddy's second letter came.

> "Dear Miss Thompson,
> I wanted you to be the first to know. I was just informed that I will be graduating first in my class. The univesity has not been easy, but I liked it.
> Very Truly Yours, Teddy Stallard"

And now today, Teddy's third letter.

> "Dear Miss Thompson,
> I wanted you to be the first to know. As of today I am Theodore Stallard, M.D. How about that!!?? I'm going to be married in July, the 27th, to be exact. I wanted to ask if you could come and sit where Mom would sit if she were here. I'll have no family there as Dad died last year.
> Very Truly Yours, Teddy Stallard"

model punished, and a third group saw no consequences. When they were moved to a room with the Bobo doll, the children who had seen the punching and kicking reinforced on the film were the most aggressive toward the doll. Those who had seen the attacks punished were the least aggressive. But when the children were promised rewards for imitating the model's aggression, all of them demonstrated that they had learned the behavior.

Thus, incentives can affect performance. Even though learning may have occurred, it may not be demonstrated until the situation is appropriate or there are incentives to perform. This might explain why some students don't perform "bad behaviors" such as swearing or smoking that they all see modeled by their peers. Personal consequences may discourage performing the behaviors. Also, children may have learned how to write the alphabet, but perform badly because their limited fine motor coordination makes neat writing impossible. Students may have learned how to simplify fractions, but perform badly on a test because they are anxious or ill or have misread the problem. In both cases, their performance is not an indication of their learning.

Recently, Bandura has focused on cognitive factors such as beliefs, self-perceptions, and expectations, so his theory is now called a **social cognitive theory** (Hill, 2002). Social cognitive theory distinguishes between enactive and vicarious learning. *Enactive learning* is learning by doing and experiencing the consequences of your actions. This may sound like operant conditioning all over again, but it is not, and the difference has to do with the role of consequences. Proponents of operant conditioning believe that consequences strengthen or weaken behavior. In enactive learning, however, consequences are seen as providing information. Our interpretations of the consequences create expectations, influence motivation, and shape beliefs (Schunk, 2000). We will see examples of enactive learning—learning by doing—later in the chapter when we consider inquiry and problem-based learning.

Vicarious learning is learning by observing others. People and animals can learn merely by observing another person or animal learn, and this fact challenges the behaviorist idea that cognitive factors are unnecessary in an explanation of learning. If people can learn by watching, they must be focusing their attention, constructing images, remembering, analyzing, and making decisions that affect learning. Thus, much is going on mentally before performance and reinforcement can even take place. Cognitive apprenticeships, discussed later in the chapter, are examples of vicarious learning—learning by observing others.

Albert Bandura expanded on behavioral theories to develop the social cognitive theory of learning.

CONNECT & EXTEND

TO THE RESEARCH
For a look at social cognitive theory and school achievement, see Schunk, D. H. (1999). Social-self interaction and achievement behavior. *Educational Psychologist, 34,* 219–227.

Learning by Observing Others

Your interview for a position in the middle school is going well. The next question is: "Who are your models as teachers? Do you hear yourself saying or see yourself doing things that other teachers have done? Are there teachers from films or books that you would like to be like?"

Through **observational learning** we learn not only how to perform a behavior but also what will happen to us in specific situations if we do perform it. Observation can be a very efficient learning process. The first time children hold hairbrushes, cups, or tennis rackets, they usually brush, drink, or swing as well as they can, given their current muscle development and coordination. Let's take a closer look at how observational learning occurs.Bandura (1986) notes that observational learning includes four elements: *paying attention, retaining information or impressions, producing behaviors,* and *being motivated* to repeat the behaviors.

Attention. In order to learn through observation, we have to pay attention. In teaching, you will have to ensure students' attention to the critical features of the lesson by making clear presentations and highlighting important points. In demonstrating a skill (for example, threading a sewing machine or operating a lathe), you may need to have students look over your shoulder as you work. Seeing your hands from the same perspective as they see their own directs their attention to the right features of the situation and makes observational learning easier.

Retention. In order to imitate the behavior of a model, you have to remember it. This involves mentally representing the model's actions in some way, probably as verbal steps ("Hwa-Rang, the eighth form in Tae Kwan Do karate, is a palm-heel block, then a middle riding stance punch, then . . ."), or as visual images, or both. Retention can be improved by mental rehearsal (imagining imitating the behavior) or by actual practice. In the retention phase of observational learning, practice helps us remember the elements of the desired behavior, such as the sequence of steps.

Production. Once we "know" how a behavior should look and remember the elements or steps, we still may not perform it smoothly. Sometimes we need a great deal of practice, feedback, and coaching about subtle points before we can reproduce the

Social cognitive theory Theory that adds concern with cognitive factors such as beliefs, self-perceptions, and expectations to social learning theory.

Observational learning Learning by observation and imitation of others.

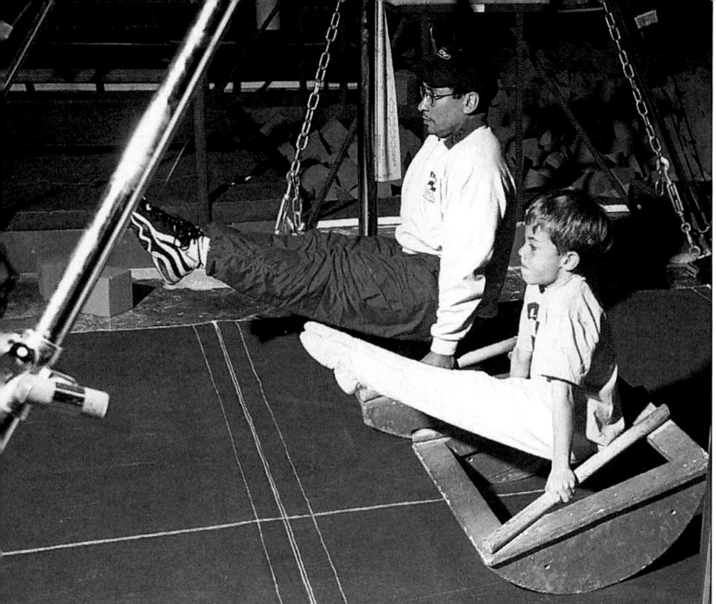

Social cognitive theories of learning consider the importance of learning by doing and learning by observing others.

behavior of the model. In the production phase, practice makes the behavior smoother and more expert.

Motivation and Reinforcement. As mentioned earlier, social learning theory distinguishes between acquisition and performance. We may acquire a new skill or behavior through observation, but we may not perform that behavior until there is some motivation or incentive to do so. Reinforcement can play several roles in observational learning. If we anticipate being reinforced for imitating the actions of a model, we may be more motivated to pay attention, remember, and reproduce the behaviors. In addition, reinforcement is important in maintaining learning. A person who tries a new behavior is unlikely to persist without reinforcement (Ollendick, Dailey, & Shapiro, 1983; Schunk, 2000). For example, if an unpopular student adopted the dress of the "in" group but was ignored or ridiculed, it is unlikely that the imitation would continue.

Bandura identifies three forms of reinforcement that can encourage observational learning. First, of course, the observer may reproduce the behaviors of the model and receive direct reinforcement, as when a gymnast successfully executes a front flip/round-off combination and the coach/model says, "Excellent!"

But the reinforcement need not be direct—it may be **vicarious reinforcement.** The observer may simply see others reinforced for a particular behavior and then increase his or her production of that behavior. For example, if you compliment two students on the attractive illustrations in their lab reports, several other students who observe your compliments may turn in illustrated lab reports next time. Most TV ads hope for this kind of effect. People in commercials become deliriously happy when they drive a particular car or drink a specific juice, and the viewer is supposed to do the same; the viewer's behavior is reinforced vicariously by the actors' obvious pleasure. Punishment can also be vicarious: You may slow down on a stretch of highway after seeing several people get speeding tickets there.

The final form of reinforcement is self-reinforcement, or controlling your own reinforcers. This sort of reinforcement is important for both students and teachers. We want our students to improve not because it leads to external rewards but because the students value and enjoy their growing competence. And as a teacher, sometimes self-reinforcement is all that keeps you going.

CONNECT & EXTEND

TO PRAXIS™ OBSERVATIONAL LEARNING (II, B2)
Identify situations in which observational learning may be a wise approach, and describe the essential elements of effective observational learning.

Factors That Influence Observational Learning. What causes an individual to learn and perform modeled behaviors and skills? Several factors play a role, as shown in Table 9.1. The developmental level of the observer makes a difference in learning. As children grow older, they are able to focus attention for longer periods of time, use memory strategies to retain information, and motivate themselves to practice. A second influence is the status of the model. Children are more likely to imitate the actions of others who seem competent, powerful, prestigious, and enthusiastic, so parents, teachers, older siblings, athletes, action heroes, rock stars, or film personalities may serve as models, depending on the age and interests of the child. Third, by watching others, we learn about what behaviors are appropriate for people like ourselves, so models who are seen as similar are more readily imitated (Pintrich & Schunk, 2002). All students need to see successful, capable models who look and sound like them, no matter what their ethnicity, socioeconomic status, or gender.

Look at Table 9.1. The last three influences involve goals and expectations. If observers expect that certain actions of models will lead to particular outcomes (such as particular practice regimens leading to improved athletic performance) and the observers value those outcomes or goals, then the observers are more likely to pay atten-

Vicarious reinforcement Increasing the chances that we will repeat a behavior by observing another person being reinforced for that behavior.

■ Table 9.1	Factors That Affect Observational Learning
Characteristic	**Effects of Modeling**
Developmental Status	Improvements with development include longer attention and increased capacity to process information, use strategies, compare performances with memorial representations, and adopt intrinsic motivators.
Model Prestige and Competence	Observers pay greater attention to competent, high-status models. Consequences of modeled behaviors convey information about functional value. Observers attempt to learn actions they believe they will need to perform.
Vicarious Consequences	Consequences to models convey information about behavioral appropriateness and likely outcomes of actions. Valued consequences motivate observers. Similarity in attributes or competence signals appropriateness and heightens motivation.
Outcome Expectations	Observers are more likely to perform modeled actions they believe are appropriate and will result in rewarding outcomes.
Goal Setting	Observers are likely to attend to models who demonstrate behaviors that help observers attain goals.
Self-efficacy	Observers attend to models when they believe they are capable of learning or performing the modeled behavior. Observation of similar models affects self-efficacy ("If they can do it, I can too").

SOURCE: From *Learning Theories: An Education Perspective* (3rd ed.), by D. H. Schunk. Published by Prentice Hall.

tion to the models and try to reproduce their behaviors. Finally, observers are more likely to learn from models if the observers have a high level of **self-efficacy**—that is, if they believe they are capable of doing the actions needed to reach the goals, or at least of learning how to do so (Bandura, 1997; Pintrich & Schunk, 2002). We will discuss goals, expectations, and self-efficacy in greater depth in Chapter 10 on motivation.

CONNECT & EXTEND

TO OTHER CHAPTERS
Sense of self-efficacy is discussed more fully in Chapter 10, as is the related concept of teacher efficacy. Background: Two books by Bandura about self-efficacy: Bandura, A. (1997). *Self-efficacy: The exercise of control.* New York: Freeman. Bandura, A. (Ed.). (1995). *Self-efficacy in changing societies.* New York: Cambridge University Press.

Observational Learning in Teaching

How would you incorporate observational leaning into your teaching? What are the skills, attitudes, and strategies in your subject that can be modeled?

There are five possible outcomes of observational learning: directing attention, encouraging existing behaviors, changing inhibitions, teaching new behaviors and attitudes, and arousing emotions. Let's look at each of these as they occur in classrooms.

Directing Attention. By observing others, we not only learn about actions, but also notice the objects involved in the actions. For example, in a preschool class, when one child plays enthusiastically with a toy that has been ignored for days, many other children may want to have the toy, even if they play with it in different ways or simply carry it around. This happens, in part, because the children's attention has been drawn to that particular toy.

Fine-Tuning Already-Learned Behaviors. All of us have had the experience of looking for cues from other people when we find ourselves in unfamiliar situations. Observing the behavior of others tells us which of our already-learned behaviors to use: the proper fork for eating the salad, when to leave a gathering, what kind of language is appropriate, and so on. Adopting the dress and grooming styles of TV or music idols is another example of this kind of effect.

Self-efficacy A person's sense of being able to deal effectively with a particular task.

What is this son learning by observing his father?

Strengthening or Weakening Inhibitions. If class members witness one student breaking a class rule and getting away with it, they may learn that undesirable consequences do not always follow rule breaking. If the rule breaker is a well-liked, high-status class leader, the effect of the modeling may be even more pronounced. This "**ripple effect**" (Kounin, 1970) can work for the teacher's benefit. When the teacher deals effectively with a rule breaker, especially a class leader, the idea of breaking this rule may be inhibited for the other students viewing the interaction. This does not mean that teachers must reprimand each student who breaks a rule, but once a teacher has called for a particular action, following through is an important part of capitalizing on the ripple effect.

Teaching New Behaviors. **Modeling** has long been used, of course, to teach dance, sports, and crafts, as well as skills in subjects such as food science, chemistry, and shop. Modeling can also be applied deliberately in the classroom to teach mental skills and to broaden horizons—to teach new ways of thinking. Teachers serve as models for a vast range of behaviors, from pronouncing vocabulary words, to reacting to the seizure of a student with epilepsy, to being enthusiastic about learning. For example, a teacher might model sound critical thinking skills by thinking "out loud" about a student's question. Or a high school teacher concerned about girls who seem to have stereotyped ideas about careers might invite women with nontraditional jobs to speak to the class.

Modeling, when applied deliberately, can be an effective and efficient means of teaching new behavior (Bandura, 1986; Schunk, 1987, 2000). Studies indicate that modeling can be most effective when the teacher makes use of all the elements of observational learning described in the previous section, especially reinforcement and practice.

> **CONNECT & EXTEND**
>
> TO **PRAXIS**™
> MODELING (II, B2)
> Teachers often utilize modeling to teach students new behaviors. Identify the characteristics that tend to make models effective in instructional contexts.

Models who are the same age as the students may be particularly effective. For example, Schunk and Hanson (1985) compared two methods for teaching subtraction to 2nd graders who had difficulties learning this skill. One group of students observed other 2nd graders learning the procedures, then participated in an instructional program on subtraction. Another group of students watched a teacher's demonstration, then participated in the same instructional program. Of the two groups, the students who observed peer models learning not only scored higher on tests of subtraction after instruction, but also gained more confidence in their own ability to learn. For students who doubt their own abilities, a good model is a low-achieving student who keeps trying and finally masters the material (Schunk, 2000).

Arousing Emotion. Finally, through observational learning people may develop emotional reactions to situations they have never experienced personally, such as flying or driving. A child who watches a friend fall from a swing and break an arm may become fearful of swings. After the terrible events of September 11th, children may be anxious when they see airplanes flying close to the ground. News reports of shark attacks have many of us anxious about swimming in the ocean. Note that hearing and reading about a situation are also forms of observation. Some terrible examples of modeling occur with "copy cat killings" in schools. When frightening things happen to people who are similar in age or circumstances to your students, they may need to talk about their emotions.

The *Guidelines* on the next page will give you some ideas about using observational learning in the classroom.

Reciprocal Determinism

In social cognitive theory both internal and external factors are important. Environmental events, personal factors, and behaviors are seen as interacting in the process of learning. Personal factors (beliefs, expectations, attitudes, and knowledge), the physical and social environment (resources, consequences of actions, other people, and physical settings), and behavior (individual actions, choices, and verbal state-

Ripple effect "Contagious" spreading of behaviors through imitation.

Modeling Changes in behavior, thinking, or emotions that occur through observing another person—a model.

GUIDELINES Using Observational Learning

Model behaviors and attitudes you want your students to learn.

Examples

1. Show enthusiasm for the subject you teach.
2. Be willing to demonstrate both the mental and the physical tasks you expect the students to perform. I once saw a teacher sit down in the sandbox while her 4-year-old students watched her demonstrate the difference between "playing with sand" and "throwing sand."
3. When reading to students, model good problem solving. Stop and say, "Now let me see if I remember what happened so far," or "That was a hard sentence. I'm going to read it again."
4. Model good problem solving—think out loud as you work through a difficult problem.

Use peers, especially class leaders, as models.

Examples

1. In group work, pair students who do well with those who are having difficulties.
2. Ask students to demonstrate the difference between "whispering" and "silence—no talking."

Make sure students see that positive behaviors lead to reinforcement for others.

Examples

1. Point out the connections between positive behavior and positive consequences in stories.
2. Be fair in giving reinforcement. The same rules for rewards should apply to the problem students as to the good students.

Enlist the help of class leaders in modeling behaviors or the entire class.

Examples

1. Ask a well-liked student to be friendly to an isolated, fearful student.
2. Let high-status students lead an activity when you need class cooperation or when students are likely to be reluctant at first. Popular students can model dialogues in foreign-language classes or be the first to tackle dissection procedures in biology.

ments) all influence and are influenced by each other. Bandura calls this interaction of forces **reciprocal determinism.**

Figure 9.1 (page 322) shows the interaction of person, environment, and behaviors in learning settings (Schunk, 1999). Social factors such as models, instructional strategies, or feedback (elements of the *environment* for students) can affect student *personal* factors such as goals, sense of efficacy for the task, attributions (beliefs about causes for success and failure), and processes of self-regulation such as planning, monitoring, and controlling distractions. For example, teacher feedback can lead students to set higher goals and increase their sense of efficacy. Social influences in the environment and personal factors encourage the *behaviors* that lead to achievement such as persistence and effort (motivation) and learning. But these behaviors also reciprocally impact personal factors. As students achieve, their sense of self-efficacy increases, for example. And behaviors also affect the social environment. For example, if students do not persist or if they seem to misunderstand, teachers may change instructional strategies or feedback.

Think for a minute about the power of reciprocal determinism in classrooms. If personal factors, behaviors, and the environment are in constant interaction, then cycles of events are progressive and self-perpetuating. Suppose a new student walks into class late. The student has a tattoo and several visible pierced body parts. The student is actually anxious and hopes to do better at this new school, but the teacher's initial reaction to the late entry and dramatic appearance is a bit hostile. The student feels insulted and responds in kind, so the teacher begins to form expectations about the student, is more vigilant and less trusting, and the student decides that this school will be just as worthless as his previous one—so why bother to try. The teacher sees the student's disengagement, invests less effort in teaching him, and the cycle continues.

Check Yourself Distinguish between social learning and social cognitive theories.

Distinguish between enactive and vicarious learning.

What are the elements of observational learning?

What is reciprocal determinism?

Reciprocal determinism An explanation of behavior that emphasizes the mutual effects of the individual and the environment on each other.

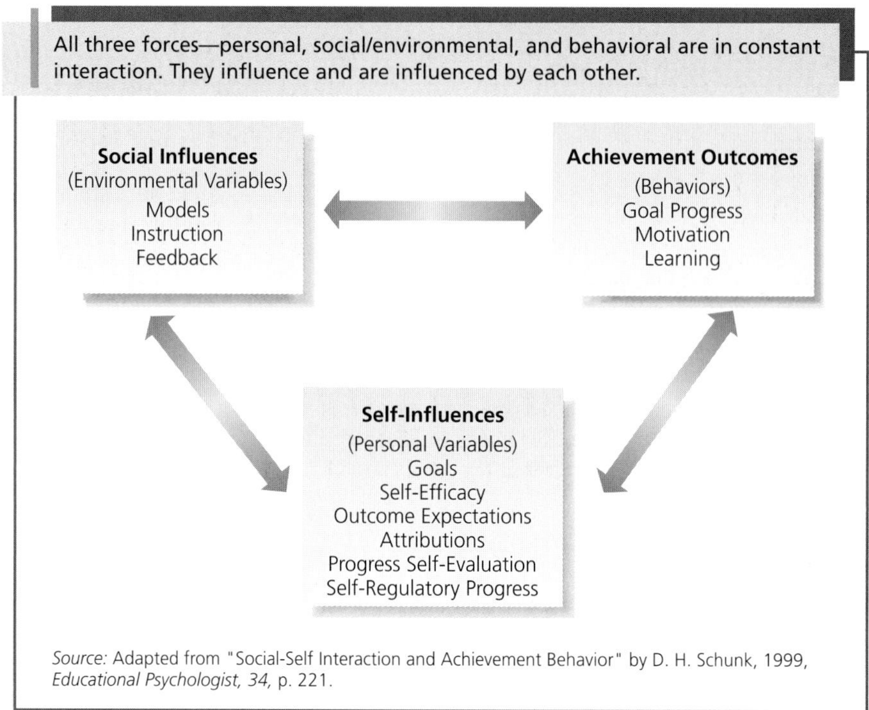

Figure 9.1 Reciprocal Influences

Social cognitive theories study the impact of social factors on individuals—the direction of the influence is from social processes *outside* the learner to the mind *inside* the learner. But there are other perspectives on learning that include a much wider range of social processes, such as cultural and historical factors, and focus on co-constructions of knowledge that occur between people, not just within them. Because these are very influential theories, we will spend the rest of the chapter learning more about them.

Constructivism and Situated Learning

Consider this situation:

> A young child who has never been to the hospital is in her bed in the pediatric wing. The nurse at the station down the hall calls over the intercom above the bed, "Hi Chelsea, how are you doing? Do you need anything?" The girl looks puzzled and does not answer. The nurse repeats the question with the same result. Finally, the nurse says emphatically, "Chelsea, are you there? Say something!" The little girl responds tentatively, "Hello wall—I'm here."

Chelsea encountered a new situation—a talking wall. The wall is persistent. It sounds like a grown-up wall. She shouldn't talk to strangers, but she is not sure about walls. She uses what she knows and what the situation provides to *construct* meaning and to act.

Here is another example of constructing meaning taken from Berk (2001, p. 31). This time a father and his 4-year-old son co-construct understandings as they walk along a California beach, collecting litter after a busy day:

> **Ben:** (running ahead and calling out) Some bottles and cans. I'll get them.
>
> **Mel:** If the bottles are broken, you could cut yourself, so let me get them. *(Catches up and holds out the bag as Ben drops items in)*

Ben: Dad, look at this shell. It's a whole one, really big. Colors all inside!

Mel: Hmmm, might be an abalone shell.

Ben: What's abalone?

Mel: Do you remember what I had in my sandwich on the wharf yesterday? That's abalone.

Ben: You eat it?

Mel: Well, you can. You eat a meaty part that the abalone uses to stick to rocks.

Ben: Ewww. I don't want to eat it. Can I keep the shell?

Mel: I think so. Maybe you can find some things in your room to put in it. *(Points to the shell's colors)* Sometimes people make jewelry out of these shells.

Ben: Like mom's necklace?

Mel: That's right. Mom's necklace is made out of a kind of abalone with a very colorful shell—pinks, purples, blues. It's called Paua. When you turn it, the colors change.

Ben: Wow! Let's look for Paua shells!

Mel: You can't find them here, only in New Zealand.

Ben: Where's that? Have you been there?

Mel: No, someone brought Mom the necklace as a gift. But I'll show you New Zealand on the globe. It's far away, halfway around the world.

Look at the knowledge being co-constructed about sea creatures and their uses for food or decoration, safety, environmental responsibility, and even geography. Constructivist theories of learning focus on how people make meaning, both on their own like Chelsea and in interaction with others like Ben.

Constructivist Views of Learning

Constructivism, "a vast and woolly area in contemporary psychology, epistemology, and education" (Von Glasersfeld, 1997, p. 204), is a broad term used by philosophers, curriculum designers, psychologists, educators, and others. Most people who use the term emphasize "the learner's contribution to meaning and learning through both individual and social activity" (Bruning, Schraw, & Ronning, 1999, p. 215). Constructivist perspectives are grounded in the research of Piaget, Vygotsky, the Gestalt psychologists, Bartlett, and Bruner as well as the educational philosophy of John Dewey, to mention just a few intellectual roots.

There is no one constructivist theory of learning. Most of the theories in cognitive science include some kind of constructivism because these theories assume that individuals construct their own cognitive structures as they interpret their experiences in particular situations (Palincsar, 1998). There are constructivist approaches in science and mathematics education, in educational psychology and anthropology, and in computer-based education. Even though many psychologists and educators use the term *constructivism,* they often mean very different things (Marshall, 1996; McCaslin & Hickey, 2001; Phillips, 1997). One way to organize constructivist views is to talk about two forms of constructivism: psychological and social construction (Palincsar, 1998; Phillips, 1997).

CONNECT & EXTEND

TO THE RESEARCH
For more on constructivism and education, see Marshall, H. H. (Ed.) (1992). *Redefining student learning: Roots of educational change.* Norwood, NJ: Ablex.

Psychological/Individual Constructivism. Psychological constructivists "are concerned with how *individuals* build up certain elements of their cognitive or emotional apparatus" (Phillips, 1997, p. 153). These constructivists are interested in individual knowledge, beliefs, self-concept, or identity, so they are sometimes called *individual* constructivists; they all focus on the inner psychological life of people. Chelsea talking to the wall in the previous section was making meaning using her own individual knowledge and beliefs.

Constructivism View that emphasizes the active role of the learner in building understanding and making sense of information.

Constructivist views of learning focus on how individuals construct their own cognitive structures as they interpret their experiences in particular learning situations.

Using these standards, the most recent information processing theories are constructivist (Mayer, 1996). Information processing approaches to learning regard the human mind as a symbol processing system. This system converts sensory input into symbol structures (propositions, images, or schemas), and then processes (rehearses or elaborates) those symbol structures so knowledge can be held in memory and retrieved. The outside world is seen as a source of input, but once the sensations are perceived and enter working memory, the important work is assumed to be happening "inside the head" of the individual (Schunk, 2000; Vera & Simon, 1993). Some psychologists, however, believe that information processing is "trivial constructivism" because the individual's only constructive contribution is to build accurate representations of the outside world (Derry, 1992; Garrison, 1995; Marshall, 1996).

In contrast, Piaget's psychological constructivist perspective is less concerned with "correct" representations and more interested in meaning as constructed by the individual. As we saw in Chapter 2, Piaget proposed a sequence of cognitive stages that all humans pass through. Thinking at each stage builds on and incorporates previous stages as it becomes more organized and adaptive and less tied to concrete events. Piaget's special concern was with logic and the construction of universal knowledge that cannot be learned directly from the environment—knowledge such as conservation or reversibility (Miller, 2002). Such knowledge comes from reflecting on and coordinating our own cognitions or thoughts, not from mapping external reality. Piaget saw the social environment as an important factor in development, but did not believe that social interaction was the main mechanism for changing thinking (Moshman, 1997). Some educational and developmental psychologists have referred to Piaget's kind of constructivism as **"first wave constructivism"** or "solo" constructivism, with its emphasis on individual meaning-making (DeCorte, Greer, and Verschaffel, 1996; Paris, Byrnes, & Paris, 2001).

Vygotsky's Social Constructivism. As you also saw in Chapter 2, Vygotsky believed that social interaction, cultural tools, and activity shape individual development and learning, just as Ben's interactions on the beach with his father shaped Ben's learning about sea creatures, safety, environmental responsibility, and geography. By participating in a broad range of activities with others, learners **appropriate** (internalize or take for themselves) the outcomes produced by working together; "they acquire new strategies and knowledge of the world and culture" (Palincsar, 1998, pp. 351–352). Putting learning in social and cultural context is **"second wave" constructivism** (Paris, Byrnes, & Paris, 2001).

Because his theory relies heavily on social interactions and the cultural context to explain learning, most psychologists classify Vygotsky as a social constructivist (Palincsar, 1998; Prawat, 1996). However, some theorists categorize him as a psychological constructivist because he was primarily interested in development within the individual (Moshman, 1997; Phillips, 1997). In a sense, Vygotsky was both. One advantage of his theory of learning is that it gives us a way to consider both the psychological and the social: He bridges both camps. For example, Vygotsky's concept of the zone of proximal development—the area where a child can solve a problem with the help (scaffolding) of an adult or more able peer—has been called a place where culture and cognition create each other (Cole, 1985). Culture creates cognition when the adult uses tools and practices from the culture (language, maps, computers, looms, or music) to steer the child toward goals the culture values (reading, writing, weaving, dance). Cognition creates culture as the adult and child together generate new practices and problem solutions to add to the cultural group's repertoire (Serpell, 1993).

CONNECT & EXTEND

TO THE RESEARCH
The 2000 Yearbook of the National Society for the Study of Education (NSSE) is devoted to the examination of constructivism. Phillips, D. C. (Ed.) (2000). *Constructivism in education: Opinions and second opinions on controversial issues.* Chicago, IL: University of Chicago Press.

First wave constructivism A focus on the individual and psychological sources of knowing, as in Piaget's theory.

Appropriate Internalize or take for yourself knowledge and skills developed in interaction with others or with cultural tools.

Second wave constructivism A focus on the social and cultural sources of knowing, as in Vygotsky's theory.

The term *constructionism* is sometimes used to talk about how public knowledge is created. Although this is not our main concern in educational psychology, it is worth a quick look.

Constructionism. Social construc*tionists* do not focus on individual learning. Their concern is how public knowledge in disciplines such as science, math, economics, or history is constructed. Beyond this kind of academic knowledge, constructionists also are interested in how common-sense ideas, everyday beliefs, and commonly held understandings about the world are communicated to new members of a sociocultural group (Gergen, 1997; Phillips, 1997). Questions raised might include who determines what constitutes history, the proper way to behave in public, or how to get elected class president. All knowledge is socially constructed, and, more important, some people have more power than others to define what constitutes such knowledge. Relationships between and among teachers, students, families, and the community are the central issues. Collaboration to understand diverse viewpoints is encouraged, and traditional bodies of knowledge often are challenged (Gergen, 1997). Vygotsky's theory, with its attention to how cognition creates culture, has some elements in common with constructionism.

A difficulty with this position is that, when pushed to the extreme of relativism, all knowledge and all beliefs are equal because they are all constructed. There are problems with this thinking for educators. First, teachers have a professional responsibility to emphasize some values, such as honesty or justice, over others such as bigotry and deception. All beliefs are not equal. As teachers, we ask students to work hard to learn. If learning cannot advance understanding because all understandings are equally good, then, as David Moshman (1997) notes, "we might just as well let students continue to believe whatever they believe" (p. 230). Also, it appears that some knowledge, such as counting and one-to-one correspondence, is not constructed but universal. Knowing one-to-one correspondence is part of being human (Geary, 1995; Schunk, 2000).

These different perspectives on constructivism raise some general questions and disagree on the answers. These questions can never be fully resolved, but different theories tend to favor different positions.

How Is Knowledge Constructed?

One tension among different approaches to constructivism is based on *how* knowledge is constructed. Moshman (1982) describes three explanations.

1. *The realities and truths of the external world direct knowledge construction.* Individuals *reconstruct* outside reality by building accurate mental representations such as propositional networks, concepts, cause-and-effect patterns, and condition-action production rules that reflect "the way things really are." Information processing holds this view of knowledge (Cobb & Bowers, 1999).

2. *Internal processes such as Piaget's organization, assimilation, and accommodation direct knowledge construction.* New knowledge is abstracted from old knowledge. Knowledge is not a mirror of reality, but rather an abstraction that grows and develops with cognitive activity. Knowledge is not true or false; it just grows more internally consistent and organized with development.

3. *Both external and internal factors direct knowledge construction.* Knowledge grows through the *interactions* of internal (cognitive) and external (environmental and social) factors. Vygotsky's description of cognitive development through the appropriation and use of cultural tools such as language is consistent with this view (Bruning, Schraw, & Ronning, 1999). Another example is Bandura's theory of reciprocal interactions among people, behaviors, and environments (Schunk, 2000). Table 9.2 on page 326 summarizes the three general explanations about how knowledge is constructed.

■ Table 9.2	How Knowledge Is Constructed	
Type	**Assumptions about Learning and Knowledge**	**Example Theories**
External Direction	Knowledge is acquired by constructing a representation of the outside world. Direct teaching, feedback, and explanation affect learning. Knowledge is accurate to the extent that it reflects the "way things really are" in the outside world.	Information processing
Internal Direction	Knowledge is constructed by transforming, organizing, and reorganizing previous knowledge. Knowledge is not a mirror of the external world, even though experience influences thinking and thinking influences knowledge. Exploration and discovery are more important than teaching.	Piaget
Both External and Internal Direction	Knowledge is constructed based on social interactions and experience. Knowledge reflects the outside world as filtered through and influenced by culture, language, beliefs, interactions with others, direct teaching, and modeling. Guided discovery, teaching, models, and coaching as well as the individual's prior knowledge, beliefs, and thinking affect learning.	Vygotsky

Knowledge: Situated or General?

A second question that cuts across many constructivist perspectives is whether knowledge is internal, general, and transferable or bound to the time and place in which it is constructed. Psychologists who emphasize the social construction of knowledge and situated learning affirm Vygotsky's notion that learning is inherently social and embedded in a particular cultural setting (Cobb & Bowers, 1999). What is true in one time and place—such as the "fact" before Columbus's time that the earth was flat—becomes false in another time and place. Particular ideas may be useful within a specific **community of practice,** such as fifteenth century navigation, but useless outside that community. What counts as new knowledge is determined in part by how well the new idea fits with current accepted practice. Over time, the current practice may be questioned and even overthrown, but until such major shifts occur, current practice will shape what is considered valuable.

Situated learning emphasizes that the real world is not like studying in school. It is more like an apprenticeship where novices, with the support of an expert guide and model, take on more and more responsibility until they are able to function independently. For those who take a situated learning view, this explains learning in factories, around the dinner table, in high school halls, in street gangs, in the business office, and on the playground.

Situated learning is often described as "enculturation," or adopting the norms, behaviors, skills, beliefs, language, and attitudes of a particular community. The community might be mathematicians or gang members or writers or students in your 8th-grade class or soccer players—any group that has particular ways of thinking and doing. Knowledge is seen *not* as individual cognitive structures but as a creation of the community over time. The practices of the community—the ways of interacting and getting things done, as well as the tools the community has created—constitute the knowledge of that community. Learning means becoming more able to participate in those practices, use the tools, and take on the identity of a member of the community (Derry, 1992; Garrison, 1995; Greeno, Collins, & Resnick, 1996; Rogoff, 1998).

At the most basic level, "situated learning . . . emphasizes the idea that much of what is learned is specific to the situation in which it is learned" (Anderson, Reder, & Simon, 1996, p. 5). Thus, some would argue, learning to do calculations in school may help students do more school calculations, but may not help them balance a checkbook, because the skills can be applied only in the context in which they were learned, namely school (Lave, 1997; Lave & Wenger, 1991). But it also appears that knowledge and skills can be applied across contexts that were not part of the initial learning situation, as when you use your ability to read and calculate to do your in-

Community of practice Social situation or context in which ideas are judged useful or true.

Situated learning The idea that skills and knowledge are tied to the situation in which they were learned and difficult to apply in new settings.

come taxes, even though income tax forms were not part of your high school curriculum (Anderson, Reder, & Simon, 1996).

Learning that is situated in school does not have to be doomed or irrelevant (Bereiter, 1997). As you saw in Chapter 8, a major question in educational psychology and education in general concerns the *transfer* of knowledge from one situation to another. How can you encourage this transfer? Help is on the way in the next section.

Common Elements of Constructivist Perspectives

What makes a lesson student-centered? List the characteristics and features that put the student in the center of learning.

We have looked at some areas of disagreement among the constructivist perspectives, but what about areas of agreement? Even though there is no single constructivist theory, many constructivist approaches recommend that educators:

- embed learning in complex, realistic, and relevant learning environments;
- provide for social negotiation and shared responsibility as a part of learning;
- support multiple perspectives and use multiple representations of content;
- nurture self-awareness and an understanding that knowledge is constructed; and
- encourage ownership in learning (Driscoll, 2000; Marshall, 1992).

Before we discuss particular teaching approaches, let's look more closely at these dimensions of constructivist teaching.

Complex Learning Environments and Authentic Tasks. Constructivists believe that students should not be given stripped down, simplified problems and basic skills drills, but instead should encounter **complex learning environments** that deal with "fuzzy," ill-structured problems. The world beyond school presents few simple problems or step-by-step directions, so schools should be sure that *every* student has experience solving complex problems. Complex problems are not simply difficult ones; they have many parts. There are multiple, interacting elements in complex problems and multiple solutions are possible. There is no one right way to reach a conclusion, and each solution may bring a new set of problems. These complex problems should be embedded in authentic tasks and activities, the kinds of situations that students will face as they apply what they are learning to the real world (Needles & Knapp, 1994; Resnick, 1987). Students may need support as they work on these complex problems, with teachers helping them find resources, keeping track of their progress, breaking larger problems down into smaller ones, and so on. This aspect of constructivist approaches is consistent with situated learning in emphasizing learning in *situations* where the learning will be applied.

Social Negotiation. Many constructivists share Vygotsky's belief that higher mental processes develop through **social negotiation** and interaction, so collaboration in learning is valued. The Language Development and Hypermedia Group (1992) suggests that a major goal of teaching is to develop students' abilities to establish and defend their own positions while respecting the positions of others and working together to negotiate or co-construct meaning. To accomplish this exchange, students must talk and listen to each other. It is a challenge for children in cultures that are individualistic and competitive, such as the United States, to adopt what has been called an **intersubjective attitude**—a commitment to build shared meaning by finding common ground and exchanging interpretations.

Multiple Perspectives and Representations of Content. When students encounter only one model, one analogy, one way of understanding complex content,

CONNECT & EXTEND

TO YOUR TEACHING/PORTFOLIO

John Cronin lists these four common misconceptions about authentic learning:

Misconception #1: If you can't take 'em to Spain, they might as well not learn Spanish at all. The fact that living with native speakers is the best way to learn Spanish does not make using the language in classroom conversations a poor alternative. Look for the small and obvious ways to make learning more authentic—especially if you can't take 'em to Spain.

Misconception #2: If you don't have your chef's license, then you'll have to starve. You don't need special training or materials to create authentic instruction. Good teachers have been doing it for years.

Misconception #3: If it isn't real fun, then it isn't real. Important learning and valuable life skills are not always fun to learn or fun to use. Self-discipline is part of growing up authentically.

Misconception #4: If you want to learn to play the piano, you must start with mastering Chopin. Not all learning has to be complicated; some important life skills are simple. From Cronin, J. F. (1993). Four misconceptions about authentic learning. *Educational Leadership, 50*(7), 78–80.

Complex learning environments Problems and learning situations that mimic the ill-structured nature of real life.

Social negotiation Aspect of learning process that relies on collaboration with others and respect for different perspectives.

Intersubjective attitude A commitment to build shared meaning with others by finding common ground and exchanging interpretations.

Constructivist approaches may involve, among other things, authentic or real-life tasks, social negotiation, and shared responsibility as part of learning.

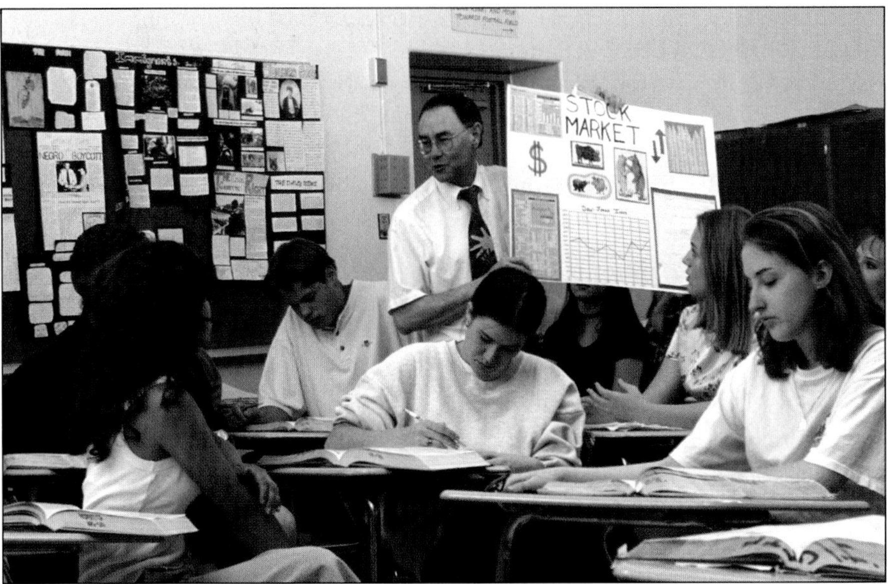

CONNECT & EXTEND

TO **PRAXIS**™
STUDENT-CENTERED LEARNING (II, A3)
Many of the major initiatives to reform content-area curricula (e.g., science, mathematics) emphasize student-centered/constructivist approaches to learning. Describe the major principles of these approaches and explain how they differ from teacher-centered approaches.

they often oversimplify as they try to apply that one approach to every situation. I saw this happen in my educational psychology class when six students were presenting an example of guided discovery learning. The students' presentation was a near copy of a guided discovery demonstration I had given earlier in the semester, but with some major misconceptions. My students knew only one way to represent discovery learning. Resources for the class should have provided **multiple representations of content** using different analogies, examples, and metaphors.

Rand Spiro and his colleagues (1991) suggest that "revisiting the same material, at different times, in rearranged contexts, for different purposes, and from different conceptual perspectives is essential for attaining the goals of advanced knowledge acquisition" (p. 28). This idea is consistent with Jerome Bruner's (1966) **spiral curriculum,** a structure for teaching that introduces the fundamental structure of all subjects—the "big ideas"—early in the school years, then revisits the subjects in more and more complex forms over time.

Understanding the Knowledge Construction Process. Constructivist approaches emphasize making students aware of their own role in constructing knowledge (Cunningham, 1992). The assumptions we make, our beliefs, and our experiences shape what each of us comes to "know" about the world. Different assumptions and different experiences lead to different knowledge. If students are aware of the influences that shape their thinking, they will be more able to choose, develop, and defend positions in a self-critical way while respecting the positions of others.

Student Ownership of Learning. "While there are several interpretations of what [constructivist] theory means, most agree that it involves a dramatic change in the focus of teaching, putting the students' own efforts to understand at the center of the educational enterprise" (Prawat, 1992, p. 357). Student ownership does not mean that the teacher abandons responsibility for instruction. Because the design of teaching is a central issue in this book, we will spend the rest of this chapter discussing examples of ownership of learning and student-centered instruction.

Check Yourself Describe three kinds of constructivism.

In what ways do constructivist views differ about knowledge sources, accuracy, and generality?

What are some common elements in most constructivist views of learning?

Multiple representations of content Considering problems using various analogies, examples, and metaphors.

Spiral curriculum Bruner's structure for teaching that introduces the fundamental structure of all subjects early in the school years, then revisits the subjects in more and more complex forms over time.

Applications of Constructivist and Situated Perspectives on Learning

In this section we will examine three specific teaching approaches that put the student at the center: inquiry and problem-based learning, dialogue and instructional conversations, and cognitive apprenticeships. Cooperative learning, another application of social constructivism, is discussed in Chapter 13 as an approach for teaching tolerance, social skills, and empathy.

Inquiry and Problem-Based Learning

John Dewey described the basic **inquiry learning** format in 1910. There have been many adaptations of this strategy, but the form usually includes these elements (Lashley, Matczynski, & Rowley, 2002). The teacher presents a puzzling event, question, or problem. The students:

- formulate hypotheses to explain the event or solve the problem,
- collect data to test the hypotheses,
- draw conclusions, and
- reflect on the original problem and the thinking processes needed to solve it.

Examples of Inquiry. In one kind of inquiry, teachers present a problem and students ask yes/no questions to gather data and test hypotheses. This allows the teacher to monitor students' thinking and guide the process. Here is an example:

1. *Teacher presents discrepant event* (after clarifying ground rules). The teacher blows softly across the top of an 8½" × 11" sheet of paper, and the paper rises. She tells students to figure out why it rises.
2. *Students ask questions* to gather more information and to isolate relevant variables. Teacher answers only "yes" or "no." Students ask if temperature is important (no). They ask if the paper is of a special kind (no). They ask if air pressure has anything to do with the paper rising (yes). Questions continue.
3. *Students test causal relationships.* In this case, they ask if the nature of the air on top causes the paper to rise (yes). They ask if the fast movement of the air results in less pressure on the top (yes). Then they test out the rule with other materials—for example, thin plastic.
4. *Students form a generalization* (principle): "If the air on the top moves faster than the air on the bottom of a surface, then the air pressure on top is lessened, and the object rises." Later lessons expand students' understanding of the principles and physical laws through further experiments.
5. The teacher leads students in a discussion of their thinking processes. What were the important variables? How did you put the causes and effects together? and so on. (Pasch et al., 1991, pp. 188–189)

CONNECT & EXTEND

TO **PRAXIS**™
INQUIRY LEARNING (II, A2, 3)
Inquiry learning is a student-centered approach to learning that pre-dates many "traditional" forms of instruction. Describe the basic structure of this approach to learning. What are its strengths and limitations? What roles does the teacher have?

Shirley Magnusson and Annemarie Palincsar have developed a teachers' guide for planning, implementing, and assessing different phases of inquiry science units (Palincsar, Magnusson, Marano, Ford, & Brown, 1998). The model, called *Guided Inquiry Supporting Multiple Literacies* or GIsML, is shown in Figure 9.2 on page 330.

The teacher first identifies a curriculum area and some general guiding questions, puzzles, or problems. For example, an elementary teacher chooses communication as the area and asks this general question: "How and why do humans and animals communicate?" Next, several specific focus questions are posed. "How do whales communicate?" "How do gorillas communicate?" The focus questions have to

Inquiry learning Approach in which the teacher presents a puzzling situation and students solve the problem by gathering data and testing their conclusions.

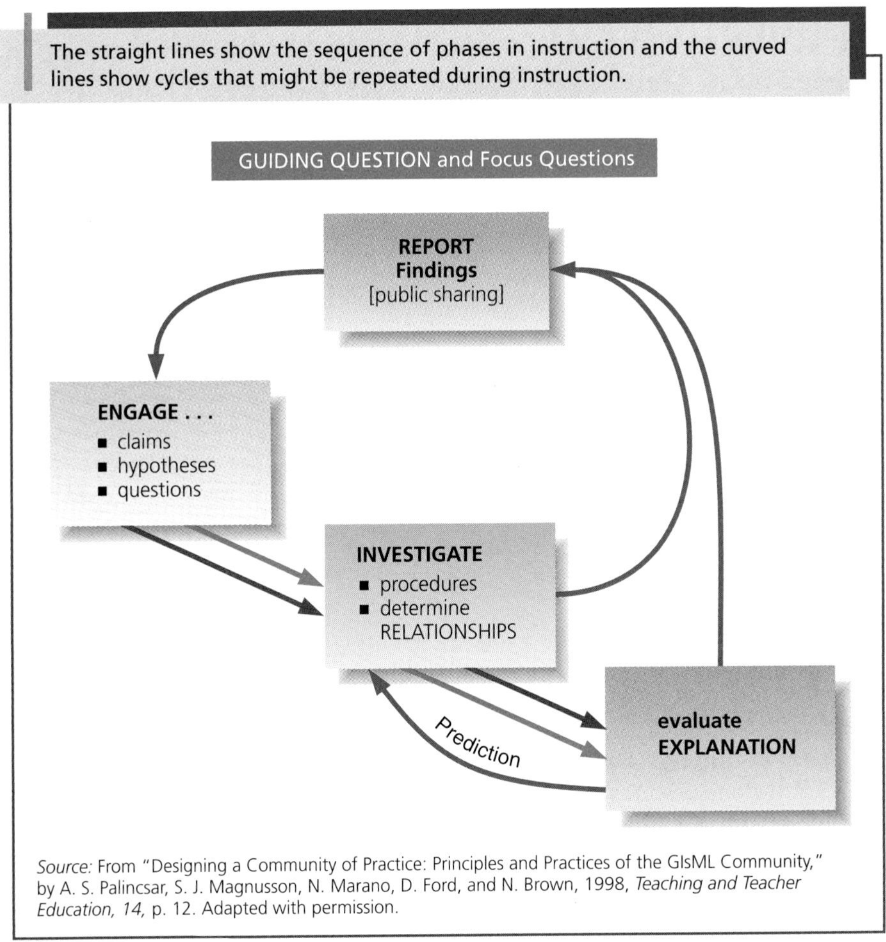

Source: From "Designing a Community of Practice: Principles and Practices of the GIsML Community," by A. S. Palincsar, S. J. Magnusson, N. Marano, D. Ford, and N. Brown, 1998, *Teaching and Teacher Education, 14,* p. 12. Adapted with permission.

■ **Figure 9.2** A Model to Guide Teacher Thinking about Inquiry-Based Science Instruction

be carefully chosen to guide students toward important understandings. One key idea in understanding animal communication is the relationship among the animal's structures, survival functions, and habitat. Animals have specific *structures* such as large ears or echo-locators, which *function* to find food or attract mates or identify predators, and these structures and functions are related to the animals' *habitats.* Thus, focus questions must ask about animals with different structures for communication, different functional needs for survival, and different habitats. Questions about animals with the same kinds of structures or the same habitats would not be good focus points for inquiry (Magnusson & Palincsar, 1995).

The next phase is to engage students in the inquiry, perhaps by playing different animal sounds, having students make guesses and claims about communication, and asking the students questions about their guesses and claims. Then the students conduct both first-hand and second-hand investigations. *First-hand investigations* are direct experiences and experiments, for example, measuring the size of bats' eyes and ears in relation to their bodies (using pictures or videos—not real bats!). In *second-hand investigations,* students consult books, the Internet, interviews with experts, and other resources to find specific information or get new ideas. As part of their investigating, the students begin to identify patterns. The curved line in Figure 9.2 shows that cycles can be repeated. In fact, students might go through several cycles of investigating, identifying patterns, and reporting results before moving on to constructing explanations and making final reports. Another possible cycle is to evaluate explanations before reporting by making and then checking predictions, applying the explanation to new situations.

Inquiry teaching allows students to learn content and process at the same time. In the examples above, students learned about the effects of air pressure, how airplanes fly, animal communication, and habitats. In addition, they learned the inquiry process itself—how to solve problems, evaluate solutions, and think critically.

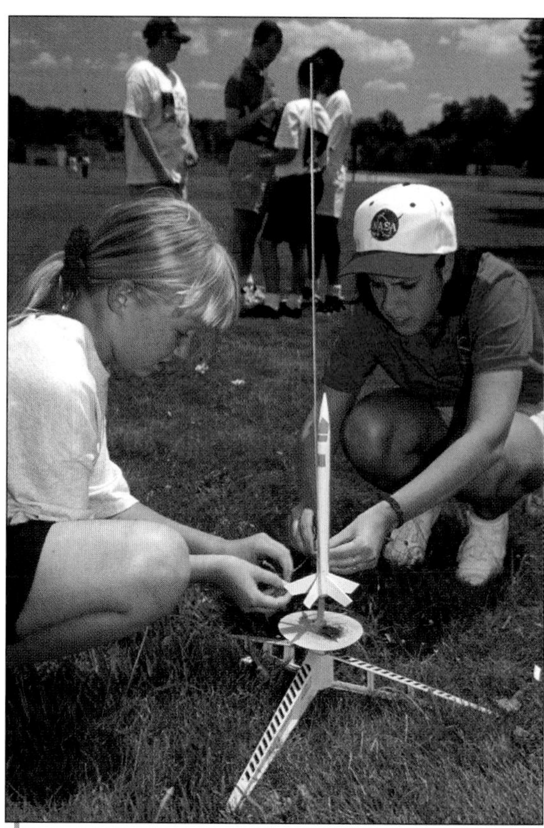

In problem-based learning students are confronted with a real problem that has meaning for them. Ideally, the problem is real, students' actions matter, and they collaborate to find solutions.

Problem-Based Learning. In **problem-based learning,** students are confronted with a real problem that has meaning for them. This problem launches their inquiry as they collaborate to find solutions. In true problem-based learning, the problem is real and the students' actions matter. In one example, a teacher capitalized on current affairs to encourage student reading, writing, and social studies problem solving:

> Cathie's elementary class learned about the Alaskan oil spill. She brought a newspaper article to class that sequenced in logbook fashion the events of the oil spill in Prince William Sound. To prepare her students to understand the article, she had her students participate in several background-building experiences. First, they used a world map, an encyclopedia, and library books to gather and share relevant information. Next, she simulated an oil spill by coating an object with oil. By then, the class was eager to read the article. (Espe, Worner, & Hotkevich, 1990, p. 45)

After they read and discussed the newspaper article, the teacher asked the class to imagine how the problem might have been prevented. Students had to explain and support their proposed solutions. The next week, the students read another newspaper article about how people in their state were helping with the cleanup efforts in Alaska. The teacher asked if the students wanted to help, and they replied with an enthusiastic "Yes!" The students designed posters and made speeches requesting donations of clean towels to be used to clean the oil-soaked animals in Prince William Sound. The class sent four large bags of towels to Alaska to help in the cleanup. The teacher's and the students' reading, writing, research, and speaking were directed toward solving a real-life problem (Espe, Worner, & Hotkevich, 1990). Other authentic problems that might be the focus for student projects are reducing pollution in local rivers, resolving student conflicts in school, raising money for class projects, or building a playground for young children. The teacher's role in problem-based learning is summarized in Table 9.3 on page 332.

Some problems are not authentic in the sense that they affect the students' lives, but they are engaging. For example, the Cognition and Technology Group at Vanderbilt University (CTGV, 1990, 1993) has developed a videodisc-based learning environment that focuses on mathematics instruction for the 5th and 6th grades. The series, called *The Adventures of Jasper Woodbury,* presents students with complex situations that require problem finding; subgoal setting; and the application of mathematics, science, history, and literature concepts to solve problems. Even though the situations are complex and lifelike, the problems can be solved using data embedded in the stories presented. Often the adventures have real-life follow-up problems that build on the knowledge developed. For example, after designing a playground for a hypothetical group of children in one Jasper adventure, students can tackle building a real playhouse for a preschool class.

The Vanderbilt group calls its problem-based approach **anchored instruction.** The *anchor* is the rich, interesting situation. This anchor provides a focus—a reason for setting goals, planning, and using mathematical tools to solve problems. The intended outcome is to develop knowledge that is useful and flexible, not inert. Inert knowledge is information that is memorized but seldom applied (CTVG, 1996; Whitehead, 1929).

Problem-based learning Methods that provide students with realistic problems that don't necessarily have "right" answers.

Anchored instruction A type of problem-based learning that uses a complex interesting situation as an anchor for learning.

Table 9.3 The Teacher's Role in Problem-Based Learning

Phase	Teacher Behavior
Phase 1 Orient students to the problem	Teacher goes over the objectives of the lesson, describes important logistical requirements, and motivates students to engage in self-selected problem-solving activity.
Phase 2 Organize students for study	Teacher helps students define and organize study tasks related to the problem.
Phase 3 Assist independent and group investigation	Teacher encourages students to gather appropriate information, conduct experiments, and search for explanations and solutions.
Phase 4 Develop and present artifacts and exhibits	Teacher assists students in planning and preparing appropriate artifacts such as reports, videos, and models and helps them share their work with others.
Phase 5 Analyze and evaluate the problem-solving process	Teacher helps students to reflect on their investigations and the processes they used.

SOURCE: From *Classroom Instruction and Management* (p. 161), by R. I. Arends. Published by McGraw-Hill.

Research on Inquiry and Problem-Based Learning. Inquiry methods are similar to discovery learning and share some of the same problems, so inquiry must be carefully planned and organized, especially for less prepared students who may lack the background knowledge and problem-solving skills needed to benefit. Some research has shown that discovery methods are ineffective and even detrimental for lower-ability students (Corno & Snow, 1986; Slavin, Karweit, & Madden, 1989). When Ted Bredderman (1983) analyzed the results of 57 comparisons of activity-based learning and more traditional approaches for teaching science, he concluded that activity-based methods were superior to content-based traditional approaches in terms of students' understanding of the scientific method and creativity, but about the same for learning science content.

In 1993, a similar comparison was made of problem-based instruction in medical school. Students learning through problem-based instruction were better at clinical skills such as problem formation and reasoning, but they were worse in their basic knowledge of science and felt less prepared in science (Albanese & Mitchell, 1993). Some students who are better at self-regulation benefit more from problem-based methods (Evensen, Salisbury-Glennon, & Glenn, 2001). The best approach may be a balance of content-focused and inquiry or problem-based methods (Arends, 2000).

For example, Eva Toth, David Klahr, and Zhe Chen (2000) tested a balanced approach for teaching 4th graders how to use the controlled variable strategy in science to design good experiments. The method had three phases: (1) in small groups, students conducted exploratory experiments to identify variables that made a ball roll farther down a ramp; (2) the teacher led a discussion, explained the controlled variable strategy, and modeled good thinking about experiment design; and (3) the students designed and conducted application experiments to isolate which variables caused the ball to roll farther. The combination of inquiry, discussion, explanation, and modeling was successful in helping the students understand the concepts.

Another constructivist approach that relies heavily on interaction is instructional conversations.

Dialogue and Instructional Conversations

One implication of Vygotsky's theory of cognitive development is that important learning and understanding require interaction and conversation. Students need to grapple with problems in their zone of proximal development, and they need the scaffolding provided by interaction with a teacher or other students. Here is a good definition of scaffolding that emphasizes the knowledge that both teacher and student bring—both are experts on something: "Scaffolding is a powerful conception of teaching and learning in which teachers and students create meaningful connections between teachers' cultural knowledge and the everyday experience and knowledge of the student" (McCaslin & Hickey, 2001, p. 137). Look back at the beach conversation between Ben and his father at the beginning of the previous section. Notice how the father used the abalone sandwich and the necklace—connections to Ben's experience and knowledge—to scaffold Ben's understanding.

Instructional conversations are *instructional* because they are designed to promote learning, but they are *conversations,* not lectures or traditional discussions. Here is a segment of conversation from a literature group in a bilingual 3rd-grade classroom (Moll & Whitmore, 1993). The conversation shows how the participants mediate each other's learning through dialogue about the shared experience.

T: *Sylvester and the Magic Pebble.* What did you think about this story?

Rita: I think they cared a lot for him.

T: What do you mean? You mean his parents?

Rita: Yes.

T: What made you think that when you read the story?

Rita: Because they really worried about him.

T: Who else wants to share something? I'd like to hear everybody's ideas. Then we can decide what we want to talk about. Sarah?

Sarah: I think he got the idea of it when he was little, or maybe one of his friends got lost or something?

T: What do you mean, he got the idea?

Sarah: He got the idea for his parents to think that Sylvester got lost.

T: You're talking about where William Steig might have gotten his ideas.

Sarah: Yes.

T: That maybe something like this happened to him or someone he knew. A lot of times authors get their ideas from real life things, don't they? Jon, what did you think about this story?

Jon: It was like a moral story. It's like you can't wish for everything. But, in a sense, everything happened to him when he was panicking.

T: When did you think he panicked?

Jon: Well, when he saw the lion, he started to panic.

Richard: And he turned himself into a rock.

Jon: Yeah. He said, "I wish I were a rock."

T: Right. And it happened, didn't it?

Richard: It was stupid of him.

T: So maybe he wasn't thinking far enough ahead? What would you have wished instead of a rock? (pp. 24–25)

The conversation continues as the students contribute different levels of interpretation of the story. The teacher notes these interpretations in her summary: "Look at all the different kinds of things you had to say. Rita talked about the characters in the

CONNECT & EXTEND

TO **PRAXIS**™
DIALOGUE AND CONVERSATION (II, A2)
Engaging discussions and instructional conversations are often students' most memorable and valuable learning experiences. Understand the principles involved in utilizing conversations and dialogue as an instructional strategy.

CONNECT & EXTEND

TO YOUR TEACHING/PORTFOLIO
For more information on instructional conversations, including examples of class transcripts and instruments to assess instructional conversations, contact: Dissemination Center, National Center for Research on Cultural Diversity and Second Language Learning, Center for Applied Linguistics, 1118 22nd Street NW, Washington, DC 20037.

Instructional conversation Situation in which students learn through interactions with teachers and/or other students.

~ Reaching Every Student ~

Lunch Learning

Even taking up lunch money can be an opportunity for an instructional conversation

During the first few minutes of the day, Ms. White asked how many children wanted hot lunches that day. Eighteen children raised their hands. Six children were going to eat cold lunches. Ms. White asked, "How many children are going to eat lunch here today?"

By starting with 18 and counting on, several children got to the answer of 24. One child got out counters and counted out a set of 18 and another set of 6. He then counted all of them and said "24."

Ms. White then asked, "How many more children are eating hot lunch than are eating cold lunch?"

Several children counted back from 18 to 12. The child with the blocks matched 18 blocks with 6 blocks and counted the blocks left over.

Ms. White asked the children who volunteered to tell the rest of the class how they got the answer. Ms. White continued asking for different solutions until no one could think of a new way to solve the problem. (Peterson, Fennema, & Carpenter, 1989, p. 45)

This teacher is creating an environment in which students can make sense of mathematics and use mathematics to make sense of the world. To accomplish these goals, teaching begins with the student's current understanding. Teachers can capitalize on the natural use of counting strategies to see how many different ways students can solve a problem. The emphasis is on mathematical thinking, not on math "facts" or on learning the one best (teacher's) way to solve the problem. The teacher is a guide, helping students construct their own understandings through dialogue (Putnam & Borko, 1997).

story and what they must be feeling. Sarah took the author's point of view. And you saw it as a particular kind of story, Jon, a moral story."

In instructional conversations, the teacher's goal is to keep everyone cognitively engaged in a substantive discussion. In the above conversation, the teacher takes almost every other turn. As the students become more familiar with this learning approach, we would expect them to talk more among themselves with less teacher talk. These conversations do not have to be long, as you can see in the *Reaching Every Student* feature.

Table 9.4 summarizes the elements of productive instructional conversations.

Cognitive Apprenticeships

Over the centuries, apprenticeships have proved to be an effective form of education. By working alongside a master and perhaps other apprentices, young people have learned many skills, trades, and crafts. Knowledgeable guides provide models, demonstrations, and corrections, as well as a personal bond that is motivating. The performances required of the learner are real and important and grow more complex as the learner becomes more competent (Collins, Brown, & Holum, 1991; Collins, Brown, & Newman, 1989; Hung, 1999). With *guided participation* in real tasks comes *participatory appropriation*—students appropriate the knowledge, skills, and values involved in doing the tasks (Rogoff, 1995, 1998). In addition, both the newcomers to learning and the old-timers contribute to the community of practice by mastering and remastering skills—and sometimes improving these skills in the process (Lave & Wenger, 1991).

Allan Collins and his colleagues (1989) suggest that knowledge and skills learned in school have become too separated from their use in the world beyond school. To correct this imbalance, some educators recommend that schools adopt many of the features of apprenticeships. But rather than learning to sculpt or dance or build a cabinet, apprenticeships in school would focus on cognitive objectives such as read-

■ Table 9.4	Elements of the Instructional Conversation
Good instructional conversations must have elements of both instruction and conversation.	
Instruction	**Conversation**
1. *Thematic focus.* Teacher selects a theme on which to focus the discussion and has a general plan for how the theme will unfold, including how to "chunk" the text to permit optimal exploration of the theme.	6. *Fewer "known-answer" questions.* Much of the discussion centers on questions for which there might be more than one correct answer.
2. *Activation and use of background knowledge.* Teacher either "hooks into" or provides students with pertinent background knowledge necessary for understanding a text, weaving the information into the discussion.	7. *Responsiveness to student contributions.* While having an initial plan and maintaining the focus and coherence of the discussion, teacher is also responsive to students' statements and the opportunities they provide.
3. *Direct teaching.* When necessary, teacher provides direct teaching of a skill or concept.	8. *Connected discourse.* The discussion is characterized by multiple, interactive, connected turns; succeeding utterances build on and extend previous ones.
4. *Promotion of more complex language and expression.* Teacher elicits more extended student contributions by using a variety of elicitation techniques: invitation to expand, questions, restatements, and pauses.	9. *Challenging, but non-threatening, atmosphere.* Teacher creates a challenging atmosphere that is balanced by a positive affective climate. Teacher is more collaborator than evaluator and students are challenged to negotiate and construct the meaning of the text.
5. *Promotion of bases for statements or positions.* Teacher promotes students' use of text, pictures, and reasoning to support an argument or position, by gently probing: "What makes you think that?" or "Show us where it says _____."	10. *General participation, including self-selected turns.* Teacher does not hold exclusive right to determine who talks; students are encouraged to volunteer or otherwise influence the selection of speaking turns.

SOURCE: From *Instructional Conversations and Their Classroom Application* (p. 7), by Claude Goldenberg, 1991, Santa Cruz, CA and Washington, DC: National Center for Research on Cultural Diversity and Second Language Learning. Copyright © 1991 by National Center for Research on Cultural Diversity and Second Language Learning. Reprinted with permission.

ing comprehension, writing, or mathematical problem solving. There are many **cognitive apprenticeship** models, but most share six features:

- Students observe an expert (usually the teacher) *model* the performance.
- Students get external support through *coaching* or tutoring (including hints, feedback, models, and reminders).
- Students receive conceptual *scaffolding,* which is then gradually faded as the student becomes more competent and proficient.
- Students continually *articulate* their knowledge—putting into words their understanding of the processes and content being learned.
- Students *reflect* on their progress, comparing their problem solving to an expert's performance and to their own earlier performances.
- Students are required to *explore* new ways to apply what they are learning—ways that they have not practiced at the master's side.

As students learn, they are challenged to master more complex concepts and skills and to perform them in many different settings (Roth & Bowen, 1995; Shuell, 1996).

How can teaching provide cognitive apprenticeships? Mentoring in teaching is one example. Another is cross-age grouping. In the Key School, an inner-city public elementary school in Indianapolis, Indiana, students of different ages work side-by-side for part of every day on a "pod" designed to have many of the qualities of an apprenticeship. The pods might focus on a craft or a discipline. Examples include gardening, architecture, and "making money." Many levels of expertise are evident in the students of different ages, so students can move at a comfortable pace, but still have the model of a master available. Community volunteers, including many parents, visit to demonstrate a skill that is related to the pod topic.

Cognitive apprenticeship A relationship in which a less experienced learner acquires knowledge and skills under the guidance of an expert.

CONNECT & EXTEND

TO THE RESEARCH

Confrey, J. (1990). What constructivism implies for teaching. In R. Davis, C. Maher, & N. Noddings (Eds.), *Constructivist views on the teaching and learning of mathematics* (pp. 107–122). Monograph 4 of the National Council of Teachers of Mathematics, Reston, VA.

Another successful example of cognitive apprenticeships, the reciprocal teaching approach for reading comprehension, is discussed in Chapter 12.

A Cognitive Apprenticeship in Learning Mathematics. Schoenfeld's (1989, 1994) teaching of mathematical problem solving is another example of the cognitive apprenticeship instructional model. Schoenfeld found that novice problem solvers began ineffective solution paths and continued on these paths even though they were not leading toward a solution. In comparison, expert problem solvers moved toward solutions using various cognitive processes such as planning, implementing, and verifying, altering their behavior based on judgments of the validity of their solution processes.

To help students become more expert problem solvers, Schoenfeld asks students three important questions: What are you doing? Why are you doing it? and How will success in what you are doing help you find a solution to the problem? These questions help students control the processes they use and build their metacognitive awareness. Here is an example:

> Problem sessions begin when I hand out a list of questions. . . . Often one student has an "inspiration". . . . My task is not to say yes or no, or even to evaluate the suggestion. Rather it is to raise the issue for discussion. . . . Typically a number of students respond [that they haven't made sense of the problem]. When we have made sense of the problem, the suggestion [X] simply doesn't make sense. . . . When this happens, I step out of my role as moderator to make the point to the whole class: If you make sure you understand the problem before you jump into a solution, you are less likely to go off on a wild goose chase. (Schoenfeld, 1987, p. 201)

This monitoring of the understanding of a problem and the problem-solving process helps students begin to think and act as mathematicians. Throughout this process, Schoenfeld repeats his three questions (What are you doing? Why? How will this help?). Each of these components is essential in helping students to be aware of and to regulate their behaviors.

CONNECT & EXTEND

TO THE RESEARCH

Perkins, D., Jay, E., & Tishman, S. (1993). New conceptions of thinking: From ontology to education. *Educational Psychologist, 28,* 67–85; see also Tishman, S., Perkins, D., and Jay, E. (1995). *The thinking classroom: Learning and teaching in a culture of thinking.* Boston: Allyn and Bacon.

Cognitive Apprenticeships in Thinking

Many educational psychologists believe that good thinking can and should be developed in school. But clearly, teaching thinking entails much more than the standard classroom practices of answering "thought" questions at the end of the chapter or participating in teacher-led discussions. What else is needed? One approach has been to focus on the development of *thinking skills,* either through **stand-alone programs** that teach skills directly, or through indirect methods that embed development of thinking in the regular curriculum.The advantage of stand-alone thinking skills programs is that students do not need extensive subject matter knowledge to master the skills. Students who have had trouble with the traditional curriculum may achieve success—and perhaps an enhanced sense of self-efficacy—through these programs. The disadvantage is that the general skills often are not used outside the program unless teachers make a concerted effort to show students how to apply the skills in specific subjects, as you can see in the *Point/Counterpoint* discussion (Mayer & Wittrock, 1996; Prawat, 1991).

The culture of a school or classroom can teach lessons about thinking by giving us models of good thinking, providing direct instruction in thinking processes, and encouraging practice of thinking processes through interactions with others.

Developing Thinking in Every Class. Another way to develop students' thinking is to provide cognitive apprenticeships in analysis, problem solving, and reasoning through the regular lessons of the curriculum. David Perkins and his colleagues (Perkins, Jay, & Tishman,

Point/Counterpoint

Should Schools Teach Critical Thinking and Problem Solving?

The question of whether schools should focus on process or content, problem-solving skills or core knowledge, higher-order thinking skills or academic information has been debated for years. Some educators suggest that students must be taught how to think and solve problems, while other educators assert that students cannot learn to "think" in the abstract. They must be thinking about something—some content. Should teachers focus on knowledge or thinking?

Point

Problem solving and higher-order thinking can and should be taught.
An article in the April, 28, 1995, issue of the *Chronicle of Higher Education* makes this claim:

> *Critical thinking is at the heart of effective reading, writing, speaking, and listening. It enables us to link together mastery of content with such diverse goals as self-esteem, self-discipline, multicultural education, effective cooperative learning, and problem solving. It enables all instructors and administrators to raise the level of their own teaching and thinking. (p. A-71)*

How can students learn to think critically? Some educators recommend teaching thinking skills directly with widely used techniques such as the Productive Thinking Program or CoRT (Cognitive Research Trust). Other researchers argue that learning computer programming languages such as LOGO will improve students' minds and teach them how to think logically. For example, Papert (1980) believes that when children learn through discovery how to give instructions to computers in LOGO, "powerful intellectual skills are developed in the process" (p. 60). Finally, because expert readers automatically apply certain metacognitive strategies, many educators and psychologists recommend directly teaching novice or poor readers how to apply these strategies. Michael Pressley's Good Strategy User model and Palincsar and Brown's (1984) reciprocal teaching approach are successful examples of direct teaching of metacognitive skills. Research on these approaches generally shows improvements in achievement and comprehension for students of all ages who participate (Pressley, Barkowski, & Schneider, 1987; Rosenshine & Meister, 1994).

Counterpoint

Thinking and problem-solving skills do not transfer.
According to E. D. Hirsch, a vocal critic of critical thinking programs:

> *But whether such direct instruction of critical thinking or self-monitoring* does *in fact improve performance is a subject of debate in the research community. For instance, the research regarding critical thinking is not reassuring. Instruction in critical thinking has been going on in several countries for over a hundred years. Yet researchers found that students from nations as varied as Israel, Germany, Australia, the Philippines, and the United States, including those who have been taught critical thinking continue to fall into logical fallacies. (1996, p. 136)*

The CoRT program has been used in over 5,000 classrooms in 10 nations. But Polson and Jeffries (1985) report that "after 10 years of widespread use we have no adequate evidence concerning . . . the effectiveness of the program" (p. 445). In addition, Mayer and Wittrock (1996) note that field studies of problem solving in real situations show that people often fail to apply the mathematical problem-solving approaches they learn in school to actual problems encountered in the grocery store or home.

Even though educators have been more successful in teaching metacognitive skills, critics still caution that there are times when such teaching hinders rather than helps learning. Robert Siegler (1993) suggests that teaching self-monitoring strategies to low-achieving students can interfere with the students' development of adaptive strategies. Forcing students to use the strategies of experts may put too much burden on working memory as the students struggle to use an unfamiliar strategy and miss the meaning or content of the lesson. For example, rather than teach students strategies for figuring out words from context, it may be helpful for students to focus on learning more vocabulary words.

What do you think? Vote online at **www.ablongman.com/woolfolk**

1993) propose that teachers do this by creating a culture of thinking in their classrooms. This means that there is a spirit of inquisitiveness and critical thinking, a respect for reasoning and creativity, and an expectation that students will learn and understand. In such a classroom, education is seen as enculturation, a broad and complex process of acquiring knowledge and understanding consistent with Vygotsky's theory of mediated learning. Just as our home culture taught us lessons about the use of language, the culture of a classroom can teach lessons about thinking by giving us models of good thinking; providing direct instruction in thinking processes;

Stand-alone thinking skills programs Programs that teach thinking skills directly without need for extensive subject matter knowledge.

and encouraging practice of those thinking processes through interactions with others.

"We did that last year—how come we have to do it again this year?"

(© W. A. Vanselow—From *Phi Delta Kappan.*)

Critical Thinking. **Critical thinking** skills are useful in almost every life situation—even in evaluating the media ads that constantly bombard us. When you see a group of gorgeous people extolling the virtues of a particular brand of orange juice as they frolic in skimpy bathing suits, you must decide if sex appeal is a relevant factor in choosing a fruit drink (remember Pavlovian advertising from Chapter 6). Table 9.5 provides a representative list of critical thinking skills.

No matter what approach you use to develop critical thinking, it is important to follow up with additional practice. One lesson is not enough. For example, if your class examined a particular historical document to determine if it reflected bias or propaganda, you should follow up by analyzing other written historical documents, contemporary advertisements, or news stories. Until thinking skills become overlearned and relatively automatic, they are not likely to be transferred to new situations. Instead, students will use these skills only to complete the lesson in social studies, not to evaluate the claims made by friends, politicians, toy manufacturers, or diet plans.

How many different words can you list that describe aspects of thinking? Try to "think" of at least 20.

The Language of Thinking. My computer's thesaurus just found over 100 more words when I highlighted "thinking." The language of thinking consists of natural language terms that refer to mental processes and mental products—"words like think, believe, guess, conjecture, hypothesis,

CONNECT & EXTEND

TO **PRAXIS**™
THINKING SKILLS (II, A1)

A nearly universal goal of educational programs across the country is the development of thinking skills. Describe what a teacher can do to cultivate these skills in the classroom. Read *Teaching Thinking Skills* (http://www.nwrel.org/scpd/sirs/6/cu11.html) for a concise overview of research, issues, and key factors related to this topic.

Table 9.5 Examples of Critical Thinking Skills

Defining and Clarifying the Problem

1. Identify central issues or problems.
2. Compare similarities and differences.
3. Determine which information is relevant.
4. Formulate appropriate questions.

Judging Information Related to the Problem

5. Distinguish among fact, opinion, and reasoned judgment.
6. Check consistency.
7. Identify unstated assumptions.
8. Recognize stereotypes and clichés.
9. Recognize bias, emotional factors, propaganda, and semantic slanting.
10. Recognize different value systems and ideologies.

Solving Problems/Drawing Conclusions

11. Recognize the adequacy of data.
12. Predict probable consequences.

SOURCE: From "California Assesses Critical Thinking," by P. Kneedler. In A. Costa (Ed.), *Developing Minds: A Resource Book for Teaching Thinking,* p. 277. Copyright © 1985 by the Association for Supervision and Curriculum Development and author. Reprinted with permission of the ASCD. All rights reserved.

Critical thinking Evaluating conclusions by logically and systematically examining the problem, the evidence, and the solution.

evidence, reasons, estimate, calculate, suspect, doubt, and theorize—to name just a few" (Tishman, Perkins, & Jay, 1995, p. 8). The classroom should be filled with a clear, precise, and rich vocabulary of thinking. Rather than saying, "What do you think about Jamie's answer?" the teacher might ask questions that expand thinking such as, "What evidence can you give to refute or support Jamie's answer?" "What assumptions is Jamie making?" "What are some alternative explanations?" Students surrounded by a rich language of thinking are more likely to think deeply about thinking. Students learn more when they engage in talk that is interpretive and that analyzes and gives explanations. Talk that just describes is less helpful in learning than talk that explains, give reasons, identifies parts, makes a case, defends a position, or evaluates evidence (Palincsar, 1998).

CONNECT & EXTEND

TO YOUR TEACHING/PORTFOLIO
List all the different words related to thinking that you hear during one of your college classes. You might contrast the "thinking language" in a class that seems to challenge you to think with that of a class that focuses on skills and facts.

An Integrated Constructivist Program: Fostering Communities of Learners

Fostering Communities of Learners (FCL) is "a system of interacting activities that results in a self-consciously active and reflective learning environment" (Brown & Campione, 1996, p. 292). This is an entire instructional program is grounded in constructivist learning theories.

CONNECT & EXTEND

TO YOUR TEACHING/PORTFOLIO
Can different formats, such as lecture or seatwork, be used in the service of different models, such as direct instruction or constructivist approaches?

It is tempting to reduce the complex processes and understandings of FCL into a simple set of steps or procedures. But the inventors, Ann Brown and Joseph Campione, themselves caution us that in considering FCL, our emphasis should be on philosophy and principles, not procedures and steps. At the heart of FCL is a three-part process: Students engage in independent and group research on one aspect of the class inquiry topic—for example, animal adaptation and survival. The goal is for the entire class to develop a deep understanding of the topic. Because the material is complex, class mastery requires that students become experts on different aspects of the larger topic and share their expertise. The sharing is motivated by a consequential task—a performance that matters. The task may be a traditional test or it may be a public performance, service project, or competition. Thus, the heart of FCL is *research,* in order to *share* information, in order to *perform* a consequential task (Brown, 1997; Brown & Campione, 1996).

This inquiry cycle may not seem that new, but what sets FCL apart, among other things, is having a variety of research-based ways of accomplishing each phase and paying careful attention to teaching students how benefit intellectually and socially from each step. *Research* can take many forms, such as reading, studying, research seminars, guided writing, consulting with experts face-to-face or electronically, or peer and cross-age tutoring. In order to do research, students are taught and coached in powerful comprehension-monitoring and comprehension-extending strategies such as summarizing and predicting for younger students, and for older students, forming analogies, giving causal explanations, providing evidence, and making sound arguments and predictions. Students are taught explicitly how to *share* information by asking for and giving help, *majoring* (developing special interest and expertise in an area), learning from each others' exhibitions, participating in cooperative groups, and joining in whole class cross-talk sessions to check the progress of the research groups. *Performing* consequential tasks includes publishing, designing, creating solutions to real problems, exhibitions, performances, tests, quizzes, and authentic assessments that can hardly be distinguished from ongoing teaching.

Thoughtful reflection and deep disciplinary content surround and support the *research, share, perform* cycle. FCL teachers create a culture of thinking—self-conscious reflection about important and complex disciplinary units. As Brown and Campione (1996) point out, we "cannot expect students to invest intellectual curiosity and disciplined inquiry on trivia" (p. 306). In FCL classrooms, the teachers' main

Fostering communities of learners (FCL) A system of interacting activities that results in a self-consciously active and reflective learning environment, and uses a research, share, perform learning cycle.

ploy is to "trap students into thinking deeply" about complex content (Brown & Campione, 1996, p. 302).

Working with Families

Not all educational reforms such as FCL are met with approval by families or the community. Many teachers using nontraditional approaches to learning find that they must explain these approaches to students' families. The *Family and Community Partnerships Guidelines* give ideas for communicating with parents about innovative constructivist teaching and learning.

Check Yourself Distinguish between inquiry and problem-based learning.

Describe six features that most cognitive apprenticeship approaches share.

What are instructional conversations?

What is meant by thinking as enculturation?

What is critical thinking?

What is FCL?

Family and Community Partnerships

Communicating about Innovations

Be confident and honest.

Examples

1. Write out your rationale for the methods you are using—consider likely objections and craft your responses.
2. Admit mistakes or oversights—explain what you have learned from them.

Treat parents as equal partners.

Examples

1. Listen carefully to parents' objections, take notes, and follow up on requests or suggestions—remember, you both want the best for the child.
2. Give parents the telephone number of an administrator who will answer their questions about a new program or initiative.
3. Invite families to visit your room or assist in the project in some way.

Communicate effectively.

Examples

1. Use plain language and avoid jargon. If you must use a technical term, define it in accessible ways. Use your best teaching skills to educate parents about the new approach.
2. Encourage local newspapers or television stations to do stories about the "great learning" going on in your classroom or school.
3. Create a lending library of articles and references about the new strategies.

Have examples of projects and assignments available for parents when they visit your class.

Examples

1. Encourage parents to try math activities. If they have trouble, show them how your students (and their child) are successful with the activities and highlight the strategies the students have learned.
2. Keep a library of students' favorite activities to demonstrate for parents.

Develop family involvement packages.

Examples

1. Once a month, send families, via their children, descriptions and examples of the math, science, or language to be learned in the upcoming unit. Include activities children can do with their parents.
2. Make the family project count, for example, as a homework grade.

SOURCE: From "Addressing Parents' Concerns over Curriculum Reform," by M. Meyer, M. Delgardelle, and J. Middleton. *Educational Leadership, 53*(7).

Enhancing Your Expertise with Technology

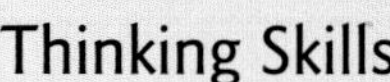

Thinking Skills

Consider this situation. Janet's first end-of-the-year evaluation was going well. The English Department supervisor noted her ability to motivate students, her willingness to participate in co-curricular activities, and her use of effective classroom management techniques. Suddenly, his tone changed. Yes, Janet would be rehired for the next school year. However, based on his classroom observations, analysis of her lesson plans, and comments from her mentoring teacher, the supervisor concluded that Janet needed to take steps to create "a stronger climate for higher-level thinking in her classes." The supervisor was not singling out Janet. Other teachers, including veterans, received the same recommendations in their evaluations.

Most of today's college students went to elementary and high school during a period of reform in the major curricular areas (e.g., science, mathematics), and efforts to reform these areas continue to the present. A common theme of these reforms has been an increased emphasis on the development and use of *higher-order thinking skills.* For some educators, the term primarily refers to inquiry skills, for others it means problem-solving skills, and for some it emphasizes critical thinking skills—so don't assume everyone means the same thing by the term *higher-order thinking.* But whatever their concept of "higher-order," many educators agree that teachers inadvertently devote too much attention to *lower-order thinking skills* (i.e, remembering, comprehending, and applying).

The Center for Critical Thinking (http://www.criticalthinking.org) provides a variety of resources to support teachers' efforts in elementary, secondary, and college classrooms to enhance students' higher-order thinking skills. (The site divides elementary and secondary resources from college resources. Whatever your level, be sure to explore each set of resources.) The resources that you will find at this site should reduce your anxieties (and Janet's) about teaching for higher-order thinking. These resources include easily implemented instructional tactics and assessment strategies to promote a culture of thinking in your classroom. Be sure you examine the typical lessons that have been revised and restructured to encourage the students' higher-order thinking skills.

You might find the following sites valuable too as you build your expertise about thinking skills:

- AEA 7 (http://edservices.aea7.k12.ia.us/framework/thinking/)
- NEA Works4Me Tips Library (http://www.nea.org/helpfrom/growing/works4me/teachtec/thinking.html)
- NRWEL (http://www.nwrel.org/scpd/sirs/6/cu11.html)
- ERIC Digests (http://www.ed.gov/databases/ERIC_Digests/index/) (Type "thinking skills" in the search box.)

Looking Back at Learning

What Would You Say? As part of your interview for a job in a large district, the superintendent asks, "What is your conception of learning? How do students learn?"

For the past four chapters we have examined different aspects of learning. We considered behavioral, information processing, social cognitive, constructivist, and situated explanations of what people learn and how they learn it. As a summary of the different theories of learning, Table 9.6 on page 342 presents several of these perspectives on learning. Rather than debating the merits of each approach, consider their contributions to understanding learning and improving teaching. Don't feel that you must choose the "best" approach—there is no such thing. Chemists, biologists, and nutritionists rely on different theories to explain and improve health. Different views of learning can be used together to create productive learning environments. Behavioral theory helps us understand the role of cues in setting the stage for behaviors and the role of consequences and practice in encouraging or discouraging behaviors. But much of humans' lives and learning is more than behaviors. Language and higher-order thinking requires complex information processing and memory—something the cognitive models of the thinker-as-computer have helped us understand. And what about the person as a creator and constructor of knowledge, not just a processor of information? Here, constructivist perspectives have much to offer.

Check Yourself What do different views of learning add to our understanding?

■ Table 9.6 Four Views of Learning

There are variations within each of these views of learning that differ in emphasis. There is also an overlap in constructivist views.

		Cognitive	Constructivist	
	Behavioral	**Information Processing**	**Psychological/Individual**	**Social/Situated**
	Skinner	J. Anderson	Piaget	Vygotsky
Knowledge	Fixed body of knowledge to acquire Stimulated from outside	Fixed body of knowledge to acquire Stimulated from outside Prior knowledge influences how information is processed	Changing body of knowledge, individually constructed in social world Built on what learner brings	Socially constructed knowledge Built on what participants contribute, construct together
Learning	Acquisition of facts, skills, concepts Occurs through drill, guided practice	Acquisition of facts, skills, concepts, and strategies Occurs through the effective application of strategies	Active construction, restructuring prior knowledge Occurs through multiple opportunities and diverse processes to connect to what is already known	Collaborative construction of socially defined knowledge and values Occurs through socially constructed opportunities
Teaching	Transmission Presentation (Telling)	Transmission Guide students toward more "accurate" and complete knowledge	Challenge, guide thinking toward more complete understanding	Co-construct knowledge with students
Role of Teacher	Manager, supervisor Correct wrong answers	Teach and model effective strategies Correct misconceptions	Facilitator, guide Listen for student's current conceptions, ideas, thinking	Facilitator, guide Co-participant Co-construct different interpretation of knowledge; listen to socially constructed conceptions
Role of Peers	Not usually considered	Not necessary but can influence information processing	Not necessary but can stimulate thinking, raise questions	Ordinary part of process of knowledge construction
Role of Student	Passive reception of information Active listener, direction-follower	Active processor of information, strategy user Organizer and reorganizer of information Rememberer	Active construction (within mind) Active thinker, explainer, interpreter, questioner	Active co-construction with others and self Active thinker, explainer, interpreter, questioner Active social participator

SOURCE: From *Reconceptualizing Learning for Restructured Schools* by H. H. Marshall. Paper presented at the Annual Meeting of the American Educational Research Association, April 1992. Copyright © Hermine H. Marshall. Adapted with permission.

Summary Table

Social Processes in Learning

(pp. 314–315)

What are some of the social factors that influence learning in school? Parents, peers, and teachers influence norms and values about school achievement. Children tend to select friends that share their orientations and interests, and these peer groups, in turn, influence children's academic motivation. But parents and teachers play a role, too. Students with authoritative parents are more likely to choose positive peer groups and to resist peer pressure for antisocial behaviors such as drug use. If students have few or no friends, being liked by the teacher can be especially important.

Social Learning and Social Cognitive Theories

(pp. 315–322)

Distinguish between social learning and social cognitive theories. Social learning theory was an early neobehavioral theory that expanded behavioral views of reinforcement and punishment. In behavioral views, reinforcement and punishment directly affect behavior. In social learning theory, seeing another person, a model, reinforced or punished can have similar effects on the observer's behavior. Social cognitive theory expands social learning theory to include cognitive factors such as beliefs, expectations, and perceptions of self.

Distinguish between enactive and vicarious learning. *Enactive learning* is learning by doing and experiencing the consequences of your actions. *Vicarious learning* is learning by observing, which challenges the behaviorist idea that cognitive factors are unnecessary in an explanation of learning. Much is going on mentally before performance and reinforcement can even take place.

What are the elements of observational learning? In order to learn through observation, we have to pay attention to aspects of the situation that will help us learn. In order to imitate the behavior of a model, you have to retain the information. This involves mentally representing the model's actions in some way, probably as verbal steps. In the production phase, practice makes the behavior smoother and more expert. Sometimes we need a great deal of practice, feedback, and coaching about subtle points before we can reproduce the behavior of the model. Finally, motivation shapes observational learning through incentives and reinforcement. We may not perform a learned behavior until there is some motivation or incentive to do so. Reinforcement can focus attention, encourage reproduction or practice, and maintain the new learning.

What is reciprocal determinism? Personal factors (beliefs, expectations, attitudes, and knowledge), the physical and social environment (resources, consequences of actions, other people, and physical settings), and behavior (individual actions, choices, and verbal statements) all influence and are influenced by each other.

Social Learning Theory: Theory that emphasizes learning through observation of others.

Social Cognitive Theory: Theory that adds concern with cognitive factors such as beliefs, self-perceptions, and expectations to social learning theory.

Observational Learning: Learning by observation and imitation of others.

Vicarious Reinforcement: Increasing the chances that we will repeat a behavior by observing another person being reinforced for that behavior.

Self-Efficacy: A person's sense of being able to deal effectively with a particular task.

Ripple Effect: "Contagious" spreading of behaviors through imitation.

Modeling: Changes in behavior, thinking, or emotions that occur through observing another person—a model.

Reciprocal Determinism: An explanation of behavior that emphasizes the mutual effects of the individual and the environment on each other.

Constructivism and Situated Learning

(pp. 322–328)

Describe three kinds of constructivism. *Psychological* constructivists such as Piaget are concerned with how *individuals* make sense of their world, based on individual knowledge, beliefs, self-concept, or identity—also called *first wave constructivism. Social* constructivists such as Vygotsky believe that social interaction, cultural tools, and activity shape individual development and learning—also called *second wave constructivism.* By participating in a broad range of activities with others, learners appropriate the outcomes produced by working together; they acquire new strategies and knowledge of their world. Finally, constructivists are interested in how public knowledge in academic disciplines is constructed as well as how everyday beliefs about the world are communicated to new members of a sociocultural group.

In what ways do constructivist views differ about knowledge sources, accuracy, and generality? Constructivists debate whether knowledge is constructed by mapping external reality, by adapting and changing internal understandings, or by an interaction of external forces and internal understandings. Most psychologists posit a role for both internal and external factors, but differ in how much they emphasize one or the other. Also, there is discussion about whether knowledge can be constructed in one situation and applied to another or whether knowledge is situated, that is, specific and tied to the context in which it was learned.

What are some common elements in most constructivist views of learning? Even though there is no single constructivist theory, many constructivist approaches recommend complex, challenging learning environments and authentic tasks; social negotiation and co-construction; multiple representations of content; understanding that knowledge is constructed; and student ownership of learning.

Constructivism: View that emphasizes the active role of the learner in building understanding and making sense of information.

First Wave Constructivism: A focus on the individual and psychological sources of knowing, as in Piaget's theory.

Appropriate: Internalize or take for yourself knowledge and skills developed in interaction with others or with cultural tools.

Second Wave Constructivism: A focus on the social and cultural sources of knowing, as in Vygotsky's theory.

Community of Practice: Social situation or context in which ideas are judged useful or true.

Situated Learning: The idea that skills and knowledge are tied to the situation in which they were learned and difficult to apply in new settings.

Complex Learning Environments: Problems and learning situations that mimic the ill-structured nature of real life.

Social Negotiation: Aspect of learning process that relies on collaboration with others and respect for different perspectives.

Intersubjective Attitude: A commitment to build shared meaning with others by finding common ground and exchanging interpretations.

Multiple Representations of Content: Considering problems using various analogies, examples, and metaphors.

Spiral Curriculum: Bruner's structure for teaching that introduces the fundamental structure of all subjects early in the school years, then revisits the subjects in more and more complex forms over time.

Applications of Constructivist and Situated Perspectives on Learning

(pp. 329–340)

Distinguish between inquiry and problem-based learning. The inquiry strategy begins when the teacher presents a puzzling event, question, or problem. The students then formulate hypotheses to explain the event or solve the problem; collect data to test the hypotheses; draw conclusions; and reflect on the original problem and the thinking processes needed to solve it. Problem-based learning may follow a similar path, but the learning begins with an authentic problem—one that matters to the students. The goal is to learn math or science or history or some other important subject while seeking a real solution to a real problem.

Describe six features that most cognitive apprenticeship approaches share. Students observe an expert (usually the teacher) *model* the performance; get external support through *coaching* or tutoring; and receive conceptual *scaffolding,* which is then gradually faded as the student becomes more competent and proficient. Students continually *articulate* their knowledge—putting into words their understanding of the processes and content being learned. They *reflect* on their progress, comparing their problem solving to an expert's performance and to their own earlier performances. Finally, students *explore* new ways to apply what they are learning—ways that they have not practiced at the master's side.

What are instructional conversations? Instructional conversations are *instructional* because they are designed to promote learning, but they are *conversations,* not lectures or traditional discussions. They are responsive to students' contributions, challenging but not threatening, connected, and interactive—involving all the students. The teacher's goal is to keep everyone cognitively engaged in a substantive discussion.

What is meant by thinking as enculturation? *Enculturation* is a broad and complex process of acquiring knowledge and understanding consistent with Vygotsky's theory of mediated learning. Just as our home culture taught us lessons about the use of language, the culture of a classroom can teach lessons about thinking by giving us *models* of good thinking; providing *direct instruction* in thinking processes; and encouraging *practice* of those thinking processes through *interactions* with others.

What is critical thinking? Critical thinking skills include defining and clarifying the problem, making judgments about the consistency and adequacy of the information related to a problem, and drawing conclusions. No matter what approach you use to develop critical thinking, it is important to follow up activities with additional practice. One lesson is not enough.

What is FCL? Fostering Communities of Learners is an approach to organizing classrooms and schools. The heart of FCL is *research,* in order to *share* information, in order to *perform* a consequential task that involves deep disciplinary content. Students engage in independent and group research so the entire class can develop an understanding of the topic. Because the material is complex, class mastery requires that students become experts on different aspects of the larger topic and share their expertise. The sharing is motivated by a consequential task—a performance that matters.

Inquiry Learning: Approach in which the teacher presents a puzzling situation and students solve the problem by gathering data and testing their conclusions.

Problem-Based Learning: Methods that provide students with realistic problems that don't necessarily have "right" answers.

Anchored Instruction: A type of problem-based learning that uses a complex interesting situation as an anchor for learning.

Instructional Conversation: Situation in which students learn through interactions with teachers and/or other students.

Cognitive Apprenticeship: A relationship in which a less experienced learner acquires knowledge and skills under the guidance of an expert.

Stand-Alone Thinking Skills Programs: Programs that teach thinking skills directly without need for extensive subject matter knowledge.

Critical Thinking: Evaluating conclusions by logically and systematically examining the problem, the evidence, and the solution.

Fostering Communities of Learners (FCL): A system of interacting activities that results in a self-consciously active and reflective learning environment and uses a research, share, perform learning cycle.

Enhancing Your Expertise with Technology: Thinking Skills

(p. 341)

Center for Critical Thinking **(http://www.criticalthinking.org)**

AEA 7 **(http://edservices.aea7.k12.ia.us/framework/thinking/)**

NEA Works4Me Tips Library **(http://www.nea.org/helpfrom/growing/works4me/teachtec/thinking.html)**

NRWEL **(http://www.nwrel.org/scpd/sirs/6/cu11.html)**

Looking Back at Learning

(Section pp. 341–342)

What do different views of learning add to our understanding? Rather than debating the merits of each approach, consider their contributions to understanding learning and improving teaching. Different views of learning can be used together to create productive learning environments. Great teachers know and use them all.

Becoming a Professional

Passing the PRAXIS™

Chapter 9 reflects many of the professional standards created by the Interstate New Teacher Assessment and Support Consortium (INTASC). These standards form the basis of the PRAXIS II™ and state-created teacher licensure exams.

One influential idea from the constructivist perspective on learning is that visiting materials in different contexts for different purposes can enhance the acquisition of knowledge. In a sense, the teacher and students "crisscross" a learning landscape. This chapter's Teachers' Casebook is a landscape especially well suited for several visits. Thoughtful learning activities about such topics as motivation, learning environments, evaluation, and instructional strategies could well be explored through the instructional challenges here.

For a first excursion through this landscape, let's examine student-centered models of instruction, one of the major topics of this chapter. A problem you seem to face in this scenario is a mismatch between the students and the curriculum that exists for them. Most of the students appear unmotivated. Perhaps they see your activities as unconnected to their lives or that they have no responsibility for their own learning. Knowledge of student centered models of instruction can help you address those concerns and draw your students into active, meaningful learning that is absent in your classroom.

Tips for PRAXIS II™

Explain the advantages and appropriate uses of major student-centered approaches to learning and instruction:

- Cooperative learning
- Inquiry method
- Problem-based learning
- Instructional conversations
- Cognitive apprenticeships

Understand important concepts related to student-centered models of instruction:

- Situated learning
- Critical thinking/Culture of thinking
- Complex learning environments
- Authentic tasks
- Multiple representations of content

Related Topics

- Tapping interests (Chapter 10)
- Objectives for learning (Chapter 12)
- Authentic assessment (Chapters 14 and 15)
- Examples of student-centered teaching in reading, mathematics, and science (Chapter 12)

Standards and Licensure Appendix: *PRAXIS II™ and INTASC*

Refer to the Appendix at the end of the book for detailed correlations to PRAXIS II™ exam topics and INTASC Standards addressed in this text.

Insights about Job Interviews: *What Would You Say?*

1. What is your conception of learning? How do students learn?
2. Who are your models as teachers? Are there teachers from films or books that you would like to be like?

Your Teaching Portfolio: *Teaching Resources*

- Use Table 9.6, "Four Views of Learning" to think about your own philosophy of learning. Would you incorporate elements from different theoretical approaches into your personal conception of learning?
- Use the *Family and Community Partnerships Guidelines* to brainstorm ideas for how you would explain your teaching innovations to families. Experiment by drafting a "Newsletter." Add Table 9.4, "Elements of an Instructional Conversation" to your **Teaching Resources** file.

VideoWorkshop Extra

If the VideoWorkshop package was included with your textbook, go to Chapter 9 of the Companion Website (www.ablongman.com/woolfolk) and click on the VideoWorkshop button. Follow the instructions for viewing *Video Clip 10: Classroom Management.* Consider this information along with what you've read in Chapter 9 while answering the following questions:

1. Explain the relationship between "active learning" and the constructivist view of learning.
2. Explain the differences among psychological constructivism, social constructivism, and sociological constructivism. Include examples.

Use the CD-ROM included in the back of your textbook to launch the "Becoming a Professional" website. The website features advice on preparing for teacher certification exams, help with getting your first job, and resources to help you perform your job well from the first day forward.

Teachers' Casebook

What Would They Do?

Here is how some practicing teachers responded to the teaching situation presented at the beginning of this chapter about the awful "book reviews."

Mark H. Smith

Teacher, Grades Nine–Twelve, *Medford High School, Medford, Massachusetts*

Experience is the best teacher. In an ideal world you can plan your course with what you think would be great material and be ready with a curriculum to meet the level you expect. But reality sets in when you see the true level of the class. High standards and expectations are great goals but they must be reasonable for the students in your class. The education profession is one that needs constant flexibility and adjustment to situations. Students learn in different ways and teachers who can adapt to classes and curricula have a better chance of succeeding.

Because this class has many different levels it will be important to find some common ground that will interest them as well as get them involved in learning. It will probably be a good idea to do different activities and even let the three top students help teach some of the others. It will not be easy to get everybody on the same page and you will probably have to spend lots of time planning, but with patience and effort you can find the level that fits and get the students to respond.

Thomas W. Newkirk

Eighth Grade Teacher, *Hamilton Heights Middle School, Arcadia, Indiana*

It would be wonderful from the outset to have a class enthralled with world literature, but you are more likely to have a class frustrated with the prospect of reading another "lame" book. Therefore, it is important to find books with themes relevant to my students. Fortunately, on the reading list there are already some selections related to recent films, and probably there are some selections related to music, television, or even commercials. The more connections I can make between the literature and my students' lives, the more likely I am to motivate them.

Jeff D. Horton

Seventh–Tenth Grade Teacher, *Colton School, Colton, Washington*

One problem may be the materials that the teacher planned to use. I do believe that students need to be introduced to the "classics" in literature. However, teachers are self-motivated to read and study these writings. We must remember that most students do not feel the same way. The teacher in this scenario must present the "classics" in a way that will hold the students' interest. Instead of reading a whole book, pick out parts that reflect the writing style or message of the author. Then present other parts of the book using other teaching tools. There are movies available that are presented in a more current style that will appeal to students. Whatever the teaching tool used, there must always be a learning activity connected to it.

While three students in the class demonstrate a sophisticated understanding of literature, every student in the class can bring a fresh insight into a discussion and be recognized for his or her contribution. In addition to class discussion, individual and group projects can be designed to encourage students to respond to the material. Considering the diversity of the class, I would evaluate student achievement with grading contracts that challenge students performing at different levels.

Michael J. Ellis

Tenth and Eleventh Grade English Teacher, *Quincy High School, Quincy, Massachusetts*

It seems the purpose behind the curriculum for this class is to expose the students to a wide array of great literature. That is a noble goal. In teaching, however, nobility must frequently give way to practicality. A teacher's first duty is to guide his students in the acquisition of necessary skills. Sometimes having them read Dickens isn't the best way to do that. The curriculum worked up over the summer will probably work well with the three standouts in the class. I'd try splintering them off from the rest. This can be a logistical nightmare and it effectively doubles your prep time for the class, but it's the best way to be sure that the students of a particular ability level don't stagnate while you cater to another group.

With the rest of the class, it's time to shift on the fly and ditch the original reading list. Emphasizing longer novels in a class dominated by poor readers is nothing less than a suicide attempt spread over 40 weeks. If you rely instead on shorter selections and young adult fiction titles with catchy plot lines, then you've at least given yourself a fighting chance at a class that actually finishes the books. It's also never a bad idea to throw video material into the mix.

Go to the Companion Website (www.ablongman.com/woolfolk) for additional case studies including audio and video cases, and examples of student work.

CHAPTER

10

Motivation in Learning and Teaching

Teachers' Casebook

What Would You Do?

It is July and you have just been hired to teach 3rd grade. This grade wasn't your first choice. Neither was this district, for that matter, but job openings were really tight, so you're pleased with your new position. You are discovering that the teaching resources in your school are slim to none; the only resources are some aging texts and the workbooks that go with them. Every idea you have suggested for software, simulation games, visual aids, or other more active teaching materials has been greeted with the same response, "There's no money in the budget for that." As you look over the texts and workbooks, you wonder how the students could be anything but bored by them. To make matters worse, the texts look pretty high-level for 3rd grade. But the objectives in the workbooks are important. Besides, the district curriculum requires these units and students will be tested on them in district-wide assessments next spring.

Critical Thinking

How would you arouse student curiosity and interest about the topics and tasks in the workbooks? How would you establish the value of learning this material? How would you handle the difficulty level of the texts? What do you need to know about motivation to solve these problems?

Collaboration

With 2 or 3 other members of your class, brainstorm what you could do to motivate your students.

Most educators agree that motivating students is one of the critical tasks of teaching. We begin with the question "What is motivation?" and examine many of the answers that have been proposed, including a discussion of intrinsic and extrinsic motivation and four general theories of motivation: behavioral, humanistic, cognitive, and sociocultural.

Next we consider more closely several personal factors that frequently appear in discussions of motivation: goal orientations; interests and emotions; and self-schemas, including the important concept of self-efficacy.

How do we put all this information together in teaching? How do we create environments, situations, and relationships that encourage motivation? First, we consider how the personal influences on motivation come together to support motivation to learn. Then, we examine how motivation is influenced by the academic work of the class, the value of the work, and the setting in which the work must be done. Finally, we discuss a number of strategies for developing motivation as a constant state in your classroom and as a permanent trait in your students.

By the time you have completed this chapter, you should be able to answer these questions:

- *What are intrinsic and extrinsic motivation and motivation to learn?*
- *How is motivation conceptualized in the behavioral, cognitive, humanistic, and sociocultural perspectives?*
- *What are the possible motivational effects of success and failure, and how do these effects relate to beliefs about ability?*
- *What are the roles of goals, interests, emotions, and beliefs about the self in motivation?*
- *What external factors can teachers influence that will encourage students' motivation to learn?*
- *What is your strategy for teaching your subject to an uninterested student?*

Days to Live by Hessam Abrishami. Original on canvas, 40″ × 30″. Reproduced with permission.

What Is Motivation?

CONNECT & EXTEND

TO THE RESEARCH
For a thorough discussion of the many terms and concepts related to motivation, see Murphy, P. K., & Alexander, P. A. (2000). A motivated exploration of motivation terminology. *Contemporary Educational Psychology, 25,* 3–53.

Motivation is usually defined as *an internal state that arouses, directs, and maintains behavior.* Psychologists studying motivation have focused on five basic questions:

1. *What choices do people make about their behavior?* Why do some students, for example, focus on their homework and others watch television?
2. *How long does it take to get started?* Why do some students start their homework right away, while others procrastinate?
3. *What is the intensity or level of involvement in the chosen activity?* Once the book bag is opened, is the student absorbed and focused or just going through the motions?
4. *What causes a person to persist or to give up?* Will a student read the entire Shakespeare assignment or just a few pages?
5. *What is the individual thinking and feeling while engaged in the activity?* Is the student enjoying Shakespeare, feeling competent, or worrying about an upcoming test (Graham & Weiner, 1996; Pintrich, Marx, & Boyle, 1993)?

CONNECT & EXTEND

TO YOUR TEACHING/PORTFOLIO

- Hopeless Henry is an example of a student experiencing *learned helplessness,* discussed later in the chapter.
- Safe Sarah is an example of a student who is motivated by *extrinsic* factors, sets *performance goals,* fears *failure,* and views *ability as fixed.* She is also a (successful) *failure-avoiding student*—discussed later in the chapter.
- Satisfied Sam is an example of a student motivated by *intrinsic* factors. He set *learning goals* in his areas of interest, but just wants to perform "OK" in other areas. These concepts are discussed later in the chapter.
- Defensive Diana is an example of a student who is motivated by extrinsic factors, sets *performance goals, fears failure,* and views *ability as fixed.* She is also a *failure-avoiding student.* Because she avoids work, she may soon become a *failure-accepting student*—discussed later in the chapter.
- Anxious Amy is an example of a student experiencing debilitating *anxiety,* discussed later in the chapter.

Meeting Some Students

As you will see in this chapter and the next, there are many factors that influence motivation. To get a sense of the complexity, let's step into a middle school general science classroom just after the teacher has given directions for a class activity. The student profiles are taken from Stipek (2002).

Hopeless Henry won't even start the assignment—as usual. He just keeps saying, "I don't understand," or "This is too hard." When he answers your questions correctly, he "guessed" and he "doesn't really know." Henry spends most of his time staring into space; he is falling farther and farther behind. Harry has trouble with question 2 above (getting started) and with question 5; during the activity he feels defeated and helpless.

Safe Sarah checks with you about every step—she wants to be perfect. You once gave her bonus points for doing an excellent color drawing of the apparatus, and now she produces a work of art for lab every time. But Sarah won't risk getting a B. If it isn't required or on the test, Sarah isn't interested. In terms of the five questions above, Sarah (1) makes good choices, (2) gets started right away, and (3) persists. But she is not really engaged and takes little pleasure in the work (4 and 5).

Satisfied Sam on the other hand, is interested in this project. In fact, he knows more than you do about it. Evidently he spends hours reading about chemistry and performing experiments. But his overall grade in your class is between B$^-$ and C$^+$ because when you were studying biology, Sam was satisfied with the C he could get on tests without even trying. In terms of the five questions about motivation, as long as he is following his own choices, Sam is prompt in getting started, engaged, persistent, and enjoys the task.

Defensive Diana doesn't have her lab manual—again, so she has to share with another student. Then she pretends to be working, but spends most of her time making fun of the assignment or trying to get answers from other students when your back is turned. She is afraid to try because if she makes an effort and fails, she fears that everyone will know she is "dumb." In terms of the five questions above, Diana makes poor choices, procrastinates, avoids engagement, and gives up easily because she is so concerned about how others will judge her.

Anxious Amy is a good student in most subjects, but she freezes on science tests and "forgets" everything she knows when she has to answer questions in class. Her parents are scientists and expect her to become one too, but her prospects

Motivation An internal state that arouses, directs, and maintains behavior.

for this future look dim. Amy's problems have to do with question 5 above—what she thinks and how she feels as she works. Her worry and anxiety may lead her to make poor choices and procrastinate, which only makes her more anxious at test time.

Each student presents a different motivational challenge, yet you have to teach the entire class. In the next few pages we will look more closely at the meaning of motivation so we can better understand these students.

Intrinsic and Extrinsic Motivation

We all know how it feels to be motivated, to move energetically toward a goal or to work hard, even if we are bored by the task. What energizes and directs our behavior? The explanation could be drives, needs, incentives, fears, goals, social pressure, self-confidence, interests, curiosity, beliefs, values, expectations, and more. Some psychologists have explained motivation in terms of personal *traits* or individual characteristics. Certain people, so the theory goes, have a strong *need* to achieve, a *fear* of tests, or an enduring *interest* in art, so they work hard to achieve, avoid tests, or spend hours in art galleries. Other psychologists see motivation more as a *state,* a temporary situation. If, for example, you are reading this paragraph because you have a test tomorrow, you are motivated (at least for now) by the situation. Of course, the motivation we experience at any given time usually is a combination of trait and state. You may be studying because you value learning *and* because you are preparing for a test.

As you can see, some explanations of motivation rely on internal, personal factors such as needs, interests, and curiosity. Other explanations point to external, environmental factors—rewards, social pressure, punishment, and so on. A classic distinction in motivation is between intrinsic and extrinsic. **Intrinsic motivation** is the natural tendency to seek out and conquer challenges as we pursue personal interests and exercise capabilities (Deci & Ryan, 1985; Reeve, 1996; Ryan & Deci, 2000). When we are intrinsically motivated, we do not need incentives or punishments, because *the activity itself is rewarding.* Satisfied Sam studies chemistry outside school simply because he loves the activity; no one makes him do it.

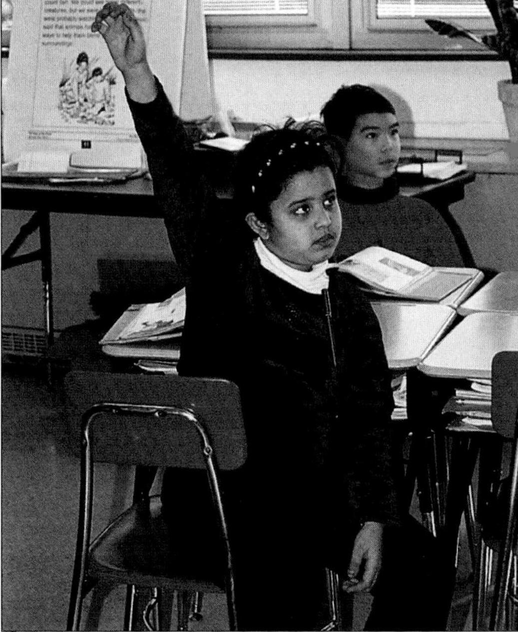

A basic question in motivation is "Where does it come from—within or outside the individual?" Why does this girl raise her hand in class—because she is interested in the subject or because she wants to earn a good grade? The answer is probably more complicated than either alternative.

In contrast, when we do something in order to earn a grade, avoid punishment, please the teacher, or for some other reason that has very little to do with the task itself, we experience **extrinsic motivation.** We are not really interested in the activity for its own sake; we care only about what it will gain us. Safe Sarah works for the grade; she has little interest in the subject itself.

According to psychologists who adopt the intrinsic/extrinsic concept of motivation, it is impossible to tell just by looking if a behavior is intrinsically or extrinsically motivated. The essential difference between the two types of motivation is the student's reason for acting, that is, whether the **locus of causality** for the action (the location of the cause) is internal or external—inside or outside the person. Students who read or practice their backstroke or paint may be reading, swimming, or painting because they freely chose the activity based on personal interests (*internal locus* of causality/intrinsic motivation), or because someone or something else outside is influencing them (*external locus* of causality/extrinsic motivation) (Reeve, 1996).

As you think about your own motivation, you probably realize that the dichotomy between intrinsic and extrinsic motivation is too simple—too all-or-nothing. One explanation is that our activities fall along a continuum from fully *self-determined* (intrinsic motivation) to fully *determined by others* (extrinsic motivation). For example, students may freely choose to work hard on activities that they don't find particularly enjoyable because they know the activities are important in reaching a valued goal—such as spending hours studying educational psychology in order to

Intrinsic motivation Motivation associated with activities that are their own reward.

Extrinsic motivation Motivation created by external factors such as rewards and punishments.

Locus of causality The location—internal or external—of the cause of behavior.

CONNECT & EXTEND

TO THE RESEARCH
To capture the difference between self- and other-determination, Richard deCharms (1976, 1983) used the metaphor of people as "origins" and "pawns." Origins perceive themselves as the origin or source of their intention to act in a certain way. As pawns, people see themselves as powerless participants in a game controlled by others. When people feel like pawns, play becomes work, leisure feels like obligation, and intrinsic motivation becomes extrinsic motivation. For example, you may have had the experience of deciding to wash the car or clean your room, only to have your motivation dampened by a parent who insists that you tackle the chore. Your chance to be an origin seems spoiled by outside attempts at control. You don't want to wash the car anymore because your sense of self-determination is taken away. DeCharms observed that students are too little governed by their own intrinsic motivation and too powerless over external controls. To deal with the issue, he developed programs to help teachers support student self-determination. The programs emphasized setting realistic goals, personal planning of activities to reach the goals, personal responsibility for actions, and feelings of self-confidence.

become a good teacher. Is this intrinsic or extrinsic motivation? Actually, it is in between—the person is freely choosing to accept outside causes such as certification requirements and then is trying to get the most benefit from the requirements. The person has *internalized an external cause.*

"What do I get for just neatness?"

(© Glenn Bernhardt)

Recently the notion of intrinsic and extrinsic motivation as two ends of a continuum has been challenged. An alternative explanation is that just as motivation can include both trait and state factors, it can also include both intrinsic and extrinsic factors. Intrinsic and extrinsic tendencies are two independent possibilities, and, at any given time, we can be motivated by some of each (Covington & Mueller, 2001). This makes sense because in school, both intrinsic and extrinsic motivation are useful. Teaching can create intrinsic motivation by connecting to students' interests and supporting growing competence. But you know this won't work all the time. Did you find long division inherently interesting? Was your curiosity piqued by irregular verbs? If teachers count on intrinsic motivation to energize all their students all of the time, they will be disappointed. There are situations where incentives and external supports are necessary. Teachers must encourage and nurture intrinsic motivation, while making sure that extrinsic motivation supports learning (Brophy, 1988; Deci, Koestner, & Ryan, 1999; Ryan & Deci, 1996). To do this, they need to know about the factors that influence motivation.

Check Yourself Define motivation.

What is the difference between intrinsic and extrinsic motivation?

How does locus of causality apply to motivation?

Four General Approaches to Motivation

Why are you reading this chapter? Are you curious about motivation and interested in the topic? Or is there a test in your near future? Do you need this course to earn a teaching certificate or to graduate? Maybe you believe that you will do well in this class, and that belief keeps you working. Perhaps it is some combination of these reasons. What motivates you to study motivation?

CONNECT & EXTEND

TO THE RESEARCH
Weiner, B. (1990). History of motivational research in education. *Journal of Educational Psychology, 82,* 616–622.

Motivation is a vast and complicated subject encompassing many theories. Some theories were developed through work with animals in laboratories. Others are based on research with humans in situations that used games or puzzles. Some theories grow out of the work done in clinical or industrial psychology. Our examination of the field will be selective; otherwise we would never finish the topic.

Behavioral Approaches to Motivation

Reward An attractive object or event supplied as a consequence of a behavior.

According to the behavioral view, an understanding of student motivation begins with a careful analysis of the incentives and rewards present in the classroom. A **reward** is an attractive object or event supplied as a consequence of a particular behavior. For example, Safe Sarah was rewarded with bonus points when she drew an excellent diagram. An **incentive** is an object or event that encourages or discourages behavior. The promise of an A$^+$ was an incentive to Sarah. Actually receiving the grade was a reward.

If we are consistently reinforced for certain behaviors, we may develop habits or tendencies to act in certain ways. For example, if a student is repeatedly rewarded with affection, money, praise, or privileges for earning letters in baseball, but receives little recognition for studying, the student will probably work longer and harder on perfecting her fastball than on understanding geometry. Providing grades, stars, stickers, and other reinforcements for learning—or demerits for misbehavior—is an attempt to motivate students by extrinsic means of incentives, rewards, and punishments.

According to Maslow's hierarchy, when the needs for love and belongingness are met, individuals can then address the so-called higher level needs of intellectual achievement and self-actualization.

Humanistic Approaches to Motivation

In the 1940s, proponents of humanistic psychology such as Carl Rogers argued that neither of the dominant schools of psychology, behavioral or Freudian, adequately explained why people act as they do. Humanistic interpretations of motivation emphasize such intrinsic sources of motivation as a person's needs for "self-actualization" (Maslow, 1970, 1968), the inborn "actualizing tendency" (Rogers & Freiberg, 1994), or the need for "self-determination" (Deci, Vallerand, Pelletier, & Ryan, 1991). So from the **humanistic perspective,** to motivate means to encourage peoples' inner resources—their sense of competence, self-esteem, autonomy, and self-actualization. Maslow's theory is a very influential humanistic explanation of motivation.

Maslow's Hierarchy. Abraham Maslow (1970) suggested that humans have a **hierarchy of needs** ranging from lower-level needs for survival and safety to higher-level needs for intellectual achievement and finally self-actualization. **Self-actualization** is Maslow's term for self-fulfillment, the realization of personal potential. Each of the lower needs must be met before the next higher need can be addressed.

Maslow (1968) called the four lower-level needs—for survival, then safety, followed by belonging, and then self-esteem—**deficiency needs.** When these needs are satisfied, the motivation for fulfilling them decreases. He labeled the three higher-level needs—intellectual achievement, then aesthetic appreciation, and finally self-actualization—**being needs.** When they are met, a person's motivation does not cease; instead, it increases to seek further fulfillment. Unlike the deficiency needs, these being needs can never be completely filled. For example, the more successful you are in your efforts to develop as a teacher, the harder you are likely to strive for even greater improvement.

Maslow's theory has been criticized for the very obvious reason that people do not always appear to behave as the theory would predict. Most of us move back and forth among different types of needs and may even be motivated by many different needs at the same time. Some people deny themselves safety or friendship in order to achieve knowledge, understanding, or greater self-esteem.

Criticisms aside, Maslow's theory does give us a way of looking at the whole student, whose physical, emotional, and intellectual needs are all interrelated. A child whose feelings of safety and sense of belonging are threatened by divorce may have little interest in learning to divide fractions. If a school is a fearful, unpredictable place where neither teachers nor students know where they stand, they are likely to be more concerned with security and less with learning or teaching. Belonging to a social group and maintaining self-esteem within that group, for example, are important to students. If doing what the teacher says conflicts with group rules, students may choose to ignore the teacher's wishes or even defy the teacher.

CONNECT & EXTEND

TO **PRAXIS**™
MASLOW (I, C1)
Consider how problems with satisfying Maslow's needs can affect student learning. Link these ideas to direct or vicarious experiences you might have had in school.

Incentive An object or event that encourages or discourages behavior.

Humanistic perspective Approach to motivation that emphasizes personal freedom, choice, self-determination, and striving for personal growth.

Hierarchy of needs Maslow's model of seven levels of human needs, from basic physiological requirements to the need for self-actualization.

Self-actualization Fulfilling one's potential.

Deficiency needs Maslow's four lower-level needs, which must be satisfied first.

Being needs Maslow's three higher-level needs, sometimes called growth needs.

CONNECT & EXTEND

TO THE RESEARCH

See the entire issue of *Educational Leadership*, September 2002 (Vol. 60, No. 1) for 14 articles on "Do Students Care About Learning?" These articles discuss how to create enthusiasm, excitement, and investment in learning.

Cognitive Approaches to Motivation

In many ways, cognitive theories of motivation also developed as a reaction to the behavioral views. Cognitive theorists believe that behavior is determined by our thinking, not simply by whether we have been rewarded or punished for the behavior in the past (Stipek, 2002). Behavior is initiated and regulated by plans (Miller, Galanter, & Pribram, 1960), goals (Locke & Latham, 1990), schemas (Ortony, Clore, & Collins, 1988), expectations (Vroom, 1964), and attributions (Weiner, 1992). One of the central assumptions in cognitive approaches is that people do not respond to external events or physical conditions such as hunger, but rather to their interpretations of these events. In cognitive theories, people are seen as active and curious, searching for information to solve personally relevant problems. Thus, cognitive theorists emphasize intrinsic motivation. Bernard Weiner's attribution theory is a good example.

CONNECT & EXTEND

TO **PRAXIS**™

ATTRIBUTION THEORY (I, C1)

Go to the *Encyclopedia of Psychology* (http://www.psychology.org/links/Environment_Behavior_Relationships/Motivation/) and follow its link for Attribution Theory to learn more about using principles derived from this theory to boost intrinsic motivation to learn.

Attribution Theory. This cognitive explanation of motivation begins with the assumption that we try to make sense of our own behavior and the behavior of others by searching for explanations and causes. To understand our own successes and failures, particularly unexpected ones, we all ask "Why?" Students ask themselves, "Why did I flunk my midterm?" or "Why did I do so well this grading period?" They may attribute their successes and failures to ability, effort, mood, knowledge, luck, help, interest, clarity of instructions, the interference of others, unfair policies, and so on. To understand the success and failures of others, we also make attributions—that the others are smart or lucky or work hard, for example. **Attribution theories** of motivation describe how the individual's explanations, justifications, and excuses about self or others influence motivation.

Bernard Weiner is one of the main educational psychologists responsible for relating attribution theory to school learning (Weiner, 1979, 1986, 1992, 1994a, 1994b, 2000; Weiner & Graham, 1989). According to Weiner, most of the attributed causes for successes or failures can be characterized in terms of three dimensions:

1. *locus* (location of the cause internal or external to the person),
2. *stability* (whether the cause stays the same or can change), and
3. *controllability* (whether the person can control the cause).

Every cause for success or failure can be categorized on these three dimensions. For example, luck is external (locus), unstable (stability), and uncontrollable (controllability). Table 10.1 shows some common attributions for success or failure on a test.

Table 10.1 Weiner's Theory of Causal Attribution

There are many explanations students can give for why they fail a test. Below are eight reasons representing the eight combinations of locus, stability, and responsibility in Weiner's model of attributions.

Dimension Classification	Reason for Failure
Internal-stable-uncontrollable	Low aptitude
Internal-stable-controllable	Never studies
Internal-unstable-uncontrollable	Sick the day of the exam
Internal-unstable-controllable	Did not study for this particular test
External-stable-uncontrollable	School has hard requirements
External-stable-controllable	Instructor is biased
External-unstable-uncontrollable	Bad luck
External-unstable-controllable	Friends failed to help

SOURCE: From *Human Motivation: Metaphors, Theories and Research*, by B. Weiner. Published by Sage Publications, Newbury Park, CA. Copyright © 1992 by Sage Publications. Adapted with permission of the publisher.

Attribution theories Descriptions of how individuals' explanations, justifications, and excuses influence their motivation and behavior.

Weiner believes that these three dimensions have important implications for motivation because they affect expectancy and value. The *stability* dimension, for example, seems to be closely related to expectations about the future. If students attribute their failure to stable factors such as the difficulty of the subject, they will expect to fail in that subject in the future. But if they attribute the outcome to unstable factors such as mood or luck, they can hope for better outcomes next time. The *internal/external locus* seems to be closely related to feelings of self-esteem (Weiner, 2000). If success or failure is attributed to internal factors, success will lead to pride and increased motivation, whereas failure will diminish self-esteem.

The *controllability* dimension is related to emotions such as anger, pity, gratitude, or shame. If we feel responsible for our failures, we may feel guilt; if we feel responsible for successes, we may feel proud. Failing at a task we cannot control can lead to shame or anger.

When failure is attributed to lack of ability, and ability is considered *uncontrollable*, the sequence of motivation is:

Failure → Lack of Ability → Uncontrollable → Not Responsible → Shame, Embarrassment → Withdraw → Performance Declines

When failure is attributed to lack of effort (a controllable cause), the sequence is:

Failure → Lack of Effort → Controllable → Responsible → Guilt → Engagement → Performance Improves

Also, feeling in control of your own learning seems to be related to choosing more difficult academic tasks, putting out more effort, using better strategies, and persisting longer in school work (Schunk, 2000; Weiner, 1994a, 1994b). Factors such as continuing discrimination against women, people of color, and individuals with special needs can affect these individuals' perceptions of their ability to control their lives (Beane, 1991; van Laar, 2000). Weiner's locus and controllability dimensions are closely related to Deci's concept of *locus of causality.*

Attributions in the Classroom. When usually successful students fail, they often make internal, controllable attributions: They misunderstood the directions, lacked the necessary knowledge, or simply did not study hard enough, for example. As a consequence, they usually focus on strategies for succeeding next time. This response often leads to achievement, pride, and a greater feeling of control (Ames, 1992).

The greatest motivational problems arise when students attribute failures to stable, uncontrollable causes. Such students may seem resigned to failure, depressed, helpless—what we generally call "unmotivated" (Weiner, 2000; Weiner, Russell, & Lerman, 1978). These students respond to failure by focusing even more on their own inadequacy; their attitudes toward schoolwork may deteriorate even further (Ames, 1992). Apathy is a logical reaction to failure if students believe the causes are stable, unlikely to change, and beyond their control. In addition, students who view their failures in this light are less likely to seek help; they believe nothing and no one can help (Ames & Lau, 1982).

Teacher Actions and Student Attributions. How do students determine the causes of their successes and failures? Remember, we also make attributions about the causes of other peoples' successes and failures. When teachers assume that student failure is attributable to forces beyond the students' control, the teachers tend to respond with sympathy and avoid giving punishments. If, however, the failures are attributed to a controllable factor such as lack of effort, the teacher's response is more likely to be irritation or anger, and reprimands may follow. These tendencies seem to be consistent across time and cultures (Weiner, 1986, 2000).

What do students make of these reactions from their teachers? Sandra Graham (1991, 1996) gives some surprising answers. There is evidence that when teachers respond to students' mistakes with pity, praise for a "good try," or unsolicited help, the students are more likely to attribute their failure to an uncontrollable cause—usually

CONNECT & EXTEND

TO YOUR TEACHING/PORTFOLIO

What are the implications of attribution theories of motivation? Consider the following, taken from Why can't Susie and Johnny do math? (1987, July). *Harvard Education Letter, Vol. 3,* No. 4, pp. 6–7.

Dale Schunk identified 40 elementary school children who were having trouble with subtraction, divided them into four groups, and set them to working. . . . A monitor . . . checked . . . groups A, B, and C every 8 minutes. To each child in the A group she commented, "You've been working hard." To children in the B group she said, "You need to work hard." Children in the C group got no comment at all, and children in the D group had contact with the proctor only when she read them instructions.

The results were unambiguous: Youngsters who were told that they had been working hard completed 63% more problems than their fellows. They got three times as many subtraction problems right on the test that followed the training.

CONNECT & EXTEND

TO YOUR TEACHING/PORTFOLIO

Read Clifford, M. M. (1990). Students need challenge, not easy success. *Educational Leadership 48*(1), 22–26. Evaluate Clifford's claim that students need some experience with failure. For whom is this experience most needed?

lack of ability. For example, Graham and Barker (1990) asked subjects of various ages to rate the effort and ability of two boys viewed on a videotape. On the tape, a teacher circulated around the class while students worked. The teacher stopped to look at the two boys' papers, did not comment to the first boy, but said to the second, "Let me give you a hint. Don't forget to carry your tens." The second boy had not asked for help and did not appear to be stumped by the problem. All the age groups watching the tapes, even the youngest, perceived the boy who received help as lower in ability than the boy who did not get help. It is as if the subjects read the teacher's behavior as saying, "You poor child, you just don't have the ability to do this hard work, so I will help."

Does this mean that teachers should be critical and withhold help? Of course not! But it is a reminder that "praise as a consolation prize" for failing (Brophy, 1985) or oversolicitous help can give unintended messages. Graham (1991) suggests that many minority group students could be the victims of well-meaning pity from teachers. Seeing the very real problems that the students face, teachers may "ease up" on requirements so the students will "experience success." But a subtle communication may accompany the pity, praise, and extra help: "You don't have the ability to do this, so I will overlook your failure." Graham says, "The . . . pertinent question for blacks is whether their own history of academic failure makes them more likely to be the targets of sympathetic feedback from teachers and thus the recipients of low-ability cues" (1991, p. 28). This kind of sympathetic feedback, even if well-intended, can be a subtle form of racism.

CONNECT & EXTEND

TO THE RESEARCH

Graham, S. (1991). A review of attribution theory in achievement contexts. *Educational Psychology Review, 3,* 5–39. This article reviews several major principles of attribution theory as they relate to achievement strivings, including the antecedents to particular self-ascriptions, the emotional consequences of causal attributions for success and failure, help seeking and help giving, peer acceptance and rejection, achievement evaluation, and attributional process in African American populations.

Expectancy × Value Theories. Theories that take into account both the behaviorists' concern with the effects or outcomes of behavior and the cognitivists' interest in the impact of individual thinking can be characterized as **expectancy × value** theories. This means that motivation is seen as the product of two main forces: the individual's expectation of reaching a goal and the value of that goal to him or her. In other words, the important questions are, "If I try hard, can I succeed?" and "If I succeed, will the outcome be valuable or rewarding to me?" Motivation is a product of these two forces, because if either factor is zero, there is no motivation to work toward the goal. For example, if I believe I have a good chance of making the basketball team (high expectation), and if making the team is very important to me (high value), then my motivation should be strong. But if either factor is zero (I believe I haven't a prayer of making the team, or I couldn't care less about playing basketball), then my motivation will be zero, too (Tollefson, 2000).

In addition, Jacqueline Eccles and Allan Wigfield add the element of *cost* to the expectancy × value equation. Values have to be considered in relation to the cost of pursuing them. How much energy will be required? What could I be doing instead? What are the risks if I fail? Will I look stupid (Eccles & Wigfield, 2001; Wigfield & Eccles, 1992)? Bandura's theory of self-efficacy, discussed later in this chapter, is an example of an expectancy × value approach to motivation (Feather, 1982; Pintrich & Schunk, 2002).

Sociocultural Conceptions of Motivation

Finish this sentence: I am a/an ________________________.
What is your identity? With what groups do you identify most strongly?

Sociocultural views of motivation emphasize participation in communities of practice. People engage in activities to maintain their identities and their interpersonal relations within the community. Thus, students are motivated to learn if they are members of a classroom or school community that values learning. Just as we learn to speak and dress and conduct ourselves in restaurants or shopping malls by being socialized—watching and learning from more capable members of the culture—we

Expectancy × value theories Explanations of motivation that emphasize individuals' expectations for success combined with their valuing of the goal.

Sociocultural views of motivation Perspectives that emphasize participation, identities, and interpersonal relations within communities of practice.

also learn to be students by watching and learning from members of our community. In other words, we learn by the company we keep (Greeno, Collins, & Resnick, 1996; Rogoff, Turkanis, & Bartlett, 2001).

The concept of identity is central in sociocultural views of motivation. When we see ourselves as soccer players, or sculptors, or engineers, or teachers, or psychologists, we have an identity within a group. Part of our socialization is moving from legitimate peripheral participation to central participation in that group. **Legitimate peripheral participation** means that beginners are genuinely involved in the work of the group, even if their abilities are undeveloped and their contributions are small. The novice weaver learns to dye wool before spinning and weaving, and the novice teacher learns to tutor one child before working with the whole group. Each task is a piece of the real work of the expert. The identities of the novice and the expert are bound up in their participation in the community. They are motivated to learn the values and practices of the community to keep their identity as community members (Lave & Wenger, 1991). *The Stories of Learning/Tributes to Teaching* feature describes how a Korean student was supported in her efforts to learn by instructors and friends.

Some classrooms are intentionally structured as learning communities. For example, Brown and Campione (1996) developed learning communities for middle school students around research projects in science, as we saw in Chapter 9. Scardamalia and Bereiter (1996) designed a learning community using a computer system called CSILE—Computer-Supported Intentional Learning Environment—that encourages collaboration among students about questions, hypotheses, and findings.

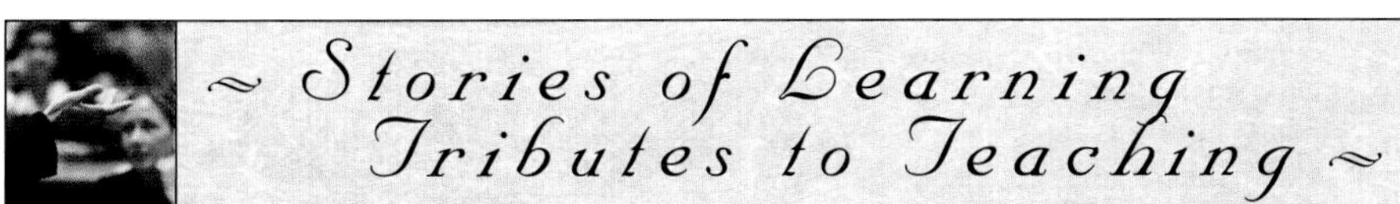

These are the words of **Lea Lee,** a Korean woman who came to the United States to become a professor and scholar. She had to be far from her family and her culture to pursue her dream, but she was supported in her efforts by instructors and friends who shared their culture and embraced hers.

> All of the school experiences were difficult for me. From taking lecture notes in class and taking exams to writing term papers, I struggled with the language barrier. I really wanted to understand the entire lecture. I understood only 30 to 40 percent of the information received during lectures during my first semester. I needed a guide who could show me how to study and how to be an outstanding student. Often, instructors don't consider that international students have special needs and require some adaptations during lectures and exams. It would have been a great help if the instructor had assigned a buddy who would have allowed me to copy lecture notes. No matter what type of problems I faced, however, I never gave up. I searched for solutions to problems so that I could achieve my goal. For example, when I could not understand a subject, I read textbooks repeatedly. I even memorized the text so that I would be able to pass the course with a good grade.
>
> After tolerating many painful years, I finally became a professor and scholar in America. My ceaseless efforts were necessary, but not sufficient to achieve my goal. Without my friends and instructors, who were encouraging and willing to give support, I know that I would not be who I am today. Many of my true friends embraced the Korean culture and encouraged me to be proud of my culture. Those friends' names and faces will live deep in my heart for a long, long time.

SOURCE: From "Six Buckets of Tears: Korean Americans' School Experiences," by Lea Lee. In Gloria Swindler-Boutte (Ed.), *Resounding Voices: School Experiences of People from Diverse Ethnic Backgrounds.* Published by Allyn & Bacon, Boston, MA.

Legitimate peripheral participation Genuine involvement in the work of the group, even if your abilities are undeveloped and contributions are small.

Table 10.2 Four Views of Motivation

	Behavioral	Humanistic	Cognitive	Sociocultural
Source of Motivation	Extrinsic	Intrinsic	Intrinsic	Intrinsic
Important Influences	Reinforcers, rewards, incentives, and punishers	Need for self-esteem, self-fulfillment, and self-determination	Beliefs, attributions for success and failure, expectations	Engaged participation in learning communities; maintaining identity through participation in activities of group
Key Theorists	Skinner	Maslow Deci	Weiner Graham	Lave Wenger

The challenge in these approaches is to be sure that all students are fully participating members of the community, because motivation comes from identity and identity comes from legitimate participation.

The behavioral, humanistic, cognitive, and sociocultural approaches to motivation are summarized in Table 10.2. These theories differ in their answers to the question, "What is motivation?" but each contributes in its own way toward a comprehensive understanding of human motivation.

To organize the many ideas about motivation in a way that is useful for teaching, let's examine three broad areas. Most contemporary explanations of motivation include a discussion of goals, interests and emotions, and self-perceptions (Murphy & Alexander, 2000).

Check Yourself What are the key factors in motivation according to a behavioral viewpoint? A humanistic viewpoint? A cognitive viewpoint? A sociocultural viewpoint?

Distinguish between deficiency needs and being needs in Maslow's theory.

What are the three dimensions of attributions in Weiner's theory?

What are expectancy × value theories?

What is legitimate peripheral participation?

Goal Orientation and Motivation

STOP THINK WRITE On a scale from 1 (Strongly Agree) to 5 (Strongly Disagree), how would you answer these questions: **I feel really pleased in school when . . .**

___ I solve problems by working hard
___ I know more than the others
___ I don't have to work hard
___ I keep busy
___ I finish first
___ All the work is easy
___ I learn something new
___ I am the only one who gets an A
___ I am with my friends

A **goal** is an outcome or attainment an individual is striving to accomplish (Locke & Latham, 1990). When students strive to read a chapter or make a 4.0 GPA, they are involved in *goal-directed behavior.* In pursuing goals, students are generally aware of some current condition (I haven't even opened my book), some ideal condition (I have understood every page), and the discrepancy between the current and ideal situations. Goals motivate people to act in order to reduce the discrepancy between

Goal What an individual strives to accomplish.

"where they are" and "where they want to be." Goal setting is usually effective for me. In addition to the routine tasks, such as eating lunch, which will happen without much attention, I often set goals for each day. For example, today I intend to finish this chapter, walk four miles, and pay my bills (I know—not too exciting). Having decided to do these things, I will feel uncomfortable if I don't complete the list.

According to Locke and Latham (1990), there are four main reasons why goal setting improves performance. Goals:

1. *Direct our attention* to the task at hand. Every time my mind wanders from this chapter, my goal of finishing helps direct my attention back to the writing.
2. *Mobilize effort.* The harder the goal, to a point, the greater the effort.
3. *Increase persistence.* When we have a clear goal, we are less likely to be distracted or to give up until we reach the goal.
4. *Promote the development of new strategies* when old strategies fall short. For example, if your goal is making an A and you don't reach that goal on your first quiz, you might try a new study approach for the next quiz, such as explaining the key points to a friend.

CONNECT & EXTEND

TO THE RESEARCH
For a synthesis of the research on goals from two founders of the theory, see: Locke, E. A., & Latham, G. P. (2002). Building a practically useful theory of goal setting and task motivation: A 35-year odyssey. *American Psychologist, 57,* 705–717.

Types of Goals and Goal Orientations

The types of goals we set influence the amount of motivation we have to reach them. Goals that are specific, moderately difficult, and likely to be reached in the near future tend to enhance motivation and persistence (Pintrich & Schunk, 2002; Stipek, 2002). Specific goals provide clear standards for judging performance. If performance falls short, we keep going. For example, I have decided to "finish this chapter" instead of deciding to "work on the book." Anything short of having the chapter ready to mail means "keep working" (looks like another late night!). Moderate difficulty provides a challenge, but not an unreasonable one. I can finish this chapter if I stay with it. Finally, goals that can be reached fairly soon are not likely to be pushed aside by more immediate concerns. Groups such as Alcoholics Anonymous show they are aware of the motivating value of short-term goals when they encourage their members to stop drinking "one day at a time."

Four Goal Orientations in School. Goals are specific targets. **Goal orientations** are patterns of beliefs about goals related to achievement in school. Goal orientations include the reasons we pursue goals and the standards we use to evaluate progress toward those goals. For example, your target might be to make an A in this course. Are you doing so in order to master educational psychology—to learn all about it, or to perform—to look good in the eyes of your friends and family? There are four main goal orientations—mastery (learning), performance (looking good), work-avoidance, and social (Murphy & Alexander, 2000; Pintrich & Schunk, 2002). In the *Stop/Think/Write* exercise above, can you tell which goal orientations are reflected in the different answers? Most of the questions were adapted from a study on students' theories about learning mathematics (Nicholls, Cobb, Wood, Yachel, Patashnick, 1990).

The most common distinction in research on students' goals is between mastery goals (also called *task goals* or *learning goals*) and performance goals (also called *ability goals* or *ego goals*) (Midgley, 2001). The point of a **mastery goal** is to improve, to learn, no matter how awkward you appear. Students who set mastery goals tend to seek challenges and persist when they encounter difficulties. Because they focus on the task at hand and are not worried about how their performance "measures up" compared to others in the class, these students have been called **task-involved learners** (Nicholls & Miller, 1984). We often say that these people "get lost in their work." In addition, they are more likely to seek appropriate help, use deeper cognitive processing strategies, apply better study strategies, and generally approach academic tasks with confidence (Butler & Neuman, 1995; Midgley, 2001; Young, 1997).

Goal orientations Patterns of beliefs about goals related to achievement in school.

Mastery goal A personal intention to improve abilities and learn, no matter how performance suffers.

Task-involved learners Students who focus on mastering the task or solving the problem.

If this girl's goal is to improve and not worry about mistakes, she may attempt more difficult pieces and welcome criticism. If her goal is to simply look good, she may avoid difficulty and criticism.

The second kind of goal is a performance goal. Students with **performance goals** care about demonstrating their ability to others. They may be focused on getting good test scores and grades, or they may be more concerned with winning and beating other students (Wolters, Yu, & Pintrich, 1996). Students whose goal is outperforming others may do things to look smart, such as reading easy books in order to "read the most books" (Young, 1997). The evaluation of their performance by others, not what they learn, is what matters. Nicholls and Miller (1984) call these students **ego-involved learners** because they are preoccupied with themselves. Deborah Stipek (2002) lists the following behaviors as indicative of a student who has a performance goal orientation:

- Cheats/copies from classmates' papers or uses short-cuts to get finished.
- Seeks attention for good performance.
- Only works hard on graded assignments.
- Is upset by and hides papers with low grades.
- Compares grades with classmates.
- Chooses tasks that are most likely to result in positive evaluations.
- Is uncomfortable with assignments that have unclear evaluation criteria and repeatedly checks with the teacher.

Wait—Are Performance Goals Always Bad? There is a similarity between intrinsic/extrinsic motivation and mastery versus performance goal orientations. Mastery-oriented students tend to be motivated by intrinsic factors whereas performance-oriented students tend to respond to extrinsic motivation. Earlier research indicated that performance goals generally were detrimental to learning, but like extrinsic motivation, a performance goal orientation may not be all bad all of the time. In fact, some research indicates that both mastery and performance goals are associated with using active learning strategies and high self-efficacy (Midgley, Kaplan, & Middleton, 2001; Midgley, 1996; Stipek, 2002). And, like intrinsic and extrinsic motivation, students can, and often do pursue mastery and performance goals at the same time.

To account for these recent findings, educational psychologists have added the distinction of approach/avoidance to the mastery/performance distinction. In other words, students may be motivated to either approach mastery or avoid misunderstanding. They may approach performance or avoid looking dumb. Look at Table 10.3 for an example of each kind of goal orientation and the effects of each. Where do you see the most problems? Do you agree that the real problems are with avoidance? Students who fear misunderstanding (mastery avoid) may be perfectionistic—focused on getting it exactly right. Students who avoid looking dumb (performance avoid) may adopt defensive, failure-avoiding strategies like Defensive Diana described earlier—they pretend not to care, make a show of "not really trying," or cheat (Jagacinski & Nicholls, 1987; Pintrich & Schunk, 2002).

Beyond Mastery and Performance. Some students don't want to learn or to look smart; they just want to avoid work. These students try to complete assignments and activities as quickly as possible without exerting much effort (Pintrich & Schunk, 2002). Nicholls called these students **work-avoidant learners**—they feel successful when they don't have to try hard, when the work is easy, or when they can "goof off."

A final category of goals becomes more important as students get older—**social goals.** As students move into adolescence, their social networks change to include more peers. Nonacademic activities such as athletics, dating, and "hanging out" compete with schoolwork (Urdan & Maehr, 1995). Social goals include a wide variety of needs and motives with different relationships to learning—some help, but some hin-

Performance goal A personal intention to seem competent or perform well in the eyes of others.

Ego-involved learners Students who focus on how well they are performing and how they are judged by others.

Work-avoidant learners Students who don't want to learn or to look smart, but just want to avoid work.

Social goals A wide variety of needs and motives to be connected to others or part of a group.

Table 10.3 Goal Orientations

Students may have either an approach or an avoidance focus for mastery and performance goal orientations.

Goal Oriention	Approach Focus	Avoidance Focus
Mastery	*Focus:* Mastering the task, learning, understanding *Standards Used:* Self-improvement, progress, deep understanding (task-involved)	*Focus:* Avoiding misunderstanding or not mastering the task *Standards Used:* Just don't be wrong, don't do it incorrectly
Performance	*Focus:* Being superior, winning, being the best *Standards Used:* Normative—getting the highest grade, winning the competition (ego-involved goal)	*Focus:* Avoiding looking stupid, avoid losing *Standards Used:* Normative—don't be the worst, get the lowest grade, or be the slowest (ego-involved goal)

SOURCE: From *Motivation in Education: Theory, Research, and Applications* (2nd ed.), by P. Pintrich and D. Schunk. Published by Prentice Hall. Copyright © 2002 by Prentice Hall. Reprinted by permission of Pearson Education, Inc., Upper Saddle River, NJ.

der learning. For example, adolescents' goal of maintaining friendly relations can get in the way of learning when cooperative learning group members don't challenge wrong answers or misconceptions because they are afraid to hurt each other's feelings (Anderson, Holland, & Palincsar, 1997). Certainly, pursuing goals such as having fun with friends or avoiding being labeled a "nerd" can get in the way of learning. But goals of bringing honor to your family or team by working hard can support learning (Urdan & Maehr, 1995).

We talk about goals in separate categories, but students have to coordinate their goals so they can make decisions about what to do and how to act. As noted above, sometimes social and academic goals are incompatible. For example, academic failure may be interpreted positively by some minority group students because noncompliance with the majority culture's norms and standards is seen as an accomplishment. Thus it would be impossible to simultaneously succeed in both school and the peer group (Ogbu, 1987; Wentzel, 1999). And succeeding in the peer group is important. The need for social relationships is basic and strong for most people.

Feedback and Goal Acceptance

Besides having specific goals and creating supportive social relationships, there are two additional factors that make goal-setting in the classroom effective. The first is *feedback.* In order to be motivated by a discrepancy between "where you are" and "where you want to be," you must have an accurate sense of both your current status and how far you have to go. There is evidence that feedback emphasizing progress is the most effective. In one study, feedback to adults emphasized either that they had accomplished 75% of the standards set or that they had fallen short of the standards by 25%. When the feedback highlighted accomplishment, the subjects' self-confidence, analytic thinking, and performance were all enhanced (Bandura, 1997).

The second factor affecting motivation to pursue a goal is *goal acceptance.* If students reject goals set by others or refuse to set their own goals, then motivation will suffer. Generally, students are more willing to adopt the goals of others if the goals seem realistic, reasonably difficult, and meaningful (Erez & Zidon, 1984) and if good reasons are given for the value of the goals. Goal acceptance might be greater (and goals more appropriate) if you work with students' families to identify and monitor the goals.

Goals: Lessons for Teachers

Students are more likely to work toward goals that are clear, specific, reasonable, moderately challenging, and attainable within a relatively short period of time. If teachers focus on student performance, high grades, and competition, they may encourage students to set performance goals. This will undermine the students' ability to learn and become task-involved (Anderman & Maehr, 1994). Students may not yet be expert at setting their own goals or keeping the goal in mind, so encouragement and accurate feedback are necessary. If you use any reward or incentive systems, be sure the goal you set is to *learn and improve* in some area, not just to perform well or look smart. And be sure the goal is not too difficult. Students, like adults, are unlikely to stick with tasks or respond well to teachers who make them feel insecure or incompetent.

Check Yourself What kinds of goals are the most motivating?

Describe mastery, performance, work-avoidant, and social goals.

What makes goal setting effective in the classroom?

Interests and Emotions

How do you feel about learning? Excited, bored, curious, fearful? Today, researchers emphasize that learning is not just about the *cold cognition* of reasoning and problem solving. Learning and information processing also are influenced by emotion, so *hot cognition* plays a role in learning as well (Miller, 2002; Pintrich, Marx, & Boyle, 1993). Students are more likely to pay attention to, learn, and remember events, images, and readings that provoke emotional responses (Alexander & Murphy, 1998; Cowley & Underwood, 1998; Reisberg & Heuer, 1992) or that are related to their interests (Renninger, Hidi, & Krapp, 1992). How can we use these findings to support learning in school?

Tapping Interests

What Would You Say? As part of your interview for a job in a large high school, the principal asks, "How would you get students interested in learning? Could you tap their interests in your teaching?"

Students' interest in and excitement about what they're learning is one of the most important factors in education.

When Walter Vispoel and James Austin (1995) surveyed over 200 middle school students, lack of interest in the topic received the highest rating as an explanation for school failures. Interest was second only to effort as a choice for explaining successes.

There are two kinds of interests—personal and situational—the trait and state distinction again. *Personal interests* are more enduring aspects of the person, such as an interest in sports, music, or ancient history. *Situational interests* are more short-lived aspects of the activity, text, or materials that catch and keep the student's attention. Both personal and situational interests are related to learning from texts—the more interest, the more deep processing and remembering of the material (Renninger, Hindi, & Krapp, 1992; Schraw & Lehman, 2001). And interests increase when students feel competent, so even if students are not initially interested in a subject or activity, they may develop interests as they experience success (Stipek, 2002).

One source of interest is fantasy. For example, Cordova and Lepper (1996) found that students learned more math facts during a computer exercise when they were challenged, as captains of star ships, to navigate through space by solving math problems. The students got to name their ships, stock the (imaginary) galley with their favorite snacks, and name all the crew members after their friends. The *Guidelines* give other ideas.

However, there are cautions in responding to students' interests, as you can see in the *Point/Counterpoint* on page 364.

GUIDELINES Building on Students' Interests

Relate content objectives to student experiences.

Examples

1. With a teacher in another school, establish pen pals across the classes. Through writing letters, students exchange personal experiences, photos, drawings, written work, and ask and answer questions ("Have you learned cursive writing yet?" "What are you doing in math now?" "What are you reading?"). Letters can be mailed in one large mailer to save stamps.
2. Identify classroom experts for different assignments or tasks. Who knows how to use the computer for graphics? How to search the Net? How to cook? How to use an index?
3. Have a "Switch Day" when students exchange roles with a school staff or support person. Students must research the role by interviewing their staff member, prepare for the job, dress the part for the day they take over, and then evaluate their success after the switch.

Identify student interests, hobbies, and extracurricular activities that can be incorporated into class lessons and discussions.

Examples

1. Have students design and conduct interviews and surveys to learn about each other's interests.
2. Keep the class library stocked with books that connect to students' interests and hobbies.

Support instruction with humor, personal experiences, and anecdotes that show the human side of the content.

Examples

1. Share your own hobbies, interests, and favorites.
2. Tell students there will be a surprise visitor; then dress up as the author of a story and tell about "yourself" and your writing.

Use original source material with interesting content or details.

Examples

1. Letters and diaries in history.
2. Darwin's notes in biology.

Create surprise and curiosity

Examples

1. Have students predict what will happen in an experiment, then show them that they are wrong.
2. Provide quotes from history and ask students to guess who said it.

Allow choices based on student interests.

Examples

1. Choice of novels or short stories.
2. Choice of project focus in science.

SOURCE: From *150 Ways to Increase Intrinsic Motivation in the Classroom,* by James P. Raffini. Published by Allyn & Bacon, Boston, MA. Copyright © 1996 by Pearson Education. Adapted by permission of the publisher. Also *Motivation in Education* (2nd ed.) by P. Pintrich and D. Schunk, 2002, Merrill/Prentice-Hall, pp. 298–299.

Point/Counterpoint

Does Making Learning Fun Make for Good Learning?

When many beginning teachers are asked about how to motivate students, they often mention making learning fun. It is true that connecting to students' interests, stimulating curiosity, and using fantasy all encourage motivation and engagement. But is it necessary for learning to be fun?

Point

Teachers should make learning fun.

When I searched "making learning fun" on Google.com, I found 10 pages of resources and references. Clearly there is interest in making learning fun. In 1987, Thomas Malone and Mark Lepper wrote a chapter on "Making Learning Fun: A Taxonomy of Intrinsic Motivations for Learning." Research shows that passages in texts that are more interesting are remembered better (Pintrich & Schunk, 2002). For example, students who read books that interested them spent more time reading, read more words in the books, and felt more positively about reading (Guthrie & Alao, 1997). Games and simulations can make learning more fun, too. For example, when my daughter was in the 8th grade, all the students in her grade spent three days playing a game her teachers had designed called ULTRA. Students were divided into groups and formed their own "countries." Each country had to choose a name, symbol, national flower, and bird. They wrote and sang a national anthem and elected government officials. The teachers allocated different resources to the countries. To get all the materials needed for the completion of assigned projects, the countries had to establish trade with one another. There was a monetary system and a stock market. Students had to work with their fellow citizens to complete cooperative learning assignments. Some countries "cheated" in their trades with other nations, and this allowed debate about international relations, trust, and war. Liz says she had fun—but she also learned how to work in a group without the teacher's supervision and gained a deeper understanding of world economics and international conflicts.

Counterpoint

Fun can get in the way of learning.

As far back as the early 1900s, educators warned about the dangers of focusing on fun in learning. None other than John Dewey, who wrote extensively about the role of interest in learning, cautioned that you can't make boring lessons interesting by mixing in fun like you can make bad chili good by adding some spicy hot sauce. Dewey wrote, "When things have to be made interesting, it is because interest itself is wanting. Moreover, the phrase itself is a misnomer. The thing, the object, is no more interesting than it was before" (Dewey, 1913, pp. 11–12). There is a good deal of research now indicating that adding interest by adding fascinating but irrelevant details actually gets in the way of learning the important information. These "seductive details," as they have been called, divert the readers' attention from the less interesting main ideas (Harp & Mayer, 1998). For example, students who read biographies of historical figures remembered more very interesting but unimportant information compared to interesting main ideas (Wade, Schraw, Buxton, & Hayes, 1993). Shannon Harp and Richard Mayer (1997) found similar results with high school science texts. These texts added emotional interest and seductive details about swimmers and golfers who are injured by lightning to a lesson on the process of lightning. They concluded that, "in the case of emotional interest versus cognitive interest, the verdict is clear. Adjuncts aimed at increasing emotional interest failed to improve understanding of scientific explanations" (p. 100). The seductive details may have disrupted students' attempts to follow the logic of the explanations and thus interfered with comprehending the text. Harp and Mayer conclude that "the best way to help students enjoy a passage is to help them understand it" (p. 100).

What do you think? Vote online at **www.ablongman.com/woolfolk**

Arousal: Excitement and Anxiety in Learning

Just as we all know how it feels to be motivated, we all know what it is like to be aroused. **Arousal** involves both psychological and physical reactions—changes in brain wave patterns, blood pressure, heart rate, and breathing rate. We feel alert, wide awake, even excited. To understand the effects of arousal on motivation, think of two extremes. The first is late at night. You are trying for the third time to understand a required reading, but you are so sleepy. Your attention drifts as your eyes droop. You decide to go to bed and get up early to study (a plan that you know seldom works). At the other extreme, imagine that you have a critical test tomorrow—one that determines whether you will get into the school you want. You feel tremendous pressure from everyone to do well. You know that you need a good night's sleep, but you are wide awake. In the first case, arousal is too low and in the second, too high.

Arousal Physical and psychological reactions causing a person to be alert, attentive, wide awake.

Psychologists have known for years that there is an optimum level of arousal for most activities (Yerkes & Dodson, 1908). Generally speaking, a higher level of arousal is helpful on simple tasks such as sorting laundry, but lower levels of arousal are better for complex tasks such as taking the GRE. Let's look for a moment at how to increase arousal by arousing curiosity.

Curiosity: Novelty and Complexity. Almost 40 years ago, psychologists suggested that individuals are naturally motivated to seek novelty, surprise, and complexity (Berlyne, 1966). Research on teaching has found that variety in teaching approaches and tasks can support learning (Brophy & Good, 1986; Stipek, 2002). For younger students, the chance to manipulate and explore objects relevant to what is being studied may be the most effective way to keep curiosity stimulated. For older students, well-constructed questions, logical puzzles, and paradoxes can have the same effect. Example: Ranchers in an area killed the wolves on their land. The following spring, they noticed that the deer population was much smaller. How could this be, since fewer wolves should mean more deer? In searching for a solution, students learn about ecology and the balance of nature: Without wolves to eliminate the weaker and sicker deer, the deer population expanded so much that the winter food supply could not sustain the deer herds. Many deer died of starvation.

CONNECT & EXTEND

TO THE RESEARCH

Lowenstein, G. (1994). The psychology of curiosity: A review and reinterpretation. *Psychological Bulletin, 117*, 75–98. This article connects curiosity to perceived gaps in information.

George Lowenstein (1994) suggests that curiosity arises when attention is focused on a gap in knowledge. "Such information gaps produce the feeling of deprivation labeled *curiosity.* The curious person is motivated to obtain the missing information to reduce or eliminate the feeling of deprivation" (p. 87). This idea is similar to Piaget's concept of disequilibrium, discussed in Chapter 2, and has a number of implications for teaching. First, students need some base of knowledge before they can experience gaps in knowledge leading to curiosity. Second, students must be aware of the gaps in order for curiosity to result. Asking students to make guesses and then providing feedback can be helpful. Also, mistakes, properly handled, can stimulate curiosity by pointing to missing knowledge. Finally, the more we learn about a topic, the more curious we may become about that subject. As Maslow (1970) predicted, fulfilling the need to know increases, not decreases, the need to know more.

As we discussed earlier, sometimes arousal is too high, not too low. Because classrooms are places where students are tested and graded, anxiety can become a factor in classroom motivation.

Anxiety in the Classroom. At one time or another, everyone has experienced **anxiety,** or a general uneasiness, a feeling of self-doubt, and sense of tension. The effects of anxiety on school achievement are clear. "From the time of the earliest work on this problem, starting with the pioneering work of Yerkes and Dodson (1908), to the present day, researchers have consistently reported a negative correlation between virtually every aspect of school achievement and a wide range of anxiety measures" (Covington & Omelich, 1987, p. 393). Anxiety can be both a cause and an effect of school failure—students do poorly because they are anxious, and their poor performance increases their anxiety. Anxiety probably is both a trait and a state. Some students tend to be anxious in many situations (trait anxiety), but some situations are especially anxiety-provoking (state anxiety) (Covington, 1992, Zeidner, 1998).

Anxiety seems to have both cognitive and affective components. The cognitive side includes worry and negative thoughts—thinking about how bad it would be to fail and worrying that you will, for example. The affective side involves physiological and emotional reactions such as sweaty palms, upset stomach, racing heartbeat, or fear (Pintrich & Schunk, 2002; Zeidner, 1995, 1998). Whenever there are pressures to perform, severe consequences for failure, and competitive comparisons among students, anxiety may be encouraged (Wigfield & Eccles, 1989).

CONNECT & EXTEND

TO THE RESEARCH

Meece, J. L., Wigfield, A., & Eccles, J. (1990). Predictors of math anxiety and its influence on young adolescents' course enrollment intentions and performance in mathematics. *Journal of Educational Psychology, 92*, 6–70. This study found that math anxiety was most directly related to students' math ability perceptions, performance expectancies, and value perceptions. Students' performance expectancies predicted subsequent math grades, whereas their value perception predicted course enrollment intentions.

Anxiety General uneasiness, a feeling of tension.

Many anxious students have poor study habits. Strategies for solving this problem might include planning a study schedule, borrowing good notes, or finding a protected place to study.

How Does Anxiety Interfere with Achievement? Anxiety interferes with learning and test performance at three points: focusing attention, learning, and testing. When students are learning new material, they must pay attention to it. Highly anxious students evidently divide their attention between the new material and their preoccupation with how worried and nervous they are feeling. Instead of concentrating, they keep noticing the tight feelings in their chest, thinking, "I'm so tense, I'll never understand this stuff!" From the beginning, anxious students may miss much of the information they are supposed to learn because their thoughts are focused on their own worries (Cassady & Johnson, 2002; Paulman & Kennelly, 1984).

But the problems do not end here. Even if they are paying attention, many anxious students have trouble learning material that is somewhat disorganized and difficult—material that requires them to rely on their memory. Unfortunately, much material in school could be described this way. In addition, many highly anxious students have poor study habits. Simply learning to be more relaxed will not automatically improve these students' performance; their learning strategies and study skills must be improved as well (Naveh-Benjamin, 1991).

Finally, anxious students often know more than they can demonstrate on a test. They may lack critical test-taking skills, or they may have learned the materials but "freeze and forget" on tests (Naveh-Benjamin, McKeachie, & Lin, 1987).

Coping with Anxiety. When students face stressful situations such as tests, they can use three kinds of coping strategies: *problem solving, emotional management,* and *avoidance.* Problem-focused strategies might include planning a study schedule, borrowing good notes, or finding a protected place to study. Emotion-focused strategies are attempts to reduce the anxious feelings, for example, by using relaxation exercises or describing the feelings to a friend. Of course, the latter might become an avoidance strategy, along with going out for pizza or suddenly launching an all out desk-cleaning attack (can't study until you get organized!). Different strategies are helpful at different points—for example, problem solving before and emotion management during an exam. Different strategies fit different people and situations (Zeidner, 1995, 1998).

Teachers should help highly anxious students to set realistic goals, because these individuals often have difficulty making wise choices. They tend to select either extremely difficult or extremely easy tasks. In the first case, they are likely to fail, which will increase their sense of hopelessness and anxiety about school. In the second case, they will probably succeed on the easy tasks, but they will miss the sense of satisfaction that could encourage greater effort and ease their fears about schoolwork. Goal cards, progress charts, or goal-planning journals may help here.

CONNECT & EXTEND

TO **PRAXIS**™
TEST ANXIETY (I, C3)
Test Taking and Anxiety (http://www.ulrc.psu.edu/studyskills/test_taking.html) provides tips and insights into addressing the problems associated with test anxiety. (And the tips might be useful for doing well on the PRAXIS™ exam!)

Interests and Emotions: Lessons for Teachers

Make efforts to keep the level of arousal right for the task at hand. If students are going to sleep, energize them by introducing variety, piquing their curiosity, surprising them, or giving them a brief chance to be physically active. Learn about their interests and incorporate these interests into lessons and assignments. If arousal is too great, follow the *Guidelines* for dealing with anxiety.

Check Yourself Do interests and emotions affect learning?

What is the role of arousal in learning?

How does anxiety interfere with learning?

GUIDELINES Coping with Anxiety

Use competition carefully.

Examples

1. Monitor activities to make sure no students are being put under undue pressure.
2. During competitive games, make sure all students involved have a reasonable chance of succeeding.
3. Experiment with cooperative learning activities.

Avoid situations in which highly anxious students will have to perform in front of large groups.

Examples

1. Ask anxious students questions that can be answered with a simple yes or no, or some other brief reply.
2. Give anxious students practice in speaking before smaller groups.

Make sure all instructions are clear. Uncertainty can lead to anxiety.

Examples

1. Write test instructions on the board or on the test itself instead of giving them orally.
2. Check with students to make sure they understand. Ask several students how they would do the first question, exercise, or sample question on a test. Correct any misconceptions.
3. If you are using a new format or starting a new type of task, give students examples or models to show how it is done.

Avoid unnecessary time pressures.

Examples

1. Give occasional take-home tests.
2. Make sure all students can complete classroom tests within the period given.

Remove some of the pressures from major tests and exams.

Examples

1. Teach test-taking skills; give practice tests; provide study guides.
2. Avoid basing most of a report-card grade on one test.
3. Make extra-credit work available to add points to course grades.
4. Use different types of items in testing because some students have difficulty with particular formats.

Develop alternatives to written tests.

Examples

1. Try oral, open-book, or group tests.
2. Have students do projects, organize portfolios of their work, make oral presentations, or create a finished product.

Teach students self-regulation strategies (Schutz & Davis, 2000)

Examples

1. Before the test: Encourage students to see the test as an important and challenging task that they have the capabilities to prepare for. Help students stay focused on the task of getting as much information as possible about the test.
2. During the test: Remind students that the test is important (but not overly important). Encourage task focus—pick out the main idea in the question, slow down, stay relaxed.
3. After the test: Think back on what went well and what could be improved. Focus on controllable attributions—study strategies, effort, careful reading of questions, relaxation strategies.

Self-Schemas

Thus far, we have talked about goals, interests, and emotions, but there is another factor that must be considered in explaining motivation. What do students believe about themselves? Let's start with a basic question—What do they believe about ability?

Beliefs about Ability

Rate these statements taken from Dweck (2000) on a scale from 1 (Strongly Agree) to 6 (Strongly Disagree).

Companion Website

___ You have a certain amount of intelligence and you really can't do much to change it.

___ You can learn new things, but you can't really change your basic intelligence.

___ No matter who you are, you can change your intelligence a lot.

___ No matter how much intelligence you have, you can always change it quite a bit.

As you saw when we discussed attribution theory, some of the most powerful attributions affecting motivation in school are beliefs about *ability*. By examining these beliefs and how they affect motivation, we will understand why some people set inappropriate, unmotivating goals; why some students adopt self-defeating strategies; and why some students seem to give up altogether.

Adults use two basic concepts of ability (Dweck, 1999, 2002). An **entity view of ability** assumes that ability is a *stable, uncontrollable* trait—a characteristic of the individual that cannot be changed. According to this view, some people have more ability than others, but the amount each person has is set. An **incremental view of ability,** on the other hand, suggests that ability is unstable and controllable—"an ever-expanding repertoire of skills and knowledge" (Dweck & Bempechat, 1983, p. 144). By hard work, study, or practice, knowledge can be increased and thus ability can be improved. If you hold an incremental view, ability changes from being stable and uncontrollable, to unstable and controllable (see Table 10.1 on p. 354). What is your view of ability? Look back at your answers in the *Stop/Think/Write* box above to see.

Young children tend to hold an exclusively incremental view of ability. Through the early elementary grades, most students believe that effort is the same as intelligence. Smart people try hard and trying hard makes you smart. If you fail, you aren't smart and you didn't try hard (Dweck, 2000; Stipek, 2002). Children are age 11 or 12 before they can differentiate among effort, ability, and performance. About this time, they come to believe that someone who succeeds without working at all must be *really* smart. This is when beliefs about ability begin to influence motivation (Anderman & Maehr, 1994).

Students who hold an entity (unchangeable) view of intelligence tend to set performance goals to avoid looking bad in the eyes of others. They seek situations where they can look smart and protect their self-esteem. Like Safe Sarah, they keep doing what they can do well without expending too much effort or risking failure, because either one—working hard or failing—indicates (to them) low ability. To work hard but still fail would be devastating. Students with learning disabilities are more likely to hold an entity view. Teachers who hold entity views are quicker to form judgments about students and slower to modify their opinions when confronted with contradictory evidence (Stipek, 2002).

Incremental theorists, in contrast, tend to set mastery goals and seek situations in which students can improve their skills, because improvement means getting smarter. Failure is not devastating; it simply indicates more work is needed. Ability is not threatened. Incremental theorists tend to set moderately difficult goals, the kind we have seen are the most motivating.

One of the most powerful influences on motivation to achieve is another kind of belief—self-efficacy.

Beliefs about Self-Efficacy

What Would You Say? The last question in your interview for the 8th grade position is, "We have some pretty discouraged students and parents because our scores were so low last year. What would you do to help students believe in their ability to learn?"

Albert Bandura (1986, 1997) suggests that predictions about possible outcomes of behavior are critical sources of motivation. "Will I succeed or fail? Will I be liked or laughed at?" These predictions are affected by **self-efficacy**—our beliefs about our personal competence or effectiveness *in a given area*. Bandura (1997) defines self-efficacy as "beliefs in one's capabilities to organize and execute the courses of action required to produce given attainments" (p. 3).

Entity view of ability Belief that ability is a fixed characteristic that cannot be changed.

Incremental view of ability Belief that ability is a set of skills that can be changed.

Self-efficacy Beliefs about personal competence in a particular situation.

Self-Efficacy, Self-Concept, and Self-Esteem. Most people assume self-efficacy is the same as self-concept or self-esteem, but it isn't. Self-efficacy is future-oriented, "a context-specific assessment of competence to perform a specific task" (Pajares, 1997, p. 15). Self-concept is a more global construct that contains many perceptions about the self, including self-efficacy. Self-concept is developed as a result of external and internal comparisons, using other people or other aspects of the self as frames of reference. But self-efficacy focuses on your ability to successfully accomplish a particular task with no need for comparisons—the question is whether you can do it, not whether others would be successful (Marsh, Walker, & Debus, 1991). Also, self-efficacy beliefs are strong predictors of behavior, but self-concept has weaker predictive power (Bandura, 1997).

Compared to self-esteem, self-efficacy is concerned with judgments of personal capabilities; self-esteem is concerned with judgments of self-worth. There is no direct relationship between self-esteem and self-efficacy. It is possible to feel highly efficacious in one area and still not have a high level of self-esteem, or vice versa. For example, I have very low self-efficacy for singing, but my self-esteem is not affected, probably because my life does not require singing. But if my self-efficacy for teaching a particular class started dropping after several bad experiences, I know my self-esteem would suffer.

Mastery experiences Our own direct experiences—the most powerful source of efficacy information.

Vicarious experiences Accomplishments that are modeled by someone else.

Social persuasion A "pep talk" or specific performance feedback—one source of self-efficacy.

Sources of Self-Efficacy. Bandura identified four sources of self-efficacy expectations: mastery experiences, physiological and emotional arousal, vicarious experiences, and social persuasion. **Mastery experiences** are our own direct experiences—the most powerful source of efficacy information. Successes raise efficacy beliefs, while failures lower efficacy. Level of arousal affects self-efficacy, depending on how the arousal is interpreted. As you face the task, are you anxious and worried (lowers efficacy) or excited and "psyched" (raises efficacy) (Bandura, 1997; Pintrich & Schunk, 2002)?

In **vicarious experiences,** someone else models accomplishments. The more closely the student identifies with the model, the greater the impact on self-efficacy. When the model performs well, the student's efficacy is enhanced, but when the model performs poorly, efficacy expectations decrease. Although mastery experiences generally are acknowledged as the most influential source of efficacy beliefs in adults, Keyser and Barling (1981) found that children (6th graders in this study) rely more on modeling as a source of self-efficacy information.

Social persuasion may be a "pep talk" or specific performance feedback. Social persuasion alone can't create enduring increases in self-efficacy, but a persuasive boost in self-efficacy can lead a student to make an effort, attempt new strategies, or try hard enough to succeed (Bandura, 1982). Social persuasion can counter occasional setbacks that might have instilled self-doubt and interrupted persistence. The potency of persuasion depends on the credibility, trustworthiness, and expertise of the persuader (Bandura, 1997).

CONNECT & EXTEND

TO THE RESEARCH

A recent study found that anxiety played a significant role in judging self-efficacy for middle school students. See Klassen, R. M. (2002). *Motivational beliefs for Indo-Canadian and Anglo-Canadian early adolescents: A cross-cultural investigation of self and collective efficacy.* Dissertation. Simon Fraser University. Burnaby, B.C., Canada.

Efficacy and Motivation. Greater efficacy leads to greater effort and persistence in the face of setbacks. Self-efficacy also influences motivation through goal setting. If we have a high sense of efficacy in a given area, we will set higher goals, be less afraid of failure, and find new strategies when old ones fail. If our sense of efficacy is low, however, we may avoid a task altogether or give up easily when problems arise (Bandura, 1993, 1997; Zimmerman, 1995).

Self-efficacy and attributions affect each other. If success is attributed to internal or controllable causes such as ability or effort, then self-efficacy is enhanced. But if success is attributed to luck or the intervention of others, then self-efficacy may not be strengthened. And efficacy affects attributions too. People with a strong

Self-efficacy is a factor in motivation. The winner of this race is likely to have a high sense of self-efficacy in the area of running, and will attribute the win to internal factors such as her own ability and effort.

sense of self-efficacy for a given task ("I'm good at math") tend to attribute their failures to lack of effort ("I should have double-checked my work"). But people with a low sense of self-efficacy ("I'm terrible at math") tend to attribute their failures to lack of ability ("I'm just dumb"). So having a strong sense of self-efficacy for a certain task encourages controllable attributions, and controllable attributions increase self-efficacy. You can see that if a student held an entity view (ability cannot be changed) and a low sense of self-efficacy, motivation would be destroyed when failures were attributed to lack of ability ("I just can't do this and I'll never be able to learn") (Bandura, 1997; Pintrich & Schunk, 2002).

There is evidence that a high sense of self-efficacy supports motivation, even when the efficacy is unrealistically high. Children and adults who are optimistic about the future, believe that they can be effective, and have high expectations are more mentally and physically healthy, less depressed, and more motivated to achieve (Flammer, 1995). After examining almost 140 studies of motivation, Sandra Graham concluded that these qualities characterize many African Americans. She found that the African Americans studied had strong self-concepts and high expectations, even in the face of difficulties (Graham, 1994, 1995).

Research indicates that performance in school is improved and self-efficacy is increased when students (a) adopt short-term goals so it is easier to judge progress; (b) are taught to use specific learning strategies such as outlining or summarizing that help them focus attention; and (c) receive rewards based on achievement, not just engagement, because achievement rewards signal increasing competence (Graham & Weiner, 1996).

Teacher Efficacy. Much of my own research has focused on a particular kind of self-efficacy—sense of efficacy in teaching (Hoy & Woolfolk, 1990, 1993; Tschannen-Moran & Woolfolk Hoy, 2001; Tschannen-Moran, Woolfolk Hoy, & Hoy, 1998; Woolfolk & Hoy, 1990; Woolfolk, Rosoff, & Hoy, 1990). **Teaching efficacy,** a teacher's belief that he or she can reach even difficult students to help them learn, appears to be one of the few personal characteristics of teachers that is correlated with student achievement. Self-efficacy theory predicts that teachers with a high sense of efficacy work harder and persist longer even when students are difficult to teach, in part because these teachers believe in themselves and in their students.

We have found that prospective teachers tend to increase in their personal sense of efficacy as a consequence of completing student teaching. Teachers' sense of personal efficacy is higher in schools where the other teachers and administrators have high expectations for students and where teachers receive help from their principals in solving instructional and management problems (Hoy & Woolfolk, 1993). Another important conclusion from our research is that efficacy grows from real success with students, not just from the moral support or cheerleading of professors and colleagues. Any experience or training that helps you succeed in the day-to-day tasks of teaching will give you a foundation for developing a sense of efficacy in your career.

The perception of control is a significant element in having a sense of efficacy. Sense of control is also an element in a current humanistic theory of motivation—self-determination.

Self-Determination

Self-determination is the need to experience choice and control in what we do and how we do it. It is the desire to have our own wishes, rather than external rewards or pressures, determine our actions (Deci & Ryan, 1985; Ryan & Deci, 2000). People strive to be in charge of their own behavior. They constantly struggle against pressure from external controls such as the rules, schedules, deadlines, orders, and limits imposed by others. Sometimes even help is rejected so that the individual can remain in command (deCharms, 1983).

Teaching efficacy A teacher's belief that he or she can reach even the most difficult students and help them learn.

Self-determination The need to experience choice and control in what we do and how we do it.

Self-Determination in the Classroom. Classroom environments that support student self-determination and autonomy are associated with greater student interest, sense of competence, creativity, conceptual learning, and preference for challenge. These relationships appear to hold from 1st grade through graduate school (Ryan & Grolnick, 1986; Williams, Wiener, Markakis, Reeve, & Deci, 1993). When students can make choices, they are more likely to believe that the work is important, even if it is not "fun." Thus, they tend to internalize educational goals and take them as their own. Ruth Garner (1998) sums up the value of self-determination: "It is through this self-determination, measured though it might be, that wise teachers allow each of their students to guide them to what the students find particularly enjoyable and worth learning" (p. 236).

In contrast to autonomy-supporting classrooms, controlling environments tend to improve performance only on rote recall tasks. When students are pressured to perform, they often seek the quickest, easiest solution. One discomforting finding, however, is that both students and parents seem to prefer more controlling teachers, even though the students learn more when their teachers support autonomy (Flink, Boggiano, & Barrett, 1990). Assuming you are willing to risk going against popular images, how can you support student autonomy? One answer is to focus on *information,* not *control,* in your interactions with students.

CONNECT & EXTEND

TO **PRAXIS**™
SELF-DETERMINATION (I, C3)
Understand how this sense can boost or diminish motivation and describe practical steps that teachers can take to establish a sense of self-determination in students.

Information and Control. Many things happen to students throughout the school day. They are praised or criticized, reminded of deadlines, assigned grades, given choices, lectured about rules, and on and on. **Cognitive evaluation theory** (Deci & Ryan, 1985; Ryan & Deci, 2000) explains how these events can influence the students' intrinsic motivation by affecting their sense of self-determination and competence. According to this theory, all events have two aspects, controlling and informational. If an event is highly controlling, that is, if it pressures students to act or feel a certain way, then students will experience less control and their *intrinsic motivation* will be diminished. If, on the other hand, the event provides information that increases the students' sense of competence and efficacy, then intrinsic motivation will increase. Of course, if the information provided makes students feel less competent, it is likely that motivation will decrease.

For example, a teacher might praise a student by saying, "Good for you! You got an A because you finally followed my instructions correctly." This is a highly controlling statement, giving the credit to the teacher and thus undermining the student's sense of self-determination and intrinsic motivation. The teacher could praise the same work by saying, "Good for you! Your understanding of the author's use of metaphors has improved tremendously. You earned an A." This statement provides information about the student's growing competence and should increase intrinsic motivation.

What can teachers do to support student autonomy? An obvious first step is to limit their controlling messages to their students and make sure the information they provide highlights students' growing competence. The *Guidelines* on page 372 give ideas about how to support students' self-determination and autonomy.

CONNECT & EXTEND

TO OTHER CHAPTERS
The concept of learned helplessness was first introduced in Chapter 4 during the discussion of learning disabilities. Learned helplessness is also an issue for at-risk students, as described in Chapter 5. Consider the many factors in a classroom that might lead to learned helplessness, including physical or cognitive disabilities, racial prejudice, sex-role stereotyping, poverty, and so on.

Learned Helplessness

Whatever the label, most theorists agree that a sense of efficacy, control, or self-determination is critical if people are to feel intrinsically motivated. When people come to believe that the events and outcomes in their lives are mostly uncontrollable, they have developed **learned helplessness** (Seligman, 1975). To understand the power of learned helplessness, consider this experiment (Hiroto & Seligman, 1975): Subjects receive either solvable or unsolvable puzzles. In the next phase of the experiment, all subjects are given a series of solvable puzzles. The subjects who struggled with unsolvable problems in the first phase of the experiment usually solve significantly fewer

Cognitive evaluation theory Suggests that events affect motivation through the individual's perception of the events as controlling behavior or providing information.

Learned helplessness The expectation, based on previous experiences with a lack of control, that all one's efforts will lead to failure.

GUIDELINES Supporting Self-Determination and Autonomy

Allow and encourage students to make choices.

Examples

1. Design several different ways to meet a learning objective (e.g., a paper, a compilation of interviews, a test, a news broadcast) and let students choose one. Encourage them to explain the reasons for their choice.
2. Appoint student committees to make suggestions about streamlining procedures such as caring for class pets or distributing equipment.
3. Provide time for independent and extended projects.

Help students plan actions to accomplish self-selected goals.

Examples

1. Experiment with goal cards. Students list their short- and long-term goals and then record 3 or 4 specific actions that will move them toward the goals. Goal cards are personal—like credit cards.
2. Encourage middle and high school students to set goals in each subject area, record them in a goal book or on a floppy disk, and check progress toward the goals on a regular basis.

Hold students accountable for the consequences of their choices.

Examples

1. If students choose to work with friends and do not finish a project because too much time was spent socializing, grade the project as it deserves and help the students see the connection between lost time and poor performance.
2. When students choose a topic that captures their imagination, discuss the connections between their investment in the work and the quality products that follow.

Provide rationales for limits, rules, and constraints.

Examples

1. Explain reasons for rules.
2. Respect rules and constraints in your own behavior.

Acknowledge that negative emotions are valid reactions to teacher control.

Examples

1. Communicate that it is okay (and normal) to feel bored waiting for a turn, for example.
2. Communicate that sometimes important learning involves frustration, confusion, weariness.

Use noncontrolling, positive feedback.

Examples

1. See poor performance or behavior as a problem to be solved, not a target of criticism.
2. Avoid controlling language, "should," "must," "have to."

SOURCE: From *150 Ways to Increase Intrinsic Motivation in the Classroom,* by James P. Raffini. Published by Allyn & Bacon, Boston, MA. Copyright © 1996 by Pearson Education. Adapted by permission of the publisher. And *Motivating Others: Nurturing Inner Motivational Resources,* by J. Reeve. Published by Allyn & Bacon, Boston, MA. Copyright © 1996 by Pearson Education. Adapted by permission of the publisher.

puzzles in the second phase. They have learned that they cannot control the outcome, so why should they even try?

Learned helplessness appears to cause three types of deficits: motivational, cognitive, and affective. Students who feel hopeless will be unmotivated and reluctant to attempt work. Like Helpless Henry described earlier, they expect to fail, so why should they even try—thus motivation suffers. Because they are pessimistic about learning, these students miss opportunities to practice and improve skills and abilities, so they develop cognitive deficits. Finally, they often suffer from affective problems such as depression, anxiety, and listlessness (Alloy & Seligman, 1979). Once established, it is very difficult to reverse the effects of learned helplessness. As we saw in Chapters 4 and 5, learned helplessness is a particular danger for students with learning disabilities and students who are the victims of discrimination.

Self-Worth

What are the connections between attributions for success and failure, and beliefs about ability, self-efficacy, and self-worth? Covington and his colleagues suggest that these factors come together in three kinds of motivational sets: *mastery-oriented, failure-avoiding,* and *failure-accepting,* as shown in Table 10.4 (Covington, 1992; Covington & Mueller, 2001; Covington & Omelich, 1987).

■ **Table 10.4** Mastery-Oriented, Failure-Avoiding, and Failure-Accepting Students

	Attitude toward Failure	Goals Set	Attributions	View of Ability	Strategies
Mastery-Oriented	Low fear of failure	Learning goals: moderately difficult and challenging	Effort, use of right strategy, sufficient knowledge is cause of success	Incremental; improvable	Adaptive strategies; e.g., try another way, seek help, practice/study more
Failure-Avoiding	High fear of failure	Performance goals; very hard or very easy	Lack of ability is cause of failure	Entity; set	Self-defeating strategies; e.g., make a feeble effort, pretend not to care
Failure-Accepting	Expectation of failure; depression	Performance goals or no goals	Lack of ability is cause of failure	Entity; set	Learned helplessness; likely to give up

Mastery-oriented students tend to value achievement and see ability as improvable (an incremental view), so they focus on mastery goals in order to increase their skills and abilities. They are not fearful of failure, because failing does not threaten their sense of competence and self-worth. This allows them to set moderately difficult goals, take risks, and cope with failure constructively. They generally attribute success to their own effort, and thus they assume responsibility for learning and have a strong sense of self-efficacy. They perform best in competitive situations, learn fast, have more self-confidence and energy, are more aroused, welcome concrete feedback (it does not threaten them), and are eager to learn "the rules of the game" so that they can succeed. All of these factors make for persistent, successful learning (Covington & Mueller, 2001; McClelland, 1985; Morris, 1991).

Failure-avoiding students tend to hold an entity view of ability, so they set performance goals. They lack a strong sense of their own competence and self-worth separate from their performance. In other words, they feel only as smart as their last test grade, so they never develop a solid sense of self-efficacy. In order to feel competent, they must protect themselves (and their self-images) from failure. If they have been generally successful, they may avoid failure like Safe Sarah, simply by taking few risks and "sticking with what they know." If, on the other hand, they have experienced some successes but also a good bit of failure then they, like Defensive Diana, may adopt self-defeating strategies such as feeble efforts, setting very low or ridiculously high goals, or claiming not to care. Just before a test a student might say, "I didn't study at all!" or "All I want to do is pass." Then, any grade above passing is a success. Procrastination is another self-protective strategy. Low grades do not imply low ability if the student can claim, "I did okay considering I didn't start the term paper until last night." Some evidence suggests that blaming anxiety for poor test performance can also be a self-protective strategy (Covington & Omelich, 1987). Very little learning is going on.

Unfortunately, failure-avoiding strategies generally lead to the very failure the students were trying to avoid. If failures continue and excuses wear thin, the students may finally decide that they are incompetent. Their sense of self-worth and self-efficacy deteriorate. They give up and thus become **failure-accepting students.** They are convinced that their problems are due to low ability. As we saw earlier, those students who attribute failure to low ability and believe ability is fixed are likely to become depressed, apathetic, and helpless. Like Hopeless Henry, they have little hope for change.

Teachers may be able to prevent some failure-avoiding students from becoming failure-accepting by helping them to find new and more realistic goals. Also, some students may need support in aspiring to higher levels in the face of sexual or ethnic stereotypes about what they "should" want or what they "should not" be able to do well. This kind of support could make all the difference. Instead of pitying or excusing these students, teachers can teach them how to learn and then hold them accountable.

CONNECT & EXTEND

TO THE RESEARCH
Graham, S., & Golan, S. (1991). Motivational influences on cognition: Task involvement, ego involvement, and depth of information processing. *Journal of Educational Psychology, 83,* 187–194.

Mastery-oriented students Students who focus on learning goals because they value achievement and see ability as improvable.

Failure-avoiding students Students who avoid failure by sticking to what they know, by not taking risks, or by claiming not to care about their performance.

Failure-accepting students Students who believe their failures are due to low ability and there is little they can do about it.

ENCOURAGING SELF-EFFICACY AND SELF-WORTH

Emphasize students' progress in a particular area.

Examples

1. Return to earlier material in reviews and show how "easy" it is now.
2. Encourage students to improve projects when they have learned more.
3. Keep examples of particularly good work in portfolios.

Make specific suggestions for improvement, and revise grades when improvements are made.

Examples

1. Return work with comments noting what the students did right, what they did wrong, and why they might have made the mistakes.
2. Experiment with peer editing.
3. Show students how their revised, higher grade reflects greater competence and raises their class average.

Stress connections between past efforts and past accomplishments.

Examples

1. Have individual goal-setting and goal-review conferences with students, in which you ask students to reflect on how they solved difficult problems.
2. Confront self-defeating, failure-avoiding strategies directly.

Set learning goals for your students, and model a mastery orientation for them.

Examples

1. Recognize progress and improvement.
2. Share examples of how you have developed your abilities in a given area and provide other models of achievement who are similar to your students—no supermen or superwomen whose accomplishments seem unattainable.
3. Read stories about students who overcame physical, mental, or economic challenges.
4. Don't excuse failure because a student has problems outside school. Help the student succeed inside school.

Self-Schemas: Lessons for Teachers

If students believe they lack the ability to deal with higher mathematics, they will probably act on this belief even if their actual abilities are well above average. These students are likely to have little motivation to tackle trigonometry or calculus, because they expect to do poorly in these areas. If students believe that failing means they are stupid, they are likely to adopt many self-protective, but also self-defeating, strategies. Just telling students to "try harder" is not particularly effective. Students need real evidence that effort will pay off, that setting a higher goal will not lead to failure, that they can improve, and that abilities can be changed. They need authentic mastery experiences. The *Guidelines* provide ideas for encouraging self-efficacy and self-worth.

Check Yourself How do beliefs about ability affect motivation?

What is self-efficacy, and how is it different from other self-schemas?

What are the sources of self-efficacy, and how does efficacy affect motivation?

How does self-determination affect motivation?

How does self-worth influence motivation?

How can we put together all this information about motivation? How can teachers create environments, situations, and relationships that encourage motivation? We address these questions next.

Motivation to Learn in School

Motivation to learn The tendency to find academic activities meaningful and worthwhile and to try to benefit from them.

Teachers are concerned about developing a particular kind of motivation in their students—the motivation to learn. Jere Brophy (1988) describes student **motivation to learn** as "a student tendency to find academic activities meaningful and worthwhile and to try to derive the intended academic benefits from them. Motivation to learn can be construed as both a general trait and a situation-specific state" (pp. 205–206). Motivation to learn involves more than wanting or intending to learn. It includes the quality of the student's mental efforts. For example, reading the text 10 times may indicate persistence, but motivation to learn implies more thoughtful, active study strategies, such as summarizing, elaborating the basic ideas, outlining in your own words, drawing graphs of the key relationships, and so on (Brophy, 1988).

It would be wonderful if all our students came to us filled with the motivation to learn, but they don't. And even if they did, work in school might still seem boring or unimportant to some students. As teachers, we have three major goals. The first is to get students productively involved with the work of the class; in other words, to create a *state* of motivation to learn. The second and longer-term goal is to develop in our students the *trait* of being motivated to learn so they will be able "to educate themselves throughout their lifetime" (Bandura, 1993, p. 136). And finally, we want our students to be cognitively engaged—to think deeply about what they study. In other words, we want them to be *thoughtful* (Blumenfeld, Puro, & Mergendoller, 1992).

In this chapter we examined the roles of intrinsic and extrinsic motivation, attributions, goals, interests, emotions, and self-schemas in motivation. Table 10.5 shows how each of these factors contributes to motivation to learn. The central questions for the remainder of the chapter are: What can teachers do to encourage and support motivation to learn? How can teachers use knowledge about attributions, goals, interests, beliefs, and self-schemas to increase motivation to learn? To organize our discussion, we will use the TARGET model.

CONNECT & EXTEND

TO YOUR TEACHING/PORTFOLIO
Relate the information in Chapter 5 to the discussion in this chapter of the challenges teachers face in helping to motivate all students.

On TARGET for Learning

Carol Ames (1990, 1992) has identified six areas where teachers make decisions that can influence student motivation to learn: the nature of the *task* that students are

CONNECT & EXTEND

TO PRAXIS™
TARGET (I, C1,2,3)
Describe the major features of the TARGET model and identify related strategies that are likely to boost motivation.

Table 10.5 Building a Concept of Motivation to Learn

Motivation to learn is encouraged when the sources of motivation are intrinsic, the goals are personally challenging, and the individual is focused on the task, has a mastery orientation, attributes successes and failures to controllable causes, and believes ability can be improved.

	Optimum Characteristics of Motivation to Learn	Characteristics That Diminish Motivation to Learn
Source of Motivation	INTRINSIC: Personal factors such as needs, interests, curiosity, enjoyment	EXTRINSIC: Environmental factors such as rewards, social pressure, punishment
Type of Goal Set	LEARNING GOAL: Personal satisfaction in meeting challenges and improving; tendency to choose moderately difficult and challenging goals	PERFORMANCE GOAL: Desire for approval for performance in others' eyes; tendency to choose very easy or very difficult goals
Type of Involvement	TASK-INVOLVED: Concerned with mastering the task	EGO-INVOLVED: Concerned with self in others' eyes.
Achievement Motivation	Motivation to ACHIEVE: mastery orientation	Motivation to AVOID FAILURE: prone to anxiety
Likely Attributions	Successes and failures attributed to CONTROLLABLE effort and ability	Success and failures attributed to UNCONTROLLABLE causes
Beliefs about Ability	INCREMENTAL VIEW: Belief that ability can be improved through hard work and added knowledge and skills	ENTITY VIEW: Belief that ability is a stable, uncontrollable trait

Students may differ in the degree to which they are willing to take risks in both classroom and social situations.

asked to do, the *autonomy* students are allowed in working, how students are *recognized* for their accomplishments, *grouping* practices, *evaluation* procedures, and the scheduling of *time* in the classroom. Epstein (1989) coined the acronym TARGET to organize these areas of possible teacher influence, as shown in Table 10.6. In the following pages we will examine each of these areas more closely.

Tasks for Learning

To understand how an **academic task** can affect students' motivation, we need to analyze the task. Tasks can be interesting or boring for students. And tasks have different values for students.

CONNECT & EXTEND

TO THE RESEARCH
Vispoel, W. P., & Austing, J. R. (1995). Success and failure in junior high school: A critical incident approach to understanding students' attributional beliefs. *American Educational Research Journal, 32,* 377–412.

CONNECT & EXTEND

TO THE RESEARCH
See the special issue on "authentic learning" in the April 1993 issue of *Educational Leadership.*

Academic tasks The work the student must accomplish, including the content covered and the mental operations required.

Attainment value The importance of doing well on a task; how success on the task meets personal needs.

Intrinsic or interest value The enjoyment a person gets from a task.

Utility value The contribution of a task to meeting one's goals.

Authentic task Tasks that have some connection to real-life problems the students will face outside the classroom.

Problem-based learning Methods that provide students with realistic problems that don't necessarily have right answers.

Task Value. As you probably recall, many theories suggest that the strength of our motivation in a particular situation is determined by our *expectation* that we can succeed and the *value* of that success to us. We can think of a task as having three kinds of value to the students (Eccles & Wigfield, 2001; Eccles, Wigfield, & Schiefele, 1998). **Attainment value** is the importance of doing well on the task. This aspect of value is closely tied to the needs of the individual (for example, the need to be competent, well-liked, athletic, etc.) and the meaning of success to that person. For instance, if someone has a strong need to appear smart and believes that a high grade on a test shows you are smart, then the test has high attainment value for that person. A second kind of value is **intrinsic** or **interest value.** This is simply the enjoyment one gets from the activity itself. Some people like the experience of learning. Others enjoy the feeling of hard physical effort or the challenge of solving puzzles. Finally, tasks have **utility value;** that is, they help us achieve a short-term or long-term goal.

You see from our discussion of task value that personal and environmental influences on motivation interact constantly. The task we ask students to accomplish is an aspect of the environment; it is external to the student. But the value of accomplishing the task is bound up with the internal needs, beliefs, and goals of the individual.

Authentic Tasks. Recently there has been a great deal written about the use of authentic tasks in teaching. An **authentic task** is one that has some connection to the real-life problems and situations that students will face outside the classroom, both now and in the future. If you ask students to memorize definitions they will never use, to learn the material only because it is on the test, or to repeat work they already understand, then there can be little motivation to learn. But if the tasks are authentic, students are more likely to see the genuine utility value of the work and are also more likely to find the tasks meaningful and interesting. **Problem-based learning** is one example of the use of authentic tasks in teaching.

An example problem presented to one group of 7th and 8th graders in Illinois was, "What should be done about a nuclear waste dump site in our area?" The students soon learned that this real problem was not a simple one. Scientists disagreed about the dangers. Environmental activists demanded that the materials be removed, even if this bankrupted the company involved—one that employed many local residents. Some members of the state assembly wanted the material taken out of state, even though no place in the country was licensed to receive the toxic materials. The

Table 10.6 The TARGET Model for Supporting Student Motivation to Learn

Teachers make decisions in many areas that can influence motivation to learn. The TARGET acronym highlights task, autonomy, recognition, grouping, evaluation, and time.

TARGET Area	Focus	Objectives	Examples of Possible Strategies
Task	How learning tasks are structured—what the student is asked to do	Enhance intrinsic attractiveness of learning tasks Make learning meaningful	Encourage instruction that relates to students' backgrounds and experience Avoid payment (monetary and other) for attendance, grades, or achievement Foster goal setting and self-regulation
Autonomy/ Responsibility	Student participation in learning/school decisions	Provide optimal freedom for students to make choices and take responsibility	Give alternatives in making assignments Ask for student comments on school life—and take them seriously Encourage students to take initiatives and evaluate their own learning Establish leadership opportunities for *all* students
Recognition	The nature and use of recognition and reward in the school setting	Provide opportunities for *all* students to be recognized for learning Recognize *progress* in goal attainment Recognize challenge seeking and innovation	Foster "personal best" awards Reduce emphasis on "honor rolls" Recognize and publicize a wide range of school-related activities of students
Grouping	The organization of school learning and experiences	Build an environment of acceptance and appreciation of all students Broaden the range of social interaction, particularly of at-risk students Enhance social skills development	Provide opportunities for cooperative learning, problem solving, and decision making Encourage multiple group membership to increase range of peer interaction Eliminate ability-grouped classes
Evaluation	The nature and use of evaluation and assessment procedures	Grading and reporting processes Practices associated with use of standardized tests Definition of goals and standards	Reduce emphasis on social comparisons of achievement Give students opportunities to improve their performance (e.g., study skills, classes) Establish grading/reporting practices that portray student progress in learning Encourage student participation in the evaluation process
Time	The scheduling of the school day	Provide opportunities for extended and significant student involvement in learning tasks Allow the learning task and student needs to dictate scheduling	Allow students to *progress at their own rate* whenever possible Encourage flexibility in the scheduling of learning experiences Give teachers greater control over time usage through, for example, block scheduling

SOURCE: From "Reinventing Schools for Early Adolescents: Emphasizing Task Goals," by M. L. Maehr and E. M. Anderman, 1993, *The Elementary School Journal, 93,* pp. 604–605.

company believed the safest solution was to leave the materials buried. The students had to research the situation, interview parties involved, and develop recommendations to be presented to state experts and community groups. "In problem-based learning

CONNECT & EXTEND

TO OTHER CHAPTERS
See Chapter 9 for a complete discussion of problem-based learning.

students assume the roles of scientists, historians, doctors, or others who have a real stake in the proposed problem. Motivation soars because students realize it's their problem" (Stepien & Gallagher, 1993, p. 26).

Supporting Autonomy and Recognizing Accomplishment

The second area in the TARGET model involves how much choice and autonomy students are allowed. Choice in schools is not the norm. Children and adolescents spend literally thousands of hours in schools where other people decide what will happen and "where raised hands are sometimes ignored, questions to teachers are fairly frequently brushed aside, and permission to go somewhere else to do something else is quite routinely refused" (Garner, 1998, p. 232). Yet we know that self-determination and a sense of internal locus of causality are critical to maintaining intrinsic motivation. What can teachers do to support choice without creating chaos?

CONNECT & EXTEND

TO THE RESEARCH

The June 1998 issue of *Educational Psychology Review,* edited by Karen Harris and Pat Alexander, has a series of articles describing models of integrated teaching that include student choice. One article by Ruth Garner (pp. 227–238) describes the power of bounded choices.

Supporting Choices. Like totally unguided discovery or aimless discussions, unstructured or unguided choices can be counterproductive for learning (Garner, 1998). For example, Dyson (1997) found that children become anxious and upset when directed by teachers to draw or write about anything they want in anyway they want. Dyson says that students see this unbounded choice as a "scary void." I know that graduate students in my classes also find it disconcerting if I ask them to design a final project that will determine their grade, just as I panic when I am asked to give a talk on "anything you want." The alternative is bounded choice—giving students a range of options that set valuable tasks for them but also allow them to follow personal interests. The balance must be just right: "too much autonomy is bewildering and too little is boring" (Guthrie et al., 1998, p. 185). The *Reaching Every Student* feature is a description of such a balance.

Students also can exercise autonomy about how they receive feedback from the teacher or from classmates. Figure 10.1 describes a strategy called "Check It Out" in which students specify the skills that they want to have evaluated in a particular assignment. Over the course of a unit, all the skills have to be "checked out," but students choose when each one is evaluated.

In addition, one study found that, compared to controlling teachers, autonomy-supporting teachers listened more, held instructional materials less, resisted giving solutions to problems, gave fewer directives, and asked more questions about what students wanted to do (Reeve, Bolt, & Cai, 1999).

Recognizing Accomplishment. The third TARGET area is *recognition* for accomplishments. Students should be recognized for improving on their own personal best, for tackling difficult tasks, for persistence, and for creativity—not just for per-

Calvin & Hobbes, January 30, 1991. Copyright © 1991 Bill Watterson. Reprinted with permission of Universal Press Syndicate.

Reaching Every Student

Bounded Choice

This example of how a student in a 5th grade class exercised her choices about researching and writing is taken from Guthrie et al. (1998). The class was studying the life cycle of the Monarch butterfly. Each child worked in a heterogeneous team and each team had a chrysalis to observe as it grew. The class had organized a library of multilevel expository books, trade books, literary books, reference books, maps, electronic data bases, and other resources. The teacher had taught specific skills that would be needed—using an index, table of contents, setting goals, writing summaries, but the students were able to choose topics and appropriate resources for crafting their own chapter.

On this day, Shawna was formulating a topic for her contribution to the class book on the Monarch's life cycle. She often thought about the different colors that her specimen was turning as it passed through the different phases of metamorphosis. She searched the class library for books to help her choose a topic. She chose three books. . . . As she studied the table of contents and looked at the pictures of he butterflies, she read that the Monarch's patches of colors on one side of the wing were quite different from on the other side of the wing. . . . She turned to her friend Jane and announced, "Hey, did you know that the coloring on the butterflies' wings helps to protect them when they are sleeping in winter?" With her notes gathered, Shawna was ready to write her chapter about how colors help in the Monarch's life cycle. (Guthrie et al., 1998, p. 186)

forming better than others. In Chapter 6 we noted that giving students rewards for activities that they already enjoy can undermine intrinsic motivation. But nothing in teaching is simple. At times, praise can have paradoxical effects. For example, if two students succeed and the teacher praises only one of them, the message, to other

Using this technique to support student autonomy, the teacher decides on a set of skills that will be developed over a unit, but the student decides which skill(s) will be evaluated on any given assignment. Over the course of the unit, all the skills have to be "checked out." This student has indicated that she wants the teacher to "check out" her creativity and verb tense.

☐ Capitals
☐ Punctuation
☐ Complete Sentences
☑ Creativity
☐ Spelling
☐ Commas
☑ Tense
☐ Semicolons
On a bitterly cold December morning, Jack set out to find the perfect cup of coffee. He had nothing in the house but instant, a gift from his mother, who was visiting over

Source: From *150 Ways to Increase Intrinsic Motivation in the Classroom,* by James P. Raffini. Published by Allyn & Bacon, Boston, MA. Copyright © 1996 by Pearson Education. Adapted by permission of the publisher.

Figure 10.1 Student Autonomy: Check It Out

children at least, may be that the praised student had less ability and had to work harder to succeed, thus earning praise. So students may use the teacher's praise or criticism as cues about capabilities—praise means I'm not very smart, so when I succeed, I deserve recognition. Criticism means my teacher thinks I'm smart and could do better (Stipek, 2002).

What sort of recognition leads to engagement? One answer comes from a study by Ruth Butler (1987). Students in the 5th and 6th grades were given interesting divergent thinking tasks followed by either individual personalized comments, standardized praise ("very good"), grades, or no feedback. Interest, performance, attributions to effort, and task involvement were higher after personal comments. Ego-involved motivation (the desire to look good or do better than others) was greater after grades and standard praise.

CONNECT & EXTEND

TO THE RESEARCH
For a thorough review of research on different forms of cooperative learning, see O'Donnell, A. M., & O'Kelly, J. (1994). Learning from peers: Beyond the rhetoric of positive results. *Educational Psychology Review, 6,* 321–350.

Grouping, Evaluation, and Time

You may remember a teacher who made you want to work hard—someone who made a subject come alive. Or you may remember how many hours you spent practicing as a member of a team, orchestra, choir, or theater troupe. If you do, then you know the motivational power of relationships with other people. David and Roger Johnson (1985) describe the power this way:

> Motivation to learn is inherently interpersonal. It is through interaction with other people that students learn to value learning for its own sake, enjoy the process of learning, and take pride in their acquisition of knowledge and development of skill. Of the interpersonal relationships available in the classroom, peers may be the most influential on motivation to learn. (p. 250)

The ways that students relate to peers are influenced by the goal structure of the activities and tasks created by the teacher.

Grouping and Goal Structures. Motivation can be greatly influenced by the ways we relate to the other people who are also involved in accomplishing a particular goal. Johnson and Johnson (1999) have labeled this interpersonal factor the **goal structure** of the task. There are three such structures: cooperative, competitive, and individualistic, as shown in Table 10.7.

Goal structure The way students relate to others who are also working toward a particular goal.

When the task involves complex learning and problem-solving skills, cooperation leads to higher achievement than competition, especially for students with lower abilities. Students learn to set attainable goals and negotiate. They become more altruistic. The interaction with peers that students enjoy so much becomes a part of the learning process. The result? The need for belonging described by Maslow is more likely to be met and motivation is increased (Johnson & Johnson, 1985; Stipek, 2002; Webb & Palincsar, 1996). There are many approaches to peer learning or group learning. We will examine these approaches in depth in Chapter 13.

Evaluation. The greater the emphasis on competitive evaluation and grading, the more students will focus on performance goals rather than mastery. And low-achieving students who have little hope of either performing well or mastering the task may simply want to get it over with. One study of 1st graders found that low-achieving students made up answers, filled in the page with patterns, or copied from other students, just to get through their seatwork. As one student said when she finished a word/definition matching exercise, "I don't know what it means, but I did it" (Anderson, Brubaker, Alleman-Brooks, & Duffy, 1985, p. 132). On closer examination, the researchers found that the work was much too hard for these students, so they connected words and definitions at random.

■ Table 10.7	Different Goal Structures		
Each goal structure is associated with a different relationship between the individual and the group. This relationship influences motivation to reach the goal.			
	Cooperative	**Competitive**	**Individualistic**
Definition	Students believe their goal is attainable only if other students will also reach the goal.	Students believe they will reach their goal if and only if other students do not reach the goal.	Students believe that their own attempt to reach a goal is not related to other students' attempts to reach the goal.
Examples	Team victories—each player wins only if all the team members win: a relay race, a quilting bee, a barn raising, a symphony, a play.	Golf tournament, singles tennis match, a 100-yard dash, valedictorian, Miss America pageant.	Lowering your handicap in golf, jogging, learning a new language, enjoying a museum, losing or gaining weight, stopping smoking.

SOURCE: From *Learning Together and Alone: Cooperation, Competition, and Individualization*, (5th ed.), by D. Johnson & R. Johnson. Published by Allyn & Bacon, Boston, MA. Copyright © 1999 by Pearson Education. Adapted by permission of the publisher.

How can teachers prevent students from simply focusing on the grade or doing the work "just to get finished"? The most obvious answer is to de-emphasize grades and emphasize learning in the class. Students need to understand the value of the work. Instead of saying, "You will need to know this for the test," tell students how the information will be useful in solving problems they want to solve. Suggest that the lesson will answer some interesting questions. Communicate that understanding is more important than finishing.

Unfortunately, many teachers do not follow this advice. Brophy (1988) reports that when he and several colleagues spent about 100 hours observing how six teachers introduced their lessons, they found that most introductions were routine, apologetic, or unenthusiastic. The introductions described procedures, made threats, emphasized finishing, or promised tests on the material. But there are exceptions. Hermine Marshall (1987) described a few elementary school teachers who seemed to establish a *learning orientation* in their classrooms. They stressed understanding instead of performing, being graded, or finishing work.

One way to emphasize learning rather than grades is to use self-evaluation. This strategy also supports autonomy. For example, the self-evaluation and goal planning sheet in Figure 10.2 on page 382 could be adapted for almost any grade.

CONNECT & EXTEND

TO THE RESEARCH

Brophy (1988) reports these examples of lesson introductions that focus on procedures and threats:

"You don't expect me to give you baby work to do every day, do you?"

"My talkers are going to get a third page to do during lunch."

"If you are done by 10 o'clock, you can go outside." (p. 204)

Time. Most experienced teachers know that there is too much work and not enough time in the school day. Even if they become engrossed in a project, students must stop and turn their attention to another subject when the bell rings or the schedule demands. Furthermore, students must progress as a group. If particular individuals can move faster or if they need more time, they may still have to follow the pace of the whole group. So scheduling often interferes with motivation by making students move faster or slower than would be appropriate or by interrupting their involvement. It is difficult to develop persistence and a sense of self-efficacy when students are not allowed to stick with a challenging activity. As a teacher, will you be able to make time for engaged and persistent learning? Some elementary classrooms have DEAR time—Drop Everything And Read—to give extended periods when everyone, even the teacher, reads. Some middle and high schools have block scheduling in which teachers work in teams to plan larger blocks of time.

CONNECT & EXTEND

TO OTHER CHAPTERS

Chapter 11 discusses how to make more time for learning by decreasing disruptions, smoothing transitions, and avoiding discipline problems.

By completing this form, students evaluate their own work in relation to their own goals and set new goals for the future.

Name ______________________ Advisor ______________

Subject ______________________ Quarter ______________

1. Self-Evaluation:

a. How am I doing in this course? ______________________

b. What difficulties have I been having? ______________________

c. How much time and effort have I been spending in this course?

d. Do I need more help in this course?________ If yes, how have I tried to get it?

2. Academic Goal

a. My goal to achieve before the end of the quarter is ______________

b. I want to work on this goal because ______________________

c. I will achieve this goal by______________________

3. Behavior or Social Goal

a. My goal to achieve before the end of the quarter is ______________

b. I want to work on this goal because ______________________

c. I will achieve this goal by______________________

Variations

Advisors may choose to use this activity at the beginning of each quarter and adapt self-evaluation and goal planning sheets to specific grade levels. Follow-up conferences are also useful for helping students evaluate their plans.

Source: From *150 Ways to Increase Intrinsic Motivation in the Classroom,* by James P. Raffini. Published by Allyn & Bacon, Boston, MA. Copyright © 1996 by Pearson Education. Adapted by permission of the publisher.

Figure 10.2 Self-Evaluation and Goals Planning

Check Yourself Define motivation to learn.

What does TARGET stand for?

How do tasks affect motivation?

Distinguish between bounded and unbounded choices.

How can recognition undermine motivation and a sense of self-efficacy?

What determines whether a goal structure is cooperative, competitive, or individualistic?

How does evaluative climate affect goal-setting?

What are some effects of time on motivation?

Bringing It All Together: Strategies to Encourage Motivation and Thoughtful Learning

Until four basic conditions are met, no motivational strategies will succeed. First, the classroom must be relatively organized and free from constant interruptions and disruptions. (Chapter 11 will give you the information you need to make sure this requirement is met.) Second, the teacher must be a patient, supportive person who never embarrasses students for mistakes. Everyone in the class should see mistakes as opportunities for learning (Clifford, 1990, 1991). Third, the work must be challenging but reasonable. If work is too easy or too difficult, students will have little motivation to learn. They will focus on finishing, not on learning. Finally, the learning tasks must be authentic (Brophy 1983; Brophy & Kher, 1986; Stipek, 1993).

Once these four basic conditions are met, the influences on students' motivation to learn in a particular situation can be summarized in three questions: Can I succeed at this task? Do I want to succeed? What do I need to do to succeed? (Eccles & Wigfield, 1985). As reflected in these questions, we want students to have confidence in their ability so they will approach learning with energy and enthusiasm. We want them to see the value of the tasks involved and work to learn, not just try to get the grade or get finished. We want students to believe that success will come when they apply good learning strategies instead of believing that their only option is to use self-defeating, failure-avoiding, face-saving strategies. When things get difficult, we want students to stay focused on the task, and not get so worried about failure that they "freeze." Table 10.8 summarizes the basic requirements and strategies for encouraging student motivation to learn, all of which are discussed at length in the next few pages.

CONNECT & EXTEND

TO **PRAXIS**™
PROMOTING INTRINSIC MOTIVATION TO LEARN (I, C2,3)
For a set of practical tips, guidelines, and suggestions for boosting and maintaining motivation to learn, go to *Increasing Student Engagement and Motivation: From Time-on-Task to Homework* (http://www.nwrel.org/request/oct00/textonly.html).

Table 10.8 Strategies to Encourage Motivation to Learn

This table refers to the entire Strategies to Encourage Motivation and Thoughtful Learning section of the text.

Fulfill basic requirements

- Provide an organized class environment
- Be a supportive teacher
- Assign challenging, but not too difficult, work
- Make tasks worthwhile

Build confidence and positive expectations

- Begin work at the students' level
- Making learning goals clear, specific, and attainable
- Stress self-comparison, not competition
- Communicate that academic ability is improvable
- Model good problem solving

Show the value of learning

- Connect the learning task to the needs of the students
- Tie class activities to the students' interests
- Arouse curiosity
- Make the learning task fun
- Make use of novelty and familiarity
- Explain connections between present learning and later life
- Provide incentives and rewards, if needed

Help students stay focused on the task

- Give students frequent opportunities to respond
- Provide opportunities for students to create a finished product
- Avoid heavy emphasis on grading
- Reduce task risk without oversimplifying the task
- Model motivation to learn
- Teach learning tactics

Can I Do It? Building Confidence and Positive Expectations

No amount of encouragement or "cheerleading" will substitute for real accomplishment. To ensure genuine progress:

1. *Begin work at the students' level and move in small steps.* The pace should be brisk, but not so fast that students have to move to the next step before they understand the previous one. This may require assigning different tasks to different students. One possibility is to have very easy and very difficult questions on every test and assignment, so all students are both successful and challenged. When grades are required, make sure all the students in class have a chance to make at least a C if they work hard.

2. *Make sure learning goals are clear, specific, and possible to reach in the near future.* When long-term projects are planned, break the work into subgoals and help students feel a sense of progress toward the long-term goal. If possible, give students a range of goals at different levels of difficulty and let them choose.

3. *Stress self-comparison, not comparison with others.* Help students see the progress they are making by showing them how to use self-management strategies such as those described in Chapter 6. Give specific feedback and corrections. Tell students what they are doing right as well as what is wrong and *why* it is wrong. Periodically, give students a question or problem that was once hard for them but now seems easy. Point out how much they have improved.

4. *Communicate to students that academic ability is improvable* and specific to the task at hand. In other words, the fact that a student has trouble in algebra doesn't necessarily mean that geometry will be difficult or that he or she is a bad English student. Don't undermine your efforts to stress improvement by displaying only the 100% papers on the bulletin board.

5. *Model good problem solving,* especially when *you* have to try several approaches to get a solution. Students need to see that learning is not smooth and error-free, even for the teacher.

Do I Want to Do It? Seeing the Value of Learning

Teachers can use intrinsic and extrinsic motivation strategies to help students see the value of the learning task.

Attainment and Intrinsic Value. To establish attainment value, we must connect the learning task with the needs of the students. First, it must be possible for students to meet their needs for safety, belonging, and achievement in our classes. The classroom should not be a frightening or lonely place. Second, we must be sure that sexual or ethnic stereotypes do not interfere with motivation. For example, we must make it clear that both women and men can be high achievers in all subjects and that no subjects are the territory of only one sex. It is not "unfeminine" to be strong in mathematics, science, shop, or sports. It is not "unmasculine" to be good in literature, art, music, or French.

There are many strategies for encouraging *intrinsic* (interest) motivation. Several of the following are taken from Brophy (1988).

1. *Tie class activities to student interests* in sports, music, current events, pets, common problems or conflicts with family and friends, fads, television and cinema personalities, or other significant features of their lives (Schiefele, 1991). But be sure you know what you are talking about. For example, if you use a verse from a Jennifer Lopez song to make a point, you had better have some knowledge of the music and the performer. When possible, give students choices of research paper or reading topics so they can follow their own interests.

2. *Arouse curiosity.* Point out puzzling discrepancies between students' beliefs and the facts. For example, Stipek (1993) describes a teacher who asked her 5th-grade class if there were "people" on some of the other planets. When the students said yes, the teacher asked if people needed oxygen to breathe. Since the students had just learned this fact, they responded yes to this question also. Then the teacher told them that there is no oxygen in the atmosphere of the other planets. This surprising discrepancy between what the children knew about oxygen and what they believed about life on other planets led to a rousing discussion of the atmospheres of other planets, the kinds of beings that could survive in these atmospheres, and so on. A straight lecture on the atmosphere of the planets might have put the students to sleep, but this discussion led to real interest in the subject.

Strategies for encouraging students' intrinsic motivation include tying class activities to student interests, arousing curiosity, and making learning tasks fun.

3. *Make the learning task fun.* Many lessons can be taught through simulations or games, as you saw in the *Point/Counterpoint* on making learning fun. Used appropriately so that the activity connects with learning, these experiences can be very worthwhile and fun, too.

4. *Make use of novelty and familiarity.* Don't overuse a few teaching approaches or motivational strategies. We all need some variety. Varying the goal structures of tasks (cooperative, competitive, individualistic) can help, as can using different teaching media. When the material being covered in class is abstract or unfamiliar to students, try to connect it to something they know and understand. For example, talk about the size of a large area, such as the Acropolis in Athens, in terms of football fields. Brophy (1988) describes one teacher who read a brief passage from *Spartacus* to personalize the unit on slavery in the ancient world.

Instrumental Value. Sometimes it is difficult to encourage intrinsic motivation, and so teachers must rely on the utility or "instrumental" value of tasks. That is, it is important to learn many skills because they will be needed in more advanced classes or because they are necessary for life outside school.

1. When these connections are not obvious, you should *explain the connections to your students.* Jeanette Abi-Nader (1991) describes one project, the PLAN program, that makes these connections come alive for Hispanic high school students. The three major strategies used in the program to focus students' attention on their future are: (1) working with mentors and models—often PLAN graduates—who give advice about how to choose courses, budget time, take notes, and deal with cultural differences in college; (2) storytelling about the achievements of former students—sometimes the college term papers of former students are posted on PLAN bulletin boards; and (3) filling the classroom with future-oriented talk such as "When you go to college, you will encounter these situations . . ." or, "You're at a parents' meeting—you want a good education for your children—and you are the ones who must speak up; that's why it is important to learn public speaking skills" (p. 548).

CONNECT & EXTEND

TO THE RESEARCH

Abi-Nader, J. (1991). Creating a vision of the future: Strategies for motivating minority students. *Phi Delta Kappan, 72,* 546–549. *Focus Questions:* Why do minority-group students sometimes find schooling unmotivating? What can be done?

2. In some situations teachers can *provide incentives and rewards for learning* (see Chapter 6). Remember, though, that giving rewards when students are already interested in the activity may undermine intrinsic motivation. If teachers began testing and grading students on their memory of the television programs they watched the previous evening, even television viewing would lose some of its intrinsic appeal (Stipek, 2002).

3. Use *ill-structured problems and authentic tasks* in teaching. Connect problems in school to real problems outside.

What Do I Need to Do to Succeed? Staying Focused on the Task

When students encounter difficulties, as they must if they are working at a challenging level, they need to keep their attention on the task. If the focus shifts to worries about performance, fear of failure, or concern with looking smart, then motivation to learn is lost. Here are some ideas for keeping the focus on learning.

CONNECT & EXTEND

TO THE RESEARCH
Thorkildsen, T. A., Nolen, S. B., & Fournier, J. (1994). What is fair? Children's critiques of practices that influence motivation. *Journal of Educational Psychology, 86*, 475–486.

Children (aged 7–12 years) were interviewed about the fairness of selected practices for influencing motivation to learn.

1. *Give students frequent opportunities to respond* through questions and answers, short assignments, or demonstrations of skills. Make sure you check the students' answers so you can correct problems quickly. You don't want students to practice errors too long. Computer learning programs give students the immediate feedback they need to correct errors before they become habits.

2. When possible, *have students create a finished product.* They will be more persistent and focused on the task when the end is in sight. We all have experienced the power of the need for closure. For example, I often begin a house-painting project thinking I will work for just an hour and then find myself still painting hours later because I want to see the finished product.

3. *Avoid heavy emphasis on grades and competition.* An emphasis on grades forces students to be ego-involved rather than task-involved. Anxious students are especially hard hit by highly competitive evaluation.

4. *Reduce task risk without oversimplifying the task.* When tasks are risky (failure is likely and the consequences of failing are grave), student motivation suffers. For difficult, complex, or ambiguous tasks, provide students with plenty of time, support, resources, help, and the chance to revise or improve work.

5. *Model motivation to learn for your students.* Talk about your interest in the subject and how you deal with difficult learning problems.

6. *Teach the particular learning tactics* that students will need to master the material being studied. Show students how to learn and remember so they won't be forced to fall back on self-defeating strategies or rote memory.

The support of families and the community can be helpful as you design strategies for your students. The *Family and Community Partnerships Guidelines* give ideas for working with families.

Check Yourself What are four conditions that must exist in a classroom before any motivational strategies can be successful?

What else can teachers do to motivate students?

Enhancing Your Expertise with Technology

Motivation to Learn

The letter stunned Judy. A parent wrote to the principal complaining that Judy was not "a good motivator." The major complaint was that Judy "failed" to participate in two reading incentive programs that year. (A pizza chain sponsored one program, and a nearby theme park sponsored the other.) Teacher participation in these programs was voluntary, and the principal never said anything about her "failure" before this letter arrived. Judy explained that she believed that these programs emphasized the quantity of reading materials over the material's quality. Like many teachers, Judy employed some forms of extrinsic motivation to learn in her classroom such as praise or certificates of achievement. But largely she relied on techniques that promote intrinsic motivation to learn.

"I agree with you, Judy, and I'll back you up," said the principal. "Let's have the parents in for a conference, but be prepared to counter their points, and explain how you deal with motivation."

Although Judy's belief about the value of intrinsic motivation is indeed supported by research, she has yet to develop

Family and Community Partnerships

Motivation to Learn

Understand family goals for children.

Examples

1. In an informal setting, around a coffee pot or snacks, meet with families individually or in small groups to listen to what they want for their children.
2. Mail out questionnaires or send response cards home with students, asking what skills the families believe their children most need to work on. Pick one goal for each child and develop a plan for working toward the goal both inside and outside school. Share the plan with the families and ask for feedback.

Identify student and family interests that can be related to goals.

Examples

1. Ask a member of the family to share a skill or hobby with the class.
2. Identify "family favorites"—favorite foods, music, vacations, sports, colors, activities, hymns, movies, games, snacks, recipes, memories. Tie class lessons to interests.

Give families a way to track progress toward goals.

Examples

1. Provide simple "progress charts" or goal cards that can be posted on the refrigerator.
2. Ask for feedback (and mean it) about parents' perceptions of your effectiveness in helping students reach goals.

Work with families to build confidence and positive expectations.

Examples

1. Avoid comparing one child in a family to another during conferences and discussions with family members.
2. Ask family members to highlight strong points of homework assignments. They might attach a note to assignments describing the three best aspects of the work and one element that could be improved.

Make families partners in showing the value of learning.

Examples

1. Invite family members to the class to demonstrate how they use mathematics or writing in their work.
2. Involve parents in identifying skills and knowledge for the children to learn in school that could be applied at home and prove helpful to the family right now, for example, keeping records on service agencies, writing letters of complaint to department stores or landlords, or researching vacation destinations.

Provide resources that build skill and will for families.

Examples

1. Give family members simple strategies for helping their children improve study skills.
2. Involve older students in a "homework hotline" telephone network for helping younger students with class assignments.

Have frequent celebrations of learning.

Examples

1. Invite families to a "museum" at the end of a unit on dinosaurs. Students create the museum in the auditorium, library, or cafeteria. After visiting the museum, families go to the classroom to examine their child's portfolio for the unit.
2. Place mini-exhibits of student work at local grocery stores, libraries, or community centers.

a wide range of such motivational techniques and strategies, and she might have some difficulty explaining their value. Judy, or any teacher in this situation, would find some immediate help with Web resources. In Web interviews, educational psychologist Carol Dweck (http://www.educationworld.com/a_curr/curr197.shtml) and journalist Alfie Kohn (http://www.webtools.familyeducation.com/article/0,1120, 3-281-0-1,00.html) discuss motivation to learn, and they provide a rationale for emphasizing the values of learning itself in contrast to the value of tangible rewards often associated with learning. The Northwest Regional Educational Laboratory (http://www.nwrel.org/request/oct00/index.html) offers a concise, authoritative Web "booklet" about motivation to learn. This booklet is essentially a novice's guide to student motivation. It contains sections about research related to the topic, affective and cognitive strategies designed to enhance intrinsic motivation to learn, suggestions for the design of engaging class activities, tips for creating motivating homework assignments, and suggestions for involving parents in those assignments.

There is one element of student motivation to learn that Judy did indeed fail to see until there was a problem: the role of parents. Whether Judy agrees with the parents or not on the issue of motivation, it is clear that she is dealing with a caring family. These parents can be valuable allies in boosting motivation. Judy might turn them into allies if she employs the suggestions for parents offered by the National Education Association (http://www.nea.org/helpfrom/connecting/tools/motivate.html).

Summary Table

What Is Motivation? (pp. 350–352)

Define motivation. Motivation is an internal state that arouses, directs, and maintains behavior. The study of motivation focuses on how and why people initiate actions directed toward specific goals, how intensively they are involved in the activity, how persistent they are in their attempts to reach these goals, and what they are thinking and feeling along the way.

What is the difference between intrinsic and extrinsic motivation? Intrinsic motivation is the natural tendency to seek out and conquer challenges as we pursue personal interests and exercise capabilities—it is motivation to do something when we don't have to. Extrinsic motivation is based on factors not related to the activity itself. We are not really interested in the activity for its own sake; we care only about what it will gain us.

How does locus of causality apply to motivation? The essential difference between intrinsic and extrinsic motivation is the person's reason for acting, that is, whether the locus of causality for the action is inside or outside the person. If the locus is internal, the motivation is intrinsic, and if the locus is external, the motivation is extrinsic. Most motivation has elements of both. In fact, intrinsic and extrinsic motivation may be two separate tendencies—both can operate at the same time in a given situation.

Motivation: An internal state that arouses, directs, and maintains behavior.

Intrinsic Motivation: Motivation associated with activities that are their own reward.

Extrinsic Motivation: Motivation created by external factors such as rewards and punishments.

Locus of Causality: The location—internal or external—of the cause of behavior.

Four General Approaches to Motivation (pp. 352–358)

What are the key factors in motivation according to a behavioral viewpoint? A humanistic viewpoint? A cognitive viewpoint? A sociocultural viewpoint? Behaviorists tend to emphasize extrinsic motivation caused by incentives, rewards, and punishment. Humanistic views stress the intrinsic motivation created by the need for personal growth, fulfillment, and self-determination. Cognitive views stress a person's active search for meaning, understanding, and competence, and the power of the individual's attributions and interpretations. Sociocultural views emphasize legitimate engaged participation and identity within a community.

Distinguish between deficiency needs and being needs in Maslow's theory. Maslow called four lower-level needs—survival, safety, belonging, and self-esteem—deficiency needs. When these needs are satisfied, the motivation for fulfilling them decreases. He labeled the three higher-level needs—intellectual achievement, aesthetic appreciation, and self-actualization—being needs. When they are met, a person's motivation does not cease; instead, it increases to seek further fulfillment.

What are the three dimensions of attributions in Weiner's theory? According to Weiner, most of the attributed causes for successes or failures can be characterized in terms of three dimensions: *locus* (location of the cause internal or external to the person), *stability* (whether the cause stays the same or can change), and *responsibility* (whether the person can control the cause). The greatest motivational problems arise when students attribute failures to stable, uncontrollable causes. These students may seem resigned to failure, depressed, helpless—what we generally call "unmotivated."

What are expectancy × value theories? Expectancy × value theories suggest that motivation to reach a goal is the product of our expectations for success and the value of the goal to us. If either is zero, our motivation is zero also.

What is legitimate peripheral participation? Legitimate peripheral participation means that beginners are genuinely involved in the work of the group, even if their abilities are undeveloped and their contributions are small. The identities of the novice and the expert are bound up in their participation in the community. They are motivated to learn the values and practices of the community to keep their identity as community members.

Reward: An attractive object or event supplied as a consequence of a behavior.

Incentive: An object or event that encourages or discourages behavior.

Humanistic Perspective: Approach to motivation that emphasizes personal freedom, choice, self-determination, and striving for personal growth.

Hierarchy of Needs: Maslow's model of seven levels of human needs, from basic physiological requirements to the need for self-actualization.

Self-Actualization: Fulfilling one's potential.

Deficiency Needs: Maslow's four lower-level needs, which must be satisfied first.

Being Needs: Maslow's three higher-level needs, sometimes called growth needs.

Attribution Theories: Descriptions of how individuals' explanations, justifications, and excuses influence their motivation and behavior.

Expectancy × Value Theories: Explanations of motivation that emphasize individuals' expectations for success combined with their valuing of the goal.

Sociocultural Views of Motivation: Perspectives that emphasize participation, identities, and interpersonal relations within communities of practice.

Legitimate Peripheral Participation: Genuine involvement in the work of the group, even if your abilities are undeveloped and contributions are small.

Goals and Motivation
(pp. 358–362)

What kinds of goals are the most motivating? Goals increase motivation if they are specific, moderately difficult, and able to be reached in the near future.

Describe mastery, performance, work-avoidant, and social goals. A mastery goal is the intention to gain knowledge and master skills, leading students to seek challenges and persist when they encounter difficulties. A performance goal is the intention to get good grades or to appear smarter or more capable than others, leading students to be preoccupied with themselves and how they appear. Students can approach or avoid these two kind of goals—the problems are greatest with avoidance. Another kind of avoidance is evident with work-avoidant learners who simply want to find the easiest way to handle the situation. Students with social goals can be supported or hindered in their learning, depending on the specific goal (i.e., have fun with friends or bring honor to the family).

What makes goal setting effective in the classroom? In order for goal setting to be effective in the classroom, students need accurate feedback about their progress toward goals and they must accept the goals set. Generally, students are more willing to adopt goals that seem realistic, reasonably difficult, and meaningful, and for which good reasons are given for the value of the goals.

Goal: What an individual strives to accomplish.
Goal orientations: Patterns of beliefs about goals related to achievement in school.
Mastery Goal: A personal intention to improve abilities and learn, no matter how performance suffers.
Task-Involved Learners: Students who focus on mastering the task or solving the problem.
Performance Goal: A personal intention to seem competent or perform well in the eyes of others.
Ego-Involved Learners: Students who focus on how well they are performing and how they are judged by others.
Work-Avoidant Learners: Students who don't want to learn or to look smart, but just want to avoid work.
Social Goals: A wide variety of needs and motives to be connected to others or part of a group.

Interests and Emotions
(pp. 362–367)

Do interests and emotions affect learning? Learning and information processing are influenced by emotion. Students are more likely to pay attention to, learn, and remember events, images, and readings that provoke emotional responses or that are related to their personal interests. However, there are cautions in responding to students' interests. "Seductive details," interesting bits of information that are not central to the learning, can hinder learning.

What is the role of arousal in learning? There appears to be an optimum level of arousal for most activities. Generally speaking, a higher level of arousal is helpful on simple tasks, but lower levels of arousal are better for complex tasks. When arousal is too low, teachers can stimulate curiosity by pointing out gaps in knowledge or using variety in activities. Severe anxiety is an example of arousal that is too high for optimal learning.

How does anxiety interfere with learning? Anxiety can be the cause or the result of poor performance; it can interfere with attention to, learning of, and retrieval of information. Many anxious students need help in developing effective test-taking and study skills.

Arousal: Physical and psychological reactions causing a person to be alert, attentive, wide awake.
Anxiety: General uneasiness, a feeling of tension.

Self-Schemas
(pp. 367–374)

How do beliefs about ability affect motivation? When people hold an entity theory of ability, that is, they believe that ability is fixed, they tend to set performance goals and strive to protect themselves from failure. When they believe ability is improvable (an incremental theory), however, they tend to set mastery goals and handle failure constructively.

What is self-efficacy, and how is it different from other self-schemas? Self-efficacy is distinct from other self-schemas in that it involves judgments of capabilities *specific to a particular task.* Self-concept is a more global construct that contains many perceptions about the self, including self-efficacy. Compared to self-esteem, self-efficacy is concerned with judgments of personal capabilities; self-esteem is concerned with judgments of self-worth.

What are the sources of self-efficacy, and how does efficacy affect motivation? Four sources are mastery experiences (direct experiences), level of arousal as you face the task, vicarious experiences (accomplishments are modeled by someone else), and social persuasion (a "pep talk" or specific performance feedback). Greater efficacy leads to greater effort, persistence in the face of setbacks, higher goals, and finding new strategies when old ones fail. If sense of efficacy is low, however, people may avoid a task altogether or give up easily when problems arise.

How does self-determination affect motivation? When students experience self-determination, they are intrinsically motivated—they are more interested in their work, have a greater sense of self-esteem, and learn more. Whether students experience self-determination depends in part on if the teacher's communications with students provide information or seek to control them. In addition, teachers must acknowledge the students' perspective, offer choices, provide rationales for limits, and treat poor performance as a problem to be solved rather than a target for criticism.

How does self-worth influence motivation? Mastery-oriented students tend to value achievement and see ability as improvable, so they focus on mastery goals, take risks, and cope with failure constructively. A low sense of self-worth seems to be linked with the failure-avoiding and failure-accepting strategies intended to protect the individual from the consequences of failure. These strategies may seem to help in the short term, but are damaging to motivation and self-esteem in the long run.

Entity View of Ability: Belief that ability is a fixed characteristic that cannot be changed.

Incremental View of Ability: Belief that ability is a set of skills that can be changed.

Self-Efficacy: Beliefs about personal competence in a particular situation.

Mastery Experiences: Our own direct experiences—the most powerful source of efficacy information.

Vicarious Experiences: Accomplishments that are modeled by someone else.

Social Persuasion: A "pep talk" or specific performance feedback—one source of self-efficacy.

Teaching Efficacy: A teacher's belief that he or she can reach even the most difficult students and help them learn.

Self-Determination: The need to experience choice and control in what we do and how we do it.

Cognitive Evaluation Theory: Suggests that events affect motivation through the individual's perception of the events as controlling behavior or providing information.

Learned Helplessness: The expectation, based on previous experiences with a lack of control, that all one's efforts will lead to failure.

Mastery-Oriented Students: Students who focus on learning goals because they value achievement and see ability as improvable.

Failure-Avoiding Students: Students who avoid failure by sticking to what they know, by not taking risks, or by claiming not to care about their performance.

Failure-Accepting Students: Students who believe their failures are due to low ability and there is little they can do about it.

■ Motivation to Learn in School

(pp. 374–382)

Define motivation to learn. Teachers are interested in a particular kind of motivation—student motivation to learn. Student motivation to learn is both a trait and a state. It involves taking academic work seriously, trying to get the most from it, and applying appropriate learning strategies in the process.

What does TARGET stand for? TARGET is an acronym for the six areas where teachers make decisions that can influence student motivation to learn: the nature of the *task* that students are asked to do, the *autonomy* students are allowed in working, how students are *recognized* for their accomplishments, *grouping* practices, *evaluation* procedures, and the scheduling of *time* in the classroom.

How do tasks affect motivation? The tasks that teachers set affect motivation. When students encounter tasks that are related to their interests, stimulate their curiosity, or are connected to real-life situations, the students are more likely to be motivated to learn. Tasks can have attainment, intrinsic, or utility value for students. Attainment value is the importance to the student of succeeding. Intrinsic value is the enjoyment the student gets from the task. Utility value is determined by how much the task contributes to reaching short-term or long-term goals.

Distinguish between bounded and unbounded choices. Like totally unguided discovery or aimless discussions, unstructured or unguided choices can be counterproductive for learning. The alternative is bounded choice—giving students a range of options that set valuable tasks for them but also allow them to follow personal interests. The balance must be just right so that students are not bewildered by too much choice or bored by too little.

How can recognition undermine motivation and a sense of self-efficacy? Recognition and reward in the classroom will support motivation to learn if the recognition is for personal progress rather than competitive victories. Praise and rewards should focus on students' growing competence. At times praise can have paradoxical effects when students use the teacher's praise or criticism as cues about capabilities.

What determines whether a goal structure is cooperative, competitive, or individualistic? How students relate to their peers in the classroom is influenced by the goal structure of the activities. Goal structures can be competitive, individualistic, or cooperative. Cooperative goal structures can encourage motivation and increase learning, especially for low-achieving students.

How does evaluative climate affect goal-setting? The more competitive the grading, the more students set performance goals and focus on "looking competent"; that is, the more they are ego-involved. When the focus is on performing rather than learning, students often see the goal of classroom tasks as simply finishing, especially if the work is difficult.

What are some effects of time on motivation? In order to foster motivation to learn, teachers should be flexible in their use of time in the classroom. Students who are forced to move faster or slower than they should or who are interrupted as they become involved in a project are not likely to develop persistence for learning.

Motivation to Learn: The tendency to find academic activities meaningful and worthwhile and to try to benefit from them.

Academic Tasks: The work the student must accomplish, including the content covered and the mental operations required.

Attainment Value: The importance of doing well on a task; how success on the task meets personal needs.

Intrinsic or Interest Value: The enjoyment a person gets from a task.

Utility Value: The contribution of a task to meeting one's goals.

Authentic Task: Tasks that have some connection to real-life problems the students will face outside the classroom.

Goal Structure: The way students relate to others who are also working toward a particular goal.

Problem-Based Learning: Methods that provide students with realistic problems that don't necessarily have right answers.

Bringing It All Together: Strategies to Encourage Motivation and Thoughtful Learning

(pp. 383–386)

What are four conditions that must exist in a classroom before any motivational strategies can be successful? Before any strategies to encourage motivation can be effective, four conditions must exist in the classroom. The classroom must be organized and free from constant disruption, the teacher must be a supportive person who never embarrasses students for making mistakes, the work must be neither too easy nor too difficult, and finally, the tasks set for students must be authentic—not busy work.

What else can teachers do to motivate students? Once these conditions are met, teachers can use strategies that help students feel confident in their abilities to improve (e.g., set challenging but reachable goals, stress self—not other—comparisons, communicate that ability is improvable), strategies that highlight the value of the learning tasks (e.g., tie tasks to student interests, arouse curiosity, show connections to the future and to real-world problems, provide incentives), and strategies that help students stay involved in the learning process without being threatened by fear of failure (e.g., provide opportunities to create a finished product, teach learning tactics, model motivation to learn for students, avoid emphasizing grades, reduce risk without oversimplifying the task).

Enhancing Your Expertise with Technology: Motivation to Learn

(pp. 386–387)

Carol Dweck
(http://www.education-world.com/a_curr/curr197.shtml)

Alfie Kohn
(http://www.webtools.familyeducation.com/article/0,1120,3-281-0-1,00.html)

The Northwest Regional Educational Laboratory
(http://www.nwrel.org/request/oct00/index.html)

National Education Association
(http://www.nea.org/helpfrom/connecting/tools/motivate.html)

Becoming a Professional

Passing the PRAXIS™

Chapter 10 reflects many of the professional standards created by the Interstate New Teacher Assessment and Support Consortium (INTASC). These standards form the basis of the PRAXIS II™ and state-created teacher licensure exams.

When you sat in your educational psychology class, you probably never connected any dots between transfer of learning and student motivation to learn. Now, however, your job status and your concerns for your future students put you in an excellent position to connect those dots. Consider these questions: How much *self-determination* did you have in choosing to work in this school district and in taking this assignment? What kinds of *expectations* are being communicated to you when you request resources? Are the curriculum and the district-wide assessments causing you to establish *goals* for yourself and your students?

Your level of self-determination, your expectations (as well those being signaled to you) for success and support, and your goals are among the many factors that will influence your motivation to be a successful teacher. Now transfer these concepts about motivation to your students. How much self-determination do they have in your classroom (or even about being in your classroom)? Will you communicate positive expectations for their success? Do they have reasonable learning goals?

Tips for PRAXIS II™

- Describe the theoretical foundations of the major approaches to motivation.
- Identify and define important terms related to motivation.
- Use your knowledge of motivation to:

  identify situations and conditions that can enhance or diminish student motivation to learn.

  design strategies to support individual and group work in the classroom.

  implement practices that help students become self-motivated.

Related Topics

- Cooperative learning (Chapter 13)
- The goals of classroom management (Chapter 11)
- Maintaining a good environment for learning (Chapter 11)
- Effects of grades and grading on students (Chapter 15)

Standards and Licensure Appendix: *PRAXIS II™ and INTASC*

Refer to the Appendix at the end of the book for detailed correlations to PRAXIS II™ exam topics and INTASC Standards addressed in this text.

Insights about Job Interview Questions: *What Would You Say?*

- As part of your interview for a job in a large high school, the principal asks, "How would you get students interested in learning? Could you tap their interests in your teaching?"
- The last question in your interview for the 8th grade position is, "We have some pretty discouraged students and parents because our scores were so low last year. What would you do to help students believe in their ability to learn?"

Your Teaching Portfolio: *Teaching Resources*

- Think about your philosophy of teaching, a question you will be asked at most job interviews. What do you believe about motivating hard-to-reach students? How can you support the development of genuine and well-founded self-efficacy in your students? (Consult the *Guidelines* for ideas.)
- Add some ideas for parent involvement from this chapter to your **Portfolio.**
- Use the section on the TARGET model (Table 10.6) to refine your teaching philosophy. How will you answer the job interview question "What would you do to motivate difficult to reach students?"
- Adapt all the *Guidelines* from the chapter for the age group you plan to teach.
- Use the TARGET model (Table 10.6) to generate motivational strategies for the grade you will teach.
- Select ideas from Table 10.7, "Strategies to Encourage Motivation to Learn" that fit your teaching and copy them into your **Teaching Resources** file.

Video**Workshop** Extra

If the Video Workshop package was included with your textbook, go to Chapter 10 of the Companion Website (www.ablongman.com/woolfolk) and click on the VideoWorkshop button. Follow the instructions for viewing *Video Clip 9: Motivation.* Consider this information along with what you've read in Chapter 10 while answering the following questions:

1. How does problem-based learning motivate students to learn?
2. Is problem-based learning a behavioral, humanistic, cognitive, or sociocultural approach to motivation?

Use the CD-ROM included in the back of your textbook to launch the "Becoming a Professional" website. The website features advice on preparing for teacher certification exams, help with getting your first job, and resources to help you perform your job well from the first day forward.

Teachers' Casebook

What Would They Do?

Here is how some practicing teachers responded to the situation presented at the beginning of this chapter about motivating students when resources are slim.

Kelly McElroy Bonin

High School Counselor, *Klein Oak High School, Spring, Texas*

Simply being excited to be working with the 3rd graders and showing interest and enthusiasm for the subject matter should arouse the students' interest and encourage them to learn. How many times have you heard it said, "Mrs. Energy was the best teacher I ever had. She took the most boring, difficult subject and made it fun and interesting." I have heard this so many times both as a student and as a teacher, and it proves my point. Just the fact that the teacher is excited about the material shows the students that this is important information that they need, plus they are curious about the material when they respect and like their teacher. If I felt like the difficulty level of the text books was too great, I would have to break the lessons down into smaller increments and use different techniques—discussion, reteaching, group projects, etc.—to enrich the students and adapt to their level of learning. When your students are motivated, they can accomplish anything—it doesn't matter what materials are available to them, what the difficulty level of the textbook is, and so on. Kids will be motivated when their teacher truly cares about them, is passionate about the material, and makes school interesting.

Pam Gaskill

Second Grade Teacher, *Riverside Elementary School, Dublin, Ohio*

Teaching is inherently creative. Use your time and creativity this summer to acquaint yourself with the required objectives and think about ways in which you can make them meaningful and relevant to your students. Explore other available resources in the community, such as libraries, speakers' bureaus, and resource centers. Plan to incorporate a variety of activities such as videos, group work, field trips, projects, and speakers so that your students will remain interested and involved. Utilize materials that your students have access to from home—books, videos, artifacts, Internet printouts. It is amazing how cooperative parents can be when asked to help in specified ways. You might even make use of the old workbook pages, not in the traditional way, but for cooperative work. You can facilitate student success by pairing weaker readers with more competent readers to discuss and complete the worksheets. Stress that everyone needs to work together to learn the material. Active participation and engagement with the materials will help your students to construct their own meanings more effectively.

Jolita Harper

Fifth Grade Teacher, *Weinland Park Elementary School, Columbus, Ohio*

The class text is just one of many means toward that end; trade books may be used as an inexpensive, user-friendly supplementary tool that enhances the curriculum. Creativity is also key. In the absence of audio-visual aids and other active teaching resources, I have made use of common materials at hand to conduct science experiments, create review games, and provide authentic opportunities for learning. No school is equipped with all the supplies that one could possibly need; thus it is essential that classroom teachers learn to utilize what is available.

I have also sought the assistance of outside agencies and organizations concerned with meeting the needs of school children. Public libraries provide specific services for educators, including the conducting of system-wide searches for class materials. Further, many book banks provide texts and beneficial teaching aids. Community organizations also present opportunities for project-based learning that are aligned with the district curriculum. My students worked with an organization that assisted them in planning and implementing the service learning projects that were a promotion requirement for the district.

Aimee Fredette

Second Grade Teacher, *Fisher Elementary School, Walpole, Massachusetts*

A very effective way that I use to get the children curious and interested is to pose a question to the class before the start of a lesson. This gives the children a focus for the lesson. As the year progresses, the children begin coming up with questions of their own. Another very successful way to spark interest and curiosity is the use of three-column activators, a brainstorming activity that the teacher and students do together. The students brainstorm WHAT WE THINK WE KNOW about the topic. The teacher records *all* responses, writing them on chart paper. Then the children brainstorm WHAT WE WANT TO KNOW about the topic. Again the teacher would record their responses. The third column, titled WHAT WE HAVE LEARNED, is added to as the theme progresses. The first two columns are referred to as the children learn about the theme.

Go to the Companion Website (www.ablongman.com/woolfolk) for additional case studies including audio and video cases, and examples of student work.

CHAPTER

11

Creating Learning Environments

Teachers' Casebook

What Would You Do?

Two boys in the middle school are terrorizing a student in one of your classes. The two are larger, stronger, and older than the boy in your class, who is small and shy. There are incidents on the bus before and after school, in the gym, and at lunch including intimidation, extortion of lunch money, tripping, shoving, and verbal taunts—"fag" is a favorite chant. You do not have the two bullies in any of your classes.

Critical Thinking

How do you handle this situation? What if the bullies were in your classes? What if the bullies and victim were girls?

Collaboration

With 2 or 3 other members of your class, role play a discussion with the boys, their teachers, their parents, or the principal—whoever you decide you should talk to. What is your plan to deal with this situation?

This chapter looks at the ways that teachers create social and physical environments for learning by examining classroom management—one of the main concerns of teachers, particularly beginning teachers. The very nature of classes, teaching, and students makes good management a critical ingredient of success; we will investigate why this is true. Successful managers create more time for learning, involve more students, and help students to become self-managing.

A positive learning environment must be established and maintained throughout the year. One of the best ways to do this is to try to prevent problems from occurring at all. But when problems arise—as they always do—an appropriate response is important. What will you do when students challenge you openly in class, when one student asks your advice on a difficult personal problem, or when another withdraws from all participation? We will examine the ways that teachers can communicate effectively with their students in these and many other situations.

By the time you have completed this chapter, you should be able to answer these questions:

- *What are the special managerial demands of classrooms and the needs of students of different ages?*
- *How will you establish a list of rules and procedures for a class?*
- *How will you arrange the physical environment of your classroom to fit your learning goals and teaching methods?*
- *What are Kounin's suggestions for preventing management problems?*
- *How would you respond to a student who seldom completes work?*
- *What are two different approaches for dealing with a conflict between a teacher and a student?*

Daffodil (1996) by Marci Forbes. Courtesy of the artist and PaintingsDIRECT (http://www.PaintingsDIRECT.com).

CONNECT & EXTEND

TO YOUR TEACHING/PORTFOLIO

Some educators object to the metaphor of teacher as manager. These critics suggest that the image brings with it notions of manipulation and detachment. Is the metaphor of manager an appropriate choice? What other metaphors can you suggest for teachers acting to maintain order and discipline? My research in this area suggests that images of group leaders (coaches, guides, etc.), problem solvers (physicians, chess players), and nurturers (mother, father, gardeners) are common for beginning teachers.

The Need for Organization

Knowledge and expertise in classroom management are marks of expertise in teaching; stress and exhaustion from managerial difficulties are precursors of burn-out in teaching (Emmer & Stough, 2001). What is it about classrooms that makes management so critical?

Classes are particular kinds of environments. They have distinctive features that influence their inhabitants no matter how the students or the desks are organized or what the teacher believes about education (Doyle, 1986). Classrooms are *multidimensional.* They are crowded with people, tasks, and time pressures. Many individuals, all with differing goals, preferences, and abilities, must share resources, accomplish various tasks, use and reuse materials without losing them, move in and out of the room, and so on. In addition, actions can have multiple effects. Calling on low-ability students may encourage their participation and thinking but may slow the discussion and lead to management problems if the students cannot answer. And events occur *simultaneously*—everything happens at once and the *pace is fast.* Teachers have literally hundreds of exchanges with students during a single day.

In this rapid-fire existence, events are *unpredictable.* Even when plans are carefully made, the overhead projector is in place, and the demonstration is ready, the lesson can still be interrupted by a burned-out bulb in the projector or a loud, angry discussion right outside the classroom. Because classrooms are *public,* the way the teacher handles these unexpected intrusions is seen and judged by all. Students are always noticing if the teacher is being "fair." Is there favoritism? What happens when a rule is broken? Finally, classrooms have *histories.* The meaning of a particular teacher's or student's actions depends in part on what has happened before. The fifteenth time a student arrives late requires a different response from the teacher than the first late arrival. In addition, the history of the first few weeks of school affects life in the class all year.

The Basic Task: Gain Their Cooperation

No productive activity can take place in a group without the cooperation of all members. This obviously applies to classrooms. Even if some students don't participate, they must allow others to do so. (We all have seen one or two students bring an entire class to a halt.) So the basic management task for teachers is to achieve order and harmony by gaining and maintaining student cooperation in class activities (Doyle, 1986). Given the multidimensional, simultaneous, fast-paced, unpredictable, public, and historical nature of classrooms, this is quite a challenge.

CONNECT & EXTEND

TO OTHER CHAPTERS

Motivation and classroom management are closely related. The motivational strategies described in Chapter 10 are good first steps in effective class management.

Gaining student cooperation means much more than dealing effectively with misbehavior. It means planning activities, having materials ready, making appropriate behavioral and academic demands on students, giving clear signals, accomplishing transitions smoothly, foreseeing problems and stopping them before they start, selecting and sequencing activities so that flow and interest are maintained—and much more. Also, different activities require different managerial skills. For example, a new or complicated activity may be a greater threat to classroom management than a familiar or simple activity.

Obviously, gaining the cooperation of kindergartners is not the same task as gaining the cooperation of high school seniors. Jere Brophy and Carolyn Evertson (1978) identified four general stages of classroom management, defined by age-related needs. During kindergarten and the first few years of elementary school, direct teaching of classroom rules and procedures is important. For children in the middle elementary years, many classroom routines have become relatively automatic, but new procedures for a particular activity may have to be taught directly and the entire system still needs monitoring and maintenance.

Toward the end of elementary school, some students begin to test and defy authority. The management challenges at this stage are to deal productively with these disruptions and to motivate students who are becoming less concerned with teachers' opinions and more interested in their social lives. By the end of high school, the challenges are to manage the curriculum, fit academic material to students' interests and abilities, and help students become more self-managing. The first few classes each semester may be devoted to teaching particular procedures for using materials and equipment, or for keeping track of and submitting assignments. But most students know what is expected.

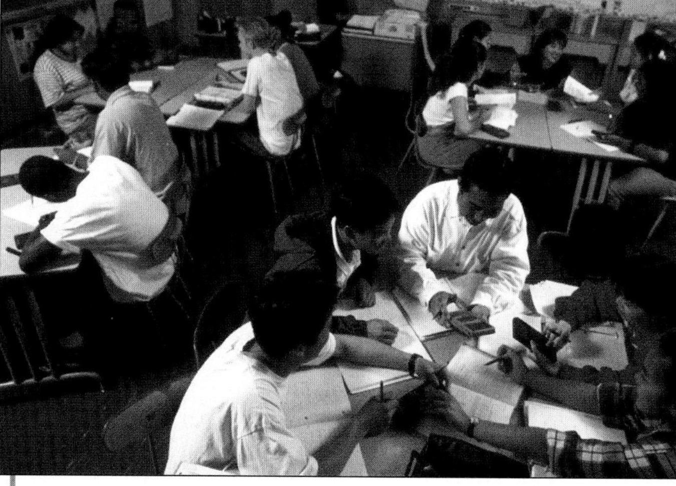

While the stereotypical classroom consists of students seated quietly in rows, their hands folded neatly on their desks, the reality is that teachers are often called on to keep track of many different activities at one time.

The Goals of Classroom Management

What Would You Say? You are interviewing for a job in a great district—it is known for innovation. The assistant principal looks at you for a moment and then asks, "What is classroom management?" How would you answer?

The aim of **classroom management** is to maintain a positive, productive learning environment. But order for its own sake is an empty goal. As we discussed in Chapter 6, it is unethical to use classroom management techniques just to keep students docile and quiet. What, then, is the point of working so hard to manage classrooms? There are at least three reasons.

More Time for Learning. As a child, I once used a stopwatch to time the commercials during a TV quiz show. I was amazed to find that half of the program was devoted to commercials. Actually, very little quizzing took place. If you used a similar approach in classrooms, timing all the different activities throughout the day, you might be surprised by how little actual teaching takes place. Many minutes each day are lost through interruptions, disruptions, late starts, and rough transitions (Karweit, 1989; Karweit & Slavin, 1981).

Obviously, students can only learn what they encounter. Almost every study examining time and learning has found a significant relationship between time spent on content and student learning (Berliner, 1988). In fact, the correlations between content studied and student learning are usually larger than the correlations between specific teacher behaviors and student learning (Rosenshine, 1979). Thus one important goal of classroom management is to expand the sheer number of minutes available for learning. This is sometimes called **allocated time.**

Simply making more time for learning will not automatically lead to achievement. To be valuable, time must be used effectively. As you saw in the chapters on cognitive learning, the way students process information is a central factor in what they learn and remember. Basically, students will learn what they practice and think about (Doyle, 1983). Time spent actively involved in specific learning tasks is often called **engaged time,** or sometimes **time on task.**

Again, however, engaged time doesn't guarantee learning. Students may be struggling with material that is too difficult or using the wrong learning strategies. When students are working with a high rate of success—really learning and understanding—we call the time spent **academic learning time.** A second goal of class management is to increase academic learning time by keeping students *actively engaged in worthwhile, appropriate learning activities.* Figure 11.1 on page 398 shows how the 1,000+ hours of time mandated for school in most states can become only about 333 hours of quality academic learning time for a typical student.

Access to Learning. Each classroom activity has its own rules for participation. Sometimes these rules are clearly stated by the teacher, but often they are implicit and

Classroom management Techniques used to maintain a healthy learning environment, relatively free of behavior problems.

Allocated time Time set aside for learning.

Engaged time Time spent actively learning.

Time on task Time spent actively engaged in the learning task at hand.

Academic learning time Time when students are actually succeeding at the learning task.

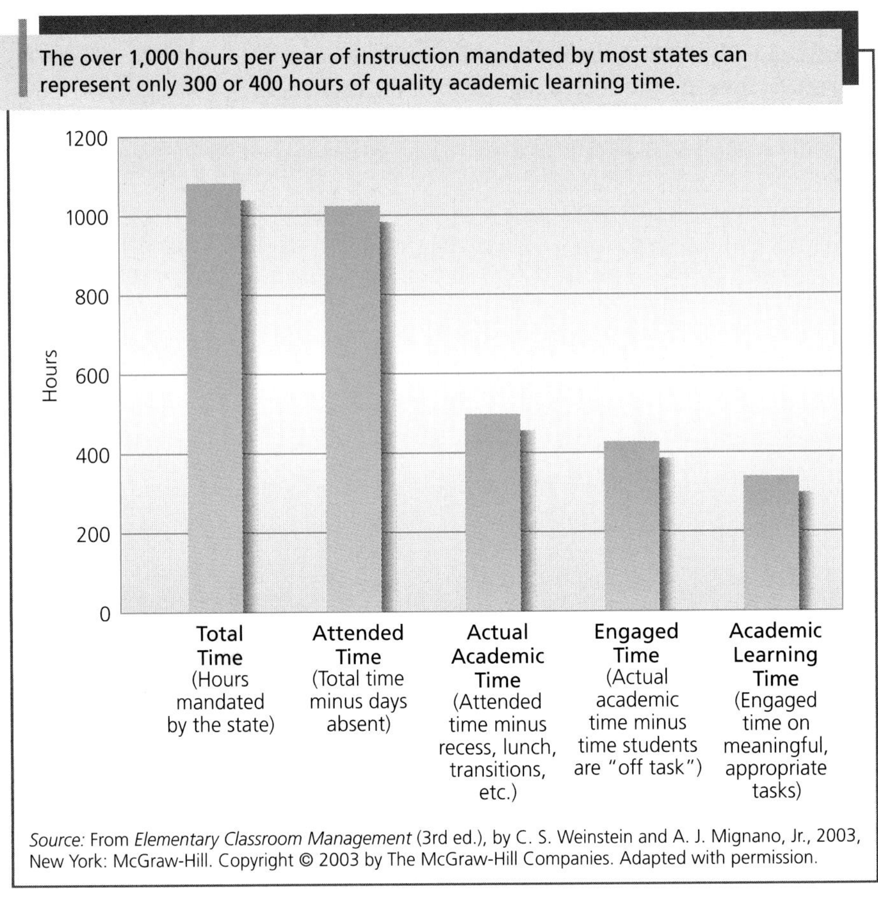

Source: From *Elementary Classroom Management* (3rd ed.), by C. S. Weinstein and A. J. Mignano, Jr., 2003, New York: McGraw-Hill. Copyright © 2003 by The McGraw-Hill Companies. Adapted with permission.

Figure 11.1 Who Knows Where the Time Goes?

unstated. Teacher and students may not even be aware that they are following different rules for different activities (Berliner, 1983). For example, in a reading group, students may have to raise their hands to make a comment, but in a show-and-tell circle in the same class, they may simply have to catch the teacher's eye.

As we saw in Chapter 5, the rules defining who can talk, what they can talk about, and when, to whom, and how long they can talk are often called **participation structures.** In order to participate successfully in a given activity, students must understand the participation structure. Some students, however, seem to come to school less able to participate than others. The participation structures they learn at home in interactions with siblings, parents, and other adults do not match the participation structures of school activities (Tharp, 1989). But teachers are not necessarily aware of this conflict. Instead, the teachers see that a child doesn't quite fit in, always seems to say the wrong thing at the wrong time, or is very reluctant to participate, and they are not sure why.

CONNECT & EXTEND

TO YOUR TEACHING/PORTFOLIO
Are there cultural differences in the verbal and nonverbal ways that students show respect, pay attention, and bid for a turn in conversation? How can cultural differences in interaction styles and expectations make classroom management more challenging?

What can we conclude? To reach the second goal of good classroom management—giving all students access to learning—you must make sure everyone knows *how to participate* in class activities. The key is awareness. What are your rules and expectations? Are they understandable, given your students' cultural backgrounds and home experiences? What unspoken rules or values may be operating? Are you clearly signaling appropriate ways to participate? For some students, particularly those with behavioral and emotional challenges, direct teaching and practicing of the important behaviors may be required (Emmer & Stough, 2001).

An example of being sensitive to participation structures was documented by Adrienne Alton-Lee and her colleagues in a classroom in New Zealand (2001). As a critical part of a unit on children in hospitals, the teacher, Ms. Nikora, planned to have one of her students, a Maori girl named Huhana, describe a recent visit to the hospi-

Participation structures Rules defining how to participate in different activities.

tal. Huhana agreed. But when the time came and the teacher asked her to come to the front of the class and share her experiences, Huhana looked down and shook her head. Rather than confront or scold Huhana, the teacher simply said, "All right. If we sit in a circle . . . Huhana might be able to tell us about what happened." When students were in a circle, the teacher said, "All right, Huhana, after Ms. Nikora called your mum and she . . . Where did she take you to?" As Huhana began to share her experience, the teacher scaffolded her participation by asking questions, providing reminders of details the teacher had learned in previous conversations with Huhana, and waiting patiently for the student's responses. Rather than perceiving the *child* as lacking competence, the teacher saw the *situation* as hindering competent expression.

Management for Self-Management. The third goal of any management system is to help students become better able to manage themselves. The movement from demanding obedience to teaching self-regulation and self-control is a fundamental shift in discussions of classroom management today (Weinstein, 1999). Tom Savage (1999) says simply, "the most fundamental purpose of discipline is the development of self-control. . . . Academic knowledge and technological skill will be of little consequence if those who possess them lack self-control" (p. 11). Through self-control, students demonstrate *responsibility*—the ability to fulfill their own needs without interfering with the rights and needs of others (Glasser, 1990). Students learn self-control by making choices and dealing with the consequences, setting goals and priorities, managing time, collaborating to learn, mediating disputes and making peace, and developing trusting relations with trustworthy teachers and classmates (Lewis, 2001; Rogers & Frieberg, 1994).

Encouraging **self-management** requires extra time, but teaching students how to take responsibility is an investment well worth the effort. When elementary and secondary teachers have very effective class management systems but neglect to set student self-management as a goal, their students often find that they have trouble working independently after they graduate from these "well-managed" classes.

Check Yourself What are the challenges of classroom management?

What are the goals of good classroom management?

CONNECT & EXTEND

TO YOUR TEACHING/PORTFOLIO

Many computer programs exist to help teachers manage their own activities inside and outside the classroom. Typical activities include online standard forms, IEPs, student home and school databases, student reports, letters to parents, archiving and locating information, electronic mail, financial planning, and scheduling. Complete classroom management systems and computer-managed instruction (CMI) are also available. For more information see: Bitter, G. G., & Pierson, M. E. (2002). *Using technology in the classroom* (5th ed.). Boston: Allyn & Bacon.

Creating a Positive Learning Environment

In making plans for your class, much of what you have already learned in this book should prove helpful. You know, for example, that problems are prevented when individual variations, such as those discussed in Chapters 2, 3, 4, and 5, are taken into account in instructional planning. Sometimes students become disruptive because the work assigned is too difficult. And students who are bored by lessons well below their ability levels may be interested in finding more exciting activities to fill their time.

In one sense, teachers prevent discipline problems whenever they make an effort to motivate students. A student involved in learning is usually not involved in a clash with the teacher or other students at the same time. All plans for motivating students are steps toward preventing problems.

CONNECT & EXTEND

TO OTHER CHAPTERS

In Chapter 12 you will learn about the importance of careful planning and clear objectives. Good planning is an important aspect of classroom management.

Some Research Results

What else can teachers do? For several years, educational psychologists at the University of Texas at Austin studied classroom management quite thoroughly (Emmer & Stough, 2001; Emmer, Evertson, & Anderson, 1980; Emmer, Evertson, & Worsham,

Self-management Management of your own behavior and acceptance of responsibility for your own actions.

CONNECT & EXTEND

TO THE RESEARCH

For a description of a study that tested the Emmer/Evertson management principles along with other approaches, such as reinforcement strategies with adolescents in several schools, see Gottfredson, D. C., Gottfredson, G. D., & Hybl, L. G. (1993). Managing adolescent behavior: A multiyear, multischool study. *American Educational Research Journal, 30,* 179–217. Generally, the application of these principles improved behavior.

2003; Evertson, 1988; Evertson, Emmer, & Worsham, 2003). Their general approach was to study a large number of classrooms, making frequent observations the first weeks of school and less frequent visits later in the year. After several months there were dramatic differences among the classes. Some had very few management problems, while others had many. The most and least effective teachers were identified on the basis of the quality of classroom management and student achievement later in the year.

Next, the researchers looked at their observation records of the first weeks of class to see how the effective teachers got started. Other comparisons were made between the teachers who ultimately had harmonious, high-achieving classes and those whose classes were fraught with problems. On the basis of these comparisons, management principles were developed. The researchers then taught these principles to a new group of teachers; the results were quite positive. Teachers who applied the principles had fewer problems; their students spent more time learning and less time disrupting; and achievement was higher. The findings of these studies formed the basis for two books on classroom management (Emmer, Evertson, & Worsham, 2003; Evertson, Emmer, & Worsham, 2003). Many of the ideas in the following pages are from these books.

Rules and Procedures Required

STOP THINK WRITE What are the three or four most important rules you will have for your classroom?

CONNECT & EXTEND

TO **PRAXIS**™
RULES (I, C4)

Fair, consistently enforced rules can have a positive effect on motivation to learn by promoting a safe and warm classroom environment. Describe how to establish and maintain effective rules. Keep in mind age-related concerns.

At the elementary school level, teachers must lead 20 to 30 students of varying abilities through many different activities each day. Without efficient rules and procedures, a great deal of time is wasted answering the same question over and over. "My pencil broke. How can I do my math?" "I'm finished with my story. What should I do now?" "Carlos hit me!" "I left my homework in my locker."

At the secondary school level, teachers must deal daily with over 100 students who use dozens of materials and often change rooms for each class. Secondary school students are also more likely to challenge teachers' authority. The effective managers studied by Emmer, Evertson, and their colleagues had planned procedures and rules for coping with these situations.

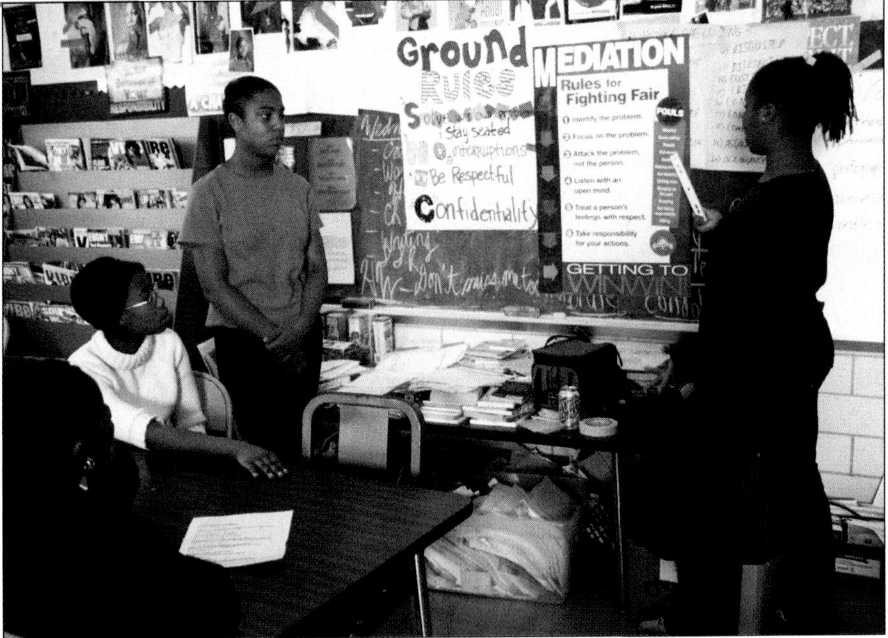

Classroom rules that are clearly understood by all students can help maintain a classroom environment that is respectful and more conducive to effective learning.

Procedures. How will materials and assignments be distributed and collected? Under what conditions can students leave the room? How will grades be determined? What are the special routines for handling equipment and supplies in science, art, or vocational classes? **Procedures** (often called routines) describe how activities are accomplished in classrooms, but they are seldom written down; they are simply the ways of getting things done in class. Carol Weinstein and Andy Mignano (Weinstein, 2003; Weinstein and Mignano, 2003) suggest that teachers establish routines to cover the following areas:

1. *Administrative routines,* such as taking attendance.
2. *Student movement,* such as entering and leaving or going to the bathroom.
3. *Housekeeping,* such as watering plants or storing personal items.
4. *Routines for accomplishing lessons,* such as how to collect assignments or return homework.
5. *Interactions between teacher and student,* such as how to get the teacher's attention when help is needed.
6. *Talk among students,* such as giving help or socializing.

You might use these six areas as a framework for planning your class procedures and routines. The *Guidelines* should help you as you plan.

CONNECT & EXTEND

TO **PRAXIS**™
PROCEDURES AND ROUTINES (I, C4)
Efficient procedures and routines reduce confusion and opportunities for misbehavior and they save time that can be devoted to learning tasks. Identify frequent activities or classroom events that would benefit from well-structured procedures or routines. Explain principles for establishing procedures and routines so that students are likely to observe them.

Procedures Prescribed steps for an activity.

GUIDELINES Establishing Class Procedures

Determine procedures for student upkeep of desks, classroom equipment, and other facilities.

Examples

1. Some teachers set aside a cleanup time each day or once a week in self-contained classes.
2. You might demonstrate and have students practice how to push chairs under the desk, take and return materials stored on shelves, sharpen pencils, use the sink or water fountain, assemble lab equipment, and so on.
3. In some classes a rotating monitor is in charge of equipment or materials.

Decide how students will be expected to enter and leave the room.

Examples

1. How will students know what they should do as soon as they enter the room? Some teachers have a standard assignment ("Have your homework out and be checking it over").
2. Under what conditions can students leave the room? When do they need permission?
3. If students are late, how do they gain admission to the room?
4. Many teachers require students to be in their seats and quiet before they can leave at the end of class. The teacher, not the bell, dismisses class.

Establish a signal and teach it to your students.

Examples

1. In the classroom, some teachers flick the lights, sound a chord on a piano or recorder, sound a bell like the "ring bell for service" at a sales counter, move to the podium and stare silently at the class, use a phrase like "Eyes, please," take out their grade books, or move to the front of the class.
2. In the halls, a raised hand, one clap, or some other signal may mean "Stop."
3. On the playground, a raised hand or whistle may mean "Line up."

Set procedures for student participation in class.

Examples

1. Will you have students raise their hands for permission to speak or simply require that they wait until the speaker has finished?
2. How will you signal that you want everyone to respond at once? Some teachers raise a cupped hand to their ear. Others preface the question with "Everyone . . . ."
3. Make sure you are clear about differences in procedures for different activities: reading group, learning center, discussion, teacher presentation, seatwork, film, peer learning group, library, and so forth.
4. How many students at a time can be at the pencil sharpener, teacher's desk, learning center, sink, book shelves, reading corner, or bathroom?

Determine how you will communicate, collect, and return assignments.

Examples

1. Some teachers reserve a particular corner of the board for listing assignments. Others write assignments in colored chalk. For younger students it may be better to prepare assignment sheets or folders, color-coding them for math workbook, reading packet, and science kit.
2. Some teachers collect assignments in a box or bin; others have a student collect work while they introduce the next activity.

No erasures? No humor!

CONNECT & EXTEND

TO YOUR TEACHING/PORTFOLIO Visit elementary school classes and note the rules posted by different teachers at the same grade level. Identify rules that are common to all or most classes, as well as those that are unusual.

Rules. **Rules** specify expected and forbidden actions in the class. They are the dos and don'ts of classroom life. Unlike procedures, rules are often written down and posted. In establishing rules, you should consider what kind of atmosphere you want to create. What student behaviors will help you teach effectively? What limits do the students need to guide their behavior? The rules you set should be consistent with school rules, and also in keeping with principles of learning. For example, we know from the research on small group learning that students benefit when they explain work to peers. They learn as they teach. A rule that forbids students to help each other may be inconsistent with good learning principles. Or a rule that says, "No erasures when writing" may make students focus more on preventing mistakes than on communicating clearly in their writing (Burden, 1995; Emmer & Stough, 2001; Weinstein & Mignano, 2003).

Having a few general rules that cover many specifics is better than listing all the dos and don'ts. But, if specific actions are forbidden, such as leaving the campus or smoking in the bathrooms, then a rule should make this clear.

Rules for Elementary School. Evertson and her colleagues (2003) give five examples of general rules for elementary school classes:

1. *Be polite and helpful.* This applies to behavior toward adults (including substitute teachers) and children. Examples of polite behavior include waiting your turn, saying "please" and "thank you," and not fighting or calling names.
2. *Respect other people's property.* This might include picking up litter; returning library books; not marking on walls, desks, or buses; and getting permission before using other people's things.
3. *Listen quietly while others are speaking.* This applies to the teacher and other students, in large-class lessons or small-group discussions.
4. *Respect and be polite to all people.* Give clear explanations of what you mean by "polite," including not hitting, fighting, or teasing. All people includes the teacher.
5. *Obey all school rules.* This reminds students that all school rules apply in your classroom. Then students cannot claim, for example, that they thought it was okay to chew gum or listen to a radio in your class, even though these are against school rules, "because you never made a rule against it for us."

Whatever the rule, students need to be taught the behaviors that the rule includes and excludes. Examples, practice, and discussion will be needed before learning is complete.

As you've seen, different activities often require different rules. This can be confusing for elementary students until they have thoroughly learned all the rules. To prevent confusion, you might consider making signs that list the rules for each activity. Then, before the activity, you can post the appropriate sign as a reminder. This provides clear and consistent cues about participation structures so all students, not just the "well-behaved," know what is expected. Of course, these rules must be explained and discussed before the signs can have their full effect.

Rules Statements specifying expected and forbidden behaviors; dos and don'ts.

Rules for Secondary School. Emmer and colleagues (2003) suggest six examples of rules for secondary students:

1. *Bring all needed materials to class.* The teacher must specify the type of pen, pencil, paper, notebook, texts, and so on.
2. *Be in your seat and ready to work when the bell rings.* Many teachers combine this rule with a standard beginning procedure for the class, such as a warm-up exercise on the board or a requirement that students have paper with a proper heading ready when the bell rings.
3. *Respect and be polite to all people.* This covers fighting, verbal abuse, and general troublemaking. All people includes the teacher.
4. *Respect other people's property.* This means property belonging to the school, the teacher, or other students.
5. *Listen and stay seated while someone else is speaking.* This applies when the teacher or other students are talking.
6. *Obey all school rules.* As with the elementary class rules, this covers many behaviors and situations, so you do not have to repeat every school rule for your class. It also reminds the students that you will be monitoring them inside and outside your class. Make sure you know all the school rules. Some secondary students are very adept at convincing teachers that their misbehavior "really isn't against the rules."

Consequences. As soon as you decide on your rules and procedures, you must consider what you will do when a student breaks a rule or does not follow a procedure. It is too late to make this decision after the rule has been broken. For many infractions, the logical consequence is having to go back and "do it right." Students who run in the hall may have to return to where they started and walk properly. Incomplete papers can be redone. Materials left out should be put back (Charles, 2002b). Sometimes consequences are more complicated. In their case studies of four expert elementary school teachers, Weinstein and Mignano (2003) found that the teachers' negative consequences fell into seven categories, as shown in Table 11.1. The main

Table 11.1 Seven Categories of Penalties for Students

1. *Expressions of disappointment.* If students like and respect their teacher, then a serious, sorrowful expression of disappointment may cause students to stop and think about their behavior.
2. *Loss of privileges.* Students can lose free time. If they have not completed homework, for example, they can be required to do it during a free period or recess.
3. *Exclusion from the group.* Students who distract their peers or fail to cooperate can be separated from the group until they are ready to cooperate. Some teachers give a student a pass for 10 to 15 minutes. The student must go to another class or study hall, where the other students and teachers ignore the offending student for that time.
4. *Written reflections on the problem.* Students can write in journals, write essays about what they did and how it affected others, or write letters of apology—if this is appropriate. Another possibility is to ask students to describe objectively what they did; then the teacher and the student can sign and date this statement. These records are available if parents or administrators need evidence of the students' behavior.
5. *Detentions.* Detentions can be very brief meetings after school, during a free period, or at lunch. The main purpose is to talk about what has happened. (In high school, detentions are often used as punishments; suspensions and expulsions are available as more extreme measures.)
6. *Visits to the principal's office.* Expert teachers tend to use this penalty rarely, but they do use it when the situation warrants. Some schools require students to be sent to the office for certain offenses, such as fighting. If you tell a student to go to the office and the student refuses, you might call the office saying the student has been sent. Then the student has the choice of either going to the office or facing the principal's penalty for "disappearing" on the way.
7. *Contact with parents.* If problems become a repeated pattern, most teachers contact the student's family. This is done to seek support for helping the student, not to blame the parents or punish the student.

SOURCE: From *Elementary Classroom Management* (3rd ed.), by C. S. Weinstein and A. J. Mignano, Jr., New York: McGraw-Hill. Copyright © 2003 by The McGraw-Hill Companies. Adapted with permission.

CONNECT & EXTEND

TO YOUR TEACHING/PORTFOLIO

Here are some tips for using consequences from Richard Curwin:

- Always implement a consequence when a rule is broken.
- Select the most appropriate consequence from the list of alternatives, taking into account the offense, situation, student involved, and the best means of helping that student.
- State the rule and consequence to the offending student. Nothing more need be said.
- Be private. Only the student(s) involved should hear.
- Do not embarrass the student.
- Do not think of the situation as win–lose. This is not a contest. Do not get involved in a power struggle.
- Control your anger. Be calm and speak quietly, but accept no excuses from the student.
- Sometimes it is best to let the student choose the consequence.
- The professional always looks for ways to help the client.

SOURCE: From Richard Curwin. *Rediscovering Hope: Our Greatest Teaching Strategy,* Copyright 1992, pp. 79–80. Permission to excerpt granted by the National Education Service, Bloomington, IN. To obtain a copy, contact the NES at 1-800-733-6786 or FAX 812-336-7790 or email NES@Bluemarble.net. All rights reserved by NES.

■ Table 11.2 A Bill of Rights for Students and Teachers

Students' Bill of Rights

Students in this class have the following rights:

To whisper when the teacher isn't talking or asking for silence.
To celebrate authorship or other work at least once a month.
To exercise outside on days there is no physical education class.
To have 2-minute breaks.
To have healthy snacks during snack time.
To participate in choosing a table.
To have privacy. Get permission to touch anyone else's possessions.
To be comfortable.
To chew gum without blowing bubbles or making a mess.
To make choices about the day's schedule.
To have free work time.
To work with partners.
To talk to the class without anyone else talking.
To work without being disturbed.

SOURCE: From *Elementary Classroom Management* (3rd ed.), by C. S. Weinstein and A. J. Mignano, Jr., New York: McGraw-Hill. Copyright © 2003 by The McGraw-Hill Companies. Adapted with permission.

point here is that decisions about penalties (and rewards) must be made early on, so students know before they break a rule or use the wrong procedure what this will mean for them. I encourage my student teachers to get a copy of the school rules and their cooperating teacher's rules, and then plan their own.

Who Sets the Rules and Consequences? In the first chapter, I described Ken, an expert teacher who worked with his students to establish a students' "Bill of Rights" instead of defining rules. These "rights" cover most situations that might require a "rule" and help the students move toward the goal of becoming self-managing. The rights for one recent year's class are listed in Table 11.2. Developing rights and responsibilities rather than rules makes a very important point to students. "Teaching children that something is wrong *because there is a rule against it* is not the same as teaching them that there is a rule against it *because it is wrong,* and helping them to understand why this is so" (Weinstein, 1999, p. 154). Students should understand that the rules are developed so that everyone can work and learn together. I might add that in recent years when Ken has had some very difficult classes, he and his students have had to establish some "laws" that protect students' rights.

Another kind of planning that affects the learning environment is designing the physical arrangement of the class furniture, materials, and learning tools.

CONNECT & EXTEND

TO THE RESEARCH

See the September 1998 issue of *Educational Leadership* for several articles on "Realizing a Positive School Climate." There are descriptions of ways to improve school climate through architecture and design, school meetings, cooperative learning, violence prevention, parent involvement, and other approaches.

Planning Spaces for Learning

Think back over all the rooms in all the schools you have attended. Which ones stand out as inviting or exciting? Which ones were cold and empty? Did one teacher have a design that let different students do different things at once?

Spaces for learning should invite and support the activities you plan in your classroom, and they should respect the inhabitants of the space. This respect begins at the classroom door for young children by helping them identify their class. One school that has won awards for its architecture paints each classroom door a different bright color, so young children can find their "home" (Herbert, 1998). Once inside, spaces can be created that invite quiet reading, group collaboration, or independent research. If students are to use materials, they should be able to reach them. In an interview with Marge Scherer (1999), Herb Kohl describes how he creates a positive environment in his classes.

> What I do is put up the most beautiful things I know—posters, games, puzzles, challenges—and let the children know these are provocations. These are ways of provoking them into using their minds. You have to create an environment that makes kids walk in and say, "I really want to see what's here. I would really like to look at this." (p. 9)

In terms of classroom arrangement, there are two basic ways of organizing space: interest areas and personal territories. These are not mutually exclusive; many teachers use a design that combines interest areas and personal territories. Individual students' desks—their territories—are placed in the center, with interest areas in the back or around the periphery of the room. This allows the flexibility needed for both large- and small-group activities. Figure 11.2 shows an elementary classroom that combines interest area and personal territory arrangements.

This 4th-grade teacher has designed a space that allows teacher presentations and demonstrations, small group work, computer interactions, math manipulatives activities, informal reading, art, and other projects without requiring constant rearrangements.

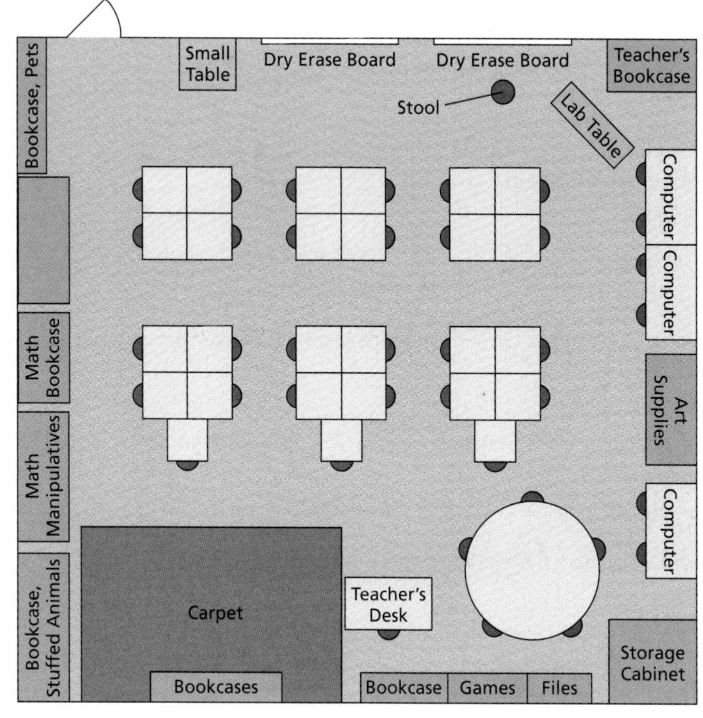

Source: From *Elementary Classroom Management* (3rd ed.), by C. S. Weinstein and A. J. Mignano, Jr., 2003, New York: McGraw-Hill. Copyright © 2003 by The McGraw-Hill Companies. Adapted with permission.

Figure 11.2 An Elementary Classroom Arrangement

Interest Areas. The design of interest areas can influence the way the areas are used by students. For example, working with a classroom teacher, Carol Weinstein (1977) was able to make changes in interest areas that helped the teacher meet her objectives of having more girls involved in the science center and having all students experiment more with a variety of manipulative materials. In a second study, changes in a library corner led to more involvement in literature activities throughout the class (Morrow & Weinstein, 1986). If you design interest areas for your class, keep the *Guidelines* on page 406 in mind.

Personal Territories. Can the physical setting influence teaching and learning in classrooms organized by territories? Front-seat location does seem to increase participation for students who are predisposed to speak in class, whereas a seat in the back will make it more difficult to participate and easier to sit back and daydream (Woolfolk & Brooks, 1983). But the **action zone** where participation is greatest may be in other areas such as on one side, or near a particular learning center (Good, 1983a; Lambert, 1994). To "spread the action around," Weinstein and Mignano (2003) suggest that teachers move around the room when possible, establish eye contact with and direct questions to students seated far away, and vary the seating so the same students are not always consigned to the back.

Horizontal rows share many of the advantages of the traditional row and column arrangements. Both are useful for independent seatwork and teacher, student, or

CONNECT & EXTEND

TO THE RESEARCH

To read three case studies describing how teachers planned the physical environments in their rooms, see Pointon, P. & Kershner, R. (2000). Making decisions about organising the primary classroom as a context for learning: The views of three experienced teachers and their pupils. *Teaching and Teacher Education, 16,* 117–127.

Action zone Area of a classroom where the greatest amount of interaction takes place.

GUIDELINES Designing Learning Spaces

Note the fixed features and plan accordingly.

Examples

1. Remember that the audiovisual center and computers need an electrical outlet.
2. Keep art supplies near the sink, small-group work by a blackboard.

Create easy access to materials and a well-organized place to store them.

Examples

1. Make sure materials are easy to reach and visible to students.
2. Have enough shelves so that materials need not be stacked.

Provide students with clean, convenient surfaces for studying.

Examples

1. Put bookshelves next to the reading area, games by the game table.
2. Prevent fights by avoiding crowded work spaces.

Make sure work areas are private and quiet.

Examples

1. Make sure there are no tables or work areas in the middle of traffic lanes; a person should not have to pass through one area to get to another.
2. Keep noisy activities as far as possible from quiet ones. Increase the feeling of privacy by placing partitions, such as bookcases or pegboards, between areas or within large areas.

Arrange things so you can see your students and they can see all instructional presentations.

Examples

1. Make sure you can see over partitions.
2. Design seating so that students can see instruction without moving their chairs or desks.

Avoid dead spaces and "racetracks."

Examples

1. Don't have all the interest areas around the outside of the room, leaving a large dead space in the middle.
2. Avoid placing a few items of furniture right in the middle of this large space, creating a "racetrack" around the furniture.

Provide choices and flexibility.

Examples

1. Establish private cubicles for individual work, open tables for group work, and cushions on the floor for whole-class meetings.
2. Give students a place to keep their personal belongings. This is especially important if students don't have personal desks.

Try new arrangements, then evaluate and improve.

Examples

1. Have a "two-week arrangement," then evaluate.
2. Enlist the aid of your students. They have to live in the room, too, and designing a classroom can be a very challenging educational experience.

CONNECT & EXTEND

TO PRAXIS™
CLASSROOM SPACE (I, C4)
The physical organization of a class has an effect on student behavior and learning. Describe how the physical layout of classrooms can affect the learning environment. Apply principles of classroom organization to enhance learning and minimize disruption.

media presentations; they encourage students to focus on the presenter and simplify housekeeping. Horizontal rows also permit students to work more easily in pairs. However, this is a poor arrangement for large-group discussion.

Clusters of four or circle arrangements are best for student interaction. Circles are especially useful for discussions but still allow for independent seatwork. Clusters permit students to talk, help one another, share materials, and work on group tasks. Both arrangements, however, are poor for whole-group presentations and may make class management more difficult.

The fishbowl or stack special formation, where students sit close together near the focus of attention (the back row may even be standing), should be used only for short periods of time, because it is not comfortable and can lead to discipline problems. On the other hand, the fishbowl can create a feeling of group cohesion and is helpful when the teacher wants students to watch a demonstration, brainstorm on a class problem, or see a small visual aid.

Getting Started: The First Weeks of Class

Determining a room design, rules, and procedures are first steps toward having a well-managed class, but how do effective teachers gain students' cooperation in those first critical days and weeks? One study carefully analyzed the first weeks' activities of effective and ineffective elementary teachers, and found striking differences (Emmer, Evertson, & Anderson, 1980).

Effective Managers for Elementary Students. In the effective teachers' classrooms, the very first day was well organized. Name tags were ready. There was something interesting for each child to do right away. Materials were set up. The teachers had planned carefully to avoid any last-minute tasks that might take them away from their students. These teachers dealt with the children's pressing concerns first. "Where do I put my things?" "How do I pronounce my teacher's name?" "Can I whisper to my neighbor?" "Where is the bathroom?" The effective teachers had a workable, easily understood set of rules and taught the students the most important rules right away. They taught the rules like any other subject—with lots of explanation, examples, and practice.

Throughout the first weeks, the effective managers continued to spend quite a bit of time teaching rules and procedures. Some used guided practice to teach procedures; others used rewards to shape behavior. Most taught students to respond to a bell or some other signal to gain their attention. These teachers worked with the class as a whole on enjoyable academic activities. They did not rush to get students into small groups or to get them started in readers. This whole-class work gave the teachers a better opportunity to continue monitoring all students' learning of the rules and procedures. Misbehavior was stopped quickly and firmly, but not harshly.

In the poorly managed classrooms, the first weeks were quite different. Rules were not workable; they were either too vague or very complicated. For example, one teacher made a rule that students should "be in the right place at the right time." Students were not told what this meant, so their behavior could not be guided by the rule. Neither positive nor negative behaviors had clear, consistent consequences. After students broke a rule, ineffective managers might give a vague criticism, such as "Some of my children are too noisy," or issue a warning, but not follow through with the threatened consequence.

In the poorly managed classes, procedures for accomplishing routine tasks varied from day to day and were never taught or practiced. Instead of dealing with these obvious needs, ineffective managers spent time on procedures that could have waited. For example, one teacher had the class practice for a fire drill the first day, but left unexplained other procedures that would be needed every day. Students wandered aimlessly and had to ask each other what they should be doing. Often the students talked to one another because they had nothing productive to do. Ineffective teachers frequently left the room. Many became absorbed in paperwork or in helping just one student. They had not made plans for how to deal with late-arriving students or interruptions. One ineffective manager tried to teach students to respond to a bell as a signal for attention, but later let the students ignore it. All in all, the first weeks in these classrooms were disorganized and filled with surprises for teachers and students alike.

Effective Managers for Secondary Students. What about getting started in a secondary school class? It appears that many of the differences between effective and ineffective elementary school teachers hold at the secondary level as well. Again, effective managers focus on establishing rules, procedures, and expectations on the first day of class. These standards for academic work and class behavior are clearly communicated to students and consistently enforced during the first weeks of class. Student behavior is closely monitored, and infractions of the rules are dealt with quickly. In classes with lower-ability students, work cycles are shorter; students are not required to spend long, unbroken periods on one type of activity. Instead, during each period they are moved smoothly through several different tasks. In general, effective teachers carefully follow each student's progress, so students cannot avoid work without facing consequences (Emmer & Evertson, 1982).

With all this close monitoring and consistent enforcement of the rules, you may wonder if effective secondary teachers have to be grim and humorless. Not necessarily. The effective managers in one study also smiled and joked more with their students (Moskowitz & Hayman, 1976). As any experienced teacher can tell you, there is much more to smile about when the class is cooperative.

CONNECT & EXTEND

TO YOUR TEACHING/PORTFOLIO

Five excellent and very practical discussions of classroom management are:

Evertson, C. M., Emmer, E. T., & Worsham, M. E. (2003). *Classroom management for elementary teachers* (6th ed.). Boston: Allyn & Bacon.

Emmer, E. T., Evertson, C. M., & Worsham, M. E. (2003). *Classroom management for secondary teachers* (6th ed.). Boston: Allyn & Bacon.

Freiberg, H. J. (Ed.). (1999). *Beyond behaviorism: Changing the classroom management paradigm.* Boston: Allyn & Bacon.

Weinstein, C. S., & Mignano, A. J., Jr. (2003). *Elementary classroom management: Lessons from research and practice* (2nd ed.). New York: McGraw-Hill.

Weinstein, C. S. (2003). *Secondary classroom management: Lessons from research and practice* (2nd ed.). New York: McGraw-Hill.

Check Yourself Distinguish between rules and procedures.

Distinguish between personal territories and interest-area spatial arrangements.

Contrast the first school week of effective and ineffective classroom managers.

Maintaining a Good Environment for Learning

A good start is just that—a beginning. Effective teachers build on this beginning. They maintain their management system by preventing problems and keeping students engaged in productive learning activities. We have discussed several ways to keep students engaged. In the chapters on motivation, for example, we considered stimulating curiosity, relating lessons to student interests, establishing learning goals instead of performance goals, and having positive expectations. What else can teachers do?

Encouraging Engagement

STOP THINK WRITE What activities keep you completely engaged—the time just seems to disappear? What is it about those activities that keeps you focused?

CONNECT & EXTEND

TO **PRAXIS**™
PROMOTING STUDENT ENGAGEMENT (I, C4)
A principle of educational psychology is that the more students are cognitively engaged in an activity, the more they are likely to learn. What tactics can teachers employ to maximize their students' cognitive engagement during learning tasks?

The format of a lesson affects student involvement. In general, as teacher supervision increases, students' engaged time also increases (Emmer & Evertson, 1981). One study, for example, found that elementary students working directly with a teacher were on task 97% of the time, whereas students working on their own were on task only 57% of the time (Frick, 1990). This does not mean that teachers should eliminate independent work for students. It simply means that this type of activity usually requires careful planning and monitoring.

When the task provides continuous cues for the student about what to do next, involvement will be greater. Activities with clear steps are likely to be more absorbing, because one step leads naturally to the next. When students have all the materials they need to complete a task, they tend to stay involved (Kounin & Doyle, 1975). If their curiosity is piqued, students will be motivated to continue seeking an answer. And, as you now know, students will be more engaged if they are involved in authentic tasks—activities that have connections to real life.

Of course, teachers can't supervise every student all the time, or rely on curiosity. Something else must keep students working on their own. In their study of elementary and secondary teachers, Evertson, Emmer, and their colleagues found that effective class managers at both levels had well-planned systems for encouraging students to manage their own work (Emmer, Evertson, & Worsham, 2003; Evertson, Emmer, & Worsham, 2003). The *Guidelines* on the next page are based on their findings.

Prevention Is the Best Medicine

The ideal way to manage problems, of course, is to prevent them in the first place. In a classic study, Jacob Kounin (1970) examined classroom management by comparing effective teachers, whose classes were relatively free of problems, with ineffective teachers, whose classes were continually plagued by chaos and disruption. Observing both groups in action, Kounin found that they were not very different in the way they handled discipline once problems arose. The difference was that the successful managers were much better at preventing problems. Kounin concluded that effective classroom managers were especially skilled in four areas: "*withitness,*" *overlapping activities, group*

GUIDELINES Keeping Students Engaged

Make basic work requirements clear.

Examples

1. Specify and post the routine work requirements for headings, paper size, pen or pencil use, and neatness.
2. Establish and explain rules about late or incomplete work and absences. If a pattern of incomplete work begins to develop, deal with it early; speak with parents if necessary.
3. Make due dates reasonable, and stick to them unless the student has a very good excuse for lateness.

Communicate the specifics of assignments.

Examples

1. With younger students, have a routine procedure for giving assignments, such as writing them on the board in the same place each day. With older students, assignments may be dictated, posted, or given in a syllabus.
2. Remind students of upcoming assignments.
3. With complicated assignments, give students a sheet describing what to do, what resources are available, due dates, and so on. Older students should also be told your grading criteria.
4. Demonstrate how to do the assignment, do the first few questions together, or provide a sample worksheet.

Monitor work in progress.

Examples

1. When you make an assignment in class, make sure each student gets started correctly. If you check only students who raise their hands for help, you will miss those who think they know what to do but don't really understand, those who are too shy to ask for help, and those who don't plan to do the work at all.
2. Check progress periodically. In discussions, make sure everyone has a chance to respond.

Give frequent academic feedback.

Examples

1. Elementary students should get papers back the day after they are handed in.
2. Good work can be displayed in class and graded papers sent home to parents each week.
3. Students of all ages can keep records of grades, projects completed, and extra credits earned.
4. For older students, break up long-term assignments into several phases, giving feedback at each point.

focusing, and *movement management* (Doyle, 1977). More recent research confirms the importance of these factors (Emmer & Stough, 2001; Evertson, 1988).

Withitness. **Withitness** means communicating to students that you are aware of everything that is happening in the classroom, that you aren't missing anything. "With-it" teachers seem to have eyes in the back of their heads. They avoid becoming absorbed or interacting with only a few students, because this encourages the rest of the class to wander. They are always scanning the room, making eye contact with individual students, so the students know they are being monitored (Charles, 2002a; Brooks, 1985).

These teachers prevent minor disruptions from becoming major. They also know who instigated the problem, and they make sure the right people are dealt with. In other words, they do not make what Kounin called *timing errors* (waiting too long before intervening) or *target errors* (blaming the wrong student and letting the real perpetrators escape responsibility for their behavior).

If two problems occur at the same time, effective managers deal with the more serious one first. For example, a teacher who tells two students to stop whispering but ignores even a brief shoving match at the pencil sharpener communicates to students a lack of awareness. Students begin to believe they can get away with almost anything if they are clever (Charles, 2002b).

Overlapping and Group Focus. **Overlapping** means keeping track of and supervising several activities at the same time. For example, a teacher may have to check the work of an individual and at the same time keep a small group working by saying, "Right, go on," and stop an incident in another group with a quick "look" or reminder (Burden, 1995; Charles, 2002b).

Maintaining a **group focus** means keeping as many students as possible involved in appropriate class activities and avoiding narrowing in on just one or two students.

Withitness According to Kounin, awareness of everything happening in a classroom.

Overlapping Supervising several activities at once.

Group focus The ability to keep as many students as possible involved in activities.

In addition to teaching subjects, teachers must be capable of managing the activities of a group of people: their attention, how they move from one place to another, and how they transition from one activity to another.

All students should have something to do during a lesson. For example, the teacher might ask everyone to write the answer to a question, then call on individuals to respond while the other students compare their answers. Choral responses might be required while the teacher moves around the room to make sure everyone is participating (Charles, 2002b). For example, during a grammar lesson the teacher might say, "Everyone who thinks the answer is *have run,* hold up the red side of your card. If you think the answer is *has run,* hold up the green side" (Hunter, 1982). This is one way teachers can ensure that all students are involved and check that they all understand the material.

Movement Management. **Movement management** means keeping lessons and the group moving at an appropriate (and flexible) pace, with smooth transitions and variety. The effective teacher avoids abrupt transitions, such as announcing a new activity before gaining the students' attention or starting a new activity in the middle of something else. In these situations, one-third of the class will be doing the new activity, many will be working on the old lesson, several will be asking other students what to do, some will be taking the opportunity to have a little fun, and most will be confused.

Another transition problem Kounin noted is the *slowdown,* or taking too much time to start a new activity. Sometimes teachers give too many directions. Problems also arise when teachers have students work one at a time while the rest of the class waits and watches. Charles (1985, p. 26) gives this example:

> During a science lesson the teacher began, "Row 1 may get up and get their beakers. Row 2 may get theirs. Now Row 3. Now, Row 1 may line up to put some bicarbonate of soda in their beakers. Row 2 may follow them," and so forth. When each row had obtained their bicarbonate of soda the teacher had them go row by row to add water. This left the remainder of the class sitting at their desks with no direction, doing nothing or else beginning to find something with which to entertain themselves.

A teacher who successfully demonstrates withitness, overlapping activities, group focus, and movement management tends to have a class filled with actively engaged students who do not escape his or her all-seeing eye. This need not be a grim classroom. It is more likely a busy place where students are actively learning and gaining a sense of self-worth rather than misbehaving in order to get attention and achieve status.

CONNECT & EXTEND

TO THE RESEARCH
Every year the September issue of *Phi Delta Kappan* contains the *"Annual Phi Delta Kappa/Gallup Poll of the Public's Attitudes Toward the Public Schools."* Questions usually ask respondents to "grade" the schools, identify the problems facing the schools, rate strategies for improvement, and give opinions about current issues such as school choice, home schooling, vouchers, and values.

Dealing with Discipline Problems

What Would You Say? You are interviewing for a job in a high school that has been in the news lately about its "zero-tolerance policy." The principal asks, "So what do you think about zero tolerance?" What is your position?

In 2002, Phi Delta Kappa published the 34th annual Gallup Poll of the public's attitude toward public schools. From 1969 until 1999, "lack of discipline" was named as the number one problem facing the schools almost every year (Rose & Gallup, 1999). In 2000 and since, lack of financial support took over the number one place, but lack of discipline was a close second every year. Clearly, the public sees discipline as an important challenge for teachers. What was your most challenging discipline problem so far and how did you handle it?

Being an effective manager does not mean publicly correcting every minor infraction of the rules. This kind of public attention may actually reinforce the misbehavior, as we saw in Chapter 6. Teachers who frequently correct students do not necessarily have the best behaved classes (Irving & Martin, 1982). The key is to know what is happening and what is important so you can prevent problems. Emmer and

Movement management Keeping lessons and the group moving at an appropriate (and flexible) pace, with smooth transitions and variety.

colleagues (2003) and Levin and Nolan (2000) suggest seven simple ways to stop misbehavior quickly, moving from least to most intrusive:

- *Make eye contact* with, or move closer to, the offender. Other nonverbal signals, such as pointing to the work students are supposed to be doing, might be helpful. Make sure the student actually stops the inappropriate behavior and gets back to work. If you do not, students will learn to ignore your signals.
- Try *verbal hints* such as "name-dropping" (simply insert the student's name into the lecture), asking the student a question, or making a humorous (not sarcastic) comment such as, "I must be hallucinating. I swear I heard someone shout out an answer, but that can't be because I haven't called on anyone yet!"
- You might also ask students *if they are aware* of the negative effects of their actions or send an "I message," described later in the chapter.
- If they are not performing a class procedure correctly, *remind the students* of the procedure and have them follow it correctly. You may need to quietly collect a toy, comb, magazine, or note that is competing with the learning activities, while privately informing the students that their possessions will be returned after class.
- In a calm, unhostile way, *ask the student to state the correct rule or procedure* and then to follow it. Glasser (1969) proposes three questions: "What are you doing? Is it against the rules? What should you be doing?"
- Tell the student in a clear, assertive, and unhostile way to *stop the misbehavior.* (Later in the chapter we will discuss assertive messages to students in more detail.) If students "talk back," simply repeat your statement.
- *Offer a choice.* For example, when a student continued to call out answers no matter what the teacher tried, the teacher said, "John, you have a choice. Stop calling out answers immediately and begin raising your hand to answer or move your seat to the back of the room and you and I will have a private discussion later. You decide" (Levin & Nolan, 2000, p. 177).

If you must impose penalties, the *Guidelines,* taken from Weinstein (2003) and Weinstein and Mignano (2003), give ideas about how to do it. The examples are taken from the actual words of the expert teachers described in their book.

CONNECT & EXTEND

TO THE RESEARCH
For a description of an extensive research project examining how teachers cope with problem behaviors, see Brophy, J., & McCaslin, M. (1992). Teachers' reports of how they perceive and cope with problem students. *Elementary School Journal, 93,* 3–68.

GUIDELINES: Imposing Penalties

Delay the discussion of the situation until you and the students involved are calmer and more objective.

Examples

1. Say calmly to a student, "Sit there and think about what happened. I'll talk to you in a few minutes," or, "I don't like what I just saw. Talk to me during your free period today."
2. Say, "I'm really angry about what just happened. Everybody take out journals; we are going to write about this." After a few minutes of writing, the class can discuss the incident.

Impose penalties privately.

Examples

1. Make arrangements with students privately. Stand firm in enforcing arrangements.
2. Resist the temptation to "remind" students in public that they are not keeping their side of the bargain.
3. Move close to a student who must be disciplined and speak so that only the student can hear.

After imposing a penalty, reestablish a positive relationship with the student immediately.

Examples

1. Send the student on an errand or ask him or her for help.
2. Compliment the student's work or give a real or symbolic "pat on the back" when the student's behavior warrants. Look hard for such an opportunity.

Set up a graded list of penalties that will fit many occasions.

Example

1. For not turning in homework: (1) receive reminder; (2) receive warning; (3) hand homework in before close of school day; (4) stay after school to finish work; (5) participate in a teacher-student-parent conference to develop an action plan.

Point/Counterpoint

Is Zero Tolerance a Good Idea?

With the very visible violence in schools today, some districts have instituted "zero-tolerance" policies for rule breaking. One result? Two 8-year old boys in New Jersey were suspended for making "terrorist threats." They had pointed paper guns at their classmates while playing. Do zero-tolerance policies make sense?

Point

Zero Tolerance means zero common sense.

An Internet search using keywords ["zero-tolerance" and schools] will locate a wealth of information about the policy—much of it against. For example, in the August 29, 2001 issue of *Salon Magazine,* Johanna Wald wrote an article entitled "The failure of zero tolerance." Here are two examples she cites

> *A 17-year-old honors student in Arkansas begins his senior year with an even more ominous cloud over his head. His college scholarship is in danger because of a 45-day sentence to an alternative school. His offense? An arbitrary search of his car by school officials in the spring revealed no drugs, but a scraper and pocketknife that his father had inadvertently left there the night before when he was fixing the rearview mirror. Despite anguished pleas of extenuating circumstances by the desperate father, the school system has so far adamantly insisted that automatic punishments for weapon possession in school are inviolate.*

> *Upon her release on bail, the National Merit scholar jailed and banned from her graduation for leaving a kitchen knife in her car commented, "They're taking away my memories." Indeed, for all of the pious talk about the need for "consequences" for students' actions, officials justifying these excesses seem curiously oblivious to the long-term impact of taking away the memories, dreams, and futures of a generation of students.*

There are many other stories available on the Web. In researching this *Point/Counterpoint* I read of a 6-year old boy in Colorado who was suspended in 1997 for giving another child a lemon drop candy. The suspension was justified using the school's zero-tolerance drug policy. Students have been suspended for playing with squirt guns, carrying key ring fobs that look like guns, using their fingers as pretend guns in a game, and drawing pictures of guns.

A 2001 Associated Press story, "ABA Recommends Dropping Zero-Tolerance in Schools," announced that the leadership of the American Bar Association voted to recommend ending zero-tolerance school policies. The article quotes a report that accompanied the resolution against zero tolerance adopted by the ABA's policy-making House of Delegates: "Zero-tolerance has become a one-size-fits-all solution to all of the problems that schools confront" (Associated Press, February 21, 2001, available online at http://www.cnn.com/2001/fyi/teachers.ednews/02/21/zero.tolerance.ap/. On this website you can post your views about zero-tolerance.

There is a caution about penalties. Never use lower achievement status (moving to a lower reading group, giving a lower grade, giving excess homework) as a punishment for breaking class rules. These actions should be done only if the benefit of the action outweighs the possible risk of harm. As Carolyn Orange (2000) notes, "Effective, caring teachers would not use low achievement status, grades, or the like as a means of discipline. This strategy is unfair and ineffective. It only serves to alienate the student" (p. 76).

There is quite a bit of discussion today about zero tolerance for rule breaking in the schools. Is this a good idea? The *Point/Counterpoint* looks at both sides.

Special Problems with Secondary Students

Many secondary students never complete their work. Besides encouraging student responsibility, what else can teachers do to deal with this frustrating problem? Because students at this age have many assignments and teachers have many students, both teacher and students may lose track of what has and has not been completed. It often helps to teach students how to use a daily planner—paper or electronic. In addition, the teacher must keep accurate records. The most important thing is to enforce the established consequences for incomplete work. Do not pass a student because you know he or she is "bright enough" to pass. Make it clear to these students that the choice is theirs: They can do the work and pass, or they

CONNECT & EXTEND

TO YOUR TEACHING/PORTFOLIO
To read about the 24 other mistakes teachers make that can cause students anxiety and trauma, see Orange, C. (2000). *25 biggest mistakes teachers make and how to avoid them.* Thousand Oakes, CA: Corwin.

Counterpoint

Zero tolerance is necessary for now.

The arguments for zero tolerance focus on school safety and the responsibilities of schools and teachers to protect the students and themselves. Of course, many of the incidents reported in the news seem like overreactions to childhood pranks or worse, over-zealous application of zero tolerance to innocent mistakes or lapses of memory. But how do school officials separate the innocent from the dangerous? For example, it has been widely reported that Andy Williams (the boy who killed two classmates in Santee, California) assured his friends before the shootings that he was only joking about "pulling a Columbine."

In response to the girl who missed her graduation ceremony because school authorities found a knife in her car, Mike Gallagher (2001), a journalist writing for NewsMax.com said:

> *I certainly understand the reason behind the e-mails of protest I received from Americans who think this is a case that went too far. It sure was a shame that this high-schooler, by all accounts a great student and fine young lady, had to miss the excitement of her commencement ceremony. But I argued that rules are rules, and zero-tolerance weapons policies were created because of parents' demands that schools be safe.*

Mr. Gallagher went on to describe a tragic event in Japan where eight young children were killed in school by madman wielding a knife just one inch longer than the one found in the student's car.

On January 13, 2003, I read a story in *USA Today* by Gregg Toppo entitled "School Violence Hits Lower Grades: Experts Who See Violent Behavior in Younger Kids Blame Parents, Prenatal Medical Problems and an Angry Society; Educators Search for Ways to Cope." The story opened with these examples: a second-grader in Indiana takes off his shoe and attacks his teacher with it, a Philadelphia kindergartner hits a pregnant teacher in the stomach, and an 8-year-old in Maryland threatens to use gasoline (he knew exactly where he would pour it) to burn down his suburban elementary school. Toppo noted, "Elementary school principals and safety experts say they're seeing more violence and aggression than ever among their youngest students, pointing to what they see as an alarming rise in assaults and threats to classmates and teachers" (p. A2). Toppo cited statistics indicating that, although the incidence of school violence has decreased overall, attacks on elementary school teachers have actually increased.

The late Albert Shanker (1995), long-time president of the American Federation of Teachers, said:

> *[S]chools must teach not only English and mathematics and reading and writing and history, but also teach that there are ways of behaving in society that are unacceptable. And when we sit back and tolerate certain types of behaviors, we are teaching youngsters that certain types of behaviors are acceptable, which eventually will end up with their being in jail or in poverty for the rest of their lives.*

What do you think? Vote online at **www.ablongman.com/woolfolk**

can refuse to do the work and face the consequences. You might also ask, in a private moment, if there is anything interfering with the student's ability to get to the work.

There is also the problem of students who continually break the same rules, always forgetting materials, for example, or getting into fights. What should you do? Seat these students away from others who might be influenced by them. Try to catch them before they break the rules, but if rules are broken, be consistent in applying established consequences. Do not accept promises to do better next time (Levin & Nolan, 2000). Teach the students how to monitor their own behavior; some of the self-management techniques described in Chapter 6 should be helpful. Finally, remain friendly with the students. Try to catch them in a good moment so you can talk to them about something other than their rule-breaking.

A defiant, hostile student can pose serious problems. If there is an outburst, try to get out of the situation as soon as possible; everyone loses in a public power struggle. One possibility is to give the student a chance to save face and cool down by saying, "It's your choice to cooperate or not. You can take a minute to think about it." If the student complies, the two of you can talk later about controlling the outbursts. If the student refuses to cooperate, you can tell him or her to wait in the hall until you get the class started on work, then step outside for a private talk. If the student refuses to leave, send another class member for the assistant principal. Again, follow through. If the student complies before help arrives, do not let him or her off the hook. If outbursts occur frequently, you might have a conference with the counselor, parents, or

CONNECT & EXTEND

TO **PRAXIS**™
STUDENT MISBEHAVIOR (I, C4)
Even the most well-managed classroom will have instances of student misbehavior. Explain the principles for dealing with common student misbehaviors. What strategies can teachers employ to deal fairly and effectively with those problems?

CONNECT & EXTEND

TO OTHER CHAPTERS
In Chapter 3 you saw a list of warning signs about violence in schools.

other teachers. If the problem is an irreconcilable clash of personalities, the student should be transferred to another teacher.

It sometimes is useful to keep records of the incidents by logging the student's name, words and actions, date, time, place, and teacher's response. These records may help identify patterns and can prove useful in meetings with administrators, parents, or special services personnel (Burden, 1995). Some teachers have students sign each entry to verify the incidents.

Violence or destruction of property is a difficult and potentially dangerous problem. The first step is to send for help and get the names of participants and witnesses. Then get rid of any crowd that may have gathered; an audience will only make things worse. Do not try to break up a fight without help. Make sure the school office is aware of the incident; usually the school has a policy for dealing with these situations. *The Stories of Learning: Tributes to Teaching* feature shows how one teacher helped two students survive a very volatile situation by keeping focused on what the students needed.

Check Yourself How can teachers encourage engagement?

Explain the factors identified by Kounin that prevent management problems in the classroom.

Describe seven levels of intervention in misbehavior.

What are some special problems and challenges in secondary classrooms?

Enhancing Your Expertise with Technology

Classroom Management

Natalie, exhausted and exasperated, went across the hallway to speak with her experienced colleague. Natalie had been hired as a long-term substitute after two others had filled in on a short-term basis. "It's almost as if law and order has broken down in that classroom," she explained. "I'm not sure where to begin. No one seems to know any rules or procedures for anything. The students have little respect for me or for each other. I dread walking down the hallway with them—it's like I'm escorting a tornado! When I try to establish a routine or a procedure, they complain that it's not Ms. Naples way." The veteran responded, "We don't know when or if Ms. Naples will be back this year. Consider it your class, and move forward from there."

Like Natalie, many novice teachers are anxious about their classroom management skills. They are encouraged to "Lay down the law on the first day!" and "Don't smile until December!"—common examples of teacher folk wisdom. The message in such bits of advice (i.e., strong disciplinarian = good teacher) may appeal to a novice who is concerned about being able to handle a class. Effective classroom management, however, requires a broad set of skills and techniques; folk wisdom offers only a little guidance.

The Center for Talented Youth (CTY) sponsored by The Johns Hopkins University (http://www.jhu.edu/gifted/teaching/classroom.htm) suggests a variety of techniques and strategies that include but go beyond discipline. Both novice and highly experienced veterans will find ideas about the following subjects valuable:

- creating rules with the class
- working with learning disabled students
- using brief activities to promote a sense of community among students
- understanding the problems of gifted students
- employing cooperative learning to foster a positive classroom atmosphere
- preventing classroom problems
- enhancing the flow of a lesson

The CTY also includes an extensive set of outside links about classroom management. Perhaps the most interesting of these sites is one that challenges you to discover your classroom management profile. Take the brief self-quiz at this site (http://education.indiana.edu/cas/tt/v1i2/what.html), and see how the results compare to your perception of yourself as a classroom manager.

~ Stories of Learning Tributes to Teaching ~

Sandy Krupinski, a chemistry teacher in New Jersey, tells how she handled a dangerous situation. Robert walked into the class, straight to Daniel's desk:

> As usual, I was standing at the doorway as the kids were coming into the classroom. I noticed Robert come in without his backpack or any books. That didn't look right, and I watched him cross the room and go over to Daniel, who was sitting at his desk. Robert picked up the desk and the leg of Daniel's chair and overturned them, cursing and screaming the whole time. I ran over. The first thing I said was "Daniel, don't raise your hands." He was on the floor on his back, and Robert was standing over him screaming. I kept saying, "Robert, look at me, look at me, look at me." Finally, he made eye contact. Then I said, "You need to come with me." We began to walk toward the door, but he turned back and started cursing again. Very quietly and firmly I told him, "You need to come with me." We began to walk toward the door, but he turned back and started cursing again. Very quietly and firmly I told him, "You need to come with me now." He followed me to the door, and as I reached the door I picked up the phone and called the office and said there was a problem and to send someone up. Then we stepped out into the hallway. Robert was angry and was going to leave, and I asked him to please stop and talk to me about what was going on, what was bothering him. I didn't yell, I didn't say, "How could you do something so stupid?" (even though that's what I felt like saying). I said, "Obviously you're upset about something. Tell me about it." It turns out that these two were friends, but Robert found out that Daniel was sleeping with his [Robert's] girlfriend. I heard a lot I didn't really want to hear, but it kept him occupied until the vice-principal came up.
>
> Once the vice-principal took Robert, I got Daniel out into the hallway and asked him if he was OK, and if he needed to go to the nurse, or needed to be out of the classroom. He said no, he was OK. I told him, "You were very smart for not raising your hands against Robert." He returned to his seat, and all the kids started saying, "Daniel, are you OK?" and crowding around him. I told them, "Robert's in the office. Daniel's OK. Let's get started on chemistry." At the end of the period, the office called for Daniel to go to the peer mediation room to have the dispute mediated.

Robert was suspended for three days, but before he left, he apologized to Sandy for his language. Sandy accepted the apology and they talked about other ways he could have handled the situation. When Robert returned after the suspension, Sandy made sure that the two boys' seats were changed so they were separated and easy for her to monitor for a while.

SOURCE: From *Secondary Classroom Management: Lessons from Research and Practice* (3rd ed.), by C. S. Weinstein. Published by McGraw-Hill.

The Need for Communication

A student says to you, "That book you assigned is really stupid—I'm not reading it!" What do you say?

Communication between teacher and students is essential when problems arise. Communication is more than "teacher talks—student listens." It is more than the words exchanged between individuals. We communicate in many ways. Our actions, movements, voice tone, facial expressions, and many other nonverbal behaviors send messages to our students. Many times, the messages we intend to send are not the messages our students receive.

CONNECT & EXTEND

TO THE RESEARCH
To read two careful studies about how children respond to ambiguous communications from teachers who appear powerless, see Bugental, D. B., Lyon, J. E., Lin, E. K., McGrath, E. P., & Bimbela, A. (1999). Children "tune out" in response to the ambiguous communication style of powerless adults. *Child Development, 70,* 214–230 and Bugental, D. B., Lewis, J. C., Lin, E., Lyon, J., & Kopeikin, H. (1999). In charge but not in control: The management of teaching relationships by adults with low perceived power. *Developmental Psychology, 35,* 1367–1378.

Message Sent—Message Received

Teacher: Carl, where is your homework?

Carl: I left it in my Dad's car this morning.

Teacher: Again? You will have to bring me a note tomorrow from your father saying that you actually did the homework. No grade without the note.

Message Carl receives: I can't trust you. I need proof you did the work.

Teacher: Sit at every other desk. Put all your things under your desk. Jane and Laurel, you are sitting too close together. One of you move!

Message Jane and Laurel receive: I expect you two to cheat on this test.

A new student comes to Ms. Lincoln's kindergarten. The child is messy and unwashed. Ms. Lincoln puts her hand lightly on the girl's shoulder and says, "I'm glad you are here." Her muscles tense, and she leans away from the child.

Message student receives: I don't like you. I think you are bad.

In all interactions, a message is sent and a message is received. Sometimes teachers believe they are sending one message, but their voices, body positions, choices of words, and gestures may communicate a different message.

Students may hear the hidden message and respond to it. For example, a student may respond with hostility if she or he feels insulted by the teacher (or by another student), but may not be able to say exactly where the feeling of being insulted came from. Perhaps it was in the teacher's tone of voice, not the words actually spoken. But the teacher feels attacked for no reason. The first principle of communication is that people respond to what they *think* was said or meant, not necessarily to the speaker's intended message or actual words.

Students in my classes have told me about one instructor who encourages accurate communication by using the **paraphrase rule.** Before any participant, including the teacher, is allowed to respond to any other participant in a class discussion, he or she must summarize what the previous speaker said. If the summary is wrong, indicating the speaker was misunderstood, the speaker must explain again. The respondent then tries again to paraphrase. The process continues until the speaker agrees that the listener has heard the intended message.

Paraphrasing is more than a classroom exercise. It can be the first step in communicating with students. Before teachers can deal appropriately with any student problem, they must know what the real problem is. A student who says, "This book is really dumb! Why did we have to read it?" may really be saying, "The book was too difficult for me. I couldn't read it, and I feel dumb."

Diagnosis: Whose Problem Is It?

As a teacher, you may find many student behaviors unacceptable, unpleasant, or troubling. It is often difficult to stand back from these problems, take an objective look, and decide on an appropriate response. According to Thomas Gordon (1981), the key to good teacher-student relationships is determining *why* you are troubled by a particular behavior and who "owns" the problem. The answer to these questions is critical. If it is really the student's problem, the teacher must become a counselor and supporter, helping the student find his or her own solution. But if the teacher "owns" the problem, it is the teacher's responsibility to find a solution through problem solving with the student.

Diagnosing who owns the problem is not always straightforward. Let's look at three troubling situations to get some practice in this skill:

1. A student writes obscene words and draws sexually explicit illustrations in a school encyclopedia.

Paraphrase rule Policy whereby listeners must accurately summarize what a speaker has said before being allowed to respond.

2. A student tells you that his parents had a bad fight and he hates his father.
3. A student quietly reads a newspaper in the back of the room.

Why are these behaviors troubling? If you cannot accept the student's behavior because it has a serious effect on you as a teacher—if you are blocked from reaching your goals by the student's action—then *you* own the problem. It is your responsibility to confront the student and seek a solution. A teacher-owned problem appears to be present in the first situation described above—the young pornographer—because teaching materials are damaged.

If you feel annoyed by the behavior because it is getting in the student's own way or because you are embarrassed for the child, but the behavior does not directly interfere with your teaching, then it is probably the student's problem. The student who hates his father would not prevent you from teaching, even though you might wish the student felt differently. The problem is really the student's, and he must find his own solution.

The third situation is more difficult to diagnose. One argument is that the teacher is not interfered with in any way, so it is the student's problem. But teachers might find the student reading the paper distracting during a lecture, so it is their problem, and they must find a solution. In a gray area such as this, the answer probably depends on how the teacher actually experiences the student's behavior. Having decided who owns the problem, it is time to act.

CONNECT & EXTEND

TO PRAXIS™
TEACHER-STUDENT COMMUNICATION (III, A)
A well-managed classroom requires a bidirectional line of communication between the teacher and students. Describe the various communication styles that teachers employ when interacting with students, and explain how those styles affect student behavior.

Counseling: The Student's Problem

Let's pick up the situation in which the student found the reading assignment "dumb." How might a teacher handle this positively?

Student: This book is really dumb! Why did we have to read it?

Teacher: You're pretty upset. This seemed like a worthless assignment to you. [Teacher paraphrases the student's statement, trying to hear the emotions as well as the words.]

Student: Yeah! Well, I guess it was worthless. I mean, I don't know if it was. I couldn't exactly read it.

Teacher: It was just too hard to read, and that bothers you.

Student: Sure, I felt really dumb. I know I can write a good report, but not with a book this tough.

Teacher: I think I can give you some hints that will make the book easier to understand. Can you see me after school today?

Student: Okay.

Here the teacher used **empathetic listening** to allow the student to find a solution. (As you can see, this approach relies heavily on paraphrasing.) By trying to hear the student and by avoiding the tendency to jump in too quickly with advice, solutions, criticisms, reprimands, or interrogations, the teacher keeps the communication lines open. Here are a few *unhelpful* responses the teacher might have made:

- I chose the book because it is the best example of the author's style in our library. You will need to have read it before your English II class next year. (The teacher justifies the choice; this prevents the student from admitting that this "important" assignment is too difficult.)
- Did you really read it? I bet you didn't do the work, and now you want out of the assignment. (The teacher accuses; the student hears, "The teacher doesn't trust me!" and must either defend herself or himself or accept the teacher's view.)
- Your job is to read the book, not ask me why. I know what's best. (The teacher pulls rank, and the student hears, "You can't possibly decide what is good

Empathetic listening Hearing the intent and emotions behind what another says and reflecting them back by paraphrasing.

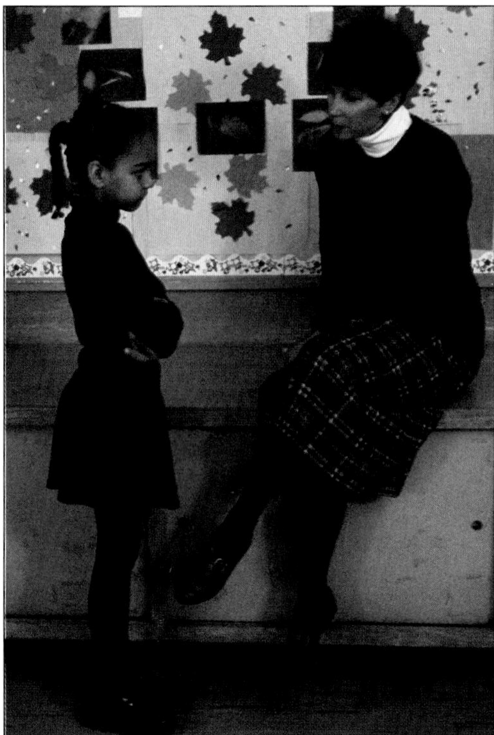
"I" messages basically mean telling a student what he or she is doing wrong, how it affects you as a teacher, and how you feel about it. This puts the onus on the student to change the behavior voluntarily.

for you!" The student can rebel or passively accept the teacher's judgment.)

Empathetic, active listening is more than a parroting of the student's words; it should capture the emotions, intent, and meaning behind them. Sokolove, Garrett, Sadker, and Sadker (1986, p. 241) have summarized the components of active listening: (1) blocking out external stimuli; (2) attending carefully to both the verbal and nonverbal messages; (3) differentiating between the intellectual and the emotional content of the message; and (4) making inferences regarding the speaker's feelings.

When students realize they really have been heard and not evaluated negatively for what they have said or felt, they feel freer to trust the teacher and to talk more openly. Sometimes the true problem surfaces later in the conversation.

Confrontation and Assertive Discipline

Now let's assume a student is doing something that actively interferes with teaching. The teacher decides the student must stop. The problem is the teacher's. Confrontation, not counseling, is required.

"I" Messages. Gordon (1981) recommends sending an **"I" message** in order to intervene and change a student's behavior. Basically, this means telling a student in a straightforward, assertive, and nonjudgmental way what she or he is doing, how it affects you as a teacher, and how you feel about it. The student is then free to change voluntarily, and often does so. Here are two "I" messages:

- If you leave your book bags in the aisles, I might trip and hurt myself.
- When you all call out, I can't concentrate on each answer, and I'm frustrated.

CONNECT & EXTEND

TO THE RESEARCH
Read Canter, L. (1989). Assertive discipline—More than names on the board and marbles in a jar. *Phi Delta Kappan, 71*(1) 41–56. Evaluate Canter's claims for his "assertive discipline" approach. What are the similarities between the criticisms of behavioral approaches to learning and the criticisms of assertive discipline? A special feature on discipline can be found in the 1989 issue of *Educational Leadership, 46*(6) 72–83. This feature presents a debate between supporters and critics of assertive discipline.

Assertive Discipline. Lee and Marlene Canter (1992; Canter, 1996) suggest other approaches for dealing with a teacher-owned problem. They call their method **assertive discipline.** Many teachers are ineffective with students because they are either wishy-washy and passive or hostile and aggressive (Charles, 2002a).

Instead of telling the student directly what to do, passive teachers tell, or often ask, the student to *try* or to *think about* the appropriate action. The passive teacher might comment on the problem behavior without actually telling the child what to do differently: "Why are you doing that? Don't you know the rules?" or "Sam, are you disturbing the class?" Or teachers may clearly state what should happen, but never follow through with the established consequences, giving the students "one more chance" every time. Finally, teachers may ignore behavior that should receive a response or they may wait too long before responding.

A *hostile response style* involves different mistakes. Teachers may make "you" statements that condemn the student without stating clearly what the student should be doing: "You should be ashamed of the way you're behaving!" or "You never listen!" or "You are acting like a baby!" Teachers may also threaten students angrily but follow through too seldom, perhaps because the threats are too vague—"You'll be very sorry you did that when I get through with you!"—or too severe. For example, a teacher tells a student in a physical education class that he will have to "sit on the bench for *three weeks.*" A few days later the team is short one member and the teacher lets the student play, never returning him to the bench to complete the three-week sentence. Often a teacher who has been passive becomes hostile and explodes when students persist in misbehaving.

In contrast with both the passive and hostile styles, an *assertive response* communicates to the students that you care too much about them and the process of

"I" message Clear, nonaccusatory statement of how something is affecting you.

Assertive discipline Clear, firm, unhostile response style.

learning to allow inappropriate behavior to persist. Assertive teachers clearly state what they expect. To be most effective, the teachers often look into a student's eyes when speaking and address the student by name. Assertive teachers' voices are calm, firm, and confident. They are not sidetracked by accusations such as "You just don't understand!" or "You don't like me!" Assertive teachers do not get into a debate about the fairness of the rules. They expect changes, not promises or apologies.

Not all educators believe that assertive discipline is useful. Earlier critics questioned the penalty-focused approach and emphasized that assertive discipline undermined student self-management (Render, Padilla, & Krank, 1989). John Covaleskie (1992) observed "What helps children become moral is not knowledge of the rules, or even obedience to the rules, but discussions about the reasons for acting in certain ways" (p. 56). These critics have had an impact. More recent versions of assertive discipline focus on teaching students "in an atmosphere of respect, trust, and support, how to behave responsibly" (Charles, 2002a, p. 47).

"They're testing you."

(By permission of James Warren. From *Phi Delta Kappan.*)

Confrontations and Negotiations. If "I" messages or assertive responses fail and a student persists in misbehaving, teacher and student are in a conflict. Several pitfalls now loom. The two individuals become less able to perceive each other's behavior accurately. Research has shown that the more angry you get with another person, the more you see the other as the villain and yourself as an innocent victim. Because you feel the other person is in the wrong, and he or she feels just as strongly that the conflict is all your fault, very little mutual trust is possible. A cooperative solution to the problem is almost impossible. In fact, by the time the discussion has gone on a few minutes, the original problem is lost in a sea of charges, countercharges, and self-defense (Baron & Byrne, 2003).

There are three methods of resolving a conflict between teacher and student. One is for the teacher to impose a solution. This may be necessary during an emergency, as when a defiant student refuses to go to the hall to discuss a public outbreak, but it is not a good solution for most conflicts. The second method is for the teacher to give in to the student's demands. You might be convinced by a particularly compelling student argument, but again, this should be used sparingly. It is generally a bad idea to be talked out of a position, unless the position was wrong in the first place. Problems arise when either the teacher or the student gives in completely.

Gordon recommends a third approach, which he calls the "no-lose method." Here the needs of both the teacher and the students are taken into account in the solution. No one person is expected to give in completely; all participants retain respect for themselves and each other. The no-lose method is a six-step, problem-solving strategy:

1. *Define the problem.* What exactly are the behaviors involved? What does each person want? (Use active listening to help students pinpoint the real problem.)
2. *Generate many possible solutions.* Brainstorm, but remember, don't allow any evaluations of ideas yet.
3. *Evaluate each solution.* Any participant may veto any idea. If no solutions are found to be acceptable, brainstorm again.
4. *Make a decision.* Choose one solution through consensus—no voting. In the end, everyone must be satisfied with the solution.
5. *Determine how to implement the solution.* What will be needed? Who will be responsible for each task? What is the timetable?
6. *Evaluate the success of the solution.* After trying the solution for a while, ask, "Are we satisfied with our decision? How well is it working? Should we make some changes?"

Many of the conflicts in classrooms are between students. These can be important learning experiences for all concerned.

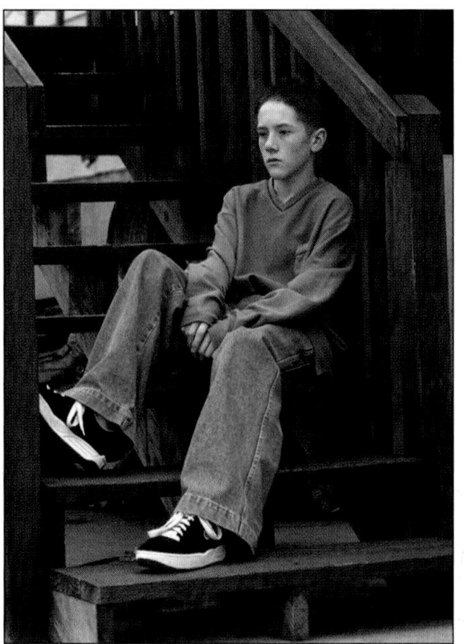

Handling conflict can be difficult for young people. Studies have shown that many conflicts among middle and high school students are resolved in destructive ways or never at all.

Student Conflicts and Confrontations

Handling conflict is difficult for most of us—for young people it can be even harder. Given the public's concern about violence in schools, it is surprising how little we know about conflicts among students (Rose & Gallup, 2001; Johnson, Johnson, Dudley, Ward, & Magnuson, 1995). There is some evidence that in elementary schools, conflicts most often center on disputes over resources (school supplies, computers, athletic equipment, or toys) and over preferences (which activity to do first or what game to play). Over 20 years ago, a large study of more than 8,000 junior and senior high students and 500 faculty from three major cities concluded that 90% of the conflicts among students are resolved in destructive ways or never resolved at all (DeCecco & Richards, 1974). The few studies conducted since that time have reached similar conclusions. Avoidance, force, and threats seem to be the major strategies for dealing with conflict (Johnson et al., 1995).

Peer Harassment. One common form of conflict in schools involves the kind of teasing and harassment described in the "What Would You Do?" situation at the beginning of this chapter. Teachers tend to underestimate the amount of bullying and harassment in schools. For example, in one survey of 8th graders, 60% of the students said that they had been harassed by a bully, but teachers in their schools estimated the number would be about 16% (Barone, 1997). A national survey found that about 33% of 6th through 10th graders had been involved in moderate or frequent bullying (Nansel et al., 2001). The line between good-natured exchanges and hostile teasing may seem thin, but a rule of thumb is that teasing someone who is less powerful or less popular or using any racial, ethnic, or religious slur should not be tolerated. When teachers are silent, students may "hear" agreement with the insult (Weinstein, 2003). Table 11.3 is a list of dos and don'ts about teasing in schools.

Table 11.3 Dos and Don'ts about Teasing

Teasing has led to some tragic situations. Talk about what to do in your class.

DO:	DON'T:
1. Be careful of others' feelings.	1. Tease someone you don't know well.
2. Use humor gently and carefully.	2. [If you are a boy] tease girls about sex.
3. Ask whether teasing about a certain topic hurts someone's feelings.	3. Tease about a person's body.
4. Accept teasing from others if you tease.	4. Tease about a person's family members.
5. Tell others if teasing about a certain topic hurts your feelings.	5. Tease about a topic when a student has asked you not to.
6. Know the difference between friendly gentle teasing and hurtful ridicule or harassment.	6. Tease someone who seems agitated or whom you know is having a bad day.
7. Try to read others' "body language" to see if their feelings are hurt—even when they don't tell you.	7. Be thin-skinned about teasing that is meant in a friendly way.
8. Help a weaker student when he or she is being ridiculed.	8. Swallow your feelings about teasing—tell someone in a direct and clear way what is bothering you.

SOURCE: From *Secondary Classroom Management: Lessons from Research and Practice* (3rd ed.), by C. S. Weinstein. Published by McGraw-Hill. Copyright © 2003 by McGraw-Hill. Adapted with permission from The McGraw-Hill Companies.

Violence in the Schools. "Even though violence in high schools is actually decreasing, interpersonal violence among youth is a concern for parent and teachers (Lowry, Sleet, Duncan, Powell, & Kolbe, 1995). Every day in America nine children or youth under age 20 are homicide victims (Children's Defense Fund, 2002). Young people ages 12 to 24 are the most likely victims of nonfatal violence in American society, and many of these attacks take place on school property. This problem has many causes; it is a challenge for every element of society. What can the schools do? Table 11.4, taken from Weinstein (2003) has some ideas for handling potentially explosive situations.

One answer is prevention. Some Chicano gang members in Chicago reported that they turned to gang activities when their teachers insulted them, called them names, humiliated them publicly, belittled their culture, ignored them in class, or blamed all negative incidents on particular students. The students reported joining gangs for security and to escape teachers who treated them badly or expected little of them because they were Latino (Padilla, 1992; Parks, 1995). Another two-year study in Ohio found that gang members respected teachers who insisted on academic performance in a caring way (Huff, 1989). I once asked a gifted educator in an urban New Jersey high school which teachers were most effective with the really tough students. He said there are two kinds, teachers who can't be intimidated or fooled and expect their students to learn, and teachers who really care about the students. When I asked, "Which kind are you?" he answered "Both!" He is an example of a "warm demander," as you will see in the next section.

Check Yourself What is meant by "empathetic listening"?

Distinguish among assertive, passive, and hostile response styles.

What are some options for dealing with student–student and student–teacher conflict?

CONNECT & EXTEND

TO THE RESEARCH

Parks, C. P. (1995). Gang behavior in the schools: Myth or reality? *Educational Psychology Review, 7*, 41–68.

ABSTRACT

The purpose of this review is to explore the nature of gang behavior in U.S. schools, with a particular focus on the extent to which such behavior affects or exacerbates the larger issue of school violence. An unanticipated finding was the absence of strong empirical support for school gang violence. The evidence does show youth gangs have changed dramatically over the last several decades and have become more violent, largely due to drugs and weapons-carrying. One major impact of this violence on schools has been the dissolving of the school as the "neutral zone," where gang activity ceased. Thus, it appears that the similar "turf" issues of the street gangs have infiltrated the schools. The review explores problems related to school gang violence definitions and literature, trends in school-related gang activity, reasons for gang membership, at-risk youth, and proposed strategies for ameliorating the problem.

Table 11.4 Handling a Potentially Explosive Situation

Here are some ideas for dealing with potential danger.

- Move slowly and deliberately toward the problem situation.
- Speak privately, quietly, and calmly. Do not threaten. Be as matter-of-fact as possible.
- Be as still as possible. Avoid pointing or gesturing.
- Keep a reasonable distance. Do not crowd the student. Do not get "in the student's face."
- Speak respectfully. Use the student's name.
- Establish eye-level position.
- Be brief. Avoid long-winded statements or nagging.
- Stay with the agenda. Stay focused on the problem at hand. Do not get sidetracked. Deal with less severe problems later.
- Avoid power struggles. Do not get drawn into "I won't, you will" arguments.
- Inform the student of the expected behavior and the negative consequence as a choice or decision for the student to make. Then withdraw from the student and allow some time for the student to decide. ("Michael, you need to return to your desk, or I will have to send for the principal. You have a few seconds to decide." The teacher then moves away, perhaps attending to other students. If Michael does not choose the appropriate behavior, deliver the negative consequences. "You are choosing to have me call the principal.") Follow through with the consequence.

SOURCE: From *Secondary Classroom Management: Lessons from Research and Practice* (3rd ed.), by C. S. Weinstein. Published by McGraw-Hill. Copyright © 2003 by McGraw-Hill. Adapted with permission from The McGraw-Hill Companies.

Summing It Up: Learning Environments for All Students

What Would You Say? You are interviewing for a job to take over a class in the middle of the school year. The lead principal asks, "In your experience with students in any capacity, what was your most challenging discipline problem so far and how did you handle it?"

We have examined a number of approaches to classroom student discipline. Are some better than others? Research provides some guidance.

Research on Different Management Approaches

Emmer and Aussiker (1990) conducted a meta-analysis of three general perspectives on management: influencing students through listening and problem-solving, as described by Gordon (1981, 1991); group management through class meetings and student discussion, as advocated by Glasser (1969, 1990), and control through rewards and punishments as exemplified by Canter and Canter (1992). No clear conclusions could be drawn about the impact of these approaches on student behaviors. However, some evaluations have found positive effects for Freiberg's (1999) Consistency Management program and for programs that use rewards and punishments (Lewis, 2001).

In a study conducted in Australia, Ramon Lewis (2001) found that recognizing and rewarding appropriate student behaviors, talking with students about how their behavior affects others, involving students in class discipline decisions, and providing nondirective hints and descriptions about unacceptable behaviors were associated with students taking greater responsibility for their own learning. It is interesting that these interventions represent all three of the general approaches reviewed by Emmer and Aussiker—influence, group management, and control. Lewis also concluded that teachers sometimes find using these interventions difficult when students are aggressive—and most in need of the approaches. When teachers feel threatened it can be difficult to do what students need, but that may be the most important time to act positively.

CONNECT & EXTEND

TO THE RESEARCH
To read more about "warm demanders," see Irvine, J. J., & Armento, B. J. (2001). *Culturally responsive teaching: Lesson planning for elementary and middle grades.* New York, NY: McGraw-Hill and Irvine, J. J., &Fraser, J. W. (1998, May). Warm demanders. *Education Week.* Available online at www.edweek.org/ew/ewstory.cfm?slug=35irvine.h17&keywords=Irvine

Culturally relevant management Taking cultural meanings and styles into account when developing management plans and responding to students.

Warm demanders Effective teachers with African American students who show both high expectations and great caring for their students.

Culturally Responsive Management

Research on discipline shows that African Americans, especially males, are punished more often and more harshly that other students. These students lose time from learning as they spend more hours in detention or suspension (Monroe & Obidah, 2002; Skiba, Michael, Nardo, & Peterson, 2000; Ferguson, 2000). Why? One explanation is a lack of cultural synchronization between teachers and students. "The language, style of walking, glances, and dress of black children, particularly males, have engendered fear, apprehension, and overreaction among many teachers and school administrators" (Irvine, 1990, p. 27). African American students may be disciplined for behaviors that were never intended to be disruptive or disrespectful. The teachers who seem to be most effective with these students practice **culturally responsive management** and have been called **"warm demanders"** (Irvine & Armento, 2001; Irvine and Fraser, 1998). Sometimes these warm demanders appear harsh to outside observers (Burke-Spero, 1999; Burke-Spero & Woolfolk Hoy, 2002). For example, results of one study indicated:

> To a person unfamiliar with African American culture of inner-city life, it could be misconstrued as intimidation or heavy handed . . . but in the minds of these informants, discipline was directly connected to caring. In fact, all viewed lack of discipline as a sign of uncaring and an apathetic teaching force. (Gordon, 1998, p. 427)

~ Reaching Every Student ~

Culturally Responsive Management

Carla Monroe and Jennifer Obidah (2002) studied Ms. Simpson, an African American teacher working with her 8th grade science class. She describes herself as having high expectations for academics and behavior in her classes—so much so that she believed her students perceived her as "mean." Yet she often used humor and dialect to communicate her expectations, as in the following exchange:

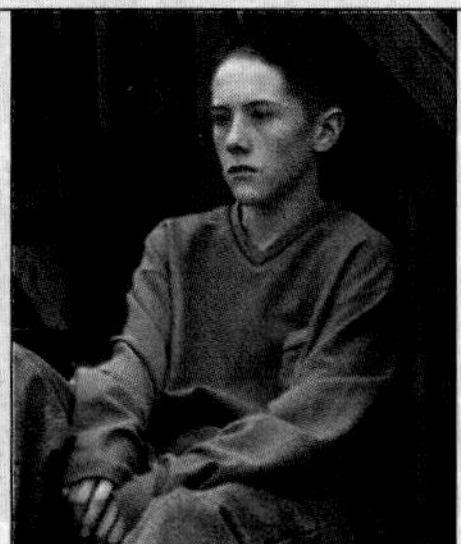

Ms. Simpson [addressing the class]: If you know you're going to act the fool just come to me and say, 'I'm going to act the fool at the pep rally,' so I can go ahead and send you to wherever you need to go. [Class laughs.]

Ms. Simpson: I'm real serious. If you know you're having a bad day, you don't want anybody touching you, you don't want nobody saying nothing to you, somebody bump into you you're going to snap—you need to come up to me and say, 'I'm going to snap and I can't go to the pep rally.' [The students start to call out various comments.]

Ms. Simpson: Now, I just want to say I expect you to have the best behavior because you're the most mature students in the building . . . don't make me stop the pep rally and ask the 8th graders to leave.

Edward: We'll have silent lunch won't we? [Class laughs.]

Ms. Simpson: You don't want to dream about what you're going to have. [Class laughs.] Ok, 15 minutes for warm ups. [The students begin their warm-up assignment.]

See the *Reaching Every Student* feature for an example.

Communicating with Families about Classroom Management

As we have seen throughout this book, families are important partners in education. This statement applies to classroom management as well. When parents and teachers share the same expectations and support each other, they can create a more positive classroom environment and more time for learning. The *Family and Community Partnerships Guidelines* on page 424 provide ideas for working with families and the community.

Besides prevention, schools can also establish mentoring programs, conflict resolution training, social skills training, more relevant curricula, and parent and community involvement programs (Padilla, 1992; Parks, 1995). One intervention that seems to be helpful is peer mediation, discussed in Chapter 13.

Check Yourself What does research say about different discipline approaches?

How does culture affect classroom management?

Family and Community Partnerships

Classroom Management

Make sure families know the expectations and rules of your class and school.

Examples

1. At a Family Fun Night, have your students do skits showing the rules—how to follow them and what breaking them "looks like" and "sounds like."
2. Make a poster for the refrigerator at home that describes, in a light way, the most important rules and expectations.
3. For older students, give families a list of due dates for the major assignments, along with tips about how to encourage quality work by pacing the effort—avoiding last minute panic.
4. Communicate in appropriate ways—use the family's first language when possible. Tailor messages to the reading level of the home.

Make families partners in recognizing good citizenship.

Examples

1. Send positive notes home when students, especially students who have had trouble with classroom management, work well in the classroom.
2. Give ideas for ways any family, even those with few economic resources, can celebrate accomplishment—a favorite food; the chance to choose a video to rent; a comment to a special person such as an aunt, grandparent, or minister; the chance to read to a younger sibling.

Identify talents in the community to help build a learning environment in your class.

Examples

1. Have students write letters to carpet and furniture stores asking for donations of remnants to carpet a reading corner.
2. Find family members who can build shelves or room dividers, paint, sew, laminate manipulatives, write stories, repot plants, or network computers.
3. Contact businesses for donations of computers, printers, or other equipment.

Seek cooperation from families when behavior problems arise.

Examples

1. Talk to families over the phone or in their home. Keep good records about the problem behavior.
2. Listen to family members and solve problems with them.

The Need for Organization
(pp. 396–399)

What are the challenges of classroom management? Classrooms are by nature multidimensional, full of simultaneous activities, fast-paced and immediate, unpredictable, public, and affected by the history of students' and teachers' actions. A manager must juggle all these elements every day. Productive classroom activity requires students' cooperation. Maintaining cooperation is different for each age group. Young students are learning how to "go to school" and need to learn the general procedures of school. Older students need to learn the specifics required for working in different subjects. Working with adolescents requires teachers to understand the power of the adolescent peer group.

What are the goals of good classroom management? The goals of effective classroom management are to make ample time for learning; improve the quality of time use by keeping students actively engaged; make sure participation structures are clear, straightforward, and consistently signaled; and encourage student self-management, self-control, and responsibility.

Classroom Management: Techniques used to maintain a healthy learning environment, relatively free of behavior problems.

Allocated Time: Time set aside for learning.

Engaged Time: Time spent actively learning.

Time on Task: Time spent actively engaged in the learning task at hand.

Academic Learning Time: Time when students are actually succeeding at the learning task.

Participation Structures: Rules defining how to participate in different activities.

Self-Management: Management of your own behavior and acceptance of responsibility for your own actions.

Creating a Positive Learning Environment
(pp. 399–408)

Distinguish between rules and procedures. Rules are the specific dos and don'ts of classroom life. They usually are written down or posted. Procedures cover administrative tasks, student movement, housekeeping, routines for running lessons, interactions between students and teachers, and interactions among students. Rules can be written in terms of rights and students may benefit from participating in establishing these rules. Consequences should be established for following and breaking the rules and procedures so that the teacher and the students know what will happen.

Distinguish between personal territories and interest-area spatial arrangements. There are two basic kinds of spatial organization, territorial (the traditional classroom arrangement) and functional (dividing space into interest or work areas). Flexibility is often the key. Access to materials, convenience, privacy when needed, ease of supervision, and a willingness to reevaluate plans are important considerations in the teacher's choice of physical arrangements.

Contrast the first school week of effective and ineffective classroom managers. Effective classroom managers spent the first days of class teaching a workable, easily understood set of rules and procedures by using lots of explanation, examples, and practice. Students were occupied with organized, enjoyable activities and learned to function cooperatively in the group. Quick, firm, clear, and consistent responses to infractions of the rules characterized effective teachers. The teachers had planned carefully to avoid any last-minute tasks that might have taken them away from their students. These teachers dealt with the children's pressing concerns first.

Procedures: Prescribed steps for an activity.

Rules: Statements specifying expected and forbidden behaviors; dos and don'ts.

Action Zone: Area of a classroom where the greatest amount of interaction takes place.

Maintaining a Good Environment for Learning
(pp. 408–414)

How can teachers encourage engagement? In general, as teacher supervision increases, students' engaged time also increases. When the task provides continuous cues for the student about what to do next, involvement will be greater. Activities with clear steps are likely to be more absorbing, because one step leads naturally to the next. Making work requirements clear and specific, providing needed materials, and monitoring activities all add to engagement.

Explain the factors identified by Kounin that prevent management problems in the classroom. To create a positive environment and prevent problems, teachers must take individual differences into account, maintain student motivation, and reinforce positive behavior. Successful problem preventers are skilled in four areas described by Kounin: "withitness," overlapping, group focusing, and movement management. When penalties have to be imposed, teachers should impose them calmly and privately.

Describe seven levels of intervention in misbehavior. Teachers can first make eye contact with the student or use other nonverbal signals, then try verbal hints such as simply inserting the student's name into the lecture. Next the teacher asks if the offender is aware of the negative effects of the actions, then reminds the student of the procedure and has her or him follow it correctly. If this does not work, the teacher can ask the student to state the correct rule or procedure and then to follow it, and then move to telling the student in a clear, assertive, and unhostile way to stop the misbehavior. If this fails too, the teacher can offer a choice—stop the behavior or meet privately to work out the consequences.

What are some special problems and challenges in secondary classrooms? Teachers working in secondary schools should be prepared to handle students who don't complete school work, repeatedly break the same rule, or openly defy teachers.

> **Withitness:** According to Kounin, awareness of everything happening in a classroom.
>
> **Overlapping:** Supervising several activities at once.
>
> **Group Focus:** The ability to keep as many students as possible involved in activities.
>
> **Movement Management:** Keeping lessons and the group moving at an appropriate (and flexible) pace, with smooth transitions and variety.

■ Enhancing Your Expertise with Technology

(p. 414)

The Center for Talented Youth (CTY)
(http://www.jhu.edu/gifted/teaching/classroom.htm)

brief self-quiz
(http://education.indiana.edu/cas/tt/v1i2/what.html)

Other Useful Websites

Classroom Management **http://scholar.coe.uwf.edu/pacee/steps/tutorial/classmanagement/main.htm#section4**

The Nova Scotia Teachers' Union has organized a set of resources on anti-violence, including reference to resources on anger management, conflict resolution, and peer mediation.
http://www.nstu.ns.ca/violence/intro.html

Excellent tutorial on classroom management.
http://scholar.coe.uwf.edu/pacee/steps/tutorial/classmanagement/main.htm#section4

Phi Delta Kappan (see the September issue for the Annual PDK/Gallup Poll of the Public's Attitudes Toward the Public Schools)
http://www.pdkintl.org/

Comprehensive guide to behavior management for bus drivers.
http://www.state.ia.us/educate/programs/transportation/special_needs/behavmod.html

Organizations

Consistency Management and Cooperative Discipline
H. Jerome Freiberg
University of Houston
College of Education
Houston, TX 77204-5872
713-743-8663

Learning Together
Roger T. Johnson and David W. Johnson
The Cooperative Learning Center
60 Peik Hall
University of Minnesota
Minneapolis, MN 55455
612-624-7031

■ The Need for Communication

(pp. 415–421)

What is meant by "empathetic listening"? Communication between teacher and student is essential when problems arise. All interactions between people, even silence or neglect, communicate some meaning. Empathetic, active listening can be a helpful response when students bring problems to teachers. Teachers must reflect back to the students what they hear them saying. This reflection is more than a parroting of words; it should capture the emotions, intent, and meaning behind them.

Distinguish among assertive, passive, and hostile response styles. The *passive style* can take several forms. Instead of telling the student directly what to do, the teacher simply comments on the behavior, asks the student to *think about* the appropriate action, or threatens but never follows through. In a *hostile response style,* teachers may make "you" statements that condemn the student without stating clearly what the student should be doing. An *assertive response* communicates to the students that the teacher cares too much about them and the process of learning to allow inappropriate behavior to persist. Assertive teachers clearly state what they expect.

What are some options for dealing with student–student and student–teacher conflict? Students need guidance in resolving conflicts. Also, classrooms need clear rules and expectations about bullying and peer harassment. No matter what the situation, the cooperation of families can help to create a positive learning environment in the classroom and school.

> **Paraphrase Rule:** Policy whereby listeners must accurately summarize what a speaker has said before being allowed to respond.
>
> **Empathetic Listening:** Hearing the intent and emotions behind what another says and reflecting them back by paraphrasing.
>
> **"I" Message:** Clear, nonaccusatory statement of how something is affecting you.
>
> **Assertive Discipline:** Clear, firm, unhostile response style.

Summing It Up: Learning Environments for All Students

(pp. 422–424)

What does research say about different discipline approaches? A combination of recognition for appropriate behavior, hints about what is unacceptable, discussion, about how behavior affects others, and student involvement in discipline decisions encourages student responsibility, but these approaches are difficult when students are aggressive.

How does culture affect classroom management? African American males are disciplined more often and more harshly in American schools. Cultural differences in behavioral expression can be the basis for misunderstandings in classroom management.

Culturally Relevant Management: Taking cultural meanings and styles into account when developing management plans and responding to students.

Warm Demanders: Effective teachers with African American students who show both high expectations and great caring for their students.

Becoming a Professional

Passing the PRAXIS™

Chapter 11 reflects many of the professional standards created by the Interstate New Teacher Assessment and Support Consortium (INTASC). These standards form the basis of the PRAXIS II™ and state-created teacher licensure exams.

After a few months in the classroom, you realize that there are practically no 100% guarantees that you can make to your students about any aspect or part of their day. Not all your lessons will be utterly engrossing. Some tests and quizzes are too easy and some are too difficult. Many of your jokes fall flat with the students (or so the groans would suggest). Nevertheless, you, like most of your colleagues in the middle school, take pride in creating school and classroom environments in which students nearly always feel safe, accepted, and respected. Now that environment is threatened—at least for one student. As a classroom manager, you have to ask yourself not only what to do to eliminate this problem for your student, but also what strategies and techniques can prevent or reduce similar problems in the future.

Tips for PRAXIS II™

Understand principles of classroom management that promote positive relationships by:

- Establishing daily procedures and routines
- Responding effectively to minor student misbehavior
- Implementing reasonable rules, penalties, and rewards
- Keeping students actively engaged in purposeful learning

Diagnose problems and prevent or reduce inappropriate behaviors by:

- Communicating with students and parents
- Addressing misbehaviors in the least intrusive way possible
- Confronting disruptive behaviors in an effective, efficient manner

Related Topics

- Self-schemas (Chapters 3 and 10)
- Behavioral approaches to teaching and management (Chapter 6)
- Methods for encouraging behaviors (Chapter 6)
- Bringing it all together: Teaching every student (Chapter 5)

Standards and Licensure Appendix: *PRAXIS II™ and INTASC*

Refer to the Appendix at the end of the book for detailed correlations to PRAXIS II™ exam topics and INTASC Standards addressed in this text.

Insights about Interview Questions: *What Would You Say?*

1. What is classroom management?
2. So what do you think about zero-tolerance?
3. In your experience with students in any capacity, what was your most challenging discipline problem so far, and how did you handle it?

Your Teaching Portfolio: *Teaching Resources*

- Think about your philosophy of teaching, a question you will be asked at most job interviews. What is your philosophy of class room management? What rules will you set and how will you establish them? (Consult the *Guidelines* for ideas.)
- Add some ideas for Parent Involvement from this chapter to your **Portfolio.**
- Adapt the rules on pages 402–403 for students you will teach.
- Add the floorplans from Figures 11.2 and 11.3 to your **Teaching Resources** file.
- Add Tables 11.3 on teasing dos and don'ts and 11.4 on handling explosive situations to your **Teaching Resources** file.

Video**Workshop** Extra

If the VideoWorkshop package was included with your textbook, go to Chapter 11 of the Companion Website (www.ablongman.com/woolfolk) and click on the VideoWorkshop button. Follow the instructions for viewing *Video Clip 8: Experiential Learning.* Consider this information along with what you've read in Chapter 11 while answering the following questions.

1. How did the instructors on this field trip promote learning? Use terminology from your text to answer this question.
2. What are the challenges of managing a lesson during a field trip?

Use the CD-ROM included in the back of your textbook to launch the "Becoming a Professional" website. The website features advice on preparing for teacher certification exams, help with getting your first job, and resources to help you perform your job well from the first day forward.

Teachers' Casebook

What Would They Do?

Here is how some practicing teachers responded to the situation presented at the beginning of this chapter about addressing problems with bullies at school.

Jolita Harper

Fifth Grade Teacher, *Weinland Park Elementary School, Columbus, OH*

I believe that the entire learning community has a clear role in preventing acts of intimidation between students, and that this is best accomplished with clear communication between all parties. Care should be taken to spread awareness between colleagues as to the nature of the situation. Classroom teachers who are alert to these instances of bullying are then able to provide an additional presence in situations, such as in hallways and the lunchroom, where this is likely to take place. Further, communication between individual classroom teachers and the victim of this bullying is essential. I would make certain to provide a sensitive ear to this student's plight as we work together to formulate alternatives toward improving the situation. Finally, in the event that the two bullying students were in my classes, I would communicate with them in such a way as to make clear the effect of their actions on others in an effort to promote empathy for their victim and, hopefully, initiate a change in their behaviors.

Keith J. Boyle

English teacher, grades 9–12, *Dunellen High School, Dunellen, NJ*

Errant behavior throughout the middle school may be indicative of future behavioral problems and, as many things in life, the more this misbehavior is allowed to exist, the longer it will have a chance to thrive. In this case of a child being continually bullied by two other children (gender having no bearing in this situation), the knowledge of this wrongdoing must not be ignored or isolated. I would interview both the victim and the bullies, separately, to glean as much information as possible. If this were a singular incident, I would attempt to handle it myself via contact with the pertinent parents. However, if this were a recurring problem, the administration must be made aware. Any administrator will acknowledge that to be left in the dark about a serious situation within the environs off his/her responsibility is precarious. The appropriate guidance counselor should also be involved. The gravity of abusive behavior toward fellow students must be emphasized to the offenders. Significant punitive action is integral in order to send a message to the entire community that their school is indeed a haven in which one can feel the uninhibited freedom to learn.

Dan Doyle

History Teacher, Grade 11, *St. Joseph's Academy, Hoffman, Illinois*

As a high school teacher I'd be especially concerned about the existence of bullying among older students. While such behavior in elementary school is hurtful and damaging, it can become downright dangerous as students get older (and bigger!). I'd also be frustrated to think that, perhaps, early warning signs among these children may have been ignored or under-addressed at the elementary level, when teachers and/or parents are better positioned to get a grip on them. My first step would be to alert school personnel, particularly those who monitor hallways, the cafeteria, and other common areas, to be on the lookout for any type of bullying behavior. I'd put those responsible in communication with the guidance counselor's office; the counselor would determine whether the parents needed to be involved from there. Events in our society in recent years preclude the option of taking this sort of behavior lightly, or assuming it will take care of itself.

Kelley Crockett

Meadowbrook Elementary School, *Fort Worth, Texas*

Bullying can not be tolerated. No school, no teacher, no administrator can afford a climate in which abusive behavior is allowed to germinate. Any incident of victimization must be immediately documented and submitted to the Principal. As well, I would schedule a conference that same day with the school counselor for my student in order to both allow another avenue of documentation and reinforce support that the problem is being aggressively addressed.

How I handle the next step depends on the administration in place but the important issue to remember is that there is a next step. The teacher must follow up with the student. Within 48 hours I would privately ask my student if there have been any further incidents. If he hesitates or acknowledges continued harassment I would direct him to write it down and I would document any questions I had asked him and his responses. I would then include his statement and my own in another report for both the Principal and the counselor.

As teachers, we hold the front line. To the children in our care we represent one of the first relationships with authority and civilize society. We can do no less than lend our voice and action to the betterment of our world.

Go to the Companion Website (www.ablongman.com/woolfolk) for additional case studies including audio and video cases, and examples of student work.

CHAPTER

12

Teaching for Academic Learning

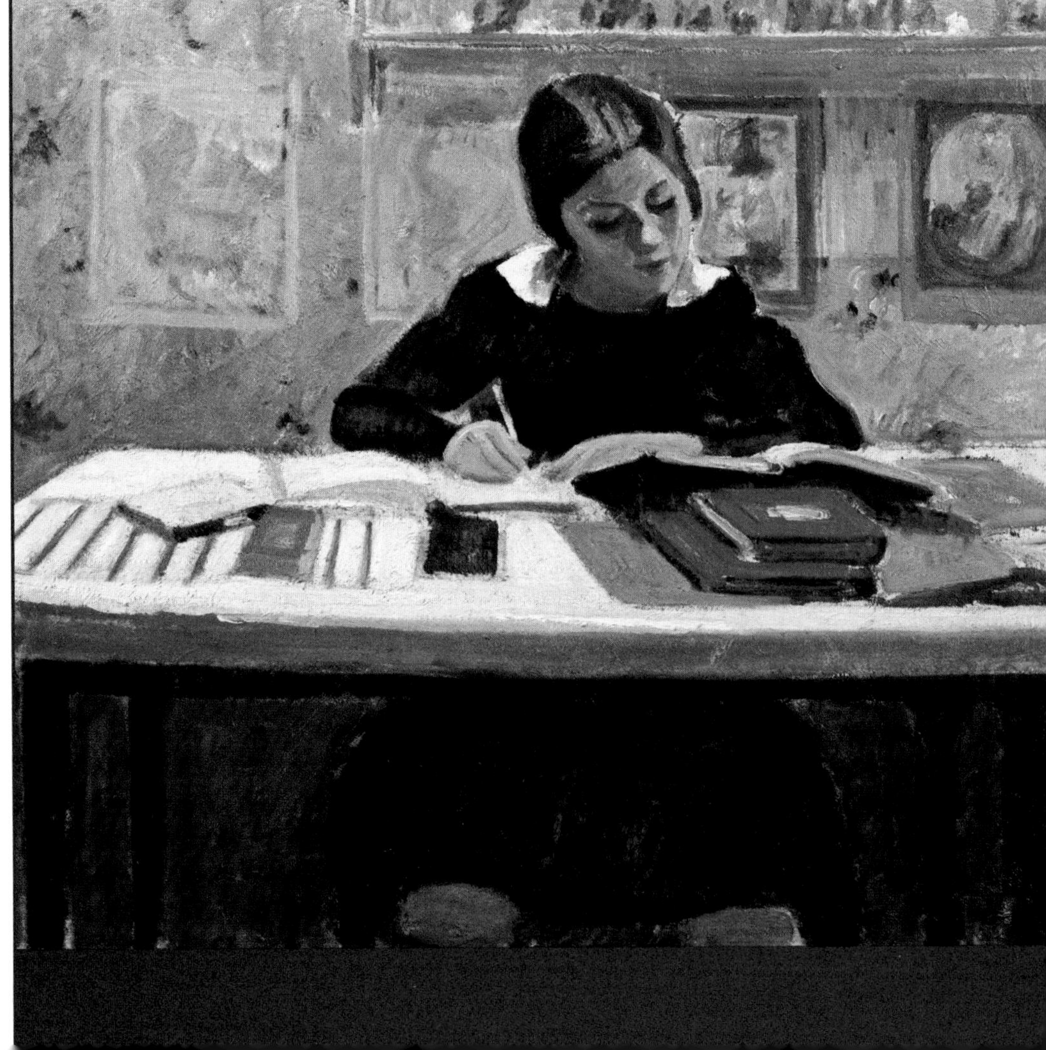

Teachers' Casebook

What Would You Do?

On the first day of your orientation for your new position as a 4th grade teacher, you are handed a long list of competencies and topics that could be covered on the 4th grade proficiency test in the spring. You learn that your new school is on a state list of districts being monitored because the test scores from previous years have been so low. You agree that many of the topics on the test list are important, but your school seems to have no plan for teaching other than drill and practice on facts and skills that might be on the test.

Critical Thinking

How will you arouse students' curiosity and interests about the topics and tasks that will be tested? How will you establish the value of learning these skills and facts? How will you get students engaged in real learning about the topics? What more do you need to know to prepare your students for this big test?

Collaboration

With 3 or 4 other students in your class, identify a key concept in your subject that is likely to be on a statewide test. Plan a way to teach that will help students understand and remember the concept.

Much of this text has been about learning and learners. In this chapter we focus on teachers and teaching. We look first at how teachers plan, including how to use taxonomies of learning objectives or themes as a basis for planning. With this foundation of knowing how to set goals and make plans, we move to a consideration of some general teacher-centered strategies: lecturing, seatwork, homework, questioning, recitation, and group discussion.

What else do we know about teachers? Are there particular characteristics that distinguish effective from ineffective teachers? Research on whole-class teaching points to the importance of several factors and we will explore them as well as the elements of effective teaching in inclusive classrooms. In the final section of this chapter, we will focus on student-centered approaches for different subjects—reading, writing, mathematics, and science. Educational psychologists have studied how people learn these subjects and identified implications for teaching.

By the time you have completed this chapter you should be able to answer these questions:

- *When and how should teachers use instructional objectives?*
- *In what situations would each of the following formats be most appropriate: lecture, seatwork and homework, questioning, and group discussion?*
- *What are the characteristics of effective teachers?*
- *How can teachers' expectations affect student learning?*
- *How does the teacher's role vary in direct and constructivist teaching approaches?*
- *What are the merits of approaches to teaching reading, mathematics, and science?*

Study or The Schoolgirl, c. 1933–1934, by Jean Puy.

The First Step: Planning

Greta Morine-Dershimer (2003) asks which of the following are true about teacher planning:

Time is of the essence.

A little goes a long way.

Plans are made to be broken.

You can do it yourself

One size fits all.

Don't look back

Companion Website

When you thought about the "What Would You Do?" challenge, you were *planning.* In the past few years, educational researchers have become very interested in teachers' planning. They have interviewed teachers about how they plan, asked teachers to "think out loud" while planning or to keep journals describing their plans, and even studied teachers intensively for months at a time. What have they found?

First, planning influences what students will learn, because planning transforms the available time and curriculum materials into activities, assignments, and tasks for students—*time is the of essence planning.* When a teacher decides to devote 7 hours to language arts and 15 minutes to science in a given week, the students in that class will learn more language than science. In fact, differences as dramatic as this do occur, with some classrooms dedicating twice as much time as others to certain subjects (Clark & Yinger, 1988; Karweitt, 1989). Planning done at the beginning of the year is particularly important, because many routines and patterns, such as time allocations, are established early. So, *a little planning does go a long way* in terms of what will be taught and what will be learned.

Second, teachers engage in several levels of planning—by the year, term, unit, week, and day. All the levels must be coordinated. Accomplishing the year's plan requires breaking the work into terms, the terms into units, and the units into weeks and days. For experienced teachers, unit planning seems to be the most important level, followed by weekly and then daily planning. As you gain experience in teaching, it will be easier to coordinate these levels of planning and incorporate the state and district curriculum requirements as well (Clark & Yinger, 1988; Morine-Dershimer, 2003).

Third, plans reduce—but do not eliminate—uncertainty in teaching. Planning must allow flexibility. There is some evidence that when teachers "overplan"—fill every minute and stick to the plan no matter what—their students do not learn as much as students whose teachers are flexible (Shavelson, 1987). So *plans are not made to be broken*—but sometimes they need to be bent a bit.

In order to plan creatively and flexibly, teachers need to have wide-ranging knowledge about students, their interests, and abilities; the subjects being taught; alternative ways to teach and assess understanding; working with groups; the expectations and limitations of the school and community; how to apply and adapt materials and texts; and how to pull all this knowledge together into meaningful activities. The plans of beginning teachers sometimes don't work because they lack knowledge about the students or the subject—they can't estimate how long it will take students to complete an activity, for example, or they stumble when asked for an explanation or a different example (Calderhead, 1996).

"And then, of course, there's the possibility of being just the slightest bit too organized."

(By permission of Glen Dines. From *Phi Delta Kappan.*)

In planning, *you can do it yourself*—but collaboration is better. Working with other teachers and sharing ideas is one of the best experiences in teaching. (Be sure to look at the websites at the end of the chapter to find additional planning resources for teachers.) But even great lesson plans taken from a terrific website on science have to be adapted to your situation. Some of the adaptation comes before you teach and some comes after. In fact, much of what experienced teachers know about planning comes from looking back—reflecting—on what worked and what didn't, so *do look back* on your plans and grow professionally in the process.

Finally, there is no one model for effective planning. *One size does not fit all* in planning. Planning is a creative problem-solving process for experienced teachers (Shavelson, 1987). These teachers know how to accomplish many lessons and to teach segments of lessons effectively. They know what to expect and how to proceed, so they don't necessarily continue to follow the detailed lesson-planning models they learned during their teacher-preparation programs. Planning is more informal—"in their heads." However, many experienced teachers think it was helpful to learn this detailed system as a foundation (Clark & Peterson, 1986).

No matter how you plan, you must have a learning goal in mind. In the next section we consider the range of goals that you might have for your students.

Objectives for Learning

We hear quite a bit today about visions, goals, outcomes, and standards. At a very general, abstract level are the grand goals society may have for graduates of public schools such as, "All children will start school ready to learn," one of the eight goals for U.S. education in *Goals 2000* (see www.ed.gov/G2K/ for all the goals). However, very general goals are meaningless as potential guidelines for instruction. States may turn these grand goals into standards, such as the South Carolina standard that students will "Develop the concept of fractions, mixed numbers, and decimals and use models to relate fractions to decimals and to find equivalent fractions." Sometimes the standards are turned into indicators such as "representing equivalent fractions objectives" (Anderson & Krathwohl, 2001, p. 18). At this level, the indicators are close to being instructional objectives.

Norman Gronlund (2000) defines **instructional objectives** as "intended learning outcomes . . . the types of performance students are expected to demonstrate at the end of instruction to show that they have learned what was expected of them" (p. 4). Objectives written by people with behavioral views focus on observable and measurable changes in the learner. **Behavioral objectives** use terms such as *list, define, add,* or *calculate.* **Cognitive objectives,** on the other hand, emphasize thinking and comprehension, so they are more likely to include words such as *understand, recognize, create,* or *apply.* Let's look at one well-developed method of writing specific objectives.

Mager: Start with the Specific. Robert Mager has developed a very influential system for writing instructional objectives. Mager's idea is that objectives ought to describe what students will be doing when demonstrating their achievement and how teachers will know they are doing it (Mager, 1975). Mager's objectives are generally regarded as *behavioral.* According to Mager, a good objective has three parts. First, it describes the intended student behavior. What must the student do? Second, it lists the conditions under which the behavior will occur: How will this behavior be recognized or tested? Third, it gives the criteria for acceptable performance on the test. Table 12.1 shows how the system works. With its emphasis on final behavior, Mager's

CONNECT & EXTEND

TO **PRAXIS**™
INSTRUCTIONAL OBJECTIVES (II, B1)
Describe the key elements of behavioral and instructional objectives. Be able to write each type of objective for a content area that you expect to teach.

CONNECT & EXTEND

TO YOUR TEACHING/PORTFOLIO
Cuban, L. (1990). Four stories about national goals for American education. *Phi Delta Kappan, 72*(4), 264–314.
Focus Questions: What should be the goals of American education? Should we have a national agenda that shapes our instructional objectives?

CONNECT & EXTEND

TO YOUR TEACHING/PORTFOLIO
Do you think behavioral objectives are really objectives in themselves, or are they a "means to an end"?

Table 12.1 Mager's Three-Part System

Robert Mager believes that a good learning objective has three parts: the students behavior, the conditions under which the behavior will be preformed, and the criteria for judging a performance.

Part	Central Question	Example
Student behavior	Do what?	Mark statements with an *F* for fact or an *O* for opinion
Conditions of performance	Under what conditions?	Given an article from a newspaper
Performance criteria	How well?	75% of the statements are correctly marked

SOURCE: From *Preparing Instructional Objectives,* by R. F. Mager. Published by David S. Lake, Belmont, CA. Copyright © 1975 by David S. Lake Publishers. Reprinted with permission.

Instructional objectives Clear statement of what students are intended to learn through instruction.

Behavioral objectives Instructional objectives stated in terms of observable behaviors.

Cognitive objectives Instructional objectives stated in terms of higher-level thinking operations.

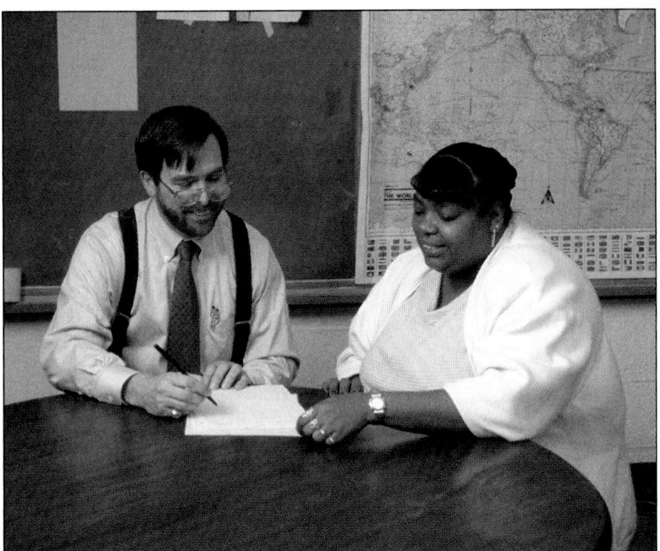

In planning, you can go it alone, but collaboration is better. Sharing ideas with colleagues can be one of the best experiences in teaching.

system requires a very explicit statement. Mager contends that often students can teach themselves if they are given well-stated objectives.

Gronlund: Start with the General. Norman Gronlund (2000) offers a different approach, which is often used for writing cognitive objectives. He believes that an objective should be stated first in general terms (*understand, solve, appreciate,* etc.). Then the teacher should clarify by listing a few sample behaviors that would provide evidence that the student has attained the objective. Look at the example in Table 12.2. The goal here really is presenting and defending a research project. A teacher could never list all the behaviors that might be involved in "presenting and defending," but stating an initial, general objective along with specific examples makes the purpose clear.

The most recent research on instructional objectives tends to favor approaches similar to Gronlund's. James Popham (2002), a former proponent of very specific objectives, makes this recommendation:

> Strive to come up with a half dozen or so truly salient, broad, yet measurable instructional objectives for your own classroom. Too many small-scope, hyperspecific objectives will be of scant value to you because, if you're at all normal, you'll soon disregard [them]. On the other hand, a small number of intellectually manageable, broad, yet measurable objectives will not only prove helpful to you instructionally but will also help you answer the what-to-assess question. (pp. 98–99)

■ **Table 12.2**	Gronlund's Combined Method for Creating Objectives

General Objective

Presents and defends the research project before a group.

Specific Examples

1. Describes the project in a well-organized manner.
2. Summarizes the findings and their implications.
3. Uses display materials to clarify ideas and relationships.
4. Answers group members' questions directly and completely.
5. Presents a report that reflects careful planning.
6. Displays sound reasoning ability through presentation and answers to questions

SOURCE: From *How to Write and Use Instructional Objectives* (6th ed.), by Norman F. Gronlund. Published by Prentice Hall.

Flexible and Creative Plans—Using Taxonomies

Think about your assignments for one of your classes. What kind of thinking is involved in doing the assignments?

Remembering facts and terms? | Analyzing a situation, task, or problem?

Understanding key ideas? | Making evaluations or giving opinions?

Applying information to solve problems? | Creating or designing something new?

What kind of thinking is involved in answering this *Stop/Think/Write* question?

Several decades ago, a group of experts in educational evaluation led by Benjamin Bloom set out to improve college and university examinations. The impact of their work has touched education at all levels around the world (Anderson & Sosniak, 1994). Bloom and his colleagues developed a **taxonomy,** or classification system, of educational objectives. Objectives were divided into three domains: cognitive, affective, and psychomotor. A handbook describing the objectives in each area was eventually published. In real life, of course, behaviors from these three domains occur simultaneously. While students are writing (psychomotor), they are also remembering or reasoning (cognitive), and they are likely to have some emotional response to the task as well (affective).

CONNECT & EXTEND

TO **PRAXIS**™
TAXONOMIES OF EDUCATIONAL OBJECTIVES (II, B1)
Taxonomies influence every aspect of instruction from textbook design to lesson planning. List the major objectives of each of the taxonomies, and describe the focus of each objective. Be able to incorporate these objectives into instructional objectives that you design.

The Cognitive Domain. Six basic objectives are listed in Bloom's taxonomy of the thinking or **cognitive domain** (Bloom, Engelhart, Frost, Hill, & Krathwohl, 1956):

1. *Knowledge:* Remembering or recognizing something without necessarily understanding, using, or changing it.
2. *Comprehension:* Understanding the material being communicated without necessarily relating it to anything else.
3. *Application:* Using a general concept to solve a particular problem.
4. *Analysis:* Breaking something down into its parts.
5. *Synthesis:* Creating something new by combining different ideas.
6. *Evaluation:* Judging the value of materials or methods as they might be applied in a particular situation.

It is common in education to consider these objectives as a hierarchy, each skill building on those below, but this is not entirely accurate (Seddon, 1978). Some subjects, such as mathematics, do not fit this structure very well (Kreitzer & Madaus, 1994). Still, you will hear many references to *lower-level* and *higher-level objectives,* with knowledge, comprehension, and application considered lower level and the other categories considered higher level. As a rough way of thinking about objectives, this can be helpful (Gronlund, 2000). The taxonomy of objectives can also be helpful in planning assessments because different procedures are appropriate for objectives at the various levels, as you will see in Chapter 15.

Bloom 2001. Bloom's taxonomy guided educators for over 40 years. It is considered one of the most significant educational writings of the 20th century (Anderson & Sosniak, 1994). In 2001, a group of educational researchers published the first major revision of the taxonomy (Anderson & Krathwohl, 2001). The new version retains the six basic levels in a slightly different order, but the names of three levels have been changed to indicate the cognitive processes involved. The six cognitive processes are remembering (knowledge), understanding (comprehension), applying, analyzing, evaluating, and creating (synthesizing). In addition, the revisers have added a new dimension to the taxonomy to recognize that cognitive processes must process something—you have to remember or understand or apply some form of knowledge. If you look at Table 12.3 you will see the result. We now have six processes—the cognitive acts of remembering, understanding, applying, analyzing, evaluating, and creating. These processes act on four kinds of knowledge—factual, conceptual, procedural, and metacognitive.

Taxonomy Classification system.

Cognitive domain In Bloom's taxonomy, memory and reasoning objectives.

Table 12.3 A Revised Taxonomy in the Cognitive Domain

	The Cognitive Process Dimension					
The Knowledge Dimension	**1. Remember**	**2. Understand**	**3. Apply**	**4. Analyze**	**5. Evaluate**	**6. Create**
A. Factual Knowledge						
B. Conceptual Knowledge						
C. Procedural Knowledge						
D. Metacognitive Knowledge						

SOURCE: From *A Taxonomy for Teaching, and Assessing,* L. Anderson and D. Krathwohl, (eds). Published by Allyn & Bacon, Boston, MA. Copyright © 2001 by Pearson Education. Reprinted by permission of the publisher.

Consider how this revised taxonomy might suggest objectives for a social studies/language arts class. An objective that targets *analyzing conceptual knowledge* is:

> After reading an historical account of the battle of the Alamo, students will be able to recognize the author's point of view or bias.

An objective for *evaluating metacognitive knowledge* might be:

> Students will reflect on their strategies for identifying the biases of the author.

The Affective Domain. The objectives in the taxonomy of the **affective domain,** or domain of emotional response, have not yet been revised from the original version. These objectives run from least committed to most committed (Krathwohl, Bloom, & Masia, 1964). At the lowest level, a student would simply pay attention to a certain idea. At the highest level, the student would adopt an idea or a value and act consistently with that idea. There are five basic objectives in the affective domain:

1. *Receiving:* Being aware of or attending to something in the environment. This is the I'll-listen-to-the-concert-but-I-won't-promise-to-like-it level.
2. *Responding:* Showing some new behavior as a result of experience. At this level a person might applaud after the concert or hum some of the music the next day.
3. *Valuing:* Showing some definite involvement or commitment. At this point a person might choose to go to a concert instead of a film.
4. *Organization:* Integrating a new value into one's general set of values, giving it some ranking among one's general priorities. This is the level at which a person would begin to make long-range commitments to concert attendance.
5. *Characterization by value:* Acting consistently with the new value. At this highest level, a person would be firmly committed to a love of music and demonstrate it openly and consistently.

Like the basic objectives in the cognitive domain, these five objectives are very general. To write specific learning objectives, you must state what students will actually be doing when they are receiving, responding, valuing, and so on. For example, an objective for a nutrition class at the valuing level (showing involvement or commitment) might be stated: After completing the unit on food contents and labeling, at least 50% of the class will commit to the junk-food boycott project by giving up candy for a month.

The Psychomotor Domain. Until recently, the **psychomotor domain,** or realm of physical ability objectives, has been mostly overlooked by teachers not directly involved with physical education. There are several taxonomies in this domain (e.g., Harrow, 1972; Simpson, 1972) that generally move from basic perceptions and reflex actions to skilled, creative movements. James Cangelosi (1990) provides a useful way to think about objec-

Affective domain Objectives focusing on attitudes and feelings.

Psychomotor domain Physical ability and coordination objectives.

tives in the psychomotor domain as either voluntary muscle capabilities that require endurance, strength, flexibility, agility, or speed, or the ability to perform a specific skill.

Objectives in the psychomotor domain should be of interest to a wide range of educators, including those in fine arts, vocational-technical education, and special education. Many other subjects, such as chemistry, physics, and biology also require specialized movements and well-developed hand and eye coordination. Using lab equipment, the "mouse" on a computer, or art materials means learning new physical skills. Here are two psychomotor objectives:

> Four minutes after completing a one-mile run in eight minutes or under, your heart rate will be below 120.
>
> Use a computer mouse effectively to "drag and drop" files.

Whatever your instructional objectives for your students, Terry TenBrink (2003, p. 67) suggests these criteria. Objectives should be:

1. Developmentally appropriate.
2. Attainable by the students within a reasonable time limit.
3. In proper sequence with other objectives (not to be accomplished until the prerequisite objectives are met).
4. In harmony with the overall goals of the course (and curriculum).
5. In harmony with the goals and values of the institution.

The *Guidelines* below should help you if you use objectives for every lesson or for just a few assignments.

Constructivist approach View that emphasizes the active role of the learner in building understanding and making sense of information.

Another View: Planning from a Constructivist Perspective

Think about the same course assignments you analyzed for thinking processes in the previous *Stop/Think/Write*. What are the big ideas that run through all those assignments? What other ways could you learn about those ideas besides the assignments?

Traditionally, it has been the teacher's responsibility to do most of the planning for instruction, but new ways of planning are developing. In **constructivist approaches,** planning is shared and negotiated. The teacher and students together make decisions

GUIDELINES Using Instructional Objectives

Avoid "word magic"—phrases that sound noble and important but say very little, such as "Students will become deep thinkers."

Examples

1. Keep the focus on specific changes that will take place in the students' knowledge of skills.
2. Ask students to explain the meaning of the objectives. If they can't give specific examples of what you mean, the objectives are not communicating your intentions to your students.

Suit the activities to the objectives.

Examples

1. If the goal is the memorization of vocabulary, give the students memory aids and practice exercises.
2. If the goal is the ability to develop well-thought-out positions, consider position papers, debates, projects, or mock trials.
3. If you want students to become better writers, give many opportunities for writing and rewriting.

Make sure your tests are related to your objectives.

Examples

1. Write objectives and rough drafts for tests at the same time—revise these drafts of tests as the units unfold and objectives change.
2. Weight the tests according to the importance of the various objectives and the time spent on each.

about content, activities, and approaches. Rather than having specific student behaviors and skills as objectives, the teacher has overarching goals—"big ideas"—that guide planning. These goals are understandings or abilities that the teacher returns to again and again.

An Example of Constructivist Planning. Vito Perrone (1994) has these goals for his secondary history students. He wants his students to be able to:

- use primary sources, formulate hypotheses, and engage in systematic study;
- handle multiple points of view;
- be close readers and active writers; and
- pose and solve problems.

The next step in the planning process is to create a learning environment that allows students to move toward these goals in ways that respect their individual interests and abilities. Perrone (1994) suggests identifying "those ideas, themes, and issues that provide the depth and variety of perspective that help students develop significant understandings" (p. 12). For a secondary history course, a theme might be "democracy and revolution," "fairness," or "slavery." In math or music, a theme might be "patterns"; in literature, "personal identity" might be the theme. Perrone suggests mapping the topic as a way of thinking about how the theme can generate learning and understanding. An example of a topic map, using the theme of "Immigrants in the United States," is shown in Figure 12.1.

With this map of the topic, "Immigrants to the United States," a history teacher can identify themes, issues, and ideas for study. Rather than "cover" the whole map, a few areas are examined in depth.

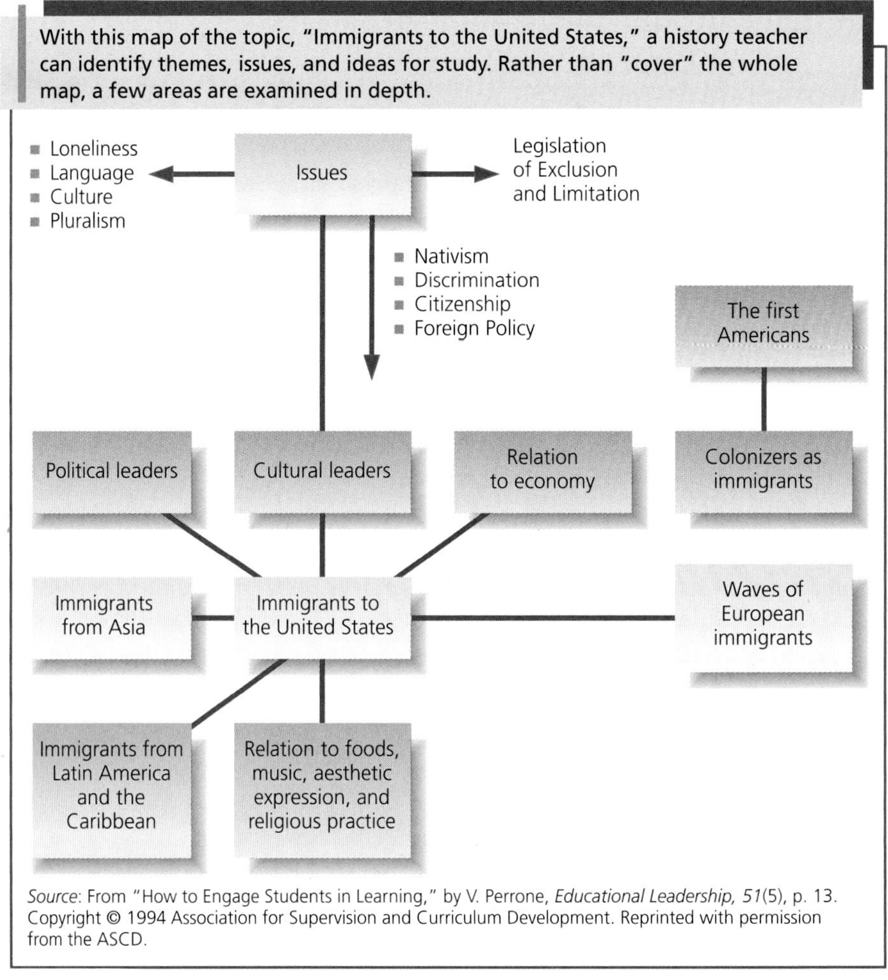

Source: From "How to Engage Students in Learning," by V. Perrone, *Educational Leadership, 51*(5), p. 13. Copyright © 1994 Association for Supervision and Curriculum Development. Reprinted with permission from the ASCD.

Figure 12.1 Planning with a Topic Map

With this topic map as a guide, teacher and students can work together to identify activities, materials, projects, and performances that will support the development of the students' understanding and abilities—the overarching goals of the class. The teacher spends less time planning specific presentations and assignments and more time gathering a variety of resources and facilitating students' learning. The focus is not so much on students' products as on the processes of learning and the thinking behind the products.

Integrated and Thematic Plans. Perrone's planning map shows a way to use the theme of immigrants to the United States to integrate issues in a history class. Today, teaching with themes and integrated content are major elements in planning and designing lessons and units, from kindergarten (Roskos & Neuman, 1995) through high school (Clarke & Agne, 1997). For example, Elaine Homestead and Karen McGinnis (middle school teachers) and Elizabeth Pate (a college professor) (1995) designed a unit on "Human Interactions" that included studying racism, world hunger, pollution, and air and water quality. Students researched issues by reading textbooks and outside sources, learning to use databases, interviewing local officials, and inviting guest speakers into class. Students had to develop knowledge in science, mathematics, and social studies. They learned to write and speak persuasively, and in the process, raised money for hunger relief in Africa.

CONNECT & EXTEND

TO PRAXIS™ PLANNING THEMATIC UNITS (II, A2)
Thematic learning units that integrate two or more content areas have become common in modern classrooms. Describe the principles involved in designing these activities, and explain how student learning can be assessed.

Elementary age students can benefit from integrated planning, too. There is no reason to work on spelling skills, then listening skills, then writing skills, and then social studies or science. All these abilities can be developed together if students work to solve authentic problems. Some ideas for integrating themes with younger children are people, friendship, communications, habitats, communities, and patterns. Possibilities for older children are given in Table 12.4.

Check Yourself What are the levels of planning and how do they affect teaching?

What is an instructional objective?

Describe the three taxonomies of educational objectives.

Describe teacher-centered and student-centered planning.

Let's assume you have an idea of *what* you want students to understand, but *how* do you teach to encourage understanding? You still need to decide what's happening on Monday. You need to design teaching that is appropriate for the objectives.

Table 12.4 Some Themes for Integrated Planning for Older Children

Courage	Time and Space
Mystery	Groups and Institutions
Survival	Work
Human Interaction	Motion
Communities of the Future	Cause and Effect
Communication/Language	Probability and Prediction
Human Rights and Responsibilities	Change and Conservation
Identity/Coming of Age	Diversity and Variation
Interdependence	Autobiography

SOURCE: Adapted from *Toward a Coherent Curriculum* by J. A. Beane (Ed.), 1995, Alexandria, VA: Association for Supervision and Curriculum Development; *Interdisciplinary High School Teaching* by J. H. Clarke and R. M. Agne, 1997, Boston: Allyn & Bacon; and *Teaching through Themes* by G. Thompson, 1991, New York: Scholastic. See Thompson for resources and strategies to develop some of these themes in elementary school and Clarke and Agne for ideas at the high school level.

CONNECT & EXTEND

TO **PRAXIS**™
TEACHER-CENTERED INSTRUCTION (II, A3)
Teacher-centered instruction is often thought of as the "traditional" approach to instruction. In what situations is this instructional format most effective? What are the basic steps involved in carrying out this form of instruction?

Teacher-Directed Instruction

What Would You Say? In your interview for the last remaining opening in the district of your dreams, the principal asks, "What is the best lesson you have taught so far? Tell me all about it and especially what made it so good."

How would you go about identifying the keys to successful teaching? You might ask students, principals, college professors of education, or experienced teachers to list the characteristics of good teachers. Or you could do intensive case studies of a few classrooms over a long period. You might observe classrooms, rate different teachers on certain characteristics, and then see which characteristics were associated with teachers whose students either achieved the most or were the most motivated to learn. (To do this, of course, you would have to decide how to assess achievement and motivation.) You could identify teachers whose students, year after year, learned more than students working with other teachers; then you could watch the more successful teachers, and note what they do. You might also train teachers to apply several different strategies to teach the same lesson and then determine which strategy led to the greatest student learning. You could videotape teachers, then ask them to view the tapes and report what they were thinking about as they taught and what influenced their decisions while teaching. You might study transcripts of classroom dialogue to learn what helped students understand.

All these approaches and more have been used to investigate teaching (Floden, 2001). Often researchers use the relationships identified between teaching and learning as the basis for developing teaching approaches and testing these approaches in design experiments (Brown, 1992; Greeno, Collins, and Resnick, 1996). Let's examine some of the specific knowledge about teaching gained from these projects.

Characteristics of Effective Teachers

Think about the most effective teacher you ever had—the one that you learned the most from. What were the characteristics of that person? What made that teacher so effective?

Some of the earliest research on effective teaching focused on the personal qualities of the teachers themselves (Medley, 1979). Results revealed some lessons about three teacher characteristics: knowledge, clarity, and warmth.

CONNECT & EXTEND

TO OTHER CHAPTERS
See Chapter 1 for a complete discussion of Darling-Hammond's study of teacher quality.

Teachers' Knowledge. Do teachers who know more about their subject have a more positive impact on their students? When we look at teachers' knowledge of facts and concepts, as measured by test scores and college grades, the relationship to student learning is unclear and may be indirect. Teachers who know more facts about their subject do not necessarily have students who learn more. But teachers who know more may make clearer presentations and recognize student difficulties more readily. They are ready for any student questions and do not have to be evasive or vague in their answers. And we know from Linda Darling-Hammond's (2000) work that the quality of teachers—as measured by whether the teachers were fully certified and had a major in their teaching field—is related to student performance. Thus, knowledge is necessary but not sufficient for effective teaching because being more knowledgeable helps teachers be clearer and more organized.

Clarity and Organization. When Barak Rosenshine and Norma Furst (1973) reviewed about 50 studies of teaching, they concluded that clarity was the most promising teacher behavior for future research on effective teaching. Teachers who provide clear presentations and explanations tend to have students who learn more and who rate their teachers more positively (Hines, Cruickshank, & Kennedy, 1985; Land, 1987). Teachers with more knowledge of the subject tend to be less vague in their

Effective teachers know how to transform their knowledge into examples, explanations, illustrations, and activities.

explanations to the class. The less vague the teacher, the more the students learn (Land, 1987). See the *Guidelines* on page 442 for ideas about how to be clear and organized in your teaching (Berliner, 1987; Evertson et al., 2003).

Warmth and Enthusiasm. As you are well aware, some teachers are much more enthusiastic than others. Some studies have found that ratings of teachers' enthusiasm for their subject are correlated with student achievement gains (Rosenshine & Furst, 1973). Warmth, friendliness, and understanding seem to be the teacher traits most strongly related to student attitudes (Murray, 1983; Ryans, 1960; Soar & Soar, 1979). In other words, teachers who are warm and friendly tend to have students who like them and the class in general. But notice, these are correlational studies. The results do not tell us that teacher enthusiasm causes student learning or that warmth causes positive attitudes, only that the two variables tend to occur together. Teachers trained to demonstrate their enthusiasm have students who are more attentive and involved, but not necessarily more successful on tests of content (Gillett & Gall, 1982). The *Guidelines* on page 442 include some ideas for communicating warmth and enthusiasm.

Beyond these general characteristics, how can teachers design instruction? The following sections describe formats or strategies—building blocks that can be used to construct lessons and units. We begin with the strategy many people associate most directly with teaching: direct instruction and explanation.

Explanation and Direct Instruction

Some studies have found that teachers' presentations take up one-sixth to one-fourth of all classroom time. Teacher explanation is appropriate for communicating a large amount of material to many students in a short period of time, introducing a new topic, giving background information, or motivating students to learn more on their own. Teacher presentations are therefore most appropriate for cognitive and affective objectives at the lower levels of the taxonomies described earlier: for remembering, understanding, applying, receiving, responding, and valuing (Arends, 2001; Kindsvatter, Wilen, & Ishler, 1992).

Direct Instruction. In the 1970s and 1980s, there was an explosion of research that focused on effective teaching. The results of all this work identified a model of

GUIDELINES Teaching Effectively

Organize your lessons carefully.

Examples

1. Provide objectives that help students focus on the purpose of the lesson.
2. Begin lessons by writing a brief outline on the board, or work on an outline with the class as part of the lesson.
3. If possible, break the presentation into clear steps or stages.
4. Review periodically.

Anticipate and plan for difficult parts in the lesson.

Examples

1. Plan a clear introduction to the lesson that tells students what they are going to learn and how they are going to learn it.
2. Do the exercises and anticipate student problems—consult the teachers' manual for ideas.
3. Have definitions ready for new terms, and prepare several relevant examples for concepts.
4. Think of analogies that will make ideas easier to understand.
5. Organize the lesson in a logical sequence; include checkpoints that incorporate oral or written questions or problems to make sure the students are following the explanations.

Strive for clear explanations.

Examples

1. Avoid vague words and ambiguous phrases: Steer clear of "the somes"—*something, someone, sometime, somehow;* "the not verys"—*not very much, not very well, not very hard, not very often;* and other unspecific fillers, such as *most, not all, sort of, and so on, of course, as you know, I guess, in fact, or whatever,* and *more or less.*
2. Use specific (and, if possible, colorful) names instead of *it, them,* and *thing.*
3. Refrain from using pet phrases such as *you know, like,* and *Okay?* Another idea is to record a lesson on tape to check yourself for clarity.
4. Give explanations at several levels so all students, not just the brightest, will understand.
5. Focus on one idea at a time and avoid digressions.

Make clear connections by using explanatory links such as because, if . . . then, or therefore.

Examples

1. "The North had an advantage in the Civil War because its economy was based on manufacturing."
2. Explanatory links are also helpful in labeling visual material such as graphs, concept maps, or illustrations.

Signal transitions from one major topic to another with phrases.

Examples

1. *"The next area . . . ," "Now we will turn to . . . ,"* or *"The second step is . . . ."*
2. Outline topics, listing key points, drawing concept maps on the board, or using an overhead projector.

Communicate an enthusiasm for your subject and the day's lesson.

Examples

1. Tell students why the lesson is important. Have a better reason than "This will be on the test" or "You will need to know it next year." Emphasize the value of the learning itself.
2. Be sure to make eye contact with the students.
3. Vary your pace and volume in speaking. Use silence for emphasis.

teaching that was related to improved student learning. Barak Rosenshine calls this approach **direct instruction** (1979) or **explicit teaching** (1986). Tom Good (1983a) uses the term **active teaching** for a similar approach.

The direct instruction model fits a specific set of circumstances because it was derived from a particular approach to research. Researchers identified the elements of direct instruction by comparing teachers whose students learned more than expected (based on entering knowledge) with teachers whose students performed at an expected or average level. The researchers focused on existing practices in American classrooms. Because the focus was on traditional forms of teaching, the research could not identify successful innovations. Effectiveness was usually defined as average improvement in standardized test scores for a whole class or school. So the results hold for large groups, but not necessarily for every student in the group. Even when the average achievement of a group improves, the achievement of some individuals may decline (Brophy & Good, 1986; Good, 1996; Shuell, 1996).

Given these conditions, you can see that direct instruction applies best to the teaching of **basic skills**—clearly structured knowledge and essential skills, such as science facts, mathematics computations, reading vocabulary, and grammar rules (Rosen-

CONNECT & EXTEND

TO YOUR TEACHING/PORTFOLIO
If you have observed in a primary grade, would you say that the teacher made use of direct instruction? Why or why not?

Direct instruction/explicit teaching Systematic instruction for mastery of basic skills, facts, and information.

Active teaching Teaching characterized by high levels of teacher explanation, demonstration, and interaction with students.

Basic skills Clearly structured knowledge that is needed for later learning and that can be taught step by step.

shine & Stevens, 1986). These skills involve tasks that are relatively unambiguous; they can be taught step-by-step and tested by standardized tests. The teaching approaches described below are not necessarily appropriate for objectives such as helping students to write creatively, solve complex problems, or mature emotionally. Weinert and Helmke (1995) describe direct instruction as having the following features:

> (a) the teacher's classroom management is especially effective and the rate of student interruptive behaviors is very low; (b) the teacher maintains a strong academic focus and uses available instructional time intensively to initiate and facilitate students' learning activities; (c) the teacher insures that as many students as possible achieve good learning progress by carefully choosing appropriate tasks, clearly presenting subject-matter information and solution strategies, continuously diagnosing each student's learning progress and learning difficulties, and providing effective help through remedial instruction. (p. 138)

How would a teacher turn these themes into actions?

Rosenshine's Six Teaching Functions. Rosenshine and his colleagues (Rosenshine, 1988; Rosenshine & Stevens, 1986) have identified six teaching functions based on the research on effective instruction. These could serve as a checklist or framework for teaching basic skills.

1. *Review and check the previous day's work.* Reteach if students misunderstood or made errors.
2. *Present new material.* Make the purpose clear, teach in small steps, and provide many examples and nonexamples.
3. *Provide guided practice.* Question students, give practice problems, and listen for misconceptions and misunderstandings. Reteach if necessary. Continue guided practice until students answer about 80% of the questions correctly.
4. *Give feedback and correctives* based on student answers. Reteach if necessary.
5. *Provide independent practice.* Let students apply the new learning on their own, in seatwork, cooperative groups, or homework. The success rate during independent practice should be about 95%. This means that students must be well prepared for the work by the presentation and guided practice and that assignments must not be too difficult. The point is for the students to practice until the skills become overlearned and automatic—until the students are confident. Hold students accountable for the work they do—check it.
6. *Review weekly and monthly* to consolidate learning. Include some review items as homework. Test often, and reteach material missed on the tests.

These six functions are not steps to be followed in a particular order, but all of them are elements of effective instruction. For example, feedback, review, or reteaching should occur whenever necessary and should match the abilities of the students. Also, keep in mind the age and prior knowledge of your students. The younger or the less prepared your students, the briefer your explanations should be. Use more and shorter cycles of presentation, guided practice, feedback, and correctives.

There are several other models of direct instruction, but most share the elements presented in Table 12.5 on page 444, which summarizes Madeline Hunter's Mastery Teaching (Hunter, 1982), another example of direct instruction.

CONNECT & EXTEND

TO THE RESEARCH

Madeline Hunter's approaches have been remarkably popular over the years, but they are not without their critics. See the November 1986 issue of *Elementary School Journal* for five articles on a four-year Madeline Hunter follow-through project. There are findings of quantitative and qualitative analysis, commentaries by Andrew Porter and Bob Slavin, and a response from Madeline Hunter. In general, the findings show some gains in the schools that used the Hunter program, but these gains were not maintained when consultation and support for the teachers were withdrawn in the final year of the program.

Why Does Direct Instruction Work? What aspects of direct instruction might explain its success? Linda Anderson (1989b) suggests that lessons that help students perceive links among main ideas will help them construct accurate understandings. Well-organized presentations, clear explanations, the use of explanatory links, and reviews as described in the clarity *Guidelines* on page 442, can all help students perceive connections among ideas. If done well, therefore, a direct instruction lesson could be a resource that students use to construct understanding. For example,

■ Table 12.5 The Hunter Mastery Teaching Program: Selected Principles

Get students set to learn.

- Make the best use of the prime time at the beginning of the lesson.
- Give students a review question or two to consider while you call the roll, pass out papers, or do other "housekeeping" chores. Follow up—listen to their answers, and correct if necessary.
- Create an *anticipatory set* to capture the students' attention. This might be an advance organizer, an intriguing question, or a brief exercise. For example, at the beginning of a lesson on categories of plants you could ask, "How is pumpkin pie similar to cherry pie but different from sweet potato pie?" Answer: Pumpkins and cherries are both fruits, unlike sweet potatoes.
- Communicate the lesson objectives (unless withholding this information for a while is part of your overall plan).

Provide information effectively.

- Determine the basic information and organize it. Use this basic structure as scaffolding for the lesson.
- Present information clearly and simply. Use familiar terms, examples, illustrations.
- Model what you mean. If appropriate, demonstrate or use analogies—"If the basketball Ann is holding were the sun, how far away do you think I would have to hold this pea to represent Pluto . . . ?"

Check for understanding, and give guided practice.

- Ask a question, and have every student signal an answer—"Thumbs up if this statement is true, down if it's false."
- Ask for a choral response: "Everyone, is this a dependent or an independent clause?"
- Sample individual responses: "Everyone, think of an example of a closed system. Jon, what's your example?"

Allow for independent practice.

- Get students started right by doing the first few questions together.
- Make independent practice brief. Monitor responses, giving feedback quickly.

reviews activate prior knowledge, so the student is ready to understand. Brief, clear presentations and guided practice avoid overloading the students' information processing systems and taxing their working memories. Numerous examples and explanations give many pathways and associations for building networks of concepts. Guided practice can also give the teacher a snapshot of the students' thinking as well as their misconceptions, so these can be addressed directly as misconceptions rather than simply as "wrong answers."

Every subject, even college English or chemistry, can require some direct instruction. Noddings (1990) reminds teachers that students may need some direct instruction in how to use various manipulative materials to get the possible benefits from them. Students working in cooperative groups may need guidance, modeling, and practice in how to ask questions and give explanations. And to solve difficult problems, students may need some direct instruction in possible problem-solving strategies.

Criticisms of Direct Instruction. Direct instruction, particularly when it involves extended teacher presentations or lectures, has some disadvantages. You may find that some students have trouble listening for more than a few minutes at a time and that they simply tune you out. Teacher presentations can put the students in a passive position by doing much of the cognitive work for them and may prevent students from asking or even thinking of questions (Freiberg & Driscoll, 1996; Gilstrap & Martin, 1975). **Scripted cooperation** is one way of incorporating active learning into lectures. Several times during the presentation, the teacher asks students to work in pairs. One person is the summarizer and the other critiques the summary. This gives students a chance to check their understanding, organize their thinking, and translate ideas into their own words. Other possibilities are described in Table 12.6.

Critics also claim that direct instruction is based on a the *wrong* theory of learning. Teachers break material into small segments, present each segment clearly, and reinforce or correct, thus *transmitting* accurate understandings from teacher to student. The student is seen as an "empty vessel" waiting to be filled with knowledge, rather than an active constructor of knowledge (Anderson, 1989a; Berg & Clough, 1991; Davis, Maher, & Noddings, 1990). These criticisms of direct instruction echo the criticisms of behavioral learning theories.

CONNECT & EXTEND

TO THE RESEARCH

For another perspective, read Berg, C. A., & Clough, M. (1991). Hunter lesson design: The wrong one for science teaching. *Educational Leadership, 48*(4), 73–78. *Focus Questions:* Why do Berg and Clough believe that the Hunter design is the wrong one for science teaching? How do students think Hunter would react? Then read Hunter, M. (1991). Hunter design helps achieve the goals of science instruction. *Educational Leadership, 48*(4), 79–81. *Focus Questions:* Evaluate Hunter's defense of her model. Do you agree that the Hunter approach can achieve the goals of science instruction?

Scripted cooperation Learning strategy in which two students take turns summarizing material and criticizing the summaries.

Table 12.6 Active Learning and Teacher Presentations

Here are some ideas for keeping students cognitively engaged in lessons. They can be adapted for many ages.

Question, All Write: Pose a question, ask everyone to jot an answer, then ask, "How many students would be willing to share their thoughts?"

Outcome Sentences: After a segment of presentation, ask students to finish a sentence such as "I learned . . . , I'm beginning to wonder . . . , I was surprised. . . ." Share as above. Students may keep their outcome sentences in a learning log or portfolio.

Underexplain with Learning Pairs: Give a brief explanation, then ask students to work in pairs to figure out the process or idea.

Voting: Ask "How many of you . . ." questions and take a count. "How many of you agree with Raschon?" "How many of you are ready to move on?" "How many of you got 48 on this problem?"

Choral Response: Have the whole class restate in unison important facts and ideas, such as "The environment is one whole system" or "A 10-sided polygon is called a decagon."

Speak-Write: Tell students you will speak briefly, for 3 or 4 minutes. They are to listen, but not take notes. At the end of the time, ask them to write the main ideas, a summary, or questions they have about what you said.

SOURCE: From *Inspiring Active Learning: A Handbook for Teachers,* by M. Harmin. Copyright © 1994 by the Association for Supervision and Curriculum Development. Reprinted with permission from the ASCD.

There is ample evidence, however, that direct instruction and explanation can help students learn actively, not passively (Leinhardt, 2001). For younger and less prepared learners, student-controlled learning without teacher direction and instruction can lead to systematic deficits in the students' knowledge. Without guidance, the understandings that students construct can be incomplete and misleading (Weinert & Helmke, 1995). Deep understanding and fluid performance—whether in dance or mathematical problem solving or reading—require models of expert performance and extensive practice with feedback (Anderson, Reder, & Simon, 1995). Guided and independent practice with feedback are at the heart of the direct instruction model.

The message for teachers is to match instructional methods to learning goals.

Seatwork and Homework

Think back to your elementary and high school days. Do you remember any homework assignments? What sticks in your mind about those assignments?

There is little research on the effects of **seatwork,** or independent classroom-desk work, but it is clear that this technique is often overused. In fact, a study found that American elementary students spend 51% of mathematics time in school working alone, while Japanese students spend 26% and Taiwanese students spend only 9% (Stigler, Lee, & Stevenson, 1987). Some educators point to these differences as part of the explanation for Asian students' superiority in mathematics.

Seatwork. Seatwork should follow up a lesson and give students supervised practice. It should not be the main mode of instruction. Unfortunately, many workbook pages and "dittos" do little to support the learning of important objectives. Before you assign work, ask yourself, "Does doing this work help students learn anything that matters?" For example, consider this task, cited in the report of the Commission on Reading of the National Institute of Education (Anderson, Hiebert, Scott, & Wilkinson, 1985):

> Read each sentence. Decide which consonant letter is used the most. Underline it each time.

What's the point? This sort of activity communicates to students that reading isn't very important or useful. Students should see the connection between the seatwork and the lesson. Tell them why they are doing the work. The objectives should be clear, all the materials that might be needed should be provided, and the work should be

CONNECT & EXTEND

TO YOUR TEACHING/PORTFOLIO Here are some more ideas for ways to involve all students actively in a lesson. Ask them to:

1. Tell the answer to a neighbor.
2. Summarize the main idea in one or two sentences, writing the summary on a piece of paper and sharing this with a neighbor, or repeat the procedures to a neighbor.
3. Write the answer on a slate, then hold up the slate.
4. Raise their hand if they know the answer (thereby allowing the teacher to check the entire class).
5. Raise their hand if they agree with an answer someone else gave.
6. Raise different colored cards when the answer is a, b, or c.

SOURCE: Taken from Rosenshine, B. (1987). Explicit teaching. In D. Berliner & B. Rosenshine (Eds.), *Talks to teachers* (pp. 75–92). New York: Random House, p. 84.

Seatwork Independent classroom work.

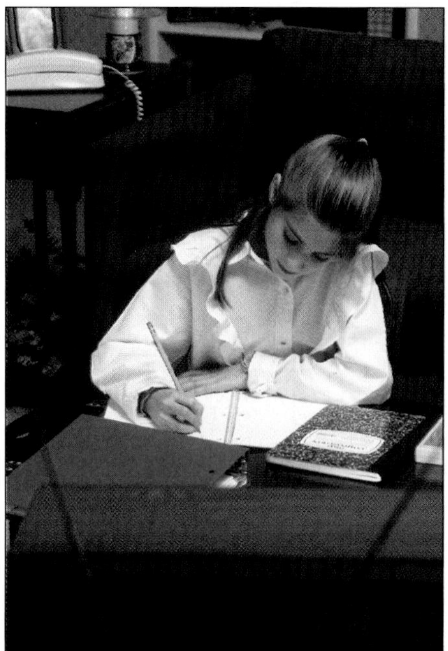

In order to make homework valuable, students must understand the assignment, especially since they may not always have someone at home to consult if they encounter problems.

easy enough that students can succeed on their own. Success rates should be high—near 100%. When seatwork is too difficult, students often resort to guessing or copying just to finish (Anderson, 1985).

Carol Weinstein and Andy Mignano (2003) describe several alternatives to workbooks and dittos, such as reading silently and reading aloud to a partner; writing for a "real" audience; writing letters or journals; transcribing conversations and punctuating them properly; making up problems; working on long-term projects and reports; solving brainteasers and puzzles; and engaging in computer activities. One of my favorites is creating a group story. Two students begin a story on the computer. Then two more add a paragraph. The story grows with each new pair's addition. The students are reading and writing, editing and improving.

Homework. In contrast to the limited research on seatwork, educators have been studying the effects of homework for over 75 years (Cooper & Valentine, 2001a, 2001b; Corno, 2000). As you can see from the *Point/Counterpoint* there continues to be a debate about the value of homework.

To benefit from individual or group seatwork or homework, students must stay involved and do the work. The first step toward involvement is getting students started correctly by making sure they understand the assignment. It may help to do the first few questions as a class, to clear up any misconceptions. This is especially important for homework assignments, because students may have no one at home to consult if they have problems with the assignment. A second way to keep students involved is to hold them accountable for completing the work correctly, not just for filling in the page. This means the work should be checked, the students given a chance to correct the errors or revise work, and the results counted toward the class grade (Brophy & Good, 1986). Expert teachers often have ways of correcting homework quickly during the first minutes of class by having students check each other's or their own work.

CONNECT & EXTEND

TO THE RESEARCH

For a current look at the research on homework, see Cooper, H., & Valentine, J. C. (Eds.) (2001). Special Issue: Homework. *Educational Psychologist, 36*(3), Summer. There are articles about parent involvement in homework, homework for students with learning disabilities, and students' views of homework.

Making Seatwork and Homework Valuable. Seatwork particularly requires careful monitoring. Being available to students doing seatwork is more effective than offering students help before they ask for it. To be available, you should move around the class and avoid spending too much time with one or two students. Short, frequent contacts are best (Brophy & Good, 1986; Rosenshine, 1977). Sometimes you may be working with a small group while other students do seatwork. In these situations it is especially important for students to know what to do if they need help. One expert teacher described by Weinstein and Mignano (2003) taught students a rule, "Ask three, then me." Students have to consult three classmates before seeking help from the teacher. This teacher also spends time early in the year showing students *how* to help each other—how to ask questions and how to explain.

AGNES

Agnes has her own ways of making homework valuable.

Point/Counterpoint — Is Homework a Valuable Use of Time?

Like so many methods in education, homework has moved in and out of favor. In the early 1900s, homework was seen as an important path to mental discipline, but by the 1940s, homework was criticized as too much drill and low-level learning. Then in the 1950s, homework was rediscovered as a way to catch up with the Soviet Union in science and mathematics, only to be seen as too much pressure on students during the more laid-back 1960s. By the 1980s, homework was in again as a way to improve the standing of American children compared to students around the world (Cooper & Valentine, 2001). Everyone has done homework—were those hours well spent?

Point

Homework does not help students learn.
No matter how interesting an activity is, students will eventually get bored with it—so why give them work both in and out of school? They will simply grow weary of learning. And important opportunities are lost for community involvement or leisure activities that would create well-rounded citizens. When parents help with homework, they can do more harm than good—sometimes confusing their children or teaching them incorrectly. And students from poorer families often must work, so they miss doing the homework; then the learning discrepancy between the rich and poor grows even greater. Besides, the research is inconsistent about the effects of homework. For example, one study found that in-class work was better than homework in helping elementary students learn (Cooper & Valentine, 2001).

Counterpoint

Well-planned homework can work for many students.
Harris Cooper and Jeffrey Valentine reviewed many studies of homework and concluded that there is little relationship between homework and learning for young students, but the relationship between homework and achievement grows progressively stronger for older students. There is recent evidence that students in high school who do more homework (and watch less television after school) have higher grades, even when other factors such as gender, grade level, ethnicity, SES, and amount of adult supervision are taken into consideration (Cooper & Valentine, 2001; Cooper, Valentine, Nye, & Lindsay, 1999). Consistent with these findings, the National PTA makes these recommendations:

> *[F]or children in grades K–2, homework is most effective when it does not exceed 10–20 minutes each day; older students, in grades 3–6, can handle 30–60 minutes a day; in junior and senior high school, the amount of homework will vary by subject. (Henderson, 1996, p. 1)*

What do you think? Vote online at **www.ablongman.com/woolfolk**

What about monitoring homework? If students get stuck on homework, they need help at home, someone who can scaffold their work without just "giving the answer" (Pressley, 1995). But many parents don't know how to help (Hoover-Dempsey et al., 2001; Hoover-Dempsey, Bassler, & Burow, 1995). The *Family and Community Partnerships Guidelines* on page 448 give ideas for helping parents help with homework.

Questioning and Recitation

Teachers pose questions, students answer. This form of teaching, sometimes called *recitation,* has been with us for many years (Stodolsky, 1988). The teacher's questions develop a framework for the subject matter involved. The pattern from the teacher's point of view consists of *initiation* (teacher asks questions), *response* (student answers), and *reaction* (praising, correcting, probing or expanding) or IRE (Burbules & Bruce, 2001). These steps are repeated over and over.

Let us consider the heart of recitation, the soliciting or *questioning* phase. Effective questioning techniques may be among the most powerful tools that teachers employ during lessons. An essential element of innovations such as cognitive apprenticeships, peer learning techniques, authentic learning activities, and nearly all other contemporary learning techniques is keeping students cognitively engaged—and that is where skillful questioning strategies are especially effective. Questions play several roles in cognition. They can help students rehearse information for effective

CONNECT & EXTEND

TO PRAXIS™
QUESTIONING (III, C)
Effective questioning skills are among the most valuable skills that a teacher can possess—and among the more difficult to develop. For guidance on asking effective questions in the classroom, read *Question Types* (http://www.unl.edu/teaching/teachquestions.html).

Family and Community Partnerships

Homework

Make sure families know what students are expected to learn.

Examples

1. At the beginning of a unit, send home a list of the main objectives, examples of major assignments, key due dates, a homework "calendar," and a list of resources available free at libraries or on the Internet.
2. Provide a clear, concise description of your homework policy—how homework is counted toward class grades; consequences for late, forgotten, or missing homework, etc.

Help families find a comfortable and helpful role in their child's homework.

Examples

1. Remind families that "helping with homework" means encouraging, listening, monitoring, praising, discussing, brainstorming—not necessarily teaching and never doing the work for their child.
2. Encourage families to set aside a quiet time and place for everyone in the family to study. Make this time a regular part of the daily routine.
3. Have some homework assignments that are fun and involve the whole family—puzzles, family albums, watching a television program together and doing a "review."
4. At parent-teacher conferences, ask families what they need to play a more helpful role in their child's homework. Check lists? Background reading? Websites? Explanations of study skills?

Solicit and use suggestions from families about homework.

Examples

1. Find out what responsibilities the child has at home—how much time is available for homework.
2. Periodically, have a "homework hotline" for call-in questions and suggestions.

If no one is at home to help with homework, set up other support systems.

Examples

1. Assign study buddies who can be available over the phone.
2. If students have computers, provide lists of Internet help lines.
3. Locate free help in public libraries and make these resources known.

Take advantage of family and community "funds of knowledge" to connect homework with life in the community and life in the community with lessons in school (Moll et al., 1992).

Examples

1. Create class lesson about how family members use math and reading in sewing and in housing construction (Epstein & Van Voorhis, 2001)
2. Design interactive homework projects that families do together to evaluate needed products for their home, for example, deciding on the best buy on shampoo or paper towels.

recall. They can work to identify gaps in one's knowledge base, and provoke curiosity and long-term interest. They can initiate cognitive conflict and promote the disequilibrium that results in a changed knowledge structure. They can serve as cues, tips, or reminders as an expert guides a novice in a learning experience. And students as well as teachers should learn to question effectively. I tell my students that the first step in doing a good research project is asking a good question.

For now we will focus on teachers' questions, to make them as helpful as possible for students. Many of the beginning teachers I work with are surprised to discover how valuable good questions can be and how difficult they are to create.

Think back to your most recent class. What kinds of questions does your professor ask? What sort of thinking is required to answer the questions? Remembering, understanding, applying, analyzing, evaluating, or creating? How long does the professor wait for an answer?

Kinds of Questions. Some educators have estimated the typical teacher asks between 30 and 120 question an hour, or about 1,5000,000 questions over a teaching career (Sadker & Sadker, 2003). What are these questions like? Many can be categorized in terms of Bloom's taxonomy of objectives in the cognitive domain. Table 12.7 offers examples of questions at the different taxonomic levels.

Table 12.7 Classroom Questions for Objectives in the Cognitive Domain

Questions can be posed that encourage thinking at every level of Bloom's taxonomy in the cognitive domain. Of course, the thinking required depends on what has gone before in the discussion.

Category	Type of Thinking Expected	Examples
Knowledge (Remembering)	Recalling or recognizing information as learned	Define . . . . What is the capital of . . . ? What did the text say about . . . ?
Comprehension (Understanding)	Demonstrating understanding of the materials; transforming, reorganizing, or interpreting	Explain in your own words . . . . Compare. . . . What is the main idea of . . . ? Describe what you saw . . . .
Application (Applying)	Using information to solve a problem with a single correct answer	Which principle is demonstrated in . . . ? Calculate the area of . . . . Apply the rule of . . . to solve . . . .
Analysis (Analyzing)	Critical thinking; identifying reasons and motives; making inferences based on specific data; analyzing conclusions to see if supported by evidence	What influenced the writings of . . . ? Why was Washington, D.C. chosen . . . ? Which of the following are facts and which are opinions . . . ? Based on your experiment, what is the chemical . . . ?
Synthesis (Creating)	Divergent, original thinking; original plan, proposal, design, or story	What's a good name for . . . ? How could we raise money for . . . ? What would the United States be like if the South had won . . . ?
Evaluation (Evaluating)	Judging the merits of ideas, offering opinions, applying standards	Which U.S. senator is the most effective? Which painting do you believe to be better? Why? Why would you favor . . . ?

SOURCE: From "Questioning Skills" by M. Sadker and D. Sadker, in J. Cooper (Ed.), *Classroom Teaching Skills: A Handbook* (3rd ed.) (pp. 143–160), 1986, Boston: D. C. Heath. Copyright © 1986 D. C. Heath. Adapted with permission.

Another way to categorize questioning is in terms of **convergent questions** (only one right answer) or **divergent questions** (many possible answers). Questions about concrete facts are convergent: "Who ruled England in 1540?" "Who wrote the original Peter Pan?" Questions dealing with opinions or hypotheses are divergent: "In this story, which character is most like you and why?" "In 100 years, which of the past five presidents will be most admired?"

Quite a bit of space in education textbooks has been devoted to urging teachers to ask a greater number of higher-level (analyzing, evaluating, and creating) and divergent questions. Is this really a better way of questioning? Research has provided several surprises.

Fitting the Questions to the Students. Both high- and low-level questions can be effective (Barden, 1995; Redfield & Rousseau, 1981). Different patterns seem to be better for different students, however. The best pattern for younger students and for lower-ability students of all ages is simple questions that allow a high percentage of correct answers, ample encouragement, help when the student does not have the correct answer, and praise. For high-ability students, the successful pattern includes harder questions at both higher and lower levels and more critical feedback (Berliner, 1987; Good, 1988; Sadker & Sadker, 2003).

Whatever their age or ability, all students should have some experience with thought-provoking questions and, if necessary, help in learning how to answer them. As we saw in Chapter 8, to master critical thinking and problem-solving skills, students must have a chance to practice the skills. They also need time to think about

Convergent questions Questions that have a single correct answer.

Divergent questions Questions that have no single correct answer.

their answers. But research shows that teachers wait an average of only one second for students to answer (Rowe, 1974). Consider the following slice of classroom life (Sadker & Sadker, 2003, p. 128):

> **Teacher:** Who wrote the poem "Stopping by Woods on a Snowy Evening"? Tom?
>
> **Tom:** Robert Frost.
>
> **Teacher:** Good. What action takes place in the poem? Sally?
>
> **Sally:** A man stops his sleigh to watch the woods get filled with snow.
>
> **Teacher:** Yes. Emma, what thoughts go through the man's mind?
>
> **Emma:** He thinks how beautiful the woods are . . . (She pauses for a second.)
>
> **Teacher:** What else does he think about? Joe?
>
> **Joe:** He thinks how he would like to stay and watch. (Pauses for a second.)
>
> **Teacher:** Yes—and what else? Rita? (Waits half a second.) Come on, Rita, you can get the answer to this. (Waits half a second.) Well, why does he feel he can't stay there indefinitely and watch the woods and the snow?
>
> **Sarah:** Well, I think it might be—(Pauses a second.)
>
> **Teacher:** Think, Sarah. (Teacher waits for half a second.) All right then—Mike? (Waits again for half a second.) John? (Waits half a second.) What's the matter with everyone today? Didn't you do the reading?

Very little thoughtful responding can take place in this situation. When teachers learn to pose a question, then wait at least 3 to 5 seconds before calling on a student to answer, students tend to give longer answers; more students are likely to participate, ask questions, and volunteer appropriate answers; student comments involving analysis, synthesis, inference, and speculation tend to increase; and the students generally appear more confident in their answers (Berliner, 1987; Rowe, 1974; Sadker & Sadker, 2003; Tobin, 1987).

This seems like a simple improvement in teaching, but 5 seconds of silence is not that easy to handle. It takes practice. You might try asking students to jot down ideas or even discuss the question with another student and formulate an answer together. This makes the wait more comfortable and gives students a chance to think. Of course, if it is clear that students are lost or don't understand the question, waiting longer will not help. When your question is met with blank stares, rephrase the question or ask if anyone can explain the confusion. However, there is some evidence that extending wait times does not affect learning in university classes (Duell, 1994), so with advanced high school students, you might conduct your own evaluation of wait time.

A word about selecting students to answer questions. If you call only on volunteers, then you may get the wrong idea about how well students understand the material. Also, the same people volunteer over and over again. Many expert teachers have some systematic way of making sure that they call on everyone: They pull names from a jar or check names off a list as each student speaks (Weinstein, 2003; Weinstein & Mignano, 2003). Another possibility is to put each student's name on an index card, then shuffle the cards and go through the deck as you call on people. You can use the card to make notes about the quality of students' answers or extra help they may need.

Responding to Student Answers. What do you do after the student answers? The most common response, occurring about 50% of the time in most classrooms, is simple acceptance—"OK" or "Uh-huh" (Sadker & Sadker, 2003). But there are better reactions, depending on whether the student's answer is correct, partially correct, or wrong. If the answer is quick, firm, and correct, simply accept the answer or ask another question. If the answer is correct but hesitant, give the student feedback about why the answer is correct: "That's right, Chris, the Senate is part of the legislative branch of government because the Senate. . . ." This allows you to explain the material again. If this student is unsure, others may be confused as well. If the answer is partially or completely wrong but the student has made an honest attempt, you should probe for more information, give clues, simplify the question, review the previous steps, or reteach the material. If the student's wrong answer is silly or careless, however, it is better simply to correct the answer and go on. (Good, 1988; Rosenshine & Stevens, 1986).

Group Discussion

Group discussion is in some ways similar to the recitation strategy, but should be more like the instructional conversations described in Chapter 9 (Tharp & Gallimore, 1991). A teacher may pose questions, listen to student answers, react, and probe for more information, but in a true group dialogue, the teacher does not have a dominant role. Students ask questions, answer each other's questions, and respond to each other's answers (Beck, McKeown, Worthy, Sandora, & Kucan, 1996; Burbules & Bruce, 2001; Parker & Hess, 2001).

There are many advantages to group discussions. The students are directly involved and have the chance to participate. Group discussion helps students learn to express themselves clearly, to justify opinions, and to tolerate different views. Group discussion also gives students a chance to ask for clarification, examine their own thinking, follow personal interests, and assume responsibility by taking leadership roles in the group. Thus, group discussions help students evaluate ideas and synthesize personal viewpoints. Discussions are also useful when students are trying to understand difficult concepts that go against common sense. As we saw in Chapters 8 and 9, many scientific concepts, such as the role of light in vision or Newton's laws of motion, are difficult to grasp because they contradict commonsense notions. By thinking together, challenging each other, and suggesting and evaluating possible explanations, students are more likely to reach a genuine understanding.

Of course, there are disadvantages. Class discussions are quite unpredictable and may easily digress into exchanges of ignorance. Some members of the group may have great difficulty participating and may become anxious if forced to speak. In addition, you may have to do a good deal of preparation to ensure that participants have a background of knowledge on which to base the discussion. And large groups are often unwieldy. In many cases, a few students will dominate the discussion while the others daydream (Arends, 2001; Kindsvatter, Wilen, & Ishler, 1988). The *Guidelines* on page 452 give some ideas for facilitating a productive group discussion.

Check Yourself What methods have been used to study teaching?

What are the general characteristics of good teaching?

What is direct instruction?

Distinguish between convergent and divergent and high-level versus low-level questions.

How can wait time affect student learning?

What are the uses and disadvantages of group discussion?

As you continue in teaching, you can continue to develop your questioning expertise.

Group discussion Conversation in which the teacher does not have the dominant role; students pose and answer their own questions.

GUIDELINES Productive Group Discussions

Invite shy children to participate.

Examples

1. "What's your opinion, Joel?" or "Does anyone have another opinion?"
2. Don't wait until there is a deadly silence to ask shy students to reply. Most people, even those who are confident, hate to break a silence.

Direct student comments and questions back to another student.

Examples

1. "That's an unusual idea, Steve. Kim, what do you think of Steve's idea?"
2. "That's an important question, John. Maura, do you have any thoughts about how you'd answer that?
3. Encourage students to look at and talk to one another rather than wait for your opinion.

Make sure that you understand what a student has said. If you are unsure, other students may be unsure as well.

Examples

1. Ask a second student to summarize what the first student said; then the first student can try again to explain if the summary is incorrect.
2. "Karen, I think you're saying. . . . Is that right, or have I misunderstood?"

Probe for more information.

Examples

1. "That's a strong statement. Do you have any evidence to back it up?"
2. "Tell us how you reached that conclusion. What steps did you go through?"

Bring the discussion back to the subject.

Examples

1. "Let's see, we were discussing . . . and Sarah made one suggestion. Does anyone have a different idea?"
2. "Before we continue, let me try to summarize what has happened thus far."

Give time for thought before asking for responses.

Examples

1. "How would your life be different if television had never been invented? Jot down your ideas on paper, and we will share reactions in a minute." After a minute: "Hiromi, will you tell us what you wrote?"

When a student finishes speaking, look around the room to judge reactions.

Examples

1. If other students look puzzled, ask them to describe why they are confused.
2. If students are nodding assent, ask them to give an example of what was just said.

Enhancing Your Expertise with Technology

Questioning Techniques

Andrew was marking his 30th year as an administrator in his K–12 school district. He had hired and supervised hundreds of teachers at every level, kindergarten through 12th grade. He had chaired dozens of committees that worked to keep the district current with modern curriculum standards, effective academic programs, and innovative instructional strategies. Early in his administrative career, Andrew observed that one of the major characteristics of expert teachers—whether they ran a teacher-centered classroom or a student-centered classroom—was the effective use of questions during lessons or learning activities. As he developed his expertise as an administrator, Andrew began to devote at least some part of a job interview with a prospective teacher or a post-observation teacher conference to questioning techniques and strategies.

The complex nature of questions and questioning techniques and strategies is reflected in the number of potential "hits" a search engine will provide for those terms. (You will also find that many of the pages and sites are designed for the corporate world. Questioning techniques are important for the employee selection process, planning business strategies, and for determining the needs of customers.) The two sites discussed here focus on different aspects of questioning, and they complement each other well. The Questioning Toolkit (http://www.fno.org/nov97/toolkit.html) sponsored by *The Educational Technology Journal* defines and illustrates the many types of questions that arise in classroom discourse. It examines the different tasks that different kinds of questions can accomplish. For example, in a stimulating learning environment, students and teachers are likely to pose a variety of organizing, hypothetical, probing, planning, and provocative questions. Expert use of the different types of questions can significantly enhance the level of cognitive activity of all those involved.

The University of Illinois at Champaign-Urbana offers an online booklet titled *Effective Classroom Questioning* (http://www.unl.edu/teaching/teachquestions.html). This booklet focuses on the use of questions as they pertain to Bloom's Taxonomy, explains the differences between open and closed questions, and higher and lower order questions. It has an excellent section that considers important components of questioning such as wait time, instructor attitude, and tips for maximizing student participation.

While we are focusing on the teacher, there is one more characteristic that affects student learning—the teacher's beliefs about the students.

Teacher Expectations

CONNECT & EXTEND

TO THE RESEARCH
Babad, E. (1995). The "Teacher's Pet" phenomenon, students' perceptions of differential behavior, and students' morale. *Journal of Educational Psychology, 87,* 361–374.

Over 30 years ago, a study by Robert Rosenthal and Lenore Jacobson (1968) captured the attention of the national media in a way that few studies by psychologists have since then. The study also caused great controversy within the professional community. Debate about the meaning of the results continues (Babad, 1995; Brophy, 1982; Good, 1988; Rosenthal, 1987, 1995; Snow, 1995).

What did Rosenthal and Jacobson say that caused such a stir? They chose several students at random in a number of elementary school classrooms, and then told the teachers that these students probably would make significant intellectual gains during the year. The students did indeed make larger gains than normal that year. The researchers presented data suggesting the existence of a "**Pygmalion effect**" or self-fulfilling prophecy in the classroom. A **self-fulfilling prophecy** is a groundless expectation that leads to behaviors that then make the original expectation come true (Merton, 1948). An example is a false belief that a bank is failing, leading to a rush to withdraw money, that then causes the bank to fail as expected.

Two Kinds of Expectation Effects

When you thought about the most effective teacher you ever had, was one of the characteristics that the teacher believed in you or demanded the best from you? How did the teacher communicate that belief?

CONNECT & EXTEND

TO THE RESEARCH
Is there any reason why teachers should not have high expectations for all of their students? What about the distinction between "high expectations" and "reasonable expectations"?

Actually, two kinds of expectation effects can occur in classrooms. In the self-fulfilling prophecy described above, the teacher's beliefs about the students' abilities have no basis in fact, but student behavior comes to match the initially inaccurate expectation. The second kind of expectation effect occurs when teachers are fairly accurate in their initial reading of students' abilities and respond to students appropriately. So far, so good. There is nothing wrong with forming and acting on accurate estimates of student ability. The problems arise when students show some improvement but teachers do not alter their expectations to take account of the improvement. This is called a **sustaining expectation effect,** because the teacher's unchanging expectation sustains the student's achievement at the expected level. The chance to raise expectations, provide more appropriate teaching, and thus encourage greater student achievement is lost. In practice, self-fulfilling prophecy effects seem to be stronger in the early grades and sustaining effects are more likely in the later grades (Kuklinski & Weinstein, 2001). And some students are more likely than others to be the recipients of sustaining expectations. For example, withdrawn children provide little information about themselves, so teachers may sustain their expectations about these children for lack of new input (Jones & Gerig, 1994).

Pygmalion effect Exceptional progress by a student as a result of high teacher expectations for that student; named for mythological king, Pygmalion, who made a statue, then caused it to be brought to life.

Self-fulfilling prophecy A groundless expectation that is confirmed because it has been expected.

Sustaining expectation effect Student performance maintained at a certain level because teachers don't recognize improvements.

Students' extracurricular activities can be sources of expectations. Teachers tend to hold higher expectations for students who participate in extracurricular activities than for students who "just hang out" after school.

Sources of Expectations

There are many possible sources of teachers' expectations (Van Matre, Valentine, & Cooper, 2000). Intelligence test scores are an obvious source, especially if teachers do not interpret the scores appropriately. Sex also influences teachers; most teachers expect more behavior problems from boys than from girls, and may have higher academic expectations for girls. The notes from previous teachers and the medical or psychological reports found in cumulative folders (permanent record files) are another obvious source of expectations. Knowledge of ethnic background also seems to have an influence, as does knowledge of older brothers and sisters. Teachers hold higher expectations for attractive students. Previous achievement, socioeconomic class, and the actual behaviors of the student are also often used as sources of information. Even the student's after-school activities can be a source of expectations. Teachers tend to hold higher expectations for students who participate in extra-curricular activities than for students who do nothing after school.

CONNECT & EXTEND

TO YOUR TEACHING/PORTFOLIO
Should you read your students' cumulative folders at the beginning of the school year? If so, how can you keep from forming low expectations?

Expectations and beliefs focus attention and organize memory, so teachers may pay attention to and remember the information that fits the initial expectations (Fiske, 1993; Hewstone, 1989). Even when student performance does not fit expectations, the teacher may rationalize and attribute the performance to external causes beyond the student's control. For example, a teacher may assume that the low-ability student who did well on a test must have cheated and that the high-ability student who failed must have been upset that day. In both cases, behavior that seems out of character is dismissed. It may take many instances of supposedly uncharacteristic behavior to change the teacher's beliefs about a particular student's abilities. Thus, expectations often remain in the face of contradictory evidence (Brophy, 1982, 1998).

Do Teachers' Expectations Really Affect Students' Achievement?

CONNECT & EXTEND

TO THE RESEARCH
For a complete discussion of teacher expectations and student learning, see Good, T., & Brophy, J. (2003). *Looking in Classrooms* (9th ed.). Boston: Allyn & Bacon.

The answer to this question is more complicated than it might seem. There are two ways to investigate the question. One is to give teachers unfounded expectations about their students and note if these baseless expectations have any effects. The other approach is to identify the naturally occurring expectations of teachers and study the effects of these expectations. The answer to the question of whether teacher expectations affect student learning depends in part on which approach is taken to study the question.

The original Rosenthal and Jacobson experiment used the first approach—giving teachers groundless expectations and noting the effects. The study was heavily criticized for the experimental and statistical methods used (Elashoff & Snow, 1971; Snow, 1995; Weinberg, 1989). A careful analysis of the results revealed that even though 1st- through 6th-grade students participated in the study, the self-fulfilling prophecy effects could be traced to just five students in grades one and two who changed dramatically. When other researchers tried to replicate the study, they did not find evidence of a self-fulfilling prophecy effect, even for children in these lower grades (Claiborn, 1969; Wilkins & Glock, 1973). After reviewing the research on teacher expectations, Raudenbush (1984) concluded that these expectations have only a small effect on student IQ scores (the outcome measure used by Rosenthal and Jacobson) and only in the early years of a new school setting—in the first years of elementary school and then again in the first years of junior high school.

But what about the second approach—naturally occurring expectations? Research shows that teachers do indeed form beliefs about students' capabilities. Many of these beliefs are accurate assessments based on the best available data and are corrected as new information is collected. Even so, some teachers do favor certain students (Babad, 1995; Rosenthal, 1987). For example, in a study of 110 students followed from age 4 to age 18, Jennifer Alvidrez and Rhona Weinstein (1999) found that teachers tended to overestimate the abilities of preschool children they rated as independent and interesting and underestimate the abilities of children seen as immature and anxious. Teachers' judgments of student ability at age 4 predicted student grade-point average at age 18. The strongest predictions were for students whose abilities were *underestimated.* If teachers decide that some students are less able, and if the teachers lack effective strategies for working with lower-achieving students, then students may experience a double threat—low expectations and inadequate teaching (Good & Brophy, 2003). The power of the expectation effect depends on the age of the students (generally speaking, younger students are more susceptible) and on how differently a teacher treats high- versus low-expectation students, an issue we turn to next (Kuklinski & Weinstein, 2001).

The *Stories of Learning/Tributes to Teaching* feature gives an example of how a teacher's expectations changed a student's perceptions of his own capabilities.

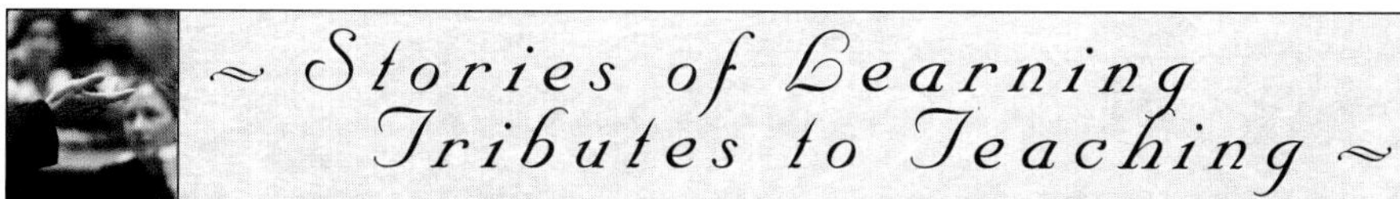

During my high school days I was a very unattentive, uninterested and underachieving student. At the beginning of my senior year I was assigned to an American history class taught by **Mrs. Field.** Although the building was old and the class was crowded, she clearly had great expectations for each student. If homework was not turned in, it was never a matter of if it would be turned in, but when. It could come in today or tomorrow, but it would come in. Mrs. Field thought we were better than we were, so we were.

One day she stopped me as I was leaving her class, waited until we were alone, looked deep in my eyes and said: "Bill Purkey, you can become a good student, I know you can." I made some sort of flip remark and went my way, but her words echoed again and again in my mind. Gradually, I began to risk some small effort in her class. Because of her belief in me, I began to put my mind in the path of learning. Perhaps she saw this as a small victory, but it was a major turning point in my life.

A dozen years later, when I received my doctorate from the University of Virginia, I made a special trip back to my old high school hoping to tell Mrs. Field what a difference she made in my life. When I arrived I learned that Mrs. Field had been killed in an automobile accident some months before. Today, when teachers tell me that there is little or nothing they can do, I tell them what I wanted to say to my most memorable teacher: "When you work with human beings, everything you do makes a difference, and every one of your accomplishments is major." There are no small victories, Mrs. Field.

—William Watson Purkey, Ed.D., LPC, Professor of Counselor Education,
University of North Carolina at Greensboro, Greensboro, North Carolina

SOURCE: From *Mentors, Masters, and Mrs. MacGregor* by J. Bluestein. Published by Health Communications. Copyright © 1995 by Health Communications. Adapted with permission of the publisher.

Table 12.8 Six Dimensions of Teaching That Can Communicate Expectations

Dimension	Students believed to be MORE capable have:	Students believed to be LESS capable have:
Task environment curriculum, procedures, task definition, pacing, qualities of environment	More opportunity to perform publicly on meaningful tasks	Less opportunity to perform publicly, especially on meaningful tasks (supplying alternate endings to a story vs. learning to pronounce a word correctly)
	More opportunity to think	Less opportunity to think, analyze (because much work is aimed at practice)
Grouping practices	More assignments that deal with comprehension, understanding (in higher-ability groups)	Less choice on curriculum assignments—more work on drill-like assignments because they are low achievers
Locus of responsibility for learning	More autonomy (more choice in assignments, fewer interruptions)	Less autonomy (frequent teacher monitoring of work, frequent interruptions)
Feedback and evaluation practices	More opportunity for self-evaluation	Less opportunity for self-evaluation
Motivational strategies	More honest/contingent feedback	Less honest/more gratuitous/less contingent feedback
Quality of teacher relationships	More respect for the learner as an individual with unique interests and needs	Less respect for the learner as an individual with unique interests and needs

SOURCE: From "Teacher Expectations: A Framework for Exploring Classrooms," by T. Good and R. Weinstein. In K. Zumwalt (Ed.), *Improving Teaching* (The ASCD 1986 Yearbook).

Teacher Behavior and Student Reaction

Table 12.8 shows six dimensions of teacher communication toward students that may be influenced by expectations. These dimensions include both instructional practices and interpersonal interactions.

Instructional Strategies. As we have seen, different grouping processes may well have a marked effect on students. And some teachers leave little to the imagination; they make their expectations all too clear. For example, Alloway (1984) recorded comments such as these directed to low-achieving groups:

"I'll be over to help you slow ones in a minute."

"The blue group will find this hard."

In these remarks the teacher not only tells the students that they lack ability, but also communicates that finishing the work, not understanding, is the goal.

Once teachers assign students to ability groups, they usually assign different learning activities. To the extent that teachers choose activities that challenge students and increase achievement, these differences are probably necessary. Activities become inappropriate, however, when students who are ready for more challenging work are not given the opportunity to try it because teachers believe they cannot handle it. This is an example of a sustaining expectation effect.

Teacher–Student Interactions. However the class is grouped and whatever the assignments, the quantity and the quality of teacher–student interactions are likely to affect the students. Students who are expected to achieve tend to be asked more and harder questions, to be given more chances and a longer time to respond, and to be interrupted less often than students who are expected to do poorly. Teachers also give these high-expectation students cues and prompts, communicating their belief that the students can answer the question (Allington, 1980; Good & Brophy, 2003; Rosenthal, 1995). When an answer on a test is "almost right," the teacher is more likely to give the benefit of the doubt (and thus the better grade) to high-achieving students (Finn, 1972). Teachers tend to smile at these students more often and show greater warmth through such nonverbal responses as leaning toward the students and nodding their heads as the students speak (Woolfolk & Brooks, 1983, 1985).

In contrast, with low-expectation students, teachers ask easier questions, allow less time for answering, and are less likely to give prompts. Teachers are more likely to respond with sympathetic acceptance or even praise to inadequate answers from low-achieving students, but to criticize these same students for wrong answers. Even more disturbing, low-achieving students receive less praise than high-achieving students for similar correct answers. This inconsistent feedback can be very confusing for low-ability students. Imagine how hard it would be to learn if your wrong answers were sometimes praised, sometimes ignored, and sometimes criticized, and your right answers received little recognition (Good 1983a, 1983b).

Of course, not all teachers form inappropriate expectations or act on their expectations in unconstructive ways (Babad, Inbar, & Rosenthal, 1982). But avoiding the problem may be more difficult than it seems. In general, low-expectation students also tend to be the most disruptive students. (Of course, low expectations can reinforce their desire to disrupt or misbehave.) Teachers may call on these students less, wait a shorter time for their answers, and give them less praise for right answers, partly to avoid the wrong, careless, or silly answers that can cause disruptions, delays, and digressions (Cooper, 1979). The challenge is to deal with these very real threats to classroom management without communicating low expectations to some students or fostering their own low expectations of themselves. And sometimes, low expectations become part of the culture of the school—beliefs shared by teachers and administrators alike (Weinstein, Madison, & Kuklinski, 1995). The *Guidelines* on page 458 may help you avoid some of these problems.

Check Yourself What are some sources of teacher expectations?

What are the two kinds of expectation effects and how do they happen?

What are the different avenues for communicating teacher expectations?

Student-Centered Teaching: Examples in Reading, Mathematics, and Science

Neither high expectations nor the appropriate use of any teaching format can *ensure* that students understand. To help students reach this goal, Eleanor Duckworth believes that teachers must pay very close attention to understanding their students' understandings (Meek, 1991). What do we know about good teaching in student-centered instruction? Table 12.9 on page 459 lists some student-centered constructivist teaching practices described by Jacqueline Grennon Brooks and M. G. Brooks (1993).

It is clear that a teacher's knowledge of the subject is critical for teaching (Ball, Lubienski, & Mewborn, 2001; Borko & Putnam, 1996). Part of that knowledge is pedagogical content knowledge, or knowing how to teach a subject to your particular students (Shulman, 1987). In the last decade, psychologists have made great progress understanding how students learn different subjects (Mayer, 1992, 1999). Based on these findings, many approaches have been developed to teach reading, writing, science, mathematics, social studies, and all the other subjects. Many of these approaches reflect the student-centered perspectives described in Chapter 9.

CONNECT & EXTEND

TO PRAXIS™
THE TEACHER'S ROLE IN STUDENT-CENTERED INSTRUCTION (II, A3)
The teacher's role in student-centered instruction is significantly different from that in teacher-centered instruction. Describe the teaching practices that are typical of student-centered instruction. Contrast them with the practices in teacher-centered instruction.

CONNECT & EXTEND

TO THE RESEARCH
See the entire issue of *Educational Leadership*, November 2002 (Vol. 60, No. 3) for 15 articles on "Reading and Writing in the Content Areas" for all grade levels.

Learning to Read and Write

For years, educators have debated whether students should be taught to read and write through code-based (phonics or skills) approaches that relate letters to sounds

GUIDELINES Avoiding the Negative Effects of Teacher Expectations

Use information about students from tests, cumulative folders, and other teachers very carefully.

Examples

1. Some teachers avoid reading cumulative folders at the beginning of the year.
2. Be critical and objective about the reports you hear from other teachers.

Be flexible in your use of grouping strategies.

Examples

1. Review work of students often and experiment with new groupings.
2. Use different groups for different subjects.
3. Use mixed-ability groups in cooperative exercises.

Make sure all the students are challenged.

Examples

1. Don't say, "This is easy, I know you can do it."
2. Offer a wide range of problems, and encourage all students to try a few of the harder ones for extra credit. Find something positive about these attempts.

Be especially careful about how you respond to low-achieving students during class discussions.

Examples

1. Give them prompts, cues, and time to answer.
2. Give ample praise for good answers.
3. Call on low achievers as often as high achievers.

Use materials that show a wide range of ethnic groups.

Examples

1. Check readers and library books. Is there ethnic diversity?
2. If few materials are available, ask students to research and create their own, based on community or family sources.

Make sure that your teaching does not reflect racial, ethnic, or sexual stereotypes or prejudice.

Examples

1. Use a checking system to be sure you call on and include all students.
2. Monitor the content of the tasks you assign. Do boys get the "hard" math problems to work at the board? Do you avoid having students with limited English give oral presentations?

Be fair in evaluation and disciplinary procedures.

Examples

1. Make sure equal offenses receive equal punishment. Find out from students in an anonymous questionnaire whether you seem to be favoring certain individuals.
2. Try to grade student work without knowing the identity of the student. Ask another teacher to give you a "second opinion" from time to time.

Communicate to all students that you believe they can learn—and mean it.

Examples

1. Return papers that do not meet standards with specific suggestions for improvements.
2. If students do not have the answers immediately, wait, probe, and then help them think through an answer.

Involve all students in learning tasks and in privileges.

Examples

1. Use some system to make sure you give each student practice in reading, speaking, and answering questions.
2. Keep track of who gets to do what job. Are some students always on the list while others seldom make it?

Monitor your nonverbal behavior.

Examples

1. Do you lean away or stand farther away from some students? Do some students get smiles when they approach your desk while others get only frowns?
2. Does your tone of voice vary with different students?

and sounds to words or through meaning-based (whole-language, literature-based, emergent literacy) approaches that do not dissect words and sentences into pieces, but instead focus on the meaning of the text (Barr, 2001; Goodman & Goodman, 1990; Smith, 1994; Stahl & Miller, 1989; Symons, Woloshyn, & Pressley, 1994).

Whole-language perspective A philosophical approach to teaching and learning that stresses learning through authentic, real-life tasks. Emphasizes using language to learn, integrating learning across skills and subjects, and respecting the language abilities of student and teacher.

Balance in Reading and Writing. Advocates of **whole-language approaches** believe that learning to read is a natural process, very much like mastering your native language. Reading is a kind of guessing game in which students sample words and make predictions and guesses about meaning based on the context of other words in the passage and on their prior knowledge. Children should be immersed in a

■ Table 12.9	Constructivist Teaching Practices

Many constructivist practices can be incorporated into any class.

1. Constructivist teachers encourage and accept student autonomy and initiative.
2. Constructivist teachers use raw data and primary sources, along with manipulative, interactive, and physical materials.
3. When framing tasks, constructivist teachers use cognitive terminology such as "classify," "analyze," "predict," and "create."
4. Constructivist teachers allow student responses to drive lessons, shift instructional strategies, and alter content.
5. Constructivist teachers inquire about students' understandings of concepts before sharing their own understandings of those concepts.
6. Constructivist teachers encourage students to engage in dialogue, both with the teacher and with one another.
7. Constructivist teachers encourage student inquiry by asking thoughtful, open-ended questions and encouraging students to ask questions of each other.
8. Constructivist teachers seek elaboration of students' initial responses.
9. Constructivist teachers engage students in experiences that might engender contradictions to their initial hypotheses and then encourage discussion.
10. Constructivist teachers allow wait-time after posing questions.
11. Constructivist teachers provide time for students to discover relationships and create metaphors.

SOURCE: From "Becoming a Constructivist Teacher." In *In Search of Understanding: The Case for Constructivist Classrooms* (pp. 101–118) by J. G. Brooks and M. G. Brooks, 1995, Association for Supervision and Curriculum Development.

print-rich environment, surrounded by books worth reading and adults who read—to the children and for themselves. When students write, they write for an audience; their goal is to communicate effectively. Vygotsky (1978) recognized the importance of authentic writing tasks: "[W]riting should be incorporated into a task that is necessary and relevant for life. Only then can we be certain that it will develop not as a matter of hand and finger habits but as a really new and complex form of speech" (p. 118).

But is whole language the whole story? There are now three decades of research demonstrating that skill in recognizing sounds and words supports reading. Advocates of code-based approaches cite research showing that being able to identify many words as you read does not depend on using context to guess meaning. In fact, it is almost the other way around—knowing words helps you make sense of context. Identifying words as you read is a highly automatic process (Byrne, Fielding-Barnsley, and Ashley, 2000; Vellutino, 1991). It is the poorest readers who resort to using context to help them understand meaning (Pressley, 1996). Alphabetic coding and awareness of letter sounds are essential skills for acquiring word identification, so some direct teaching of the alphabet and phonics is helpful in learning to read.

The best approach probably makes use of both phonics and whole language. After all, we want our students to be both fluent and enthusiastic readers and writers (Bus & van IJzendoorn, 1999; Pressley, 1998). If students need help cracking the phonics code—give them what they need. Don't let ideology get in the way. You will just send more students to private tutors—if their families can afford it. But don't forget that reading and writing are for a purpose. Surround students with good literature and create a community of readers and writers. In Table 12.10 on page 460, the Center for Early Reading describes 10 principles that capture this balanced approach to teaching.

CONNECT & EXTEND

TO THE RESEARCH
See the special section on "Reading" in *Phi Delta Kappan,* 2002, Vol. 83, No. 10, pp. 740–757 for three perspectives on teaching reading.

Table 12.10 Improving the Reading Achievement of America's Children: CIERA's 10 Research-Based Principles

CIERA (the Center for the Improvement of Early Reading Achievement) has reviewed the research on learning to read and distilled the best findings into these 10 principles. Read the expanded version of the principles on their Website—www.ciera.org—under free information.

1. **Home language and literacy experiences** support the development of key print concepts and a range of knowledge prepares students for school-based learning. Programs that help families initiate and sustain these experiences show positive benefits for children's reaching achievement.

   Examples: Joint reading with a family member, parental modeling of good reading habits, monitoring homework and television viewing.

2. **Preschool programs** are particularly beneficial for children who do not experience informal learning opportunities in their homes. Such preschool experiences lead to improved reading achievement, with some effects lasting through grade 3.

   Examples: Listening to and examining books, saying nursery rhymes, writing messages, and seeing and talking about print.

3. **Skills that predict later reading success** can be promoted in kindergarten and grade 1. The two most powerful of these predictors are letter-name knowledge and phonemic awareness. Instruction in these skills has demonstrated positive effects on primary grade reading achievement, especially when it is coupled with letter-sound instruction.

   Examples: Encourage children to hear and blend sound through oral renditions of rhymes, poems, and songs, as well as writing messages and in journals.

4. **Primary-level instruction** that supports successful reading acquisition is consistent, well-designed, and focused.

   Examples: Systematic word recognition instruction on common, consistent letter-sound relationships and important but often unpredictable high-frequency words, such as *the* and *what;* teaching children to monitor the accuracy of their reading as well as their understanding of texts through strategies such as predicting, inferencing, clarifying misunderstandings, and summarizing; promoting word recognition and comprehension through repeated reading of text, guided reading and writing, strategy lessons, reading aloud with feedback, and conversations about texts children have read.

5. **Primary-level classroom environments** in successful schools provide opportunities for students to apply what they have learned in teacher-guided instruction to everyday reading and writing.

   Examples: Teachers read books aloud and hold follow-up discussions, children read independently every day, and children write stories and keep journals. These events are monitored frequently by teachers, ensuring that time is well spent and that children receive feedback on their efforts. Teachers design and revise these events based on information from ongoing assessment of children's strengths and needs.

6. **Cultural and linguistic diversity** among America's children reflects the variations within their communities and homes. This diversity is manifest in differences in the children's dispositions toward and knowledge about topics, language, and literacy.

   Examples: Effective instruction includes assessment, integration, and extension of relevant background knowledge and the use of texts that recognize diverse backgrounds. Build on the children's language when children are learning to speak, listen to, write, and read English. When teachers capitalize on the advantages of bilingualism or biliteracy, second language reading acquisition is significantly enhanced.

7. **Children who are identified as having reading disabilities** profit from the same sort of well-balanced instructional programs that benefit all children who are learning to read and write, including systematic instruction *and* meaningful reading and writing.

   Examples: Intensive one-on-one or small-group instruction, attention to both comprehension and word recognition processes, thoroughly individualized assessment and instructional planning, and extensive experiences with many types of texts.

8. **Proficient reading in third grade** and above is sustained and enhanced by programs that adhere to four fundamental features:

   Features: (1) deep and wide opportunities to read, (2) acquiring new knowledge and vocabulary, through wide reading and through explicit instruction about networks of new concepts, (3) emphasizing the influence on understanding of kinds of text (e.g., stories versus essays) and the ways writers organize particular texts, and (4) assisting students in reasoning about text.

9. **Professional opportunities** to improve reading achievement are prominent in successful schools and programs.

   Examples: Opportunities for teachers and administrators to analyze instruction, assessment, and achievement; to set goals for improvement; to learn about effective practices; and to participate in ongoing communities that deliberately try to understand both successes and persistent problems.

10. **Entire school staffs,** not just first-grade teachers, are involved in bringing children to high levels of achievement.

    Examples: In successful schools, reading achievement goals are clear, expectations are high, instructional means for attaining goals are articulated, and shared assessments monitor children's progress. Even though they might use different materials and technologies, successful schools maintain a focus on reading and writing and have programs to involve parents in their children's reading and homework. Community partnerships, including volunteer tutoring programs, are common.

SOURCE: From www.ciera.org.

Comprehension Monitoring and Reading: Reciprocal Teaching. The goal of **reciprocal teaching** is to help students understand and think deeply about what they read (Palincsar, 1986; Palincsar & Brown, 1984, 1989). To accomplish this goal, students in small reading groups learn four strategies: *summarizing* the content of a passage, *asking a question* about the central point, *clarifying* the difficult parts of the material, and *predicting* what will come next. These are strategies that skilled readers apply almost automatically, but poor readers seldom do—or they don't know how. To use the strategies effectively, poorer readers need direct instruction, modeling, and practice in actual reading situations.

First, the teacher introduces these strategies, perhaps focusing on one strategy each day. The teacher explains and models each strategy and encourages students to practice. Next, the teacher and the students read a short passage silently. Then the teacher again provides a model by summarizing, questioning, clarifying, or predicting based on the reading. Everyone reads another passage, and the students gradually begin to assume the teacher's role. The teacher becomes a member of the group, and may finally leave, as the students take over the teaching. Often the students' first attempts are halting and incorrect. But the teacher gives clues, guidance, encouragement, support in doing parts of the task (such as providing question stems), models, and other forms of scaffolding to help the students master these strategies. The goal is for students to learn to apply these strategies independently as they read so they can make sense of text.

Applying Reciprocal Teaching. Although reciprocal teaching seems to work with almost any age student, most of the research has been done with younger adolescents who can read aloud fairly accurately, but who are far below average in reading comprehension. After 20 hours of practice with this approach, many students who were in the bottom quarter of their class moved up to the average level or above on tests of reading comprehension. Palincsar has identified three guidelines for effective reciprocal teaching ("When Student Becomes Teacher," 1986):

1. *Shift gradually.* The shift from teacher control to student responsibility must be gradual.
2. *Match demands to abilities.* The difficulty of the task and the responsibility must match the abilities of each student and grow as these abilities develop.
3. *Diagnose thinking.* Teachers should carefully observe the "teaching" of each student for clues about how the student is thinking and what kind of instruction the student needs.

In reciprocal teaching, Palincsar and Brown first remind us that procedures for fostering and monitoring comprehension must be taught—not all students develop these strategies on their own. Second, they focus attention on 4 rather than 40 or more strategies, as some sources have suggested. Third, they emphasize practicing these 4 strategies in the context of actual reading—reading literature and reading texts. Finally, they develop the idea of scaffolding and gradually moving the student toward independent and fluid reading comprehension (Rosenshine & Meister, 1994).

Learning and Teaching Mathematics

Think back to the ways that you were taught mathematics. What were your math classes like in elementary school? High school?

Some of the most compelling support for constructivist approaches to teaching comes from mathematics education. Critics of direct instruction believe that traditional mathematics instruction often teaches students an unintended lesson—that

Reciprocal teaching A method, based on modeling, to teach reading comprehension strategies.

CONNECT & EXTEND

TO THE RESEARCH

Another example of how students solve mathematics problems by applying rules is taken from Merseth, K. K. (1993). How old is the shepherd? An essay about mathematics education. *Phi Delta Kappan, 74*, 548–554. Merseth cites findings from research showing that three out of four students will produce some numerical answer to the problem: There are 125 sheep and 5 dogs in a flock. How old is the shepherd? Here is how one child reached an answer. Notice that logic and reasoning play a role: "125 + 5 = 130 . . . this is too big, and 125 – 5 = 120 is still too big . . . while 125/5 = 25. That works! I think the shepherd is 25 years old!"

they "cannot understand mathematics," or worse, that mathematics doesn't have to make sense, you just have to memorize the formulas. Arthur Baroody and Herbert Ginsburg (1990, p. 62) give this example:

> Sherry, a junior high student, explained that her math class was learning how to convert measurements from one unit to another. The interviewer gave Sherry the following problem:
>
> > To feed data into the computer, the measurements in your report have to be converted to one unit of measurement: feet. Your first measurement, however, is 3 feet 6 inches. What are you going to feed into the computer?
>
> Sherry recognized immediately that the conversion algorithm taught in school applied. . . . However, because she really did not understand the rationale behind the conversion algorithm, Sherry had difficulty in remembering the steps and how to execute them. After some time she came up with an improbable answer (it was less than 3 feet). Sherry knew she was in trouble and became flustered. At this point, the interviewer tried to help by asking her if there was any other way of solving the problem. Sherry responded sharply, "No!" She explained, "That's the way it has to be done." The interviewer tried to give Sherry a hint: "Look at the numbers in the problem, is there another way we can think about them that might help us figure out the problem more easily?" Sherry grew even more impatient, "This is the way I learned in school, so it has to be the way."

Sherry believed that there was only one way to solve a problem. Though Sherry knew that 6 inches was one-half a foot and that the fraction one-half was equivalent to the decimal expression .5, she did not use this knowledge to solve the problem informally and quickly ("3 feet 6 inches is 3½ feet, or 3.5 feet"). Her beliefs prevented her from effectively using her existing mathematical knowledge to solve the problem. Sherry had probably been taught to memorize the steps to convert one measurement to another. How would a constructivist approach teach the same material?

The following excerpt shows how a 3rd-grade teacher, Ms. Coleman, uses a constructivist approach to teach negative numbers. Notice the use of dialogue and the way the teacher asks students to justify and explain their thinking. The class has been considering one problem: –10 + 10 = ? A student, Marta, has just tried to explain, using a number line, why –10 + 10 = 0:

> **Teacher:** Marta says that negative ten plus ten equals zero, so you have to count ten numbers to the right. What do you think, Harold?
>
> **Harold:** I think it's easy, but I don't understand how she explained it.
>
> **Teacher:** OK. Does anybody else have a comment or a response to that? Tessa? (Peterson, 1992, p. 165)

CONNECT & EXTEND

TO THE RESEARCH

See the special section on "The Math Wars" in *Phi Delta Kappan*, (2001), Vol. 83, No. 3, pp. 255–272 for a look at controversies in math teaching.

As the discussion progresses, Ms. Coleman encourages students to talk directly to each other:

> **Teacher:** You said you don't understand what she is trying to say?
>
> **Chang:** No.
>
> **Teacher:** Do you want to ask her?
>
> **Chang:** What do you mean by counting to the right?

This dialogue reveals three things about learning and teaching in a constructivist classroom: The thinking processes of the students are the focus of attention; one topic is considered in depth rather than attempting to "cover" many topics; and assessment is ongoing and mutually shared by teacher and students.

Jere Confrey (1990b) analyzed an expert mathematics teacher in a class for high school girls who had difficulty with mathematics. Confrey identified five components in a model of this teacher's approach to teaching. These components are summarized in Table 12.11.

Table 12.11 A Constructivist Approach to Mathematics: Five Components

1. Promote students' autonomy and commitment to their answers
   Examples:
   - Question both right and wrong student answers.
   - Insist that students at least try to solve a problem and be able to explain what they tried.
2. Develop students' reflective processes
   Examples:
   - Question students to guide them to try different ways to resolve the problem.
   - Ask students to restate the problem in their own words; to explain what they are doing and why; and to discuss what they mean by the terms they are using.
3. Construct a case history of each student
   Examples:
   - Note general tendencies in the way the student approaches problems, as well as common misconceptions and strengths.
4. If the student is unable to solve a problem, intervene to negotiate a possible solution with the student
   Examples:
   - Based on the case study and your understanding of how the student is thinking about a problem, guide the student to think about a possible solution.
   - Ask questions such as "Is there anything you did in the last one that will help you here?" or "Can you explain your diagram?"
   - If the student is becoming frustrated, ask more direct, product-oriented questions.
5. When the problem is solved, review the solution
   Examples:
   - Encourage students to reflect on what they did and why.
   - Note what students did well and build confidence.

SOURCE: From "What Constructivism Implies for Teaching," by J. Confrey, 1990, in *Constructivist Views on the Teaching and Learning of Mathematics* by R. Davis, C. Maher, and N. Noddings (Eds.). Monograph 4 of the National Council of Teachers of Mathematics, Reston, VA. Copyright © 1990 National Council of Teachers of Mathematics. Adapted with permission.

Learning Science

We have seen a number of times that by high school many students have "learned" some unfortunate lessons in school. Like Sherry described in the preceding section, they have learned that math is impossible to understand and you just have to apply the rules to get the answers. Or they may have developed some misconceptions about the world, such as the belief that the earth is warmer in the summer because it is closer to the sun.

Many educators note that the key to understanding in science is for students to directly examine their own theories and confront the shortcomings (Hewson, Beeth, & Thorley, 1998). For **conceptual change** to take place, students must go through six stages: initial discomfort with their own ideas and beliefs, attempts to explain away inconsistencies between their theories and evidence presented to them, attempts to adjust measurements or observations to fit personal theories, doubt, vacillation, and finally conceptual change (Nissani & Hoefler-Nissani, 1992). You can see Piaget's notions of assimilation, disequilibrium, and accommodation operating here. Students try to make new information fit existing ideas (assimilation), but when the fit simply won't work and disequilibrium occurs, then accommodation or changes in cognitive structures follow.

The goal of conceptual change teaching in science is to help students pass through these six stages of learning. The two central features of conceptual change teaching are:

- Teachers are committed to teaching for student understanding rather than "covering the curriculum."
- Students are encouraged to make sense of science using their current ideas—they are challenged to describe, predict, explain, justify, debate, and defend the adequacy of their understanding. Dialogue is key. Only when intuitive ideas prove inadequate can new learning take hold (Anderson & Roth, 1989).

Conceptual change teaching has much in common with cognitive apprenticeships and inquiry learning described in Chapter 9—with scaffolding and dialogue playing

Conceptual change teaching in science A method that helps students understand (rather than memorize) concepts in science by using and challenging the students' current ideas.

These students are testing the endurance of a straw tower during an outdoor science class project. The teacher hopes that this interactive approach to teaching scientific concepts will be more meaningful to her students than if she simply "talked" about them in class.

key roles (Shuell, 1996). The *Guidelines* below, adapted from Hewson, Beeth, and Thorley (1998), give some ideas for teaching for conceptual change.

How would these guidelines look in practice? One answer comes from Michael Beeth's study of a 5th-grade classroom. Table 12.12 is a list of learning goals that the teacher presented to her students. In this classroom, the teacher typically began instruction with a question such as, "Do you have ideas? Can you talk about them? Bring them out into the open? Why do you like your ideas? Why are you attracted to

GUIDELINES: Teaching for Conceptual Change

Encourage students to make their ideas explicit.

Examples

1. Ask students to make predictions that might contradict their naïve conceptions.
2. Ask students to state their ideas in their own words, including the attractions and limitations of the ideas for them.
3. Have students explain their ideas using physical models or illustrations.

Help students see the differences among ideas.

Examples

1. Have students summarize or paraphrase each other's ideas.
2. Encourage comparing ideas by presenting and comparing evidence.

Encourage metacognition.

Examples

1. Give a pretest before starting a unit; then have students discuss their own responses to the pretest. Group similar pretest responses together and ask students to discover what is a more general concept underlying the responses.
2. At the end of lessons, ask students: "What did you learn?" "What do you understand?" "What do you believe about the lesson?" "How have your ideas changed?"

Explore the status of ideas. Status is an indication of how much students know and accept ideas and find them useful.

Examples

1. Ask direct questions about how intelligible, plausible, and fruitful an idea is. That is, do you know what the idea means, do you believe it, and can you achieve some valuable outcome using the idea?
2. Plan activities and experiments that support and question the students' ideas such as showing successful applications or pointing out contradictions.

Ask students for justifications of their ideas.

Examples

1. Teach students to use terms such as *logical, consistent, inconsistent,* and *coherent* in giving justifications.
2. Ask students to share and analyze each other's justifications.

■ Table 12.12	One Teacher's Learning Goals for Conceptual Change Teaching

The teacher in one 5th grade class gives these questions to her students to support their thinking about science.

1. Can you state your own ideas?
2. Can you talk about why you are attracted to your ideas?
3. Are your ideas consistent?
4. Do you realize the limitations of your ideas and the possibility they might need to change?
5. Can you try to explain your ideas using physical models?
6. Can you explain the difference between understanding an idea and believing in an idea?
7. Can you apply intelligible and plausible to your own ideas?

SOURCE: Adapted from "Teaching Science in Fifth Grade: Instructional Goals that Support Conceptual Change," by M. E. Beeth, 1998, *Journal of Research in Science Teaching*, *35*, p. 1093.

them?" (Beeth, 1998, p. 1095). During her teaching she constantly asked questions that required explanation and justifications. She summarized the students' answers, and sometimes challenged, "But do you really believe what you say?" Studies of the students in the teacher's classroom over the years showed that they had a sophisticated understanding of science concepts.

Beyond the Debates to Outstanding Teaching

In spite of the criticisms and debates, there is no one best way to teach. Different goals require different methods. Direct instruction leads to better performance on achievement tests, whereas the open, informal methods such as discovery learning or inquiry approaches are associated with better performance on tests of creativity, abstract thinking, and problem solving. In addition, the open methods are better for improving attitudes toward school and for stimulating curiosity, cooperation among students, and lower absence rates (Walberg, 1990). According to these conclusions, when the goals of teaching involve problem solving, creativity, understanding, and mastering processes, many approaches besides direct instruction should be effective. These guidelines are in keeping with Tom Good's conclusion that teaching should become less direct as students mature and when the goals involve affective development and problem solving or critical thinking (Good, 1983a).

CONNECT & EXTEND

TO THE RESEARCH
The May 1993 issue of *Educational Leadership* has over a dozen articles on the changing curriculum, including several on the ways that mathematics education has been changed by the National Council of Teachers of Mathematics (NCME) Curriculum and Evaluation Standards for School Mathematics.

Check Yourself Describe the debate about learning to read.

Describe the use of dialogue in reciprocal teaching.

Describe student-centered constructivist approaches to mathematics and science teaching.

Contrast teaching in direct and student-centered instruction.

Effective Teaching in Inclusive Classrooms

When you think about teaching in an inclusive classroom, what are your concerns? Do you have enough training? Will you get the support you need from school administrators or specialists? Will working with the students with disabilities take time away from your other responsibilities?

These questions are common ones, and sometimes concerns are justified. But effective teaching for exceptional students does not require a unique set of skills. It is a combination of good teaching practices and sensitivity to all your students. Students with disabilities need to *learn the academic material,* and they need to be *full participants in the day-to-day life of the classroom.*

To accomplish the first goal of academic learning, Larrivee (1985) concluded that effective teachers of mainstreamed students do the following:

1. Use time efficiently by having smooth management routines, avoiding discipline problems, and planning carefully.
2. Ask questions at the right level of difficulty.
3. Give supportive, positive feedback to students, helping them figure out the right answer if they are wrong but on the right track.

In addition, students with learning disabilities appear to benefit from and using extended practice distributed over days and weeks and from *advanced organizers* such as focusing students on what they already know or stating clear objectives (Swanson, 2001).

To accomplish the second goal of integrating students with disabilities into the day-to-day life of the classroom, Ferguson, Ferguson, and Bogdan (1987) give the following guidelines:

1. Mix students with disabilities into groups with students who do not have special needs. Avoid resegregating the students with disabilities into separate groups.
2. Instead of sending students out for special services such as speech therapy, remedial reading, or individualized instruction, try to integrate the special help into the class setting, perhaps during a time when the other students are working independently too.
3. Make sure your language and behavior toward students with disabilities is a good model for everyone.
4. Teach about differences among people as part of the curriculum. Let students become familiar with aids for individuals with disabilities, such as hearing aids, sign language, communication boards, and so on. And give students many different ways to show their ability—writing, talking, organizing, drawing, diagramming, planning, demonstrating, helping, or performing, for example.
5. Have students work together in cooperative groups or on special projects such as role plays, biographical interviews, or lab assignments.
6. Try to keep similar schedules and activity patterns for all students.

The *Reaching Every Student* feature has other ideas about effective teaching in inclusive classrooms.

Working with Individual Students

What Would You Say? The last person to interview you for your first teaching job is the coordinator of special services for the school. This is the question: "How do you accommodate different learning challenges and abilities in your teaching? Do you make use of community resources or technology? How?"

When students have special needs, they may be referred to specialists such as child study teams, school psychologists, or teachers of students with special needs for evaluation (see Table 4.8 on page 136 for guidelines about referring students for evaluation). The outcome of this process sometimes includes the preparation of an individualized education program or IEP, as described in Chapter 4.

≈ Reaching Every Student ≈

Resource Rooms, Collaborative Consultation, and Cooperative Teaching

Many schools provide additional help for classroom teachers who work with students with disabilities. A resource room is a classroom with special materials and equipment and a specially trained teacher. Students may come to the resource room each day for several minutes or several hours and receive instruction individually or in small groups. The rest of the day, the students are in regular education classes. Besides working with students directly, a resource teacher may also work with them indirectly by giving the general education teacher ideas, materials, or actual demonstrations of teaching techniques.

Increasingly, special and general education teachers are working together, collaborating to assume equal responsibility for the education of students with disabilities. The collaboration may work through consultation, planning, and problem solving about how to teach specific students, or the special education teacher might work directly alongside the general education teacher in a class made up of students with and without disabilities. The latter is called *cooperative teaching.* The teachers assume different roles, depending on the age of the students and their needs. For example, in a secondary class, the general education teacher might be responsible for academic content, while the special education instructor teaches study skills and learning strategies. In another classroom, the general education teacher might deal with core content, while the special teacher provides remediation, enrichment, or reteaching when necessary. The two teachers might also try team teaching, where each is responsible for different parts of the lesson.

When using cooperative teaching, it is important that general education students and students with disabilities aren't resegregated in the class, with the general education teacher always working with the "general education" students and the special education teacher always working with the "mainstreamed" students. I observed one class in which the students with disabilities worked only with the special education teacher but often looked longingly over their shoulders at the activities of their classmates working with the general education teacher. Rather than integrating the students with disabilities into the class, this cooperative teaching arrangement accentuated their separateness. Figure 12.2 shows different ways to implement cooperative teaching.

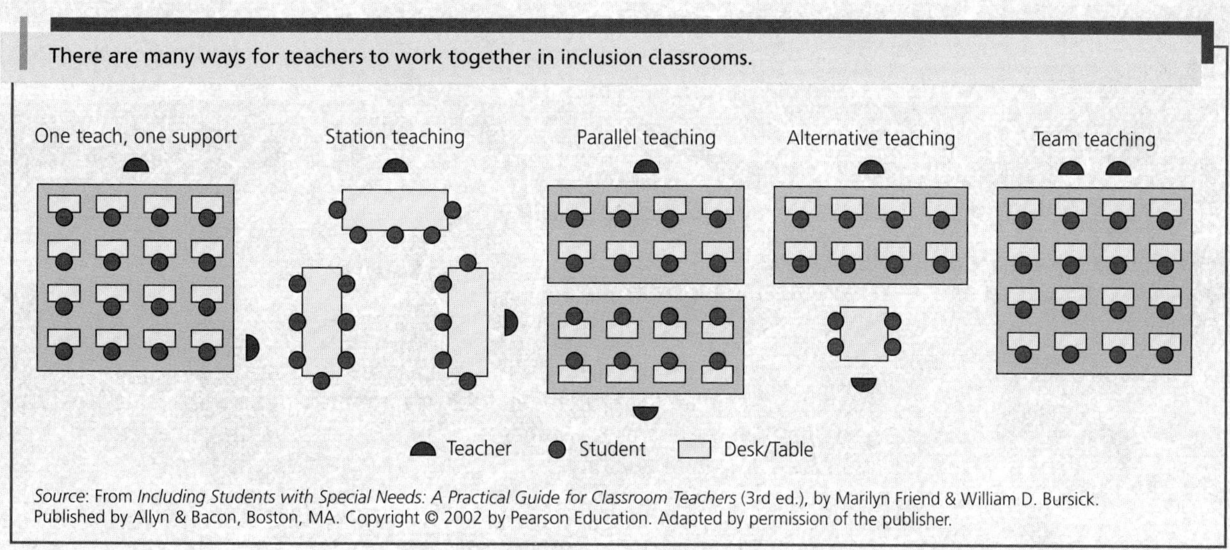

Source: From *Including Students with Special Needs: A Practical Guide for Classroom Teachers* (3rd ed.), by Marilyn Friend & William D. Bursick. Published by Allyn & Bacon, Boston, MA. Copyright © 2002 by Pearson Education. Adapted by permission of the publisher.

Figure 12.2 Cooperative and Co-Teaching Approaches

This IEP (Individualized Education Program) was developed for a 9-year-old girl. This section of the plan focuses on following the teacher's directions and reading.

Student: Amy North Age: 9 Grade: 1 Date: Oct. 17, 1995

1. Unique Characteristics or Needs: Noncompliance
Frequently noncompliant with teacher's instructions.

1. Present Levels of Performance
Complies with about 50% of teacher's requests/commands.

2. Special Education, Related Services, and Modifications
Implemented immediately, strong reinforcement for compliance with teacher's instructions (Example: "Sure I will" plan including precision requests and reinforcer menu for points earned for compliance, as described in *The Tough Kid Book,* by Rhode, Jenson, and Reavis, 1992); within 3 weeks, training of parents by school psychologists to use precision requests and reinforcement at home.

3. Objectives (Including Procedures, Criteria, and Schedule)
Within one month, will comply with teacher requests/commands 90% of the time; compliance monitored weekly by the teacher.

4. Annual Goals
Will become compliant with teacher's requests/commands.

2. Unique Characteristics or Needs: Reading
2a. Very slow reading rate. 2c. Limited phonics skills
2b. Poor comprehension 2d. Limited sight-word vocabulary

1. Present Levels of Performance
2a. Reads stories of approximately 100 words of first-grade level at approximately 40 words per minute.
2b. Seldom can recall factual information about stories immediately after reading them.
2c. Consistently confuses vowel sounds, often misidentifies consonants, and does not blend sounds.
2d. Has sight-word vocabulary of approximately 150 words.

2. Special Education, Related Services, and Modifications
2a-2c. Direct instruction 30 minutes daily in vowel discrimination, consonant identification, and sound blending: begin immediately, continue throughout school year.
2a&2d. Sight word drill 10 minutes daily in addition to phonics instruction and daily practice; 10 minutes practice in using phonics and sight-word skills in reading a story at the level; begin immediately, continue for school year.

3. Objectives (Including Procedures, Criteria, and Schedule)
2a. Within 3 months, will read stories at her level at 60 words per minute with 2 or fewer errors per story; within six months, 80 words with 2 or fewer errors; performance monitored daily by teacher or aide.
2b. Within 3 months, will answer oral and written comprehension questions requiring recall or information from stories she has just read with 90% accuracy (e.g., Who is in the story? What happened? When? Why?) and be able to predict probable outcomes with 80% accuracy; performance monitored daily by teacher or aide.
2c. Within 3 months, will increase sight-word vocabulary to 200 words, within 6 months to 250 words, assessed by flashcard presentation.

4. Annual Goals
2a-2c. Will read fluently and with comprehension at begining-second-grade level.

Source: From *Exceptional Learners: Introduction to Special Education* (3rd ed.), by D. P. Hallahan & J. M. Kauffman. Published by Allyn & Bacon, Boston, MA. Copyright © 1995 by Pearson Education. Reprinted by permission of the publisher.

Figure 12.3 An Excerpt from an Individualized Education Program (IEP)

Figure 12.3 is an excerpt from the IEP of a 9-year-old girl with mild retardation. This section of the plan focuses on one behavior problem and reading. You may help to develop these programs for students in your classes. The programs should provide guidance for you in teaching.

Technology and Exceptional Students

Computers have improved the education of exceptional children in countless ways. Given the record keeping and program planning needed to meet federal regulations, teachers can use computers to manage instruction. For students who require small steps and many repetitions to learn a new concept, computers are the perfect patient tutors, repeating steps and lessons as many times as necessary. A well-designed computer instructional program is engaging and interactive—two important qualities for students with problems paying attention or with a history of failure that has eroded motivation. For example, a math or spelling program might use images, sounds, and gamelike features to maintain the attention of a student with an attention-deficit disorder. Interactive videodisc programs are being developed to help hearing people use sign language. Many programs do not involve sound, so students with hearing impairments can get the full benefit from the lessons. Students who have trouble reading can use programs that will "speak" a word for them if they touch the unknown word with a light pen or the cursor. With this immediate access to help, the students are much more likely to get the reading practice they need to prevent falling farther and farther behind. Other devices actually convert printed pages and typed texts to spoken words for students who are blind or others who benefit from hearing information.

Technology can be an enormous boon for students with disabilities. This student is blind, but uses an abacus with a Braille 'n' Speak in order to take a math test alongside his sighted peers in a general education classroom.

For the student with a learning disability whose writing can't be read, word processors produce perfect penmanship so the ideas can finally get on paper. Once the ideas are on paper, the student can reorganize and improve the writing without the agony of rewriting by hand (Hallahan & Kauffman, 2003; Hardman, Drew, & Egan, 1996; Reynolds & Birch, 1988).

With these tremendous advances in technology have come new barriers, however. Many computers have graphic interfaces. To manipulate the programs requires precise "mouse movements," as you may remember when you first learned to point and click. These maneuvers are difficult for students with motor problems or visual impairments. And the information available on the Internet often is unusable for students with visual problems. Researchers are working on the problem—trying to devise ways for people to access the information nonvisually, but the adaptations are not perfected yet (Hallahan & Kauffman, 2003). One current trend is **universal design**—considering the needs of all users as new tools, or learning programs, or websites (Pisha & Coyne, 2001).

For gifted students, computers can be a connection with databases and computers in universities, museums, and research labs. Computer networks allow students to work on projects and share information with others across the country. It is also possible to have gifted students write programs for students and teachers. Quite a few principals around the country rely on their students to make the technology in the school work. These are just a few examples of what technology can do. Check with the resource teachers in your district to find out what is available in your school.

Check Yourself What characterizes effective teaching for exceptional students?

What resources do teachers have to work effectively with exceptional children?

Universal design Considering the needs of all users as new tools, or learning programs, or websites.

Summary Table

■ The First Step: Planning

(pp. 432–439)

What are the levels of planning and how do they affect teaching? Teachers engage in several levels of planning—by the year, term, unit, week, and day. All the levels must be coordinated. Accomplishing the year's plan requires breaking the work into terms, the terms into units, and the units into weeks and days. The plan determines how time and materials will be turned into activities for students. There is no single model of planning, but all plans should allow for flexibility. Planning is a creative problem-solving process for experienced teachers. They know how to accomplish many lessons and segments of lessons. They know what to expect and how to proceed, so they don't necessarily continue to follow the detailed lesson-planning models they learned during their teacher-preparation programs. Planning is more informal—"in their heads."

What is an instructional objective? An instructional objective is a clear and unambiguous description of your educational intentions for your students. Mager's influential system for writing behavioral objectives states that a good objective has three parts—the intended student behavior, the conditions under which the behavior will occur, and the criteria for acceptable performance. Gronlund's alternative approach suggests that an objective should be stated first in general terms, then the teacher should clarify by listing sample behaviors that would provide evidence that the student has attained the objective. The most recent research on instructional objectives tends to favor approaches similar to Gronlund's.

Describe the three taxonomies of educational objectives. Bloom and others have developed taxonomies categorizing basic objectives in the cognitive, affective, and psychomotor domains. In real life, of course, behaviors from these three domains occur simultaneously. A taxonomy encourages systematic thinking about relevant objectives and ways to evaluate them. Six basic objectives are listed in the cognitive domain: knowing, understanding, applying, analyzing, evaluating, and creating. A recent revision of this taxonomy adds that these processes can act on four kinds of knowledge—factual, conceptual, procedural, and metacognitive. Objectives in the affective domain run from least committed to most committed. At the lowest level, a student would simply pay attention to a certain idea. At the highest level, the student would adopt an idea or a value and act consistently with that idea. Objectives in the psychomotor domain generally move from basic perceptions and reflex actions to skilled, creative movements.

Describe teacher-centered and student-centered planning. In teacher-centered approaches, teachers select learning objectives and plan how to get students to meet those objectives. Teachers control the "what" and "how" of learning. In contrast, planning is shared and negotiated in student-centered, or constructivist, approaches. Rather than having specific student behaviors as objectives, the teacher has overarching goals or "big ideas" that guide planning. Integrated content and teaching with themes are often part of the planning. Assessment of learning is ongoing and mutually shared by teacher and students.

Instructional Objectives: Clear statement of what students are intended to learn through instruction.

Behavioral Objectives: Instructional objectives stated in terms of observable behaviors.

Cognitive Objectives: Instructional objectives stated in terms of higher-level thinking operations.

Taxonomy: Classification system.

Cognitive Domain: In Bloom's taxonomy, memory and reasoning objectives.

Affective Domain: Objectives focusing on attitudes and feelings.

Psychomotor Domain: Physical ability and coordination objectives.

Constructivist Approach: View that emphasizes the active role of the learner in building understanding and making sense of information.

■ Teacher-Directed Instruction

(pp. 440–452)

What methods have been used to study teaching? For years, researchers have tried to unravel the mystery of effective teaching using classroom observation, case studies, interviews, experimentation with different methods, stimulated recall (teachers view videotapes and explain their teaching), analysis of lesson transcripts, and other approaches to study teaching in real classrooms.

What are the general characteristics of good teaching? Teacher knowledge of the subject is necessary but not sufficient for effective teaching because being more knowledgeable helps teachers be clearer and more organized. Teachers who provide clear presentations and explanations tend to have students who learn more and who rate their teachers more positively. Teacher warmth, friendliness, and understanding seem to be the traits most strongly related to positive student attitudes.

What is direct instruction? Direct instruction is appropriate for teaching basic skills and explicit knowledge. It includes the teaching functions of review/overview, presentation, guided practice, feedback and correctives (with reteaching if necessary), independent practice, and periodic reviews. The younger or less able the students, the shorter the presentation should be with more cycles of practice and feedback.

Distinguish between convergent and divergent and high-level versus low-level questions. Convergent questions have only one right answer. Divergent questions have many possible answers. Higher-level questions require analysis, synthesis, and evaluation—students have to think for themselves. The best pattern for younger students and for lower-ability students of all ages is simple questions that allow a high percentage of correct answers, ample encouragement, help when the student does not have the correct answer, and praise. For high-ability students, the successful pattern includes harder questions at both higher and lower levels and more critical feedback. Whatever their age or ability, all students should have some experience with thought-provoking questions and, if necessary, help in learning how to answer them.

How can wait time affect student learning? Teacher responses to answers should not be too hasty in most cases and should provide appropriate feedback. When teachers learn to pose a question, then wait at least 3 to 5 seconds before calling on a student to answer, students tend to give longer answers; more students are likely to participate, ask questions, and volunteer appropriate answers; student comments involving analysis, synthesis, inference, and speculation tend to increase; and the students generally appear more confident in their answers.

What are the uses and disadvantages of group discussion? Group discussion helps students participate directly, express themselves clearly, justify opinions, and tolerate different views. Group discussion also gives students a chance to ask for clarification, examine their own thinking, follow personal interests, and assume responsibility by taking leadership roles in the group. Thus, group discussions help students evaluate ideas and synthesize personal viewpoints. However, discussions are quite unpredictable and may easily digress into exchanges of ignorance.

Direct Instruction/Explicit Teaching: Systematic instruction for mastery of basic skills, facts, and information.

Active Teaching: Teaching characterized by high levels of teacher explanation, demonstration, and interaction with students.

Basic Skills: Clearly structured knowledge that is needed for later learning and that can be taught step by step.

Scripted Cooperation: Learning strategy in which two students take turns summarizing material and criticizing the summaries.

Seatwork: Independent classroom work.

Convergent Questions: Questions that have a single correct answer.

Divergent Questions: Questions that have no single correct answer.

Group Discussion: Conversation in which the teacher does not have the dominant role; students pose and answer their own questions.

Enhancing Your Expertise with Technology

(pp. 452–453)

The Questioning Toolkit **http://www.fno.org/nov97/toolkit.html**

Effective Classroom Questioning
http://www.unl.edu/teaching/teachquestions.html

Other Useful Websites

Yahoo directory of K–12 lesson plans **http://dir.yahoo.com/Education/K_12/Teaching/Lesson_Plans/**

Teacher's Net, Lesson Bank
http://www.teachers.net/lessons/posts/posts/html

Chemistry resources
http://198.110.10.57/Chem/Chem1Docs/Index.html

National standards
http://www.mcrel.org/standards-benchmarks/index.asp

AskEric Lesson plans **http://ericir.syr.edu/VirtualLessons/**

New York Times education resources
http://www.nytimes.com/learning/

Funbrain games for lessons **http://www.funbrain.com**

JDL Technologies: Resources for students and teachers
http://www.k-12world.com

Teacher Expectations

(pp. 453–457)

What are some sources of teacher expectations? Sources include intelligence test scores, gender, notes from previous teachers and the medical or psychological reports found in cumulative folders, ethnic background, knowledge of older brothers and sisters, physical characteristics, previous achievement, socioeconomic class, and the actual behaviors of the student.

What are the two kinds of expectation effects and how do they happen? The first is the self-fulfilling prophecy when the teacher's beliefs about the students' abilities have no basis in fact, but student behavior comes to match the initially inaccurate expectation. The second is a sustaining expectation effect when teachers are fairly accurate in their initial reading of students' abilities and respond to students appropriately. The problems arise when students show some improvement but teachers do not alter their expectations to take account of the improvement. When this happens, the teacher's unchanging expectation can sustain the student's achievement at the expected level. In practice, sustaining effects are more common than self-fulfilling prophecy effects.

What are the different avenues for communicating teacher expectations? Some teachers tend to treat students differently, depending on their own views of how well the students are likely to do. Differences in treatment toward low-expectation students may include setting less challenging tasks, focusing on lower-level learning, giving fewer choices, providing inconsistent feedback, and communicating less respect and trust. Students may behave accordingly, fulfilling teachers' predictions or staying at an expected level of achievement.

Pygmalion Effect: Exceptional progress by a student as a result of high teacher expectations for that student; named for mythological king, Pygmalion, who made a statue, then caused it to be brought to life.

Self-Fulfilling Prophecy: A groundless expectation that is confirmed because it has been expected.

Sustaining Expectation Effect: Student performance maintained at a certain level because teachers don't recognize improvements.

Student-Centered Teaching: Examples in Reading, Mathematics, and Science

(pp. 457–465)

Describe the debate about learning to read. Today there is an ongoing debate between advocates of whole-language approaches to reading and writing and balanced approaches that include direct teaching of skills and phonics. Advocates of whole language believe children learn best when they are surrounded by good literature and read and write for authentic purposes. Advocates of a balanced approach cite extensive research indicating that skill in recognizing sounds and words—phonemic awareness—is fundamental in learning to read. Excellent primary teachers use a balanced approach combining authentic reading with skills instruction when needed.

Describe the use of dialogue in reciprocal teaching. The goal of reciprocal teaching is to help students understand and think deeply about what they read. To accomplish this goal, students in small reading groups learn four strategies: *summarizing* the content of a passage, *asking a question* about the central point, *clarifying* the difficult parts of the material, and *predicting* what will come next. These strategies are practiced in a classroom dialogue about the readings. Teachers first take a central role, but as the discussion progresses, the students take more and more control.

Describe student-centered constructivist approaches to mathematics and science teaching. Constructivist approaches to teaching mathematics and science emphasize deep understanding of concepts (as opposed to memorization), discussion and explanation, and exploration of students' implicit understandings. Many educators note that the key to understanding in science is for students to directly examine their own theories and confront the shortcomings. For change to take place, students must go through six stages: initial discomfort with their own ideas and beliefs, attempts to explain away inconsistencies between their theories and evidence presented to them, attempts to adjust measurements or observations to fit personal theories, doubt, vacillation, and finally conceptual change.

Contrast teaching in direct and student-centered instruction. In direct instruction, the teacher gives well-organized presentations, clear explanations, carefully delivered prompts, and feedback. These actions can be resources for students as they construct understanding. In student-centered approaches, the teacher designs authentic tasks, monitors student thinking, ask questions, and prods inquiry. Both kinds of teaching may be appropriate at different times.

Whole-Language Perspective: A philosophical approach to teaching and learning that stresses learning through authentic, real-life tasks. Emphasizes using language to learn, integrating learning across skills and subjects, and respecting the language abilities of student and teacher.

Reciprocal Teaching: A method, based on modeling, to teach reading comprehension strategies.

Conceptual Change Teaching in Science: A method that helps students understand (rather than memorize) concepts in science by using and challenging the students' current ideas.

Effective Teaching in Inclusive Classrooms

(pp. 465–469)

What characterizes effective teaching for exceptional students? Effective teaching for exceptional students does not require a unique set of skills. It is a combination of good teaching practices and sensitivity to all students. Students with disabilities need to learn the academic material, and they need to be full participants in the day-to-day life of the classroom.

What resources do teachers have to work effectively with exceptional children? When students have special needs they may be referred to specialists such as child study teams, school psychologists, or teachers of students with special needs for evaluation. The outcome of this process sometimes includes the preparation of an individualized educational program or IEP, as described in Chapter 4, which will have teaching ideas and guidelines. Many schools provide additional help for classroom teachers working with students with disabilities, such as a resource room with special materials and equipment and a specially trained teacher. Increasingly, special and regular educators are working together to teach specific students or the special education teacher might work directly alongside the regular teacher in a class made up of students with and without disabilities.

Universal Design: Considering the needs of all users as new tools, or learning programs, or websites

Becoming a Professional

Passing the PRAXIS™

Chapter 12 reflects many of the professional standards created by the Interstate New Teacher Assessment and Support Consortium (INTASC). These standards form the basis of the PRAXIS II™ and state-created teacher licensure exams.

Recent policy changes in many states as well as the federal Leave No Child Behind Act will probably have a strong influence on your new career as a teacher. Schools that fail to promote or maintain strong student learning—as measured by various tests—will face a variety of actions. The test scores of your students will receive increased scrutiny from administrators, boards of education, and state education departments. Teachers will have to adjust to these new circumstances.

In some ways you may be better prepared for these changes than veteran colleagues. Many newer tests emphasize skills and knowledge that are learned most effectively through a variety of student-centered instructional strategies that you have encountered in this textbook and your educational psychology class.

Tips for PRAXIS II™

Develop plans for instruction and consider:

- The role of objectives in instruction
- Writing behavioral and cognitive objectives
- The use of educational taxonomies to design effective objectives
- The role of independent practice (i.e., seatwork and homework)

Understand the basic principles of teacher-centered and student-centered forms of instruction, including:

- Appropriate uses and limitations
- The role of the teacher
- Effective questioning techniques
- Whole group discussions
- Recitation
- Cooperative learning
- Thematic/interdisciplinary instruction

Related Topics

- The TARGET Model for supporting motivation to learn (Chapter 10)
- Learning and teaching about concepts (Chapter 8)
- Creating culturally compatible classrooms (Chapter 5)
- New directions in standardized testing (Chapter 14)
- Innovations in assessment (Chapters 14 and 15)

Standards and Licensure Appendix: *PRAXIS II™ and INTASC*

Refer to the Appendix at the end of the book for detailed correlations to PRAXIS II™ exam topics and INTASC Standards addressed in this text.

Insights about Job Interview Questions: *What Would You Say?*

1. What is the best lesson you have taught so far? Tell me all about it and especially what made it so good.
2. How do you accommodate different learning challenges and abilities in your teaching? Do you make use of community resources or technology? How?

Your Teaching Portfolio: *Teaching Resources*

- What is your approach to planning? How will you match teaching approaches to learning goals?
- Add some ideas for parent involvement in homework from this chapter to your **Portfolio.**
- Include a summary of the cognitive, affective, and psychomotor taxonomies in your **Teaching Resources** file.
- Include Table 12.6, "Active Learning and Teacher Presentations," in your file.
- If you will teach elementary school, include Table 12.10, "Improving Reading: CIERA's 10 Research-Based Principles."

Video**Workshop** Extra

If the VideoWorkshop package was included with your textbook, go to Chapter 12 of the Companion Website (www.ablongman.com/woolfolk) and click on the VideoWorkshop button. Follow the instructions for viewing *Video Clip 4: Adaptions in the Inclusive Classroom.* Consider this information along with what you've read in Chapter 12 while answering the following questions:

1. How are the teachers in this video adapting this classroom, lessons, and testing to make them more accessible for special needs students? Imagine you are a 5th-grade teacher with a partially sighted student in your classroom. What kinds of accommodations might you make for this student?
2. How does a teacher determine how to modify a classroom for a student with special needs?

Use the CD-ROM included in the back of your textbook to launch the "Becoming a Professional" website. The website features advice on preparing for teacher certification exams, help with getting your first job, and resources to help you perform your job well from the first day forward.

Teachers' Casebook

What Would They Do?

Here is how some practicing teachers responded to the teaching situation presented at the beginning of this chapter about preparing students for proficiency tests.

Sandra Gill

Sixth Grade Teacher, *Hudson Middle School, Hudson, New York*

Since the topics on the upcoming proficiency test are important ones, I would use them to form the core of my own curriculum. The curriculum would augment individual assignments with a hefty dose of group challenges in which students would work collaboratively in doing projects involving the examination of the world outside of school. These challenges would culminate in written reports as well as group presentations, incorporating both visual and verbal elements, for classmates and others. I would choose the members of each group based on the personalities and learning styles of the students. The competencies and topics that pertained to the proficiency test would be identified in the plan for each group challenge, and they would be repeated in subsequent challenges in order to reinforce them.

Julie Mohok

Classroom Teacher, *Ponam Primary School, Manus Island, Papua New Guinea* (currently a doctoral student at Queensland University of Technology)

The first thing I would do is try to understand the situation. Perhaps through conversing with other teachers, and analyzing past records I could quickly learn of the contributing factors to the present low school performance. In addition, I would find out what the reasons are for the school's decision to resort to drill and practice on facts and skills. This may be a situation analysis. This understanding would assist me in planning my teaching for the first few weeks without overtly challenging the school administration.

I would proceed to plan and teach on the principle that learning and developing skills is for usage in the real world and not merely for passing some important test. This may include experiments, simulations, role plays, watching a video clip on a specific topic, etc. These activities should motivate students by arousing curiosity and interest in learning. Drilling and practice of key concepts and skills can follow enjoyable segments. In the process, I would inform the school's administration of my teaching program. Perhaps I might even suggest that they conduct a mid-test within the school to find out if my teaching makes a difference to the students' success rate as they prepare for the big test.

Margaret Doolan

Year Three, *St. Michael's School, Gordonvale QLD 4865, Australia*

What a challenge!

The first few weeks would be spent in becoming familiar with my students and the standard of work of each. I would then enlist the help of my teacher-aide and as many parents as possible to help with individual and small-group study.

Throughout the year we would cover all test topics using all forms of information available—books, library visits, excursions, guest speakers, newspapers, computers, and displays. We would read, write, talk, write poems, illustrate, and integrate with science, math, and the arts wherever possible. I would present these topics as normal curriculum learning, without mentioning "test" to the class at this stage. Finally, in order to prepare the class for the actual test itself, I would obtain copies of previous papers and practice going through them. If necessary to create enthusiasm, I would graph class results (not individual) and attempt to achieve a higher rate of successful answers each time.

Jennifer Hudson Thomas

Armidale High School, Armidale, Australia

Although the importance of the 4th grade proficiency test cannot be overlooked from both the student's and school's point of view, it should not impede the process of "real" teaching and learning. Developing an enthusiasm for the learning required should be the greatest priority for any group of learners. Listing the mandatory topics to be covered and voting on the order in which these topics will be undertaken will give the learners some ownership of the direction that their learning will take over the year. Further involvement in planning the course and outcomes of such units of work will also increase students' commitment to their learning. Relating the learning within each topic to the real-life situations and interests of the group of learners will also help promote and "sell" the learning required. As the teacher, it will be my responsibility to incorporate as many of the required competencies as often as possible in all learning undertaken. This should ensure that the facts and skills required for that proficiency test become consolidated learning and form the basis of an automatic and well-rehearsed response repertoire. With such a learning background, my students should be able to generalize their skills and approach the proficiency test in the spring with confidence.

Go to the Companion Website (www.ablongman.com/woolfolk) for additional case studies including audio and video cases, and examples of student work.

CHAPTER

13

Teaching for Self-Regulation, Creativity, and Tolerance

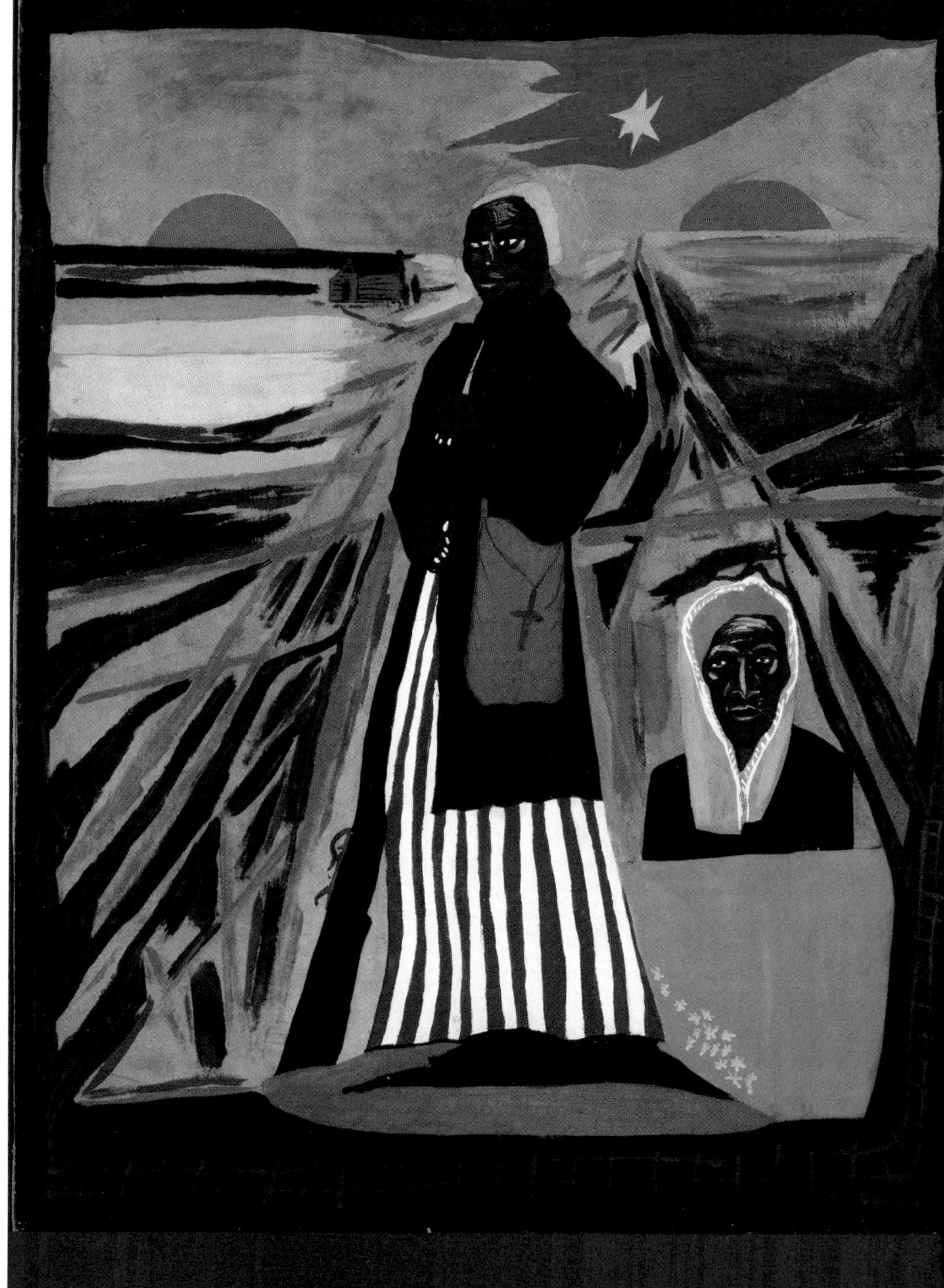

Teachers' Casebook

What Would You Do?

When a terrible tragedy strikes, such as the events of 9/11 or a shooting in a school, how would you handle the situation? Assume you are in class on a Tuesday in the winter. It is late morning and you have just gone to lunch when you hear that a few students in a nearby high school have taken some teachers and other students hostage. Rumors are flying about whether the students have guns, what they want, who is involved, how many hostages there are, and when the incident began. Some students and teachers in your school have friends and relatives in this neighboring district.

Critical Thinking

What is your immediate response? What will you do over the next few weeks and months to respond to the students' concerns and fears about such frightening events?

Collaboration

With 2 other members of your class, draft what you would say to your class.

Even with all the concern about academic standards, performance on proficiency tests, and international comparisons of student achievement, schooling has always been about more than academic learning. Of course academics are the prime directive, "but schools have major responsibilities for other aspects of students' development as well, such as helping students develop the attitudes, skills, and orientations needed to lead humane lives and act effectively as citizens to sustain democratic institutions" (Battistich, Watson, Solomon, Lewis, & Schaps, 1999).

In addition, an education that prepares students to live humane lives has value in the corporate marketplace:

> Most corporations are looking for employees who are not only good at the mastery of a particular set of academic skills but who also have the ability to work harmoniously with a wide variety of coworkers as a cooperative team, to demonstrate initiative and responsibility, and to communicate effectively. (Aronson, 2000, p. 91)

In this chapter we look at several important nonacademic outcomes of schooling that are critical for success in and out of school. We begin with a basic ability—self-regulation—being able to manage your own emotions, thinking, learning, and actions.

By the time you have completed this chapter, you should be able to answer the following questions.

- *What are the factors that facilitate self-regulated learning?*
- *How would you define creativity, and what are sources and some ideas about creativity?*
- *What is emotional intelligence, and what are social and emotional learning?*
- *Why is compassion and tolerance important in schools?*
- *How can you create a learning community in your classroom?*
- *How can cooperative learning strategies promote academic and social development?*

Self-Regulation and Agency

STOP THINK WRITE How are you studying right now? What goals have you set for your reading today? What is your plan for learning, and what strategies are you using right now to learn? How did you learn those strategies?

Barry Zimmerman (2002) defines **self-regulation** as the process we use to activate and sustain our thoughts, behaviors, and emotions in order to reach our goals. When the goals involve learning, we talk about self-regulated learning.

Today, people change jobs an average of seven times before they retire. Many of these career changes require new learning that must be self-initiated and self-directed (Martinez-Pons, 2002; Weinstein, 1994). Thus, one goal of teaching should be to free students from the need for teachers so the students can continue to learn independently throughout their lives. To continue learning independently throughout life, you must be a self-regulated learner. **Self-regulated learners** have a combination of academic learning skills and self-control that makes learning easier, so they are more motivated; in other words, they have the *skill* and the *will* to learn (McCombs & Marzano, 1990; Murphy & Alexander, 2000). Self-regulated learners transform their mental abilities, whatever they are, into academic skills (Zimmerman, 2002).

CONNECT & EXTEND

TO THE RESEARCH

The Spring 2002 issue of *Theory Into Practice* is devoted to "Becoming a Self-Regulated Learner." The editors for this volume were Stephen Pape, Barry Zimmerman, and Frank Pajares—three of the top researchers in the area of self-regulated learning. There are articles about what classroom teachers can do to help students learn how to learn; self-regulation in math, reading, and writing; gender differences in self-regulation; and other useful topics. See http://www.coe.ohio-state.edu/TIP/

What Influences Self-Regulation?

The concept of self-regulated learning integrates much of what is known about effective learning and motivation. Three factors influence skill and will: knowledge, motivation, and self-discipline or volition.

CONNECT & EXTEND

TO **PRAXIS**™

SELF-REGULATION (II, A1)

Take a look at *The Learning Base* (http://www.allkindsofminds.org/library/challenges/GTPSelfregulatingLearning.htm) for tips to help students develop the goals, metacognitive skills, and self-regulatory practices that can support a lifelong devotion to learning.

Knowledge. To be self-regulated learners, students need *knowledge* about themselves, the subject, the task, strategies for learning, and the contexts in which they will apply their learning. "Expert" students know about *themselves* and how they learn best. For example, they know their preferred learning styles, what is easy and what is hard for them, how to cope with the difficult parts, what their interests and talents are, and how to use their strengths (see Chapter 4 of this book). These experts also know quite a bit about the *subject* being studied—and the more they know, the easier it is to learn more (Alexander, 1997). They probably understand that different *learning tasks* require different approaches on their part. A simple memory task, for example, might require a mnemonic strategy (see Chapter 7) whereas a complex comprehension task might be approached by means of concept maps of the key ideas (see Chapter 8). Also, these self-regulated learners know that learning is often difficult and knowledge is seldom absolute; there usually are different ways of looking at problems as well as different solutions (Pressley, 1995; Winne, 1995).

These expert students not only know what each task requires; they also can apply the *strategy* needed. They can skim or read carefully. They can use memory strategies or reorganize the material. As they become more knowledgeable in a field, they apply many of these strategies automatically. In short, they have mastered a large, flexible repertoire of learning strategies and tactics (see Chapter 8).

Finally, expert learners think about the *contexts* in which they will apply their knowledge—when and where they will use their learning—so they can set motivating goals and connect present work to future accomplishments (Wang & Palincsar, 1989; Weinstein, 1994; Winne, 1995).

Motivation. Self-regulated learners are *motivated* to learn (see Chapter 10). They find many tasks in school interesting because they value learning, not just performing well in the eyes of others. But even if they are not intrinsically motivated by a particular task, they are serious about getting the intended benefit from it. They know *why* they are studying, so their actions and choices are self-determined and not controlled by others. However, knowledge and motivation are not always enough. Self-

Self-regulation Process of activating and sustaining thoughts, behaviors, and emotions in order to reach goals.

Self-regulated learners Have a combination of academic learning skills and self-control that makes learning easier.

Volition Will power; self-discipline.

Family and Community Partnerships

Parents Supporting Self-Regulation

Help parents model self-regulation.

Examples

1. Ask parents to show their children how they set goals for the day or week, write to-do lists, or keep appointment books.
2. Encourage parents to model self-evaluation as they focus on areas they want to improve.

Emphasize the value of encouragement.

Examples

1. Target small steps for improving an academic skill.
2. Tell parents about the areas that are most challenging for their child—the areas that will be the most in need of encouragement.

Make families a source of good strategy ideas.

Examples

1. Have short, simple materials describing a "strategy of the month" that students can practice at home.
2. Create a lending library of books about goal setting, motivation, learning, and time-management strategies for students.
3. Encourage families to help their children focus on problem-solving processes and not turn immediately to the answers at the back of the book when doing homework.

Provide self-evaluation guidelines for families.

Examples

1. Give families ideas about assignment or record-keeping sheets.
2. For parent conferences, have examples of materials other families have successfully used to keep track of progress.

regulated learners need volition or self-discipline. "Where motivation denotes commitment, volition denotes follow-through" (Corno, 1992, p. 72).

Volition. It is Friday night. I have been writing almost all day and my cold is getting worse. I want to keep writing because the deadline for this chapter is very near. I have knowledge and motivation, but to keep going I need a good dose of volition. **Volition** is an old-fashioned word for will-power. Self-regulated learners know how to protect themselves from distractions—where to study, for example, so they are not interrupted. They know how to cope when they feel anxious, drowsy, or lazy (Corno, 1992, 1995; Snow, Corno, & Jackson, 1996). And they know what to do when tempted to stop working and take a nap—the temptation I'm facing now—that, and a large bowl of (low-fat) chips and salsa.

Parents can teach and support self-regulated learning through modeling and encouragement at home. There are also ways that teachers can work with parents to help students become more self-regulating.

Family Influences. Children begin to learn self-regulation in their homes. Parents can teach and support self-regulated learning through modeling, encouragement, facilitation, and rewarding of goal setting, good strategy use, and other processes described in the next section (Martinez-Pons, 2002). The *Family and Community Partnership Guidelines* give some ideas for working with parents to help students become more self-regulating.

Obviously, not all of your students will be self-regulated learners. In fact, some psychologists suggest that you think of this capacity as an individual difference characteristic (Snow, Corno, & Jackson, 1996). Some students are much better at it than others. How can you help more students become self-regulated learners? What is involved in being self-regulated?

CONNECT & EXTEND

TO THE RESEARCH
See the entire issue of *Educational Leadership,* September 2002 (Vol. 60, No. 1) for 14 articles on "Do Students Care About Learning?" These articles discuss how to create enthusiasm, excitement, and investment in learning.

Self-Regulation Processes

Students today are faced with constant distractions. Barry Zimmerman (2002, p. 64) describes Tracy, a high-school student who is devoted to MTV:

> An important mid-term math exam is two weeks away, and she had begun to study while listening to popular music "to relax her." Tracy has not set any study goals for herself—instead she simply tells herself to do as well as she can on the test. She uses no specific learning strategies for condensing and memorizing important material and does not plan out her study time, so she ends up cramming for a few hours before the test. She has only vague self-evaluative standards and cannot gauge her academic preparation accurately. Tracy attributes her learning difficulties to an inherent lack of mathematical ability and is very defensive about her poor study methods. However, she does not ask for help from others because she is afraid of "looking stupid," or seek out supplementary materials from the library because she "already has too much to learn." She finds studying to be anxiety-provoking, has little self-confidence in achieving success, and sees little intrinsic value in acquiring mathematical skill.

Clearly, Tracy is unlikely to do well on the test. What would help? Look at Figure 13.1 and you will see the phases of self-regulation—processes that would help Tracy learn math. In the forethought phase, Tracy needs to set clear, reasonable goals and plan a few strategies for accomplishing those goals. And Tracy's beliefs about motivation make a difference at this point too. If Tracy had a sense of self-efficacy for doing the

The phases of self-regulation are forethought, performance, and self-reflection—linked in a continuing cycle.

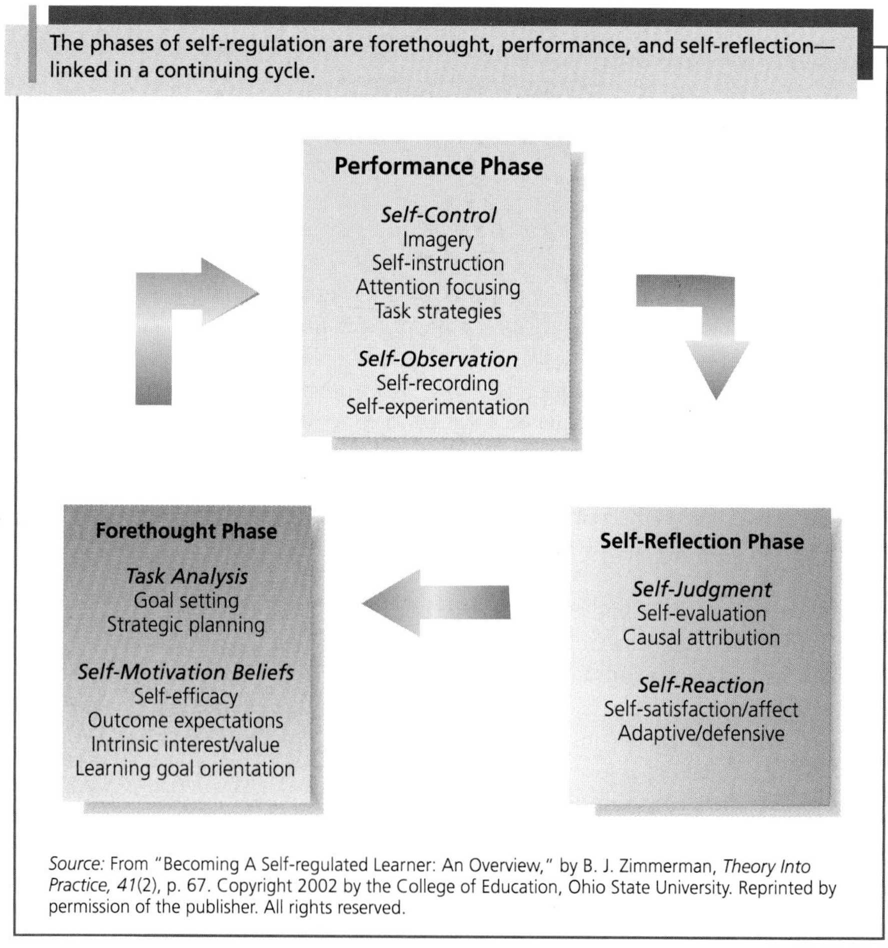

Source: From "Becoming A Self-regulated Learner: An Overview," by B. J. Zimmerman, *Theory Into Practice, 41*(2), p. 67.

Figure 13.1 The Cycle of Self-Regulated Learning

strategies that she planned, if she believed that using those strategies would lead to math learning and success on the test, if she saw some connections between her own interests and the math learning, and if she were trying to master the material—not just look good or avoid looking bad—then she would be on the road to self-regulated learning.

Moving from the forethought to the performance phase brings new challenges. Now Tracy must have a repertoire of self-control (volitional) and learning strategies, including using imagery, mnemonics, attention focusing, and other techniques such as those described in Chapter 7 (Kiewra, 2002). She also will need to self-observe, that is, monitor how things are going so she can change strategies if needed. Actual recording of time spent, problems solved, or pages written may provide clues about when or how to make the best use of study time.

Finally, Tracy needs to look back on her performance and reflect on what happened. It will help her develop a sense of efficacy if she attributes successes to effort and good strategy use and avoids self-defeating actions such as making weak efforts or pretending not to care. All of these self-regulation strategies can be learned and improved through direct teaching, modeling, coaching, and practice (Butler, 2002; Pape & Smith, 2002). Table 13.1 shows how a teacher might work with individuals, small groups, and the whole class to learn self-monitoring, self-evaluation, and positive self-perceptions.

Check Yourself What factors are involved in self-regulated learning? What is the self-regulated learning cycle?

■ Table 13.1 Teaching Students To Be Self-Regulated Learners

Here is how a teacher might work with individuals, small groups, and the whole class to learn self-monitoring, self-evaluation, and positive self-perceptions.

Instructional Targets	General Instructional Principles	Individual Instruction	Small-Group Instruction	Whole-Class Instruction
Self-monitoring, self-evaluation, and positive self-perceptions	■ Teacher assists students to (a) compare outcomes to task criteria, (b) interpret and use instructor feedback, (c) revise ineffective approaches, (d) link success to effortful strategy use, (e) articulate personalized strategies for monitoring. ■ Students record revisions to strategies in their own words for reference and ongoing strategy development.	■ Student completes work and/or brings in an assignment with teacher feedback. ■ Teacher asks questions that guide student to (a) self-evaluate work quality, (b) analyze teacher feedback, (c) recognize successes, (d) identify problems and needed solutions. ■ Student revises his or her strategy sheet with advice to him- or herself about what to do in the future.	■ Teacher facilitates small-group discussions. ■ Teacher guides students to evaluate outcomes, either in process or after receiving feedback from teachers. ■ Students work together to compare outcomes to task demands. ■ Students share ideas about how to revise approaches to build on successes but overcome challenges. ■ Students record revisions to their personalized strategies in their own words.	■ Teacher asks students to self-evaluate work prior to submission. ■ Teacher provides feedback to students that references task criteria. ■ Teacher requires students to interpret and learn from instructor feedback as part of the assignment. ■ Teacher facilitates small- and/or large-group discussions in which students evaluate outcomes (anonymous) against task goals. ■ Teacher provides feedback on products and the process of self-monitoring.

SOURCE: From "Individualizing Instruction in Self-Regulated Learning," by D. L. Butler, *Theory Into Practice, 41*(2), p. 88.

Creativity

Consider this student. He had severe dyslexia—a learning disability that made reading and writing exceedingly difficult. He described himself as an "underdog." In school, he knew that if the reading assignment would take others an hour, he had to allow two or three hours. He knew that he had to keep a list of all his most frequently misspelled words in order to be able to write at all. He spent hours alone in his room. Would you expect his writing to be creative?

The person in the box above is John Irving, celebrated author of what one critic called "wildly inventive" novels such as *The World According to Garp, The Cider House Rules,* and *A Prayer for Owen Meany* (Amabile, 2001). How do we explain his amazing creativity? Let's start by asking: What is creativity?

Defining Creativity

CONNECT & EXTEND

TO YOUR TEACHING/PORTFOLIO
For a wonderful story of a first year teacher with truly creative ideas see Codell, E. R. (2001). *Educating Esme: Diary of a teacher's first year.* Chapel Hill, NC: Algonquin Books.

Howard Gardner defines the creative individual as "a person who regularly solves problems, fashions products, or defines new questions in a domain in a way that is initially considered novel but that ultimately becomes accepted in a particular cultural setting" (Gardner, 1993a, p. 35). The notion of solving problems that are important for a particular culture is also part of his definition of intelligence. So creativity, talent, and intelligence are related; they allow us to solve important problems (Robinson & Clinkenbeard, 1998).

Creativity is the ability to produce work that is original, but still appropriate and useful (Berk, 2002). Most psychologists agree that there is no such thing as "all-purpose creativity"; people are creative *in a particular area,* as John Irving was in writing fiction. But to be creative, the "invention" must be intended. An accidental spilling of paint that produces a novel design is not creative unless the artist recognizes the potential of the "accident" or uses the spilling technique intentionally to create new works (Weisberg, 1993). Although we frequently associate the arts with creativity, any subject can be approached in a creative manner.

What Is the Source of Creativity?

Researchers have studied cognitive processes, personality factors, motivational patterns, and background experiences to explain creativity (Simonton, 2000). But to truly understand creativity, we must look to the social environment too. Both intrapersonal (cognition, personality) and social factors support creativity (Amabile, 1996; 2001; Simonton, 2000). Teresa Amabile (1996) proposes a three-component model of creativity:

1. *Domain-relevant skills* including talents and competencies that are valuable for working in the domain. An example would be Michelangelo's skills in shaping stone, developed when he lived with a stonecutter's family as a child.
2. *Creativity-relevant processes* including work habits and personality traits such as a John Irving's habits of working 10-hour days to write and rewrite and rewrite until he perfected his stories.
3. *Intrinsic task motivation* or a deep curiosity and fascination with the task. This aspect of creativity can be greatly influenced by the social environment (as we saw in Chapter 10), by supporting autonomy, stimulating curiosity, encouraging fantasy, and providing challenge.

Another social factor that influences creativity is whether the field is ready and willing to acknowledge the creative contribution (Nakamura & Csikszentmihalyi, 2001). History is filled with examples of creative breakthroughs rejected at the time (for

Creativity Imaginative, original thinking or problem solving.

example, Galileo's theory of the sun at the center of the solar system) and of rivalries between creators that led each to push the edges of creativity (the friendly and productive rivalry between Picasso and Matisse).

Creativity and Cognition. Having a rich store of knowledge in an area is the basis for creativity, but something more is needed. For many problems, that "something more" is the ability to break set—**restructuring** the problem to see things in a new way, which leads to a sudden insight. Often this happens when a person has struggled with a problem or project, then sets it aside for a while. Some psychologists believe that time away from the problem allows for *incubation,* a kind of unconscious working through the problem. It is more likely that leaving the problem for a time interrupts rigid ways of thinking so you can restructure your view of the situation (Gleitman, Fridlund, & Reisberg, 1999). So it seems that creativity requires extensive knowledge, flexibility, and the continual reorganizing of ideas. And we saw that motivation, persistence, and social support play important roles in the creative process as well.

The focus of creativity research and writing in the past has been on white males. This underrepresents and misunderstands the nature of creativity in women and ethnic minority groups.

Creativity and Diversity. Even though creativity has been studied for centuries, as Dean Simonton said, "Psychologists still have a long way to go before they come anywhere close to understanding creativity in women and minorities" (2000, p. 156). The focus of creativity research and writing over the years has been white males. Patterns of creativity in other groups are complex—sometimes matching and sometimes diverging from patterns found in traditional research. Keep this in mind as you read the findings discussed in the next few sections. Women and ethnic minority groups have been underrepresented in many of these studies.

In another connection between creativity and culture, research suggests that being on the outside of mainstream society, being bilingual, or being exposed to other cultures might encourage creativity (Simonton, 1999, 2000). In fact, true innovators often break rules. "Creators have a desire to shake things up. They are restless, rebellious, and dissatisfied with the status quo" (Winner, 2000, p. 167).

Assessing Creativity

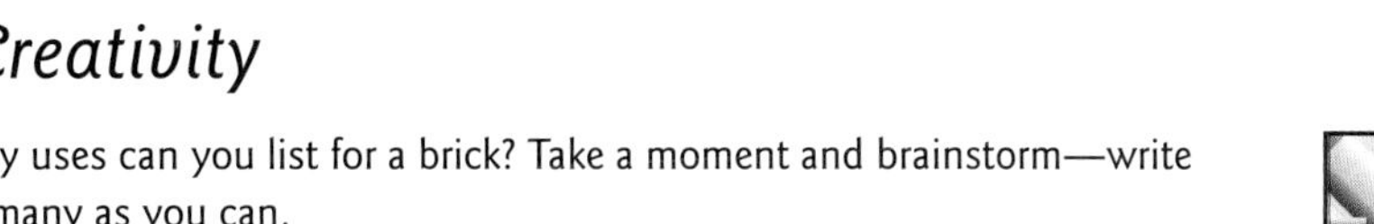

STOP THINK WRITE How many uses can you list for a brick? Take a moment and brainstorm—write down as many as you can.

How shall we assess creativity? One answer has been to equate creativity with divergent thinking. **Divergent thinking** is the ability to propose many different ideas or answers. **Convergent thinking** is the more common ability to identify only one answer.

Agnes is able to think divergently.

Restructuring Conceiving of a problem in a new or different way.

Divergent thinking Coming up with many possible solutions.

Convergent thinking Narrowing possibilities to a single answer.

The titles she gave her drawings, from left to right, are as follows: "Dracula," "one-eyed monster," "pumpkin," "Hula-Hoop," "poster," "wheelchair," "earth," "moon," "planet," "movie camera," "sad face," "picture," "stoplight," "beach ball," "the letter O," "car," "glasses."

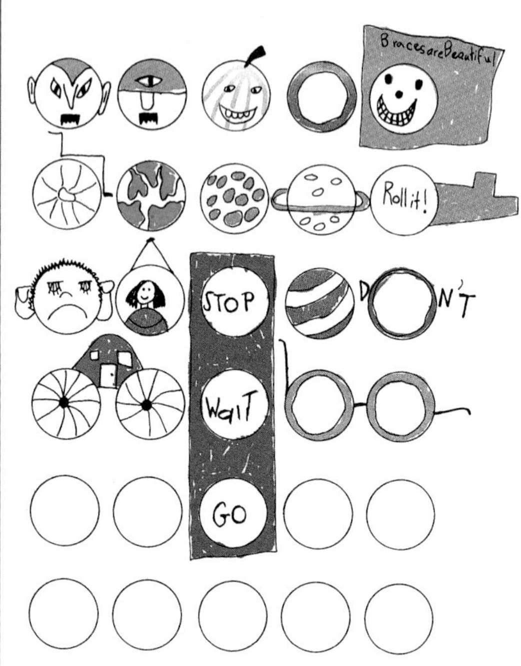

Source: Test form copyright © 1980 by Scholastic Testing Service, Inc. Reprinted by permission of Scholastic Testing Service, Inc., Bensenville, IL 60106 from *The Torrance Tests of Creative Thinking* by E. P. Torrance.

■ **Figure 13.2** A Graphic Assessment of the Creativity of an Eight-Year-Old

E. P. Torrance has developed two types of creativity tests: verbal and graphic (Torrance, 1972; Torrance & Hall, 1980). In the verbal test, you might be instructed to think up as many uses as possible for a brick (as you did above) or asked how a particular toy might be changed to make it more fun. On the graphic test, you might be given 30 circles and asked to create 30 different drawings, each drawing including at least one circle. Figure 13.2 shows the creativity of an 8-year-old girl in completing this task.

Responses to all these tasks are scored for originality, fluency, and flexibility, three aspects of divergent thinking. *Originality* is usually determined statistically. To be original, a response must be given by fewer than 5 or 10 people out of every 100 who take the test. *Fluency* is the number of different responses. *Flexibility* is generally measured by the number of different categories of responses. For instance, if you listed 20 uses of a brick, but each was to build something, your fluency score might be high, but your flexibility score would be low. Of the three measures, fluency—the number of responses—is the best predictor of divergent thinking, but there is more to real-life creativity than divergent thinking (Bjorklund, 1989).

Teachers are not always the best judges of creativity. In fact, Torrance (1972) reports data from a 12-year follow-up study indicating no relationship between teachers' judgments of their students' creative abilities and the actual creativity these students revealed in their adult lives. A few possible indicators of creativity in your students are curiosity, concentration, adaptability, high energy, humor (sometimes bizarre), independence, playfulness, nonconformity, risk taking, attraction to the complex and mysterious, willingness to fantasize and daydream, intolerance for boredom, and inventiveness (Sattler, 1992).

Creativity in the Classroom

Today's and tomorrow's complex problems require creative solutions. How can teachers promote creative thinking? All too often, in the crush of day-to-day classroom life, teachers stifle creative ideas without realizing what they are doing. Teachers are in an excellent position to encourage or discourage creativity through their acceptance or rejection of the unusual and imaginative. The *Guidelines* on the next page, adapted from Frederiksen (1984) and Sattler (1992), describe other possibilities for encouraging creativity.

Brainstorming. In addition to encouraging creativity through everyday interactions with students, teachers can try **brainstorming.** The basic tenet of brainstorming is to separate the process of creating ideas from the process of evaluating them because evaluation often inhibits creativity (Osborn, 1963). Evaluation, discussion, and criticism are postponed until all possible suggestions have been made. In this way, one idea inspires others; people do not withhold potentially creative solutions out of fear of criticism. John Baer (1997, p. 43) gives these rules for brainstorming:

1. Defer judgment.
2. Avoid ownership of ideas. When people feel that an idea is "theirs," egos sometimes get in the way of creative thinking. They are likely to be more defensive later when ideas are critiqued, and they are less willing to allow their ideas to be modified.

CONNECT & EXTEND

TO **PRAXIS**™
CREATIVITY (II, A3)
Describe techniques that teachers can use to enhance creative thinking in the classroom. Go to *Mind Tools* (http://www.demon.co.uk/mindtool/brainstm.html) for tips about implementing effective brainstorming procedures.

Brainstorming Generating ideas without stopping to evaluate them.

GUIDELINES ENCOURAGING CREATIVITY

Accept and encourage divergent thinking.

Examples

1. During class discussion, ask: "Can anyone suggest a different way of looking at this question?"
2. Reinforce attempts at unusual solutions to problems, even if the final product is not perfect.

Tolerate dissent.

Examples

1. Ask students to support dissenting opinions.
2. Make sure nonconforming students receive an equal share of classroom privileges and rewards.

Encourage students to trust their own judgment.

Examples

1. When students ask questions you think they can answer, rephrase or clarify the questions and direct them back to the students.
2. Give ungraded assignments from time to time.

Emphasize that everyone is capable of creativity in some form.

Examples

1. Avoid describing the feats of great artists or inventors as if they were superhuman accomplishments.
2. Recognize creative efforts in each student's work. Have a separate grade for originality on some assignments.

Be a stimulus for creative thinking.

Examples

1. Use a class brainstorming session whenever possible.
2. Model creative problem solving by suggesting unusual solutions for class problems.
3. Encourage students to delay judging a particular suggestion for solving a problem until all the possibilities have been considered.

3. Feel free to "hitchhike" on other ideas. This means that it's okay to borrow elements from ideas already on the table, or to make slight modifications of ideas already suggested.
4. Encourage wild ideas. Impossible, totally unworkable ideas may lead someone to think of other, more possible, more workable ideas. It's easier to take a wildly imaginative bad idea and tone it down to fit the constraints of reality than to take a boring bad idea and make it interesting enough to be worth thinking about.

Individuals as well as groups may benefit from brainstorming. In writing this book, for example, I have sometimes found it helpful to list all the different topics that could be covered in a chapter, then leave the list and return to it later to evaluate the ideas.

Take Your Time—and Play! Years ago, Sigmund Freud (1959) linked creativity and play: "Might we not say that every child at play behaves like a creative writer, in that he creates a world of his own, or, rather, rearranges the things of his world in a new way which pleases him? . . . The creative writer does the same as the child at play. He creates a world of phantasy which he takes very seriously—that is, which he invests with large amounts of emotion" (pp. 143–144). There is some evidence that preschool children who spend more time in fantasy and pretend play are more creative. In fact, playing

CONNECT & EXTEND

TO THE RESEARCH

For recent research on brainstorming, see: Brown, V. R., & Paulus, P. B. (2002). Making group brainstorming more effective: Recommendations from an associative memory perspective. *Current Directions in Psychological Science, 11,* 208–212.

DILBERT

Dilbert leads his coworkers in brainstorming.

before taking a creativity test resulted in higher scores on the test for the young students in one study (Berk, 2001; Bjorklund, 1989). Teachers can encourage students of all ages to be more reflective—to take time for ideas to grow, develop, and be restructured.

The Big C: Revolutionary Innovation

Do you remember the children in Terman's study of giftedness described in Chapter 4? These students all had IQ scores over 140—in the top 1% of the population. The students grew up to be experts and high-achieving professionals—but they did not innovate. They lacked what Ellen Winner (2000) calls the "big-C creativity" or innovation that establishes a new field or revolutionizes an old one. Even child prodigies do not necessarily become adult innovators. Prodigies have mastered well-established domains very early, but innovators change the entire domain. Innovators often are rebellious, restless, dissatisfied, courageous, and independent. "Individuals who ultimately make creative breakthroughs tend from their earliest days to be explorers, innovators, and tinkerers. . . . Often this adventurousness is interpreted as insubordination, though more fortunate tinkerers receive from teachers or peers some form of encouragement for their experimentation" (Gardner, 1993a, pp. 32–33). What can parents and teachers do to encourage these potential creators? Winner (2000) lists four dangers to avoid:

1. Avoid pushing so hard that the child's intrinsic passion to master a field becomes a craving for extrinsic rewards.
2. Avoid pushing so hard that the child later looks back on a missed childhood.
3. Avoid freezing the child into a safe, technically perfect way of performing that has led to lavish rewards.
4. Be aware of the psychological wounds that can follow when the child who can perform perfectly becomes the forgotten adult who can do nothing more than continue to perform perfectly—without ever creating something new.

Finally, teachers and parents can encourage students with outstanding abilities and creative talents to give back to the society that has provided the extra support and resources that they needed. Service learning, discussed later in the chapter, is one opportunity.

Check Yourself What is creativity and how is it assessed?

How can teachers support creativity in the classroom?

Social and Emotional Learning

CONNECT & EXTEND

TO YOUR TEACHING/PORTFOLIO
For a full description of several programs and strategies that support social emotional learning, see Cohen, J. (Ed.) (1999). *Educating minds and hearts: Social emotional learning and the passage into adolescence.* New York: Teachers College Press.

You may remember in Chapter 4 we examined Howard Gardner's theory of multiple intelligences, including intrapersonal and interpersonal intelligences. In this section we look briefly at the learning that is related to these areas. We begin with the individual and the concept of emotional intelligence.

Emotional Intelligence

What Would You Say? As part of the interview process for a job in a middle school, you are asked the following: "What do you think about the idea of emotional intelligence? Would you teach that in your class?"

Emotional intelligence (EQ) The ability to process emotional information accurately and efficiently.

We all know people who are academically or artistically talented, but unsuccessful. They have problems in school, in relationships, and on the job, but can't improve the situations. According to some psychologists, the source of the difficulties may be a lack of **emotional intelligence,** first defined by Peter Salovey and John Mayer as the ability to process emotional information accurately and efficiently (Mayer & Cobb,

2000; Mayer & Salovey, 1997; Roberts, Zeidner, & Matthews, 2001). Daniel Goleman (1995) popularized the idea of emotional intelligence (E-IQ or EQ) in his best-selling book based on the work of Salovey and Mayer. Goleman's ideas even made the cover of *Time* magazine (Gibbs, 1995) and were featured in publications for principals and teachers including the magazine *Education Leadership.*

Success in life requires more than cognitive skills; it is important to be emotionally "smart" as well. Teachers can help students develop emotional as well as cognitive intelligence.

What Is EQ? At the center of emotional intelligence are four broad abilities: perceiving, integrating, understanding, and managing emotions (Mayer & Cobb, 2000). If you can't *perceive* what you are feeling, how can you make good choices about jobs, relationships, time management, or even entertainment (Baron, 1998)? Individuals who can *perceive* and *understand* emotions in others (usually by reading the nonverbal cues) and respond appropriately are more successful in working with people and often emerge as leaders (Wood & Wood, 1999). If you can't *integrate* your emotions into your thinking about situations and *understand* your own emotions, how can you communicate your feelings to others accurately? Friends keep asking, "What's wrong?" and you keep saying, "Nothing!"

Finally, you must *manage* your emotions, particularly negative emotions such as anger or depression. The goal is not to suppress feelings, but not to be overwhelmed by them either. Managing emotions includes the ability to focus energy, persist, control impulses, and delay immediate gratification. Emotional management is critical in school. For example, compared to 4-year-old students who act on their impulses immediately, 4-year-old children who can delay instant gratification to work toward a goal become much better students in high school (Shoda, Mischel, & Peake, 1990).

Some researchers have criticized the notion of EQ, saying that emotional intelligence is not a cluster of capabilities but rather a set of personality traits or the application of general intelligence to social situations (Izard, 2001; Nestor-Baker, 1999). Does intelligence inform emotion so we are "smart" about managing our feelings and impulses or does emotion inform intelligence so we make good decisions and understand other people? Probably both are true. The major point is that success in life requires more than cognitive skills, and teachers are important influences in helping students develop all of these capabilities.

EQ Goes to School. In less than a decade, the subject of emotional intelligence and competency has become a topic of increasing interest to educators as they interact with students affected by stresses and challenges of a complex world. Some research suggests that programs that help students build their emotional competencies have beneficial effects, including an increase in cooperative behaviors and a reduction in anti-social activities like the use of slurs and bullying. For example, Norma Feshbach (1989, 1997) developed a 36-hour program for helping elementary students become more empathetic. The program included exercises such as deciding what each person in your family would like most as a birthday present or determining how the world would appear to you if you were a cat. Students also retold stories from the perspective of the different characters in a story, then played the role of each character on videotaped performances of the stories. Students learned to analyze how people looked and sounded as they played each role. Sandra Graham's (1996) program for helping aggressive boys learn to read the intentions of others also included role plays and practice in reading the emotions of others. The educational advantages of decreased student aggression and increased empathy are obvious, but these skills also prepare students for life outside the classroom.

Cautions. One of the problems with innovations in educational psychology is that they are often inadvertently misinterpreted or ill-described in the popular media by writers and reporters who have limited backgrounds in both psychology and education. The concept of emotional intelligence is one innovation that seems to be facing that fate. For authoritative information on this topic you will find it useful to turn to these sources:

> ***Emotional Intelligence Home Page:*** Basic assumptions of emotional intelligence, different perspectives, and tests of EQ
> **(http://www.emotionaliq.com/Gdefault.htm)**

Edutopia: This online journal devotes an entire issue to emotional intelligence and learning, including research, practices, and resources. **(http://glef.org/EdutopiaPDF/Spring01.pdf)**

New Hampshire Public Radio: Listen to an interview with John D. Mayer, one of the creators of the concept of emotional intelligence. **(http://www.nhpr.org/content/fullmonty_view.php/2368/)**

Social Skills

As we saw in Chapter 3, having stable, supportive relationships with friends who are socially competent and mature enhances social development, especially during difficult times (Hartup & Stevens, 1999). Rejected children often have more problems as adults, such as dropping out of school or committing crimes (Coie et al., 1995; Coie & Dodge, 1998). Many social skills are important for learning as well. For example, listening is valuable in relationships, in classes, and on the job. See the *Reaching Every Student* feature for an example of one teacher who taught her students how to listen.

~ Reaching Every Student ~

Learning to Listen

Ms. Perez and her fourth-grade class are working on a unit on social skills in social studies. They are learning the skill of listening to someone who is talking by doing the following:

1. Look at the person who is talking.
2. Remember to sit quietly.
3. Think about what is being said.
4. Say yes or nod your head.
5. Ask a question about the topic to find out more.

Jeanine, a student in the class, has just practiced these listening skills in front of the class by role-playing the part of a student who is talking to her teacher about an assignment. In the role-play, Ms. Perez played herself. The class is now giving Jeanine feedback on her performance.

Ms: Perez: First, did Jeanine look at me when I was talking? Before you answer, can someone tell me why it's important to look at the person who is talking?

Lorna: You don't want the other person to think you're not listening even though you are. So you really have to show them you are listening.

Ms. Perez: That's right, Lorna. Well, how did Jeanine do on this one?

Charles: Well, she looked at you at first but while you were explaining the assignment she looked down at her feet. It kind of looked like she wasn't listening.

Jeanine: I was listening, but I guess I should have kept good eye contact all the way through.

Ms. Perez: Yes, Jeanine. To be honest, if I didn't know you better, I would have thought that you didn't care about what I was saying. You need to work harder on that step. The next step is to remember to sit quietly. How did Jeanine do with this one?

Milton: I think she did well. She remembered not to laugh, fidget, or play with anything while you were talking.

Ms. Perez: I agree, Milton. Nice work, Jeanine. Now, can someone tell me what the next listening step is?

Kyrie: It's to think about what the person is saying.

Ms. Perez: Right, Kyrie. Let's let Jeanine evaluate herself on this one.

Jeanine: Well, I tried to think about what you were saying. Once I felt my mind start to wander, but I followed your suggestion and started thinking about a question that I could ask you.

Ms. Perez: Good, Jeanine. Trying to think of a question to ask can be very helpful. How did you think you did on the next step? Did you nod your head or say yes to show you were following me?

Jeanine: I think I did.

Ms. Perez: What do the rest of you think? Did Jeanine nod her head or say yes?

Tara: Well, I saw her nod a little, but it was hard to tell. Maybe she needs to nod more clearly.

Ms. Perez: Jeanine, you need to nod more strongly or the teacher won't realize you are doing it.

SOURCE: From *Including Students with Special Needs: A Practical Guide for Classroom Teachers* (3rd ed.), by Marilyn Friend & William D. Bursick. Published by Allyn & Bacon, Boston, MA. Copyright © 2002 by Pearson Education. Adapted by permission of the publisher.

Different social skills are important at different ages. Table 13.2 gives examples of the Social Development Program sequence from the New Haven Public Schools for grades K–3, 6, and 11 taken from Shriver, Schwab-Stone, and DeFalco (1999). For example, in the 6th grade, students are taught a six-step problem-solving process keyed to a traffic light poster:

RED	STOP, CALM DOWN, and THINK before you act
YELLOW	Say the PROBLEM and how you FEEL Set a POSITIVE GOAL Think of lots of SOLUTIONS Think ahead of the CONSEQUENCES
GREEN	GO ahead and TRY the BEST PLAN

Life Skills: Preventing High-Risk Behaviors

The statistics are frightening. By age 13, 40% of children have at least experimented with alcohol. Eating disorders emerge in early in adolescence, even as young as age 10. Sixteen percent of 13-year-olds have had sexual intercourse, but for many girls, their first experience was not voluntary. In fact, the estimates are that adult men (20 or older) are the fathers of two-thirds of babies born to teenage girls. Because problems begin early and because beliefs about personal vulnerability and health risks change little from ages 12 to 18, lessons about healthy living have to begin before middle school (Stipek, de la Sota, & Weishaupt, 1999).

■ Table 13.2 Social Development Programs

Here is the social development program sequence from the New Haven Public Schools for grades K–3, 6, and 11

K–3rd grade	6th Grade	11th Grade
36–55 lessons taught in each grade 2–3 times a week for the school year	45 lessons taught 3 times a week for 2 marking periods as a Life Skills Class	37 lessons integrated in U.S. History II throughout the year and 3 lessons taught in English
Project Charlie ■ Self-awareness ■ Relationships ■ Decision making ■ Chemical use in society ■ Violence prevention **Building Blocks: An AIDS Curriculum for Early Elementary Educators (4–6 lessons taught with Project Charlie)** ■ Germs ■ Communicable diseases ■ Staying healthy ■ Sickness and medicine ■ Immune system ■ Seeking health information ■ Being different ■ HIV/AIDS	**Social Problem Solving** ■ Self-control ■ Stress management ■ Problem solving ■ Decision making ■ Communication ■ Violence prevention **Substance Use Prevention** ■ Peer pressure resistance **Human Growth and Development, AIDS Prevention, and Teen Pregnancy Prevention** ■ Puberty ■ Reproduction ■ Relationships without sex ■ HIV/AIDS	**A World of Difference (taught in History)** ■ Beliefs and values ■ Prejudice, stereotyping, and discrimination ■ Scapegoating and racism ■ Violence prevention **Substance Use Prevention (taught in History)** ■ Effects of drug use in pregnancy and video *Innocent Addicts* **HIV/AIDS Education and Prevention (taught in English)** ■ Review of basic facts about HIV ■ Barriers to prevention ■ Living with AIDS

SOURCE: From *Educating Minds and Hearts: Social Emotional Learning and the Passage into Adolescence,* by J. Cohen. Published by Teachers College Press.

But what works? Providing information or "scare" tactics such as the DARE drug prevention program seem to have little positive effect and may even encourage curiosity and experimentation (Dusenbury & Falco, 1995; Tobler & Stratton, 1997). The most effective programs include developmentally appropriate language and concepts, teach students to resist social pressure, provide accurate information about rates of behavior (*not* everyone is doing it), use interactive teaching methods such as role-playing or small groups, provide training in skills that help in many situations such as the 6-step problem solving strategy described above, give thorough coverage of the topic with follow-up, and practice cultural sensitivity.

Debra Stipek and her colleagues (1999) describe many ways that teachers embed life lessons into school subjects and informal discussions. For example, class rules emphasize respect ("there are no stupid questions"), students learn to give "put ups" not "put downs," the lives of historical figures provide opportunities to discuss choices and how to deal with stresses, and student conflicts become life lessons in relationships. In addition, students are given a "Toolbox of Coping Skills" that contains concrete objects to be used to address problems. The Toolbox includes Post-it® notes to record student concerns and troubling situations, so that the incidents can be dealt with at an appropriate time. Exit and U-turn signs remind students that the best strategy may be to "exit" the situation. "Exiting to a safe place, without explanation, is taught as one appropriate face-saving, and possibly life-saving, response" (Stipek et al., 1999, p. 443). Early indicators are that students do learn to use these skills.

Check Yourself What is emotional intelligence?

How can social skills be taught?

What are the elements of effective risk prevention programs?

We now turn to other approaches for developing social skills that confront hatred and intolerance.

Compassion and Tolerance

What did your high school do in reaction to the series of shootings that occurred in the late 1990s? Do you remember your thoughts and feelings?

In the weeks and months after the killings at Columbine High School, educators, parents, psychologists, politicians, and journalists struggled to explain what happened—and to understand how to prevent recurrences. How could two above-average students from stable families commit such heinous crimes? The book, *No One Left to Hate: Teaching Compassion After Columbine,* by the eminent social psychologist, Elliot Aronson (2000), is the best explanation I have found for what happened that day and what can be done now. In the book and in the research described are some fundamental lessons for all educators.

The events at Columbine High School in the spring of 1999 still resonate deeply with teachers, students, and parents. Who or what is to blame? What are the solutions to the problems, the lessons to be learned?

As Aronson recounts, the tragic events of that day have been blamed on the emotional pathology of the shooters, easy access to guns in the United States, the absence of good security and surveillance in the school, and violence in the media and in video games. The solutions suggested have included early identification of potential troublemakers through student informants or searches of student property and web postings, metal detectors in schools, better gun control, and censorship of violence in the media. Clearly these issues deserve attention.

Each of these "solutions" might improve the situation in some schools, but each has problems. Eric Harris and Dylan Klebold, the shooters at Columbine, stood out in their appearance in school, but they functioned reasonably well, did their homework, and had decent grades. There are literally thousands of students like them in schools across the country. Metal detectors might be useful, but in some schools the atmosphere created could undermine the learning community teachers are trying to establish. And some school shooters have waited outside the schools to attack. Metal detectors would not detect those guns. Gun control has been difficult to accomplish politically and may never solve the problem of children's easy access to guns. Censorship brings with it threats to individual rights. None of these approaches gets at the true causes of the tragedy at Columbine. Aronson (2000, p. 88) points out that:

> Looking for root causes in individual pathology is an approach that seems sensible on the surface, but it does not get to the root of the problem. What is it about the atmosphere in the schools themselves that makes these young people so desperate, diabolical, and callous? Why do they seek revenge, or a twisted notion of glory, by shooting their classmates? In what ways have they felt rejected, ignored, humiliated, or treated unfairly at school? Are the schools doing the best they can to develop students' characters as well as their intellects? Can schools do better at creating inclusive, caring communities with positive role models for students?

Not everyone agrees that character and compassion should be taught in schools, as you can see in the *Point/Counterpoint.*

Point/Counterpoint

Should Schools Teach Character and Compassion?

Not all educators believe that schools should teach compassion, tolerance, or other aspects of character and morality. Here are the two contrasting opinions.

Point

Schooling should include character education.
Proponents of character education point to violence in the schools, teenage pregnancy, and drug use among young people as evidence that educators need to address issues of morality and virtue. They argue that families are no longer doing a good job in this area, so schools must assume the burden. Thomas Lickona (2002) describes character education as the deliberate effort to cultivate personal qualities such as wisdom, honesty, kindness, and self-discipline. The goals of character education are to produce good people (who can work and love), good schools (that are caring and conducive to learning), and a good society (that deals effectively with problems such as violence and poverty). To accomplish these goals, Lickona believes that students need knowledge and moral reasoning capabilities, emotional qualities such as self-respect and empathy, and skills such as cooperation and communication. Character education strategies include modeling kindness and cooperation, creating a classroom community that is democratic and supportive, using cooperative learning strategies, including reflection on moral issues in the curriculum, and teaching conflict resolution.

Counterpoint

Character education is ineffective and dangerous.
Alfie Kohn (2002) cautions that the term "character education" has two meanings. The first is the general concern shared by most parents and educators that students grow into good, caring, honest people. The second is a narrow set of programs and strategies for teaching a particular set of values. Few people disagree with the general concern, but there is disagreement about the narrower programs. For example, Kohn (2002) says:

> *What goes by the name of character education nowadays is, for the most part, a collection of exhortations and extrinsic inducements designed to make children work harder and do what they're told. Even when other values are also promoted—caring or fairness, say—the preferred method of instruction is tantamount to indoctrination. The point is to drill students in specific behaviors rather than engage them in deep, critical reflection about certain ways of being. (p. 138)*

Kohn suggests that rather than try to "fix" students' character, we should fix the structure of schools to make them more just and caring.

What do you think? Vote online at **www.ablongman.com/woolfolk**

CONNECT & EXTEND

TO THE RESEARCH
For a complete discussion of the debate about character education, see Abbeduto, L. (Ed.) (2002). *Taking sides: Clashing on controversial issues in educational psychology* (pp. 128–155). Guilford, CT: McGraw-Hill/Duskin.

As a teacher you may have little to say about violence on television, metal detectors, or gun control—but you have much to say about the way students treat each other and the sense of community created in your classes. You can teach tolerance and compassion through direct and indirect means. For example, Esme Codell (2001, p. 34) describes how she used literature to teach about the pain of being teased. Esme's 5th grade class had read *The Hundred Dresses*, a story about a poor immigrant girl who was teased mercilessly by other girls in her class. After reading the story, one student, Ashworth, whispered in Esme's ear that he had something he wanted to tell the class:

> I faced him toward the class and put my hands on his shoulders. He was trembling terribly. "Ashworth has something personal to share with you. I hope you will keep in mind *The Hundred Dresses* when he tells you."
>
> "I . . . I only have nine and a half fingers," he choked. "Please don't tease me about it." He held up his hands.
>
> The class hummed, impressed, then was silent as Ashworth shifted on his feet. Finally, Billy called out, "I'll kick the ass of anyone who makes fun of you!"
>
> "Yeah, me too!" said Kirk.
>
> "Yeah, Ash! You just tell us if anyone from another class messes with you, we'll beat their ass up and down!"
>
> Yeah, yeah, yeah! The class became united in the spirit of ass-kicking. Ashworth sighed and smiled at me. The power of literature!

Another approach to encourage compassion is the jigsaw classroom—a strategy Elliot Aronson invented when he was a professor of social psychology (and I was a student) at the University of Texas at Austin. Some of my friends worked on his research team. Jigsaw is one approach to cooperative learning. We turn to that topic now.

Group Work and Cooperation in Learning

CONNECT & EXTEND

TO YOUR TEACHING/PORTFOLIO
Cooperative learning (1986, September). *Harvard Education Letter, 2*(5), 4–6. One advantage of cooperative learning, as noted by Nel Noddings of Stanford University, is that "children solve problems at a more thoughtful, deliberate pace than they do when working as a class. Without any teacher to approve or reject a proposed solution, they debate strategies for some time." Noting how often children in groups call out, "Wait, wait!" Noddings wonders how many would like to slow down the pace of full-class instruction so they could feel that they really understood.

For the past three decades, researchers have examined cooperative learning. Although there are some inconsistencies, the majority of the studies indicate that truly cooperative groups have positive effects on students' empathy, tolerance for differences, feelings of acceptance, friendships, self-confidence, and even school attendance (Solomon, Watson, & Battistich, 2001).

The terms *group learning* and *cooperative learning* often are used as if they meant the same thing. Actually, group work is simply several students working together—they may or may not be cooperating. Many activities can be completed in groups. For example, students can work together in conducting local surveys. How do people feel about the plan to build a new mall that will bring more shopping and more traffic? Would the community support or oppose the building of a nuclear power plant? If students must learn 10 new definitions in a biology class, why not let students divide up the terms and definitions and teach one another? Be sure, however, that everyone in the group can handle the task. Sometimes a group effort ends with one or two students doing the work of the entire group.

Group work can be useful, but true cooperative learning requires much more than simply putting students in groups.

Beyond Groups to Cooperation. Collaboration and **cooperative learning** have a long history in American education. In the early 1900s, John Dewey criticized the use of competition in education and encouraged educators to structure schools as democratic learning communities. These ideas fell from favor in the 1940s and 1950s, and were replaced by a resurgence of competition. In the 1960s, there was a swing back to individualized and cooperative learning structures, stimulated in part by concern for civil rights and interracial relations (Webb & Palincsar, 1996). Today, evolving constructivist perspectives on learning fuel interest in collaboration and cooperative learning and "there is a heightened interest in situations where elaboration, interpretation, explanation, and argumentation are integral to the activity of the group and where learning is supported by other individuals" (Webb & Palincsar, 1996, p. 844).

Cooperative learning Arrangement in which students work in mixed-ability groups and are rewarded on the basis of the success of the group.

Different learning theory approaches favor cooperative learning for different reasons (O'Donnell, 2002; O'Donnell & O'Kelly, 1994). Information processing theorists point to the value of group discussion in helping participants rehearse, elaborate, and expand their knowledge. As group members question and explain, they have to organize their knowledge, make connections, and review—all processes that support information processing and memory. Advocates of a Piagetian perspective suggest that the interactions in groups can create the cognitive conflict and disequilibrium that lead an individual to question his or her understanding and try out new ideas—or, as Piaget (1985) said, "to go beyond his current state and strike out in new directions" (p. 10). Those who favor Vygotsky's theory suggest that social interaction is important for learning because higher mental functions such as reasoning, comprehension, and critical thinking originate in social interactions and are then internalized by individuals. Children can accomplish mental tasks with social support before they can do them alone. Thus cooperative learning provides the social support and scaffolding that students need to move learning forward. Table 13.3 summarizes the functions of cooperative learning from different theoretical perspectives, and describes some of the elements of each kind of group.

To benefit from the dimensions of cooperative learning listed in Table 13.3, groups must *be cooperative*—all members must participate. But, as any teacher or parent knows, cooperation is not automatic when students are put into groups. Angela O'Donnell and Jim O'Kelly, colleagues of mine at Rutgers University, describe a teacher who claimed to be using "cooperative learning" by asking students to work in pairs on a paper, each writing one part. Unfortunately, the teacher allowed no time to work together and provided no guidance or preparation in cooperative social skills. Students got a grade for their individual part and a group grade for the whole project. One student received an A for his part, but a C for the group project because his partner earned an F—he never turned in any work. So one student was punished with a C for a situation he could not control while the other was rewarded with a C for doing no work at all. This was not cooperative learning—it wasn't even group work (O'Donnell & O'Kelly, 1994). Let's look at what can go wrong with cooperative learning—then we can consider how to avoid these problems.

What Can Go Wrong: Misuses of Group Learning. Without careful planning and monitoring by the teacher, group interactions can hinder learning and reduce rather than improve social relations in classes. For example, if there is pressure in a

Table 13.3 Different Forms of Cooperative Learning for Different Purposes

Different forms of cooperative learning (Elaboration, Piagetian, and Vygotskian) fit different purposes, need different structures, and have their own potential problems and possible solutions.

Considerations	Elaboration	Piagetian	Vygotskian
Group size	Small (2–4)	Small	Dyads
Group composition	Heterogeneous/homogeneous	Homogeneous	Heterogeneous
Tasks	Rehearsal/integrative	Exploratory	Skills
Teacher role	Facilitator	Facilitator	Model/guide
Potential problems	Poor help-giving Unequal participation	Inactive No cognitive conflict	Poor help-giving Providing adequate time/dialogue
Averting problems	Direct instruction in help-giving Modeling help-giving Scripting interaction	Structuring controversy	Direct instruction in help-giving Modeling help-giving

SOURCE: From "Learning from Peers: Beyond the Rhetoric of Positive Results," by A. M. O'Donnell and J. O'Kelly, 1994, *Educational Psychology Review, 6*, p. 327.

CONNECT & EXTEND

TO **PRAXIS**™
CHARACTERISTICS OF COOPERATIVE LEARNING (II, A2)
Many instructional strategies labeled as "cooperative learning" lack one or more qualities that are essential components of such techniques. List those essential qualities and explain the role of each.

group for conformity—perhaps because rewards are being misused or one student dominates the others—interactions can be unproductive and unreflective. Misconceptions might be reinforced or the worst, not the best, ideas may be combined to construct a superficial understanding (Battistich, Solomon, & Delucci, 1993). Also, the ideas of low status students may be ignored or even ridiculed while the contributions of high status students are accepted and reinforced, regardless of the merit of either set of ideas (Anderson, Holland, & Palincsar, 1997; Cohen, 1986). Mary McCaslin and Tom Good (1996) list several other disadvantages of group learning:

- Students often value the process or procedures over the learning. Speed and finishing early take precedence over thoughtfulness and learning.
- Rather than challenging and correcting misconceptions, students support and reinforce misunderstandings.
- Socializing and interpersonal relationships may take precedence over learning.
- Students may simply shift dependency from the teacher to the "expert" in the group—learning is still passive and what is learned can be wrong.
- Status differences may be increased rather than decreased. Some students learn to "loaf" because the group progresses with or without their contributions. Others become even more convinced that they are unable to understand without the support of the group.

The next sections examine how teachers can avoid these problems and encourage true cooperation.

Making Cooperative Learning Work

What Would You Say? As part of the interview process for a job in an elementary school, you are asked the following: "Do you use group work in your teaching? Why or why not? How would you use it in this school?"

David and Roger Johnson (1999) list five elements that define true cooperative learning groups:

- Face-to-face interaction
- Positive interdependence
- Individual accountability
- Collaborative skills
- Group processing

Students *interact face-to-face* and close together, not across the room. Group members experience *positive interdependence*—they need each other for support, explanations, and guidance. Even though they work together and help each other, members of the group must ultimately demonstrate learning on their own; they are held *individually accountable* for learning, often through individual tests or other assessments. *Collaborative skills* are necessary for effective group functioning. Often these skills, such as giving constructive feedback, reaching consensus, and involving every member, must be taught and practiced before the groups tackle a learning task. Finally, members monitor *group processes* and relationships to make sure the group is working effectively and to learn about the dynamics of groups. They take time to ask, "How are we doing as a group? Is everyone working together?"

CONNECT & EXTEND

TO THE RESEARCH
Cooperative Learning (1990, special section). *Educational Leadership, 47*(4), 4–67, and Cooperative Learning (1991, special section). *Educational Leadership, 48,* 71–95.

CONNECT & EXTEND

TO THE RESEARCH
The Winter 2002 issue of *Theory Into Practice* is devoted to "Promoting Thinking Through Peer Learning." The editor for this volume was Angella O'Donnell, one of the top researchers in the area of cooperative learning. There are articles by Noreen Webb, Alison King, Annemarie Palincsar, and others.

Setting Up Cooperative Groups. How large should a cooperative group be? The answer depends on your learning goals. If the purpose is for the group members to review, rehearse information, or practice, 4 to 5 or 6 students is about the right size. But if the goal is to encourage each student to participate in discussions, problem solving, or computer learning, then groups of 2 to 4 members work best. Also, in setting up cooperative groups, it often makes sense to balance the number of boys and girls. Some research indicates that when there are just a few girls in a group, they tend to be left out of the discussions unless they are the most able or assertive members.

By contrast, when there are only one or two boys in the group, they tend to dominate and be "interviewed" by the girls unless these boys are less able than the girls or are very shy. In general, for very shy and introverted students, individual learning may be a better approach (O'Donnell & O'Kelly, 1994; Webb, 1985; Webb & Palincsar, 1996). Whatever the case, teachers must monitor groups to make sure everyone is contributing and learning.

In setting up cooperative groups, it often makes sense to balance the number of boys and girls in order to promote equal participation by each member.

Giving and Receiving Explanations. In practice, the effects of learning in a group vary, depending on what actually happens in the group and who is in it. If only a few people take responsibility for the work, these people will learn, but the nonparticipating members probably will not. Students who ask questions, get answers, and attempt explanations are more likely to learn than students whose questions go unasked or unanswered. In fact, there is evidence that the more a student provides elaborated, thoughtful explanations to other students in a group, the more the *explainer* learns. Giving good explanations appears to be even more important for learning than receiving explanations (Webb, Farivar, & Mastergeorge, 2002; Webb & Palincsar, 1996). In order to explain, you have to organize the information, put it into your own words, think of examples and analogies (which connect the information to things you already know), and test your understanding by answering questions. These are excellent learning strategies (King, 1990, 2002; O'Donnell & O'Kelly, 1994).

Good explanations are relevant, timely, correct, and elaborated enough to help the listener correct misunderstandings; the best explanations tell why (Webb et al., 2002). For example, in a middle school mathematics class, students worked in groups on the following problem:

> Find the cost of a 30-minute telephone call to the prefix 717 where the first minute costs $0.22 and each additional minute costs $0.13.

The level of explanation and help students received was significantly related to learning; the higher the level, the more learning. Table 13.4 shows the different levels of help. Of course, the students must pay attention to and use the help to learn. And the help-receiver also has responsibilities if learning is to go well. For example, if a helper says, "13 times 29" then the receiver should say, "Why is it 29?" Asking good questions and giving clear explanations are critical, and usually these skills must be taught.

Table 13.4 Levels of Help in Cooperative Groups

Students are more likely to learn if they give and get higher level help.

Level	Description and Example
Highest	
6	Verbally labeled explanation of how to solve part or all of the problem ("Multiply 13 cents by 29, because 29 minutes are left after the first minute.")
5	Numerical rule with no verbal labels for the numbers ("This is 30, so you minus 1.")
4	Numerical expression or equation ("13 times 29.")
3	Numbers to write or copy ("Put 13 on top, 29 on the bottom. Then you times it.")
2	Answer to part or all of the problem ("I got $3.77.")
1	Non-content or non-informational response ("Just do it the way she said.")
0	No response
Lowest	

SOURCE: From "Productive Helping in Cooperative Groups," by N. M. Webb, S. H. Farivar, and A. M. Mastergeorge, *Theory Into Practice, 41*(1), p. 14. Copyright © 2002 by the College of Education, Ohio State University. Reprinted by permission of the publisher.

Assigning Roles. Some teachers assign roles to students to encourage cooperation and full participation. Several roles are described in Table 13.5 on page 496. If you use roles, be sure that the roles support learning. In groups that focus on social skills, roles should support listening, encouragement, and respect for differences. In groups that focus on practice, review, or mastery of basic skills, roles should support persistence, encouragement, and participation. In groups that focus on higher-order problem solving or complex learning, roles should encourage thoughtful discussion, sharing of explanations and insights, probing, brainstorming,

Table 13.5 Possible Student Roles in Cooperative Learning Groups

Depending on the purpose of the group and the age of the participants, having these assigned roles might help students cooperate and learn. Of course, students may have to be taught how to enact each role effectively, and roles should be rotated so students can participate in different aspects of group learning.

Role	Description
Encourager	Encourages reluctant or shy students to participate
Praiser/Cheerleader	Shows appreciation of other's contributions and recognizes accomplishments
Gate Keeper	Equalizes participation and makes sure no one dominates
Coach	Helps with the academic content, explains concepts
Question Commander	Makes sure all students' questions are asked and answered
Checker	Checks the group's understanding
Taskmaster	Keeps the group on task
Recorder	Writes down ideas, decisions, and plans
Reflector	Keeps group aware of progress (or lack of progress)
Quiet Captain	Monitors noise level
Materials Monitor	Picks up and returns materials

SOURCE: From *Cooperative Learning* by S. Kagan. Published by Kagan Publishing, San Clemente, CA. Copyright © 1994 by Kagan Publishing. Adapted with permission. 1-800-WEE CO-OP.

and creativity. Make sure that you don't communicate to students that the major purpose of the groups is simply to do the procedures—the roles. Roles are supports for learning, not ends in themselves (Woolfolk Hoy & Tschannen-Moran, 1999).

Often, cooperative learning strategies include group reports to the entire class. If you have been on the receiving end of these class reports, you know that they can be deadly dull. To make the process more useful for the audience as well as the reporters, Annemarie Palincsar and Leslie Herrenkohl (2002) taught the class members to use intellectual roles as they listened to reports. These roles were based on the scientific strategies of predicting and theorizing, summarizing results, and relating predictions and theories to results. Some audience members were assigned the role of checking the reports for clear relationships between predictions and theories. Other students in the audience listened for clarity in the findings. And the rest of the students were responsible for evaluating how well the group reports linked prediction, theories, and findings. Research shows that using these roles promotes class dialogue, thinking and problem solving, and conceptual understanding (Palincsar & Herrenkohl, 2002).

Strategies for Cooperation

We now turn to different strategies that build in structures to support both social and cognitive learning.

Jigsaw. An early format for cooperative learning that emphasizes high interdependence is **Jigsaw.** This structure was invented by Elliot Aronson and his graduate students in 1971 in Austin, Texas: " . . . as a matter of absolute necessity to help defuse a highly explosive situation" (Aronson, 2000, p. 137). The Austin schools had just been desegregated by court order. White, African American, and Hispanic students were together in classrooms for the first time. Hostility and turmoil ensued with fistfights in corridors and classrooms. Aronson's answer was the Jigsaw classroom.

In Jigsaw, each group member is given part of the material to be learned by the whole group and becomes an "expert" on his or her piece. Students have to teach each other, so everyone's contribution is important. A more recent version, Jigsaw II, adds expert groups in which the students who have the same material from each learning group confer to make sure they understand their assigned part and then plan ways to teach the information to their learning group members. Next, students return to their learning groups, bringing their expertise to the sessions. In the end, students take an individual test covering all the material and earn points for their learning team score. Teams can work for rewards or simply for recognition (Aronson, 2000; Slavin, 1995).

Judy Pitts (1992) describes a lesson about how to do library research that has a jigsaw format. The overall project for each group is to educate the class about a different country. Groups have to decide what information to present and how to make it interesting for their classmates. In the library, each group member is responsible for mastering a particular resource (*Readers' Guide, NewsBank,* reference sets, almanacs, etc.) and teaching other group members how to use it, if the need arises. Students

Jigsaw A cooperative structure in which each member of a group is responsible for teaching other members one section of the material.

learning about each resource meet first in expert groups to be sure all the "teachers" know how to use the resource.

In this class, students confront complex, real-life problems, and not simplified worksheets. They learn by doing and by teaching others. The students must take positions and argue for them—how should our group educate the class about Turkey, for example—while being open to the ideas of others. They may encounter different representations of the same information—graphs, databases, maps, interviews, or encyclopedia articles—and have to integrate information from different sources. This lesson exemplifies many of the characteristics of constructivist approaches described in Chapter 9. The students have a good chance of learning how to do library research by actually doing it. But in Aronson's eyes, an even greater lesson is learned about tolerance and compassion. The *Stories of Learning/Tributes to Teaching* feature tells about a student who was in one of those early Jigsaw classes in Austin.

Reciprocal Questioning. Another cooperative approach can be used with a wide range of ages and subjects. **Reciprocal questioning** requires no special materials or testing procedures. After a lesson or presentation by the teacher, students work in pairs or triads to ask and answer questions about the material (King, 1990, 1994,

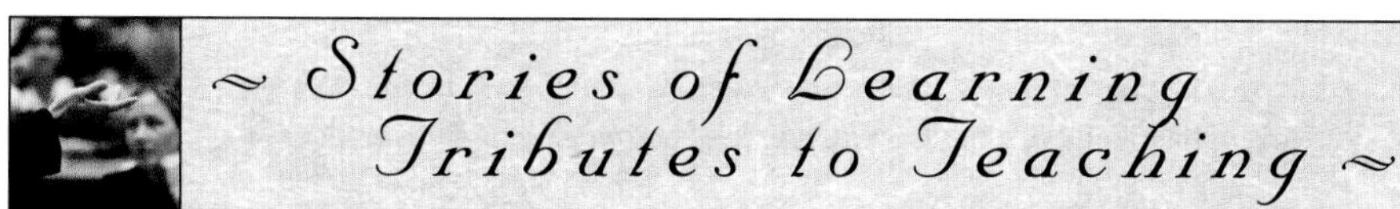

Years after inventing the Jigsaw strategy, Elliot Aronson received the following letter:

Dear Professor Aronson:

I am a senior at —— University. Today I got a letter admitting me to the Harvard Law School. This may not seem odd to you but, let me tell you something. I am the sixth of seven children my parents had—and I am the only one who ever went to college, let alone graduate, or go to law school.

By now, you are probably wondering why this stranger is writing to you and bragging to you about his achievements. Actually, I'm not a stranger although we never met. You see, last year I was taking a course in social psychology and we were using a book you wrote called *The Social Animal,* and when I read about prejudice and jigsaw it all sounded very familiar—and then, I realized that I was in that very first class you ever did jigsaw in—when I was in the 5th grade in Austin. And as I read on, it dawned on me that I was the boy that you called **Carlos.** And then I remembered you when you first came to our classroom and how I was scared and how I hated school and how I was so stupid and didn't know anything. And you came in—it all came back to me when I read your book—you were very tall—about 6½ feet—and you had a big black beard and you were funny and made us all laugh.

And, most important, when we started to do work in jigsaw groups, I began to realize that I wasn't really that stupid. And the kids I thought were cruel and hostile became my friends and the teacher acted friendly and nice to me and I actually began to love school, and I began to love to learn things and now I'm about to go to Harvard Law School.

You must get a lot of letters like this but I decided to write anyway because let me tell you something. My mother tells me that when I was born I almost died. I was born at home and the cord was wrapped around my neck and the midwife gave me mouth to mouth and saved my life. If she were still alive, I would write to her too, to tell her that I grew up smart and good and I'm going to law school. But she died a few years ago. I'm writing to you because, no less than her, you saved my life too.

SOURCE: From *Nobody Left to Hate: Teaching Compassion after Columbine,* by E. Aronson. Published by Worth Publishers.

Reciprocal questioning Approach where groups of two or three students ask and answer each other's questions after a lesson or presentation.

CONNECT & EXTEND

TO THE RESEARCH

King, A. (1990). Enhancing peer interaction and learning in the classroom through reciprocal questioning. *American Educational Research Journal, 27,* 664–687.

2002). The teacher provides question stems (see Table 13.6), then students are taught how to develop specific questions on the lesson material using the generic question stems. The students create questions, then take turns asking and answering. This process has proved more effective than traditional discussion groups because it seems to encourage deeper thinking about the material. Questions such as those in Table 13.6, which encourage students to make connections between the lesson and previous knowledge or experience, seem to be the most helpful. For example, using the question stems in Table 13.6, a small group in Mr. Garcia's 9th-grade world cultures class had the following discussion about the concept of "culture":

Sally: In your own words, what does *culture* mean?

Jim: Well, Mr. Garcia said in the lesson that a culture is the knowledge and understandings shared by the members of a society. I guess it's all the things and beliefs and activities that people in a society have in common. It includes things like religion, laws, music, medical practices . . . stuff like that.

Sally: And dance, art, family roles.

Barry: Knowledge includes language. So, I guess cultures includes language, too.

Jim: I guess so. Actually, I have a question about that: How does a culture influence the language of a society?

Barry: Well, for one thing, the language is made up of words that are important to the people of that culture. Like, the words name things that the people care about, or need, or use. And so, different cultures would have different vocabularies. Some cultures may not even have a word for *telephone,* because they don't have any. But, phones are important in our culture, so we have lots of different words for phones, like *cell phone, digital phone, desk phone, cordless phone, phone machine,* and. . . .

Jim (laughing): I'll bet desert cultures don't have any words for *snow* or *skiing.*

Sally (turning to Barry): What's your question?

Barry: I've got a great question! You'll never be able to answer it. What would happen if there was a group somewhere without any spoken language? Maybe they were all born not being able to speak, or something like that. How would that affect their culture, or could there even *be* a culture?

Sally: Well, it would mean they couldn't communicate with each other.

Jim: And they wouldn't have any music! Because they wouldn't be able to sing.

Table 13.6 Question Stems to Encourage Dialogue in Reciprocal Questioning

After studying materials or participating in a lesson, students use these stems to develop questions and share answers.

What is a new example of . . . ?	Why is . . . important?
How would you use . . . to . . . ?	How are . . . and . . . similar? How are . . . and . . . different?
What would happen if . . . ?	What is the best . . . and why?
What are the strengths and weaknesses of . . . ?	Compare . . . and . . . with regard to . . .
How does . . . tie in with what we learned before?	What do you think causes . . . ?
Explain why . . . Explain how . . .	What conclusions can you draw about . . . ?
How does . . . affect . . . ?	Do you agree or disagree with this statement . . . ? Support your answer.
What is the meaning of . . . ?	

SOURCE: From "Structuring Peer Interaction to Promote High-Level Cognitive Processing," by A. King, *Theory Into Practice, 41*(1), p. 34–35. Copyright 2002 by the College of Education, Ohio State University. Reprinted by permission of the publisher. All rights reserved.

Barry: But wait! Why couldn't they communicate? Maybe they would develop a nonverbal language system, you know, the way people use hand signals, or the way deaf people use sign language. . . .

(King, 2002, pp. 34–35)

Scripted Cooperation. Donald Dansereau and his colleagues have developed a method for learning in pairs called **scripted cooperation.** Students work together on almost any task, including reading a selection of text, solving math problems, or editing writing drafts. In reading, for example, both partners read a passage, then one student gives an oral summary. The other partner comments on the summary, noting omissions or errors. Next, the partners work together to elaborate on the information—create associations, images, mnemonics, ties to previous work, examples, analogies, and so on. The partners switch roles of summarizer and listener for the next section of the reading, and then continue to take turns until they finish the assignment (Dansereau, 1985; O'Donnell & O'Kelly, 1994).

STAD. Some cooperative methods emphasize increasing motivation through teamwork and interteam competition. Robert Slavin and his associates have developed a system for overcoming the disadvantages of the cooperative goal structure (lack of focus, off-task behaviors, unfair division of work) while maintaining its advantages. The system is called Student Teams–Achievement Divisions, or STAD (Slavin, 1995). Each team has about five members with a mix of abilities, ethnic backgrounds, and sexes. The teacher calculates an individual learning expectation (ILE) score, or base score, for each team member. This score represents the student's average level of performance. Details about how to determine the base scores are given in Table 13.7.

Students work in their teams to study and prepare for twice-weekly quizzes, but they take the quizzes individually, just as in a regular class. Based on test performance, each team member can earn from one to three points for the group. Table 13.7 shows how points are awarded by comparing each student's current test score to his or her base (ILE) score (Slavin, 1995). As you can see from the table, every student has an equal chance to contribute the maximum number of points to the team total. Thus, every student, not just the most able or motivated, has reason to work hard. This system avoids the problem of students' unequal contributions to a group project. Every

CONNECT & EXTEND

TO PRAXIS™
FORMS OF COOPERATIVE LEARNING (II, A2)
STAD, Jigsaw, and TGT are just three of many cooperative learning techniques, each designed for certain instructional purposes. Go to *Cooperative Learning* (http://www.utc.edu/Teaching-Resource-Center/CoopLear.html), sponsored by the University of Tennessee at Chattanooga, to learn about techniques and uses for cooperative learning.

Table 13.7 Using Individual Learning Expectations

The idea behind individual learning expectations, or ILEs, is that students ought to be judged in relation to their own abilities and not compared to others. The focus is on improvement, not on comparisons among students.

To calculate an ILE score, the teacher simply averages the student's grades or test scores from previous work. These scores are usually on a 100-point scale. Letter grades can be converted to points based on the school's system—for example, A = 90 points, B = 80 points, and so on. The student's average score is her or his initial base score. The ILE score becomes the standard for judging each student's work.

If the teacher is using the STAD system of cooperative learning, then students earn points for their group based on the following system:

Test Score	Points Earned for Group
A perfect score	3
10 or more points above ILE score	3
5 to 9 points above ILE score	2
4 points below to 4 points above ILE score	1
5 or more points below ILE score	0

Scripted cooperation A learning strategy in which two students take turns summarizing material and critiquing the summaries.

week the group earning the greatest number of points is declared the winner. Team accomplishments should be recognized in a class newsletter or a bulletin board display.

Every few weeks, the teams can be changed so that students have a chance to work with many different class members. Every two weeks or so, the teacher must recompute each student's ILE score by averaging the old base score with grades on the recent tests. With this system, improvement pays off for all students. Those with less ability can still earn the maximum for their team by scoring 10 or more points above their own base score. Those with greater ability are still challenged because they must score well above their own average or make a perfect score to contribute the maximum to the group total.

The *Guidelines* give you ideas for incorporating cooperative learning in to your classes.

Check Yourself What are the learning theory underpinnings of cooperative learning?

Describe five elements that define true cooperative learning.

What are some possible strategies for cooperative learning?

As you gain teaching experience, you can continue to develop your expertise.

GUIDELINES Using Cooperative Learning

Fit group size and composition to your learning goals.

Examples

1. For social skills and team-building goals, use groups of 2–5, common interest groups, mixed groups, or random groups.
2. For structured fact and skill-based practice and review tasks, use groups of 2–4, mixed ability such as high-middle and middle-low or high-low and middle-middle group compositions.
3. For higher-level conceptual and thinking tasks, use groups of 2–4; select members to encourage interaction.

Assign appropriate roles.

Examples

1. For social skills and team-building goals, assign roles to monitor participation and conflict; rotate leadership of the group.
2. For structured fact and skill-based practice and review tasks, assign roles to monitor engagement and insure low-status students have resources to offer, as in Jigsaw.
3. For higher-level conceptual and thinking tasks, assign roles only to encourage interaction, divergent thinking, and extended, connected discourse, as in debate teams, group facilitator. Don't let roles get in the way of learning.

Make sure you assume a supporting role as the teacher.

Examples

1. For social skills and team-building goals, be a model and encourager.
2. For structured fact and skill-based practice and review tasks, be a model, director, or coach.
3. For higher-level conceptual and thinking tasks, be a model and facilitator.

Move around the room and monitor the groups.

Examples

1. For social skills and team-building goals, watch for listening, turn-taking, encouraging, and managing conflict.
2. For structured fact and skill-based practice and review tasks, watch for questioning, giving multiple elaborated explanations, attention, and practice.
3. For higher-level conceptual and thinking tasks, watch for questioning, explaining, elaborating, probing, divergent thinking, providing rationales, synthesizing, using and connecting knowledge sources.

Start small and simple until you and the students know how to use cooperative methods.

Examples

1. For social skills and team-building goals, try one or two skills, such as listening and paraphrasing.
2. For structured fact and skill-based practice and review tasks, try pairs of students quizzing each other.
3. For higher-level conceptual and thinking tasks, try reciprocal questioning using pairs and just a few question stems.

SOURCE: Adapted from "Implications of Cognitive Approaches to Peer Learning for Teacher Education" by A. Woolfolk Hoy and M. Tschannen-Moran, 1999. In A. O'Donnell & A. King (Eds.), *Cognitive Perspectives on Peer Learning* (pp. 257–284). Mahwah, NJ: Lawrence Erlbaum.

Enhancing Your Expertise with Technology

Cooperative Learning

Following her mentor's advice, at her first Back-to-School Night, Juanita explained to the parents that for the first several months of the school year, she would be taking a traditional approach that utilized whole- and small-group instructional activities along with a few independent projects. But by mid-year, Juanita felt that it was time to expand her instructional repertoire and develop expertise in using cooperative learning techniques. Juanita and her mentor developed a modest set of Jigsaw activities based on content and skills from a chapter in the social studies book. The activities seemed to go well. The students were actively engaged with research on the Internet and encyclopedias. The groups hummed with questioning, explaining, and elaborating. Juanita administered the test supplied by the textbook publisher, and, to her relief, the test scores were in line with previous tests. With practice and refinement, she was certain that her students would nudge up the test scores.

Then the controversy began. A few parents of children who scored poorly on the test complained that it is the teacher who should do the teaching, not other students, and they wanted a meeting with the principal to emphasize that point. Could Juanita justify her choices? Could you?

Most classrooms are highly complex, dynamic environments that demand the use of techniques or strategies that help students accomplish a variety of instructional or learning tasks. Research has established that well-designed, carefully monitored cooperative approaches to learning can be effective means to such ends. Some techniques, such as STAD, are effective in helping students rehearse and maintain basic knowledge of content matter. Other techniques, such as reciprocal questioning, are effective in helping students develop essential reading skills.

Choices about which techniques to employ for various activities require a level of expertise that novice teachers can attain through knowledge, guidance, and reflection. Visits to the following sites can aid in building the knowledge necessary to implement effective cooperative learning groups in a sophisticated, thoughtful way.

Jigsaw Classroom provides a comprehensive and detailed description of Jigsaw, one of the earliest effective cooperative learning techniques. The site contains an overview of Jigsaw, steps for the classroom use of Jigsaw, tips for avoiding some of the potential pitfalls of the technique, and example lessons. There are excellent links to other cooperative learning sites as well (http://www.jigsaw.org/).

The Cooperative Learning Center focuses on the research and work of Roger T. Johnson and David W. Johnson of the University of Minnesota. Newsletters, essays, and a cooperative learning Questions & Answer section are available (http://www.clcrc.com/).

The International Association for the Study of Cooperation in Education is an organization that supports the research and use of cooperative learning techniques. The site contains links to other sites about cooperative learning, a set of newsletters, and contact information to local cooperative learning advocacy associations (http://www.iasce.net/).

Cooperative and Collaborative Learning The Disney Learning Partnership and Channel 13 (New York City's PBS station) have collaborated on an excellent site that offers a wide set of resources, including video clips of cooperative learning in action. Particularly valuable are insights from teachers about the implementation of these techniques, and discussions about how cooperative techniques relate to such topics as multiple intelligences, inquiry learning, and state and national standards (http://www.thirteen.org/edonline/concept2class/month5/).

Creating a Learning Community

Teachers can have no impact on students who are physically or psychologically absent from school. Some of our students come to us with a deep commitment to education; others see little value in academic learning. From the 1970s through the 1980s, the high school dropout rate declined, but since 1990, the rate has held constant at about 11% of the 16- to 24-year olds in the United States. These rates vary by ethnicity, with the rate for Asians and Pacific Islanders at 3.8%, Whites at 6.9%, African Americans at 13%, and Hispanic Americans at 28% (National Center for Educational Statistics, 2002). Schools are challenged to help all students see the value of education, but we have been especially unsuccessful in reaching some groups of students.

When students perceive their schools as competitive places where they are treated differently based on race, gender, or ethnicity, then they are more likely to act out or withdraw altogether. But when they feel that they have choices, that the emphasis is

Schools are challenged to help all students see the value of education. When students feel they have choices, individual improvement rather than comparison to others is emphasized; when they feel respected and supported by teachers and other students, they are more likely to bond with their school.

on personal improvement and not comparisons, and when they feel respected and supported by teachers, students are more likely to bond with schools (Roeser, Eccles, & Sameroff, 1999). We have talked in other chapters about encouraging student engagement and positive attitudes toward education. We saw that culturally responsive teaching can provide access to learning for more students. We looked at authentic tasks and problem-based learning as ways to connect with students' lives and interests. We examined the TARGET model for ideas about building motivation to learn. Here we examine building caring communities.

Nel Noddings (1992, 1995) has written about the need to create caring educational environments where students take more responsibility for governing their school and classroom. Students are more intrinsically motivated when they feel that their teachers care about them (Grolnick, Ryan, & Deci, 1991). Historically, however, American schools have emphasized regulating students' behavior through rules, not relationships. This is not true in every culture, however. For example, in the book, *Learning to Teach in Two Cultures*, Shimahara and Sakai (1995) observe that the Japanese approach to classroom management emphasizes such interpersonal bonds as emotional ties, relationships, and character. Success of the Japanese system "does not depend on many rules, but on a sense of trust and interdependency between the classroom teacher and his or her students and among the students" (Shimahara & Sakai, 1995, p. 79).

Classroom Community

Companion Website

STOP THINK WRITE

Consider this situation, described by Aronson (2000, p. 171). You are a high school social studies teacher. Just as you are opening a topic for discussion, Dave, a struggling student, says, "I've decided one thing anyway. I don't want to be an American. As soon as I get the chance, I'm leaving!" What would you do?

David and Roger Johnson (1999) describe three Cs for safe and productive schools: cooperative community, constructive conflict resolution, and civic values (Johnson & Johnson, 1999). At the heart of the community is the idea of positive interdependence—individuals working together to achieve mutual goals. Constructive conflict resolution is essential in the community because conflicts are inevitable and even necessary for learning. Piaget's theory of development and the research on conceptual change teaching tell us that true learning requires cognitive conflict. And indi-

Table 13.8 Academic and Interpersonal Conflict and Learning

Conflict, if handled well, can support learning. Academic conflicts can lead to critical thinking and conceptual change. Conflicts of interest are unavoidable, but can be handled so no one is the loser.

Academic Controversy	Conflicts of Interest
One person's ideas, information, theories, conclusions, and opinions are incompatible with those of another, and the two seek to reach an agreement.	The actions of one person attempting to maximize benefits prevents, blocks or interferes with another person maximizing her or his benefits.
Controversy Procedure	*Integrative (Problem-Solving) Negotiations*
Research and prepare positions	Describe wants
Present and advocate positions	Describe feelings
Refute opposing position and refute attacks on own position	Describe reasons for wants and feelings
Reverse perspectives	Take other's perspective
Synthesize and integrate best evidence and reasoning from all sides	Invent three optional agreements that maximize joint outcomes
	Choose one and formalize agreement

SOURCE: From "The Three Cs of School and Classroom Management," by D. Johnson and R. Johnson. In H. J. Freiberg (Ed.) *Beyond Behaviorism: Changing the Classroom Management Paradigm.* Boston: Allyn & Bacon. Copyright © 1999 by Allyn & Bacon. Adapted with permission.

viduals trying to exist in groups will have interpersonal conflicts, which also can lead to learning. Table 13.8 shows how academic and interpersonal conflicts can be positive forces in a learning community. One study of 10th graders found that students who were wrong, but for different reasons, were sometimes able to correct their misunderstandings if they argued together about their conflicting wrong answers (Schwarz, Neuman, & Biezuner, 2000). Later in this chapter we will talk more about conflict resolution in schools.

The last C is civic values—the understandings and beliefs that hold the community together. Values are learned through direct teaching, modeling, literature, group discussions, and the sharing of concerns. Some teachers have a "Concerns Box" where students can put written concerns and comments. The box is opened once a week at a class meeting and the concerns are discussed. Johnson and Johnson (1999) give the example of a class meeting about respect. One student tells her classmates that she felt hurt during recess the day before because no one listened when she was trying to teach them the rules to a new game. The students discussed what it means to be respectful and why respect is important. Then the students shared personal experiences of times when they felt respected versus not respected.

Respect begins with the teacher. In response to Dave's statement above about not wanting to be an American, his teacher Ms. Santos, modeled respect:*

> "Do you have another country in mind, Dave?"
>
> It turns out that Dave does have two or three countries in mind, but when he mentions them, some of the other students respond by bringing up specific problems in those countries. A lively and vigorous discussion ensues. Dave holds his own, but, as the discussion continues, he appears increasingly willing to listen to and to think about the views being expressed by some of the other students. Throughout most of this discussion, Ms. Santos does not take an active part, but sits still, leans forward, and listens attentively.
>
> After a while, Ms. Santos asks, "Do you want to live in a country without problems?" Her tone is calm, but the question is provocative. She has directed her

CONNECT & EXTEND

TO OTHER CHAPTERS
The need for belonging is the third level of Maslow's hierarchy, discussed in Chapter 10. The need to maintain relationships is strong. I was reminded of this when my daughter was reprimanded by her 4th-grade teacher for passing notes during class. Liz's explanation was that there had been a fight during lunch, ". . . and we had to work it out!"

**Source:* Adapted from *Nobody left to hate: Teaching compassion after Columbine* by E. Aronson, 2000, New York: Worth, pp. 171–173.

question to Dave, in the context of the discussion, but the question embraces all of the students. Several of them begin to address the implications of that question. The teacher then helps the students think through the potential value of living in a country that can be considered "a work in progress"; that is, a country where there is still important and worthwhile work to be done. The students are inspired. They begin to come up with examples of people who have taken up that challenge—the challenge of working to make the country a better place for all of its citizens: Eleanor Roosevelt, Martin Luther King, Jr., Cesar Chavez, and the like. After a while, Dave comes up with an example himself. His voice has taken on a tone of interest and excitement. He seems less anguished, less disillusioned, more hopeful.

Getting Started on Community

Here is how a 7th grade teacher described her experiences working with one English class to establish rules and procedures together (Freiberg, 1999, p. 171):

> I began with my first-period class. We started slowly, with my asking them about what it would take for the class to work for them. I then told them what it would take for the class to work for me. I was amazed at the overlap. They wanted to know up front what I expected in terms of tests, quantity and quality of work, late assignments, talking in class, and amount and how often they would have homework, where they could sit, grading and whether classroom participation counted. We talked about the best classes and the worst classes. We talked about respect and the need to respect ideas and each other, to listen to and be willing to be an active participant without [verbally] running over other people in the class or being run over. I talked about "my teacher time" and their "student time." Well, this was five months ago and I am amazed at the level of cooperation. I am well ahead of last year in the curriculum; we have class meetings once a week to see how things are going and adjust as needed. We created a classroom constitution and had a constitutional convention when we felt it needed to be changed. I didn't believe it would make a difference, the students really surprised me with their level of maturity and responsibility and I surprised myself with my own willingness to change. This has been a great year and I am sorry to see it end and my students leave to another grade level. I am considering asking my principal to move me to eighth grade so I could have the same students again. I have been teaching for fourteen years and this has been my best year. I feel supported by my students and my students told me they feel supported by me.

Another example of respect for students and their lives comes from Esme Codell, the wonderful first year teacher we met in Chapter 1. "Madame Esme" (the name she preferred) had a morning ritual:

> In the morning, three things happen religiously. I say good morning, real chipper, to every single child and make sure they say good morning back. Then I collect "troubles" in a "Trouble Basket," a big green basket into which the children pantomime unburdening their home worries so they can concentrate on school. Sometimes a kid has no troubles. Sometimes a kid piles it in, and I in turn pantomime bearing the burden. This way, too, I can see what disposition the child is in when he or she enters. Finally, before they can come in, they must give me a word, which I print on a piece of tagboard and keep in an envelope. It can be any word, but preferably one that they heard and don't really know or one that is personally meaningful . . . We go over the words when we do our private reading conferences. (Codell, 2001, p. 30)

Conflict and Negotiation

In every community there are conflicts. David Johnson and his colleagues (1995) provided conflict resolution training to 227 students in 2nd through 5th grade. Students learned a five-step negotiating strategy:

1. Jointly define the conflict. Separate the person from the problem and the actions involved, avoid win–lose thinking, and get both parties' goals clear.
2. Exchange positions and interests. Present a tentative proposal and make a case for it; listen to the other person's proposal and feelings; and stay flexible and cooperative.
3. Reverse perspectives. See the situation from the other person's point of view and reverse roles and argue for that perspective.
4. Invent at least three agreements that allow mutual gain. Brainstorm, focus on goals, think creatively, and make sure everyone has power to invent solutions.
5. Reach an integrative agreement. Make sure both sets of goals are met. If all else fails, flip a coin, take turns, or call in a third party—a mediator.

In addition to learning conflict resolution, all students in Johnson and Johnson's study were trained in mediation strategies. The role of the mediator was rotated—every day the teacher chose two students to be the class mediators and to wear the mediators' T-shirts. Johnson and his colleagues found that students learned the conflict resolution and mediation strategies and used them successfully, both in school and at home, to handle conflicts in a more productive way. For details of the strategies, see Johnson and Johnson (1994), Miller (1994), or Smith (1993).

Peer mediation has also been successful with older students and those with serious problems (Sanchez & Anderson, 1990). In one program, selected gang members were given mediation training, then all members were invited to participate voluntarily in the mediation process, supervised by school counselors. Strict rules governed the process leading to written agreements signed by gang representatives. Sanchez and Anderson (1990) found that gang violence in the school was reduced to a bare minimum—"The magic of the mediation process was communication" (p. 56).

Even if you do not have formal peer mediation training in your school, you can help your students handle conflict more productively. For example, Madame Esme taught her 5th graders a simple four-step process and posted the steps on a bulletin board: "1. Tell person what you didn't like. 2. Tell person how it made you feel. 3. Tell person what you want in the future. 4. Person responds with what they can do. Congratulations! You are a Confident Conflict Conqueror!" (p. 23).

CONNECT & EXTEND

TO PRAXIS™
CONFLICT RESOLUTION (II, A2)
For guidelines and concrete actions for achieving cooperation in classrooms, read *Cooperation, Conflict, Resolution, and School Violence: A Systems Approach* (http://iume.tc.columbia.edu/choices/briefs/choices05.html).

Respect and Protect

One system that has been developed to combat violence in the schools is Respect and Protect from the Johnson Institute, Minneapolis, Minnesota. The program is founded on five ideas: First, everyone is obliged to respect and protect the rights of others. Second, violence is not acceptable. Third, the program targets the violence-enabling behaviors of staff, students, and parents such as denying, rationalizing, justifying, or blaming others for violence. Fourth, there is a clear definition of what constitutes violence that distinguishes two kinds of violence—bully/victim violence and violence that arises from normal conflicts. Finally, the program has both adult-centered prevention that improves the school climate and student-centered interventions that give students choices and clear consequences (Rembolt, 1998). Table 13.9 on page 506 gives an overview of the levels of choices and consequences.

CONNECT & EXTEND

TO YOUR TEACHING/PORTFOLIO
A good resource for teachers about bullying and peer relations is Keith Sullivan's *The Anti-Bullying Handbook* (Oxford University Press, 2002).

Table 13.9 Respect and Protect

This table shows measured responses to each level of violence.

Overview of Choices, Consequences, and Contracts Intervention Process

Violence Level	Level One	Level Two	Level Three	Level Four	Level Five
Violation	Rule Violation (Minor infraction)	Misuse of Power (Repeat violation)	Abuse of Power (Serious)	Continued Abuse (Severe)	Pathology (Intractable)
Staff Action	Confront behavior Stop violence Deal with problem File intervention report Review No Violence rule Suggest anger management, conflict resolution, peer mediation, or class meeting	Confront behavior Stop violence Refer to office File intervention report Try to assess type of conflict Evaluate for talk with parent	Confront behavior Stop violence Refer to office File intervention report Try to assess type of conflict Parent conference Suggest parenting program	Confront behavior Stop violence Refer to office File intervention report Assess type of conflict Do psychosocial evaluation Hold parent conference Mandate parenting program Suggest family counseling	Confront behavior Stop violence Refer to office File intervention report Follow psychosocial recommendations Hold parent conference Mandate parenting program Suggest intensive therapy or treatment for student
Student Consequences	Review of activity for violence Parent notified (optional) Restitution Legal action	Office referral Life Skills worksheet Parent notified Restricted until worksheet finished Restitution Legal action	Office referral Parent notified Minimum time-out Violence Group Anger management Connections Empowerment Restitution Legal action	Office referral Parent notified Maximum time-out Violence Group Reconnections Restitution Legal action	Office referral Parent notified Maximum time-out Placement into an alternative setting Restitution Legal action
Contracts*	Verbal Promise	Simple Contract	Turf Contract I	Turf Contract II	Bottom-Line Contract

Students are placed at Levels 1–5 depending on the frequency and severity of their violent behavior. Students may stay at a particular level as the situation warrants. Any violent act that is racial, sexual, involves physical fighting, or is committed against staff results in the student being placed immediately at Level 3 or higher. The program manual provides lists of behaviors that correlate with each level of violence.

*See source for a complete description of the different contracts.

SOURCE: From "Making Violence Unacceptable," by C. Rembolt, *Educational Leadership, 56*(1), p. 36. Copyright © 1998 Association for Supervision and Curriculum Development. Reprinted with permission from the ASCD.

Another approach that builds tolerance and moves outside the classroom is service learning.

Community Outside the Classroom: Service Learning

Service learning An approach to combining academic learning with personal and social development.

Service learning is another approach to combining academic learning with personal and social development for secondary and college students (Johnson & Notah, 1999;

Woolfolk Hoy, Demerath, & Pape, 2002). The Alliance for Service Learning in Education Reform (1993) lists several characteristics of service learning. The activities:

- Are organized and meet actual community needs,
- Are integrated into the student's curriculum,
- Provide time to reflect and write about the service experience,
- Provide opportunities to apply newly learned academic skills and knowledge,
- Enhance both academic learning and a sense of caring for others.

Service learning activities may involve direct service (tutoring, serving meals at homeless shelters), indirect service (collecting food for shelters, raising money), or advocacy (design and distribute posters about a food drive, write newspaper articles) (Johnson & Notah, 1999).

Participation in community service learning can promote political and moral development for adolescents. Through service learning projects, adolescents experience their own competence and agency by working with others in need. Students see themselves as political and moral agents, rather than as merely good citizens (Youniss & Yates, 1997). In addition, community service learning can help adolescents think in new ways about their relationships with people who are unlike them, and thus can lead them to become more tolerant of difference (Tierney, 1993). Finally, service learning experiences foster an "ethic of care" that can result in a growing commitment to confront difficult social problems (Rhodes, 1997). In this sense, student involvement in community service learning can motivate and empower adolescents to critically reflect on their role in society (Woolfolk Hoy, Demerath, & Pape, 2002; Claus & Ogden, 1999).

Some schools now have participation in service learning as a graduation requirement. At least three of these school requirements have been challenged in court, but so far the requirements have been upheld (Johnson & Notah, 1999). Studies of service learning have produced mixed results. Some studies have found modest gains on measures of social responsibility, tolerance for others, empathy, attitude toward adults, and self-esteem (Solomon et al., 2001).

A case study at an urban parochial high school describes a successful service-learning experience (Youniss & Yates, 1999). This program was required for juniors at the school and was part of a year-long course on social justice. In the class, students examined the moral implications of current events such as homelessness, poverty, exploitation of immigrant laborers, and urban violence. Students also were required to serve four times (approximately 20 hours) at an inner-city soup kitchen. The researchers concluded that students emerged from the course with, "a deeper awareness of social injustice, a greater sense of commitment to confront these injustices, and heightened confidence in their abilities overall" (Yates & Youniss, 1999, p. 64).

Check Yourself What are Johnson and Johnson's three Cs of establishing a classroom community?

What are some options for resolving conflicts in schools?

What is service learning?

Summary Table

■ Self-Regulation and Agency

(pp. 478–481)

What factors are involved in self-regulated learning? One important goal of teaching is to prepare students for lifelong learning. To reach this goal, students must be self-regulated learners; that is, they must have a combination of the knowledge, motivation to learn, and volition that provides the skill and will to learn independently and effectively. Knowledge includes an understanding of self, subject, task, learning strategy, and contexts for application. Motivation to learn provides the commitment, and volition is the follow-through that combats distraction and protects persistence.

What is the self-regulated learning cycle? In this cycle, students move through three phases: forethought (which includes setting goals, making plans, self-efficacy, and motivation); performance (which involves self-control and self-monitoring); and reflection (which includes self-evaluation and adaptations, leading to the forethought/planning phase again).

Self-Regulation: Process of activating and sustaining thoughts, behaviors, and emotions in order to reach goals.

Self-Regulated Learners: Have a combination of academic learning skills and self-control that makes learning easier.

Volition: Will power; self-discipline.

■ Creativity

(pp. 482–486)

What is creativity and how is it assessed? Creativity is a process that involves independently restructuring problems to see things in new, imaginative ways. Creativity is difficult to measure, but tests of divergent thinking can assess originality, fluency, and flexibility. Originality is usually determined statistically. To be original, a response must be given by fewer than 5 or 10 people out of every 100 who take the test. Fluency is the number of different responses. The number of different categories of responses measures flexibility. Teachers can encourage creativity by providing opportunities for play, using brainstorming techniques, and accepting divergent ideas.

What can teachers do to support creativity in the classroom? Teachers can encourage creativity in their interactions with students by accepting unusual, imaginative answers, modeling divergent thinking, using brainstorming, and tolerating dissent.

Creativity: Imaginative, original thinking or problem solving.

Restructuring: Conceiving of a problem in a new or different way.

Divergent Thinking: Coming up with many possible solutions.

Convergent Thinking: Narrowing possibilities to a single answer.

Brainstorming: Generating ideas without stopping to evaluate them.

■ Social and Emotional Learning

(pp. 486–490)

What is emotional intelligence? Emotional Intelligence is the ability to process emotional information accurately and efficiently. At the center of emotional intelligence are four broad abilities: perceiving, integrating, understanding, and managing emotions.

How can social skills be taught? Social skills can be taught through direct instruction, modeling, practice, and integration of the skills into the daily life of the school.

What are the elements of effective risk-prevention programs? The most effective programs include developmentally appropriate language and concepts, teaching students to resist social pressure, accurate information about rates of behavior, interactive teaching such as role-playing or small groups, training in skills that help in many situations such as problem-solving strategies, thorough coverage of the topic with follow-up, and cultural sensitivity.

Emotional Intelligence (EQ): The ability to process emotional information accurately and efficiently.

■ Compassion and Tolerance

(pp. 490–500)

What are the learning theory underpinnings of cooperative learning? Learning can be enhanced in cooperative groups through rehearsal and elaboration (information processing theories), creation and resolution of disequilibrium (Piaget's theory), or scaffolding of higher mental processes (Vygotsky's theory).

Describe five elements that define true cooperative learning. Students *interact face-to-face* and close together, not across the room. Group members experience *positive interdependence*—they need each other for support, explanations, and guidance. Even though they work together and help each other, members of the group must ultimately demonstrate learning on their own—they are held *individually accountable* for learning, often through individual tests or other assessments. If necessary, the *collaborative skills* important for effective group functioning, such as giving constructive feedback, reaching consensus, and involving every member, are taught and practiced before the groups tackle a learning task. Finally, members monitor *group processes* and relationships to make sure the group is working effectively and to learn about the dynamics of groups.

What are some possible strategies for cooperative learning? Strategies include Jigsaw, reciprocal questioning, scripted cooperation, STAD (student teams–achievement divisions), and many others.

Cooperative Learning: Arrangement in which students work in mixed-ability groups and are rewarded on the basis of the success of the group.

Jigsaw: A cooperative structure in which each member of a group is responsible for teaching other members one section of the material.

Reciprocal Questioning: Approach where groups of two or three students ask and answer each other's questions after a lesson or presentation.

Scripted Cooperation: A learning strategy in which two students take turns summarizing material and critiquing the summaries.

Enhancing Your Expertise with Technology: Cooperative Learning

(p. 501)

http://www.jigsaw.org/
http://www.clcrc.com/
http://www.iasce.net/
http://www.thirteen.org/edonline/concept2class/month5/

Other Useful Websites

http://edweb.sdsu.edu/webquest/webquest.html
http://www.math.purdue.edu~ccc/
http://www2.ncsu.edu/unity/lockers/users/f/felder/public/Cooperative_Learning.html
http://www.cde.ca.gov/iasa/cooplrng2.html
http://google.yahoo.com/bin/query?p=cooperative+learning&hc=1&hs=19
http://global.cscc.edu/deved/_private/New_Folder3/New_Folder/Default.htm

Creating a Learning Community

(pp. 501–507)

What are Johnson and Johnson's three Cs of establishing a classroom community? The three Cs are cooperative community, constructive conflict resolution, and civic values. Classroom management begins by establishing a community based on cooperative learning. At the heart of the community is the idea of positive interdependence—individuals working together to achieve mutual goals. Constructive conflict resolution is essential in the community because conflicts are inevitable and even necessary for learning. The last C is civic values—the understandings and beliefs that hold the community together. Values are learned through direct teaching, modeling, literature, group discussions, and the sharing of concerns.

What are some options for resolving conflicts in schools? Possibilities include teaching students to solve their conflicts with words and clear communication, peer mediation, conflict resolution strategies, and school-wide programs such as Protect and Respect.

What is service learning? Service learning activities are organized and meet actual community needs. They are integrated into the student's curriculum, and provide time for the student to reflect about the service experience and to apply newly learned academic skills and knowledge.

Service Learning: An approach to combining academic learning with personal and social development.

Becoming a Professional

Passing the PRAXIS™

Chapter 13 reflects many of the professional standards created by the Interstate New Teacher Assessment and Support Consortium (INTASC). These standards form the basis of the PRAXIS II™ and state-created teacher licensure exams.

Your generation of teachers may influence the profession more than any generation before it. The folk wisdom, institutional memory, and history of teaching in this country provide little guidance for working with millions of students who have the shared experiences—vicarious or actual—of school shootings, terrorist bombings, and sniper attacks. An earlier generation of teachers conducted air raid drills to protect students from dangers from afar; the next generation of teachers will conduct "lock-downs" to protect students from dangers from within our country.

These events will affect students' emotions and how they interact with you and each other, the ways in which educators manage classrooms and schools, and the values that teachers emphasize in their classrooms and curricula. (One apparent early trend, for example, is that schools will emphasize the responsibilities of citizens toward their communities.) You and your colleagues will have significant roles in shaping the responses that schools and communities make to the realities of modern life.

Tips for PRAXIS II™

Focus on these major topics:

- The role of the school in the community
- Community environments and conditions that affect students' lives and learning
- Events outside the immediate school or community environment that may influence student behavior

Related Topics

Family and Community Partnerships (in each chapter)

- How teachers motivate students (Chapter 10)

Standards and Licensure Appendix: *PRAXIS II™ and INTASC*

Refer to the Appendix at the end of the book for detailed correlations to PRAXIS II™ exam topics and INTASC Standards addressed in this text.

Insights about Interview Questions: *What Would You Say?*

1. As part of the interview process for a job in a middle school, you are asked the following: "What do you think about the idea of emotional intelligence? Would you teach that in your class?"
2. As part of the interview process for a job in an elementary school, you are asked the following: "Do you use group work in your teaching? Why or why not? How would you use it in this school?"

Your Teaching Portfolio: *Teaching Resources*

- Add the websites for EQ to your **Portfolio.**
- Add examples of how you would use cooperative learning structures to your **Portfolio.**
- Add Tables 13.1, "Teaching Students to be Self-Regulated Learners," 13.5, "Possible Student Roles in Cooperative Learning Groups," 13.6, "Question Stems to Encourage Dialogue in Reciprocal Questioning," 13.7, "Using Individual Learning Expectations," 13.8, "Academic and Interpersonal Conflict and Learning," and 13.9, "Respect and Protect" to your file of **Teaching Resources.**

Use the CD-ROM included in the back of your textbook to launch the "Becoming a Professional" website. The website features advice on preparing for teacher certification exams, help with getting your first job, and resources to help you perform your job well from the first day forward.

Teachers' Casebook

What Would They Do?

Here is how some practicing teachers responded to the situation presented at the beginning of this chapter about helping students deal with traumatic situations.

William Rodney Allen

11th and 12th grades, *Louisiana School for Math, Science, and the Arts, Natchitoches, Louisiana*

I had a class on the morning of September 11, and I made the decision to take my students to our auditorium, where we saw on our large-screen TV the World Trade Center Towers collapse. In the days ahead, we talked both about the terrorism itself and our reactions to it. Some students seemed deeply troubled by September 11, while others seemed to take it in stride. I found that my discussions of tragic events in America's past—slavery, the horrors in the trenches of World War I, the pandemic of AIDS in Africa—seemed to be more affecting to students who had just lived through a great national tragedy of their own.

If there were a hostage situation at a near-by school, I would have to get a sense of how much and how immediately my students needed to know about the situation. Our students, being mostly from other cities, would be fairly unlikely to know anyone involved. I can't see much in the way of "historical interest" in a local hostage situation, in contrast to the events of 9/11, so I would probably be less likely to dismiss class and have them watch things unfold on CNN. After the fact, I would encourage students, both in class and during my office hours, to express any concerns they had about the event. We also have three counselors who are available to help students deal with emotional problems. As the parent of two daughters, I know that teenagers sometimes like to act as though nothing can bother them too much—even when that's far from the case. It helps teens a great deal just to have a sympathetic adult listen to their problems.

Suzi E. Young

5th Grade Teacher, *York Middle School, York, Maine*

If a tragedy were to strike where teachers and students were being held hostage, I am sure that the principal of our school would have the school make some sort of statement about whatever had happened. I would have to wait for direction from her to see what I am allowed to say or not say for that day.

After that initial response from the school, I would try to gather all of the facts that I could about the incident. Then, if my 5th grade students were to ask me questions directly or wish to discuss the matter, I would make sure that they understood the event. I have found in the past that my 5th graders just usually want clarification because they just don't understand what happened. I tell them everything that I know and point out anything that may be an opinion. Because we study facts and opinions, I point out facts versus opinions in news reporting and others telling the events as they see them. I tell them my opinion when they want it. Fifth graders want truth, honesty, and they also want to move on. I feel that when I have shared my fears with them, they tend to be grateful because they may be feeling the same way, or they have heard their parents say some of the same things. They are not as scared when they know that others may be having the same feelings that they are.

Students don't like to belabor the situation, no matter how tragic it may be. They like normalcy. I have found that if I make any conversation safe to talk about, we talk about anything they need to discuss for as long as they need to discuss it, and then move on.

Keith J. Boyle

English Teacher, grades 9–12, *Dunellen, New Jersey*

Such a situation warrants a firm voice of reason amid what would likely be an extremely intense atmosphere. I would attempt to quell any dissemination of further rumors and find out the facts as quickly as possible. In the aftermath of the event, communication is paramount. The best way to try to gain some understanding of the event and its emotional or psychological impact upon one's students is simply to talk things out. Also, allow students to take any path of vocalizing their concerns, be that through written exercises or just allowing students to vent. Everyone needs an outlet; allow the students a level of freedom to exercise their outlets.

Go to the Companion Website (www.ablongman.com/woolfolk) for additional case studies including audio and video cases, and examples of student work.

CHAPTER

14

Standardized Testing

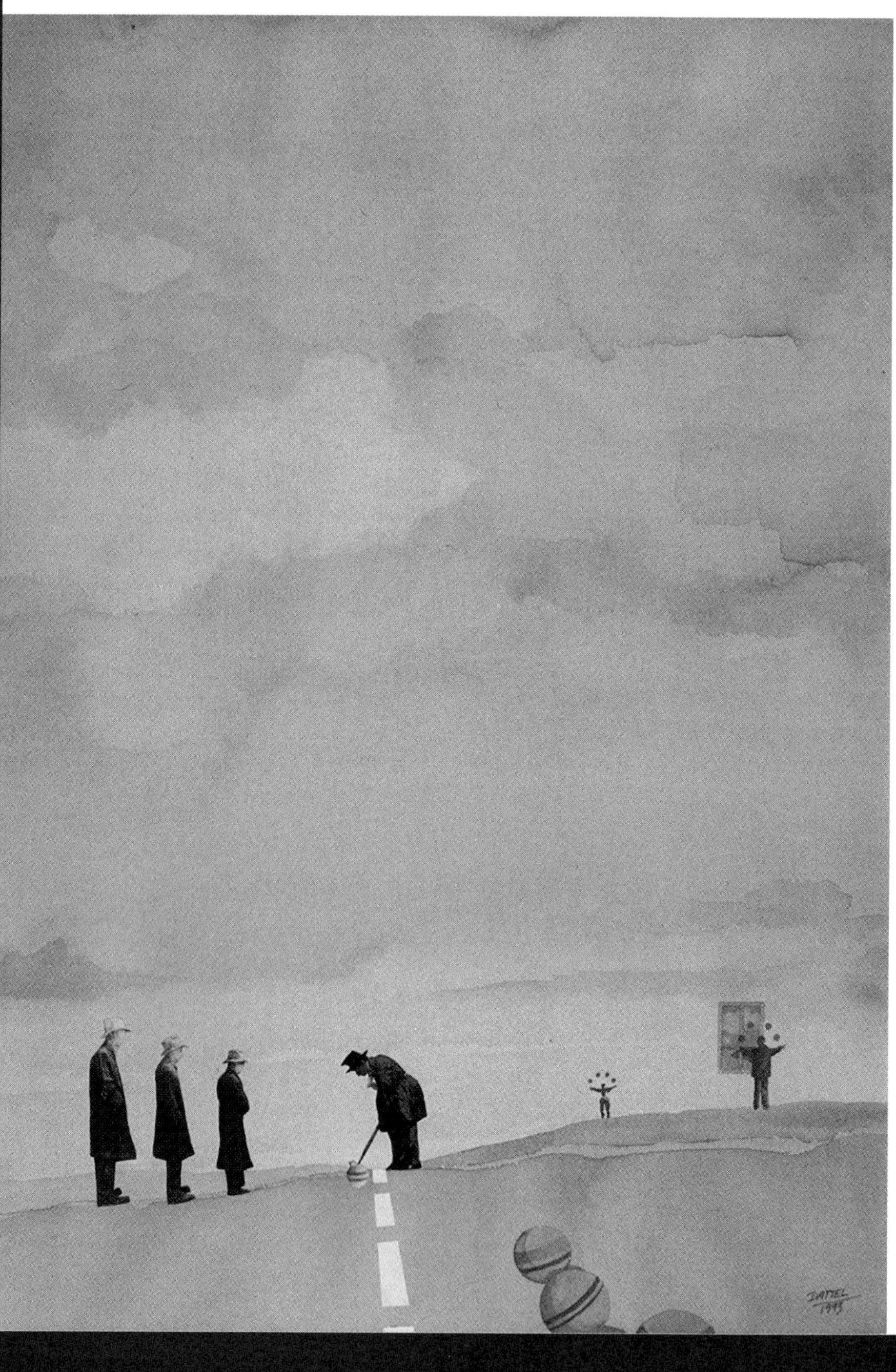

Teachers' Casebook

What Would You Do?

It is nearing the end of school and the 9th grade achievement test results are finally in. The parents' report form went home last Friday, and Monday morning you get a call from the principal during your planning period. The parents of one of your math students are in the office and have asked to speak with you and the principal immediately. The father is a prominent businessman and the mother is a lawyer. Their daughter received a grade-equivalent score of 11.8 on her standardized math test. The girl has been making Bs and Cs in your class—she seldom completes homework and has trouble with your conceptual approach to math. She just wants to know the "steps" to solve the problems so she can finish. You have tried several times to get the parents to come in to talk about ways to support the girl's learning, but they never seem to have had the time—until today.

You smile as you enter the principal's office, but the parents are not smiling. As soon as you sit down, the father says, "Well, you can see from our daughter's scores that you have been totally wrong in the grades you have given her this year. We thought she was just weak in math, but now it is clear you have something against her! Or maybe you just don't know how to teach math to bright girls."

The mother chimes in, "Yes, we expect you to reconsider her final grades for the year in light of her obvious ability. In fact," she glances at the principal and then glares at you again, "we believe she should get credit for the 10th grade class you teach as well, because she obviously knows the material already."

Critical Thinking

What would you say to the parents? What do you need to know about tests to deal with this situation? How will you approach working with this student? How will these issues affect the grade levels you will teach?

Collaboration

With 3 other members of your class, role play this conference.

Would it surprise you to learn that published tests, such as the college entrance exams and IQ tests, are creations of the 20th century? In the 19th and early 20th centuries, college entrance was generally based on grades, essays, and interviews. From your own experience, you know that testing has come a long way since then—too far, say some critics. They want to revise testing as a way of reshaping the curriculum and reforming education. We will explore these new ideas in this chapter.

In spite of the criticisms, schools still use many standardized tests, so teachers must be knowledgeable about testing. This chapter focuses on preparing for and interpreting standardized tests. Understanding how standardized test scores are determined, what they really mean, and how they can be used (or misused) provides you a framework for ensuring that the tests you give are appropriate.

First, we consider testing in general, including the various methods of interpreting test scores. Then, we look at the different kinds of standardized tests used in schools. Finally, we examine the criticisms of testing and the alternatives being proposed. By the time you have completed this chapter, you should be able to answer these questions:

- *How do you calculate mean, median, mode, and standard deviation?*
- *What are percentile ranks, standard deviations,* z *scores,* T *scores, and stanine scores?*
- *How can you improve reliability and validity in testing?*
- *What do results of achievement, aptitude, and diagnostic tests tell teachers?*
- *How would you prepare students (and yourself) for taking standardized tests?*
- *What are the strengths and weaknesses of alternative forms of assessment such as portfolios?*

Evaluation, Measurement, and Assessment

A member of your 7th grade class does poorly in the arithmetic reasoning section of a standardized test. How would your interpretation of the results differ if the test were a criterion-referenced type as opposed to a norm-referenced type? Explain.

CONNECT & EXTEND

TO YOUR TEACHING/PORTFOLIO
Both subjective judgments and objective measurements are used in evaluation. Are both equally valid in making educational decisions?

All teaching involves **evaluation.** At the heart of evaluation is judgment, making decisions based on values. In the process of evaluation, we compare information to criteria and then make judgments. Teachers must make all kinds of judgments. "Should we use a different text this year?" "Is this film appropriate for my students?" "Will Sarah do better if she repeats the 1st grade?" "Should Terry get a B^- or a C^+ on the project?"

Measurement is evaluation put in quantitative terms—the numeric description of an event or characteristic. Measurement tells how much, how often, or how well by providing scores, ranks, or ratings. Instead of saying, "Sarah doesn't seem to understand addition," a teacher might say, "Sarah answered only 2 of the 15 problems correctly in her addition homework." Measurement also allows a teacher to compare one student's performance on one particular task with either a standard or the performances of the other students.

Not all the evaluative decisions made by teachers involve measurement. Some decisions are based on information that is difficult to express numerically: student preferences, information from parents, previous experiences, even intuition. But measurement does play a large role in many classroom decisions, and, when properly done, it can provide unbiased data for evaluations.

Increasingly, evaluation and measurement specialists are using the term **assessment** to describe the process of gathering information about students' learning. Assessment is broader than testing and measurement because it includes all kinds of ways to sample and observe students' skills, knowledge, and abilities. Assessment is "any of a variety of procedures used to obtain information about student performance" (Linn & Gronlund, 2000, p. 32). Assessments can be formal, such as unit tests, or informal, such as observing who emerges as a leader in group work. Assessments can be designed by classroom teachers or by local, state, or national agencies such as school districts or the Educational Testing Service. And today, assessments can go well beyond paper-and-pencil exercises to observations of performances, the development of portfolios, or the creation of artifacts (Linn & Gronlund, 2000; Popham, 2002). In this chapter, we focus on formal assessments designed by groups and agencies outside the classroom. These assessments usually involve testing and the reporting of scores.

CONNECT & EXTEND

TO **PRAXIS**™
CRITERION-/NORM-REFERENCED TESTS (II, C5)
The ERIC Digest *Norm- and Criterion-Referenced Testing* (http://www.ed.gov/databases/ERIC_Digests/ed410316.html) describes the purposes, content, and issues related to criterion- and norm-referenced tests.

The answers given on any type of test have no meaning by themselves; we must make some kind of comparison to interpret test results. There are two basic types of comparison: In the first, a test score is compared to the scores obtained by other people who have taken the same test. (This is called a *norm-referenced* comparison.) The second type is *criterion-referenced.* Here, the comparison is to a fixed standard or minimum passing score.

Evaluation Decision making about student performance and about appropriate teaching strategies.

Measurement An evaluation expressed in quantitative (number) terms.

Assessment Procedures used to obtain information about student performance.

Norm-referenced testing Testing in which scores are compared with the average performance of others.

Norm groups A group whose average score serves as a standard for evaluating any student's score on a test.

Norm-Referenced Tests

In **norm-referenced testing,** the people who have taken the test provide the *norms* for determining the meaning of a given individual's score. You can think of a norm as being the typical level of performance for a particular group. By comparing the individual's raw score (the actual number correct) to the norm, we can determine if the score is above, below, or around the average for that group. There are at least three types of **norm groups** (comparison groups) in education—the class or school itself, the school district, and national samples.

Norm-referenced tests cover a wide range of general objectives rather than assessing a limited number of specific objectives. Norm-referenced tests are especially useful in measuring the overall achievement of students who have come to understand complex material by different routes. Norm-referenced tests are also appropriate when only the top few candidates can be admitted to a program.

However, norm-referenced measurement has its limitations. The results of a norm-referenced test do not tell you whether students are ready to move on to more advanced material. For instance, knowing that a student is in the top 3% of the class on a test of algebraic concepts will not tell you if he or she is ready to move on to advanced math; everyone in the class may have a limited understanding of the algebraic concepts.

Norm-referenced tests are useful in measuring overall achievement, but are not necessarily predictive of student readiness to move to more advanced work in an area.

Nor are norm-referenced tests particularly appropriate for measuring affective and psychomotor objectives. To measure individuals' psychomotor learning, you need a clear description of standards. (Even the best gymnast in school performs certain exercises better than others and needs specific guidance about how to improve.) In the affective area, attitudes and values are personal; comparisons among individuals are not really appropriate. For example, how could we measure an "average" level of political values or opinions? Finally, norm-referenced tests tend to encourage competition and comparison of scores. Some students compete to be the best. Others, realizing that being the best is impossible, may compete to be the worst. Either goal has its casualties.

Criterion-Referenced Tests

When test scores are compared, not to those of others, but to a given criterion or standard of performance, this is **criterion-referenced testing.** To decide who should be allowed to drive a car, it is important to determine just what standard of performance is appropriate for selecting safe drivers. It does not matter how your test results compare to the results of others. If your performance on the test was in the top 10% but you consistently ran through red lights, you would not be a good candidate for receiving a license, even though your score was high.

Criterion-referenced tests measure the mastery of very specific objectives. The results of a criterion-referenced test should tell the teacher exactly what the students can and cannot do, at least under certain conditions. For example, a criterion-referenced test would be useful in measuring the ability to add three-digit numbers. A test could be designed with 20 different problems, and the standard for mastery could be set at 17 correct out of 20. (The standard is often somewhat arbitrary and may be based on such things as the teacher's experience.) If two students receive scores of 7 and 11, it does not matter that one student did better than the other because neither met the standard of 17. Both need more help with addition.

In teaching basic skills there are many instances where comparison to a preset standard is more important than comparison to the performance of others. It is not very comforting to know, as a parent, that your child is better in reading than most of the students in class if none of the students is reading at grade level. Sometimes standards for meeting the criterion must be set at 100% correct. You would not like to have your appendix removed by a surgeon who left surgical instruments inside the body *only* 10% of the time.

Criterion-referenced tests are not appropriate for every situation, however. Many subjects cannot be broken down into a set of specific objectives. Moreover, although standards are important in criterion-referenced testing, they can often be arbitrary, as you have already seen. When deciding whether a student has mastered the addition of three-digit numbers comes down to the difference between 16 or 17 correct

CONNECT & EXTEND

TO YOUR TEACHING/PORTFOLIO
Giving accurate feedback to parents is part of a teacher's job. When talking with a parent about a child's abilities, do you think the use of norm-referenced or criterion-referenced test results is more desirable?

Criterion-referenced testing Testing in which scores are compared to a set performance standard.

■ Table 14.1	Deciding on the Type of Test to Use

Norm-referenced tests may work best when you are
- Measuring general ability in certain areas, such as English, algebra, general science, or American history.
- Assessing the range of abilities in a large group.
- Selecting top candidates when only a few openings are available.

Criterion-referenced tests may work best when you are
- Measuring mastery of basic skills.
- Determining if students have prerequisites to start a new unit.
- Assessing affective and psychomotor objectives.
- Grouping students for instruction.

answers, it seems difficult to justify one particular standard over another. Finally, at times it is valuable to know how the students in your class compare to other students at their grade level both locally and nationally. Table 14.1 offers a comparison of norm-referenced and criterion-referenced tests. You can see that each type of test is well suited for certain situations, but each also has its limitations.

Check Yourself Distinguish among evaluation, measurement, and assessment.

Distinguish between norm-referenced and criterion-referenced tests.

CONNECT & EXTEND

TO **PRAXIS**™
CONCEPTS OF STANDARDIZED TESTING (II, C5)
Be able to define norming samples, frequency distributions, measures of central tendency, standard deviation, normal distribution, reliability, and validity, and explain their roles in standardized tests.

What Do Test Scores Mean?

Standardized tests are those official-looking pamphlets and piles of forms purchased by school systems and administered to students. More specifically, the tests are called *standardized* because "the same directions are used for administering them in all classrooms and standard procedures are used for scoring and interpreting them" (Carey, 1994, p. 443). Standard methods of developing items, administering the test, scoring it, and reporting the scores are all implied by the term *standardized test.*

Basic Concepts

STOP THINK WRITE Guess the mean, median, and mode for these two sets of scores:

50, 45, 55, 55, 45, 50, 50 Mean _______ Median _______ Mode _______

100, 0, 50, 90, 10, 50, 50 Mean _______ Median _______ Mode _______

Which set of scores has the largest standard deviation?

In standardized testing, the test items and instructions have been tried out to make sure they work and then rewritten and retested as necessary. The final version of the test is administered to a **norming sample,** a large sample of subjects as similar as possible to the students who will be taking the test in school systems throughout the country. This norming sample serves as a comparison group for all students who take the test.

The test publishers provide one or more ways of comparing each student's raw score (number of correct answers) with the norming sample. Let's look at some of the measurements on which comparisons and interpretations are based.

Standardized tests Tests given, usually nationwide, under uniform conditions and scored according to uniform procedures.

Norming sample Large sample of students serving as a comparison group for scoring standardized tests.

Frequency distribution Record showing how many scores fall into set groups.

Frequency Distributions. A **frequency distribution** is simply a listing of the number of people who obtain each score or fall into each range of scores on a test or other measurement procedure. For example, on a spelling test, 19 students made these scores: 100, 95, 90, 85, 85, 85, 80, 75, 75, 75, 70, 65, 60, 60, 55, 50, 50, 45, 40. A graph, in this case a **histogram** (bar graph), of the spelling test scores is shown in Figure 14.1 where one axis (the *x*, or horizontal, axis) indicates the possible scores and the other axis (the *y*, or vertical, axis) indicates the number of subjects who attained each score.

Over one million standardized tests are given each school day in the United States, on average.

Measurements of Central Tendency and Standard Deviation. You have probably had a great deal of experience with means. A **mean** is simply the arithmetical average of a group of scores. To calculate the mean, you add the scores and divide the total by the number of scores in the distribution. For example, the total of the 19 spelling scores is 1,340, so the mean is 1,340/19, or 70.53. The mean offers one way of measuring **central tendency,** the score that is typical or representative of the whole distribution of scores.

Two other measures of central tendency are the median and the mode. The **median** is the middle score in the distribution, the point at which half the scores are larger and half are smaller. The median of the 19 scores is 75. Nine scores in the distribution are greater than or equal to 75, and nine are less. The **mode** is the score that occurs most often. The distribution in Figure 14.1 actually has two modes, 75 and 85, because each of these scores occurred three times. This makes it a *bimodal distribution.*

The measure of central tendency gives a score that is representative of the group of scores, but it does not tell you anything about how the scores are distributed. Two groups of scores may both have a mean of 50 but be alike in no other way. One group might contain the scores 50, 45, 55, 55, 45, 50, 50; the other group might contain the scores 100, 0, 50, 90, 10, 50, 50—the groups in the *Stop/Think/Write* question at the beginning of this section. In both cases the mean, median, and mode are all 50, but the distributions are quite different.

The **standard deviation** is a measure of how widely the scores vary from the mean. The larger the standard deviation, the more spread out the scores in the distribution.

CONNECT & EXTEND

TO YOUR TEACHING/PORTFOLIO

At a PTA meeting, parents were complaining because half of the students in the district scored below the district average on the achievement tests that were given. Is this a valid complaint?

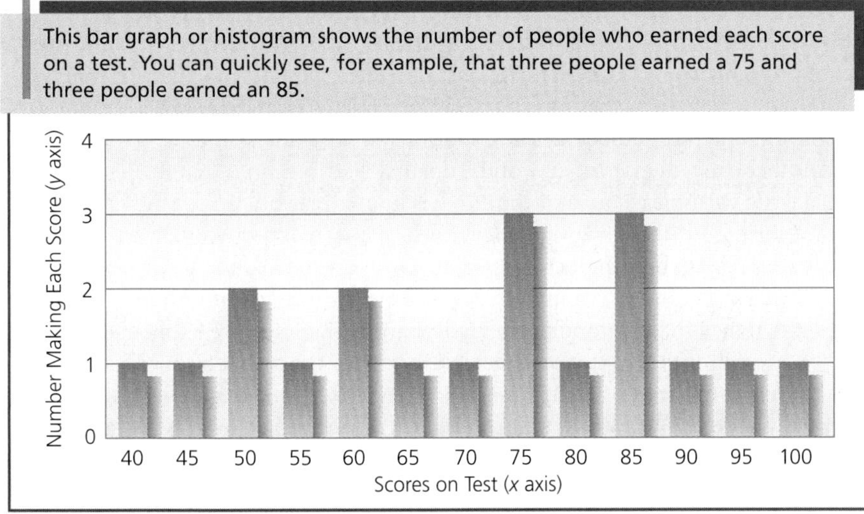
This bar graph or histogram shows the number of people who earned each score on a test. You can quickly see, for example, that three people earned a 75 and three people earned an 85.
Number Making Each Score (y axis)
0
1
2
3
4
40 45 50 55 60 65 70 75 80 85 90 95 100
Scores on Test (x axis)

■ **Figure 14.1** Histogram of a Frequency Distribution

Histogram Bar graph of a frequency distribution.

Mean Arithmetical average.

Central tendency Typical score for a group of scores.

Median Middle score in a group of scores.

Mode Most frequently occurring score.

Standard deviation Measure of how widely scores vary from the mean.

CONNECT & EXTEND

TO YOUR TEACHING/PORTFOLIO
Which math class, A or B, is probably easier to teach, judging from the following standard score results (50 = national average)?

Class A: Mean = 55 SD = 13 or
Class B: Mean = 53 SD = 4

(*Answer:* Probably Class B because the range of achievement levels is not as great as in Class A.)

The smaller the standard deviation, the more the scores are clustered around the mean. For example, in the distribution 50, 45, 55, 55, 45, 50, 50, the standard deviation is much smaller than in the distribution 100, 0, 50, 90, 10, 50, 50. Another way of saying this is that distributions with very small standard deviations have less **variability** in the scores.

The standard deviation is relatively easy to calculate if you remember your high school math. It does take time, however. The process is similar to taking an average, but you use square roots. To calculate the standard deviation, you follow these steps:

1. Calculate the mean (written as $\bar{X}$) of the scores.
2. Subtract the mean from each of the scores. This is written as $(X - \bar{X})$.
3. Square each difference (multiply each difference by itself). This is written $(X - \bar{X})^2$.
4. Add all the squared differences. This is written $\Sigma(X - \bar{X})^2$.
5. Divide this total by the number of scores. This is written $\frac{\Sigma(X - \bar{X})^2}{N}$.
6. Find the square root. This is written $\sqrt{\frac{\Sigma(X - \bar{X})^2}{N}}$, which is the formula for calculating the standard deviation.

Knowing the mean and the standard deviation of a group of scores gives you a better picture of the meaning of an individual score. For example, suppose you received a score of 78 on a test. You would be very pleased with the score if the mean of the test were 70 and the standard deviation were 4. In this case, your score would be 2 standard deviations above the mean, a score well above average.

Consider the difference if the mean of the test had remained at 70, but the standard deviation had been 20. In the second case, your score of 78 would be less than 1 standard deviation from the mean. You would be much closer to the middle of the group, with a score above average, but not high. Knowing the standard deviation tells you much more than simply knowing the **range** of scores. No matter how the majority scored on the tests, one or two students may do very well or very poorly and thus make the range very large.

The Normal Distribution. Standard deviations are very useful in understanding test results. They are especially helpful if the results of the tests form a **normal distribution.** You may have encountered the normal distribution before. It is the bell-shaped curve, the most famous frequency distribution because it describes many naturally occurring physical and social phenomena. Many scores fall in the middle, giving the curve its puffed appearance. You find fewer and fewer scores as you look out toward the end points, or *tails,* of the distribution. The normal distribution has been thoroughly analyzed by statisticians. The mean of a normal distribution is also its midpoint. Half the scores are above the mean, and half are below it. In a normal distribution, the mean, median, and mode are all the same point.

Another convenient property of the normal distribution is that the percentage of scores falling within each area of the curve is known, as you can see in Figure 14.2. A person scoring within 1 standard deviation of the mean obviously has company. Many scores pile up here. In fact, 68% of all scores are located in the area from 1 standard deviation below to 1 standard deviation above the mean. About 16% of the scores are higher than 1 standard deviation above the mean. Of this higher group, only 2% are better than 2 standard deviations above the mean. Similarly, only about 16% of the scores are less than 1 standard deviation below the mean, and of that group only about 2% are worse than 2 standard deviations below the mean. At 2 standard deviations from the mean in either direction, the scorer has left the pack.

The SAT college entrance exam is one example of a normal distribution. The mean of the SAT is 500 and the standard deviation is 100. If you know people who made scores of 700, you know they did very well. Only about 2% of the people who

Variability Degree of difference or deviation from mean.

Range Distance between the highest and the lowest scores in a group.

Normal distribution The most commonly occurring distribution, in which scores are distributed evenly around the mean.

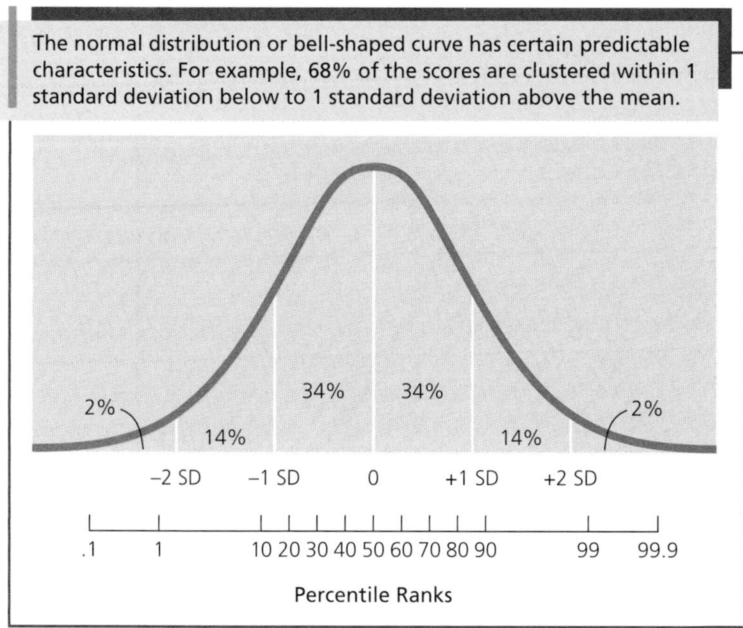

Figure 14.2 The Normal Distribution

take the test do that well, because only 2% of the scores are better than 2 standard deviations above the mean in a normal distribution.

Types of Scores

At your first parent conference, a mother and father are concerned about their child's percentile rank of 86. They say that they expect their child to "get close to 100 percent. We know she should be able to do that because her grade-equivalent score is half a year above her grade!" What would you say? Do they understand the meaning of these scores?

Now you have enough background for a discussion of the different kinds of scores you may encounter in reports of results from standardized tests—scores these parents don't seem to understand.

Percentile Rank Scores. The concept of ranking is the basis for one very useful kind of score reported on standardized tests, a percentile rank score. In **percentile ranking,** each student's raw score is compared with the raw scores of the students in the norming sample. The percentile rank shows the percentage of students in the norming sample that scored *at or below* a particular raw score. If a student's score were the same as or better than three-quarters of the students in the norming sample, the student would score in the 75th percentile or have a percentile rank of 75. You can see that this does *not* mean that the student had a raw score of 75 correct answers or even that the student answered 75% of the questions correctly. Rather, the 75 refers to the percentage of people in the norming sample whose scores on the test were equal to or below this student's score. A percentile rank of 50 means that a student has scored as well as or better than 50% of the norming sample and has achieved an average score.

Figure 14.3 on page 520 illustrates one caution in interpreting percentile scores. Differences in percentile ranks do not mean the same thing in terms of raw score points in the middle of the scale as they do at the fringes. The graph shows Joan's and Alice's percentile scores on the fictitious Test of Excellence in Language and Arithmetic. Both students are about average in arithmetic skills. One equaled or surpassed 50% of the norming sample; the other, 60%. However, because their scores are in the

Percentile rank Percentage of those in the norming sample who scored at or below an individual's score.

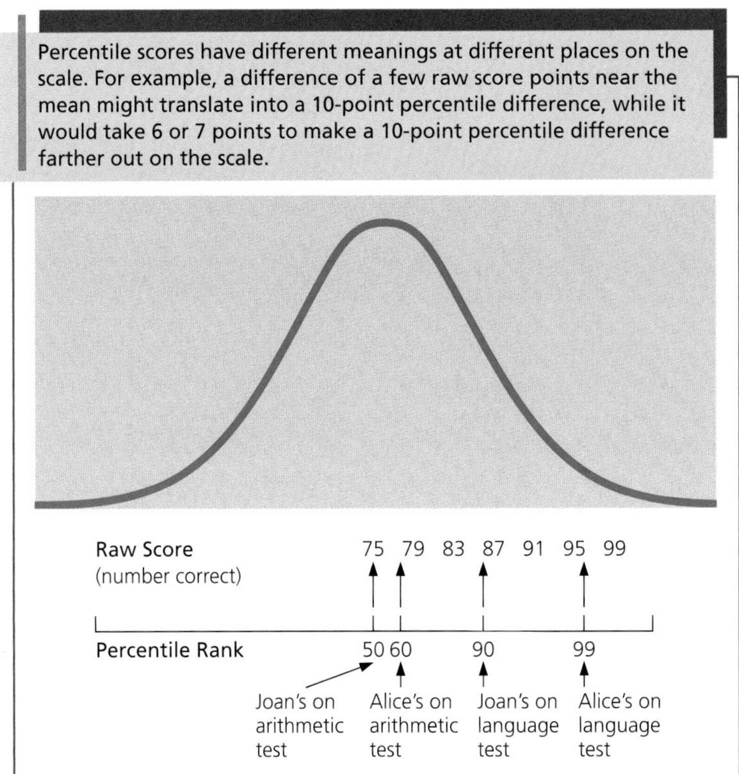
Percentile scores have different meanings at different places on the scale. For example, a difference of a few raw score points near the mean might translate into a 10-point percentile difference, while it would take 6 or 7 points to make a 10-point percentile difference farther out on the scale.
Raw Score
(number correct)
75 79 83 87 91 95 99
Percentile Rank
50 60 90 99
Joan's on arithmetic test
Alice's on arithmetic test
Joan's on language test
Alice's on language test

Figure 14.3 Percentile Ranking on a Normal Distribution Curve

middle of the distribution, this difference in percentile ranks means a raw score difference of only a few points. Their raw scores were actually 75 and 77. In the language test, the difference in percentile ranks seems to be about the same as the difference in arithmetic, since one ranked at the 90th percentile and the other at the 99th. But the difference in their raw scores on the language test is much greater. It takes a greater difference in raw score points to make a difference in percentile rank at the extreme ends of the scale. On the language test the difference in raw scores is about 10 points.

Grade-Equivalent Scores. **Grade-equivalent scores** are generally obtained from separate norming samples for each grade level. The average of the scores of all the 10th graders in the norming sample defines the 10th-grade equivalent score. Suppose the raw-score average of the 10th grade norming sample is 38. Any student who attains a raw score of 38 on that test will be assigned a grade-equivalent score of 10th grade. Grade-equivalent scores are generally listed in numbers such as 8.3, 4.5, 7.6, 11.5, and so on. The whole number gives the grade. The decimals stand for tenths of a year, but they are usually interpreted as months.

Suppose a student with the grade-equivalent score of 10 is a 7th grader. Should this student be promoted immediately? Probably not. Different forms of tests are used at different grade levels, so the 7th grader may not have had to answer items that would be given to 10th graders. The high score may represent superior mastery of material at the 7th-grade level rather than a capacity for doing advanced work. Even though an average 10th grader could do as well as our 7th grader on this particular test, the 10th grader would certainly know much more than this test covered. Also, grade-equivalent score units do not mean the same thing at every grade level. For example, a 2nd grader reading at the 1st-grade level would have more trouble in school than an 11th grader who reads at the 10th-grade level.

Grade-equivalent score Measure of grade level based on comparison with norming samples from each grade.

Because grade-equivalent scores are misleading and are often misinterpreted, especially by parents, most educators and psychologists strongly believe they should not be used at all. There are several other forms of reporting available that are more appropriate.

Standard scores Scores based on the standard deviation.

***z* score** Standard score indicating the number of standard deviations above or below the mean.

***T* score** Standard score with a mean of 50 and a standard deviation of 10.

Stanine scores Whole number scores from 1 to 9, each representing a wide range of raw scores.

Standard Scores. As you may remember, one problem with percentile ranks is the difficulty in making comparisons among ranks. A discrepancy of a certain number of raw-score points has a different meaning at different places on the scale. With standard scores, on the other hand, a difference of 10 points is the same everywhere on the scale.

Standard scores are based on the standard deviation. A very common standard score is called the ***z* score.** A *z* score tells how many standard deviations above or below the average a raw score is. In the example described earlier, in which you were fortunate enough to get a 78 on a test where the mean was 70 and the standard deviation was 4, your *z* score would be +2, or 2 standard deviations above the mean. If a person were to score 64 on this test, the score would be 1.5 standard deviation units *below* the mean, and the *z* score would be –1.5. A *z* score of 0 would be no standard deviations above the mean—in other words, right on the mean.

To calculate the *z* score for a given raw score, subtract the mean from the raw score and divide the difference by the standard deviation. The formula is:

$$z = \frac{X - \overline{X}}{SD}$$

Because it is often inconvenient to use negative numbers, other standard scores have been devised to eliminate this difficulty. The ***T* score** has a mean of 50 and uses a standard deviation of 10. Thus a *T* score of 50 indicates average performance. If you multiply the *z* score by 10 (which eliminates the decimal) and add 50 (which gets rid of the negative number), you get the equivalent *T* score as the answer. The person whose *z* score was –1.5 would have a *T* score of 35.

First multiply the *z* score by 10: $-1.5 \times 10 = -15$

Then add 50: $-15 + 50 = 35$

The scoring of the SAT test is based on a similar procedure. The mean of the scores is set at 500, and a standard deviation of 100 is used.

Before we leave this section on types of scores, we should mention one other widely used method. **Stanine scores** (the name comes from "standard nine") are standard scores. There are only nine possible scores on the stanine scale, the whole numbers 1 through 9. The mean is 5, and the standard deviation is 2. Each unit from 2 to 8 is equal to half a standard deviation.

Stanine scores provide a method of considering a student's rank, because each of the nine scores includes a specific range of percentile scores in the normal distribution. For example, a stanine score of 1 is assigned to the bottom 4% of scores in a distribution. A stanine of 2 is assigned to the next 7%. Of course, some raw scores in this 7% range are better than others, but they all get a stanine score of 2.

Each stanine score represents a wide range of raw scores. This has the advantage of encouraging teachers and parents to view a student's score in more general terms instead of making fine distinctions based on a few points. Figure 14.4 compares the four

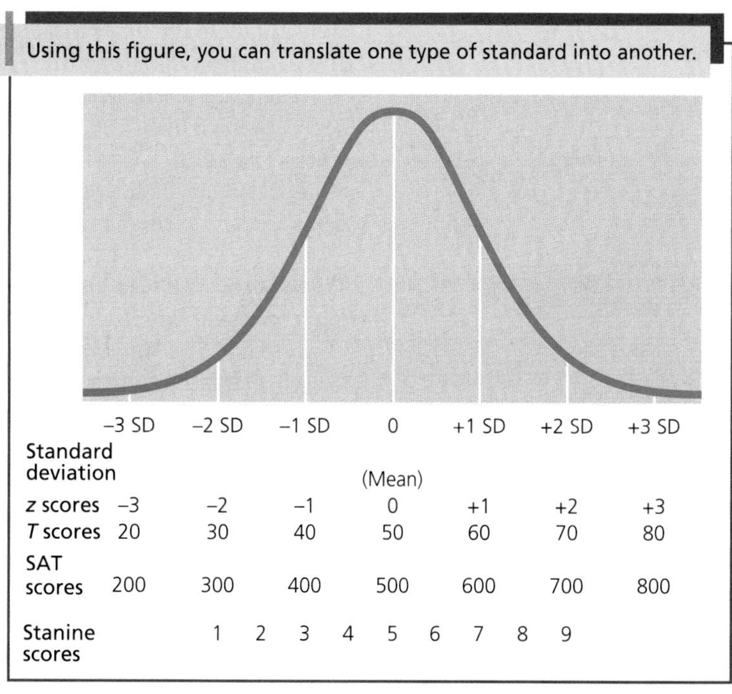

Figure 14.4 Four Types of Standard Scores on a Normal Distribution Curve

types of standard scores we have considered, showing how each would fall on a normal distribution curve.

Interpreting Test Scores

What Would You Say? As part of the interview process for a job in a high school, you are asked the following: "How would you interpret the test scores of minority group students?"

One of the most common problems with the use of tests is misinterpretation of scores. This often happens because of the belief that numbers are precise measurements of a student's ability. No test provides a perfect picture of a person's abilities; a test is only one small sample of behavior. Three factors are important in developing good tests and interpreting results: reliability, validity, and absence of bias.

Reliability. If you took a standardized test on Monday, then took the same test again a week later, and you received about the same score each time, you would have reason to believe the test was reliable. If 100 people took the test one day, then repeated it the following week, and the ranking of the individual scores was about the same for both tests, you would be even more certain the test was reliable. (Of course, this assumes that no one looks up answers or studies before the second test.) A reliable test gives a consistent and stable "reading" of a person's ability from one occasion to the next, assuming the person's ability remains the same. A reliable thermometer works in a similar manner, giving you a reading of 100°C each time you measure the temperature of boiling water. Measuring a test's **reliability** this way, by giving the test on two different occasions, indicates *stability* or *test-retest reliability.* If a group of people takes two equivalent versions of a test and the scores on both tests are comparable, this indicates *alternate-form reliability.*

Reliability can also refer to the internal consistency or the precision of a test. This type of reliability, known as *split-half reliability,* is calculated by comparing performance on half of the test questions with performance on the other half. If, for example, someone did quite well on all the odd-numbered items and not at all well on the even-numbered items, we could assume that the items were not very consistent or precise in measuring what they were intended to measure.

There are several ways to compute reliability, but all the possibilities give numbers between 0.0 and 1.0, like a correlation coefficient. Above .90 is considered very reliable; .80 to .90 is good, and below .80 is not very good reliability for standardized tests (Haladyna, 2002). The most effective way to improve reliability is to add more items to a test. Generally speaking, longer tests are more reliable than shorter ones.

True Score. All tests are imperfect estimators of the qualities or skills they are trying to measure. There are errors in every testing situation. Sometimes the errors are in your favor and you score higher than your ability might warrant; perhaps you reviewed a key section just before the test. Sometimes the errors go against you—you are sick, sleepy, or focused on the wrong material in your review. But if you could be tested over and over again without becoming tired and without memorizing the answers, your good luck and bad luck would even out, and the average of the test scores would bring you close to a **true score.** In other words, we can think of a student's true score as the mean of all the scores the student would receive if the test were repeated many times.

In reality, however, students take a test only once. So the score each student receives is made up of the hypothetical *true score* plus some amount of *error.* How can error be reduced so that the actual score can be brought closer to a true score? As you might guess, this returns us to the question of reliability. The more reliable the test, the less error in the score actually obtained. On standardized tests, test developers take this into consideration and make estimations of how much the students' scores

CONNECT & EXTEND

TO YOUR TEACHING/PORTFOLIO
There are many sources of error in testing: personal (e.g., misreading directions, illness, reviewing wrong material, anxiety); test-related (e.g., unclear directions, excessive length, too-high reading level); and context-related (too-competitive situation, noise, mistakes by test administrator).

Reliability Consistency of test results.

True score Hypothetical average of all of an individual's scores if repeated testing under ideal conditions were possible.

would probably vary if they were tested repeatedly. This estimation is called the **standard error of measurement.** It represents the *standard deviation* of the distribution of scores from our hypothetical repeated testings. Thus a reliable test can also be defined as one with a small standard error of measurement. In their interpretation of tests, teachers must also take into consideration the margin for error.

Confidence Interval. Never base an opinion of a student's ability or achievement on the exact score the student obtains. Many test companies now report scores using a **confidence interval,** or "standard error band," that encloses the student's actual score. This makes use of the standard error of measurement and allows a teacher to consider the range of scores that might include a student's true score.

Let us assume, for example, that two students in your class take a standardized achievement test in Spanish. The standard error of measurement for this test is 5. One student receives a score of 79 and the other, a score of 85. At first glance, these scores seem quite different. But when you consider the standard error bands around the scores, not just the scores alone, you see that the bands overlap. The first student's true score might be anywhere between 74 and 84 (that is, the actual score of 79 plus and minus the standard error of 5). The second student's true score might be anywhere between 80 and 90. It is crucial to keep in mind the idea of standard error bands when selecting students for special programs. No child should be rejected simply because the obtained score missed the cutoff by one or two points. The student's true score might well be above the cutoff point.

Validity. If a test is sufficiently reliable, the next question is whether it is valid, or more accurately, whether the judgments and decisions based on the test are valid. To have **validity,** the decisions and inferences based on the test must be supported by evidence. This means that validity is judged in relation to a particular use or purpose, that is, in relation to the actual decision being made and the evidence for that decision (Linn & Gronlund, 2000; Popham, 2002). A particular test might be valid for one purpose, but not for another.

There are different kinds of evidence to support a particular judgment. If the purpose of a test is to measure the skills covered in a course or unit, then we would hope to see test questions on all the important topics and not on extraneous topics. If this condition is met, we would have *content-related evidence of validity.* Have you ever taken a test that dealt only with a few ideas from one lecture or just a few pages of the textbook? Then decisions based on that test (like your grade) certainly lacked content-related evidence of validity.

Some tests are designed to predict outcomes. The SATs, for example, are intended to predict performance in college. If SAT scores correlate with academic performance in college as measured by, say, grade-point average in the first year, then we have *criterion-related evidence of validity* for the use of the SAT in admissions decisions.

Most standardized tests are designed to measure some psychological characteristic or "construct" such as reasoning ability, reading comprehension, achievement motivation, intelligence, creativity, and so on. It is a bit more difficult to gather *construct-related evidence of validity,* yet this is a very important requirement, probably the most important. Construct-related evidence of validity is gathered over many years. It is indicated by a pattern of scores. For example, older children can answer more questions on intelligence tests than younger children can. This fits with our construct of intelligence. If the average 5-year-old answered as many questions correctly on a test as the average 13-year-old, we would doubt that the test really measured intelligence. Construct-related evidence for validity can also be demonstrated when the results of a test correlate with the results of other well-established, valid measures of the same construct.

Today, many psychologists suggest that construct validity is the broadest category and that gathering content- and criterion-related evidence is another way of determining if the test measures the construct it was designed to measure. Nearly thirty

CONNECT & EXTEND

TO THE RESEARCH
Messick, S. (1995). Standards of validity and the validity of standards in performance assessment. *Educational Measurement: Issues and Practice, 14*(4), 5–8.

CONNECT & EXTEND

TO YOUR TEACHING/PORTFOLIO
Can you answer these questions taken from Popham, W. J. (1988). *Educational evaluation* (2nd ed.). Englewood Cliffs, NJ: Prentice-Hall, p. 127?

Indicate which of the following types of validity evidence is being gathered.

a. Subject-matter experts have been summoned to rate the consonance of a test's items with the objectives the test is supposed to measure.
b. A correlation is computed between a new test of student self-esteem and a previously validated and widely used test of student self-esteem.
c. Scores on a screening test (used to assign sophomores to standard or enriched English classes) are correlated with English competence of college juniors (as reflected by grades assigned at the close of junior year English classes).

Answers: a. content b. construct c. criterion

Standard error of measurement Hypothetical estimate of variation in scores if testing were repeated.

Confidence interval Range of scores within which an individual's particular score is likely to fall.

Validity Degree to which a test measures what it is intended to measure.

GUIDELINES — Increasing Reliability and Validity

Make sure the test actually covers the content of the unit of study.

Examples

1. Compare test questions to course objectives. Make sure that there is good overlap.
2. Use local achievement tests and local norms when possible.
3. Check to see if the test is long enough to cover all important topics.
4. Are there any difficulties your students experience with the test, such as not enough time, level of reading, and so on? If so, discuss these problems with appropriate school personnel.

Make sure students know how to use all the test materials.

Examples

1. Several days before the testing, do a few practice questions with a similar format.
2. Demonstrate the use of the answer sheets, especially computer-scored answer sheets.
3. Check with new students, shy students, slower students, and students who have difficulty reading to make sure they understand the questions.
4. Make sure students know if and when guessing is appropriate.

Follow instructions for administering the test exactly.

Examples

1. Practice giving the test before you actually use it.
2. Follow the time limits exactly.

Make students as comfortable as possible during testing.

Examples

1. Do not create anxiety by making the test seem like the most important event of the year.
2. Help the class relax before beginning the test, perhaps by telling a joke or having everyone take a few deep breaths. Don't be tense yourself!
3. Make sure the room is quiet.
4. Discourage cheating by monitoring the room. Don't become absorbed in your own paperwork.

Remember that no test scores are perfect.

Examples

1. Interpret scores using bands instead of a single score.
2. Ignore small differences between scores.

years ago Sam Messick (1975) raised two important questions to consider in making any decisions about using a test: Is the test a good measure of the characteristic it is assumed to assess? Should the test be used for the proposed purpose? The first question is about construct validity; the second is about ethics and values (Moss, 1992).

A test must be reliable in order to be valid. For example, if, over a few months, an intelligence test yields different results each time it is given to the same child, then by definition it is not reliable. Certainly it couldn't be a valid measure of intelligence because intelligence is assumed to be fairly stable, at least over a short period of time. However, reliability will not guarantee validity. If that intelligence test gave the same score every time for a particular child but didn't predict school achievement, speed of learning, or other characteristics associated with intelligence, then performance on the test would not be a true indicator of intelligence. The test would be reliable—but invalid. The *Guidelines* should help you increase the reliability and validity of the standardized tests you give.

CONNECT & EXTEND

TO REAL LIFE
A woman aims her gun at the bull's-eye on a target and shoots five times. All five shots hit in the upper right-hand corner. Is the gun reliable? Is it valid? What are some possible sources of error?

Absence of Bias. Reliability and validity have long been criteria for judging assessments. But over the past 20 years, educators and psychologists realized that another criterion should be added—absence of bias. **Assessment bias** "refers to qualities of an assessment instrument that offend or unfairly penalize a group of students because of the students' gender, ethnicity, socioeconomic status, religion, or other such group-defining characteristic" (Popham, 2002, p. 73). Biases are aspects of the test such as content, language, or examples that might distort the performance of a group—either for better or for worse. For example, if a reading test used passages that described boxing or football scenarios, we might expect males on average to do better than females.

Assessment bias Qualities of an assessment instrument that offend or unfairly penalize a group of students because of the students' gender, SES, race, ethnicity, etc.

Two forms of assessment bias are unfair penalization and offensiveness. The reading assessment with heavy sports content is an example of *unfair penalization*—

girls may be penalized for their lack of boxing or football knowledge. *Offensiveness* occurs when a particular group might be insulted by the content of the assessment. Offended, angry students may not perform at their best.

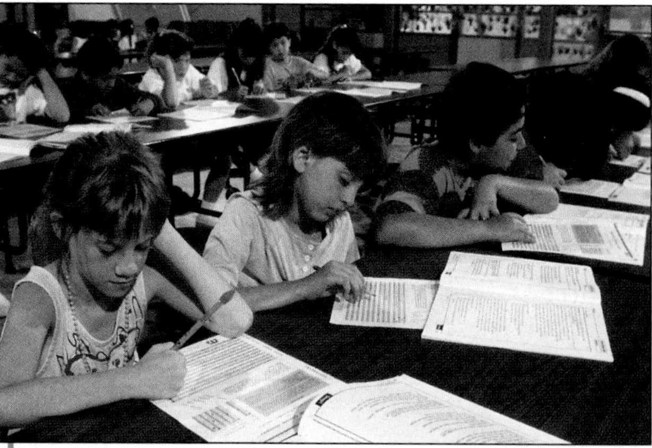

Assessment bias refers to testing that offends or unfairly penalizes a group of students because of their gender, ethnicity, socioeconomic status, religion, or other group characteristic.

Are tests such as the individual measures of intelligence or college admissions tests fair assessments for minority group students? This is a complex question. Research on test bias shows that most standardized tests predict school achievement equally well across all groups of students. Items that might appear on the surface to be biased against minorities are not necessarily more difficult for minorities to answer correctly (Sattler, 2001). Even though standardized aptitude and achievement tests are not biased against minorities in predicting school performance, many people believe that the tests still can be unfair. Tests may not have *procedural fairness;* that is, some groups may not have an equal opportunity to show what they know on the test. Here are a few examples:

1. The language of the test and the tester is often different from the languages of the students.
2. Answers that support middle-class values are often rewarded with more points.
3. On individually administered intelligence tests, being very verbal and talking a lot is rewarded. This favors students who feel comfortable in that particular situation.

Also, tests may not be fair, because different groups have had different *opportunities to learn* the material tested. The questions asked tend to center on experiences and facts more familiar to the dominant culture than to minority group students.

Concern about cultural bias in testing has led some psychologists to try to develop **culture-fair** or **culture-free tests.** These efforts have not been very successful. On many of the so-called culture-fair tests, the performance of students from lower socioeconomic backgrounds and ethnic groups has been the same as or worse than their performance on the standard Wechsler and Binet Intelligence scales (Sattler, 2001).

Today most standardized tests are checked carefully for assessment bias, but teacher-made tests may have biased content as well. It makes sense to have colleagues check your tests for bias, especially when you are getting started in teaching (Popham, 2002).

The *Guidelines* on page 526 might help all your students take tests.

Check Yourself Describe the key features of a standardized test. What are mean, median, mode, and standard deviation? Describe different kinds of scores. What is test reliability? What is test validity? What is absence of bias?

CONNECT & EXTEND

TO **PRAXIS**™
TYPES OF STANDARDIZED TESTS (II, C1)
Teachers, learning specialists, and school psychologists use a variety of tests. Distinguish among achievement, diagnostic, and aptitude tests. Describe the purposes for each.

Types of Standardized Tests

Several kinds of standardized tests are used in schools today. If you have seen the cumulative folders that include testing records for individual students over several years, then you know the many ways students are tested in this country. There are three broad categories of standardized tests: achievement, diagnostic, and aptitude (including interest). As a teacher, you will probably encounter achievement and aptitude tests most frequently.

Culture-fair/culture-free test A test without cultural bias.

Becoming an Expert Test-Taker

Use the night before the test effectively.

Examples

1. Study the night before the exam, ending with a final look at a summary of the key points, concepts, and relationships.
2. Get a good night's sleep. If you know you generally have trouble sleeping the night before an exam, try getting extra sleep on several previous nights.

Set the situation so you can concentrate on the test.

Examples

1. Give yourself plenty of time to eat and get to the exam room.
2. Don't sit near a friend. It may make concentration difficult. If your friend leaves early, you may be tempted to do so, too.

Make sure you know what the test is asking.

Examples

1. Read the directions carefully. If you are unsure, ask the instructor or proctor for clarification.
2. Read each question carefully to spot tricky words, such as *not, except, all of the following but one.*
3. On an essay test, read every question first, so you know the size of the job ahead of you and can make informed decisions about how much time to spend on each question.
4. On a multiple-choice test, read every alternative, even if an early one seems right.

Use time effectively.

Examples

1. Begin working right away and move as rapidly as possible while your energy is high.
2. Do the easy questions first.
3. Don't get stuck on one question. If you are stumped, mark the question so you can return to it easily later, and go on to questions you can answer more quickly.
4. If you are unsure about a question, answer it, but mark it so you can go back if there is time.
5. On a multiple-choice test, if you know you will not have time to finish, fill in all the remaining questions with the same letter if there is no penalty for guessing.
6. If you are running out of time on an essay test, do not leave any questions blank. Briefly outline a few key points to show the instructor you knew the answer but needed more time.

Know when to guess on multiple-choice or true-false tests.

Examples

1. Always guess when only right answers are scored.
2. Always guess when you can eliminate some of the alternatives.
3. Don't guess if there is a penalty for guessing, unless you can confidently eliminate at least one alternative.
4. Are correct answers always longer? shorter? in the middle? more likely to be one letter? more often true than false?
5. Does the grammar give the right answer away or eliminate any alternatives?

Check your work.

Examples

1. Even if you can't stand to look at the test another minute, reread each question to make sure you answered the way you intended.
2. If you are using a machine-scored answer sheet, check occasionally to be sure the number of the question you are answering corresponds to the number of the answer on the sheet.

On essay tests, answer as directly as possible.

Examples

1. Avoid flowery introductions. Answer the question in the first sentence and then elaborate.
2. Don't save your best ideas till last. Give them early in the answer.
3. Unless the instructor requires complete sentences, consider listing points, arguments, and so on by number in your answer. It will help you organize your thoughts and concentrate on the important aspects of the answer.

Learn from the testing experience.

Examples

1. Pay attention when the teacher reviews the answers. You can learn from your mistakes, and the same question may reappear in a later test.
2. Notice if you are having trouble with a particular kind of item; adjust your study approach next time to handle this type of item better.

Achievement Tests: What Has the Student Learned?

Look at the test printout in Figure 14.5 on page 528. What are this student's strengths and weaknesses? How do you know?

Achievement tests Standardized tests measuring how much students have learned in a given content area.

The most common standardized tests given to students are **achievement tests.** These are meant to measure how much a student has learned in specific content areas such

Table 14.2 Content Comparisons for Several Common Group Standardized Achievement Tests (Early Elementary Grades)

The most common testing programs cover similar topics, but be sure the test that your school uses matches your important curricular goals.

	ITBS	MAT-7	SAT-9	CAT	CTBS
Full name	Iowa Test of Basic Skills	Metropolitan Achievement Test, 7th ed	Stanford Achievement Tests, 9th edition	TerraNova CAT	TerraNova CTBS
Reading	Vocabulary Comprehension Word Analysis	Vocabulary Comprehension Word Recognition	Vocabulary Comprehension Word study skills	Vocabulary Comprehension Word Analysis	Vocabulary Comprehension Word Analysis
Mathematics	Concepts Problems Computation	Concepts and problem solving Procedures	Problem solving Procedures	Concepts and Application Computation	Mathematics Computation
Language	Language Listening	Language	Language Spelling Listening	Mechanics Expression	Mechanics Spelling
Other	Science Social Studies Sources of information	Science Social Studies	Environment	Science Social Studies	Science Social Studies
Publisher	Riverside Publishing	Harcourt Brace Educational Measurement	Harcourt Brace Educational Measurement	CBT McGraw-Hill	CBT McGraw-Hill
Website	www.riverpub.com	www.hbtpc.com/	www.hbtpc.com/	www.ctb.com/	www.ctb.com/

SOURCE: From *Essentials of Standardized Achievement Testing: Validity and Accountability,* by T. H. Haladyna. Published by Allyn & Bacon, Boston, MA. Copyright © 2002 by Pearson Education. Adapted by permission of the publisher.

as reading comprehension, language usage, computation, science, social studies, mathematics, and logical reasoning. There are achievement tests for both individuals and groups. Individual tests include, for example, the Wide-Range Achievement Test, Peabody Individual Achievement Test, and the KeyMath Diagnostic Tests. Common group tests are shown in Table 14.2. These tests vary in their reliability and validity. Group tests can be used for screening—to identify children who might need further testing or as a basis for grouping students according to achievement levels. Individual achievement tests are given to determine a child's academic level more precisely, or to help diagnose learning problems.

Using Information from a Norm-Referenced Achievement Test. What specific information can teachers expect from achievement test results? Test publishers usually provide individual profiles for each student, showing scores on each subtest. Figure 14.5 is an example of an individual profile for a 4th grader, Ken Jones, on the *TerraNova,* Second Edition. Note that the Individual Profile Report has two pages. The first page (Performance on Objectives) attempts to paint a picture of the student's mastery of different objectives in *Reading, Language, Mathematics, Science,* and *Social Studies.* For example, under *Reading* are the objectives of "basic understanding," "analyze text," "evaluate/extend meaning," and "identify reading strategies." Beside each objective are several different ways of reporting Ken's score.

Raw Score/Student OPI Score: Under the first column labeled "Student" is the number of items (out of 100) that Ken answered correctly for that objective. But

CONNECT & EXTEND

TO THE RESEARCH

Turner, M. D., Baldwin, L., Kleinert, H. L., & Kearns, J. F. (2000). The relation of a statewide alternate assessment for students with severe disabilities to other measures of instructional effectiveness. *Journal of Special Education, 34,* 69–76.

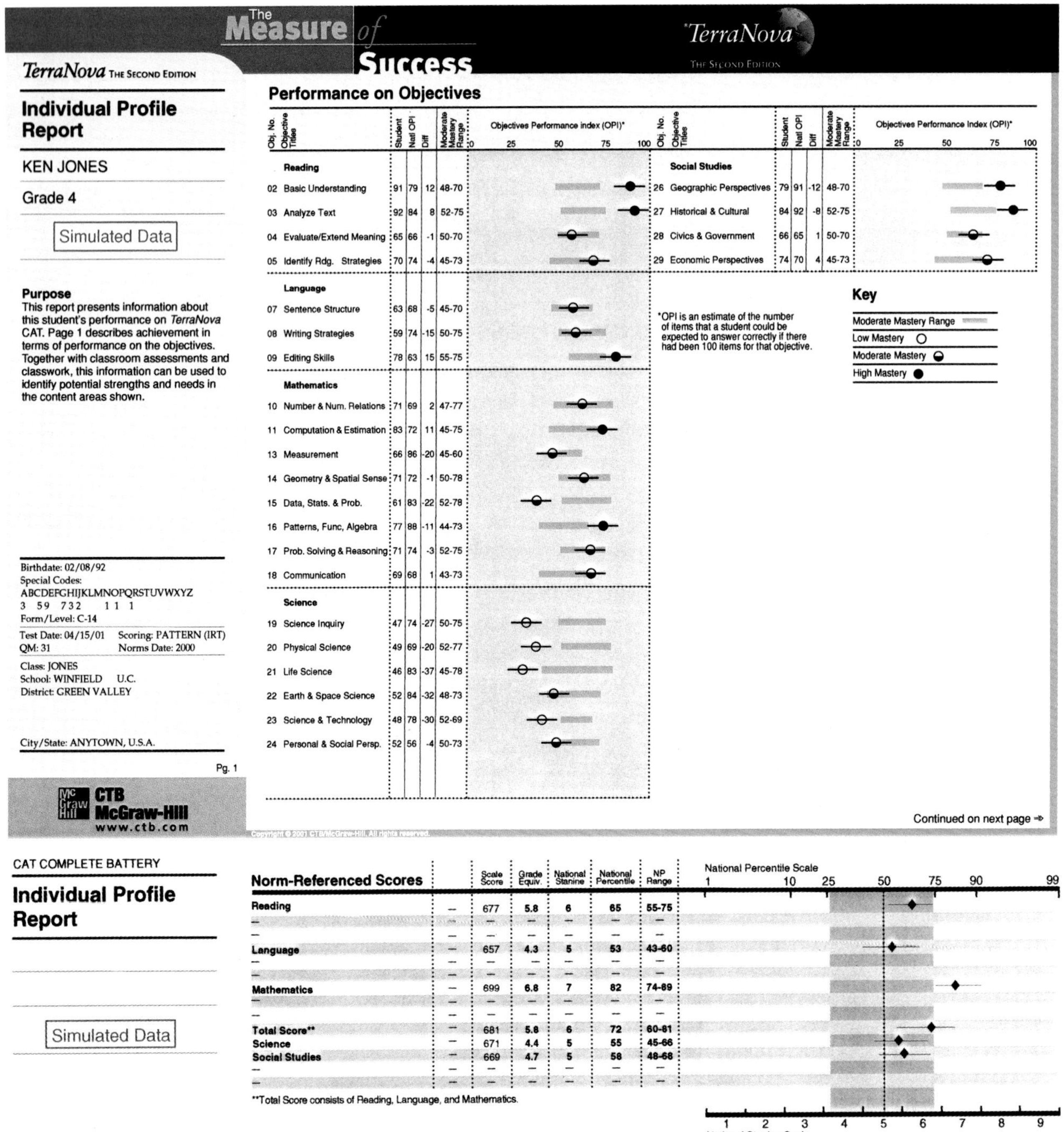

TerraNova THE SECOND EDITION

The Measure of Success

TerraNova THE SECOND EDITION

Individual Profile Report

KEN JONES

Grade 4

Simulated Data

Purpose
This report presents information about this student's performance on *TerraNova* CAT. Page 1 describes achievement in terms of performance on the objectives. Together with classroom assessments and classwork, this information can be used to identify potential strengths and needs in the content areas shown.

Birthdate: 02/08/92
Special Codes:
ABCDEFGHIJKLMNOPQRSTUVWXYZ
3 59 732 1 1 1
Form/Level: C-14
Test Date: 04/15/01 Scoring: PATTERN (IRT)
QM: 31 Norms Date: 2000
Class: JONES
School: WINFIELD U.C.
District: GREEN VALLEY
City/State: ANYTOWN, U.S.A.

Pg. 1

CTB McGraw-Hill www.ctb.com

Performance on Objectives

Obj. No.	Objective Titles	Student	Nat'l OPI	Diff	Moderate Mastery Range
	Reading				
02	Basic Understanding	91	79	12	48-70
03	Analyze Text	92	84	8	52-75
04	Evaluate/Extend Meaning	65	66	-1	50-70
05	Identify Rdg. Strategies	70	74	-4	45-73
	Language				
07	Sentence Structure	63	68	-5	45-70
08	Writing Strategies	59	74	-15	50-75
09	Editing Skills	78	63	15	55-75
	Mathematics				
10	Number & Num. Relations	71	69	2	47-77
11	Computation & Estimation	83	72	11	45-75
13	Measurement	66	86	-20	45-60
14	Geometry & Spatial Sense	71	72	-1	50-78
15	Data, Stats. & Prob.	61	83	-22	52-78
16	Patterns, Func, Algebra	77	88	-11	44-73
17	Prob. Solving & Reasoning	71	74	-3	52-75
18	Communication	69	68	1	43-73
	Science				
19	Science Inquiry	47	74	-27	50-75
20	Physical Science	49	69	-20	52-77
21	Life Science	46	83	-37	45-78
22	Earth & Space Science	52	84	-32	48-73
23	Science & Technology	48	78	-30	52-69
24	Personal & Social Persp.	52	56	-4	50-73
	Social Studies				
26	Geographic Perspectives	79	91	-12	48-70
27	Historical & Cultural	84	92	-8	52-75
28	Civics & Government	66	65	1	50-70
29	Economic Perspectives	74	70	4	45-73

*OPI is an estimate of the number of items that a student could be expected to answer correctly if there had been 100 items for that objective.

Key
Moderate Mastery Range
Low Mastery
Moderate Mastery
High Mastery

Continued on next page

CAT COMPLETE BATTERY

Individual Profile Report

Simulated Data

Norm-Referenced Scores

		Scale Score	Grade Equiv.	National Stanine	National Percentile	NP Range
Reading	—	677	5.8	6	65	55-75
—	—	—	—	—	—	—
—	—	—	—	—	—	—
Language	—	657	4.3	5	53	43-60
—	—	—	—	—	—	—
—	—	—	—	—	—	—
Mathematics	—	699	6.8	7	82	74-89
—	—	—	—	—	—	—
—	—	—	—	—	—	—
Total Score**	—	681	5.8	6	72	60-81
Science	—	671	4.4	5	55	45-66
Social Studies	—	669	4.7	5	58	48-68
—	—	—	—	—	—	—
—	—	—	—	—	—	—

**Total Score consists of Reading, Language, and Mathematics.

■ **Figure 14.5** A Typical Score Report

Source: Individual Profile Report from TERRANOVA, The Second Edition. Published by McGraw-Hill. Copyright © 2001 by McGraw-Hill. Adapted with permission from The McGraw-Hill Companies.

be aware, the test probably did not have 100 items to assess that objective, so this is an adjusted number (an OPI score) based on the actual number of items presented and the number Ken got right. The OPI score is an estimate of the number of items that Ken could be expected to get correct *if* there had been 100 items for that objective. A caution—on many standardized tests, some of these specific skill areas may be measured with only a few items each, and the fewer the items, the more potential problems there can be with reliability.

National OPI: The average OPI score for the national standardization sample completed in 2000.

Difference: The difference between the student's score and the national average—is the student below or above the national average and by how much? You can see that Ken is 15 points below the national average on writing strategies and 15 points above on editing skills.

Moderate Mastery Range: Indicates middle level mastery for this objective. For analyzing text, the range is 52 to 75 and Ken's score is above that range.

OPI Graph: On the graph to the right of the scores, a completely filled in circle indicates high mastery (see Ken's score on analyzing text in reading), a half-filled in circle is in the moderate mastery range (see Ken's score on sentence structure), and an empty circle indicates low mastery (science inquiry).

On page 2 of the report (Norm-Referenced Scores) Ken's scores are compared to students in the national standardization sample, completed in 2000.

Scale Score: The basic score used to derive all the other scores, sometimes called a growth score because it describes growth in achievement that typically occurs as students move through the grades.

Grade Equivalent Score: This indicates that Ken's scale score is the same as an average student in that grade and month of school. Beware of the problems with grade-equivalent scores described earlier.

National Stanine: This is Ken's stanine score based on a national norming sample comparison group.

National Percentile Score: This score tells us where he stands in relation to students at his grade level across the country.

National Percentile Range: The range of national percentile scores in which Ken's true score is likely to fall. You may remember from our discussion of true scores that this range, or confidence interval, is determined by adding and subtracting the standard error of the test from Ken's actual score. There is a 95% chance that Ken's true score is within this range.

Beside the scores is a graph showing Ken's national percentile and stanine scores, with the standard error bands indicated around the scores.

CONNECT & EXTEND

TO **PRAXIS**™ INTERPRETING ACHIEVEMENT TESTS (II, C4)

Accurate information from the teacher is essential for students' academic progress. The ERIC Digest *Explaining Test Results to Parents* (http://www.ed.gov/databases/ERIC_Digests/ed302559.html) will help with this task.

CONNECT & EXTEND

TO YOUR TEACHING/PORTFOLIO

If you have access to your own records, locate copies of standardized tests you have taken and interpret the scores as if you were your own teacher.

Diagnostic Tests: What Are the Student's Strengths and Weaknesses?

If teachers want to identify specific learning problems, they may need to refer to results from the various **diagnostic tests** that have been developed. Most diagnostic tests are given to students individually by a highly trained professional. The goal is usually to identify the specific problems a student is having. Achievement tests, both standardized and teacher-made, identify weaknesses in academic content areas such as mathematics, computation, or reading. Individually administered diagnostic tests identify weaknesses in learning processes. There are diagnostic tests to assess the ability to hear differences among sounds, remember spoken words or sentences, recall a sequence of symbols, separate figures from their background, express relationships, coordinate eye and hand movements, describe objects orally, blend sounds to form words, recognize details in a picture, coordinate movements, and many other abilities needed to learn, remember, and communicate learning. Elementary school teachers are more likely than secondary school teachers to receive information from diagnostic tests. High school students are more likely to take aptitude tests.

CONNECT & EXTEND

TO YOUR TEACHING/PORTFOLIO

Some diagnostic tests, for example, the Detroit Tests of Learning Aptitude (4th ed.) and Part I of the Woodcock-Johnson Psycho-Educational Battery: Tests of Cognitive Ability, measure a student's ability in a variety of areas. Others, however, assess a student's ability in a more specific area. Tests of motor skills include Developmental Tests of Visual Motor Integration. For assessing specific areas of perception, commonly used tests include the Wepman Auditory Discrimination Test, the Goldman-Fristoe-Woodcock Test of Auditory Discrimination, the Tests of Learning and Memory, and the Motor-Free Visual Perception Test.

Diagnostic tests Individually administered tests to identify special learning problems.

CONNECT & EXTEND

TO YOUR TEACHING/PORTFOLIO
Choose a partner to role play a parent–teacher conference. The teacher should interpret the scores to the parent and make judgments or recommendations about the child's future educational experiences. The parent should feel free to ask questions concerning the interpretation and the recommendations.

Terry: 3rd grade, scores based on national norm.

Math Computation: 6.0 (grade-equivalent score)

Math Reasoning: 3.5 (grade-equivalent score)

Reading Vocabulary: 85th percentile

Reading Comprehension: 53rd percentile

Group IQ score: 79 (test was given the day before Terry's birthday)

Bobbie: 10th grade, scores based on local norms.

Math Computation: 5 (stanine score)

Math Reasoning: 4 (stanine score)

Reading Vocabulary: 53 (*T* score)

Reading Comprehension: 38 (*T* score)

WISC III Verbal = 121

WISC III Performance = 130

WISC III Total = 125

Aptitude Tests: How Well Will the Student Do in the Future?

Think back to your college entrance examination. What test did you take? How did you prepare? Did your score surprise you? How would you help your students prepare for this kind of test?

Both achievement and aptitude tests measure developed abilities. Achievement tests may measure abilities developed over a short period of time, such as during a week-long unit on map reading, or over a longer period of time, such as a semester. **Aptitude tests** are meant to measure abilities developed over many years and to predict how well a student will do in the future at learning unfamiliar material. The greatest difference between the two types of tests is that they are used for different purposes. Achievement tests measure final performance (and perhaps give grades), and aptitude tests predict how well people will do in particular programs such as college or professional school (Anastasi, 1988).

IQ and Scholastic Aptitude. In Chapter 4, we discussed one of the most influential aptitude tests of all, the IQ test. The IQ test as we know it could well be called a test of scholastic aptitude. Now that you understand the concept of standard deviation, you will be able to appreciate several statistical characteristics of the tests. For example, the IQ score is really a standard score with a mean of 100 and a standard deviation of 15 or 16, depending on the test. Thus about 68% of the general population would score between +1 and –1 standard deviations from the mean, or between about 85 and 115.

A difference of a few points between two students' IQ scores should not be viewed as important. Scores between 90 and 109 are within the average range. In fact, scores between 80 and 119 are considered within the range of low average to high average. To see the problems that may arise, consider the following conversation:

> **Parent:** We came to speak with you today because we are shocked at our son's IQ score. We can't believe he has only a 99 IQ when his sister scored much higher on the same test. We know they are about the same. In fact, Sam has better marks than Lauren did in the 5th grade.
>
> **Teacher:** What was Lauren's score?
>
> **Parent:** Well, she did much better. She scored a 103!

Clearly, brother and sister have both scored within the average range. Although the standard error of measurement on the WISC-III (Weschler Intelligence Scale for Children, third edition) varies slightly from one age to the next, the average standard error for the total score is 3.2. So the bands around Sam's and Lauren's IQ scores—about 96 to 102 and 100 to 106—are overlapping. Either child could have scored 100, 101, or 102.

Discussing Test Results with Families. At times, you will be expected to explain or describe test results to your students' families. *The Family and Community Partnerships Guidelines* give some ideas.

CONNECT & EXTEND

TO **PRAXIS**™
STANDARDIZED TESTING: MAJOR ISSUES (II, C5)
Since their inception, there have been controversies regarding the use of standardized tests in the schools. Familiarize yourself with the major issues that underlie these controversies. Explain the positions of the different camps in these controversies.

Check Yourself What are three kinds of standardized tests?

Issues in Standardized Testing

What Would You Say? As part of the interview process for a job in an elementary school, you are asked the following: "What should we do to raise our test scores in this school?"

Educators increasingly are expected to use standardized test scores to make judgments about students, curricula, and school performance. This trend is likely to continue. Recently enacted federal law, for example, requires each state to categorize its

Aptitude tests Tests meant to predict future performance.

Family and Community Partnerships

Explaining and Using Test Results

Be ready to explain, in nontechnical terms, what each type of score on the test report means.

Examples

1. If the test is norm-referenced, know if the comparison group was national or local. Explain that the child's score shows how he or she performed *in relation to* the other students in the comparison group.
2. If the test is criterion-referenced, explain that the child's scores show how well he or she performs in specific areas.

If the test is norm-referenced, focus on the percentile scores. They are the easiest to understand.

Examples

1. Percentile scores tell what percent of students in the comparison group made the same score or lower—higher percentiles are better and 99 is as high as you can get. 50 is average.
2. Remind parents that percentile scores do not tell the "percent correct," so scores that would be bad on a classroom test (say 65% to 75% or so) are above average—even good—as percentile scores.

Avoid using grade-equivalent scores.

Examples

1. If parents want to focus on the "grade level" of their child, tell them that high grade-equivalent scores reflect a thorough understanding of the current grade level and NOT the capacity to do higher grade-level work.
2. Tell parents that the same grade-equivalent score has different meanings in different subjects—reading versus mathematics, for example.

Be aware of the error in testing.

Examples

1. Encourage parents to think of the score not as a single point but as a range or band that includes the score.
2. Ignore small differences between scores.
3. Note that sometimes individual skills on criterion-referenced tests are measured with just a few (2 or 3) items. Compare test scores to actual class work in the same areas.

Use conference time to plan a learning goal for the child that families can support.

Examples

1. Have example questions, similar to those on the test, to show parents what their child can do easily and what kinds of questions he or she found difficult.
2. Be prepared to suggest an important skill to target.

public schools based on results from such tests. This enhanced status of standardized testing requires teachers to be far more knowledgeable about every aspect of these tools. We begin with a basic question—just how much testing is going on?

How Widespread Is Standardized Testing?

You are a rare individual if you did not experience several standardized tests during your elementary and secondary education. In the United States, all 50 states and the District of Columbia have policies on statewide testing. In 48 of the 50 states and the District of Columbia, these tests include multiple-choice questions. Short-answer questions are on tests in 34 states. Only 18 states have tests that require students to construct longer responses such as essays (Doherty, 2002). Table 14.3 on page 532 has a few examples of the testing programs from several states.

For as long as I can remember, educators and policy makers have been concerned about the test performance of American students on these standardized tests. In 1983 the National Commission on Excellence in Education published *A Nation at Risk: The Imperative for Educational Reform.* According to this report, standardized test scores were at a 25-year low. More recently, politicians point to the Third International Mathematics and Science Study (TIMSS) showing that the United States appeared to be behind many other developed countries in math and science test scores. Part of the response to these headlines has been more testing. In 2001, the U.S. Congress passed the *No Child Left Behind Act* that requires each state to create content standards in reading and mathematics and assessments to measure student learning and knowledge linked to those standards. Science content standards and assessments

CONNECT & EXTEND

TO THE RESEARCH

See the March 2002 issue of *Phi Delta Kappan* for two articles on high-stakes testing in Alaska:

High-stakes testing in Alaska poses special problems for Alaska Natives and for students with disabilities—the same kinds of problems that high-stakes testing poses for similar groups in other locales.

"Equity for Alaska Natives: Can High-Stakes Testing Bridge the Chasm Between Ideals and Realities?" by Ken Jones and Paul Ongtooguk.

"High-Stakes Testing for Students with Special Needs," by Toni K. McDermott and Donald F. McDermott.

CONNECT & EXTEND

TO THE RESEARCH

McNeil, L. M., & Valenzuela, A. (2000). *The harmful impact of the TASS system of testing in Texas: Beneath the accountability rhetoric.* Cambridge, MA: Harvard University Civil Rights Project (www.law.harvard.edu/groups/civilrights/testing.html)

■ **Table 14.3** Examples of Testing Programs Sponsored by States

Many states have their own testing programs. See the websites below for more information. Does your state have a program?

State/Web	Brief Description
Arizona ade.state.az.us	Arizona Academic Standards are assessed using the Arizona Instrument to Measure Standards. Tests are given in reading, writing, and mathematics in grades 3, 5, and 7. The high school test will be used for pass/fail decisions affecting graduation. The state also administers the Stanford–9.
Colorado cde.state.co.us	Colorado's K–12 Academic Standards is assessed via the Colorado Student Assessment Program, which measures reading, writing, mathematics, and science in grades 3, 4, 5, 7, and 8.
Florida firn.edu/doe	The Florida Statewide Assessment Program was started in 1971 and currently is designed to assess its Sunshine State Standards in reading (grades 4, 8, and 10) and in mathematics (grades 5, 8, and 10). Florida also gives the SAT–9.
Kansas ksbe.state.ks.us	Kansas Curricular Standards includes reading, writing, and mathematics, variously assessed in grades 4, 5, 6, 7, 8, 10, and 11. Science and social studies are scheduled to be assessed.
Michigan http://www. meritaward.state.mi.us/	The Michigan Educational Assessment Program (MEAP) is based on the state's Model Core Curriculum Outcomes and the Content Standards. MEAP's purposes include comparing actual achievement to expected achievement and charting improvement over time. Michigan intends to target academic help where it's needed, mainly in poor communities. The state uses benchmark standards to chart progress of students and schools.
Minnesota cfl.state.mn.us	Minnesota Comprehensive Assessment measures the Basic and High Standards in reading and mathematics. Minnesota has a two-tier graduation standard. School districts have an option to use a publisher's nationally normed test. School districts can also develop their own tests, as long as the test measures state content standards.
Nebraska nde.state.us	School-Based, Teacher-Led Assessment and Reporting System uses Nebraska's content standards (Leading Educational Achievement Through Nebraska Standards). Reading/writing, mathematics, science, and social studies/history are covered. There is no state-mandated testing.
Ohio ode.state.oh.us	Standards for Ohio Schools drives Ohio's assessment program, which tests in grades 4, 6, and 9. Legislation has been passed making grade-level tests for promotion, with the caveat of providing remedial programs.
Oregon ode.state.or.us	Oregon has its Academic Content Standards and currently offers tests in reading, writing, mathematics, and science in grades 3, 5, and 7. The Certificate of Initial Mastery is a high school certification based on a high school test battery.

SOURCE: From *Essentials of Standardized Achievement Testing: Validity and Accountability*, by T. H. Haladyna. Published by Allyn & Bacon, Boston, MA. Copyright © 2002 by Pearson Education. Adapted by permission of the publisher.

will be developed next (Linn, Baker, & Betebenner, 2002). These assessments must be taken every year by every child in grades 3 through 8 and once in high school. To keep up with the law, see http://www.ed.gov/offices/OESE/esea/summary.html.

Given all this testing, how are the results used?

Accountability and High-Stakes Testing

High-stakes testing Standardized tests whose results have powerful influences when used by school administrators, other officials, or employers to make decisions.

Accountable Making teachers and schools responsible for student learning, usually by monitoring learning with high-stakes tests.

Test scores may affect "admission" to 1st grade, promotion from one grade to the next, high school graduation, access to special programs, placement in special education classes, teacher certification and tenure, and school funding. Because the decisions affected by test scores are so critical, many educators call this process **high-stakes testing.** One of the high-stakes uses for test results is to hold teachers, schools, and administrators **accountable** for student performance. For example, teacher bonuses might be tied to their students' achievement or schools funding' may be affected by testing results. One of the provisions in the *No Child Left Behind Act* is that states must develop adequate yearly progress (AYP) objectives for all students and for specific groups such as students from major ethnic and racial groups, students with disabilities, and students whose English is limited. These AYP objectives must be set with the goal that all students are proficient or better by the 2013–2014 school year. Schools that fail to meet their AYP objectives for two years will be identified for improvement (Linn, Baker, & Betebenner, 2002). The students in these "failing schools" can transfer. If the school's scores don't improve after three years, the school curriculum and/or staff can be replaced.

Is it reasonable to hold teachers and schools accountable for student achievement? The *Point/Counterpoint* shows that people disagree.

As you can tell from the *Point/Counterpoint,* high-stakes testing is a complex and controversial practice. To be valuable, testing programs must have a number of characteristics. Of course, the tests used must be reliable, valid for the purposes used, and free of bias. In addition, the a testing program must:

1. *Match the content standards of district*—this is a vital part of validity.
2. *Be part of the larger assessment plan.* No one test provides all the necessary information about student achievement. It is critical that schools avoid making pass/fail decisions based on a single test.
3. *Test complex thinking,* not just skills and factual knowledge.
4. *Provide alternate assessment strategies* for students with identifiable disabilities.
5. *Provide opportunities for restesting* when the stakes are high.

Making high-stakes testing even more stressful.

Point/Counterpoint

Should Tests Be Used to Hold Teachers Accountable?

There are two possible meanings for accountability. The first has to do with gathering information so that we can make good educational decisions about programs, policies, and resources. The second is holding someone responsible for student learning—usually the school or the teacher (Haladyna, 2002).

Point

The public needs information.

The argument for this kind of accountability is that the public has a right to know how their schools are doing, especially because public money is used to finance schools. Testing may help to raise expectations for the lowest-performing schools and give educators the information they need to improve the programs in their schools (Doherty, 2002). And people who make decisions about which reading programs to adopt or how to allocate resources need information about student achievement. The *No Child Left Behind Act of 2002* mandates annual assessment in reading and math for every student in grades 3–8. One goal is "to empower parents, citizens, educators, administrators, and policy makers with data from those annual assessments. The data will be available in annual report cards on school performance and on statewide progress. They will give parents information about the quality of their children's schools, the qualifications of teachers, and their children's progress in key subjects" (U.S. Department of Education, *No Child Left Behind* Fact Sheet, 2002).

Counterpoint

Using test scores to hold teachers and schools accountable does not make sense.

Will results of standardized tests really give parents information about the "quality of their children's schools" or the "qualifications of teachers"? If the test matches important objectives of the curriculum, is given to students who actually studied the curriculum for a reasonable period of time, is free of bias, fits the students' language capabilities, and was administered properly, then test results provide some information about the effectiveness of the school.

But studies of the actual tests in action show troubling consequences. Testing narrows the curriculum. For example, using the *Texas Assessment of Academic Skills* has led to curriculum changes that overemphasize what is tested and neglect other areas. The test of mathematics appears to also be a test of reading. Students with poor reading ability have trouble with the math test, especially if their first language is not English. And an unintended consequence of the early warning testing in elementary school is to "push out" students who leave school because they decide they are going to fail the high school graduation test—so why should they bother (McNeil & Valenzuela, 2000).

What do you think? Vote online at **www.ablongman.com/woolfolk**

CONNECT & EXTEND

TO THE RESEARCH

The Winter 2003 issue of *Theory Into Practice* on "The Impact of High-Stakes Testing" is edited by Marguerite Clarke and Kelvin Gregory and has the following articles:

"High-Stakes Testing and the Curriculum" by Marguerite Clarke

"High-Stakes Testing and Teachers" by George Madaus, Lisa Abrams, and Joseph Pedulla

"High-Stakes Testing and Students" by Catherine Horn, Harvard University

"Preparing for High-Stakes Testing" by Cengiz Gulek

"Lessons from Abroad: International Practices in High-Stakes Testing" by Kelvin Gregory

"Where to From Here?" by Naomi Chudowsky and James Pellegrino

6. *Include all students* in the testing, but also provide informative reports of the results that make the students' situations clear if they have special challenges or circumstances such as disabilities.
7. *Provide appropriate remediation* when students fail.
8. Make sure all students taking the test *have adequate opportunities to learn* the material being tested.
9. *Take into account the student's language.* Students who have difficulty reading or writing in English will not perform well on tests that require English.
10. *Use test results for children, not against them* (Haladyna, 2002).

This is important, so I repeat: Standardized achievement tests must be chosen so that the items on the test actually measure knowledge gained in the classes. This match is absent more often than we might assume: One group of teachers in St. Louis found that fewer than 10% of the items in their curriculum overlapped in both the textbooks and the standardized tests they were using (Fiske, 1988). Also, students must have the necessary skills to take the test. If students score low on a science test not because they lack knowledge about science, but because they have difficulty reading the questions, don't speak English, or have too little time to finish, then the test is not a valid measure of science achievement for those students.

No matter how good the test, some uses of high-stakes tests are not appropriate. Table 14.4 describes these problem uses.

CONNECT & EXTEND

TO THE RESEARCH

Linn, R. L. (2000). Assessments and accountability. *Educational Researcher, 29*(2), 4–16.

Testing Teachers

All states require some kind of licensing in order to be a teacher, and testing is a big part of that process. There is no national test yet, but the PRAXIS™ series is used by 35 states.

Table 14.4 Inappropriate Uses for High-Stakes Test Results

Beware of some uses for standardized test results. Tests were not designed for these purposes.

Pass/Fail Decisions	In order to deny students graduation from any grade, there must be strong evidence that the test used is valid, reliable, and free of bias. Some tests, for example, the *Texas Assessment of Academic Skills* (TAAS), have been challenged in the courts and found to meet these standards, but not all tests are good enough to make pass/fail decisions.
State-to-State Comparisons	You cannot really compare states using standardized test scores. States do not have the same curriculum, tests, resources, or challenges. If comparisons are made, they usually tell us what we already know—some states have more funding for schools and families with higher incomes or education levels.
Evaluation of Teachers or Schools	Many influences on test scores—family and community resources—are outside the control of teachers and schools. Often students move from school to school, so many students taking a test in spring may have been in the school only for a few weeks.
Identifying Where to Buy a House	Generally speaking, the schools with the highest test scores are in the neighborhoods where families have the highest levels of education and income. They may not be the "best schools" in terms of teaching, programs, or leadership, but they are the schools lucky enough to have the "right" students.

SOURCE: From *Essentials of Standardized Achievement Testing: Validity and Accountability,* by T. H. Haladyna. Published by Allyn & Bacon, Boston, MA. Copyright © 2002 by Pearson Education. Adapted by permission of the publisher.

CONNECT & EXTEND

TO THE RESEARCH

Smith, M. L. (1991). Put to the test: The effects of external testing on teachers. *Educational Researcher, 20*(5), 8–11.

PRAXIS™. This three-phase set of tests developed by the Educational Testing Service is an example of testing programs for teachers. Early in the prospective teacher's education program, *PRAXIS I™: Academic Skills Assessment* tests basic skills such as reading, writing, and mathematics. A computer-based package is available to remediate any weak areas identified by the test. *PRAXIS II™: Subject Assessments,* given at the end of the undergraduate program, test subject matter knowledge and also Principles of Teaching and Learning. *PRAXIS III™: Classroom Performance Assessments* is based on the particular licensing requirements for each participating state. This assessment is conducted by trained local evaluators, mostly through classroom observations. Within each *PRAXIS™* phase there are several modules from which to choose. States can require any one—or a combination of two or all three—of the PRAXIS™ phases for licensure (Danielson & Dwyer, 1995; Dwyer & Villegas, 1993).

Like the alternatives to standardized tests we will examine shortly, the *PRAXIS Series™* makes greater use of authentic performances and products. In the *PRAXIS™ Principles of Teaching and Learning* test, teacher candidates analyze case studies and suggest solutions to teaching problems. In *PRAXIS III™,* teachers might complete a lesson-planning exercise and then be interviewed about what they planned and why. They might be asked to submit a portfolio containing an overview of a unit, details of two consecutive lessons, copies of student handouts, lists of the resources selected for background, a videotape of teaching samples showing both large- and small-group lessons, and other examples of their actual work. Some states have developed systems for assessing beginning teachers that also rely on portfolios, including samples of teachers' writing, student work, and videotaped segments of classroom instruction, as shown in Table 14.5. Results of these assessments can be used to determine eligibility for a provisional teaching license as well as to provide feedback for continuing professional development (Lomask, Pecheone, & Baron, 1995).

CONNECT & EXTEND

TO YOUR TEACHING/PORTFOLIO
Find out what the requirements are for licensure tests in your state. Check the Website for the Educational Testing Service: www.ets.org.

National Board Certification. In addition to assessing beginning teachers, there is growing interest in setting standards for accomplished teaching. In 1986 the

Table 14.5 An Overview of a Science Teaching Portfolio

These are the entries expected in the portfolio of a beginning science teacher in Connecticut. Decisions about provisional certification as well as suggestions for improvement are based on the portfolio.

Task I—Planning for student learning

- Description of major concepts and goals for a two-week unit.
- Description of student characteristics relevant to learning this unit.
- Day-to-day journal entries for the unit.

Task II—Facilitating student learning

- Description of one student-centered lab activity during the unit.
- Description of one unit's topic dealing with science, technology, and society issues.
- Three 15-minute video segments of lab activity, post-lab discussion, and science-technology-society lesson.

Task III—Evaluation of student learning

- Entire work of three students during the unit.
- Detailed analysis of these students' learning.
- General analysis of whole class work and learning.
- Analysis of teaching and suggestions for future changes.

SOURCE: "Assessing New Science Teachers," by M. S. Lomask, R. L. Pecheone, and J. B. Baron, 1995, *Educational Leadership, 52*(6), p. 63. Copyright © 1995 by Connecticut State Department of Education. Adapted with permission.

Carnegie Task Force on Teaching as a Profession called for the creation of a National Board for Professional Teaching Standards (NBPTS). This Board will offer experienced teachers advanced certification in more than 30 fields, categorized by subject matter and developmental level of students. Standards in all areas will be grounded in five general propositions about accomplished practice (Yinger, 1999):

1. Teachers are committed to students and their learning.
2. Teachers know the subjects they teach and how to teach those subjects to their students.
3. Teachers are responsible for managing and monitoring student learning.
4. Teachers think systematically about their practice and learn from experience.
5. Teachers are members of learning communities.

The process, which relies on portfolio assessment, is voluntary and still being refined. At the time of this writing, the cost to the teacher being evaluated was $2000, but schools often help teachers cover the expense. In about 31 states, teachers who meet the standards for national teacher certification earn bonus pay (Haladyna, 2002). If you become a teacher, assessment awaits you at several points in your career.

The Uses of Testing in American Society

How has standardized testing affected your life so far? What opportunities have been opened or closed to you based on test scores? Was the process fair?

CONNECT & EXTEND

TO THE RESEARCH
Background: For an argument that American standards and students are not in crisis, see Berliner, D., & Biddle, B. (1996). *The manufactured crisis: Myths, frauds, and the attack on America's public schools.* White Plains, NY: Longman. For the counterargument, see Ravitch, D. (1995). *National standards in American education: A citizen's guide.* Washington, DC: Brookings Institution.

As you have seen, tests are not simply procedures used in research. Every day, there are many decisions made about individuals that are based on the results of tests. Should Emily be issued a driver's license? How many and which students from the 8th grade would benefit from an accelerated program in science? Who belongs in a remedial class? Who will be admitted to college or professional school? Who will get a teaching license? In answering these questions, it is important to distinguish between the quality of the test itself and the way the test is used. Even the best instruments can be, and have been, misused. In earlier years, for example, using otherwise valid and reliable individual intelligence tests, many students were inappropriately identified as having mental retardation. The problem was not with the tests, but with the fact that the test score was the only information used to classify students. Much more information must be considered.

Behind all the statistics and terminology are issues related to values and ethics. Who will be tested? What are the consequences of choosing one test over another for a particular purpose with a given group? What is the effect of the testing on the students? How will the test scores of minority group students be interpreted? What do we really mean by intelligence, competence, and scholastic aptitude? Do our views agree with those implied by the tests we use to measure these constructs? How will test results be integrated with other information about the individual to make judgments? Answering these questions requires choices based on values, as well as accurate information about what tests can and cannot tell us.

CONNECT & EXTEND

TO THE RESEARCH
See the May, 2002 issue of *Phi Delta Kappan* for "The Human Face of the High-Stakes Testing Story," by Linda Nathan.

> Schools like the Boston Arts Academy are desperately trying to keep the Massachusetts Comprehensive Assessment System from destroying their very fabric, Ms. Nathan says. She intends to make it through the MCAS mania by continuing to fight for a rich and rigorous arts and academic curriculum, taught by highly qualified and committed teachers in an atmosphere of respect and high expectations.

Available online http://www.pdkintl.org/kappan/k0204nat.htm.

Preparing for Tests

Two types of training can make a difference in test scores. One is simple familiarity with the procedures of standardized tests. Students who have extensive experience with standardized tests do better than those who do not. Some of this advantage may be the result of greater self-confidence, less tendency to panic, familiarity with different kinds of questions (for example, analogies such as house : garage : : —— : car), and practice with the various answer sheets (Anastasi, 1988). Even brief orientations about how to take tests can help students who lack familiarity and confidence.

A second type of training that appears to be very promising is instruction in general cognitive skills such as solving problems, carefully analyzing questions, considering all alternatives, noticing details and deciding which are relevant, avoiding impulsive answers, and checking work. These are the kinds of metacognitive and study skills we have discussed before. Training in these skills is likely to generalize to many tasks (Anastasi, 1988; Popham, 2002). The *Stories of Learning/Tributes to Teaching* feature is an example of a teacher who taught her students how to tackle tests.

Check Yourself What are some current issues in testing?

Can students become better test-takers?

~ Stories of Learning / Tributes to Teaching ~

A 6th grade class in Illinois used their statewide testing as an opportunity for problem-based learning (Ewy with student authors, 1997). This class read a newspaper article about the upcoming test and the less than stellar school performance in previous years. They took on the following problem: How could they improve their own test scores on the IGAP (Illinois Goal Assessment Program)? The students talked about why the problem was important and how to solve it, generating the problem analysis chart below.

Problem Analysis Chart

Problem: How can we improve our performance on the IGAP test in such a way that we (1) keep improving each year, (2) set a good example for our school, (3) make preparing for IGAP more fun?

Our Ideas

- Pay attention in class
- Hold fundraiser to get books and computer program
- Look at actual IGAP book format
- Practice: Use computer games
- Get someone who knows how to coach IGAP: teacher, parent, friend, brother/sister
- Tackle one subject at a time
- Find out who wants to know

Facts We Know

- Test on reading, writing, and math
- You get better when you practice
- You might read questions wrong
- Fill in circles
- Writing is scored by time, spelling, sentence structure

Our Questions

- When is IGAP?
- How long is the test?
- How long should we practice?
- What should we practice (math, reading, writing)?
- How many problems?
- How is the test scored (math, reading, writing)?
- How much time is given for math, reading, writing?
- How did I do on the last IGAP test?

Our Action Plan

- Ask principal, teacher, tutor
- Ask person who made test
- Work with teacher to set up schedule
- Look for resources for practice
- Ask parents and principal to help

Then the students divided into groups to do different tasks: schedule practice times, look for resources, make up questions and interview experts, and set up a tutoring program. The result? The students met or exceeded the state reading, writing, and mathematics goals. Later that year, when they had to take the math placement test for junior high, these students researched the test: What are the cutoff points, the possible range of scores, and the evaluation criteria?

Perhaps you can take on a similar problem with your students. The *Becoming An Expert Test-Taker Guidelines* might help as part of the program.

SOURCE: Excerpted from "Kids Take on 'the Test,'" by C. Ewy & student authors, *Educational Leadership*, 54(4), p. 77.

Enhancing Your Expertise with Technology

Standardized Testing

A true story: Dan's mentor, Mr. Snell, had advised him in September that he would witness a lot of amazing events during his first year of teaching. The mentor was right, and an amazing event was occurring right now. It was a few minutes after school dismissal. Dan had given each student in his 6th grade class an envelope that enclosed a copy of the results from the achievement tests that were administered just a few weeks before. Moments after students exited the school building, many parents anxiously opened the envelopes, and read the results. Some parents hugged their children; other parents appeared visibly upset. A group of parents gathered and seemed to be comparing the reports. The next morning Dan checked his voice mail. He had six requests from parents for conferences to discuss the results of the tests. Dan immediately contacted Mr. Snell for advice.

Interests and concerns about standardized testing are among the most serious and sensitive ones that face teachers and other educators. Parents become understandably upset when their children bring home low test scores. Scores help teachers to determine which students would benefit from supplemental assistance. Like most powerful tools, standardized tests can be used for purposes for which they are suited (e.g., helping educators identify weak areas in the curriculum) or they can be misused (e.g., judging the relative quality of school systems).

The online journal *Practical Assessment, Research and Evaluation* (http://ericae.net/pare/), published by ERIC Clearinghouse on Assessment and Evaluation, is a rich, authoritative, and comprehensive source of information about standardized testing (as well as other topics related to assessment and evaluation). Most of the articles are written for practitioners, primarily teachers and administrators, but some of them are targeted at other concerned audiences—parents, students, and researchers, for example. (And as we have discovered about student-centered learning, it is often valuable to explore a topic from more than one perspective.) Here are some sample titles of the dozens of journal articles that have been published since 1988:

- Explaining Tests Results to Parents
- Preparing Students to Take Standardized Tests
- Norm- and Criterion-Referenced Tests
- Questions to Ask When Evaluating Tests
- Using State Standards and Tests to Improve Instruction
- The Concept of Statistical Significance Testing

CONNECT & EXTEND

TO **PRAXIS**™
ALTERNATIVES TO STANDARDIZED TESTING (II, C1)
For an overview of the major forms of authentic testing, go to Teachervision.com (http://www.teachervision.com/lesson-plans/lesson-6385.html).

New Directions in Standardized Testing

Standardized tests continue to be controversial. In response to dissatisfaction with traditional forms of assessment, new approaches have emerged to deal with some of the most common testing problems.

Authentic Assessment

As the public and government demanded greater accountability in education in the 1980s and 1990s and as traditional standardized tests became the basis for high-stakes decisions, pressure to do well led many teachers and schools to "teach to the test." This tended to focus student learning on basic skills and facts. Even more troubling, say critics, the traditional tests assess skills that have no equivalent in the real world. Students are asked to solve problems or answer questions they will never encounter again; they are expected to do so alone, without relying on any tools or resources and while working under extreme time limits. Real life just isn't like this. Important problems take time to solve and often require using resources, consulting other people, and integrating basic skills with creativity and high-level thinking (Kirst, 1991a; Popham, 2002; Wolf, Bixby, Glenn, & Gardner, 1991).

In response to these criticisms, the **authentic assessment** movement was born. The goal was to create standardized tests that assess complex, important, real-life outcomes. The approach is also called *direct assessment, performance assessment,* or *alternative assessment.* These terms refer to procedures that are alternatives to traditional multiple-choice standardized tests because they directly assess student perfor-

Authentic assessment Measurement of important abilities using procedures that simulate the application of these abilities to real-life problems.

mance on "real-life" tasks (Hambleton, 1996; Popham, 2002). Some states are developing procedures to conduct authentic assessments. For example, in 1990, Kentucky passed the Educational Reform Act. The act identifies six objectives for students, including such goals as applying knowledge from mathematics, the "hard" sciences, arts, humanities, and the social sciences to problems the students will encounter throughout their lives as they become self-sufficient individuals and responsible members of families, work groups, and communities.

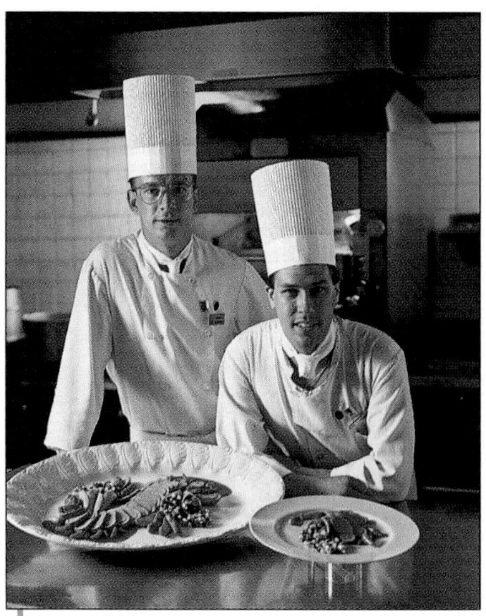

In many subjects the most reliable test is to demonstrate the ability to produce a finished product.

Many of the suggestions for improving standardized tests will require new forms of testing, more thoughtful and time-consuming scoring, and perhaps new ways of judging the quality of the tests themselves. Standardized tests of the future may be more like the writing sample you may have submitted for college entrance and less like the multiple-choice college entrance tests you also had to take. Newer tests will feature more **constructed-response** formats. This means that students will create responses (essays, problem solutions, graphs, diagrams), rather than simply selecting the (one and only) correct answer. This will allow tests to measure higher-level and divergent thinking.

In the excitement about authentic assessment, it is important to be sensible. Just being different from traditional standardized tests will not guarantee that the alternative tests are better. Many questions have to be answered. Assume, for example, that a new assessment requires students to complete a hands-on science project. If the student does well on one science project, does this mean the student "knows" science and would do well on other projects? One study found that students' performance on three different science tasks was quite variable: A student who did well on the absorbency experiment, for example, might have trouble with the electricity task. Thus, it was hard to generalize about a student's knowledge of science based on just the three tasks. Many more tasks would be needed to get a good sense of science knowledge, but a performance assessment with many different tasks would be expensive and time-consuming (Shavelson, Gao, & Baxter, 1993).

CONNECT & EXTEND

TO OTHER CHAPTERS
Chapter 15 includes a discussion of alternatives for authentic assessment, including portfolios and exhibitions.

In addition, if high-stakes decisions are based on performance assessments, will teachers begin to "teach to the assessment" by giving students practice in these particular performances? Will being a good writer bias judges in favor of a performance? Will this make performance assessments even more prone to discriminate against some groups? And how will the projects be judged? Will different judges agree on the quality? When researchers examined the results of the 1992 Vermont Portfolio Assessment Program, they found that scorers assessing the same portfolio often gave very different ratings (Kotrez, Stecher, & Diebert, 1993). In other words, will judgments based on alternative assessments be reliable and valid? Will the assessment results generalize to tasks beyond those on the test itself? Will the new assessments have a positive effect on learning (Hambleton, 1997; Moss, 1992)? Because this is a new area, it will take time to develop high-quality alternative assessments for use by whole school districts or states. Until more is known, it may be best to focus on authentic assessment at the classroom level, as we will discuss in the next chapter.

Is this "performance assessment"?

Changes in the SAT

Developments in assessment have had an impact on the SAT college entrance examination. Starting in 2005, the SAT (renamed the SAT I) will have a 20- to 30-minute essay, similar to the written essay that now appears on the SAT II. This will add a more authentic assessment of writing. The SAT Verbal Exam will become the SAT Critical Reading Exam with short reading sections added to the longer reading

Constructed-response format Assessment procedures that require the student to create an answer instead of selecting an answer from a set of choices.

Reaching Every Student

Accommodations in Testing

Accommodations in testing may be made in the setting of the test, timing and scheduling, test presentation, and student response modes. Schools have to keep good records about what is done, because these accommodations have to be documented. Here are some examples of possible accommodations taken from Spinelli, 2002 (pp. 151–152).

Examples of Setting Accommodations

Conditions of Setting

- Minimal distractive elements (e.g., books, artwork, window views)
- Special lighting
- Special acoustics
- Adaptive or special furniture
- Individual student or small group of students rather than large group

Location

- Study carrel
- Separate room (including special education classroom)
- Seat closest to test administrator (teacher, proctor, etc.)
- Home
- Hospital
- Correctional institution

Examples of Timing Accommodations

Duration

- Changes in duration can be applied to selected subtests of an assessment or to the assessment overall
- Extended time (i.e., extra time)
- Unlimited time

Organization

- Frequent breaks during parts of the assessment (e.g., during subtests)
- Extended breaks between parts of assessment (e.g., subtests) so that assessments can be administered in several sessions

Examples of Scheduling Accommodations

Time

- Specific time of day (e.g., morning, midday, afternoon, after ingestion of medication)
- Specific day of week
- Over several days

Organization

- In a different order from that used for most students (e.g., longer subtest first, shorter later; math first, English later)
- Omit questions that cannot be adjusted for an accommodation (e.g., graph reading for student using Braille) and adjust for missing scores

passages. These reading passages will cover a wider range of subject areas such as science, the humanities, and history. The old venerable analogies section will be eliminated and multiple-choice grammar questions will be added. The quantitative exam will become the SAT Math Exam, with coverage broadened to include three years of high school mathematics—Algebra 1, Algebra 2, geometry, and other higher-level math courses. The quantitative comparisons section will be dropped in favor of these higher-level questions.

The changes in the SAT are likely to have at least two effects. High school curricula will target preparation for the tests—students will be encouraged to take as much math as possible before taking the SAT. Writing may receive more emphasis. But the second effect probably will be that commercial test preparation courses will see increases in enrollment (Cavanagh, 2002).

CONNECT & EXTEND

TO THE RESEARCH

For a complete discussion of performance assessment, see Hambleton, R. K. (1996). Advances in assessment models, methods, and practices. In D. C. Berliner & R. C. Calfee (Eds.), *Handbook of educational psychology.* New York: Macmillan.

Accommodating Diversity in Testing

With high-stakes testing have come concerns about who should take tests. IDEA (the Individuals with Disabilities Education Act) mandates that students with disabilities must be included in general testing, but with accommodations or appropriate

Examples of Presentation Accommodations

Format Alterations

- Braille edition
- Large-print version
- Larger bubbles on answer sheet
- One complete sentence per line in reading passage
- Bubbles to side of choices in multiple-choice exams
- Key words or phrases highlighted
- Increased spacing between lines
- Fewer number of items per page

Procedure Changes

- Use sign language to give directions to student
- Reread directions
- Write helpful verbs in directions on board or on separate piece of paper
- Simplify language, clarify or explain directions
- Provide extra examples
- Prompt student to stay focused on test, move ahead, read entire item
- Explain directions to student during test

Assistive Devices

- Audiotape of directions
- Computer reads directions and/or items
- Magnification device
- Amplification device (e.g., hearing aid)
- Noise buffer
- Templates to reduce visible print
- Markers or masks to maintain place
- Dark or raised lines
- Pencil grips

Examples of Response Accommodations

Format Alterations

- Mark responses in test booklet rather than record on separate page
- Respond on different paper, such as graph paper, wide-lined paper, paper with wide margins

Procedural Changes

- Use reference materials (e.g. dictionary, arithmetic tables)
- Give response in different mode (e.g., pointing, oral response to tape recorders, sign language)

Assistive Devices

- Word processor or computer to responses
- Amanuensis (proctor-scribe writes student responses)
- Slant board or wedge
- Calculator or abacus
- Brailler
- Other communication device (e.g., symbol board)
- Spell checker

modifications if needed (Spinelli, 2002). The IEP (Individualized Education Program) team generally makes the decisions about who should have accommodations and what these might be, so as a teacher you might participate in these discussions. The *Reaching Every Student: Accommodations in Testing* feature gives some ideas.

Check Yourself What is authentic assessment?

What are the changes in the SAT and how might they affect schools?

What are accommodations in testing?

CONNECT & EXTEND

TO THE RESEARCH

See *Phi Delta Kappan* June, 2002 article, "Assessment Crisis: The Absence of Assessment *FOR* Learning," By Richard J. Stiggins, taken from the June, 2002 issue.

> If we wish to maximize student achievement in the U.S., we must pay far greater attention to the improvement of classroom assessment, Mr. Stiggins warns. Both assessment of learning and assessment for learning are essential. But one is currently in place, and the other is not.

Available online at http://www.pdkintl.org/kappan/k0206sti.htm

Summary Table

Evaluation, Measurement, and Assessment (pp. 514–516)

Distinguish among evaluation, measurement, and assessment. In the process of evaluation, we compare information to criteria and then make judgments. Measurement is evaluation put in quantitative terms. Assessment includes measurement, but is broader because it includes all kinds of ways to sample and observe students' skills, knowledge, and abilities.

Distinguish between norm-referenced and criterion-referenced tests. In norm-referenced tests, a student's performance is compared to the average performance of others. In criterion-referenced tests, scores are compared to a preestablished standard. Norm-referenced tests cover a wide range of general objectives. However, results of norm-referenced tests do not tell whether students are ready for advanced material, and they are not appropriate for affective and psychomotor objectives. Criterion-referenced tests measure the mastery of very specific objectives.

Evaluation: Decision making about student performance and about appropriate teaching strategies.

Measurement: An evaluation expressed in quantitative (number) terms.

Assessment: Procedures used to obtain information about student performance.

Norm-Referenced Testing: Testing in which scores are compared with the average performance of others.

Norm Groups: A group whose average score serves as a standard for evaluating any student's score on a test.

Criterion-Referenced Testing: Testing in which scores are compared to a set performance standard.

What Do Test Scores Mean? (pp. 516–525)

Describe the key features of a standardized test. Standardized tests are most often norm-referenced. They have been pilot-tested, revised, and then administered in final form to a norming sample, which becomes the comparison group for scoring.

What are mean, median, mode, and standard deviation? The mean (arithmetical average), median (middle score), and mode (most common score) are all measures of central tendency. The standard deviation reveals how scores spread out around the mean. A normal distribution is a frequency distribution represented as a bell-shaped curve. Many scores cluster in the middle; the farther from the midpoint, the fewer the scores.

Describe different kinds of scores. There are several basic types of standardized test scores: percentile rankings, which indicate the percentage of others who scored at or below an individual's score; grade-equivalent scores, which indicate how closely a student's performance matches average scores for a given grade; and standard scores, which are based on the standard deviation. *T* and *z* scores are both common standard scores. A stanine score is a standard score that incorporates elements of percentile rankings.

What is test reliability? Some tests are more reliable than others; that is, they yield more stable and consistent estimates. Care must be taken in the interpretation of test results. Each test is only a sample of a student's performance on a given day. The score is only an estimate of a student's hypothetical true score. The standard error of measurement takes into account the possibility for error and is one index of test reliability.

What is test validity? The most important consideration about a test is the validity of the decisions and judgments that are based on the test results. Evidence of validity can be related to content, criterion, or construct. Construct-related evidence for validity is the broadest category and encompasses the other two categories of content and criterion. Tests must be reliable to be valid, but reliability does not guarantee validity.

What is absence of bias? Tests must be free of assessment bias. Bias occurs when tests include material that offends or unfairly penalizes a group of students because of the students' gender, SES, race, ethnicity. Culture-fair tests have not proved to solve the problem of assessment bias.

Standardized Tests: Tests given, usually nationwide, under uniform conditions and scored according to uniform procedures.

Norming Sample: Large sample of students serving as a comparison group for scoring standardized tests.

Frequency Distribution: Record showing how many scores fall into set groups.

Histogram: Bar graph of a frequency distribution.

Mean: Arithmetical average.

Central Tendency: Typical score for a group of scores.

Median: Middle score in a group of scores.

Mode: Most frequently occurring score.

Standard Deviation: Measure of how widely scores vary from the mean.

Variability: Degree of difference or deviation from mean.

Range: Distance between the highest and the lowest scores.

Normal Distribution: The most commonly occurring distribution, in which scores are distributed evenly around the mean.

Percentile Rank: Percentage of those in the norming sample who scored at or below an individual's score.

Grade-Equivalent Score: Measure of grade level based on comparison with norming samples from each grade.

Standard Scores: Scores based on the standard deviation.

***z* Score:** Standard score indicating the number of standard deviations above or below the mean.

***T* Score:** Standard score with a mean of 50 and a standard deviation of 10.

Stanine Scores: Whole number scores from 1 to 9, each representing a wide range of raw scores.

Reliability: Consistency of test results.

True Score: Hypothetical average of all of an individual's scores if repeated testing under ideal conditions were possible.

Standard Error of Measurement: Hypothetical estimate of variation in scores if testing were repeated.

Confidence Interval: Range of scores within which an individual's particular score is likely to fall.

Validity: Degree to which a test measures what is intended.

Assessment Bias: Qualities of an assessment instrument that offend or unfairly penalize a group of students because of the students' gender, SES, race, ethnicity, etc.

Culture-Fair/Culture-Free Test: A test without cultural bias.

Types of Standardized Tests
(pp. 525–530)

What are three kinds of standardized tests? Three kinds of standardized tests are used frequently in schools: achievement, diagnostic, and aptitude. Profiles from norm-referenced achievement tests can also be used in a criterion-referenced way. Diagnostic tests usually are given individually to elementary school students when learning problems are suspected. Aptitude tests are designed to predict how a student will perform in the future. For example, the Scholastic Assessment Test (SAT) predicts performance in the first year of college.

Achievement Tests: Standardized tests measuring how much students have learned in a given content area.

Diagnostic Tests: Individually administered tests to identify special learning problems.

Aptitude Tests: Tests meant to predict future performance.

Issues in Standardized Testing
(pp. 530–537)

What are some current issues in testing? Controversy over standardized testing has focused on the role and interpretation of tests, the widespread use of tests to evaluate schools, the problems with accountability based on test scores, and the testing of teachers. If the test matches important objectives of the curriculum, is given to students who actually studied the curriculum for a reasonable period of time, is free of bias, fits the students' language capabilities, and was administered properly, then test results provide some information about the effectiveness of the school. But studies of the actual tests in action show troubling consequences such as narrowing the curriculum and pushing some students out of school early. Teachers should use results to improve instruction, not to stereotype students or justify lowered expectations.

Can students become better test-takers? Performance on standardized tests can be improved if students gain experience with this type of testing and are given training in study skills and problem solving. Many students can profit from direct instruction about how to prepare for and take tests. Involving students in designing these test preparation programs can be helpful.

High-Stakes Testing: Standardized tests whose results have powerful influences when used by school administrators, other officials, or employers to make decisions.

Accountable: Making teachers and schools responsible for student learning, usually by monitoring learning with high-stakes tests.

Enhancing Your Expertise with Technology: Standardized Testing
(p. 538)

The online journal *Practical Assessment, Research and Evaluation* **(http://ericae.net/pare/)**

New Directions in Standardized Testing
(pp. 538–541)

What is authentic assessment? Authentic assessments are procedures that assess students' abilities to solve important real-life problems, think creatively, and act responsibly. Such approaches assume that assessment should reveal the potential for future learning and help identify interventions for realizing that potential. Standardized tests of the future will be more varied and will use more constructed-response formats, requiring students to generate (rather than select) answers.

What are the changes in the SAT, and how might they affect schools? Starting in 2005, the SAT will include a written essay, more critical reading, and higher-level mathematics (Algebra 2, geometry, and other advanced math). Analogies and quantitative comparisons will be eliminated.

What are accommodations in testing? The IEP team usually decides if students covered by an IEP will participate in school-wide testing and if so, with what adaptations or accommodations. These could include changes in the setting of testing, timing and scheduling, presentation mode of the test, and/or student's mode of response.

Authentic Assessment: Measurement of important abilities using procedures that simulate the application of these abilities to real-life problems.

Constructed-Response Format: Assessment procedures that require the student to create an answer instead of selecting an answer from a set of choices.

Becoming a Professional

Passing the PRAXIS™

Chapter 14 reflects many of the professional standards created by the Interstate New Teacher Assessment and Support Consortium (INTASC). These standards form the basis of the PRAXIS II™ and state-created teacher licensure exams.

Your need to be knowledgeable about standardized testing is well-illustrated in this chapter's Teachers' Casebook. Parents and students frequently misunderstand the results of these instruments, often attributing the wrong meaning to various types of scores. Teachers who possess that knowledge are in a position to serve their students well by being able to use test results in ways that are consistent with the purposes of specific tests and that recognize the strengths and limitations of those tests. With that knowledge, teachers, parents, and students can use information provided by the tests to make informed educational decisions.

Tips for PRAXIS II™

Understand the major concepts related to measurement theory, including:

- Norming samples
- Percentile rank, grade-equivalent scores, stanine scores, *T* and *z* scores
- Standard deviation, mean, mode, median, standard error of measurement, and confidence intervals
- Reliability and validity

Describe the characteristics and purposes of major types of tests:

- Criterion-referenced and norm-referenced tests
- Achievement, aptitude, and diagnostic tests

Explain the major issues related to concerns about standardized testing, including:

- High-stakes testing
- Bias in testing
- Test-taking programs

Related Topics

- SES and achievement (Chapter 5)
- How intelligence is measured (Chapter 4)
- Innovations in assessment (Chapters 14 and 15)

Standards and Licensure Appendix: *PRAXIS II™ and INTASC*

Refer to the Appendix at the end of the book for detailed correlations to PRAXIS II™ exam topics and INTASC Standards addressed in this text.

Insights about Interview Questions: *What Would You Say?*

1. As part of the interview process for a job in a high school, you are asked the following: "How would you interpret the test scores of minority group children?"
2. As part of the interview process for a job in an elementary school, you are asked the following: "What should we do to raise our test scores in this school?"

Your Teaching Portfolio: *Teaching Resources*

- What do you believe about the uses of testing for children?
- Add some ideas for parent involvement from this chapter.
- Using the *Guidelines* for preparing for a test, prepare a testing guide sheet for the grades you will teach.
- Add Figure 14.2, Figure 14.3, Figure 14.4, and the *Stories of Learning/Tributes to Teaching,* "Taking on 'The Test': Problem-Based Learning" to your **Teaching Resources** file.

VideoWorkshop Extra

If the VideoWorkshop package was included with your textbook, go to Chapter 14 of the Companion Website (www.ablongman.com/woolfolk) and click on the VideoWorkshop button. Follow the instructions for viewing *Video Clip II: Standardized Tests.* Consider this information along with what you've read in Chapter 14 while answering the following questions:

1. According to the speaker on this video, what are the problems with using criterion-referenced tests? When would criterion-referenced testing be an appropriate means of assessment? Give examples and explain.
2. "Tests now are being used in ways that the originators of tests never foresaw." Explain this statement and its consequences.

Use the CD-ROM included in the back of your textbook to launch the "Becoming a Professional" website. The website features advice on preparing for teacher certification exams, help with getting your first job, and resources to help you perform your job well from the first day forward.

Teachers' Casebook

What Would They Do?

Here is how some practicing teachers respond to the teaching situation presented at the beginning of this chapter about the parents who want their daughter to skip a grade in math.

Mark H. Smith

Teacher, *Grades Nine through Twelve, Medford High School, Medford, Massachusetts*

I understand that many parents will choose the side of their child over the side of a teacher. This definitely happened in this case, because the parents would not come in to talk about their daughter's learning until they had something they thought would give them ammunition against the teacher. As a teacher all you can do is explain your grading procedure, what the curriculum is, and what is expected of the students in your class. When you have clear and reasonable expectations for all of your students, then it becomes the responsibility of the student to achieve.

Thomas W. Newkirk

Eighth Grade Teacher, *Hamilton Heights Middle School, Arcadia, Indiana*

The grade a student receives in a class is sometimes not so much a measure of intelligence as it is a measure of performance. Bright students who are disorganized may bring assignments in days past a due date. Bright students who are distracted may not bring assignments in at all. Bright students who have been absent several days may be overwhelmed by the work waiting for them.

The grade a student receives in a class often requires an explanation in order that the students and the parents understand the basis for the evaluation. It is important that the teacher maintain a record of comments and correspondence for parents and teachers to review.

While it is wonderful that the student has a grade-equivalent of 11.8 on the achievement test, her daily class performance does not meet the established standard for an A. Whether a student's achievement test results are high or low, it would be unfair to reconsider a final grade based on one score.

Unless the school has a policy for receiving credit for classes based on achievement tests, the parents and the student should be encouraged to maintain the lines of communication as she enters the 10th grade class.

Thomas O'Donnell

Social Studies Chairperson, *Grades Seven through Twelve, Malden High School, Malden, Massachusetts*

The math achievement the girl took might not be a good device for measuring one's ability to go beyond high school math to the more abstract, conceptual approach needed for college-level math. You must explain your grading system to parents so they understand the needed combination of effort and achievement to achieve top grades.

Since the parent statements include two serious charges against you, make it clear you expect respect from them, but that this issue will have no impact on your work with the student. You must reject their expectations of changing grades and credits.

Suzy L. Boswell

Art Teacher, *Grades Six through Eight, Pickens County Middle School, Jasper, Georgia*

One of the most challenging aspects of a teacher's job is often the task of communicating with the parents. Unfortunately, most parents begin to lose contact with the school system and the children's teachers when their child enters middle school or junior high. Parents may think that they are no longer needed or that their child prefers them to remain anonymous, so as not to embarrass them. However, the motivation and learning process are still very much a shared responsibility of school and home.

The parents did not volunteer their time to listen to a lecture. In this particular case they may actually be coming to the school to give the teacher a lecture and to "set her straight." It may require a great deal of diplomacy to turn this into a positive and productive meeting, but we as teachers deal with unwilling students almost daily and this situation is not any different.

Once the tone is set and the parents are receptive, it may be helpful to explain to them the characteristics of the tests, including the various methods that are used to measure the results of the test. It is important to note that students may have the aptitude to learn and to perform in the classroom and yet simply choose not to apply themselves. Therefore, these students are still not meeting the requirements necessary to earn credit for a particular class.

Go to the Companion Website (www.ablongman.com/woolfolk) for additional case studies including audio and video cases, and examples of student work.

CHAPTER

15

Classroom Assessment

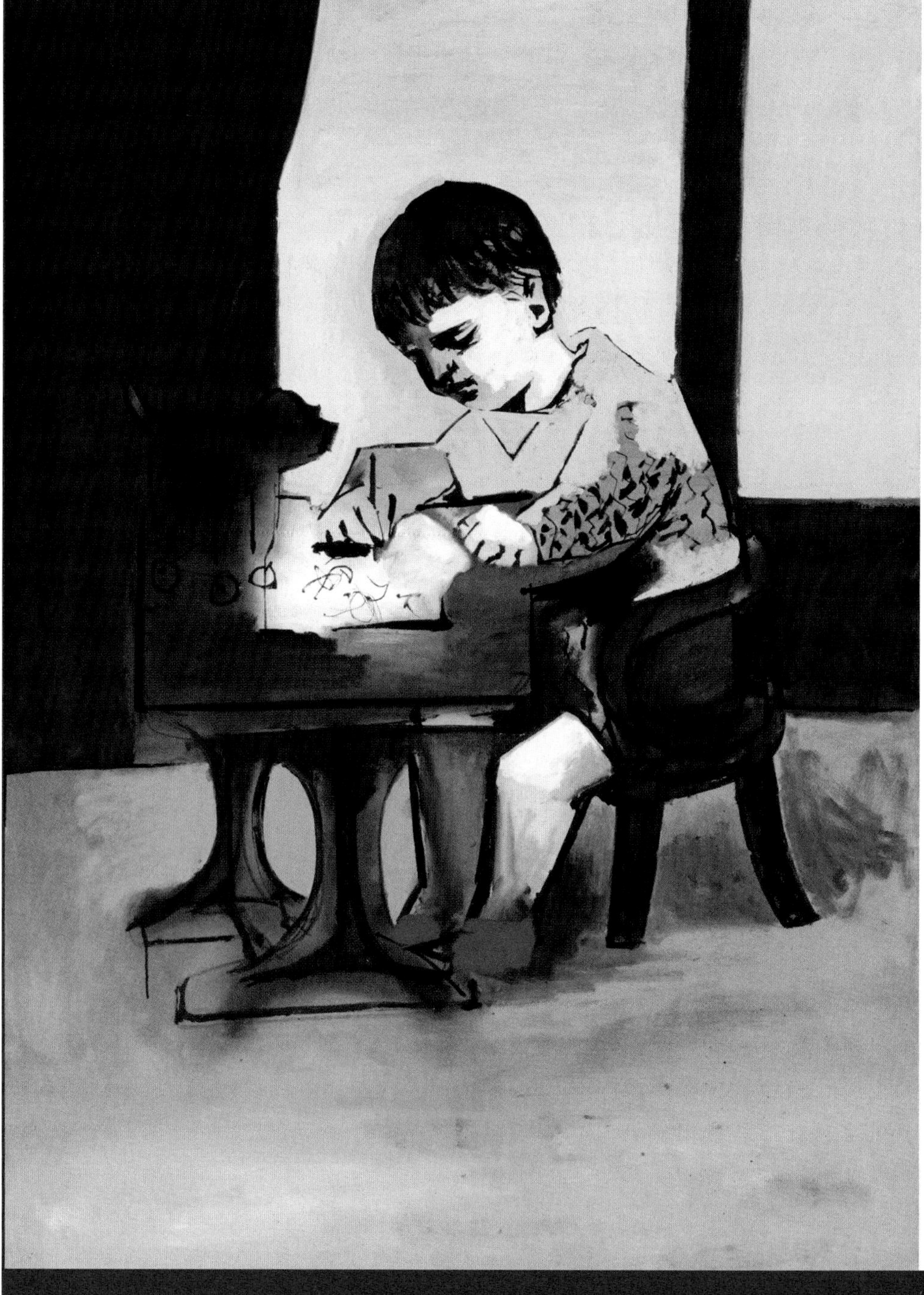

Teachers' Casebook

What Would You Do?

Your school requires that you give letter grades to your class. You can use any method you want, as long as an A, B, C, D, or F appears for each of the subject areas on every student's report card, every grading period. Some teachers are using worksheets, quizzes, homework, and tests. Others are assigning group work and portfolios. A few teachers are individualizing standards by grading on progress and effort more than final achievement. Some are trying contract approaches and experimenting with longer term projects, while others are relying almost completely on daily class work. Two teachers who use group work are considering giving credit toward grades for being a "good group member" or competitive bonus points for the top-scoring group. Others are planning to use improvement points for class rewards, but not for grades. Your only experience with grading was using written comments and a mastery approach that rated the students as making satisfactory or unsatisfactory progress toward particular objectives. You want a system that is fair and manageable, but also encourages learning, not just performance.

Critical Thinking

What would be your major graded assignments and projects? Would you include credit for behaviors such as group participation or effort? How would you put all the elements together to determine a grade for every student for every marking period? How would you justify your system to the principal and to the parents? How will these issues affect the grades you will teach?

Collaboration

With 2 or 3 other members of your class, develop a section of a class handbook that describes your grading policy. Be prepared to defend the policy.

In this chapter, we will look at both tests and grades, focusing not only on the effects they are likely to have on students, but also on practical means of developing more efficient methods for testing and grading.

We begin with a consideration of the many types of tests teachers prepare each year and approaches to assessment that don't rely on traditional testing. Then we examine the effects grades are likely to have on students. Because there are so many grading systems, we also spend some time identifying the advantages and disadvantages of one system over another. Finally, we turn to the very important topic of communication with students and parents. How will you justify the grades you give?

By the time you have completed this chapter, you should be able to answer these questions:

- *How will you test students on a unit of work?*
- *How can you evaluate tests that accompany textbooks and teachers' manuals?*
- *How should you create multiple-choice and essay test items for your subject area?*
- *Will you use authentic assessment approaches, including portfolios, performances, exhibitions, and scoring rubrics?*
- *What are the potential positive and negative effects of grades on students?*
- *What are examples of criterion-referenced and norm-referenced grading systems?*
- *How will you explain your grading system to parents who do not understand their child's grades?*

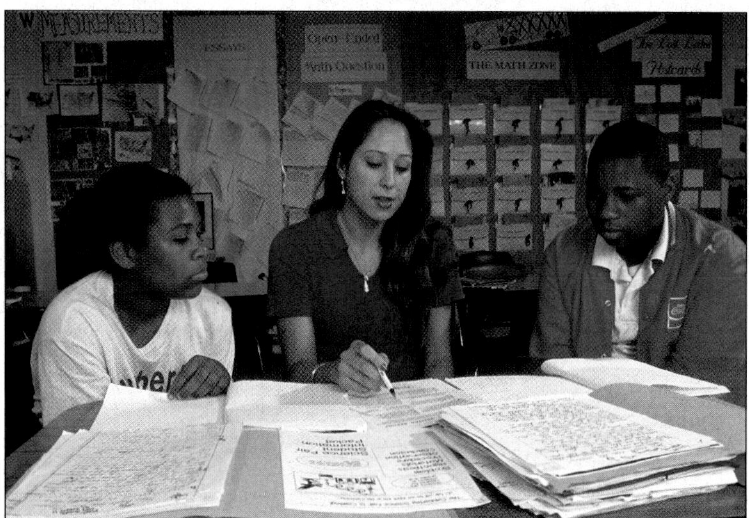

Formative testing is used to *form* instruction. The purpose is to guide teacher planning and help students identify areas that need work.

Formative and Summative Assessment

As a teacher, you may or may not help in designing the grading system for your school or your class. Many school districts have a standard approach to grading. Still, you will have choices about how you use your district's grading system and how you assess your students' learning. Will you give tests? How many? What kinds? Will students do projects or keep portfolios of their work? How will homework influence grades? Will you use journals, and if so, will you "grade" them?

There are two general uses or functions for assessment: formative and summative. **Formative assessment** occurs before or during instruction. The purposes of formative assessment are to guide the teacher in planning and to help students identify areas that need work. In other words, formative assessment helps *form* instruction. Often students are given a formative test prior to instruction, a **pretest** that helps the teacher determine what students already know. Sometimes a test is given during instruction to see what areas of weakness remain so teaching can be directed toward the problem areas. This is generally called a **diagnostic test,** but should not be confused with the standardized diagnostic tests of more general learning abilities discussed in the previous chapter. A classroom diagnostic test identifies a student's areas of achievement and weakness in a particular subject. Older students are often able to apply the information from diagnostic tests to "reteach" themselves. Pretests and diagnostic tests are not graded. And because formative tests do not count toward the final grade, students who tend to be very anxious about "real" tests may find this low-pressure practice in test-taking especially helpful.

CONNECT & EXTEND

TO YOUR TEACHING/PORTFOLIO
What are some specific ways in which formative evaluation can be implemented in the classroom?

Summative assessment occurs at the end of instruction. Its purpose is to let the teacher and the students know the level of accomplishment attained. Summative assessment, therefore, provides a *summary* of accomplishment. The final exam is a classic example.

The distinction between formative and summative assessment is based on how the results are used. The same assessment procedure can be used for either purpose. If the goal is to obtain information about student learning for planning purposes, the assessment is formative. If the purpose is to determine final achievement (and help determine a course grade), the assessment is summative.

CONNECT & EXTEND

TO **PRAXIS**™
TYPES OF ASSESSMENT (II, C1, 4)
Understand the purposes of formative and summative assessment. Explain how teachers and students can make effective use of the information generated by each type of test.

Check Yourself What are two kinds of classroom assessment?

Formative assessment Ungraded testing used before or during instruction to aid in planning and diagnosis.

Pretest Formative test for assessing students' knowledge, readiness, and abilities.

Diagnostic test Formative test to determine students' areas of weakness.

Summative assessment Testing that follows instruction and assesses achievement.

Getting the Most from Traditional Assessment Approaches

STOP THINK WRITE Think back to your most recent test. What was the format? Did you feel that the test results were an accurate reflection of your knowledge or skills? Have you ever had to design a test? What makes a good, fair test?

When most people think of assessment, they usually think of testing. As you will see shortly, teachers today have many other options, but testing is still a significant activity in most classrooms. Let's consider your options for assessing students using the traditional testing approach. In this section we will examine how to plan effective tests, evaluate the tests that accompany standard curriculum materials, and write your own test questions.

Planning for Testing

Both instruction and assessment are most effective when they are well organized and planned. When you have a good plan, you are in a better position to judge the tests provided in teachers' manuals and texts and to write tests yourself.

When to Test? Frank Dempster (1991) examined the research on reviews and tests and reached these useful conclusions for teachers:

1. Frequent testing encourages the retention of information and appears to be more effective than a comparable amount of time spent reviewing and studying the material.
2. Tests are especially effective in promoting learning if you give students a test on the material soon after they learn it, then retest on the material later. The retestings should be spaced farther and farther apart.
3. The use of cumulative questions on tests is a key to effective learning. Cumulative questions ask students to apply information learned in previous units to solve a new problem.

Unfortunately, the curriculum in many schools is so full that there is little time for frequent tests and reviews. Dempster argues that students will learn more if we "teach them less," that is, if the curriculum includes fewer topics, but explores those topics in greater depth and allows more time for review, practice, testing, and feedback (Dempster, 1993).

Judging Textbook Tests. Most elementary and secondary school texts today come complete with supplemental materials such as teaching manuals, handout masters, and ready-made tests. Using these tests can save time, but is this good teaching practice? The answer depends on your objectives for your students, the way you taught the material, and the quality of the tests provided (Airasian, 2001). If the textbook test matches your testing plan and the instruction you actually provided for your students, then it may be the right test to use. Table 15.1 gives key points to consider in evaluating textbook tests.

What if there are no tests available for the material you want to cover, or the tests provided in your teachers' manuals are not appropriate for your students? Then it's

CONNECT & EXTEND

TO THE RESEARCH

- Dempster, F. (1991). Synthesis of research on reviews and tests. *Educational Leadership, 48*(7), 71–76. *Focus Question:* How can tests and reviews be used to encourage student learning?
- Dempster, F. N. (1993). Exposing our students to less should help them learn more. *Phi Delta Kappan, 74,* 432–437.

Table 15.1 Key Points to Consider in Judging Textbook Tests

The decision to use a textbook test must come *after* a teacher identifies the objectives that he or she taught and now wants to assess.

Textbook tests are designed for the typical classroom, but since few classrooms are typical, most teachers deviate somewhat from the text in order to accommodate their pupils' needs.

The more classroom instruction deviates from the textbook objectives and lesson plans, the less valid the textbook tests are likely to be.

The main consideration in judging the adequacy of a textbook test is the match between its test questions and what pupils were taught in their classes:

- Are questions similar to the teacher's objectives and instructional emphases?
- Do questions require pupils to perform the behaviors they were taught?
- Do questions cover all or most of the important objectives taught?
- Is the language level and terminology appropriate for pupils?
- Does the number of items for each objective provide a sufficient sample of pupil performance?

SOURCE: From *Assessment in the Classroom* (p. 190), by P. Airasian, 1996, New York: McGraw-Hill.

time for you to create your own tests. We will consider the two major kinds of traditional tests—objective and essay.

Objective Testing

CONNECT & EXTEND

TO **PRAXIS**™
TRADITIONAL ASSESSMENT
(II C1, 2, 4)
Objective and essay tests continue to have important roles in effective assessment and evaluation programs. Describe the appropriate uses of these types of tests. Identify the advantages and limitations of each.

Multiple-choice questions, matching exercises, true/false statements, and short-answer or fill-in items are all types of **objective testing.** The word "objective" in relation to testing means "not open to many interpretations," or "not subjective." The scoring of these types of items is relatively straightforward compared to the scoring of essay questions because the answers are more clear-cut than essay answers.

The guiding principle for deciding which item format is best is to use the one that gives you the most direct measure of the learning outcome you intended for your students (Gronlund, 2003). In other words, if you want to see how well students can write a letter, have them write a letter, don't ask multiple-choice questions about letters. But if many different item formats will work equally well, then use multiple-choice questions because they are easier to score fairly and can cover many topics. Switch to other formats if writing good multiple-choice items for the material is not possible or appropriate. For example, if related concepts such as terms and definitions need to be linked, then a matching item is a better format than multiple-choice. If it is difficult to come up with several wrong answers for a multiple-choice item, try a true/false question instead. Alternatively, ask the student to supply a short answer that completes a statement (fill in the blank). Variety in objective testing can lower students' anxiety because the entire grade does not depend on one type of question that a particular student may find difficult. Here we look closely at the multiple-choice format because it is the most versatile—and the most difficult to use well.

CONNECT & EXTEND

TO OTHER CHAPTERS
See Chapter 12 for a discussion of Bloom's taxonomy of objectives in the cognitive domain and a recent revision of this taxonomy.

Using Multiple-Choice Tests. People often assume that multiple-choice items are appropriate only for asking factual questions. But multiple-choice items can test higher-level objectives as well, although writing higher-level items is difficult. A multiple-choice item can assess more than recall and recognition if it requires the student to deal with new material by *applying* or *analyzing* the concept or principle being tested (Gronlund, 2003; Popham, 2002). For example, the following multiple-choice item is designed to assess students' ability to recognize unstated assumptions, one of the skills involved in analyzing an idea:

> An educational psychology professor states, "A z score of +1 on a test is equivalent to a percentile rank of approximately 84." Which of the following assumptions is the professor making?
>
> 1. The scores on the test range from 0 to 100.
> 2. The standard deviation of the test scores is equal to 3.4.
> 3. The distribution of scores on the test is normal. (correct answer)
> 4. The test is valid and reliable.

Writing Multiple-Choice Questions. All test items require skillful construction, but good multiple-choice items are a real challenge. Some students jokingly refer to multiple-choice tests as "multiple-guess" tests—a sign that these tests are often poorly designed. Your goal in writing test items is to design them so that they measure student achievement, not test-taking and guessing skills.

The **stem** of a multiple-choice item is the part that asks the question or poses the problem. The choices that follow are called *alternatives.* The wrong answers are called **distractors** because their purpose is to distract students who have only a partial understanding of the material. If there were no good distractors, students with only a vague understanding would have no difficulty in finding the right answer.

The *Guidelines,* adapted from Gronlund (2003), Popham (2002), and Smith, Smith, & De Lisi (2001) should make writing multiple-choice and other objective test questions easier.

Objective testing Multiple-choice, matching, true/false, short-answer, and fill-in tests; scoring answers does not require interpretation.

Stem The question part of a multiple-choice item.

Distractors Wrong answers offered as choices in a multiple-choice item.

GUIDELINES Writing Objective Test Items

The stem should be clear and simple, and present only a single problem. Unessential details should be left out.

Poor

There are several different kinds of standard or derived scores. An IQ score is especially useful because . . .

Better

An advantage of an IQ score is . . .

The problem in the stem should be stated in positive terms. Negative language is confusing. If you must use words such as *not, no,* or *except,* underline them or type them in all capitals.

Poor

Which of the following is not a standard score?

Better

Which of the following is NOT a standard score?

Do not expect students to make extremely fine discrimination among answer choices.

Poor

The percentage of area in a normal curve falling between +1 and −1 standard deviations is about:

a. 66% b. 67% c. 68% d. 69%.

Better

The percentage of area in a normal curve falling between +1 and −1 standard deviations is about:

a. 14% b. 34% (c.) 68% d. 95%.

As much wording as possible should be included in the stem so that phrases will not have to be repeated in each alternative.

Poor

A percentile score

a. indicates the percentage of items answered correctly.
b. indicates the percentage of correct answers divided by the percentage of wrong answers.
c. indicates the percentage of people who scored at or above a given raw score.
d. indicates the percentage of people who scored at or below a given raw score.

Better

A percentile score indicates the percentage of

a. items answered correctly.
b. correct answers divided by the percentage of wrong answers.
c. people who scored at or above a given raw score.
(d.) people who scored at or below a given raw score.

Each alternative answer should fit the grammatical form of the stem, so that no answers are obviously wrong.

Poor

The Stanford-Binet test yields an

a. IQ score. c. vocational preference.
b. reading level. d. mechanical aptitude.

Better

The Stanford-Binet is a test of

(a.) intelligence. c. vocational preference.
b. reading level. d. mechanical aptitude.

Categorical words such as *always, all, only,* or *never* should be avoided unless they can appear consistently in all the alternatives. Most smart test takers know that categorical answers are usually wrong.

Poor

A student's true score on a standardized test is

a. never equal to the obtained score.
b. always very close to the obtained score.
c. always determined by the standard error of measurement.
d. usually within a band that extends from +1 to −1 standard errors of measurement on each side of the obtained score.

Better

Which one of the statements below would most often be correct about a student's true score on a standardized test?

a. It equals the obtained score.
b. It will be very close to the obtained score.
c. It is determined by the standard error of measurement.
(d.) It could be above or below the obtained score.

You should also avoid including two distractors that have the same meaning. If only one answer can be right and if two answers are the same, then these two must both be wrong. This narrows down the choices considerably.

Poor

The most frequently occurring score in a distribution is called the

a. mode. c. arithmetical average.
b. median. d. mean.

Better

The most frequently occurring score in a distribution is called the

(a.) mode. c. standard deviation.
b. median. d. mean.

Avoid using the exact wording found in the textbook. Poor students may recognize the answers without knowing what they mean.

Avoid overuse of *all of the above* and *none of the above.* Such choices may be helpful to students who are simply guessing. In addition, using *all of the above* may trick a quick student who sees that the first alternative is correct and does not read on to discover that the others are correct, too.

Obvious patterns on a test also aid students who are guessing. The position of the correct answer should be varied, as should its length.

CONNECT & EXTEND

TO YOUR TEACHING/PORTFOLIO
Some students prefer essay tests because they can write down something, even if it doesn't answer the question, and receive at least partial credit for the question. Do you think that granting partial credit is a common grading practice among teachers? Considering that essay questions sample only a limited amount of material, does the practice seem commendable or defensible?

Essay Testing

The best way to measure some learning objectives is to require students to create answers on their own. An essay question is appropriate in these cases. The most difficult part of essay testing is judging the quality of the answers, but writing good, clear questions is not particularly easy, either. We will look at writing, administering, and grading essay tests, with most of the specific suggestions taken from Gronlund (2003). We will also consider factors that can bias the scoring of essay questions and ways you can overcome these problems.

Evaluate these two essay questions from Popham (2002, pp. 169–170):

1. (High school level) You have just viewed a videotape containing three widely seen television commercials. What is the one classic propaganda technique present in all three commercials?

2. (Middle school level) Thinking back over the mathematics lesson and homework assignments you had during the past 12 weeks, what conclusions can you draw? Take no more than one page for your response.

Constructing Essay Tests. Because answering takes time, true essay tests cover less material than objective tests. Thus, for efficiency, essay tests should be limited to the assessment of more complex learning outcomes.

An essay question should give students a clear and precise task and should indicate the elements to be covered in the answer. (Are the questions above clear and precise?) The students should know how extensive their answer should be and about how much time they should spend on each question. Question 2 above gives a page limit, but would you know what is being asked?

Students should be given ample time for answering. If more than one essay is being completed in the same class period, you may want to suggest time limits for each. Remember, however, that time pressure increases anxiety and may prevent accurate assessment of some students. Whatever your approach, do not try to make up for the limited amount of material an essay test can cover by including a large number of essay questions. It would be better to plan on more frequent testing than to include more than two or three essay questions in a single class period. Combining an essay question with a number of objective items is one way to avoid the problem of limited sampling of course material (Gronlund, 2003).

Evaluating Essays: Dangers. In 1912, Starch and Elliot began a classic series of experiments that shocked educators into critical consideration of subjectivity in testing. These researchers wanted to find out the extent to which teachers were influenced by personal values, standards, and expectations in scoring essay tests. For their initial study, they sent copies of English examination papers written by two high school students to English teachers in 200 high schools. Each teacher was asked to score the papers according to his or her school's standards. A percentage scale was to be used, with 75% as a passing grade.

The results? Neatness, spelling, punctuation, and communicative effectiveness were all valued to different degrees by different teachers. The scores on one of the papers ranged from 64% to 98%, with a mean of 88.2. The average score for the other paper was 80.2, with a range between 50% and 97%. The following year, Starch and Elliot (1913a, 1913b) published similar findings in a study involving history and geometry papers. The most important result of these studies was the discovery that the problem of subjectivity in grading was not confined to any particular subject area. The main difficulties were the individual standards of the grader and the unreliability of scoring procedures.

Evaluating Essays: Methods. Gronlund (2003) offers several strategies for grading essays that avoid problems of subjectivity and inaccuracy. When possible, a good first step is to construct a model answer. Even when students are given some choice in testing, teachers can decide what type of information should be in a model answer. Here is an example from TenBrink (2003, p. 326).

> *Question:* Defend *or* refute the following statement: Civil wars are necessary to the growth of a developing country. Cite reasons for your argument, and use examples from history to help substantiate your claim.
>
> *Model answer:* All answers, regardless of the position taken, should include (1) a clear statement of the position, (2) at least five logical reasons, (3) at least four examples from history that *clearly* substantiate the reasons given.

Once you have a model answer, you can assign points to its various parts. You might also give points for the organization of the answer and the internal consistency. You can then assign grades such as 1 to 5 or A, B, C, D, and F, and sort the papers into piles by grade. As a final step, skim the papers in each pile to see if they are comparable in quality. These techniques will help ensure fairness and accuracy in grading.

When grading essay tests with several questions, it makes sense to grade all responses to one question before moving on to the next. This helps prevent the quality of a student's answer to one question from influencing your reaction to the student's other answers. After you finish reading and scoring the first question, shuffle the papers so that no students end up having all their questions graded first, last, or in the middle.

You may achieve greater objectivity if you ask students to put their names on the back of the paper, so that grading is anonymous. A final check on your fairness as a grader is to have another teacher who is equally familiar with your goals and subject matter grade your tests without knowing what grades you have assigned. This can give you valuable insights into areas of bias in your grading practices.

Now that we have examined both objective and essay testing, we can compare examples of the different approaches. Table 15.2 presents a summary of the advantages and disadvantages of each.

Problems with grading essay tests include subjectivity and inaccuracy. It is difficult to understand or control the degree to which the grading of essay tests might be influenced by a teacher's personal values.

Check Yourself How should teachers plan for assessment?

Describe two kinds of traditional testing.

Table 15.2 Advantages and Disadvantages of Different Kinds of Test Items

No kind of item is perfect. A mix of kinds may be the best approach.

Type	Advantages	Disadvantages
Short answer	Can test many facts in a short time. Fairly easy to score. Excellent format for math. Tests recall.	Difficult to measure complex learning. Often ambiguous.
Essay	Can test complex learning. Can assess thinking process and creativity.	Difficult to score objectively. Uses a great deal of testing time. Subjective.
True/False	Tests the most facts in shortest time. Easy to score. Tests recognition. Objective.	Difficult to measure complex learning. Difficult to write reliable items. Subject to guessing.
Matching	Excellent for testing associations and recognition of facts. Although terse, can test complex learning (especially concepts). Objective.	Difficult to write effective items. Subject to process of elimination.
Multiple choice	Can assess learning at all levels of complexity. Can be highly reliable, objective. Tests fairly large knowledge base in short time. Easy to score.	Difficult to write. Somewhat subject to guessing.

SOURCE: From *Classroom Teaching Skills* (7th ed.), by James Cooper. Published by Houghton-Mifflin. Copyright © 2003 by Houghton Mifflin Company. Adapted with permission of the publisher.

CONNECT & EXTEND

TO THE RESEARCH
For ideas about making classroom assessment better, see Stiggins, R. J. (2001). Assessment crisis: The absence of assessment *FOR* learning, *Phi Delta Kappan, 83,* 758–765. Available online at http://www.pdkintl.org/kappan/k0206sti.htm

Innovations in Assessment

We have been considering how to make traditional testing more effective; now let's look at a few current approaches to classroom assessment. One of the main criticisms of standardized tests—that they control the curriculum, emphasizing recall of facts instead of thinking and problem solving—is a major criticism of classroom tests as well. Few teachers would dispute these criticisms. Even if you follow the guidelines we have been discussing, traditional testing can be limiting. What can be done? Should innovations in classroom assessment make traditional testing obsolete? The *Point/Counterpoint* addresses this question.

Point/Counterpoint

Which Is Better—Traditional Tests or Authentic Assessments?

We have seen the advantages and disadvantages of standardized tests, but what about classroom testing? Are traditional multiple-choice and essay tests useful in classroom assessment?

Point

Traditional tests are a poor basis for classroom assessment.
In his article "Standards, Not Standardization: Evoking Quality Student Work," Grant Wiggins (1991) makes a strong case for giving students standards of excellence against which they can judge their accomplishments. But these standards should not be higher scores on multiple-choice tests. When scores on traditional tests become the standard, the message to students is that only right answers matter and the thinking behind the answers is unimportant. Wiggins notes:

> *We do not judge Xerox, the Boston Symphony, the Cincinnati Reds, or Dom Perignon vineyards on the basis of indirect, easy to test, and common indicators. Nor would the workers in those places likely produce quality if some generic, secure test served as the only measure of their success in meeting a standard. Demanding and getting quality, whether from students or adult workers, means framing standards in terms of the work that we undertake and value. And it means framing expectations about that work which make quality a necessity, not an option. Consider:*
>
> - *the English teacher who instructs peer-editors to mark the place in a student paper where they lost interest in it or found it slapdash and to hand it back for revision at that point;*
> - *the professor who demands that all math homework be turned in with another student having signed off on it, where one earns the grade for one's work and the grade for the work that each person (willingly!) countersigned. (p. 22)*

In a more recent article, Wiggins continues to argue for assessment that makes sense, that tests knowledge as it is applied in real-world situations. Understanding cannot be measured by tests that ask students to use skills and knowledge out of context. "In other words, we cannot be said to understand something unless we can employ our knowledge wisely, fluently, flexibly, and aptly in particular and diverse contexts" (Wiggins, 1993, p. 200).

Counterpoint

Traditional tests can play an important role.
Most psychologists and educators would agree with Wiggins that setting clear, high, authentic standards is important, but many also believe that traditional tests are useful in this process. Learning may be more than knowing the right answers, but right answers are important. While schooling is about learning to think and solve problems, it is also about knowledge. Students must have something to think about—facts, ideas, concepts, principles, theories, explanations, arguments, images, opinions. Well-designed traditional tests can evaluate students' knowledge effectively and efficiently (Airasian, 1996; Kirst, 1991b). Some educators believe that traditional testing should play an even greater role than it currently does. Educational policy analysts suggest that American students, compared to students in many other developed countries, lack essential knowledge because American schools emphasize process—critical thinking, self-esteem, problem solving—more than content. In order to teach more about content, teachers will need to determine how well their students are learning the content, and traditional testing provides useful information about content learning.

Tests are also valuable in motivating and guiding students' learning. There is research evidence that frequent testing encourages learning and retention (Nungester & Duchastel, 1982). In fact, students generally learn more in classes with more rather than fewer tests (Dempster, 1991).

What do you think? Vote online at **www.ablongman.com/woolfolk**

SOURCE: From "Standards Not Standardization," by G. Wiggins, 1991, *Educational Leadership, 48,*(5), pp. 18–25. Copyright © 1991 by the Association for Supervision and Curriculum Development. Reprinted with permission.

One solution that has been proposed to solve the testing dilemma is to apply the concept of authentic assessment to classroom testing.

Authentic assessments Assessment procedures that test skills and abilities as they would be applied in real-life situations.

Authentic Classroom Assessment

What Would You Say? In your interview with the search team in an elementary school known for innovation, one of the teachers asks, "What do you know about using portfolios, performances, projects, and rubrics to assess learning?"

Authentic assessments ask students to apply skills and abilities as they would in real life. For example, they might use fractions to enlarge or reduce recipes. Grant Wiggins made this argument over a decade ago:

> If tests determine what teachers actually teach and what students will study for—and they do—then the road to reform is a straight but steep one: test those capabilities and habits we think are essential, and test them in context. Make [tests] replicate, within reason, the challenges at the heart of each academic discipline. Let them be—authentic. (1989, p. 41)

CONNECT & EXTEND

TO **PRAXIS**™
AUTHENTIC TESTS (II, C1, 2, 4)
The emphasis on student-centered learning has been accompanied by an emphasis on authentic tests. Understand the purpose, value, and advantages of these forms of assessment. Describe their characteristics and the potential problems with their use.

Wiggins goes on to say that if our instructional goals for students include the abilities to write, speak, listen, create, think critically, do research, solve problems, or apply knowledge, then our tests should ask students to write, speak, listen, create, think, research, solve, and apply. How can this happen?

Many educators suggest we look to the arts and sports for analogies to solve this problem. If we think of the "test" as being the recital, exhibition, game, mock court trial, or other performance, then teaching to the test is just fine. All coaches, artists, and musicians gladly "teach" to these "tests" because performing well on these tests is the whole point of instruction. Authentic assessment asks students to perform. The performances may be thinking performances, physical performances, creative performances, or other forms.

CONNECT & EXTEND

TO THE RESEARCH
Aschbacher, P. (1997). New directions in student assessment [Special Issue]. *Theory Into Practice, 36*(4), 194–272.

It may seem odd to talk of thinking as a performance, but there are many parallels. Serious thinking is risky, because real-life problems are not well defined. Often the outcomes of our thinking are public—others evaluate our ideas. Like a dancer auditioning for a Broadway show, we must cope with the consequences of being evaluated. Like a sculptor looking at a lump of clay, a student facing a difficult problem must experiment, observe, redo, imagine and test solutions, apply both basic skills and inventive techniques, make interpretations, decide how to communicate results to the intended audience, and often accept criticism and improve the solution (Eisner, 1999; Herman, 1997). Table 15.3 on page 556 lists some characteristics of authentic tests.

"I hate taking a test without an eraser."

(© *Martha Campbell*)

Performance in Context: Portfolios and Exhibitions

The concern with authentic assessment has led to the development of several approaches based on the goal of *performance in context.* Instead of circling answers to "factual" questions on nonexistent situations, students are required to solve real problems. Facts are used in a context where they apply—for example, the student uses grammar facts to write a persuasive letter to a software company requesting donations for the class computer center. The following example of a test of performance is taken from the Connecticut Core of Common Learning:

> Many local supermarkets claim to have the lowest prices. But what does this really mean? Does it mean that every item in their store is priced lower, or just some of them? How can you really tell which supermarket will save

■ Table 15.3	Characteristics of Authentic Tests

A. Structure and Logistics

1. Are more appropriately public; involve an audience, a panel, and so on.
2. Do not rely on unrealistic and arbitrary time constraints.
3. Offer known, not secret, questions or tasks.
4. Are more like portfolios or a *season* of games (not one-shot).
5. Require some collaboration with others.
6. Recur—and are *worth* practicing for, rehearsing, and retaking.
7. Make assessment and feedback to students so central that school schedules, structures, and policies are modified to support them.

B. Intellectual Design Features

1. Are "essential"—not needlessly intrusive, arbitrary, or contrived to "shake out" a grade.
2. Are "enabling"—constructed to point the student toward more sophisticated use of the skills or knowledge.
3. Are contextualized, complex intellectual challenges, not "atomized" tasks, corresponding to isolated "outcomes."
4. Involve the student's own research or use of knowledge, for which "content" is a means.
5. Assess student habits and repertoires, not mere recall or plug-in skills.
6. Are *representative* challenges—designed to emphasize *depth* more than breadth.
7. Are engaging and educational.
8. Involve somewhat ambiguous ("ill-structured") tasks or problems.

C. Grading and Scoring Standards

1. Involve criteria that assess essentials, not easily counted (but relatively unimportant) errors.
2. Are graded not on a "curve" but in reference to performance standards (criterion-referenced, not norm-referenced).
3. Involve demystified criteria of success that appear to *students* as inherent in successful activity.
4. Make self-assessment a part of the assessment.
5. Use a multifaceted scoring system instead of one aggregate grade.
6. Exhibit harmony with shared schoolwide aims—a *standard.*

D. Fairness and Equity

1. Ferret out and identify (perhaps hidden) strengths.
2. Strike a *constantly* examined balance between honoring achievement and native skill or fortunate prior training.
3. Minimize needless, unfair, and demoralizing comparisons.
4. Allow appropriate room for student learning styles, aptitudes, and interests.
5. Can be—should be—attempted by *all* students, with the test "scaffolded up," not "dumbed down," as necessary.

SOURCE: From "Teaching to the Authentic Test," by G. W. Wiggins, 1989, *Educational Leadership,* 45(7), p. 44. Copyright © 1989 by the Association of Supervision and Curriculum Development. Reprinted with permission.

> you the most money? Your assignment is to design and carry out a study to answer this question. What items and prices will you compare and why? How will you justify the choice of your "sample"? How reliable is the sample, etc.? (Wolf, Bixby, Glenn, & Gardner, 1991, p. 61)

Students completing this "test" will use mathematical facts and procedures in the context of solving a real-life problem. In addition, they will have to think critically and write persuasively. The *Stories of Learning/Tributes to Teaching* feature gives another example from my own education.

Portfolios and exhibitions are two approaches to assessment that require performance in context. With these approaches, it is difficult to tell where instruction stops and assessment starts because the two processes are interwoven (Smith, Smith, & De Lisi, 2001).

Portfolios. For years photographers, artists, models, and architects have had portfolios to display their skills and often to get jobs. A **portfolio** is a systematic collection of work, often including work in progress, revisions, student self-analyses, and reflections on what the student has learned (Popham, 2002). One student's self-reflection is presented in Figure 15.1.

Written work or artistic pieces are common contents of portfolios, but students might also include graphs, diagrams, snapshots of displays, peer comments, audio- or videotapes, laboratory reports, and computer programs—anything that demonstrates learning in the area being taught and assessed (Belanoff & Dickson, 1991; Camp, 1990; Wolf, Bixby, Glenn, & Gardner, 1991). There is a distinction between

Portfolio A collection of the student's work in an area, showing growth, self-reflection, and achievement.

~ Stories of Learning Tributes to Teaching ~

When I was in graduate school in Texas, the standard doctoral candidacy examination was three days worth of closed book, handwritten, blue-book-filled answers to questions. Candidates were examined in three areas of educational psychology: social/developmental; learning/cognition; and statistics/research methodology. This was a "high-stakes," make-or-break three days that determined whether you had to leave school with a "terminal Master's" (sounds deadly doesn't it!), instead of being allowed to go on to your doctoral research. By the time we took the exam, we had completed our coursework and internships. All that remained to earn the Ph.D was to design, complete, analyze, and write up an independent research project—the dissertation. This is a complex bit of work that takes many students months or even years to finish successfully.

Now this was the 70s—a time in Texas of protest. It was a time when students were more active in asserting their rights. And I was part of that spirit. I was certain that the three-day test was not a good assessment of our learning. I asked the faculty, "When will we have to sit down for three days and answer multiple-choice questions, write essays without any resources, or solve statistics problems that are not related to our research questions?" I wanted a more "authentic" assessment—something connected to our learning and our future. I talked to other students, wrote position papers, and lobbied professors. Finally I was asked to speak at a faculty meeting about the situation.

To my amazement and gratitude, the faculty voted to allow an option to the three-day test. Candidates could write a research proposal that examined a significant research question from the perspectives of social/developmental and learning/cognition in educational psychology. In addition, we were required to design a study that used appropriate methodology and statistics. I chose this option (after making all that fuss, I almost had to). Some of my friends said that I was crazy because I spent months preparing my proposal while they crammed a few weeks for their traditional exam. But then I used my proposal, with some improvements, to do my dissertation and finished a year ahead of them. I got a grant to do it, based on the thinking and writing that went into completing the option of that "authentic" assessment project. At my alma mater, the alternative candidacy exam is still in place today, and that is the form I use for my graduate students at Ohio State—thanks to the willingness of a **good faculty** to entertain student suggestions over 30 years ago.

Not only has this student's writing improved, but the student has become a more self-aware and self-critical writer.

2

Today I looked at all my stories in my writing folder I read some of my writing since September I noticed that I've improved some stuff. Now I edit my stories, and revise. Now I use periods, quotation mark. Sometimes my stories are langer I used to misspell my words and now I look in a dictionary or ask a friend and now I write exciting and scary stories and now I have very good endings. Now I use capitals I used to leave out words and write short simple stories.

Source: From "What Makes a Portfolio a Portfolio?" by F. L. Paulson, P. Paulson, and C. Meyers, 1991, *Educational Leadership, 48, 5,* p. 63. Copyright © 1991 by the Association for Supervision and Curriculum Development. Reprinted with permission.

■ **Figure 15.1** A Student Reflects on Learning: Self-Analysis of Work in a Portfolio

CONNECT & EXTEND

TO THE RESEARCH

Paulson, F. L., Paulson, P. R., & Meyer, C. A. (1991). What makes a portfolio a portfolio? *Educational Leadership, 48*(5), 60–63. *Focus Question:* Describe five entries that they might include in portfolios for their students.

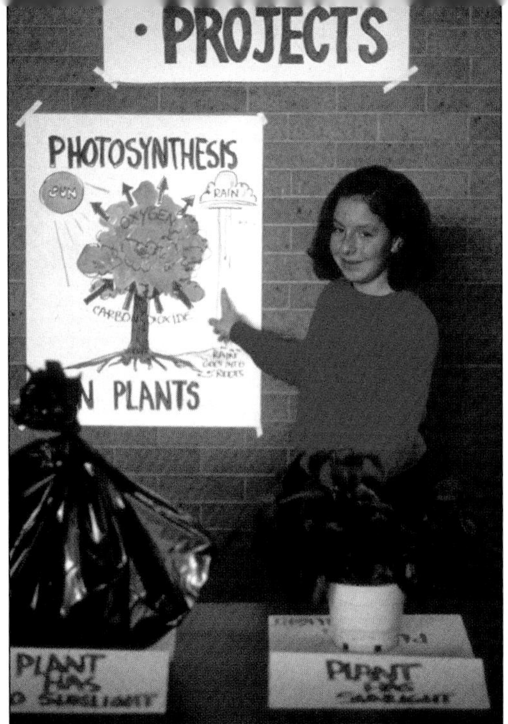

Student exhibitions are a type of performance test that requires students to use good communication, and are likely to involve many hours of preparation. Exhibitions help students appreciate high quality work.

process portfolios and final or "best work" portfolios. The distinction is similar to the difference between formative and summative evaluation. Process portfolios document learning and show progress. Best works portfolios showcase final accomplishments (Johnson & Johnson, 2002). Table 15.4 shows some examples for both individuals and groups.

Exhibitions. An **exhibition** is a performance test that has two additional features. First, it is public, so students preparing exhibitions must take the audience into account; communication and understanding are essential. Second, an exhibition often requires many hours of preparation, because it is the culminating experience of a whole program of study. Thomas Guskey and Jane Bailey (2001) suggest that exhibits help students understand the qualities of good work and recognize those qualities in their own productions and performances. Students also benefit when they select examples of their work to exhibit and articulate their reasons for the selections. Being able to judge quality can encourage student motivation by setting clear goals.

The *Guidelines* give some ideas for using portfolios and exhibits in your teaching.

Table 15.4 Process and Best Works Portfolios for Individuals and Groups

Here are a few examples of how to use portfolios in different subjects.

The Process Portfolio

Subject Area	Individual Student	Cooperative Group
Science	Documentation (running records or logs) of using the scientific method to solve a series of laboratory problems	Documentation (observation checklists) of using the scientific method to solve a series of laboratory problems
Mathematics	Documentation of mathematical reasoning through double-column mathematical problem solving (computations on the left side and running commentary explaining thought processes on the right side)	Documentation of complex problem solving and use of higher-level strategies
Language Arts	Evolution of compositions from early notes through outlines, research notes, response to others' editing, and final draft	Rubrics and procedures developed to ensure high-quality peer editing

The Best Works Portfolio

Subject Area	Individual Student	Cooperative Group
Language Arts	The best compositions in a variety of styles—expository, humor/satire, creative (poetry, drama, short story), journalistic (reporting, editorial columnist, reviewer), and advertising copy	The best dramatic production, video project, TV broadcast, newspaper, advertising display
Social Studies	The best historical research paper, opinion essay on historical issue, commentary on current event, original historical theory, review of a historical biography, account of academic controversy participated in	The best community survey, paper resulting from academic controversy, oral history compilation, multidimensional analysis of historical event, press corps interview with historical figure
Fine Arts	The best creative products such as drawings, paintings, sculptures, pottery, poems, thespian performance	The best creative products such as murals, plays written and performed, inventions thought of and built

SOURCE: From *Meaningful Assessment: A Meaningful and Cooperative Process,* by D. W. Johnson, R. T. Johnson. Published by Allyn & Bacon, Boston, MA. Copyright © 2002 by Pearson Education. Adapted by permission of the publisher.

GUIDELINES Creating Portfolios

Students should be involved in selecting the pieces that will make up the portfolio.

Examples

1. During the unit or semester, ask each student to select work that fits certain criteria, such as "my most difficult problem," "my best work," "my most improved work," or "three approaches to. . . ."
2. For their final submissions, ask students to select pieces that best show how much they have learned.

A portfolio should include information that shows student self-reflection and self-criticism.

Examples

1. Ask students to include a rationale for their selections.
2. Have each student write a "guide" to his or her portfolio, explaining how strengths and weaknesses are reflected in the work included.
3. Include self- and peer critiques, indicating specifically what is good and what might be improved.
4. Model self-criticism of your own productions.

The portfolio should reflect the students' activities in learning.

Examples

1. Include a representative selection of projects, writings, drawings, and so forth.
2. Ask students to relate the goals of learning to the contents of their portfolios.

The portfolio can serve different functions at different times of the year.

Examples

1. Early in the year, it might hold unfinished work or "problem pieces."
2. At the end of the year, it should contain only what the student is willing to make public.

Portfolios should show growth.

Examples

1. Ask students to make a "history" of their progress along certain dimensions and to illustrate points in their growth with specific works.
2. Ask students to include descriptions of activities outside class that reflect the growth illustrated in the portfolio.

Teach students how to create and use portfolios.

Examples

1. Keep models of very well done portfolios as examples, but stress that each portfolio is an individual statement.
2. Examine your students' portfolios frequently, especially early in the year when they are just getting used to the idea. Give constructive feedback.

Evaluating Portfolios and Performances

Checklists, rating scales, and scoring rubrics are helpful when you assess performances, because assessments of performances, portfolios, and exhibitions are criterion-referenced, not norm-referenced. In other words, the students' products and performances are compared to established public standards, not ranked in relation to other students' work (Cambourne & Turbill, 1990; Wiggins, 1991). For example, Figure 15.2 on page 560 gives three alternatives—numerical, graphic, and descriptive—for rating an oral presentation.

Scoring Rubrics. A checklist or rating scale gives specific feedback about elements of a performance. **Scoring rubrics** are rules that are used to determine the quality of a student performance (Mabry, 1999). For example, a rubric describing an excellent oral presentation might be:

> Pupil consistently faces audience, stands straight, and maintains eye contact; voice projects well and clearly; pacing and tone variation appropriate; well-organized; points logically and completely presented; brief summary at end. (Airasian, 1996, p. 155)

It is often helpful to have students join in the development of rating scales and scoring rubrics. When students participate, they are challenged to decide what quality work looks or sounds like in a particular area. They know in advance what is expected. As students gain practice in designing and applying scoring rubrics, their work and their learning often improve. Figure 15.3 on page 561 is an evaluation form for self- and peer assessment of contributions to cooperative learning groups.

CONNECT & EXTEND

TO **PRAXIS**™
PORTFOLIO ASSESSMENT
(II, C1, 2)
For a discussion of the advantages, limitations, design, and implementation of portfolio programs, and to examine samples of portfolio checklists, go to Teachervison.com (http://www.teachervision.com/lesson-plans/lesson-4536.html).

Exhibition A performance test or demonstration of learning that is public and usually takes an extended time to prepare.

Scoring rubrics Rules that are used to determine the quality of a student performance.

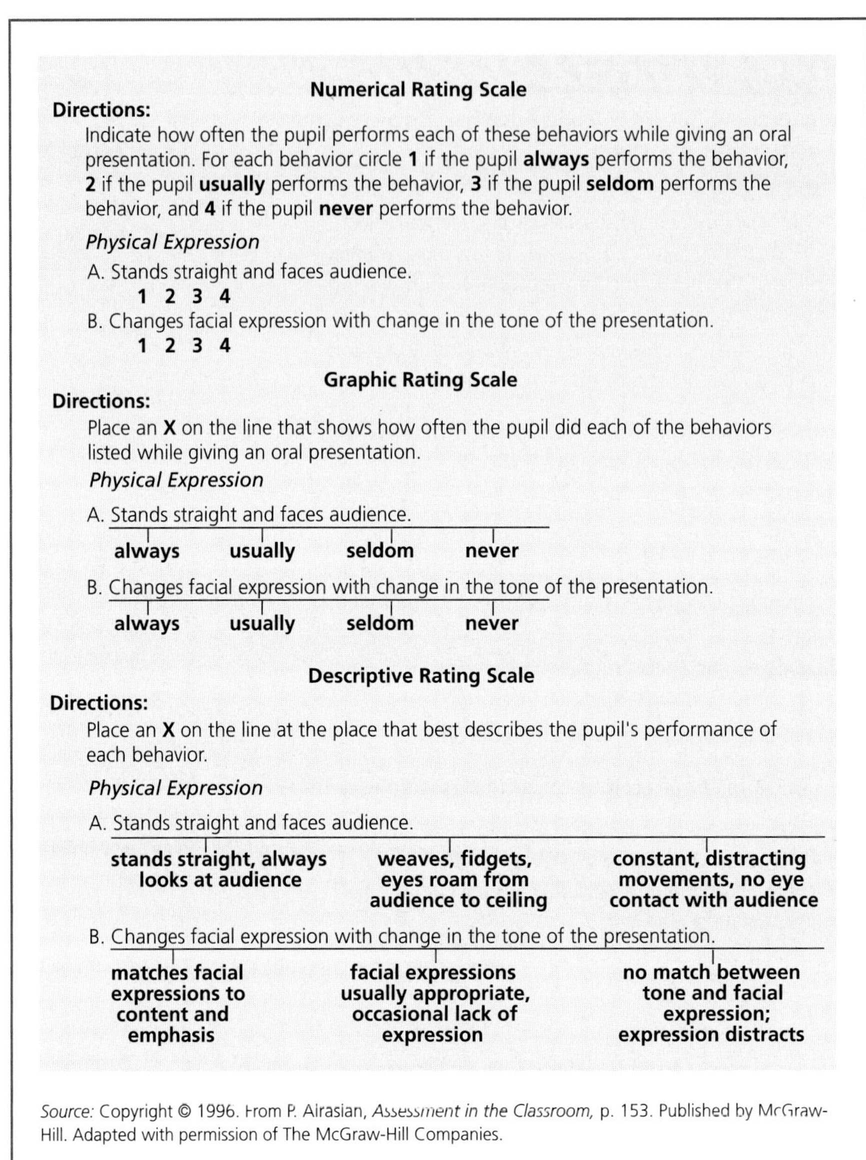

Numerical Rating Scale

Directions:

Indicate how often the pupil performs each of these behaviors while giving an oral presentation. For each behavior circle **1** if the pupil **always** performs the behavior, **2** if the pupil **usually** performs the behavior, **3** if the pupil **seldom** performs the behavior, and **4** if the pupil **never** performs the behavior.

Physical Expression

A. Stands straight and faces audience.

1 2 3 4

B. Changes facial expression with change in the tone of the presentation.

1 2 3 4

Graphic Rating Scale

Directions:

Place an **X** on the line that shows how often the pupil did each of the behaviors listed while giving an oral presentation.

Physical Expression

A. Stands straight and faces audience.

always **usually** **seldom** **never**

B. Changes facial expression with change in the tone of the presentation.

always **usually** **seldom** **never**

Descriptive Rating Scale

Directions:

Place an **X** on the line at the place that best describes the pupil's performance of each behavior.

Physical Expression

A. Stands straight and faces audience.

stands straight, always looks at audience	**weaves, fidgets, eyes roam from audience to ceiling**	**constant, distracting movements, no eye contact with audience**

B. Changes facial expression with change in the tone of the presentation.

matches facial expressions to content and emphasis	**facial expressions usually appropriate, occasional lack of expression**	**no match between tone and facial expression; expression distracts**

Source: Copyright © 1996. From P. Airasian, *Assessment in the Classroom,* p. 153. Published by McGraw-Hill. Adapted with permission of The McGraw-Hill Companies.

Figure 15.2 Three Ways of Rating an Oral Presentation

Performance assessment requires careful judgment on the part of teachers and clear communication to students about what is good and what needs improving. In some ways the approach is similar to the clinical method first introduced by Binet to assess intelligence: It is based on observing the student perform a variety of tasks and comparing his or her performance to a standard. Just as Binet never wanted to assign a single number to represent the child's intelligence, teachers who use authentic assessments do not try to assign one score to the student's performance. Even if rankings, ratings, and grades have to be given, these judgments are not the ultimate goals—improvement of learning is. Some of the following *Guidelines* for developing rubrics are taken from Goodrich (1997)and Johnson and Johnson (2002).

CONNECT & EXTEND

TO THE RESEARCH

For a positive view of using portfolios as a state-wide assessment process, see Ambruscato, J. (1993). Early results and tentative implications from the Vermont Portfolio Project. *Phi Delta Kappan, 74,* 474–477.

Reliability, Validity, Generalizability. Because judgment plays such a central role in evaluating performances, issues of reliability, validity, and generalizability are critical considerations. As we saw in the previous chapter, judges assessing the Vermont Portfolios often have not agreed on ratings, so reliability may not be adequate. When raters are experienced and scoring rubrics are well developed and refined, however,

STUDENT SELF- AND PEER EVALUATION FORM

This form will be used to assess the members of your learning group. Fill one form out on yourself. Fill one form out on each member of your group. During the group discussion, give each member the form you have filled out on them. Compare the way you rated yourself with the ways your groupmates have rated you. Ask for clarification when your rating differs from the ratings given you by your groupmates. Each member should set a goal for increasing his or her contribution to the academic learning of all group members.

Person Being Rated: ______________________________

Write the number of points earned by the group member:
(4 = Excellent, 3 = Good, 2 = Poor, 1 = Inadequate)

____ On time for class.
____ Arrives prepared for class.
____ Reliably completes all assigned work on time.
____ Work is of high quality.
____ Contributes to groupmates' learning daily.
____ Asks for academic help and assistance when it is needed.
____ Gives careful step-by-step explanations (doesn't just tell answers).
____ Builds on others' reasoning.
____ Relates what is being learned to previous knowledge.
____ Helps draw a visual representation of what is being learned.
____ Voluntarily extends a project.

Source: From "The Role of Cooperative Learning in Assessing and Communicating Student Learning," by D.W. Johnson and R.T. Johnson. In *ASCD 1996 Yearbook: Communicating Student Learning* (p. 41), T. Guskey (Ed.).

Figure 15.3 Self- and Peer Evaluation of Group Learning

reliability may improve (Herman & Winters, 1994; LeMahieu, Gitomer, & Eresh, 1993). Some of this improvement in reliability occurs because a rubric focuses the raters' attention on a few dimensions of the work and gives limited scoring levels to choose from. If scorers can give only a rating of 1, 2, 3, or 4, they are more likely to

CONNECT & EXTEND

TO **PRAXIS**™
SCORING RUBRICS (II, C3)
Kathy Schrock's Guide for Educators (http://school.discovery.com/schrockguide/assess.html) provides information about every aspect of the use of scoring rubrics in the classroom as well as an extensive collection of rubrics that can be used or adapted by teachers.

GUIDELINES: Developing a Rubric

1. *Look at models:* Show students examples of good and not-so-good work. Identify the characteristics that make the good ones good and the bad ones bad.
2. *List criteria:* Use the discussion of models to begin a list of what counts in quality work.
3. *Articulate gradations of quality:* Describe the best and worst levels of quality, then fill in the middle levels based on your knowledge of common problems and the discussion of not-so-good work.
4. *Practice on models:* Have students use the rubrics to evaluate the models you gave them in Step. 1.
5. *Use self- and peer assessment:* Give students their task. As they work, stop them occasionally for self- and peer-assessment.
6. *Revise:* Always give students time to revise their work based on the feedback they get in Step 5.
7. *Use teacher assessment:* Use the same rubric students used to assess their work yourself.
8. A number of *websites* provide examples of rubrics in different subjects and grades or will allow teachers generate their own rubrics.
   http://ericae.net/pare/getvn.asp?v=7&n=25
   http://rubistar.4teachers.org/
   http://www.teach-nology.com/web_tools/rubrics/

Note: Step 1 may be necessary only when you are asking students to engage in a task with which they are unfamiliar. Steps 3 and 4 are useful but time-consuming; you can do these on your own, especially when you've been using rubrics for a while. A class experienced in rubric-based assessment can streamline the process so that it begins with listing criteria, after which the teacher writes out the gradations of quality, checks them with the students, makes revisions, then uses the rubric for self-, peer, and teacher assessment.

agree than if they could score based on a 100-point scale. So the rubrics may achieve reliability not because they capture underlying agreement among raters, but because the rubrics limit options and thus limit variability in scoring (Mabry, 1999).

In terms of validity, there is some evidence that students who are classified as "master" writers on the basis of portfolio assessment are judged less capable using standard writing assessment. Which form of assessment is the best reflection of enduring qualities? There is so little research on this question, it is hard to say (Herman & Winters, 1994). In addition, when rubrics are developed to assess specific tasks, the results of applying the rubric may not predict performance on anything except very similar tasks, so what do we actually know about students' learning more generally (Haertel, 1999; Herman, 1997)?

CONNECT & EXTEND

TO THE RESEARCH
For a description of one school's graduation exhibitions and a thoughtful analysis of the use of exhibitions in teaching, see McDonald, J. P. (1993). Three pictures of an exhibition: Warm, cool, and hard. *Phi Delta Kappan, 74,* 480–485.

Diversity and Equity in Performance Assessment. Equity is an issue in all assessment and no less so with performances and portfolios. With a public performance, there could be bias effects based on a student's appearance and speech or the student's access to expensive audio, video, or graphic resources. Performance assessments have the same potential as other tests to discriminate unfairly against students who are not wealthy or who are culturally different (McDonald, 1993). And the extensive group work, peer editing, and out-of-class time devoted to portfolios means that some students may have access to more extensive networks of support and outright help. Many students in your classes will have families with sophisticated computer graphics and desktop publishing capabilities. Others may have little support from home. These differences can be sources of bias and inequity.

Assessing Learning Potential: Dynamic Assessment

One criticism of traditional forms of intelligence testing is that such tests are merely samples of performance at one particular point in time; they fail to capture the child's potential for future learning. An alternative view of cognitive assessment is based on the assumption that the goal of assessment is to reveal potential for learning and to identify the psychological and educational interventions that will help the person realize this potential. Procedures developed by Joe Campione and Ann Brown give graduated prompts as a child works to solve a problem. The prompts are scripted, beginning with a general hint and ending with a detailed instruction for how find the answer. The way the child uses the prompt and learns within the testing situation gives evidence of learning potential (Feuerstein, 1979; Kozulin & Falik, 1995).

Campione and Brown's techniques reflect Vygotsky's ideas about the zone of proximal development—the range of functioning where a child cannot solve problems independently but can benefit from guidance. Results of these tests offer a thought-provoking and radically different approach to testing. Rather than focusing on where a child is, these approaches point toward where the child could go and give guidance for the journey (Grigorenko & Sternberg, 1998).

Look at Table 15.5. It summarizes the possibilities and limitations of aligning different assessment tools with their targets. One major message in this chapter is to match the type of assessment tools use to the target—what is being assessed.

Check Yourself What is authentic assessment?

Describe portfolios and exhibitions.

What are the issues of reliability, validity, and equity with portfolios and performance assessment?

What is learning potential assessment?

■ **Table 15.5** Aligning Different Assessment Tools with Their Targets

Different learning outcomes require different assessment methods.

Target to Be Assessed	Assessment Method: Selected Response	Essay	Performance Assessment	Personal Communication
Knowledge Mastery	Multiple choice, true/false, matching, and fill-in can sample mastery of elements of knowledge	Essay exercises can tap understanding of relationships among elements of knowledge	Not a good choice for this target—three other options preferred	Can ask questions, evaluate answers, and infer mastery—but a time-consuming option
Reasoning Proficiency	Can assess understanding of basic patterns of reasoning	Written descriptions of complex problem solutions can provide a window into reasoning proficiency	Can watch students solve some problems and infer about reasoning proficiency	Can ask student to "think aloud" or can ask follow-up questions to probe reasoning
Skills	Can assess mastery of the prerequisites of skillful performance—but cannot tap the skill itself	Can assess mastery of the prerequisites of skillful performance—but cannot tap the skill itself	Can observe and evaluate skills as they are being performed	Strong match when skill is oral communication proficiency; also can assess mastery of knowledge prerequisite to skillful performance
Ability to Create Products	Can assess mastery of knowledge prerequisite to the ability to create quality products—but cannot assess the quality of products themselves	Can assess mastery of knowledge prerequisite to the ability to create quality products—but cannot assess the quality of products themselves	A strong match can assess: (a) proficiency in carrying out steps in product development and (b) attributes of the product itself	Can probe procedural knowledge and knowledge of attributes of quality products—but not product quality

SOURCE: From "Where Is Our Assessment Future and How Can We Get There?" by R. J. Stiggins. In R. W. Lissitz, W. D. Schafer (Eds.), *Meaningful Assessment: A meaningful and Cooperative Process.* Published by Allyn & Bacon, Boston, MA. Copyright © 2002 by Pearson Education. Adapted by permission of the publisher.

Enhancing Your Expertise with Technology

Assessment

Robin was one of several teachers from her high school (and the only first-year teacher) to be invited to serve on the special district committee for assessment and evaluation. The superintendent created the committee in reaction to a report by a team of monitors from the state department of education. The report was generally favorable, but the team criticized the district's high schools for their near-exclusive use of traditional tools for assessing and evaluating students. The committee would make recommendations for revamping the district's approach to assessment and evaluation. Many of the veteran educators were looking to Robin for guidance—these experienced teachers were basically novices about the intricacies of recent innovations.

Assessment is one of the most complex tasks of teaching. Innovative instructional techniques have enriched the scope of how students learn in school, while innovations in assessment provide teachers rich insights into the complexity of what their students have learned and what they can do with their knowledge. Just as an architect needs to be knowledgeable of materials, construction techniques, client needs, and aesthetics, and understand how they affect the use of a building, a teacher needs to be knowledgeable of the purposes, uses, and values of different assessment techniques, and understand how they affect the learner.

At the first meeting of the special committee on assessment, Robin would find it valuable to introduce other committee members to the section of Edutopia Online (http://www.glef.org) that is devoted to assessment. The sponsor of this site, The George Lucas Foundation, has tapped into the expertise of many of the leading scholars on assessment to provide a rich set of resources devoted to the knowledgeable use of alternative forms of assessment in the classroom.

(continued)

(Many of the resources offered at Edutopia are in video and audio formats as well as in text.) A list of the assessment topics examined by Edutopia could serve very well as the committee's agenda:

- Classroom, school, and district-wide examples of alternative assessment programs
- Interviews with assessment experts
- Using portfolios (including the use of digital portfolios), performances, projects, and exhibitions for assessment
- Current research on assessment and testing
- The teacher's role in assessment
- Student reflections and journals
- Strategies and resources that parents, policy makers, teachers, administrators, and community members can use to educate the public about K–12 assessment

Effects of Grades and Grading on Students

Think back on your report cards and grades over the years. Did you ever receive a grade that was lower than you expected? How did you feel about yourself, the teacher, the subject, and school in general as a result of the lower grade? What could the teacher have done to help you understand and profit from the experience?

When we think of grades, we often think of competition. Highly competitive classes may be particularly hard on anxious students, students who lack self-confidence, and students who are less prepared. So, although high standards and competition do tend to be generally related to increased academic learning, it is clear that a balance must be struck between high standards and a reasonable chance to succeed.

CONNECT & EXTEND

TO YOUR TEACHING/PORTFOLIO
Classroom evaluation is frequently referred to as the "grading game." What aspects of grading resemble a game from the student's point of view?

Effects of Failure

It may sound as though low grades and failure should be avoided in school. But the situation is not that simple. After reviewing many years of research on the effects of failure from several perspectives, Margaret Clifford (1990, 1991) concluded that failure can have both positive and negative effects on subsequent performance, depending on the situation and the personality of the students involved.

CONNECT & EXTEND

TO **PRAXIS**™
GRADING
Be able to define criterion- and norm-referenced grading systems, identify examples of each, and explain the advantages and disadvantages of each system. Describe the possible effects of grades on students.

For example, one study required subjects to complete three sets of problems. On the first set, the experimenters arranged for subjects to experience either 0%, 50%, or 100% success. On the second set, it was arranged for all subjects to fail completely. On the third set of problems, the experimenters merely recorded how well the subjects performed. Those who had succeeded only 50% of the time before the failure experience performed the best. It appears that a history of complete failure or 100% success may be bad preparation for learning to cope with failure—something we must all learn. Some level of failure may be helpful for most students, especially if teachers help the students see connections between hard work and improvement. Efforts to protect students from failure and to guarantee success may be counterproductive. Clifford (1990) gives this advice to teachers:

> It is time for educators to replace easy success with challenge. We must encourage students to reach beyond their intellectual grasp and allow them the privilege of learning from mistakes. There must be a tolerance for error-making in every classroom, and gradual success rather than continual success must become the yardstick by which learning is judged. (p. 23)

The more able your students, the more challenging and important it will be to help them learn to "fail successfully" (Foster, 1981).

So far, we have been talking about the effects of failing a test or perhaps a course. But what about the effect of failing an entire grade—that is, of being "held back"? Almost 20% of seniors have repeated at least one grade since kindergarten, usually in the earlier grades (Kelly, 1999). Some researchers believe that being held back injures students' self-esteem and increases the chances that they will drop out of school (Grissom & Smith, 1989; Roderick, 1994). In their view, students generally do better academically when promoted. For example, in a longitudinal study of 29 retained and 50 low-achieving but promoted students, Shane Jimerson (1999) found that the retained students had poorer educational and employment outcomes than the promoted students years later. The retained students dropped out more often, had lower paying jobs, and received lower competence ratings from employers. In addition, the low-achieving but promoted students were comparable to a control group in all employment outcomes at age 20.

Other researchers have found some advantage for more emotionally immature children of average or above average ability who are retained in 1st, 2nd, or 3rd grade (Kelly, 1999; Pierson & Connell, 1992), but the advantage may not last. In one study that followed many students for several years, children who could have been retained, but who were promoted, did about as well as similar children who were held back, and sometimes better (Reynolds, 1992).

No matter what, students who are having trouble should get help, whether they are promoted or retained. Just covering the same material again in the same way won't solve the students' academic or social problems. As Jeannie Oakes (1999) has said, "No sensible person advocates social promotion as it is currently framed—simply passing incompetent students on to the next grade" (p. 8). The best approach may be to promote the students along with their peers, but to give them special remediation during the summer or the next year (Mantzicopoulos & Morrison, 1992; Shepard & Smith, 1989). An even better approach would be to prevent the problems before they occur by providing extra resources such as tutoring, as happens in the *Reading Recovery* program or Slavin's *Success for All* (McCoy & Reynolds, 1999).

CONNECT & EXTEND

TO THE RESEARCH

Harvard Graduate School of Education. (1999, January/February). Retention vs. social promotion: Schools search for alternatives. *Harvard Education Newsletter, 15*(1), 1–3. *Focus Question:* What are the effects of retention on students? Can you propose alternatives?

CONNECT & EXTEND

TO THE RESEARCH

Here are several studies of retentions:

Mantzicopolous, P., & Morrison, D. (1992). Kindergarten retention: Academic and behavioral outcomes through the end of second grade. *American Educational Research Journal, 29,* 182–198.

Pierson, L. H., & Connell, J. P. (1992). Effect of grade retention on self-system processes, school engagement, and academic performance. *Journal of Educational Psychology, 84,* 300–307.

Shepard, L. A., & Smith, M. L. (1990). Synthesis of research on grade retention. *Educational Leadership, 47*(8), 84–88.

McCoy, A. R., & Reynolds, A. J. (1999). Grade retention and school performance: An extended investigation. *Journal of School Psychology, 37,* 273–298.

Vitaro, F., Brendgen, M., & Tremblay, R. E. (1999). Prevention of school dropout through the reduction of disruptive behaviors and school failure in elementary school. *Journal of School Psychology, 37,* 205–226.

Effects of Feedback

The results of several studies of feedback fit well with the notion of "successful" or constructive failure. These studies have concluded that it is more helpful to tell students *why* they are wrong so they can learn more appropriate strategies (Bangert-Drowns, Kulik, Kulik, & Morgan, 1991). Students often need help figuring out why their answers are incorrect. Without such feedback, they are likely to make the same mistakes again. Yet this type of feedback is rarely given. In one study, only about 8% of the teachers noticed a consistent type of error in a student's arithmetic computation and informed the student (Bloom & Bourdon, 1980).

What are the identifying characteristics of effective written feedback? With older students (late elementary through high school), written comments are most helpful when they are personalized and when they provide constructive criticism. This means the teacher should make specific comments on errors or faulty strategies, but balance this criticism with suggestions about how to improve, as well as comments on the positive aspects of the work (Butler & Nisan, 1986; Guskey & Bailey, 2001). Working with 6th grade teachers, Elawar and Corno (1985) found that feedback was dramatically improved when the teachers used these four questions as a guide: "What is the key error? What is the probable reason the student made this error? How can I guide the student to avoid the error in the future? What did the student do well that could be noted?" (p. 166). Here are some examples of teachers' written comments that proved helpful (Elawar & Corno, 1985, p. 164):

> Juan, you know how to get a percent, but the computation is wrong in this instance. . . . Can you see where? (Teacher has underlined the location of errors.)

> You know how to solve the problem—the formula is correct—but you have not demonstrated that you understand how one ffraction multiplied by another can give an answer that is smaller than either ($\frac{1}{2} \times \frac{1}{2} = \frac{1}{4}$).

Comments like these should help students correct errors and recognize good work, progress, and increasing skill.

Grades and Motivation

> **CONNECT & EXTEND**
>
> **TO OTHER CHAPTERS**
> See Chapter 6 for a discussion of how to use praise effectively. These guidelines apply to written feedback as well.

> **CONNECT & EXTEND**
>
> **TO YOUR TEACHING/PORTFOLIO**
> Given the various roles of evaluation, what is the disadvantage of a teacher giving a test and not returning the results until several weeks later? What is the disadvantage of merely posting the grade without returning the actual test? What is the disadvantage of returning the students' scored answer sheets without reviewing the correct answers?

"If you find yourself relying on counting assessments toward grades as a primary means of motivating students to work in the class, it is time to do a thorough reevaluation of what is happening in your classroom . . . there are more serious problems than those involving assessment" (Smith, Smith, & De Lisi, 2001, p. 27). Educators agree that assessment should motivate students to learn—not just to work for a grade.

Is there really a difference between working for a grade and working to learn? The answer depends in part on how a grade is determined. As a teacher, you can use grades to motivate the kind of learning you intend students to achieve in your course. If you test only at a simple but detailed level of knowledge, you may force students to choose between complex learning and a good grade. But when a grade reflects meaningful learning, working for a grade and working to learn become the same thing. Finally, while high grades may have some value as rewards or incentives for meaningful engagement in learning, low grades generally do not encourage greater efforts. Students receiving low grades are more likely to withdraw, blame others, decide that the work is "dumb," or feel responsible for the low grade but helpless to make improvements. Rather than give a failing grade, you might consider the work incomplete and give students support in revising or improving. Maintain high standards and give students a chance to reach them (Guskey, 1994; Guskey & Bailey, 2001).

Another effect on motivation occurs in high schools in the race for valedictorian. Sometimes students and parents find clever ways to move ahead of the competition—but the strategies have little to do with learning. As Tom Guskey and Jane Bailey (2001) note, when a valedictorian wins by a 1/1,000 of decimal point, how meaningful is the learning behind the difference? Some high schools now name multiple valedictorians—as many as meet the highest standards of the school—because they believe that the educators' job is "not to *select* talent, but, rather, to *develop* talent (Guskey & Bailey, 2001, p. 39).

The *Guidelines* summarize the effects grades can have on students.

Check Yourself How can failure support learning?

Which is better, social promotion or being "held back"?

Can feedback, including grades, promote learning and motivation?

Grading and Reporting: Nuts and Bolts

Think about the other courses you are taking this term besides this one. How are your grades calculated in those courses?

In determining a final grade, the teacher must make a major decision. Should a student's grade reflect the amount of material learned and how well it has been learned, or should the grade reflect the student's status in comparison with the rest of the class? In other words, should grading be criterion-referenced or norm-referenced?

GUIDELINES: Minimizing the Detrimental Effects of Grades

Avoid reserving high grades and high praise for answers that conform to your ideas or to those in the textbook.

Examples

1. Give extra points for correct and creative answers.
2. Withhold your opinions until all sides of an issue have been explored.
3. Reinforce students for disagreeing in a rational, productive manner.
4. Give partial credit for partially correct answers.

Make sure each student has a reasonable chance to be successful, especially at the beginning of a new task.

Examples

1. Pretest students to make sure they have prerequisite abilities.
2. When appropriate, provide opportunities for students to retest to raise their grades, but make sure the retest is as difficult as the original.
3. Consider failing efforts as "incomplete" and encourage students to revise and improve.

Balance written and oral feedback.

Examples

1. Consider giving short, lively written comments with younger students and more extensive written comments with older students.
2. When the grade on a paper is lower than the student might have expected, be sure the reason for the lower grade is clear.
3. Tailor comments to the individual student's performance; avoid writing the same phrases over and over.
4. Note specific errors, possible reasons for errors, ideas for improvement, and work done well.

Make grades as meaningful as possible.

Examples

1. Tie grades to the mastery of important objectives.
2. Give ungraded assignments to encourage exploration.
3. Experiment with performances and portfolios.

Base grades on more than just one criterion.

Examples

1. Use essay questions as well as multiple-choice items on a test.
2. Grade oral reports and class participation.

Criterion-Referenced versus Norm-Referenced Grading

In **criterion-referenced grading,** the grade represents a list of accomplishments. If clear objectives have been set for the course, the grade may represent a certain number of objectives met satisfactorily. When a criterion-referenced system is used, criteria for each grade generally are spelled out in advance. It is then up to the student to earn the grade she or he wants to receive. Theoretically, in this system all students can achieve an A if they reach the criteria.

In **norm-referenced grading,** the major influence on a grade is the student's standing in comparison with others who also took the course. If a student studies very hard and almost everyone else does too, the student may receive a disappointing grade, perhaps a C or D.

Criterion-Referenced Systems. Criterion-referenced grading has the advantage of relating judgments about a student to the achievement of clearly defined instructional goals. Some school districts have developed reporting systems where report cards list objectives along with judgments about the student's attainment of each. Reporting is done at the end of each unit of instruction. The elementary school report card shown in Figure 15.4 on page 568 demonstrates the relationship between assessment and the goals of the unit.

Norm-Referenced Systems. One common type of norm-referenced grading is called **grading on the curve.** How you feel about this approach probably depends on where your grades generally fell along that "curve." There is good evidence that this type of grading damages the relationships among students and between teachers and students (Krumboltz & Yeh, 1996). When you think about it, if the curve arbitrarily

CONNECT & EXTEND

TO THE RESEARCH
For a summary of the considerations in developing a grading plan, see Frisbie, D. A., & Waltmen, K. K. (1992). Developing a personal grading plan. *Educational Measurement: Issues and practices* (pp. 35–42). Washington, DC: National Council on Measurement in Education.

Criterion-referenced grading Assessment of each student's mastery of course objectives.

Norm-referenced grading Assessment of students' achievement in relation to one another.

Grading on the curve Norm-referenced grading that compares students' performance to an average level.

This is one example of a criterion-referenced report card. Other forms are possible, but all criterion-referenced reports indicate student progress toward specific goals.

LINCOLN ELEMENTARY SCHOOL
GRADE 5

Student ________ Teacher ________ Principal Muriel Simms Quarter 2 3 4

E = Excellent S = Satisfactory P = Making Progress N = Needs improvement

READING PROGRAM

Materials Used: ________

___ Reads with understanding
___ Is able to write about what is read
___ Completes reading group work accurately and on time
___ Shows interest in reading

Reading Skills
___ Decodes new words
___ Understands new words

Independent Reading Level
Below/At Grade Level/Above

LANGUAGE ARTS
___ Uses oral language effectively
___ Listens carefully
___ Masters weekly spelling

Writing skills
___ Understands writing as process
___ Creates a rough draft
___ Makes meaningful revisions
___ Creates edited, legible final draft

Editing skills
___ Capitalizes
___ Punctuates
___ Uses complete sentences
___ Uses paragraphs
___ Demonstrates dictionary skills

Writing skill level:
Below/At Grade Level/Above

MATHEMATICS

Problem Solving
___ Solves teacher-generated problems
___ Solves self-/student-generated problems
___ Can create story problems

Interpreting Problems
___ Uses appropriate strategies
___ Can use more than one strategy
___ Can explain strategies in written form
___ Can explain strategies orally

Math Concepts

Understands Base Ten
Beginning/Developing/Sophisticated

Multiplication, Basic facts
Beginning/Developing/Sophisticated

2-Digit Multiplications
Beginning/Developing/Sophisticated

Division
Beginning/Developing/Sophisticated

Geometry
Beginning/Developing/Sophisticated

Overall Math Skill Level:
Beginning/Developing/Sophisticated

Attitude/Work Skills
___ Welcomes a challenge
___ Persistent
___ Takes advantage of learning from others
___ Listens to others
___ Participates in discussion

It Figures
Is working on: ________

Goals: ________
Is working on achieving goal: ________

SOCIAL STUDIES
___ Understands subject matter
___ Shows curiosity and enthusiasm
___ Contributes to class discussions
___ Uses map skills
___ Demonstrates control of reading skills by interpreting text

Topics covered: individual cultures, Columbus–first English colonies

SCIENCE
___ Shows curiosity about scientific subject matter
___ Asks good scientific questions
___ Shows knowledge of scientific method
___ Uses knowledge of scientific method to help set up and run experiment(s)
___ Makes good scientific observations
___ Has researched scientific topic(s)
Topic(s) ________

I Wonder
Is currently working on ________

WORKING SKILLS
___ Listens carefully
___ Follows directions
___ Works neatly and carefully
___ Checks work
___ Completes work on time
___ Uses time wisely
___ Works well independently
___ Works well in a group
___ Takes risks in learning
___ Welcomes a challenge

HOMEWORK
___ Self-selects homework
___ Completes work accurately
___ Completes work on time

PRESENTATIONS/PROJECTS
____

HUMAN RELATIONS
___ Shows courtesy
___ Respects rights of others
___ Shows self-control
___ Interacts well with peers
___ Shows a cooperative and positive attitude in class
___ Shows a cooperative attitude when asked to work with other students
___ Is willing to help other students
___ Works well with other adults (subs, student teacher, parents, etc.)

Attendance

	1st	2nd	3rd	4th
Present				
Absent				
Tardy				

Placement for next year: ________

Source: From "Reporting Methods in Grades K–8," by K. Lake and K. Kafka. In *ASCD 1996 Yearbook: Communicating Student Learning* (p. 104), T. Guskey (Ed.).

Figure 15.4 A Criterion-Referenced Report Card

limits the number of good grades that can be given, then, in the game of grading, most students will be losers (Guskey & Bailey, 2001; Haladyna, 2002; Kohn, 1996). Over 20 years ago, Benjamin Bloom (of Bloom's taxonomy) and his colleagues (1981) pointed out the fallacy of grading on the curve:

> There is nothing sacred about the normal curve. It is the distribution most appropriate to chance and random activity. Education is a purposeful activity, and we seek to have students learn what we have to teach. If we are effective in our instruction, the distribution of achievement should be very different from

Table 15.6 Comparing Norm-Referenced and Criterion-Referenced Standards for Grading

Norm-referenced systems use the performance of the rest of the class as the standard for determining grades. Criterion-referenced systems use standards of subject mastery and learning to determine grades.

Grade	Criterion-referenced	Norm-referenced
A	Firm command of knowledge domain High level of skill development Exceptional preparation for later learning	Far above class average
B	Command of knowledge beyond the minimum Advanced development of most skills Has prerequisites for later learning	Above class average
C	Command of only the basic concepts of knowledge Demonstrated ability to use basic skills Lacks a few prerequisites for later learning	At the class average
D	Lacks knowledge of some fundamental ideas Some important skills not attained Deficient in many of the prerequisites for later learning	Below class average
F	Most of the basic concepts and principles not learned Most essential skills cannot be demonstrated Lacks most prerequisites needed for later learning	Far below class average

SOURCE: From "Developing a Personal Grading Plan," by D. A. Frisbie and K. K. Waltmen, 1992, *Educational Measurement: Issues and Practices*, p. 37. Copyright © 1992 by the National Council on Measurement in Education. Reprinted with permission.

> the normal curve. In fact, we may even insist that our educational efforts have been *unsuccessful* to the extent that the distribution of achievement approximates the normal distribution. (pp. 52–53)

Table 15.6 compares descriptions of a student's performance using criterion-referenced and norm-referenced standards and suggests a way to translate these descriptions into grades.

In the following paragraphs we examine a few popular systems for calculating grades.

The Point System and Percentage Grading

One popular system for combining grades from many assignments is a point system. Each test or assignment is given a certain number of total points, depending on its importance. A test worth 40% of the grade could be worth 40 points. A paper worth 20% could be worth 20 points. Points are then awarded on the test or paper based on specific criteria. An A+ paper, one that meets all the criteria, could be given the full 20 points; an average paper might be given 10 points. If tests of comparable importance are worth the same number of points, are equally difficult, and cover a similar amount of material, this system can be fair and practical. But in most schools, these points still must be converted into some form of final grade. So the teacher has to decide the standards for assigning grades.

Using another approach, **percentage grading,** the teacher can assign grades based on how much knowledge each student has mastered—what percentage of the total knowledge he or she understands. To do this, the teacher might score tests and other classwork with percentage scores (based on how much is correct—50%, 85%, etc.) and then average these scores to reach a course score. These scores can then be converted into letter grades according to predetermined cutoffs. Any number of

CONNECT & EXTEND

TO YOUR TEACHING/PORTFOLIO
Can grades be used as motivators for all students? What determines whether a grade is motivating? How can a teacher use grades so that they tend to be motivating instead of discouraging?

Percentage grading System of converting class performances to percentage scores and assigning grades based on predetermined cutoff points.

students can earn any grade. This procedure is very common; you may have experienced it yourself as a student. Let us look at it more closely, because it has some frequently overlooked problems.

The grading symbols of A, B, C, D, and F are probably the most popular means of reporting at the present time. School systems often establish equivalent percentage categories for each of these symbols. The percentages vary from school district to school district, but two typical ones are as follows:

90–100% = A; 80–89% = B; 70–79% = C; 60–69% = D; below 60% = F

94–100% = A; 85–93% = B; 76–83% = C; 70–75% = D; below 70% = F

As you can see, although both districts have an A to F five-point grading system, the average achievement required for each grade is different.

Can we really say what is the total amount of knowledge available in, for example, 8th grade science? Are we sure we can accurately measure what percentage of this body of knowledge each student has attained? To use percentage grading appropriately, we would have to know exactly what there was to learn and exactly how much of that knowledge each student had learned (Popham, 2002). These conditions are seldom met, even though teachers use the cutoff points to assign grades as if measurement were so accurate that a one-point difference was meaningful: "In spite of decades of research in educational and psychological measurement, which has produced more defensible methods, the concept [of percentage grading], once established, has proved remarkably resistant to change" (Zimmerman, 1981, p. 178).

Any grading system prescribed or suggested by the school can be influenced by particular concerns of the teacher and the difficulty of the task. So don't be fooled by the seeming security of points or absolute percentages. Your own grading philosophy will continue to operate, even in this system. Because there is more concern today with specifying objectives and criterion-referenced assessment, especially at the elementary grade levels, several alternative methods for evaluating student progress against predetermined criteria have evolved.

The Contract System and Grading Rubrics

When applied to the whole class, the **contract system** indicates the type, quantity, and quality of work required for each number or letter grade in the system. Rubrics describe the performance expected for each level. Students agree, or "contract," to work for particular grades by meeting the specified requirements and performing at the level specified. For example, the following standards might be established:

F: Not coming to class regularly or not turning in the required work.

D: Coming to class regularly and turning in the required work on time.

C: Coming to class regularly, turning in the required work on time, and receiving a check mark on all assignments to indicate they are satisfactory.

B: Coming to class regularly, turning in the required work on time, and receiving a check mark on all assignments except at least three that achieve a check-plus, indicating superior achievement.

A: As above, plus a successful oral or written report on one of the books listed for supplementary reading.

This example calls for more subjective judgment than would be ideal. However, contract systems reduce student anxiety about grades. The contract system can be applied to individual students, in which case it functions much like an independent study plan.

Unfortunately, the system can lead to overemphasis on the quantity of work. Teachers may be too vague about the standards that differentiate acceptable from unacceptable work. This is where scoring rubrics for each assignment can be helpful. If

CONNECT & EXTEND

TO YOUR TEACHING/PORTFOLIO
How would you solve the following problem? You are using a contract system in one of your classes. One of the requirements for an A is "to write a book report." However, some students are reporting on books that you think they read last year, and some are handing in short, superficial reports. How can you structure the contract system so that the students will do a better quality of work?

CONNECT & EXTEND

TO OTHER CHAPTERS
See Chapter 6 for a discussion of behavior management contracts.

Contract system System in which each student works for a particular grade according to agreed-upon standards.

clear and well-developed rubrics describe the performances expected for each assignment, and if students learn to use the rubrics to evaluate their own work, then quality, not quantity, will be at the center of grading. You can modify the contract system by including a **revise option.** For example, a check mark might be worth 75 points and a check-plus 90 points; a check-plus earned after revision could be worth 85 points—more than a check, but less than a check-plus earned the first time around. This system allows students to improve their work, but also rewards students for getting it right the first time. In addition, the teacher may be less reluctant to judge a project unsatisfactory because students can improve their work (King, 1979). But beware, if a school system requires a five-point grading scale and all students contract for and achieve the highest grade (before or after revising), the teacher will wish that the principal had been consulted about the system before the grades came out. The *Guidelines* give ideas for using any grading system in a fair and reasonable way.

Revise option In a contract system, the chance to revise and improve work.

GUIDELINES Using Any Grading System

Explain your grading policies to students early in the course and remind them of the policies regularly.

Examples

1. Give older students a handout describing the assignments, tests, grading criteria, and schedule.
2. Explain to younger students in a low-pressure manner how their work will be evaluated.

Set reasonable standards.

Examples

1. Discuss workload and grading standards with more experienced teachers.
2. Give a few formative tests to get a sense of your students' abilities before you give a graded test.
3. Take tests yourself first to gauge the difficulty of the test and to estimate the time your students will need.

Base your grades on as much objective evidence as possible.

Examples

1. Plan in advance how and when you will test.
2. Keep a portfolio of student work. This may be useful in student or parent conferences.

Be sure students understand test directions.

Examples

1. Outline the directions on the board.
2. Ask several students to explain the directions.
3. Go over a sample question first.

Correct, return, and discuss test questions as soon as possible.

Examples

1. Have students who wrote good answers read their responses for the class; make sure they are not the same students each time.
2. Discuss why wrong answers, especially popular wrong choices, are incorrect.
3. As soon as students finish a test, give them the answers to questions and the page numbers where answers are discussed in the text.

As a rule, do not change a grade.

Examples

1. Make sure you can defend the grade in the first place.
2. DO change any clerical or calculation errors.

Guard against bias in grading.

Examples

1. Ask students to put their names on the backs of their papers.
2. Use an objective point system or model papers when grading essays.

Keep pupils informed of their standing in the class.

Examples

1. Write the distribution of scores on the board after tests.
2. Schedule periodic conferences to go over work from previous weeks.

Give students the benefit of the doubt. All measurement techniques involve error.

Examples

1. Unless there is a very good reason not to, give the higher grade in borderline cases.
2. If a large number of students miss the same question in the same way, revise the question for the future and consider throwing it out for that test.

SOURCE: From *Problems in Middle and High School Teaching: A Handbook for Student Teachers and Beginning Teachers* (pp. 182–187), by A. M. Drayer, 1979, Boston: Allyn & Bacon. Copyright © 1979 by Allyn & Bacon. Adapted by permission of the author and publisher.

"I hope this isn't another ploy to up your grade, Haskell."

(© *Art Bouthillier*)

Grading on Effort and Improvement

Grading on effort and improvement is not really a complete grading system, but rather a theme that can run through most grading methods. Should teachers grade students based on how much they learn or on the final level of learning? One problem with using improvement as a standard for grading is that the best students improve the least, because they are already the most competent. Do you want to penalize these students because they knew quite a bit initially, and the teaching and testing have limited how much learning they can demonstrate? After all, unless you assign extra work, these students will run out of things to do (Airsian, 2001; Guskey & Bailey, 2001).

One solution is to use the **individual learning expectation (ILE)** system described on page 499. With this system, students earn improvement points on tests or assignments for scoring above their personal base (average) score or for making a perfect score. The teacher can count these improvement points when figuring a final grade or simply use them as a basis for giving other classroom rewards. Another option is to recognize good student effort through oral or written comments, notes to parents, or other recognition. See the *Reaching Every Student* feature for one example.

Cautions: Being Fair

Individual learning expectation (ILE) Personal average score.

Halo effect The tendency for a general impression of a person to influence our perception of any aspect of that person.

The attributions a teacher makes about the causes of student successes or failures can affect the grades that students receive. Teachers are more likely to give higher grades for effort (a controllable factor) than for ability (an uncontrollable factor). Lower grades are more likely when teachers attribute a student's failure to lack of effort instead of lack of ability (Weiner, 1979). It is also possible that grades can be influenced by a **halo effect**—that is, by the tendency to view particular aspects of a student based on a general impression, either positive or negative. As a teacher, you may find it dif-

Reaching Every Student

Using Technology to Recognize Improvement

An elementary school principal we know uses her cell phone to communicate to parents what she calls "The Good News." She carries her phone with her as she walks through the hallways, visits the cafeteria, supervises the playground, and observes teachers' classes. When she sees a student performing well in class, assisting a classmate, or helping to improve the school, she immediately calls that student's parent or guardian on her phone and announces, "Hello, this is Ms. Johnson, the principal at Judd Elementary School. I just saw Tonya . . ." After explaining what she observed and complimenting the child, she hands the phone to the child so that he or she can talk briefly with the parent or guardian. Everyone leaves with a big smile.

When asked about calls to parents concerning student problems, Ms. Johnson explains, "Those I save for after school. Often, I have to think more carefully about what I'm going to say and what strategies I'm going to recommend. When I see a child doing something wonderful, however, I want to let the parents know about that right away. And I never have to weigh my words. Plus, I think it means more to the child."

The principal's phone calls have completely altered the culture of this school. Parent involvement and participation in school events is at an all-time high, and their regard for Ms. Johnson and the school staff is exceptionally positive. It's a small thing, but it has made a big difference.

SOURCE: From *Developing Grading and Reporting Systems for Student Learning*, by T. R. Guskey & J. M. Bailey. Copyright © 2001 by Corwin Press, Inc. Reprinted by permission of the publisher.

■ Table 15.7	Possible Grading Accommodations for Students with Special Needs

What can you do to make grading more appropriate for students with special needs? Here are some possibilities.

Adaptation	Example
Change Grading Criteria	
Vary grading weights assigned to different activities or products.	Increase credit for participation in classroom group activities and decrease credit for essay examinations.
Grade on improvement by assigning extra points.	Change a *C* to a *B* if the student's total points have increased significantly from the previous marking period.
Modify or individualize curriculum expectations.	Indicate in the IEP that the student will work on subtraction while the other students work on division.
Use contracts and modified course requirements for quality, quantity, and timelines.	State in the contract that student will receive a *B* for completing all assignments at 80% quantity, and timelines. accuracy, attending all classes, and completing one extra-credit report.
Provide Supplemental Information	
Add written comments to clarify details about the criteria used.	Write on the report card that the student's grade reflects performance on IEP objectives and not on the regular classroom curriculum.
Add information from student activity log.	Note that while the student's grade was the same this marking period, daily records show the student completed math assignments with less teacher assistance.
Add information about effort, progress, and achievement from portfolios or performance-based assignments.	State that the student's written language showed an increase in word variety, sentence length, and quality of ideas.
Use Other Grading Options	
Use checklists of skills and show the number or percentage of objectives met.	Attach a checklist to the report card indicating that during the marking period, the student mastered addition facts, two-digit addition with regrouping, and counting change to one dollar.
Use pass/fail grades.	Students receive a "pass" for completing 80% of daily work with at least 70% accuracy, and attending 90% of class sessions.

SOURCE: From T. R. Guskey & J. M. Bailey, *Developing Grading and Reporting Systems for Student Learning*, p. 118. Copyright © 2001. Reprinted by permission of Corwin Press, Inc.

ficult to avoid being affected by positive and negative halos. A very pleasant student who seems to work hard and causes little trouble may be given the benefit of the doubt (B– instead of C+), whereas a very difficult student who seems to refuse to try might be a loser at grading time (D instead of C–).

Diversity and Grading

In assigning and reporting grades, how do you make accommodations for students with special needs? Table 15.7 gives some options.

It may be up to you as the teacher to decide how to calculate the grades of students with special needs and students whose first language is not English, but be sure to check whether there are school or district policies already in place. Also, some schools now offer families a choice of the languages for the report card itself. The form is the same, just the language is different (Guskey & Bailey, 2001).

Check Yourself Describe two kinds of grading.

What is the point system?

Describe some alternatives to traditional grading.

What are some sources of bias in grading?

CONNECT & EXTEND

TO YOUR TEACHING/PORTFOLIO
Often, teachers tend to blame certain students for classroom disturbances even though they may not be guilty. Is this an example of the halo effect? Can you think of other examples?

CONNECT & EXTEND

TO THE RESEARCH
Munk, D. D., & Bursuck, W. D. (2001). Preliminary findings on personalized grading plans for middle school students with learning disabilities. *Exceptional Children, 67,* 211–234.

Beyond Grading: Communication

What Would You Say? During your interview for a job in a very diverse district, the department chair asks you, "How will you communicate with families about your homework and grading policies?"

No number or letter grade conveys the totality of a student's experience in a class or course. Both students and teachers sometimes become too focused on the end point—the grade. But children and adolescents spend the majority of their waking hours for many months of the year in school, where teachers are the relevant adults. This gives teachers the opportunity and the responsibility to know their students as people.

There are a number of ways to communicate with and report to families. Many teachers I know have a beginning-of-the-year newsletter or student handbook that communicates homework, behavior, and grading policies to families. Other options described by Guskey & Bailey (2001) are:

- Notes attached to report cards
- Phone calls, especially "Good News" calls
- School open houses
- Conferences, including student-led conferences
- Portfolios or exhibits of student work
- Homework Hotlines
- School or class Web Pages
- Home visits

Conferences with parents are often expected of teachers in elementary school and can be equally important in junior high and high school. Clearly, the more skilled teachers are at communicating, the more effective they will be at conducting these conferences. Listening and problem-solving skills such as those discussed in Chapter 11 can be particularly important. When you are dealing with parents or students who are angry or upset, make sure you really hear the concerns of the participants, not just their words. The atmosphere should be friendly and unrushed. Any observations about the student should be as factual as possible, based on observation or information from assignments. Information gained from a student or a parent should be kept confidential. The *Family and Community Partnerships Guidelines* offer some helpful ideas for planning and conducting conferences.

An important federal law, the Buckley Amendment, may affect you as a teacher. Also called the Family Educational Rights and Privacy Act of 1974 and the Educational Amendments Act of 1974, this law states that all educational agencies must make test results and any other information in students' records available to the students and/or their parents. If the records contain information students or parents believe is incorrect, they can challenge such entries and have the information removed if they win the challenge. This means that the information in a student's records must be based on firm, defensible evidence. Tests must be valid and reliable. Your grades must be justified by thorough assessment and observation. Comments and anecdotes about students must be accurate and fair.

Conferences with parents will be more successful if the teacher is able to use effective communication skills. Listening is an important element.

Check Yourself How can communication with families support learning?

Family and Community Partnerships

Conferences

Plan ahead.

Examples

What are your goals?

Problem solving?

Sharing test results?

Asking questions that you want answered?

Providing information you want to share? Emphasize the positive.

Describing your "next steps" in the classroom?

Making suggestions for use at home?

Begin with a positive statement.

Examples

"Howard has a great sense of humor."

"Giselle really enjoys materials that deal with animals."

"Sandy is sympathetic when somebody has a problem."

Listen actively.

Examples

Empathize with the parents.

Accept their feelings: "You seem to feel frustrated when Lee doesn't listen."

Establish a partnership.

Examples

Ask parents to follow through on class goals at home: "If you ask to see the homework checklist and go over it at home with Iris, I'll review it and chart her progress at school."

Plan follow-up contacts.

Examples

Write notes or make phone calls to share successes.

Keep parents informed *before* problems develop.

End with a positive statement.

Examples

"José has made several friends this year."

"Courtney should be a big help in the social studies play that her group is developing."

SOURCE: From *The Successful Classroom: Management Strategies for Regular and Special Education Teachers,* (p. 181) by D. P. Fromberg & M. Driscoll. Published by Teachers College, Columbia University. Reprinted by permission of the publisher.

Summary Table

Formative and Summative Assessment
(p. 548)

What are two kinds of classroom assessment? Most teachers must assess students and assign grades. Many schools have established policies about testing and grading practices, but individual teachers decide how these practices will be carried out. In the classroom, assessment may be formative (ungraded, diagnostic) or summative (graded). Formative assessment helps form instruction, and summative assessment summarizes students' accomplishments.

Formative Assessment: Ungraded testing used before or during instruction to aid in planning and diagnosis.

Pretest: Formative test for assessing students' knowledge, readiness, and abilities.

Diagnostic Test: Formative test to determine students' areas of weakness.

Summative Assessment: Testing that follows instruction and assesses achievement.

Getting the Most from Traditional Assessment Approaches
(pp. 548–553)

How should teachers plan for assessment? Assessment requires planning. Learning is supported by frequent testing using cumulative questions that ask students to apply and integrate knowledge. With the goals of assessment in mind, teachers are in a better position to design their own tests or evaluate the tests provided by textbook publishers.

Describe two kinds of traditional testing. Two traditional formats for testing are the objective test and the essay test. Objective tests, which can include multiple-choice, true/false, fill-in, and matching items, should be written with specific guidelines in mind. Writing and scoring essay questions requires careful planning, in addition to criteria to discourage bias in scoring. Essay tests are susceptible to biases such as grading essays higher when they are longer or written in elaborate prose.

Objective Testing: Multiple-choice, matching, true/false, short-answer, and fill-in tests; scoring answers does not require interpretation.

Stem: The question part of a multiple-choice item.

Distractors: Wrong answers offered as choices in a multiple-choice item.

Innovations in Assessment
(pp. 554–563)

What is authentic assessment? Critics of traditional testing believe that teachers should use authentic tests and other authentic assessment procedures. Authentic assessment requires students to perform tasks and solve problems that are similar to the real-life performances that will be expected of them outside of school.

Describe portfolios and exhibitions. Portfolios and exhibitions are two examples of authentic assessment. A portfolio is a collection of the student's work, sometimes chosen to represent growth or improvement or sometimes featuring "best work." Exhibitions are public performances of the student's understandings. With portfolios and exhibitions there is an emphasis on performing real-life tasks in meaningful contexts. Evaluating alternative assessments requires judgment and attention to validity, reliability, generalizability, and equity, just as with all assessment.

What are the issues of reliability, validity, and equity with portfolios and performance assessment? Using authentic assessments does not guarantee reliability, validity, and equity (absence of bias). In fact, without clear standards and training, raters can reach very different conclusions about portfolios and performances. Using rubrics is one way to make assessment more reliable and valid. But the results from assessment based on rubrics may not predict performance on related tasks. Also, rater bias based on the appearance, speech, or behavior of minority group students or a lack of resources may place minority group students at a disadvantage in performance assessments or projects.

What is learning potential assessment? An alternative goal of assessment is to reveal potential for learning and identify the psychological and educational interventions that will help the individual realize this potential. Procedures give graduated prompts as a child works to solve a problem—beginning with a general hint and ending with a detailed instruction for how to find the answer. The way the child uses the prompt and learns within the testing situation gives evidence of learning potential.

Authentic Assessments: Assessment procedures that test skills and abilities as they would be applied in real-life situations.

Portfolio: A collection of the student's work in an area, showing growth, self-reflection, and achievement.

Exhibition: A performance test or demonstration of learning that is public and usually takes an extended time to prepare.

Scoring Rubrics: Rules that are used to determine the quality of a student performance.

Enhancing Your Expertise with Technology
(pp. 563–564)

Edutopia Online **(http://www.glef.org)**

Effects of Grades and Grading on Students

(pp. 564–566)

How can failure support learning? Students need experience in coping with failure, so standards must be high enough to encourage effort. Occasional failure can be positive if appropriate feedback is provided. Students who never learn how to cope with failure and persist in learning may give up quickly when their first efforts are unsuccessful.

Which is better, social promotion or being "held back"? Simply retaining or promoting a student who is having difficulty will not guarantee that the student will learn. Unless the student is very young or emotionally immature compared to others in the class, the best approach may be to promote, but provide extra support such as tutoring or summer school sessions.

Can feedback, including grades, promote learning and motivation? Written or oral feedback that includes specific comments on errors or faulty strategies, but that balances this criticism with suggestions about how to improve, along with comments on the positive aspects of the work, increases learning. Grades can encourage students' motivation to learn if they are tied to meaningful learning.

Grading and Reporting: Nuts and Bolts

(pp. 566–573)

Describe two kinds of grading. Grading can be either criterion-referenced or norm-referenced. Criterion-referenced report cards usually indicate how well each of several objectives has been met by the individual student. One popular norm-referenced system is grading on the curve, based on a ranking of students in relation to the average performance level. This is not recommended.

What is the point system? Tests and papers are often scored on a point system. Many schools use percentage grading systems, but the difficulty of the tests and the scoring criteria often influence the results. The difference between a B and a C may only be a matter of one or two points on paper, but the effect of the difference can be large for a student.

Describe some alternatives to traditional grading. Alternatives to traditional grading are the contract and ILE. Whatever system you use, you will have to decide whether you want to grade on effort, improvement, or some combination and whether you want to limit the number of good grades available.

What are some sources of bias in grading? Many factors besides quality of work can influence grades: the teacher's beliefs about the student's ability or effort or the student's general classroom behavior, for example. There are many appropriate accommodations that teachers can make to insure that grading is fair.

Criterion-Referenced Grading: Assessment of each student's mastery of course objectives.

Norm-Referenced Grading: Assessment of students' achievement in relation to one another.

Grading on the Curve: Norm-referenced grading that compares students' performance to an average level.

Percentage Grading: System of converting class performances to percentage scores and assigning grades based on predetermined cutoff points.

Contract System: System in which each student works for a particular grade according to agreed-upon standards.

Revise Option: In a contract system, the chance to revise and improve work.

Individual Learning Expectation (ILE): Personal average score.

Halo Effect: The tendency for a general impression of a person to influence our perception of any aspect of that person.

Beyond Grading: Communication

(pp. 574–575)

How can communication with families support learning? Not every communication from the teacher needs to be tied to a grade. Communication with students and parents can be important in helping a teacher understand students and present effective instruction by creating a consistent learning environment. Students and parents have a legal right to see all the information in the students' records, so the contents of files must be appropriate, accurate, and supported by evidence.

Becoming a Professional

Passing the PRAXIS™

Chapter 15 reflects many of the professional standards created by the Interstate New Teacher Assessment and Support Consortium (INTASC). These standards form the basis of the PRAXIS II™ and state-created teacher licensure exams.

You are on the right course! A useful grading system possesses the qualities that you have identified: fairness, manageability, and supportive of learning. The system will be perceived as one that is based on merit, provides useful information about achievement, and serves to direct future learning. A system with these qualities is essential, for you will be making evaluations of your students' growth as learners. These evaluations serve as feedback to your students. This feedback may affect their future achievement, motivation to learn, self-esteem, and, possibly, opportunities beyond school.

In order to provide feedback that will affect those potential outcomes in the most advantageous ways, you must become familiar with the complexities of classroom assessment. And just as you have learned that there has been much research-based innovation when it comes to instruction, there has been much research-based innovation when it comes to classroom assessment that promises to add new understandings to what and how your students are learning.

Tips for PRAXIS II™

Understand major concepts related to classroom assessment and grading:

- Formative and summative assessment
- Reliability and validity
- Criterion-referenced and norm-referenced grading

Describe the characteristics, uses, and limitations of major assessment techniques, including:

- Multiple-choice items
- Essays
- Portfolios
- Exhibitions

Design a scoring rubric for an authentic learning task that possesses:

- Validity
- Reliablity
- Generalizability
- Equity

Standards and Licensure Appendix: *PRAXIS II™ and INTASC*

Refer to the Appendix at the end of the book for detailed correlations to PRAXIS II™ exam topics and INTASC Standards addressed in this text.

Insights about Interview Questions: *What Would You Say?*

1. What do you know about using portfolios, performances, projects, and rubrics to assess learning?
2. How will you communicate with families about your homework and grading policies?

Your Teaching Portfolio: *Teaching Resources*

- Think about your philosophy of teaching. What do you believe about testing and grading? How will you assign grades? (Consult the *Guidelines* for ideas.)
- Develop a grading plan for the grade level you want to teach and add it to your **Portfolio.**
- Add some ideas for parent involvement from this chapter to your **Portfolio.**
- Adapt the *Guidelines* for developing rubrics for the age group you plan to teach.
- Add Table 15.1, "Key Points to Consider in Judging Textbook Tests," Table 15.3, "Characteristics of Authentic Tests," and Table 15.7, "Possible Grading Accommodations for Students with Special Needs" to your **Teaching Resources** file.

Use the CD-ROM included in the back of your textbook to launch the "Becoming a Professional" website. The website features advice on preparing for teacher certification exams, help with getting your first job, and resources to help you perform your job well from the first day forward.

Teachers' Casebook

What Would They Do?

Here is how some practicing teachers responded to the teaching situation presented at the beginning of this chapter about setting up a system to give letter grades.

Katie Churchill

Third Grade Teacher, *Oriole Parke Elementary School, Chicago, Illinois*

I would use a combination of assessment tools to evaluate my students. Using a rubric that students and parents alike are familiar with provides an easy-to-follow and understand grading system. The rubric needs to remain in a focal area in the classroom as a constant reminder to the students of what their expectations are.

By differentiating instruction consistently to cover all learning styles and modalities, the students would hopefully become more involved and invested in their own learning and, as a result, produce better quality work and exceed expectations.

Several factors would play a part in obtaining a particular letter grade. The letter grade would be earned through a combination of group work, completing objectives, and following the rubric quidelines for quality work.

Madya Ayala

High School Teacher of Preperatoria Eugenio Garza Lagüera, *Campus Garza Sada, Monterrey, N.L. Mexico*

I think it is important to assess a cross-section of student work. First, portfolios can be a useful way to gather various types of work throughout the year. Using a portfolio, a teacher can then attach a letter grade to student progress and achievement. It is important to grade children not only on progress, but also on their understanding of material. I would use meaningful, written assessments to test for retention and understanding of my students' knowledge. Finally, I would grade various projects and experiments so that the students who are better project-based learners will be graded fairly. I also like the idea of using a rubric system to grade students on writing or projects. Under a rubric system, a teacher allocates a certain number of points to each content area. It is then easy to attach a letter grade based on the number of points received.

Katie Piel

Kindergarten–Sixth Grade Teacher, *West Park School, Moscow, Idaho*

Students should be given the latitude to express achievement in different ways like group projects, daily class work, tests, and individual projects. All students would be held accountable for demonstrating their own learning. With each teacher grading on a different standard, the teachers must also take on the responsibility of collaborating with their peers. Communicating to other teachers the skills a student can be expected to bring with him or her to the next level is crucial.

Aimee Fredette

Second Grade Teacher, *Fisher Elementary School, Walpole, Massachusetts*

I believe that students are not all smart in the same ways. I give the students a variety of ways to demonstrate their knowledge. I also focus on the students' ability to take their knowledge and integrate it into other subject areas across the curriculum.

I use a student portfolio for each child, compiled throughout the year and used to show growth and development. Each time I correct papers I choose a couple of pieces of work that each child has done. I put these papers in the portfolio folder. I try to choose a variety of work, not necessarily their "prize work." At the end of the year the children receive the entire folder to keep.

Allan Osborne

Assistant Principal, *Snug Harbor Community School, Quincy, Massachusetts*

Any grading system should consider a student's progress and effort. Grading systems also should be individualized to account for a student's unique strengths and weaknesses. Thus, a mainstreamed special education student should not be held to the same expectations as a gifted student.

The most critical aspect of any successful grading system is that it is fair. Fairness dictates that students and their parents be given information in advance about class requirements and expectations, along with a description of grading criteria. A system that is fair can be easily justified. It is also important to keep accurate and detailed records of student progress. In addition to recording grades on tests, quizzes, and projects, anecdotal records describing a student's typical performance should be kept. These records can be valuable if a report card grade is questioned.

Although group assignments can be an important learning experience, I would be reluctant to place too much emphasis on a group project grade. As we all know, each member of the group does not participate equally, and thus, a group grade does not reflect the contribution of each individual member.

Go to the Companion Website (www.ablongman.com/woolfolk) for additional case studies including audio and video cases, and examples of student work.

Standards and Licensure: PRAXIS II™ and INTASC

James B. O'Kelly, Ed.D.

Rutgers University and Sayreville Public Schools

Each state in the country has its own set of licensure requirements that new teachers must meet in order to work in the classroom. An increasing number of states are basing their requirements on standards developed by INTASC (Interstate New Teacher Assessment and Support Consortium). These standards are based on ten principles of effective teaching that INTASC has identified as essential for optimal student learning. Many states assess new teachers' knowledge of those principles through the use of tests from the PRAXIS II™ series published by the Educational Testing Service. Within the PRAXIS II™ series are three *Principles of Learning and Teaching* (PLT) tests, one each for grades K–6, 5–9, and 7–12. Each PLT test assesses students' knowledge of educational psychology and its application in the classroom. (Also, INTASC is presently developing its own *Test for Teaching Knowledge.* INTASC reports that this test will focus on "child development, theories of teaching and learning, diagnostic skills, the role of student background in the learning process, and other foundational knowledge and skills essential to the profession of teaching.")

This Appendix is designed to help you study for your PLT test and meet the Knowledge standards for each of INTASC's ten principles of effective teaching. The left-hand column of the table lists the topics assessed in a PLT test. The right-hand column contains INTASC's Knowledge standards. In the center column, you will find the chapters, sections, and pages that correspond to the PLT tests and INTASC standards. The Woolfolk Website includes additional features to assist you with your efforts to meet licensure requirements, including a set of weblinks to sites that address the demands of the PLT test and INTASC standards.

I suggest that you carefully develop a plan to meet these requirements. A major step would be to familiarize yourself with the challenges of the PRAXIS II™ series, especially the PLT tests, and to understand the rationale and features of the INTASC standards. These Websites will help you to accomplish that goal:

- The PRAXIS™ Series: Professional Assessments for Beginning Teachers™ (www.ets.org/praxis)
- PRAXIS™ test requirements for specific states (www.ets.org/praxis/prxstate.html)
- Test at a Glance (Overviews of PLT tests prepared by ETS)
    - PLT: Grades K–6 (www.ets.org/praxis/taags/prx0522.html)
    - PLT: Grades 5–9 (www.ets.org/praxis/taags/prx0523.html)
    - PLT: Grades 7–12 (www.ets.org/praxis/taags/prx0524.html)
- INTASC Standards for New Teacher Licensure (www.ccsso.org/intascst.html)

Use the "Becoming a Professional" CD-ROM included in the back of your textbook to open the "Appendix Online" file, which inludes a set of weblinks correlated to the PRAXIS II™ exam.

PRAXIS™ Topics	Woolfolk Text Connections	INTASC Principles
I. Students as Learners	*Chapters 2, 6–9* (entire chapters)	
A. Student Development and the Learning Process		
1. Theoretical foundations about how learning occurs: how students construct knowledge, acquire skills, and develop habits of mind		2A. The teacher understands how learning occurs—how students construct knowledge, acquire skills, and develop habits of mind—and knows how to use instructional strategies that promote student learning.
■ Examples of important theorists:		
• Jean Piaget	*Chapter 2*/Piaget's Theory of Cognitive Development (pp. 30–40)	
• Lev Vygotsky	*Chapter 2*/Vygotsky's Sociocultural Perspective (pp. 44–50)	
• Howard Gardner	*Chapter 4*/Multiple Intelligences (pp. 108–111)	
• Robert Sternberg	*Chapter 4*/Intelligence as a Process (pp. 111–113)	
• Albert Bandura	*Chapter 9*/Social Learning and Social Cognitive Theories (pp. 315–322)	
■ Important terms that relate to learning theory:		
• Adaptation	*Chapter 2*/Basic Tendencies in Thinking (pp. 30–31)	
• Conservation	*Chapter 2*/Basic Tendencies in Thinking (pp. 30–31)	
• Constructivism	*Chapter 2*/Implications of Piaget's Theory for Teachers (pp. 40–44); Implications of Vygotsky's Theory for Teachers (pp. 50–53) *Chapter 9*/Constructivism and Situated Learning (pp. 322–328); Applications of Constructivist and Situated Learning (pp. 329–341)	
• Equilibration	*Chapter 2*/Basic Tendencies in Thinking (pp. 30–31)	
• Co-constructed process	*Chapter 2*/The Social Sources of Individual Thinking (pp. 45–46)	
• Private speech	*Chapter 2*/Basic Tendencies in Thinking (pp. 30–31)	
• Scaffolding	*Chapter 2*/Assisted Learning (p. 51); Guidelines: Applying Vygotsky' Ideas in Teaching (p. 53); *Reaching Every Student:* Scaffold Learning (p. 51) *Chapter 9*/Dialogue and Instructional Conversations (pp. 333–334); Cognitive Apprenticeships (pp. 334–336)	
• Zone of proximal development	*Chapter 2*/The Zone of Proximal Development (pp. 52–53) *Chapter 9*/Dialogue and Instructional Conversations (pp. 333–334)	

PRAXIS™ Topics	Woolfolk Text Connections	INTASC Principles
• Learning	*Chapter 6*/Understanding Learning (pp. 198–200) *Chapter 7*/Comparing Cognitive and Behavioral Views (pp. 236–237) *Chapter 9*/Constructivism and Situated Learning (pp. 322–325)	
• Knowledge	*Chapter 2*/The Social Sources of Individual Thinking (pp. 45–46); Activity and Constructing Knowledge (pp. 41–42) *Chapter 7*/The Importance of Knowledge in Learning (pp. 237–238); Becoming Knowledgeable: Some Basic Principles (pp. 260–266) *Chapter 9*/How Is Knowledge Constructed? (p. 325); Knowledge: Situated or General? (p. 326)	
• Memory	*Chapter 7*/Sensory Memory (pp. 240–242); Working Memory (pp. 242–246); Long-Term Memory (pp. 246–255)	
• Schemas	*Chapter 7*/Schemas (pp. 250–251)	
• Transfer	*Chapter 8*/Defining Transfer (p. 303); A Contemporary View of Transfer (p. 303)	
2. Human development in the physical, social, emotional, moral, and cognitive domains		2C. The teacher is aware of expected developmental progressions and ranges of individual variation within each domain (physical, social, emotional, moral, and cognitive), can identify levels of readiness in learning, and understands how development in any one domain may affect performance in others.
■ Contributions of important theorists:		
• Jean Piaget	*Chapter 2*/Piaget's Theory of Cognitive Development (pp. 28–40)	
• Lev Vygotsky	*Chapter 2*/Vygotsky's Sociocultural Perspective (pp. 44–50)	
• Erik Erikson	*Chapter 3*/The Work of Erikson (pp. 66–70)	
• Lawrence Kohlberg	*Chapter 3*/Kohlberg's Stages of Moral Development (pp. 80–82)	
• Carol Gilligan	*Chapter 3*/Diversity in Reasoning: The Morality of Caring (pp. 82–83)	
■ Major progressions in each developmental domain and the ranges of individual variation within each domain	*Chapter 2*/Four Stages of Cognitive Development (pp. 31–40); Some Limitations of Piaget's Theory (pp. 42–44); Cognitive Development and Information Processing (p. 43); The Social Sources of Individual Thinking (pp. 45–46); The Development of Language (pp. 53–56) *Chapter 3*/The Preschool Years: Trust, Autonomy, and Initiative (p. 67); Elementary and Middle School Years (p. 67); Adolescence: The Search for Identity (pp. 67–69) Kohlberg's Stages of Moral Development (pp. 80–82)	2B. The teacher understands that students' physical, social, emotional, moral and cognitive development influence learning and knows how to address these factors when making instructional decisions.

PRAXIS™ Topics	Woolfolk Text Connections	INTASC Principles
■ Impact of students' physical, social, emotional, moral, and cognitive development on their learning and how to address these factors when making decisions	*Chapter 2*/Four Stages of Cognitive Development (p. 31); Some Limitations of Piaget's Theory (pp. 42–43); *Guidelines:* Teaching the Preoperational Child (p. 35); *Guidelines:* Teaching the Concrete-Operational Child (p. 37); *Guidelines:* Helping Students to Use Formal Operations (p. 40); The Social Sources of Individual Thinking (pp. 45–46); The Development of Language (pp. 53–56); Assisted Learning (p. 51); The Zone of Proximal Development (pp. 52–53); *Enhancing Your Expertise with Technology:* Emotional and Social Development (p. 57) *Chapter 3*/The Preschool Years: Trust, Autonomy, and Initiative (p. 67); Elementary and Middle School Years (p. 67); Adolescence: The Search for Identity (pp. 67–69); Kohlberg's Stages of Moral Development (pp. 80–82); Self-Concept and Self-Esteem (pp. 70–73); School Life and Self-Esteem (pp. 73–75); Gender, Ethnicity, and Self-Esteem (pp. 75–78) *Chapter 11*/Effective Managers for Elementary Students (p. 407); Effective Managers for Secondary Students (p. 407); Special Problems with Secondary Students (pp. 412–414)	
■ How development in one domain, such as physical, may affect performance in another domain, such as social	*Chapter 2*/General Principles of Development (p. 24); The Brain and Cognitive Development (pp. 24–28); Influences on Development (p. 30) *Chapter 3*/*Guidelines:* Supporting Personal and Social Development (p. 91); Navigating Transitions (pp. 91–93)	
B. Students as Diverse Learners 1. Differences in the ways students learn and perform	*Chapter 4*/Learner Differences and Learner Needs (entire chapter) *Chapter 5*/Culture and Community (entire chapter)	3A. The teacher understands and can identify differences in approaches to learning and performance, including different learning styles, multiple intelligences, and performance modes, and can design instruction that helps use students' strengths as the basis for growth.
■ Learning styles	*Chapter 4*/Cognitive and Learning Styles (pp. 118–121) *Chapter 5*/Learning Styles (pp. 182–183)	
■ Multiple intelligences	*Chapter 4*/Multiple Intelligences (pp. 108–111) *Chapter 5*/Learning Styles (pp. 182–183)	

PRAXIS™ Topics	Woolfolk Text Connections	INTASC Principles
■ Performance modes		
• Concrete operational thinking	*Chapter 2*/Late Elementary to the Middle School Years: The Concrete-Operational Stage (pp. 34–37); *Guidelines:* Teaching the Concrete-Operational Child (p. 37) *Chapter 5*/Learning Styles (pp. 182–183)	
• Visual and aural learners	*Chapter 4*/Students with Learning Disabilities (pp. 124–126) *Chapter 5*/Learning Styles (pp. 182–183) *Chapter 7*/*Reaching Every Student:* A Picture and a Few Hundred Words (p. 248)	
■ Gender differences	*Chapter 3*/Gender, Ethnicity, and Self-Esteem (pp. 75–78); Diversity in Reasoning: The Morality of Caring (pp. 82–83) *Chapter 5*/Females and Males: Differences in the Classroom; *Guidelines:* Avoiding Sexism in Teaching (p. 174)	
■ Cultural expectations and styles	*Chapter 5*/Today's Multicultural Classroom (pp. 154–157); Ethnic and Racial Differences (pp. 161–169); *Guidelines:* Culturally Relevant Teaching (p. 188) *Chapter 12*/Teacher Expectations (pp. 453–456)	
2. Areas of exceptionality in students' learning	*Chapter 4*/Learner Differences and Learner Needs (entire chapter)	3B. The teacher knows about areas of exceptionality in learning—including learning disabilities, visual and perceptual difficulties, and special physical or mental challenges.
■ Special physical or sensory challenges	*Chapter 4*/Students with Communication Disorders (p. 126–128); Students with Health Impairments (pp. 133–134); Students Who Are Deaf and Hard of Hearing (pp. 134–135); Students with Low Vision and Blindness (pp. 135–136)	
■ Learning disabilities	*Chapter 4*/Students with Learning Disabilities (pp. 124–126); Individual Education Programs (pp. 122–123); Section 504 Protections for Students (pp. 136–137)	
■ ADHD	*Chapter 4*/Students with Hyperactivity and Attention Disorders (pp. 137–138); Treating and Teaching Students with ADHD (pp. 138–140)	
■ Functional and mental retardation	*Chapter 4*/Students with Mental Retardation (pp. 128–131); *Guidelines:* Teaching Students with Mild Retardation (p. 130)	

PRAXIS™ Topics	Woolfolk Text Connections	INTASC Principles
3. Legislation and institutional responsibilities relating to exceptional students		
■ Americans with Disabilities Act (ADA), Individuals with Disabilities Education Act (IDEA); Section 504 Protections for Students	*Chapter 4*/Changes in the Law: Integration and Inclusion (pp. 121–124); Section 504 Protections for Students (pp. 136–140)	10C. The teacher understands and implements laws related to students' rights and teacher responsibilities (e.g., for equal education, appropriate education for handicapped students, confidentiality, privacy, appropriate treatment of students, reporting in situations related to possible child abuse).
■ Inclusion, mainstreaming, and "least restrictive environment"	*Chapter 4*/Changes in the Law: Integration and Inclusion (pp. 121–124) *Chapter 12*/Effective Teaching in Inclusive Classrooms (pp. 465–469)	
4. Approaches for accommodating various learning styles, intelligences, or exceptionalities		
■ Differentiated instruction	*Chapter 4*/Learner Differences and Learner Needs (entire chapter); focus on: Multiple Intelligences Goes to School (pp. 110–111); Ability Differences and Teaching (pp. 115–118); Teaching Students Who Are Gifted and Talented (pp. 140–145); Changes in the Law: Integration and Inclusion (pp. 121–124); Prevalent Problems and Mild Disabilities (pp. 124–132); Students with Mental Retardation (pp. 128–131) *Chapter 5*/Learning Styles (pp. 182–183) *Chapter 12*/Effective Teaching in the Inclusive Classroom (pp. 465–469); *Reaching Every Student:* Resource Rooms, Collaboration, Consultation, and Cooperative Teaching (p. 467)	3A. The teacher understands and can identify differences in approaches to learning and performance, including different learning styles, multiple intelligences, and performance modes, and can design instruction that uses students' strengths as the basis for growth.
■ Alternative assessment	*Chapter 15*/Assessing Learning Potential: Dynamic Assessment (p. 562); Authentic Assessment (p. 555); Authentic Classroom Tests (p. 555); Performance in Context: Portfolios and Exhibition (pp. 555–558); *Guidelines:* Creating Portfolios (p. 559); Scoring Rubrics (pp. 559–560); *Guidelines:* Developing a Rubric (p. 561)	
■ Testing modifications	*Chapter 14*/Reaching Every Student: Accommodations in Testing (p. 540)	
5. Process of second language acquisition and strategies to support the learning of students	*Chapter 5*/Dialects (pp. 174–176); Bilingualism (pp. 176–181); *Guidelines:* Dialects in the Classroom (p. 177)	3C. The teacher knows about the process of second language acquisition and about strategies to support the learning of students whose first language is not English.

PRAXIS™ Topics	Woolfolk Text Connections	INTASC Principles
6. Understanding of influences of individual experiences, talents, and prior learning, as well as language, culture, family, and community values on students' learning		
■ Multicultural backgrounds	*Chapter 5*/American Cultural Diversity (pp. 156–157); Ethnic and Racial Differences (pp. 161–169); The Changing Demographics: Cultural Differences (pp. 161–163); *Enhancing Your Expertise with Technology:* Teaching Every Student (p. 189)	3D. The teacher understands how students' learning is influenced by individual experiences, talents, and prior learning, as well as language, culture, family and community values. 3E. The teacher has a well-grounded framework for understanding cultural and community diversity and knows how to learn about and incorporate students' experiences, cultures, and community resources into instruction.
■ Age-appropriate knowledge and behaviors	*Chapter 2*/Four Stages of Cognitive Development (pp. 31–40); Implications of Piaget's Theory for Teachers (pp. 40–44); Vygotsky's Sociocultural Perspective (pp. 44–50); Implications of Vygotsky's Theory for Teachers (pp. 50–53); Language Development in the School Years (pp. 54–56); *Enhancing Your Expertise with Technology:* Language and Literacy Development (p. 57) *Chapter 3*/entire chapter—focus on: The Preschool Years: Trust, Autonomy, and Initiative (p. 67); Elementary and Middle School Years: Industry versus Inferiority (p. 67); Adolescence: The Search for Identity (pp. 67–69); Moral Development (pp. 80–87); Navigating Transitions (pp. 91–93)	
■ The student culture at the school	*Chapter 3*/Peer Relationships and Peer Cultures (pp. 88–90) *Chapter 5*/Peer Influences and Resistance Cultures (p. 159) *Chapter 10*/Learned Helplessness (pp. 371–372)	6A. The teacher understands communication theory, language development, and the role of language in learning.
■ Family backgrounds	*Chapter 3*/American Families Today (p. 88)	
■ Linguistic patterns and differences	*Chapter 2*/The Development of Language (pp. 53–57) *Chapter 4*/Students with Communication Disorders (pp. 126–128) *Chapter 5*/Dialects (pp. 174–176); Bilingualism (pp. 176–181); Childrearing Styles (p. 160)	

PRAXIS™ Topics	Woolfolk Text Connections	INTASC Principles
■ Cognitive patterns and differences	*Chapter 4*/Cognitive and Learning Styles (pp. 118–121); Learning Styles and Preferences (pp. 120–121) *Chapter 7*/Individual Differences and Working Memory (pp. 258–259); Long-Term Memory (pp. 259–260)	
■ Social and emotional issues	*Chapter 3*/Taking the Perspective of Others (p. 78); Moral Behavior (pp. 83–87) *Chapter 4*/Students with Emotional and Behavioral Disorders (pp. 131–132) *Chapter 13*/Emotional Intelligence (pp. 486–488)	
C. Student Motivation and the Learning Environment		5A. The teacher can use knowledge about human motivation and behavior drawn from the foundational sciences of psychology, anthropology, and sociology to develop strategies for organizing and supporting individual and group work.
1. Theoretical foundations about human motivation and behavior	*Chapter 10*/Behavioral Approaches to Motivation (pp. 352–353); Humanistic Approaches to Motivation (p. 353); Cognitive Approaches to Motivation (pp. 354–356); Sociocultural Conceptions of Motivation (pp. 356–358)	
■ Important terms that relate to motivation and behavior	*Chapter 6*/Operant Conditioning: Trying New Responses (pp. 202–208); Reinforcement (pp. 204–205); Punishment (p. 205); Reinforcement Schedules (pp. 205–207) *Chapter 10*/Motivation in Learning and Teaching (entire chapter): *Reaching Every Student:* Bounded Choice (p. 379); *Enhancing Your Expertise with Technology:* Motivation to Learn (pp. 386–387) *Chapter 10*/On TARGET for Learning (pp. 375–378); *Family and Community Partnerships:* Motivation to Learn (p. 387) *Chapter 12*/Teacher Expectations (pp. 453–457)	
2. How knowledge of human emotion and behavior should influence strategies for organizing and supporting individual and group work in the classroom	*Chapter 10*/Arousal: Excitement and Anxiety in Learning (pp. 364–366); On TARGET for Learning (pp. 375–378); Bringing It All Together: Strategies to Encourage Motivation and Thoughtful Learning (pp. 383–386); *Guidelines:* Coping with Anxiety (p. 367); *Guidelines:* Supporting Self-Determination and Autonomy (p. 372) *Chapter 12*/Teacher Expectations (pp. 453–457)	5A. The teacher can use knowledge about human motivation and behavior drawn from the foundational sciences of psychology, anthropology, and sociology to develop strategies for organizing and supporting individual and group work.

PRAXIS™ Topics	Woolfolk Text Connections	INTASC Principles
3. Factors and situations that are likely to promote or diminish students' motivation to learn, and how to help students to become self-motivated		5E. The teacher recognizes factors and situations that are likely to promote or diminish intrinsic motivation and knows how to help students become self-motivated.
4. Principles of effective management and strategies to promote positive relationships, cooperation, and purposeful learning		5D. The teacher understands the principles of effective classroom management and can use a range of strategies to promote positive relationships, cooperation, and purposeful learning in the classroom.
■ Establishing daily procedures and routines ■ Establishing classroom rules, punishments, and rewards	*Chapter 6*/Methods for Encouraging Behavior (pp. 209–213); *Guidelines*: Encouraging Positive Behavior (p. 213); Coping with Undesirable Behavior (pp. 213–216); *Reaching Every Student:* Students with Learning and Behavior Problems (p. 218) *Chapter 11*/Rules and Procedures Required (pp. 400–404); *Guidelines:* Establishing Class Procedures (p. 401); Prevention is the Best Medicine (pp. 408–410); *Enhancing Your Expertise with Technology:* Classroom Management (p. 414); *Reaching Every Student:* Culturally Responsive Management (p. 423) *Chapter 12*/Teacher Expectations (pp. 453–457)	
■ Giving timely feedback	*Chapter 6*/*Guidelines:* Using Praise Appropriately (p. 210) *Chapter 11*/The Need for Communication (pp. 415–421) *Chapter 12*/Responding to Student Answers (pp. 450–451) *Chapter 15*/Effects of Feedback (pp. 565–566)	
■ Maintaining accurate records	*Chapter 15*/Portfolios (pp. 556–558); *Guidelines:* Creating Portfolios (p. 559); Evaluating Portfolios and Performances (pp. 559–562); Grading and Reporting: Nuts and Bolts (pp. 566–573)	
■ Communicating with parents and caregivers	*Chapters 2–15*/Family and Community Partnerships (one per chapter)	
■ Using objective behavior descriptions	*Chapter 6*/Applied Behavior Analysis (pp. 209–216)	
■ Responding to student misbehavior	*Chapter 6*/Coping with Undesirable Behavior (pp. 213–216); *Guidelines:* Using Punishment (p. 216); Group Consequences (pp. 217–218) *Chapter 11*/Dealing with Discipline Problems (pp. 410–412); Special Problems with Secondary Students (pp. 412–414); *Guidelines:* Imposing Penalties (p. 411); Counseling: The Students' Problem (pp. 417–418); Confrontation and Assertive Discipline (pp. 418–419); Student Conflict and Confrontation (pp. 420–421)	

PRAXIS™ Topics	Woolfolk Text Connections	INTASC Principles
■ Arranging classroom space	*Chapter 11*/Planning Spaces for Learning (pp. 404–406); *Guidelines:* Designing Learning Spaces (p. 406)	
■ Pacing and the structure of the lesson	*Chapter 11*/Encouraging Engagement (p. 408); *Guidelines:* Keeping Students Engaged (p. 409); Withitness (p. 409); Overlapping and Group Focus (pp. 409–410); Movement Management (p. 410) *Chapter 12*/Clarity and Organization (pp. 440–441); *Guidelines:* Teaching Effectively (p. 442)	
II. Instruction and Assessment		
A. Instructional Strategies		
1. Major cognitive processes associated with student learning		
■ Critical thinking	*Chapter 9*/Critical Thinking (p. 338)	
■ Creative thinking	*Chapter 1*/Reaching Every Student: Creativity in an Urban School (p. 9) *Chapter 13*/Creativity (pp. 482–486); *Guidelines:* Encouraging Creativity (p. 485)	4A. The teacher understands the cognitive processes associated with various kinds of learning (e.g., critical and creative thinking, problem structuring and problem solving, invention, memorization and recall) and how these processes can be stimulated.
■ Inductive and deductive thinking	*Chapter 8*/Structure and Discovery (pp. 280–281)	
■ Problem structuring and problem solving	*Chapter 8*/Structure and Discovery (pp. 280–281); Translation and Schema Training (pp. 286–287); *Guidelines:* Problem Solving (p. 294)	
■ Invention	*Chapter 13*/Creativity (pp. 482–486)	
■ Memorization and recall	*Chapter 7*/Cognitive Views of Learning (focus on sections related to memory); *Enhancing Your Expertise with Technology:* Memory Techniques (p. 267)	
2. Major categories, advantages, and appropriate uses of instructional strategies		4B. The teacher understands principles and techniques, along with advantages and limitations, associated with various instructional strategies (e.g., cooperative learning, direct instruction, discovery learning, whole-group discussion, independent study, interdisciplinary instruction).
■ Cooperative learning	*Chapter 13*/Group Work and Cooperation in Learning (pp. 492–494); Making Cooperative Learning Work (pp. 494–496); Strategies for Cooperation (pp. 496–500); *Guidelines:* Using Cooperative Learning (p. 500); *Enhancing Your Expertise with Technology:* Cooperative Learning (p. 501)	

PRAXIS™ Topics	Woolfolk Text Connections	INTASC Principles
■ Direct instruction (often referred to as *teacher-centered instruction*)	*Chapter 12*/Explanation and Direct Instruction (pp. 441–445), focus on: Why Does Direct Instruction Work? (pp. 443–444); Criticisms of Direct Instruction (pp. 444–445)	1B. The teacher understands how students' conceptual frameworks and their misconceptions for an area of knowledge can influence their learning.
■ Discovery learning	*Chapter 8*/Teaching Concepts through Discovery (pp. 280–281); *Guidelines:* Applying Bruner's Ideas (p. 281) *Chapter 9*/Inquiry and Problem-Based Learning (pp. 329–332)	
■ Whole-group discussion	*Chapter 12*/Group Discussion (p. 451); *Guidelines:* Productive Group Discussions (p. 452)	
■ Independent study	*Chapter 8*/Learning Strategies and Tactics (pp. 296–298); *Guidelines:* Becoming an Expert Student (p. 301) *Chapter 13*/Self-Regulation and Agency (pp. 478–481)	
■ Interdisciplinary instruction (sometimes referred to as *thematic instruction*)	*Chapter 9*/Problem-Based Learning (pp. 331–332) *Chapter 12*/Integrated and Thematic Planning (p. 439)	
■ Questioning	*Chapter 12*/Kinds of Questions (pp. 448–449); Questioning and Recitation (pp. 447–451); *Enhancing Your Expertise with Technology:* Questioning Techniques (pp. 452–453) *Chapter 13*/Reciprocal Questioning (pp. 497–499)	
3. Principles, techniques, and methods associated with major instructional strategies		4B. The teacher understands principles and techniques, along with advantages and limitations, associated with various instructional strategies (e.g., cooperative learning, direct instruction, discovery learning, whole-group discussion, independent study, interdisciplinary instruction).
■ Direct instruction (*often referred to as teacher-centered instruction*)	*Chapter 6*/Mastery Learning (p. 217) *Chapter 8*/Teaching Concepts through Exposition (pp. 281–283); *Guidelines:* Applying Ausubel's Ideas (p. 283) *Chapter 12*/Explanation and Direct Instruction (pp. 441–445); Questioning and Recitation (pp. 447–451); Group Discussions (p. 451); Rosenshine's Six Teaching Functions (p. 443)	
■ Student-centered models	*Chapter 8*/Teaching Concepts through Discovery (pp. 280–281); *Guidelines:* Applying Bruner's Ideas (p. 281) *Chapter 9*/Common Elements of Constructivist Perspectives (pp. 327–328); Inquiry and Problem-Based Learning (pp. 329–332); Cognitive Apprenticeships (pp. 334–336)	

PRAXIS™ Topics	Woolfolk Text Connections	INTASC Principles
4. Methods for enhancing student learning through the use of a variety of resources and materials		
■ Computers, Internet resources, Web pages, email ■ Audiovisual technologies such as videotapes and compact discs ■ Local experts ■ Primary documents ■ Field trips ■ Libraries ■ Service learning	*Chapter 3*/*Reaching Every Student:* Safety on the Internet (p. 95) *Chapter 5*/*Reaching Every Student:* Access to Technology (p. 178) *Chapter 12*/Technology and Exceptional Students (pp. 468–469) *Chapter 13*/Service Learning (p. 506)	4C. The teacher knows how to enhance learning through the use of a wide variety of materials as well as human and technological resources (e.g., computers, audio-visual technologies, videotapes and discs, local experts, primary documents and artifacts, texts, reference books, literature, and other print resources).
B. Planning Instruction		
1. Techniques for planning instruction to meet curriculum goals, including the incorporation of learning theory, subject matter, curriculum development, and student development		7A. The teacher understands learning theory, subject matter, curriculum development, and student development and knows how to use this knowledge in planning instruction to meet curriculum goals.
■ National and state learning standards ■ State and local curriculum frameworks ■ State and local curriculum guides ■ Scope and sequence in specific disciplines ■ Units and lessons ■ Behavioral objectives: affective, cognitive, and psychomotor ■ Learner objectives and outcomes	*Chapter 12*/The First Step: Planning (pp. 432–439); Another View: Planning from a Constructivist Perspective (pp. 437–439); focus on: An Example of Constructivist Planning (pp. 438–439); Integrated and Thematic Plans (p. 439) *Chapter 12*/Objectives for Learning (pp. 433–437); The Cognitive Domain (p. 435); Bloom 2001 (pp. 435–436); The Affective Domain (p. 436); The Psychomotor Domain (pp. 436–437); *Guidelines:* Using Instructional Objectives (p. 437)	7B. The teacher knows how to take contextual considerations (instructional materials, individual student interests, needs, and aptitudes, and community resources) into account in planning instruction that creates an effective bridge between curriculum goals and students' experiences.
2. Techniques for creating effective bridges between curriculum goals and students' experiences		
■ Modeling	*Chapter 9*/Learning by Observing Others (pp. 317–319), focus on: Factors That Influence Observational Learning (pp. 318–319), focus on: Teaching New Behaviors (p. 320); *Guidelines:* Using Observational Learning (p. 321)	
■ Guided practice	*Chapter 2*/Assisted Learning (p. 51) *Chapter 6*/Cognitive Behavior Modification and Self-Instruction (pp. 223–225) *Chapter 9*/Cognitive Apprenticeships (pp. 331–334) *Chapter 12*/Rosenshine's Six Teaching Functions (p. 443)	

PRAXIS™ Topics	Woolfolk Text Connections	INTASC Principles
■ Independent practice, including homework	*Chapter 12*/Seatwork and Homework (pp. 445–447) *Chapter 13*/Self-Regulation and Agency (pp. 478–481); *Family and Community Partnerships:* Parents Supporting Self-Regulation (p. 479)	
■ Transitions	*Chapter 11*/Overlapping and Group Focus (pp. 409–410); Movement Management (p. 410); *Guidelines:* Keeping Students Engaged (p. 409)	
■ Activating students' prior knowledge	*Chapter 7*/The Importance of Knowledge in Learning (pp. 237–238); Capacity and Duration and Contents of Long-Term Memory (pp. 246–247) *Chapter 8*/Advance Organizers (p. 282); The Results of Problem Representation, focus on: schema-driven problem solving (pp. 285–287)	
■ Anticipating preconceptions	*Chapter 8*/Views of Concept Learning (pp. 276–277); Strategies for Teaching Concepts (pp. 276–277), focus on: Undergeneralization and Overgeneralization; Factors That Hinder Problem Solving (pp. 277–280)	
■ Encouraging exploration and problem solving	*Chapter 2*/Implications of Piaget's Theory for Teachers (pp. 40–44) *Chapter 8*/Problem Solving (pp. 283–295); *Enhancing Your Expertise with Technology:* Problem Solving (p. 295) *Chapter 13*/Self-Regulation and Agency (pp. 478–481); Creativity and Cognition (p. 483); Creativity in the Classroom (pp. 484–486)	
■ Building new skills on those previously acquired	*Chapter 2*/Basic Tendencies in Thinking (pp. 30–31) *Chapter 4*/Students with Mental Retardation (pp. 128–131); *Guidelines:* Teaching Students with Mild Retardation (p. 130) *Chapter 6*/Mastery Learning (p. 217) *Chapter 7*/The Importance of Knowledge in Learning (pp. 237–238); Capacity and Duration and Contents of Long-Term Memory (pp. 246–247); *Guidelines:* Using Information Processing Ideas in the Classroom (p. 256); Development of Declarative Knowledge (pp. 260–263); Becoming an Expert: Procedural and Conditional Knowledge (pp. 264–266) *Chapter 9*/Observational Learning in Teaching (pp. 319–320)	

PRAXIS™ Topics	Woolfolk Text Connections	INTASC Principles
C. Assessment Strategies		8A. The teacher understands the characteristics, uses, advantages, and limitations of different types of assessments (e.g., criterion-referenced and norm-referenced instruments, traditional standardized and performance-based tests, observation systems, and assessments of student work) for evaluating how students learn, what they know and are able to do, and what kinds of experiences will support their further growth and development.
1. Types of assessments	*Chapter 14*/Norm-Referenced Tests (pp. 514–515); Criterion-Referenced Tests (pp. 515–516); Achievement Tests: What Has the Student Learned? (pp. 526–529); Diagnostic Tests: What Are the Student's Strengths and Weaknesses? (p. 529); Aptitude Tests: How Well Will the Students Do in the Future? (p. 530); Authentic Assessment (pp. 538–539) *Chapter 15*/Formative and Summative Assessment (p. 548); Objective Testing (pp. 550–551); Essay Tests (pp. 552–553); Performance in Context: Portfolios and Exhibitions (pp. 555–559); Assessing Learning Potential: Dynamic Assessment (p. 562); *Enhancing Your Expertise with Technology:* Assessment (p. 563)	
2. Characteristics of assessments	*Chapter 14*/Reliability (p. 522); Validity (pp. 523–524); *Guidelines:* Increasing Reliability and Variability (p. 524) *Chapter 15*/Writing Multiple-Choice Questions (p. 550); *Guidelines:* Writing Objective Test Items (p. 551); Constructing Essays (p. 552); Reliability, Variability, Generalizability, (pp. 560–562); *Guidelines:* Developing a Rubric (p. 561)	8B. The teacher knows how to select, construct, and use assessment strategies and instruments appropriate to the learning outcomes being evaluated and to other diagnostic purposes.
3. Scoring assessments	*Chapter 15*/Using Multiple-Choice Tests (p. 550); Evaluating Essays: Dangers (p. 552); Evaluating Essays: Methods (pp. 552–553); Evaluating Portfolios and Performances (pp. 559–562); *Guidelines:* Developing a Rubric (p. 561)	
4. Uses of assessments	*Chapter 14*/Norm-Referenced Tests (pp. 514–515); Criterion-Referenced Tests (pp. 515–516); Using Information from a Norm-Referenced Achievement Test (pp. 528–529); Interpreting Test Scores (pp. 522–525); IQ and Scholastic Aptitude (p. 530); Accountability and High Stakes (pp. 532–534); The Uses of Testing in American Society (p. 536) *Chapter 15*/Formative and Summative Assessment (p. 548); Getting the Most from Traditional Assessment Approaches (pp. 548–553); Innovations in Assessment (pp. 554–564)	

PRAXIS™ Topics	Woolfolk Text Connections	INTASC Principles
5. Understanding of measurement theory and assessment-related issues	*Chapter 14*/Norm-Referenced Tests (pp. 514–515); Criterion-Referenced Tests (pp. 515–516); What Do Test Scores Mean? (pp. 516–524); New Directions in Standardized Testing (pp. 538–541); *Enhancing Your Expertise with Technology:* Standardized Testing (p. 538)	8C. The teacher understands measurement theory and assessment-related issues, such as validity, reliability, bias, and scoring concerns.
III. Communication Techniques		
A. Basic, effective verbal and nonverbal communication techniques	*Chapter 10*/Can I Do It? Building Confidence and Positive Expectations (p. 384) *Chapter 12*/Teacher Expectations (pp. 453–457) *Chapter 11*/The Need for Communication (pp. 415–421) *Chapter 15*/*Reaching Every Student:* Using Technology to Recognize Improvement (p. 572)	6C. The teacher recognizes the importance of nonverbal as well as verbal communication. 6D. The teacher knows about and can use effective verbal, nonverbal, and media communication techniques.
B. Effect of cultural and gender differences on communications in the classroom	*Chapter 5*/Language Differences in the Classroom (pp. 174–181); Sociolinguistics (pp. 183–184)	6B. The teacher understands how cultural and gender differences can affect communication in the classroom.
C. Types of questions that can stimulate discussion in different ways for different purposes	*Chapter 9*/Dialogue and Instructional Conversations (pp. 333–334) *Chapter 12*/Questioning and Recitation (pp. 447–451)	6D. The teacher knows about and can use effective verbal, nonverbal, and media communication techniques.
■ Probing for learner understanding	*Chapter 9*/Dialogue and Instructional Conversations (pp. 333–334) *Chapter 12*/Questioning and Recitation (pp. 447–451)	
■ Helping students articulate their ideas and thinking processes	*Chapter 9*/Dialogue and Instructional Conversations (pp. 333–334); *Enhancing Your Expertise with Technology:* Thinking Skills (p. 341) *Chapter 12*/Group Discussion (p. 451); *Guidelines:* Teaching for Conceptual Change (p. 464)	
■ Promoting risk-taking and problem solving	*Chapter 8*/*Guidelines:* Problem Solving (p. 295) *Chapter 12*/*Guidelines:* Teaching for Conceptual Change (p. 464)	
■ Facilitating factual recall	*Chapter 12*/Comprehension Monitoring and Reading: Reciprocal Teaching (p. 461); Applying Reciprocal Teaching (p. 461); Questioning and Recitation (pp. 447–451) *Chapter 13*/Reciprocal Questioning (pp. 497–499)	

PRAXIS™ Topics	Woolfolk Text Connections	INTASC Principles
■ Encouraging convergent and divergent thinking	*Chapter 13*/Assessing Creativity (p. 483) *Chapter 12*/Kinds of Questions (pp. 448–449)	
■ Stimulating curiosity	*Chapter 10*/Tapping Interests (pp. 362–363); *Guidelines:* Building on Students' Interests (p. 363); Curiosity: Novelty and Complexity (p. 365)	
■ Helping students to question	*Chapter 12*/Fitting the Questions to the Students (pp. 449–450) *Chapter 12*/Questioning and Recitation (pp. 447–451); Comprehension Monitoring and Reading: Reciprocal Teaching (p. 461); Applying Reciprocal Teaching (p. 461) *Chapter 13*/Reciprocal Questioning (pp. 497–499)	
IV. Profession and Community		
A. The Reflective Practitioner		
1. Types of resources available for professional development and learning		9B. The teacher is aware of major areas of research on teaching and of resources available for professional learning (e.g., professional literature, colleagues, professional associations, professional development activities).
■ Professional literature	*Chapters 2–15*/Margin Notes: *Connect and Extend* to the research (various places in each chapter); *Connect and Extend* to professional journals (various places in each chapter)	
■ Colleagues	*Chapters 2–15*/*Teachers' Casebook* (opening and closing sections of each chapter)	
■ Professional associations ■ Professional development activities	*Chapter 1*/*Enhancing Your Expertise with Technology:* Professional Development (p. 17) *Chapters 1–15*/Teaching Resources (at back of each chapter)	1A. The teacher understands major concepts, assumptions, debates, processes of inquiry, and ways of knowing that are central to the discipline(s) s/he teaches.
2. Ability to read and understand articles about current views, ideas, and debates regarding best teaching practices	*Chapter 1*/Using Research to Understand and Improve Teaching (pp. 11–15) *Chapters 2–15*/*Point/Counterpoint* (one per chapter)	9B. The teacher is aware of major areas of research on teaching and of resources available for professional learning (e.g., professional literature, colleagues, professional associations, professional development activities).
3. Why personal reflection on teaching practices is critical, and approaches that can be used to achieve this	*Chapter 1*/Point/Counterpoint (p. 7) *Chapters 1–15*/*Becoming a Professional* (at back of each chapter)	9A. The teacher understands methods of inquiry that provide him/her with a variety of self- assessment and problem-solving strategies for reflecting on his/her practice, its influences on students' growth and learning, and the complex interactions between them.

PRAXIS™ Topics	Woolfolk Text Connections	INTASC Principles
B. The Larger Community		
1. Role of the school as a resource to the larger community	*Chapter 5*/Culture and Community (entire chapter)	10A. The teacher understands schools as organizations within the larger community context and understands the operations of the relevant aspects of the system(s) within which s/he works.
2. Factors in the students' environment outside of school (family circumstances, community environments, health, and economic conditions) that may influence students' life and learning	*Chapter 3*/American Families Today (p. 88); Peer Relationships and Peer Cultures (pp. 88–90); Challenges for Children (pp. 91–97); *Guidelines:* Helping Children of Divorce (p. 89) *Chapter 4*/Prevalent Problems and Mild Disabilities (pp. 124–132); Less Prevalent Problems and More Severe Disabilities (pp. 133–136) *Chapter 5*/Culture and Community (entire chapter) *Chapters 2–15*/*Family and Community Partnerships:* (one in each chapter)	10B. The teacher understands how factors in the students' environment outside of school (e.g., family circumstances, community environments, health and economic conditions) may influence students' life and learning.
3. Basic strategies for involving parents/guardians and leaders in the community in the educational process	*Chapter 5*/Culture and Community (entire chapter)	
4. Major laws related to students' rights and teacher responsibilities	*Chapter 4*/Changes in the Law: Integration and Inclusion (pp. 121–124)	10C. The teacher understands and implements laws related to students' rights and teacher responsibilities (e.g., for equal education, appropriate education for handicapped students, confidentiality, privacy, appropriate treatment of students, reporting in situations related to possible child abuse).
▪ Equal education ▪ Appropriate education for handicapped children ▪ Confidentiality and privacy ▪ Appropriate treatment of students	*Chapter 4*/The Rights of Students and Families (pp. 123–124) *Chapter 15*/Beyond Grading: Communication (focus on: Buckley Amendment) (pp. 574–575) *Chapter 11*/The Need for Communication (pp. 415–421)	
▪ Reporting situations related to possible child abuse	*Chapter 3*/Children and Youth at Risk (pp. 93–97)	

Absence seizure A seizure involving only a small part of the brain that causes a child to lose contact briefly.
Academic learning time Time when students are actually succeeding at the learning task.
Academic tasks The work the student must accomplish, including the content covered and the mental operations required.
Accommodation Altering existing schemes or creating new ones in response to new information.
Accountable Making teachers and schools responsible for student learning, usually by monitoring learning with high-stakes tests.
Achievement tests Standardized tests measuring how much students have learned in a given content area.
Acronym Technique for remembering names, phrases, or steps by using the first letter of each word to form a new, memorable word.
Action research Systematic observations or tests of methods conducted by teachers or schools to improve teaching and learning for their students.
Action zone Area of a classroom where the greatest amount of interaction takes place.
Activation spreading Retrieval of pieces of information based on their relatedness to one another. Remembering one bit of information activates (stimulates) recall of associated information.
Active teaching Teaching characterized by high levels of teacher explanation, demonstration, and interaction with students.
Adaptation Adjustment to the environment.
Adolescent egocentrism Assumption that everyone else shares one's thoughts, feelings, and concerns.
Advance organizer Statement of inclusive concepts to introduce and sum up material that follows.
Affective domain Objectives focusing on attitudes and feelings.
Algorithm Step-by-step procedure for solving a problem; prescription for solutions.
Allocated time Time set aside for learning.
Americans with Disabilities Act (ADA) Legislation prohibiting discrimination against persons with disabilities in employment, transportation, public access, local government, and telecommunications.
Analogical instruction Teaching new concepts by making connections (analogies) with information that the student already understands.
Analogical thinking Heuristic in which one limits the search for solutions to situations that are similar to the one at hand.
Anchored instruction A type of problem-based learning that uses a complex interesting situation as an anchor for learning.
Androgynous Having some typically male and some typically female characteristics apparent in one individual.
Anorexia nervosa Eating disorder characterized by very limited food intake.
Antecedents Events that precede an action.
Anxiety General uneasiness, a feeling of tension.
Applied behavior analysis The application of behavioral learning principles to understand and change behavior.
Appropriate Internalize or take for yourself knowledge and skills developed in interaction with others or with cultural tools.
Aptitude tests Tests meant to predict future performance.
Arousal Physical and psychological reactions causing a person to be alert, attentive, wide awake.
Articulation disorders Any of a variety of pronunciation difficulties, such as the substitution, distortion, or omission of sounds.
Assertive discipline Clear, firm, unhostile response style.
Assessment bias Qualities of an assessment instrument that offend or unfairly penalize a group of students because of the students' gender, SES, race, ethnicity, etc.
Assessment Procedures used to obtain information about student performance.
Assimilation Fitting new information into existing schemes.
Assisted learning Providing strategic help in the initial stages of learning, gradually diminishing as students gain independence.
Attainment value The importance of doing well on a task; how success on the task meets personal needs.
Attention Focus on a stimulus.
Attention-deficit/hyperactivity disorder Current term for disruptive behavior disorders marked by overactivity, excessive difficulty sustaining attention, or impulsiveness.
Attribution theories Descriptions of how individuals' explanations, justifications, and excuses influence their motivation and behavior.
Authentic assessments Measurement of important abilities using procedures that simulate the application of these abilities to real-life problems. Also, assessment procedures that test skills and abilities as they would be applied in real-life situations.
Authentic task Tasks that have some connection to real-life problems the students will face outside the classroom.
Authoritarian personality Rigidly conforming to the belief that society is naturally competitive, with "better" people reaping its rewards.
Automated basic skills Skills that are applied without conscious thought.
Automaticity The ability to perform thoroughly learned tasks without much mental effort. Also the result of learning to perform a behavior or thinking process so thoroughly that the performance is automatic and does not require effort.

Autonomy Independence.
Aversive Irritating or unpleasant.
Basic skills Clearly structured knowledge that is needed for later learning and that can be taught step by step.
Behavior modification Systematic application of antecedents and consequences to change behavior.
Behavioral learning theories Explanations of learning that focus on external events as the cause of changes in observable behaviors.
Behavioral objectives Instructional objectives stated in terms of observable behaviors.
Being needs Maslow's three higher-level needs, sometimes called growth needs.
Between-class ability grouping/tracking System of grouping in which students are assigned to classes based on their measured ability or their achievements.
Bilingualism Speaking two languages fluently.
Blended families Parents, children, and stepchildren merged into families through remarriages.
Bottom-up processing Perceiving based on noticing separate defining features and assembling them into a recognizable pattern.
Brainstorming Generating ideas without stopping to evaluate them.
Bulimia Eating disorder characterized by overeating, then getting rid of the food by self-induced vomiting or laxatives.
CAPS A strategy that can be used in reading literature *Characters, Aim* of story, *Problem, Solution.*
Case study Intensive study of one person or one situation.
Central executive The part of working memory that is responsible for monitoring and directing attention and other mental resources.
Central tendency Typical score for a group of scores.
Cerebral palsy Condition involving a range of motor or coordination difficulties due to brain damage.
Chain mnemonics Memory strategies that associate one element in a series with the next element.
Chunking Grouping individual bits of data into meaningful larger units.
Classical conditioning Association of automatic responses with new stimuli.
Classification Grouping objects into categories.
Classroom management Techniques used to maintain a healthy learning environment, relatively free of behavior problems.
Co-constructed process A social process in which people interact and negotiate (usually verbally) to create an understanding or to solve a problem. The final product is shaped by all participants.
Code-switching Successful switching between cultures in language, dialect, or nonverbal behaviors to fit the situation.
Cognitive apprenticeship A relationship in which a less experienced learner acquires knowledge and skills under the guidance of an expert.
Cognitive behavior modification Procedures based on both behavioral and cognitive learning principles for changing your own behavior by using self-talk and self-instruction.
Cognitive development Gradual orderly changes by which mental processes become more complex and sophisticated.
Cognitive domain In Bloom's taxonomy, memory and reasoning objectives.
Cognitive evaluation theory Suggests that events affect motivation through the individual's perception of the events as controlling behavior or providing information.
Cognitive objectives Instructional objectives stated in terms of higher-level thinking operations.
Cognitive styles Different ways of perceiving and organizing information.
Cognitive view of learning A general approach that views learning as an active mental process of acquiring, remembering, and using knowledge.
Collective monologue Form of speech in which children in a group talk but do not really interact or communicate.
Collective self-esteem Beliefs about the worth of the groups you belong to.
Community of practice Social situation or context in which ideas are judged useful or true.
Compensation The principle that changes in one dimension can be offset by changes in another.
Complex learning environments Problems and learning situations that mimic the ill-structured nature of real life.
Concept mapping Student's diagram of his or her understanding of a concept.
Concept A general category of ideas, objects, people, or experiences whose members share certain properties.
Conceptual change teaching in science A method that helps students understand (rather than memorize) concepts in science by using and challenging the students' current ideas.
Concrete operations Mental tasks tied to concrete objects and situations.
Conditional knowledge "Knowing when and why" to use declarative and procedural knowledge.
Conditioned response (CR) Learned response to a previously neutral stimulus.
Conditioned stimulus (CS) Stimulus that evokes an emotional or physiological response after conditioning.
Confidence interval Range of scores within which an individual's particular score is likely to fall.
Consequences Events that follow an action.
Conservation Principle that some characteristics of an object remain the same despite changes in appearance.
Constructed-response format Assessment procedures that require the student to create an answer instead of selecting an answer from a set of choices.
Constructivism/Constructivst approach View that emphasizes the active role of the learner in building understanding and making sense of information.
Context The physical or emotional backdrop associated with an event.
Contiguity Association of two events because of repeated pairing.
Contingency contract A contract between the teacher and a student specifying what the student must do to earn a particular reward or privilege.
Continuous reinforcement schedule Presenting a reinforcer after every appropriate response.
Contract system System in which each student works for a particular grade according to agreed-upon standards.
Convergent questions Questions that have a single correct answer.
Convergent thinking Narrowing possibilities to a single answer.

Cooperative learning Arrangement in which students work in mixed-ability groups and are rewarded on the basis of the success of the group.

Correlations Statistical descriptions of how closely two variables are related.

Creativity Imaginative, original thinking or problem solving.

Criterion-referenced grading Assessment of each student's mastery of course objectives.

Criterion-referenced testing Testing in which scores are compared to a set performance standard.

Critical thinking Evaluating conclusions by logically and systematically examining the problem, the evidence, and the solution.

Crystallized intelligence Ability to apply culturally approved problem-solving methods.

Cueing Providing a stimulus that "sets up" a desired behavior.

Cultural deficit model A model that explains the school achievement problems of ethnic minority students by assuming that their culture is inadequate and does not prepare them to succeed in school.

Cultural tools The real tools (computers, scales, etc.) and symbol systems (numbers, language, graphs) that allow people in a society to communicate, think, solve problems, and create knowledge.

Culturally compatible classrooms Classrooms in which procedures, rules, grouping strategies, attitudes, and teaching methods do not cause conflicts with the students' culturally influenced ways of learning and interacting.

Culturally relevant management Taking cultural meanings and styles into account when developing management plans and responding to students.

Culturally relevant pedagogy Excellent teaching for students of color that includes academic success, developing/maintaining cultural competence, and developing a critical consciousness to challenge the status quo.

Culture The knowledge, values, attitudes, and traditions that guide the behavior of a group of people and allow them to solve the problems of living in their environment.

Culture-fair/Culture-free test A test without cultural bias.

Decay The weakening and fading of memories with the passage of time.

Decentering Focusing on more than one aspect at a time.

Declarative knowledge Verbal information; facts; "knowing that" something is the case.

Deductive reasoning Drawing conclusions by applying rules or principles; logically moving from a general rule or principle to a specific solution.

Deficiency needs Maslow's four lower-level needs, which must be satisfied first.

Defining attributes Distinctive features shared by members of a category.

Descriptive studies Studies that collect detailed information about specific situations, often using observation, surveys, interviews, recordings, or a combination of these methods.

Development Orderly, adaptive changes we go through from conception to death.

Developmental crisis A specific conflict whose resolution prepares the way for the next stage.

Deviation IQ Score based on statistical comparison of an individual's performance with the average performance of others in that age group.

Diagnostic tests Formative tests to determine students' areas of weakness. Also, individually administered tests to identify special learning problems.

Dialect Rule-governed variation of a language spoken by a particular group.

Direct instruction/explicit teaching Systematic instruction for mastery of basic skills, facts, and information.

Disability The inability to do something specific such as walk or hear.

Discovery learning Bruner's approach, in which students work on their own to discover basic principles.

Discrimination Responding differently to similar, but not identical stimuli. Also, treating particular categories of people unequally.

Disequilibrium In Piaget's theory, the "out-of-balance" state that occurs when a person realizes that his or her current ways of thinking are not working to solve a problem or understand a situation.

Distractors Wrong answers offered as choices in a multiple-choice item.

Distributed practice Practice in brief periods with rest intervals.

Distributive justice Beliefs about how to divide materials or privileges fairly among members of a group; follows a sequence of development from equality to merit to benevolence.

Divergent questions Questions that have no single correct answer.

Divergent thinking Coming up with many possible solutions.

Domain-specific knowledge Information that is useful in a particular situation or that applies mainly to one specific topic.

Domain-specific strategies Consciously applied skills to reach goals in a particular subject or problem area.

Educational psychology The discipline concerned with teaching and learning processes; applies the methods and theories of psychology and has its own as well.

Educationally blind Needing Braille materials in order to learn.

Egocentric Assuming that others experience the world the way you do.

Ego-involved learners Students who focus on how well they are performing and how they are judged by others.

Elaboration Adding and extending meaning by connecting new information to existing knowledge.

Elaborative rehearsal Keeping information in working memory by associating it with something else you already know.

Emotional intelligence (EQ) The ability to process emotional information accurately and efficiently.

Empathetic listening Hearing the intent and emotions behind what another says and reflecting them back by paraphrasing.

Engaged time Time spent actively learning.

English as a second language (ESL) Designation for programs and classes to teach English to students who are not native speakers of English.

Entity view of ability Belief that ability is a fixed characteristic that cannot be changed.

Epilepsy Disorder marked by seizures and caused by abnormal electrical discharges in the brain.

Episodic memory Long-term memory for information tied to a particular time and place, especially memory of the events in a person's life.

Equilibration Search for mental balance between cognitive schemes and information from the environment.

Ethnic pride A positive self-concept about one's racial or ethnic heritage.

Ethnicity A cultural heritage shared by a group of people.

Ethnography A descriptive approach to research that focuses on life within a group and tries to understand the meaning of events to the people involved.

Evaluation Decision making about student performance and about appropriate teaching strategies.

Exceptional students Students who have abilities or problems so significant that they require special education or other services to reach their potential.

Executive control processes Processes such as selective attention, rehearsal, elaboration, and organization that influence encoding, storage, and retrieval of information in memory.

Exemplar A specific example of a given category that is used to classify an item.

Exhibition A performance test or demonstration of learning that is public and usually takes an extended time to prepare.

Expectancy × value theories Explanations of motivation that emphasize individuals' expectations for success combined with their valuing of the goal.

Experimentation Research method in which variables are manipulated and the effects recorded.

Expert teachers Experienced, effective teachers who have developed solutions for common classroom problems. Their knowledge of teaching process and content is extensive and well organized.

Explicit memory Long-term memories that involve deliberate or conscious recall.

Expository teaching Ausubel's method—teachers present material in complete, organized form, moving from broadest to more specific concepts.

Extinction Gradual disappearance of a learned response.

Extrinsic motivation Motivation created by external factors such as rewards and punishments.

Failure-accepting students Students who believe their failures are due to low ability and there is little they can do about it.

Failure-avoiding students Students who avoid failure by sticking to what they know, by not taking risks, or by claiming not to care about their performance.

Field dependence Cognitive style in which patterns are perceived as wholes.

Field independence Cognitive style in which separate parts of a pattern are perceived and analyzed.

First wave constructivism A focus on the individual and psychological sources of knowing, as in Piaget's theory.

Fluid intelligence Mental efficiency, nonverbal abilities grounded in brain development.

Formal operations Mental tasks involving abstract thinking and coordination of a number of variables.

Formative assessment Ungraded testing used before or during instruction to aid in planning and diagnosis.

Fostering communities of learners (FCL) A system of interacting activities that results in a self-consciously active and reflective learning environment, and uses a research, share, perform learning cycle.

Frequency distribution Record showing how many scores fall into set groups.

Full inclusion The integration of all students, including those with severe disabilities, into regular classes.

Functional fixedness Inability to use objects or tools in a new way.

Gender biases Different views of males and females, often favoring one gender over the other.

Gender schemas Organized networks of knowledge about what it means to be male or female.

Gender-role identity Beliefs about characteristics and behaviors associated with one sex as opposed to the other.

General knowledge Information that is useful in many different kinds of tasks; information that applies to many situations.

Generalization Responding in the same way to similar stimuli.

Generalized seizure A seizure involving a large portion of the brain.

Generativity Sense of concern for future generations.

Gestalt German for *pattern* or *whole;* Gestalt theorists hold that people organize their perceptions into coherent wholes.

Gifted student A very bright, creative, and talented student.

Goal orientations Patterns of beliefs about goals related to achievement in school.

Goal structure The way students relate to others who are also working toward a particular goal.

Goal What an individual strives to accomplish.

Goal-directed actions Deliberate actions toward a goal.

Good behavior game Arrangement where a class is divided into teams and each team receives demerit points for breaking agreed-upon rules of good behavior.

Grade-equivalent score Measure of grade level based on comparison with norming samples from each grade.

Grading on the curve Norm-referenced grading that compares students' performance to an average level.

Group consequences Rewards or punishments given to a class as a whole for adhering to or violating rules of conduct.

Group discussion Conversation in which the teacher does not have the dominant role; students pose and answer their own questions.

Group focus The ability to keep as many students as possible involved in activities.

Guided discovery An adaptation of discovery learning, in which the teacher provides some direction.

Halo effect The tendency for a general impression of a person to influence our perception of any aspect of that person.

Handicap A disadvantage in a particular situation, sometimes caused by a disability.

Heuristic General strategy used in attempting to solve problems.

Hierarchy of needs Maslow's model of seven levels of human needs, from basic physiological requirements to the need for self-actualization.

High-road transfer Application of abstract knowledge learned in one situation to a different situation.

High-stakes testing Standardized tests whose results have powerful influences when used by school administrators, other officials, or employers to make decisions.

Histogram Bar graph of a frequency distribution.

Hostile aggression Bold, direct action that is intended to hurt someone else; unprovoked attack.

Humanistic perspective Approach to motivation that emphasizes personal freedom, choice, self-determination, and striving for personal growth.

Hypothetico-deductive reasoning A formal-operations problem-solving strategy in which an individual begins by identifying all the factors that might affect a problem and then deduces and systematically evaluates specific solutions.
"I" message Clear, nonaccusatory statement of how something is affecting you.
Identity Principle that a person or object remains the same over time. Also, the complex answer to the question, "Who am I?"
Identity achievement Strong sense of commitment to life choices after free consideration of alternatives.
Identity diffusion Uncenteredness; confusion about who one is and what one wants.
Identity foreclosure Acceptance of parental life choices without consideration of options.
Images Representations based on the physical attributes—the appearance—of information.
Implicit memory Knowledge that we are not conscious of recalling, but influences behavior or thought without our awareness.
Impulsive Characterized by cognitive style of responding quickly but often inaccurately.
Incentive An object or event that encourages or discourages behavior.
Incremental view of ability Belief that ability is a set of skills that can be changed.
Individual Learning Expectation (ILE) Personal average score.
Individualized Education Program (IEP) Annually revised program for an exceptional student, detailing present achievement level, goals, and strategies, drawn up by teachers, parents, specialists, and (if possible) the student.
Individuals with Disabilities Education Act (IDEA) Amendment to PL 94-142.
Inductive reasoning Formulating general principles based on knowledge of examples and details.
Industry Eagerness to engage in productive work.
Information processing The human mind's activity of taking in, storing, and using information.
Initiative Willingness to begin new activities and explore new directions.
Inquiry learning Approach in which the teacher presents a puzzling situation and students solve the problem by gathering data and testing their conclusions.
Insight Sudden realization of a solution. Also, the ability to deal effectively with novel situations.
Instructional conversation Situation in which students learn through interactions with teachers and/or other students.
Instructional objectives Clear statement of what students are intended to learn through instruction.
Instrumental aggression Strong actions aimed at claiming an object, place, or privilege—not intended to harm, but may lead to harm.
Integrity Sense of self-acceptance and fulfillment.
Intelligence quotient (IQ) Score comparing mental and chronological ages.
Intelligence Ability or abilities to acquire and use knowledge for solving problems and adapting to the world.
Interference The process that occurs when remembering certain information is hampered by the presence of other information.
Intermittent reinforcement schedule Presenting a reinforcer after some but not all responses.
Internalize Process whereby children adopt external standards as their own.
Intersubjective attitude A commitment to build shared meaning with others by finding common ground and exchanging interpretations.
Interval schedule Length of time between reinforcers.
Intrinsic motivation Motivation associated with activities that are their own reward.
Intrinsic or interest value The enjoyment a person gets from a task.
Intuitive thinking Making imaginative leaps to correct perceptions or workable solutions.
Jigsaw A cooperative structure in which each member of a group is responsible for teaching other members one section of the material.
Keyword method System of associating new words or concepts with similar-sounding cue words and images.
KWL A strategy to guide reading and inquiry Before—What do I already *know?* What do I *want* to know? After—What have I *learned?*
Lateralization The specialization of the two hemispheres (sides) of the brain cortex.
Learned helplessness The expectation, based on previous experiences with a lack of control, that all one's efforts will lead to failure.
Learning disability Problem with acquisition and use of language; may show up as difficulty with reading, writing, reasoning, or math.
Learning preferences Preferred ways of studying and learning, such as using pictures instead of text, working with other people versus alone, learning in structured or in unstructured situations, and so on.
Learning strategies General plans for approaching learning tasks.
Learning styles Characteristic approaches to learning and studying.
Learning tactics Specific techniques for learning, such as using mnemonics or outlining a passage.
Learning Process through which experience causes permanent change in knowledge or behavior.
Least restrictive placement Placement of each child in as normal an educational setting as possible.
Legitimate peripheral participation Genuine involvement in the work of the group, even if your abilities are undeveloped and contributions are small.
Levels of processing theory Theory that recall of information is based on how deeply it is processed.
Licensure tests In many states, teachers are required to take standardized tests, such as the PRAXIS™ series designed by the Educational Testing Service, in order to be certified or licensed as a teacher.
Limited English proficiency (LEP) Descriptive term for students who have limited mastery of English.
Loci method Technique of associating items with specific places.
Locus of causality The location—internal or external—of the cause of behavior.
Long-term memory Permanent store of knowledge.
Long-term working memory: Holds the strategies for pulling information from long-term memory into working memory.

Low vision Vision limited to close objects.
Low-road transfer Spontaneous and automatic transfer of highly practiced skills.
Mainstreaming Teaching children with disabilities in regular classes for part or all of their school day.
Maintenance rehearsal Keeping information in working memory by repeating it to yourself.
Massed practice Practice for a single extended period.
Mastery experiences Our own direct experiences—the most powerful source of efficacy information.
Mastery goal A personal intention to improve abilities and learn, no matter how performance suffers.
Mastery learning Teaching approach in which students must learn one unit and pass a test at a specified level before moving to the next unit.
Mastery-oriented students Students who focus on learning goals because they value achievement and see ability as improvable.
Maturation Genetically programmed, naturally occurring changes over time.
Mean Arithmetical average.
Meaningful verbal learning Focused and organized relationships among ideas and verbal information.
Means-ends analysis Heuristic in which a goal is divided into subgoals.
Measurement An evaluation expressed in quantitative (number) terms.
Median Middle score in a group of scores.
Melting pot A metaphor for the absorption and assimilation of immigrants into the mainstream of society so that ethnic differences vanish.
Mental age In intelligence testing, a score based on average abilities for that age group.
Mental retardation Significantly below-average intellectual and adaptive social behavior, evident before age 18.
Metacognition Knowledge about our own thinking processes.
Metalinguistic awareness Understanding about one's own use of language.
Microgenetic studies Detailed observation and analysis of changes in a cognitive process as the process unfolds over a several day or week period of time.
Minority group A group of people who have been socially disadvantaged—not always a minority in actual numbers.
Mnemonics Techniques for remembering; also, the art of memory.
Mode Most frequently occurring score.
Modeling Changes in behavior, thinking, or emotions that occur through observing another person—a model.
Moral dilemmas Situations in which no choice is clearly and indisputably right.
Moral realism Stage of development wherein children see rules as absolute.
Moral reasoning The thinking process involved in judgments about questions of right and wrong.
Morality of cooperation Stage of development wherein children realize that people make rules and people can change them.
Moratorium Identity crisis; suspension of choices because of struggle.
Motivation to learn The tendency to find academic activities meaningful and worthwhile and to try to benefit from them.
Motivation An internal state that arouses, directs, and maintains behavior.
Movement management Keeping lessons and the group moving at an appropriate (and flexible) pace, with smooth transitions and variety.
Multicultural education Education that teaches the value of cultural diversity.
Multiple representations of content Considering problems using various analogies, examples, and metaphors.
Myelination The process by which neural fibers are coated with a fatty sheath called *myelin* that makes message transfer more efficient.
Negative correlation A relationship between two variables in which a high value on one is associated with a low value on the other. Example: height and distance from top of head to the ceiling.
Negative reinforcement Strengthening behavior by removing an aversive stimulus when the behavior occurs.
Neo-Piagetian theories More recent theories that integrate findings about attention, memory, and strategy use with Piaget's insights about children's thinking and the construction of knowledge.
Neutral stimulus Stimulus not connected to a response.
Nongraded elementary school/The Joplin plan Arrangement wherein students are grouped by ability in particular subjects, regardless of their ages or grades.
Norm groups A group whose average score serves as a standard for evaluating any student's score on a test.
Normal distribution The most commonly occurring distribution, in which scores are distributed evenly around the mean.
Norming sample Large sample of students serving as a comparison group for scoring standardized tests.
Norm-referenced grading Assessment of students' achievement in relation to one another.
Norm-referenced testing Testing in which scores are compared with the average performance of others.
Object permanence The understanding that objects have a separate, permanent existence.
Objective testing Multiple-choice, matching, true/false, short-answer, and fill-in tests; scoring answers does not require interpretation.
Observational learning Learning by observation and imitation of others.
Operant conditioning Learning in which voluntary behavior is strengthened or weakened by consequences or antecedents.
Operants Voluntary (and generally goal-directed) behaviors emitted by a person or an animal.
Operations Actions a person carries out by thinking them through instead of literally performing the actions.
Organization Ongoing process of arranging information and experience into mental systems or categories. Also, ordered and logical network of relations.
Overgeneralization Inclusion of nonmembers in a category; overextending a concept.
Overlapping Supervising several activities at once.
Overlearning Practicing a skill past the point of mastery.
Overt aggression A form of hostile aggression that involves physical attack.
Paraphrase rule Policy whereby listeners must accurately summarize what a speaker has said before being allowed to respond.

Part learning Breaking a list of rote learning items into shorter lists.
Participant observation A method for conducting descriptive research in which the researcher becomes a participant in the situation in order to better understand life in that group.
Participation structures Rules defining how to participate in different activities. Also, the formal and informal rules for how to take part in a given activity.
Peg-type mnemonics Systems of associating items with cue words.
Percentage grading System of converting class performances to percentage scores and assigning grades based on predetermined cutoff points.
Percentile rank Percentage of those in the norming sample who scored at or below an individual's score.
Perception Interpretation of sensory information.
Performance goal A personal intention to seem competent or perform well in the eyes of others.
Personal development Changes in personality that take place as one grows.
Perspective-taking ability Understanding that others have different feelings and experiences.
Phonological loop Part of working memory. A memory rehearsal system for verbal and sound information of about 1.5 to 2 seconds.
Physical development Changes in body structure and function over time.
Portfolio A collection of the student's work in an area, showing growth, self-reflection, and achievement.
Positive correlation A relationship between two variables in which the two increase or decrease together. Example: calorie intake and weight gain.
Positive practice Practicing correct responses immediately after errors.
Positive reinforcement Strengthening behavior by presenting a desired stimulus after the behavior.
PQ4R A method for studying text that involves six steps *Preview, Question, Read, Reflect, Recite, Review.*
Pragmatics The rules for when and how to use language to be an effective communicator in a particular culture.
Prejudice Prejudgment, or irrational generalization about an entire category of people.
Premack principle Principle stating that a more-preferred activity can serve as a reinforcer for a less-preferred activity.
Preoperational The stage before a child masters logical mental operations.
Presentation punishment Decreasing the chances that a behavior will occur again by presenting an aversive stimulus following the behavior; also called Type I punishment.
Pretest Formative test for assessing students' knowledge, readiness, and abilities.
Priming Activating a concept in memory or the spread of activation from one concept to another.
Principle Established relationship between factors.
Private speech Children's self-talk, which guides their thinking and action. Eventually these verbalizations are internalized as silent inner speech.
Problem Any situation in which you are trying to reach some goal and must find a means to do so.
Problem solving Creating new solutions for problems.
Problem-based learning Methods that provide students with realistic problems that don't necessarily have "right" answers.
Procedural knowledge Knowledge that is demonstrated when we perform a task; "knowing how."
Procedural memory Long-term memory for how to do things.
Procedures Prescribed steps for an activity.
Productions The contents of procedural memory; rules about what actions to take, given certain conditions.
Prompt A reminder that follows a cue to make sure the person reacts to the cue.
Propositional network Set of interconnected concepts and relationships in which long-term knowledge is held.
Prototype Best representative of a category.
Psychomotor domain Physical ability and coordination objectives.
Psychosocial Describing the relation of the individual's emotional needs to the social environment.
Punishment Process that weakens or suppresses behavior.
Pygmalion effect Exceptional progress by a student as a result of high teacher expectations for that student; named for mythological king, Pygmalion, who made a statue, then caused it to be brought to life.
Race A group of people who share common biological traits that are seen as self-defining by the people of the group.
Random Without any definite pattern; following no rule.
Range Distance between the highest and the lowest scores in a group.
Ratio schedule Reinforcement based on the number of responses between reinforcers.
READS A five-step reading strategy *Review* headings; *Examine* boldface words; *Ask*, "What do I expect to learn?"; *Do* it—Read; *Summarize* in your own words.
Reciprocal determinism An explanation of behavior that emphasizes the mutual effects of the individual and the environment on each other.
Reciprocal questioning Approach where groups of two or three students ask and answer each other's questions after a lesson or presentation.
Reciprocal teaching A method, based on modeling, to teach reading comprehension strategies.
Reconstruction Recreating information by using memories, expectations, logic, and existing knowledge.
Reflective Thoughtful and inventive. Reflective teachers think back over situations to analyze what they did and why and to consider how they might improve learning for their students. Also, characterized by cognitive style of responding slowly, carefully, and accurately.
Regular education initiative An educational movement that advocates giving regular education teachers, not special education teachers, responsibility for teaching mildly (and sometimes moderately) handicapped students.
Reinforcement Use of consequences to strengthen behavior.
Reinforcer Any event that follows a behavior and increases the chances that the behavior will occur again.
Relational aggression A form of hostile aggression that involves verbal attacks and other actions meant to harm social relationships.
Reliability Consistency of test results.
Removal punishment Decreasing the chances that a behavior will occur again by removing a pleasant stimulus following the behavior; also called Type II punishment.

Reprimands Criticisms for misbehavior; rebukes.
Resistance culture Group values and beliefs about refusing to adopt the behaviors and attitudes of the majority culture.
Respondents Responses (generally automatic or involuntary) elicited by specific stimuli.
Response cost Punishment by loss of reinforcers.
Response set Rigidity; tendency to respond in the most familiar way.
Response Observable reaction to a stimulus.
Restructuring Conceiving of a problem in a new or different way.
Retrieval Process of searching for and finding information in long-term memory.
Reversibility A characteristic of Piagetian logical operations—the ability to think through a series of steps, then mentally reverse the steps and return to the starting point; also called *reversible thinking.*
Reversible thinking Thinking backward, from the end to the beginning.
Revise option In a contract system, the chance to revise and improve work.
Reward An attractive object or event supplied as a consequence of a behavior.
Ripple effect "Contagious" spreading of behaviors through imitation.
Rote memorization Remembering information by repetition without necessarily understanding the meaning of the information.
Rules Statements specifying expected and forbidden behaviors; dos and don'ts.
Satiation Requiring a person to repeat a problem behavior past the point of interest or motivation.
Scaffolding Support for learning and problem solving. The support could be clues, reminders, encouragement, breaking the problem down into steps, providing an example, or anything else that allows the student to grow in independence as a learner.
Schema-driven problem solving Recognizing a problem as a "disguised" version of an old problem for which one already has a solution.
Schemata (singular, **schema**) Basic structures for organizing information; concepts.
Schemes Mental systems or categories of perception and experience.
Scoring rubrics Rules that are used to determine the quality of a student performance.
Script Schema or expected plan for the sequence of steps in a common event such as buying groceries or ordering take-out pizza.
Scripted cooperation Learning strategy in which two students take turns summarizing material and criticizing the summaries.
Seatwork Independent classroom work.
Second wave constructivism A focus on the social and cultural sources of knowing, as in Vygotsky's theory.
Section 504 A part of civil rights law that prevents discrimination against people with disabilities in programs that receive federal funds, such as public schools.
Self-actualization Fulfilling one's potential.
Self-concept Our perceptions about ourselves.
Self-determination The need to experience choice and control in what we do and how we do it.
Self-efficacy A person's sense of being able to deal effectively with a particular task. Also, beliefs about personal competence in a particular situation.
Self-esteem The value each of us places on our own characteristics, abilities, and behaviors.
Self-fulfilling prophecy A groundless expectation that is confirmed because it has been expected.
Self-instruction Talking oneself through the steps of a task.
Self-management Management of your own behavior and acceptance of responsibility for your own actions. Also, use of behavioral learning principles to change your own behavior.
Self-regulated learners Have a combination of academic learning skills and self-control that makes learning easier.
Self-regulation Process of activating and sustaining thoughts, behaviors, and emotions in order to reach goals.
Self-reinforcement Providing yourself with positive consequences, contingent on accomplishing a particular behavior.
Semantic memory Memory for meaning.
Semilingual Not proficient in any language; speaking one or more languages inadequately.
Semiotic function The ability to use symbols—language, pictures, signs, or gestures—to represent actions or objects mentally.
Sensorimotor Involving the senses and motor activity.
Sensory memory System that holds sensory information very briefly.
Serial-position effect The tendency to remember the beginning and the end but not the middle of a list.
Seriation Arranging objects in sequential order according to one aspect, such as size, weight, or volume.
Service learning An approach to combining academic learning with personal and social development through doing volunteer service.
Shaping Reinforcing each small step of progress toward a desired goal or behavior.
Short-term memory Component of memory system that holds information for about 20 seconds.
Single-subject experimental studies Systematic interventions to study effects with one person, often by applying and then withdrawing a treatment.
Situated learning The idea that skills and knowledge are tied to the situation in which they were learned and difficult to apply in new settings.
Social cognitive theory Theory that adds concern with cognitive factors such as beliefs, self-perceptions, and expectations to social learning theory.
Social development Changes over time in the ways we relate to others.
Social goals A wide variety of needs and motives to be connected to others or part of a group.
Social isolation Removal of a disruptive student for 5 to 10 minutes.
Social learning theory Theory that emphasizes learning through observation of others.
Social negotiation Aspect of learning process that relies on collaboration with others and respect for different perspectives.
Social persuasion A "pep talk" or specific performance feedback—one source of self-efficacy.
Socialization The ways in which members of a society encourage positive development for the immature individuals of the group.
Sociocultural theory Emphasizes role in development of cooperative dialogues between children and more knowledgeable

members of society. Children learn the culture of their community (ways of thinking and behaving) through these interactions.

Sociocultural views of motivation Perspectives that emphasize participation, identities, and interpersonal relations within communities of practice.

Socioeconomic status (SES) Relative standing in the society based on income, power, background, and prestige.

Sociolinguistics The study of the formal and informal rules for how, when, about what, to whom, and how long to speak in conversations within cultural groups.

Spasticity Overly tight or tense muscles, characteristic of some forms of cerebral palsy.

Speech disorder Inability to produce sounds effectively for speaking.

Spiral curriculum Bruner's structure for teaching that introduces the fundamental structure of all subjects early in the school years, then revisits the subjects in more and more complex forms over time.

Stand-alone thinking skills programs Programs that teach thinking skills directly without need for extensive subject matter knowledge.

Standard deviation Measure of how widely scores vary from the mean.

Standard error of measurement Hypothetical estimate of variation in scores if testing were repeated.

Standard scores Scores based on the standard deviation.

Standard speech The most generally accepted and used form of a given language.

Standardized tests Tests given, usually nationwide, under uniform conditions and scored according to uniform procedures.

Stanine scores Whole number scores from 1 to 9, each representing a wide range of raw scores.

Statistically significant Not likely to be a chance occurrence.

Stem The question part of a multiple-choice item.

Stereotype threat The extra emotional and cognitive burden that your performance in an academic situation might confirm a stereotype that others hold about you.

Stereotype Schema that organizes knowledge or perceptions about a category.

Stimulus control Capacity for the presence or absence of antecedents to cause behaviors.

Stimulus Event that activates behavior.

Story grammar Typical structure or organization for a category of stories.

Subjects People or animals studied.

Successive approximations Small components that make up a complex behavior.

Summative assessment Testing that follows instruction and assesses achievement.

Sustaining expectation effect Student performance maintained at a certain level because teachers don't recognize improvements.

Synapses The tiny space between neurons—chemical messages are sent across these gaps.

Syntax The order of words in phrases or sentences.

***T* score** Standard score with a mean of 50 and a standard deviation of 10.

Tacit knowledge Knowing how rather than knowing that—knowledge that is more likely to be learned during everyday life than through formal schooling.

Task analysis System for breaking down a task hierarchically into basic skills and subskills.

Task-involved learners Students who focus on mastering the task or solving the problem.

Taxonomy Classification system.

Teaching efficacy A teacher's belief that he or she can reach even the most difficult students and help them learn.

Teaching portfolio A depiction of you as a teacher, usually including a curriculum vitae, statement of teaching philosophy, examples of your teaching plans and activities, example assignments and tests, students' work, and even videos or CD excerpts of teaching.

Theory of multiple intelligences In Gardner's theory of intelligence, a person's eight separate abilities logical-mathematical, verbal, musical, spatial, bodily-kinesthetic, interpersonal, intrapersonal, and naturalist.

Theory Integrated statement of principles that attempts to explain a phenomenon and make predictions.

Time on task Time spent actively engaged in the learning task at hand.

Time out Technically, the removal of all reinforcement. In practice, isolation of a student from the rest of the class for a brief time.

Token reinforcement system System in which tokens earned for academic work and positive classroom behavior can be exchanged for some desired reward.

Top-down processing Perceiving based on the context and the patterns you expect to occur in that situation.

Tracking Assignment to different classes and academic experiences based on achievement.

Transfer Influence of previously learned material on new material.

Transition programming Gradual preparation of exceptional students to move from high school into further education or training, employment, or community involvement.

Triarchic theory of intelligence A three-part description of the mental abilities (thinking processes, coping with new experiences, and adapting to context) that lead to more or less intelligent behavior.

True score Hypothetical average of all of an individual's scores if repeated testing under ideal conditions were possible.

Unconditioned response (UR) Naturally occurring emotional or physiological response.

Unconditioned stimulus (US) Stimulus that automatically produces an emotional or physiological response.

Undergeneralization Exclusion of some true members from a category; limiting a concept.

Universal design Considering the needs of all users as new tools, or learning programs, or websites.

Untracking Redesigning schools to teach students in classes that are not grouped by ability.

Utility value The contribution of a task to meeting one's goals.

Validity Degree to which a test measures what it is intended to measure.

Variability Degree of difference or deviation from mean.

Verbalization Putting your problem-solving plan and its logic into words.

Vicarious experiences Accomplishments that are modeled by someone else.

Vicarious reinforcement Increasing the chances that we will repeat a behavior by observing another person being reinforced for that behavior.

Visuospatial sketchpad Part of working memory. A holding system for visual and spatial infromation.

Voicing problems Inappropriate pitch, quality, loudness, or intonation.

Volition Will power; self-discipline.

Warm demanders Effective teachers with African American students who show both high expectations and great caring for their students.

Whole-language perspective A philosophical approach to teaching and learning that stresses learning through authentic, real-life tasks. Emphasizes using language to learn, integrating learning across skills and subjects, and respecting the language abilities of student and teacher.

Within-class ability grouping System of grouping in which students in a class are divided into two or three groups based on ability in an attempt to accommodate student differences.

Withitness According to Kounin, awareness of everything happening in a classroom.

Work-avoidant learners Students who don't want to learn or to look smart, but just want to avoid work.

Working memory The information that you are focusing on at a given moment.

Working-backward strategy Heuristic in which one starts with the goal and moves backward to solve the problem.

***z* score** Standard score indicating the number of standard deviations above or below the mean.

Zone of proximal development Phase at which a child can master a task if given appropriate help and support.

AAMD Ad Hoc Committee on Terminology and Classification. (1992). *Mental retardation: Definition, classification, and systems of support* (9th ed.). Washington, DC: American Association on Mental Retardation.

Abi-Nader, J. (1991). Creating a vision of the future: Strategies for motivating minority students. *Phi Delta Kappan, 72,* 546–549.

Aboud, F., & Skerry, S. (1984). The development of ethnic identification: A critical review. *Journal of Cross-Cultural Psychology, 15,* 3–34.

Ackerman, P. L., Bowen, K. R., Beier, M., & Kanfer, R. (2001). Determinants of individual differences and gender differences in knowledge. *Journal of Educational Psychology, 93,* 797–825.

Airasian, P. W. (1996). *Assessment in the classroom.* New York: McGraw-Hill.

Airasian, P. W., & Walsh, M. E. (1997). Constructivist cautions. *Phi Delta Kappan, 78,* 444–449.

Airasian, P. W. (2001). *Classroom assessment: Concepts and applications* (4th ed.). New York: McGraw-Hill.

Albanese, M. A., & Mitchell, S. A. (1993). Problem-based learning: A review of literature on its outcomes and implementation issues. *Academic Medicine, 68,* 52–81.

Alberto, P., & Troutman, A. C. (1990). *Applied behavior analysis for teachers: Influencing student performance* (3rd ed.). Columbus, OH: Merrill.

Alberto, P., & Troutman, A. C. (2003). *Applied behavior analysis for teachers: Influencing student performance* (6th ed.). Saddle River, NJ: Prentice-Hall/Merrill.

Alexander, P. A. (1992). Domain knowledge: Evolving themes and emerging concerns. *Educational Psychologist, 27,* 33–51.

Alexander, P. A. (1995). Superimposing a situation-specific and domain-specific perspective on an account of self-regulated learning. *Educational Psychologist, 30,* 189–194.

Alexander, P. A. (1995, April). Stages and phases of domain learning: The dynamics of subject-matter knowledge, strategy knowledge, and motivation. In R. Garner (Chair), *Toward a multidimensional model of domain learning.* Symposium presented at the annual meeting of the American Educational Research Association, San Francisco.

Alexander, P. A. (1996). The past, present, and future of knowledge research: A reexamination of the role of knowledge in learning and instruction. *Educational Psychologist, 31,* 89–92.

Alexander, P. A. (1997). Mapping the multidimensional nature of domain learning: The interplay of cognitive, motivational, and strategic forces. *Advances in Motivation and Achievement, 10,* 213–250.

Alexander, P. A., & Jetton, T. L. (1996). The role of importance and interest in the processing of text. *Educational Psychology Review, 8,* 89–121.

Alexander, P. A., Kulikowich, J. M., & Schulze, S. K. (1994). How subject-matter knowledge affects recall and interest. *American Educational Research Journal, 31,* 313–337.

Alexander, P. A., & Murphy, P. K. (1998). The research base for APA's Learner-Centered Psychological Principles. In N. Lambert & B. McCombs (Eds.), *How students learn: Reforming schools through learner-centered education* (pp. 33–60). Washington, DC: American Psychological Association.

Alliance for Service Learning in Education Reform. (1993). Standards of quality for school based service learning. *Equity and Excellence in Education, 26*(2), 71–77.

Allington, R. (1980). Teacher interruption behaviors during primary-grade oral reading. *Journal of Educational Psychology, 71,* 371–377.

Alloway, N. (1984). *Teacher expectations.* Paper presented at the meetings of the Australian Association for Research in Education, Perth, Australia.

Alloy, L. B., & Seligman, M. E. P. (1979). On the cognitive component of learned helplessness and depression. *The Journal of Learning and Motivation, 13,* 219–276.

Alton-Lee, A., Diggins, C., Klenner, L., Vine, E., & Dalton, N. (2001). Teacher management of the learning environment during a social studies discussion in a new-entrant classroom in New Zealand. *The Elementary School Journal, 101,* 549–566.

Alvidrez, J., & Weinstein, R. S. (1999). Early teacher perceptions and later student academic achievement. *Journal of Educational Psychology, 91,* 731–746.

Alwin, D., & Thornton, A. (1984). Family origins and schooling processes: Early versus late influence of parental characteristics. *American Sociological Review, 49,* 784–802.

Amabile, T. M. (1996). *Creativity in context.* Boulder, CO: Westview Press.

Amabile, T. M. (2001). Beyond talent: John Irving and the passionate craft of creativity. *American Psychologist, 56,* 333–336.

Amato, L. F., Loomis, L. S., & Booth, A. (1995). Parental divorce, marital conflict, and offspring well-being during early adulthood. *Social Forces, 73,* 895–915.

American Association of University Women (AAUW). (1991). *Shortchanging girls, shortchanging America.* Washington, DC: Author.

American Psychological Association. (2002). Warning signs. Retrieved April 16, 2002, from http://helping.apa.org/warningsigns

Ames, C. (1990). Motivation: What teachers need to know. *Teachers College Record, 91,* 409–421.

Ames, C. (1992). Classrooms: Goals, structures, and student motivation. *Journal of Educational Psychology, 84,* 261–271.

Ames, R., & Lau, S. (1982). An attributional analysis of student help-seeking in academic settings. *Journal of Educational Psychology, 74,* 414–423.

Anastasi, A. (1988). *Psychological testing* (6th ed.). New York: Macmillan.

Anderman, E. M., & Maehr, M. L. (1994). Motivation and schooling in the middle grades. *Review of Educational Research, 64,* 287–310.

Anderson, C. W., & Roth, K. J. (1989). Teaching for meaningful and self-regulated learning of science. In J. Brophy (Ed.), *Advances in research on teaching* (Vol. 1, pp. 265–306). Greenwich, CT: JAI Press.

Anderson, C. W., & Smith, E. L. (1983, April). *Children's conceptions of light and color: Developing the concept of unseen rays.* Paper presented at the annual meeting of the American Educational Research Association, Montreal.

Anderson, C. W., & Smith, E. L. (1987). Teaching science. In V. Richardson-Koehler (Ed.), *Educators' handbook: A research perspective* (pp. 84–111). New York: Longman.

Anderson, C. W., Holland, J. D., & Palincsar, A. S. (1997). Canonical and sociocultural approaches to research and reform in science education: The story of Juan and his group. *The Elementary School Journal, 97,* 359–384.

Anderson, J. R. (1993). Problem solving and learning. *American Psychologist, 48,* 35–44.

Anderson, J. R. (1995a). *Cognitive psychology and its implications* (4th ed.). New York: Freeman.

Anderson, J. R. (1995b). *Learning and memory.* New York: John Wiley & Sons.

Anderson, J. R., Reder, L. M., & Simon, H. A. (1995). Applications and misapplication of cognitive psychology to mathematics education. Unpublished manuscript. Available online at http://www.psy.cmu.edu/~mm4b/misapplied.html

Anderson, J. R., Reder, L. M., & Simon, H. A. (1996). Situated learning and education. *Educational Researcher, 25,* 5–11.

Anderson, L. M. (1985). What are students doing when they do all that seatwork? In C. Fisher & D. Berliner (Eds.), *Perspectives on instructional time* (pp. 189–202). New York: Longman.

Anderson, L. M. (1989a). Learners and learning. In M. Reynolds (Ed.), *Knowledge base for beginning teachers* (pp. 85–100). New York: Pergamon.

Anderson, L. M. (1989b). Classroom instruction. In M. Reynolds (Ed.), *Knowledge base for beginning teachers* (pp. 101–116). New York: Pergamon.

Anderson, L. M., Brubaker, N. L., Alleman-Brooks, J., & Duffy, G. G. (1985). A qualitative study of seatwork in first-grade classrooms. *Elementary School Journal, 86,* 123–140.

Anderson, L. W., & Krathwohl, D. R. (Eds.). (2001). *A taxonomy for learning, teaching, and assessing: A revision of Bloom's taxonomy of educational objectives.* New York: Longman.

Anderson, L. W., & Sosniak, L. A. (Eds.). (1994). *Bloom's taxonomy: A forty-year retrospective.* Ninety-third yearbook for the National Society for the Study of Education: Part II. Chicago: University of Chicago Press.

Anderson, P. J., & Graham, S. M. (1994). Issues in second-language phonological acquisition among children and adults. *Topics in Language Disorders, 14,* 84–100.

Anderson, R., Hiebert, E., Scott, J., & Wilkinson, I. (1985). *Becoming a nation of readers: The report of the commission on reading.* Washington, DC: National Institute of Education.

Anderson, R. C., Nguyen-Jahiel, K., McNurlen, B., Archodidou, A., Kim, S-Y., Reznitskaya, A., et al. (2001). The snowball phenomenon: Spread of ways of talking and ways of thinking across groups of children. *Cognition and Instruction, 19,* 1–46.

Anderson, S. M., Klatzky, R. L., & Murray, J. (1990). Traits and social stereotypes: Efficiency differences in social information processing. *Journal of Personality and Social Psychology, 59,* 192–201.

Anglin, J. M. (1993). Vocabulary development: A morphological analysis. *Monographs of the Society for Research in Child Development, 58*(10, Serial No. 238).

Anyon, J. (1980). Social class and the hidden curriculum of work. *Journal of Education, 162,* 67–92.

APA Board of Educational Affairs. (1995). *Learner-centered psychological principles: A framework for school redesign and reform.* Washington, DC: American Psychological Association.

Archer, S. L., & Waterman, A. S. (1990). Varieties of identity diffusions and foreclosures: An exploration of the subcategories of the identity statuses. *Journal of Adolescent Research, 5,* 96–111.

Arends, R. I. (2001). *Learning to teach* (5th ed.). New York: McGraw-Hill.

Arlin, M. (1984). Time, equality, and mastery learning. *Review of Educational Research, 54,* 65–86.

Armbruster, B. B., & Anderson, T. H. (1981). Research synthesis on study skills. *Educational Leadership, 39,* 154–156.

Armstrong, L. S. (1991, January 16). Racial, ethnic prejudice still prevalent, survey finds. *Education Week,* 7.

Arnold, M. L. (2000). Stage, sequence, and sequels: Changing conceptions of morality, post-Kohlberg. *Educational Psychology Review, 12,* 365–383.

Aronson, E. (2000). *Nobody left to hate: Teaching compassion after Columbine.* New York: Worth.

Aronson, J. (2002). Stereotype threat: Contending and coping with unnerving expectations. In J. Aronson & D. Cordova (Eds.), *Improving education: Classic and contemporary lessons from psychology* (pp. 279–301). New York: Academic Press.

Aronson, J., Fried, C. B., & Good, C. (2002). Reducing the effects of stereotype threat on African American college students: The role of theories of intelligence. *Journal of Experimental Social Psychology, 33,* 113–125.

Aronson, J., Lustina, M. J., Good, C., Keough, K., Steele, C. M., & Brown, J. (1999). When White men can't do math: Necessary and sufficient factors in stereotype threat. *Journal of Experimental Social Psychology, 35,* 29–46.

Aronson, J., & Salinas, M. F. (1998). Stereotype threat, attributional ambiguity, and Latino underperformance. Unpublished manuscript, University of Texas at Austin.

Aronson, J., Steele, C. M., Salinas, M. F., & Lustina, M. J. (1999). The effect of stereotype threat on the standardized test performance of college students. In E. Aronson (Ed.), *Readings about the social animal* (8th ed.). New York: Freeman.

Artman, L., & Cahan, S. (1993). Schooling and the development of transitive inference. *Developmental Psychology, 29,* 753–759.

Ashcraft, M. H. (2002). *Cognition* (3rd ed.). Upper Saddle River, NJ: Prentice-Hall.

Association for the Gifted. (2001). *Diversity and developing gifts and talents: A national action plan.* Arlington, VA: Author.

Associated Press. (2001, February 21). ABA recommends dropping zero-tolerance in schools. Available online at http://www.cnn.com/2001/fyi/teachers.ednews/02/21/zero.tolerance.ap. Downloaded on January 23, 2003.

Association for Supervision and Curriculum Development. (1990). Effective teaching redux. *ASCD Update, 32*(6), 5.

Association for Supervision and Curriculum Development. (1991). Issue. *ASCD Update, 33*(3), 7.

Atkinson, R. C., & Shiffrin, R. M. (1968). Human memory: A proposed system and its control processes. In K. Spence & J. Spence (Eds.), *The psychology of learning and motivation* (Vol. 2, pp. 89–195). New York: Academic Press.

Atkinson, R. K., Levin, J. R., Kiewra, K. A., Meyers, T., Atkinson, L. A., Renandya, W. A., & Hwang, Y. (1999). Matrix and mnemonic text-processing adjuncts: Comparing and combining their components. *Journal of Educational Psychology, 91,* 242–257.

Au, K. H. (1980). Participation structures in a reading lesson with Hawaiian children: Analysis of a culturally appropriate instructional event. *Anthropology and Education Quarterly, 11,* 91–115.

Ausubel, D. P. (1963). *The psychology of meaningful verbal learning.* New York: Grune and Stratton.

Ausubel, D. P. (1977). The facilitation of meaningful verbal learning in the classroom. *Educational Psychologist, 12,* 162–178.

Ausubel, D. P. (1982). Schemata, advance organizers, and anchoring ideas: A reply to Anderson, Spiro, and Anderson. *Journal of Structural Learning, 7,* 63–73.

Avramidis, E., Bayliss, P., & Burden, R. (2000). Student teachers' attitudes toward the inclusion of children with special education needs in the ordinary school. *Teaching and Teacher Education, 16,* 277–293.

Ayres, N. (2002). Calculators in the classroom. Retrieved on August 16, 2002, from http://www.math.twsu.edu/history/topics/calculators.html#calc

Babad, E. Y. (1995). The "Teachers' Pet" phenomenon, students' perceptions of differential behavior, and students' morale. *Journal of Educational Psychology, 87,* 361–374.

Babad, E. Y., Inbar, J., & Rosenthal, R. (1982). Pygmalion, Galatea, and the Golem: Investigations of biased and unbiased teachers. *Journal of Educational Psychology, 74,* 459–474.

Baddeley, A. D. (1986). *Working memory.* Oxford, UK: Clarendon Books.

Baddeley, A. (1998). *Human memory: Theory and practice* (Rev. ed.). Boston: Allyn and Bacon.

Baddeley, A. D. (2001). Is working memory still working? *American Psychologist, 56,* 851–864.

Baer, J. (1997). *Creative teachers, creative students.* Boston: Allyn and Bacon.

Bailey, S. M. (1993). The current status of gender equity research in American Schools. *Educational Psychologist, 28,* 321–339.

Baillargeon, R., & DeVos, J. (1991). Object permanence in young infants: Further evidence. *Child Development, 62,* 1227–1246.

Baker, C. (1993). *Foundations of bilingual education and bilingualism.* Clevedon, England: Multilingual Matters.

Baker, D. (1986). Sex differences in classroom interaction in secondary science. *Journal of Classroom Interaction, 22,* 212–218.

Bakerman, R., Adamson, L. B., Koner, M., & Barr, R. G. (1990). !Kung infancy: The social context of object exploration. *Child Development, 61,* 794–809.

Ball, D. L. (1997). What do students know? Facing challenges of distance, context, and desire in trying to hear children. In B. J. Biddle, T. L. Good, & I. F. Goodson (Eds.), *The international handbook of teachers and teaching* (pp. 769–818). Dordrecht, the Netherlands: Kluwer.

Ball, D. L., Lubienski, S. T., & Mewborn, D. S. (2001). Research on teaching mathematics: The unsolved problem of teachers' mathematical knowledge. In V. Richardson (Ed.), *Handbook of research on teaching* (4th ed., pp. 433–456). Washington, DC: American Educational Research Association.

Bandura, A. (1965). Influence of models' reinforcement contingencies on the acquisition of imitative responses. *Journal of Personality and Social Psychology, 1,* 589–595.

Bandura, A. (1977). *Social learning theory.* Englewood Cliffs, NJ: Prentice-Hall.

Bandura, A. (1982). Self-efficacy mechanisms in human agency. *American Psychologist, 37,* 122–147.

Bandura, A. (1986). *Social foundations of thought and action.* Englewood Cliffs, NJ: Prentice-Hall.

Bandura, A. (1993). Perceived self-efficacy in cognitive development and functioning. *Educational Psychologist, 28,* 117–148.

Bandura, A. (1997). *Self-efficacy: The exercise of control.* New York: Freeman.

Bandura, A., Ross, D., & Ross, S. A. (1963). Vicarious reinforcement and imitative learning. *Journal of Abnormal and Social Psychology, 67,* 601–607.

Bangert-Drowns, R. L., Kulik, C. C., Kulik, J. A., & Morgan, M. (1991). The instructional effect of feedback in test-like events. *Review of Educational Research, 61,* 213–238.

Banks, J. A. (1993). Multicultural education: Characteristics and goals. In J. Banks & C. McGee Banks (Eds.), *Multicultural education: Issues and perspectives* (2nd ed.) (pp. 2–26). Boston: Allyn and Bacon.

Banks, J. A. (1993). Multicultural education: Development, dimensions, and challenges. *Phi Delta Kappan, 75,* 22–28.

Banks, J. A. (1994). *Multiethnic education: Theory and practice.* Boston: Allyn and Bacon.

Banks, J. A. (1997). *Teaching strategies for ethnic studies* (6th ed.). Boston: Allyn and Bacon.

Banks, J. A. (2002). *An introduction to multicultural education* (3rd ed.). Boston: Allyn and Bacon.

Barden, L. M. (1995). Effective questioning and the ever-elusive higher-order question. *American Biology Teacher, 57,* 423–426.

Bargh, J. A., & Chartrand, T. L. (1999). The unbearable automaticity of being. *American Psychologist, 54,* 462–479.

Baron, R. A. (1998). *Psychology* (4th ed.). Boston: Allyn and Bacon.

Baron, R. A., & Byrne, D. (2003). *Social psychology* (10th ed.). Boston: Allyn and Bacon.

Barone, F. J. (1997). Bullying in school: It doesn't have to happen. *Phi Delta Kappan, 79,* 80–82.

Baroody, A. R., & Ginsburg, H. P. (1990). Children's learning: A cognitive view. In R. Davis, C. Maher, & N. Noddings (Eds.), *Constructivist views on the teaching and learning of mathematics* (pp. 51–64). Monograph 4 of the National Council of Teachers of Mathematics, Reston, VA.

Barr, R. (2001). Research on the teaching of reading. In V. Richardson (Ed.), *Handbook of research on teaching* (4th ed., pp. 390–415). Washington, DC: American Educational Research Association.

Bartlett, F. C. (1932). *Remembering: A study in experimental and social psychology.* New York: Macmillan.

Battistich, V., Solomon, D., & Delucci, K. (1993). Interaction processes and student outcomes in cooperative groups. *Elementary School Journal, 94,* 19–32.

Basow, S. A., & Rubin, L. R. (1999). Gender influences on adolescent development. In N. G. Johnson, M. C. Roberts, & J. Worell (Eds.), *Beyond appearance: A new look at adolescent girls* (pp. 25–52). Washington, DC: American Psychological Association.

Battistich, V., Watson, M., Solomon, D., Lewis, C., & Schaps, E. (1999). Beyond the three R's: A broad agenda for school reform. *The Elementary School Journal, 99,* 415–432.

Beane, J. A. (1991). Sorting out the self-esteem controversy. *Educational Leadership, 49*(1), 25–30.

Beane, J. A. (1995). (Ed.). *Toward a coherent curriculum.* Alexandria, VA: Association for Supervision and Curriculum Development.

Beck, I. L., McKeown, M. G., Worthy, J., Sandora, C. A., & Kucan, L. (1996). Questioning the author: A yearlong classroom implementation to engage students with text. *The Elementary School Journal, 96,* 385–414.

Becker, W. C., Engelmann, S., & Thomas, D. R. (1975). *Teaching 1: Classroom management.* Chicago: Science Research Associates.

Bee, H. (1981). *The developing child* (3rd ed.). New York: Harper & Row.

Bee, H. (1992). *The developing child* (6th ed.). New York: Harper & Row.

Beeth, M. E. (1998). Teaching science in fifth grade: Instructional goals that support conceptual change. *Journal of Research in Science Teaching, 35,* 1091–1101.

Beezer, B. (1985). Reporting child abuse and neglect: Your responsibilities and your protections. *Phi Delta Kappan, 66,* 434–436.

Belanoff, P., & Dickson, M. (1991). *Portfolios: Process and product.* Portsmouth, NH: Heinemann, Boynton/Cook.

Belfiore, P. J., & Hornyak, R. S. (1998). Operant theory and the application of self-monitoring to adolescents. In D. Schunk & B. Zimmerman (Eds.), *Self-regulated learning: From theory to self-reflective practice* (pp. 184–202). New York: Guilford.

Benenson, J. F. (1993). Greater preference among females than males for dyadic interaction in early childhood. *Child Development, 64,* 544–555.

Benjafield, J. G. (1992). *Cognition.* Englewood Cliffs, NJ: Prentice-Hall.

Bennett, C. I. (1995). *Comprehensive multicultural education: Theory and practice* (3rd ed.). Boston: Allyn and Bacon.

Bennett, C. I. (1999). *Comprehensive multicultural education: Theory and practice* (4th ed.). Boston: Allyn and Bacon.

Bereiter, C. (1997). Situated cognition and how I overcome it. In D. Kirshner & J. A. Whitson (Eds.), *Situated cognition: Social, semiotic, and psychological perspectives* (pp. 281–300). Mahwah, NJ: Lawrence Erlbaum.

Berg, C. A., & Clough, M. (1991). Hunter lesson design: The wrong one for science teaching. *Educational Leadership, 48*(4), 73–78.

Berger, K. S. (2000). *The developing person: Through childhood and adolescence.* New York: Worth.

Berger, K. S. (2003). *The developing person through childhood and adolescence* (6th ed.). New York: Worth Publishers.

Berger, K. S., & Thompson, R. A. (1995). *The developing person through childhood and adolescence.* New York: Worth.

Berk, L. (2002). *Infants, children, and adolescents* (4th ed.). Boston: Allyn and Bacon.

Berk, L. E. (1997). *Child development* (4th ed.). Boston: Allyn and Bacon.

Berk, L. E. (2001). *Awakening children's minds: How parents and teachers can make a difference.* New York: Oxford University Press.

Berk, L. E., & Spuhl, S. T. (1995). Maternal interaction, private speech, and task performance in preschool children. *Early Childhood Research Quarterly, 10,* 145–169.

Berliner, D. (1983). Developing concepts of classroom environments: Some light on the T in studies of ATI. *Educational Psychologist, 18,* 1–13.

Berliner, D. (1987). But do they understand? In V. Richardson-Koehler (Ed.), *Educators' handbook: A research perspective* (pp. 259–293). New York: Longman.

Berliner, D. (1988). Simple views of effective teaching and a simple theory of classroom instruction. In D. Berliner & B. Rosenshine (Eds.), *Talks to teachers* (pp. 93–110). New York: Random House.

Berliner, D. (1992).Telling the stories of educational psychology. *Educational Psychologist, 27,* 143–152.

Berliner, D., & Biddle, B. (1997). *The manufactured crisis: Myths, frauds, and the attack on America's public schools.* White Plains: Longman.

Berlyne, D. (1966). Curiosity and exploration. *Science, 153,* 25–33.

Berndt, T. J., & Keefe, K. (1995). Friends' influence on adolescents' adjustment to school. *Child Development, 66,* 1312–1329.

Betancourt, H., & Lopez, S. R. (1993). The study of culture, ethnicity, and race in American psychology. *American Psychologist, 48,* 629–637.

Bhatia, T. K., & Richie, W. C. (1999). The bilingual child: Some issues and perspectives. In W. C. Richie & T. K. Bhatia (Eds.), *Handbook of child language acquisition.* San Diego: Academic Press.

Bialystok, E. (1999). Cognitive complexity and attentional control in the bilingual child. *Child Development, 70,* 636–644.

Biggs, J. (2001). Enhancing learning: A matter of style of approach. In R. Sternberg & L. Zhang (Eds.), *Perspectives on cognitive, learning, and thinking styles* (pp. 73–102). Mahwah, NJ: Lawrence Erlbaum.

Bivens, J. A., & Berk, L. E. (1990). A longitudinal study of elementary school children's private speech. *Merrill-Palmer Quarterly, 36,* 443–463.

Bjorklund, D. F. (1989). *Children's thinking: Developmental function and individual differences.* Pacific Grove, CA: Brooks/Cole.

Block, J. H. (1983). Differential premises arising from differential socialization of the sexes: Some conjectures. *Child Development, 54,* 1335–1354.

Block, J. H., & Anderson, L. W. (1975). *Mastery learning in classroom instruction.* New York: Macmillan.

Bloom, B. S. (1968). *Learning for mastery. Evaluation Comment, 1(2).* Los Angeles: University of California, Center for the Study of Evaluation of Instructional Programs.

Bloom, B. S. (1981). *All our children learning: A primer for parents, teachers, and other educators.* New York: McGraw-Hill.

Bloom, B. S. (1982). The role of gifts and markers in the development of talent. *Exceptional Children, 48,* 510–522.

Bloom, B. S., Engelhart, M. D., Frost, E. J., Hill, W. H., & Krathwohl, D. R. (1956). *Taxonomy of educational objectives. Handbook I: Cognitive domain.* New York: David McKay.

Bloom, R., & Bourdon, L. (1980). Types and frequencies of teachers' written instructional feedback. *Journal of Educational Research, 74,* 13–15.

Bluestein, J. (1995). *Mentors, masters, and Mrs. MacGregor.* Deerfield Beach, FL: Health Communications.

Blumenfeld, P. C., Puro, P., & Mergendoller, J. R. (1992). Translating motivation into thoughtfulness. In H. Marshall (Ed.), *Redefining student learning: Roots of educational change* (pp. 207–240). Norwood, NJ: Ablex.

Boggiano, A. K., Flink, C., Shields, A., Seelbach, A., & Barrett, M. (1993). Use of techniques promoting students' self-determination: Effects on students' analytic problem-solving skills. *Motivation and Education, 17,* 319–336.

Boldizar, J. P. (1991). Assessing sex typing and androgyny in children: The children's sex inventory. *Developmental Psychology, 27,* 505–515.

Boom, J., Brugman, D., & van der Heijden, P. G. (2001). Hierarchical structure of moral stages assessed by a sorting task. *Child Development, 72,* 535–548.

Borko, H. (1989). Research on learning to teach: Implications for graduate teacher preparation. In A. Woolfolk (Ed.), *Research perspectives on the graduate preparation of teachers* (pp. 69–87). Boston: Allyn and Bacon.

Borko, H., & Putnam, R. (1996). Learning to teach. In D. Berliner & R. Calfee (Eds.), *Handbook of educational psychology* (pp. 673–708). New York: Macmillan.

Borko, H., & Livingston, C. (1989). Cognition and improvisation: Differences in mathematics instruction by expert and novice teachers. *American Educational Research Journal, 26,* 473–498.

Borkowski, J. G., Johnston, M. B., & Reid, M. K. (1986). Metacognition, motivation, and the transfer of control processes. In S. J. Ceci (Ed.), *Handbook of cognition: Social and neurological aspects of learning disabilities.* Hillsdale, NJ: Lawrence Erlbaum.

Bos, C. S., & Reyes, E. I. (1996). Conversations with a Latina teacher about education for language-minority students with special needs. *The Elementary School Journal, 96,* 344–351.

Boutte, G. S. (Ed.). (2002). *Resounding voices: School experiences of people from diverse ethnic backgrounds.* Boston: Allyn and Bacon.

Braddock, J., II, & Slavin, R. E. (1993). Why ability grouping must end: Achieving excellence and equity in American education. *Journal of Intergroup Relations, 20*(2), 51–64.

Brannon, L. (2002). *Gender: Psychological perspectives* (3rd ed.). Boston: Allyn and Bacon.

Bransford, J. D., & Stein, B. S. (1993). *The IDEAL problem solver: A guide for improving thinking, learning, and creativity* (2nd ed.). New York: Freeman.

Bredderman, T. (1983). Effects of activity-based elementary science on student outcomes: A qualitative synthesis. *Review of Educational Research, 53,* 499–518.

Bredekamp, S., & Copple, C. (1997). *Developmentally appropriate practice in early childhood programs.* Washington, DC: National Association for the Education of Young Children.

Bretherton, I., & Waters, E. (1985). Growing points of attachment theory and research. *Monographs of the Society for Research in Child Development, 50* (1, 2, Serial No. 209).

Brice, A. E. (2002). *The Hispanic child: Speech, language, culture, and education.* Boston: Allyn and Bacon.

Brody, L. (1999). *Gender, emotion, and the family.* Cambridge, MA: Harvard University Press.

Bronfenbrenner, U., McClelland, P., Wethington, E., Moen, P., & Ceci, S. (1996). *The state of Americans: This generation and the next.* New York: Free Press.

Brooks, D. (1985). Beginning the year in junior high: The first day of school. *Educational Leadership, 42,* 76–78.

Brooks, J. G., & Brooks, M. G. (1993). *In search of understanding: The case for constructivist classrooms.* Alexandria, VA: Association for Supervision and Curriculum Development.

Brophy, J. (1998). *Motivating students to learn.* New York: McGraw-Hill.

Brophy, J. E. (1981). Teacher praise: A functional analysis. *Review of Educational Research, 51,* 5–21.

Brophy, J. E. (1982, March). *Research on the self-fulfilling prophecy and teacher expectations.* Paper presented at the annual meeting of the American Educational Research Association, New York.

Brophy, J. E. (1983). Conceptualizing student motivation to learn. *Educational Psychologist, 18,* 200–215.

Brophy, J. E. (1985). Teacher–student interaction. In J. Dusek (Ed.), *Teacher expectancies* (pp. 303–328). Hillsdale, NJ: Lawrence Erlbaum.

Brophy, J. E. (1988). On motivating students. In D. Berliner & B. Rosenshine (Eds.), *Talks to teachers* (pp. 201–245). New York: Random House.

Brophy, J. E., & Evertson, C. (1978). Context variables in teaching. *Educational Psychologist, 12,* 310–316.

Brophy, J. E., & Good, T. (1986). Teacher behavior and student achievement. In M. Wittrock (Ed.), *Handbook of research on teaching* (3rd ed.) (pp. 328–375). New York: Macmillan.

Brophy, J. E., & Kher, N. (1986). Teacher socialization as a mechanism for developing student motivation to learn. In R. Feldman (Ed.), *Social psychology applied to education* (pp. 256–288). New York: Cambridge University Press.

Brown, A. (1987). Metacognition, executive control, self-regulation, and other more mysterious mechanisms. In F. Weinert & R. Kluwe (Eds.), *Metacognition, motivation, and understanding* (pp. 65–116). Hillside, NJ: Lawrence Erlbaum.

Brown, A. (1997). Transforming schools into communities of thinking and learning about serious matters. *American Psychologist, 52,* 399–413.

Brown, A. L. (1992). Design experiments: Theoretical and methodological challenges in creating complex interventions in classroom settings. *Journal of the Learning Sciences, 2,* 141–178.

Brown, A. L., Bransford, J., Ferrara, R., & Campione, J. (1983). Learning, remembering, and understanding. In P. Mussen (Ed.), *Handbook of child psychology* (Vol. 3, pp. 515–629). New York: Wiley.

Brown, A. L., & Campione, J. C. (1996). Psychological theory and the design of innovative learning environments: On procedures, principles, and systems. In L. Schauble & R. Glaser (Eds.), *Innovations in learning: New environments for education* (pp. 289–325). Mahwah, NJ: Lawrence Erlbaum.

Brown, J. S., & Burton, R. R. (1979). Diagnostic models for procedural bugs in basic mathematical skills. *Cognitive Science, 2,* 155–192.

Brown, M. (2000). Access, instruction, and barriers. *Remedial and Special Education, 21,* 182–192.

Bruer, John T. (1999). In search of . . . brain-based education. *Phi Delta Kappan, 80,* 648–657.

Bruner, J. (1986). *Actual minds, possible worlds.* Cambridge, MA: Harvard University Press.

Bruner, J. S. (1960). *The process of education.* New York: Vintage Books.

Bruner, J. S. (1966). *Toward a theory of instruction.* New York: Norton.

Bruner, J. S. (1971). *The relevance of education.* New York: Norton.

Bruner, J. S. (1973). *Beyond the information given: Studies in the psychology of knowing.* New York: Norton.

Bruner, J. S., Goodnow, J. J., & Austin, G. A. (1956). *A study of thinking.* New York: Wiley.

Bruning, R. H., Schraw, G. J., & Ronning, R. R. (1999). *Cognitive psychology and instruction* (3rd ed.). Columbus, OH: Merrill.

Buenning, M., & Tollefson, N. (1987). The cultural gap hypothesis as an explanation for the achievement patterns of Mexican-American students. *Psychology in the Schools, 14,* 264–271.

Bugental, D. B., Lewis, J. C., Lin, E., Lyon, J., & Kopeikin, H. (1999). In charge but not in control: The management of teaching relationships by adults with low perceived power. *Developmental Psychology, 35,* 1367–1378.

Bugental, D. B., Lyon, J. E., Lin, E. K., McGrath, E. P., & Bimbela, A. (1999). Children "tune out" in response to the ambiguous communication style of powerless adults. *Child Development, 70,* 214–230.

Bulgren, J. A., Deshler, D. D., Schumaker, J. B., & Lenz, B. K. (2000). The use and effectiveness of analogical instruction in diverse secondary content classrooms. *Journal of Educational Psychology, 92,* 426–441.

Burbules, N. C., & Bruce, B. C. (2001). Theory and research on teaching as dialogue. In V. Richardson (Ed.), *Handbook of research on teaching* (4th ed., pp. 1102–1121). Washington, DC: American Educational Research Association.

Burden, P. R. (1995). *Classroom management and discipline: Methods to facilitate cooperation and instruction.* White Plains, NY: Longman.

Burton, R. V. (1963). The generality of honesty reconsidered. *Psychological Review, 70,* 481–499.

Burke-Spero, R. (1999). Toward a model of "civitas" through an ethic of care: A qualitative study of preservice teachers' perceptions about learning to teach diverse populations (Doctoral dissertation, The Ohio State University, 1999). *Dissertation Abstracts International, 60,* 11A, 3967.

Burke-Spero, R., & Woolfolk Hoy, A. (2002). *The need for thick description: A qualitative investigation of developing teacher efficacy.* Unpublished manuscript, University of Miami.

Bus, A. G., & van Ijzendoorn, M. H. (1999). Phonological awareness and early reading: a meta-analysis of experimental training studies. *Journal of Educational Psychology, 91,* 403–414.

Buss, D. M. (1995). Psychological sex differences: Origin through sexual selection. *American Psychologist, 50,* 164–168.

Butler, D. L. (2002). Individualized instruction in self-regulated learning. *Theory Into Practice, 41,* 81–92.

Butler, R. (1987). Task-involving and ego-involving properties of evaluation: Effects of different feedback conditions on motivational perceptions, interest, and performance. *Journal of Educational Psychology, 79,* 474–482.

Butler, R., & Neuman, O. (1995). Effects of task and ego achievement goals on help-seeking behaviors and attitudes. *Journal of Educational Psychology, 87,* 261–271.

Butler, R., & Nisan, M. (1986). Effects of no feedback, task-related comments, and grades on intrinsic motivation and performance. *Journal of Educational Psychology, 78,* 210–224.

Byrne, B., Fielding-Barnsley, R., & Ashley, L. (2000). Effects of preschool phoneme identity training after six years: Outcome level distinguished from rate of response. *Journal of Educational Psychology, 92,* 659–667.

Byrne, B. M., & Shavelson, R. J. (1996). On the structure of social self-concept for pre-, early, and late adolescents: A test of the Shavelson model. *Journal of Personality and Social Psychology, 70,* 599–613.

Byrne, B. M., & Worth Gavin, D. A. (1996). The Shavelson model revisited: Testing for structure of academic self concept across pre-, early, and late adolescents. *Journal of Educational Psychology, 88,* 215–229.

Byrnes, J. P. (1996). *Cognitive development and learning in instructional contexts.* Boston: Allyn and Bacon.

Byrnes, J. P., & Fox, N. A. (1998). The educational relevance of research in cognitive neuroscience. *Educational Psychology Review, 10,* 297–342.

Caine, R. N., & Caine, G. (1991). *Making connections: Teaching and the human brain.* Alexandria, VA: Association for Supervision and Curriculum Development.

Calderhead, J. (1996). Teacher: Beliefs and knowledge. In D. Berliner & R. Calfee (Eds.), *Handbook of educational psychology* (pp. 709–725). New York: Macmillan.

Callahan, C. M., Tomlinson, C. A., & Plucker, J. (1997). *Project STATR using a multiple intelligences model in identifying and promoting talent in high-risk students.* Storrs, CT: National Research Center for Gifted and Talented. University of Connecticut Technical Report.

Calmore, J. A. (1986). National housing policy and black America: Trends, issues, and implications. In *The state of black America 1986* (pp. 115–149). New York: National Urban League.

Cambourne, B., & Turbill, J. (1990). Assessment in whole-language classrooms: Theory into practice. *Elementary School Journal, 90,* 337–349.

Cameron, J., & Pierce, W. D. (1994). Reinforcement, reward, and intrinsic motivation: A meta-analysis. *Review of Educational Research, 64,* 363–423.

Cameron, J., & Pierce, W. D. (1996). The debate about rewards and intrinsic motivation: Protests and accusations do not alter the results. *Review of Educational Research, 66,* 39–52.

Camp, R. (1990, Spring). Thinking together about portfolios. *The Quarterly of the National Writing Project, 27,* 8–14.

Campbell, L., Campbell, B., & Dickinson, D. (1999). *Teaching and learning through multiple intelligences* (2nd ed.). Boston: Allyn and Bacon.

Cangelosi, J. S. (1990). *Designing tests for evaluating student achievement.* New York: Longman.

Canter, L. (1996). First the rapport—then the rules. *Learning, 24*(5), 12+.

Canter, L., & Canter, M. (1992). *Lee Canter's Assertive Discipline: Positive behavior management for today's classroom.* Santa Monica: Lee Canter and Associates.

Carey, L. M. (1994). *Measuring and evaluating school learning* (2nd ed.). Boston: Allyn and Bacon.

Carey, S., & Gellman, R. (Eds.). (1991). *The epigenesis of mind: Essays on biology and cognition.* Cambridge, MA: MIT Press.

Cariglia-Bull, T., & Pressley, M. (1990). Short-term memory differences between children predict imagery effects when sentences are read. *Journal of Experimental Child Psychology, 49,* 384–398.

Carnegie Council on Adolescent Development. (1995). *Great transitions: Preparing adolescents for a new century.* New York: Carnegie Corporation of New York.

Carnegie Forum on Education and the Economy. (1986). *A nation prepared: Teachers for the 21st century.* Washington, DC: Author.

Carnegie Foundation for the Advancement of Teaching (1987). *1987 national survey of public school teachers.* Princeton, NJ: Author.

Carney, R. N., & Levin, J. R. (2000). Mnemonic instruction, with a focus on transfer. *Journal of Educational Psychology, 92,* 783–790.

Carney, R. N., & Levin, J. R. (2002). Pictorial illustrations *still* improve students' learning from text. *Educational Psychology Review, 14,* 5–26.

Carpendale, J. I. M. (2000). Kohlberg and Piaget on stages and moral reasoning. *Developmental Review, 20,* 181–205.

Carroll, J. (1993). *Human cognitive abilities: A survey of factor analytic studies.* Cambridge, England: Cambridge University Press.

Carroll, J. B. (1997). The three-stratum theory of cognitive abilities. In D. P. Flanagan, J. L. Genshaft, & P. L. Harrison (Eds.), *Con-*

temporary intellectual assessment: Theories, tests, and issues (pp. 122–130). New York: Guilford.

Carter, K. (1984). Do teachers understand principles of writing tests? *Journal of Teacher Education, 35,* 57–60.

Casanova, U. (1987). Ethnic and cultural differences. In V. Richardson-Koehler (Ed.), *Educators' handbook: A research perspective* (pp. 370–393). New York: Longman.

Case, R. (1985a). *Intellectual development: Birth to adulthood.* New York: Academic Press.

Case, R. (1985b). A developmentally-based approach to the problem of instructional design. In R. Glaser, S. Chipman, & J. Segal (Eds.), *Teaching thinking skills* (Vol. 2, pp. 545–562). Hillsdale, NJ: Lawrence Erlbaum.

Case, R. (1992). *The mind's staircase: Exploring the conceptual underpinnings of children's thought and knowledge.* Mahwah, NJ: Lawrence Erlbaum.

Case, R. (1998). The development of conceptual structures. In D. Kuhn & R. S. Siegler (Eds.), *Handbook of child psychology: Vol. 2: Cognition, perception, and language* (pp. 745–800). New York: Wiley.

Cassady, J. C., & Johnson, R. E. (2002). Cognitive anxiety and academic performance. *Contemporary Educational Psychology 27,* 270–295.

Cattell, R. B. (1963). Theory of fluid and crystallized intelligence: A critical experiment. *Journal of Educational Psychology, 54,* 1–22.

Cauley, K., & Tyler, B. (1989). The relationship of self-concept to prosocial behavior in children. *Early Childhood Research Quarterly, 4,* 51–60.

Cavanagh, S. (2002, July 10). Overhauled SAT could shake up school curricula. *Education Week on the Web.* Retrieved August 5, 2002 from http://edweek.org/ew/newstory.cfm?slug=42sat.h21

Cazden, C. B. (1988). *Classroom discourse: The language of teaching and learning.* Portsmouth, NH: Heinemann.

Ceci, S. J. (1991). How much does schooling influence intelligence and its cognitive components? A reassessment of the evidence. *Developmental Psychology, 27,* 703–720.

Ceci, S. J., & Roazzi, A. (1994). The effects of context on cognition: Postcards from Brazil. In R. J. Sternberg (Ed.), *Mind in context* (pp. 74–101). New York: Cambridge University Press.

Chambers, B., & Abrami, P. C. (1991). The relationship between student team learning outcomes and achievement, causal attributions, and affect. *Journal of Educational Psychology, 83,* 140–146.

Chamot, A. U., & O'Malley, J. M. (1996). The Cognitive Academic Language Learning Approach: A model for linguistically diverse classrooms. *The Elementary School Journal, 96,* 259–274.

Chan, C. K., & Sachs, J. (2001). Beliefs about learning in children's understanding of science texts. *Contemporary Educational Psychology, 26,* 192–210.

Chance, P. (1991). Backtalk: a gross injustice. *Phi Delta Kappan, 72,* 803.

Chance, P. (1992). The rewards of learning. *Phi Delta Kappan, 73,* 200–207.

Chance, P. (1993). Sticking up for rewards. *Phi Delta Kappan, 74,* 787–790.

Chapman, J. W., Tunmer, W. E., & Prochnow, J. E. (2000). Early reading-related skills and performance, reading self-concept, and the development of academic self-concept: A longitudinal study. *Journal of Educational Psychology, 92,* 703–708.

Chapman, M., Zahn-Waxler, C., Cooperman, G., & Iannotti, R. (1987). Empathy and responsibility in the motivation of children's helping. *Developmental Psychology, 23,* 140–145.

Charles, C. M. (1985). *Building classroom discipline: From models to practice* (2nd ed.). New York: Longman.

Charles, C. M. (2002a). *Essential elements of effective discipline.* Boston: Allyn and Bacon.

Charles, C. M. (2002b). *Building classroom discipline* (7th ed.). Boston: Allyn and Bacon.

Chi, M. T. H. (1978). Knowledge structures and memory development. In R. Siegler (Ed.), *Children's thinking: What develops?* (pp. 73–96). Hillsdale, NJ: Lawrence Erlbaum.

Chi, M. T. H., Glaser, R., & Farr, M. (Eds.). (1988). *The nature of expertise.* Hillsdale, NJ: Lawrence Erlbaum.

Chi, M. T. H., & Koeske, R. D. (1983). Network representation of a child's dinosaur knowledge. *Developmental Psychology, 19,* 29–39.

Children's Defense Fund. (2002). *The state of America's children: Yearbook 2002.* Washington, DC: Author.

Claiborn, W. L. (1969). Expectancy effects in the classroom: A failure to replicate. *Journal of Education Psychology, 60,* 377–383.

Clark, C. M. (1983). Personal communication.

Clark, C. M., & Peterson, P. L. (1986). Teachers' thought processes. In M. Wittrock (Ed.), *Handbook of research on teaching* (3rd ed.) (pp. 255–296). New York: Macmillan.

Clark, C. M., & Yinger, R. (1988). Teacher planning. In D. Berliner & B. Rosenshine (Eds.), *Talks to teachers* (pp. 342–365). New York: Random House.

Clark, J. M., & Paivio, A. (1991). Dual coding theory and education. *Educational Psychology Review, 3,* 149–210.

Clark, K., & Clark, M. (1939). The development of consciousness of self and the emergence of racial identification in Negro preschool children. *Journal of Social Psychology, 10,* 591–599.

Clark, R., Anderson, N. B., Clark, V. R., & Williams, D. R. (1999). Racism as a stressor for African Americans. *American Psychologist, 54,* 805–816.

Clarke, J. H., & Agne, R. M. (1997). *Interdisciplinary high school teaching.* Boston: Allyn and Bacon.

Claus, J., & Ogden, C. (1999). Service learning for youth empowerment and social change: An introduction. In J. Claus & C. Ogden (Eds.), *Service learning for youth empowerment and social change.* New York: Peter Lang.

Clement, S. L. (1978). Dual marking system: Simple and effective. *American Secondary Education, 8,* 49–52.

Clifford, M. M. (1984). Educational psychology. In *Encyclopedia of Education* (pp. 413–416). New York: Macmillan.

Clifford, M. M. (1990). Students need challenge, not easy success. *Educational Leadership, 48*(1), 22–26.

Clifford, M. M. (1991). Risk taking: Empirical and educational considerations. *Educational Psychologist, 26,* 263–298.

Cobb, P., & Bowers, J. (1999). Cognitive and situated learning: Perspectives in theory and practice. *Educational Researcher, 28*(2), 4–15.

Codell, E. R. (2001). *Educating Esme: Diary of a teacher's first year.* Chapel Hill, NC: Algonquin Books.

Cognition and Technology Group at Vanderbilt. (1990). Anchored instruction and its relations to situated cognition. *Educational Researcher, 19*(6), 2–10.

Cognition and Technology Group at Vanderbilt. (1993). Anchored instruction and situated learning revisited. *Educational Technology, 33*(3), 52–70.

Cognition and Technology Group at Vanderbilt. (1996). Looking at technology in context: A framework for understanding technology and educational research. In D. Berliner & R. Calfee

(Eds.), *Handbook of educational psychology* (pp. 807–840). New York: Macmillan.

Cohen, E. G. (1986). *Designing groupwork: Strategies for the heterogeneous classroom.* New York: Teachers College Press.

Cohen, J. (Ed.). (1999). *Educating minds and hearts: Social emotional learning and the passage into adolescence.* New York: Teachers College Press.

Coie, J. D., & Dodge, K. A. (1998). Aggression and antisocial behavior. In N. Eisenberg (Ed.), *Handbook of child psychology: Vol. 3. Social, emotional, and personality development* (5th ed.) (pp. 779–862). New York: Wiley.

Coie, J. D., Terry, R., Lenox, K., Lochman, J., & Hyman, C. (1995). Childhood peer rejection and aggression as predictors of stable patterns of adolescent disorder. *Development and Psychopathology, 7,* 697–714.

Cole, D. A., Martin, J. M., Peeke, L. A., Seroczynski, A. D., & Fier, J. (1999). Children's over- and underestimation of academic competence: A longitudinal study of gender differences, depression, and anxiety. *Child Development, 70,* 459–473.

Cole, M. (1985). The zone of proximal development: Where culture and cognition create each other. In J. V. Wertsch (Ed.), *Culture, communication, and cognition: Vygotskian perspectives* (pp. 146–161). Cambridge: Cambridge University Press.

Coleman, J. S. (1966). *Equality of educational opportunity.* Washington DC: U.S. Government Printing Office.

Coles, R. (1990, September). Teachers who made a difference. *Instructor,* 58–59.

Collins, A., Brown, J. S., & Holum, A. (1991). Cognitive apprenticeship: Making thinking visible. *American Educator, 15*(3), 38–39.

Collins, A., Brown, J. S., & Newman, S. E. (1989). Cognitive apprenticeship: Teaching the crafts of reading, writing, and mathematics. In L. B. Resnick (Ed.), *Knowing, learning, and instruction: Essays in honor of Robert Galser* (pp. 453–494). Hillsdale, NJ: Lawrence Erlbaum.

Collins, A., & Ferguson, W. (1993). Epistemic forms and epistemic games: Structures and strategies to guide inquiry. *Educational Psychologist, 28,* 35.

Collins, W. A., Maccoby, E. E., Steinberg, L., Hetherington, E. M., & Bornstein, M. H. (2000). Contemporary research on parenting: The case for nature and nurture. *American Psychologist, 55,* 218–232.

Confrey, J. (1990a). A review of the research on students' conceptions in mathematics, science, and programming. *Review of Research in Education, 16,* 3–56.

Confrey, J. (1990b). What constructivism implies for teaching. In R. Davis, C. Maher, & N. Noddings (Eds.), *Constructivist views on the teaching and learning of mathematics* (pp. 107–122). Monograph 4 of the National Council of Teachers of Mathematics, Reston, VA.

Conger, R. D., Conger, K. J., & Elder, G. (1997). Family economic hardship and adolescent academic performance: Mediating and moderating processes. In G. Duncan & J. Brooks-Gunn (Eds.), *Consequences of growing up poor* (pp. 288–310). New York: Russell Sage Foundation.

Connell, R. W. (1996). Teaching the boys: New research on masculinity, and gender strategies for schools. *Teachers College Record, 98,* 206–235.

Cooke, B. L., & Pang, K. C. (1991). Recent research on beginning teachers: Studies of trained and untrained novices. *Teaching and Teacher Education, 7,* 93–110.

Cooper, C. R. (1998). *The weaving of maturity: Cultural perspectives on adolescent development.* New York: Oxford University Press.

Cooper, C. R., & Denner, J. (1998). Theories linking culture and psychology: Universal and community-specific processes. In J. T. Spence, J. M. Darley, & D. J. Foss (Eds.), *Annual review of psychology* (pp. 559–584). Palo Alto, CA: Annual Reviews.

Cooper, G., & Sweller, J. (1987). Effects of schema acquisition and rule automation on mathematical problem-solving transfer. *Journal of Educational Psychology, 79,* 347–362.

Cooper, H., & Valentine, J. C. (Eds.). (2001a). Special Issue: Homework. *Educational Psychologist, 36*(3), Summer.

Cooper, H., & Valentine, J. C. (2001b). Using research to answer practical questions about homework. *Educational Psychologist, 36,* 143–153.

Cooper, H. M. (1979). Pygmalion grows up: A model for teacher expectation communication and performance influence. *Review of Educational Research, 49,* 389–410.

Cooper, H. M., & Good, T. (1983). *Pygmalion grows up: Studies in the expectation communication process.* New York: Longman.

Cooper, H. M., Valentine, J. C., Nye, B., & Kindsay, J. J. (1999). Relationships between five after-school activities and academic achievement. *Journal of Educational Psychology, 91,* 369–683.

Copi, I. M. (1961). *Introduction to logic.* New York: Macmillan.

Cordova, D. I., & Lepper, M. R. (1996). Intrinsic motivation and the process of learning: Beneficial effects of contextualization, personalization, and choice. *Journal of Educational Psychology, 88,* 715–730.

Corenblum, B., & Annis, R. C. (1987). Racial identity and preference among Canadian Indian and White children: Replication and extension. *Canadian Journal of Behavioural Science, 19,* 254–265.

Corkill, A. J. (1992). Advance organizers: Facilitators of recall. *Educational Psychology Review, 4,* 33–67.

Corno, L. (1992). Encouraging students to take responsibility for learning and performance. *The Elementary School Journal, 93,* 69–84.

Corno, L. (1995). Comments on Winne: Analytic and systemic research are both needed. *Educational Psychologist, 30,* 201–206.

Corno, L. (1995). The principles of adaptive teaching. In A. Ornstein (Ed.), *Teaching: Theory into practice.* (pp. 98–115). Boston: Allyn and Bacon.

Corno, L. (2000). Looking at homework differently. *Elementary School Journal, 100,* 529–548.

Corno, L., & Snow, R. E. (1986). Adapting teaching to individual differences in learners. In M. Wittrock (Ed.), *Handbook of research on teaching* (3rd ed.) (pp. 605–629). New York: Macmillan.

Covaleskie, J. F. (1992). Discipline and morality: Beyond rules and consequences. *The Educational Forum, 56*(2), 56–60.

Covington, M. V. (1992). *Making the grade: A self-worth perspective on motivation and school reform.* New York: Holt, Rinehart, & Winston.

Covington, M. V., & Mueller, K. J. (2001). Intrinsic versus extrinsic motivation: An approach/avoidance reformulation. *Education Psychology Review, 13,* 157–176.

Covington, M. V., & Omelich, C. L. (1984). An empirical examination of Weiner's critique of attribution research. *Journal of Educational Psychology, 76,* 1214–1225.

Covington, M. V., & Omelich, C. (1987). "I knew it cold before the exam": A test of the anxiety-blockage hypothesis. *Journal of Educational Psychology, 79,* 393–400.

Cowley, G., & Underwood, A. (1998, June 15). Memory. *Newsweek, 131*(24), 48–54.

Craik, F. I. M., & Lockhart, R. S. (1972). Levels of processing: A framework for memory research. *Journal of Verbal Learning and Verbal Behavior, 11,* 671–684.

Crawford, J. (1997). *Best evidence: Research foundations of the Bilingual Education Act.* Washington, DC: National Clearinghouse for Bilingual Education.

Crick, N. R., Casas, J. F., & Mosher M. (1997). Relational and overt aggression in preschool. *Developmental Psychology, 33,* 579–588.

Crisci, P. E. (1986). The Quest National Center: A focus on prevention of alienation. *Phi Delta Kappan, 67,* 440–442.

Cronin, J. F. (1993). Four misconceptions about authentic learning. *Educational Leadership, 50*(7), 78–80.

Crosson-Tower, C. (2002). *When children are abused: An educator's guide to intervention.* Boston: Allyn and Bacon.

Cummins, D. D. (1991). Children's interpretation of arithmetic word problems. *Cognition and Instruction, 8,* 261–289.

Cummins, J. (1984). *Bilingualism and special education.* San Diego: College Hill Press.

Cummins, J. (1994). *The acquisition of English as a second language.* In K. Spangenberg-Urbschat & R. Prichard (Eds.), *Kids come in all languages: Reading instruction for ESL students* (pp. 36–62). Newark, DE: International Reading Association.

Cunningham, D. J. (1992). Beyond educational psychology: Steps toward an educational semiotic. *Educational Psychology Review, 4,* 165–194.

Current Directions in Psychological Science. (1993). Special Section: Controversies, 2, 1–12.

Damon, W. (1994). Fair distribution and sharing: The development of positive justice. In B. Puka (Ed.), Fundamental research in moral development (pp. 189–254). *Moral development: A compendium, Vol. 2.* New York: Garland Publishing.

Danielson, C., & Dwyer, C. (1995). How Praxis III supports beginning teachers. *Educational Leadership, 52*(6), 66–67.

Dansereau, D. F. (1985). Learning strategy research. In J. Segal, S. Chipman, & R. Glaser (Eds.), *Thinking and learning skills. Vol. I: Relating instruction to research* (pp. 209–239). Hillsdale, NJ: Lawrence Erlbaum.

Dark, V. J., & Benbow, C. P. (1991). Differential enhancement of working memory with mathematical versus verbal precocity. *Journal of Educational Psychology, 83,* 48–60.

Darling-Hammond, L. (2000). Teacher quality and student achievement: A review of state policy evidence. *Educational Policy Analysis Archives, 8,* 1–48. Retrieved January 20, 2002 from http://epaa.asu.edu/epaa/v8n1/

Das, J. P. (1995). Some thoughts on two aspects of Vygotsky's work. *Educational Psychologist, 30,* 93–97.

Davidson, J. (1982). The group mapping activity for instruction in reading and thinking. *Journal of Reading, 26,* 52–56.

Davis, G. A., & Rimm, S. B. (1985). *Education of the gifted and talented.* Englewood Cliffs, NJ: Prentice-Hall.

Davis, J. K. (1991). Educational implications of field-dependence—independence. In S. Wapner & J. Demick (Eds.), *Field-dependence—independence: Cognitive styles across the life span* (pp. 149–176). Hillsdale, NJ: Lawrence Erlbaum.

Davis, R. B., Maher, C. A., & Noddings, N. (Eds.). (1990). Constructivist views on the teaching and learning of mathematics. *Monograph 4 of the National Council of Teachers of Mathematics,* Reston, VA.

Davis-Kean, P. E., & Sandler, H. M. (2001). A meta-analysis of measures of self-esteem for young children: A framework for future measurers. *Child Development, 72,* 887–906.

De Corte, E., & Verschaffel, L. (1985). Beginning first graders' initial representation of arithmetic word problems. *Journal of Mathematical Behavior, 4,* 3021.

De Corte, E., Greer, B., & Verschaffel, L. (1996). Mathematics learning and teaching. In D. Berliner & R. Calfee (Eds.), *Handbook of educational psychology* (pp. 491–549). New York: Macmillan.

Deaux, K. (1993). Commentary: Sorry, wrong number: A reply to Gentile's call. *Psychological Science, 4,* 125–126.

DeCecco, J., & Richards, A. (1974). *Growing pains: Uses of school conflicts.* New York: Aberdeen.

deCharms, R. (1976). *Enhancing motivation.* New York: Irvington.

deCharms, R. (1983). Intrinsic motivation, peer tutoring, and cooperative learning: Practical maxims. In J. Levine & M. Wang (Eds.), *Teacher and student perceptions: Implications for learning* (pp. 391–398). Hillsdale, NJ: Lawrence Erlbaum.

Deci, E. L. (1975). *Intrinsic motivation.* New York: Plenum.

Deci, E. L., Koestner, R., & Ryan, R. M. (1999). A meta-analytic review of experiments examining the effects of extrinsic rewards on intrinsic motivation. *Psychological Bulletin, 125,* 627–668.

Deci, E. L., & Ryan, R. M. (1985). *Intrinsic motivation and self-determination in human behavior.* New York: Plenum.

Deci, E. L., & Ryan, R. M. (2000). The "what" and "why" of goal pursuits: Human needs and the self-determination of behavior. *Psychological Inquiry, 11,* 227–268.

Deci, E. L., Vallerand, R. J., Pelletier, L. G., & Ryan, R. M. (1991). Motivation and education: The self-determination perspective. *Educational Psychologist, 26,* 325–346.

Delpit, L. (1995). *Other people's children: Cultural conflict in the classroom.* New York: The New York Press.

Dempster, F. N. (1991). Synthesis of research on reviews and tests. *Educational Leadership, 48*(7), 71–76.

Dempster, F. N. (1993). Exposing our students to less should help them learn more. *Phi Delta Kappan, 74,* 432–437.

Derry, S. J. (1989). Putting learning strategies to work. *Educational Leadership, 47*(5), 4–10.

Derry, S. J. (1991). Strategy and expertise in solving word problems. In C. McCormick, G. Miller, & M. Pressley (Eds.), *Cognitive strategies research: From basic research to educational applications.* New York: Springer-Verlag.

Derry, S. J. (1992). Beyond symbolic processing: Expanding horizons for educational psychology. *Journal of Educational Psychology, 84,* 413–419.

Derry, S. J., & Murphy, D. A. (1986). Designing systems that train learning ability: From theory to practice. *Review of Educational Research, 56,* 1–39.

Deshler, D. D., & Schumaker, J. B. (1986). Learning strategies: An instructional alternative for low-achieving adolescents. *Exceptional Children, 52,* 583–590.

Dewey, J. (1910). *How we think.* Boston: D.C. Heath.

Dewey, J. (1913). *Interest and effort in education.* Cambridge, MA: Houghton-Mifflin.

Diamond, M., & Hobson, J. (1998). *Magic trees of the mind.* New York: Dutton.

Diaz, R. M., & Berk, L. E. (Eds.). (1992). *Private speech: From social interaction to self-regulation.* Hillsdale, NJ: Lawrence Erlbaum.

Diaz-Rico, L. T., & Weed, K. Z. (2002). *The crosscultural, language, and academic development handbook* (2nd ed.). Boston: Allyn and Bacon.

Diller, L. (1998). *Running on ritalin.* New York: Bantam Books.

Dinnel, D., & Glover, J. A. (1985). Advance organizers: Encoding manipulations. *Journal of Educational Psychology, 77,* 514–522.

DiVesta, F. J., & Di Cintio, M. J. (1997). Interactive effects of working memory span and text comprehension on reading comprehension and retrieval. *Learning and Individual Differences, 9,* 215–231.

DiVesta, F. J., & Gray, G. S. (1972). Listening and notetaking. *Journal of Educational Psychology, 63,* 8–14.

Dochy, F., Segers, M., & Buehl, M. M. (1999). The relation between assessment practices and outcome studies: The case of research on prior knowledge. *Review of Educational Research, 69,* 145–186.

Doctorow, M., Wittrock, M. C., & Marks, C. (1978). Generative processes in reading comprehension. *Journal of Educational Psychology, 70,* 109–118.

Dodge, K. A., & Somberg, D. R. (1987). Hostile attributional biases among aggressive boys are exacerbated under conditions of threats to the self. *Child Development, 58,* 213–224.

Doherty, K. M. (2002, July 12). Assessment. *Education Week on the Web.* Retrieved August 5, 2002 from http://edweek.org/context/topics/issuespage.cmf?id=41

Dole, J. A., Duffy, G. G., Roehler, L. R., & Pearson, P. D. (1991). Moving from the old to the new: Research on reading comprehension instruction. *Review of Educational Research, 61,* 239–264.

Dorval, R., & Eckerman, C. O. (1984). Developmental trends in the quality of conversation achieved by small groups of acquainted peers. *Monographs of the Society for Research in Child Development, 49* (2, Serial No. 206).

Doyle, W. (1977). The uses of nonverbal behaviors: Toward an ecological model of classrooms. *Merrill-Palmer Quarterly, 23,* 179–192.

Doyle, W. (1983). Academic work. *Review of Educational Research, 53,* 159–200.

Doyle, W. (1986). Classroom organization and management. In M. C. Wittrock (Ed.), *Handbook of research on teaching* (3rd ed.) (pp. 392–431). New York: Macmillan.

Driscoll, M. P. (1994). *Psychology of learning for instruction.* Boston: Allyn and Bacon.

Driscoll, M. P. (2000). *Psychology of learning for instruction* (2nd ed.). Boston: Allyn and Bacon.

Duchastel, P. (1979). Learning objectives and the organization of prose. *Journal of Educational Psychology, 71,* 100–106.

Duckitt, J. (1992). Psychology and prejudice: A historical analysis and integrative framework. *American Psychologist, 47,* 1182–1193.

Duckitt, J. (1994). *The social psychology of prejudice.* Westport, CT: Praeger.

Duell, O. K. (1994). Extended wait time and university student achievement. *American Educational Research Journal, 31,* 397–414.

Duncan, G. J., & Brooks-Gunn, J. (2000). Family poverty, welfare reform, and child development. *Child Development, 71,* 188–196.

Duncker, K. (1945). On solving problems. *Psychological Monographs, 58*(5, Whole No. 270).

Dunn, K., & Dunn, R. (1978). *Teaching students through their individual learning styles.* Reston, VA: National Council of Principals.

Dunn, K., & Dunn, R. (1987). Dispelling outmoded beliefs about student learning. *Educational Leadership, 44*(6), 55–63.

Dunn, R. (1987). Research on instructional environments: Implications for student achievement and attitudes. *Professional School Psychology, 2,* 43–52.

Dunn, R., Beaudry, J. S., & Klavas, A. (1989). Survey of research on learning styles. *Educational Leadership, 47*(7), 50–58.

Dunn, R., Dunn, K., & Price, G. E. (1984). *Learning Style Inventory.* Lawrence, KS: Price Systems.

Durbin, D. L., Darling, N., Steinberg, L., & Brown, B. B. (1993). Parenting style and peer group membership among European-American adolescents. *Journal of Research on Adolescence, 3,* 87–100.

Dusenbury, L., & Falco, M. (1995). Eleven components of effective drug abuse prevention curricula. *Journal of School Health, 65,* 420–425.

Dweck, C. (2000). *Self-theories: Their role in motivation, personality, and development.* Philadelphia: Routledge Press.

Dweck, C. (2002). The development of ability conceptions. In A. Wigfield & J. Eccles (Eds.), *The development of achievement motivation.* San Diego, CA: Academic Press.

Dweck, C. S. (1986). Motivational processes affecting learning. *American Psychologist, 41,* 1040–1047.

Dweck, C. S. (1999). *Self-theories: Their role in motivation, personality, and development.* Philadelphia: Psychology Press.

Dweck, C. S., & Bempechat, J. (1983). Children's theories on intelligence: Consequences for learning. In S. Paris, G. Olson, & W. Stevenson (Eds.), *Learning and motivation in the classroom* (pp. 239–256). Hillsdale, NJ: Lawrence Erlbaum.

Dwyer, C. A., & Villegas, A. M. (1993, January). *Guiding conceptions and assessment principles for the Praxis Series: Professional assessments for beginning teachers.* Princeton, NJ: Educational Testing Service.

Dyson, A. H. (1997). *Writing superheroes: Contemporary childhood, popular culture, and classroom literacy.* New York: Teachers College Press.

Eaton, J. F., Anderson, C. W., & Smith, E. L. (1984). Students' misconceptions interfere with science learning: Case studies of fifth-graders. *Elementary School Journal, 84,* 365–379.

Eccles, J., & Wigfield, A. (1985). Teacher expectations and student motivation. In J. Dusek (Ed.), *Teacher expectancies* (pp. 185–226). Hillsdale, NJ: Lawrence Erlbaum.

Eccles, J., Wigfield, A., & Schiefele, U. (1998). Motivation to succeed. In W. Damon (Series Ed.) & N. Eisenberg (Volume Ed.), *Handbook of child psychology: Vol. 3. Social, emotional, and personality development* (5th ed., pp. 1017–1095). New York: Wiley.

Egan, S. K., Monson, T. C., & Perry, D. G. (1998). Social-cognitive influences on change in aggression over time. *Developmental Psychology, 34,* 996–1006.

Eggen, P. D., & Kauchak, D. P. (2001). *Strategies for teachers: Teaching content and thinking skills* (4th ed.). Boston: Allyn and Bacon.

Eisenberg, N., & Fabes, R. A. (1998). Prosocial development. In W. Damon (Series Ed.) & N. Eisenberg (Vol. Ed.), *Handbook of child psychology: Vol. 3. Social, emotional, and personality development* (5th ed., pp. 701–778). New York: Wiley.

Eisenberg, N., Martin, C. L., & Fabes, R. A. (1996). Gender development and gender effects. In D. Berliner & R. Calfee (Eds.), *Handbook of educational psychology* (pp. 358–396). New York: Macmillan.

Eisenberg, N., & Miller, P. A. (1987). The relation of empathy to prosocial and related behaviors. *Psychological Bulletin, 101,* 91–119.

Eisenberg, N., Shell, R., Pasernack, J., Lennon, R., Beller, R., & Mathy, R. M. (1987). Prosocial development in middle childhood: A longitudinal study. *Developmental Psychology, 23,* 712–718.

Eisenberg, R., Pierce, W. D., & Cameron, J. (1999). Effects of rewards on intrinsic motivation—Negative, neutral, and positive:

Comment on Deci, Koestner, and Ryan (1999). *Psychological Bulletin, 125,* 677–691.

Eisner, E. W. (1999). The uses and limits of performance assessments. *Phi Delta Kappan, 80,* 658–660.

Elashoff, J. D., & Snow, R. E. (1971). *Pygmalion reconsidered.* Worthington, OH: Charles A. Jones.

Elawar, M. C., & Corno, L. (1985). A factorial experiment in teachers' written feedback on student homework: Changing teacher behavior a little rather than a lot. *Journal of Educational Psychology, 77,* 162–173.

Elkind, D. (1981). Obituary—Jean Piaget (1896–1980). *American Psychologist, 36,* 911–913.

Elrich, M. (1994). The stereotype within. *Educational Leadership, 51*(8), 12–15.

Emery, R. E. (1989). Family violence. *American Psychologist, 44,* 321–328.

Emmer, E. T., & Aussiker, A. (1990). School and classroom discipline problems: How well do they work? In O. Moles (Ed.), *Student discipline strategies: Research and practice.* Albany, NY: SUNY Press.

Emmer, E. T., & Evertson, C. M. (1981). Synthesis of research on classroom management. *Educational Leadership, 38,* 342–345.

Emmer, E. T., & Evertson, C. M. (1982). Effective classroom management at the beginning of the school year in junior high school classes. *Journal of Educational Psychology, 74,* 485–498.

Emmer, E. T., Evertson, C. M., & Anderson, L. M. (1980). Effective classroom management at the beginning of the school year. *Elementary School Journal, 80,* 219–231.

Emmer, E. T., Evertson, C. M., & Worsham, M. E. (2003). *Classroom management for secondary teachers* (6th ed.). Boston: Allyn and Bacon.

Emmer, E. T., & Stough, L. M. (2001). Classroom management: A critical part of educational psychology with implications for teacher education. *Educational Psychologist, 36,* 103–112.

Engle, R. W. (2001). What is working memory capacity? In H. Roediger, J. Nairne, I. Neath, & A. Suprenant (Eds.), *The nature of remembering: Essays in honor of Robert G. Crowder* (pp. 297–314). Washington, DC: American Psychological Association.

Entwisle, D. R., & Alexander, K. L. (1998). Facilitating the transition to first grade: The nature of transition and research on factors affecting it. *The Elementary School Journal, 98,* 351–364.

Entwisle, D. R., Alexander, K., & Olson, L. (1997). *Children, schools, and inequality.* Boulder, CO: Westview Press.

Epanchin, B. C., Townsend, B., & Stoddard, K. (1994). *Constructive classroom management: Strategies for creating positive learning environments.* Pacific Grove, CA: Brooks/Cole.

Epstein, H. (1978). Growth spurts during brain development: Implications for educational policy and practice. In J. Chall & A. Mirsky (Eds.), *Education and the brain. The seventy-seventh yearbook of the National Society for the Study of Education, Part II* (pp. 343–370). Chicago: University of Chicago Press.

Epstein, H. (1980). EEG developmental stages. *Developmental Psychobiology, 13,* 629–631.

Epstein, J. L. (1989). Family structure and student motivation. In R. E. Ames & C. Ames (Eds.), *Research on motivation in education: Vol 3. Goals and cognitions* (pp. 259–295). New York: Academic Press.

Epstein, J. L. (1995). School/Family/Community partnerships: Caring for the children we share. *Phi Delta Kappan, 76,* 701–712.

Epstein, J. L., & MacIver, D. J. (1992). *Opportunities to learn: Effects on eighth graders of curriculum offerings and instructional approaches.* (Report No. 34). Baltimore: Center for Research on Elementary and Middle Schools, Johns Hopkins University.

Epstein, J. L., & Van Voorhis, F. L. (2001). More than minutes: Teachers' roles in designing homework. *Educational Psychologist, 36,* 181–193.

Erez, M., & Zidon, I. (1984). Effects of goal acceptance on the relationship of goal difficulty to performance. *Journal of Applied Psychology, 69,* 69–78.

Erickson, F., & Shultz, J. (1982). *The counselor as gatekeeper: Social interaction in interviews.* New York: Academic Press.

Ericsson, K. A. (1999). Expertise. In R. Wilson & F. Keil (Eds.), *The MIT encyclopedia of the cognitive sciences* (pp. 298–300). Cambridge, MA: MIT Press.

Ericsson, K. A., & Charness, N. (1999). Expert performance: Its structure and acquisition. In S. Ceci & W. Williams (Eds.), The nature-nurture debate: The essential readings. *Essential readings in developmental psychology.* Malden, MA: Blackwell.

Ericsson, K. A., & Smith, J. (Eds.). (1991). *Toward a general theory of expertise.* Cambridge, UK: Cambridge University Press.

Erikson, E. H. (1963). *Childhood and society* (2nd ed.). New York: Norton.

Erikson, E. H. (1968). *Identity, youth, and crisis.* New York: Norton.

Erikson, E. H. (1980). *Identity and the life cycle* (2nd ed.). New York: Norton.

Espe, C., Worner, C., & Hotkevich, M. (1990). Whole language—What a bargain. *Educational Leadership, 47*(6), 45.

Evans, E. D., & Craig, D. (1990). Adolescent cognitions for academic cheating as a function of grade level and achievement status. *Journal of Adolescent Research, 5,* 325–345.

Evans, L., & Davies, K. (2000). No sissy boys here: A content analysis of the representation of masculinity in elementary school reading texts. *Sex Roles, 42,* 255–270.

Evensen, D. H., Salisbury-Glennon, J. D., & Glenn, J. (2001). A qualitative study of six medical students in a problem-based curriculum: Toward a situated model of self-regulation. *Journal of Educational Psychology, 93,* 659–676.

Evertson, C. M. (1988). Managing classrooms: A framework for teachers. In D. Berliner & B. Rosenshine (Eds.), *Talks to teachers* (pp. 54–74). New York: Random House.

Evertson, C. M., Emmer, E. T., & Worsham, M. E. (2003). *Classroom management for elementary teachers* (6th ed.). Boston: Allyn and Bacon.

Ewy, C., . & student authors. (1997). Kids take on "the test." *Educational Leadership, 54*(4), 76–78.

Fagot, B. I., & Hagan, R. (1991). Observations of parent reactions to sex-stereotyped behaviors: Age and sex effects. *Child Development, 62,* 617–628.

Fagot, B. I., Hagan, R., Leinbach, M. D., & Kronsberg, S. (1985). Differential reactions to assertive and communicative acts of toddler boys and girls. *Child Development, 56,* 1499–1505.

Fantuzzo, J., Davis, G., & Ginsburg, M. (1995). Effects of parent involvement in isolation or in combination with peer tutoring on student self-concept and mathematics achievement. *Journal of Educational Psychology, 87,* 272–281.

Farnaham-Diggory, S. (1994). Paradigms of knowledge and instruction. *Review of Educational Research, 64,* 463–477.

Feather, N. T. (1982). *Expectations and actions: Expectancy-value models in psychology.* Hillsdale, NJ: Lawrence Erlbaum.

Feiman-Nemser, S. (1983). Learning to teach. In L. Shulman & G. Sykes (Eds.), *Handbook of teaching and policy* (pp. 150–170). New York: Longman.

Fennema, E., & Peterson, P. (1988). Effective teaching for boys and girls: The same or different? In D. Berliner & B. Rosenshine (Eds.), *Talks to teachers* (pp. 111–127). New York: Random House.

Ferguson, A. A. (2000). *Bad boys: Public schools and the making of Black masculinity.* Ann Arbor, MI: University of Michigan Press.

Ferguson, D. L., Ferguson, P. M., & Bogdan, R. C. (1987). If mainstreaming is the answer, what is the question? In V. Richardson-Koehler (Ed.), *Educators' handbook: A research perspective* (pp. 394–419). New York: Longman.

Feshbach, N. (1997). Empathy: The formative years—Implications for clinical practice. A. Bohart & L. Greenberg (Eds.), *Empathy reconsidered: New directions in psychotherapy* (pp. 33–59). Washington, DC: American Psychological Association.

Feshbach, N. (1998). Aggression in the schools: Toward reducing ethnic conflict and enhancing ethnic understanding. In P. Trickett & C. Schellenbach (Eds.), *Violence against children in the family and the community* (pp. 269–286). Washington, DC: American Psychological Association.

Feuerstein, R. (1979). *The dynamic assessment of retarded performers: The Learning Potential Assessment Device, theory, instruments, and techniques.* Baltimore: University Park Press.

Feuerstein, R. (1990). The theory of structural cognitive modifiability. In B. Presseisen (Ed.), *Learning and thinking styles: Classroom interaction* (pp. 68–134). Washington, DC: National Education Association.

Finn, J. (1972). Expectations and the educational environment. *Review of Educational Research, 42,* 387–410.

Fischer, K. W., & Pare-Blagoev, J. (2000). From individual differences to dynamic pathways of development. *Child Development, 71,* 850–853.

Fiske, E. B. (1988, April 10). America's test mania. *New York Times* (Education Life Section), pp. 16–20.

Fiske, S. T. (1993). Social cognition and social perception. *Annual Review of Psychology, 44,* 155–194.

Fitts, P. M., & Posner, M. I. (1967). *Human performance.* Belmont, CA: Brooks Cole.

Fitzgerald, J. (1995). English-as-a-second-language learners' cognitive reading process: A review of the research in the United States. *Review of Educational Research, 62,* 145–190.

Flammer, A. (1995). Developmental analysis of control beliefs. In A. Bandura, (Ed.), *Self-efficacy in changing societies* (pp. 69–113). New York: Cambridge University Press.

Flavell, J. H. (1985). *Cognitive development* (2nd ed.). Englewood Cliffs, NJ: Prentice-Hall.

Flavell, J. H., Friedrichs, A. G., & Hoyt, J. D. (1970). Developmental changes in memorization processes. *Cognitive Psychology, 1,* 324–340.

Flavell, J. H., Green, F. L., & Flavell, E. R. (1995). Young children's knowledge about thinking. *Monographs of the Society for Research in Child Development, 60*(1) (Serial No. 243).

Flink, C. F., Boggiano, A. K., & Barrett, M. (1990). Controlling teaching strategies: Undermining children's self-determination and performance. *Journal of Personality and Social Psychology, 59,* 916–924.

Floden, R. E. (2001). Research on effects of teaching: A continuing model for research on teaching. In V. Richardson (Ed.), *Handbook of research on teaching* (4th ed., pp. 3–16). Washington, DC: American Educational Research Association.

Floden, R. E., & Klinzing, H. G. (1990). What can research on teacher thinking contribute to teacher preparation? A second opinion. *Educational Researcher, 19*(4), 15–20.

Ford, D. Y. (2000). *Infusing multicultural content into the curriculum for gifted students.* (ERIC EC Digest #E601). Arlington, VA: The ERIC Clearinghouse on Disabilities and Gifted Education.

Foster, W. (1981, August). *Social and emotional development in gifted individuals.* Paper presented at the Fourth World Conference on Gifted and Talented, Montreal.

Fox, L. H. (1981). Identification of the academically gifted. *American Psychologist, 36,* 1103–1111.

Frable, D. E. S. (1997). Gender, Racial, ethnic, and class identities. In J. T., Spence, J. M. Darley, & D. J. Foss (Eds.), *Annual Review of Psychology* (pp. 139–162). Palo Alto, CA: Annual Reviews.

Frank, S. J., Pirsch, L. A., & Wright, V. C. (1990). Late adolescents' perceptions of their parents: Relationships among deidealization, autonomy, relatedness, and insecurity and implications for adolescent adjustment and ego identity status. *Journal of Youth and Adolescence, 19,* 571–588.

Frederiksen, N. (1984). Implications of cognitive theory for instruction in problem solving. *Review of Educational Research 54,* 363–407.

Freiberg, H. J. (1999). Sustaining the paradigm. In H. J. Freiberg (Ed.), *Beyond behaviorism: Changing the classroom management paradigm* (pp. 164–173). Boston: Allyn and Bacon.

Freiberg, H. J. (Ed.). (1999). *Beyond behaviorism: Changing the classroom management.* Boston: Allyn and Bacon.

Freiberg, H. J., & Driscoll, A. (1996). *Universal teaching strategies* (2nd ed.). Boston: Allyn and Bacon.

Freud, S. (1959). Creative writers and daydreaming. In J. Strachey (Ed.), *The standard edition of the complete psychological works of Sigmund Freud* (Vol. 9). London: Hogarth Press.

Frick, T. W. (1990). Analysis of patterns in time: A method of recording and quantifying temporal relations in education. *American Educational Research Journal, 27,* 180–204.

Friend, M., & Bursuck, W. (1996). *Including students with special needs: A practical guide for classroom teachers.* Boston: Allyn and Bacon.

Friend, M., & Bursuck, W. D. (2002). *Including students with special needs* (3rd ed.). Boston: Allyn and Bacon.

Fuchs, L. S., Fuchs, D., Hamlett, C. L., & Karns, K. (1998). High-achieving students' interactions and performance on complex mathematical tasks as a function of homogeneous and heterogeneous pairings. *American Educational Research Journal, 35,* 227–268.

Fulk, C. L., & Smith, P. J. (1995). Students' perceptions of teachers' instructional and management adaptations for students with learning or behavior problems. *The Elementary School Journal, 95,* 409–419.

Fuller, F. G. (1969). Concerns of teachers: A developmental conceptualization. *American Educational Research Journal, 6,* 207–226.

Furstenberg, F. F., & Cherlin, A. J. (1991). *Divided families.* Cambridge: Harvard University Press.

Gage, N. L. (1991). The obviousness of social and educational research results. *Educational Researcher, 20*(A), 10–16.

Gagné, E. D. (1985). *The cognitive psychology of school learning.* Boston: Little, Brown.

Gagné, E. D., Yekovich, C. W., & Yekovich, F. R. (1993). *The cognitive psychology of school learning* (2nd ed.). New York: HarperCollins.

Gagné, R. M. (1985). *The conditions of learning and theory of instruction* (4th ed.). New York: Holt, Rinehart & Winston.

Galambos, S. J., & Goldin-Meadow, S. (1990). The effects of learning two languages on metalinguistic development. *Cognition, 34,* 1–56.

Gallagher, M. (2001, June 11). More on zero-tolerance in schools. *NewsMax.com.* Available online at http://www.newsmax.com/archives/articles/2001/6/11/123253.shtml. Downloaded on January 23, 2003.

Gallimore, R., & Goldenberg, C. (2001). Analyzing cultural models and settings to connect minority achievement and school improvement research. *Educational Psychologist, 36,* 45–56.

Gallini, J. K. (1991). Schema-based strategies and implications for instructional design in strategy training. In C. McCormick, G. Miller, & M. Pressley (Eds.), *Cognitive strategies research: From basic research to educational applications.* New York: Springer-Verlag.

Gamoran, A. (1987). The stratification of high school learning opportunities. *Sociology of Education, 60,* 135–155.

Garcia, E. (2002). *Student cultural diversity: Understanding the meaning and meeting the challenge.* Boston: Houghton Mifflin.

Garcia, E. E. (1992). "Hispanic" children: Theoretical, empirical, and related policy issues. *Educational Psychology Review, 4,* 69–94.

Garcia, R. L. (1991). *Teaching in a pluralistic society: Concepts, models, and strategies.* New York: HarperCollins.

Garcia, T., & Pintrich, P. (1994). Regulating motivation and cognition in the classroom: The role of self-schemas and self-regulatory strategies. In B. J. Zimmerman & D. Schunk (Eds.), *Self-regulation of learning and performance: Issues and educational applications* (pp. 127–153). Hillsdale, NJ: Lawrence Erlbaum.

Gardner, H. (1982). *Developmental psychology* (2nd ed.). Boston: Little, Brown.

Gardner, H. (1983). *Frames of mind: The theory of multiple intelligences.* New York: Basic Books.

Gardner, H. (1993a). *Creating minds: An anatomy of creativity seen through the lives of Freud, Einstein, Picasso, Stravinsky, Elliot, Graham, and Gandhi.* New York: Basic Books.

Gardner, H. (1993b). *Educating the unschooled mind: A science and public policy seminar.* Washington, DC: American Educational Research Association.

Gardner, H. (1998). Reflections on multiple intelligences: Myths and messages. In A. Woolfolk (Ed.), *Readings in educational psychology* (2nd ed.) (pp. 61–67). Boston: Allyn and Bacon.

Gardner, H. (1999). Are there additional intelligences? In J. Kane (Ed.), *Education, information, and transformation: Essays on learning and thinking* (pp. 111–131). Upper Saddle River, NJ: Prentice-Hall.

Gardner, H. (1999, August). *Who owns intelligence?* Invited address at the Annual Meeting of the American Psychological Association, Boston.

Gardner, H., & Hatch, T. (1989). Multiple intelligences go to school. *Educational Researcher, 18*(8), 4–10.

Gardner, R., Brown, R., Sanders, S., & Menke, D. J. (1992). "Seductive details" in learning from text. In K. A. Renninger, S. Hidi, & A. Krapp (Eds.), *The role of interest in learning and development* (pp. 239–254). Hillsdale, NJ: Lawrence Erlbaum.

Gargarian, G. (1996). The art of design. In Y. Kafai & M. Resnick (Eds.), *Constructivism in practice: Designing, thinking, and learning in a digital world* (pp. 125–160). Mahwah, NJ: Lawrence Erlbaum.

Garmon, A., Nystrand, M., Berends, M., & LePore, P. C. (1995). An organizational analysis of the effects of ability grouping. *American Educational Research Journal, 32,* 687–715.

Garmoran, A. (1987). The stratification of high school learning opportunities. *Sociology of Education, 60,* 135–155.

Garner, R. (1990). When children and adults do not use learning strategies: Toward a theory of settings. *Review of Educational Psychology, 60,* 517–530.

Garner, R. (1998). Choosing to learn and not-learn in school. *Educational Psychology Review, 10,* 227–238.

Garrison, J. (1995). Deweyan pragmatism and the epistemology of contemporary social constructivism. *American Educational Research Journal, 32,* 716–741.

Garrod, A., Beal, C., & Shin, P. (1990). The development of moral orientation in elementary school children. *Sex Roles, 22,* 13–27.

Gartner, A., & Lipsky, D. K. (1987). Beyond special education: Toward a quality system for all students. *Harvard Educational Review, 57,* 367–395.

Gay, G. (2000). *Culturally responsive teaching: Theory, research, and practice.* New York: Teachers College Press.

Geary, D. C. (1995). Sexual selection and sex differences in spatial cognition. *Learning and Individual Differences, 7,* 289–303.

Geary, D. C. (1998). What is the function of mind and brain? *Educational Psychologist, 10,* 377–388.

Geary, D. C. (1999). Evolution and developmental sex differences. *Current Directions in Psychological Science, 8,* 115–120.

Gelman, R. (1979). Preschool thought. *American Psychologist, 34,* 900–905.

Gelman, R., & Baillargeon, R. (1983). A review of some Piagetian concepts. In P. Mussen (Ed.), *Carmichael's manual of child psychology. Vol. 3: Cognitive development* (E. Markman & J. Flavell, Volume Eds.). New York: Wiley.

Gelman, S. A., & Ebeling, K. S. (1989). Children's use of nonegocentric standards in judgments of size. *Child Development, 60,* 920–932.

Gentner, D. (1975). Evidence for the psychological reality of semantic components: The verbs of possession. In D. Norman & D. Rumelhart (Eds.), *Explorations in cognition* (pp. 211–246). San Francisco: Freeman.

Gerbner, G., Gross, L. Signorelli, N., & Morgan, M. (1986). *Television's mean world: Violence Profile No. 14–15.* Philadelphia: Annenberg School of Communication, University of Pennsylvania.

Gergen, K. J. (1997). Constructing constructivism: Pedagogical potentials. *Issues in Education: Contributions from Educational Psychology, 3,* 195–202.

Gersten, R. (1996a). The language-minority students in transition: Contemporary instructional research. *The Elementary School Journal, 96,* 217–220.

Gersten, R. (1996b). Literacy instruction for language-minority students: The transition years. *The Elementary School Journal, 96,* 217–220.

Gibbs, J. W., & Luyben, P. D. (1985). Treatment of self-injurious behavior: Contingent versus noncontingent positive practice overcorrection. *Behavior Modification, 9,* 3–21.

Gibbs, N. (1995, October 2). The EQ factor. *Time,* 60–68.

Gick, M. L. (1986). Problem-solving strategies. *Educational Psychologist, 21,* 99–120.

Gick, M. L., & Holyoak, K. L. (1983). Schema induction and analogical transfer. *Cognitive Psychology, 15,* 1–38.

Gillett, M., & Gall, M. (1982, March). *The effects of teacher enthusiasm on the at-task behavior of students in the elementary grades.*

Paper presented at the annual meeting of the American Educational Research Association, New York.

Gilligan, C. (1982). *In a different voice: Psychological theory and women's development.* Cambridge, MA: Harvard University Press.

Gilligan, C., & Attanucci, J. (1988). Two moral orientations: Gender differences and similarities. *Merrill-Palmer Quarterly, 34,* 223–237.

Gilstrap, R. L., & Martin, W. R. (1975). *Current strategies for teachers: A resource for personalizing education.* Pacific Palisades, CA: Goodyear.

Ginsburg, H., & Opper, S. (1988). *Piaget's theory of intellectual development* (3rd ed.). Englewood Cliffs, NJ: Prentice-Hall.

Girls' math achievement: What we do and don't know. (1986, January). *Harvard Education Letter, 2*(1), 1–5.

Glaser, R. (1981). The future of testing: A research agenda for cognitive psychology and psychometrics. *American Psychologist, 36,* 923–936.

Glasgow, K. L., Dornbusch, S. M., Troyer, L., Steinberg, L., & Ritter, P. L. (1997). Parenting styles, adolescents' attributions, and educational outcomes in nine heterogeneous high schools. *Child Development, 68,* 507–523.

Glasser, W. (1969). *Schools without failure.* New York: Harper & Row.

Glasser, W. (1990). *The quality school: Managing students without coercion.* New York: Harper & Row.

Glassman, M. (2001). Dewey and Vygotsky: Society, experience, and inquiry in educational practice. *Educational Researcher, 30*(4), 3–14.

Gleitman, H., Fridlund, A. J., & Reisberg, D. (1999). *Psychology* (5th ed.). New York: Norton.

Goldenberg, C. (1996). The education of language-minority students: Where are we, and where do we need to go? *The Elementary School Journal, 96,* 353–361.

Goleman, D. (1988, April 10). An emerging theory on blacks' I.Q. scores. *New York Times* (Education Life Section), pp. 22–24.

Goleman, D. (1995). *Emotional intelligence.* New York: Bantam.

Gollnick, D. A., & Chinn, P. C. (1994). *Multicultural education in a pluralistic society* (4th ed.). New York: Merrill.

Good, T., & Brophy, J. (2003). *Looking in classrooms* (9th ed.). Boston: Allyn and Bacon.

Good, T. L. (1983a). Classroom research: A decade of progress. *Educational Psychologist, 18,* 127–144.

Good, T. L. (1983b). Research on classroom teaching. In L. Shulman & G. Sykes (Eds.), *Handbook of teaching and policy* (pp. 42–80). New York: Longman.

Good, T. L. (1988). Teacher expectations. In D. Berliner & B. Rosenshine (Eds.), *Talks to teachers* (pp. 159–200). New York: Random House.

Good, T. L. (1996). Teaching effects and teacher evaluation. In J. Sikula (Ed.), *Handbook of research on teacher education* (pp. 617–665). New York: Macmillan.

Good, T. L., Grouws, D., & Ebmeier, H. (1983). *Active mathematics teaching.* New York: Longman.

Goodman, Y. M., & Goodman, K. S. (1990). Vygotsky in a whole-language perspective. In L. Moll (Ed.), *Vygotsky and education: Instructional implications and applications of sociohistorical psychology* (pp. 223–250). New York: Cambridge University Press.

Goodrich, H. (1997). Understanding rubrics. *Educational Leadership, 54*(4), 14–17.

Gordon, D. (2001, June, 18). The dominator. *Newsweek,* 42–47.

Gordon, E. W. (1991). Human diversity and pluralism. *Educational Psychologist, 26,* 99–108.

Gordon, J. A. (1998). Caring through control: Reaching urban African American youth. *Journal for a Just and Caring Education, 4,* 418–440.

Gordon, T. (1974). *Teacher effectiveness training.* New York: Peter H. Wyden.

Gordon, T. (1981). Crippling our children with discipline. *Journal of Education, 163,* 228–243.

Graber, J. A., & Brooks-Gunn, J. (1996). Transitions and turning points: Navigating the passage from childhood through adolescence. *Developmental Psychology, 32,* 768–776.

Graham, S. (1991). A review of attribution theory in achievement contexts. *Educational Psychology Review, 3,* 5–39.

Graham, S. (1994). Motivation in African Americans. *Review of Educational Research, 64,* 55–117.

Graham, S. (1995). Narrative versus meta-analytic reviews of race differences in motivation. *Review of Educational Research, 65,* 509–514.

Graham, S. (1996). How causal beliefs influence the academic and social motivation of African-American children. In G. G. Brannigan (Ed.), *The enlightened educator: Research adventures in the schools* (pp. 111–126). New York: McGraw-Hill.

Graham, S. (1998). Self-blame and peer victimization in middle school: An attributional analysis. *Developmental Psychology, 34,* 587–599.

Graham, S., & Barker, G. (1990). The downside of help: An attributional developmental analysis of helping behavior as a low ability cue. *Journal of Educational Psychology, 82,* 7–14.

Graham, S., Taylor, A., & Hudley, C. (1998). Exploring achievement values among ethnic minority early adolescents. *Journal of Educational Psychology, 90,* 606–620.

Graham, S., & Weiner, B. (1996). Theories and principles of motivation. In D. Berliner & R. C. Calfee (Eds.), *Handbook of educational psychology* (pp. 63–84). New York: Macmillan.

Grant, C. A., & Sleeter, C. E. (1989). Race, class, gender, exceptionality, and educational reform. In J. Banks & C. McGee Banks (Eds.), *Multicultural education: Issues and perspectives* (pp. 49–66). Boston: Allyn and Bacon.

Gray, P. (2002). *Psychology* (4th ed.). New York: Worth.

Greeno, J. G., Collins, A. M., & Resnick, L. B. (1996). Cognition and learning. In D. Berliner & R. Calfee (Eds.), *Handbook of educational psychology* (pp. 15–46). New York: Macmillan.

Greenough, W. T., Black, J. E., & Wallace, C. S. (1987). Experience and brain development. *Child Development, 58,* 539–559.

Gregorc, A. F. (1982). *Gregorc Style Delineator: Development, technical, and administrative manual.* Maynard, MA: Gabriel Systems.

Gresham, F. (1981). Social skills training with handicapped children. *Review of Educational Research, 51,* 139–176.

Grigorenko, E. L., & Sternberg, R. J. (1998). Dynamic testing. *Psychological Bulletin, 124,* 75–111.

Grigorenko, E. L., & Sternberg, R. J. (2001). Analytical, creative, and practical intelligence as predictors of self-reported adaptive functioning: A case study in Russia. *Intelligence, 29,* 57–73.

Grinder, R. E. (1981). The "new" science of education: Educational psychology in search of a mission. In F. H. Farley & N. J. Gordon (Eds.), *Psychology and education: The state of the union* (pp. 354–366). Berkeley, CA: McCutchan.

Grissom, J. B., & Smith, L. A. (1989). Repeating and dropping out of school. In L. Shepard & M. Smith (Eds.), *Flunking grades:*

Research and policies on retention (pp. 34–63). Philadelphia: Falmer Press.

Grolnick, W. S., Ryan, R. M., & Deci, E. L. (1991). Inner resources for school achievement: Motivational mediators of children's perceptions of their parents. *Journal of Educational Psychology, 83,* 508–517.

Gronlund, N. E. (2000). *How to write and use instructional objectives* (6th ed.). Columbus: OH: Merrill.

Gronlund, N. E. (2003). *Assessment of student achievement* (7th ed.). Boston: Allyn and Bacon.

Gross, M. U. M. (1992). The use of radical acceleration in cases of extreme intellectual precocity. *Gifted Child Quarterly, 36,* 91–99.

Grossman, H., & Grossman, S. H. (1994). *Gender issues in education.* Boston: Allyn and Bacon.

Grotevant, H. D. (1998). Adolescent development in family contexts. In N. Eisenberg (Ed.), *Handbook of child psychology: Vol 3. Social, emotional, and personality development* (5th ed.) (pp. 1097–1149). New York: Wiley.

Guilford, J. P. (1988). Some changes in the Structure-of-Intellect model. *Educational and Psychological Measurement, 48,* 1–4.

Guitierrez, R., & Slavin, R. E. (1992). Achievement effects of the nongraded elementary school: A best evidence synthesis. *Review of Educational Research, 62,* 333–376.

Gunn Morris, V., & Morris, C. L. (2002). No more cotton picking: African American voices from a small southern town. In G. S. Boutte (Ed.), *Resounding voices: School experiences of people from diverse ethnic backgrounds* (pp. 17–42). Boston: Allyn and Bacon.

Gurian, M., & Henley, P. (2001). *Boys and girls learn differently: A guide for teachers and parents.* San Francisco: Jossey-Bass.

Guskey, T. R. (1994). Making the grade: What benefits students? *Educational Leadership, 52*(2), 14–21.

Guskey, T. R., & Bailey, J. M. (2001). *Developing grading and reporting systems for student learning.* Thousand Oaks, CA: Corwin Press.

Guskey, T. R., & Gates, S. L. (1986). Synthesis of research on mastery learning. *Education Leadership, 43,* 73–81.

Gustafsson, J-E., & Undheim, J. O. (1996). Individual differences in cognitive functioning. In D. Berliner & R. Calfee (Eds.), *Handbook of educational psychology* (pp. 186–242). New York: Macmillan.

Guthrie, J. T., & Alao, S. (1997). Designing contexts to increase motivations of reading. *Educational Psychologist, 32,* 95–105.

Guthrie, J. T., Cox, K. E., Anderson, E., Harris, K., Mazzoni, S., & Rach, L. (1998). Principles of integrated instruction for engagement in reading. *Educational Psychology Review, 10,* 227–238.

Haertel, E. H. (1999). Performance assessment and educational reform. *Phi Delta Kappan, 80,* 662–666.

Hagborg, W. J. (1993). Rosenberg Self-Esteem Scale and Harter's Self-Perception Profile for Adolescents: A concurrent validity study. *Psychology in Schools, 30,* 132–136.

Hakuta, K. (1986). *Mirror of language: The debate on bilingualism.* New York: Basic Books.

Hakuta, K., & Garcia, E. E. (1989). Bilingualism and education. *American Psychologist, 44,* 374–379.

Hakuta, K., & Gould, L. J. (1987). Synthesis of research on bilingual education. *Educational Leadership, 44*(6), 38–45.

Haladyna, T. H. (2002). *Essentials of standardized achievement testing: Validity and accountability.* Boston: Allyn and Bacon.

Hale-Benson, J. E. (1986). *Black children: Their roots, culture, and learning styles* (rev. ed.). Baltimore: Johns Hopkins University Press.

Halford, J. M. (1999). A different mirror: A conversation with Ronald Takaki. *Educational Leadership, 56*(7), 8–13.

Hall, J. W. (1991). More on the utility of the keyword method. *Journal of Educational Psychology, 83,* 171–172.

Hallahan, D. P., & Kauffman, J. M. (2003). *Exceptional learners: Introduction to special education* (9th ed.). Boston: Allyn and Bacon.

Hallahan, D. P., Kauffman, J. M., & Lloyd, J. W. (1999). *Introduction to learning disabilities* (4th ed.). Boston: Allyn and Bacon.

Hallowell, E. M., & Ratey, J. J. (1994). *Driven to distraction.* New York: Pantheon Books.

Halpern, D. F. (2000). *Sex differences in cognitive abilities.* Mahwah, NJ: Lawrence Erlbaum.

Halpern, D. F., & LaMay, M. L. (2000). The smarter sex: A critical review of sex differences in intelligence. *Educational Psychology Review, 12,* 229–246.

Hambleton, R. K. (1996). Advances in assessment models, methods, and practices. In D. C. Berliner & R. C. Calfee (Eds.), *Handbook of educational psychology* (pp. 899–925). New York: Macmillan.

Hamilton, R. J. (1985). A framework for the evaluation of the effectiveness of adjunct questions and objectives. *Review of Educational Research, 55,* 47–86.

Hamm, J. (2000). Do birds of a feather flock together? The variable bases for African American, Asian America, and European American adolescents' selection of similar friends. *Developmental Psychology, 36,* 209–219.

Hamman, D., Berthelot, J., Saia, J., & Crowley, E. (2000). Teachers' coaching of learning and its relation to students' strategic learning. *Journal of Educational Psychology, 92,* 342–348.

Hamre, B. K., & Pianta, R. C. (2001). Early teacher–child relationships and the trajectory of children's school outcomes through eighth grade. *Child Development, 72,* 625–638.

Hansen, R. A. (1977). Anxiety. In S. Ball (Ed.), *Motivation in education.* New York: Academic Press.

Hardiman, P. T., Dufresne, R., & Mestre, J. P. (1989). The relation between problem categorization and problem solving among experts and novices. *Memory & Cognition, 17,* 627–638.

Hardman, M. L., Drew, C. J., & Egan, M. W. (1999). *Human exceptionality: Society, school, and family* (6th ed.). Boston: Allyn and Bacon.

Harp, S. F., & Mayer, R. E. (1998). How seductive details do their damage: A theory of cognitive interest in science learning. *Journal of Educational Psychology, 90,* 414–434.

Harris, J. R. (1998). *The nurture assumption: Why children turn out the way they do; parents matter less than you think and peers matter more.* New York: Free Press.

Harris, K. R. (1990). Developing self-regulated learners: The role of private speech and self-instruction. *Educational Psychologist, 25,* 35–50.

Harris, K. R., & Graham, S. (1996). Memo to constructivist: Skills count too. *Educational Leadership, 53*(5), 26–29.

Harris, K. R., Graham, S., & Pressley, M. (1991). Cognitive-behavioral approaches in reading and written language: Developing self-regulated learners. In N. N. Singh & I. L. Beale (Eds.), *Learning disabilities: Nature, theory, and treatment* (pp. 415–451). New York: Springer-Verlag.

Harris, K. R., & Pressley, M. (1991). The nature of cognitive strategy instruction: Interactive strategy construction. *Exceptional Children, 57,* 392–404.

Harris, K. R., Graham S., & Pressley, M. (1992). Cognitive-behavioral approaches in reading and written language: Developing self-regulated learners. In N. N. Singh & I. L. Beale (Eds.), *Learning disabilities: Nature, theory, and treatment* (pp. 415–451). New York: Springer-Verlag.

Harrow, A. J. (1972). *A taxonomy of the psychomotor domain: A guide for developing behavior objectives.* New York: David McKay.

Harter, S. (1990). Issues in the assessment of self-concept of children and adolescents. In A. LaGreca (Ed.), *Through the eyes of a child* (pp. 292–325). Boston: Allyn and Bacon.

Harter, S. (1998). The development of self-representations. In N. Eisenberg (Ed.), *Handbook of child psychology: Vol 3. Social, emotional, and personality development* (5th ed.) (pp. 553–618). New York: Wiley.

Hartup, W. W., & Stevens, N. (1999). Friendships and adaptation across the lifespan. *Current Directions in Psychological Science, 8,* 76–79.

Hayes, S. C., Rosenfarb, I., Wulfert, E., Munt, E. D., Korn, Z., & Zettle, R. D. (1985). Self-reinforcement effects: An artifact of social standard setting? *Journal of Applied Behavior Analysis, 18,* 201–214.

Henderson, M. (1996). *Helping your students get the most of homework* [Brochure]. Chicago: National Parent–Teacher Association.

Herbert, E. A. (1998). Design matters: How school environment affects children. *Educational Leadership, 56*(1), 69–71.

Herman, J. (1997). Assessing new assessments: How do they measure up? *Theory Into Practice, 36,* 197–204.

Herman, J. L., Aschbacher, P. R., & Winters, L. (1992). *A practical guide to alternative assessment.* Alexandria, VA: Association for Supervision and Curriculum Development.

Herman, J., & Winters. L. (1994). Portfolio research: A slim collection. *Educational Leadership, 52*(2), 48–55.

Hernshaw, L. S. (1987). *The shaping of modern psychology: A historical introduction from dawn to present day.* London: Routledge & Kegan Paul.

Hess, R., & McDevitt, T. (1984). Some cognitive consequences of maternal intervention techniques. A longitudinal study. *Child Development, 55,* 1902–1912.

Hess, R., Chih-Mci, C., & McDevitt, T. M. (1987). Cultural variation in family beliefs about children's performance in mathematics: Comparisons among People's Republic of China, Chinese-American, and Caucasian-American families. *Journal of Educational Psychology, 79,* 179–188.

Hess, R. D., & Shipman, V. C. (1965). Early experience and the socialization of cognitive modes in children. *Child Development, 36,* 869–886.

Hetherington, E. M. (1999). Should we stay together for the sake of the children? In E. Hetherington (Ed.), *Coping with divorce, single-parenting, and remarriage: A risk and resilience perspective* (pp. 93–116). Hillsdale, NJ: Lawrence Erlbaum.

Hetherington, E. M., & Kelly, J. (2002). *For better or for worse: Divorce reconsidered.* New York: W. W. Norton.

Heward, W. L., & Orlansky, M. D. (1992). *Exceptional children* (4th ed.). Columbus, OH: Charles E. Merrill.

Hewson, P. W., Beeth, M. E., & Thorley, N. R. (1998). Teaching for conceptual change. In B. J. Fraserr & K. G. Tobin (Eds.), *International handbook of science education* (pp. 199–218). New York: Kluwer.

Hewstone, M. (1989). Changing stereotypes with disconfirming information. In D. Bar-Tal, C. Graumann, A. Kruglanski, & W. Stroebe (Eds.), *Stereotyping and prejudice: Changing conceptions* (pp. 207–223). New York: Springer-Verlag.

Hilgard, E. R., Atkinson, R. L., & Atkinson, R. C. (1979). *Introduction to psychology* (7th ed.). New York: Harcourt Brace Jovanovich.

Hill, W. F. (2002). *Learning: A survey of psychological interpretations* (7th ed.). Boston: Allyn and Bacon.

Hines, C. V., Cruickshank, D. R., & Kennedy, J. J. (1985). Teacher clarity and its relation to student achievement and satisfaction. *American Educational Research Journal, 22,* 87–99.

Hiroto, D. S., & Seligman, M. E. P. (1975). Generality of learned helplessness in man. *Journal of Personality and Social Psychology, 31,* 311–327.

Hodges, E. V. E., & Perry, D. G. (1999). Personal and interpersonal antecedents and consequences of victimization by peers. *Journal of Personality and Social Psychology, 76,* 677–685.

Hofer, B. K., & Pintrich, P. R. (1997). The development of epistemological theories: Beliefs about knowledge and knowing and their relation to learning. *Review of Educational Research, 67,* 88–140.

Hoffman, L. W. (1984). Work, family, and the socialization of the child. In R. Parke (Ed.), *Review of child development research* (Vol. 7, pp. 223–282). Chicago: University of Chicago Press.

Hoffman, M. L. (2000). *Empathy and moral development.* New York: Cambridge University Press.

Hoge, D. R., Smit, E. K., & Hanson, S. L. (1990). School experiences predicting changes in self-esteem of sixth- and seventh-grade students. *Journal of Educational Psychology, 82,* 117–126.

Holahan, C., & Sears, R. (1995). *The gifted group in later maturity.* Stanford, CA: Stanford University Press.

Holden, G. W., & Ritchie, K. L. (1991). Linking extreme marital discord, child rearing practices, and child behavior problems: Evidence from battered women. *Child Development, 62,* 311–327.

Hoover-Dempsey, K. V., Bassler, O. C., & Burow, R. (1995). Parents' reported involvement in students' homework: Strategies and practices. *The Elementary School Journal, 95,* 435–450.

Hoover-Dempsey, K. V., Battiato, A. C., Walker, J. M. T., Reed, R. P., DeJong, J. M., & Jones, K. P. (2001). Parental involvement in homework, *Educational Psychologist, 36,* 195–209.

Horgan, D. D. (1995). *Achieving gender equity: Strategies for the classroom.* Boston: Allyn and Bacon.

Horn, J. L. (1998). A basis for research on age differences in cognitive capabilities. In J. J. McArdle & R. W. Woodcock (Eds.), *Human cognitive theories in theory and practice* (pp. 57–87). Mahwah, NJ: Lawrence Erlbaum.

Horowitz, B. (2002, April 22). Gen Y: A tough crowd to sell. *USA Today,* pp. B1–2.

Howard, K. (1990, Spring). Making the writing portfolio real. *The Quarterly of the National Writing Project, 27,* 4–8.

Howe, M. J. A., Davidson, J. W., & Sloboda, J. A. (1998). Innate talents: Reality or myth? *Behavioral and Brain Sciences, 21,* 399–406.

Hoy, W. K., & Woolfolk, A. E. (1990). Organizational socialization of student teachers. *American Educational Research Journal, 27,* 279–300.

Hoy, W. K., & Woolfolk, A. E. (1993). Teachers' sense of efficacy and the organizational health of schools. *Elementary School Journal, 93,* 355–372.

Huessman, L. R., Eron, L. D., Klein, R., Brice, P., & Fischer, P. (1983). Mitigating the imitation of aggressive behaviors by changing children's attitudes about media violence. *Journal of Personality and Social Psychology, 44,* 899–910.

Huff, C. R. (1989). Youth gangs and public policy. *Crime & Delinquency, 35,* 524–537.

Hughes, D. R. (1998). *Kids online: Protecting your children in cyberspace.* Grand Rapids, MI: Fleming H. Revell.

Hundert, J., & Bucher, B. (1978). Pupil's self-scored arithmetic performance: A practical procedure for maintaining accuracy. *Journal of Applied Behavior Analysis, 11,* 304.

Hung, D. W. L. (1999). Activity, apprenticeship, and epistemological appropriation: Implications from the writings of Michael Polanyi. *Educational Psychologist, 34,* 193–205.

Hunt, E. (2000). Let's hear it for crystallized intelligence. *Learning and Individual Differences, 12,* 123–129.

Hunt, J. McV. (1961). *Intelligence and experience.* New York: Ronald.

Hunt, N., & Marshall, K. (2002). *Exceptional children and youth: An introduction to special education* (3rd ed.). Boston: Houghton Mifflin.

Hunt, R. R., & Ellis, H. C. (1999). *Fundamentals of cognitive psychology* (6th ed.). New York: McGraw-Hill College.

Hunter, M. (1982). *Mastery teaching.* El Segundo, CA: TIP Publications.

Hymowitz, K. S. (2001, April 18). "Zero Tolerance" is schools' first line of defense. *Newsday.*

Iran-Nejad, A. (1990). Active and dynamic self-regulation of learning processes. *Review of Educational Research, 60,* 573–602.

Irvine, J. J., (1990). *Black students and school failure: Policies, practices, and prescriptions.* New York: Praeger.

Irvine, J. J., & Armento, B. J. (2001). *Culturally responsive teaching: Lesson planning for elementary and middle grades.* New York: McGraw-Hill.

Irvine, J. J., & Fraser, J. W. (1998, May). Warm demanders. *Education Week.* Available online at http://www.edweek.org/ew/ewstory.cfm?slug=35irvine.h17&keywords=Irvine

Irving, O., & Martin, J. (1982). Withitness: The confusing variable. *American Educational Research Journal, 19,* 313–319.

Irwin, J. W. (1991). *Teaching reading comprehension* (2nd ed.). Boston: Allyn and Bacon.

Isabella, R., & Belsky, J. (1991). Interactional synchrony and the origins of infant–mother attachment: A replication study. *Child Development, 62,* 373–384.

Izard, C. E. (2001). Emotional intelligence or adaptive emotions? *Emotion, 1,* 249–257.

Jacklin, C. N., DiPietro, J. A., & Maccoby, E. E. (1984). Sex-typing behavior and sex-typing pressure in child–parent interactions. *Sex Roles, 13,* 413–425.

Jacobs, J. E., Lanza, S., Osgood, D. W., Eccles, J. S., & Wigfield, A. (2002). Changes in children's self-competence and values: Gender and domain differences across grades one through twelve. *Child Development, 73,* 509–527.

Jagacinski, C. M., & Nicholls, J. G. (1987). Competence and affect in task involvement and ego involvement: The impact of social comparison information. *Journal of Educational Psychology, 76,* 107–114.

James, W. (1890). *The principles of psychology* (Vol. 2). New York: Holt.

James, W. (1912). *Talks to teachers on psychology: And to students on some of life's ideals.* New York: Holt.

Jarrett, R. (1995). Growing up poor: The family experiences of socially mobile youth in low-income African American neighborhoods. *Journal of Adolescent Research, 10,* 111–135.

Jehng, J. C., Johnson, S., & Anderson, R. C. (1993). Schooling and students' epistemological beliefs about learning. *Contemporary Educational Psychology, 18,* 23–35.

Jensen, L. A., Arnett, J. J., Feldman, S. S., & Cauffman, E. (2002). It's wrong but everybody does it: Academic dishonesty among high school and college students. *Contemporary Educational Psychology, 27,* 209–228.

Jenson, W. R., Sloane, H. N., & Young, K. R. (1988). *Applied behavior analysis in education: A structured teaching approach.* Englewood Cliffs, NJ: Prentice-Hall.

Jimenez, R. T., & Gersten, R. (1999). Lessons and dilemmas derived from the literacy instruction of two Latina/o teachers. *American Educational Research Journal, 36,* 265–302.

Jimerson, S. R. (1999). On the failure of failure: Examining the association between early grade retention and education and employment outcomes during late adolescence. *Journal of School Psychology, 37,* 243–272.

John-Steiner, V., & Mahn, H. (1996). Sociocultural approaches to learning and development: A Vygotskian framework. *Educational Psychologist, 31,* 191–206.

Johnson, A. M., & Notah, D. J. (1999). Service learning: History, literature, review, and a pilot study of eighth graders. *The Elementary School Journal, 99,* 453–467.

Johnson, D. W., & Johnson, R. (1985). Motivational processes in cooperative, competitive, and individualistic learning situations. In C. Ames & R. Ames (Eds.), *Research on motivation in education. Vol. 2: The classroom milieu* (pp. 249–286). New York: Academic Press.

Johnson, D. W., & Johnson, R. (1999). *Learning together and alone: Cooperation, competition, and individualization* (5th ed.). Boston: Allyn and Bacon.

Johnson, D. W., & Johnson, R. (1999). The three Cs of school and classroom management. In H. J. Freiberg (Ed.), *Beyond behaviorism: Changing the classroom management paradigm* (pp. 119–144). Boston: Allyn and Bacon.

Johnson. D. W., & Johnson, R. T. (1996). The role of cooperative learning in assessing and communicating student learning. In T. Guskey (Ed.), *ASCD 1996 Yearbook: Communicating student learning* (pp. 25–46). Alexandria, VA: Association for Supervision and Curriculum Development.

Johnson, D. W., & Johnson, R. T. (2002). *Meaningful assessment: A meaningful and cooperative process.* Boston: Allyn and Bacon.

Johnson, D. W., Johnson, R., Dudley, B., Ward, M., & Magnuson, D. (1995). The impact of peer mediation training on the management of school and home conflicts. *American Educational Research Journal, 32,* 829–844.

Jones, E. D., & Southern, W. T. (1991). Conclusions about acceleration: Echoes of a debate. In W. Southern & E. Jones (Eds.), *The academic acceleration of gifted children* (pp. 223–228). New York: Teachers College Press.

Jones, M. G., & Gerig, T. M. (1994). Silent sixth-grade students: Characteristics, achievement, and teacher expectations. *Elementary School Journal, 95,* 169–182.

Jones, M. S., Levin, M. E., Levin, J. R., & Beitzel, B. D. (2000). Can vocabulary-learning strategies and pair-learning formats be profitably combined? *Journal of Educational Psychology, 92,* 256–262.

Jordan, N., & Goldsmith-Phillips, J. (1994). *Assessment of learning disabilities.* Boston: Allyn and Bacon.

Joshua, S., & Dupin, J. J. (1987). Taking into account students' conceptions in instructional strategy: An example in physics. *Cognition and Instruction, 4,* 117–135.

Joyce, B. R., Weil, M., & Calhoun, E. (2000). *Models of teaching* (6th ed.). Boston: Allyn and Bacon.

Jurden, F. H. (1995). Individual differences in working memory and complex cognition. *Journal of Educational Psychology, 87,* 93–102.

Kagan, S. (1983). Social orientation among Mexican-American children: A challenge to traditional classroom structures. In E. Garcia (Ed.), *The Mexican-American child: Language, cognition, and social development.* Tempe, AZ: Center for Bilingual Education.

Kagan, S. (1994). *Cooperative learning.* San Juan Capistrano, CA: Kagan Cooperative Learning.

Kail, R., & Hall, L. K. (1999). Sources of developmental change in children's word-problem performance. *Journal of Educational Psychology, 91,* 600–668.

Kalyuga, S., Chandler, P., Tuovinen, J., & Sweller, J. (2001). When problem solving is superior to studying worked examples. *Journal of Educational Psychology, 93,* 579–588.

Kanfer, F. H., & Gaelick, L. (1986). Self-management methods. In F. Kanfer & A. Goldstein (Eds.), *Helping people change: A textbook of methods* (3rd ed.). New York: Pergamon.

Kantor, H., & Lowe, R. (1995). Class, race, and the emergence of federal education policy: From the New Deal to the Great Society. *Educational Researcher, 24*(3), 4–11.

Kaplan, J. S. (1991). *Beyond behavior modification* (2nd ed.). Austin, TX: Pro-Ed.

Kardash, C. M., & Howell, K. L. (2000). Effects of epistemological beliefs and topic-specific beliefs on undergraduates' cognitive and strategic processing of dual-positional text. *Journal of Educational Psychology, 92,* 524–535.

Kardash, C. M., & Scholes, R. J. (1996). Effects of preexisting beliefs, epistemological beliefs, and need for cognition on interpretation of controversial issues. *Journal of Educational Psychology, 88,* 260–271.

Karpov, Y. V., & Bransford, J. D. (1995). L. S. Vygotsky and the doctrine of empirical and theoretical learning. *Educational Psychologist, 30,* 61–66.

Karpov, Y. V., & Haywood, H. C. (1998). Two ways to elaborate Vygotsky's concept of mediation implications for instruction. *American Psychologist, 53,* 27–36.

Karweit, N. (1989). Time and learning: A review. In R. E. Slavin (Ed.), *School and classroom organization* (pp. 69–95). Hillsdale, NJ: Lawrence Erlbaum.

Karweit, N., & Slavin, R. (1981). Measurement and modeling choices in studies of time and learning. *American Educational Research Journal, 18,* 157–171.

Kazdin, A. E. (1984). *Behavior modification in applied settings.* Homewood, IL: Dorsey Press.

Kazdin, A. E. (2001). *Behavior modification in applied settings* (6th ed.). Belmont, CA: Wadsworth.

Keefe, J. W. (1982). Assessing student learning styles: An overview. In *Student learning styles and brain behavior.* Reston, VA: National Association of Secondary School Principals.

Keefe, J. W., & Monk, J. S. (1986). *Learning style profile examiner's manual.* Reston, VA: National Association of Secondary School Principals.

Kelly, K. (1999). Retention vs. social promotion: Schools search for alternatives. *Harvard Education Letter, 15*(1), 1–3.

Keogh, B. K., & MacMillan, D. L. (1996). Exceptionality. In D. Berliner & R. Calfee (Eds.), *Handbook of educational psychology* (pp. 311–330). New York: Macmillan.

Kerckhoff, A. C. (1986). Effects of ability grouping in British secondary schools. *American Sociological Review, 51,* 842–858.

Keyser, V., & Barling, J. (1981). Determinants of children's self-efficacy beliefs in an academic environment. *Cognitive Therapy and Research, 5,* 29–40.

Kiewra, K. A. (1985). Investigating notetaking and review: A depth of processing alternative. *Educational Psychologist, 20,* 23–32.

Kiewra, K. A. (1988). Cognitive aspects of autonomous note taking: Control processes, learning strategies, and prior knowledge. *Educational Psychologist, 23,* 39–56.

Kiewra, K. A. (1989). A review of note-taking: The encoding storage paradigm and beyond. *Educational Psychology Review, 1,* 147–172.

Kiewra, K. A. (2002). How classroom teachers can help students learn and teach them how to learn. *Theory Into Practice, 41,* 71–80.

Kindsvatter, R., Wilen, W., & Ishler, M. (1992). *Dynamics of effective teaching* (2nd ed.). New York: Longman.

King, A. (1990). Enhancing peer interaction and learning in the classroom through reciprocal questioning. *American Educational Research Journal, 27,* 664–687.

King, A. (1994). Guiding knowledge construction in the classroom: Effects of teaching children how to question and how to explain. *American Educational Research Journal, 31,* 338–368.

King, A. (2002). Structuring peer interactions to promote high-level cognitive processing. *Theory Into Practice, 41,* 31–39.

King, G. (1979, June). Personal communication. University of Texas at Austin.

King, K. M., & Kitchener, K. S. (1994). *Developing reflective judgement: Understanding and promoting intellectual growth and critical thinking in adolescents and adults.* San Francisco: Jossey-Bass.

Kintsch, W. (1998). *Comprehension: A paradigm for cognition.* New York: Cambridge University Press.

Kirk, S., Gallagher, J. J., & Anastasiow, N. J. (1993). *Educating exceptional children* (7th ed.). Boston: Houghton Mifflin.

Kirst, M. (1991a). Interview on assessment issues with Lorrie Shepard. *Educational Researcher, 20*(2), 21–23.

Kirst, M. (1991b). Interview on assessment issues with James Popham. *Educational Researcher, 20*(2), 24–27.

Klausmeier, H. J. (1976). Instructional design and the teaching of concepts. In J. Levin & V. Allen (Eds.), *Cognitive learning in children: Theories and strategies* (pp. 191–218). New York: Academic Press.

Klausmeier, H. J. (1992). Concept learning and concept teaching. *Educational Psychologist, 27,* 267–286.

Klein, P. (2002). Multiplying the problem of intelligence by eight. In L. Abbeduto (Ed.), *Taking sides: Clashing on controversial issues in educational psychology* (pp. 219–232). Guilford, CT: McGraw-Hill/Duskin.

Kling, K. C., Hyde, J. S., Showers, C. J., & Buswell, B. N. (1999). Gender differences in self-esteem: A meta-analysis. *Psychological Bulletin, 125,* 470–500.

Knapp, M., Turnbull, B. J., & Shields, P. M. (1990). New directions for educating children of poverty. *Educational Leadership, 48*(1), 4–9.

Kogan, N. (1983). Stylistic variation in childhood and adolescence: Creativity, metaphor, and cognitive style. In P. Mussen (Ed.),

Handbook of child psychology (4th ed.) (Vol. 3, pp. 630–706). New York: Wiley.

Kohlberg, L. (1963). The development of children's orientations toward moral order: Sequence in the development of moral thought. *Vita Humana, 6,* 11–33.

Kohlberg, L. (1975). The cognitive-developmental approach to moral education. *Phi Delta Kappan, 56,* 670–677.

Kohlberg, L. (1981). *The philosophy of moral development.* New York: Harper & Row.

Kohlberg, L. (1984). *Essays on moral development.* San Francisco: Harper & Row.

Kohlberg, L., Yaeger, J., & Hjertholm, E. (1969). Private speech: Four studies and a review of theories. *Child Development, 39,* 691–736.

Kohn, A. (1991). Caring kids: The role of the schools. *Phi Delta Kappan, 72,* 496–506.

Kohn, A. (1993). Rewards versus learning: A response to Paul Chance. *Phi Delta Kappan, 74,* 783–787.

Kohn, A. (1996). By all available means: Cameron and Pierce's defense of extrinsic motivators. *Review of Educational Research, 66,* 1–4.

Kohn, A. (2002). How not to teach values. In L. Abbeduto (Ed.), *Taking sides: Clashing on controversial issues in educational psychology* (pp. 138–153). Guilford, CT: McGraw-Hill/Duskin.

Kokko, K., & Pulkkinen, L. (2000). Aggression in childhood and long-term unemployment in adulthood: A cycle of maladaptation and some protective factors. *Developmental Psychology, 36,* 463–472.

Kolb, G., & Whishaw, I. Q. (1998). Brain plasticity and behavior. In J. T. Spence, J. M. Darley, & D. J. Foss (Eds.), *Annual Review of Psychology* (pp. 43–64). Palo Alto, CA: Annual Reviews.

Korenman, S., Miller, J., & Sjaastad, J. (1995). Long-term poverty and child development in the United States: Results from the NLSY. *Children and Youth Services Review, 17,* 127–155.

Korf, R. (1999). Heuristic search. In R. Wilson & F. Keil (Eds.), *The MIT encyclopedia of the cognitive sciences* (pp. 372–273). Cambridge, MA: MIT Press.

Koriat, A., Goldsmith, M., & Pansky, A. (2000). Toward a psychology of memory accuracy. In S. Fiske (Ed.), *Annual review of psychology* (pp. 481–537). Palo Alto, CA: Annual Reviews.

Kosslyn, S. M., & Koenig, O. (1992). *Wet mind: The new cognitive neuroscience.* New York: Free Press.

Kotrez, D., Stecher, B., & Diebert, E. (1993). *The reliability of scores from the 1992 Vermont Portfolio Assessment Program.* CSE Technical Report 355. Los Angeles: UCLA Center for the Study of Evaluation.

Kounin, J. S. (1970). *Discipline and group management in classrooms.* New York: Holt, Rinehart & Winston.

Kounin, J. S., & Doyle, P. H. (1975). Degree of continuity of a lesson's signal system and task involvement of children. *Journal of Educational Psychology, 67,* 159–164.

Kozulin, A. (1990). *Vygotsky's psychology: A biography of ideas.* Cambridge, MA: Harvard University Press.

Kozulin, A., & Falik, L. (1995). Dynamic cognitive assessment of the child. *Current Directions, 4,* 192–195.

Kozulin, A., & Presseisen, B. Z. (1995). Mediated learning experience and psychological tools: Vygotsky's and Feuerstein's perspectives in a study of student learning. *Educational Psychologist, 30,* 67–75.

Krathwohl, D. R., Bloom, B. S., & Masia, B. B. (1964). *Taxonomy of educational objectives. Handbook II: Affective domain.* New York: David McKay.

Kreitzer, A. E., & Madaus, G. F. (1994). Empirical investigations of the hierarchical structure of the taxonomy. In L. W. Anderson & L. A. Sosniak (Eds.), *Bloom's taxonomy: A forty-year retrospective.* Ninety-third yearbook for the National Society for the Study of Education: Part II (pp. 64–81). Chicago: University of Chicago Press.

Kroger, J. (1995). The differentiation of "firm" and "developmental" foreclosure identity statuses: A longitudinal study. *Journal of Adolescent Research, 10,* 317–337.

Krumboltz, J. D., & Krumboltz, H. B. (1972). *Changing children's behavior.* Englewood Cliffs, NJ: Prentice-Hall.

Krumboltz, J. D., & Yeh, C. J. (1996). Competitive grading sabotages good teaching. *Phi Delta Kappan, 78,* 324–326.

Kuhn, D. (1991). *The skills of argument.* New York: Cambridge University Press.

Kuklinski, M. R., & Weinstein, R. S. (2001). Classroom and developmental differences in a path model of teacher expectancy effects. *Child Development, 72,* 1554–1578.

Kulik, C. C., & Kulik, J. A. (1982). Effects of ability grouping on secondary school students: A meta-analysis of evaluation findings. *American Educational Research Journal, 19,* 415–428.

Kulik, J. A., & Kulik, C. C. (1984). Effects of accelerated instruction on students. *Review of Educational Research, 54,* 409–425.

Kulik, J. A., & Kulik, C. L. (1997). Ability grouping. In N. Colangelo & G. Davis (Eds.), *Handbook of gifted education* (2nd ed., pp. 230–242). Boston: Allyn and Bacon.

Ladson-Billings, G. (1990). Like lightning in a bottle: Attempting to capture the pedagogical excellence of successful teachers of Black students. *Qualitative Studies in Education, 3,* 335–344.

Ladson-Billings, G. (1992). Culturally relevant teaching: The key to making multicultural education work. In C.A. Grant (Ed.), *Research and multicultural education* (pp. 106–121). London: Falmer Press.

Ladson-Billings, G. (1994). *The dream keepers.* San Francisco: Jossey-Bass.

Ladson-Billings, G. (1995). But that is just good teaching! The case for culturally relevant pedagogy. *Theory Into Practice, 34,* 161–165.

Lambert, (1995). Stereotypes and social judgment: The consequences of group variability. *Journal of Personality and Social Psychology, 68,* 388–403.

Lambert, N. M. (1994). Seating arrangement in classrooms. *The International Encyclopedia of Education* (2nd ed.) *9,* 5355–5359.

Lamon, M., Chan, C. K. K., Scardamalia, M., Burtis, J., & Brett, C. (1993, April). *Beliefs about learning and constructive processes in reading: Effects of a computer supported intentional learning environment.* Paper presented at the annual meeting of the American Educational Research Association, Atlanta.

Land, M. L. (1987). Vagueness and clarity. In M. Dunkin (Ed.), *The international encyclopedia of teaching and teacher education* (pp. 392–397). New York: Pergamon.

Langer, E. J. (1993). A mindful education. *Educational Psychologist, 28,* 43–51.

Language Development and Hypermedia Group. (1992). "Open" software design: A case study. *Educational Technology, 32,* 43–55.

Larrivee, B. (1985). *Effective teaching behaviors for successful mainstreaming.* New York: Longman.

Lashley, T. J., II, Matczynski, T. J., & Rowley, J. B. (2002). *Instructional models: Strategies for teaching in a diverse society* (2nd ed.). Belmont, CA: Wadsworth/Thomson Learning.

Lave, J. (1988). *Cognition in practice: Mind, mathematics, and culture in everyday life.* New York: Cambridge University Press.

Lave, J. (1997). The culture of acquisition and the practice of understanding. In D. Kirshner & J. A. Whitson (Eds.), *Situated cognition: Social, semiotic, and psychological perspectives* (pp. 17–35). Mahwah, NJ: Lawrence Erlbaum.

Lave, J., & Wenger, E. (1991). *Situated learning: Legitimate peripheral participation.* Cambridge, MA: Cambridge University Press.

Lee, A. Y., & Hutchinson, L. (1998). Improving learning from examples through reflection. *Journal of Experimental Psychology: Applied, 4,* 187–210.

Leinhardt, G. (1988). Situated knowledge and expertise in teaching. In J. Calderhead (Ed.), *Teachers' professional learning* (pp. 146–168). London: Farmer Press.

Leinhardt, G. (2001). Instructional explanations: A commonplace for teaching and location for contrasts. In V. Richardson (Ed.), *Handbook of research on teaching* (4th ed., pp. 333–357). Washington, DC: American Educational Research Association.

LeMahieu, P., Gitomer, D. H., & Eresh, J. T. (1993). *Portfolios in large-scale assessment: Difficult but not impossible.* Unpublished manuscript, University of Delaware.

Leming, J. S. (1981). Curriculum effectiveness in value/moral education. *Journal of Moral Education, 10,* 147–164.

Lepper, M. R. (1988). Motivational considerations in the study of instruction. *Cognition and Instruction, 5,* 289–309.

Lepper, M. R., & Greene, D. (1978). *The hidden costs of rewards: New perspectives on the psychology of human motivation.* Hillsdale, NJ: Lawrence Erlbaum.

Lepper, M. R., Keavney, M., & Drake, M. (1996). Intrinsic motivation and extrinsic reward: A commentary on Cameron and Pierce's meta-analysis. *Review of Educational Research, 66,* 5–32.

Lerner, R. M., & Galambos, N. L. (1998). Adolescent development: Challenges and opportunities for research, programs, and policies. In J. T. Spence, J. M. Darley, & D. J. Foss (Eds.), *Annual Review of Psychology* (pp. 413–446). Palo Alto, CA: Annual Reviews.

Levin, J. R. (1994). Mnemonic strategies and classroom learning: A twenty-year report card. *Elementary School Journal, 94,* 235–254.

Levin, J. R., & Nolan, J. F. (2000). *Principles of classroom management: A professional decision-making model.* Boston: Allyn and Bacon.

Lewinsohn, P. M., Rohde, P., & Seeley, J. R. (1994). Psychological risk factors for future attempts. *Journal of Consulting and Clinical Psychology, 62,* 297–305.

Lewis, R. (2001). Classroom discipline and student responsibility: The students' view. *Teaching and Teacher Education, 17,* 307–319.

Liben, L. S., & Signorella, M. L. (1993). Gender-schematic processing in children: The role of initial interpretations of stimuli. *Developmental Psychology, 29,* 141–149.

Lickona, T. (2002). Character education: Seven crucial issues. In L. Abbeduto (Ed.), *Taking sides: Clashing on controversial issues in educational psychology* (pp. 130–137). Guilford, CT: McGraw-Hill/Duskin.

Lindsay, P. H., & Norman, D. A. (1977). *Human information processing: An introduction to psychology* (2nd ed.). New York: Academic Press.

Linley, L. (1999). Multi-age classes and high ability students. *Review of Educational Research, 69,* 187–221.

Linn, M. C., & Hyde, J. S. (1989). Gender, mathematics, and science. *Educational Researcher, 18,* 17–27.

Linn, R. L. (1986). Educational testing and assessment: Research needs and policy issues. *American Psychologist, 41,* 1153–1160.

Linn, R. L. (2000). Assessments and accountability. *Educational Researcher, 29*(2), 4–16.

Linn, R. L., Baker, E. L., & Betebenner, D. W. (2002). Accountability systems: Implications of the requirements of the No Child Left Behind Act of 2001. *Educational Researcher, 31*(6), 3–16.

Linn, R. L., & Gronlund, N. E. (2000). *Measurement and assessment in education* (8th ed.). Columbus, OH: Merrill.

Lipscomb, T. J., MacAllister, H. A., & Bregman, N. J. (1985). A developmental inquiry into the effects of multiple models on children's generosity. *Merrill-Palmer Quarterly, 31,* 335–344.

Locke, E. A., & Latham, G. P. (1990). *A theory of goal setting and task performance.* Englewood Cliffs, NJ: Prentice-Hall.

Locke, E. A., & Latham, G. P. (2002). Building a practically useful theory of goal setting and task motivation: A 35-year odyssey. *American Psychologist, 57,* 705–717.

Loftus, E., & Palmer, J. C. (1974). Reconstruction of automobile destruction: An example of the interaction between language and memory. *Journal of Verbal Learning and Verbal Behavior, 13,* 585–589.

Lomask, M. S., Pecheone, R. L., & Baron, J. B. (1995). Assessing new science teachers. *Educational Leadership, 52*(6), 62–65.

Lonka, K., Joram, E., & Bryson, M. (1996). Conceptions of learning and knowledge: Does training make a difference? *Contemporary Educational Psychology, 21,* 240–260.

Lorch, R. F., Lorch, E. P., Ritchey, K., McGovern, L., & Coleman, D. (2001). Effects of headings on text summarization. *Contemporary Educational Psychology 26,* 171–191.

Lord, S., Eccles, J., & McCarthy, K. (1994). Surviving the junior high school transition: Family processes and self-perceptions as protective factors. *Journal of Early Adolescence, 14,* 162–199.

Louis, B., Subotnik, R. F., Breland, P. S., & Lewis, M. (2000). Establishing criteria for high ability versus selective admission to gifted programs: Implications for policy and practice. *Educational Psychology Review, 12,* 295–314.

Loveless, T. (1998). The tracking and ability grouping debate. *Fordham Report, 2*(88), 1–27.

Loveless, T. (1999). Will tracking reform promote social equity? *Educational Leadership, 56*(7), 28–32.

Lovett, M. W., et al. (2000). Components of effective remediation for developmental disabilities: Combining phonological and strategy-based instruction to improve outcomes. *Journal of Educational Psychology, 92,* 263–283.

Lowenstein, G. (1994). The psychology of curiosity: A review and reinterpretation. *Psychological Bulletin, 117,* 75–98.

Lowry, R., Sleet, D., Duncan, C., Powell, K., & Kolbe, L. (1995). Adolescents at risk for violence. *Educational Psychology Review, 7,* 7–40.

Luiten, J., Ames, W., & Ackerson, G. (1980). A meta-analysis of the effects of advance organizers on learning and retention. *American Educational Research Journal, 17,* 211–218.

Ma, X., & Kishor, N. (1997). Attitude toward self, social factors, and achievement in mathematics: A meta-analytic review. *Educational Psychology Review, 9,* 89–120.

Mabry, L. (1999). Writing to the rubrics: Lingering effects of traditional standardized testing on direct writing assessment. *Phi Delta Kappan, 80,* 673–679.

Maccoby, E. E. (1998). *The two sexes: Growing up apart, coming together.* Cambridge, MA: Belknap/Harvard University Press.

Maccoby, E. E., & Jacklin, C. N. (1974). *The psychology of sex differences.* Stanford, CA: Stanford University Press.

Mace, F. C., Belfiore, P. J., & Hutchinson, J. M. (2001). Operant theory and research on self-regulation. In B. Zimmerman & D. Schunk (Eds.), *Self-regulated learning and academic achievement: Theoretical perspectives* (2nd ed.). Mahwah, NJ: Lawrence Erlbaum.

Macionis, J. J. (2003). *Sociology* (9th ed.). Upper Saddle River, NJ: Prentice-Hall.

Macrae, C. N., Milne, A. B., & Bodenhausen, C. V. (1994). Stereotypes as energy-saving devices: A peek inside the cognitive toolbox. *Journal of Personality and Social Psychology, 66,* 37–47.

Madsen, C. H., Becker, W. C., & Thomas, D. R. (1968). Rules, praise, and ignoring: Elements of elementary classroom control. *Journal of Applied Behavior Analysis, 1,* 139–150.

Madsen, C. H., Becker, W. C., Thomas, D. R., Koser, L., & Plager, E. (1968). An analysis of the reinforcing function of "sit down" commands. In R. K. Parker (Ed.), *Readings in educational psychology.* Boston: Allyn and Bacon.

Maehr, M. L., & Anderman, E. M. (1993). Reinventing schools for early adolescents: Emphasizing task goals. *The Elementary School Journal, 93,* 593–610.

Mager, R. (1975). *Preparing instructional objectives* (2nd ed.). Palo Alto, CA: Fearon.

Magnusson, S. J., & Palincsar, A. S. (1995). The learning environment as a site of science reform. *Theory Into Practice, 34,* 43–50.

Maier, N. R. F. (1933). An aspect of human reasoning. *British Journal of Psychology, 24,* 144–155.

Major, B., & Schmader, T. (1998). Coping with stigma through psychological disengagement. In J. Swim & C. Stangor (Eds.), *Stigma: The target's perspective* (pp. 219–241). New York: Academic Press.

Maker, C. J. (1987). Gifted and talented. In V. Richardson-Koehler (Ed.), *Educators' handbook: A research perspective* (pp. 420–455). New York: Longman.

Malone, T. W., & Lepper, M. (1987). Making learning fun: A taxonomy of intrinsic motivations for learning. In R. E. Snow and M. J. Farr (Eds.), *Aptitude, learning and instruction, Volume 3: Cognitive and affective process analysis* (pp. 223–253). Hillsdale, NJ: Lawrence Erlbaum.

Mangione, P. L., & Speth, T. (1998). The transition to elementary school: A framework for creating early childhood continuity through home, school, and community partnerships. *The Elementary School Journal, 98,* 381–397.

Manning, B. H. (1991). *Cognitive self-instruction of classroom processes.* Albany, NY: State University of New York Press.

Manning, B. H., & Payne, B. D. (1996). *Self-talk for teachers and students: Metacognitive strategies for personal and classroom use.* Boston: Allyn and Bacon.

Manning, M. L., & Baruth, L. G. (1996). *Multicultural education of children and adolescents* (2nd ed.). Boston: Allyn and Bacon.

Mantzicopolos, P., & Morrison, D. (1992). Kindergarten retention: Academic and behavioral outcomes through the end of second grade. *American Educational Research Journal, 29,* 182–198.

Marcia, J. E. (1987). The identity status approach to the study of ego identity development. In T. Honess & K. Yardley (Eds.), *Self and identity: Perspectives across the life span* (pp. 161–171). London: Routledge & Kegan Paul.

Marcia, J. E. (1991). Identity and self development. In R. Lerner, A. Peterson, & J. Brooks-Gunn (Eds.), *Encyclopedia of Adolescence* (Vol. 1). New York: Garland.

Marcia, J. E. (1994). The empirical study of ego identity. In H. Bosma, T. Graafsma, H. Grotebanc, & D. DeLivita (Eds.), *The identity and development.* Newbury Park, CA: Sage.

Marcia, J. E. (1999). Representational thought in ego identity, psychotherapy, and psychosocial development. In I. E. Sigel (Ed.), *Development of mental representation: Theories and applications.* Mahwah, NJ: Lawrence Erlbaum.

Marcus, N., Cooper, M., & Sweller, J. (1996). Understanding instructions. *Journal of Educational Psychology, 88,* 49–63.

Marinova-Todd, S., Marshall, D., & Snow, C. (2000). Three misconceptions abut age and L2 learning. *TESOL Quarterly, 34*(1), 9–34.

Markman, E. (1992). Constraints on word learning: Speculations about their nature, origins, and domain specificity. In M. Gunnar & M. Maratsos (Eds.), *Minnesota symposium on child psychology* (Vol. 25, pp. 59–101). Hillsdale, NJ: Lawrence Erlbaum.

Markman, E. M. (1977). Realizing that you don't understand: A preliminary investigation. *Child Development, 48,* 986–992.

Markman, E. M. (1979). Realizing that you don't understand: Elementary school children's awareness of inconsistencies. *Child Development, 50,* 643–655.

Markstrom-Adams, C. (1992). A consideration of intervening factors in adolescent identity formation. In G. R. Adams, R. Montemayor, & T. Gullotta (Eds.), *Advances in adolescent development: Vol. 4. Adolescent identity formation* (pp. 173-192). Newbury Park, CA: Sage.

Marsh, H. W. (1987). The big-fish-little-pond effect on academic self-concept. *Journal of Educational Psychology, 79,* 280–295.

Marsh, H. W. (1990). Influences of internal and external frames of reference on the formation of math and English self-concepts. *Journal of Educational Psychology, 82,* 107–116.

Marsh, H. W. (1994). Using the National Longitudinal Study of 1988 to evaluate theoretical models of self-concept: The Self-Description Questionnaire. *Journal of Educational Psychology, 86,* 439–456.

Marsh, H. W., Chessor, D., Craven, R., & Roche, L. (1995). The effects of gifted and talented programs on academic self-concept: The big fish strikes again. *American Educational Research Journal, 32,* 285–321.

Marsh, H. W., & Holmes, I. W. M. (1990). Multidimensional self-concepts: Construct validation of responses by children. *American Educational Research Journal, 27,* 89–118.

Marsh, H. W., Kong, C., & Hau, K. (2000). Longitudinal multilevel models of the big-fish-little-pond effect on academic self-concept: Counterbalancing contrast and reflected-glory effects in Hong Kong schools. *Journal of Personality & Social Psychology, 78,* 337–349.

Marsh, H. W., Parada, R. H., Yeung, A. S., & Healey, J. (2001). Aggressive school troublemakers and victims: A longitudinal model examining the pivotal role of self-concept. *Journal of Educational Psychology, 93,* 411–419.

Marsh, H. W., & Shavelson, R. (1985). Self-concept: Its multifaceted, hierarchical structure. *Educational Psychologist, 20,* 107–123.

Marsh, H. W., & Yeung, A. S. (1997). Coursework selection: Relation to academic self-concept and achievement. *American Educational Research Journal, 34,* 691–720.

Marsh, H. W., Walker, R., & Debus, R. (1991). Subject-specific components of academic self-concept and self-efficacy. *Contemporary Educational Psychology, 16,* 331–345.

Marshall, H. (1996). Implications of differentiating and understanding constructivist approaches. *Journal of Educational Psychology, 31,* 235–240.

Marshall, H. H. (1987). Motivational strategies of three fifth-grade teachers. *Elementary School Journal, 88,* 135–150.

Marshall, H. H. (Ed.). (1992). *Redefining student learning: Roots of educational change.* Norwood, NJ: Ablex.

Martin, C. L. (1989). Children's use of gender-related information in making social judgments. *Developmental Psychology, 25,* 80–88.

Martin, C. L., & Little, J. K. (1990). The relation of gender understanding to children's sex-typed preferences and gender stereotypes. *Child Development, 61,* 1427–1439.

Martin, G., & Pear, J. (1992). *Behavior modification: What it is and how to do it* (4th ed.). Englewood Cliffs, NJ: Prentice-Hall.

Martindale, C. (1991). *Cognitive psychology: A neural-network approach.* Pacific Grove, CA: Brooks/Cole.

Martinez-Pons, M. (2002). A social cognitive view of parental influence on student academic self-regulation. *Theory Into Practice, 61,* 126–131.

Martinez-Pons, M. (2002). Parental influences on children's academic self-regulatory development. *Theory Into Practice, 41,* 126–131.

Maslow, A. H. (1968). *Toward a psychology of being* (2nd ed.). New York: Van Nostrand.

Maslow, A. H. (1970). *Motivation and personality* (2nd ed.). New York: Harper and Row.

Mason, D. A., & Good, T. L. (1993). Effects of two-group and whole-class teaching on regrouped elementary students' mathematics achievement. *American Educational Research Journal, 30,* 328–360.

Matlin, M. W., & Foley, H. J. (1997). *Sensation and perception* (4th ed.). Boston: Allyn and Bacon.

Mautone, P. D., & Mayer, R. E. (2001). Signaling as a cognitive guide in multimedia learning. *Journal of Educational Psychology, 93,* 377–389.

Mayer, J. D., & Cobb, C. D. (2000). Educational policy on emotional intelligence: Does it make sense? *Educational Psychology Review, 12,* 163–183.

Mayer, J. D., & Salovey, P. (1997). What is emotional intelligence? In P. Salovey & D. Sluyter (Eds.), *Emotional development, emotional literacy, and emotional intelligence.* New York: Basic Books.

Mayer, J. D., Salovey, P., & Caruso, D. R. (2000). Competing models of emotional intelligence. In Sternberg, R. J. (Ed.), *Handbook of human intelligence* (2nd ed., pp. 396–420). New York: Cambridge University Press.

Mayer, R. E. (1983a). Can you repeat that? Qualitative and quantitative effects of repetition and advance organizers on learning from science prose. *Journal of Educational Psychology, 75,* 40–49.

Mayer, R. E. (1983b). *Thinking, problem solving, cognition.* San Francisco: Freeman.

Mayer, R. E. (1984). Twenty-five years of research on advance organizers. *Instructional Science, 8,* 133–169.

Mayer, R. E. (1992). Cognition and instruction: Their historic meeting within educational psychology. *Journal of Educational Psychology, 84,* 405–412.

Mayer, R. E. (1992). *Thinking, problem solving, cognition* (2nd ed.). New York: Freeman.

Mayer, R. E. (1996). Learners as information processors: Legacies and limitations of educational psychology's second metaphor. *Journal of Educational Psychology, 31,* 151–161.

Mayer, R. E. (1997). Multimedia learning: Are we asking the right questions? *Educational Psychologist, 32,* 1–19.

Mayer, R. E. (1999). Multimedia aids to problem-solving transfer. *International Journal of Educational Research, 31,* 611–623.

Mayer, R. E. (1999). *The promise of educational psychology: Learning in the content areas.* Upper Saddle River, NJ: Prentice-Hall.

Mayer, R. E. (2001). *Multimedia learning.* New York: Cambridge University Press.

Mayer, R. E., & Gallini, J. K. (1990). When is an illustration worth ten thousand words? *Journal of Educational Psychology, 82,* 715–726.

Mayer, R. E., & Sims, V. K. (1994). For whom is a picture worth a thousand words? Extensions of a dual-coding theory of multimedia learning. *Journal of Educational Psychology, 86,* 389–401.

Mayer, R. E., & Wittrock, M. C. (1996). Problem-solving transfer. In D. Berliner & R. Calfee (Eds.), *Handbook of educational psychology* (pp. 47–62). New York: Macmillan.

McCaslin, M., & Good, T. (1996). The informal curriculum. In D. Berliner & R. Calfee (Eds.), *Handbook of educational psychology* (pp. 622–670). New York: Macmillan.

McCaslin, M., & Hickey, D. T. (2001). Self-regulated learning and academic achievement: A Vygotskian view. In B. Zimmerman & D. Schunk (Eds.), *Self-regulated learning and academic achievement: Theoretical perspectives* (2nd ed., pp. 227–252). Mahwah, NJ: Lawrence Erlbaum.

McClelland, D. (1985). *Human motivation.* Glenview, IL: Scott, Foresman.

McClelland, D. C. (1993). Intelligence is not the best predictor of job performance. *Current Directions in Psychological Science, 2,* 5–6.

McCoach, D. B., Kehle, T. J., Bray, M. L., & Siegle, D. (2001). Best practices in the identification of gifted students with learning disabilities. *Psychology in the Schools, 38,* 403–411.

McCombs, B. L., & Marzano, R. J. (1990). Putting the self in self-regulated learning: The self as agent in integrating skill and will. *Educational Psychologist, 25,* 51–70.

McCormick, C. B., & Levin, J. R. (1987). Mnemonic prose-learning strategies. In M. Pressley & M. McDaniel (Eds.), *Imaginary and related mnemonic processes* (pp. 407–427). New York: Springer-Verlag.

McCoy, A. R., & Reynolds, A. J. (1999). Grade retention and school performance: An extended investigation. *Journal of School Psychology, 37,* 273–298.

McDevitt, T. M., & Ormrod, J. E. (2002). *Child development and education.* Upper Saddle River, NJ: Merrill/Prentice-Hall.

McDonald, J. P. (1993). Three pictures of an exhibition: Warm, cool, and hard. *Phi Delta Kappan, 6,* 480–485.

McGoey, K. E., & DuPaul, G. J. (2000). Token reinforcement and response cost procedures: Reducing disruptive behavior of children with attention-deficit/hyperactivity disorder. *School Psychology Quarterly, 15,* 330–343.

McLaughlin, T. F., & Gnagey, W. J. (1981, April). *Self-management and pupil self-control.* Paper presented at the annual meeting of the American Educational Research Association, Los Angeles.

McLoyd, V. C. (1998). Economic disadvantage and child development. *American Psychologist, 53,* 185–204.

McNeil, L. M., & Valenzuela, A. (2000). *The harmful impact of the TAAS system of testing in Texas: Beneath the accountability rhetoric.* Cambridge, MA: Harvard University Civil Rights Project. Available online at www.law.harvard.edu/groups/civilrights/testing.html

McNemar, Q. (1964). Lost: Our intelligence? Why? *American Psychologist, 19,* 871–882.

Mediascope. (1996). *National television violence study: Executive summary 1994–1995.* Studio City, CA: Author.

Medley, D. M. (1979). The effectiveness of teachers. In P. Peterson & H. Walberg (Eds.), *Research on teaching: Concepts, findings, and implications* (pp. 11–27). Berkeley, CA: McCutchan.

Meece, J. L. (1997). *Child and adolescent development for educators.* New York: McGraw-Hill.

Meece, J. L. (2002). *Child and adolescent development for educators* (2nd ed.). New York: McGraw-Hill.

Meece, J. L., & Kurtz-Costes, B. (2001). Introduction: The schooling of ethnic minority children and youth. *Educational Psychologist, 36,* 1–7.

Meichenbaum, D. (1977). *Cognitive behavior modification: An integrative approach.* New York: Plenum.

Meichenbaum, D. (1986). Cognitive behavior modification. In F. Kanfer & A. Goldstein (Eds.), *Helping people change: A textbook of methods* (3rd ed.) (pp. 346–380). New York: Pergamon.

Meichenbaum, D., Burland, S., Gruson, L., & Cameron, R. (1985). Metacognitive assessment. In S. Yussen (Ed.), *The growth of reflection in children* (pp. 1–30). Orlando, FL: Academic Press.

Mendell, P. R. (1971). Retrieval and representation in long-term memory. *Psychonomic Science, 23,* 295–296.

Merton, R. K. (1948). The self-fulfilling prophecy. *Antioch Review, 8,* 193–210.

Messick, S. (1975). The standard problem: Meaning and values in measurement and evaluation. *American Psychologist, 35,* 1012–1027.

Messick, S. (1994). The matter of style: Manifestations of personality in cognition, learning, and teaching. *Educational Psychologist, 29,* 121–136.

Metcalfe, B. (1981). Self-concept and attitude toward school. *British Journal of Educational Psychology, 51,* 66–76.

Metcalfe, J., & Shimamura, A. P. (Eds.). (1994). *Metacognition: Knowledge about knowing.* Cambridge, MA: MIT Press.

Midgley, C. (2001). A goal theory perspective on the current status of middle level schools. In T. Urdan & F. Pajares (Eds.), *Adolescence and education* (pp. 33–59). Volume I. Greenwich, CT: Information Age Publishing.

Midgley, C., Kaplan, A., & Middleton, M. (2001). Performance-approach goals: Good for what, for whom, under what circumstances, and at what cost? *Journal of Educational Psychology, 93,* 77–86.

Mifflin, M. (1999, December 13). Singing the pink blues. Mothers who think. Retrieved March 16, 2002, from http://www.salon.com/mwt/feature/1999/12/13/toys/

Miller, E. (1994). Peer mediation catches on, but some adults don't. *Harvard Education Letter, 10*(3), 8.

Miller, G. A. (1956). The magical number seven, plus or minus two: Some limits on our capacity for processing information. *Psychological Review, 63,* 81–97.

Miller, G. A., Galanter, E., & Pribram, K. H. (1960). *Plans and the structure of behavior.* New York: Holt, Rinehart & Winston.

Miller, K., & Gelman, R. (1983). The child's representation of number: A multidimensional scaling analysis. *Child Development, 54,* 1470–1479.

Miller, P. H. (2002). *Theories of developmental psychology* (4th ed.). New York: Worth.

Miller, R. B. (1962). Analysis and specification of behavior for training. In R. Glaser (Ed.), *Training research and education: Science edition.* New York: Wiley.

Mills, J. R., & Jackson, N. E. (1990). Predictive significance of early giftedness: The case of precocious reading. *Journal of Educational Psychology, 82,* 410–419.

Mitchell, B. M. (1984). An update on gifted and talented education in the U.S. *Roeper Review, 6,* 161–163.

Moerk, E. L. (1992). *A first language taught and learned.* Baltimore: Paul H. Brookes.

Moll, L. C., & Whitmore, K. F. (1993). Vygotsky in classroom practice: Moving from individual transmission to social transaction. In E. Forman, N. Minick, & C. A. Stone (Eds.), *Contexts for learning: Sociocultural dynamics in children's development* (pp. 19–42). New York: Oxford University Press.

Moll, L. C., Amanti, C., Neff, D., & Gonzalez, N. (1992). Funds of knowledge: Using a qualitative approach to connect homes and classrooms. *Theory Into Practice, 31,* 132–141.

Monroe, C. R., & Obidah, J. E. (2002, April). *The impact of cultural synchronization on a teacher's perceptions of disruption: A case study of an African American middle school classroom.* Paper presented at the American Educational Research Association, New Orleans, LA.

Monteleone, J. A. (1998). *Child abuse.* St. Louis, MO: G.W. Medical Publisher.

Morin, V. A., & Miller, S. P. (1998). Teaching multiplication to middle school students with mental retardation. *Education & Treatment of Children, 21,* 22–36.

Morrine-Dershimer, G. (2003). Instructional planning. In J. Cooper (Ed.), *Classroom teaching skills* (7th ed., pp. 19–51). Boston: Houghton-Mifflin.

Morris, C. G. (1991). *Psychology: An introduction* (7th ed.). Englewood Cliffs, NJ: Prentice-Hall.

Morris, P. F. (1990). Metacognition. In M. W. Eysenck, (Ed.), *The Blackwell dictionary of cognitive psychology* (pp. 225–229). Oxford, UK: Basil Blackwell.

Morrow, L. M. (1983). Home and school correlates of early interest in literature. *Journal of Educational Research, 76,* 221–230.

Morrow, L. M., & Weinstein, C. (1986). Encouraging voluntary reading: The impact of a literature program on children's use of library centers. *Reading Research Quarterly, 21,* 330–346.

Moshman, D. (1982). Exogenous, endogenous, and dialectical constructivism. *Developmental Review, 2,* 371–384.

Moshman, D. (1997). Pluralist rational constructivism. *Issues in Education: Contributions from Educational Psychology, 3,* 229–234.

Moshman, D., Glover, J. A., & Bruning, R. H. (1987). *Developmental psychology.* Boston: Little, Brown.

Moskowitz, G., & Hayman, M. L. (1976). Successful strategies of inner-city teachers: A year-long study. *Journal of Educational Research, 69,* 283–289.

Moss, P. A. (1992). Shifting conceptions of validity in educational measurement: Implications for performance assessment. *Review of Educational Research, 62,* 229–258.

Mueller, C. M., & Dweck, C. S. (1998). Praise for intelligence can undermine children's motivation and performance. *Journal of Personality and Social Psychology, 75,* 33–52.

Mumford, M. D., Costanza, D. P., Baughman, W. A., Threlfall, V., & Fleishman, E. A. (1994). Influence of abilities on performance during practice: Effects of massed and distributed practice. *Journal of Educational Psychology, 86,* 134–144.

Murdock, T. B., Hale, N. M., & Weber, M. J. (2001). Predictors of cheating among early adolescents: Academic and social motivations. *Contemporary Educational Psychology, 26,* 96–115.

Murphy, P. K., & Alexander, P. A. (2000). A motivated exploration of motivation terminology. *Contemporary Educational Psychology, 25,* 3–53.

Murray, H. G. (1983). Low inference classroom teaching behavior and student ratings of college teaching effectiveness. *Journal of Educational Psychology, 75,* 138–149.

Mussen, P., Conger, J. J., & Kagan, J. (1984). *Child development and personality* (6th ed.). New York: Harper & Row.

Muth, K. D., & Alverman, D. E. (1999). *Teaching and learning in the middle grades.* Boston: Allyn and Bacon.

Nakamura, J., & Csikszentmihalyi, M. (2001). Catalytic creativity: The case of Linus Pauling. *American Psychologist, 56,* 337–341.

Nansel, T. R., Overbeck, M., Pilla, R. S., Ruan, W. J., Simons-Morton, B., & Schiedt, P. (2001). Bullying behavior among US youth: Prevalence and association with psychosocial adjustment. *Journal of the American Medical Association, 285*(16), 2094–2100.

National Assessment of Educational Progress. (1997). Washington, DC: National Center for Educational Statistics. Available online at http://www.nces.ed.gov/nationsreportcard/about/

National Center for Educational Statistics. (2002). Reports available online at http://nces.ed.gov/pubsearch/majorpub.asp

National Council of Teachers of Mathematics (NCTM). (1991). *Professional standards for teaching mathematics.* Reston, VA: Author.

National Joint Committee on Learning Disabilities (NJCLD). (1989). *Letter from NJCLD to member organizations. Topic: Modifications to the NJCLD definition of learning disabilities.* Washington, DC: Author.

National Science Foundation (NSF). (1988). *Women and minorities in science and engineering* (NSF 88-301). Washington, DC: Author.

National Science Foundation. (1996, December 31). *Women and underrepresented minority scientists and engineers have lower levels of employment in business and industry, 1996* (14). Available at http://www.nsf.gov/sbe/srs/databrf/sdb96331.htm

Naveh-Benjamin, M. (1991). A comparison of training programs intended for different types of test-anxious students: Further support for an information-processing model. *Journal of Educational Psychology, 83,* 134–139.

Naveh-Benjamin, M., McKeachie, W. J., & Lin, Y. (1987). Two types of test-anxious students: Support for an information processing model. *Journal of Educational Psychology, 79,* 131–136.

Needles, M., & Knapp, M. (1994). Teaching writing to children who are undeserved. *Journal of Educational Psychology, 86,* 339–349.

Neimark, E. (1975). Intellectual development during adolescence. In F. D. Horowitz (Ed.), *Review of child development research* (Vol. 4). Chicago: University of Chicago Press.

Neisser, U. (1976). *Cognition and reality.* San Francisco: Freeman.

Neisser, U., Boodoo, G., Bouchard, A., Boykin, W., Brody, N., Ceci, S. J., Halpern, D. F., Loehlin, J. C., Perloff, R., Sternberg, R. J., & Urbina, S. (1996). Intelligence: Knowns and unknowns. *American Psychologist, 51,* 77–101.

Nelson, G. (1993). Risk, resistance, and self-esteem: A longitudinal study of elementary school-aged children from mother-custody and two-parent families. *Journal of Divorce and Remarriage, 19,* 99–119.

Nelson, K. (1986). *Event knowledge.* Hillsdale, NJ: Lawrence Erlbaum.

Nelson, T. O. (1996). Consciousness and metacognition. *American Psychologist, 51,* 102–116.

Nestor-Baker, N. S. (1999). *Tacit knowledge in the superintendency: An exploratory analysis.* Unpublished doctoral dissertation, The Ohio State University, Columbus, OH.

Newcombe, N., & Baenninger, M. (1990). The role of expectations in spatial test performance: A meta-analysis. *Sex Roles, 16,* 25–37.

Newmann, F. M., & Wehlage, G. G. (1993). Five standards of authentic instruction. *Educational Leadership, 50*(7), 8–12.

Newstead, S. E., Franklyn-Stokes, A., & Armstead, P. (1996). Individual differences in student cheating. *Journal of Educational Psychology, 88,* 229–241.

Nicholls, J., Cobb, P., Wood, T., Yachel, E., & Patashnick, M. (1990). Assessing student's theories of success in mathematics: Individual and classroom differences. *Journal for Research in Mathematics Education, 21,* 109–122.

Nicholls, J. G., & Miller, A. (1984). Conceptions of ability and achievement motivation. In R. Ames & C. Ames (Eds.), *Research on motivation in education. Vol. 1: Student Motivation* (pp. 39–73). New York: Academic Press.

Nicholls, J. G., Nelson, J. R., & Gleaves, K. (1995). Learning facts versus learning that most questions have many answers: Students' evaluations of contrasting curricula. *Journal of Educational Psychology, 87,* 253–260.

Nissani, M., & Hoefler-Nissani, D. M. (1992). Experimental studies of belief dependence of observations and of resistance to conceptual change. *Cognition and Instruction, 9,* 97–111.

Noddings, N. (1990). Constructivism in mathematics education. In R. Davis, C. Maher, & N. Noddings (Eds.), *Constructivist views on the teaching and learning of mathematics* (pp. 7–18). Monograph 4 of the National Council of Teachers of Mathematics, Reston, VA.

Noddings, N. (1992). *The challenge to care in schools: An alternative approach to education.* New York: Teachers College Press.

Noddings, N. (1995). Teaching themes of care. *Phi Delta Kappan, 76,* 675–679.

Norman, D. P. (1982). *Learning and memory.* San Francisco: Freeman.

Norton, P., & Sprague, D. (2001). *Technology for teaching.* Boston: Allyn and Bacon.

Novak, J. D., & Musonda, D. (1991). A twelve-year longitudinal study of science concept learning. *American Educational Research Journal, 28,* 117–154.

Nungester, R. J., & Duchastel, P. C. (1982). Testing versus review: Effects on retention. *Journal of Educational Psychology, 74,* 18–22.

Nylund, D. (2000). *Treating Huckleberry Finn: A new narrative approach to working with kids diagnosed ADD/ADHD.* San Francisco: Jossey-Bass.

O'Boyle, M. W., & Gill, H. S. (1998). On the relevance of research findings in cognitive neuroscience to educational practice. *Educational Psychology Review, 10,* 397–410.

O'Connor, C. (1997). Dispositions toward (collective) struggle and educational resilience in the inner city: A case analysis of six African American high school students. *American Educational Research Journal, 34,* 593–629.

O'Donnell, A. (Ed.). (2002, Winter). Promoting thinking through peer learning. Special issue of *Theory Into Practice, 61*(1).

O'Donnell, A. M., & O'Kelly, J. (1994). Learning from peers: Beyond the rhetoric of positive results. *Educational Psychology Review, 6,* 321–350.

O'Leary, K. D. (1980). Pills or skills for hyperactive children? *Journal of Applied Behavior Analysis, 13,* 191–204.

O'Leary, K. D., & O'Leary, S. (Eds.). (1977). *Classroom management: The successful use of behavior modification* (2nd ed.). Elmsford, NY: Pergamon.

O'Leary, K. D., & Wilson, G. T. (1987). *Behavior therapy: Application and outcome.* Englewood Cliffs, NJ: Prentice-Hall.

O'Leary, K. D., Kaufman, K. F., Kass, R. E., & Drabman, R. S. (1970). The effects of loud and soft reprimands on the behavior of disruptive students. *Exceptional Children, 37,* 145–155.

O'Leary, S. (1995). Parental discipline mistakes. *Current Directions in Psychological Science, 4,* 11–13.

O'Leary, S. G., & O'Leary, K. D. (1976). Behavior modification in the schools. In H. Leitenberg (Ed.), *Handbook of behavior modification and behavior therapy.* Englewood Cliffs, NJ: Prentice-Hall.

O'Neil, J. (1990). Link between style, culture proves divisive. *Educational Leadership, 48*(2), 8.

Oakes, J. (1985). *Keeping track.* New Haven: Yale University Press.

Oakes, J. (1990a). Opportunities, achievement, and choice: Women and minority students in science and math. *Review of Research in Education, 16,* 153–222.

Oakes, J. (1990b). *Multiplying inequities: The effects of race, social class, and tracking on opportunities to learn mathematics and science.* Santa Monica, CA: Rand.

Oakes, J. (1999). Promotion or retention: Which one is social? *Harvard Education Letter, 15*(1), 8.

Oakes, J., & Wells, A. S. (1998). Detracking for high student achievement. *Educational Leadership, 55*(6), 38–41.

Oakes, J., & Wells, A. S. (2002). Detracking for high student achievement. In L. Abbeduto (Ed.), *Taking sides: Clashing views and controversial issues in educational psychology* (2nd ed., pp. 26–30). Guilford, CT: McGraw-Hill Duskin.

Ogbu, J. U. (1987). Variability in minority school performance: A problem in search of an explanation. *Anthropology and Education Quarterly, 18,* 312–334.

Ogbu, J. U. (1997). Understanding the school performance of urban blacks: Some essential background knowledge. In H. Walberg, O. Reyes, & R. P. Weissberg (Eds.), *Children and youth: Interdisciplinary perspectives* (pp. 190–140). Norwood, NJ: Ablex.

Ogbu, J. U. (1999). Beyond language: Ebonics, Proper English, and identity in a Black-American speech community. *American Educational Research Journal, 36,* 147–184.

Ogden, J. E., Brophy, J. E., & Evertson, C. M. (1977, April). *An experimental investigation of organization and management techniques in first-grade reading groups.* Paper presented at the annual meeting of the American Educational Research Association, New York.

Okagaki, L. (2001). Triarchic model of minority children's school achievement. *Educational Psychologist, 36,* 9–20.

Ollendick, T. H., Dailey, D., & Shapiro, E. S. (1983). Vicarious reinforcement: Expected and unexpected effects. *Journal of Applied Behavior Analysis, 16,* 485–491.

Olsen, L. (1988). *Crossing the schoolhouse border: Immigrant students and the California public schools.* San Francisco: California Tomorrow.

Onslow, M. (1992). Choosing a treatment program for early stuttering: Issues and future directions. *Journal of Speech and Hearing Research, 35,* 983–993.

Orange, C. (2000). *25 biggest mistakes teachers make and how to avoid them.* Thousand Oaks, CA: Corwin.

Orlando L., & Machado, A. (1996). In defense of Piaget's theory: A reply to 10 common criticisms. *Psychological Review, 103,* 143–164.

Ormrod, J. E. (1999). *Human learning* (3rd ed.). Upper Saddle River: NJ: Merrill/Prentice-Hall.

Ortony, A., Clore, G. L., & Collins, A. (1988). *The cognitive structure of emotions.* Cambridge: Cambridge University Press.

Osborn, A. F. (1963). *Applied imagination* (3rd ed.). New York: Scribner's.

Osborne, J. W. (2001). Testing stereotype threat: Does anxiety explain race and sex differences in achievement? *Contemporary Educational Psychology, 26,* 291–310.

Ovando, C. J. (1989). Language diversity and education. In J. Banks & C. McGee Banks (Eds.), *Multicultural education: Issues and perspectives* (pp. 208–228). Boston: Allyn and Bacon.

Ovando, C. J., & Collier, V. P. (1998). *Bilingual and ESL classrooms: Teaching in multicultural contexts* (2nd ed.). Boston: McGraw-Hill.

Owens, R. (1999). *Language disorders: A functional approach to assessment and intervention* (3rd ed.). Boston: Allyn and Bacon.

Padilla, F. M. (1992). *The gang as an American enterprise.* New Brunswick, NJ: Rutgers University Press.

Paivio, A. (1971). *Imagery and verbal processes.* New York: Holt, Rinehart & Winston.

Paivio, A. (1986). *Mental representations: A dual-coding approach.* New York: Oxford University Press.

Pajares, F. (1997). Current directions in self-efficacy research. In M. L. Maehr & P. R. Pintrich (Eds.), *Advances in motivation and achievement* (Vol. 10, pp. 1–49). Greenwich, CT: JAI Press.

Palincsar, A. S. (1986). The role of dialogue in providing scaffolded instruction. In J. Levin & M. Pressley (Eds.), *Educational Psychologist, 21* (Special issue on learning strategies), 73–98.

Palincsar, A. S. (1998). Social constructivist perspectives on teaching and learning. In J. T. Spence, J. M. Darley, & D. J. Foss (Eds.), *Annual Review of Psychology* (pp. 345–375). Palo Alto, CA: Annual Reviews.

Palincsar, A. S., & Brown, A. L. (1984). Reciprocal teaching of comprehension-fostering and monitoring activities. *Cognition and Instruction, 1,* 117–175.

Palincsar, A. S., & Brown, A. L. (1989). Classroom dialogues to promote self-regulated comprehension. In J. Brophy (Ed.), *Advances in research on teaching* (Vol. 1, pp. 35–67). Greenwich, CT: JAI Press.

Palincsar, A. S., & Herrenkohl, L. R. (2002). Designing collaborative learning contexts. *Theory Into Practice, 61,* 26–32.

Palincsar, A. S., Magnuson, S. J., Marano, N., Ford, D., & Brown, N. (1998). Designing a community of practice: Principles and practices of the GIsML community. *Teaching and Teacher Education, 14,* 5–19.

Panksepp, J. (1998). Attention deficit hyperactivity disorders, psychostimulants, and intolerance of playfulness: A tragedy in the making? *Current Directions in Psychological Science, 7,* 91–98.

Pape, S. J., & Smith, C. (2002). Self-regulating mathematics skills. *Theory Into Practice, 41,* 93–101.

Papert, S. (1980). *Mindstorms; Children, computers, and powerful ideas.* New York: Basic Books.

Papert, S. (1993). *The children's machine: Rethinking school in the age of the computer.* New York: Basic Books.

Paris, S. (1988, April). *Fusing skill and will: The integration of cognitive and motivational psychology.* Paper presented at the annual meeting of the American Educational Research Association, New Orleans.

Paris, S. G., Byrnes, J. P., & Paris, A. H. (2001). Constructing theories, identities, and actions of self-regulated learners. In B. J. Zimmerman & D. H. Schunk (Eds.), *Self-regulated learning and academic achievement: Theoretical perspectives* (2nd ed., pp. 253–287). Mahwah, NJ: Lawrence Erlbaum.

Paris, S. G., & Cunningham, A. E. (1996). Children becoming students. In D. Berliner & R. Calfee, (Eds.), *Handbook of Educational Psychology* (pp. 117–146). New York: Macmillan.

Paris, S. G., Lipson, M. Y., & Wixson, K. K. (1983). Becoming a strategic reader. *Contemporary Educational Psychology, 8,* 293–316.

Parker, W. C., & Hess, D. (2001). Teaching with and for discussion. *Teaching and Teacher Education, 17,* 273–289.

Parks, C. P. (1995). Gang behavior in the schools: Myth or reality? *Educational Psychology Review, 7,* 41–68.

Pasch, M., Sparks-Langer, G., Gardner, T. G., Starko, A. J., & Moody, C. D. (1991). *Teaching as decision making: Instructional practices for the successful teacher.* New York: Longman.

Pate, P. E., Homestead, E. R., & McGinnis, K. L. (1997). *Making integrated curriculum work: Teachers, students, and the quest for coherent curriculum.* New York: Teachers College Press.

Pate, P. E., McGinnis, K., & Homestead, E. (1995). Creating coherence through curriculum integration. In M. Harmin (1994). *Inspiring active learning: A handbook for teachers* (pp. 62–70). Alexandria, VA: Association for Supervision and Curriculum Development.

Paulman, R. G., & Kennelly, K. J. (1984). Test anxiety and ineffective test taking: Different names, same construct? *Journal of Educational Psychology, 76,* 279–288.

Payne, K. J., & Biddle, B. J. (1999). Poor school funding, child poverty, and mathematics achievement. *Educational Researcher, 28*(6), 4–12.

Pelham, W. E. (1981). Attention deficits in hyperactive and learning-disabled children. *Exceptional Education Quarterly, 2,* 13–23.

Pellegrini, A. D., Bartini, M., & Brooks, F. (1999). School bullies, victims, and aggressive victims: Factors relating to group affiliation and victimization in early adolescence. *Journal of Educational Psychology, 91,* 216–224.

Penuel, W. R., & Wertsch, J. V. (1995). Vygotsky and identity formation: A sociocultural approach. *Educational Psychologist, 30,* 83–92.

Peng, S., & Lee, R. (1992, April). *Home variables, parent–child activities, and academic achievement: A study of 1988 eighth graders.* Paper presented at the annual meeting of the American Educational Research Association, San Francisco.

Perkins, D. N., Jay, E., & Tishman, S. (1993). New conceptions of thinking: From ontology to education. *Educational Psychologist, 28,* 67–85.

Perkins, D. N., & Salomon, G. (1989). Are cognitive skills context-bound? *Educational Researcher, 18,* 16–25.

Perner, J. (2000). Memory and theory of mind. In E. Tulving & F. I. M. Craik (Eds.), *The Oxford handbook of memory* (pp. 297–312). New York: Oxford.

Perrone, V. (1994). How to engage students in learning. *Educational Leadership, 51*(5), 11–13.

Perry, N. E., VandeKamp, K., & Mercer, L. (2000, April). *Investigating teacher-student interactions that foster self-regulated learning.* In N. E. Perry (Chair), Symposium conducted at the meeting of the American Educational Research Association, New Orleans.

Peterson, J. L., & Newman, R. (2000). Helping to curb youth violence: The APA-MTV "Warning Signs" initiative. *Professional Psychology: Research & Practice, 31,* 509–514.

Peterson, P. L. (1992). Revising their thinking: Keisha Coleman and her third-grade mathematics class. In H. Marshall (Ed.), *Redefining student learning: Roots of educational change* (pp. 151–176). Norwood, NJ: Ablex.

Peterson, P. L., & Comeaux, M. A. (1989). Assessing the teacher as a reflective professional: New perspectives on teacher evaluation. In A. Woolfolk (Ed.), *Research perspectives on the graduate preparation of teachers* (pp. 132–152). Englewood Cliffs, NJ: Prentice-Hall.

Peterson, P. L., Fennema, E., & Carpenter, T. (1989). Using knowledge of how students think about mathematics. *Educational Leadership, 46*(4), 42–46.

Petrill, S. A., & Wilkerson, B. (2000). Intelligence and achievement: A behavioral genetic perspective. *Educational Psychology Review, 12,* 185–199.

Pettigrew, T. (1998). Intergroup contact theory. In J. T. Spence, J. M. Darley, & D. J. Foss (Eds.), *Annual Review of Psychology* (pp. 65–85). Palo Alto, CA: Annual Reviews.

Pfeffer, C. R. (1981). Developmental issues among children of separation and divorce. In I. Stuart & L. Abt (Eds.), *Children of separation and divorce.* New York: Van Nostrand Reinhold.

Pfiffner, L. J., & O'Leary, S. G. (1987). The efficacy of all positive management as a function of the prior use of negative consequences. *Journal of Applied Behavior Analysis, 20,* 265–271.

Pfiffner, L. J., Rosen, L. A., & O'Leary, S. G. (1985). The efficacy of an all-positive approach to classroom management. *Journal of Applied Behavior Analysis, 18,* 257–261.

Phillips, D. (1995). The good, the bad, and the ugly: The many faces of constructivism. *Educational Researcher, 24*(7), 5–12.

Phillips, D. (1997). How, why, what, when, and where: Perspectives on constructivism and education. *Issues in Education: Contributions from Educational Psychology, 3,* 151–194.

Phillips, D., & Zimmerman, M. (1990). The developmental course of perceived competence and incompetence among competent children. In R. Sternberg & J. Kolligian (Eds.), *Competence considered* (pp. 41–66). New Haven, CT: Yale University Press.

Phye, G. D. (1992). Strategic transfer: A tool for academic problem solving. *Educational Psychology Review, 4,* 393–421.

Phye, G. D. (2001). Problem-solving instruction and problem-solving transfer: The correspondence issue. *Journal of Educational Psychology, 93,* 571–578.

Phye, G. D., & Sanders, C. E. (1994). Advice and feedback: Elements of practice for problem solving. *Contemporary Educational Psychology, 17,* 211–223.

Piaget, J. (1954). *The construction of reality in the child* (M. Cook, Trans.). New York: Basic Books.

Piaget, J. (1962). *Comments on Vygotsky's critical remarks concerning "The language and thought of the child" and "Judgment and reasoning in the child."* Cambridge, MA: MIT Press.

Piaget, J. (1963). *Origins of intelligence in children.* New York: Norton.

Piaget, J. (1964). Development and learning. In R. Ripple & V. Rockcastle (Eds.), *Piaget rediscovered* (pp. 7–20). Ithaca, NY: Cornell University Press.

Piaget, J. (1965). *The moral judgment of the child.* New York: Free Press.

Piaget, J. (1965/1995). *Sociological studies.* New York: Routledge. (Original work published in 1965.)

Piaget, J. (1969). *Science of education and the psychology of the child.* New York: Viking.

Piaget, J. (1970a). Piaget's theory. In P. Mussen (Ed.), *Handbook of child psychology* (3rd ed.) (Vol. 1, pp. 703–732). New York: Wiley.

Piaget, J. (1970b). *The science of education and the psychology of the child.* New York: Orion Press.

Piaget, J. (1974). *Understanding causality* (D. Miles and M. Miles, Trans.). New York: Norton.

Piaget, J. (1985). *The equilibrium of cognitive structures: The central problem of intellectual development* (T. Brown & K. L. Thampy, Trans.). Chicago: University of Chicago Press.

Pierson, L. H., & Connell, J. P. (1992). Effect of grade retention on self-system processes, school engagement, and academic performance. *Journal of Educational Psychology, 84,* 300–307.

Pintrich, P. R. (1994). Continuities and discontinuities: Future directions for research in educational psychology. *Educational Psychologist, 29,* 137–148.

Pintrich, P. R. (2000). Educational psychology a the millennium: A look back and a look forward. *Educational Psychologist, 35,* 221–226.

Pintrich, P. R., Marx, R. W., & Boyle, R. A. (1993). Beyond cold conceptual change: The role of motivational beliefs and classroom contextual factors in the process of conceptual change. *Review of Educational Research, 63,* 167–199.

Pintrich, P. R., & Schrauben, B. (1992). Students' motivational beliefs and their cognitive engagement in academic tasks. In D. Schunk & J. Meece (Eds.), *Students' perceptions in the classroom: Causes and consequences* (pp. 149–183). Hillsdale, NJ: Lawrence Erlbaum.

Pintrich, P. R., & Schunk, D. H. (2002). *Motivation in education: Theory, research, and applications* (2nd ed.). Upper Saddle River, NJ: Merrill/Prentice-Hall.

Pisha, B., & Coyne, P. (2001). Smart for the start: The promise of universal design for learning. *Remedial and Special Education, 22,* 197–203.

Pitts, J. M. (1992). Constructivism: Learning rethought. In J. B. Smith & J. C. Coleman, Jr. (Eds.), *School Library Media Annual* (Vol. 10, pp. 14–25). Englewood, CO: Libraries Unlimited.

Pointon, P., & Kershner, R. (2000). Making decisions about organising the primary classroom as a context for learning: The views of three experienced teachers and their pupils. *Teaching and Teacher Education, 16,* 117–127.

Polson, P. G., & Jeffries, R. (1985). Instruction in general problem-solving skills: An analysis of four approaches. In J. Segal, S. Chipman, & R. Glaser (Eds.), *Thinking and learning skills* (Vol. 1, pp. 417–455). Mahwah, NJ: Lawrence Erlbaum.

Popham, W. J. (1999). *Classroom assessment: What teachers need to know.* Boston: Allyn and Bacon.

Popham, W. J. (2002). *Classroom assessment: What teachers need to know.* (3rd ed.). Boston: Allyn and Bacon.

Posner, M. I. (1973). *Cognition: An introduction.* Glenview, IL: Scott, Foresman.

Prawat, R. S. (1991). The value of ideas: The immersion approach to the development of thinking. *Educational Researcher, 20,* 3–10.

Prawat, R. S. (1992). Teachers beliefs about teaching and learning: A constructivist perspective. *American Journal of Education, 100,* 354–395.

Prawat, R. S. (1996). Constructivism, modern and postmodern. *Issues in Education: Contributions from Educational Psychology, 3,* 215–226.

Premack, D. (1965). Reinforcement theory. In D. Levine (Ed.), *Nebraska symposium on motivation* (Vol. 13, pp. 123–180). Lincoln, NE: University of Nebraska Press.

Pressley, M. (1986). The relevance of the good strategy user model to the teaching of mathematics. In J. Levin & M. Pressley (Eds.), *Educational Psychologist, 21* (Special issue on learning strategies), 139–161.

Pressley, M. (1991). Comparing Hall (1988) with related research on elaborative mnemonics. *Journal of Educational Psychology, 83,* 165–170.

Pressley, M. (1995). More about the development of self-regulation: complex, long-term, and thoroughly social. *Educational Psychologist, 30,* 207–212.

Pressley, M. (1996, August). *Getting beyond whole language: Elementary reading instruction that makes sense in light of recent psychological research.* Paper presented at the Annual meeting of the American Psychological Association, Toronto.

Pressley, M. (1998). *Reading instruction that works: The case for balanced teaching.* New York: The Guilford Press.

Pressley, M., Barkowski, J. G., & Schneider, W. (1987). Cognitive strategies: Good strategy users coordinate metacognition and knowledge. In R. Vasta & G. Whitehurst (Eds.), *Annals of Child Development,* (Vol. 5, pp. 89–129). Greenwich, CT: JAI Press.

Pressley, M., Levin, J., & Delaney, H. D. (1982). The mnemonic keyword method. *Review of Research in Education, 52,* 61–91.

Price, G., & O'Leary, K. D. (1974). *Teaching children to develop high performance standards.* Unpublished manuscript. State University of New York at Stony Brook.

Price, W. F., & Crapo, R. H. (2002). *Cross-cultural perspectives in introductory psychology* (4th ed.). Pacific Grove, CA: Wadsworth.

Public Agenda Foundation. (1994). *First things first: What Americans expect from public schools.* New York: Author.

Putnam, R., & Borko, H. (2000). What do new views of knowledge and thinking have to say about research on teacher learning? *Educational Researcher, 29*(1), 4–15.

Putnam, R. T., & Borko, H. (1997). Teacher learning: Implications of new views of cognition. In B. J. Biddle, T. L. Good, & I. F. Goodson (Eds.), *The international handbook of teachers and teaching* (Vol. 2, pp. 1223–1296). Dordrecht, the Netherlands: Kluwer.

Qian, G., & Alvermann, D. E. (2000). Relationship between epistemological beliefs and conceptual change learning. *Reading & Writing Quarterly: Overcoming Learning Difficulties, 16,* 59–74.

Quay, H. C., & Peterson, D. R. (1987). *Manual for the revised behavior problem checklist.* Coral Cables, FL: Author.

Rachlin, H. (1991). *Introduction to modern behaviorism* (3rd ed.), New York: W. H. Freeman.

Raffini, J. P. (1996). *150 ways to increase intrinsic motivation in the classroom.* Boston: Allyn and Bacon.

Range, L. M. (1993). Suicide prevention: Guidelines for schools. *Educational Psychology Review, 5,* 135–154.

Rathus, S. A. (1988). *Understanding child development.* New York: Holt, Rinehart & Winston.

Raudenbush, S. (1984). Magnitude of teacher expectancy effects on pupil IQ as a function of the credibility of expectancy induction: A synthesis of findings from 18 experiments. *Journal of Educational Psychology, 76,* 85–97.

Raudsepp, E., & Haugh, G. P. (1977). *Creative growth games.* New York: Harcourt Brace Jovanovich.

Rauscher, F. H., & Shaw, G. L. (1998). Key components of the Mozart effect. *Perceptual and Motor Skills, 86,* 835–841.

Ravitch, D. (1995). *National standards in American education: A citizens's guide.* Washington, DC: Brookings Institution.

Recht, D. R., & Leslie, L. (1988). Effect of prior knowledge on good and poor readers' memory of text. *Journal of Educational Psychology, 80,* 16–20.

Reder, L. M. (1996). Different research programs on metacognition: Are the boundaries imaginary? *Learning and Individual Differences, 8,* 383–390.

Redfield, D. L., & Rousseau, E. W. (1981). A meta-analysis of experimental research on teacher questioning behavior. *Review of Educational Research, 51,* 181–193.

Reed, S., & Sautter, R. C. (1990). Children of poverty: The status of 12 million Americans. *Phi Delta Kappan, 71*(10), K1–K12.

Reeve, J. (1996). *Motivating others: Nurturing inner motivational resources.* Boston: Allyn and Bacon.

Reeve, J., Bolt, E., & Cai, Y. (1999). Autonomy-supportive teachers: How they teach and motivate students. *Journal of Educational Psychology, 91,* 537–548.

Reich, P. A. (1986). *Language development.* Englewood Cliffs, NJ: Prentice-Hall.

Reid, M. K., & Borkowski, J. G. (1987). Causal attributions of hyperactive children: Implications for teaching strategies and self control. *Journal of Educational Psychology, 79,* 296–307.

Reimann, P., & Chi, M. T. H. (1989). Human expertise In K. J. Gilhooly (Ed.), *Human and machine problem solving* (pp. 161–191). New York: Plenum Press.

Reis, S. M., Kaplan, S. N., Tomlinson, C. A., Westberg, K. L., Callahan, C. M., & Cooper, C. R. (2002). Equal does not mean identical. In L. Abbeduto (Ed.), *Taking sides: Clashing on controversial issues in educational psychology* (pp. 31–35). Guilford, CT: McGraw-Hill/Duskin.

Reisberg, D., & Heuer, F. (1992). Remembering the details of emotional events. In E. Winograd & U. Neisser (Eds.), *Affect and accuracy in recall: Studies of "flashbulb" memories.* Cambridge, England: Cambridge University Press.

Rembolt, C. (1998). Making violence unacceptable. *Educational Leadership, 56*(1), 32–38.

Render, G. F., Padilla, J. N. M., & Krank, H. M. (1989). What research really shows about assertive discipline. *Educational Leadership, 46*(6), 72–75.

Rennie, L. J., & Parker, L. H. (1987). Detecting and accounting for gender differences in mixed-sex and single-sex groupings in science lessons. *Educational Review, 39*(1), 65–73.

Renninger, K. A., Hidi, S., & Krapp, A. (Eds.). (1992). *The role of interest in learning and development.* Hillsdale, NJ: Lawrence Erlbaum.

Renzulli, J. S., & Reis, S. M. (1991). The schoolwide enrichment model: A comprehensive plan for the development of creative productivity. In N. Colangelo & G. Davis (Eds.), *Handbook of gifted education* (pp. 111–141). Boston: Allyn and Bacon.

Renzulli, J. S., & Smith, L. H. (1978). *The Learning Styles Inventory: A measure of student preferences for instructional techniques.* Mansfield Center, CT: Creative Learning Press.

Resnick, L. B. (1981). Instructional psychology. *Annual Review of Psychology, 32,* 659–704.

Resnick, L. B. (1987). Learning in school and out. *Educational Researcher, 16*(9), 13–20.

Resnick, L. B., & Nolan, K. (1995). Where in the world are world-class standards? *Educational Leadership, 52*(6), 6–11.

Reynolds, A. (1992). Grade retention and school adjustment: An explanatory analysis. *Educational Evaluation and Policy Analysis, 14*(2), 101–121.

Reynolds, M. C., & Birch, J. W. (1988). *Adaptive mainstreaming: A primer for teachers and principals* (3rd ed.). New York: Longman.

Reynolds, W. M. (1980). Self-esteem and classroom behavior in elementary school children. *Psychology in the Schools, 17,* 273–277.

Rhodes, R. A. (1997). *Community service and higher learning: Explorations of the caring self.* Albany: State University of New York Press.

Rice, F. P., & Dolgin, K. G. (2002). *The adolescent: Development, relationships, and culture* (10th ed.). Boston: Allyn and Bacon.

Ricciardelli, L. A. (1992). Bilingualism and cognitive development: Relation to threshold theory. *Journal of Psycholinguistic Research, 21,* 301–316.

Richardson, T. M., & Benbow, C. P. (1990). Long-term effects of acceleration on the social-emotional adjustment of mathematically precocious youths. *Journal of Educational Psychology, 82,* 464–470.

Roberts, R. D., Zeidner, M., & Matthews, G. (2001). Does emotional intelligence meet traditional standards for an intelligence? Some new data and conclusions. *Emotion, 1,* 196–231.

Robinson, A., & Clinkenbeard, P. R. (1998). Giftedness: An exceptionality examined. In J. T. Spence, J. M. Darley, & D. J. Foss (Eds.), *Annual Review of Psychology* (pp. 117–139). Palo Alto, CA: Annual Reviews.

Robinson, D. H. (1998). Graphic organizers as aids to test learning. *Reading Research and Instruction, 37,* 85–105.

Robinson, D. H., & Kiewra, K. A. (1995). Visual argument: Graphic outlines are superior to outlines in improving learning from text. *Journal of Educational Psychology, 87,* 455–467.

Roderick, M. (1994). Grade retention and school dropout: Investigating an association, *American Educational Research Journal, 31,* 729–760.

Roeser, R. W., Eccles, J. S., & Sameroff, A. J. (2000). School as a context of early adolescents' academic and social-emotional development: A summary of research findings. *Elementary School Journal, 100,* 443–471.

Rogers, C. R. (1969). *Freedom to learn.* Columbus, OH: Charles E. Merrill.

Rogers, C. R., & Freiberg, H. J. (1994). *Freedom to learn* (3rd ed.). Columbus, OH: Charles E. Merrill.

Rogoff, B. (1990). *Apprenticeship in thinking: Cognitive development in social context.* New York: Oxford University Press.

Rogoff, B. (1995). Observing sociocultural activity on three planes: Participatory appropriation, guided participation, and apprenticeship. In J. Wertsch, P. del Rio, & A. Alverez (Eds.), *Sociocultural studies of mind.* (pp. 139–164). Cambridge, England: Cambridge University Press.

Rogoff, B. (1998). Cognition as a collaborative process. In W. Damon (Series Ed.) and D. Kuhn, & R. S. Siegler (Vol. Eds.), *Handbook of child psychology: Vol. 2.* (5th ed., pp. 679–744). New York: Wiley.

Rogoff, B., & Chavajay, P. (1995). What's become of the research on the cultural basis of cognitive development? *American Psychologist, 50,* 859–877.

Rogoff, B., & Morelii, G. (1989). Perspectives on children's development from cultural psychology. *American Psychologist, 44,* 343–348.

Rogoff, B., Turkanis, C. G., & Bartlett, L. (2001). *Learning together: Children and adults in a school community.* New York: Oxford.

Rogoff, B., & Wertsch, J. V. (Eds.). (1984). *Children's learning in the "zone of proximal development."* San Francisco: Jossey-Bass.

Rohwer, W. D., Jr., & Sloane, K. (1994). Psychological perspectives. In L. Anderson & L. Sosniak (Eds.), *Bloom's taxonomy: A forty-year retrospective.* Ninety-third yearbook for the National Society for the Study of Education: Part II (pp. 41–63). Chicago: University of Chicago Press.

Rop, C. (1997/1998). Breaking the gender barrier in the physical sciences. *Educational Leadership, 55*(4), 58–60.

Rosch, E. H. (1973). On the internal structure of perceptual and semantic categories. In T. Moore (Ed.), *Cognitive development and the acquisition of language* (pp. 111–144). New York: Academic Press.

Rose, L. C., . & Gallup, A. M. (1999). The 31st annual Phi Delta Kappa/Gallup Poll of the public's attitude toward the public schools. *Phi Delta Kappan, 81*(1), 41–58.

Rose, L. C., & Gallup, A. M. (2001). The 33rd annual Phi Delta Kappa/Gallup Poll of the public's attitude toward the public schools. *Phi Delta Kappan, 83*(1), 41–58.

Rosenberg, M. (1979). *Conceiving the self.* New York: Basic Books.

Rosenshine, B. (1977, April). *Primary grades instruction and student achievement.* Paper presented at the annual meeting of the American Educational Research Association, New York.

Rosenshine, B. (1979). Content, time, and direct instruction. In P. Peterson & H. Walberg (Eds.), *Research on teaching: Concepts, findings, and implications* (pp. 28–56). Berkeley, CA: McCutchan.

Rosenshine, B. (1986). Synthesis of research on explicit teaching. *Educational Leadership, 43*(7), 60–69.

Rosenshine, B. (1988). Explicit teaching. In D. Berliner & B. Rosenshine (Eds.), *Talks to teachers* (pp. 75–92). New York: Random House.

Rosenshine, B., & Furst, N. (1973). The use of direct observation to study teaching. In R. Travers (Ed.), *Second handbook of research on teaching.* Chicago: Rand McNally.

Rosenshine, B., & Meister, C. (1992, April). *The uses of scaffolds for teaching less structured academic tasks.* Paper presented at the annual meeting of the American Educational Research Association, San Francisco.

Rosenshine, B., & Meister, C. (1994). Reciprocal teaching: A review of the research. *Review of Educational Research, 64,* 479–530.

Rosenshine, B., & Stevens, R. (1986). Teaching functions. In M. Wittrock (Ed.), *Handbook of research on teaching* (3rd ed.) (pp. 376–391). New York: Macmillan.

Rosenthal, R. (1987). Pygmalion effects: Existence, magnitude and social importance. A reply to Wineburg. *Educational Researcher, 16,* 37–41.

Rosenthal, R. (1995). Critiquing Pygmalion: A 25-year perspective. *Current Directions in Psychological Science, 4,* 171–172.

Rosenthal, R., & Jacobson, L. (1968). *Pygmalion in the classroom.* New York: Holt, Rinehart, Winston.

Roskos, K., & Neuman, S. B. (1993). Descriptive observation of adults' facilitation of literacy in young children's play. *Early Childhood Research Quarterly, 8,* 77–98.

Roskos, K., & Neuman, S. B. (1998). Play as an opportunity for literacy. In O. N. Saracho & B. Spodek (Eds.), *Multiple perspectives on play in early childhood education* (pp. 100–115). Albany: State University of New York Press.

Rosser, R. (1994). *Cognitive development: Psychological and biological perspectives.* Boston: Allyn and Bacon.

Roth, W-M., & Bowen, G. M. (1995). Knowing and interacting: A study of culture, practices, and resources in a grade 8 open-inquiry science guided by an apprenticeship metaphor. *Cognition and Instruction, 13,* 73–128.

Rotherham-Borus, M. J. (1994). Bicultural reference group orientations and adjustment. In M. Bernal & G. Knight (Eds.), *Ethnic identity.* Albany, NY: State University of New York Press.

Rowe, M. B. (1974). Wait-time and rewards as instructional variables: Their influence on language, logic, and fate control. Part 1: Wait-time. *Journal of Research in Science Teaching, 11,* 81–94.

Rudolph, K. D., Lambert, S. F., Clark, A. G., & Kurlakowsky, K. D. (2001). Negotiating the transition to middle school: The role of self-regulatory processes. *Child Development, 72,* 926–946.

Rumelhart, D., & Ortony, A. (1977). The representation of knowledge in memory. In R. Anderson, R. Spiro, & W. Montague (Eds.), *Schooling and the acquisition of knowledge* (pp. 99–135). Hillsdale, NJ: Lawrence Erlbaum.

Ruopp, F., & Driscoll, M. (1990, January/February). Access to algebra. *Harvard Education Letter,* 6(A), 4–5.

Ryan, R. M., & Deci, E. L. (1996). When paradigms clash: Comments on Cameron and Pierce's claim that rewards do not undermine intrinsic motivation. *Review of Educational Research, 66,* 33–38.

Ryan, R. M., & Deci, E. L. (2000). Intrinsic and extrinsic motivation: Classic definitions and new directions. *Contemporary Educational Psychology, 25,* 54–67.

Ryan, R. M., & Grolnick, W. S. (1986). Origins and pawns in the classroom: Self-report and projective assessments of individual differences in the children's perceptions. *Journal of Personality and Social Psychology, 50,* 550–558.

Ryans, D. G. (1960). *Characteristics of effective teachers, their descriptions, comparisons and appraisal: A research study.* Washington, DC: American Council on Education.

Saarni, C. (2002). *The development of emotional competence.* New York: Guilford.

Sadker, M., & Sadker, D. (1986). Sexism in the classroom: From grade school to graduate school. *Phi Delta Kappan, 68,* 512.

Sadker, M., & Sadker, D. (1994). *Failing at fairness: How America's schools cheat girls.* New York: Scribner.

Sadker, M., & Sadker, D. (2003). Questioning skills. In J. Cooper (Ed.), *Classroom teaching skills* (7th ed., pp. 101–147). Boston: Houghton-Mifflin.

Sadker, M., Sadker, D., & Klein, S. (1991). The issue of gender in elementary and secondary education. *Review of Research in Education, 17,* 269–334.

Sagvolden, T. (1999). Attention deficit/hyperactive disorder. *European Psychologist, 4,* 109–114.

Salomon, G., & Perkins, D. N. (1989). Rocky roads to transfer: Rethinking mechanisms of a neglected phenomenon. *Educational Psychologist, 24,* 113–142.

Sanchez, F., & Anderson, M. L. (1990, May). Gang mediation: A process that works. *Principal,* 54–56.

Sanders, W. L., & Rivers, J. C. (1996). *Cumulative and residual effects of teachers on student academic achievement.* University of Tennessee Value-Added Research and Assessment Center, Knoxville, Tennessee.

Sandrock, J. W. (1996). *Adolescence.* Dubuque, IA: Brown & Benchmark.

Sattler, J. (1992). *Assessment of children* (3rd ed. rev.). San Diego: Jerome M. Sattler.

Sattler, J. M. (2001). *Assessment of children: Cognitive applications* (4th ed.). San Diego, CA: Jerome M. Sattler, Inc.

Savage, T. V. (1999). *Teaching self-control through management and discipline.* Boston: Allyn and Bacon.

Sawyer, R. J., Graham, S., & Harris, K. R. (1992). Direct teaching, strategy instruction, and strategy instruction with explicit self-regulation: Effects on the composition skills and self-efficacy of learning disabled students. *Journal of Educational Psychology, 84,* 340–352.

Scardamalia, M., & Bereiter, C. (1996). Adaptation and understanding: A case for new cultures of schooling. In S. Vosniado, E. De Corte, R. Glasse, & H. Mandl (Eds.), *International perspectives on the design of technology-supported learning environments* (pp. 149–163). Hillsdale, NJ: Lawrence Erlbaum.

Scarr, S., & Carter-Saltzman, L. (1982). Genetics and intelligence. In R. Sternberg (Ed.), *Handbook of human intelligence* (pp. 792–896). New York: Cambridge University Press.

Scherer, M. (1993). On savage inequalities: A conversation with Jonathan Kozol. *Educational Leadership, 50*(4), 4–9.

Scherer, M. (1999). The discipline of hope: A conversation with Herb Kohl. *Educational Leadership, 56*(1), 8–13.

Schiefele, U. (1991). Interest, learning, and motivation. *Educational Psychologist, 26,* 299–324.

Schneider, W., & Bjorklund, D. F. (1992). Expertise, aptitude, and strategic remembering. *Child Development, 63,* 416–473.

Schoenfeld, A. H. (1987). What's all the fuss about metacognition? In A. H. Scoenfeld (Ed.), *Cognitive science and mathematics education* (pp. 189–215). Hillsdale, NJ: Lawrence Erlbaum.

Schoenfeld, A. H. (1989). Teaching mathematical thinking and problem solving. In L. B. Resnick & L. E. Klopfer (Eds.), *Toward the thinking curriculum: Current cognitive research* (pp. 83–103). Alexandria, VA: ASCD.

Schoenfeld, A. H. (1994). *Mathematics thinking and problem solving.* Hillsdale, NJ: Lawrence Erlbaum.

Schofield, J. W. (1991). School desegregation and intergroup relations. *Review of Research in Education, 17,* 235–412.

Schofield, J. W. (1995). Review of research on school desegregation's impact on elementary and secondary school students. In J. A. Banks & C. Banks (Eds.), *Handbook of research on multicultural education.* New York: Macmillan.

Schommer, M. (1997). The development of epistemological beliefs among secondary students: A longitudinal study. *Journal of Educational Psychology, 89,* 37–40.

Schommer-Aikins, M. (2002). An evolving theoretical framework for an epistemological belief system. In B. K. Hofer & P. R. Pintrich (Eds.), *Personal epistemology: The psychology of beliefs about knowledge and knowing* (pp. 103–118). Mahwah, NJ: Lawrence Erlbaum.

Schon, D. (1983). *The reflective practitioner.* New York: Basic Books.

Schraw, G., & Lehman, S. (2001). Situational Interest: A review of the literature and directions for future research. *Educational Psychology Review, 13,* 23–52.

Schraw, G., & Moshman, D. (1995). Metacognitive theories. *Educational Psychology Review, 7,* 351–371.

Schraw, G., & Olafson, L. (in press). Teachers' epistemological world views and educational practice. *Issues in Education: Contributions from Educational Psychology.*

Schuder, T. (1994). The genesis of transactional strategies for at-risk students. *Elementary School Journal, 94,* 235–254.

Schunk, D. H. (1987). Peer models and children's behavioral change. *Review of Educational Research, 57,* 149–174.

Schunk, D. H. (1999). Social-self interaction and achievement behavior. *Educational Psychologist, 34,* 219–227.

Schunk, D. H. (2000). *Learning theories: An educational perspective* (3rd ed.). Columbus, OH: Merrill/Prentice-Hall.

Schunk, D. H., & Hanson, A. R. (1985). Peer models: Influence on children's self-efficacy and achievement. *Journal of Educational Psychology, 77,* 313–322.

Schutz, P. A., & Davis, H. A. (2000). Emotions and self-regulations during test-taking. *Educational Psychologist, 35,* 243–256.

Schwartz, B., & Reisberg, D. (1991). *Learning and memory.* New York: Norton.

Schwartz, B., & Robbins, S. J. (1995). *Psychology of learning and behavior* (4th ed.). New York, Norton.

Schwartz, B., Wasserman, E. A., & Robbins, S. J. (2002). *Psychology of learning and behavior* (5th ed.). New York: W. W. Norton.

Schwarz, B. B., Neuman, Y., & Biezuner, S. (2000). Two wrongs may make a right . . . if they argue together! *Cognition and Instruction, 18,* 461–494.

Seddon, G. M. (1978). The properties of Bloom's taxonomy of educational objectives for the cognitive domain. *Review of Educational Research, 48,* 303–323.

Seifert, K. L., & Hoffnung, R. J. (1991). *Child and adolescent development.* Boston: Houghton Mifflin.

Seligman, M. E. P. (1975). *Helplessness: On depression, development, and death.* San Francisco: Freeman.

Selman, R. L. (1980). *The growth of interpersonal understanding.* New York: Academic Press.

Semb, G. B., & Ellis, J. A. (1994). Knowledge taught in school: What is remembered? *Review of Educational Research, 64,* 253–286.

Serpell, R. (1993). Interface between sociocultural and psychological aspects of cognition. In E. Forman, N. Minick, & C. A. Stone (Eds.), *Contexts for learning: Sociocultural dynamics in children's development* (pp. 357–368). New York: Oxford University Press.

Shanker, A. (1995, May 15). Restoring the connection between behavior and consequences. *Vital speeches of the day.* Washington, DC: America Federation of Teachers.

Shavelson, R. J. (1987). Planning. In M. Dunkin (Ed.), *The international encyclopedia of teaching and teacher education* (pp. 483–486). New York: Pergamon Press.

Shavelson, R. J., & Bolus, R. (1982). Self-concept: The interplay of theory and methods. *Psychology, 74,* 3–17.

Shavelson, R. J., Gao, X., & Baxter, G. (1993). *Sampling variability of performance assessments.* CSE Technical Report 361. Los Angeles: UCLA Center for the Study of Evaluation.

Shepard, L. A., & Smith, M. L. (1989). Academic and emotional effects of kindergarten retention. In L. Shepard & M. Smith (Eds.), *Flunking grades: Research and policies on retention* (pp. 79–107). Philadelphia: Falmer Press.

Sherman, A. (1994). *Wasting America's future: The Children's Defense Fund report on the costs of child poverty.* Boston: Beacon Press.

Sherman, J. G., Ruskin, R. S., & Semb, G. B. (Eds.). (1982). *The Personalized System of Instruction: 48 seminal papers.* Lawrence, KS: TRI Publications.

Sherman, J. W., & Bessenoff, G. R. (1999). Stereotypes as source-monitoring cues: On the interaction between episodic and semantic memory. *Psychological Science, 10,* 106–110.

Shields, P., Gordon, J., & Dupree, D. (1983). Influence of parent practices upon the reading achievement of good and poor readers. *Journal of Negro Education, 52,* 436–445.

Shimahara, N. K., & Sakai, A. (1995). *Learning to teach in two cultures.* New York: Garland.

Shoda, Y., Mischel, W., & Peake, P. K. (1990). Predicting adolescent cognitive and self-regulatory competencies from preschool delay of gratification. *Developmental Psychology, 26,* 978–986.

Shriver, T. P., Schwab-Stone, M., & DeFalco, K. (1999). Why SEL is the better way: The New Haven Social Development Program. In J. Cohen (Ed.), *Education minds and hearts: Social emotional learning and the passage into adolescence* (pp. 43–60). New York: Teachers College Press.

Shuell, T. J. (1986). Cognitive conceptions of learning. *Review of Educational Research, 56,* 411–436.

Shuell, T. J. (1990). Phases of meaningful learning. *Review of Educational Psychology, 60,* 531–548.

Shuell, T. J. (1996). Teaching and learning in a classroom context. In D. Berliner & R. Calfee (Eds.), *Handbook of educational psychology* (pp. 726–764). New York: Macmillan.

Shulman, L. S. (1987). Knowledge and teaching: Foundations of the new reform. *Harvard Educational Review, 19*(2), 4–14.

Shulman, L. S. (1992). Toward a pedagogy of cases. In J. Shulman (Ed.), *Case method in teacher education* (pp. 1–30). New York: Teachers College Press.

Shultz, J., & Florio, S. (1979). Stop and freeze: The negotiation of social and physical space in a kindergarten/first grade classroom. *Anthropology and Education Quarterly, 10,* 166–181.

Siddle Walker, V. (2001). African American teaching in the South: 1940–1960. *Review of Educational Research, 38,* 751–779.

Siegel, J., & Shaughnessy, M. F. (1994). Educating for understanding: An interview with Howard Gardner. *Phi Delta Kappan, 75,* 536–566.

Siegler, R. S. (1993). Adaptive and non-adaptive characteristics of low-income children's mathematical strategy use. In B. Penner (Ed.), *The challenge in mathematics and science education: Psychology's response* (pp. 341–366). Washington, DC: American Psychological Association.

Siegler, R. S. (1998). *Children's thinking* (3rd ed.). Upper Saddle River, NJ: Prentice-Hall.

Siegler, R. S. (2000). The rebirth of children's learning. *Child Development, 71,* 26–35.

Siegler, R. S., & Crowley, K. (1991). The microgenetic method: A direct means for studying cognitive development. *American Psychologist, 56,* 606–620.

Simon, D. P., & Chase, W. G. (1973). Skill in chess. *American Scientist, 61,* 394–403.

Simon, H. A. (1995). The information-processing view of mind. *American Psychologist, 50,* 507–508.

Simon, P. (1980). *The tongue-tied American: Confronting the foreign language crisis.* New York: Continuum.

Simonton, D. K. (1999). Creativity from a historiometric perspective. In R. J. Sternberg (Ed.), *Handbook of creativity* (116–133). New York: Cambridge University Press.

Simonton, D. K. (2000). Creativity: Cognitive, personal, developmental, and social aspects. *American Psychologist, 55,* 151–158.

Simpson, E. J. (1972). The classification of educational objectives in the psychomotor domain. *The Psychomotor Domain. Vol. 3.* Washington: Gryphon House.

Singley, K., & Anderson, J. R. (1989). *The transfer of cognitive skill.* Cambridge, MA: Harvard University Press.

Sisk, D. A. (1988). Children at risk: The identification of the gifted among the minority. *Gifted Education International, 5,* 138–141.

Skiba, R. J., Michael, R. S., Nardo, A. C., & Peterson, R. (2000). *The color of discipline: Sources of racial and gender disproportionality in school punishment* (Report #SRS1). Bloomington, IN: Indiana Education Policy Center.

Skinner, B. F. (1950). Are theories of learning necessary? *Psychological Review, 57,* 193–216.

Skinner, B. F. (1953). *Science and human behavior.* New York: Macmillan.

Skinner, B. F. (1989). The origins of cognitive thought. *American Psychologist, 44,* 13–18.

Skoe, E. E. A. (1998). The ethic of care: Issues in moral development. In E. E. A. Skoe & A. L. von der Lippe (Eds.), *Personality development in adolescence* (pp. 143–171). London: Routledge.

Skoe, E. E., Pratt, M. W., Matthews, M., & Curror, S. E. (1996). The ethic of care: Stability over time, gender differences, and correlates in mid-to late adulthood. *Psychology and Aging, 11,* 280–292.

Slaby, R. G., Roedell, W. C., Arezzo, D., & Hendrix, K. (1995). *Early violence prevention.* Washington, DC: National Association for the Education of Young Children.

Slater, L. (2002, February 3). The trouble with self-esteem. *The New York Times Magazine,* pp. 44–47.

Slavin, R. E. (1987). Ability grouping and student achievement in elementary schools: A best-evidence synthesis. *Review of Educational Research, 57,* 293–336.

Slavin, R. E. (1990). Achievement effects of ability grouping in secondary schools: A best-evidence synthesis. *Review of Educational Research, 60,* 471–500.

Slavin, R. E. (1995). *Cooperative learning* (2nd ed.). Boston: Allyn and Bacon.

Sleeter, C. E. (1995). Curriculum controversies in multicultural education. In E. Flaxman & H. Passow (Eds.), *94th Yearbook of the National Society for the Study of Education: Part II: Changing populations, changing schools* (pp. 162–185). Chicago: University of Chicago Press.

Smetana, J. G. (2000). Middle-class African American adolescents' and parents' conceptions of parental authority and parenting practices: A longitudinal investigation. *Child Development, 71,* 1672–1686.

Smith, C. B. (Moderator). (1994). *Whole language: The debate.* Bloomington, IN: EDINFO Press.

Smith, D. D. (1998). *Introduction to special education: Teaching in an age of challenge* (3rd ed.). Boston: Allyn and Bacon.

Smith, F. (1975). *Comprehension and learning: A conceptual framework for teachers.* New York: Holt, Rinehart & Winston.

Smith, J. D., & Caplan, J. (1988). Cultural differences in cognitive style development. *Developmental Psychology, 24,* 46–52.

Smith, J. K., Smith, L. F., & De Lisi, R. (2001). *Natural classroom assessment: Designing seamless instruction and assessment.* Thousand Oaks, CA: Corwin Press.

Smith, M. (1993). Some school-based violence prevention strategies. *NASSP Bulletin, 77*(557), 70–75.

Smith, M. L. (1991). Put to the test: The effects of external testing on teachers. *Educational Researcher, 20*(5), 8–11.

Smith, S. M., Glenberg, A., & Bjork, R. A. (1978). Environmental context and human memory. *Memory and Cognition, 6,* 342–353.

Snider, V. E. (1990). What we know about learning styles from research in special education. *Educational Leadership, 48*(2), 53.

Snow, C. E. (1987). Beyond conversation: Second language learners' acquisition of description and explanation. In J. P. Lantolf & A. Labarca (Eds.), *Research in second language learning: Focus on the classroom* (pp. 3–16). Norwood, NJ: Ablex.

Snow, C. E. (1993). Families as social contexts for literacy development. In C. Daiute (Ed.), *New directions for child development* (No. 61, pp. 11–24). San Francisco: Jossey-Bass.

Snow, M. A. (1986). *Innovative second language education: Bilingual immersion programs* (Education Report 1). Los Angeles: Center of Language Education and Research, University of California.

Snow, R. E. (1995). Pygmalion and intelligence. *Current Directions in Psychological Science, 4,* 169–171.

Snow, R. E., Corno, L., & Jackson, D. (1996). Individual differences in affective and cognitive functions. In D. Berliner & R. Calfee (Eds.), *Handbook of educational psychology* (pp. 243–310). New York: Macmillan.

Snowman, J. (1984). Learning tactics and strategies. In G. Phye & T. Andre (Eds.), *Cognitive instructional psychology* (pp. 243–275). Orlando, FL: Academic Press.

Soar, R. S., & Soar, R. M. (1979). Emotional climate and management. In P. Peterson & H. Walberg (Eds.), *Research on teaching: Concepts, findings, and implications* (pp. 97–119). Berkeley, CA: McCutchan.

Sobesky, W. E. (1983). The effects of situational factors on moral judgment. *Child Development, 54,* 575–584.

Sokolove, S., Garrett, J., Sadker, D., & Sadker, M. (1986). Interpersonal communications skills. In J. Cooper (Ed.), *Classroom teaching skills: A handbook* (pp. 233–278). Lexington, MA: D. C. Heath.

Solomon, D., Watson, M. S., & Battistich, V. A. (2001). Teaching and schooling effects on moral/prosocial development. In V. Richardson (Ed.), *Handbook of research on teaching* (4th ed., pp. 566–603). Washington, DC: American Educational Research Association.

Sotillo, S. M. (2002). Finding our voices, finding ourselves: Becoming bilingual and bicultural. In G. S. Boutte (Ed.), *Resounding voices: School experiences of people from diverse ethnic backgrounds* (pp. 275–307). Boston: Allyn and Bacon.

Spearman, C. (1927). *The abilities of man: Their nature and measurement.* New York: Macmillan.

Spector, J. E. (1992). Predicting progress in beginning reading: Dynamic assessment of phonemic awareness. *Journal of Educational Psychology, 84,* 353–363.

Spence, J. T., & Buckner, C. E. (2000). Instrumental and expressive traits, trait stereotypes, and sexist attitudes: What do they signify? *Psychology of Women Quarterly, 24,* 44–62.

Spencer, M. B., & Markstrom-Adams, C. (1990). Identity processes among racial and ethnic-minority children in America. *Child Development, 61,* 290–310.

Spencer, S. J., Steele, C. M., & Quinn, D. M. (1999). Stereotype threat and women's math performance. *Journal of Experimental Social Psychology, 35,* 4–28.

Spinelli, C. G. (2002). *Classroom assessment for students with special needs in inclusive classrooms.* Upper Saddle River, NJ: Merrill/Prentice-Hall.

Spiro, R. J., Feltovich, P. J., Jacobson, M. L., & Coulson, R. L. (1991). Cognitive flexibility, constructivism, and hypertext: Random access instruction for advanced knowledge acquisition in ill-structured domains. *Educational Technology, 31*(5), 24–33.

Stahl, S. A. (2002). Different strokes for different folks? In L. Abbeduto (Ed.), *Taking sides: Clashing on controversial issues in educational psychology* (pp. 98–107). Guilford, CT: McGraw-Hill/Duskin.

Stahl, S. A., & Miller, P. D. (1989). Whole language and language experience approaches for beginning reading: A quantitative research synthesis. *Review of Educational Research, 59,* 87–116.

Stainback, S., & Stainback, W. (1992). Schools as inclusive communities. In W. Stainback & S. Stainback (Eds.), *Controversial issues confronting special education: Divergent perspectives* (pp. 29–43). Boston: Allyn and Bacon.

Stanovich, K. E. (1992). *How to think straight about psychology* (3rd ed.). Glenview, IL: Scott, Foresman.

Stanovich, K. E. (1994). Constructivism in reading. *Journal of Special Education, 28,* 259–274.

Stanovich, K. E. (1998). Cognitive neuroscience and educational psychology: What season is it? *Educational Psychology Review, 10,* 419–426.

Starch, D., & Elliot, E. C. (1912). Reliability of grading high school work in English. *Scholastic Review, 20,* 442–457.

Starch, D., & Elliot, E. C. (1913a). Reliability of grading work in history. *Scholastic Review, 21,* 676–681.

Starch, D., & Elliot, E. C. (1913b). Reliability of grading work in mathematics. *Scholastic Review, 21,* 254–259.

Starr, R. H., Jr. (1979). Child abuse. *American Psychologist, 34,* 872–878.

Steele, C. M., & Aronson, J. (1995). Stereotype threat and the intellectual test performance of African Americans. *Journal of Personality and Social Psychology, 69,* 797–811.

Steele, K. M., Bass, K. E., & Crook, M. D. (1999). The mystery of the Mozart effect: Failure to replicate. *Psychological Science, 10,* 366–368.

Steinberg, L. (1996). *Beyond the classroom: Why schools are failing and what parents need to do.* New York: Simon & Schuster.

Steinberg, L. (1998). Standards outside the classroom. In D. Ravitch (Ed.), *Brookings papers on educational policy* (pp. 319–358). Washington, DC: Brookings Institute.

Steinberg, L., Dornbusch, S. M., & Brown, B. B. (1992). Ethnic differences in adolescent achievement: An ecological perspective. *American Psychologist, 47,* 723–729.

Stephen, J., Fraser, E., & Marcia, J. E. (1992). Moratorium achievement (Mama) cycles in life span identity development: Vale orientations and reasoning system correlates. *Journal of Adolescence, 15,* 283–300.

Stepien, W., & Gallagher, S. (1993). Problem-based learning: As authentic as it gets. *Educational Leadership, 50*(7), 25–28.

Sternberg, R. J. (1985). *Beyond IQ: A triarchic theory of human intelligence.* New York: Cambridge University Press.

Sternberg, R. J. (1986). *Intelligence applied: Understanding and increasing your own intellectual skills.* New York: Harcourt Brace Jovanovich.

Sternberg, R. J. (1990). *Metaphors of mind: Conceptions of the nature of intelligence.* New York: Cambridge University Press.

Sternberg, R. J. (1998). Myths, countermyths, and truths about intelligence. In A. Woolfolk (Ed.), *Readings in educational psychology* (2nd ed.) (pp. 53–60). Boston: Allyn and Bacon.

Sternberg, R. J. (1999). *Cognitive psychology* (2nd ed.). Ft. Worth, TX: Harcourt Brace.

Sternberg, R. J. (1999). A propulsion model of types of creative contribution. *Review of General Psychology, 3,* 83–100.

Sternberg, R. J. (2000). *Handbook of human intelligence.* New York: Cambridge University Press.

Sternberg, R. J., & Davidson, J. (1982, June). The mind of the puzzler. *Psychology Today,* 37–44.

Sternberg, R. J., & Detterman, D. L. (Eds.). (1986). *What is intelligence? Contemporary viewpoints on its nature and definition.* Norwood, NJ: Ablex.

Sternberg, R. J., & Kaufman, J. C. (1998). Human abilities. In J. T. Spence, J. M. Darley, & D. J. Foss (Eds.), *Annual Review of Psychology* (pp. 479–502). Palo Alto, CA: Annual Reviews.

Sternberg, R. J., & Wagner, R. K. (1993). The geocentric view of intelligence and job performance is wrong. *Current Directions in Psychological Science, 2,* 1–5.

Sternberg, R. J., Wagner, R. K., Williams, W. M., & Horvath, J. A. (1995). Testing common sense. *American Psychologist, 50,* 912–927.

Stevenson, H. W., & Stigler, J. (1992). *The learning gap.* New York: Summit Books.

Stiggins, R. J. (2002). Where is our assessment future and how can we get there? In R. W. Lissitz & W. D. Schafer (Eds.), *Assessment in educational reform: Both means and ends* (pp. 18–48). Boston: Allyn and Bacon.

Stigler, J. W., Lee, S., & Stevenson, H. W. (1987). Mathematics classrooms in Japan, Taiwan, and the United States. *Child Development, 58,* 1272–1285.

Stipek, D., de la Sota, A., & Weishaupt, L. (1999). Life lessons: An embedded classroom approach to preventing high-risk behaviors among preadolescents. *The Elementary School Journal, 99,* 433–451.

Stipek, D. J. (1993). *Motivation to learn* (2nd ed.). Boston: Allyn and Bacon.

Stipek, D. J. (1998). *Motivation to learn* (3rd ed.). Boston: Allyn and Bacon.

Stipek, D. J. (2002). *Motivation to learn: Integrating theory and practice* (4th ed.). Boston: Allyn and Bacon.

Stodolsky, S. S. (1988). *The subject matters: Classroom activity in math and social studies.* Chicago: University of Chicago Press.

Stormont, M., Stebbins, M. S., & Holliday, G. (2001). Characteristics and educational support needs of underrepresented gifted adolescents. *Psychology in the Schools, 38,* 413–423.

Stormshak, E. A., Bierman, K. L., Bruschi, C., Dodge, K. A., Coie, J. D., et al. (1999). The relation between behavior problems and peer preference in different classrooms. *Child Development, 70,* 169–182.

Stumpf, H. (1995). Gender differences on test of cognitive abilities: Experimental design issues and empirical results. *Learning and Individual Differences, 7,* 275–288.

Sullivan, M. A., & O'Leary, S. G. (1990). Maintenance following reward and cost token programs. *Behavior Therapy, 21,* 139–149.

Sulzby, E., & Teale, W. (1991). Emergent literacy. In R. Barr, M. L. Kamil, P. B. Mosenthal, & P. D. Pearson (Eds.), *Handbook of reading research, Vol. II* (pp. 727–758). New York: Longman.

Sulzer-Azaroff, B., & Mayer, G. R. (1986). *Achieving educational excellence using behavioral strategies.* New York: Holt, Rinehart & Winston.

Sunburst Software. (1999). *A Field Trip to the Sea.*

Suzuki, B. H. (1983). The education of Asian and Pacific Americans: An introductory overview. In D. Nakanishi & M. Hirano-Nakanishi (Eds.), *The education of Asian and Pacific Americans: Historical perspectives and prescriptions for the future* (pp. 1–14). Phoenix, AZ: Oryx Press.

Svoboda, J. S. (2001). Review of *Boys and girls learn differently.* The Men's Resource Network. Retrieved May 18, 2002 from http://www.themenscenter.com/mensight/reviews/Svoboda/boysandgirls.htm

Swanson, H. L. (1990). The influence of metacognitive knowledge and aptitude on problem solving. *Journal of Educational Psychology, 82,* 306–314.

Swanson, H. L. (2001). Research on interventions for adolescents with learning disabilities: A meta-analysis of outcomes related to higher-order processing. *The Elementary School Journal, 101,* 332–348.

Swanson, H. L., O'Conner, J. E., & Cooney, J. B. (1990). An information processing analysis of expert and novice teachers' problem solving. *American Educational Research Journal, 27,* 533–556.

Sweeney, W. J., Salva, E., Cooper, J. O., & Talbert-Johnson, C. (1998). Using self-evaluation to improve difficult to read handwriting for secondary students. *Journal of Behavioral Education, 3,* 427–443.

Sweller, J., van Merrienboer, J. J. G., & Paas, F. G. W. C. (1998). Cognitive architecture and instructional design. *Educational Psychology Review, 10,* 251–296.

Symons, S., Woloshyn, V., & Pressley, M. (1994). The scientific evaluation of the whole language approach to literacy development [Special issue]. *Educational Psychologist, 29*(4).

Tait, H., & Enwistle, N. J. (in press). Identifying students at risk through ineffective study strategies. *Higher Education.*

Talbot, M. (2002, February 24). Girls just want to be mean. *The New York Times Magazine,* pp. 24–29+.

Tavris, C. (1998, September 13). Peer pressure. [Review of the book *The nurture assumption: Why children turn out the way they do; parents matter less than you think and peers matter more*]. *New York Review of Books,* 14–15.

Taylor, J. B. (1983). Influence of speech variety on teachers' evaluation of reading comprehension. *Journal of Educational Psychology, 75,* 662–667.

Taylor, E. (1998). Clinical foundation of hyperactivity research. *Behavioural Brain Research, 94,* 11–24.

TenBrink, T. D. (2003). Assessment. In J. Cooper (Ed.), *Classroom teaching skills* (7th ed., pp. 311–353). Boston: Houghton-Mifflin.

Tennyson, R. D. (1981, April). *Concept learning effectiveness using prototype and skill development presentation forms.* Paper presented at the annual meeting of the American Educational Research Association, Los Angeles.

Terman, L. M., & Oden, M. H. (1947). The gifted child grows up. In L. M. Terman (Ed.), *Genetic studies of genius* (Vol. 4). Stanford, CA: Stanford University Press.

Terman, L. M., & Oden, M. H. (1959). The gifted group in mid-life. In L. M. Terman (Ed.), *Genetic studies of genius* (Vol. 5). Stanford, CA: Stanford University Press.

Terman, L. M., Baldwin, B. T., & Bronson, E. (1925). Mental and physical traits of a thousand gifted children. In L. M. Terman (Ed.), *Genetic studies of genius* (Vol. 1). Stanford, CA: Stanford University Press.

Tesser, A., Stapel, D. A., & Wood, J. V. (2002). *Self and motivation: Emerging psychological perspectives.* Washington, DC: American Psychological Association.

Tharinger, D. J., Lambert, N. M., Bricklin, P. M., Feshbach, N., Johnson, N. F., Oakland, T. D., Paster, V. S., & Sanchez, W. (1996). Education reform: Challenges for psychology and psychologists. *Professional Psychology: Research & Practice, 27,* 24–33.

Tharp, R. G. (1989). Psychocultural variables and constants: Effects on teaching and learning in schools. *American Psychologist, 44,* 349–359.

Tharp, R. G., & Gallimore, R. (1988). *Rousing minds to life: Teaching, learning, and schooling in social context.* New York: Cambridge University Press.

Tharp, R. G., & Gallimore, R. (1991). *The instructional conversation: Teaching and learning in social activity.* Washington, DC: National Center for Research on Cultural Diversity and Second Language Learning.

Theodore, L. A., Bray, M. A., Kehle, T. J., & Jenson, W. R. (2001). Randomization of group contingencies and reinforcers for reduce classroom disruptive behavior. *Journal of School Psychology, 39,* 267–277.

Third International Mathematics and Science Study. (1998). Washington, DC: National Center for Educational Statistics. Available online at http://nces.ed.gov/timss/

Thomas, E. L., & Robinson, H. A. (1972). *Improving reading in every class: A sourcebook for teachers.* Boston: Allyn and Bacon.

Thompson, R. A., & Wyatt, J. M. (1999). Current research on child maltreatment: Implications for educators. *Educational Psychology Review, 11,* 173–202.

Thorndike, E. L. (1913). *Educational psychology: Vol. 2. The psychology of learning.* New York: Teachers College, Columbia University.

Thorndike, R., Hagen, E., & Sattler, J. (1986). *The Stanford-Binet Intelligence Scale* (4th ed.). Chicago: Riverside.

Tierney, R. J., Readence, J. E., & Dishner, E. K. (1990). *Reading strategies and practices: A compendium* (3rd ed.). Boston: Allyn and Bacon.

Tierney, W. G. (1993). *Building communities of difference: Higher education in the twenty-first century.* Westport, CT: Bergin and Garvey.

Timmer, S. G., Eccles, J., & O'Brien, K. (1988). How children use time. In F. Juster & F. Stafford (Eds.), *Time, goods, and well-being.* Ann Arbor, MI: Institute for Social Research, University of Michigan.

Tishman, S., Perkins, D., & Jay, E. (1995). *The thinking classroom: Creating a culture of thinking.* Boston: Allyn and Bacon.

Tobin, K. (1987). The role of wait time in higher cognitive learning. *Review of Educational Research, 56,* 69–95.

Tobler, N., & Stratton, H. (1997). Effectiveness of school-based drug prevention programs: A metaanalysis of the research. *Journal of Primary Prevention, 18,* 71–128.

Tollefson, N. (2000). Classroom applications of cognitive theories of motivation. *Education Psychology Review, 12,* 63–83.

Tomasello, M., Kruger, A. C., & Ratner, H. H. (1993). Cultural learning. *Behavioral and Brain Sciences, 16,* 495–552.

Tomlinson-Keasey, C. (1990). Developing our intellectual resources for the 21st century: Educating the gifted. *Journal of Educational Psychology, 82,* 399–403.

Tomlinson-Keasey, C., & Little, T. D. (1990). Predicting educational attainment, occupational achievement intellectual skill, and personal adjustment among gifted men and women. *Journal of Educational Psychology, 82,* 442–455.

Toppo, G. (2003, January 13). School violence hits lower grades: Experts who see violent behavior in younger kids blame parents, prenatal medical problems and an angry society; educators search for ways to cope. *USA Today.* Available at http://www.usatoday.com/educate/college/education/articles/20030119.htm. Downloaded on January 23, 2003.

Torrance, E. P. (1972). Predictive validity of the Torrance tests of creative thinking. *Journal of Creative Behavior, 6,* 236–262.

Torrance, E. P. (1986). Teaching creative and gifted learners. In M. Wittrock (Ed.), *Handbook of research on teaching* (3rd ed.) (pp. 630–647). New York: Macmillan.

Torrance, E. P., & Hall, L. K. (1980). Assessing the future reaches of creative potential. *Journal of Creative Behavior, 14,* 1–19.

Toth, E., Klahr, D., & Chen, Z. (2000). Bridging research and practice: A cognitively based classroom intervention for teaching experimentation to elementary school children. *Cognition and Instruction, 18,* 423–459.

Tschannen-Moran, M., & Woolfolk Hoy, A. (2001). Teacher efficacy: Capturing an elusive construct. *Teaching and Teacher Education, 17,* 783–805.

Tschannen-Moran, M., Woolfolk Hoy, A., & Hoy, W. K. (1998). Teacher efficacy: Its meaning and measure. *Review of Educational Research, 68,* 202–248.

Turiel E. (1983). *The development of social knowledge: Morality and convention.* New York: Cambridge University Press.

Turiel, E. (1998). The development of morality. In W. Damon (Series Ed.) & N. Eisenberg (Vol. Ed.), *Handbook of child psychology: Vol. 3. Social, emotional, and personality development* (5th ed., pp. 863–932). New York: Wiley.

Twenge, J. M., & Campbell, W. K. (2001). Age and birth cohort differences in self-esteem: A cross temporal meta-analysis. *Journal of Personality and Social Psychology Review, 5,* 321–344.

U.S. Census Bureau. www.census.gov/Press-Release/www/2001/cb01-158.html

U.S. Department of Education. (1993). *National excellence: A case for developing America's talent.* Washington DC: Author.

U.S. Department of Education (2002). *No Child Left Behind* Fact Sheet. Retrieved August 5, 2002 from http://www.ed.gov/offices/OESE/esea/factsheet.html

U.S. Department of Health and Human Services. (1997). *Youth risk behavior surveillance—U.S., 1995.* MMWR, 45 (No. SS-4).

Urdan, T. C., & Maehr, M. L. (1995). Beyond a two-goal theory of motivation and achievement: A case for social goals. *Review of Educational Research, 65,* 213–243.

Van Houten, R., & Doleys, D. M. (1983). Are social reprimands effective? In S. Axelrod & J. Apsche (Eds.), *The effects of punishment on human behavior.* San Diego: Academic Press.

van Laar, C. (2000). The paradox of low academic achievement but high self-esteem in African American students: An attributional account. *Educational Psychology Review, 12,* 33–61.

Van Matre, J. C., Valentine, J. C., & Cooper, H. (2000). Effect of students' after-school activities on teachers' academic expectations. *Contemporary Educational Psychology, 25,* 167–183.

Van Meter, P. (2001). Drawing construction as a strategy for learning from text. *Journal of Educational Psychology, 93,* 129–140.

Van Meter, P., Yokoi, L., & Pressley, M. (1994). College students' theory of note-taking derived from their perceptions of note-taking. *Journal of Educational Psychology, 86,* 323–338.

Vasquez, J. A. (1990). Teaching to the distinctive traits of minority students. *The Clearing House, 63,* 299–304.

Vaughn, S., Bos, C. S., & Schumm, J. S. (1996). *Teaching mainstreamed, diverse, and at-risk students in the general education classroom.* Boston: Allyn and Bacon.

Veenman, S. (1984). Perceived problems of beginning teachers. *Review of Educational Research, 54,* 143–178.

Veenman, S. (1997). Combination classes revisited. *Educational Research and Evaluation, 65*(4), 319–381.

Vellutino, F. R. (1991). Introduction to three studies on reading acquisition: Convergent findings on theoretical foundations of code-oriented versus whole-language approaches to reading instruction. *Journal of Educational Psychology, 83,* 437–443.

Vera, A. H., & Simon, H. A. (1993). Situated action: A symbolic interpretation. *Cognitive Science, 17,* 7–48.

Viadero, D. (1990). Battle over multicultural education rises in intensity. *Education Week, 10*(13), 1, 11, 13, 14.

Vispoel, W. P. (1995). Self-concept inartistic domains: An extension of the Shavelson, Hubmner, and Stanton (1976) model. *Journal of Educational Psychology, 87,* 134–153.

Vispoel, W. P., & Austin, J. R. (1995). Success and failure in junior high school: A critical incident approach to understanding students' attributional beliefs. *American Educational Research Journal, 32,* 377–412.

von Glaserfeld, E. (1995). A constructivist approach to teaching. In L. Steffe & J. Gale (Eds.), *Constructivism in education* (p. 5). Hillsdale, NJ: Lawrence Erlbaum.

von Glaserfeld, E. (1997). Amplification of a constructivist perspective. *Issues in Education: Contributions from Educational Psychology, 3,* 203–210.

Vroom, V. (1964). *Work and motivation.* New York: Wiley.

Vygotsky, L. S. (1978). *Mind in society: The development of higher mental process.* Cambridge, MA: Harvard University Press.

Vygotsky, L. S. (1986). *Thought and language.* Cambridge, MA: MIT Press.

Vygotsky, L. S. (1987). *Problems of general psychology.* New York: Plenum.

Vygotsky, L. S. (1993). *The collected works of L. S. Vygotsky: Vol. 2* (J. Knox & C. Stevens, Trans.). New York: Plenum.

Vygotsky, L. S. (1997). *Educational psychology* (R. Silverman, Trans.). Boca Raton, FL: St. Lucie.

Wade, S. E., Schraw, G., Buxton, W. M., & Hayes, M. T. (1993). Seduction of the strategic reader: Effects of interest on strategies and recall. *Reading Research Quarterly, 28,* 3–24.

Waits, B. K., & Demana, F. (2000). Calculators in mathematics teaching and learning: Past, present, future. In M. J. Burke & F. R. Curcio (Eds.), *Learning mathematics for a new century: NCTM 2000 Yearbook* (pp. 51–66). Reston, VA: National Council of Teachers of Mathematics.

Walberg, H. J. (1984). Improving the productivity of America's schools. *Educational Leadership, 41,* 19–27.

Walberg, H. J. (1990). Productive teaching and instruction: Assessing the knowledge base. *Phi Delta Kappan, 72,* 470–478.

Walker, L. J. (1991). Sex differences in moral reasoning. In W. M. Kurtines & J. L. Gewirtz (Eds.), *Handbook of moral behavior and development* (Vol. 2, pp. 333–362). Hillsdale, NJ: Lawrence Erlbaum.

Walker, L. J., & Pitts, R. C. (1998). Naturalistic conceptions of moral maturity. *Developmental Psychology, 34,* 403–419.

Walker, L. J., Pitts, R. C., Hennig, K. H., & Matsuba, M. K. (1995). Reasoning about morality and real-life moral problems. In M. Killen & D. Hart (Eds.), *Morality in everyday life: Developmental perspectives* (pp. 371–407). Cambridge, England: Cambridge University Press.

Walton, G. *Identification of the intellectually gifted children in the public school kindergarten.* Unpublished doctoral dissertation, University of California, Los Angeles, 1961.

Wang, A. Y., & Thomas, M. H. (1995). Effects of keywords on long-term retention: Help or hindrance? *Journal of Educational Psychology, 87,* 468–475.

Wang, A. Y., Thomas, M. H., & Ouellette, J. A. (1992). Keyword mnemonic and retention of second-language vocabulary words. *Journal of Educational Psychology, 84,* 520–528.

Wang, M. C., & Palincsar, A. S. (1989). Teaching students to assume an active role in their learning. In M. Reynolds (Ed.), *Knowledge base for the beginning teacher* (pp. 71–84). New York: Pergamon.

Wasserman, E. A., & Miller, R. R. (1997). What's elementary about associative learning. In J. T. Spence, J. M. Darley, & D. J. Foss (Eds.), *Annual Review of Psychology* (pp. 573–607). Palo Alto, CA: Annual Reviews.

Waterman, A. S. (1992). Identity as an affect of optimal psychological functioning. In G. Adams, T. Gullota, & R. Montemayoor (Eds.), *Adolescent identity formation.* Newbury Park, CA: Sage.

Waters, H. F. (1993, July 12). Networks under the gun. *Newsweek,* 64–66.

Webb, N. (1985). Verbal interaction and learning in peer-directed groups. *Theory Into Practice, 24,* 32–39.

Webb, N., & Palincsar, A. (1996). Group processes in the classroom. In D. C. Berliner & R. C. Calfee (Eds.), *Handbook of educational psychology* (pp. 841–876). New York: Macmillan.

Webb, N. M., Farivar, S. H., & Mastergeorge, A. M. (2002). Productive helping in cooperative groups. *Theory Into Practice, 41,* 13–20.

Weiland, A., & Coughlin, R. (1979). Self-identification and preferences: A comparison of White and Mexican-American first- and third-graders. *Journal of Cross-Cultural Psychology, 10,* 356–365.

Weinberg, R. A. (1989). Intelligence and IQ. *American Psychologist, 44,* 98–104.

Weinberger, D. (2001, March 10). A brain too young for good judgment. *The New York Times,* p. A13.

Weiner, B. (1979). A theory of motivation for some classroom experiences. *Journal of Educational Psychology, 71,* 3–25.

Weiner, B. (1986). *An attributional theory of motivation and emotion.* New York: Springer.

Weiner, B. (1990). History of motivational research in education. *Journal of Educational Psychology, 82,* 616–622.

Weiner, B. (1992). *Human motivation: Metaphors, theories, and research.* Newbury Park, CA: Sage.

Weiner, B. (1994a). Ability versus effort revisited: The moral determinants of achievement evaluation an achievement as a moral system. *Educational Psychologist, 29,* 163–172.

Weiner, B. (1994b). Integrating social and persons theories of achievement striving. *Review of Educational Research, 64,* 557–575.

Weiner, B. (2000). Interpersonal and intrapersonal theories of motivation from an attributional perspective. *Educational Psychology Review, 12,* 1–14.

Weiner, B., & Graham, S. (1989). Understanding the motivational role of affect: Lifespan research from an attributional perspective. *Cognition and Emotion, 4,* 401–419.

Weiner, B., Russell, D., & Lerman, D. (1978). Affective consequences of causal ascriptions. In J. H. Harvey, W. J. Ickes, & R. F. Kidd (Eds.), *New directions in attribution research* (Vol. 2). Hillsdale, NJ: Lawrence Erlbaum.

Weinert, F. E., & Helmke, A. (1995). Learning from wise mother nature or big brother instructor: The wrong choice as seen from an educational perspective. *Educational Psychologist, 30,* 135–143.

Weinstein, C. E. (1994). Learning strategies and learning to learn. *Encyclopedia of Education.*

Weinstein, C. S. (1977). Modifying student behavior in an open classroom through changes in the physical design. *American Educational Research Journal, 14,* 249–262.

Weinstein, C. S. (1999). Reflections on best practices and promising programs: Beyond assertive classroom discipline. In H. J. Freiberg (Ed.), *Beyond behaviorism: Changing the classroom management paradigm* (pp. 147–163). Boston: Allyn and Bacon.

Weinstein, C. S. (2003). *Secondary classroom management: Lessons from research and practice* (2nd ed.). New York: McGraw-Hill.

Weinstein, C. S., & Mignano, A. (2003). *Elementary classroom management: Lessons from research and practice* (3rd ed.). New York: McGraw-Hill.

Weinstein, R. S., Madison, S. M., & Kuklinski, M. R. (1995). Raising expectations in schools: Obstacles and opportunities for change. *American Educational Research Journal, 32,* 121–159.

Weisberg, R. W. (1993). *Creativity: Beyond the myth of genius.* New York: W. H. Freeman.

Weiss, G., & Hechtman, L. T. (1993). *Hyperactive children grow up: ADHD in children, adolescents, and adults* (2nd ed.). New York: Guilford Press.

Wells, A. S., & Crain, R. L. (1994). Perpetuation theory and the long-term effects of school desegregation. *Review of Educational Research, 64,* 531–55.

Wentzel, K. R. (1999). Social-motivational processes and interpersonal relations: Implications for understanding motivation in school. *Journal of Educational Psychology, 91,* 76–97.

Wentzel, K. R., & Battle, A. A. (2001). Social relationships and school adjustment. In T. Urdan & F. Pajares (Eds.), *Adolescence education: General issues in the education of adolescents* (Vol. 1, pp. 93–118). Greenwich, CT: Information Age.

Wertsch, J. V. (1991). *Voices of the mind: A sociocultural approach to mediated action.* Cambridge, MA: Harvard University Press.

Wertsch, J., & Tulviste, P. (1992). L. S. Vygotsky and contemporary developmental psychology. *Developmental Psychology, 28,* 548–557.

Wessells, M. G. (1982). *Cognitive psychology.* New York: Harper & Row.

Westberg, K. L., Archambault, F. X., Dodyns, S. M., & Slavin, T. J. (1993). The classroom practices observation study. *Journal of the Education of the Gifted, 16*(2), 120–146.

Wheelock, A. (1992). *Crossing the tracks: How untracking can save America's schools.* New York: the New Press.

When the student becomes the teacher. (1986, March). *Harvard Education Letter, 2*(3), 5–6.

White, K. R. (1982). The relation between socioeconomic status and academic achievement. *Psychological Bulletin, 91*(3), 461–481.

White, S., & Tharp, R. G. (1988, April). *Questioning and wait-time: A cross cultural analysis.* Paper presented at the annual meeting of the American Educational Research Association, New Orleans.

Whitehead, A. N. (1929). *The aims of education.* New York: Macmillan.

Whitehurst, G. J., Epstein, J. N., Angell, A. L., Payne, A. C., Crone, D. A., & Fischel, J. E. (1994). Outcomes of an emergent literacy program in headstart. *Journal of Educational Psychology, 86,* 542–555.

Wigfield, A., & Eccles, J. (1989). Test anxiety in elementary and secondary school students. *Educational Psychologist, 24,* 159–183.

Wigfield, A., & Eccles, J. S. (2002). Students' motivation during the middle school years. In J. Aronson (Ed.), *Improving academic development: Impact of psychological factors in education.* New York: Academic Press.

Wigfield, A., Eccles, J., MacIver, D., Rueman, D., & Midgley, C. (1991). Transitions at early adolescence: Changes in children's domain-specific self-perceptions and general self-esteem across the transition to junior high school. *Developmental Psychology, 27,* 552–565.

Wigfield, A., Eccles, J. S., & Pintrich, P. R. (1996). Development between the ages of 11 and 25. In D. Berliner & R. Calfee, (Eds.), *Handbook of Educational Psychology* (pp. 148–185). New York: Macmillan.

Wiggins, G. (1989). Teaching to the authentic test. *Educational Leadership, 46*(7), 41–47.

Wiggins, G. (1991). Standards, not standardization: Evoking quality student work. *Educational Leadership, 48*(5), 18–25.

Wiggins, G. (1993). Assessment, authenticity, context, and validity. *Phi Delta Kappan, 75,* 200–214.

Wiig, E. H. (1982). Communication disorders. In H. Haring (Ed.), *Exceptional children and youth* (pp. 81–110). Columbus, OH: Charles E. Merrill.

Wilder, A. A., & Williams, J. P. (2001). Students with severe learning disabilities can learn higher order comprehension skills. *Journal of Educational Psychology, 93,* 268–278.

Wilgenbusch, T., & Merrell, K. W. (1999). Gender differences in self-concept among children and adolescents: A meta-analysis of multidimensional studies. *School Psychology Quarterly, 14,* 101–120.

Wilkins, W. E., & Glock, M. D. (1973). *Teacher expectations and student achievement: A replication and extension.* Ithaca, NY: Cornell University Press.

Willcutt, E. G., Pennington, B. F., Boada, R., Ogline, J. S., Tunick, R. A., Chhabidas, N. A., & Olson, R. K. (2001). A comparison of the cognitive deficits in reading disability and attention-deficit/hyperactivity disorder. *Journal of Abnormal Psychology, 110,* 157–172.

Willerman, L. (1979). *The psychology of individual and group differences.* San Francisco: Freeman.

Williams, C., & Bybee J. (1994). What do children feel guilty about? Developmental and gender differences. *Developmental Psychology, 30,* 617–623.

Williams, G. C., Wiener, M. W., Markakis, K. M., Reeve, J., & Deci, E. L. (1993). Medical student motivation for internal medicine. *Annals of Internal Medicine.*

Williams, J. P. (2002). Using the Theme Scheme to improve story comprehension. In C. C. Block and M. Pressley (Eds.), Comprehension instruction: Research-based best practices (pp. 126–139). New York: Guilford.

Williams, W., Blythe, T., White, N., Li, J., Sternberg, R., & Gardner, H. (1996). *Practical Intelligence in school.* New York: HarperCollins.

Willingham, W. W., & Cole, N. S. (1997). *Gender and fair assessment.* Mahwah, NJ: Lawrence Erlbaum.

Willis, P. (1977). *Learning to labor.* Lexington, MA: D.C. Heath.

Willoughby, T., Porter, L., Belsito, L., & Yearsley, T. (1999). Use of elaboration strategies by grades two, four, and six. *Elementary School Journal, 99,* 221–231.

Wilson, C. W., & Hopkins, B. L. (1973). The effects of contingent music on the intensity of noise in junior high home economics classes. *Journal of Applied Behavior Analysis, 6,* 269–275.

Wilson, M. (2001). The case for sensorimotor coding in working memory. *Psychonomic Bulletin and Review, 8,* 44–57.

Winett, R. A., & Winkler, R. C. (1972). Current behavior modification in the classroom: Be still, be quiet, be docile. *Journal of Applied Behavior Analysis, 15,* 499–504.

Wingate, N. (1986). Sexism in the classroom. *Equity and Excellence, 22,* 105–110.

Wink, J., & Putney, L. (2002). *A vision of Vygotsky.* Boston: Allyn and Bacon.

Winne, P. H. (1995). Inherent details in self-regulated learning. *Educational Psychologist, 30,* 173–188.

Winne, P. H. (2001). Self-regulated learning viewed from models of information processing. In B. J. Zimmerman & D. H. Schunk (Eds.), *Self-regulated learning and academic achievement: Theoretical perspectives* (2nd ed., pp. 153–189). Mahwah, NJ: Lawrence Erlbaum.

Winner, E. (2000). The origins and ends of giftedness. *American Psychologist, 55,* 159–169.

Winograd, P., & Johnston, P. (1982). Comprehension monitoring and the error-detection paradigm. *Journal of Reading Behavior, 14,* 61–76.

Winsler, A., Diaz, R. M., Espinosa, L., & Rodriquez, J. L. (1999). When learning an second language does not mean losing the first: Bilingual lan-guage development in low-income, Spanish-speaking children attending bilingual preschool. *Child Development, 70,* 349–362.

Witkin, H. A., Moore, C. A., Goodenough, D. R., & Cox, R. W. (1977). Field-dependent and field-independent cognitive styles and their educational implications. *Review of Educational Research, 47,* 1–64.

Wittrock, M. (Ed.). (1986). *Handbook of research on teaching* (3rd ed.). New York: Macmillan.

Wittrock, M. C. (1982, March). *Educational implications of recent research on learning and memory.* Paper presented at the annual meeting of the American Educational Research Association, New York.

Wittrock, M. C. (1992). An empowering conception of educational psychology. *Educational Psychologist, 27,* 129–142.

Wolf, D., Bixby, J., Glenn, J., III, & Gardner, H. (1991). To use their minds well: New forms of student assessment. *Review of Research in Education, 17,* 31–74.

Wolters, C. A., Yu, S. L., & Pintrich, P. R. (1996). The relation between goal orientation and students' motivational beliefs and self-regulated learning. *Learning and Individual Differences, 8,* 211–238.

Women on Words and Images. (1975). *Dick and Jane as victims: Sex stereotyping in children's readers.* Available from author, P.O. Box 2163, Princeton, NJ.

Wong, L. (1987). Reaction to research findings: Is the feeling of obviousness warranted? *Dissertation Abstracts International,* 48/12, 3709B (University Microfilms #DA 8801059).

Wood, D., Bruner, J., & Ross, S. (1976). The role of tutoring in problem solving. *British Journal of Psychology, 66,* 181–191.

Wood, S. E., & Wood, E. G. (1999). *The world of psychology* (3rd ed.). Boston: Allyn and Bacon.

Woolfolk, A. E., & Brooks, D. (1983). Nonverbal communication in teaching. In E. Gordon (Ed.), *Review of research in education* (Vol. 10, pp. 103–150). Washington, DC: American Educational Research Association.

Woolfolk, A. E., & Brooks, D. (1985). The influence of teachers' nonverbal behaviors on students' perceptions and performance. *Elementary School Journal, 85,* 514–528.

Woolfolk, A. E., & Hoy, W. K. (1990). Prospective teachers' sense of efficacy and beliefs about control. *Journal of Educational Psychology, 82,* 81–91.

Woolfolk, A. E., Rosoff, B., & Hoy, W. K. (1990). Teachers' sense of efficacy and their beliefs about managing students. *Teaching and Teacher Education, 6,* 137–148.

Woolfolk, A. E., & Woolfolk, R. L. (1974). A contingency management technique for increasing student attention in a small group. *Journal of School Psychology, 12,* 204–212.

Woolfolk Hoy, A., Demerath, P., & Pape, S. (2002). Teaching adolescents: Engaging developing selves. In T. Urdan & F. Pajares (Eds.), *Adolescence and education* (pp. 119–169). Volume I. Greenwich, CT: Information Age Publishing.

Woolfolk Hoy, A., & Murphy, P. K. (2001). Teaching educational psychology to the implicit mind. In R. Sternberg & B. Torff (Eds.), *Understanding and teaching the implicit mind* (pp. 145–185). Mahwah, NJ: Lawrence Erlbaum.

Woolfolk Hoy, A., & Tschannen-Moran. M. (1999). Implications of cognitive approaches to peer learning for teacher education. In A. O'Donnell & A. King (Eds.), *Cognitive perspectives on peer learning* (pp. 257–284). Mahwah, NJ: Lawrence Erlbaum.

Wright, S. C., & Taylor, D. M. (1995). Identity and the language of the classroom: Investigating the impact of heritage versus second language instruction on personal and collective self-esteem. *Journal of Educational Psychology, 87,* 241–252.

Wyler, R. S. (1988). Social memory and social judgment. In P. Solomon, G. Goethals, C. Kelly, & B. Stephans (Eds.), *Perspectives on memory research.* New York: Springer-Verlag.

Yates, M., & Youniss, J. (1999). Promoting identity development: Ten ideas for school-based service-learning programs. In J. Claus & C. Ogden (Eds.), *Service learning for youth empowerment and social change* (pp. 43–67). New York: Peter Lang.

Yee, A. H. (1992). Asians as stereotypes and students: Misperceptions that persist. *Educational Psychology Review, 4,* 95–132.

Yell, M. L. (1990). The use of corporal punishment, suspension, expulsion, and timeout with behaviorally disordered students in public schools: Legal considerations. *Behavioral Disorders, 15,* 100–109.

Yerkes, R. M., & Dodson, J. D. (1908). The relation of strength of stimulus to rapidity of habit formation. *Journal of Comparative Neurology, 18,* 459–482.

Yetman, N. R. (1999). *Majority and minority: The dynamics of race and ethnicity in American life.* (6th ed.). Boston: Allyn and Bacon.

Yeung, A. S., McInerney, D. M., Russell-Bowie, D., Suliman, R., Chui, H., & Lau, I. C. (2000). Where is the hierarchy of academic self-concept? *Journal of Educational Psychology, 92,* 556–567.

Yinger, R. (1999). The role of standards in teaching and teacher education. In G. Griffin (Ed.), *The education of teachers: Ninety-eighth yearbook of the National Society for the Study of Education (Part 1)* (pp. 85–113). Chicago: University of Chicago Press.

You and the system. (1991, April). *Teacher Magazine,* 32H.

Young, A. J. (1997). I think, therefore I'm motivated: The relations among cognitive strategy use, motivational orientation, and classroom perceptions over time. *Learning and Individual Differences, 9,* 249–283.

Youniss, J., & Yates, M. (1997). *Community service and social responsibility in youth.* Chicago: University of Chicago Press.

Zeidner, M. (1995). Adaptive coping with test situations. *Educational Psychologist, 30,* 123–134.

Zeidner, M. (1998). *Test anxiety: The state of the art.* New York: Plenum.

Zelli, A., Dodge, K. A., Lochman, J. E., & Laird, R. D. (1999). The distinction between beliefs legitimizing aggression and deviant processing of social cues: Testing measurement validity and the hypothesis that biased processing mediates the effects of beliefs on aggression. *Journal of Personality and Social Psychology, 77,* 150–166.

Zigmond, N., Jenkins, J., Fuchs, D., Deno, S., & Fuchs, L. S. (1995). When students fail to achieve satisfactorily: A reply to Leskey and Waldron. *Phi Delta Kappan, 77,* 303–306.

Zimmerman, B. J. (1990). Self-regulated learning and academic achievement: An overview. *Educational Psychologist, 21,* 3–18.

Zimmerman, B. J. (1995). Self-efficacy and educational development. In A. Bandura (Ed.), *Self-efficacy in changing societies* (pp. 202–231). New York: Cambridge University Press.

Zimmerman, B. J. (2002). Becoming a self-regulated learner: An overview. *Theory Into Practice, 41,* 64–70.

Zimmerman, B. J., & Schunk, D. H. (Eds.). (2001). *Self-regulated learning and academic achievement: Theoretical perspectives* (2nd ed.). Mahwah, NJ: Lawrence Erlbaum.

Zimmerman, D. W. (1981). On the perennial argument about grading "on the curve" in college courses. *Educational Psychologist, 16,* 175–178.

SUBJECT INDEX

PHOTO CREDITS

p. 6, Will Hart; p. 8, Kelly Hoy, Arlington Writers; pp. 9, 50, 178, 300, 334, 488, David Young-Wolff/Getty Images/Stone p. 10, Bob Daemmrich/The Image Works; p. 30, Anderson/Monkmeyer; p. 34, Brian Smith; p. 36, Brian Smith; p. 42, Bill Bachmann/The Image Works; p. 43, Elena Rooraid/PhotoEdit; p. 45, James V. Wertsch/Washington University; p. 47, Lindfors Photography; pp. 51, 248, 351, 379, 572, Kelly Hoy, Arlington Writers; p. 54, Billy E. Barnes/PhotoEdit; p. 56, Michael Newman/PhotoEdit; p. 66, Ted Streshinsky/Corbis; p. 67, Lindfors Photography; p. 73, Michael Newman/PhotoEdit; p. 77, Esbin Anderson/The Image Works; p. 82, Courtesy of Carol Gilligan; p. 84, David Young-Wolff/PhotoEdit; p. 89, Ellen Senisi/The Image Works; p. 92, Myrleen Ferguson Cate/PhotoEdit; pp. 95, 218, 420, 423, Nancy Richmond/The Image Works; p. 106, Tony Freeman/PhotoEdit; p. 109, Tom Herde/Boston Globe; p. 111, AP/Wide World Photos; p. 114, Bob Daemmrich/The Image Works; p. 123, Courtesy of National Easter Seals Society; pp. 127, 467, 515, Will Hart; p. 128, Bob Daemmrich/The Image Works; p. 130, Paul Conklin/PhotoEdit; p. 142 Will Hart; p. 160, Lindfors Photography; p. 162, Michael Newman/PhotoEdit; p. 165, Carl Iwasaki/Life Magazine © Time, Inc.; p. 170, John Boykin/PhotoEdit; p. 180, Billy E. Barnes/PhotoEdit; p. 182, Lindfors Photography; p. 199, Lindfors Photography; p. 203, Falk/Monkmeyer; p. 207, Elizabeth Crews; p. 209, Will Hart; p. 217, Ellen Senisi/The Image Works; p. 236, Li-Hua Lan/Syracuse Newspapers/The Image Works; p. 242, Lindfors Photography; p. 246, Ellen Senisi/The Image Works; p. 257, Michael Newman/PhotoEdit; p. 261, Lindfors Photography; p. 265, Spencer Grant/PhotoEdit; p. 279, Lindfors Photography; p. 282, © Syracuse Newspapers/Michelle Gabel/The Image Works; p. 289, Walter Hodges/Stone; p. 292, Kimimasa Mayama/Reuters NewMedia Inc. CORBIS; p. 298, Stephen Marks; p. 299, Lindfors Photography; p. 304, Lindfors Photography; p. 314, Will Hart; p. 317, Stanford University News Service; p. 318, Tony Freeman/PhotoEdit; p. 324, Will Hart; p. 328, Will Hart/PhotoEdit; p. 331 Jeff Greenberg/PhotoEdit; p. 336, Lindfors Photography; p. 353, Bob Daemmrich/The Image Works; p. 360, Andy Sacks/Stone; p. 362, Robert Harbison; p. 366, Tom McCarthy/PhotoEdit; p. 369, Jeff Greenberg/PhotoEdit; p. 376, Bill Bachmann/The Image Works; p. 385, Jose Galvez/PhotoEdit; p. 397, Bonnie Kamin/PhotoEdit; p. 400, Lindfors Photography; p. 410, Kelly Hoy, Arlington Writers; p. 418, Ellen Senisi/The Image Works; p. 434, Brian Smith; p. 441, Lindfors Photography; p. 446 Comstock Royalty Free Division; p. 454, Peter Hvizdak/The Image Works; p. 464, Robert Harbison; p. 469, Robin Sachs/PhotoEdit; p. 479, Jeff Greenberg/PhotoEdit; p. 483, Michael Newman/PhotoEdit; p. 487, Ellen Senisi/The Image Works; p. 490, Hal Stoelzle/Rocky Mountain News/CORBIS/Sygma; p. 495, Nancy Sheeham/PhotoEdit; p. 502, Myrleen Ferguson/PhotoEdit; p. 517, Bob Daemmrich/The Image Works; p. 525, Bob Daemmrich/Stock Boston; p. 539, Ed Lallo/Liaison Agency; p. 548, Will Hart/PhotoEdit; p. 553, David Young-Wolff/PhotoEdit; p. 558, Richard Hutchings/PhotoEdit; p. 574, Robert E. Daemmrich/Stone